MANAGERIAL ECONOMICS

THE IRWIN SERIES IN ECONOMICS

Appleyard and Field
INTERNATIONAL ECONOMICS
second edition

Appleyard and Field
INTERNATIONAL TRADE
second edition

Appleyard and Field
INTERNATIONAL MONETARY THEORY
second edition

Baily and Friedman
MACROECONOMICS, FINANCIAL MARKETS, AND THE INTERNATIONAL SECTOR
second edition

Barron and Lynch
ECONOMICS
third edition

Baye and Beil
MANAGERIAL ECONOMICS AND BUSINESS STRATEGY

Blair
URBAN AND REGIONAL ECONOMICS

Bornstein
COMPARATIVE ECONOMIC SYSTEMS: MODELS AND CASES
sixth edition

Brown and Moore
READINGS, ISSUES, AND PROBLEMS IN PUBLIC FINANCE
fourth edition

Colander
ECONOMICS
second edition

Colander
MICROECONOMICS
second edition

Colander
MACROECONOMICS
second edition

Denzau
MICROECONOMIC ANALYSIS: MARKETS & DYNAMICS

Fisher
STATE AND LOCAL PUBLIC FINANCE

Hadjimichalakis and Hadjimichalakis
CONTEMPORARY MONEY, BANKING, AND FINANCIAL MARKETS

Hyman
ECONOMICS
third edition

Hyman
MICROECONOMICS
third edition

Hyman
MACROECONOMICS
third edition

Hyman
MODERN MICROECONOMICS: ANALYSIS AND APPLICATIONS
third edition

Katz and Rosen
MICROECONOMICS
second edition

Lehmann
REAL WORLD ECONOMIC APPLICATIONS: THE WALL STREET JOURNAL WORKBOOK
fourth edition

Lindert
INTERNATIONAL ECONOMICS
ninth edition

Maurice and Phillips
ECONOMIC ANALYSIS: THEORY AND APPLICATION
sixth edition

Maurice and Thomas
MANAGERIAL ECONOMICS
fifth edition

Nadler and Hansen
MICROCOMPUTER MACROECONOMICS WITH IBM DISK

O'Sullivan
URBAN ECONOMICS
second edition

O'Sullivan
ESSENTIALS OF URBAN ECONOMICS

Peterson
PRINCIPLES OF ECONOMICS: MICRO
eighth edition

Peterson
PRINCIPLES OF ECONOMICS: MACRO
eighth edition

Prager
APPLIED MICROECONOMICS: AN INTERMEDIATE APPROACH

Rima
DEVELOPMENT OF ECONOMIC ANALYSIS
fifth edition

Roger and Daniel
PRINCIPLES OF ECONOMICS SOFTWARE SIMULATION

Rosen
PUBLIC FINANCE
fourth edition

Schwarz and Van Dyken
MANAGER: MANAGERIAL ECONOMICS SOFTWARE

Seo
MANAGERIAL ECONOMICS: TEXT, SHORT CASES
seventh edition

Sharp, Register, and Leftwich
ECONOMICS OF SOCIAL ISSUES
eleventh edition

Shepherd
PUBLIC POLICIES TOWARD BUSINESS
eighth edition

Shugart
THE ORGANIZATION OF INDUSTRY

Slavin
INTRODUCTION TO ECONOMICS
fourth edition

Streifford
ECONOMIC PERSPECTIVE

Walton and Wykoff
UNDERSTANDING ECONOMICS TODAY
fourth edition

MANAGERIAL ECONOMICS

FIFTH EDITION

S. CHARLES MAURICE
Professor of Economics
Texas A&M University

CHRISTOPHER R. THOMAS
Associate Professor of Economics
University of South Florida

IRWIN

Chicago • Bogota • Boston • Buenos Aires • Caracas
London • Madrid • Mexico City • Sydney • Toronto

IRWIN
Concerned About Our Environment

In recognition of the fact that our company is a large end-user of fragile yet replenishable resources, we at IRWIN can assure you that every effort is made to meet or exceed Environmental Protection Agency (EPA) recommendations and requirements for a "greener" workplace.

To preserve these natural assets, a number of environmental policies, both companywide and department-specific, have been implemented. From the use of 50% recycled paper in our textbooks to the printing of promotional materials with recycled stock and soy inks to our office paper recycling program, we are committed to reducing waste and replacing environmentally unsafe products with safer alternatives.

Senior sponsoring editor: *Gary Nelson*
Developmental editor: *Amy Winston*
Senior marketing manager: *Ron Bloecher*
Project editor: *Beth Yates*
Production manager: *Ann Cassady*
Designer: *Heidi J. Baughman*
Cover designer: *Katherine Farmer*
Cover photographer: *William Warren/Westlight*
Art studio: *Steadman Gibson Corporate Design, Inc.*
Compositor: *Weimer Graphics, Inc.*
Typeface: *10/12 Palatino*
Printer: *R. R. Donnelley & Sons Company*

Library of Congress Cataloging-in-Publication Data

Maurice, S. Charles.
Managerial economics. — 5th ed. / S. Charles Maurice, Christopher R. Thomas.
p. cm.
Includes bibliographical references and index.
ISBN 0-256-16055-4
1. Managerial economics. I. Thomas, Christopher R. II. Title.
HD30.22.M39 1995
338.5'024658—dc20 94-26272

inted in the United States of America
3 4 5 6 7 8 9 0 DO 1 0 9 8 7 6 5

To Niccie and Shelly

PREFACE

Our Underlying Philosophy

Three main goals have guided the development of this book from its conception through this newly revised fifth edition.

- Our primary objective has always been to develop and set forth the fundamentals of microeconomic theory while focusing on the use of theory in managerial decision making. Our purpose is to teach business students the economic way of thinking when making business and personal decisions.
- Another related fundamental goal of this text is to show students (future entrepreneurs and business managers) how the theoretical concepts can actually be used and implemented in real-world decision making.
- Finally, our text demonstrates the relation of managerial economics to other courses in a business school curriculum, such as finance, marketing, business policy, and quantitative analysis. Our aim is to reinforce what students have learned in other courses and provide a foundation of analysis for future coursework.

Indeed, these three objectives illuminate the primary distinguishing characteristics of our approach to managerial economics.

Audience

Managerial Economics is essentially an economics text designed especially for business students. A majority of students, including both undergraduates and students in MBA programs, will enroll in courses with the same title as this book. However, many instructors and students use this text for courses in applied microeconomics.

This text can stand alone in the sense that it contains all of the principles of microeconomics theory needed to understand specific managerial economics concepts; no supplemental text is necessary. By presenting the basic theory and the specific managerial economics constructs together, we demonstrate that managerial economics is simply an application of microeconomics.

Coverage, Pedagogy, and Changes to the Fifth Edition

We stress that the theoretical principles of microeconomics are useful for managerial decision makers. In order to make this crucial point, we emphasize that the principles of microeconomics will invariably enable a manager to make decisions that will lead to economically efficient solutions, maximize profits, or maximize the value of the firm. Using simple numerical examples, we show that the implementation of microeconomic principles is not all that hard. We do point out that the information used in these examples is more complete than would probably be available to actual business decision makers. These examples of the implementation of the theory are designed to teach the economic way of obtaining solutions to problems if complete information is available. In this way, we develop analytical tools that will be useful when making decisions based upon information that is not so complete. To reinforce further the economic way of thinking about business problems, we draw upon articles in publications such as *The Wall Street*

Journal in order to show that actual managers really do use the theoretical principles set forth in the text when making decisions on a day-to-day basis. Almost every one of the chapters includes at least one of these illustrations.

We often relate managerial economics to other courses in business; for example, we use concepts from finance courses in the development of the theories of maximizing the value of the firm and investment. We use marketing concepts in developing the principles of demand forecasting and the effects of advertising. We rely extensively on the concepts developed in courses on quantitative analysis when implementing the theoretical principles of microeconomics.

Because the previous edition of *Managerial Economics* represented a major revision that included a reorganization and some change of emphasis, this edition was not revised as extensively as the last. We have, however, made a few important changes that we believe will make the text easier to follow and more accessible to students. We have also made some additions that we feel are useful. First, we have added a chapter on the fundamentals of risk and uncertainty in the preliminary material (Chapter 6). In that chapter we discuss risk analysis and decision making under uncertainty and risk. We then implement this analysis at several points throughout the text. All of the material on decision making under risk or uncertainty is presented separately so that those who wish to omit it may do so without any loss of continuity. We do think, however, this new material gives an added flavor to the other material on managerial decision making.

The chapters on production and cost have been reorganized in order to present short-run production and cost together in Chapter 10, and long-run production and cost together in Chapter 11. With this restructuring, we can show more easily and directly the relation between a firm's production function and its cost function. This linkage is often not set forth and demonstrated in such a straightforward manner. We have expanded and reorganized the introductory chapter on demand, supply, and market equilibrium. Our aim is to show how ordinary demand and supply functions are derived from the generalized form of these functions that include variables other than price. Although much of the material in this chapter will be a review for most students, the discussion of the relation between demand curves and the generalized form will give considerable insight into the chapters on demand and supply estimation and forecasting, which include exogenous variables in the equations.

We have also streamlined and tightened most of the material throughout the text. Chapter 4, which discusses optimization theory, has been tightened a great deal. For example, we have dropped the discussion on unconstrained minimization and instead demonstrate that all unconstrained problems can be cast as maximization problems. The emphasis upon optimization as the fundamental underpinning of most managerial decision making is introduced in Chapter 4 and is carried throughout much of the remainder of the text. Chapter 12, which discusses production and cost estimation, has been streamlined primarily by moving Cobb-Douglas estimation to the appendix and using instead the traditional U-shaped or inverted U-shaped functions, which conform to the theoretical functions, as the function to be estimated. Cubic and quadratic functions are used exclusively in the chapters on implementation of the theory of the firm.

We have also placed more emphasis on estimation of firm demand functions rather than market demand function. This type of estimation is more relevant to managerial decision making and does not necessitate the use of the more complex two-stage least squares. Finally, we have made many minor but beneficial changes throughout all of the chapters; for example, we have dropped many out-of-date illustrations and have added a number of new ones to illustrate and reinforce the theoretical and empirical material.

Notwithstanding these changes, many—or perhaps most—aspects of the text remain unchanged, as we continue to focus upon the use of economic theory and empirical analysis in decision making. As noted, we continue to stress the importance of optimization theory and the importance of marginal benefits and marginal cost in decision making. The text continues to focus on the use, understanding, and interpretation of statistical analysis rather than on calculating the statistical results. We continue to relegate mathematical proofs of the theories and some of the more complex theoretical and empirical estimation to the appendixes. Although the theoretical analysis in the text is rigorous and thorough, only graphical, verbal, and algebraic analysis is used in developing the theories. In this development we frequently refer students back to the fundamentals of the theory of optimization, which provides the foundation of those theories.

We frequently implement the theories using numerical examples in order to reinforce students' understanding and demonstrate that these theories are useful and relevant for business decision making. Many adopters of previous editions have told us that the problems at the end of each chapter are one of the most useful parts of the text, and so we have revised many of these problems. We continue to use technical problems to help students learn mechanics. The applied problems emphasize the use of economics in business decision making and frequently require the use of hypothetical data to obtain solutions to relevant business problems. In order to make the material less abstract, we continue to use numbers rather than letters in much of the graphical analysis of the theoretical material.

In addition to all changes noted here, we have tried to make improvements in every chapter. These changes are generally designed to reinforce the focus of text, which is that managerial economics is extremely useful for decision making, and to make the material more accessible and easier to digest.

We would like to thank many adopters of the previous edition of this text for useful comments and suggestions. In particular, we want to thank Dr. Ki Soo Kim of the Pusan Fisheries University for his help on the development and exposition of the new material on risk and uncertainty.

S. Charles Maurice
Christopher R. Thomas

BRIEF CONTENTS

CONTENTS

What is Business?

An Economic Activity

How? What? Who? and for Whom?

C H A P T E R

1

The Scope of Managerial Economics

The fundamental task of a manager is to make decisions. Every type of manager in every type of organization must continually make decisions that affect the performance of the organization. The best—or more precisely, the most successful—managers are those who make decisions that enable the organization to achieve its goals. The objective of managerial economics is to provide a framework for analyzing business decisions. Instead of presenting a detailed list of rules for specific decision-making problems, such as how to design a successful laundry detergent advertisement or how to obtain venture capital, managerial economics addresses the larger economic forces that shape day-to-day decision making. By applying economic theory to business problems, managerial economics develops general principles that can be applied to business decision making. Although economic theory is not the only tool used by successful managers, it is a powerful and essential tool. The objective of this text is to show you how managers can use economics in making decisions that will achieve the firm's goals—in particular, maximization of profit.

As the subtitle of the text suggests, managerial economics focuses on the application of *microeconomic* theory, a basic tool used by economists. Microeconomics is the study and analysis of the behavior of individual segments of the economy: individual consumers, workers and owners of resources, individual firms, industries, and markets for goods, services, and productive resources. Microeconomics is concerned with topics such as how consumers choose the goods and services they purchase and how firms make hiring, pricing, production, and advertising decisions. Let us emphasize at the beginning that while these theories are relatively simple, they are the same theoretical methods used by real-world decision makers.

In other words, although the economic theory used in this text is relatively simple, it is sophisticated enough to be used in actual managerial decision making.

This text uses economic theory to analyze economic problems that are relevant to firms. You will learn to analyze decision-making problems similar to those currently being considered by analysts in the nation's largest firms. It is not our intention to make you into a professional economist. This text is designed to help you learn basic economic theory and to allow you to practice using economics in order to become a competent professional decision maker and manager. The basic theoretical tools, the fundamental methods of analysis, and the approaches to problem solving used by professional economists and business analysts are those you will learn to use.

The major reason for studying managerial economics is that it is useful. Every manager—in fact, every person—makes economic decisions every day. We will always face problems of scarcities and consequently must make choices. A knowledge of economics helps people make wise choices. Therefore, all students will find managerial economics useful in both their professional and private lives.

Students who choose business as a career will find economics particularly useful. (Note that people who become doctors, lawyers, or other professionals are in business also.) Economics is extremely useful in making decisions designed to increase the firm's profit and to enable the firm to operate more efficiently. Economics is useful in helping decision makers decide how to adapt to external changes in economic variables. The appropriate level of advertising and the investment decision are economic decisions, and an understanding of economic theory helps managers make the most profitable decisions.

A knowledge of economics is useful also to people who work for government agencies or nonprofit institutions. Although the goals of these agencies and institutions do not include profit maximization, they do involve economic efficiency. For example, a government agency may be required to allocate a given budget to attain the maximum benefit—in education, health care, and so forth—permitted by the size of the budget. Or it may be charged with attaining a certain goal at the lowest possible cost. These are economic problems, and managerial economics provides the tools needed to solve these problems. Just as it helps business managers, economics helps these managers of nonprofit organizations adapt to changes in the economic environment in the most efficient manner.

We have barely skimmed the surface, mentioning only a few types of decisions for which economic reasoning is useful. We will discuss many such examples throughout the text. You will be able to increase your ability to analyze and solve decision-making problems through practice. The better your understanding of economic theory and the more you practice applying the theory, the better prepared you will be for carrying out the tasks of managers.

1.1 THE ROLE OF MANAGERS

Making decisions and processing information are the two primary tasks of managers. We separate these two tasks for analytical purposes; but in reality, they are inseparable. In order to make intelligent decisions, managers must be able to obtain, process, and use information. Economic theory helps managers know what information should be obtained, how to process the information, and how to use it.

The task of organizing and processing information in conjunction with basic economic theory can take two general forms. The first involves a specific decision that must be made by the manager. The second general form involves using readily available information to carry out a course of action that furthers the goals of the organization.

Examples of the first type of decisions that managers might have to make are (1) whether or not to close down a branch of the firm, (2) whether or not a store or restaurant should stay open more hours a day, (3) how a government agency can be reorganized to be more efficient, (4) how a hospital can treat more patients without a decrease in patient care, and (5) whether to install an in-house computer rather than pay for outside computing services. These and a myriad of other managerial decisions require the use of basic economics. Economic theory helps decision makers know what information is necessary to make the decision and how to process and use that information. In other words, an important purpose of economic theory is to indicate what information will be useful in solving problems and enabling firms to operate more efficiently. After obtaining the desired information, managers must then analyze this information and use it in connection with the theoretical and statistical tools available to make the best decision possible under the circumstances.

The second general form of managerial decision making involves using readily available information to carry out a course of action that furthers the goals of the organization. Basic economic theory is extremely useful to managers in this task also. Managers receive useful information every day from many sources. Some of these sources are *The Wall Street Journal,* business magazines such as *Business Week,* local newspapers, television, private newsletters, and conversations with others. Successful managers know how to pick out the useful information from the vast amount of information they receive. They know how to evaluate this information and act on it in order to further the goals of their organizations.

Of course, a manager must know the goals of the organization. As we mentioned above, managerial economics is useful not only to managers in profit-maximizing firms but also to managers in government and in nonprofit organizations. The primary goal of a manufacturing firm would be to maximize profits. The primary goal of a foundation could be to further some cause. A public hospital could have the goal of treating as many patients as possible—subject, of course, to certain standards. A state university could have the goal of educating, above a certain standard, as many students as possible.

We should emphasize, however, that the tasks of managers in practically all of these situations are the same. Each goal involves an optimization problem. The manager attempts either to maximize or minimize some objective function (possibly subject to some constraint). And, for all goals that involve an optimization problem, the same general economic principles apply, a point we will stress in a forthcoming chapter.

In addition to the goal of maximizing profit, economists have considered a number of alternatives to profit maximization as the manager's objective. For example, the salaries of some managers are closely linked to the level of sales of their company. These managers may be more likely to pursue a policy of maximizing sales or market share rather than focusing on profits alone. Alternatively, managers may mix objectives. Maximizing sales while keeping profits above some minimum target level allows a manager to pursue a higher salary while still satisfying the shareholders' interest in profits. Numerous other managerial goals have also been examined. While some of these other managerial objectives may have merit in some cases, the assumption of profit maximization more accurately predicts the pattern of managerial decision making than any other assumption. Indeed, a manager who fails to see the firm's role as earning profits will quite likely be replaced—either by stockholders or through a takeover.

1.2 MANAGERIAL ECONOMICS AND BUSINESS CAREERS[1]

Managerial economics deals with the decisions a manager must make in the course of maximizing profits or pursuing another goal. The microeconomic theory and the various empirical skills that you will learn in this course can begin to prepare you for a variety of interesting and challenging careers. Knowledge of managerial economics can be part of the preparation for at least four different career paths: business, government, finance, or public administration.

Business Careers

Many students taking a course in managerial economics are planning on careers in business management. Some small businesses and virtually all large and medium businesses rely on business forecasts to make operating decisions, to plan strategies for product development and marketing, and to make capital investment decisions. Businesses may wish to forecast sales, prices, interest rates, personal incomes, or even exchange rates. A manager needs to know how to interpret and use these economic forecasts. The best decisions usually require the manager to combine the forecasts of others with the manager's own forecasts. One of the most important things we will teach you is how to interpret forecasts.

Training for a career in business decision making will generally involve developing three basic sets of skills: a thorough understanding of economic theory, a strong set of statistical and mathematical skills, and effective communication skills. In addition to these basic skills, your preparation for a business career will require learning the principles and techniques from other disciplines in the business curriculum, especially accounting, finance, business computing science, marketing, and management. As you will see, the study of managerial economics will strengthen both your understanding of microeconomic theory and your ability to apply quantitative tools to business decision making.

[1]This section draws heavily from the "1991 Guide to Careers in Economics and Business," published by *The Margin* magazine, January/February 1991.

Careers in Government

You probably will not be surprised to learn that federal, state, and local government agencies offer vast employment opportunities. At the federal level of government, the departments of agriculture, commerce, labor, and state are the largest employers. The types of jobs in government agencies range across the fields of agriculture, business, finance, international trade, transportation, urban economics, and utilities.

Many of the jobs in government involve economic analysis. Government economists typically analyze and forecast the impact of changes in laws and public policies. For example, economists at the Federal Trade Commission analyze specific industries in order to help enforce antitrust laws, which are designed to make and keep markets competitive in nature. At the Bureau of Labor Statistics (BLS), economists study prices, wages, productivity, and employment in the national economy. The Commerce Department studies data on production, distribution, and consumption of goods and services. College preparation for a job in government should emphasize economic theory and quantitative skills. Course work in accounting, mathematics, statistics, computer science, sampling theory and survey design will enhance your chances of getting a government job.

The BLS predicts little change in the employment of economists by the federal government while predicting a small increase in state and local government employment. Nearly 40 percent of all economists in the United States work for government agencies.

Careers in Finance

The field of financial economics offers a number of different career paths; a course in managerial economics can help prepare you for any of them. You might choose a job as an investment banker, a commercial banker, a corporate financial manager, a stockbroker, a trader, or a financial securities analyst. The field is so broad that it is difficult to summarize salaries in these jobs. *The Wall Street Journal* frequently reports extremely high salaries for the high-level positions at various financial institutions. Stockbrokers, commodities brokers, and investment bankers work on a commission basis. The BLS forecasts a significant increase in job opportunities for all sectors of financial employment.

Investment bankers help corporations finance business transactions, raise venture capital, and make investments. Many investment banking firms require a Master of Business Administration (MBA) for employment. Commercial banks perform various financial services for both consumers and businesses. Most commercial banks provide their own training programs for newly hired graduates. Nevertheless, courses in accounting, finance, and economics will enhance your chances of getting a job at a commercial bank. Corporate financial managers work with budgeting, cash management, investment financing, international finance, and mergers and acquisitions. Usually, an undergraduate degree in finance or business is required. Stockbrokers provide financial counseling to help clients build portfolios of securities that best match their risk and return profiles. Traders work on the floor of the stock exchanges where they buy and sell financial securities for their brokerage firms. Security analysts work for brokerage firms and other investment organizations. Their job is to use various types of market, financial, and trend analyses to evaluate various financial securities. All of the tools you will learn in managerial economics will help prepare you for a career as a securities analyst. In addition, you will find courses in accounting, finance, computer science, and statistics to be extremely valuable.

Careers in Public Administration

Careers in public administration involve producing public policy rather than profit. The tools of managerial economics apply not only to profit-maximizing firms but also to nonprofit organizations, including government agencies. Management opportunities in public administration include administrative managers, legislators, and chief executives. Administrative managers direct operations of various government agencies. They manage secretarial services, oversee data processing, direct materials scheduling and distribution, and manage personnel. Upper-level public administrators set goals and make plans for various agencies. Salaries for administrative managers vary widely.

Legislative jobs include becoming a US senator or representative, a state senator or representative, or a member of a city council. Training to become a legislator may involve any one of several fields of study. The most common are business, law, and political science. You may find that many positions require a master's degree in public administration (MPA), which trains students for leadership careers in local, state, and federal agencies, as well as for careers in nonprofit organizations. Regardless of which one of the many paths you might choose in public administration, training in managerial economics will provide you with analytical skills that are absolutely essential for producing quality public policy.

1.3 PURPOSE OF ECONOMIC THEORY

Economics is a logical system for using and processing information, and therefore provides a useful way of thinking about problems. Because a large part of this text is devoted to the use of economic theory in addressing economic problems, we want to explain briefly how and why economic theory is used to analyze problems. No doubt you have heard statements such as, "That's OK in theory, but what about the real world?" or, "I don't want ivory tower theorizing, I want the hard facts." The hard fact is that economic theory is designed to enable people to understand the functioning of the real world, which is often far too complex to comprehend without making the simplifying assumptions used in theories. Theory allows people to gain insights into complicated problems that would be impossible to understand without a theoretical structure.

Economic theory is an abstract generalization or simplification that gives a picture of the economic behavior of individuals or institutions that will explain real-world phenomena and make predictions about that behavior. The real world is an extraordinarily complicated place. The purpose of economic theory is to make sense out of confusion, to turn complexity into relative simplicity. A huge number of variables or external forces can affect behavior—some are important but most relatively insignificant. Many of these variables change frequently. Economic theory is concerned with determining which variables are important to the issue at hand. Economists use theory to concentrate on a few important forces and ignore the large number of variables that are unimportant. By abstracting away from the irrelevant, economists can make predictions and explanations that are valid in the real world, even though the theory may ignore most actual characteristics of the real world.

Using economic theory is in many ways analogous to using a road map. A road map abstracts away from nonessential characteristics and concentrates on what is relevant for the task at hand. Suppose you wanted to drive from Tampa to Houston. If you had never made that trip before, you would probably want a map. But you would not want a map that showed every road or street, no matter how small, in every city and town along the way. More likely you would obtain maps of Florida, Alabama, Mississippi, Louisiana, and Texas, showing only the interstate highways and other major roads. These maps abstract away from all nonessential thoroughfares and are therefore not a totally realistic picture of the landscape along the way, but they would certainly be adequate for the task. Actually, a more realistic map that showed every road, no matter how insignificant, would probably be too unwieldy to be of much use and you might get lost.

Suppose that you decide to stop along the way in New Orleans and spend a couple days sightseeing in the city. Now you would need a more complicated map that showed all or most of the city streets, and perhaps gave some information about the location of points of interest to tourists. This more complex map would abstract away from most characteristics of the city but it would be more detailed than the state road maps.

Economic theory is similar to a map. A theory should be only as complex as is necessary for the desired task. Any nonessential characteristics of the economy should be omitted because they are not needed. For example, to understand and explain the behavior of firms in general, economists use broad general assumptions in their theories and ignore the specific characteristics that describe actual firms or groups of firms. These individual characteristics are not necessary to understand firm behavior in general; they would complicate the analysis and make it less general. When economists want to analyze the behavior of specific groups of firms, such as public utility monopolies or large firms that face competition from only a few others, they would add some additional assumptions that would make the theory more specific but also somewhat more complex. Economic theories, like road maps, are designed for the tasks at hand.

The theories set forth and explained here will be extremely general, although the examples that illustrate their use will be more specific to individual firms and markets. The theories are not designed to apply to any individual firm, and will therefore use broad general assumptions that are not meant to be realistic. They are designed to explain firm and management behavior in general—to apply to no one individual firm, but to all firms.

It would actually be impossible for us to set forth a theory designed to apply to a particular managerial position in which you might find yourself in the future. You may be the CEO of IBM (at the time of writing, one is needed), or you might manage a small farm, or you might manage the European branch of an automobile manufacturer, or you might be the chief administrator of a metropolitan hospital, or you might be the administrator of some not-yet-enacted national health care plan, or you might be in any one of thousands of positions, some of which haven't even been thought of yet. We don't know what you are going to do in the future, and you probably don't either.

Therefore, we can only present theories that illustrate a general picture of the behavior of firms and markets. We do believe, however, that this theoretical structure will be useful no matter what you choose to do. Each person will have to adapt the structure in order to use it for, and apply it to, the particular task at hand at the time.

To summarize, economic theory allows managers to ignore all factors unimportant or irrelevant for a particular problem, in order to come to grips with that problem without becoming entangled in insignificant issues. One can deduce conclusions, using simple assumptions, while ignoring factors that could have an effect on the outcome, but in all likelihood will not. Therefore, when carrying out analysis, remember that, while everything depends in some way on everything else, most things depend in an essential way upon only a few other things. Economists generally concentrate on the close interdependence of a few variables.

Furthermore, the ability to use theory to abstract and ignore unimportant factors helps managers know what information is useful in making decisions and what is not. As we noted previously, a major role of managers is obtaining, processing, and using information. As we will show, economic theory helps indicate what information is relevant to a decision and how to use that information.

1.4 THE PURPOSE OF EMPIRICAL ANALYSIS

We sometimes hear that we are living in an age of information. It seems as though we are constantly being inundated with all kinds of information. More data are available than anyone could possibly use or digest. Yet we have emphasized that a major role or function of managers is to obtain and process information in order to make wise decisions that further the goals of the organization. Such decisions are frequently impossible without good information.

Decision makers must have some way of making sense out of the confusion in the real world. This task often requires statistical data. But simply collecting the data—much of which is readily available—is not enough. A decision maker or manager should know what information is relevant and useful for a particular purpose or decision. As noted above, economic theory can be extremely useful in determining what information should be collected and used. A manager must also organize and process the previously disorganized data in such a way that economic theory can be used in making a decision.

In several places throughout the text, we will describe the way managers can use empirical (or quantitative) analysis to organize and process information in the form of statistical data, and use the information to make decisions. The principal type of empirical analysis to be used is *regression analysis,* which, as those of you who have taken an introductory statistics course may recall, is a technique used to determine how one or more explanatory variables affect the value of a dependent variable.

While we will concentrate on regression analysis as a means of organizing data, this is not the only method that can be used. We stress regression analysis simply because it is a widely used technique and because space limitations preclude a comprehensive discussion of all available empirical techniques. At this point, let us mention something that we will stress throughout the text: Our purpose is *not* to teach you how to do statistics or to calculate the regression. That task is appropriately left to courses in statistics, quantitative business analysis, or econometrics. Rather our objective is to show how empirical analysis can be used in managerial decision making. Our emphasis is on the way regressions are interpreted and used, not how they are calculated.

We will discuss two uses of empirical analysis that are closely related. In one type of discussion we describe how to interpret regressions in order to obtain estimates and forecasts of demand and cost conditions facing a firm. These are the conditions that a manager should know in order to make decisions that maximize profit or promote other goals of the organization. Again, we emphasize that our intention is not to show you how to calculate regression estimates. Rather, the goal is to show how to interpret regression results, and how to decide what specific type of regression to use.

In a second type of empirical discussion, we use numerical examples to show how managers with complete information can use estimations of demand and cost conditions to achieve the goal of the organization—in most cases profit maximization. Although no firm ever has such ideal data and estimations, we follow this approach for two reasons: We want to reinforce the theory that has been presented, and we want to provide a blueprint that can be modified and adapted for use under conditions that are not ideal.

Although we have discussed the purpose of economic theory and the purpose of empirical analysis separately, we must emphasize that these tools are complements, not substitutes, in managerial decision making. Wise decision making requires that both be used together. Economic theory indicates how to approach a given problem, and what type of information and what variables are important. Empirical analysis helps a decision maker organize and process the information and put it into a form that is consistent with the theory. Therefore, the emphasis of this text is on using economic theory in conjunction with empirical analysis, to make optimizing decisions consistent with the goals of the firm.

1.5 STRUCTURE OF THE TEXT

The text is divided into seven parts. Part I sets forth the fundamentals of price determination in competitive markets. We first discuss market demand, market supply, market equilibrium, and causes of changes in equilibrium price and quantity in Chapter 2. Then, in Chapter 3, we explore the concept of elasticity and how elasticity affects the changes in equilibrium. There is a high probability that the material in Part I will be largely a review of material that you have learned in principles classes. This material is reviewed because it is so important in all courses in economics, including graduate courses; you will encounter it throughout the text. It is practically impossible to learn new topics in economics without a thorough understanding of market demand, supply, and equilibrium.

Part II will present some tools of analysis that you will find useful as you progress through the text. The theory of optimization, set forth in Chapter 4, provides the theoretical foundation for (1) the theory of consumer behavior—why people choose to purchase what they purchase; (2) the theory of production—how firms choose the optimal combination of inputs to produce their product; (3) the theory of the firm—how firms choose their output, price, and other variables to maximize their profits; and (4) the theory of input choice—how firms choose the amount of inputs that will maximize profit. These four theories make up a very large portion of the theoretical material in the text. If you understand the simple rules of optimization set forth in Chapter 4, you should have little difficulty with later theoretical material. Chapter 5 describes the estimation techniques (regression analysis in particular) that will be used in later empirical analysis. Again, the emphasis here is on interpretation, not calculation. Chapter 6 is concerned with the concepts of risk and uncertainty. Here you will encounter the basic principles that will be used later in situations in which a decision maker does not have complete information about all variables relevant to a decision.

Part III contains both theoretical and empirical material. We first describe the theory of consumer behavior and how consumers choose their purchases in Chapter 7; then, in Chapters 8 and 9, we show how managers can estimate and forecast their demand. Part IV, dealing with production and cost, is also both theoretical and empirical. Chapters 10 and 11 develop the theories of production and discuss how this structure is related to cost. An empirical analysis of production and cost estimation is included in Chapter 12.

Part V is the first of three parts dealing with what is generally called the theory of the firm. We begin with the theory of perfectly competitive firms and industries in Chapter 13; firms attempt to maximize their profits when they have no control over the price they charge. Chapter 14 describes the way such firms can use price and cost estimates to implement the profit-maximizing decision. Part VI examines the behavior of firms with market power—firms that have the freedom to set the price of the product they sell. Chapters 15 and 16 develop, respectively, the theory of monopoly firms—firms with no close competitors—and the theory of imperfectly competitive firms—firms with varying degrees of competition from other firms. Chapter 17 discusses how firms with market power can use cost and demand estimates to implement their profit-maximizing decisions. Part VI ends with a discussion of the behavior of firms that produce in more than one plant, sell in more than one market, and produce more than one type of product. Chapter 18 examines these special topics.

Until this point in the text we were concerned with single-period analysis—firms make decisions that relate to only one period of time. This framework of analysis is extremely useful for most topics in microeconomics, particularly as a first approach. Firms do however make decisions that are relevant over more than one period. This extension, decision making over time, is the subject matter of Part VII. Chapter 19 introduces the tools necessary to include a time dimension into the decision-making process and discusses some topics for which time is an important element. Chapter 20 is concerned with the firm's capital investment decisions and the way these are made.

As you will see, a large portion of this text is devoted to the development of theoretical techniques and analyses, but much of it is also devoted to the application of these techniques and analyses to decision-making problems. Many of these applications are discussed within the main body of the text. We also set off separately many "Illustrations" that are designed to show the relevance of the text material to real firms and industries. The illustrations were taken primarily from articles that appeared in *The Wall Street Journal* during the last few years, although some are from other publications. These illustrations are designed to do precisely what the word implies—to illustrate the importance of economics in understanding how firms behave, and in making managerial decisions. We believe that you will find many of these illustrations interesting and informative.

We want to end this introductory chapter with two final points. First, we want to stress that the text does not assume that students have a background in calculus. The only mathematical training required is a little elementry algebra and the rudiments of geometry—what a graph is and what a line on a graph means—plus some addition, subtraction, multiplication, and division. However, for students with more mathematical background, we provide mathematical expositions in the appendixes to the relevant chapters.

Second, we want to give you a hint to help you learn economics. Economics is best learned by doing economics, in addition to reading and listening. "Doing economics" means working economics problems for yourself. We strongly recommend that, when you are reading graphical or numerical material, you actually work along with the textual exposition as we set forth this material. This approach will provide you with a better understanding of the material than by simply reading it. We also suggest that you work some of the problems provided at the end of each chapter. These problems are designed to reinforce the important concepts presented in the text. Answers are provided for some of the problems at the end of the book.

In closing, we hope you enjoy your course in managerial economics, and even more importantly, we hope you will find it useful in your future professional life.

PART

I

Price Determination in Competitive Markets

CHAPTER 2

Demand, Supply, and Market Equilibrium

CHAPTER 3

Elasticity and Demand

CHAPTER

2 Demand, Supply, and Market Equilibrium

This chapter discusses and analyzes one of the most important topics in economics, and one of the most important concepts for managers: How prices and quantities sold are determined in markets. This topic comes up in all levels of economics courses, from beginning principles to graduate theory courses. A thorough understanding of how markets function and how prices are determined in markets should be a key part of any manager's economics training. You will come across the concepts set forth in this chapter throughout the rest of this text.

market
A formal or informal arrangement in which people exchange goods, services, or productive resources.

Because markets can take on a variety of forms, we suggest an extremely general definition of a market: A **market** is a formal or informal arrangement in which people exchange goods, services, or productive resources. Some examples of formal markets are stock exchanges, bond markets, and commodity markets, in which exchange takes place between people at one location or people linked to that location by telephone or computer. Less formal markets are the clothing market in a particular city, the world automobile market, the real estate market in a state or region, or the national market for beginning accountants. There are a myriad of other markets, more and less organized, broad geographically, and diverse in the type of products exchanged. The important point is that markets exist when exchange takes place between buyers and sellers.

This chapter focuses primarily on the way markets for consumer goods and services function, although the basic concepts apply also to markets for resources, such as labor, land, raw materials, and capital equipment. Supply and demand analysis applies to markets characterized by many buyers and sellers and markets in which a homogeneous or relatively nondifferentiated good or

competitive markets
A market characterized by many buyers and sellers in which a homogeneous good or service is sold.

service is sold. Such markets are called **competitive markets**. As you will see later in the text, many of the principles of competitive markets apply to markets that do not exactly meet all of the specifications of a competitive market.

We begin the analysis of competitive markets by describing the buyer side of the market—called the demand side of the market. Next we describe the seller side—called the supply side. We then put the demand side and the supply side together to show how prices and quantities sold are determined in a market. Finally, we show how forces on the demand side or the supply side of the market can change and thereby affect the price and the quantity sold in a market.

2.1 DEMAND

quantity demanded
The amount of a good or service consumers are willing and able to purchase during a given period of time (week, month, etc.).

The amount of a good or service that consumers in a market are willing and able to purchase during a given period of time (e.g., a week, a month) is called **quantity demanded**. Although economists emphasize the importance of price in purchasing decisions, as we will do, they also recognize that a multitude of factors other than price affect the amount of a good or service people will purchase. However, in order to simplify market analysis and make it manageable, economists ignore those many factors that have an insignificant effect on purchases and concentrate only upon the most important factors. Indeed, only six factors are considered sufficiently important to be included in most studies of market demand.

This section develops two types of demand relations: (1) *generalized demand functions,* which show how quantity demanded is related to product price and five other factors that affect demand, and (2) *ordinary demand functions,* which show the relation between quantity demanded and the price of the product when all other variables affecting demand are held constant at specific values. As you will see in this chapter, ordinary demand functions are derived from generalized demand functions. Traditionally, economists have referred to ordinary demand functions simply as "demand functions" or "demand." We shall follow this tradition.

The Generalized Demand Function

generalized demand function
The relation between quantity demanded and the six factors that affect quantity demanded: $Q_d = f(P, M, P_R, \mathcal{T}, P_e, N)$.

The six principal variables that influence the quantity demanded of a good or service are (1) the price of the good or service, (2) the incomes of consumers, (3) the prices of related goods and services, (4) the tastes or preference patterns of consumers, (5) the expected price of the product in future periods, and (6) the number of consumers in the market. The relation between quantity demanded and these six factors is referred to as the **generalized demand function** and is expressed as follows:

$$Q_d = f(P, M, P_R, \mathcal{T}, P_e, N)$$

where f means "is a function of" or "depends on," and

Q_d = the quantity demanded of the good or service,
P = the price of the good or service,

M = the consumers' income (generally per capita),
P_R = the price of related goods or services,
$\mathscr{T}$ = the taste patterns of consumers,
P_e = the expected price of the good in some future period,
N = the number of consumers in the market.

The generalized demand function shows how all six variables *jointly* determine the quantity demanded. In order to discuss the *individual* effect that any one of these six variables has on Q_d, we must explain how changing just that one variable *by itself* influences Q_d. To isolate the individual effect of a single variable requires that all other variables that affect Q_d be held constant. Thus, whenever we speak of the effect that a particular variable has on quantity demanded, we mean the individual effect *holding all other variables constant*.

We now discuss each of the six variables to show how they are related to the amount of a good or service consumers buy. We begin by discussing the effect of changing the price of a good while holding the other five variables constant. As you would expect, consumers are willing and able to buy more of a good the lower the *price* of the good and will buy less of a good the higher the price of the good. Price and quantity demanded are negatively (inversely) related because, when the price of a good rises, consumers tend to shift from that good to other goods that are now relatively cheaper. Conversely, when the price of a good falls, consumers tend to purchase more of that good and less of other goods that are now relatively more expensive. Price and quantity demanded are inversely related when all other factors are held constant. This relation between price and quantity demanded is so important that we will discuss it in more detail later in this chapter and again in Chapter 7.

normal good
A good or service for which an increase (decrease) in income causes consumers to demand more (less) of the good, holding all other variables in the generalized demand function constant.

inferior good
A good or service for which an increase (decrease) in income causes consumers to demand less (more) of the good, all other factors held constant.

Next consider changes in *income,* again holding constant the rest of the variables that influence consumers. An increase in income can cause the amount of a commodity consumers purchase either to increase or to decrease. If an increase in income causes consumers to demand more of a good, when all other variables in the generalized demand function are held constant, we refer to such a commodity as a **normal good**. A good is also a normal good if a *decrease* in income causes consumers to demand less of the good, all other things held constant. There are some goods and services for which an increase in income would *reduce* consumer demand, other variables held constant. This type of commodity is referred to as an **inferior good**. In the case of inferior goods, rising income causes consumers to demand *less* of the good, and falling income causes consumers to demand *more* of the good. Some examples of goods and services that might be inferior include mobile homes, shoe repair services, generic food products, and used cars.

Commodities may be *related in consumption* in either of two ways—as substitutes or as complements. In general, goods are *substitutes* if one good can be used in the place of the other; an example might be Toyotas and Chryslers. If two goods are substitutes, an increase in the price of one good will increase the demand for the other good. If the price of Toyotas rises while the price of Chryslers remains constant, we would expect consumers to purchase more Chryslers—holding all other factors constant. If an increase in the price of a

substitutes
Two goods are substitutes if an increase (decrease) in the price of one of the goods causes consumers to demand more (less) of the other good, holding all other factors constant.

complements
Two goods are complements if an increase (decrease) in the price of one of the goods causes consumers to demand less (more) of the other good, all other things held constant.

related good causes consumers to demand more of a good, then the two goods are **substitutes**. Similarly, two goods are substitutes if a decrease in the price of one of the goods causes consumers to demand less of the other good, all other things constant.

Goods are said to be *complements* if they are used in conjunction with each other. Examples might be cameras and film, lettuce and salad dressing, or baseball games and hot dogs. A decrease in the price of tickets to the baseball game will increase demand for hot dogs at the game, all else constant. If the demand for one good decreases when the price of a related good increases, the two goods are **complements**. Similarly, two goods are complements if a decrease in the price of one of the goods causes consumers to demand more of the other good, all other things constant.[1]

Expectations of consumers also influence consumers' decisions to purchase goods and services. More specifically, consumers' expectations about the future price of a commodity can change their current purchasing decisions. If consumers expect the price to be higher in a future period, demand will probably rise in the current period. On the other hand, expectations of a price decline in the future will cause some purchases to be postponed—thus, demand in the current period will fall. An example of this can be seen in the automobile industry. Automakers often announce price increases for the next year's models several months before the cars are available in showrooms in order to stimulate demand for the current year's cars.

A change in consumer tastes can change demand for a good or service. Obviously, taste changes could either increase or decrease consumer demand. While consumer tastes are not directly measurable (as are the other variables in the generalized demand function), you may wish to view the variable $\mathscr{T}$ as an index of consumer tastes; $\mathscr{T}$ takes on larger values as consumers perceive a good becoming higher in quality, more fashionable, more healthful, or more desirable in any way. A decrease in $\mathscr{T}$ corresponds to a change in consumer tastes away from a good or service as consumers perceive falling quality, or displeasing appearance, or diminished healthfulness. Consequently, when all other variables in the generalized demand function are held constant, a movement in consumer tastes toward a good or service will increase demand. A movement in consumer tastes away from a good will decrease demand for the good. A change in consumer tastes or preferences occurs when, for example, the *New England Journal of Medicine* publishes research findings that show a higher incidence of cancer among people who regularly eat bacon. This causes the demand for bacon to decrease (the taste index $\mathscr{T}$ declines), all other factors remaining constant.

Finally, an increase in the number of consumers in the market will increase the demand for a good, and a decrease in the number of consumers will decrease the demand for a good, all other factors held constant. In markets that

[1]Not all commodities are either substitutes or complements in consumption. Many commodities are essentially independent. For example, we would not expect the price of lettuce to significantly influence the demand for automobiles. Thus, we can treat these commodities as independent and ignore the price of lettuce when evaluating the demand for automobiles.

experience a growth in the number of buyers—such as the health care industry as the population matures, or Florida during the tourist season—we would expect demand to increase.

The generalized demand function set forth above is expressed in the most general mathematical form. Economists and market researchers often express the generalized demand function in a more specific mathematical form in order to show more precisely the relation between quantity demanded and some of the more important variables that affect demand. They frequently express the generalized demand function in a linear functional form. The following equation is an example of a linear form of the generalized demand function:

$$Q_d = a + bP + cM + dP_R + e\mathcal{T} + fP_e + gN$$

where Q_d, P, M, P_R, $\mathcal{T}$, P_e, and N are as defined above, and a, b, c, d, e, f, and g are parameters.

slope parameters Parameters in a linear function that measure the effect on the dependent variable (Q_d) of changing one of the independent variables (P, M, P_R, $\mathcal{T}$, P_e, and N), while holding the rest of these variables constant.

The intercept parameter a shows the value of Q_d when the variables P, M, P_R, $\mathcal{T}$, P_e, and N are all simultaneously equal to zero. The other parameters b, c, d, e, f, and g are called **slope parameters**: they measure the effect on quantity demanded of changing one of the variables P, M, P_R, $\mathcal{T}$, P_e, or N while holding the rest of these variables constant. The slope parameter b, for example, measures the change in quantity demanded per unit change in price, that is, $b = \Delta Q_d/\Delta P$.[2] As stressed above, Q_d and P are inversely related, and b is negative because ΔQ_d and ΔP have opposite algebraic signs.

The slope parameter c measures the effect on the amount purchased of a one-unit change in income ($c = \Delta Q_d/\Delta M$). For normal goods, sales increase when income rises, so c is positive. If the good is inferior, sales decrease when income rises, so c is negative. The parameter d measures the change in the amount consumers want to buy per unit change in P_R ($d = \Delta Q_d/\Delta P_R$). If an increase in P_R causes sales to rise, the goods are substitutes and d is positive. If an increase in P_R causes sales to fall, the two goods are complements and d is negative. Since $\mathcal{T}$, P_e, and N are each directly related to the amount purchased, the parameters e, f, and g are all positive.[3]

Relation When the generalized demand function is expressed in linear form:

$$Q_d = a + bP + cM + dP_R + e\mathcal{T} + fP_e + gN$$

the slope parameters (b, c, d, e, f, and g) measure the effect on the amount of the good purchased of changing one of the variables (P, M, P_R, $\mathcal{T}$, P_e, and N) while holding the rest of the variables constant. For example, b ($=\Delta Q_d/\Delta P$) measures the change in quantity demanded per unit change in price holding M, P_R, $\mathcal{T}$, P_e, and N constant. When the slope parameter of a specific variable is positive (negative) in sign, quantity demanded is directly (inversely) related to that variable.

[2]The symbol "Δ" means "change in." Thus if quantity demanded rises (falls), then ΔQ_d is positive (negative). Similarly, if price rises (falls), ΔP is positive (negative). In general, the ratio of the change in Y divided by the change in X ($\Delta Y/\Delta X$) measures the change in Y per unit change in X.

[3]Since consumer tastes are not directly measurable as are the other variables, you may wish to view $\mathcal{T}$ as an index of consumer tastes that ranges in value from 0, if consumers think a product is worthless, to a value of 10 if they think the product is extremely desirable. In this case, the parameter e shows the effect on quantity demanded of a one-unit change in the taste index ($\mathcal{T}$), and e is positive.

TABLE 2.1
Summary of the Generalized (linear) Demand Function
$Q_d = a + bP + cM + dP_R + e\mathcal{T} + fP_e + gN$

Variable	Relation to quantity demanded	Sign of slope parameter
P	Inverse	$b = \Delta Q_d/\Delta P$ is negative
M	Direct for normal goods	$c = \Delta Q_d/\Delta M$ is positive
	Inverse for inferior goods	$c = \Delta Q_d/M$ is negative
P_R	Direct for substitute goods	$d = \Delta Q_d/P_R$ is positive
	Inverse for complement goods	$d = \Delta Q_d/\Delta P_R$ is negative
$\mathcal{T}$	Direct	$e = \Delta Q_d/\Delta \mathcal{T}$ is positive
P_e	Direct	$f = \Delta Q_d/\Delta P_e$ is positive
N	Direct	$g = \Delta Q_d/\Delta N$ is positive

Table 2.1 summarizes this discussion of the generalized demand function. Each of the six factors that affect quantity demanded are listed, and the table shows whether the quantity demanded varies directly or inversely with each variable and gives the sign of the slope parameters. Again let us stress that these relations are in the context of all other things being equal. An increase in the price of the commodity will lead to a decrease in quantity demanded as long as the other variables—income, the price of related commodities, consumer tastes, price expectations, and the number of customers—remain constant.

Demand Functions

demand function
A table, graph, or an equation that shows how quantity demanded is related to product price, holding constant the five other variables that influence demand.

The relation between price and quantity demanded per period of time when all other factors that affect consumer demand are held constant, is called a **demand function** or simply **demand**. Demand gives, for various prices of a good, the corresponding quantities that consumers are willing and able to purchase at each of those prices, all other things held constant. The "other things" that are held constant for a specific demand function are the five variables other than price that can affect demand. Demand functions can be expressed as an equation, a schedule or table, or a graph. We begin with a demand equation.

A demand function can be expressed in the most general form as the equation:

$$Q_d = f(P)$$

which means that the quantity demanded is a function of (depends on) the price of the good, holding all other variables constant. A demand function is obtained by holding all the variables in the generalized demand function constant except price:

$$Q_d = f(P;\ M',\ P_R',\ P_e',\ \mathcal{T}',\ N') = f(P)$$

where the prime on the variables to the right of the semicolon means that those variables are held constant at some specified amount no matter what value the product price takes.

Relation A demand function expresses quantity demanded as a function of product price only: $Q_d = f(P)$. Demand functions—whether expressed as equations, tables, or graphs—give the quantity demanded at various prices holding constant the effects of income, price of related goods, consumer tastes, expected price, and the number of consumers. Demand functions are derived from generalized demand functions by holding all the variables in the generalized demand function constant except price.

To illustrate the derivation of a demand function from the generalized demand function, suppose the generalized demand function is

$$Q_d = 280 - 20P + 60M - 50P_R + 20\mathscr{T} + 10P_e + 4N$$

To derive a demand function, $Q_d = f(P)$, the variables M, P_R, $\mathscr{T}$, P_e, and N must be assigned fixed values. Suppose consumer income is $15 (measured in thousands of dollars), the price of a related good is $10, an index of consumer tastes is 8 (perhaps on a scale from one to ten), the expected future price is $6, and the number of consumers in this market is 100 (measured in thousands of buyers). To find the demand function, the fixed values of M, P_R, $\mathscr{T}$, P_e, and N are substituted into the generalized demand function:

$$\begin{aligned} Q_d &= 280 - 20P + 60(15) - 50(10) + 20(8) + 10(6) + 4(100) \\ &= 280 - 20P + 900 - 500 + 160 + 60 + 400 \\ &= 1{,}300 - 20P \end{aligned}$$

Thus the demand function is expressed in the form of a linear demand equation, $Q_d = 1{,}300 - 20P$. The intercept parameter, 1,300, is the amount of the good consumers would demand if price is zero. The slope of this demand function ($= \Delta Q_d/\Delta P$) is –20 and indicates that a $1 increase in price causes quantity demanded to decrease by 20 units. Although not all demand functions are linear, you will see later in the text that the linear form is a frequently used specification for estimating and forecasting demand functions.

The above linear demand equation satisfies all the conditions set forth in the definition of demand. All variables other than product price are held constant—income at $15,000, the price of a related good at $10, tastes at 8, expected price at $6, and the number of consumers at 100,000. At each price, the equation gives the amount that consumers would purchase at that price. For example, if price is $50,

$$Q_d = 1{,}300 - (20 \times 50) = 300$$

or if price is $40,

$$Q_d = 1{,}300 - (20 \times 40) = 500$$

demand schedule
A table showing a list of possible product prices and the corresponding quantities demanded.

A **demand schedule** (or table) shows a list of several prices and the quantity demanded per period of time at each of the prices, again holding all variables other than price constant. Seven prices and their corresponding quantities demanded are shown in Table 2.2. Each of the seven combinations of price and quantity demanded is derived from the demand function exactly as shown above. (You may check this for yourself.)

demand curve A graph showing the relation between quantity demanded and price when all other variables influencing quantity demanded are held constant.

As noted above, the final way of showing a demand function is in a graph. A graphical demand function is called a **demand curve**. The seven price–quantity demanded combinations in Table 2.2 are plotted in Figure 2.1, and these points are connected with the straight line D_0, which is the demand curve associated with the demand equation $Q_d = 1{,}300 - 20P$. This demand curve meets the specifications of the definition of demand. All variables other than price are held constant. The demand curve D_0 gives the value of quantity demanded (on the horizontal axis) for every value of price (on the vertical axis).

TABLE 2.2

The Demand Schedule for the Demand Function D_0: $Q_d = 1{,}300 - 20P$

Price	Quantity demanded
$65	0
60	100
50	300
40	500
30	700
20	900
10	1,100

FIGURE 2.1

A Demand Curve ($Q_d = 1{,}300 - 20P$)

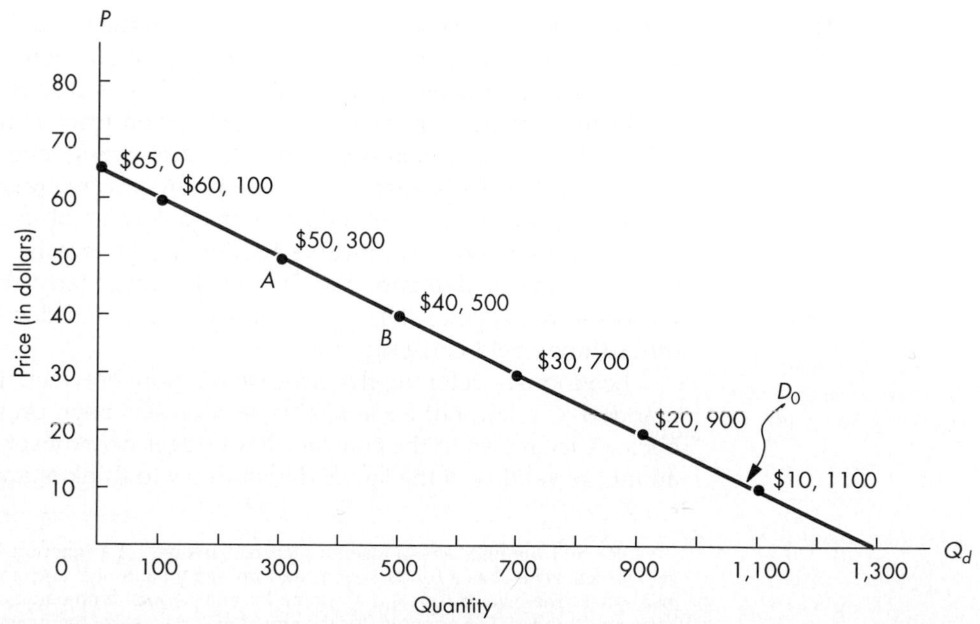

Note that in the graph of the demand equation, $Q_d = 1{,}300 - 20P$, the independent variable P is plotted along the vertical axis, and the dependent variable Q_d is plotted along the horizontal axis. This switch is traditional among economists. Thus the equation plotted in the figure is the inverse of the above demand equation: $P = 65 - 1/20Q_d$.[4] The vertical intercept is 65, indicating that at a price of \$65, consumers will demand zero units of the good. The horizontal intercept is 1,300, which is the maximum amount of the good buyers will take when the good is given away ($P = 0$). The slope of the graphed inverse demand is −1/20, indicating that if quantity demanded rises by one unit, price must fall 1/20 of a dollar (or 5 cents). This inverse, as you can see, yields price-quantity combinations identical to those given by the above demand equation.

Although demand is generally interpreted as indicating the amount that consumers will buy at each price, sometimes managers and market researchers wish to know the highest price that can be charged for any given amount of the product. As it turns out, a point on a demand curve can be interpreted in either of two ways: (1) the maximum amount of a good that will be purchased if a given price is charged, or (2) the maximum price that consumers will pay for a specific amount of a good. Consider, for example, point A (\$50, 300) on the demand curve in Figure 2.1. If the price of the good is \$50, the maximum amount consumers will purchase is 300 units. Equivalently, \$50 is the highest price that consumers can be charged in order to sell 300 units. Sometimes \$50 is called the **demand price** for 300 units, and each price on demand can be called the demand price for the corresponding quantity on the horizontal axis.

demand price
The maximum price consumers can be charged in order to sell a given amount of a good.

The Law of Demand

Before moving on to an analysis of changes in the variables that are held constant when deriving a demand function, we want to reemphasize the relation between price and quantity demanded, which was discussed earlier in this chapter. In the demand equation, the parameter on price is negative; in the demand schedule, price and quantity demanded are inversely related; and in the graph, the demand curve is negatively sloped. This inverse relation between price and quantity demanded is not simply a characteristic of the specific demand function discussed here. This inverse relation is so pervasive that economists refer to it as the **law of demand**: The law of demand states that quantity demanded increases when price falls and quantity demanded decreases when price rises, other things held constant.

law of demand
Quantity demanded increases when price falls, and quantity demanded decreases when price rises, other things held constant.

Economists refer to the inverse relation between price and quantity demanded as a law, not because this relation has been proven mathematically, but because examples to the contrary have never been observed. If you have doubts about the validity of the law of demand, try to think of any goods or services that

[4]Recall from high school algebra that the "inverse" of a function $Y = f(X)$ is the function $X = g(Y)$ which gives X as a function of Y, and the same pairs of Y and X values that satisfy $Y = f(X)$ also satisfy the inverse function $X = g(Y)$. In other words, both equations express the same relation between Y and X. For example, for the equation $Y = 10 + 2X$, the inverse function, $X = 1/2Y - 5$, is found by solving algebraically for X in terms of Y.

you would buy more of if the price were higher, other things being equal. Or, can you imagine someone going to the grocery store expecting to buy one six-pack of Pepsi for $2.50, then noticing that the price is $5.00, and deciding to buy two or three six-packs? You don't see stores advertising higher prices when they want to increase sales or get rid of unwanted inventory.

The principal reason for the inverse relation between price and quantity demanded is that all goods have substitutes. When the price of one good rises, consumers can shift some of their purchases to other goods that serve a similar function. The only electric company in a city faces competition from the gas company in many uses. Even when AT&T was the only long distance telephone company, people could substitute mail for telephone calls, and now AT&T faces intense competition from other long distance phone companies. We believe it will be difficult for you to think of a product that you are now consuming for which there is absolutely no available substitute. We explore in much greater depth the concept of substitution and its relation to the law of demand in Chapter 7.

change in quantity demanded
A movement along a given demand curve that occurs when the price of the good changes, all else constant.

Once a demand function, $Q_d = f(P)$, is derived from a generalized demand function, a **change in quantity demanded** can only be caused by a change in price. The other five variables that influence demand in the generalized demand function (M, P_R, $\mathcal{T}$, P_e, and N) are fixed in value for any particular demand equation. A change in price is represented on a graph by a movement along a fixed demand curve. In Figure 2.1, if price falls from $50 to $40 (and the other variables remain constant), a change in quantity demanded from 300 to 500 units occurs and is illustrated by a movement along D_0 from point A to point B.

Relation For a demand function $Q_d = f(P)$, a change in price causes a change in quantity demanded. The other five variables that influence demand in the generalized demand function (M, P_R, $\mathcal{T}$, P_e, and N) are fixed in value for any particular demand equation. On a graph, a change in price causes a movement along a demand curve from one price to another price.

Shifts in Demand

When any one of the five variables held constant when deriving a demand function from the generalized demand relation changes value, a new demand function results, causing the entire demand curve to *shift* to a new location. To illustrate this extremely important concept, we will show how a change in one of these five variables, such as income, affects a demand schedule.

We begin with the demand schedule from Table 2.2 which is reproduced in columns 1 and 2 of Table 2.3. Recall that the quantities demanded for various product prices were obtained by holding all variables except price constant in the generalized demand function. If income increases from $15,000 to $20,000, quantity demanded increases *at each and every price,* as shown in column 3. When the price is $30, for example, consumers will buy 700 units if their income is $15,000 but will buy 1,000 units if their income is $20,000. In Figure 2.2, D_0 is the demand curve associated with an income level of $15,000, and D_1 is the demand curve after income rises to $20,000. Since the increase in income caused quantity demanded to increase *at every price,* the demand curve shifts to the right from D_0

TABLE 2.3
Three Demand Schedules

(1) Price	(2) D_0 Quantity demanded (M = \$15)	(3) D_1 Quantity demanded (M = \$20)	(4) D_2 Quantity demanded (M = \$10)
\$65	0	300	0
60	100	400	0
50	300	600	0
40	500	800	200
30	700	1,000	400
20	900	1,200	600
10	1,100	1,400	800

increase in demand
A change in the demand function that causes an increase in quantity demanded at every price and is reflected by a rightward shift in the demand curve.

decrease in demand
A change in the demand function that causes a decrease in quantity demanded at every price and is reflected by a leftward shift in the demand curve.

determinants of demand
Variables that change the quantity demanded at each price and that determine where the demand curve is located: M, P_R, $\mathcal{T}$, P_e, and N.

change in demand
A shift in demand, either leftward or rightward, that occurs only when one of the five determinants of demand change.

to D_1 in Figure 2.2. Everywhere along D_1 quantity demanded is greater than along D_0 for equal prices. This change in the demand function is called an **increase in demand.**

A **decrease in demand** occurs when a change in one or more of the variables M, P_R, $\mathcal{T}$, P_e, or N causes the quantity demanded to decrease at every price and the demand curve shifts to the left. Column 4 in Table 2.3 illustrates a decrease in demand caused by income falling to \$10,000. At every price, quantity demanded in column 4 is less than quantity demanded when income is either \$15,000 or \$20,000 (columns 2 and 3, respectively, in Table 2.3). The demand curve in Figure 2.2 when income is \$10,000 is D_2, which lies to the left of D_0 and D_1.

While we have illustrated shifts in demand caused by changes in income, a change in any one of the five variables that are held constant when deriving a demand function will cause a shift in demand. These five variables—M, P_R, $\mathcal{T}$, P_e, and N—are called the **determinants of demand** because they determine where the demand curve is located. A **change in demand** occurs when one or more of the determinants of demand change. Think of M, P_R, $\mathcal{T}$, P_e, and N as the five "demand-shifting" variables. The demand curve shifts to a new location only when one or more of these demand-shifting variables changes.

Relation An increase in demand means that, at each price, more is demanded; a decrease in demand means that, at each price, less is demanded. Demand changes, or shifts, when one of the determinants of demand changes. These determinants of demand are income, prices of related goods, consumer tastes, expected future price, and the number of consumers.

The shifts in demand illustrated in Figure 2.2 were derived mathematically from the generalized demand function. Recall that the demand function D_0 (Q_d = 1,300 – 20P) was derived from the generalized demand function

$$Q_d = 280 - 20P + 60M - 50P_R + 20\mathcal{T} + 10P_e + 4N$$

where the five determinants of demand were held constant at values of $M = 15$, $P_R = 10$, $\mathcal{T} = 8$, $P_e = 6$, and $N = 100$. When income increases from 15 to 20 (that is, from \$15,000 to \$20,000), the new demand equation at this higher income is

FIGURE 2.2
Shifts in Demand

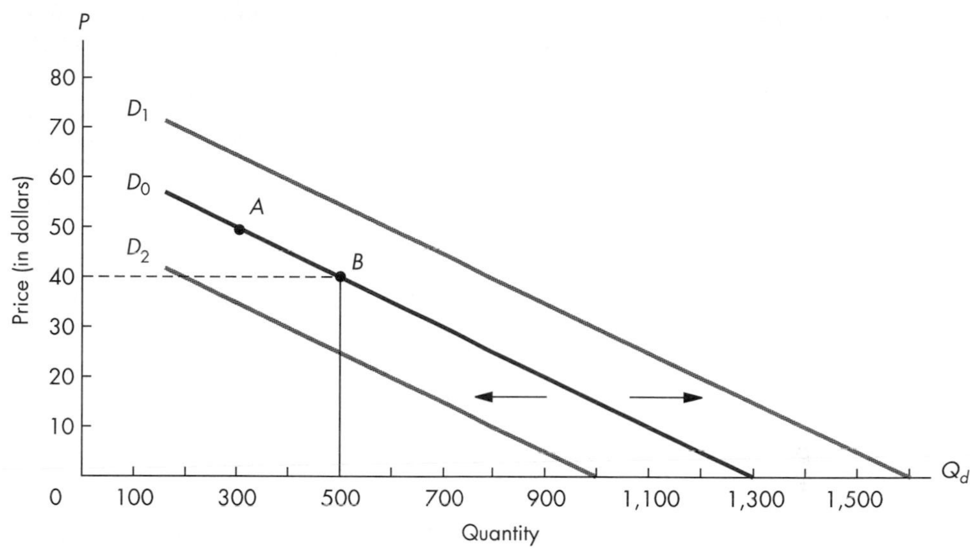

found by substituting $M = 20$ into the generalized demand function and solving for the new demand function:

$$\begin{aligned} Q_d &= 280 - 20P + (60 \times 20) - 500 + 160 + 60 + 400 \\ &= 1{,}600 - 20P \end{aligned}$$

In Figure 2.2, this demand function is shown by the demand curve D_1. At every price, quantity demanded increases by 300 units (1,600 – 1,300 = 300). Each of the quantities in column 3 of Table 2.2 was calculated from the new demand equation $Q_d = 1{,}600 - 20P$. As you can see, every quantity in column 3 is 300 units larger than the corresponding quantity in column 2. Thus, the increase in income has caused an increase in demand.

When income falls from $15,000 to $10,000, demand shifts from D_0 to D_2. We leave the derivation of the demand function for D_2 as an exercise. The procedure, however, is identical to the process set forth above.

From the preceding discussion, you may have noticed that the direction in which demand shifts when one of the five demand determinants changes depends upon the sign of the slope parameter on that variable in the generalized demand function. The increase in income caused quantity demanded to rise for all prices because $\Delta Q_d/\Delta M$ (= +60) is positive, which indicates that a $1,000 increase in income causes a 60-unit increase in quantity demanded at every price level. Since income increased by $5,000 in this example ($M$ increases from 15 to 20), quantity demanded increases by 300 units (= 5 × 60). Thus, when the slope parameter on M is positive in the generalized demand function, an increase in income causes an increase in demand. As explained earlier, when income and quantity demanded are positively related *in the generalized demand*

TABLE 2.4
Summary of Demand Shifts

Determinants of demand	Demand increases*	Demand decreases†	Sign of slope parameter‡
1. Income (M)			
Normal good	M rises	M falls	$c > 0$
Inferior good	M falls	M rises	$c < 0$
2. Price of related good (P_R)			
Substitute good	P_R rises	P_R falls	$d > 0$
Complement good	P_R falls	P_R rises	$d < 0$
3. Consumer tastes ($\mathcal{T}$)	$\mathcal{T}$ rises	$\mathcal{T}$ falls	$e > 0$
4. Expected price (P_e)	P_e rises	P_e, falls	$f > 0$
5. Number of consumers (N)	N rises	N falls	$g > 0$

*Demand increases when the demand curve shifts rightward.
†Demand decreases when the demand curve shifts leftward.
‡This column gives the sign of the corresponding slope parameter in the generalized demand function.

function, the good is a normal good. If the parameter on M is negative, an increase in income causes a decrease in demand, and the good is an inferior good.[5]

Consider now the slope parameter on the price of a related good. Returning once more to the previous numerical example, recall that the slope parameter for P_R in the generalized demand function is equal to –50, which means that a one-dollar increase in the price of the related good causes quantity demanded to decrease by 50 units at every product price. In other words, an increase in the price of the related good causes the demand curve to shift to the left. As explained earlier, when P_R and Q_d are inversely related in the generalized demand function, the two goods are complements. Had the parameter for P_R been positive, the price of the related good and quantity demanded would be directly related, an increase in the price of the related good would shift demand to the right, and the two goods would be substitutes.

For $\mathcal{T}$, P_e, and N the slope parameters are all positive in the generalized demand function, and an increase in any one of these variables causes demand to increase. A decrease in either $\mathcal{T}$, P_e, or N causes a decrease in demand. Table 2.4 summarizes this discussion for all five of the determinants of demand.

2.2 SUPPLY

The amount of a good or service offered for sale in a market depends upon an extremely large number of variables. Similar to the case of demand, economists ignore all of the relatively unimportant variables in order to concentrate upon those variables that have the greatest effect on quantity supplied. In general,

[5]It is only correct to speak of a change in income affecting *quantity demanded* when referring to the generalized demand function. Once income has been held constant to derive a demand function, a change in income causes a change in demand (a shift in the demand curve), not a change in quantity demanded. The same distinction holds for the other determinants of demand P_R, $\mathcal{T}$, P_e, and N.

economists assume that the quantity of a good offered for sale depends upon six major variables:

1. The price of the good itself.
2. The price of the inputs used to produce the good.
3. The prices of goods related in production.
4. The level of available technology.
5. The expectations of the producers concerning the future price of the good.
6. The number of firms producing the good.

The Generalized Supply Function

generalized supply function The relation between quantity supplied and the six factors that jointly affect quantity supplied: $Q_s = g(P, P_i, P_r, T, P_e, F)$.

The **generalized supply function** shows how all six of these variables *jointly* determine the quantity supplied. The generalized supply function is expressed mathematically as

$$Q_s = g(P, P_i, P_r, T, P_e, F)$$

The quantity of a good or service offered for sale (Q_s) is determined not only by the price of the good or service (P), but also by the prices of the inputs used in production (P_i), the prices of goods that are related in production (P_r), the level of available technology (T), the expectations of producers concerning the future price of the good (P_e), and the number of firms (F). The symbol g is used as "a function of" to distinguish the supply relation from the generalized demand function.

Now we consider how each of the six variables is related to the quantity of a good or service firms produce. We begin by discussing the effect of a change in the price of a good while holding the other five variables constant. Typically, the higher the price of the product, the greater the quantity firms wish to produce and sell, all other things being equal. Conversely, the lower the price, the smaller the quantity firms will wish to produce and sell. Producers are induced by higher prices to produce and sell more, while lower prices tend to discourage production. Thus, price and quantity supplied are, in general, directly related.

An increase in the price of one or more of the inputs used to produce the product will obviously increase the cost of production. If the cost rises, the good becomes less profitable, and producers will want to supply a smaller quantity at each price. Conversely, a decrease in the price of one or more of the inputs used to produce the product will decrease the cost of production. When cost falls, the good becomes more profitable, and producers will want to supply a larger amount at each price. Therefore, an increase in the price of an input causes a decrease in production, while a decrease in the price of an input would cause an increase in production.

substitutes in production Goods for which an increase in the price of one good relative to the price of another good causes producers to increase production of the now higher priced good and decrease the production of the other good.

Changes in the prices of goods that are related in production may affect producers in either one of two ways, depending on whether the goods are substitutes or complements in production. Two goods, X and Y, are **substitutes in production** if an increase in the price of good X relative to good Y causes pro-

ILLUSTRATION 2.1

Effects of Changes in Determinants of Demand on Price and Sales

Much of the discussion of demand theory in this chapter concerned the effects of changes in the determinants of demand, or demand-shifting variables, on demand functions, and the consequent effects of these shifts on prices and sales. Some actual examples of these effects, all of which were reported in recent issues of *The Wall Street Journal*, should illustrate and reinforce this theoretical analysis. These examples illustrate the consequences of changes in income for both normal and inferior goods, changes in the price of a related good (both substitutes and complements), changes in taste, and changes in expectations. These examples also provide some insight into the way that managers can adjust to such changes in a way that benefits the firm.

Changes in Income

During the fall of 1991 and the spring of 1992, the US economy was in a slump or recession. During a recession, people who lose their jobs obviously suffer reduced income, as do many people who are able to continue their employment. In January 1992 the *Journal* noted that, while the furniture business is typically hard hit by a recession, the downturn of 1991 was even worse for furniture stores. The layoffs had ". . . devastated white-collar workers, usually furniture stores' best customers, because they have the most discretionary income. And many professionals who haven't lost their jobs are too nervous to splurge on [high-priced furniture]."

In the first 10 months of 1991, furniture sales fell 6 percent and more than 1,800 stores went out of business, up 21 percent from store failures in the same period the previous year. And it wasn't just the smaller stores that closed. Several large chains went bankrupt and others drastically reduced their number of stores. Many survivors were barely hanging on.

Furniture is a normal good that is extremely sensitive to income changes. The *Journal* pointed out an important, but probably obvious reason for the extreme sensitivity of furniture sales to income. Furniture purchases can generally be postponed until financial conditions improve. As one corporate executive noted, "If it's not a necessity, people are waiting for values."

If firms selling normal goods are harmed by a slump in the economy, one might expect firms selling inferior goods to prosper. Two days after the above article on declining furniture sales the *WSJ* reported, "Housewares entrepreneurs are finding a way to thrive in the recession: hitch your star to the back-to-basics trend . . . While sales of furniture and big-ticket appliances suffer, some business owners find their customers are actually stepping up purchases of inexpensive housewares." Several manufacturers were reporting large increases in sales and some chains were opening new stores.

The owner of one such firm said his items were hot, ". . . because consumers are eating out less to save money and want things to make cooking at home easier." A marketing professor agrees, noting that, "Consumers tell themselves, 'If I'm going to stay at home, I want it to be enjoyable. Why suffer?' "

Another group of firms that benefited when the recession led many people to cut down on eating out were restaurants that featured takeout services. Families, particularly two-career couples, that decreased their visits to sit-down restaurants often did not want to cook dinner, so opted for something that was less expensive than dining out and easier than cooking. The *WSJ* reported that the "sit-down" share of the restaurant business was shrinking while the takeout share was increasing rapidly. Restaurants that competed in both markets were finding that their off-premises sales were rising while their on-premises sales were falling. Even restaurants that had not previously offered takeout service were now being practically forced into this segment of the market.

These two examples of goods that experienced an increase in sales as incomes fell illustrate that inferior goods do not necessarily mean that the good or service is somehow undesirable or inferior in quality. Most people purchase housewares and takeout food orders from time to time. But when a decrease in income causes people to purchase less of some thing, such as furniture or full-service restaurant meals, they frequently buy more of a lower priced good that they consider a substitute.

Changes in Price of Related Goods

Rail and air transportation provide excellent illustrations of the relation between the sales of one product and the price of a substitute product. The *WSJ* reported that in the summer of 1992 ridership on Amtrak dropped dramatically, falling 13 percent in June, the largest monthly decrease since 1980. Amtrak estimated that a large part of the summer decline was due to the lower fares offered by airlines. According to the *Journal*, "At the beginning of the '90s, travelers outraged with high airfares flocked to the railroad; ridership hit an all-time high in 1990 and was at its second highest ever in 1991." In October 1993, the *Journal* noted that train travel had increased and Amtrak was expected to achieve sales close to those in the record year 1990. Amtrak's explanation for the increase—an increase in business trips and higher airfares.

While the relation between gasoline prices and automobile travel is obvious, bicycles and gasoline are related also, but in a different way. In 1991, the *WSJ* reported that the number of people who were biking to work had more than doubled. While environmental and health concerns had played a role in the increase, "Rising fuel and public transportation costs are the main reason commuters are bicycling more." Thus bicycles appear to be substitutes for gasoline and public transportation.

In January 1992, rumors that the Bush administration was close to a deal that would send large quantities of meat to the Commonwealth of Independent States (the former Soviet republics) spurred cattle futures prices. According to the rumors, the bulk of the meat to be shipped was pork. As the *WSJ* noted, "One quirk amid yesterday's export speculation was that although it involved pork, it had a stronger impact on cattle futures. Analysts attributed this to demand relationships between the cash markets for cattle and pork that have little to do with the supply of cattle available at the moment." The analysts recognized that pork and beef are probably substitutes. The reduction in the domestic supply of pork after the large shipment would probably increase the price of pork, and consequently increase the demand for beef, which at that time was relatively weak. Therefore, cattle futures prices rose based upon the rumor.

Changes in Taste

As we stressed, consumer taste is an important determinant of demand. An important determinant of the consumer tastes in an economy is the age structure of people in the economy (obvious, once it is pointed out, but perhaps not so obvious otherwise). As people age, their income and spending rise through middle age, then decline thereafter. Thus, an economy consisting of a large proportion of people in middle age would purchase more goods and services than another economy with a much younger population, other things equal.

Apart from income alone, however, people in different age groups have different spending patterns. The *WSJ* pointed out some of these differences. People in the 45 to 55 age group, who are likely to have grown children either in college or working and living at home, spend more than any other group on food eaten away from home, transportation, entertainment, and education. They also contribute more to charity and spend more on pensions and insurance. People in the 55 to 64 group spend less than those 45 to 55 in most categories, with the notable exception being health care. People in the 35 to 45 group, who are likely to have school-age children at home, outspend all other groups on food used at home, housing, and clothing. They also spend more on alcohol. It follows, therefore, that as the age structure in a city, a region, or a country changes, the demands for different goods and services shift, reflecting the influence of the shifting taste patterns.

Changes in Price Expectations

One would expect that expectations about the future price of a good would have an insignificant effect on the price of some goods, such as bread, movies, pizza, and other goods that are not durable or expensive. Price expectations would have a stronger effect on the demand for more durable, higher-priced goods, such as automobiles, jewelry, and major appliances. In a 1992 article about the bankruptcy of a huge Canadian real estate company, the *Journal* stated, "More than any other business, real estate is dependent upon people's expectations about the future. When those

ILLUSTRATION 2.1

(*concluded*)

expectations are hopeful, . . . the value of real estate soars. When those expectations turn gloomy, . . . real estate values crash."

Later in the article, the *Journal* asked, "But where do these expectations come from? There is a tendency to dismiss them as irrational, mere 'animal spirits'." The answer: "Most of the time, though, expectations come from the market's sifting of the best judgments of tens of thousands of highly intelligent people. And the best judgments are drab and dismal compared to those of the middle 1980s."

These illustrations should give you some idea of the way that changes in the determinants of demand actually shift the demand for goods and services and how such shifts affect the price and sales of the products. They should also give an insight into how managers can forecast and react to such changes in a manner that furthers the goals of the organization.

Sources: Jeffrey Taylor, "Cattle Prices Rise, Boosted by Rumors that US Is Close to Setting Deal to Send Meat to C.I.S.," *The Wall Street Journal*, 1992. "How Spending Changes during Middle Age," *The Wall Street Journal*, 1992. David Frum, "Real Estate, Victim of the '90s," *The Wall Street Journal*, 1992. Jeffrey Taylor, "Pork-Belly Market Is Seeing Leaner Days," *The Wall Street Journal*, 1992. Suzanne Alexander, "Riding a Bike to Work Gains in Popularity," *The Wall Street Journal*, 1992. "Amtrak's Ridership Is Back on the Rails," *The Wall Street Journal*, 1993. "Good News for Planes, Bad News for Trains," *The Wall Street Journal*, 1992. James S. Hirsch, "Tough Economic Times Are Knocking Stuffing Out of Many Furniture Stores," *The Wall Street Journal*, 1993. Kevin Helliker, "Forget Candlelight, Flowers—and Tips: More Restaurants Tout Takeout Service," *The Wall Street Journal*, 1992. Barbara Marsh, "Recession Apparently Spares Housewares Industry," *The Wall Street Journal*, 1992.

ducers to increase production of good X and decrease production of good Y. For example, if the price of corn increases, while the price of wheat remains the same, some farmers may change from growing wheat to growing corn, and less wheat will be supplied. In the case of manufactured goods, firms can switch resources from the production of one good to the production of a substitute (in production) commodity when the price of the substitute rises. Alternatively, two goods X and Y, are **complements in production** if an increase in the price of good X causes producers to supply more of good Y. For example, crude oil and natural gas often occur in the same oil field, making natural gas a by-product of producing crude oil, or vice versa. If the price of crude oil rises, petroleum firms produce more oil, so the output of natural gas also increases. Other examples of complements in production include nickel and copper (which occur in the same deposit), beef and leather hides, and bacon and pork chops.

complements in production Goods for which an increase in the price of one good, relative to the price of another good, causes producers to increase production of both goods.

technology The state of knowledge concerning the combination of resources to produce goods and services.

Next consider changes in the level of available technology. **Technology** is that state of knowledge concerning how to combine resources to produce goods and services. An improvement in the state of technology would lower the costs of production, which would increase the supply of the good to the market, all other things remaining the same. Even though measuring technology is rather complicated, you can view advances in technology as leading to lower costs and greater supply of the good.

A firm's decision about its level of production depends not only on the current price of the good but also upon the firm's *expectation* about the future price

TABLE 2.5
Summary of the Generalized (linear) Supply Function
$Q_s = h + kP + lP_i + mP_r + nT + rP_e + sF$

Variable	Relation to quantity supplied	Sign of slope parameter
P	Direct	$k = \Delta Q_s/\Delta P$ is positive
P_i	Inverse	$l = \Delta Q_s/\Delta P_i$ is negative
P_r	Inverse for substitutes in production (wheat and corn)	$m = \Delta Q_s/P_r$ is negative
	Direct for complements in production (oil and gas)	$m = \Delta Q_s/\Delta P_r$ is positive
T	Direct	$n = \Delta Q_s/\Delta T$ is positive
P_e	Inverse	$r = \Delta Q_s/\Delta P_e$ is negative
F	Direct	$s = \Delta Q_s/\Delta F$ is positive

of the good. If firms expect the price of a good they produce to rise in the future, they may withhold some of the good, thereby reducing supply of the good in the current period. Finally, if the number of firms in the industry increases, more of the good or service will be supplied at each price. Conversely, a decrease in the number of firms in the industry decreases the supply of the good, all other things remaining constant.

As in the case of demand, economists often find it useful to express the generalized supply function in linear functional form:

$$Q_s = h + kP + lP_i + mP_r + nT + rP_e + sF,$$

where Q_s, P, P_i, P_r, T, P_e, and F are defined as above, h is an intercept parameter, and k, l, m, n, r, and s are slope parameters. Table 2.5 summarizes this discussion of the generalized supply function. Each of the six factors that affect production are listed along with the relation to quantity supplied (direct or inverse). Let us again stress that, just as in the case of demand, these relations are in the context of all other things being equal.

supply function
A table, graph, or an equation that shows how quantity supplied is related to product price, holding constant the five other variables that influence supply.

determinants of supply
Variables that cause a change in supply (i.e., a shift in the supply curve).

change in quantity supplied
A movement along a given supply curve that occurs when the price of a good changes.

Supply Functions

Just as demand functions are derived from the generalized demand function, supply functions are derived from the generalized supply function. A **supply function** shows the relation between Q_s and P holding the **determinants of supply** (P_i, P_r, T, P_e, and F) constant:

$$Q_s = g(P; P_i', P_r', T', P_e', F') = g(P)$$

where the "prime" means the determinants of supply are held constant at some specified value. Once a supply function $Q_s = g(P)$ is derived from a generalized supply function, a **change in quantity supplied** can only be caused by a change in price.

Relation A supply function expresses quantity supplied as a function of product price only: $Q_s = g(P)$. Supply functions give the quantity supplied for various prices holding constant the effects of input prices, prices of goods related in production, the state of technology, expected price, and the number of firms in the industry. Supply functions are derived from generalized supply functions by holding all the variables in the generalized supply function constant except price.

To illustrate the derivation of a supply function from the generalized supply function, suppose the generalized supply function is

$$Q_s = 50 + 10P - 8P_i + 5F$$

Technology, the prices of goods related in production, and the expected price of the product in the future have been omitted to simplify this illustration. Suppose the price of an important input is $50, and there are currently 90 firms in the industry producing the product. To find the supply function, the fixed values of P_i and F are substituted into the generalized supply function:

$$\begin{aligned} Q_s &= 50 + 10P - 8(50) + 5(90) \\ &= 100 + 10P \end{aligned}$$

The linear supply function gives the quantity supplied for various product prices, holding constant the other variables that affect supply. For example, if the price of the product is $20,

$$Q_s = 100 + 10(20) = 300$$

or if the price is $50,

$$Q_s = 100 + 10(50) = 600$$

supply schedule
A table showing a list of possible product prices and the corresponding quantities supplied.

supply curve
A graph showing the relation between quantity supplied and price, when all other variables influencing quantity supplied are held constant.

A **supply schedule** (or table) shows a list of several prices and the quantity supplied at each of the prices, again holding all variables other than price constant. Table 2.6 shows seven prices and their corresponding quantities supplied. Each of the seven price–quantity supplied combinations are derived, as shown above, from the supply equation $Q_s = 100 + 10P$, which was derived from the generalized supply function by setting $P_i = \$50$ and $F = 90$. Figure 2.3 graphs the **supply curve** associated with this supply equation and supply schedule. As with

TABLE 2.6
The Supply Schedule for the Supply Function S_0: $Q_s = 100 + 10P$

Price	Quantity supplied
$65	750
60	700
50	600
40	500
30	400
20	300
10	200

demand curves, price is shown on the vertical axis and quantity on the horizontal axis. Thus the equation plotted in the figure is the inverse of the supply equation: $P = -10 + 1/10Q$. The slope of this inverse supply equation graphed in Figure 2.3 is $\Delta P/\Delta Q_s$, which equals 1/10 and is the reciprocal of the slope parameter k (= $\Delta Q_s/\Delta P = 10$).

Any particular combination of price and quantity supplied on a supply curve can be interpreted in either of two equivalent ways. A point on the supply schedule indicates either (1) the maximum amount of a good or service that will be offered for sale at a specific price, or (2) the minimum price necessary to induce producers voluntarily to offer a given quantity for sale. This minimum price is sometimes referred to as the **supply price** for that level of output.

supply price
The minimum price necessary to induce producers voluntarily to offer a given quantity for sale.

change in quantity supplied
A movement along a given supply curve that occurs when the price of the good changes, all else constant.

As in the case of a demand function, once a supply equation, $Q_s = g(P)$, is derived from a generalized supply function, a **change in quantity supplied** can only be caused by a change in price. A change in quantity supplied represents a movement along a given supply curve. Consider the supply curve S_0 in Figure 2.3. If product price rises from \$20 to \$30, the quantity supplied increases from 300 to 400 units, a movement from point R to point S along the supply curve S_0.

Relation For a supply function $Q_s = g(P)$, a change in price causes a change in quantity supplied. The other five variables that affect supply in the generalized supply function (P_i, P_r, T, P_e, F) are fixed in value for any particular supply equation. On a graph, a change in price causes a movement along a supply curve from one price to another price.

FIGURE 2.3
A Supply Curve ($Q_s = 100 + 10P$)

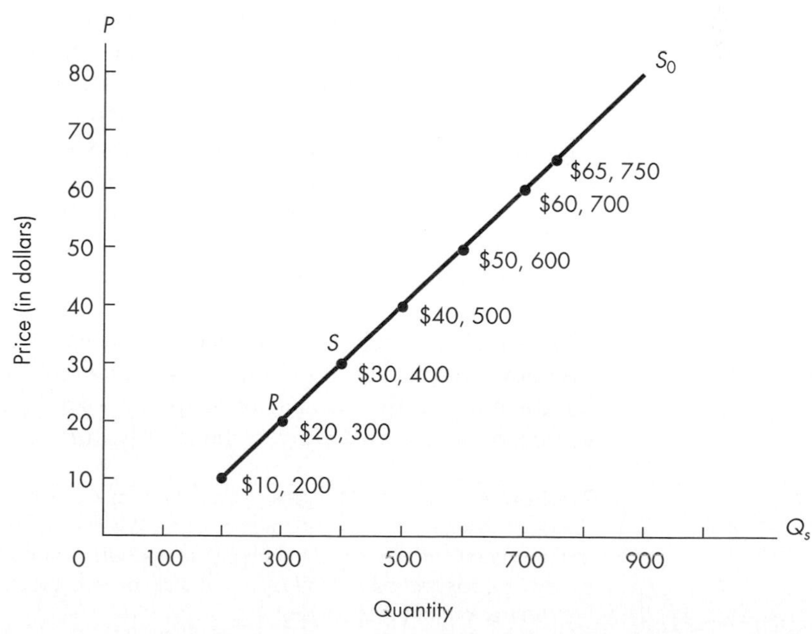

TABLE 2.7
Three Supply Schedules

(1) Price	(2) S_0 Quantity supplied $Q_s = 100 + 10P$ (P_i = \$50, F = 90)	(3) S_1 Quantity supplied $Q_s = 250 + 10P$ (P_i = \$31.25, F = 90)	(4) S_2 Quantity supplied $Q_s = -200 + 10P$ (P_i = \$50, F = 30)
\$65	750	900	450
60	700	850	400
50	600	750	300
40	500	650	200
30	400	550	100
20	300	450	0
10	200	350	0

Shifts in Supply

As we differentiate between a change in quantity demanded due to a change in price and a shift in demand because of a change in one of the determinants of demand, we must make the same distinction with supply. A shift in supply occurs only when one of the five determinants of supply (P_i, P_r, T, P_e, F) changes value. An increase in the number of firms in the industry, for example, causes the quantity supplied to increase at every price so that the supply curve shifts to the right, and this circumstance is called an **increase in supply**. A decrease in the number of firms in the industry causes a **decrease in supply**, and the supply curve shifts to the left. We can illustrate shifts in supply by examining the effect on the supply function of changes in the values of the determinants of supply.

increase in supply
A change in the supply function that causes an increase in quantity supplied at every price, and is reflected by a rightward shift in the supply curve.

decrease in supply
A change in the supply function that causes a decrease in quantity supplied at every price, and is reflected by a leftward shift in the supply curve.

Table 2.6 is reproduced in columns 1 and 2 of Table 2.7. If the price of the input falls to \$31.25, the new supply function is $Q_s = 250 + 10P$, and the quantity supplied increases *at each and every price* as shown in column 3. This new supply curve when the price of the input falls to \$31.25 is shown as S_1 in Figure 2.4 and lies to the right of S_0 at every price. Thus, the decrease in P_i causes the supply curve to shift rightward, which illustrates an increase in supply. To illustrate a decrease in supply, suppose the price of the input remains at \$50, but the number of firms in the industry decreases to 30 firms. The supply function is now $Q_s = -200 + 10P$, and quantity supplied decreases *at every price* as shown in column 4. The new supply curve in Figure 2.4, S_2, lies to the left of S_0 at every price. Thus, the decrease in the number of firms causes a decrease in supply which is represented by a leftward shift in the supply curve.

Relation An increase in supply means that, at each price, more of the good is supplied; a decrease in supply means that, at each price, less is supplied. Supply changes (or shifts) when one of the determinants of supply changes. These determinants of supply are the price of inputs, the price of goods related in production, the state of technology, the expected price in the future, and the number of firms in the industry.

FIGURE 2.4
Shifts in Supply

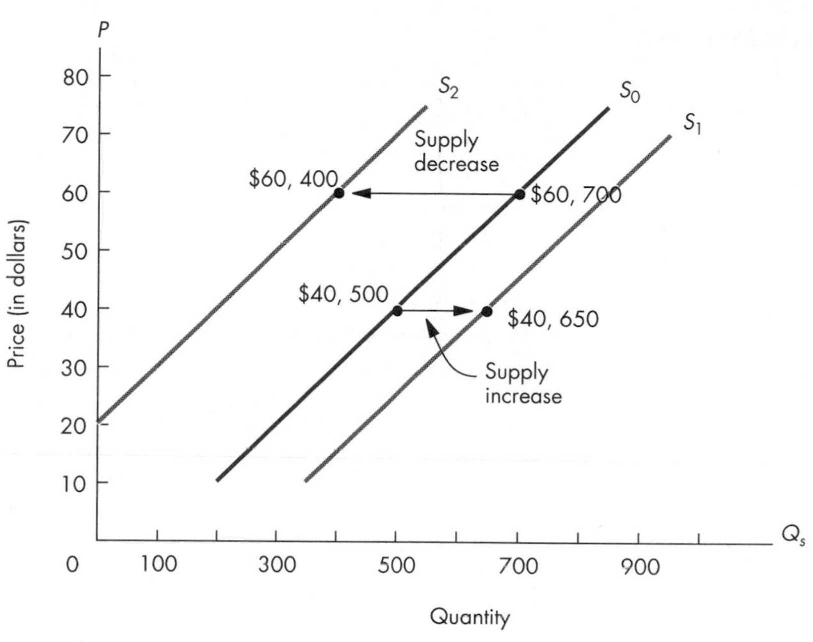

As in the case of demand, the direction in which a supply curve shifts when one of the determinants of supply changes value depends upon the sign of the slope parameter in the generalized supply function. In the above example, when the input price falls to $31.25, quantity supplied increases for every price because the slope parameter for P_i is negative ($l = -8$). Thus, a fall in the price of the input causes an increase in supply. Table 2.8 summarizes this discussion of shifts in supply.

2.3 MARKET EQUILIBRIUM

market equilibrium
A situation in which, at the prevailing price, consumers can buy all of a good they wish and producers can sell all of the good they wish. The price at which $Q_d = Q_s$.

equilibrium price
The price at which $Q_d = Q_s$.

equilibrium quantity
The amount of a good bought and sold in market equilibrium.

Demand and supply provide an analytical framework for the analysis of the behavior of buyers and sellers in markets. Demand shows how buyers respond to changes in price and other variables that determine quantities buyers are willing and able to purchase. Supply shows how sellers respond to changes in price and other variables that determine quantities offered for sale. The interaction of buyers and sellers in the marketplace leads to **market equilibrium**. Market equilibrium is a situation in which, *at the prevailing price*, consumers can buy all of a good they wish and producers can sell all of the good they wish. In other words, equilibrium occurs when price is at a level for which quantity demanded equals quantity supplied. In equilibrium, the price is called **equilibrium price** and the quantity sold is called **equilibrium quantity**.

To illustrate how market equilibrium is achieved, we can use the demand and supply schedules set forth in the preceeding sections. Table 2.9 shows both

TABLE 2.8
Summary of Supply Shifts

Determinants of supply	Supply increases*	Supply decreases†	Sign of slope parameter‡
1. Price of inputs (P_i)	P_i falls	P_i rises	$l < 0$
2. Price of goods related in production (P_r)			
Substitute good	P_r falls	P_r rises	$m < 0$
Complement good	P_r rises	P_r falls	$m > 0$
3. State of technology (T)	T rises	T falls	$n > 0$
4. Expected price (P_e)	P_e falls	P_e rises	$r < 0$
5. Number of firms in industry (F)	N rises	N falls	$s > 0$

*Supply increases when the supply curve shifts rightward.
†Supply decreases when the supply curve shifts leftward.
‡This column gives the sign of the corresponding slope parameter in the generalized supply function.

TABLE 2.9
Market Equilibrium

(1) Price	(2) S_0 Quantity supplied ($Q_s = 100 + 10P$)	(3) D_0 Quantity demanded ($Q_d = 1{,}300 - 20P$)	(4) Excess supply (+) or excess demand (–) ($Q_s - Q_d$)
$65	750	0	+750
60	700	100	+600
50	600	300	+300
40	500	500	0
30	400	700	–300
20	300	900	–600
10	200	1,100	–900

excess supply (surplus) Exists when quantity supplied exceeds quantity demanded.

excess demand (shortage) Exists when quantity demanded exceeds quantity supplied.

the demand schedule for D_0 (given in Table 2.2) and the supply schedule for S_0 (given in Table 2.6). As the table shows, equilibrium in the market occurs when price is $40 and both quantity demanded and quantity supplied are equal to 500 units. At every price above $40, quantity supplied is greater than quantity demanded. **Excess supply** or a **surplus** exists when the quantity supplied exceeds the quantity demanded. The first three entries in column 4 of Table 2.9 show the excess supply or surplus at each price above $40. At every price below $40, quantity supplied is less than quantity demanded. A situation in which quantity demanded exceeds quantity supplied is called **excess demand** or a **shortage.** The last three entries in column 4 of the table show the excess demand or shortage at each price below the $40 equilibrium price. Excess demand and excess supply equal zero only in equilibrium. In equilibrium the market "clears" in the sense that buyers can purchase all they want and sellers can sell all they want at the equilibrium price. Because of this clearing of the market, equilibrium price is sometimes called the **market clearing price**.

market clearing price
The price of a good at which buyers can purchase all they want and sellers can sell all they want at that price. This is another name for the equilibrium price.

Before moving on to a graphical analysis of equilibrium, we want to reinforce the concepts illustrated in Table 2.9 by using the demand and supply functions from which the table was derived. To this end, recall that the demand equation is $Q_d = 1{,}300 - 20P$, and the supply equation is $Q_s = 100 + 10P$. Since equilibrium requires that $Q_d = Q_s$, in equilibrium,

$$1{,}300 - 20P = 100 + 10P$$

Solving this equation for equilibrium price,

$$1{,}200 = 30P$$
$$P = \$40$$

At the market clearing price of $40,

$$Q_d = 1{,}300 - (20 \times 40) = 500$$
$$Q_s = 100 + (10 \times 40) = 500$$

As expected, these mathematically derived results are identical to those presented in Table 2.9.

According to Table 2.9, when price is $50, there is a surplus of 300 units. Using the demand and supply equations, when $P = 50$,

$$Q_d = 1{,}300 - (20 \times 50) = 300$$
$$Q_s = 100 + (10 \times 50) = 600$$

Therefore, when price is $50,

$$Q_s - Q_d = 600 - 300 = 300$$

which is the result shown in column 4.

To express the equilibrium solution graphically, Figure 2.5 shows the demand curve D_0 and the supply curve S_0 associated with the schedules in Table 2.9. These are also the demand and supply curves previously shown in Figures 2.1 and 2.3. Clearly, $40 and 500 units are the equilibrium price and quantity. Only at a price of $40 does quantity demanded equal quantity supplied.

Market forces will drive price toward $40. If price is $50, producers want to supply 600 units while consumers only demand 300 units. An excess supply of 300 units develops. Producers must lower price in order to keep from accumulating unwanted inventories. At any price above $40, excess supply results, and producers will lower price.

If price is $20, consumers are willing and able to purchase 900 units, while producers offer only 300 units for sale. An excess demand of 600 units results. Since their demands are not satisfied, consumers bid the price up. Any price below $40 leads to an excess demand, and the shortage induces consumers to bid up the price.

Given no outside influences that prevent price from being bid up or down, an equilibrium price and quantity is attained. This equilibrium price is the price

FIGURE 2.5
Market Equilibrium

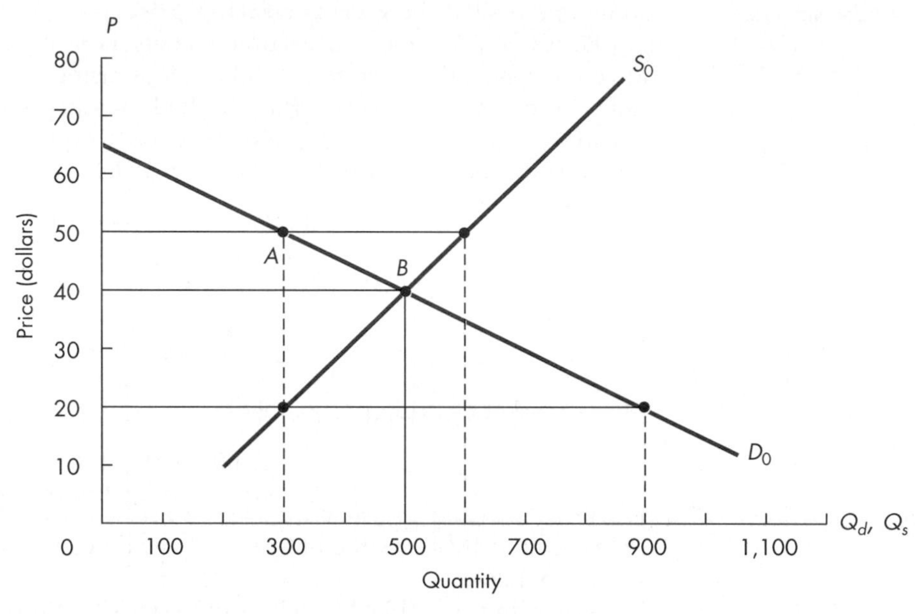

that clears the market; both excess demand and excess supply are zero in equilibrium. Equilibrium is attained in the market because of the following:

Principle The equilibrium price is that price at which quantity demanded is equal to quantity supplied. When the current price is above the equilibrium price, quantity supplied exceeds quantity demanded. The resulting excess supply induces sellers to reduce price in order to sell the surplus. If the current price is below equilibrium, quantity demanded exceeds quantity supplied. The resulting excess demand causes the unsatisfied consumers to bid up price. Since prices below equilibrium are bid up by consumers and prices above equilibrium are lowered by producers, the market will converge to the equilibrium price-quantity combination.

A final point about market equilibrium should be made before moving on to changes in equilibrium in the next section. It is crucial for you to understand that in the analysis of demand and supply there will never be either a permanent shortage or surplus as long as price is allowed to adjust freely to the equilibrium level. In other words, assuming that market price adjusts *quickly* to the equilibrium level, surpluses or shortages do not occur in free markets. In the absence of impediments to the adjustment of prices (such as government imposed price ceilings or floors), the market is always assumed to clear. This assumption greatly simplifies demand and supply analysis. Indeed, how many instances of surpluses or shortages have you seen in markets where prices can adjust freely? The duration of any surpluses or shortages is generally short enough that we can reasonably ignore the adjustment period for purposes of demand and supply analysis.

ILLUSTRATION 2.2

Do Buyers Really Bid Up Prices?

We have emphasized that when a surplus exists unwanted inventories accumulate and sellers lower prices. And, when there is a shortage, consumers, unable to buy all they want at the going price, bid up the price. It's easy to see that a surplus would induce sellers to lower the price. But do consumers actually bid up the price during a shortage?

An article in *The Wall Street Journal* describes how the bidding process actually took place in housing markets in many areas of the country. During the spring of 1986 a huge influx of home buyers, lured by lower mortgage rates, began offering sellers $100 to $45,000 extra for scarce houses in desirable suburbs or prestigious urban neighborhoods. *The Wall Street Journal* reported that bidding contests were breaking out in a growing number of hot housing markets for the first time since the late 1970s. The trend began in Boston and upstate New York, then appeared in most of the Northeast, suburbs of Chicago, Detroit, Minneapolis, parts of Ohio, and major California cities. The connection is that all of these areas were experiencing substantial economic growth at the time.

While overbidding wasn't the norm, it occurred in 25 percent of home sales in some booming areas. As the *Journal* noted, "Its pervasiveness is helping to drive house prices sky high."

The median price of existing homes in April 1986 was 8.4 percent higher than the year before, the biggest year-to-year gain in five years. (The increase in price was only 4.3 percent in 1985.) One economist predicted an additional gain of 8 to 10 percent during the rest of the year. He said, "There is too much overbidding to hold down prices."

The article reports several specific examples. A New York couple offered $2,000 above the $181,000 asking price for a New Jersey home that needed a new furnace, a repainted garage, and extensive bathroom repairs. They made the offer to win a bidding war with two other buyers. And they said they were happy because they knew people who had paid as much as $10,000 above the asking price.

A Washington, DC, couple paid $4,500 above the asking price for a home in a fashionable neighborhood, after simply driving by. Many people were even giving up some purchase conditions, such as demanding structural inspection for hidden flaws, in order to win bidding contests. A California couple reported paying $135,000 for a two-bedroom house priced at $120,000. An Alexandria, Virginia, lawyer, after she was outbid for another home, paid $170,000 for a $167,000 house that needed $25,000 in repairs. A real estate agent in Albany, New York, said that one fourth of the homes in the area priced between $65,000 and $170,000 sold for more than the asking price.

A statement by a senior vice president of a securities firm sums up the process: "The baby-boom generation wants suburban housing. The drop in interest rates sort of really got the process going. Given the current scarcity of suburban homes, this [overbidding] could last longer than the rates dropping."

Translated into demand and supply, when interest rates fell and as more people wanted to live in the suburbs, the demand for homes in many suburban areas increased substantially. Quantity demanded exceeded quantity supplied at the old equilibrium price. Consumers, not able to get all the houses they wanted at that price, bid the price up. Not until the new price reaches the new higher equilibrium will overbidding cease.

It is interesting to note that by mid-1990 the boom in housing had turned into a slump. In many areas there was a surplus of homes on the market, forcing sellers to reduce prices, sometimes drastically. In January 1992, *The Wall Street Journal* reported that one large real estate firm was prospering during the slump, and, incidentally, that prices were being bid down not by the sellers directly, but by the real estate brokers. In 1991, Schweppe & Co. sold more homes than it had during the boom of 1986. This firm was not only soliciting home owners to put their homes on the market, but aggressively trying to convince these owners that they must reduce their prices significantly if they wished to sell. The *WSJ* quotes Jay Schweppe, "I have to sit in your living room and say, 'I know you bought this property three years ago, but you've lost $35,000. Sorry." No longer are the three most important words in real estate: location, location, and location. In the current real estate slump, they are: price, price, and price.

Sources: Joann S. Lublin, "Eager Home Buyers Bid up Prices in Rising Numbers of Hot Markets," *The Wall Street Journal*, 1986. Cynthia Crossen, "A Realtor Stays Hot in a Cold Market by Going for Blood," *The Wall Street Journal*, 1992.

2.4 CHANGES IN MARKET EQUILIBRIUM

If demand and supply never changed, equilibrium price and quantity would remain the same forever, or at least for a very long time, and market analysis would be extremely uninteresting and totally useless for managers. In reality, the variables held constant when deriving demand and supply curves do change. Consequently, demand and supply curves shift, and equilibrium price and quantity change. Using demand and supply, managers may make either qualitative forecasts or quantitative forecasts. A **qualitative forecast** predicts only the *direction* in which an economic variable, such as price or quantity, will move. A **quantitative forecast** predicts both the *direction* and the *magnitude* of the change in an economic variable.

qualitative forecast
A forecast that predicts only the direction in which an economic variable will move.

quantitative forecast
A forecast that predicts both the direction and the magnitude of the change in an economic variable.

For instance, if you read in *The Wall Street Journal* that Congress is considering a tax cut, demand and supply analysis enables you to forecast whether the price and sales of a particular product will increase or decrease. If you forecast that price will rise and sales will fall, you have made a qualitative forecast about price and quantity. Alternatively, you may have sufficient data on the exact nature of demand and supply to be able to predict that price will rise by $1.10 and sales will fall by 7,000 units. This is a quantitative forecast. Obviously, a manager would get more information from a quantitative forecast than from a qualitative forecast. But managers may not always have sufficient data to make quantitative forecasts. In many instances just being able to predict correctly whether price will rise or fall can be extremely valuable to a manager.

Thus, an important function and challenging task for managers is predicting the effect, especially the effect on market price, of specific changes in the variables that determine the position of demand and supply curves. We will first discuss the process of adjustment when something causes demand to change while supply remains constant, then the process when supply changes while demand remains constant.

Changes in Demand (supply constant)

To illustrate the effects of changes in demand when supply remains constant, we have reproduced D_0 and S_0 in Figure 2.6. Equilibrium occurs at $40 and 500 units, shown as point *A* in the figure. The demand curve D_1, showing an increase in demand, and the demand curve D_2, showing a decrease in demand, are reproduced from Figure 2.2. Recall that the shift from D_0 to D_1 was caused by an increase in income from $15,000 to $20,000. The shift from D_0 to D_2 resulted from the decrease in income from $15,000 to $10,000.

Begin in equilibrium at point *A*. Now let demand increase to D_1 as shown. At the original $40 price consumers now demand 800 units with the new demand. Since firms are still willing to supply only 500 units at $40, a shortage of 300 units results. As described in the previous section, the shortage causes the price to rise to a new equilibrium where quantity demanded equals quantity supplied. This new equilibrium, where D_1 crosses S_0, occurs when price is $50 and quantity sold is 600 units (point *B*). Therefore the increase in demand increases both equilibrium price and quantity.

FIGURE 2.6
Demand Shifts (supply constant)

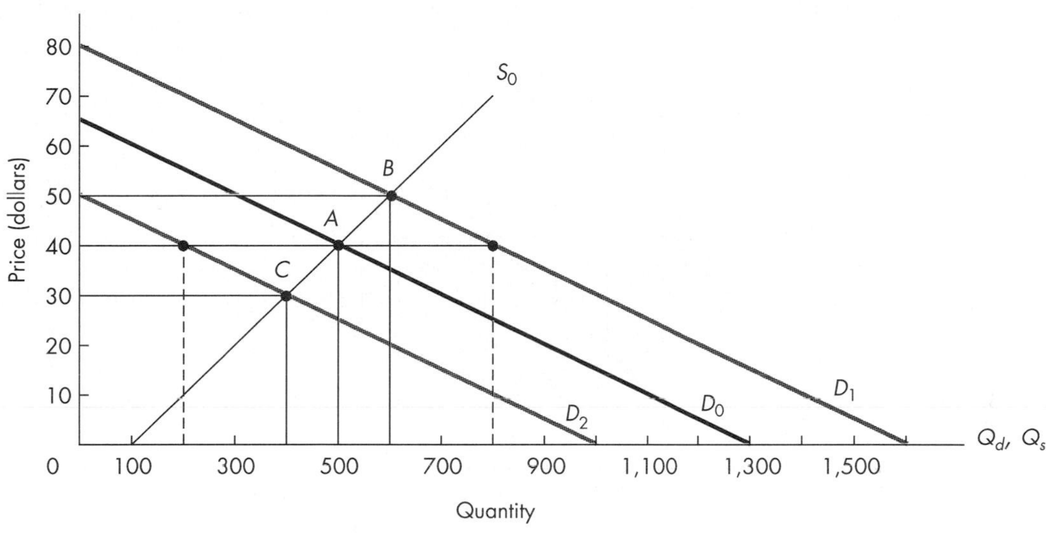

To illustrate the effect of a decrease in demand, supply held constant, we return to the original equilibrium at point *A* in the figure. Now we decrease the demand to D_2. At the original equilibrium price of $40, firms still want to supply 500 units, but now consumers want to purchase only 200 units. Thus, there is a surplus of 300 units at $40. As already explained, a surplus causes price to fall. In this example, the market returns to equilibrium only when price decreases to $30 and quantity sold is 400 (point *C*). Therefore the decrease in demand decreases both equilibrium price and quantity. We have now established the following principle:

Principle When demand increases and supply is constant, equilibrium price and quantity both rise. When demand decreases and supply is constant, equilibrium price and quantity both fall.

Changes in Supply (demand constant)

To illustrate the effects of changes in supply when demand remains constant, we reproduce D_0 and S_0 in Figure 2.7. The supply curve S_1, showing an increase in supply, and the supply curve S_2, showing a decrease in supply, are reproduced from Figure 2.4. Recall that the shift from S_0 to S_1 was caused by a decrease in the price of an input from $50 to $31.25. The shift from S_0 to S_2 resulted from a decrease in the number of firms in the industry from 90 firms to 30 firms.

Begin in equilibrium at point *R*. Let supply first increase to S_1 as shown. At the original $40 price consumers still want to purchase 500 units, but sellers now wish to sell 650 units, causing a surplus or excess supply of 150 units. The surplus causes price to fall, which induces sellers to supply less and buyers to

FIGURE 2.7
Supply Shifts (demand constant)

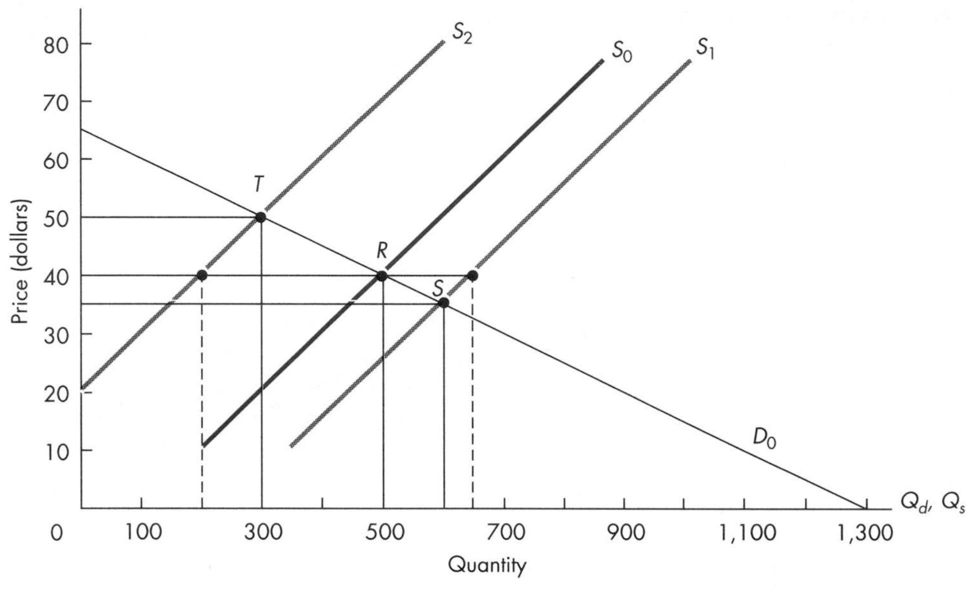

demand more. Price continues to fall until the new equilibrium is attained at a price of $35 and a quantity sold of 600 units (point *S*). At this new equilibrium, quantity demanded equals quantity supplied. Thus, when supply increases and demand remains constant, equilibrium price will fall and equilibrium quantity will increase.

To demonstrate the effect of a supply decrease, we return to the original input price, $50, to obtain the original supply curve S_0 and the original equilibrium at P = $40 and Q = 500 units (point *R*). Let the number of firms in the industry decrease from 90 to 30, causing supply to shift from S_0 to S_2 in Figure 2.7. At the original $40 price, consumers still want to buy 500 units, but now sellers wish to sell only 200 units, as shown in the figure. This leads to a shortage or excess demand of 300 units. Shortages cause price to rise. The increase in price induces sellers to supply more and buyers to demand less, thereby reducing the shortage. Price will continue to increase until it attains the new equilibrium at a price of $50 and 300 units of output being sold (point *T*). At the new equilibrium, S_2 intersects D_0 and quantity supplied equals quantity demanded. Therefore, when supply decreases while demand remains constant, price will rise and quantity sold will decrease. We have now established the following principle:

Principle When supply increases and demand is constant, equilibrium price falls and equilibrium quantity rises. When supply decreases and demand is constant, equilibrium price rises and equilibrium quantity falls.

FIGURE 2.8
Simultaneous Shifts in Demand and Supply: Demand and Supply Both Increase

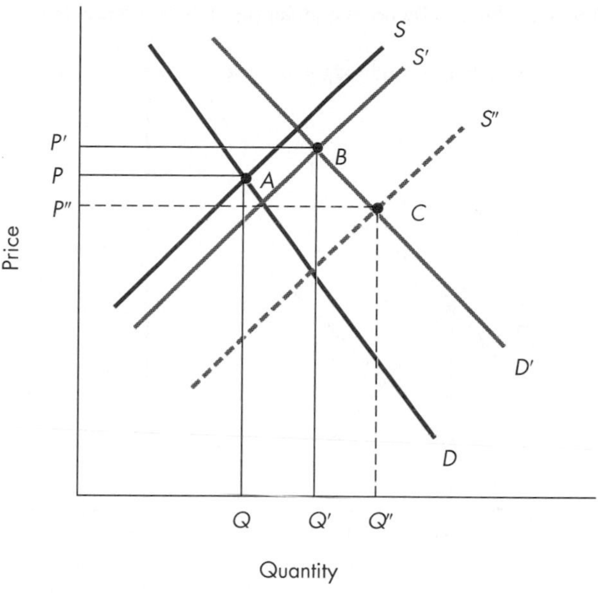

Simultaneous Shifts in Both Demand and Supply

To this point, we have examined changes in demand or supply holding the other curve constant. In both cases, the effect on equilibrium price and quantity can be predicted. In situations involving both a shift in demand along with a shift in supply, it is possible to predict either the direction in which price changes, or the direction in which quantity changes, *but not both.* When it is not possible to predict the direction of change in a variable, the change in that variable is said to be **indeterminate**. The change in either equilibrium price or quantity will be indeterminate when the direction of change depends upon the relative magnitudes of the shifts in the demand and supply curves.

indeterminate
The change in either equilibrium price or quantity will be indeterminate when the direction of change depends upon the relative magnitude of the shifts in the demand and supply curves.

In Figure 2.8, D and S are, respectively, demand and supply, and equilibrium price and quantity are P and Q (point A). Suppose demand increases to D' and supply increases to S'. Equilibrium quantity increases to Q', and equilibrium price rises from P to P' (point B). Suppose, however, that supply had increased even more to the dashed supply S'' so that the new equilibrium occurs at point C instead of at point B. Comparing point A to point C, equilibrium quantity still increases (Q to Q''), but now equilibrium price *decreases* from P to P''. In the case where both demand and supply increase, a *small* increase in supply relative to demand causes price to rise, while a *large* increase in supply relative to demand causes price to fall. In the case of a simultaneous increase in both demand and supply, equilibrium output always increases, but the change in equilibrium price is indeterminate.

FIGURE 2.9

Summary of Simultaneous Shifts in Demand and Supply: The Four Possible Cases

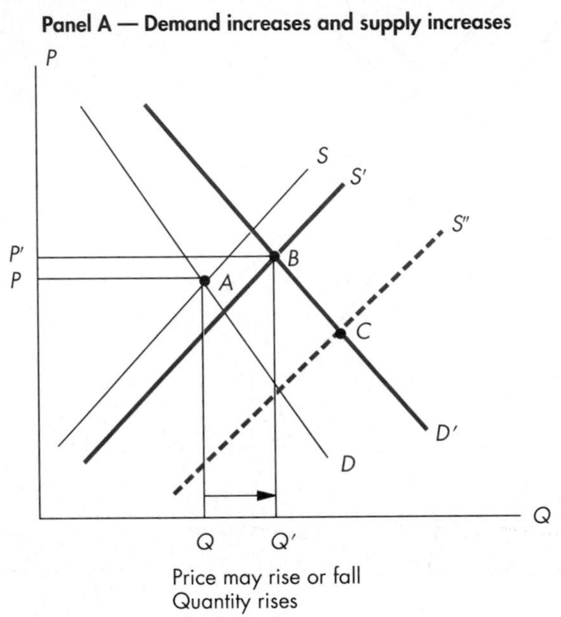

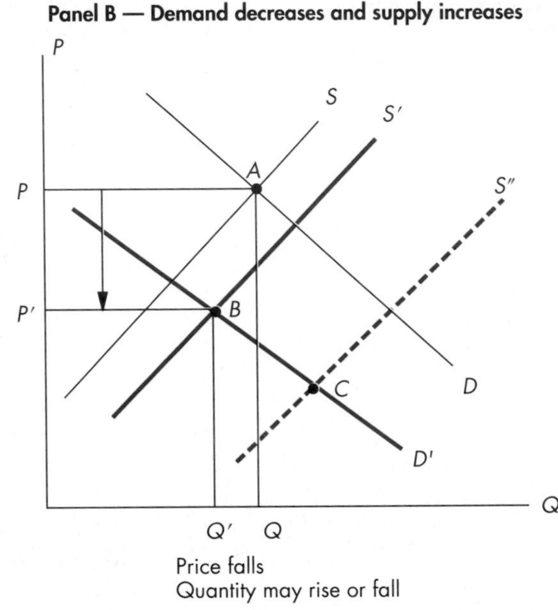

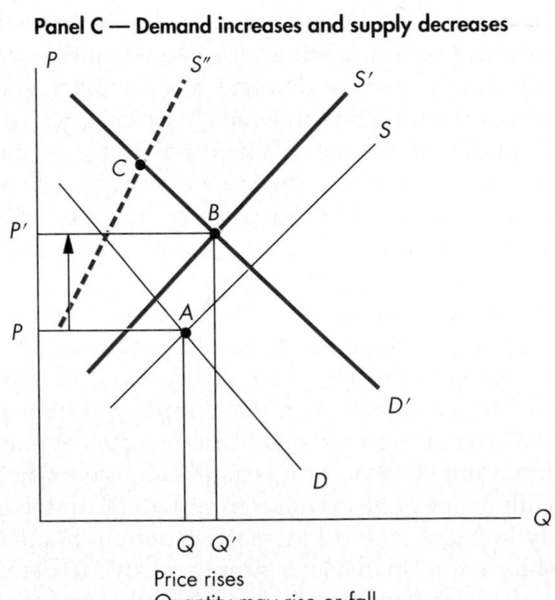

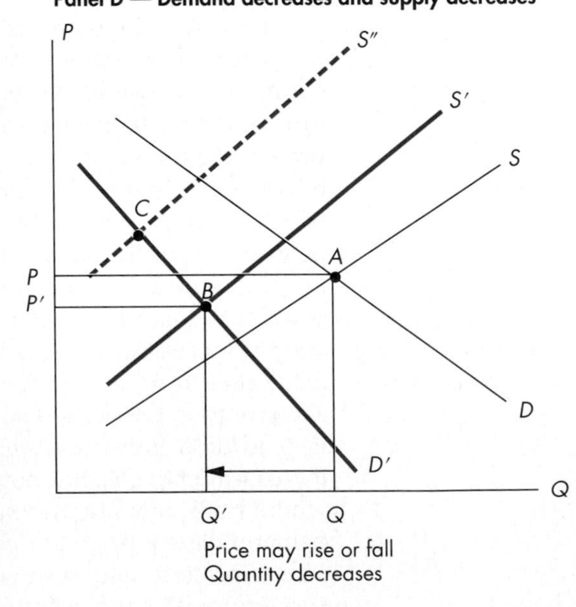

When both demand and supply shift together, either (1) the change in quantity can be predicted and the change in price is indeterminate, or (2) the change in quantity is indeterminate and the change in price can be predicted. Figure 2.9 summarizes the four possible outcomes when demand and supply both shift. In each of the four panels in Figure 2.9, point *C* shows an alternative point of equilibrium that reverses the direction of change in one of the variables, price or quantity. You should use the reasoning process set forth above to verify the conclusions presented for each of the four cases. We have established the following principle:

Principle When demand and supply both shift simultaneously, if the change in quantity (price) can be predicted, the change in price (quantity) is indeterminate. The change in equilibrium quantity or price is indeterminate when the variable can either rise or fall depending upon the relative magnitudes by which demand and supply shift.

Predicting the Direction of Change in Airfares: A Qualitative Analysis

Suppose you manage the travel department for a large US corporation, and your sales force makes heavy use of air travel to call on customers. The president of the corporation wants you to reduce travel expenditures for 1995. The extent to which you will need to curb air travel in 1995 will depend upon what happens to the price of air travel. If airfares fall in 1995, you can satisfy both the wants of the president, who wants expenditures cut, and the sales personnel, who would be hurt by travel restrictions. Clearly, you need to predict what will happen to airfares in 1995. You have recently read in *The Wall Street Journal* about the following two events that you expect will affect the airline industry in 1995:

1. A number of new, small airlines have recently entered the industry and others are expected to enter in 1995.
2. Teleconferencing is becoming a popular, cost-effective alternative to business travel for many US corporations. The trend is expected to accelerate in 1995 as telecommunications firms begin cutting prices on teleconferencing rates.

We can use Figure 2.10 to analyze how these events would affect the price of air travel in 1995. The current demand and supply curves in the domestic market are D_{1994} and S_{1994}. Equilibrium airfare in 1994 is denoted P_{1994} at point *A* in Figure 2.10.

An increase in the number of airlines causes supply to increase. The increase in supply is shown in Figure 2.10 by the shift in supply to S_{1995}. Since teleconferencing and air travel are substitutes, a reduction in the price of teleconferencing causes a decrease in demand. The decrease in demand is shown in Figure 2.10 by the shift in demand to D_{1995}. Thus, you must analyze a situation in which demand and supply shift simultaneously. The decrease in demand combined with the increase in supply leads you to predict a fall in airfares in 1995 to P_{1995} (point *B* in Figure 2.10). While you can predict that airfares will definitely fall when demand decreases and supply increases, you cannot predict whether equi-

FIGURE 2.10
Demand and Supply for Air Travel

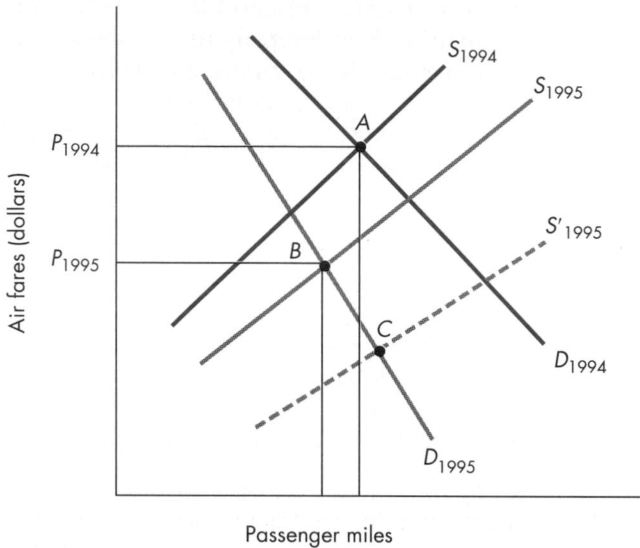

librium quantity will rise or fall in this situation (as shown by the shift to S'_{1995} in Figure 2.10). The change in quantity is indeterminate. The predicted fall in airfares is good news for you, but bad news for the financially troubled airline industry.

This analysis of the air travel market is an example of qualitative analysis. You only predicted the *direction* of the price change, not the magnitude of the change. Managers are certainly interested in whether price will increase or decrease. They are also interested in *how much* price will increase or decrease. Determining how much price will rise involves quantitative analysis. In order to carry out quantitative analysis, either you must be given the exact specification of the market demand and supply equations or you must estimate them from market data. In later chapters we will show you how to estimate demand and supply from market data. We will look now at an example of quantitative analysis where the demand and supply equations have already been estimated for you.

Advertising and the Price of Potatoes: A Quantitative Analysis

The Potato Growers Association of America estimates that next year the demand and supply functions facing US potato growers will be

$$Q_d = 28 - 0.04\,P$$
$$Q_s = -2 + 0.16\,P$$

where quantity demanded and quantity supplied are measured in trillions of hundredweight (a measure equal to 100 pounds) per year, and price is measured in cents per hundredweight. First, we will predict the price of potatoes next year and how many potatoes will be sold. The market clearing price is easily determined by setting quantity demanded equal to quantity supplied and solving algebraically for equilibrium price:

$$Q_d = Q_s$$
$$28 - 0.04\ P = -2 + 0.16\ P$$
$$30 = 0.20\ P$$
$$150 = P_E$$

Thus the equilibrium price of potatoes next year will be 150 cents ($1.50) per hundredweight. The equilibrium level of potato production is determined by substituting the market price of 150 cents into either the demand or supply function to get Q_E:

$$Q_d = Q_s = Q_E$$
$$28 - (0.04 \times 150) = -2 + (0.16 \times 150) = 22$$

Thus the equilibrium output of potatoes will be 22 trillion hundredweight per year.

Even though that's a lot of potatoes, the Potato Growers Association plans to begin a nationwide advertising campaign to promote potatoes by informing consumers of the nutritional benefits of potatoes. The association estimates that the advertising campaign, which will make consumers want to eat more potatoes, will increase demand to:

$$Q_d = 40 - 0.05\ P$$

Assuming that supply is unaffected by the advertising, you would obviously predict the market price of potatoes will rise as a result of the advertising and the resulting increase in demand. However, to determine the actual market clearing price, you must equate the new quantity demanded with the quantity supplied:

$$40 - 0.05\ P = -2 + 0.16\ P$$
$$P_E = 200$$

The price of potatoes will increase to 200 cents ($2.00) with the advertising campaign. Consequently, the prediction is that the national advertising campaign will increase the market price of potatoes by 50 cents per hundredweight. This is an example of a quantitative forecast since the forecast involves both the magnitude and the direction of change in price. To make a quantitative forecast about the impact of the ads on the level of potato production, you simply substitute the new market price of 200 cents into either the demand or supply function to obtain the new Q_E:

$$Q_d = Q_s = Q_E$$
$$40 - (0.05 \times 200) = -2 + (0.16 \times 200) = 30$$

ILLUSTRATION 2.3

Price Ceilings, Coupons, and Gasoline Rationing

In the winter of 1991, events in the Persian Gulf culminated in the outbreak of war. During the fall leading up to the war, consumers saw prices at the gas pumps rise steadily from an average of about $1.05 per gallon to nearly $1.40 per gallon. On several evenings, the television newscasters interviewed so-called experts, who were predicting that the price of gasoline might soar to $2 or more a gallon.

President Bush declared that he would not pump crude oil from the Strategic Petroleum Reserve just to lower gasoline prices; the President's decision drew bitter criticism. Some members of Congress argued that Bush's failure to dip into the nation's oil reserves would force the nation to employ gasoline rationing. Congress seemed willing to return to price ceilings and impose gasoline rationing rather than allow higher market-determined prices to allocate gasoline among buyers. The war ended rather rapidly, so rationing was not imposed.

Let's return now to 1974 and examine one of the bureaucratic rationing plans that was proposed to deal with the gasoline shortages created by government price ceilings in effect then. In 1974 the price ceilings imposed by the federal government were creating widespread shortages of gasoline. Long lines of cars waiting hours to get gasoline were commonplace. The figure shows how the price ceilings created shortages. Notice in the graph that the ceiling price, 75 cents per gallon, was below the market (equilibrium) price, 95 cents per gallon, creating a shortage of 8 billion gallons of gasoline per month.

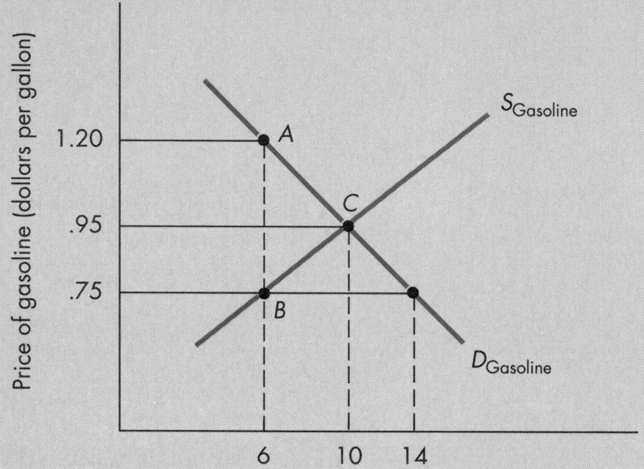

In an attempt to eliminate the shortage of gasoline, the US government printed 4.8 billion gasoline rationing coupons of various denominations. Each owner of a registered vehicle was to receive a monthly allotment of coupons. To buy one gallon of gasoline, a consumer would pay a price of 75 cents and a one-unit coupon. The government would only allocate a total of 6 billion coupons per month to match the amount of gasoline available.

2.5 CEILING AND FLOOR PRICES

Shortages and surpluses *can* occur after a shift in demand or supply, but as we have stressed, these shortages and surpluses are sufficiently short in duration that they can reasonably be ignored in demand and supply analysis. In other words, markets are assumed to adjust fairly rapidly and we concern ourselves only with the comparison of equilibriums before and after a shift in supply or demand. There are, however, some types of shortages and surpluses that market forces do not eliminate. These are more permanent in nature and result from government interferences with the market mechanism, which prevent prices from freely moving up or down to clear the market.

Under this plan each car owner was to receive the same number of coupons. Some drivers would want more gasoline, others less gasoline, than their monthly allotment of coupons would allow. To accommodate differing gasoline demands, the government planned to allow drivers to buy and sell coupons. The price of the coupons would be determined by the market forces of demand and supply. Therefore, the "full" price paid for a gallon of gasoline (P_F) would be equal to 75 cents plus the market-determined price paid for a one-gallon coupon (P_c) (i.e., $P_F = \$0.75 + P_c$). The coupons that drivers would receive for their monthly allotment were not costless to use. The opportunity cost of using them to purchase gasoline rather than selling them in the coupon market would be P_c, the amount that could be obtained by selling the coupons in the market.

Under a coupon-rationing scheme, the price of coupons will be bid up by consumers until the quantity demanded of gasoline *at the full price of* P_F just equals the quantity supplied by producers at the price of 75 cents. (Note that producers will only produce 6 billion gallons of gasoline per month because they receive only $0.75 per gallon.) Therefore, the equilibrium price of a coupon would be bid up to 45 cents ($P_c = AB$). At point *A* in the figure, the total price of a gallon of gasoline just clears the market and no shortage exists. The coupon-rationing scheme successfully eliminates the shortage caused by the government imposed price ceiling. The question is, does a price ceiling on gasoline coupled with a coupon-rationing scheme really make consumers better off? Unfortunately for consumers, the answer is no.

Comparing points *A* and *C* in the figure indicates that the full price of gasoline would be 25 cents lower and gasoline consumption 4 billion gallons per month higher if the government simply let the price of gasoline rise to the free-market level of 95 cents. In addition, it should be noted that the printing cost alone for the coupons was more than $10 million (in 1974 dollars).

For reasons that will probably never be known, government officials decided not to implement coupon rationing. Instead gasoline was rationed by using license plate numbers to dictate which day a driver could buy gasoline, but the shortages continued. The shortage of gasoline eventually disappeared with the removal of price ceilings. No shortage has since been reported. Even the Persian Gulf War, with bombings of oil fields and refineries, colossal oil spills, and unprecedented supply disruptions on a daily basis, failed to result in consumers not being able to purchase all the gasoline they desired at the going market price.

Source: See Jane Kidwell, "Motorists on Their Own if US Hit with Gas Shortage," *Tampa Tribune-Times*, October 7, 1990, p. 17-A.

Typically these more permanent shortages and surpluses are caused by government imposing legal restrictions on the movement of prices. Shortages and surpluses can be created simply by legislating a price below or above equilibrium. Governments have decided in the past, and will surely decide in the future, that the price of a particular commodity, is "too high" or "too low" and proceed to set a "fair price." Without evaluating the desirability of such interference, we can use demand and supply curves to analyze the economic effects of these two types of interference: the setting of minimum and maximum prices.

ceiling price
The maximum price the government permits sellers to charge for a good. When this price is below equilibrium, a shortage occurs.

If the government imposes a maximum price, or **ceiling price**, on a good, the effect is to cause a shortage of that good. In Panel A of Figure 2.11, a ceiling price of $1 is set on some good *X*. No one can legally sell *X* for more than $1, and $1 is less than the equilibrium (market clearing) price of $2. At the ceiling price of $1, the maximum amount that producers are willing to supply is 22 units. At $1, consumers wish to purchase 62 units. A shortage of 40 units results from the imposition of the $1 price ceiling. Market forces will not be permitted to bid up the price to eliminate the shortage because producers cannot sell the good for more than $1. This type of shortage will continue until government eliminates the price ceiling or until shifts in either supply or demand cause the equilibrium price to fall to $1 or lower. It is worth noting that "black" (illegal) markets usually arise in such cases. Some consumers are willing to pay more than $1 for good X rather than do without it, and some producers are willing to sell good X for more than $1 rather than forego the extra sales. In most cases the law is not a sufficient deterrent to the illegal trade of a good at prices above the ceiling.

floor price
The minimum price the government permits sellers to charge for a good. When this price is above equilibrium, a surplus occurs.

Alternatively, the government may believe that the suppliers of the good are not earning as much income as they deserve and, therefore, sets a minimum price or **floor price**. You can see the results of such actions in Panel B of Figure 2.11. Dissatisfied with the equilibrium price of $2 and equilibrium quantity of 50, the government sets a minimum price of $3. Since the government cannot repeal the law of demand, consumers reduce the amount they purchase to 32 units. Producers, of course, are going to increase their production of X to 84 units in response to the $3 price. Now a surplus of 52 units exists. Because the government is not allowing the price of X to fall, this surplus is going to continue until it is either eliminated by the government or demand or supply shifts cause

FIGURE 2.11
Ceiling and Floor Prices

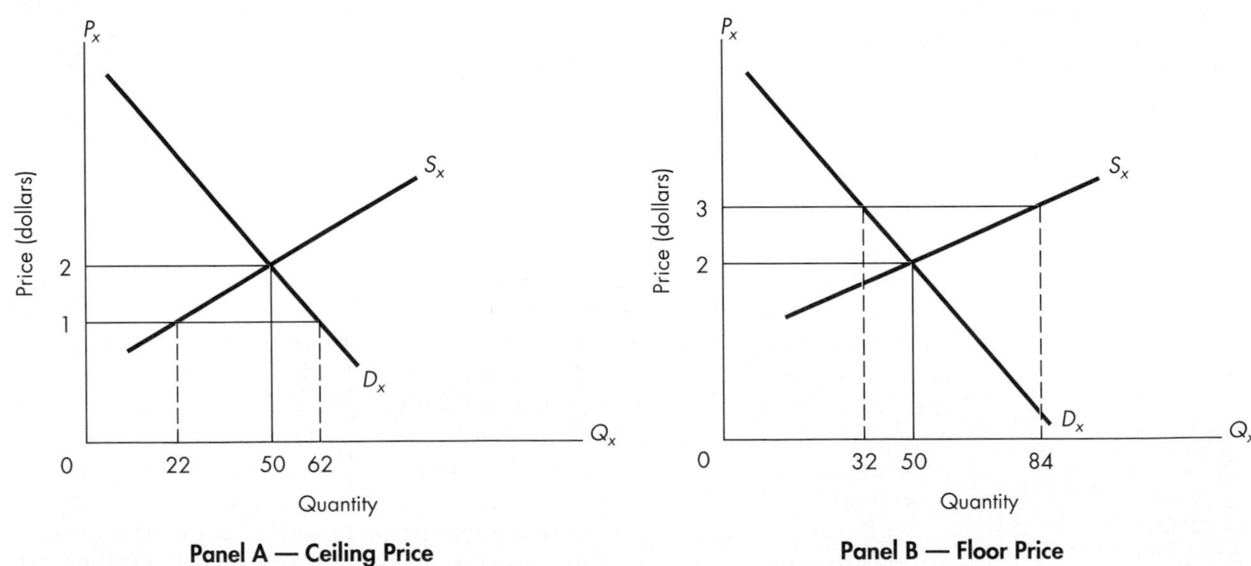

market price to rise to $3 or higher. In order for the government to ensure that producers do not illegally sell their surpluses for less than $3, the government must either restrict the production of X to 32 units or be willing to buy (and store or destroy) the 52 surplus units.

This section can be summarized by the following principle:

Principle When the government sets a ceiling price below the equilibrium price, a shortage or excess demand results because consumers wish to buy more units of the good than producers are willing to sell at the ceiling price. If the government sets a floor price above the equilibrium price, a surplus or excess supply results because producers offer for sale more units of the good than buyers wish to consume at the floor price.

For managers to make successful decisions by watching for changes in economic conditions, they must be able to predict how these changes will affect the market. As we hope you have seen, this is precisely what economic analysis is designed to do. This ability to use economics to make predictions is one of the topics we will emphasize throughout the text.

2.6 SUMMARY

In this chapter we presented the basic framework of demand and supply analysis. The market was divided into two different groups of participants—consumers and producers. Demand analysis focuses on the behavior of consumers, while supply analysis examines the behavior of producers. The demand and supply curves together determine the price and output that occur in a market. The impact of changing market circumstances upon equilibrium price and output is determined by making the appropriate shifts in either demand or supply, and comparing equilibriums before and after the change.

The generalized demand function specifies how the quantity demanded of a good is related to six variables that jointly determine the amount of a good or service consumers are willing and able to buy. By holding constant the five determinants of demand—income, the price of related goods, consumer tastes, expected price, and the number of consumers—and letting only the price of the good vary, a demand function is derived. The law of demand states that quantity demanded and price are inversely related, all other variables influencing demand held constant. Whenever the price of a good changes, a "change in quantity demanded" occurs, which is represented by a movement along a fixed demand curve. A point on the demand curve shows either the maximum amount of a good that will be purchased if a given price is charged or the maximum price consumers will pay for a specific amount of the good.

The five determinants of demand (M, P_R, T, P_e, and N) are also called the demand shifting variables because their values determine the location of the demand curve. If any of these five variables changes, the demand curve shifts either leftward (demand decreases) or rightward (demand increases), and a change in demand is said to have occurred. Table 2.4 summarizes how demand curves shift when each of the determinants of demand changes value.

For producers, the generalized supply function shows how six variables—the price of the product, the price of inputs, the prices of goods related in production, the state of technology, the expected price of the good, and the number of firms—jointly determine the amount of a good or service producers are willing to supply. Quantity supplied and price are directly related, all other variables influencing supply held constant. When the price of a good changes, a change in quantity supplied occurs, which is represented by a movement along a fixed supply curve. A point on the supply curve shows either the maximum amount of a good that will be offered for sale at a given price or the minimum price (the supply price) necessary to induce producers voluntarily to offer a particular quantity for sale.

The five determinants of supply (P_i, P_r, T, P_e, and F) are also called the supply-shifting variables because

FIGURE 2.12
Summary of Demand Shifts (supply constant) and Supply Shifts (demand constant)

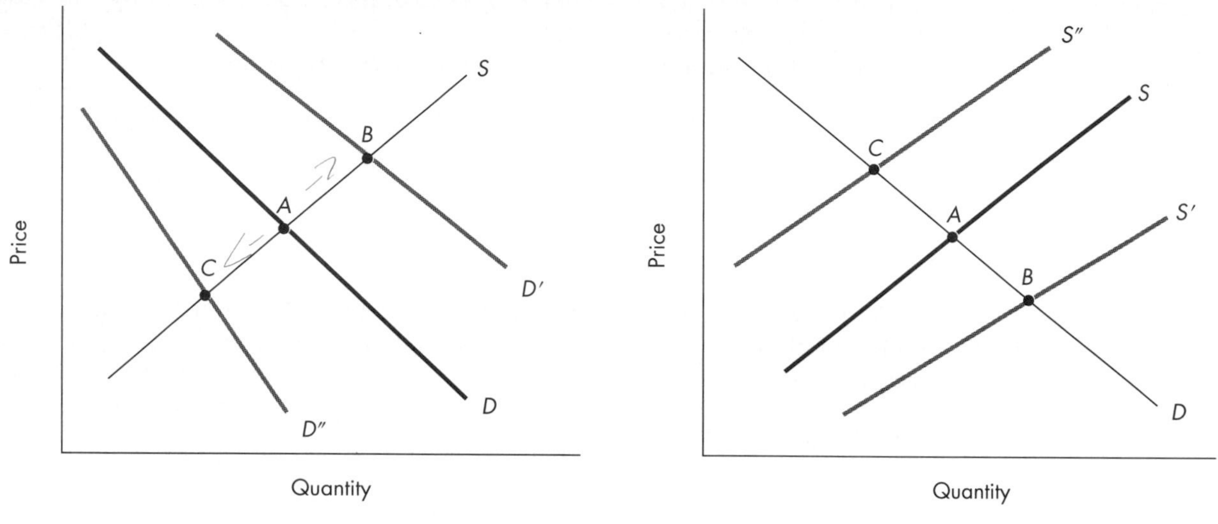

Panel A — Shifts in demand (supply constant)

Panel B — Shifts in supply (demand constant)

their values determine the location of the supply curve. If any one of these five variables changes, the supply curve shifts either leftward (supply decreases) or rightward (supply increases), and a change in supply is said to have occurred. Table 2.8 summarizes how supply curves shift when each of the determinants of supply changes value.

The equilibrium price and quantity in a market are determined by the intersection of demand and supply curves. At the point of intersection, quantity demanded equals quantity supplied, and the market clears. Since the location of the demand and supply curves is determined by the five determinants of demand and the five determinants of supply, a change in any one of these ten variables will result in a new equilibrium point. Figure 2.12 summarizes the results when either demand or supply shifts while the other curve remains constant. When demand increases and supply remains constant, price and quantity sold both rise, as shown by the movement from point *A* to *B* in Panel A of Figure 2.12. A decrease in demand, supply constant, causes both price and quantity sold to fall, as shown by the movement from point *A* to *C*. When supply increases and demand remains constant, price falls and quantity sold rises, as shown by the movement from point *A* to *B* in Panel B of Figure 2.12. A decrease in supply, demand constant, causes price to rise and quantity sold to fall, as shown by the movement from point *A* to *C* in Panel B.

When both supply and demand shift simultaneously, it is possible to predict either the direction in which price changes or the direction in which quantity changes, but not both. The change in equilibrium quantity or price is said to be indeterminate when the direction of change depends upon the relative magnitudes by which demand and supply shift. The four possible cases for simultaneous shifts in demand and supply are summarized in Figure 2.9.

Demand and supply analysis allows managers to make either qualitative or quantitative forecasts. A forecast is qualitative in nature when only the direction of change in market equilibrium is predicted. If enough quantitative information is available, managers can make quantitative forecasts to predict both the direction and magnitude of changes in equilibrium values of price and quantity. Never underestimate the value of qualitative forecasts. Correctly predicting the direction of change in price or sales can be an extremely valuable skill for any manager.

Sometimes the government imposes either a ceiling price or a floor price, which interferes with the market mechanism and prevents price from freely moving up or down to clear the market. When government sets a ceiling price below the equilibrium price, a shortage results because consumers wish to buy more of the good than producers are willing to sell at the ceiling price. If government sets a floor price above the equilibrium price, a surplus results because producers offer for sale more of the good than buyers wish to purchase at the higher floor price.

In this chapter we had two purposes. The first was to show you how managers can use economic theory to make predictions about the effect of exogenous events upon prices. We attempted to show what to expect about price and quantity in specific markets when certain variables change or are expected to change. As we will show in later chapters, the ability to make correct forecasts under difficult conditions separates good (successful) managers from those who are not so good (unsuccessful).

The second purpose was to prepare you for the material we will present in the following chapters. These chapters will show how demand and supply functions are derived from the behavior of consumers and firms and how these functions can be estimated. A thorough understanding of the material set forth in this chapter is essential to developing the ability to use and interpret demand and supply estimations and make accurate forecasts about the future.

TECHNICAL PROBLEMS

An asterisk indicates the answer is provided at the end of the book

1. Suppose the demand curve for good *X* passes through the point $P = \$2$, $Q_d = 35$. Give two interpretations of this point on the demand curve.
2. Using a graph, explain carefully the difference between a movement along a demand curve and a shift in the demand curve.

* 3. What happens to *demand* when the following changes occur?
   - *a.* The price of the commodity falls.
   - *b.* Income increases and the commodity is normal.
   - *c.* Income increases and the commodity is inferior.
   - *d.* The price of a substitute good increases.
   - *e.* The price of a substitute good decreases.
   - *f.* The price of a complement good increases.
   - *g.* The price of a complement good decreases.
   - *h.* The price of the good is expected to increase.
   - *i.* The price of the good is expected to decrease.

4. Suppose the supply curve for good *X* passes through the point $P = \$25$, $Q_s = 500$. Give two interpretations of this point on the supply curve.
5. Using a graph, explain carefully the difference between a movement along a supply curve and a shift in the supply curve.
6. Other things remaining the same, what would happen to the *supply* of a particular commodity if the following changes occur?
   - *a.* The price of the commodity decreases.
   - *b.* A technological breakthrough enables the good to be produced at a significantly lower cost.
   - *c.* The prices of inputs used to produce the commodity increase.
   - *d.* The price of a commodity that is a substitute in production decreases.
   - *e.* The managers of firms that produce the good expect the price of the good to rise in the near future.

7. Suppose that the generalized demand function for good X is:

$$Q_d = 60 - 2P_X + 10M + 7P_R$$

where
Q_d = the quantity of X demanded
P_X = the price of X
M = the (average) consumer income (in thousands of dollars), and
P_R = the price of a related good R.

a. Is good X normal or inferior? Explain.
b. Are goods X and R substitutes or complements? Explain.
Suppose that $M = \$40$, $P_R = \$20$.
c. What is the demand function for good X?
Suppose the supply function is

$$Q_s = -600 + 10P_X$$

d. What are equilibrium price and quantity?
e. What happens to equilibrium price and quantity if other things remain the same as in part *d*, but income increases to \$52?
f. What happens to equilibrium price and quantity if other things remain the same as in part *d*, but the price of good R decreases to \$14?
g. What happens to equilibrium price and quantity if other things remain the same, income and the price of the related goods are at their original levels, and supply shifts to $Q_s = -360 + 10P_X$?

8. Determine the effect upon equilibrium price and quantity sold if the following changes occur in a particular market:
a. Consumers' income increases and the good is normal.
b. The price of a substitute good (in consumption) increases.
c. The price of a substitute good (in production) increases.
d. The price of a complement good (in consumption) increases.
e. The price of inputs used to produce the good increases.
f. Consumers expect that the price of the good will increase in the near future.
g. It is widely publicized that consumption of the good is hazardous to health.
h. Cost-reducing technological change takes place in the industry.

9. The following general supply relation shows the quantity of good X that producers offer for sale (Q_s):

$$Q_s = 19 + 20P_X - 10P_i + 6T - 32P_r - 20P_e + 5F$$

where P_X is the price of X, P_i is the price of labor, T is an index measuring the level of technology, P_r is the price of a good R that is related in production, P_e is the expected future price of good X, and F is the number of firms in the industry.
a. Determine the equation of the supply curve for X when $P_i = 8$, $T = 4$, $P_r = 4$, $P_e = 5$, and $F = 47$. Plot this supply curve on a graph.
b. Suppose the price of labor increases from 8 to 9. Find the equation of the new supply curve. Plot the new supply curve on a graph.
c. Is the good related in production a complement or a substitute in production? Explain.
d. What is the correct way to interpret each of the coefficients in the supply relation given above?

10. Use the graph that follows to answer the following questions.

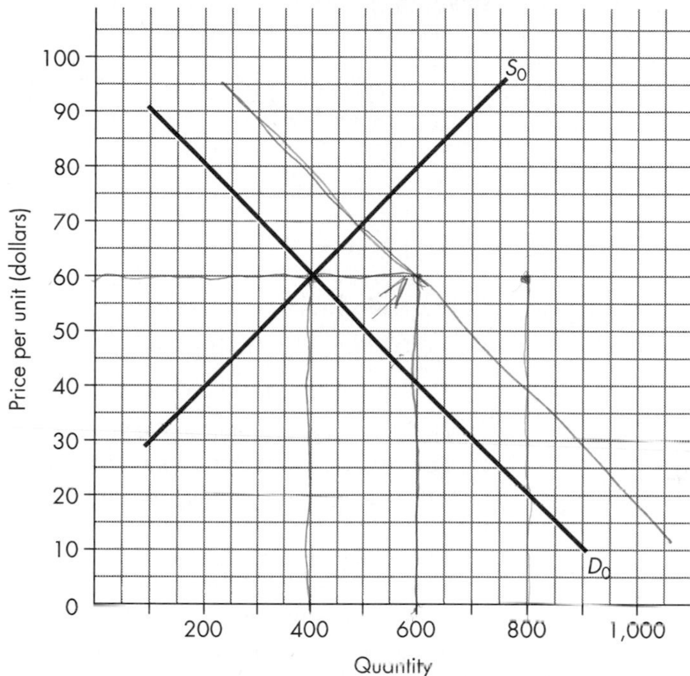

a. What is the equilibrium price and quantity?
b. What is the effect of a ceiling price of $40?
c. What is the effect of a floor price of $50? A floor price of $70?
d. Suppose income increases and consumers are willing and able to buy 100 more units at each price. Construct the new demand curve and label it D_1. What is the new equilibrium price and quantity?
e. Suppose input prices fall and suppliers are willing to offer for sale 200 more units at each price. Construct the new supply curve, and label it S_1. Suppose instead, when input prices fall, supply price falls by $20 for each level of output. Verify that the new supply curve is exactly the same in either case. What are the new equilibrium price and output when the supply and demand curves are D_1 and S_1?

* 11. Suppose that the demand and supply functions for good *X* are:

$$Q_d = 50 - 8P$$
$$Q_s = -17.5 + 10P$$

a. What are equilibrium price and quantity?
b. What is the market outcome if price is $2.75? What do you expect to happen? Why?
c. What is the market outcome if price is $4.25? What do you expect to happen? Why?
d. What happens to equilibrium price and quantity if the demand function becomes $Q_d = 59 - 8P$?
e. What happens to equilibrium price and quantity if the supply function becomes $Q_s = -40 + 10P$ (demand is $Q_d = 50 - 8P$)?

12. The table below presents the demand and supply schedules for apartments in a small US city:

Monthly rental rate (dollars per month)	Quantity demanded (number of units per month)	Quantity supplied (number of units per month)
$300	130,000	35,000
350	115,000	37,000
400	100,000	41,000
450	80,000	45,000
500	72,000	52,000
550	60,000	60,000
600	55,000	70,000
650	48,000	75,000

a. The equilibrium rental rate is $________ per month.
b. The equilibrium number of apartments rented is ________ per month.

Suppose the city council decides rents are too high and imposes a rent ceiling of $400.

c. The ceiling on rent causes a ________ of ________ apartments per month.
d. How many *more* renters would have found an apartment in this city if the ceiling had not been imposed?

Suppose instead of a ceiling price, the city council places a floor of $600 on rental rates.

e. The floor on rent causes a ________ of ________ apartments per month.

13. In the graph that follows, the original demand and supply curves for movies are D_0 and S_0 and the market is in equilibrium at price P_0 and output Q_0. For each of the following events, draw an appropriate new supply or demand curve for movies.

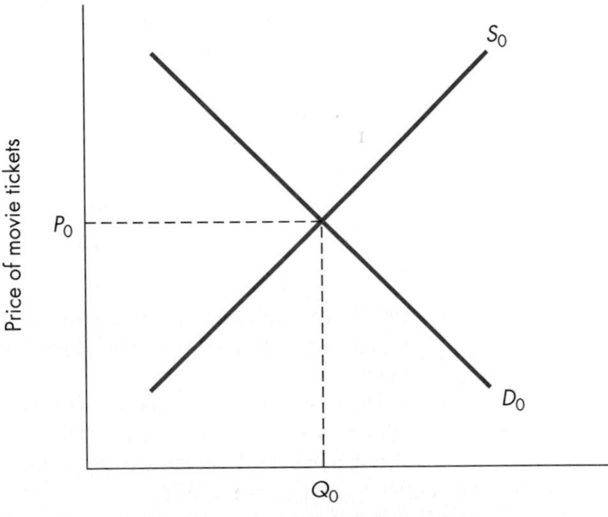

a. Movie theaters double the price of soft drinks and popcorn.
b. A national video rental chain cuts its rental rate by 25 percent.
c. Cable television begins offering pay-per-view movies.
d. The screenwriter's guild ends a 10-month strike.
e. Kodak reduces the price it charges Hollywood producers for motion picture film.

What do you predict will happen to the price of a movie ticket and sales of movie tickets as a result of each of these events?

14. According to an article in *The Wall Street Journal,* many cities were reporting a substantial decrease in the amount of garbage being collected after they changed from levying a tax on each household to pay for the pickup, to charging a fee for each bag or can picked up. Would this have been the result of a change in demand? If so why, or if not, why not? If not, what was the probable reason?

APPLIED PROBLEMS

1. Suppose you are the manager of a California winery. How would you expect the following events to affect the price you receive for a bottle of wine?
   a. The price of comparable French wines decreases.
   b. One hundred new wineries open in California.
   c. The unemployment rate in the United States decreases.
   d. The price of cheese increases.
   e. The price of a glass bottle increases significantly due to new government antishatter regulations.
   f. Researchers discover a new wine-making technology that reduces production costs.
   g. The price of wine vinegar, which is made from the leftover grape mash, increases.
   h. The average age of consumers increases, and older people drink less wine.
2. Citrus Speculation and Forecasting, Inc., has been hired by a private consortium of orange growers to predict what will happen to the price and output of oranges under the conditions below. What are your predictions?
   a. The price of grapefruit falls.
   b. A major freeze destroys a large number of the orange trees in Florida.
   c. The scientists in the agricultural extension service of the University of Florida discover a way to double the number of oranges produced by each orange tree.
   d. The American Medical Association announces that orange juice can reduce the risk of heart attack.
3. Morgan Realty is considering investing in an apartment complex in Tampa. After considerable research, managers at Morgan Realty discover some events that may influence their decision to buy. Tampa is growing steadily. Inflation is running at about 5 to 7 percent, but wages in Tampa are not keeping up. The rate of interest has risen to about 10 percent, but, because of the easy money policy undertaken by the Federal Reserve System, most authorities expect the interest rate to fall. Various new service-oriented industries, which will employ a large proportion of white-collar workers, are moving to the city. Finally, the University of South Florida in Tampa is undertaking a massive dormitory construction project, which is expected to increase the number of dormitory rooms by 45 percent over the next two years.

Analyze the effect of each of these influences on the demand for apartments in Tampa. Show the effects of each graphically.

4. Several economics faculty members were standing in line in the student union cafeteria for lunch. One was heard to say, "I sure wish the union would raise their food prices." The others agreed. What in the world would motivate such a wish?
5. In October 1990, rising jet fuel prices led most major US airlines to raise fares by a total of 15.3 percent after the August invasion of Kuwait by Saddam Hussein. Explain how this substantial increase in airfares would affect the following:
   a. The demand for air travel.
   b. The demand for hotels.
   c. The demand for rental cars.
   d. The supply of overnight mail.
6. Toys-Were-Us, a toy retailing company, has just filed for protection under Chapter 11 bankruptcy law. Apparently management frequently raised toy prices when they should have been reduced and cut prices when they should have been raised. How would managers know when their prices are too high? How would they know if their prices were too low?
7. Some firms experience extreme seasonal fluctuation in the demand for the goods or services produced by their firms. Some examples are air-conditioning repair services, toy retailers, and tax accounting firms.
   a. What problems would evolve from such seasonal fluctuations in demand?
   b. What can managers of such types of firms do to help solve these problems?
   c. Would the problem and/or solutions be different if the extreme fluctuations in demand were not seasonal or regular? An example might be a firm that manufactures a product for which demand is extremely sensitive to general economic conditions.
8. Suppose you are a stock market analyst specializing in the stocks of theme parks, and you are examining Disneyland's stock. *The Wall Street Journal* reports that tourism has slowed down in the United States. At Six Flags Magic Mountain in Valencia, California, a new Viper roller coaster is now operating and another new ride, Psyclone, will be opening this year. Using demand and supply analysis, predict the impact of these events on ticket prices and attendance at Disneyland. As reported in *The Wall Street Journal*, Disneyland has slashed ticket prices and admitted that attendance was somewhat lower. Is this consistent with your prediction using demand and supply analysis? In light of the fact that both price and output are falling at Disneyland, is the law of demand being violated in the world of fantasy?
9. The Council on Economic Priorities recently published "Shopping for a Better World," a guide that rates 168 companies on their social performance. The aim of the Council is to "make progressive policies profitable" by informing consumers about such questions as which pasta producer also makes cigarettes, which companies have women in executive management positions, which companies give to charity, and so on. Using demand and supply analysis, explain how disseminating this type of information can translate into higher profits for "socially responsible" firms.
10. California voters, in an attempt to halt the rapid increase in the state's automobile insurance rates, approved Proposition 103. The measure proposes to roll back auto insurance rates by 20 percent and freeze them for at least a year. Using a graph,

show the impact of Proposition 103 on the market for automobile insurance in California. As the costs of providing insurance continue to rise, what do you predict will happen over time in the California market for auto insurance? How would your prediction change if Proposition 103 is defeated?

11. In January 1993, *The Wall Street Journal* reported that recent law school graduates were having a very difficult time obtaining jobs in the legal profession. Many law schools said that 10 to 20 percent of their 1992 graduates still had not found a job. The historical average had been 6 to 8 percent. Many recent graduates were taking jobs outside of law at much lower wages than were typically paid to beginning lawyers. Based on this information, what would be your prediction about lawyers' salaries for the future? The next year? The next six years?

CHAPTER

3 Elasticity and Demand

While it is extremely important for managers to recognize that quantity demanded and price are inversely related, it is equally—or perhaps even more—important to know *by how much* sales will change for a given change in price. A 10 percent decrease in price that leads to a 2 percent increase in quantity demanded differs greatly in effect from a 10 percent decrease in price that causes a 50 percent increase in quantity demanded. There is a substantial difference in the effect on total consumer expenditure, and hence total revenue to the firm, between these two responses to a change in price. Certainly, when making pricing decisions, managers should have a good idea about how responsive consumers will be to any price changes and whether revenues will rise or fall.

The majority of this chapter is devoted to the concept of *demand elasticity,* a measure of the responsiveness of quantity demanded to a change in price along a demand curve, and an indicator of the effect of a price change on total consumer expenditure on a product. The concept of demand elasticity provides managers, economists, and policymakers a framework for understanding why consumers in some markets are extremely responsive to changes in price while consumers in other markets are not. This understanding is useful in many types of managerial decisions. As noted, demand elasticity is so crucial to managerial decision making that we have devoted most of this chapter to examining this concept.

We will begin by defining the coefficient of demand elasticity, and then show how to use demand elasticities to find the percentage changes in price or quantity that result from movements along a demand curve. Next, the relation between elasticity and the total revenue received by firms from the sale of a product is examined in detail. Then we discuss three factors that determine the degree of responsiveness of consumers, and hence the elasticity of demand. We also show how to compute the elasticity of demand either over an interval or at a point on demand, and how to compute two other important elasticities—income and cross-price elasticities. The last section of this chapter introduces the concept of marginal revenue and demonstrates the relation among demand, marginal revenue, and elasticity.

3.1 THE COEFFICIENT OF DEMAND ELASTICITY

demand elasticity
A measure of the responsiveness of consumers to changes in the price of a good.

price elasticity and own-price elasticity
Other names for demand elasticity.

coefficient of demand elasticity (*E*)
The percentage change in quantity demanded, divided by the percentage change in price. *E* is always a negative number because *P* and *Q* are inversely related.

As noted above, **demand elasticity** measures the responsiveness or sensitivity of consumers to changes in the price of a good or service. Demand elasticity is sometimes referred to as **price elasticity** or **own-price elasticity** to distinguish this elasticity from income and cross-price elasticities—two other elasticities we will examine later in this chapter. We will begin this section by presenting a formal (mathematical) definition of demand elasticity, and then show how demand elasticity is related to the issue of whether total revenue rises or falls after a change in the price of a good or service.

Consumer responsiveness to a price change is measured by the **coefficient of demand elasticity (*E*)**, defined as

$$E = \frac{\%\Delta Q}{\%\Delta P} = \frac{\text{Percentage change in quantity demanded}}{\text{Percentage change in price}}$$

Since price and quantity demanded are inversely related by the law of demand, the numerator and denominator always have opposite algebraic signs, and the coefficient of demand elasticity is always negative. The elasticity coefficient is calculated for movements along a given demand curve (or function) as price changes and all other factors affecting quantity demanded are held constant. Suppose a 10 percent price decrease ($\%\Delta P = -10\%$) causes consumers to increase their purchases by 30 percent ($\%\Delta Q = +30\%$). The coefficient of demand elasticity is equal to –3 (= +30%/–10%) in this case. In contrast, if the 10 percent decrease in price causes only a 5 percent increase in sales, the elasticity coefficient would equal –0.5 (= +5%/–10%). Clearly, the smaller (absolute) value of *E* indicates less sensitivity on the part of consumers to a change in price.

elastic
Demand is elastic when $|E| > 1$.

inelastic
Demand is inelastic when $|E| < 1$.

When a change in price causes consumers to respond so strongly that the percentage by which they adjust their consumption *exceeds* (in absolute value) the percentage change in price, demand is said to be **elastic** over that price interval. In mathematical terms, demand is elastic when $|\%\Delta Q|$ exceeds $|\%\Delta P|$, and thus $|E|$ is greater than 1. When a change in price causes consumers to respond so weakly that the percentage by which they adjust their consumption is *less than* (in absolute value) the percentage change in price, demand is said to be **inelastic** over that price interval. In other words, demand is inelastic when the numerator is smaller than the denominator (in absolute value), and thus $|E|$ is less than 1. In the special instance in which the percentage change in quantity *just equals* the percentage change in price (in absolute value), de-

TABLE 3.1
The Coefficient of Demand Elasticity (E)
$$E = \frac{\%\Delta Q}{\%\Delta P}$$

Elasticity	Responsiveness	Coefficient of demand elasticity
Elastic	$\|\%\Delta Q\| > \|\%\Delta P\|$	$\|E\| > 1$
Unitary elastic	$\|\%\Delta Q\| = \|\%\Delta P\|$	$\|E\| = 1$
Inelastic	$\|\%\Delta Q\| < \|\%\Delta P\|$	$\|E\| < 1$

Note: The symbol "| |" denotes the absolute value.

unitary elastic
Demand is unitary elastic when $|E| = 1$.

mand is said to be **unitary elastic**, and $|E|$ is equal to 1. Table 3.1 summarizes this discussion.

Suppose a manager knows the coefficient of demand elasticity for a company's product is equal to –2.5 over the range of prices currently being considered by the firm's marketing department. The manager is considering decreasing price by 8 percent and wishes to predict the percentage by which quantity demanded will increase. From the definition of the coefficient of demand elasticity, it follows that

$$-2.5 = \frac{\%\Delta Q}{-8\%},$$

so,

$$-2.5 \times -8\% = \%\Delta Q,$$

and,

$$\%\Delta Q = +20\%$$

Thus, the manager can increase sales by 20 percent by lowering price 8 percent.

Alternatively, suppose a manager of a different firm faces a coefficient of demand elasticity equal to –0.5 over the range of prices it would consider charging for its product. This manager wishes to stimulate sales by 15 percent. The manager is willing to lower price to accomplish the increase in sales but needs to know the percentage amount by which price must be lowered to obtain the 15 percent increase in sales. Again using the definition of the coefficient of demand elasticity, it follows that

$$-0.5 = \frac{+15\%}{\%\Delta P}$$

so,

$$\begin{aligned}\%\Delta P &= 15\%/-0.5\\ &= -30\%\end{aligned}$$

Thus, this manager must lower price by 30 percent in order to increase sales by 15 percent.

As you can see, the concept of demand elasticity is rather simple. Demand elasticity is nothing more than a mathematical measure of how sensitive quantity demanded is to changes in price. We will now apply the concept of demand elasticity to a crucial question facing managers. How does a change in the price of the firm's product affect the total revenue received?

3.2 ELASTICITY AND TOTAL REVENUE

total revenue (*TR*)
The total amount paid to producers for a good or service ($TR = P \times Q$).

Managers of firms, as well as industry analysts, government policymakers, and academic researchers, are frequently interested in how total revenue changes when there is a movement along the demand curve. **Total revenue (*TR*)**, which also equals the total expenditure by consumers on the commodity, is simply the price of the commodity times quantity demanded, or

$$TR = P \times Q$$

As we have emphasized, price and quantity demanded move in opposite directions along a demand curve: If price rises, quantity falls; if price falls, quantity rises. The change in price and the change in quantity have opposite effects on total revenue. Consider a price increase. A higher price would, by itself, tend to increase *TR*. However, the resulting decrease in quantity demanded would, by itself, tend to decrease *TR*. The relative strengths of these two effects will determine the overall effect on *TR*. We will examine these two effects separately, then combine them to establish the relation between elasticity and total revenue.

The Price Effect and the Quantity Effect of a Price Change

Figure 3.1 illustrates how a change in price affects total revenue. Both panels show the same linear demand curve. We begin in Panel A, which illustrates the change in total revenue for a region of demand in which the quantity effect dominates the price effect. Suppose a manager initially sets a price of $18 and sells 600 units of the good (point *a*). Now let the price be reduced to $16, which causes a movement down the demand curve from point *a* to *b* so that quantity demanded increases to 800 units. The change in total revenue is

$$\begin{aligned}\Delta TR &= TR_b - TR_a = P_bQ_b - P_aQ_a = (\$16 \times 800) - (\$18 \times 600)\\ &= \$12{,}800 - \$10{,}800\\ &= +\$2{,}000\end{aligned}$$

Thus, total revenue rises by $2,000 when price is lowered from $18 to $16.

price effect
The effect on total revenue of a change in price, holding output constant.

quantity effect
The effect on total revenue of a change in output, holding price constant.

This increase in total revenue is the overall effect of a *price effect* and a *quantity effect.* The effect on total revenue of changing price, holding output constant, is called the **price effect**. Since price is *reduced* by $2 (= $18 – $16) for each of the 600 units that can be sold at $18, the price effect is –$1,200 (= –$2 × 600) and is represented by area A in Panel A. By itself, the reduction in price reduces total revenue by $1,200. The effect on total revenue of changing output, holding price constant, is called the **quantity effect**. Since quantity is *increased* by 200 units, and each of these extra 200 units can be sold for $16, the quantity effect is +$3,200 (= $16 × 200), and is represented by area B in Panel A. By itself, the increase in quantity causes total revenue to rise by $3,200. Over the interval from point *a* to *b*, the quantity effect dominates the price effect since area B is larger than area A ($3,200 > $1,200).

FIGURE 3.1
Changes in Total Revenue from a Price Change

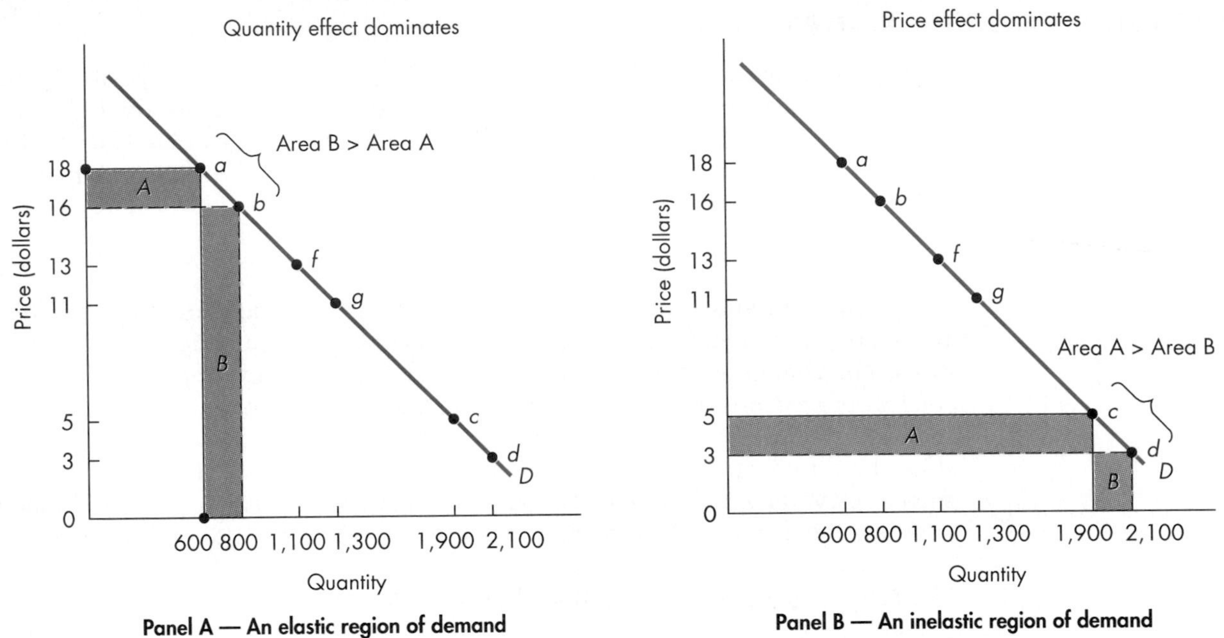

Panel A — An elastic region of demand

Panel B — An inelastic region of demand

The overall change in total revenue caused by reducing price from \$18 to \$16 is equal to the sum of the price effect and the quantity effect:

$$\begin{aligned}\Delta TR &= \text{Price effect} + \text{Output effect}\\ &= -\$1{,}200 + \$3{,}200\\ &= +\$2{,}000\end{aligned}$$

As expected, this amount is identical to the change in total revenue computed earlier by taking the difference between the total revenues at points *a* and *b* ($TR_b - TR_a$). Thus when the quantity effect dominates the price effect, a decrease in price causes total revenue to rise because quantity (the dominant variable) increases. It is easy to verify that, in this case, an *increase* in price would cause total revenue to fall because quantity (the dominant variable) decreases.[1] To

[1]Reversing the direction of movement along the demand curve (now from point *b* to *a*) causes total revenue to *fall*. The price effect is positive (+\$1,200) and the quantity effect is now negative (−\$3,200). The combined impact of these two effects causes total revenue to fall when price rises from \$16 to \$18:

$$\begin{aligned}\Delta TR &= +\$1{,}200 + (-\$3{,}200)\\ &= -\$2{,}000\end{aligned}$$

Again, *TR* moves in the same direction *Q* moves since the quantity effect outweighs the price effect over the interval *a* to *b* on the demand curve.

summarize the situation when the quantity effect dominates the price effect (area B > area A), a change in price causes total revenue to move in the same direction that quantity moves. In other words, an increase in *Q* (caused by a decrease in *P*) results in higher total revenue, and a decrease in *Q* (caused by an increase in *P*) results in lower total revenue.

Now we examine a different portion of the same demand curve where the price effect dominates the quantity effect. This situation is illustrated in Panel B of Figure 3.1. Suppose a manager lowers price from \$5 to \$3, causing quantity to rise from 1,900 to 2,100 units. Total revenue changes from \$9,500 (= \$5 × 1,900) to \$6,300 (= \$3 × 2,100) for a decrease of \$3,200. Since price is reduced by \$2 for each of the 1,900 units that can be sold at \$5, the price effect is –\$3,800 (= –\$2 × 1,900) and is represented by area A in Panel B. Since quantity is increased by 200 units, and each of these 200 additional units can be sold for \$3, the quantity effect is +\$600 (= \$3 × 200) and is represented by area B in Panel B. Over the interval of demand from point *c* to *d*, the price effect dominates the quantity effect (i.e., area A > area B). The reduction in price from \$5 to \$3 causes total revenue to *fall* by \$3,200:

$$\begin{aligned}\Delta TR &= \text{Price effect} + \text{Quantity effect}\\ &= -\$3{,}800 + \$600\\ &= -\$3{,}200\end{aligned}$$

As before, this amount is identical to the difference between total revenue at prices of \$5 and \$3 (–\$3,200). Thus, when the price effect dominates the quantity effect, a decrease in price causes total revenue to fall because price (the dominant variable) decreases. You should verify that an *increase* in price from \$3 to \$5 would cause total revenue to rise because price (the dominant variable) increases. To summarize the situation when the price effect dominates the quantity effect (area A > area B), a change in price causes total revenue to move in the same direction that price moves. An increase in *P* results in higher total revenue, and a decrease in *P* results in lower total revenue.

The price effect and quantity effect exactly offset one another when area A equals area B, which implies the two effects are equal (but opposite in sign). When neither the price effect nor the quantity effect outweighs the other, a change in price (either an increase or a decrease) leaves total revenue unchanged. Such a situation is illustrated over the interval from point *f* to *g* in Figure 3.1. You should verify that total revenue is the same at both points *f* and *g* and that the price effect and quantity effect are equal but opposite in sign.

Relation The overall impact of raising or lowering price on total revenue ($TR = P \times Q$) is equal to the sum of the price effect and quantity effect of a change in price:

$$\Delta TR = \text{Price effect} + \text{Quantity effect}$$

When the price effect dominates the quantity effect, the direction of movement of price determines the direction of movement of *TR*. If *P* rises (falls), *TR* rises (falls). When the quantity effect dominates the price effect, the direction of movement of quantity determines the direction of movement of *TR*. If *Q* rises (falls) when price is decreased (increased), *TR* rises (falls). If neither the price effect nor the quantity effect dominates the other, *TR* does not change when price either rises or falls.

The Coefficient of Elasticity and Total Revenue

With the information about the price and quantity effects of a price change, relating the coefficient of elasticity and the effect of changes in price on total revenue is simple and straightforward. As we pointed out, if the quantity effect is greater than the price effect (in absolute value) over a range of demand, total revenue moves in the same direction as the change in quantity over that range. Recall that when demand is elastic, $|E| > 1$ and $|\%\Delta Q| > |\%\Delta P|$. This means that the quantity effect is greater than the price effect when demand is elastic. It follows that over an elastic range of demand, the change in total revenue moves in the same direction as the change in quantity, and in the opposite direction from the change in price. That is, when demand is elastic, if price falls and quantity demanded rises, total revenue must rise; when price rises and quantity demanded falls, total revenue must fall.

Now consider a range of demand where the price effect dominates the quantity effect, and, consequently, total revenue moves in the same direction as the change in price. Since the price effect dominates the quantity effect, it follows that $|\%\Delta Q| < |\%\Delta P|$, $|E| < 1$, and demand is inelastic over this range of demand. Thus, when demand is inelastic, if price falls and quantity demanded rises, total revenue must fall; when price rises and quantity demanded falls, total revenue must rise.

When the price effect just offsets the quantity effect, $|\%\Delta Q| = |\%\Delta P|$, $|E| = 1$, and demand is unitary elastic over this range of demand. When demand is unitary elastic, total revenue remains unchanged for either an increase in price or a decrease in price. This discussion is summarized in Table 3.2 and in the following relation:

Relation If the percentage change in quantity demanded exceeds the percentage change in price ($|\%\Delta Q| > |\%\Delta P|$) over a range of demand, demand is elastic over this range, and an increase (decrease) in price causes total revenue to decrease (increase). If the percentage change in price exceeds the percentage change in quantity demanded ($|\%\Delta P| > |\%\Delta Q|$) over a range of demand, demand is inelastic over this range, and an increase (decrease) in price causes total revenue to increase (decrease).

Note in Figure 3.1 that demand is elastic over the \$16 to \$18 price range, but inelastic over the \$3 to \$5 price range. In general, the elasticity of demand varies along any particular demand curve, even one that is linear. It is generally incorrect to say a demand curve is either elastic or inelastic. You can only say that a

TABLE 3.2
Relations between Demand Elasticity and Total Revenue (*TR*)

	Elastic $|\%\Delta Q| > |\%\Delta P|$ *Q*-effect dominates	Unitary elastic $|\%\Delta Q| = |\%\Delta P|$ No dominant effect	Inelastic $|\%\Delta Q| < |\%\Delta P|$ *P*-effect dominates
Price rises	*TR* falls	No change in *TR*	*TR* rises
Price falls	*TR* rises	No change in *TR*	*TR* falls

demand curve is elastic or inelastic *over a particular price range.* For example, it is correct to say that demand curve D in Figure 3.1 is elastic over the \$16 to \$18 price range and inelastic over the \$3 to \$5 price range.

3.3 FACTORS AFFECTING DEMAND ELASTICITY

Demand elasticity plays such an important role in business decision making that managers should understand not only how to use the concept to obtain information about the demand for the products they sell, but also how to recognize the factors that affect demand elasticity. We will now discuss the four factors that make the demand for some products more elastic than the demand for other products.

Availability of Substitutes

The availability of substitutes is by far the most important determinant of demand elasticity. The better the substitutes for a given good or service, the more elastic is the demand for that good or service. When the price of a good or service rises, consumers will substantially reduce consumption of that good or service if they perceive that close substitutes are readily available. Naturally, consumers will be less responsive to a price increase if they perceive that only poor substitutes are available. When there are many close substitutes for a good and the price of that good falls, the price of these other substitute goods is higher relative to the now lower-priced good. Many people will switch if they think the lower-priced product will easily substitute for the relatively higher-priced goods. If there are not particularly close substitutes available, only a few people will switch to the lower-priced good.

Thus, the greater the consumers' ability to find satisfactory substitutes for a particular good, the more responsive they will be to a change in the price of the good, whether the price of the good rises or falls. This means the elasticity of demand is higher, the greater the availability of close substitutes. Some goods for which demand is rather elastic include fruit, corporate jets, and cafeteria meals. Alternatively, goods for which consumers perceive few or no good substitutes have low elasticities of demand. Wheat, salt, and gasoline tend to have low elasticities because there are only poor substitutes available—for instance, corn, pepper, and diesel fuel, respectively.

The definition of the market for a good greatly affects the number of substitutes and thus its elasticity of demand. For example, if all of the gasoline stations in a city raised the price of gasoline by 10 cents per gallon, total sales of gasoline would undoubtedly fall—but probably not by much. If, on the other hand, only the Exxon stations raised price by 10 cents, the sales of Exxon gasoline would probably fall substantially. There are many good substitutes for Exxon gasoline at the higher price, but there are not as many substitutes for gasoline in general. Moreover, if only one service station raised its price, that station's sales would be expected to fall almost to zero in the long run. The availability of so many easily accessible substitutes would encourage most customers to trade elsewhere, since the cost of finding a substitute service station is so small.

Percent of Consumer's Budget

The percentage of the consumer's budget that is spent on the commodity is also important in the determination of price elasticity. All other things equal, we would expect the price elasticity to be directly related to the percentage of consumers' budgets spent on the good. For example, the demand for refrigerators is probably more price elastic than the demand for toasters, since the expenditure required to purchase a refrigerator would make up a larger percentage of the budget of a "typical" consumer. Note that we are not saying that price elasticity is determined by the price of the good. Rather, price elasticity is influenced by the relation between total expenditure on the good and the budget of potential consumers of the commodity.

Product Durability

All other things equal, durable goods tend to be more price elastic than nondurable commodities. This relation results simply from the fact that the purchase of a durable good may be postponed. If the price of a durable commodity rises, quantity demanded would be expected to fall by a larger percentage than would be the case for nondurables because many potential buyers would have the option of making do with their existing durables. Returning to the earlier example, the demand for refrigerators would be more elastic than that for toasters since the refrigerator is more durable. The consumer can make do with the old refrigerator longer while searching for the lowest price.

Time Period of Adjustment

The length of the time period used in measuring the price elasticity affects the magnitude of the elasticity coefficient. In general, the longer the time period of measurement, the larger (the more elastic) the coefficient of demand elasticity will be. This relation is the result of consumers having more time to adjust to the price change.

Consider, for example, the way consumers would adjust to an increase in the price of milk. Suppose the dairy farmers' association is able to convince all producers of milk nationwide to raise their milk prices by 15 percent. During the first week the price increase takes effect, consumers come to the stores with their grocery lists already made up. Shoppers notice the higher price of milk but have already planned their meals for the week. While a few of the shoppers will react immediately to the higher milk prices and reduce the amount of milk they purchase, many shoppers will go ahead and buy the same amount of milk they purchased the week before. If the dairy association collects sales data and measures the elasticity of demand for milk after the first week of the price hike, they will be happy to see that the 15 percent increase in the price of milk caused only a modest reduction in milk sales.

Over the coming weeks, however, consumers begin looking for ways to consume less milk. They substitute foods that have similar nutritional composition to milk; consumption of cheese, eggs, and yogurt all increase. Some consumers will even switch to powdered milk for some of their less urgent milk needs—

perhaps to feed the cat or to use in cooking. Six months after the price increase, the dairy association again measures the demand elasticity of milk. Now the coefficient of demand elasticity is probably much larger (more elastic) since it is measured over a six-month time period instead of a one-week time period.

For all goods and services, given a longer time period to adjust, the demand for the commodity exhibits more responsiveness to changes in price—the demand becomes more elastic. Of course, we can treat the effect of time on elasticity within the framework of the effect of available substitutes. The greater the time period available for consumer adjustment, the more substitutes become available and economically feasible. As we stressed above, the more available are substitutes, the more elastic is demand.

3.4 CALCULATING DEMAND ELASTICITY

The coefficient of demand elasticity can be calculated either (1) over an interval (or arc) along demand, or (2) at a point on a demand curve. The choice of whether to measure demand elasticity at a point on demand or over an interval depends upon the particular application. In both cases, E still measures the sensitivity of consumers to changes in the price of the commodity.

Computing Elasticity over an Interval

arc elasticity
The coefficient of demand elasticity calculated over an interval of a demand curve.

When the coefficient of demand elasticity is calculated over an interval of a demand curve or schedule, the coefficient is called the **arc elasticity**. For example, in Figure 3.2, the elasticities measured over the intervals RS, ST, TU—or any other *price range* that might be of interest—are all referred to as arc elasticities.[2] Between any two points on demand, the percentage changes in quantity demanded and price are calculated as

$$\%\Delta Q = \frac{\Delta Q}{Q_{base}} \times 100$$

$$\%\Delta P = \frac{\Delta P}{P_{base}} \times 100$$

where Q_{base} and P_{base} represent the "base" upon which the percentage changes are computed. When taking the ratio of the two percentage changes, the factor of 100 cancels out of the numerator and denominator, and the arc elasticity of demand can be expressed as

$$E = \frac{\dfrac{\Delta Q}{Q_{base}}}{\dfrac{\Delta P}{P_{base}}}$$

[2]The arc between any two points on a demand *curve* corresponds to a movement between any two prices in a demand *schedule*. Thus, the elasticity coefficient calculated between two prices in a demand schedule is also called an arc elasticity.

FIGURE 3.2
Calculating Arc Elasticity

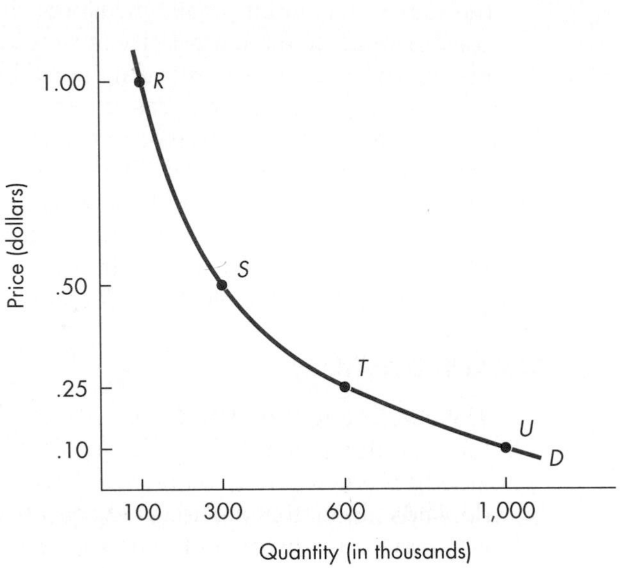

The only thing that could possibly complicate the above calculation is the choice of the base price and base quantity. The mathematical convention is to use the "initial" values of P and Q as the base upon which to measure the percentage changes. This convention, however, requires a minor modification in the way arc elasticities are computed. If we use the initial price and quantity as base values for computing elasticity, we get two different values of E for the same interval, depending on whether the movement is up or down over the interval. In fact, the interval may be so wide that moving up demand (price rises) produces one value of E that indicates demand is elastic while moving down demand (price falls) produces another value of E that indicates demand is inelastic.

For example, at point R (P = \$1 and Q = 100) in Figure 3.2 total revenue is \$100, and at point S (P = \$0.50 and Q = 300) total revenue is \$150. Thus, over the interval RS, total revenue rises when price falls, and demand must be elastic over this interval. Using R as the initial (base) point and moving *down* to S, the calculated elasticity is –4:

$$E = \frac{\dfrac{300 - 100}{100}}{\dfrac{.50 - 1.00}{1.00}} = \frac{2}{-\dfrac{1}{2}} = -4$$

If we compute the elasticity for the same interval of demand by using S as the initial (base) point and moving *up* the interval to R. The calculated elasticity is now equal to $-\frac{2}{3}$:

TABLE 3.3
Computing Arc Elasticities

Interval	Price falls from	Total revenue (when P falls)	Arc elasticity (E)
RS	\$1 to \$.50	TR rises	$\frac{(100-300)/200}{(1.00-.50)/.75} = -1.5$
ST	\$.50 to \$.25	TR unchanged	$\frac{(300-600)/450}{(.50-.25)/.375} = -1$
TU	\$.25 to \$.10	TR falls	$\frac{(600-1{,}000)/800}{(.25-.10)/.175} = -0.583$

$$E = \frac{\frac{100-300}{300}}{\frac{1.00-.50}{.50}} = \frac{-\frac{2}{3}}{1} = -\frac{2}{3}$$

Not only is $-\frac{2}{3}$ not equal to –4, but demand now appears to be inelastic. The reason for the difference lies in the fact that we computed elasticity over a wide range of the demand curve, and the base values lie at opposite ends of the arc.

The correct approximation of arc elasticity is obtained by using the average (or midpoint) values of quantity and price as the base for computing percentage changes.[3] When measuring arc elasticities over an interval of a demand curve, the following arc formula should be used:

$$E = \frac{\frac{\Delta Q}{Q_{\text{base}}}}{\frac{\Delta P}{P_{\text{base}}}} = \frac{\frac{\Delta Q}{\text{Average } Q}}{\frac{\Delta P}{\text{Average } P}}$$

We will use this formula (here and throughout the rest of the text) to compute the arc elasticity of demand over the interval RS as shown in Figure 3.2:

$$E = \frac{\frac{100-300}{200}}{\frac{1.00-.50}{.75}} = \frac{-1}{\frac{2}{3}} = -\frac{3}{2} = -1.5$$

The arc elasticity equals –1.5 no matter whether the computation is made moving up or down interval RS. Since $|-1.5|$ is greater than 1, demand is, in fact, elastic as expected from the previously noted change in total revenue. Table 3.3 shows the computations for the three intervals RS, ST, and TU in Figure 3.2. We have established the following principle:

[3]The average values of P and Q are also the mid-point values between the initial values and the new values. For example, if Q is initially 300 units and the new value is 100, the mid-point value is 200, which is also the average value [(300 + 100)/2 =200].

ILLUSTRATION 3.1

Texas Calculates Elasticity

In addition to its regular license plates, the state of Texas, as do other states, sells personalized or "vanity" license plates. To raise additional revenue, the state will sell a vehicle owner a license plate saying whatever the owner wants as long as it uses six letters (or numbers), no one else has the same license as the one requested, and it isn't obscene. For this service, the state charges a higher price than the price for standard licenses. Many people are willing to pay this higher price rather than display a license of the standard form such as 387 BRC.

For example, an opththalmologist announces his practice with the license MYOPIA. Others tell their personalities with COZY-1 and ALL MAN. A rabid Star Trek fan has BM ME UP.

In 1986, Texas increased the price for such plates from $25 to $75. The *Houston Post,* October 19, 1986, reported that before the price increase about 150,000 cars in Texas had personalized licenses. After the increase in price, only 60,000 people ordered the vanity plates. As it turned out, demand was rather inelastic over this range. As you can calculate, the own-price elasticity is –.86. Thus revenue rose after the price increase, from $3,750,000 to $4,500,000.

But the *Houston Post* article quoted the assistant director of the Texas Division of Motor Vehicles as saying, "Since the demand dropped* the state didn't make money from the higher fees, so the price for next year's personalized plates will be $40." If the objective of the state is to make money from these licenses and if the numbers in the article are correct, this is the wrong thing to do. It's hard to see how the state lost money by increasing the price from $25 to $75—the revenue increased and the cost of producing plates must have decreased since fewer were produced. So the move from $25 to $75 was the right move.

Moreover, let's suppose that the elasticity between $75 and $40 is essentially the same as that calculated for the movement from $25 to $75 (–.86). We can use this estimate to calculate what happens to revenue if the state drops the price to $40. We must first find what the new quantity demanded will be at $40. Using the arc elasticity formula and the elasticity of –.86,

$$E = \frac{\Delta Q/\text{Average } Q}{\Delta P/\text{Average } P}$$

$$= \frac{(60{,}000 - Q)/[(60{,}000 + Q)/2]}{(75 - 40)/[(75 + 40)/2]} = -.86$$

where Q is the new quantity demanded. Solving this equation for Q, the estimated sales are 102,000 (rounded) at a price of $40. With this quantity demanded and price, total revenue would be $4,080,000 representing a decrease of $420,000 from the revenue at $75 a plate. If the state's objective is to raise revenue by selling vanity plates, it should increase rather than decrease price.

This application actually makes two points. First, even decision makers in organizations that are not run for profit, such as government agencies, should be able to use economic analysis. Second, managers whose firms are in business to make a profit should make an effort to know (or at least have a good approximation for) the elasticity of demand for the products they sell. Only with this information will they know what price to charge.

*It was, of course, quantity demanded that decreased, not demand.

Source: This illustration is based upon Barbara Boughton, "A License for Vanity," *Houston Post*, October 19, 1986, pp. 1G, 10G.

Principle When calculating the elasticity of demand over an interval of demand, use the arc elasticity formula:

$$E = \frac{\Delta Q}{\text{Average } Q} \Big/ \frac{\Delta P}{\text{Average } P}$$

Computing Elasticity at a Point

point elasticity
A measurement of demand elasticity calculated at a point on the demand curve, rather than over an interval.

As noted, it is sometimes useful to measure elasticity at a point on the demand curve rather than over an interval. When elasticity is computed at a point on demand it is called **point elasticity** of demand. Computing elasticity at a point on demand is no more difficult than computing arc elasticity. We begin with the case of a linear demand.

If the demand curve is linear, it can be expressed in intercept-slope form as $P = a + bQ$, where a is the P-intercept and b is the inverse of the slope of the demand function ($\Delta P/\Delta Q$), which is negative because P and Q are negatively related along demand. The elasticity of demand at a given point on demand is

$$E = \%\Delta Q/\%\Delta P = P/(P - a)$$

where P is the value of price at the given point on demand.[4] Now consider the linear demand curve in Panel A of Figure 3.3 At a price of \$100 (point L), the elasticity of demand is –5 [=100/(100 – 120)] since the intercept, a, equals 120. At a price of \$60 (point M), demand is unitary elastic [E = –1 = 60/(60 – 120)]. When price is \$40 (point N), demand is inelastic [E = –.5 = 40/(40 – 120)].

We now use Panel B of Figure 3.3 to show how to compute demand elasticity at a point on a *curvilinear* demand. To compute elasticity of demand for a price of \$100, first construct the line tangent to point R on the demand curve, extending the tangent line until it touches the price axis. Since P, Q, and slope are identical for the linear demand and the curvilinear demand at R, their elasticities are identical at R. Therefore, to calculate the elasticity of the curved demand at R, compute the point elasticity as for a linear demand curve, using the price-intercept of the tangent line as the value of a. At \$100, the elasticity of demand is –2.5 [= 100/(100 – 140)]. At \$40, the elasticity of demand is –.8 [= 40/(40 – 90)].

Elasticity (generally) Varies along a Demand Curve

In general, different intervals or points along the same demand curve have differing elasticities of demand, even when the demand curve is linear. When demand is linear, the slope of the demand curve is constant. Even though the *absolute* rate at which quantity demanded changes as price changes ($\Delta Q/\Delta P$) remains constant,

[4]The proof of this formula is relatively simple. Let the inverse of the demand function be expressed as $P = a + bQ$; and, solving for demand, $Q = -a/b + (1/b)P$. Since we do not have to worry about averaging the bases P and Q at a *point* on demand, the elasticity formula can be written as

$$E = \frac{\Delta Q/Q}{\Delta P/P} = \frac{\Delta Q}{\Delta P} \cdot \frac{P}{Q}$$

The slope of demand, $\Delta Q/\Delta P$ equals $1/b$. Therefore,

$$E = \frac{1}{b} \cdot \frac{P}{Q} = \frac{1}{b} \cdot \frac{P}{\left(\frac{a}{-b} + \frac{1}{b}P\right)} = \frac{P}{P - a}$$

See Appendix 3A for a derivation of this result using calculus.

FIGURE 3.3
Calculating Point Elasticity

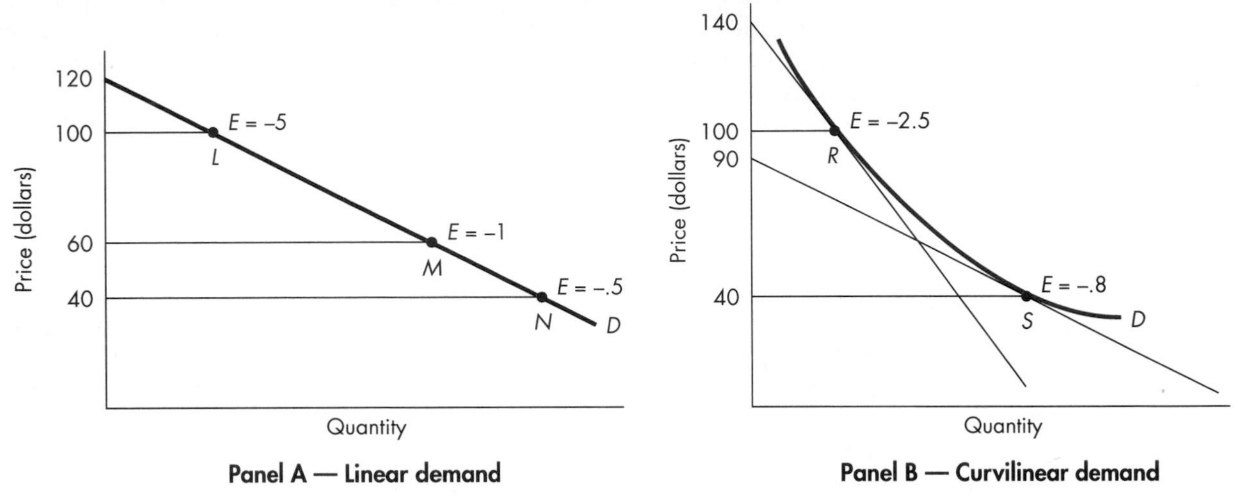

Panel A — Linear demand **Panel B — Curvilinear demand**

the *proportional* rate of change in Q as P changes ($\%\Delta Q/\%\Delta P$) varies along a linear demand curve. To see why, rewrite the coefficient of elasticity as

$$E = \frac{\Delta Q/Q}{\Delta P/P}$$

or

$$E = \frac{\Delta Q}{\Delta P} \cdot \frac{P}{Q}$$

Moving along a linear demand does not cause the term $\Delta Q/\Delta P$ to change, but elasticity does vary because the proportionality term P/Q changes. Compare intervals *ab* and *cd* in Panel A of Figure 3.1. Over both intervals, $\Delta Q/\Delta P = -200/2 = -100$; that is, a \$1 decrease in price causes quantity demanded to increase by 100 units. The computed elasticities,

$$E_{ab} = -100 \cdot \frac{17}{700} = -2.43, \text{ and}$$

$$E_{cd} = -100 \cdot \frac{4}{2{,}000} = -0.2$$

differ because the proportionality term P/Q becomes smaller when moving down the demand curve. Note that demand elasticity decreases when moving down a linear demand curve, *regardless* of whether elasticity is measured over an interval or at a point (see Panel A, Figure 3.3). Thus, price and demand elasticity vary *directly* along a linear demand curve.

In the case of curvilinear demand, price and demand elasticity also vary, except in one special case. When the demand equation takes the form $Q = aP^b$, the elasticity is *constant* along the demand curve and is equal to b.[5] We mention this special case here simply to be complete.

Relation In general, the elasticity of demand varies along a demand curve. For a linear demand, price and elasticity vary directly: the higher the price, the more elastic is demand. For a curvilinear demand, there is no general rule about the relation between price and elasticity, except for the special case of $Q = aP^b$, which has a constant demand elasticity (equal to b) for all prices.

3.5 OTHER ELASTICITIES

income elasticity (E_M) Measures the responsiveness of quantity demanded to changes in income, holding all other variables in the generalized demand function constant.

cross-price elasticity (E_{XY}) Measures the responsiveness of quantity demanded to changes in the price of a related good, when all the other variables in the generalized demand function remain constant.

Sometimes economists and business decision makers are interested in measuring the sensitivity of consumers to changes in either income or the price of a related good. **Income elasticity** measures the responsiveness of quantity demanded to changes in income, holding all other variables in the generalized demand function constant. **Cross-price elasticity** measures the responsiveness of quantity demanded to changes in the price of a related good, when all the other variables in the generalized demand function remain constant. In this section we show how to calculate and interpret these two elasticities.

Income Elasticity

As noted, income elasticity measures the responsiveness of quantity purchased when income changes, all else constant. Income elasticity, E_M, is the percentage change in quantity demanded divided by the percentage change in income, holding all other variables in the generalized demand function constant, including the good's own price:

$$E_M = \frac{\%\Delta Q}{\%\Delta M} = \frac{\Delta Q/Q}{\Delta M/M} = \frac{\Delta Q}{\Delta M} \cdot \frac{M}{Q}$$

As you can see, the sign of E_M depends upon the sign of $\Delta Q/\Delta M$, which may be positive (if the good is normal) or negative (if the good is inferior). Thus, if the good is normal, the income elasticity is positive. If the good is inferior, the income elasticity is negative.

To illustrate the computation of income elasticity, consider Metro Ford, a new-car dealership in Atlanta. The manager of Metro Ford expects average household income in Fulton County to increase from $22,000 to $25,000 annually when the current recession ends, causing an increase in the demand for new cars. At a constant average price of $15,000 per car, the increase in income will cause sales to rise from 800 to 1,400 units per month. Panel A in Figure 3.4 illustrates this situation. The increase in income shifts the demand for new cars rightward—a new car is a normal good. To calculate the income elasticity of demand, we use the arc elasticity method of computing percentage changes over an interval. The income elasticity of demand in Panel A is

[5]See Appendix 3B for a proof of this result.

FIGURE 3.4
Calculating Income Elasticity of Demand

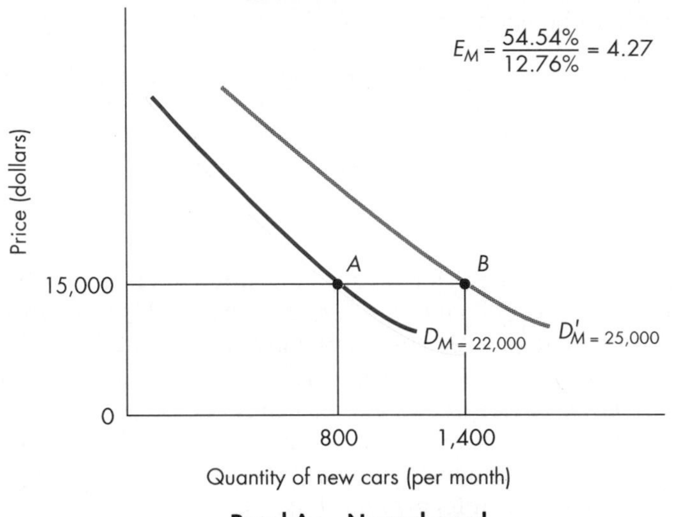

Panel A — Normal good

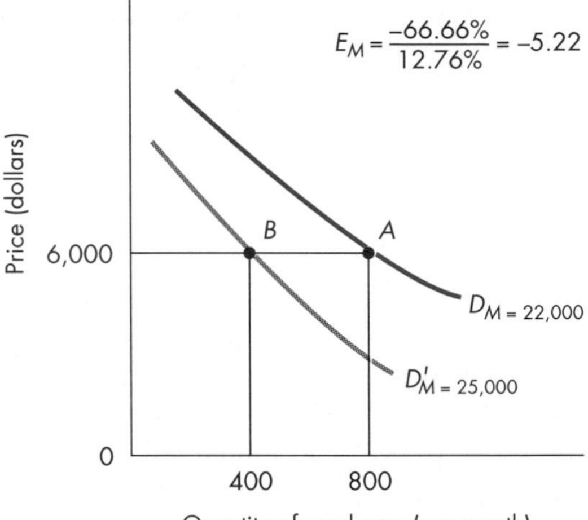

Panel B — Inferior good

$$E_M = \frac{\%\Delta Q}{\%\Delta M} = \frac{\dfrac{600}{1{,}100}}{\dfrac{3{,}000}{23{,}500}} = \frac{54.55\%}{12.77\%} = 4.27$$

We should mention that the choice of $15,000 as the price at which to measure income elasticity is arbitrary. The manager at Metro Ford probably chose a price of $15,000 as a typical new-car price.

Now consider Lemon Motors, a used-car dealership in Atlanta. Panel B in Figure 3.4 depicts the demand for used cars at Lemon Motors. The increase in household income in Fulton County causes a decrease in demand for used cars from D to D'—used cars are assumed to be inferior goods in this example. Holding used-car prices at $6,000, sales at the used-car dealership fall from 800 to 400 units per month. Again using the arc method of computing percentage changes, the income elasticity of demand is

$$E_M = \frac{\%\Delta Q}{\%\Delta M} = \frac{\dfrac{-400}{600}}{\dfrac{3{,}000}{23{,}500}} = \frac{-66.67\%}{12.77\%} = -5.22$$

As expected, the income elasticity is negative for an inferior good.

Relation The income elasticity measures the responsiveness of consumers to changes in income when the price of the good and all other determinants of demand are held constant. The income elasticity is positive (negative) for normal (inferior) goods.

Cross-Price Elasticity

The cross-price elasticity of a good, as already noted, measures the responsiveness of quantity demanded of one good to changes in the price of another good, when all the other variables in the generalized demand function remain constant. The cross-price elasticity between the good in question (X) and another good (Y)—denoted E_{XY}—is calculated by taking the ratio of the percentage change in the quantity demanded of good X ($\%\Delta Q_X$) and dividing by the percentage change in the price of the other good Y ($\%\Delta P_Y$):

$$E_{XY} = \frac{\%\Delta Q_X}{\%\Delta P_Y} = \frac{\Delta Q_X/Q_X}{\Delta P_Y/P_Y} = \frac{\Delta Q_X}{\Delta P_Y} \cdot \frac{P_Y}{Q_X}$$

Note that the sign of E_{XY} depends upon the sign of $\Delta Q_X/\Delta P_Y$, which can be positive or negative. Recall from Chapter 2 that if an increase in the price of one good causes the quantity purchased of another good to increase, the goods are substitutes (i.e., $\Delta Q_X/\Delta P_Y > 0$). If the rise in the price of one good causes the quantity purchased of another good to fall, the goods are complements (i.e., $\Delta Q_X/\Delta P_Y < 0$). If there is no change in the quantity purchased of the other good, the two goods are independent (i.e., $\Delta Q_X/\Delta P_Y = 0$). Thus, E_{XY} is positive when X and Y are substitutes; E_{XY} is negative when X and Y are complements.[6]

Suppose the commissioner of the Tampa Sports Authority is studying the pricing of Tampa Bay Buccaneer football tickets. Of particular concern is the sensitivity of football fans to the price of soccer tickets (P_S) and the price of parking at Tampa Stadium (P_P), a substitute good and a complementary good, respectively, for football games. If Buccaneer fans are quite responsive to changes in the prices of soccer and parking, the commissioner may be able to improve attendance at Bucs' home games by recommending to the Sports Authority an increase in the price of soccer and a decrease in the price of parking at the stadium. If football fans are rather insensitive to the price of soccer and the price of parking, there is not much the commissioner of the Sports Authority can do to stimulate sales—only improved performance of the team or a reduction in the price of football tickets is likely to enhance attendance.

As illustrated in Panel A in Figure 3.5, an increase from \$9 to \$10 in the price of Rowdies' tickets (Tampa's soccer team) will cause the demand for football tickets to shift rightward from D to D'. At a constant price of \$24 for football tickets, sales of football tickets (Q_F) increase from 48,000 to 50,000 (point A to point B). The cross-price elasticity between football and soccer (E_{FS}) is computed using the arc formula:

[6] We should note that the cross-price elasticity of X for Y need not equal the cross-price elasticity of Y for X.

FIGURE 3.5
Calculating Cross-Price Elasticity of Demand

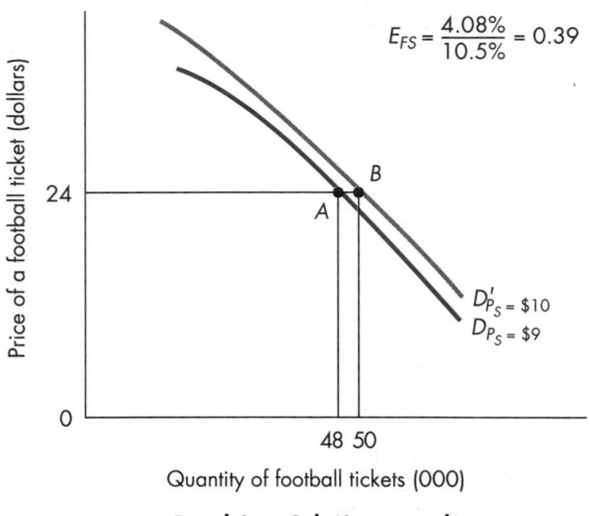

Panel A — Substitute goods

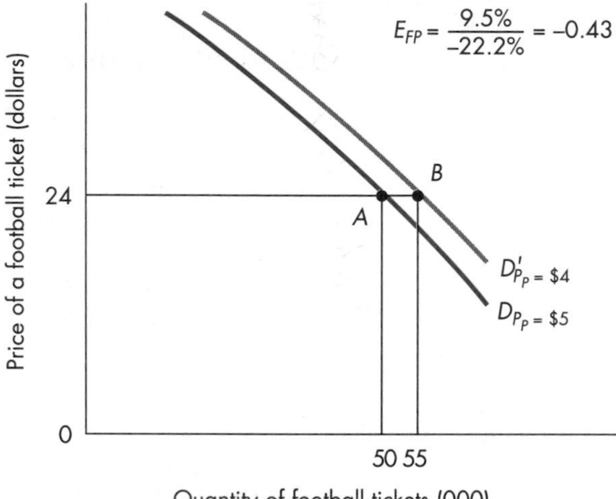

Panel B — Complementary goods

$$E_{FS} = \frac{\%\Delta Q_F}{\%\Delta P_S} = \frac{\frac{2}{49}}{\frac{1}{9.5}} = \frac{4.08\%}{10.53\%} = 0.39$$

Note that the cross-price elasticity between football and soccer is positive (for substitutes), but rather small, indicating football and soccer are rather weak substitutes.

Panel B in Figure 3.5 shows that decreasing the price of parking (P_P) from $5 to $4 causes an increase in the demand for football tickets from *D* to *D′*. At a constant $24 price of football tickets, sales of football tickets increase from 50,000 to 55,000, as a result of reducing the parking fees at the stadium. The cross-price elasticity between football and parking (E_{FP}) is computed as:

$$E_{FP} = \frac{\%\Delta Q_F}{\%\Delta P_P} = \frac{\frac{5}{52.5}}{\frac{-1}{4.5}} = \frac{9.52\%}{-22.22\%} = -0.43$$

The cross-price elasticity between football and parking is negative (as expected for complements), but small, indicating that football fans are not particularly responsive to changes in the price of parking. Because of the small absolute values of the cross-price elasticities, the Tampa Sports Authority is not likely to have much impact on attendance at Bucs games if it raises soccer prices and lowers parking fees.

ILLUSTRATION 3.2

Empirical Elasticities of Demand*

Using the appropriate data and statistical techniques, it is possible to estimate own-price, income, and cross-price elasticities from actual demand schedules. We have collected a sample of estimated demand elasticities from a variety of sources and present them in the table below. In the chapter on empirical demand functions, we will show how to estimate actual demand elasticities.

Looking at the own-price elasticities presented in the table, note that the demand for basic agricultural products such as beef and eggs is inelastic. Fruit, for which consumers can find many substitutes, has a much more elastic demand than beef or eggs. For any particular make and model of automobile, consumers can find plenty of readily available substitutes. Consequently, the demand elasticity for General Motors' Pontiac Catalina is very large. Another factor affecting own-price elasticity is the length of time consumers have to adjust to a price change. It is interesting that gasoline demand is inelastic in the short run, but elastic in the long run.

We explained in the text that cross price elasticities are positive for substitutes and negative for complements. All three pairs of goods in the table are substitutes ($E_{XY} > 0$). Beef and chicken are weak substitutes, while margarine and butter seem to be rather strong substitutes. The extremely high cross-price elasticity of demand between Pontiac Catalinas and Chevrolet Impalas suggests that these two cars were virtually identical in the eyes of consumers.

Normal goods have positive income elasticities of demand (E_M); and inferior goods have negative income elasticities. Potatoes are inferior goods since E_M is negative. Beef is more strongly normal than chicken, indicating that a given percentage increase in income causes an almost fourfold greater increase in beef consumption than chicken consumption. The high income elasticity of demand for foreign travel indicates that consumer demand for foreign travel is quite responsive to changes in income. Furniture demand, on the other hand, appears to be rather insensitive to changes in income.

Table of Empirical Elasticities of Demand

Own-price elasticities of demand (E)	
Beef	−0.956
Eggs	−0.263
Fruit	−3.021
GM Pontiac Catalina	−16.99
Gasoline (short run)	−0.43
Gasoline (long run)	−1.50
Cross-price elasticities of demand (E_{XY})	
Beef and chicken	0.350
Margarine and butter	1.526
Catalinas and Impalas	19.3
Income elasticities of demand (E_M)	
Beef	1.27
Chicken	0.33
Potatoes	−0.81
Foreign travel by U.S. citizens	3.09
Furniture	0.53

*For our own-price, cross-price, and income elasticities for all agricultural products, see Dale Heien, "The Structure of Food Demand: Interrelatedness and Duality," *American Journal of Agricultural Economics,* May 1982. For automobile own-price and cross-price elasticities, see F. Owen Irvine, Jr., "Demand Equations for Individual New Car Models Estimated Using Transaction Prices with Implications for Regulatory Issues," *Southern Economic Journal,* January 1983. For short-run and long-run gasoline elasticities, see, respectively Robert Archibald and Robert Gillingham, "An Analysis of Short-Run Consumer Demand for Gasoline Using Household Survey Data," *Review of Economics and Statistics,* November 1980, and James Griffin and Henry Steele, *Energy Economics and Policy,* Academic Press, 1980, p. 232. For foreign travel and furniture income economics, see Hendrik Houghakker and Lester Taylor, *Consumer Demand in the United States; Analyses and Projections,* Harvard University Press, 1970.

Relation The cross-price elasticity measures the responsiveness of the quantity demanded of one good when the price of another good changes, holding the price of the good and all other determinants of demand constant. Cross-price elasticity is positive (negative) when the two goods are substitutes (complements).

3.6 MARGINAL REVENUE, DEMAND, AND ELASTICITY

The responsiveness of consumers to changes in the price of a good must be considered by managers when making pricing and output decisions. The elasticity of demand gives managers essential information about how total revenue will be affected by a change in price. As it turns out, an equally important concept for pricing and output decisions is *marginal revenue.* **Marginal revenue** is the addition to total revenue attributable to selling one additional unit of output,

marginal revenue (MR)
The addition to total revenue attributable to selling one additional unit of output.

$$MR = \Delta TR/\Delta Q$$

Marginal revenue is related to demand elasticity because marginal revenue, like demand elasticity, involves changes in total revenue caused by movements along a demand curve.

Marginal Revenue and Demand

As noted, marginal revenue is related to the way changes in price and output affect total revenue along a demand curve. To see the relation between marginal revenue and price, consider the following numerical example. The demand schedule for a product is presented in columns 1 and 2 of Table 3.4. Price times quantity gives the total revenue obtainable at each level of sales, shown in column 3.

Marginal revenue, shown in column 4, indicates the change in total revenue from an additional unit of sales. Note that marginal revenue equals price only for the first unit sold. For the first unit sold, total revenue is the demand price for one unit. The first unit sold adds $4—the price of the first unit—to total revenue, and the marginal revenue of the first unit sold equals $4; that is, $MR = P$ for the first unit. If two units are sold, the second unit should contribute $3.50 (the price of the second unit) to total revenue. But total revenue for two units is only $7, indicating that the second unit adds only $3 (= $7 – $4) to total revenue. Thus the marginal revenue of the second unit is not equal to price, as it was for the first unit. Indeed, examining columns 2 and 4 in Table 3.4 indicates that $MR < P$ for all but the first unit sold.

TABLE 3.4
Demand and Marginal Revenue

(1) Unit sales	(2) Price	(3) Total revenue	(4) Marginal revenue ($\Delta TR/\Delta Q$)
0	$4.50	$ 0	—
1	4.00	4.00	$4.00
2	3.50	7.00	3.00
3	3.10	9.30	2.30
4	2.80	11.20	1.90
5	2.40	12.00	0.80
6	2.00	12.00	0
7	1.50	10.50	−1.50

inframarginal units
Units of output that could have been sold at a higher price had a firm not lowered its price to sell the marginal unit.

Marginal revenue is less than price ($MR < P$) for all but the first unit sold because price must be lowered in order to sell more units. Not only is price lowered on the marginal (additional) unit sold, but price is also lowered for all the inframarginal units sold. The **inframarginal units** are those units that could have been sold at a higher price had the firm not lowered price to sell the marginal unit. Marginal revenue for any output level can be expressed as:

$$MR = \text{Price} - \frac{\text{Revenue lost by lowering price}}{\text{on the inframarginal units}}$$

The second unit of output sells for \$3.50. By itself, the second unit contributes \$3.50 to total revenue. But, marginal revenue is not equal to \$3.50 for the second unit because in order to sell the second unit, price on the first unit is lowered from \$4 to \$3.50. In other words, the first unit is an inframarginal unit, and the \$0.50 lost on the first unit must be subtracted from the price. The net effect on total revenue of selling the second unit is \$3 (= \$3.50 – \$0.50), the same value as shown in column 4 of Table 3.4.

If the firm is currently selling two units and wishes to sell three units, it must lower price from \$3.50 to \$3.10. The third unit increases total revenue by its price, \$3.10. In order to sell the third unit, the firm must lower price on the two units that could have been sold for \$3.50 if only two units were offered for sale. The revenue lost on the two inframarginal units is \$0.80 (= \$0.40 × 2). Thus the marginal revenue of the third unit is \$2.30 (= \$3.10 – \$0.80), and marginal revenue is less than the price of the third unit.

It is now easy to see why $P = MR$ for the first unit sold. For the first unit sold, price is not lowered on any inframarginal units. Since price must fall in order to sell additional units, marginal revenue must be less than price at every other level of sales (output).

As shown in column 4, marginal revenue declines for each additional unit sold. Notice that it is positive for each of the first five units sold. However, marginal revenue is zero for the sixth unit sold, and marginal revenue becomes negative thereafter. That is, the seventh unit sold actually causes total revenue to decline. Marginal revenue is positive when the effect of lowering price on the inframarginal units is less than the revenue contributed by the added sales at the lower price. Marginal revenue is negative when the effect of lowering prices on the inframarginal units is greater than the revenue contributed by the added sales at the lower price.

Relation Marginal revenue must be less than price for all units sold after the first, because the price must be lowered in order to sell more units. When marginal revenue is positive, total revenue increases when quantity increases. When marginal revenue is negative, total revenue decreases when quantity increases. Marginal revenue is zero when total revenue is maximized.

Figure 3.6 shows graphically the relations among demand, marginal revenue, and total revenue for the demand schedule in Table 3.4. As noted above, MR is below price (in Panel A) at every level of output except the first. When total revenue (in Panel B) begins to decrease, marginal revenue becomes negative. Demand and marginal revenue are both negatively sloped.

Sometimes the interval over which marginal revenue is measured is greater than one unit of output. After all, managers don't necessarily increase output by just one unit at a time. Suppose in Table 3.4 that we want to compute marginal revenue when output increases from 2 units to 5 units. Over the interval, the change in total revenue is \$5 (= \$12 – \$7), and the change in output is 3 units. Marginal revenue is \$1.67 (= $\Delta TR/\Delta Q$ = \$5/3) per unit change in output; that is, each of the 3 units contributes (on average) \$1.67 to total revenue. As a general rule, whenever the interval over which marginal revenue is being measured is more than a single unit, divide ΔTR by ΔQ to obtain the marginal revenue for each of the units of output in the interval.

As mentioned in Chapter 2, demand equations are frequently specified to be linear in form for purposes of empirical estimation and forecasting. The relation between a linear demand equation and its marginal revenue function is no different than the relation set forth in the above relation. The case of a linear demand curve is special because the relation between demand and marginal revenue has some additional properties that do not hold for nonlinear demand curves.

When demand is linear, marginal revenue lies halfway between demand and the vertical axis. This implies that marginal revenue must be twice as steep

FIGURE 3.6

Demand, Marginal Revenue, and Total Revenue

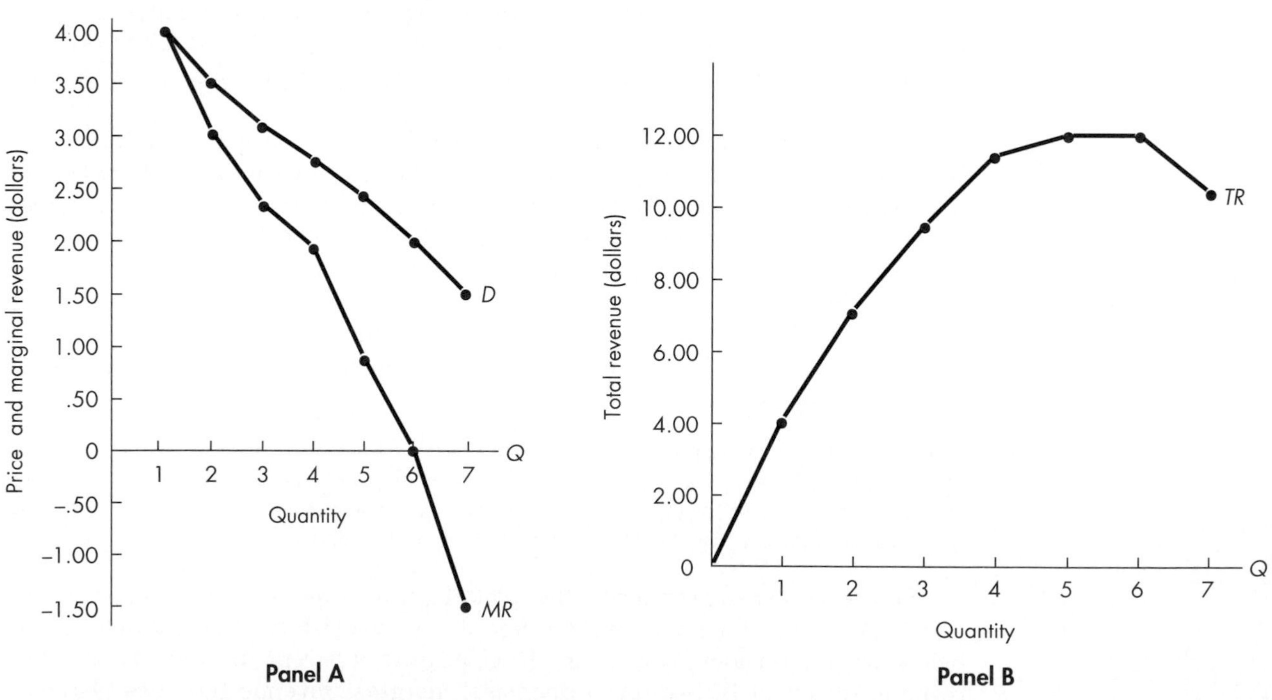

as demand. The mathematical relation between demand and marginal revenue in the case of a linear demand is derived in Appendix A.

Relation When demand is linear, $P = a + bQ$, marginal revenue is also linear, intersects the vertical (price) axis at the same point demand does, and is twice as steep as demand. The equation of the linear marginal revenue curve is $MR = a + 2bQ$.

Figure 3.7 shows the linear demand curve $P = 6 - 0.05Q$. (Remember that b is negative because P and Q are inversely related.) The associated marginal reve-

FIGURE 3.7
Linear Demand, Marginal Revenue, and Elasticity

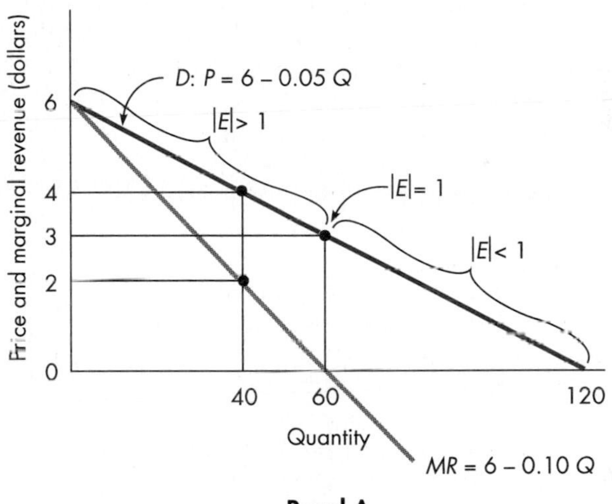

Panel A

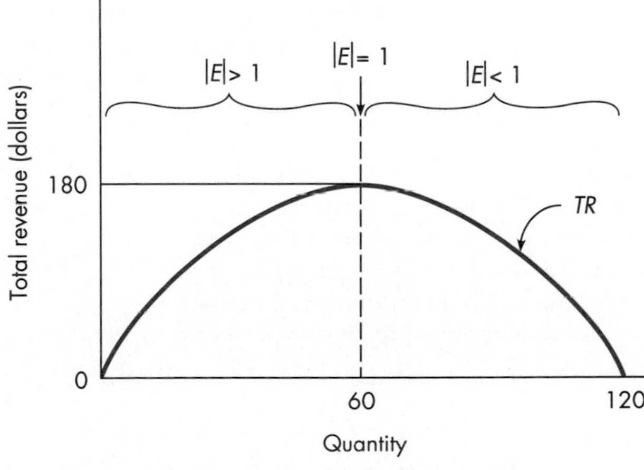

Panel B

ILLUSTRATION 3.3

Cigarette Taxes and Demand Elasticity

In 1993, President Clinton appeared to be leaning toward a large tax increase on cigarettes, and possibly alcohol, to finance part of his proposed health care plan. *The Wall Street Journal* (April 14, 1993) pointed out a problem with such "sin taxes." The chairwoman of the President's Council of Economic Advisors noted that such taxes are designed to do two things at once: (1) raise revenue for the government, and (2) discourage drinking, smoking, and other activities considered harmful to people's health. As the *Journal* pointed out, the two goals may conflict. If the administration proves too successful in discouraging alcohol and tobacco consumption, there might not be enough money to pay for the health plan.

The director of the Congressional Budget Office believed that if the White House imposed a tobacco tax of $1 to $2 per pack, the tendency would be to "overestimate the amount of revenue that would come in." An industry analysis of the federal liquor tax in 1985 concluded that the government had expected to raise $14 billion in revenue over three years but only $11 billion came in. The president of the Distilled Spirits Council stated that after the tax on liquor was raised in 1991, the government actually collected 2.3 percent less in tax revenue.

On the other hand, the director of the Alcohol Policies Project at the Center for Science in the Public Interest argued that the falloff in revenues after the last tax increase was temporary, and stated, "To say that raising taxes doesn't raise more money is nonsense." A lawyer with the Nonsmokers' Rights Association of Canada pointed to the Canadian experience with "sin taxes" by arguing that tax increases on tobacco over the past decade had lifted the average price of a pack of cigarettes in Canada to $4.43 (US) from $1.74. At the same time Canadians were smoking 40 percent fewer cigarettes and yet, overall tobacco tax revenue soared to $5.6 billion from $1.6 billion.

As you probably realize, the effect on government revenue from an excise tax on tobacco, alcohol, or any other good depends in large part on the elasticity of demand for that good. Consider the above statement saying that raising taxes doesn't raise more money is just total nonsense. Obviously, if the government imposes a tax on a good that had not been previously taxed, tax receipts must rise if sales do not fall to zero after the price increase resulting from the tax. However, a tax increase over an existing tax may either increase or decrease tax revenue, depending on demand elasticity.

The following figure illustrates this point. Assume that in this cigarette market there is already a tax on cigarettes of $1 per pack. The relevant current supply is shown by the supply curve labeled $S_{\$1\text{ tax}}$. Two possible demand curves in equilibrium are D_1 and D_2. At the point of equilibrium, D_1 is more elastic than D_2, since any given percentage change in price will cause a larger percentage change in quantity demanded along D_1 than along D_2. When a $1-per-pack tax is levied, equilibrium price is $2 and sales are 700 million packs per month. Government's tax receipts from the $1-per-pack tax are therefore $700 million.

Now let the tax increase to $2 per pack, and the cigarette supply curve shifts upward (a decrease in supply) to the curve labeled $S_{\$2\text{ tax}}$. If D_2 (the less elastic demand) is the relevant demand curve, price rises to approximately $2.75 and sales fall to 530 million packs per month. After the tax increase, tax receipts *rise* to $1,060 million (= $2 × 530 million packs). Also note that the elasticity of demand over the range of the price increase is

$$E = \frac{\Delta Q/\text{Average } Q}{\Delta P/\text{Average } P} = \frac{-170/615}{.75/2.375} = -.875$$

Demand is inelastic over this range.

nue curve is also linear, intersects the price axis at $6, and is twice as steep as the demand curve. Because it is twice as steep, marginal revenue intersects the quantity axis at 60 units, which is half the output level for which demand intersects the quantity axis. The equation for marginal revenue has the same vertical intercept, but twice the slope: $MR = 6 - 0.10Q$.

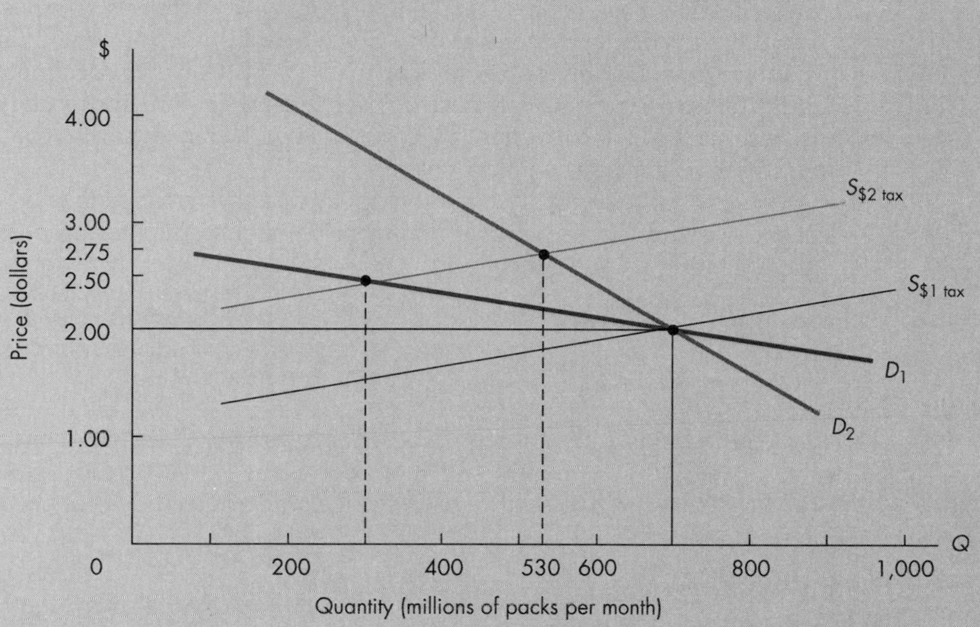

Now assume that D_1 (the more elastic demand) is the relevant demand curve. The shift in supply after the tax increase causes price to increase to \$2.50 and sales to decrease to 300 million. Tax receipts now *fall* from \$700 million at the \$1 tax to \$600 million (= \$2 × 300 million packs) at the \$2 tax. Demand elasticity over this range is

$$E = \frac{\Delta Q/\text{Average } Q}{\Delta P/\text{Average } P} = \frac{-400/500}{.50/2.25} = -3.60$$

This time demand is quite elastic over the range.

This exercise demonstrates two points: (1) The effect on government tax revenue of an increase in taxes on cigarettes or alcohol depends on the demand elasticity for the good; and (2) If demand is sufficiently elastic—not just elastic—the tax increase could actually *decrease,* not increase, government revenue.

There is substantial empirical evidence that demand for cigarettes is relatively inelastic (see Grossman, et al., 1993). Elasticity estimates vary by age group: −1.20 for youths aged 12–17, −.74 for young smokers aged 20–25, −.44 for smokers between 26 and 35 years old, and −.15 for smokers over 35 years old. Virtually all studies of federal cigarette tax revenues assume an inelastic demand for cigarettes, and therefore, they predict higher tax revenues from tax hikes. In a recent study, a tax rate of \$1.26 a pack was predicted to maximize tax revenue at \$16 billion, while a \$2 tax hike was predicted to yield only \$11 billion in tax revenues.

Sources: Rick Wartzman, "Clinton's Proposal for 'Sin Taxes' May Stumble by Turning Too Many Americans into Saints," *The Wall Street Journal,* April 14, 1993. Michael Grossman, Jody Sindelar, John Mullahy, and Richard Andersen, "Alcohol and Cigarette Taxes," *Journal of Economic Perspectives,* Fall 1993.

Marginal Revenue and Elasticity

Using Figure 3.7, we now examine the relation of own-price elasticity to demand and marginal revenue. Recall that if total revenue increases when price falls and quantity rises, demand is elastic; if total revenue decreases when price falls and quantity rises, demand is inelastic. When marginal revenue is positive in Panel A, from a quantity of zero until 60, total revenue increases as price declines in Panel B; thus demand is elastic over this range. Conversely, when marginal revenue is negative, at quantities greater than 60, total revenue declines when price falls; thus demand must be inelastic over this range. Finally, if marginal revenue is zero, at 60, total revenue does not change when quantity changes, so the elasticity of demand is unitary at 60.

Except for marginal revenue being linear and twice as steep as demand, all of the above relations hold for nonlinear demands. Thus for all demand curves the following relation must hold.

Relation Marginal revenue is less than price at every level of output after the first unit. When MR is positive (negative), total revenue increases (decreases) as quantity increases, and demand is elastic (inelastic). When MR is zero, the elasticity of demand is unitary.

The relation among marginal revenue, elasticity of demand, and price at any quantity can be expressed still more precisely. As shown in Appendix C, the relation between marginal revenue, price, and elasticity, *for linear or curvilinear demands,* is:

$$MR = P(1 + 1/E)$$

where E is the own-price elasticity of demand and P is product price. When demand is elastic ($|E| > 1$), $|1/E|$ is less than one, $1 + 1/E$ is positive, and marginal revenue is positive. When demand is inelastic ($|E| < 1$), $|1/E|$ is greater than one, $1 + 1/E$ is negative, and marginal revenue is negative. In the case of unitary elasticity ($|E| = 1$), $1 + 1/E$ is zero, and marginal revenue is zero.

To illustrate the relation between MR, P, and E numerically, we calculate marginal revenue at 40 units of output for the demand curve shown in Panel A of Figure 3.7. At 40 units of output, the point elasticity of demand is equal to -2 [$= P/(P - a) = 4/(4 - 6)$]. Using the formula presented above, MR is equal to 2 [$= 4(1 - 1/2)$]. This is the same value for marginal revenue that is obtained by substituting $Q = 40$ into the equation for marginal revenue: $MR = 6 - 0.1(40) = 2$.

Relation For any demand curve, when demand is elastic ($|E| > 1$), marginal revenue is positive. When demand is inelastic ($|E| < 1$), marginal revenue is negative. When demand is unitary elastic ($|E| = 1$), marginal revenue is zero. For all demand and marginal revenue curves:

$$MR = P(1 + 1/E)$$

where E is the own-price elasticity of demand.

3.7 SUMMARY

Demand elasticity—the own-price elasticity of demand—measures the responsiveness or sensitivity of consumers to changes in the price of a good. The elasticity of demand is the ratio of the percentage change in quantity demanded to the percentage change in the price of the good. Over a specified price range, demand is said to be either elastic, unitary elastic, or inelastic according to whether the elasticity coefficient is greater than, equal to, or less than one, respectively. In the case of linear demand, moving down the demand curve causes demand elasticity to get smaller.

An extremely important relation in economic analysis relates the change in total revenue (due to a movement along demand) and the elasticity of demand. If demand is elastic for a given change in price, an increase in price causes total revenue to fall. A decrease in price causes total revenue to rise if demand is elastic over the price range. If demand is inelastic for a given price change, an increase in price causes total revenue to rise, while a decrease in price causes total revenue to fall.

Several factors affect the own-price elasticity of demand. The most important of these is the availability of close substitutes. The better and more numerous the substitutes for a good, the more elastic is the demand for the good. Demand elasticity is directly related to the percentage of the consumers' budgets spent on the good and the durability of the product. Also, the longer the time period that consumers have to adjust to price changes, the more responsive they will be, and the more elastic is demand.

Demand elasticities are calculated either for intervals along the demand curve or at points on the demand curve. The arc elasticity formula is used to calculate elasticity along an arc (or interval) of demand. The arc elasticity formula uses the average or mid-point values of price and quantity, rather than the initial values, for the purpose of computing percentage changes. Specifically, the arc elasticity of demand (E) is

$$E = \frac{\Delta Q}{\text{Average } Q} \Big/ \frac{\Delta P}{\text{Average } P}$$

In contrast to the arc elasticity, the point elasticity of demand measures elasticity at a point. When demand is linear, the point elasticity is calculated as

$$E = P/(P - a)$$

where a is the price-intercept of the demand curve. The point elasticity of demand for a curvilinear demand is computed by constructing the tangent line to the curve at the point of measure. Extend the tangent line until it intersects the price axis. Compute the point elasticity as for a linear demand, using the price-intercept of the tangent line as the value of a.

When comparing elasticities along a particular demand curve, demand elasticity generally varies directly with price: demand is more elastic at higher prices and less elastic at lower prices. An exception to this rule is the special demand curve $Q = aP^b$, which has a constant elasticity equal to the value of b throughout its entire range of prices.

Two other important elasticities are income elasticity, which measures the responsiveness of quantity purchased to changes in income, and cross-price elasticity, which measures the responsiveness of quantity purchased to changes in the price of related goods (substitutes or complements). Both of these elasticities are measured using the arc (averaging) method to compute percentage changes. In the case of income elasticity, the elasticity measure is positive if the good is normal, negative if the good is inferior. In the case of cross-price elasticity, the elasticity measure is positive if the two goods are substitutes, negative if they are complements.

Marginal revenue is the change in total revenue resulting from the sale of an additional unit of output. Marginal revenue declines as output increases and is less than price for every quantity except for the first unit, in which case marginal revenue equals price. When MR is positive, TR is rising. When MR is negative, TR is falling. When MR is zero, TR is neither rising nor falling: It is at its maximum value. In the case of linear demand, where demand is expressed as $P = a + bQ$, marginal revenue is also linear, and is expressed as $MR = a + 2bQ$. In other words, marginal revenue is also linear, intersects the price axis at the same point as demand, and is twice as steep as demand.

For any demand, linear or curvilinear, marginal revenue can be expressed as $MR = P(1 + 1/E)$, where E is the own-price elasticity of demand. Hence, if demand is elastic, marginal revenue is positive. If demand is inelastic, marginal revenue is negative. When demand is unitary elastic, marginal revenue is equal to zero.

TECHNICAL PROBLEMS

1. If quantity demanded decreases 8 percent, when price increases 10 percent, what is the own-price elasticity of demand?
   a. Given the own-price elasticity of demand calculated above, what would happen to quantity demanded if price now decreases 4 percent?

b. Based on the above own-price elasticity of demand, what must have happened to price if quantity demanded increases 6 percent?

2. Fill in the blanks.
   a. Total revenue rises when price ________ over a region of demand that is elastic, or when price ________ over a region of demand that is inelastic.
   b. Over an elastic region of demand, total revenue falls when price ________. Over an inelastic region of demand, total revenue falls when price ________.
   c. An increase or decrease in price in the unitary elastic region of demand causes total revenue to ________.

* 3. Use the graph that follows to answer the following questions.
   a. The arc elasticity of demand over the price range $3 to $5 is ________.
   b. Let price rise from $3 to $5. The price effect of raising price is $________. The quantity effect of raising price is $________. The net effect is to ________ total revenue by $________.
   c. Total revenue when price is $5 is $________. Total revenue when price is $3 is $________. The change in output when price falls from $5 to $3 is ________. Therefore, marginal revenue is $________.
   d. Marginal revenue is ________ and $|E|$ is ________ than one.
   e. Using average price for *P*, verify that $MR = P(1 + 1/E)$.

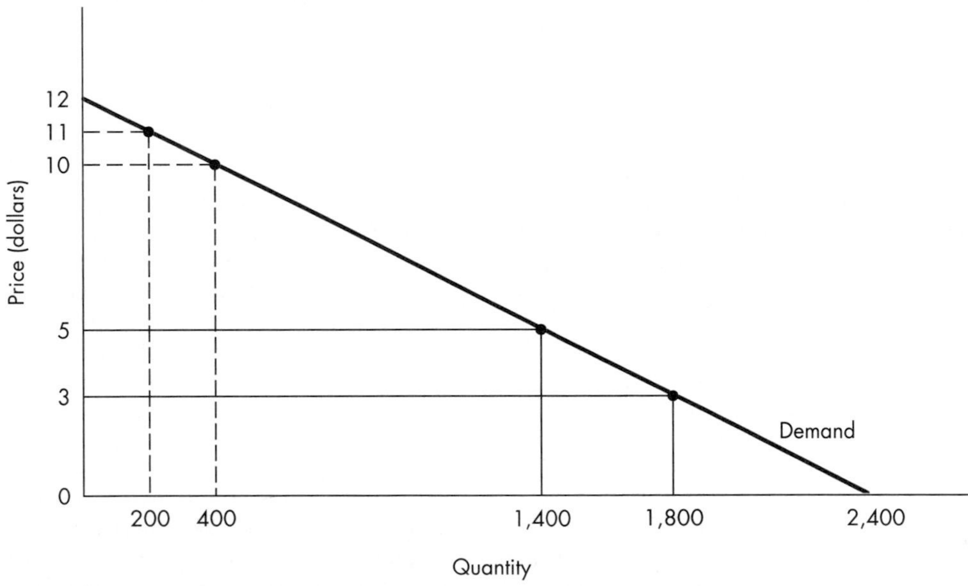

4. Use the graph in problem 3 to answer the following questions:
   a. The arc elasticity of demand over the price range $10 to $11 is ________.
   b. Let price fall from $11 to $10. The price effect of reducing price is $________. The quantity effect of reducing price is $________. The net effect is to ________ total revenue by $________.
   c. Total revenue when price is $10 is $________. Total revenue when price is $11 is $________. The change in output when price falls from $11 to $10 is ________. Therefore, marginal revenue is $________.

d. Marginal revenue is ________ and E is ________ than one.
e. Using the average price for P, verify that $MR = P(1 + 1/E)$.

5. Use the linear demand curve shown on the following page to answer the following questions.
   a. The point elasticity of demand at a price of $800 is ________.
   b. The point elasticity of demand at a price of $200 is ________.
   c. Demand is unitary elastic at a price of $________.
   d. As price rises, $|E|$ ________ (gets larger, gets smaller, stays the same) for a linear demand curve.

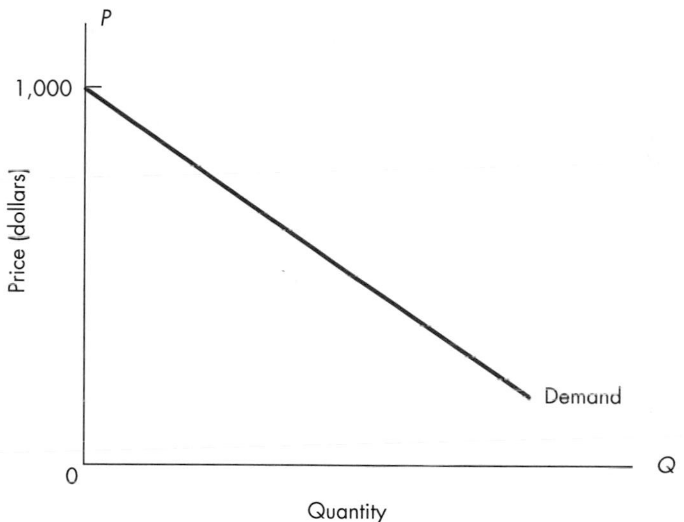

6. Use the information in the following table and the arc formula to calculate the own-price, income, and cross-price elasticities of demand. (Recall that each elasticity is calculated holding all other variables constant.)
   a. Is demand elastic or inelastic?
   b. Is X a normal or an inferior good?
   c. Are X and Y substitutes or complements?
   d. If the price of X increases 5 percent, what will happen to the quantity of X demanded? What will happen to total expenditure on X?
   e. If income increases 10 percent, what will happen to the quantity of X demanded?
   f. If the price of Y decreases 20 percent, what will happen to the quantity of X demanded?

Price of X	Quantity demanded of X	Income ($1,000)	Price of related good Y
$20	200	$25	$4
20	300	25	8
20	280	23	4
10	400	25	4

7. Using the following demand schedule, calculate total revenue, marginal revenue, and own-price elasticity of demand. Then show the relation among marginal revenue, price, and elasticity of demand.

Price	Quantity demanded	Total revenue	Marginal revenue	Elasticity of demand
$60	8	_____		
50	16	_____	_____	_____
40	24	_____	_____	_____
30	32	_____	_____	_____
20	40	_____	_____	_____
10	48	_____	_____	_____

8. Use the graph below to answer the questions.

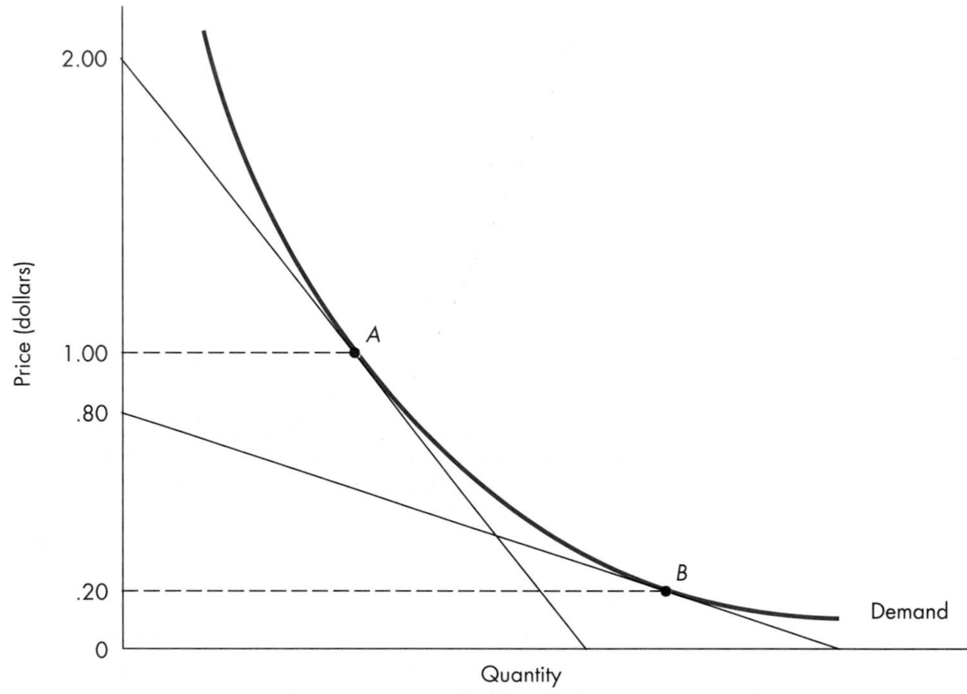

a. What are the elasticities of demand at prices of $0.20 and $1.00?
b. What happens to total revenue if price increases by a small amount at point *A*? At point *A*, is marginal revenue positive, negative, or zero?
c. What happens to total revenue if price decreases by a small amount at point *B*? At point *B*, is marginal revenue positive, negative, or zero?

9. In the graph on the next page, the shift in the demand for *X* from D_X^0 to D_X^1 is caused by the price of a related good *Y* changing from $10 to $14. Compute the cross-price elasticity of demand when P_X = $8. Are goods *X* and *Y* substitutes or complements? What sign does E_{XY} have?

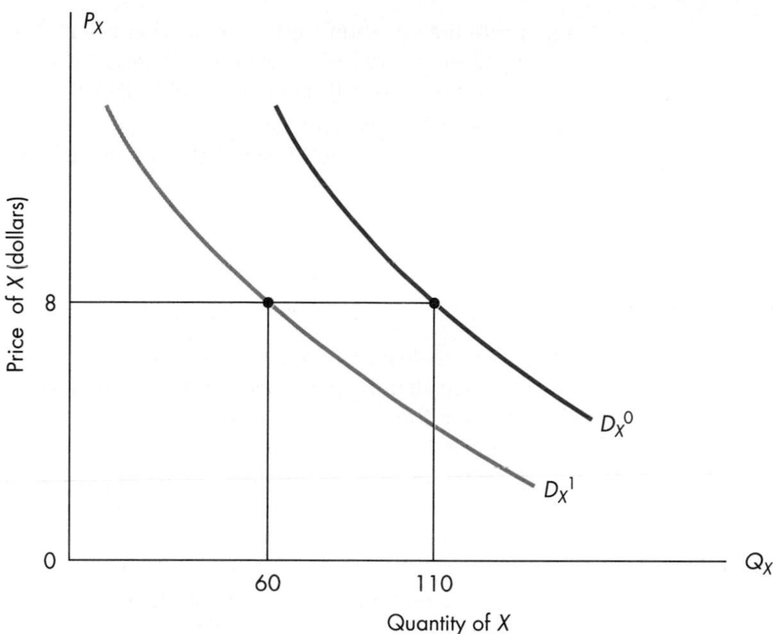

10. In the following graph, the shift in the demand for X from D_X^0 to D_X^1 is caused by a decrease in income from \$5,000 to \$4,000 when P_X = \$110. Compute the income elasticity of demand. Is good X normal or inferior? What sign does E_M have?

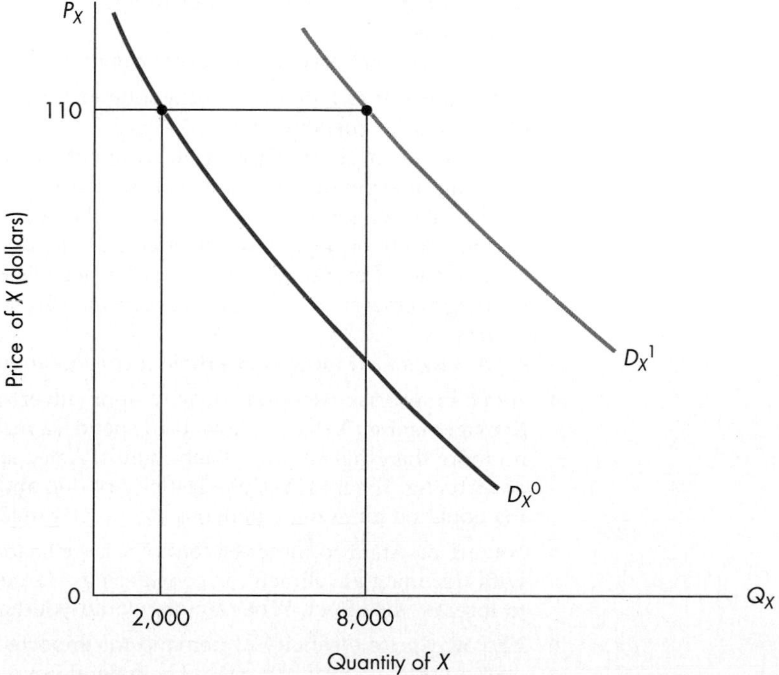

* 11. Write the equation for the demand curve in the graph for problem 3. What is the equation for marginal revenue? At what price is demand unitary elastic? At what output is marginal revenue equal to zero?

12. Suppose the demand for good X is $Q = 20/P$. What is total revenue when $P = \$1$? When $P = \$2$? When $P = \$4$? What is the elasticity of demand for this demand curve? Why?

APPLIED PROBLEMS

1. In an article about the financial problems of *USA Today*, *Newsweek* (April 27, 1992) reported that the paper was losing about $20 million a year. A Wall Street analyst said that the paper should raise its price from 50 cents to 75 cents, which he estimated would bring in an additional $65 million a year. The paper's publisher rejected the idea, saying that circulation could drop sharply after a price increase, citing the *The Wall Street Journal*'s experience after it increased its price to 75 cents. What implicit assumptions are the publisher and the analyst making about demand elasticity?
2. Assume that the demand for plastic surgery is price inelastic. Are the following statements true or false? Explain.
   a. When the price of plastic surgery increases, the number of operations decreases.
   b. The percentage change in the price of plastic surgery is less than the percentage change in quantity demanded.
   c. Changes in the price of plastic surgery do not affect the number of operations.
   d. Quantity demanded is quite responsive to changes in price.
   e. If more plastic surgery is performed, expenditures on plastic surgery will decrease.
   f. The marginal revenue of another operation is negative.
3. What effect, if any, do each of the following events have on the own-price elasticity of demand for corporate jets?
   a. Reduced corporate earnings lead to cuts in travel budgets and increase the share of expenditures on private jet travel.
   b. Further deregulation of the commercial airlines industry substantially increases the variety of departure times and destinations offered by commercial airlines.
   c. The cost of manufacturing corporate jets rises.
   d. Improvements in jet engine design increases the expected lifetime of corporate jets.
   e. A new, much more fuel-efficient corporate jet is introduced.
4. Aztec Enterprises depends heavily upon advertising to sell its products. Management at Aztec is allowed to spend $2 million monthly on advertising, but no more than this amount. Each month, Aztec spends exactly $2 million on advertising. What is Aztec's elasticity of demand for advertising? Can you write the equation for Aztec's demand for advertising?
5. You are assistant to the president of a large state university. The university, faced with declining enrollment, is considering a large decrease in tuition. You are asked to forecast the effect. What factors would you have to consider? Explain.
6. The own-price elasticity of demand for imported whiskey is estimated to be -0.20 over a wide interval of prices. The federal government decides to raise the import

tariff on foreign whiskey causing its price to rise by 20 percent. Will sales of whiskey rise or fall, and by what percentage amount?

7. As manager of Citywide Racquet Club, you must determine the best price to charge for locker rentals. Assume that the (marginal) cost of providing lockers is zero. The monthly demand for lockers is estimated to be:

$$Q = 100 - 2P$$

where P is the monthly rental price, and Q is the number of lockers rented per month.
   a. What price would you charge?
   b. How many lockers are rented monthly at this price?
   c. Explain why you chose this price.

8. The demand curve for haircuts at Terry Bernard's Hair Design is

$$P = 15 - 0.15Q$$

where Q is the number of cuts per week, and P is the price of a haircut. Terry is considering raising her price above the current price of \$9. Terry is unwilling to raise price if the price hike will cause revenues to fall.
   a. Should Terry raise the price of haircuts above \$9? Why or why not?
   b. Suppose demand for Terry's haircuts increases to $P = 22 - 0.22Q$. At a price of \$9, should Terry raise the price of her haircuts? Why or why not?

9. As part of his plan to reduce the budget deficit, President Clinton proposed raising the excise tax on gasoline by 50 cents per gallon. While passage of this proposal was blocked by Congress, what would have happened to the sales of gasoline if the price of gasoline were to rise by 45 cents per gallon? (Producers cannot pass the entire 50-cent tax increase on to consumers.) Assume that the average price of gasoline is now \$1.30 per gallon and use the short-run price elasticity for gasoline presented in Illustration 3.2 to answer this question. Would you have expected total expenditure on gasoline by consumers to have risen or fallen had Clinton's proposed 50-cent-per-gallon excise tax been enacted? Explain.

10. *The Wall Street Journal* (Feb. 13, 1992) reported that movie attendance dropped 8 percent in 1991 as ticket prices rose a little more than 5 percent. What is the elasticity of demand for movie tickets? Could demand elasticity be somewhat overestimated from these figures? That is, could other things have changed, accounting for some of the decline in attendance?

APPENDIX 3A Linear Demand, Elasticity, and Marginal Revenue

Linear Demand and Marginal Revenue

For a straight line demand, marginal revenue is twice as steep and has the same vertical intercept as demand. A general straight line demand has the form

$$P = a + bQ, \text{ where } a > 0, b < 0$$

Total revenue (TR) is therefore

$$TR = P \cdot Q = (a + bQ)\,Q = aQ + bQ^2$$

Marginal revenue (MR) is

$$MR = \frac{dTR}{dQ} = a + 2bQ$$

In absolute value, the slope of MR, $2b$, is twice as great as the slope of demand, b. Both curves have the same vertical intercept, a. This relation is shown in Figure A3.1.

FIGURE A3.1
Linear Demand and Marginal Revenue

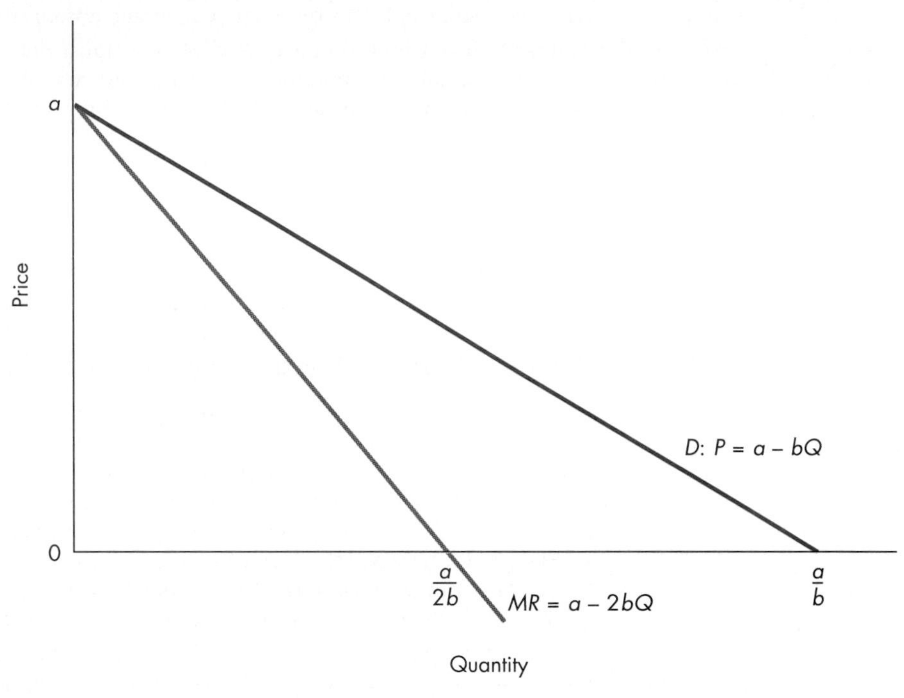

Linear Demand and Point Elasticity

The point elasticity of demand can be expressed as

$$E = \frac{dQ}{dP} \cdot \frac{P}{Q}$$

For the inverse demand $P = a + bQ$, the demand function is $Q = -a/b + (1/b)P$. Thus,

$$\frac{dQ}{dP} = 1/b,$$

and

$$E = \frac{1}{b} \frac{P}{\frac{1}{b}(-a + P)} = \frac{P}{(P - a)}$$

The point elasticity of demand varies inversely with price along a linear demand curve:

$$\frac{dE}{dP} = \frac{-a}{(P - a)^2} < 0$$

As price falls along a linear demand, E gets larger (i.e., less negative), $|E|$ gets smaller, and demand becomes less elastic. Similarly, as price rises, $|E|$ gets larger, and demand becomes more elastic.

APPENDIX 3B The Special Case of Constant Elasticity of Demand: $Q = aP^b$

When demand takes the form $Q = aP^b$, the elasticity of demand is constant and equal to b:

$$E = \frac{dQ}{dP} \cdot \frac{P}{Q} = baP^{b-1}\left(\frac{P}{aP^b}\right) = b.$$

For example, when $Q = aP^{-1}$, demand is unitary elastic for all prices.

APPENDIX 3C Derivation of $MR = P(1 + 1/E)$

The relation between marginal revenue, price, and demand elasticity can be derived quite easily using calculus. We begin with the relation between price, quantity, and total revenue:

$$TR = P \cdot Q$$

Thus,

$$MR = \frac{dTR}{dQ} = P + \frac{dP}{dQ}Q$$

Factoring out P,

$$MR = P\left(1 + \frac{dP}{dQ}\frac{Q}{P}\right)$$

Since

$$E = \frac{dQ}{dP}\frac{P}{Q}$$

$$MR = P\left(1 + \frac{1}{E}\right)$$

PART

II

Some Preliminaries

CHAPTER

4 Theory of Optimizing Behavior

Economic decision makers, whether they are managers of a firm, household consumers, or administrators in government or nonprofit organizations, all make decisions that they believe will lead to the best outcome in a given situation. The decision-making process by which "best solutions" are found involves applying principles from the theory of optimization. For example, managers may want to find the level of output that maximizes the profit of the firm or to determine how much labor, capital, and raw material inputs to use to produce a given amount of output at the lowest possible cost. Consumers search, within the constraints imposed by prices and their income, for the combination of goods and services that will yield the highest level of satisfaction. The mayor of a city decides how to allocate limited tax revenues among various city services to maximize the well-being of the citizens.

This chapter develops the simple rules of optimization that form the underpinnings of the theories of consumer choice, production, input usage, and profit maximization for firms. These rules of optimization are pervasive throughout the study of economics and are essential for understanding the behavior of economic decision makers. Managers should understand the principles of optimization because it will enable them to make better decisions. Furthermore, understanding how other people, possibly potential customers, make their decisions helps managers obtain and use information that furthers the goals of their firm.

We begin the analysis of optimization theory by explaining some terminology that you will encounter in this chapter and throughout a large part of the text. We then derive two rules for making optimal decisions. If you thoroughly understand these two rules, you will have little difficulty with the theories that are developed later in the text.

4.1 CONCEPTS AND TERMINOLOGY

Before we begin to develop the theory of optimizing behavior, we must present some concepts and terminology that you should be familiar with in order to understand the development and application of the principles of optimization. In addition to their use in this chapter, these concepts are used throughout the text when setting forth theoretical concepts.

Objective Functions

objective function The function the decision maker seeks to maximize or minimize.

Optimizing behavior on the part of a decision maker involves trying to maximize or minimize an **objective function**. For a manager of a firm, the objective function is usually profit, which is to be maximized. For a consumer, the objective function is the satisfaction derived from consumption of goods, which is to be maximized. For the mayor of a city seeking to provide adequate law enforcement services, the objective function might be cost, which is to be minimized. For the manager of the marketing division of a large corporation, the objective function is usually sales, which are to be maximized. In other words, the objective function measures whatever it is that the particular decision maker wishes to either maximize or minimize.

maximization problem An optimization problem that involves maximizing the objective function.

minimization problem An optimization problem that involves minimizing the objective function.

If the decision maker seeks to *maximize* an objective function, the optimization problem is called a **maximization problem**. Alternatively, if the objective function is to be minimized, the optimization problem is called a **minimization problem**. As a general rule, when the objective function measures a benefit, the decision maker seeks to maximize this benefit and is solving a maximization problem. When the objective function measures a cost, the decision maker seeks to minimize this cost, and is solving a minimization problem. As you will see later in this chapter, the rules for solving maximization and minimization problems are identical.

Activities or Choice Variables

activities or choice variables Determine the value of the objective function.

The value of the objective function is determined by the level of one or more **activities** or **choice variables**. For example, the value of profit depends upon the number of units of output produced and sold. The production of units of the good is the activity that determines the value of the objective function, which in this case is profit. The decision maker controls the value of the objective function by choosing the level of the activities or choice variables.

Objective functions may be a function of more than one activity. Consider the cost of producing a good or service. If just two inputs—labor and capital—are used in production, the cost function (objective function) can be expressed as

$$\begin{aligned} C &= wL + rK \\ &= f(L, K) \end{aligned}$$

where C is the cost of production, w is the price of a unit of labor services, L is the amount of labor services employed, r is the price of a unit of capital services, and K is the amount of capital services employed. The cost function has two choice variables, L and K. For any given level of output, a manager will choose L and K to minimize the cost of production.

discrete choice variable
A choice variable that can take only specific integer values.

The choice variables in the optimization problems discussed in this text will at times vary discretely and at other times vary continuously. A **discrete choice variable** can only take on specified integer values, such as 1, 2, 3, . . . or 10, 20, 30, ... An example of a discrete choice variable is Table 3.4 in Chapter 3, in which quantity sold varies in units of one. All examples of discrete choice variables will be presented in tables.

continuous choice variable
A choice variable that can take on any value between two end points.

A **continuous choice variable** can take on any value between two end points. For example, a continuous variable that can vary between zero and ten can take on the value 2, 2.345, 7.9, 8.999, or any one of the infinite number of values between the two limits. An example of a continuous choice variable is Figure 3.7 in Chapter 3, in which quantity sold can take on any value along the horizontal axis between zero and 120 units. Examples of continuous choice variables will usually be presented graphically, but will sometimes be shown by equations. As it turns out, the optimization rules differ only slightly in the discrete and continuous cases.

Unconstrained and Constrained Optimization

unconstrained optimization
An optimization problem in which the decision maker can choose the level of activity from an unrestricted set of values.

In addition to categorizing optimization problems as either maximization or minimization problems, optimization problems are also categorized according to whether the decision maker can choose the values of the choice variables in the objective function from an *unconstrained* or *constrained* set of values. **Unconstrained optimization** problems occur when a decision maker can choose the level of activity from an unrestricted set of values in order to maximize the objective function. In this text, we only show how to solve unconstrained *maximization* problems because all of the *unconstrained* decision problems we address are maximization problems.[1] In managerial decision making, the most important type of unconstrained maximization problem arises when an activity generates both benefits and costs, and the decision maker must maximize the net benefit of the activity, where the net benefit is the difference between the total benefit and the total cost of the activity.

An example of an unconstrained optimization problem that you will encounter throughout this text is a firm that chooses the level of sales—or resource usage or advertising—to maximize its profit. Increased sales increase the firm's revenues, which is the benefit. Increased sales also increase the firm's costs. The inputs used to produce the increased output must be paid. Profit, which is calculated as the difference between total revenue and total cost, is the net benefit from the firm's sales. The firm chooses the level of sales that gives the maximum

[1]As it turns out, all unconstrained minimization problems can be transformed into unconstrained maximization problems just by multiplying the objective function by –1. The value of the choice variable that minimizes the objective function is exactly equal to the value of the choice variable that maximizes the objective function (after it has been multiplied by –1).

net benefits or profits. The profit maximization problem is considered an *unconstrained* optimization problem because the manager can choose any level of output in order to maximize net benefit. In the pursuit of the highest possible profit, the manager is bound by no external restrictions on how much output the firm may produce.[2]

constrained optimization Optimization problems in which the decision maker can choose values for the choice variables from a restricted set of values.

constrained maximization A maximization problem where the activities must be chosen to satisfy a side constraint that the total cost of the activities be held to a specific amount.

Constrained optimization problems involve choosing the levels of two or more activities that generate both benefits and costs to a decision maker. In this text, we examine both constrained maximization and constrained minimization problems. A **constrained maximization** problem occurs when a decision maker chooses the levels of two or more activities so as to maximize the total benefits, subject to the side constraint that the total (combined) cost of these activities be held to a specific amount. The objective function is the total benefit function, and the constraint is the total cost function. Since total cost is held to a specific level, the choice of activity levels is constrained to the various combinations of activity levels, whose combined cost just equals the specified constraint on cost. An example of a constrained maximization problem would be a corporate advertising director who can spend only $10,000 per month, in total, on advertising in various media. The advertising director must choose, for example, the level of advertising on radio, newspapers, and billboards in order to maximize monthly sales. The maximization problem is a constrained problem because the combined cost of radio, newspaper, and billboard advertising cannot exceed $10,000.

constrained minimization A minimization problem where the activities must be chosen to satisfy a side constraint that the total benefit of the activities be held to a specific amount.

A **constrained minimization** problem occurs when a decision maker chooses the levels of two or more activities so as to minimize the total costs from the activities, subject to the side constraint that the total (combined) benefits of these activities are held to a specific amount. In this case, the objective function is the total cost function, and the total benefit function is now the constraint. Holding total benefits constant restricts the choice of activity levels. An example of a constrained minimization problem would be a manager who wishes to find the combination of inputs to hire in order to produce 300 units of output per week at the lowest possible total cost. The objective function is the total cost of the combination of inputs chosen to produce 300 units of output. While there are many combinations of inputs that can be used to produce 300 units of the good, the decision maker must choose from the subset of all input combinations that will produce exactly 300 units of output, which is the constraint.

As we will show later in this chapter, the constrained maximization and the constrained minimization problems have one simple rule for the solution. Therefore, you will only have one rule to learn for all constrained optimization problems.

marginal analysis An analytical tool for solving optimization problems that involves changing the value(s) of the choice variable(s) by a small amount to see if the objective function can be further increased (for maximization problems) or further decreased (for minimization problems).

Marginal Analysis

Even though there are a huge number of possible maximizing or minimizing decisions, you will see that all optimization problems can be solved using a powerful analytical tool called **marginal analysis**. Marginal analysis involves

---

[2]As long as there exits a range of output over which the firm can earn positive profit, a rational manager will obviously avoid the ranges of output where profit is negative. Since the decision maker *chooses* not to select values of the choice variable in the range of negative profit, no *external* constraint is present, and the optimization problem is an unconstrained one.

changing the value(s) of the choice variable(s) by a small amount to see if the objective function can be further increased (in the case of maximization problems) or further decreased (in the case of minimization problems). If so, the manager continues to make incremental adjustments in the choice variables until no further improvements are possible. Marginal analysis leads to two simple rules for solving optimization problems, one for unconstrained decisions and one for constrained decisions. We turn first to the unconstrained decision.

4.2 UNCONSTRAINED MAXIMIZATION

As noted above, an unconstrained maximization problem arises when a decision maker chooses the level of an activity so as to obtain the maximum possible net benefit from the activity, where net benefit (*NB*) is the difference between total benefit (*TB*) and total cost (*TC*):

$$NB = TB - TC$$

optimal level of the activity The level of activity that maximizes net benefit.

The level of activity that maximizes net benefit is called the **optimal level of the activity**. In this section we develop the simple rule for finding the optimal level of an activity: Increase the activity when another unit of the activity creates greater *additional* benefits than *additional* costs, and decrease the level of the activity when one less unit of the activity creates a greater reduction in costs than benefits.

Maximization with a Discrete Choice Variable

We will begin the analysis of unconstrained maximization with a discrete choice variable problem. Table 4.1 shows a schedule of total benefits and total costs for various levels of some activity, called *A*, expressed in integers between zero and eight. Note that both total benefit (column 2) and total cost (column 3) increase as the activity is increased. The net benefit for each level of activity is computed by subtracting column 3 from column 2. Clearly, the net benefit changes as the level of the activity changes. In this optimization problem, the activity level (*A*) is the choice variable because it is the variable that determines the level of net benefit.

TABLE 4.1
Unconstrained Maximization: The Case of a Discrete Choice Variable

(1) Level of activity *A*	(2) Total benefit of activity *TB*	(3) Total cost of activity *TC*	(4) Net benefit of activity *NB*	(5) Marginal benefit *MB*	(6) Marginal cost *MC*
0	$ 0	$ 0	$ 0	—	—
1	16	2	14	16	2
2	30	6	24	14	4
3	40	11	29	10	5
4	48	20	28	8	9
5	54	30	24	6	10
6	58	45	13	4	15
7	61	61	0	3	16
8	63	80	−17	2	19

It is obvious from Table 4.1 that the optimal level of activity is three units, because the net benefit associated with three units ($29) is higher than that associated with any other level. Therefore, if the level of the activity is less than three, an increase in A increases the net benefit. If the level of the activity is greater than three, a decrease in A also increases the net benefit. Note that at the optimal level of the activity, the total benefit is not maximized nor is the total cost minimized. The solution to an unconstrained maximization problem maximizes the *net* benefit.

We can find the optimal level of the activity by using *marginal analysis*. As noted earlier, marginal analysis involves examining the effects of small changes in the level of an activity to see if such changes increase or decrease the net benefit of the activity. Marginal analysis is based on the following simple principle:

Principle If, at a given level of activity, a small increase or decrease in the level of that activity causes *net benefit* to increase, then that level of the activity is not optimal. The activity is increased or decreased in order to obtain the highest net benefit. The optimal level of the activity is attained when no further increases in net benefit are possible for any changes in the activity.

marginal benefit (MB)
The addition to total benefit attributable to increasing the activity by a small amount.

marginal cost (MC)
The addition to total cost attributable to increasing the activity by a small amount.

The marginal analysis solution to optimization problems involves comparing the **marginal benefit (MB)** of a change in an activity and the **marginal cost (MC)** of the change. Marginal benefit is the addition to total benefit that occurs when the level of an activity is increased by a small amount. Marginal benefit also measures the *reduction* in total benefit when the activity level is *decreased* by a small amount. Marginal cost is the increase in total cost that occurs when the level of an activity is increased by a small amount. Marginal cost also measures the decrease in total cost when the level of the activity is decreased by a small amount. Expressed more formally, marginal benefit and marginal cost are defined as

$$MB = \frac{\text{Change in total benefit}}{\text{Change in activity}} = \frac{\Delta TB}{\Delta A}$$

and

$$MC = \frac{\text{Change in total cost}}{\text{Change in activity}} = \frac{\Delta TC}{\Delta A}$$

where the symbol "Δ" means "the change in" and A denotes the level of the activity. Thus, marginal benefit and marginal cost are the changes in benefits and costs *per unit* change in the activity.

Columns 5 and 6 in Table 4.1 show the marginal benefit and marginal cost for each change in the level of the activity. The marginal benefit of the third unit of the activity is $10 because increasing A from two to three units increases total benefit from $30 to $40. The marginal benefit also indicates how much total benefit decreases if A is reduced by a small amount. Reducing A from three to two units decreases total benefit by $10. Thus $10 is the amount that the third unit adds to the total benefit and is also the amount by which the total benefit falls when the third unit is given up.

TABLE 4.2
Relations between Marginal Benefit (*MB*), Marginal Cost (*MC*), and Net Benefit (*NB*)

	$MB > MC$	$MB < MC$
Increase activity	*NB* rises	*NB* falls
Decrease activity	*NB* falls	*NB* rises

You can determine whether net benefit (*NB*) is rising or falling simply by comparing marginal benefit (*MB*) and marginal cost (*MC*), without even computing net benefit. Begin by assuming that at some current level of the activity, an increase in the activity causes marginal benefit to exceed marginal cost ($MB > MC$). If *A* increases by one unit, two things occur. Total benefit (*TB*) rises and total cost (*TC*) rises. Whether or not net benefit (*NB*) rises depends on how much total benefit rises relative to how much total cost rises. Since by assumption marginal benefit exceeds marginal cost, total benefit must rise by more than total cost rises; thus, net benefit must rise. In Table 4.1, the marginal benefit of the third unit of the activity is $10, and the marginal cost is $5. Since the third unit adds $10 to total benefit and only $5 to total cost, net benefit rises by $5 (from $24 to $29, as shown in column 4). Suppose the decision maker mistakenly decreases the activity when *MB* exceeds *MC*. In this case, total benefit falls by more than total cost, and net benefit declines. For example, at three units of the activity, reducing the activity level to two units causes total benefits to fall by $10 (*MB*) and total cost to fall by $5 (*MC*). Net benefit falls by $5 (from $29 to $24) when *A* is decreased from three to two units.

Now suppose marginal benefit is less than marginal cost ($MB < MC$). Increasing *A* causes total benefit to rise by less than total cost, and net benefit *falls*. In Table 4.1 the marginal benefit from adding the fifth unit is $6, and the marginal cost is $10. Increasing *A* from four to five units causes total benefit to rise by only $6, while total cost rises by $10; net benefit must fall by $4 (from $28 to $24). *Decreasing A* from five to four units will cause net benefit to *rise*. Total benefit falls by only $6, while total cost falls by $10, causing net benefit to rise by $4 (from $24 to $28). The relation between marginal benefit, marginal cost, and net benefit is summarized in Table 4.2.

The relation between marginal benefit, marginal cost, and net benefit provides the keys to finding the optimal level of an activity using marginal analysis. If marginal benefit exceeds marginal cost, increasing the activity results in higher net benefits. The decision maker continues to increase the activity until the last unit is reached for which marginal benefit exceeds marginal cost (any further increase in activity causes *MC* to exceed *MB*). Refer again to Table 4.1. When considering the first unit of the activity, the decision maker increases the activity from zero to one because $16 (*MB*) is greater than $2 (*MC*). The decision maker should also add the second unit of activity, because the second unit adds $14 to total benefit and only $4 to total cost. Since the marginal benefit of the third unit ($10) is greater than the marginal cost ($5), the third unit will be added. The fourth unit of activity should not be added since it adds only $8 to total benefit, while adding $9 to total cost. If the decision maker mistakenly

ILLUSTRATION 4.1

Is Cost-Benefit Analysis Really Useful?

We have extolled the usefulness of optimization theory—often referred to as "cost-benefit analysis"—in business decision making as well as decision making in everyday life. This process involves weighing the marginal benefits and marginal costs of an activity while ignoring all previously incurred or sunk costs. The principal rule is to increase the level of an activity if marginal benefits exceed marginal costs and decrease the level if marginal costs exceed marginal benefits. This simple rule, however, flies in the face of many honored traditional principles such as "never give up" or "anything worth doing is worth doing well" or "waste not, want not." So you might wonder if cost-benefit analysis is as useful as we have said it is.

It is, at least according to an article in *The Wall Street Journal* titled "Economic Perspective Produces Steady Yields." In this article, a University of Michigan research team concludes, "Cost-benefit analysis pays off in everyday living." This team quizzed Michigan seniors and faculty members on such questions as how often they walk out on a bad movie, refuse to finish a bad novel, start over on a weak term paper, or abandon a research project that no longer looks promising. They believe that people who cut their losses this way are following sound economic rules: calculating the net benefits of alternative courses of action, writing off past costs that can't be recovered, and weighing the opportunity to use future time and effort more profitably elsewhere.*

The findings: Among faculty members, those who use cost-benefit reasoning in this fashion had higher salaries relative to their age and departments. Economists were more likely to apply the approach than professors of humanities or biology. Among students, those who have learned to use cost-benefit analysis frequently are apt to have far better grades than their SAT scores would have predicted. The more economics courses the students had taken, the more likely they were to apply cost-benefit analysis outside the classroom. The director of the University of Michigan study did concede that for many Americans, cost-benefit rules often appear to conflict with traditional principles such as those we previously mentioned. Notwithstanding these probable conflicts, the study provides evidence that decision makers do indeed prosper by following the logic of marginal analysis.

*"Economic Perspective Produces Steady Yields," *The Wall Street Journal*, March 31, 1992.

undertakes the fourth unit of activity, net benefit falls by $1. Thus, the optimal level of the activity is three units. Marginal analysis leads to the conclusion that three units of activity maximize net benefit without ever having to calculate net benefit at each level of the activity. Even more important, you obtain the same solution to the optimization problem by using either the total benefit approach or the marginal analysis approach, and marginal analysis is simpler and more general.

Up to this point, we have discussed unconstrained maximization problems in which the choice variable is discrete. The results are summarized in the following principle:

Principle When a decision maker faces an unconstrained maximization problem and must choose among discrete levels of an activity, the activity should be increased if $MB > MC$ and decreased if $MB < MC$. Thus, the optimal level of the activity is attained—net benefit is maximized—when the level of the activity is the last level for which marginal benefit exceeds marginal cost.

Maximization with a Continuous Choice Variable

When a choice variable can vary continuously, marginal analysis is used in exactly the same manner as when the choice variable is discrete. However, when the choice variable is continuous, the incremental adjustments in the activity can be extremely small, and the decision maker will need to adjust the level of activity until marginal benefit *exactly equals* marginal cost. Figure 4.1 illustrates the situation graphically.

Assume that increasing the level of some activity, A, increases both total benefit and total cost, both of which are expressed in dollars. Thus, marginal benefit and marginal cost are positive for each increase in the activity. Panel A of the figure shows the net benefit (total benefit minus total cost) for all relevant

FIGURE 4.1
Unconstrained Maximization: The Case of a Continuous Choice Variable

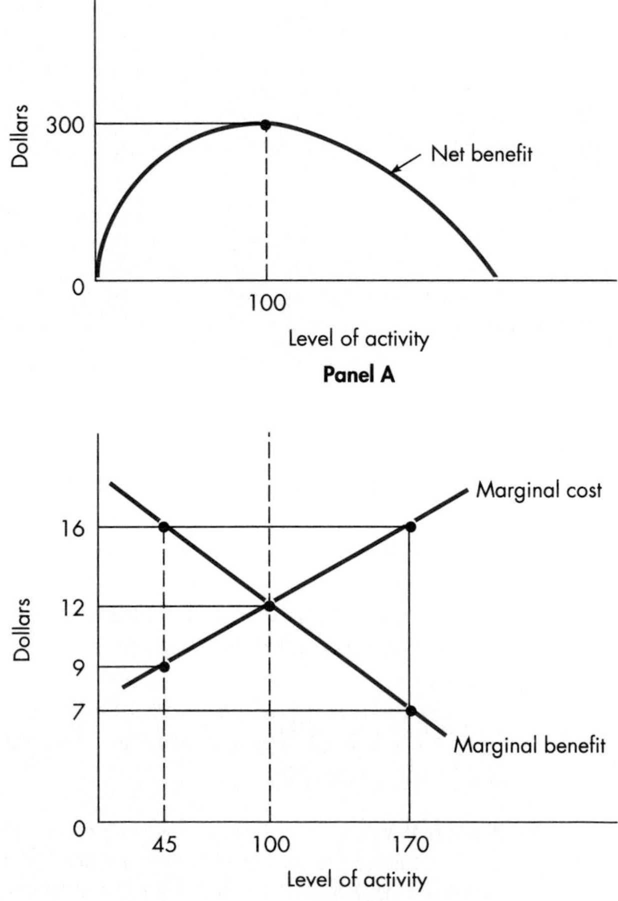

levels of the activity. As you can see, the maximum net benefit ($300) is obtained from using 100 units of the activity. Now we will show that marginal analysis (comparing marginal benefit and marginal cost) leads to the identical solution for the optimal level of activity.

In Panel B, the positively sloped marginal cost curve shows the marginal cost from small increases in the activity over the relevant range. The negatively sloped marginal benefit curve shows the marginal benefit for small increases in the activity. As emphasized above, a decision maker should increase the activity level as long as each additional unit of the activity adds more to total benefit than to total cost. From the graph, for each additional unit of the activity from zero to 100 units, the marginal benefit exceeds the marginal cost. For example, the 45th unit of the activity provides a marginal benefit of $16 but is obtained at a marginal cost of only $9. Thus, the 45th unit added $7 (= $16 – $9) to net benefit. Similarly, the 46th unit would add slightly less than $16 to total benefit, slightly more than $9 to total cost, and, as a result, slightly less than $7 to net benefit. By an identical argument, every unit up to 100 units adds more to benefit than to cost and, therefore, should be added.

Alternatively, suppose the decision maker mistakenly chooses to use 170 units of the activity, at which marginal cost ($16) exceeds marginal benefit ($7). Reducing the activity level by one unit (from 170 to 169) reduces total benefit by $7 but reduces total cost by $16. This one-unit reduction causes net benefit to increase $9 ($16 – $7). For every one-unit decrease in the activity back to 100 units, net benefit rises because *MB* is less than *MC* over this range.

Therefore, by showing that *NB* can be further increased at every other level of activity, we have shown that only 100 units, where marginal benefit equals marginal cost at $12, results in the maximum level of net benefit. It is important to note that to find the optimal level of an activity, the decision maker needs to have information only on *marginal* benefit and *marginal* cost. Information on net benefit is not necessary.

Thus we have established the following principle:

Principle When a decision maker wishes to obtain the maximum net benefit from an activity that is continuously variable, the optimal level of the activity is that level at which the marginal benefit equals the marginal cost (*MB* = *MC*).

Profit Maximization at Austin Semiconductor: An Unconstrained Maximization Problem

Suppose you have been hired to manage Austin Semiconductor, a medium-size electronics manufacturing firm that produces a highly specialized semiconductor device used exclusively in the manufacture of laptop computers. Your first goal is to adjust the production level of the firm to maximize profit, the difference between the firm's total revenue (what it takes in) and total cost (what it pays out). Austin Semiconductor is currently producing 2,999 semiconductor units per month. You want to determine if this is the optimal (profit-maximizing) level of output. If not, you must determine whether the firm should increase or decrease production and by how much. You know that these questions can be

FIGURE 4.2
Marginal Revenue and Marginal Cost at Austin Semiconductor

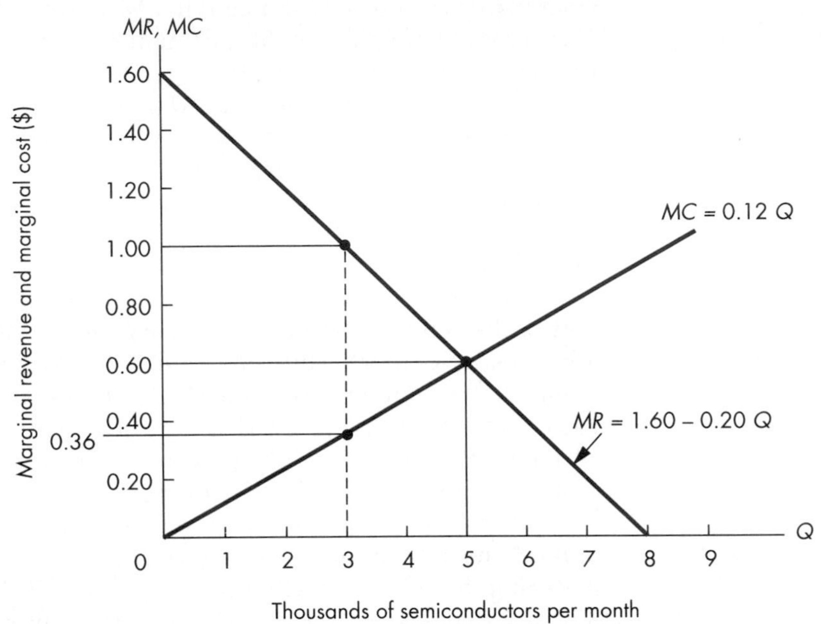

easily answered if you have information on the firm's marginal revenue (benefit) and marginal cost of production.

You ask your marketing research department to estimate the marginal revenue from sales of additional units, and your production engineers to estimate the marginal cost of producing additional units. Figure 4.2 shows the marginal revenue (*MR*) and marginal cost (*MC*) curves they provide you. From the graph, you see that the 3,000th semiconductor produced each month would add $1 to monthly total revenue, while the 3000th unit adds $0.36 to monthly total cost.[3] Obviously, Austin Semiconductor can increase profit by $0.64 by increasing production from 2,999 to 3,000 units per month. And the firm should continue to increase production until marginal revenue just equals marginal cost. In Figure 4.2, marginal revenue equals marginal cost at 5,000 units per month. Note that you found the profit-maximizing level of output without knowing either total revenue, total cost, or profit. To determine how much profit the firm makes at 5,000 units per month, you would need to know the total revenue and the total cost. We will develop these functions later in the text.

Had your marketing department and production engineers given you marginal revenue and marginal cost *equations* instead of graphs, you still could find

[3]When interpreting numerical values for marginal benefit and marginal cost, remember that the values refer to, or are associated with, a particular unit of activity. In this example, marginal cost is equal to $0.36 for the *3000th* unit. Strictly speaking, it is incorrect to say "marginal cost is $0.36 for *3,000 units*." At 3,000 units of production, the marginal cost is $0.36 *for the last unit produced* (i.e., the 3,000th unit).

the optimal level of semiconductor production. The equations for marginal revenue and marginal cost shown in Figure 4.2 are, respectively,

$$MR = 1.60 - 0.20Q$$
$$MC = 0.12Q$$

where Q is measured in thousands of semiconductor units produced each month. To determine the profit-maximizing level of output, you set marginal revenue equal to marginal cost and solve for Q^* (the profit-maximizing level of output):

$$1.60 - 0.20Q = 0.12Q$$
$$Q^* = 5 \text{ (thousand) units}$$

As expected, this is the same level of output obtained by finding the intersection of the MR and MC curves in Figure 4.2.

More Than One Choice Variable

To this point, we have considered only one choice variable. However, when decision makers wish to maximize the net benefits from several activities, precisely the same principle applies: The firm maximizes net benefits when the marginal benefit from each activity equals the marginal cost of that activity. The problem is somewhat more complicated because the marginal benefit or return from increasing one activity may depend on the levels of the other activities. The same can be said for the marginal cost. This complication, however, does not change the fundamental principle that, at the optimal choice, the marginal benefit from each activity equals its marginal cost.

To illustrate this point, let us now alter the profit maximization problem to include advertising as well as output as decision variables that are chosen simultaneously. Increased advertising increases the quantity of a good demanded, and hence the revenue obtained, at each price. Suppose that, at a given level of output and advertising, the marginal revenue from an increase in output equals its marginal cost ($MR_Q = MC_Q$). Suppose also that, at these levels of output and advertising, the marginal revenue from an increase in advertising exceeds its marginal cost ($MR_A > MC_A$). The firm should clearly increase its level of advertising in order to increase its profits. (Since additional expenditures on advertising add more to revenue than to cost, additional advertising will lead to higher profits.) But the increase in advertising will change the firm's level of sales and output because increased advertising leads to an increase in demand. When output changes, the marginal revenue and marginal costs associated with output are no longer equal. For instance, with the increase in output, it may be that $MR_Q < MC_Q$, so that the firm would want to decrease output. Then, if output is decreased, the marginal revenue and marginal costs associated with advertising may again change. The point is that the firm will have to adjust both output and advertising until the marginal benefits equal the marginal costs in both activities; the firm will have to equate marginal revenue and marginal cost for output and advertising simultaneously.

Another example of unconstrained optimization with several choice variables occurs when a profit-maximizing firm uses several inputs in the produc-

ILLUSTRATION 4.2

How Much Sulfur Dioxide Emission Is Optimal?

The Clean Air Act of 1990, signed into law by President Bush on November 15, 1990, represents the nation's first major reform of laws in two decades governing the control of pollution. One of the provisions of the bill, which addresses the acid rain problem, requires reduction of sulfur dioxide emissions (SO_2) by 10 million tons annually by the year 2000. The bill identifies 111 electric power plants with the worst SO_2 emissions. These plants must meet an intermediate pollution reduction goal by 1995, then fully comply by 2000.

Acid rain refers to the elevated level of acidity in rain caused primarily by emissions of SO_2 from coal-burning electric utility plants. Sulfur dioxide reacts with hydrogen peroxide in clouds to form sulfuric acid, which is dissolved in raindrops.* Originally, policymakers and environmentalists thought acid rain was killing aquatic life in many of the lakes in Northeastern United States and in parts of Canada. Additionally, environmentalists were concerned over damage to forests, agricultural land, and buildings. Emissions of SO_2 also are thought to affect atmospheric visibility and human health.

To assess the damage of acid rain, Congress commissioned a ten-year, $500 million study in 1980 called the National Acid Precipitation Assessment Program (NAPAP). According to NAPAP, the impact and costs of acid rain are much smaller than environmentalists originally thought. Fewer lakes have been damaged by acid rain than were believed, agriculture appears to be unaffected by acid rain, and damage to forests was minimal. Several studies found aesthetic benefits from reducing the level of SO_2 emissions. While it appears that controlling SO_2 has some benefits, the magnitude of such benefits is not widely agreed upon. Paul Portney estimates that the benefits from controlling SO_2, as set forth by the Clean Air Act, will be in the range of $2 billion to $9 billion annually.†

Portney also estimates that the costs of compliance with the Clean Air Act will exceed $30 billion annually (and may rise substantially by the year 2000). The compliance expenditures do not include other indirect social costs of pollution control, such as job losses, higher prices, and lower product quality. Given these costs and benefits, Portney asks "If these estimates are even close to correct, . . . costs may exceed benefits by a considerable margin." Why is this so? Could it be that government policymakers do not understand marginal analysis? After all, at the level of SO_2 emissions allowed under the Clean Air Act, not only is the marginal cost of pollution abatement much greater than marginal benefit, but total cost exceeds total benefit—that is, net benefit from pollution control is negative.

Portney believes that this nonoptimal level of pollution control results from misperceptions about both the benefits and costs of controlling SO_2 emissions. Regardless of how a policymaker perceives costs and benefits, the optimal level of SO_2 emissions is the level at which spending one more dollar on reducing SO_2 generates exactly one more dollar of additional benefits. Policymakers would avoid being lured into possibly buying too much pollution control by mistakenly considering only the increase in total benefits of reduced emissions if they (correctly) compared marginal benefits and marginal costs. This is only one example of government policy that could benefit from the use of marginal analysis.

*See Laurence Kulp, "Acid Rain: Causes, Effects, and Control," *Regulation*, Winter 1990.

†See Paul R. Portney, "Economics and the Clean Air Act," *Journal of Economic Perspectives*, Fall 1990.

tion process (when the level of output depends on the levels of usage of several inputs). The firm would hire the amount of each input at which the marginal benefit (increased revenue) from each input equals its marginal cost (e.g., the wage rate in the case of labor). The complication is that the marginal revenue generated by any one input depends on the level of usage of the other inputs. Therefore, if for any one input, marginal revenue is not equal to marginal cost, the firm will have to adjust (increase or decrease) its usage of that input: and, since this change in the usage of that input will change the marginal revenues from the other inputs, their levels of usage must also be adjusted until equilibrium is reached. Again, the complication of multiple choice variables does not change the principle of unconstrained optimization. Each choice variable is determined such that $MR = MC$. The only difference is that the several optimization conditions must be met simultaneously.

4.3 CONSTRAINED OPTIMIZATION

While many of the decisions facing a manager involve unconstrained choice of an activity (or activities) in order to maximize net benefit, on many occasions a manager will face situations in which the choice of activity levels is constrained by the circumstances surrounding the maximization or minimization problem. These constrained optimization problems can be solved, as in the case of unconstrained maximization, using the logic of marginal analysis. As noted in Section 4.1, even though constrained optimization problems can be either maximization or minimization problems, the optimization rule is the same for both types.

A crucial concept for solving constrained optimization problems is the concept of marginal benefit per dollar spent on an activity. Before you can understand how to solve constrained optimization problems, you must first understand how to interpret the ratio of the marginal benefit of an activity divided by the price of the activity. We turn now to a discussion of marginal benefit per dollar, then show how to use this concept to find the optimal levels of the activities in constrained optimization problems.

Marginal Benefit per Dollar Spent on an Activity

Retailers frequently advertise that their products give "more value for your money." People don't usually interpret this as the best product in its class or the one with the highest value. Neither do they interpret it as the cheapest. The advertiser wants to get across the message that customers will get more for their money or more value for each dollar spent on the product. When product rating services (such as *Consumer Reports*) rate a product a "best buy" they don't mean it is the best product, or the cheapest; they mean that consumers will get more value per dollar spent on that product. When firms want to fill a position, they don't necessarily hire the person who would be the most productive in that job—that person may cost too much. Neither do they necessarily hire the person who would work for the lowest wages—that person may not be very productive. They want the employee who can do the job and give the highest productivity for the wages paid.

In the above examples, phrases such as "most value for your money" and "best buy" mean that a particular activity yields the highest marginal benefit per dollar spent. To illustrate this concept, suppose you are the office manager for an expanding law firm, and you find that you need an extra copy machine in the office—the one copier you have is being overworked. You shop around and find three brands of office copy machines (brands A, B, and C) that have virtually identical features. The three brands do differ, however, in price and in the number of copies the machines will make before they wear out. Brand *A*'s copy machine costs \$2,500 and will produce about 500,000 copies before it wears out. The marginal benefit of this machine is 500,000 ($MB_A = 500{,}000$) since the machine provides the law office with the ability to produce 500,000 additional copies. To find the marginal benefit *per dollar spent* on copy machine *A*, marginal benefit is divided by price ($P_A = 2{,}500$):

$$\begin{aligned} MB_A/P_A &= 500{,}000 \text{ copies } / \text{ } 2{,}500 \text{ dollars} \\ &= 200 \text{ copies/dollar} \end{aligned}$$

You get 200 copies for each of the dollars spent to purchase copy machine *A*. Now compare machine *A* with machine *B* that will produce 600,000 copies and costs \$4,000. The marginal benefit is greater, but so is the price. To determine how "good a deal" you get with machine *B*, compute the marginal benefit per dollar spent on machine *B*:

$$\begin{aligned} MB_B/P_B &= 600{,}000 \text{ copies } / \text{ } 4{,}000 \text{ dollars} \\ &= 150 \text{ copies/dollar} \end{aligned}$$

Even though machine *B* provides a higher marginal benefit, its marginal benefit per dollar spent is lower than for machine *A*. Machine *A* is a "better deal" than machine *B* because it yields higher marginal benefit per dollar. The third copy machine produces 580,000 copies over its useful life and costs \$2,600. Machine *C* is neither the best machine (580,000 < 600,000 copies) nor is it the cheapest machine (\$2,600 > \$2,500), but of the three machines, machine *C* provides the greatest marginal benefit per dollar spent:

$$\begin{aligned} MB_C/P_C &= 580{,}000 \text{ copies } / \text{ } 2{,}600 \text{ dollars} \\ &= 223 \text{ copies/dollar} \end{aligned}$$

A consumer of copy machines would rank machine *C* first, machine *A* second, and machine *B* third.

When choosing among different activities, a decision maker compares the marginal benefits per dollar spent on each of the activities, *not* the marginal benefits of the activities. Marginal benefit, by itself, does not provide sufficient information for decision making purposes. It is marginal benefit per dollar spent that matters in decision making.

Constrained Maximization

The general constrained maximization problem involves a manager or decision maker choosing the levels of two or more activities in order to maximize a total benefit (objective) function subject to a constraint in the form of a budget that restricts the amount that can be spent. To illustrate how marginal analysis can be employed to find the optimal levels of activities for a constrained maximization problem, consider a situation in which there are two activities, *A* and *B*. Each unit of activity *A* costs \$4 to undertake and each unit of activity *B* costs \$2 to undertake. The manager faces a constraint that allows a total expenditure of only \$100 on activities *A* and *B* combined. The manager wishes to allocate the \$100 between activities A and B so that the total benefits from both activities combined is maximized.

The manager is currently choosing to engage in 20 units of activity A and 10 units of activity B. The constraint is met for the combination 20A and 10B since (\$4 × 20) + (\$2 × 10) = \$100. For this combination of activities, suppose that the marginal benefit of the last unit of activity A is 40 units of additional benefit, and the marginal benefit of the last unit of B is 10 units of additional benefit. In this situation, the marginal benefit per dollar spent on activity A exceeds the marginal benefit per dollar spent on activity B:

$$MB_A/P_A = 40/4 = 10 > 5 = 10/2 = MB_B/P_B$$

Spending an additional dollar on activity A increases total benefit by 10 units, while spending an additional dollar on activity B increases total benefit by 5 units. Since the marginal benefit per dollar spent is greater for activity A, it provides "more for the money" or is a "better deal" at this combination of activities.

To take advantage of this fact, the manager can increase activity A by 1 unit and decrease activity B by 2 units (now, $A = 21$ and $B = 8$). This combination of activities still costs just \$100 [(\$4 × 21) + (\$2 × 8) = \$100]. Purchasing one more unit of activity A causes total benefit to rise by 40 units, while purchasing two less units of activity B causes total benefit to fall by 20 units. The combined total benefit from activities A and B *rises* by 20 units (= 40 – 20) *and* the new combination of activities ($A = 21$ and $B = 8$) costs the same amount, \$100, as the old combination ($A = 20$ and $B = 10$). The decision maker has succeeded in increasing total benefit without spending any more than \$100 on the activities.

Naturally, the manager will continue to increase spending on activity A and reduce spending on activity B so long as MB_A/P_A exceeds MB_B/P_B. In most situations, the marginal benefit of an activity declines as the activity increases.[4] Consequently, as activity A is increased, MB_A gets smaller. As activity B is decreased, MB_B gets larger. Thus, as spending on A rises and spending on B falls, MB_A/P_A falls and MB_B/P_B rises. As the manager increases activity A and decreases activity B, a point is eventually reached at which activity A is no longer a "better deal" than activity B; that is, MB_A/P_A equals MB_B/P_B. At this point, total benefit is maximized subject to the constraint that only \$100 is spent on the two activities.

If the original allocation of spending on activities A and B had been such that

$$MB_A/P_A < MB_B/P_B$$

the manager would recognize that activity B is the "better deal." In this case, total benefit could be increased by spending more on activity B and less on

[4]Decreasing marginal benefit is quite common. As you drink several cans of Coke in succession, you get ever smaller amounts of additional satisfaction from successive cans. As you continue studying for an exam, each additional hour of study increases your expected exam grade by ever smaller amounts. In such cases, marginal benefit is inversely related to the level of the activity. Increasing the activity level causes marginal benefit to fall, and decreasing the activity level causes marginal benefit to rise.

activity A, while maintaining the \$100 budget. Activity B would be increased by 2 units for every 1 unit decrease in activity A (in order to satisfy the \$100 spending constraint) until the marginal benefit per dollar spent is equal for both activities:

$$MB_A/P_A = MB_B/P_B$$

We have developed the following rule for finding the optimal activity levels for constrained maximization problems:

Principle In order to maximize total benefits subject to a constraint on the level of activities, choose the level of each activity so that the marginal benefit per dollar spent is equal for all activities.

$$MB_A/P_A = MB_B/P_B$$

and at the same time, the chosen level of activities must also satisfy the constraint.

The Optimal Allocation of Advertising Expenditures: A Constrained Maximization Problem

To illustrate how a firm can use the technique of constrained maximization to allocate its advertising budget, suppose a manager of a small retail firm wants to maximize the effectiveness (in total sales) of the firm's weekly advertising budget of \$2,000. The manager has the option of advertising on the local television station or on the local AM radio station. As a class project, a managerial economics class at a nearby college estimated the impact on the retailer's sales of varying levels of advertising in the two different media. The manager wants to maximize the number of units sold; thus the total benefit is measured by the total number of units sold. The estimates of the *increases* in weekly sales (the marginal benefits) from increasing the levels of advertising on television and radio are as follows:

	Increase in units sold	
Number of ads	MB_{TV}	MB_{radio}
1	400	360
2	300	270
3	280	240
4	260	225
5	240	150
6	200	120

Television ads are more "powerful" than radio ads in the sense that the marginal benefits from additional TV ads tend to be larger than those for more radio ads. However, since the manager is constrained by the limited advertising budget, the relevant measure is not simply marginal benefit, but rather marginal benefit per dollar spent on advertising. The price of television ads is \$400 per ad, and the price of radio ads is \$300 per ad. Although the first TV ad dominates the first radio ad in terms of its marginal benefit (increased sales), the marginal benefit per dollar's worth of expenditure for the first radio ad is greater than for the first television ad:

	Marginal benefit/price	
	Television	Radio
Ad 1	400/400 = 1.00	360/300 = 1.2

This indicates that sales rise by 1 unit per dollar spent on the first television ad and 1.2 units on the first radio ad. Therefore, when allocating the budget, the first ad selected by the manager will be a radio ad—the activity with the largest marginal benefit per dollar spent. Following the same rule, the $2,000 advertising budget would be allocated as follows:

Decision	MB/P	Ranking of MB/P	Cumulative expenditures
Buy radio ad 1	360/300 = 1.20	1	$ 300
Buy TV ad 1	400/400 = 1.00	2	$ 700
Buy radio ad 2	270/300 = 0.90	3	$1,000
Buy radio ad 3	240/300 = 0.80	4	$1,300
Buy TV ad 2	300/400 = 0.75	5 (tie)	$1,700
Buy radio ad 4	225/300 = 0.75	5 (tie)	$2,000

By selecting two television ads and four radio ads, the manager of the firm has maximized sales subject to the constraint that only $2,000 can be spent on advertising activity. Note that for the optimal levels of television and radio ads (2 TV and 4 radio):

$$\frac{MB_{TV}}{P_{TV}} = \frac{MB_{radio}}{P_{radio}} = 0.75$$

The fact that the preceding application used artificially simplistic numbers shouldn't make you think that the problem is artificial. If we add a few zeros and make the price of the 30-second TV ad $400,000 rather than $400, we have the real-world situation faced by advertisers.

Constrained Minimization

Constrained minimization problems involve minimizing a total cost function (the objective function) subject to a constraint that the levels of activities be chosen such that a given level of total benefit is achieved. To illustrate how marginal analysis is applied to constrained minimization problems, consider a manager that must minimize the total cost of two activities, *A* and *B*, subject to the constraint that 3,000 units of benefit are to be generated by activities *A* and *B*. The price of activity *A* is $5 per unit, and the price of activity *B* is $20 per unit. Suppose the manager is currently using 100 units of activity *A* and 60 units of activity *B*, and this combination of activity generates total benefit equal to 3,000. At this combination of activities, the marginal benefit of activity *A* is 30 and the marginal benefit of activity *B* is 60. In this situation, the marginal benefit per dollar spent on activity *A* exceeds the marginal benefit per dollar spent on activity *B*:

$$MB_A/P_A = 30/5 = 6 > 3 = 60/20 = MB_B/P_B$$

Since the marginal benefit per dollar spent is greater for activity *A* than for activity *B*, activity *A* gives "more for the money."

To take advantage of activity A, the manager can reduce activity B by one unit, which causes total benefit to fall by 60 units and reduces cost by \$20. To hold total benefit constant, the 60 units of lost benefit can be made up by increasing activity A by 2 units. The additional units of activity A cause total cost to rise by \$10. By reducing activity B by one unit and increasing activity A by two units, the manager *reduces* total cost by \$10 (= \$20 – 10) without reducing total benefit.

As long as $MB_A/P_A > MB_B/P_B$, the manager will continue to increase activity A and decrease activity B at the rate that holds TB constant until

$$MB_A/P_A = MB_B/P_B$$

This is the same condition that must be met in the case of constrained maximization. If there are more than two activities in the objective function, the condition is expanded to require that the marginal benefit per dollar spent be equal for all activities:

$$MB_A/P_A = MB_B/P_B = MB_C/P_C = \cdots = MB_Z/P_Z$$

We can express the principle of constrained optimization as follows:

Principle An objective function is maximized or minimized subject to a constraint if, for all of the activities in the objective function, the ratios of marginal benefit to price are equal, and the constraint is satisfied.

The Optimal Combination of Inputs: A Constrained Minimization Problem

Cyber Corporation is currently producing 10,000 units of output using two inputs, capital and labor. At the existing input usage level, the marginal product of capital is 300 (the last unit of capital increased output by 300 units), and the marginal product of labor is 150 (the last worker hired increased output by 150 units per year). Cyber wishes to produce 10,000 units at the lowest possible total cost.

The current wage rate (w) is \$30,000 per year, and the annual cost of using a unit of capital (r) is \$80,000 per year. Comparing the marginal benefits per dollar spent on labor and capital reveals that Cyber Corporation is currently using too much capital and too little labor:

$$\frac{MP_K}{r} = \frac{300}{\$80{,}000} < \frac{150}{\$30{,}000} = \frac{MP_L}{w}$$

If Cyber reduces capital usage by one unit, output would fall by 300 units per year, and annual cost would decline by \$80,000. Then, to hold output at 10,000 units per year, the 300 units per year lost from the reduction in capital could be produced by employing two more workers, at a cost of only \$60,000, because the marginal product of each worker is approximately 150 units of output and each of the two additional workers costs the firm \$30,000. The following table summarizes the transaction:

Action	Cost	Output
Reduce capital by one unit	–\$80,000	–300
Employ two additional workers	+\$60,000	+300
Net change	–\$20,000	0

As this example indicates, the firm can save $20,000 while continuing to produce 10,000 units per year by replacing some of its capital with labor. Cyber would continue reducing its capital and adding labor, holding output constant, as long as the above inequality held. As capital is reduced, MP_K rises; as labor increases, MP_L falls. Eventually a point is reached where MP_L/w equals MP_K/r, and no further reallocations will lower cost.

Alternatively, if the firm had originally been using levels of capital and labor at which $MP_K/r > MP_L/w$, the firm could reduce total cost by substituting some capital for labor at a rate that keeps output constant. Only in the case in which $MP_K/r = MP_L/w$ is there no reallocation between capital and labor that would reduce cost.

4.4 SUMMARY

In this chapter we have given you the key to the kingdom of microeconomic analysis: marginal analysis. Virtually all of microeconomics involves solutions to optimization problems. The most interesting and challenging problems facing a manager involve trying either to maximize or minimize particular objective functions. Regardless of whether the optimization involves maximization or minimization, or constrained or unconstrained choice variables, all optimization problems are solved by using marginal analysis. No other tool in managerial economics is more powerful than the ability to attack problems by using the logic of marginal analysis.

The results of this chapter fall neatly into two categories: the solution to unconstrained and constrained optimization problems. When the values of the choice variables are *not* restricted by constraints such as limited income, limited expenditures, or limited time, the optimization problem is said to be unconstrained. One of the most important unconstrained optimization problems facing managers is selecting the set of variables that will maximize the profit of the firm. This problem and all other unconstrained maximization problems can be solved by following this simple rule. To maximize an objective function, the value of which depends on certain activities or choice variables, each activity is carried out until the marginal benefit from an increase in the activity equals the marginal cost of the increased activity:

$$MB_A = MC_A, MB_B = MC_B, \cdots, MB_Z = MC_Z$$

When the choice variables are not continuous but discrete, it may not be possible to precisely equate benefit and cost at the margin. For discrete choice variables, the decision maker simply carries out the activity up to the point where *any further* increases in the activity result in marginal cost exceeding marginal benefit.

In many instances, managers face limitations on the range of values that the choice variables can take. For example, budgets may limit the amount of labor and capital managers may purchase. Time constraints may limit the number of hours managers can allocate to certain activities. Such constraints are common and require modifying the solution to optimization problems. To maximize or minimize an objective function subject to a constraint, the ratios of the marginal benefit to price must be equal for all activities,

$$\frac{MB_A}{P_A} = \frac{MB_B}{P_B} = \cdots = \frac{MB_Z}{P_Z}$$

and the values of the choice variables must meet the constraint. One of the most important constrained optimization problems facing a manager is the task of producing a given output at the least possible total cost.

The two decision rules presented in this chapter will be used throughout this text. If you remember these rules, economic analysis will be clear and straightforward. These two rules, although simple, are the essential tools for making economic decisions. And, as the rules emphasize, *marginal changes* are the keys to optimization decisions.

TECHNICAL PROBLEMS

1. Fill in the blanks in the following table. Then use the table to answer the questions:

X	*TB*	*TC*	*NB*	*MB*	*MC*
0	$ 0	$____	$ 0		
1	____	____	27	$35	$____
2	65	____	____	____	10
3	85	30	____	____	____
4	____	____	51	____	14
5	____	60	____	8	____
6	____	____	____	5	20

a. If activity *X* is increased from 2 to 3 units, total benefit ________ by ________ dollars.
b. If X is increased from 2 to 3 units, total cost ________ by ________ dollars, and net benefit ________ by ________ dollars.
c. If X is decreased from 5 to 4 units, total benefit ________ by ________ dollars.
d. If X is decreased from 5 to 4 units, total cost ________ by ________ dollars, and net benefit ________ by ________ dollars.
e. The optimal level of activity is ________ units of this activity, and net benefit is ________ dollars.

2. Use the graph that follows to answer the following questions.

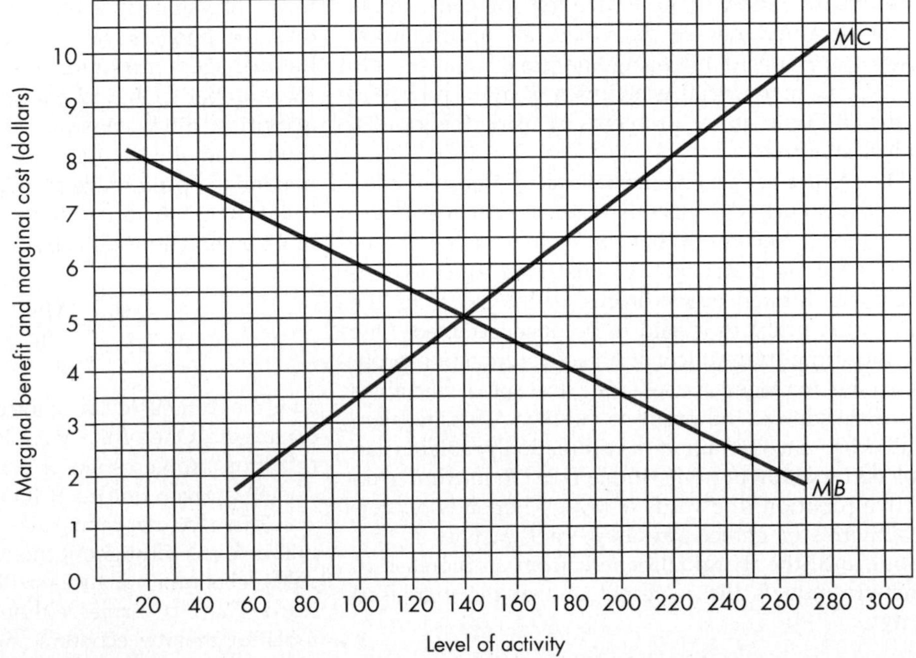

a. At 60 units of the activity, marginal benefit is \$ ________ and marginal cost is \$ ________ .

b. Adding the 60th unit of the activity causes net benefit to ________ (increase, decrease) by \$ ________ .

c. At 180 units of the activity, marginal benefit is \$ ________ and marginal cost is \$ ________ .

d. Subtracting the 180th unit of the activity causes net benefit to ________ (increase, decrease) by \$ ________ .

e. The optimal level of the activity is ________ units. At the optimal level of the activity, marginal benefit is \$ ________ and marginal cost is \$ ________ .

3. Fill in the blanks in the following statements:

   a. In an unconstrained maximization problem, the activity should be decreased when ________ is greater than ________ . If the activity is a continuous variable, the optimal level of activity occurs when ________ equals ________ . If the activity is a discrete variable, the optimal level of activity is the last level of activity for which ________ exceeds ________ .

   b. In a constrained maximization (or minimization) problem involving two activities *A* and *B*, activity *A* should be decreased and activity *B* increased when ________ is less than ________ . When the activities are continuous variables, the optimal levels of activities *A* and *B* occur where ________ equals ________ , and the ________ is satisfied.

* 4. Activity *A* has the following marginal benefit (*MB*) and marginal cost (*MC*) functions:

$$MB = 50 - 0.025A$$

and

$$MC = 40 + 0.025A$$

where *MB* and *MC* are measured in dollars.

   a. The 100th unit of the activity increases total benefit by \$ ________ and increases total cost by \$ ________ . Since marginal benefit is ________ (greater, less) than marginal cost, adding the 100th unit of the activity ________ (increases, decreases) net benefit by \$ ________ .

   b. The 400th unit of the activity increases total benefit by \$ ________ and increases total cost by \$ ________ . Since marginal benefit is ________ (greater, less) than marginal cost, subtracting the 400th unit of the activity ________ (increases, decreases) net benefit by \$ ________ .

   c. The optimal level of the activity is ________ units. At the optimal level of activity, marginal benefit is \$ ________ and marginal cost is \$ ________ .

   The total benefit (*TB*) and total cost (*TC*) functions for the activity are:

$$TB = 50A - 0.0125A^2$$

and

$$TC = 40A + 0.0125A^2$$

where *TB* and *TC* are measured in dollars.

   d. For the optimal level of the activity in part *c*, the total benefit is \$ ________ , the total cost is \$ ________ , and the net benefit is \$ ________ .

   e. Compute the net benefit for the activity levels 0, 100, 200, 300, 400, and 500 units. Graph the net benefit function. Does it reach its maximum value at the level of activity that was optimal in part *c*?

5. Fill in the blanks in the following statement:
If marginal benefit exceeds marginal cost, then ________ (increasing, decreasing) the level of activity by one unit ________ (increases, decreases) ________ (total, marginal, net) benefit by more than it ________ (increases, decreases) ________ (total, marginal) cost. Therefore, ________ (increasing, decreasing) the level of activity by one unit must increase net benefit. The manager should continue to ________ (increase, decrease) the level of activity until marginal benefit and marginal cost are ________ (zero, equal).

6. A decision maker wishes to maximize the total benefit associated with three activities, X, Y, and Z. The price per unit of activities X, Y, and Z is \$1, \$2, and \$3 respectively. The following table gives the ratio of the marginal benefit to the price of the activities for various levels of each activity:

Level of activity	$\frac{MB_X}{P_X}$	$\frac{MB_Y}{P_Y}$	$\frac{MB_Z}{P_Z}$
1	10	22	14
2	9	18	12
3	8	12	10
4	7	10	9
5	6	6	8
6	5	4	6
7	4	2	4
8	3	1	2

a. If the decision maker chooses to use one unit of X, one unit of Y, and one unit of Z, the total benefit that results is \$________.

b. For the fourth unit of activity Y, each dollar spent increases total benefit by \$________. The fourth unit of activity Y increases total benefit by \$________.

c. Suppose the decision maker can spend a total of only \$18 on the three activities. What is the optimal level of X, Y, and Z? Why is the combination 1X, 4Y, and 3Z not optimal? Why is the combination 2X, 2Y, and 4Z not optimal?

d. Now suppose the decision maker has \$33 to spend on the three activities. What is the optimal level of X, Y, and Z? If the decision maker has \$35 to spend, what is the optimal combination? Explain.

7. Correct the following statement:
"The optimal level of any activity is that level for which marginal benefit exceeds marginal cost by the greatest possible amount."

* 8. Suppose a firm is considering two different activities, activities X and Y, which yield the total benefits presented in the schedule below. The price of X is \$2 per unit, and the price of Y is \$10 per unit.

Level of activity	Total benefit of activity X TB_X	Total benefit of activity Y TB_Y
0	0	0
1	\$30	\$100
2	54	190
3	72	270
4	84	340
5	92	400
6	98	450

a. The firm places a budget constraint of \$26 on expenditures on activities X and Y. What is the level of X and Y that maximizes total benefit subject to the budget constraint?

b. What is the total benefit associated with the optimal level of X and Y in part a?

c. Now let the budget constraint increase to \$58. What is the optimal level of X and Y now? What is the total benefit when the budget constraint is \$58?

9. "At the optimal level of the activity, further increases in the activity necessarily decrease *total* benefit." Evaluate.

10. In Illustration 4.1 we noted that the rule for maximization set forth in the text contradicts some honored traditional principles such as "never give up" or "anything worth doing is worth doing well," or "waste not, want not." Explain the contradiction for each of these rules.

APPLIED PROBLEMS

1. Using optimization theory, analyze the following quotations:
   a. "The optimal number of traffic deaths in the United States is zero."
   b. "Any pollution is too much pollution."
   c. "We cannot pull US troops out of Somalia. We have committed so much already."
   d. "If Congress cuts out the NASA space station, we will have wasted all of the resources that we have already spent on it. Therefore, we must continue funding it."
   e. "If the 55 mile-per-hour speed limit has reduced traffic deaths, we should reduce the speed limit even more."

2. Appalachian Coal Mining believes that it can increase labor productivity and, therefore, net revenue by reducing air pollution in its mines. It estimates that the marginal cost function for reducing pollution by installing additional capital equipment is

$$MC = 40P$$

where P represents a reduction of one unit of pollution in the mines. It also feels that for every unit of pollution reduction the marginal increase in revenue (MR) is

$$MR = 1{,}000 - 10P$$

How much pollution reduction should Appalachian Coal Mining undertake?

3. The business section of the *International Herald Tribune* carried a story with the headline "Hark! The Herald Angels Sing of Teleconferencing" (Peter H. Lewis, New York Times Service). The story described how video teleconferencing—two-way telecasts—is gaining popularity with businesses. Indeed, it was reported that some firms are regarding teleconferencing as an effective substitute for in-person conferences. And the cost has been declining to the point where it is comparable to "having four or five executives jump on a plane to go to a common point."

   Your boss asked you to evaluate teleconferencing as an alternative to the six global conferences the firm is currently holding each year. In his instructions to you, he said that "it looks like we might be able to realize substantial savings without reducing the impact of the conferences."

   Set up a plan for solving this optimization problem. What are the benefits? What are the costs? Should this problem be treated as a constrained or unconstrained optimization problem? Why?

4. Twentyfirst Century Electronics has discovered a theft problem at its warehouse and has decided to hire security guards. The firm wants to hire the optimal number of security guards. The following table shows how the number of security guards affects the number of radios stolen per week.

Number of security guards	Number of radios stolen per week
0	50
1	30
2	20
3	14
4	8
5	6

   a. If each security guard is paid \$200 a week and the cost of a stolen radio is \$25, how many security guards should the firm hire?
   b. If the cost of a stolen radio is \$25, what is the most the firm would be willing to pay to hire the first security guard?
   c. If each security guard is paid \$200 a week and the cost of a stolen radio is \$50, how many security guards should the firm hire?

5. Suppose that Future World Marketing Research Group develops a machine that can measure the increase in an individual's happiness as a person consumes more of a product. Using this machine on one of their office employees who consumes only beer and sandwiches, they found that this employee's additional happiness function—call it a marginal happiness function—for beer is

$$MH_B = 25 - 2B$$

   That is, the first beer gives 23 extra units of happiness, the second gives 21 extra units, the third 19, and so on. Likewise, the employee's additional happiness function for sandwiches is

$$MH_S = 36 - 4S$$

   If the price of beer is \$1.50 per bottle, the price of sandwiches is \$2.00 each, and if the employee has a daily budget of \$15.50, how much of each of these commodities will this person consume each day?

6. In an article on after-Christmas retail pricing, *The Wall Street Journal* (January 27, 1993) quotes a consumer researcher who "expects shoppers to adjust to buying more merchandise at full price rather than hunting bargains." He stated,
   a. "Consumers will trade shorter shopping trips for the higher cost of goods." How does this fit into the framework of optimization theory? What problem is the consumer trying to solve?
   b. And, "Such a consumer behavior pattern usually takes hold as recessions yield to prosperity." Is he probably correct? Why or why not?

7. Janice Waller, the manager of the customer service department at First Bank of Jefferson County, can hire employees with a high school diploma for \$20,000 annually and employees with a bachelor's degree for \$30,000. She wants to maximize the

number of customers served, given a fixed payroll. The table below shows how the total number of customers served varies with the number of employees.

Number of employees	Total number of customers served	
	High school diploma	Bachelor's degree
1	120	100
2	220	190
3	300	270
4	370	330
5	430	380
6	470	410

a. If Ms. Waller has a payroll of $160,000, how should she allocate this budget in order to maximize the number of customers served?

b. If she has a budget of $150,000 and currently hires three people with high school diplomas and three with bachelor's degrees, is she making the correct decision? Why or why not? If not, what should she do? (Assume she can hire part-time workers.)

c. If her budget is increased to $240,000, how should she allocate this budget?

8. Government spending on education is one of the issues that all candidates in national elections generally address. Ignoring the politics of this issue for the moment, is it possible for government to spend too much on educating America's children? Explain.

9. Rob Spana, southeast sales manager for Manufacturer's Aluminum Supply, makes most of his outside sales by playing either golf or tennis with potential clients. From much past experience, he estimates that various levels of playing golf and tennis generate the following amounts of additional sales (*MB*):

Number of rounds of golf (*G*)	Additional sales generated (MB_G)	Number of tennis matches (*T*)	Additional sales generated (MB_T)
1	$2,500	1	$2,400
2	2,000	2	2,250
3	1,750	3	2,100
4	1,375	4	1,800
5	1,250	5	1,500
6	1,200	6	1,050
7	1,125	7	750
8	1,100	8	600

One round of golf (18 holes) takes 5 hours to play (including a half-hour stop at the clubhouse) and one tennis match (best two out of three sets) takes 3 hours to complete. Rob can only get away from the office to play golf and tennis 20 hours each week.

a. What is the optimal number of rounds of golf to play and the optimal number of tennis matches to play?

b. Suppose Rob gets sick one week and can only get in 12 hours of golf and tennis. What level of golf and tennis play is optimal?

10. Bavarian Crystal Works designs and produces lead crystal wine decanters for export to international markets. The production manager of Bavarian Crystal Works estimates total and marginal production costs to be

$$TC = 10{,}000 + 40Q + 0.0025Q^2$$

and

$$MC = 40 + 0.005Q$$

where costs are measured in US dollars, and Q is the number of wine decanters produced annually. Because Bavarian Crystal Works is only one of many crystal producers in the world market, it can sell as many of the decanters as it wishes for \$70 apiece. Total and marginal revenue are

$$TR = 70Q$$

and

$$MR = 70$$

where revenues are measured in US dollars, and Q is annual decanter production.

a. What is the optimal level of production of wine decanters? What is the marginal revenue from the last wine decanter sold?

b. What is the total revenue, total cost, and net benefit (profit) from selling the optimal number of wine decanters?

c. At the optimal level of production of decanters, an extra decanter can be sold for \$70, thereby increasing total revenue by \$70. Why does the manager of this firm *not* produce and sell one more unit?

11. Joy Land Toys, a toy manufacturer, is experiencing quality problems on its assembly line. The marketing division estimates that each defective toy that leaves the plant costs the firm \$10, on average, for replacement or repair. The engineering department recommends hiring quality inspectors to sample for defective toys. In this way many quality problems can be caught and prevented before shipping. After visiting other companies, a management team derives the following schedule showing the approximate number of defective toys that would be produced for several levels of inspection.

Number of inspectors	Average number of defective toys (per day)
0	92
1	62
2	42
3	27
4	17
5	10
6	5

The daily wage of inspectors is \$70.

a. How many inspectors should the firm hire?

b. What would your answer be if the wage rate is \$90?

c. What if the average cost of a defective toy is \$5 and the wage rate of inspectors is \$70?

APPENDIX

Unconstrained Maximization

Consider an activity, the level of which is denoted by x. The activity generates benefits (B),

$$B = B(x)$$

and costs (C),

$$C = C(x)$$

The objective is to maximize net benefit (NB), which is defined as the difference between total benefit and total cost:

$$NB = NB(x) = B(x) - C(x)$$

From differential calculus, we know that the necessary condition for maximization of the net benefit function is that the derivative of the net benefit function with respect to the choice variable be equal to zero:

$$\frac{dNB}{dx} = \frac{dB(x)}{dx} - \frac{dC(x)}{dx} = 0$$

Hence, net benefit is maximized when

$$\frac{dB(x)}{dx} = \frac{dC(x)}{dx}$$

Since dB/dx represents marginal benefit and dC/dx represents marginal cost, net benefit is maximized when marginal benefit equals marginal cost.

Constrained Maximization

Consider a total benefit function which is a function of n activities, $x_1, x_2, \ldots, x_n$:

$$B = B(x_1, x_2, \cdots, x_n)$$

The partial derivatives of the total benefit function, $\partial B/\partial x_i$ ($i = 1, 2, \ldots, n$) represent the marginal benefit associated with activity x_i. For convenience, we can denote the ith marginal benefit as MB_i ($= \partial B/\partial x_i$).

The constraint on the n activities can be expressed as

$$p_1x_1 + p_2x_2 + \cdots + p_nx_n = M$$

where $p_1, p_2, \ldots, p_n$ are the prices of each of the n activities and M is the total amount that can be spent on all activities combined.

To find the optimal levels of $x_1, x_2, \ldots, x_n$, the following Lagrangian function is maximized:

$$L = B(x_1, x_2, \ldots, x_n) - \lambda[M - p_1x_1 - p_2x_2 - \cdots - p_nx_n]$$

The first-order necessary condition for maximization requires that the partial derivatives of the Lagrangian function all equal zero:

$$\frac{\partial L}{\partial x_1} = \frac{\partial B}{\partial x_1} - \lambda p_1 = 0$$
$$\frac{\partial L}{\partial x_2} = \frac{\partial B}{\partial x_2} - \lambda p_2 = 0$$
$$\vdots \qquad \vdots$$
$$\frac{\partial L}{\partial x_n} = \frac{\partial B}{\partial x_n} - \lambda p_n = 0$$
$$\frac{\partial L}{\partial \lambda} = p_1x_1 + p_2x_2 + \cdots + p_nx_n - M = 0$$

Rearranging the first n of these equations, the first-order condition for maximization requires

$$\frac{\partial B}{\partial x_1} = \lambda p_1 \qquad \frac{MB_1}{p_1} = \lambda$$
$$\frac{\partial B}{\partial x_2} = \lambda p_2 \quad \text{or} \quad \frac{MB_2}{p_2} = \lambda$$
$$\vdots \qquad \vdots$$
$$\frac{\partial B}{\partial x_n} = \lambda p_n \qquad \frac{MB_n}{p_n} = \lambda$$

Thus, it follows that $x_1, x_2, \ldots, x_n$ must be chosen such that

$$\frac{MB_1}{p_1} = \frac{MB_2}{p_2} = \cdots = \frac{MB_n}{p_n}$$

for a constrained maximum to be achieved. The condition that $\partial L/\partial \lambda = 0$ adds the additional requirement that the constraint be met.

Constrained Minimization

Consider a total cost function, which is the sum of the expenditures on n activities, $x_1, x_2, \ldots, x_n$:

$$C = p_1x_1 + p_2x_2 + \cdots + p_nx_n$$

The prices of the activities, $p_1, p_2, \ldots, p_n$ are the partial derivatives $\partial C/\partial x_i = p_i$ ($i = 1, 2, \ldots, n$).

The constraint requires that the activities generate a given level of total benefit ($\overline{B}$)

$$\overline{B} = B(x_1, x_2, \cdots, x_n),$$

where $B(x_1\ x_2, \ldots, x_n)$ is the total benefit from the n activities.

To find the optimal levels of $x_1, x_2, \ldots, x_n$, the following Lagrangian equation is minimized:

$$L = p_1x_1 + p_2x_2 + \cdots + p_nx_n + \lambda\,[\,\overline{B} - B(x_1, x_2, \cdots, x_n)]$$

The first-order necessary condition for minimization requires that the partial derivatives of the Lagrangian function all equal zero:

$$\frac{\partial L}{\partial x_1} = p_1 - \lambda\frac{\partial B}{\partial x_1} = 0$$

$$\frac{\partial L}{\partial x_2} = p_2 - \lambda\frac{\partial B}{\partial x_2} = 0$$

$$\vdots \qquad \vdots$$

$$\frac{\partial L}{\partial x_n} = p_n - \lambda\frac{\partial B}{\partial x_n} = 0$$

$$\frac{\partial L}{\partial \lambda} = \overline{B} - B(x_1, x_2, \ldots, x_n) = 0$$

Rearranging the first n of these equations, the first-order condition for *minimization* requires

$$p_1 = \lambda\frac{\partial B}{\partial x_1} \qquad \frac{MB_1}{p_1} = \frac{1}{\lambda}$$

$$p_2 = \lambda\frac{\partial B}{\partial x_2} \quad \text{or} \quad \frac{MB_2}{p_2} = \frac{1}{\lambda}$$

$$\vdots \qquad \vdots$$

$$p_n = \lambda\frac{\partial B}{\partial x_n} \qquad \frac{MB_n}{p_n} = \frac{1}{\lambda}$$

Thus, it follows that $x_1, x_2, \ldots x_n$ must be chosen such that

$$\frac{MB_1}{p_1} = \frac{MB_2}{p_2} = \cdots = \frac{MB_n}{p_n}$$

Notice that this condition for minimization is the same as the condition for maximization. The condition that $\partial L/\partial\lambda = 0$ adds the additional requirement that the constraint be met.

CHAPTER

5 Basic Estimation Techniques

In order to implement the various techniques discussed in this text, managers must be able to determine the mathematical relation between the economic variables that make up the various functions used in managerial economics—demand functions, production functions, cost functions, and others. For example, managers often must determine the total cost of producing various levels of output. As you will see in Chapter 12, the relation between total cost (C) and quantity (Q) can be specified as

$$C = a + bQ + cQ^2 + dQ^3$$

parameters
The coefficients in an equation that determine the exact mathematical relation among the variables.

where a, b, c, and d are the *parameters* of the cost equation. **Parameters** are coefficients in an equation that determine the exact mathematical relation among the variables in the equation. Once the numerical values of the parameters are determined, the manager then knows the quantitative relation between output and total cost. For example, suppose the values of the parameters of the cost equation are determined to be $a = 1{,}262$, $b = 1.0$, $c = -0.03$, and $d = 0.005$. The cost equation can now be expressed as:

$$C = 1{,}262 + 1.0Q - 0.03Q^2 + 0.005Q^3$$

This equation can now be used to compute the total cost of producing various levels of output. If, for example, the manager wishes to produce 30 units of output, the total cost can be calculated as

$$C = 1{,}262 + 30 - 0.03(30)^2 + 0.005(30)^3 = \$1{,}400$$

Thus, in order for the cost function to be useful for decision making, the manager must know the numerical values of the parameters.

The process of finding estimates of the numerical values of the parameters of an equation is called **parameter estimation**. Although there are several techniques for estimating parameters, the values of the parameters are often obtained by using a technique called **regression analysis**. Regression analysis uses data on economic variables to determine a mathematical equation that describes the relation between the economic variables. Regression analysis involves both the estimation of parameter values and testing for statistical significance.

parameter estimation
The process of finding estimates of the numerical values of the parameters of an equation.

regression analysis
A statistical technique for estimating the parameters of an equation and testing for statistical significance.

In this chapter, we will set forth the *basics* of regression analysis. We want to stress that throughout the discussion of regression analysis, in this chapter and the chapters that follow, we are not as much interested in your knowing the ways the various statistics are calculated, as we are in your knowing how these statistics can be interpreted and used. We will often rely on intuitive explanations, leaving formal derivations for the appendixes at the end of the chapter.

5.1 THE SIMPLE LINEAR REGRESSION MODEL

Regression analysis is a technique used to determine the mathematical relation between a **dependent variable** and one or more **explanatory variables**. The explanatory variables are the economic variables that are thought to affect the value of the dependent variable. In the **simple linear regression model**, the dependent variable Y is related to only *one* explanatory variable X, and the relation between Y and X is linear:

$$Y = a + bX$$

dependent variable
The variable whose variation is to be explained.

explanatory variables
The variables that are thought to cause the dependent variable to take on different values.

simple linear regression model
A linear regression model with one explanatory variable: $Y = a + bX$.

This is the equation for a straight line, with X plotted along the horizontal axis and Y along the vertical axis. The parameter a is called the **intercept parameter** because it gives the value of Y at the point where the regression line crosses the Y-axis. (X is equal to zero at this point.) The parameter b is called the **slope parameter** because it gives the slope of the regression line. The slope of a line measures the rate of change in Y as X changes ($\Delta Y/\Delta X$); it is therefore the change in Y per unit change in X.

intercept parameter
The parameter that gives the value of Y at the point where the regression line crosses the Y-axis.

slope parameter
The slope of the regression line, $b = \Delta Y/\Delta X$, or the change in Y associated with a one-unit change in X.

Note that Y and X are linearly related in the regression model; that is, the effect of a change in X on the value of Y is constant. More specifically, a one-unit change in X causes Y to change by a constant b units. The simple regression model is based on a linear relation between Y and X, in large part because estimating the parameters of a linear model is relatively simple statistically. As it turns out, assuming a linear relation is not overly restrictive. For one thing, many variables are actually linearly related or very nearly linearly related. For those cases where Y and X are instead related in a curvilinear fashion, you will see that a simple transformation of the variables often makes it possible to model nonlinear relations within the framework of the linear regression model. You will see how to make these simple transformations later in this chapter.

A Hypothetical Regression Model

true (or actual) relation
The true or actual underlying relation between Y and X that is unknown to the researcher but is to be discovered by analyzing the sample data.

To illustrate the simple regression model, consider a statistical problem facing the Tampa Bay Travel Agents' Association. The Association wishes to determine the mathematical relation between the dollar volume of sales of travel packages (S) and the level of expenditure on newspaper advertising (A) for travel agents located in the Tampa–St. Petersburg metropolitan area. Suppose that the **true (or actual) relation** between sales and advertising expenditures is

$$S = 10{,}000 + 5A$$

where S measures monthly sales in dollars, and A measures monthly advertising expenditures in dollars. The true relation between sales and advertising is unknown to the analyst; it must be "discovered" by analyzing data on sales and advertising. Researchers are never able to know with certainty the exact nature of the underlying mathematical relation between the dependent variable and the explanatory variable, but regression analysis does provide a method for estimating the true relation.

Figure 5.1 shows the true or actual relation between sales and advertising expenditures. If an agency chooses to spend nothing on newspaper advertising, its sales are expected to be $10,000 per month. If an agency spends $3,000 monthly on ads, it can expect sales of $25,000 (= 10,000 + 5 × 3,000). Because $\Delta S/\Delta A$ equals 5, for every $1 of additional expenditure on advertising, the travel

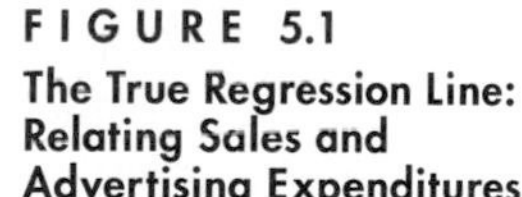
FIGURE 5.1
The True Regression Line: Relating Sales and Advertising Expenditures

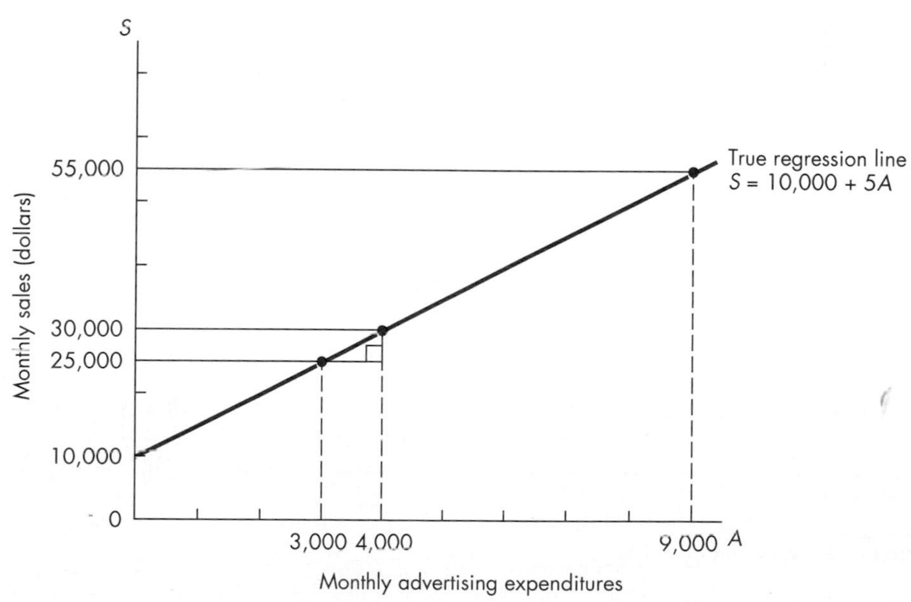

agency can expect a $5 increase in sales. For example, increasing outlays from $3,000 to $4,000 per month causes expected monthly sales to rise from $25,000 to $30,000, as shown in the figure.

The Random Error Term

The regression equation (or line) shows the level of expected sales for each level of advertising expenditure. As noted, if a travel agency spends $3,000 monthly on ads, it can expect on average to have sales of $25,000. We should stress that $25,000 should not be interpreted as the exact level of sales that a firm will experience when advertising expenditures are $3,000, but only as an average level. To illustrate this point, suppose that three travel agencies in the Tampa–St. Petersburg area each spend exactly $3,000 on advertising. Will all three of these firms experience sales of precisely $25,000? This is *not* likely. While each of these three firms spends exactly the same amount on advertising, each firm experiences certain *random* effects that are peculiar to that firm. These random effects cause the sales of the various firms to deviate from the expected $25,000 level of sales.

Table 5.1 illustrates the impact of random effects on the actual level of sales achieved. Each of the three firms in Table 5.1 spent $3,000 on advertising in the month of January. According to the true regression equation, each of these travel agencies would be expected to have sales of $25,000 in January. As it turns out, the manager of the Tampa Travel Agency used the advertising agency owned and managed by her brother, who gave better than usual service. This travel agency actually sold $30,000 worth of travel packages in January—$5,000 more than the expected or average level of sales. The manager of Buccaneer Travel Service was on a ski vacation in early January and did not start spending money on advertising until the middle of January. Buccaneer Travel Service's sales were only $21,0000—$4,000 less than the regression line predicted. In January nothing unusual happened to Happy Getaway Tours, and its sales of $25,000 exactly matched what the average travel agency in Tampa would be expected to sell when it spends $3,000 on advertising.

Because of these random effects, the level of sales for a firm cannot be *exactly* predicted. The regression equation shows only the *average* or *expected* level of sales when a firm spends a given amount on advertising. The exact level of sales for any particular travel agency (such as the ith agency) can be expressed as:

$$S_i = 10{,}000 + 5A_i + e_i$$

TABLE 5.1
The Impact of Random Effects on January Sales

Firm	Advertising expenditure	Actual sales	Expected sales	Random effect
Tampa Travel Agency	$3,000	$30,000	$25,000	$5,000
Buccaneer Travel Service	3,000	21,000	25,000	–4,000
Happy Getaway Tours	3,000	25,000	25,000	0

where S_i and A_i are, respectively, the sales and advertising levels of the ith agency and e_i is the random effect experienced by the ith travel agency. Since e_i measures the amount by which the *actual* level of sales differs from the average level of sales, e_i is called an *error term*, or a *random error*. The **random error term** captures the effects of all the minor, unpredictable factors that cannot reasonably be included in the model as explanatory variables.

random error term
An unobservable term added to a regression model to capture the effects of all the minor, unpredictable factors that affect *Y* but cannot reasonably be included as explanatory variables.

Because the *true* regression line is unknown, the first task of regression analysis is to obtain estimates of *a* and *b*. To do this, data on monthly sales and advertising expenditures must be collected from Tampa Bay area travel agents. Using these data, a regression line is then fitted. Before turning to the task of fitting a regression line to the data points in a sample, we summarize the simple regression model in the following statistical relation:

Relation The simple linear regression model relates a dependent variable *Y* to a single independent explanatory variable *X* in a linear equation called the true regression line:

$$Y = a + bX$$

where *a* is the *Y*-intercept, and *b* is the slope of the regression line ($\Delta Y/\Delta X$). The regression line shows the average or expected value of *Y* for each level of the explanatory variable *X*.

5.2 FITTING A REGRESSION LINE

The purpose of regression analysis is twofold: (1) to estimate the parameters (*a* and *b*) of the true regression line, and (2) to test whether the estimated values of the parameters are statistically significant. (We will discuss the meaning of statistical significance later.) We turn now to the first task—the estimation of *a* and *b*. You will see that estimating *a* and *b* is equivalent to fitting a straight line through a scatter of data points plotted on a graph. Regression analysis provides a way of finding the line that "best fits" the scatter of data points.

To estimate the parameters of the regression equation, an analyst first collects data on the dependent and explanatory variables. The data could be collected over time for a specific firm (or a specific industry). This type of data set is called a **time-series**. Alternatively, the data could be collected from several different firms or industries at a given time; this type of data set is called a **cross-sectional** data set. No matter how the data are collected, the result would be a scatter of data points (called a **scatter diagram**) through which a regression line would be fitted.

time-series
A data set in which the data for the dependent and explanatory variables are collected over time for a specific firm.

cross-sectional
A data set in which the data on the dependent and explanatory variables are collected from many different firms or industries at a given point in time.

scatter diagram
A graph of the data points in a sample.

To show how the parameters are estimated, we refer once again to the Tampa Bay Travel Agents' Association. Suppose the association asks seven agencies (out of the total 475 agencies located in the Tampa–St. Petersburg area) for data on their sales and advertising expenditures during the month of January. These data (a cross-sectional data set) are presented in Table 5.2 and are plotted in a scatter diagram in Figure 5.2. Each dot in the figure refers to a specific sales-expenditure combination in the table. The data seem to indicate that a positive relation exists between sales and advertising—the higher the level of advertising, the higher (on average) the level of sales. The objective of regression analysis is to find the straight line that "best fits" the scatter of data points. Since fitting a line through

TABLE 5.2
Sales and Advertising Expenditures for a Sample of Seven Travel Agencies

Firm	Sales	Advertising expenditure
A	$15,000	$2,000
B	30,000	2,000
C	30,000	5,000
D	25,000	3,000
E	55,000	9,000
F	45,000	8,000
G	60,000	7,000

FIGURE 5.2
The Sample Regression Line: Relating Sales and Advertising Expenditures

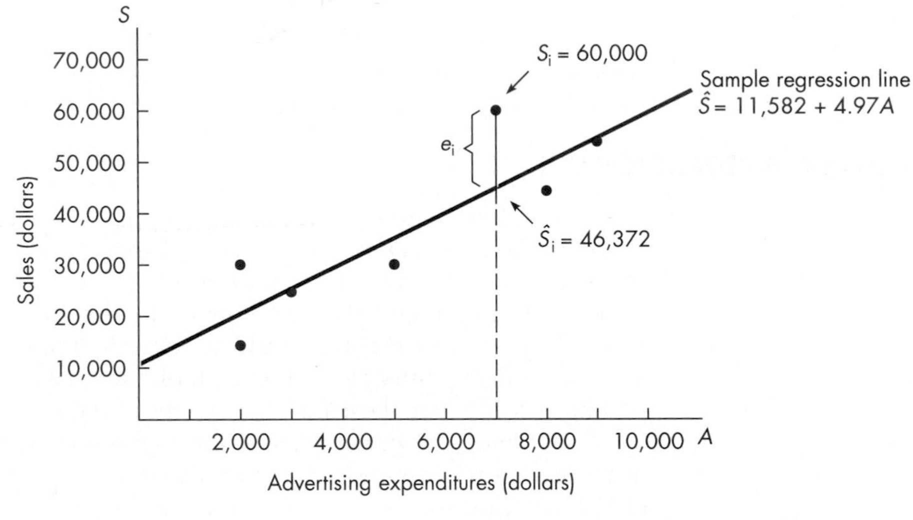

a scatter of data points simply involves choosing values of the parameters *a* and *b*, fitting a regression line and estimation of parameters are conceptually the same thing.

population regression line The equation or line representing the true (or actual) underlying relation between the dependent variable and the explanatory variable(s).

sample regression line The line that best fits the scatter of data points in the sample and provides an estimate of the population regression line.

The association wants to use the data in the sample to estimate the true regression line, also called the **population regression line**. The line that best fits the data in the sample is called the **sample regression line**. Since the sample contains information on only seven out of the total 475 travel agencies, it is highly unlikely that the sample regression line will be exactly the same as the true regression line. The sample regression line is only an estimate of the true regression line. If one is able to collect data on *every* member of the population—all 475 travel agencies in this example—the sample regression line would converge to the true regression line. Because data collection is costly, an analyst seldom has data on every member of a population. Naturally, the larger the size of the sample, the more accurately the sample regression line will estimate the true regression line.

In Figure 5.2, the sample regression line that best fits the seven sample data points presented in Table 5.2 is given by:

$$\hat{S} = 11{,}582 + 4.97A$$

method of least-squares
A method of estimating the parameters of a linear regression equation by finding the line that minimizes the sum of the squared distances from each sample data point to the sample regression line.

fitted or predicted value
The predicted value of Y (denoted $\hat{Y}$) associated with a particular value of X, which is obtained by substituting that value of X into the sample regression equation.

residual
The difference between the actual value of Y and the fitted (or predicted) value of Y: $Y_i - \hat{Y}_i$.

estimators
The formulas by which the estimates of parameters are computed.

estimates
The estimated values of parameters obtained by substituting sample data into estimators.

where $\hat{S}$ is called the fitted or predicted value of S. Regression analysis uses the **method of least-squares** to find the sample regression line that best fits the data in the sample. The principle of least-squares is based on the idea that the sample regression line that is most likely to match the *true* regression line is the line that minimizes the sum of the squared distances from each sample data point to the *sample* regression line.

Look at the sample data point for advertising expenditures of $7,000 and sales of $60,000 in Figure 5.2. The sample regression equation indicates that advertising expenditures of $7,000 will result in $46,372 (= 11,582 + 4.97 × 7,000) of sales. The value $46,372 is called the **fitted or predicted value** of sales, which we denote as $\hat{S}_i$. The difference between the actual value of sales and the fitted (predicted) value, $S_i - \hat{S}_i$, is called the **residual** and is equal to the vertical distance between the data point and the fitted regression line (denoted e_i in Figure 5.2). The residual for the data point at ($7,000, $60,000) is $13,628 (= $60,000 − 46,372). Regression analysis selects the straight line (i.e., chooses a and b), in order to minimize the sum of the squared residuals (Σe_i^2), which is why it is often referred to as least-squares analysis.

We are not concerned with teaching you the details involved in computing the least-squares estimates of a and b since computers are almost always used in regression analysis for this purpose. Nevertheless, it might be informative for you to see how the computer can calculate estimates of a and b. The formulas by which the estimates of a and b are computed are frequently called **estimators**. The formulas for computing the least-squares estimates of a and b (denoted $\hat{a}$ and $\hat{b}$ to indicate that these are **estimates** and not the true values) are

$$\hat{b} = \frac{\Sigma(X_i - \overline{X})(Y_i - \overline{Y})}{\Sigma(X_i - \overline{X})^2}$$

and

$$\hat{a} = \overline{Y} - \hat{b}\overline{X}$$

where $\overline{Y}$ and $\overline{X}$ are, respectively, the sample means of the dependent variable and independent variable, and X_i and Y_i are the observed values for the ith observation. While our central concern is that you understand how to interpret regression analysis, we have provided the mathematical derivation of the least-squares formulas for $\hat{a}$ and $\hat{b}$ in Appendix 5A at the end of this chapter for those who wish to see a formal derivation. So you can appreciate the tedious nature of the arithmetic involved in computing least-squares estimates, Appendix 5A illustrates the computations that will be done for you by a computer. We can now summarize least-squares estimation with the following statistical relation:

Relation Estimating the parameters of the true regression line is equivalent to fitting a line through a scatter diagram of the sample data points. The sample regression line, which is found using the method of least-squares, is the line that best fits the sample:

$$\hat{Y} = \hat{a} + \hat{b}X$$

where $\hat{a}$ and $\hat{b}$ are the least-squares estimates of the true (population) parameters a and b. The sample regression line estimates the true regression line.

We now turn to the task of testing hypotheses about the true values of a and b—which are unknown to the researcher—using the information contained in the sample. These tests involve determining whether the dependent variable is truly related to the independent variable or whether the relation as estimated from the sample data is due only to the randomness of the sample.

5.3 TESTING FOR STATISTICAL SIGNIFICANCE

Once the parameters of an equation are estimated, the analyst must address the question of whether or not the parameter estimates ($\hat{a}$ and $\hat{b}$) are significantly different from zero. If the estimated coefficient is far enough away from zero—either sufficiently greater than zero (a positive estimate) or sufficiently less than zero (a negative estimate)—the estimated coefficient is said to be **statistically significant**. The question of statistical significance arises because the estimates are themselves random variables. The parameter estimates are random because they are calculated using values of Y and X that are collected in a random fashion (remember, the sample is a random sample). Since the values of the parameters are *estimates* of the true parameter values, the estimates are rarely equal to the true parameter values. In other words, the estimates calculated by the computer are almost always going to be either "too large" or "too small."

statistically significant
An estimated parameter is statistically significant if there is sufficient evidence from the sample to believe that the true value of the coefficient is not zero.

Because the estimated values of the parameters ($\hat{a}$ and $\hat{b}$) are unlikely to be the true values (a and b), it is possible that a parameter could truly be equal to zero even though the computer calculates a parameter estimate that is *not* equal to zero. Fortunately, statistical techniques exist that provide a tool for making probabilistic statements about the true values of the parameters. This tool is called **hypothesis testing**.

hypothesis testing
A statistical technique for making a probabilistic statement about the true value of a parameter.

To understand fully the concept of hypothesis testing, you would need to take at least one course, and probably two, in statistics. In this text we intend only to motivate through intuition the *necessity* and *process* of performing a test of statistical significance. Our primary emphasis will be to show you how to test the hypothesis that Y is truly related to X. If Y is indeed related to X, the true value of the slope parameter b will be either a positive or negative number. (Remember, if $b = \Delta Y/\Delta X = 0$, no change in Y occurs when X changes.) Thus, the explanatory variable X has a statistically significant effect on the dependent variable Y when $b \neq 0$.[1]

[1]Testing for statistical significance of the intercept parameter a is typically of secondary importance to testing for significance of the slope parameters. As you will see, it is the slope parameters rather than the intercept parameter that provide the most essential information for managerial decision making. Nevertheless, it is customary to test the intercept parameter for statistical significance in exactly the same manner as the slope parameter is tested.

We will now discuss the procedure for testing for statistical significance by describing how to measure the accuracy, or precision, of an estimate. Then we will introduce and explain a statistical test (called a t-test) that can be used to make a probabilistic statement about whether or not Y is truly related to the explanatory variable X—that is, whether or not the true value of the parameter b is zero.

The Relative Frequency Distribution for $\hat{b}$

As noted, the necessity of testing for statistical significance arises because the analyst does not know the true values of a and b—they are estimated from a random sample of observations on Y and X. Consider again the relation between sales of travel packages and advertising expenditures estimated in the previous section. The least-squares estimate of the slope parameter b from the sample of seven travel agencies shown in Table 5.2 is 4.97. Suppose you collected a new sample by randomly selecting seven other travel agencies and use their sales and advertising expenditures to estimate b. The estimate for b will probably not equal 4.97 for this second sample. Remember, $\hat{b}$ is computed using the values of S and A in the sample. Because of randomness in sampling, different samples generally result in different values of S and A, and thus different estimates of b. Therefore, $\hat{b}$ is a random variable—its value varies in repeated samples.

relative frequency distribution
The distribution (and relative frequency) of values $\hat{b}$ can take because observations on Y and X come from a random sample.

The relative frequency with which $\hat{b}$ takes on different values provides information about the *accuracy* of the parameter estimates. Even though researchers seldom have the luxury of taking repeated samples, statisticians have been able to determine theoretically the **relative frequency distribution** of values that $\hat{b}$ would take in repeated samples. Figure 5.3 shows the relative frequency, or likelihood, that $\hat{b}$ takes on different values in repeated samples, *when the true value of* b *is equal to 5.*

FIGURE 5.3
Relative Frequency Distribution for $\hat{b}$ When $b = 5$

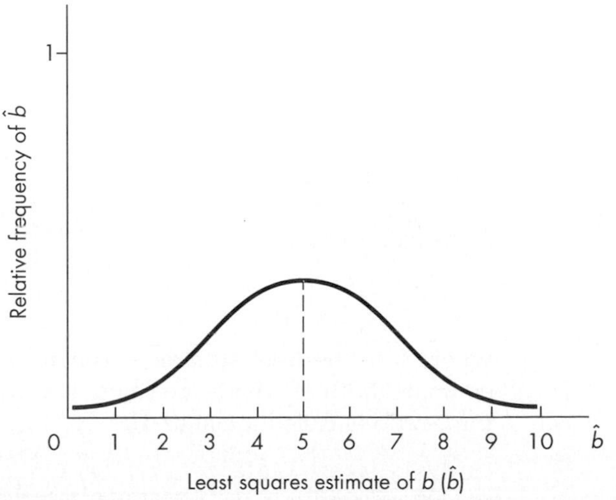

Notice that the distribution of values that $\hat{b}$ might take in various samples is centered around the true value of 5. Even though the probability of drawing a sample for which $\hat{b}$ exactly equals 5 is extremely small, the average (mean or expected) value of all possible values of $\hat{b}$ is 5. The estimator $\hat{b}$ is said to be an **unbiased estimator** if the average (mean or expected) value of the estimator is equal to the true value of the parameter. Statisticians have demonstrated that the least-squares estimators of a and b ($\hat{a}$ and $\hat{b}$) are unbiased estimators in a wide variety of statistical circumstances. Unbiasedness does not mean that any one estimate equals the true parameter value. Unbiasedness only means the estimates tend to be centered around the true value.

unbiased estimator
An estimator that produces estimates of a parameter that are on average equal to the true value of the parameter.

The smaller the dispersion of $\hat{b}$ around the true value, the more likely it is that an estimate of $\hat{b}$ is close to the true value. In other words, the smaller the variance of the distribution of $\hat{b}$, the more accurate estimates are likely to be. Not surprisingly, the variance of the estimate of b plays an important role in the determination of statistical significance. The square root of the variance of $\hat{b}$ is called the **standard error of the estimate**, which we will denote $S_{\hat{b}}$.[2] All computer regression routines compute standard errors for the parameter estimates.

standard error of the estimate
The square root of the variance of a relative frequency distribution of an estimator.

The Concept of a *t*-Ratio

When we regressed sales on advertising expenditures for the seven travel agencies in Table 5.2, we obtained an estimate of b equal to 4.97. Since 4.97 is not equal to zero, this seems to suggest that the level of advertising does indeed affect sales. (Remember that if $b = 0$, there is no relation between sales and advertising.) As explained above, the estimate of b calculated using a random sample may take on a range of values. Even though 4.97 is greater than zero, it is possible that the true value of b is zero. In other words, the analyst runs some risk that the true value of b is zero even when $\hat{b}$ is not calculated to be zero.

The probability of drawing a sample for which the estimate of b is "much larger" than zero is very small when the true value of b is actually zero. How large does $\hat{b}$ have to be in order to be quite sure that b is not really zero (i.e., advertising does play a significant role in determining sales)? The answer to this question is obtained by performing a hypothesis test. The hypothesis that one normally tests is that $b = 0$. Statisticians use a ***t*-test** to make a probabilistic statement about the likelihood that the true parameter value b is not equal to zero. Using the *t*-test, it is possible to determine statistically how large $\hat{b}$ must be in order to conclude that b is not equal to zero.

***t*-test**
A statistical test used to test the hypothesis that the true value of a parameter is equal to some specific number, usually zero ($b = 0$).

In order to perform a *t*-test for statistical significance, we form what statisticians call a ***t*-ratio**:

$$t = \frac{\hat{b}}{S_{\hat{b}}}$$

***t*-ratio**
The ratio of an estimated regression parameter divided by the standard error of the estimate.

where $\hat{b}$ is the least squares estimate of b, and $S_{\hat{b}}$ is the standard error of the estimate, both of which are calculated by the computer. The numerical value of the *t*-ratio is called a ***t*-statistic**.

***t*-statistic**
The numerical value of the *t*-ratio.

[2]More correctly, the standard error of the estimate is the square root of the *estimated* variance of $\hat{b}$.

By combining information about the size of $\hat{b}$ (in the numerator) and the accuracy or precision of the estimate (in the denominator), the t-ratio indicates how much confidence one can have that the true value of b is actually larger than (significantly different from) zero. The larger the t-ratio, the more confident one can be that the true value of b is greater than zero. To show why this is true, we must examine both the numerator and denominator of the t-ratio. Consider the numerator. When b actually is zero, drawing a random sample that will produce an estimate of b that is much larger than zero is unlikely. Thus, the larger the numerator of the t-ratio, the less likely it is that b really does equal zero. Turning now to the denominator of the t-ratio, recall that $S_{\hat{b}}$, the standard error of the estimate, measures the accuracy of the estimate of b. The smaller the standard error of $\hat{b}$ (and thus the more accurate $\hat{b}$ is), the smaller the error in estimation is likely to be. Consequently, the farther from zero is $\hat{b}$ (i.e., the larger the numerator) and the smaller the standard error of the estimate (i.e., the smaller the denominator), the larger the t-ratio, and the more sure we are that the true value of b is greater than zero.

If we had estimated $\hat{b}$ to be negative (for example, if we had estimated the relation between profits and shoplifting), we would be more certain that b was really negative if the t-ratio had a more negative magnitude. Regardless of whether $\hat{b}$ is positive or negative, the following important statistical relation is established:

Relation The larger the absolute value of $\frac{\hat{b}}{S_{\hat{b}}}$ (the t-ratio), the more probable it is that the true value of b is not equal to zero.

Performing a *t*-Test for Statistical Significance

critical value of *t*
The value that the t-statistic must exceed in order to reject the hypothesis that $b = 0$.

The t-statistic is used to test the hypothesis that the true value of b equals zero. If the calculated t-statistic or t-ratio is greater than the **critical value of *t*** (to be explained later), then the hypothesis that $b = 0$ is rejected in favor of the alternative hypothesis that $b \neq 0$. When the calculated t-statistic exceeds the critical value of t, b is significantly different from zero, or equivalently, b is statistically significant.

level of risk
The probability that a statistical test will reject a hypothesis when in fact the hypothesis is correct.

Although performing a t-test is the correct way to assess the statistical significance of a parameter estimate, there is always some risk that the t-test will indicate $b \neq 0$ when in fact the true value is zero. The **level of risk** associated with a t-test is the probability that the t-test will indicate $b \neq 0$ when in fact, b *is* equal to zero. Stated differently, the risk level is the probability of finding the parameter to be statistically significant, when in fact it is not. The risk level gives the probability of making such a mistake. In regression analysis, t-tests are generally conducted at either a 1 percent, 5 percent, or 10 percent level of risk. The lower the level of risk at which the t-test is conducted, the higher the critical value of t associated with the test. (Remember, a large t-ratio is required to be almost certain that the true value of b is not equal to zero.)

level of confidence
The probability that a statistical test will reject a hypothesis when the hypothesis is incorrect. The level of confidence is equal to one minus the level of risk.

A concept closely related to the level of risk is the *level of confidence*. If the level of risk chosen for conducing a t-test is 5 percent, then the **level of confidence** for the test is 95 percent, which means that the t-ratio is large enough that we can be 95 percent confident that the true value of b is not equal to zero. The

ILLUSTRATION 5.1

How Confident Is "Confident Enough"?

We have emphasized that the choice of confidence level in a statistical analysis depends on the judgment of the analyst and the perceived consequences of making an error. We want to tell you two stories to better illustrate this important point.

During the first days of the Persian Gulf War, the world was stunned by the success rate of the bombing attacks against military targets in Iraq. In his first news briefing at the outbreak of the Persian Gulf War, General Normal Schwarzkopf reported that 80 percent of the nearly 15,000 sorties flown had successfully hit their intended target. Many of the correspondents in attendance were highly suspicious about such an extraordinary success rate, but two reporters, Barbara Smith and Heraldo Jones, decided to test the general's assertion that the true success rate was 80 percent. They obtained a list of the locations of 100 of the 15,000 targets, then enlisted the help of a pilot of a three-seater Stealth fighter to fly them over each of the 100 targets to see how many were damaged by bombs. Smith and Jones counted 65 bomb-damaged targets, indicating only a 65 percent success rate, as opposed to the reported 80 percent.

Each reporter had to decide whether 65 percent was far enough away from 80 percent to refute the Schwarzkopf assertion. Both realized the inherent randomness of sampling and that the 100 targets may not have exactly reflected the population of 15,000 targets, known only to the general and his staff.

Smith was tempted to report to her news director that she had discovered compelling evidence that General Schwarzkopf incorrectly reported the success rate of the air war. If correct, she would probably become famous and win a Pulitzer Prize; but if wrong, she would be ruined professionally. Smith was not willing to take more than a 5 percent risk that she was wrong and General Schwarzkopf was correct; that is, she had to be 95 percent confident before she was willing to conclude that the 80 percent figure was incorrect. Smith decided that 65 percent was not far enough below 80 percent to make her feel 95 percent confident that 80 percent was an exaggeration. Therefore, she did not report her findings.

Jones, in contrast to Smith, badly wanted to be an anchor. He was willing to bet his career by taking a 75 percent risk that he was wrong and the general was right; that is, he was comfortable with only a 25 percent level of confidence. At the 25 percent level of confidence, Jones viewed a 65 percent success rate as being far enough away from the asserted 80 percent success rate that he rejected the general's assertion. Jones called his news anchor with startling evidence that General Schwarzkopf had misinformed the public about the success of the air war. Jones's network reported his story on national news, and upon hearing this news report, General Schwarzkopf decided to reveal the list of the initial 15,000 sorties. Using the entire population of 15,000 targets, the Middle East press corps verified that 80 percent of the targets were indeed damaged by bombs. As it turned out, Barbara Smith was later promoted to anchor at her network. Heraldo Jones was fired and now hosts a talk show at an obscure radio station in College Station, Texas.

level of confidence equals one hundred minus the level of risk (95 = 100 – 5). The appropriate confidence level is determined by the analyst on the basis of the cost of making an error. For example, if you will lose your job if you make a mistake, you will probably want to use a high-confidence level (a low risk level).

The t-test is simple to perform. First, calculate the t-statistic (t-ratio) from the parameter estimate and its standard error, both of which are calculated by the computer. Next, find the appropriate critical value of t for the chosen level of confidence or risk. The critical value of t is provided in the t-table at the end of this book along with explanatory text. The critical value of t is defined by the level of confidence and the appropriate *degrees of freedom*. The **degrees of freedom** for a t-test is equal to $n - k$, where n is the number of observations in the

degrees of freedom
The number of observations in the sample minus the number of parameters being estimated by the regression analysis ($n - k$).

We should note that this story is entirely undocumented and based completely on hearsay evidence. The next story about the importance of choosing the correct level of confidence is, however, documented in *The Wall Street Journal*, "Statisticians Occupy Front Lines in Battle over Passive Smoking," July 28, 1993.

The article begins, "In the controversy over passive smoking, the difference between 90 and 95 percent has become a matter of life and death." The US Environmental Protection Agency (EPA) reported that there is a 90 percent probability that the risk of lung cancer is somewhere between 4 percent and 35 percent higher for passive smokers than for those who are not exposed to environmental smoke. This calculation is called by statisticians a "90 percent confidence interval," which means that they are 90 percent sure that the *true* risk of lung cancer for passive smokers lies between 4 and 35 percent higher. The director of the Health Policy Center, a frequent consultant and expert witness for the tobacco industry, countered, "Ninety-nine percent of all epidemiological studies use a 95 percent confidence interval." As the *Journal* reported, "These five percentage points will haunt the coming [court] battle . . . in which tobacco interests led by Philip Morris and RJR Nabisco have sued the EPA's report convicting environmental tobacco smoke of causing lung cancer in nonsmokers." The companies had charged that the EPA's finding was "manipulated."

The EPA evidence was based upon studies that led it to conclude that nonsmoking women who live with smokers have, on average, a 19 percent higher risk of developing lung cancer than women who live in a smoke-free home. Tobacco lawyers and statisticians have attacked the 19 percent figure as being so small as to be canceled out by other unknowns and based upon bad sampling procedures.

An independent statistical consultant, however, calculated that the 19 percent figure is statistically significant at the 5 percent level of confidence. He noted that a second calculation of a 90 percent probability that the lung-cancer-risk range is between 4 percent and 35 percent higher for passive smokers than those who aren't exposed to smoking was added to the report "to give reviewers a better feeling for the reliability of the calculations." The director of the HPC asserted that the reason a 95 percent confidence level was not used is that it would be so wide it might hint that passive smoking actually reduced the risk of lung cancer. That is, the higher the probability of being correct, the broader the range must be. The *Journal* noted that a 95 percent calculation might show, for instance, that passive smokers' risk of lung cancer ranges from say, 15 percent *lower* to 160 percent higher than the risk run by those in a smoke-free environment. An EPA consultant admitted that using a 95 percent confidence interval would hint that passive smoking might reduce the risk of cancer, and, he said, that was the reason it wasn't used. Any such hint in the report "would be meaningless and confusing."

Of course, we do not want to participate here in the smoking-effect controversy. We only want to emphasize how important the choice of a confidence level can be in statistical analysis.

sample and k is the number of parameters estimated. (In the advertising example, there are $7 - 2 = 5$ degrees of freedom since we have seven observations and estimated two parameters, a and b.)

Once the critical value of t is found for, say the 95 percent level of confidence, the *absolute value* of the calculated t-statistic is compared to the critical value of t. If the absolute value of the t-statistic is greater than the critical value of t, we say that, with 95 percent confidence, the estimated parameter is (statistically) significantly different from zero. If the *absolute value* of the calculated t-statistic is less than the critical value of t, the estimated value of b cannot be treated as being significantly different from zero, and X plays no statistically significant role in determining the value of Y.

We now test to see if 4.97 is significantly different from zero. The standard error of $\hat{b}$, which is calculated by the computer, is equal to 1.23. Thus, the t-statistic is equal to 4.04 (= 4.97/1.23). Next we compare 4.04 to the critical value of t, using a 95 percent confidence level (a 5 percent risk level). As noted above, there are 5 degrees of freedom. If you turn to the table of critical t-values at the end of the text, you will find that the critical value of t for 5 degrees of freedom and a 95 percent confidence level is 2.571. Since 4.04 is larger than 2.571, we reject the hypothesis that b is zero and can now say that 4.97 ($\hat{b}$) is significantly different from zero. This means that advertising expenditure is a statistically significant variable in determining the level of sales. If 4.04 had been less than the critical value, we would not have been able to reject the hypothesis that b is zero, and we would not have been able to conclude that advertising plays a significant role in determining the level of sales.

The procedure for testing for statistical significance of a parameter estimate is summarized in the following statistical principle:

Principle In order to test for statistical significance of a parameter estimate $\hat{b}$, compute the t-ratio

$$t = \frac{\hat{b}}{S_{\hat{b}}}$$

where $S_{\hat{b}}$ is the standard error of the estimate $\hat{b}$. Next, find the critical t value in the t-table at the end of the text. Choose the critical t-value with $n - k$ degrees of freedom for the desired level of confidence. If the absolute value of the t-ratio is greater (less) than the critical t-value, then $\hat{b}$ is (is not) statistically significant.

5.4 EVALUATION OF THE REGRESSION EQUATION

Once the individual parameter estimates $\hat{a}$ and $\hat{b}$ have been tested for statistical significance using t-tests, researchers often wish to evaluate the *complete* estimated regression equation, $\hat{Y} = \hat{a} + \hat{b}X$. Evaluation of the regression equation involves determining how well the estimated regression equation "explains" the variation in Y. Two statistics are frequently employed to evaluate the overall acceptability of a regression equation. The first is called the *coefficient of determination*, normally denoted as "R^2" and pronounced "R-squared." The second is the *F-statistic*, which is used to test whether the *overall* equation is statistically significant.

The Coefficient of Determination (R^2)

coefficient of determination (R^2) The fraction of total variation in the dependent variable explained by the regression equation.

The **coefficient of determination (R^2)** measures the fraction of the total variation in the dependent variable that is explained by the regression equation. In terms of the example used earlier, it is the fraction of the variation in sales that is explained by variation in advertising expenditures. Therefore, the value of R^2 can range from 0 (the regression equation explains none of the variation in Y) to 1 (the regression equation explains all of the variation in Y). While the R^2 is printed out as a decimal value by most computers, the R^2 is often spoken of in terms of a percentage. For example, if the calculated R^2 is 0.7542, we could say that approximately 75 percent of the variation in Y is explained by the model.

FIGURE 5.4
High and Low Correlation

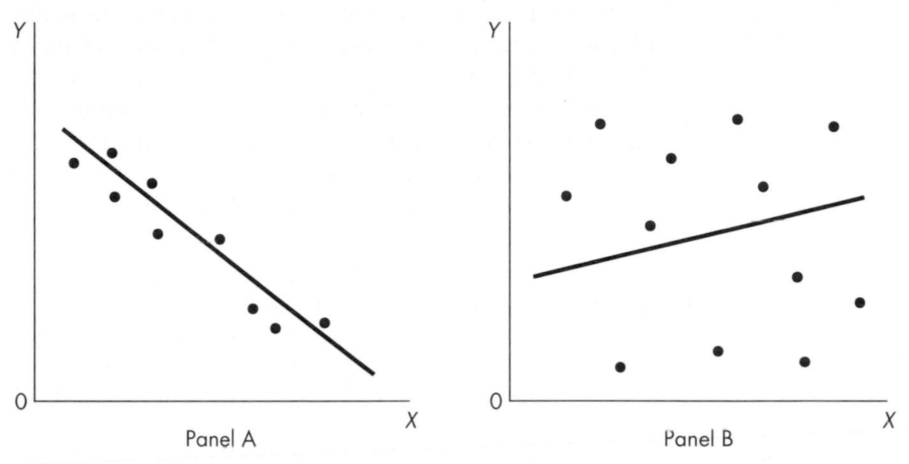

If the value of R^2 is high, there is high correlation between the dependent and independent variables; if it is low, there is low correlation. For example, in Figure 5.4, Panel A, the observations in the scatter diagram all lie rather close to the regression line. Since the deviations from the line are small, the correlation between X and Y is high and the value of R^2 will be high. In the extreme case when all of the observations lie on a straight line, R^2 will be equal to 1. In Panel B, the observations are scattered widely around the regression line. The correlation between X and Y in this case is much less than in Panel A, so the value of R^2 is rather small.

We must caution you that high correlation between two variables (or even a statistically significant regression coefficient) does not necessarily mean the variation in the dependent variable Y is *caused by* the variation in the independent variable X. It might be the case that variation in Y is caused by variation in Z, but X happens to be correlated to Z. Thus Y and X will be correlated even though variation in X does not cause Y to vary. A high R^2 does not prove that Y and X are causally related, only that Y and X are correlated. We summarize this discussion with a statistical relation:

Relation The coefficient of determination (R^2) measures the fraction of the total variation in Y that is explained by the variation in X. R^2 ranges in value from 0 (the regression explains none of the variation in Y) to 1 (the regression explains all of the variation in Y). A high R^2 indicates Y and X are highly correlated and the scatter diagram tightly fits the sample regression line.

The *F*-Statistic

F-statistic
A statistic used to test whether the overall regression equation is statistically significant.

Although the R^2 is a widely used statistic, it is subjective in the sense of how much explained variation—explained by the regression equation—is enough to view the equation as being statistically significant. An alternative is the ***F*-statistic**. In very general terms, this statistic provides a measure of the ratio of explained variation (in the dependent variable) to unexplained variation. To test whether the overall equation is significant, this statistic is compared to a critical F-value obtained from an F-table (at the end of this text). The critical F-value is identified by two separate degrees of freedom and the confidence level. The first of the degrees of freedom is $k - 1$ (i.e., the number of independent variables) and the second is $n - k$. If the value for the calculated F-statistic exceeds the critical F-value, the regression equation is statistically significant at the specified confidence level. The discussion of the F-statistic is summarized in a statistical relation:

Relation The F-statistic is used to *test* whether the regression equation as a whole explains a significant amount of the variation in Y. The test involves comparing the F-statistic to the critical F-value with $k - 1$ and $n - k$ degrees of freedom and the chosen level of confidence. If the F-statistic exceeds the critical F-value, the regression equation is statistically significant.

All of the statistics you will need in order to analyze a regression—the coefficient estimates, the standard errors, the t-ratios, R^2, and the F-statistic—are automatically calculated and printed by most available regression programs. As mentioned before, our objective is not that you understand how these statistics are calculated. Rather, we want you to know how to set up a regression and interpret the results. We now provide you with a hypothetical example of a regression analysis that might be performed by a manager of a firm.

Controlling Product Quality at SLM: A Regression Example

Specialty Lens Manufacturing (SLM) produces contact lenses for patients who are unable to wear standard contact lenses. These specialty contact lenses must meet extraordinarily strict standards. The production process is not perfect, however, and some lenses have slight flaws. Patients receiving flawed lenses almost always detect the flaws, and the lenses are returned to SLM for replacement. Returned lenses are costly, both in terms of redundant production costs and diminished corporate reputation for SLM. Inspectors using high-powered microscopes examine many, but not all, of the lenses before they are shipped to doctors.

Management at SLM decided to measure the effectiveness of its inspection process using regression analysis. During a 22-week time period, SLM collected weekly data on the percentage of lenses shipped that were returned by doctors due to flaws (F), and the number of hours per week inspectors spent examining lenses (H). The manager estimated the regression equation

$$F = a + bH$$

using the 22 weekly observations on F and H. The computer printed out the following output:

DEPENDENT VARIABLE: F		F-RATIO:	16.54
OBSERVATIONS: 22		R-SQUARED:	0.8651
VARIABLES	PARAMETER ESTIMATE	STANDARD ERROR	T-RATIO
INTERCEPT	9.0	2.57	3.50
H	-0.10	0.04	-2.50

As expected, $\hat{a}$ is positive and $\hat{b}$ is negative. If no inspection is done ($H = 0$), then the percentage of shipped lenses that are returned as defective is expected to be 9 percent. The estimate of b ($\hat{b} = \Delta F/\Delta H = -0.10$) indicates that each additional hour per week spent inspecting lenses will decrease the percentage of lenses that are flawed by 0.1 percent. Thus, it takes 10 extra hours of inspection of decrease flaws by 1 percent.

In order to determine if the parameter estimates $\hat{a}$ and $\hat{b}$ are significantly different from zero, the manager must conduct a t-test on each estimated parameter. The t-ratios for $\hat{a}$ and $\hat{b}$ are 3.50 and –2.50, respectively:

$$t_{\hat{a}} = 9.0/2.57 = 3.50 \text{ and } t_{\hat{b}} = -0.10/0.04 = -2.50$$

The critical t-value is found in the table at the end of the book. There are 22 observations and 2 parameters, so the degrees of freedom are $n - k = 22 - 2 = 20$. Choosing the 95 percent level of confidence (a 5 percent level of risk), the critical t-value is 2.086. Since the absolute value of $t_{\hat{a}}$ and $t_{\hat{b}}$ both exceed 2.086, both $\hat{a}$ and $\hat{b}$ are statistically significant.

Overall, the equation explains about 86 percent of the total variation in the dependent variable (F). To test for significance of the entire equation, an F-test is used. The critical F-value is obtained from the table at the end of the book. Since $k - 1 = 2 - 1 = 1$, and $n - k = 22 - 2 = 20$, $F_{1,20}$ at the 95 percent confidence level is 4.35. The F-statistic calculated by the computer is 16.54, exceeds 4.35, and the entire equation is statistically significant.

Using the estimated equation, $\hat{F} = 9.0 - 0.10H$, the manager can estimate the percentage of flawed lenses that will be shipped for various hours of weekly inspection. For example, if inspectors spend 60 hours per week examining lenses, SLM can expect 3 percent ($= 9.0 - 0.1 \times 60$) of the lenses shipped to be flawed.

5.5 MULTIPLE REGRESSION

Thus far we have discussed simple regressions involving a linear relation between the dependent variable Y and a *single* explanatory variable X. In many problems, however, the variation in Y depends upon more than one explanatory variable. There may quite a few variables needed to adequately explain the

ILLUSTRATION 5.2

R&D Expenditures and the Value of the Firm

In order to determine how much to spend on research and development (R&D) activities, a manager may wish to know how R&D expenditures affect the value of the firm. To investigate the relation between the value of a firm and the amount the firm spends on R&D, Wallin and Gilman* use simple regression analysis to estimate the model

$$V = a + bR$$

where the value of the firm (V) is measured by the price-to-earnings ratio, and the level of expenditures on R&D (R) is measured by R&D expenditures as a percentage of the firm's total sales.

Wallin and Gilman collected a cross-sectional data set on the 20 firms with the largest R&D expenditures in the 1981–82 time period. The computer output from a regression program and a scatter diagram showing the 20 data points with the sample regression line are presented below:

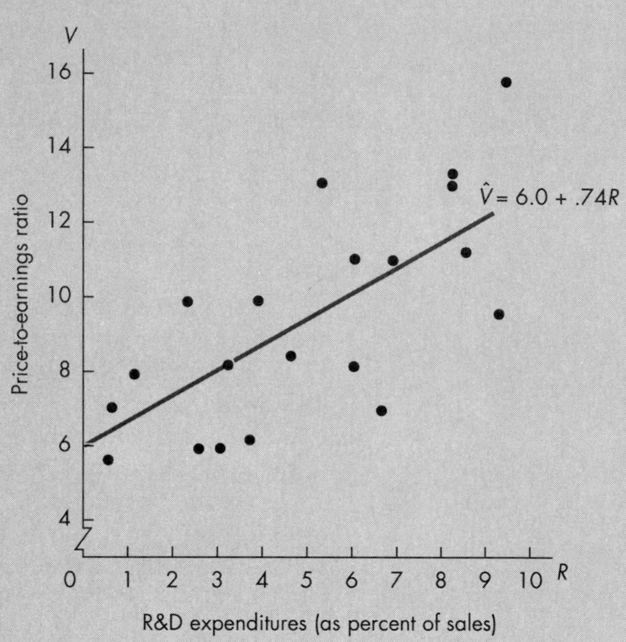

DEPENDENT VARIABLE: V		F-RATIO: 20.090	
OBSERVATIONS: 20		R-SQUARE: 0.5274	
VARIABLE	PARAMETER ESTIMATE	STANDARD ERROR	T-RATIO
INTERCEPT	6.00	0.917	6.54
R	0.74	0.165	4.48

multiple regression models Regression models that use more than one explanatory variable to explain the variation in the dependent variable.

variation in the dependent variable. **Multiple regression models** use two or more explanatory variables to explain the variation in the dependent variable. In this section we will show you how to use and interpret multiple regression models.

The Multiple Regression Model

A typical multiple regression equation might take the form

$$Y = a + bX + cW + dZ$$

First let's test to see if the estimate of a is statistically significant. Although the parameter estimate is positive (6.00), is it large enough that we can be sure the true value of a is not equal to zero? After all, even if a actually is zero, the random nature of the least-squares estimate of a means it is possible that $\hat{a}$ could in fact be positive even if a is actually equal to zero. To test for statistical significance, use the t-value for $\hat{a}$, which the computer has calculated for you as the ratio of the parameter estimate to its standard error:

$$t_{\hat{a}} = \frac{6.00}{.917} = 6.54$$

and compare this value to the critical value of t. We will use a 95 percent confidence level (a 5 percent risk level). Since there are 20 observations and two parameters are estimated, there are 20 – 2 = 18 degrees of freedom. The table at the end of the text (critical t-values) gives us a critical value of 2.101. The calculated t-value for $\hat{a}$ is larger than 2.101; so, we conclude that $\hat{a}$ is significantly different from zero. In terms of the estimated equation, this means that a firm that spends nothing on R&D, on average, has a price-to-earnings ratio of 6.0.

The estimate of b (.74) is also positive. The calculated t-ratio is 4.48, which is greater than the critical value of t. The interpretation of $\hat{b}$ is that if a firm increases R&D expenditures by one percent (of sales), the firm can expect its value (as measured by the P/E ratio) to rise by .74.

The R^2 for the regression equation indicates that about 53 percent of the total variation in the value of a firm is explained by the regression equation; that is, 53 percent of the variation in V is explained by the variation in R. The regression equation does not explain 47 percent of the variation in the value of the firm.

The F-ratio is used to test for significance of the entire equation. To determine the critical value of F (with a 95 percent confidence level), it is necessary to determine the degrees of freedom. In this case, $k - 1 = 2 - 1 = 1$ and $n - k = 20 - 2 = 18$ degrees of freedom. In the table of values of the F-statistic at the end of the text, you can look down the $k - 1 = 1$ column until you get to the 18th row ($n - k = 18$) and read the value 4.41. Since the calculated F-value (20.090) exceeds 4.41, the regression equation is significant at the 95 percent confidence level.

*C Wallin and J Gilman, "Determining the Optimal Level for R&D Spending," *Research Management* 14, 5 (September/October 1986), pp. 19–24.

Source: This illustration is adapted from a regression problem presented in William Mendenhall and Terry Sincich, *A Second Course in Business Statistics: Regression Analysis* (San Francisco: Dellen, 1989).

In this equation, Y is the dependent variable, a is the intercept parameter, X, W, and Z are the explanatory variables, and b, c, and d are the slope parameters for each of these explanatory variables.

As in simple regression, the slope parameters b, c, and d measure the change in Y associated with a one-unit change in one of the explanatory variables, holding the rest of the explanatory variables constant. If, for example, $c = 3.00$, then a one-unit increase in W results in a three-unit increase in Y, holding X and Z constant.

Estimation of the parameters of a multiple regression equation is accomplished by finding a linear equation that best fits the data. As in simple regression, a computer is used to obtain the parameter estimates, their individual standard errors, the *F*-statistic, and the R^2. The statistical significance of the individual parameters and of the equation as a whole can be determined by *t*-tests and an *F*-test, respectively. The R^2 is interpreted as the fraction of the variation in Y explained by the *entire set* of explanatory variables taken together. Indeed, the only real complication introduced by multiple regression is that there are more *t*-tests to perform. Although (as you may know from courses in statistics) the *calculation* of the parameter estimates become much more difficult as additional independent variables are added, the manner in which they are *interpreted* does not change. Consider the following example.

A Multiple Regression Consumption Function

Suppose you work for the state legislature, and you wish to project sales tax revenues for the coming year. Since a primary source of sales tax revenue comes from levies on household consumption, you will need to estimate a consumption function. Suppose you believe the variation in household consumption expenditures can be adequately explained by using two independent variables—family income and the number of children in the household. The multiple regression equation can be specified as

$$C = a + bI + cN$$

where C is monthly consumption expenditures, I is monthly income, and N is the number of children. Since income and consumption are expected to be positively related, you would expect b to be positive. Likewise, c is expected to be positive. Furthermore, you would also expect a to be positive since it reflects the consumption expenditures for a family with no children and no income. The intercept parameter is often referred to as the "minimum subsistence level of consumption."

In order to estimate a, b, and c you could obtain data from a sample of families. Suppose that such data were obtained from 30 families and used in an available regression program. The output from the estimation of your simple consumption function is

DEPENDENT VARIABLE: C F-RATIO: 141.4

OBSERVATIONS: 30 R-SQUARED: 0.8350

VARIABLE	PARAMETER ESTIMATE	STANDARD ERROR	T-RATIO
INTERCEPT	443.0	125.0	3.54
I	0.810	0.06	13.50
N	132.50	68.8	1.93

As expected, the estimates of *a*, *b*, and *c* are all positive. The intercept parameter indicates that a family with no income (I = 0) and no children (N = 0) is expected to spend $443 per month on consumption. The estimate of *b* indicates that households will spend 81 cents on consumption out of each additional dollar of income received. Each additional child is estimated to add $132.50 to monthly consumption expenditure. (Presumably, the average household saves 19 cents of each additional dollar of income.)

In order to determine if the parameter estimates are significantly different from zero, *t*-tests must be conducted on each of the three parameter estimates. The *t*-ratios for $\hat{a}$, $\hat{b}$, and $\hat{c}$ are calculated as the ratio of the estimated parameter to its standard error, a calculation which is made for you by most computer programs (see the "*T*-ratio" column in the computer printout). Next, the critical value of *t* is found in the table at the end of the book. Since there are 30 observations and 3 parameters are estimated, the degrees of freedom are $n - k = 30 - 3 = 27$. Using a 5 percent level of risk (a 95 percent confidence level), the critical value of *t* is found to be 2.052.

Comparing the calculated *t*-statistics shown in the computer printout with the critical *t*, you can see that the absolute values of $t_{\hat{a}}$ (= 3.54) and $t_{\hat{b}}$ (= 13.50) exceed the critical value of 2.052. Thus, the estimates of *a* and *b* are statistically significant—that is, we can be 95 percent sure that the true values of *a* and *b* are not equal to zero. In the case of $\hat{c}$, however, the *t*-statistic (1.93) is not greater than 2.052, and we cannot say with 95 percent confidence that *c* is not equal to zero. As you can confirm, $\hat{c}$ is statistically significant at the 90 percent level of confidence (or 10 percent level of risk). In order to reject the hypothesis that $c = 0$, a higher level of risk is required. Thus, the statistical evidence that the number of children affects consumption expenditure is weaker than the evidence that income affects consumption expenditure.[3]

Turning now to the overall equation, the value of R^2 indicates that 83.5 percent of the total variation in consumption is explained by the regression equation (i.e., by the variation in I and N). To test for significance of the entire equation, it is necessary to use the *F*-statistic. To obtain the critical *F*-value, note there are $k - 1 = 3 - 1 = 2$ and $n - k = 30 - 3 = 27$ degrees of freedom. From the table of *F*-statistics at the end of the text, the critical *F*-value for $F_{2,27}$ at the 5 percent risk level is 3.35. Since the *F*-statistic (141.4) exceeds this value, you can say that the regression equation is statistically significant.

5.6 NONLINEAR REGRESSION ANALYSIS

While linear regression models can be applied to a wide variety of economic relations, there are also many economic relations that are nonlinear in nature. Nonlinear regression models are used when the underlying relation between Y and X plots as a curve, rather than a straight line. An analyst generally chooses a

[3]When the coefficient on a particular explanatory variable is not statistically significant at an acceptable level of confidence (say 90 or 95 percent), researchers typically drop this explanatory variable from the regression equation and estimate a new equation including only the explanatory variables that play a statistically significant role in explaining the variation in Y.

ILLUSTRATION 5.3

Do Auto Insurance Premiums Really Vary with Costs?

In an article examining the impact of Proposition 103 on auto insurance rates in California, Benjamin Zycher noted that in 1988 an adult male with no citations or at-fault accidents who lived in Hollywood could expect to pay an annual insurance premium of $1,817. The same adult male driver would have to pay only $862 if he lived in Monrovia, only $697 in San Diego, and only $581 in San Jose. Zycher explains that this variability in premiums exists because insurers obviously determine premiums by considering the individual's driving record, type of car, sex, age, and various other factors that are "statistically significant predictors of an individual driver's future losses."

Also important in the determination of insurance premiums is the geographic location of the driver's residence. Future losses are likely to be smaller in rural areas compared to urban areas because of lower vehicle densities, reduced theft, smaller repair costs, etc. Using data on bodily injury premiums for 20 California counties, we investigated the relation between insurance premiums and two explanatory variables—the number of claims and the average dollar cost of a claim in the various counties. Specifically, we wanted to determine if the variation in premiums across counties can be adequately explained by cost differences across the counties.

Using the data shown in the table in the next column, we estimated the following multiple regression equation:

$$P = a + b_1N + b_2C$$

where P is the average bodily insurance premium paid per auto, N is the number of claims per thousand insured vehicles, and C is the average dollar amount of each bodily injury claim.

Bodily Injury in California: Claims, Costs, and Premiums

County	N Claims*	C Cost†	P Annual premium‡
Los Angeles	23.9	$10,197	$319.04
Orange	19.5	9,270	255.00
Ventura	16.7	9,665	225.51
San Francisco	16.3	8,705	208.95
Riverside	15.2	8,888	200.16
San Bernadino	15.6	8,631	196.22
San Diego	16.0	8,330	191.80
Alameda	14.4	8,654	191.46
Marin	13.0	8,516	190.78
San Mateo	14.1	7,738	189.01
Sacramento	15.3	7,881	181.42
Santa Clara	14.4	7,723	179.74
Contra Costa	13.2	8,702	177.92
Santa Barbara	10.7	9,077	176.65
Sonoma	10.6	9,873	171.38
Fresno	14.7	7,842	168.11
Kern	11.9	7,717	160.97
Humboldt	12.2	7,798	151.02
Butte	11.1	8,783	129.84
Shasta	9.7	9,803	126.34

*Per thousand insured vehicles.

†Average per claim.

‡Average premium income per insured auto.

Source: Western Insurance information service.

nonlinear regression model when the scatter diagram shows a curvilinear pattern. In some cases, economic theory will strongly suggest that Y and X are related in a nonlinear fashion, and the analyst can expect to see a curvilinear pattern in the scatter of data points. Later in this text, we will introduce you to several important economic relations that are nonlinear in nature. You will need

The computer output for this multiple regression equation is:

DEPENDENT VARIABLE: P		F-RATIO: 87.659	
OBSERVATIONS: 20		R-SQUARE: 0.9116	
VARIABLE	PARAMETER ESTIMATE	STANDARD ERROR	T-RATIO
INTERCEPT	-74.139	34.612	-2.14
N	11.320	0.953	11.88
C	0.011	0.004	2.75

There is evidence from these parameter estimates that bodily injury premiums in a particular county are positively related to both the number of claims in that county and the average cost of those claims. Specifically, an additional claim per thousand vehicles in a county tends to increase yearly premiums by $11.32. A $1,000 increase in the average cost of claims in a county tends to increase premiums by about $11 annually. The intercept in this regression has no meaningful interpretation.

To determine whether N and C are indeed significant explanatory variables, we use the following t-values, which are calculated by the computer:

$$t_{\hat{b}_1} = \frac{11.320}{0.953} = 11.88$$

$$t_{\hat{b}_2} = \frac{0.011}{0.004} = 2.75$$

The critical t-value for this regression is 2.110 (17 degrees of freedom and a 95 percent confidence level). Since both t-values exceed the critical value, we concluded that N and C both play statistically significant roles in determining the level of premiums charged for bodily injury insurance.

Notice also that the R^2 is 0.9116, indicating that 91 percent of the variation in premiums is explained by variables N and C. The F-ratio also provides more statistical evidence that the relation between the dependent variable P and the explanatory variables N and C is quite strong. The critical F-value for $F_{2,17}$ at a 95 percent level of confidence is 3.59. Since the F-statistic exceeds this value by a large amount, the regression equation is statistically significant.

It is interesting to note how well the level of premiums can be explained using only two explanatory variables. Indeed, this regression analysis supports Benjamin Zycher's claim that the substantial statewide variation in California auto insurance premiums can be attributed to geographic differences in the costs incurred by insurers.

Source: See Benjamin Zycher, "Automobile Insurance Regulation, Direct Democracy, and the Interests of Consumers," *Regulation* (Summer 1990).

to know how to estimate the parameters of a nonlinear economic relation using the techniques of regression analysis.

In this section, we will show you two forms of nonlinear regression models for which the parameters can be estimated using *linear* regression analysis. The trick to using *linear* regression to estimate the parameters in *nonlinear* models is to transform the nonlinear relation into one that is linear and can be estimated by the techniques of least-squares. Two extremely useful forms of nonlinear models that you will encounter later in the text are (1) quadratic regression models, and (2) log-linear regression models. As you will see, using either one of these two nonlinear models does not complicate the analysis much at all.

Quadratic Regression Models

quadratic regression model A nonlinear regression model of the form: $Y = a + bX + cX^2$.

One of the most useful nonlinear forms for managerial economics is the **quadratic regression model**, which can be expressed as

$$Y = a + bX + cX^2$$

In a number of situations later in this book, theoretical relations between economic variables will graph as either a U- or an inverted U-shaped curve. You may recall from your high-school algebra class that quadratic functions have graphs that are either U- or ∩-shaped, depending upon the signs of b and c. If b is negative and c is positive, the quadratic function is U-shaped. If b is positive and c is negative, the quadratic function is ∩-shaped. Thus, a U-shaped quadratic equation ($b < 0$ and $c > 0$) is appropriate when, as X increases, Y first falls, eventually reaches a minimum, and then rises thereafter. Alternatively, an inverted U-shaped quadratic equation ($b > 0$ and $c < 0$) is appropriate if, as X increases, Y first rises, eventually reaches a peak, and then falls thereafter.

In order to estimate the three parameters of the quadratic relation (a, b, and c), the equation must be transformed into a linear form that can be estimated using linear regression analysis. This task is accomplished by creating a new variable Z, defined as $Z = X^2$, then substituting Z for X^2 to transform the quadratic model into a linear model:

$$\begin{aligned} Y &= a + bX + cX^2 \\ &= a + bX + cZ \end{aligned}$$

The slope parameter for Z (c) is identical to the slope parameter for X^2 (c).

This simple transformation is accomplished by having the computer create a new variable Z by squaring the values of X for each observation. You then regress Y on X and Z. The computer will generate an intercept parameter estimate ($\hat{a}$), a slope parameter estimate for X ($\hat{b}$), and a slope parameter estimate for Z ($\hat{c}$). The estimated slope parameter for Z is $\hat{c}$, which, of course, is the slope parameter on X^2. We illustrate this procedure with an example.

Figure 5.5 shows a scatter diagram for 12 observations on Y and X (shown by the table in the figure). Looking at the scatter of data points, it is clear that fitting a straight line through the data points would produce a "poor" fit, but fitting a U-shaped curve will produce a much better fit. To estimate the parameters of a quadratic regression equation, a new variable Z (= X^2) is generated on the computer. The actual data used in the regression are presented in Figure 5.5. The computer printout from the regression of Y on X and Z is

FIGURE 5.5
A Quadratic Regression Equation

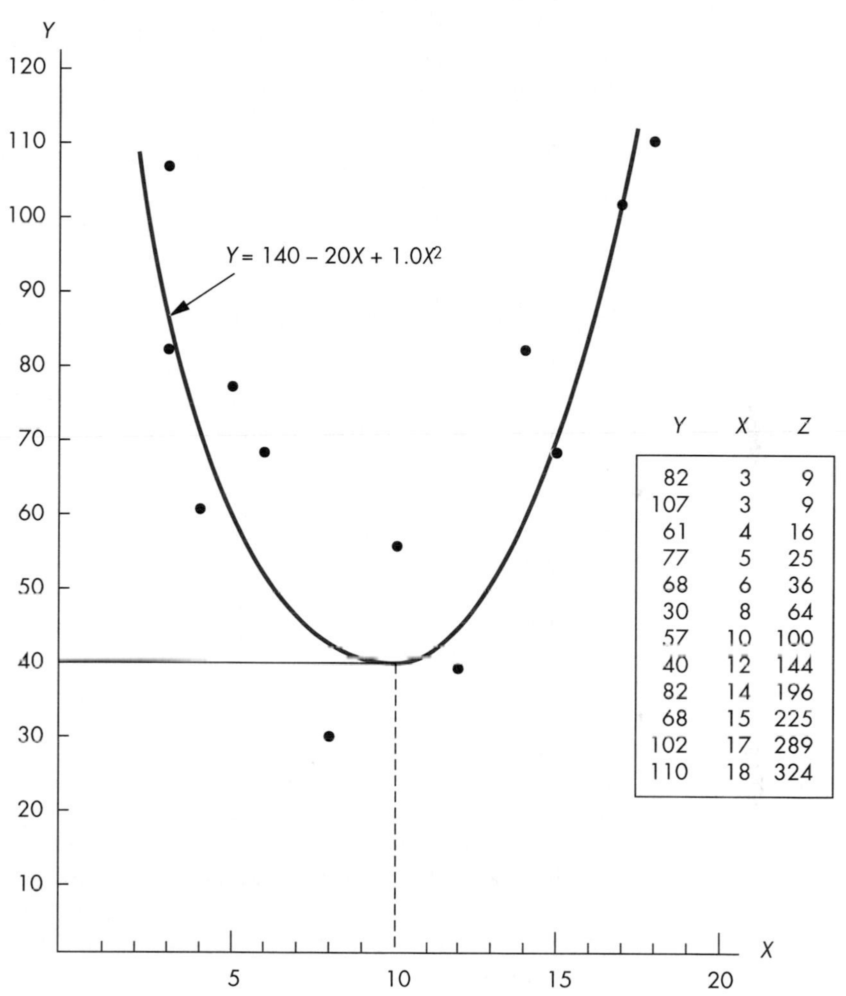

Y	X	Z
82	3	9
107	3	9
61	4	16
77	5	25
68	6	36
30	8	64
57	10	100
40	12	144
82	14	196
68	15	225
102	17	289
110	18	324

```
DEPENDENT VARIABLE:  Y        F-RATIO:   13.11

OBSERVATIONS:  12             R-SQUARED:  0.750

                PARAMETER          STANDARD
VARIABLE        ESTIMATE            ERROR               T-RATIO

INTERCEPT         140.0             17.14                  8.17
X                 -20.0              4.14                 -4.83
Z                   1.0              0.50                  2.00
```

Thus, the estimated quadratic regression equation is

$$Y = 140 - 20X + 1.0X^2$$

The estimated slope parameter for Z is 1.0. As explained above, 1.0 is also the slope parameter estimate for X^2. The estimated equation can be used to estimate the value of Y for any particular value of X. For example, if X is equal to 10, the quadratic regression equation predicts that Y will be equal to 40 (= $140 - 20 \times 10 + 10^2$). In any multiple regression equation, the estimated parameters are tested for statistical significance by performing the usual t-tests as discussed above.

Log-Linear Regression Models

log-linear regression model A nonlinear regression model of the form $Y = aX^bZ^c$. This model is estimated by regressing the logarithm of the dependent variable on the logarithms of each of the explanatory variables. The coefficients b and c are elasticities.

Another kind of nonlinear equation that can be estimated by transforming the equation into a linear form is a **log-linear regression model** in which Y is related to one or more explanatory variables in a multiplicative fashion:

$$Y = aX^bZ^c$$

This nonlinear functional form is particularly useful because the parameters b and c are elasticities:

$$b = \frac{\text{Percentage change in } Y}{\text{Percentage change in } X}$$

$$c = \frac{\text{Percentage change in } Y}{\text{Percentage change in } Z}$$

Using this form of nonlinear regression, the elasticities are estimated directly—the parameter estimates associated with each explanatory variable are elasticities. (The parameter a, however, is not an elasticity.)

In order to estimate the parameters of this nonlinear equation, it must be transformed into a linear form. This is accomplished by taking natural logarithms of both sides of the equation. Taking the logarithm of the function $Y = aX^bZ^c$ results in

$$\log Y = (\log a) + b(\log X) + c(\log Z)$$

So, if we define

$$\begin{aligned} Y' &= \log Y \\ X' &= \log X \\ Z' &= \log Z \\ a' &= \log a \end{aligned}$$

the regression equation is linear:

$$Y' = a' + bX' + cZ'$$

Once estimates have been obtained, tests for statistical significance and evaluation of the equation are done precisely as we described earlier. The only difference is that the intercept parameter estimate provided by the computer is not a;

rather it is equal to log a. To obtain the parameter estimate for a, we must take the antilog of the parameter estimate $\hat{a}'$:

$$\text{antilog}\ (\hat{a}') = e^{a'}$$

The antilog of a number can be found using the "e^x" key found on most hand calculators. We illustrate the log-linear regression model with an example.

Panel A of Figure 5.6 shows a scatter diagram of 12 observations on Y and X. The scatter diagram in Panel A suggests a curvilinear model will fit these data better than a linear model. Suppose we use a log-linear model with one explanatory variable: $Y = aX^b$. Since Y is positive at all points in the sample, the parameter a is expected to be positive. Since Y is decreasing as X increases, the parameter on X (b) is expected to be negative. The actual values of Y and X plotted in the scatter diagram in Panel A are shown in the box in Panel A.

To estimate the parameters a and b in the nonlinear equation, we transform the equation by taking logarithms:

$$\log Y = \log a + b \log X$$

Thus, the curvilinear model in Panel A is transformed into an equivalent model that is linear when the variables are expressed in logarithms. In Panel B, the transformed variables, log Y and log X, are obtained by instructing the computer to take logarithms of Y and X, respectively. The 12 observations, in terms of logarithms, are displayed in Panel B. Regressing log Y on log X results in the following computer printout:

DEPENDENT VARIABLE: LOGY		F-RATIO: 70.0	
OBSERVATIONS: 12		R-SQUARE: 0.875	
VARIABLE	PARAMETER ESTIMATE	STANDARD ERROR	T-RATIO
INTERCEPT	11.06	0.48	23.04
LOGX	-0.96	0.11	-8.73

As the F-ratio and R^2 indicate, a log-linear model does a quite reasonable job of explaining the variation in Y. The t-ratios for the intercept and slope parameters are 23.04 (= 11.06/0.48) and –8.73 (= –0.96/0.11), respectively. Both parameter estimates are statistically significant at the 99 percent level of confidence since both t-statistics exceed the critical t-value of 3.169.

Panel B of Figure 5.6 illustrates why this model is called a log-linear model. Notice that when the data points in Panel A are converted to logarithms (log Y and log X), the *logarithms* of Y and X exhibit a linear relation, as indicated by the scatter diagram shown in Panel B. The estimated log-linear regression equation is plotted in Panel B to show you how a straight line fits the logarithms of Y and X.

FIGURE 5.6
A Log-Linear Regression Equation

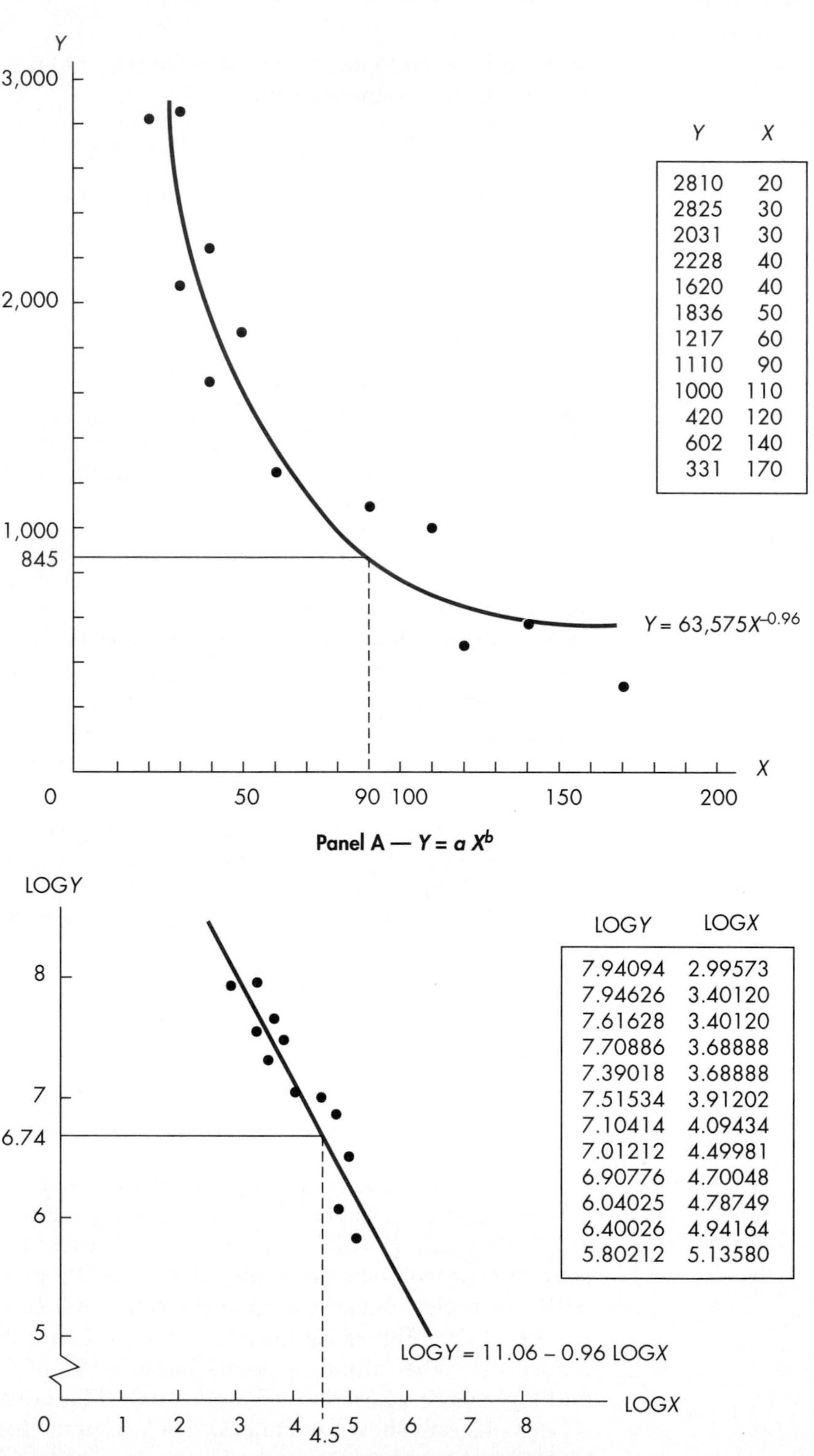

Panel A — $Y = a X^b$

Panel B — $\text{LOG}Y = \text{LOG}a + b\text{LOG}X$

To obtain the parameter estimates a and b in the nonlinear equation $Y = aX^b$, note that the slope parameter on log X is also the exponent on X in the nonlinear equation ($\hat{b} = -0.96$). Since b is an elasticity, the estimated elasticity is –0.96. Thus, a 10 percent increase in X results in a 9.6 percent decrease in Y. To obtain an estimate of a, we take the antilog of the estimated value of the intercept parameter:

$$\hat{a} = \text{antilog}\ (11.06) = e^{11.06} = 63{,}575.$$

In order to show that the two models are mathematically equivalent, we have calculated the predicted value of log Y when log X is equal to 4.5. Using the estimated log-linear regression equation, we find that when log $X = 4.5$, log $Y = 6.74$ [= 11.06 – 0.96(4.5)]. Taking antilogs of log Y and log X, we get the point $X = 90$ and $Y = 845$ [$= 63{,}575(90)^{-0.96}$]. Thus, the two equations are equivalent representations of the mathematical relation between Y and X.

5.7 REGRESSION ANALYSIS IN MANAGERIAL DECISION MAKING

We hope you have seen from this brief overview that regression analysis is extremely useful because it offers managers a way of estimating the functions they need for managerial decision making. While we will have much more to say about specific applications of regression analysis in later chapters, at this point we want you simply to understand that regression techniques are actually used in managerial decision making.

As Robert F. Soergel (general marketing manager, E. L. Weingard Division, Emerson Electric Company) put it, "regression analysis can be extremely helpful, and it's not as difficult as its name suggests."[4] Regression analysis is simply a tool to provide the information necessary for a manager to make decisions that maximize profits, or as Mr. Soergel observed, "the computer is a tool, not a master." We will use this tool to find estimates of the various functions we will describe later in the text. It's not that hard, and we would agree with Mr. Soergel's conclusion of "the best part: it's not expensive."

The statistical analyses (or, if you wish, econometrics) that we are going to use in this text are really rather simple. Our two major objectives are also simple:

1. We want you to be able to set up a regression equation that could subsequently be estimated by using one of the readily available regression packages.
2. We want you to be able to use the output of a regression to examine those economic issues that are of interest to the manager of an enterprise.

Hence, in terms of the field of study known as econometrics, we will concentrate our attention on helping you to avoid what are called *specification errors*. In simple terms, this means that we will show you how to set up an estimation equation that is appropriate for the use to which it is to be put. Specification errors—

[4]"Probing the Past for the Future," *Sales & Marketing Management*, March 14, 1983.

such as excluding important explanatory variables or using an inappropriate form for the equation—are serious; they can result in the estimates being *biased*.

In addition to specification errors, there are other problems that can be encountered in regression analysis. These problems, which are more difficult than the material we want to cover in this text, are reviewed briefly in the appendix to this chapter.

5.8 SUMMARY

This chapter sets forth the basic principles of regression analysis—estimation and testing for statistical significance. The emphasis of the chapter was on explaining how to interpret the results of regression analysis, rather than on the mathematics of regression analysis. A mathematical derivation of the statistical techniques is presented in the appendixes at the end of the chapter.

The simple linear regression model relates a dependent variable to a single explanatory variable in a linear fashion: $Y = a + bX$. The parameter a is the Y-intercept—the value of Y when X is zero. The parameter b is the slope of the regression line; it measures the rate of change in Y as X changes ($\Delta Y/\Delta X$). Because the variation in Y is affected not only by variation in X, but also by various random effects, we cannot predict exactly the actual value of Y. Thus, you should interpret the regression equation as giving the average or expected value of Y for any particular value of X.

Parameter estimates are obtained by choosing values of a and b that minimize the sum of the squared residuals. The residual is the difference between the actual value of Y and the fitted value of Y ($Y_i - \hat{Y}_i$). This method of estimating a and b is called the method of least-squares. The estimated regression line, $Y = \hat{a} + \hat{b}X$, *is called the sample regression line. The sample regression line is an estimate of the true regression line.*

The estimates $\hat{a}$ and $\hat{b}$ do not, in general, equal the true values of a and b. Since $\hat{a}$ and $\hat{b}$ are computed from the data in the random sample, the estimates themselves are random variables. Statisticians have shown that the distribution of values that the estimates might take is centered around the true value of the parameter. An estimator is *unbiased* if the mean value of the estimator is equal to the true value of the parameter. The method of least-squares produces unbiased estimates of a and b.

It is the randomness of the parameter estimates that necessitates testing for statistical significance. Just because the estimate $\hat{b}$ is not equal to zero does *not* mean the true value of b is not actually equal to zero. Even when b *does* equal zero, it is still possible that the sample of Y and X values will produce a least-squares estimate $\hat{b}$ that is different from zero. It is necessary to determine statistically if there is sufficient evidence in the sample to indicate that Y is truly related to X (i.e., $b \neq 0$). This is called testing for statistical significance.

The t-test is used to test for statistical significance of parameter estimates. The larger the absolute value of the t-ratio,

$$t = \frac{\hat{b}}{S_{\hat{b}}}$$

the more probable it is that the true value of b is not equal to zero ($S_{\hat{b}}$ is the standard error of the parameter estimate). To test for statistical significance of an individual parameter estimate, compute the t-ratio as defined above. Then find the critical t-value in the t-table. Choose the critical t-value with $n - k$ degrees of freedom for the desired level of confidence. If the absolute value of the t-ratio is greater than the critical t-value, $\hat{b}$ is statistically significant. If the absolute value is less than the critical t-value, $\hat{b}$ is not statistically significant.

To measure how well the sample regression line fits the data, the R^2 statistic (also called the coefficient of determination) is computed. The R^2 measures the fraction of the total variation in Y that is explained by the variation in X. The value of R^2 ranges from 0 (the regression equation explains none of the variation in Y) to 1 (the regression equation explains all of the variation in Y). A high R^2 indicates Y and X are highly correlated, and the scatter diagram tightly fits the sample regression line.

The F-statistic is used to *test* whether the equation as a whole explains a significant amount of the variation in Y. To test whether the overall equation is significant, the F-statistic is compared to the critical F-value with $k - 1$ and $n - k$ degrees of freedom and the chosen level of confidence. If the value for the calculated F-statistic exceeds the critical F-value, the regression equation is statistically significant.

Multiple regression models use two or more explanatory variables to explain the variation in the dependent variable. The coefficient on each of the explanatory variables measures the degree of variation in Y associated with variation in that explanatory variable, holding all other explanatory variables constant. As in the case of simple regression, each coefficient is tested for significance by using the t-test. The F-statistic is used to test the overall equation for significance. The R^2 measures the fit of the equation.

Many economic relations of interest to managers are *nonlinear* in nature. Two types of nonlinear models are presented in this chapter: (1) quadratic regression models, and (2) log-linear regression models. The quadratic regression model is appropriate when the curve fitting the scatter diagram is either U-shaped or an inverted U-shaped. The quadratic equation, $Y = a + bX + cX^2$, is transformed into a linear form by computing a new variable, $Z = X^2$, and substituting for X^2 to get a linear form: $Y = a + bX + cZ$. A second type of nonlinear model presented in this chapter is the log-linear model. In this nonlinear model, the dependent variable is related to one or more explanatory variables in a multiplicative fashion. The log-linear model for two explanatory variables takes the form: $Y = aX^bZ^c$. A particularly useful feature of this specification is that the parameters b and c are elasticities. For example, b measures the percent change in Y that results when X changes by one percent. By taking logarithms, the logarithm of Y can be expressed as a linear function of the logarithms of the explanatory variables: $\log Y = \log a + b \log X + c \log Z$. Once this transformation is made, estimation and tests of statistical significance proceed as usual.

We must emphasize again that all of the statistics needed for regression analysis are automatically computed when using a computerized regression routine. The purpose of this chapter was to show you how to interpret and use the regression statistics produced by the computer.

TECHNICAL PROBLEMS

1. Compare and contrast the following terms:
   a. Dependent and explanatory variables.
   b. Time-series and cross-sectional data sets.
   c. Simple regression and multiple regression.
   d. T-statistics and F-statistics
   e. R^2 and F-tests.
   f. Linear and nonlinear equations.
   g. Parameter estimation and fitting a regression line.
   h. True regression lines and sample regression lines.
   i. Y and $\hat{Y}$, a and $\hat{a}$, b and $\hat{b}$.
2. Regression analysis is often referred to as least-squares regression. Why is this name appropriate?
3. Why must you test your parameter estimates to see if they are statistically significant? What does it mean to say an estimated regression coefficient is statistically significant at a 95 percent level of confidence?
4. The graph below shows a scatter diagram of 10 data points on Y and X. The computer output from the regression analysis using these data is

DEPENDENT VARIABLE: Y		F-RATIO: 8.747	
OBSERVATIONS: 10		R-SQUARED: 0.5223	
VARIABLE	PARAMETER ESTIMATE	STANDARD ERROR	T-RATIO
INTERCEPT	800.0	106.724	7.496
X	-2.5	0.874	-2.860

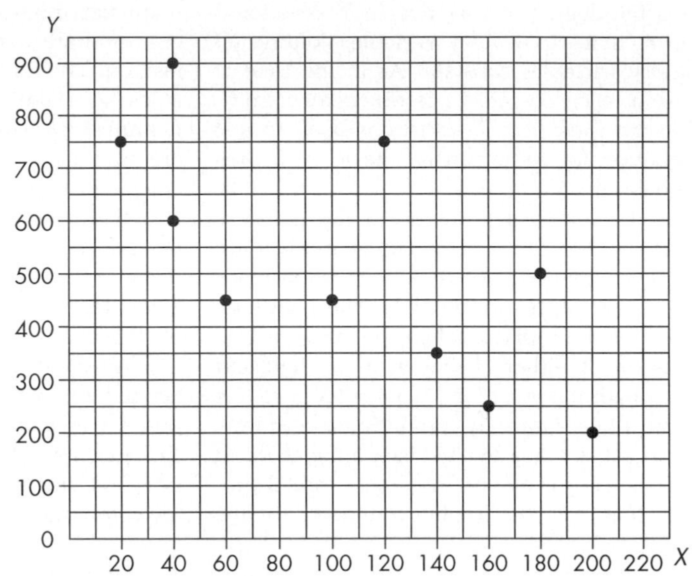

a. What is the equation of the sample regression line?
b. Draw the sample regression line on the figure.
c. Test the intercept and slope estimates for statistical significance at the 99 percent confidence level. Explain how you performed this test and present your results.
d. Test the overall equation for statistical significance at the 99 percent confidence level. Explain how you performed this test and present your results.
e. If X equals 140, what is the fitted (or predicted) value of Y? Compute the residual for this data point. Explain intuitively why residuals occur. Can you explain how it might happen that the two data points for $X = 40$ have different Y values?
f. What fraction of the total variation in Y is explained by the regression?

5. Evaluate each of the following statements:
   a. "The more precise the estimate of $\hat{b}$ (i.e., the smaller the standard error of $\hat{b}$), the higher the t-ratio will be."
   b. "In a multiple regression model, the coefficients on the explanatory variables measure the percent of the total variation in the dependent variable Y explained by that explanatory variable."
   c. "The more degrees of freedom in the regression, the more likely it is that a given t-ratio exceeds the critical t-value."
   d. "The coefficient of determination (R^2) can only be exactly equal to one when the sample regression line passes through each and every data point."
   e. "If $\hat{b}$ is an unbiased estimate of b, then $\hat{b}$ equals the true value of b."
6. *A simple regression model, $Y = a + bX$, is estimated by a computer program, which produces the following computer output:
   a. How many degrees of freedom does this regression analysis have?
   b. What is the critical value of t at the 95 percent level of confidence?
   c. Test to see if the estimates of a and b are statistically significant.

DEPENDENT VARIABLE: Y F-RATIO: 141.391

OBSERVATIONS: 25 R-SQUARED: 0.8347

VARIABLE	PARAMETER ESTIMATE	STANDARD ERROR	T-RATIO
INTERCEPT	443.72	124.82	3.55
X	0.80572	0.06776	11.89

d. How much of the total variation in Y is explained by this regression equation? How much of the total variation in Y is unexplained by this regression equation?

e. What is the critical value of the F-statistic at a 95 percent level of confidence? Is the overall regression equation statistically significant?

f. If X equals 100, what value do you expect Y will take? If X equals zero?

* 7. A manager wants to determine the relation between a firm's sales and its advertising levels in newspapers and on radio. The manager estimates the following multiple regression equation:

$$S = a + bN + cR$$

where S is sales, N is dollar expenditure on newspaper ads, and R is dollar expenditure on radio ads.

a. What do the parameters a, b, and c measure in this problem?

b. What signs do you expect each of the three parameters to have?

Suppose the manager instead wishes to estimate the following relation:

$$S = aN^bR^c$$

c. What do the parameters a, b, and c measure now?

d. Transform this nonlinear equation so that it can be estimated using linear regression.

8. A multiple regression model, $R = a + bW + cX + dZ$ is estimated by a computer package, which produces the following output:

DEPENDENT VARIABLE: R F-RATIO: 3.50

OBSERVATIONS: 36 R-SQUARED: 0.2470

VARIABLE	PARAMETER ESTIMATE	STANDARD ERROR	T-RATIO
INTERCEPT	12.6	8.33	1.51
W	22.0	3.61	6.09
X	4.1	1.65	2.48
Z	16.3	4.45	3.66

a. How many degrees of freedom does this regression analysis have?
b. What is the critical value of t at the 99 percent level of confidence?
c. Test to see if the estimates of a, b, c, and d are statistically significant.
d. How much of the total variation in R is explained by this regression equation? How much of the total variation in R is unexplained by this regression equation?
e. What is the critical value of the F-statistic at a 99 percent level of confidence? Is the overall regression equation statistically significant?
f. If W equals 10, X equals 5, and Z equals 30, what value do you predict R will take? If W, X, and Z are all equal to zero?

9. A manager estimates the relation between cost of production and the level of output by specifying the following equation:

$$C = a + bQ$$

where C is total cost of production, and Q is the level of output. Unfortunately, some of the variation in cost (C) is due to changes in the prices of labor and capital. The true (or correct) specification of the model should have included the prices of labor and capital as explanatory variables. What kinds of problems does this mistake cause?

10. Suppose Y is related to R and S in the following nonlinear way:

$$Y = aR^bS^c$$

a. How can this nonlinear equation be transformed into a linear form that can be analyzed by using multiple regression analysis?

Ninety observations are used to obtain the following regression results:

DEPENDENT VARIABLE:	LOG Y	F-RATIO:	132.0
OBSERVATIONS:	90	R-SQUARED:	0.750
VARIABLE	PARAMETER ESTIMATE	STANDARD ERROR	T-RATIO
INTERCEPT	-1.386	0.830	-1.670
LOG R	0.452	0.175	2.583
LOG S	0.300	0.098	3.061

b. Test each estimated coefficient for statistical significance at the 95 percent level of confidence (5 percent risk level).
c. Test the overall equation for statistical significance at the 95 percent level of confidence (5 percent risk level).
d. How well does this model fit the data?
e. Using the estimated value of the intercept, compute an estimate of a.
f. If R = 200 and S = 1,500, compute the expected value of Y.
g. What is the estimated elasticity of R? Of S?

APPLIED PROBLEMS

1. The director of marketing at Vanguard Corporation believes that sales of the company's Bright Side laundry detergent (S) are related to Vanguard's own advertising expenditures (A), as well as the combined advertising expenditures of its three biggest rival detergents (R). The marketing director collects 36 weekly observations on S, A, and R to estimate the following multiple regression equation:

$$S = a + bA + cR$$

where S, A, and R are measured in thousands of dollars per week.

a. What sign does the marketing director expect a, b, and c to have?

b. Interpret the coefficients a, b, and c.

The regression output from the computer is

DEPENDENT VARIABLE: S		F-RATIO: 4.781	
OBSERVATIONS: 36		R-SQUARED: 0.2246	
VARIABLE	PARAMETER ESTIMATE	STANDARD ERROR	T-RATIO
INTERCEPT	1750.86	638.21	2.74
A	8.55	3.25	2.63
R	-3.61	1.64	-2.20

c. Does Vanguard's advertising expenditure have a statistically significant effect on the sales of Bright Side detergent? Explain.

d. Does advertising by its three largest rivals affect sales of Bright Side detergent in a statistically significant way? Explain.

e. What fraction of the total variation in sales of Bright Side remains unexplained? What can the marketing director do to increase the explanatory power of the sales equation? What other explanatory variables might be added to this equation?

f. What is the expected level of sales each week when Vanguard spends $40,000 per week and the combined advertising expenditures for the three rivals is $100,000 per week?

2. In his analysis of California's Proposition 103 (see Illustration 5.3), Benjamin Zycher notes that one of the most important provisions of this proposition is eliminating the practice by insurance companies of basing premiums (in part) on the geographic location of drivers. Prohibiting the use of geographic location to assess the risk of a driver creates a substantial implicit subsidy from low-loss counties to high-loss counties, such as Los Angeles, Orange, and San Francisco counties. Zycher hypothesizes that the percent of voters favoring Proposition 103 in a given county (V) is inversely related to the (average) percentage change in auto premiums (P) that the proposition confers upon the drivers of that county.

The data in the table below were presented by Zycher to support his contention that V and P are inversely related.

County	V Percent for Proposition 103	P Change in average premium
Los Angeles	62.8	−21.4
Orange	51.7	−8.2
San Francisco	65.2	−0.9
Alameda	58.9	+8.0
Marin	53.5	+9.1
Santa Clara	51.0	+11.8
San Mateo	52.8	+12.6
Santa Cruz	54.2	+13.0
Ventura	44.8	+1.4
San Diego	44.1	+10.7
Monterey	41.6	+15.3
Sacramento	39.3	+16.0
Tulare	28.7	+23.3
Sutter	32.3	+37.1
Lassen	29.9	+46.5
Siskiyou	29.9	+49.8
Modoc	23.2	+57.6

Sources: California Department of Insurance and Office of the California Secretary of State.

Using the data in the table, we estimated the regression equation:

$$V = a + bP$$

to see if voting behavior is related to the change in auto insurance premiums in a statistically significant way. The regression output from the computer is

```
DEPENDENT VARIABLE:  V          F-RATIO:  42.674

OBSERVATIONS:  17               R-SQUARED: 0.7399

                PARAMETER       STANDARD
VARIABLE        ESTIMATE        ERROR           T-RATIO

INTERCEPT        53.682          2.112          25.418
P                -0.528          0.081          -6.519
```

a. Does this regression equation provide evidence of a statistically significant relation between voter support for Proposition 103 in a county and changes in average auto premiums affected by Proposition 103 in that county? Perform an *F*-test at the 95 percent level of confidence.

b. Test the intercept estimate for significance at the 95 percent confidence level. If Proposition 103 has no impact on auto insurance premiums in any given county, what percent of voters do you expect will vote for the proposition?

c. Test the slope estimate for significance at the 95 percent confidence level. If *P* increases by 10 percent, by what percent does the vote for Proposition 103 decline?

3. A security analyst specializing in the stocks of the motion picture industry wishes to examine the relation between the number of movie theater tickets sold in December and the annual level of earnings in the motion picture industry. Time-series data for the last 15 years are used to estimate the regression model

$$E = a + bN$$

where E is total earnings of the motion picture industry measured in millions, and N is the number of tickets sold in December measured in hundred thousand units. The regression output is

DEPENDENT VARIABLE: E		F-RATIO: 63.96	
OBSERVATIONS: 15		R-SQUARED: 0.8311	
VARIABLE	PARAMETER ESTIMATE	STANDARD ERROR	T-RATIO
INTERCEPT	250.42	201.31	1.24
N	32.31	8.54	3.78

a. How well do movie ticket sales in December explain the level of earnings for the entire year? Present statistical evidence to support your answer.

b. On average, what effect does a 100,000-ticket increase in December sales have on the annual earnings in the movie industry?

c. Sales of movie tickets in December 1993 are expected to be approximately 950,000. According to this regression analysis, what do you expect earnings for 1993 to be?

4. The manager of Collins Import Autos believes the number of cars sold in a day (Q) depends upon two factors: (1) the number of hours the dealership is open (H), and (2) the number of salespersons working that day (S). After collecting data for two months (58 days), the manager estimates the following log-linear model:

$$Q = aH^bS^c$$

a. Explain how to transform this log-linear model into a linear form that can be estimated using multiple regression analysis.

The computer output for the multiple regression analysis is

DEPENDENT VARIABLE:	LOG Q	F-RATIO:	29.97
OBSERVATIONS:	58	R-SQUARED:	0.5215
VARIABLE	PARAMETER ESTIMATE	STANDARD ERROR	T-RATIO
INTERCEPT	0.9162	0.2413	3.797
LOG H	0.3517	0.1021	3.445
LOG S	0.2550	0.0785	3.248

b. How do you interpret coefficients b and c? If the dealership increases the number of salespersons by 20 percent, what will be the percentage increase in daily sales?
c. Test the overall model for statistical significance at the 5 percent risk level (95 percent confidence level).
d. What percent of the total variation in daily auto sales is explained by this equation? What could you suggest to increase this percentage?
e. Test the intercept for statistical significance at the 5 percent level of risk (95 percent confidence level). If H and S both equal zero, are sales expected to be zero? Explain why or why not.
f. Test the estimated coefficient b for statistical significance. If the dealership decreases its hours of operation by 10 percent, what is the expected impact on daily sales?

APPENDIX 5A Least-Squares Parameter Estimation

Consider the sample regression line

(1) $\hat{Y}_i = a + \hat{b}X_i$

where $\hat{a}$ and $\hat{b}$ are estimates of the population parameters a and b. The goal of least-squares regression is to find estimates of $\hat{a}$ and $\hat{b}$ that minimize the sum of the squared residuals (denoted ESS) for the sample of n observations on Y and X:

$$(2)\ ESS = \sum_{i=1}^{n} e_i^2 = \sum_{i=1}^{n} (Y_i - \hat{Y}_i)^2 = \sum_{i=1}^{n} (Y_i - \hat{a} - \hat{b}X_i)^2$$

Notice that ESS is a function of the estimates $\hat{a}$ and $\hat{b}$. To find the values of the estimates that minimize ESS, partially differentiate equation 2 with respect to $\hat{a}$ and $\hat{b}$, and then set the two partial derivatives equal to zero:

$$(3)\ \frac{\partial ESS}{\partial \hat{a}} = -2\,\Sigma\,(Y_i - \hat{a} - \hat{b}X_i) = 0$$

$$(4)\ \frac{\partial ESS}{\partial \hat{b}} = -2\,\Sigma\,X_i\,(Y_i - \hat{a} - \hat{b}X_i) = 0$$

Multiplying and rearranging terms:

(3A) $\Sigma Y_i = n\hat{a} + \hat{b}\,\Sigma X_i$

(4A) $\Sigma Y_i X_i = \hat{a}\,\Sigma\,X_i + \hat{b}\,\Sigma\,X_i^2$

Now solve 3A and 4A simultaneously for $\hat{a}$ and $\hat{b}$. To do this, multiply 3A by ΣX_i and 4A by n:

(3B) $\Sigma X_i \Sigma Y_i = n\hat{a}\,\Sigma X_i + \hat{b}\,(\Sigma X_i)^2$

(4B) $n\,\Sigma Y_i X_i = n\hat{a}\,\Sigma X_i + \hat{b}\,n\,\Sigma\,X_i^2$

Next, subtract 3B from 4B:

(5) $n\,\Sigma Y_i X_i - \Sigma X_i \Sigma Y_i = \hat{b}\,[n\,\Sigma X^2 - (\Sigma X_i)^2]$

and it follows that

$$(6)\ \hat{b} = \frac{n\,\Sigma X_i Y_i - \Sigma X_i \Sigma Y_i}{n\,\Sigma X_i^2 - (\Sigma X_i)^2}$$

TABLE 5A.1

Computing the Least-Squares Estimates $\hat{a}$ and $\hat{b}$ for the Sample of Seven Travel Agencies

Sales Y_i	Advertising expenditure X_i	$X_i - \overline{X}$	$(X_i - \overline{X})^2$	$Y_i - \overline{Y}$	$(X_i - \overline{X})(Y_i - \overline{Y})$
15,000	2,000	−3,143	9,878,449	−22,143	69,595,449
30,000	2,000	−3,143	9,878,449	−7,143	22,450,449
30,000	5,000	−143	20,449	−7,143	1,021,449
25,000	3,000	−2,143	4,592,449	−12,143	26,022,449
55,000	9,000	3,857	14,876,449	17,857	68,874,449
45,000	8,000	2,857	8,162,449	7,857	22,447,449
60,000	7,000	1,857	3,448,449	22,857	42,445,449
Σ 260,000	36,000		50,857,143		252,857,143

$\overline{Y} = 260{,}000/7 = 37{,}143$
$\overline{X} = 36{,}000/7 = 5{,}143$
$\hat{b} = \Sigma(X_i - \overline{X})(Y_i - \overline{Y})/\Sigma(X_i - \overline{X})^2 = 252{,}857{,}143/50{,}857{,}143 = 4.97$
$\hat{a} = \overline{Y} - \hat{b}\overline{X} = 37{,}143 - (4.97 \times 5{,}143) = 11{,}582$

where $\overline{X}$ and $\overline{Y}$ are the sample means of X and Y. After finding $\hat{b}$, $\hat{a}$ is calculated as

(7) $\hat{a} = \overline{Y} - \hat{b}\overline{X}$

To illustrate how the computer uses equations 6 and 7 to estimate a and b, Table 5A.1 shows the computations that will be done for you by a computer. Table 5A.1 calculates the parameter estimates for the sample regression line that best fits the data in Table 5.2.

APPENDIX 5B Derivation of the Coefficient of Determination (R^2)

The coefficient of determination, denoted R^2, measures how well the overall equation explains the variation in the dependent variable Y. The total variation in Y can be attributed to one of two things: variation due to changes in the explanatory variable(s) or variation due to random influences. R^2 is derived by decomposing the variation in Y into these two component parts.

Statisticians measure the variation in the dependent variable as $Y_i - \overline{Y}$, the variation in Y about the sample mean ($\overline{Y}$). To motivate why the sample mean is used, recall that if Y_i does not vary at all in the sample (i.e., Y_i is constant for all observations), Y_i equals Y for every observations in the sample. The sample mean, then, provides a point of reference about which the variation in Y_i can be measured. The amount by which the value of Y predicted by the regression ($\hat{Y}_i$) deviates from the sample mean ($\overline{Y}$) is referred to as the explained variation, and is denoted $\hat{Y}_i - \overline{Y}$. The unexplained variation in Y_i is the residual amount, $Y_i - \hat{Y}_i$. Figure 5B.1 shows how the variation in Y_i is decomposed for one particular observation in the sample.

The total variation in Y_i in the sample is computed by squaring the total variation in Y_i and summing across all observations in the sample:

$$\text{Total variation} = \Sigma(Y_i - \overline{Y})^2$$

Given the decomposition discussed above, the total variation in Y can also be expressed as the sum of the explained and unexplained variation in Y:

Total variation in Y = Total explained variation + Total unexplained variation

$$\Sigma(Y_i - \overline{Y})^2 = \Sigma(\hat{Y}_i - \overline{Y})^2 + \Sigma(Y_i - \hat{Y}_i)^2$$

The coefficient of determination measures the fraction of total variation explained by the regression:

$$R^2 = \frac{\text{Total explained variation}}{\text{Total variation in } Y} = \frac{\Sigma(\hat{Y}_i - \overline{Y})^2}{\Sigma(Y_i - \overline{Y})^2}$$

Thus it follows that R^2 can vary from 0 to 1 in value.

FIGURE 5B.1
Decomposition of Total Variation in Y

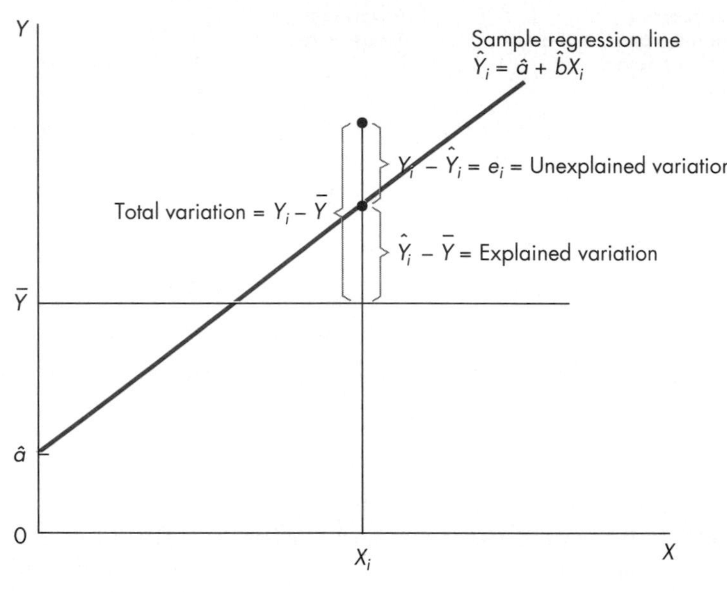

APPENDIX 5C Some Additional Problems in Regression Analysis

Multicollinearity

When using regression analysis, we assume that the explanatory (right-hand side) variables are linearly independent of one another. If this assumption is violated, we have the problem of multicollinearity. Under normal circumstances, multicollinearity will result in the estimated standard errors being larger than their true values. This means, then, that if multicollinearity exists, finding statistical significance will be more difficult. More specifically, if moderate multicollinearity is present, the estimate of the coefficient, $\hat{b}$, will be unbiased; but the estimated standard error, $S_{\hat{b}}$, will be increased. Thus, the t-coefficient, $t = \hat{b}/S_{\hat{b}}$, will be reduced, and it will be more difficult to find statistical significance.

Multicollinearity is not unusual. The question is what to do about it. As a general rule, the answer is *nothing*. To illustrate, consider the following function that denotes some true relation,

$$Y = a + bX + cZ$$

If X and Z are not linearly independent—if X and Z are collinear—the standard errors of the estimates for b and c will be increased. Shouldn't we just drop one? Not in the normal instance. If Z is an important explanatory variable, the exclusion of Z would be a *specification error* and would result in biased estimates of the coefficients—a much more severe problem.

Heteroscedasticity

The problem of heteroscedasticity is encountered when the variance of the error term is not constant. It can be encountered when there exists some relation between the error term and one or more of the explanatory variables—for example, when there exists a positive relation between X and the errors (i.e., large errors are associated with large values of X).

In such a case, the estimated parameters are still unbiased, but the standard errors of the coefficients are biased; so the calculated t-ratios are unreliable. This problem, most normally encountered in cross-section studies, can sometimes be corrected by performing a transformation on the data or equation. Otherwise, it becomes necessary to employ a technique called weighted least-squares estimation.

Autocorrelation

The problem of autocorrelation, associated with time-series data, occurs when the errors are not independent over time. For example, it could be the case that a high error in one period tends to promote a high error in the following period.

With autocorrelation (sometimes referred to as serial correlation) the estimated parameters are unbiased, but the standard errors are again biased, resulting in unreliability of the calculated *t*-ratios. Tests for determining if autocorrelation is present (most notably the Durbin-Watson test) are included in most of the available regression packages. Furthermore, most packages also include techniques for estimating an equation in the presence of autocorrelation.

CHAPTER

6 Decision Making under Uncertainty and Risk

In Chapter 4 we set forth the theory of optimizing behavior, the foundation of managerial decision making, under the assumption that a decision maker knows with certainty the marginal benefits and marginal costs as well as the consequences of a decision. Most of the theoretical analysis in this text is also developed under this assumption. While many decisions managers make do involve considerable certainty, managers must frequently make decisions in situations where the outcome of a decision cannot be known in advance. A manager may decide, for example, to invest in a new production facility with the expectation that the new technology and equipment will reduce production costs. Even after studying hundreds of technical reports, a manager may still not know with certainty the cost-savings of the new plant until the plant is built and operating. In other words, the outcome of the manager's decision to build the new plant is random because the reduction in costs (the outcome) is not known with certainty at the time the manager makes the decision to build the new plant.

In this chapter we present some basic rules that managers, and for that matter all decision makers, can and do use to help make decisions under conditions of uncertainty and risk. In the next section, we explain the difference between decision making under *uncertainty* and decision making under *risk*. The remainder of this chapter is devoted to some rules for decision making in the absence of certainty. As you will see, these rules provide only *guidelines* for making decisions when outcomes are not certain. No single rule for making decisions under uncertainty or risk is, or can be, universally employed by all managers at all times. Nevertheless, the rules presented give an overview of some of the methods of analyzing uncertainty and risk that can help managers make decisions under conditions of less than complete certainty.

Before plunging into our presentation of decision making under uncertainty and risk, we want to address a question that may be concerning you: Why do we devote such a large portion of this text to managerial decision making under certainty or complete information, knowing full well that a huge proportion of managerial decisions are made with incomplete information—that is, under uncertainty or risk? There are two good reasons. First, the theory of optimization, weighing marginal benefits and marginal costs, as explained in Chapter 4, provides the basic foundation for all decision making regardless of the amount of information available to a decision maker about the potential outcomes of various actions. In order to learn how to do something under less than ideal conditions, one should first learn how to do it under ideal conditions. Second, even though a decision maker does not have complete information about the marginal benefits and marginal costs of all levels of an activity or choice variable, the *MB*/*MC* rule from Chapter 4 is the most productive approach to profit-maximization decisions under many, if not most, relevant circumstances. We will return to these two points and develop them in some detail in the final part of this chapter.

6.1 DISTINCTIONS BETWEEN RISK AND UNCERTAINTY

risk
A decision is made under risk when a manager can list all outcomes and assign probabilities to each outcome.

objective probabilities
Probabilities on outcomes that are determined by analyzing data on actual experiences a manager has had in similar situations.

subjective probabilities
Probabilities on outcomes that are based on hunches or "gut feelings."

uncertainty
Exists when a decision maker cannot list all possible outcomes and/or cannot assign probabilities to the various outcomes.

states of nature
Future events or conditions that can influence an outcome or payoff but which cannot be controlled by the decision maker.

When the outcome of a decision is not known with certainty, a manager faces a decision making problem under either conditions of risk or conditions of uncertainty. A decision is made under conditions of **risk** when a manager can make a list of all possible random outcomes associated with a decision and assign a probability of occurrence to each one of the outcomes. The process of assigning probabilities to outcomes sometimes involves rather sophisticated analysis based upon the manager's extensive experience in similar situations or on other data. Probabilities assigned in this way are **objective probabilities**. In other circumstances, in which the manager has little experience with a particular decision situation and little or no relevant historical data, the probabilities assigned to the outcomes are derived in a subjective way and are called **subjective probabilities**. Subjective probabilities are based upon hunches, "gut feelings," or personal experiences rather than on scientific data.

An example of a decision made under risk might be the following. A manager decides to spend $1,000 on a magazine ad believing there are three possible outcomes for the ad: a 20 percent chance the ad will have only a small effect on sales, a 60 percent chance of a moderate effect, and a 20 percent chance of a very large effect. This decision is made under risk because the manager can list each potential outcome and determine the probability of each outcome occurring.

In contrast to risk, **uncertainty** exists when a decision maker cannot list all possible outcomes and/or cannot assign probabilities to the various outcomes. When faced with uncertainty, a manager would know only the different decision options available and the different possible *states of nature*. The **states of nature** are the future events or conditions that can influence the final outcome or payoff of a decision, but cannot be controlled or affected by the manager. Even though both risk and uncertainty involve less than complete information, there is more information known under risk than under uncertainty.

An example of a decision made under uncertainty would be a manager of a pharmaceutical company deciding whether or not to spend $3 million on the research and development of a new medication for high blood pressure. The payoff from the research and development spending will depend upon whether or not the President's new health plan imposes price regulations on new drugs. The two states of nature facing the manager in this problem are (1) government does impose price regulations or (2) government does *not* impose price regulations. While the manager knows the payoff that will occur under either state of nature, the manager has no idea of the probability that price regulations will be imposed on drug companies. Under such conditions, a decision is made under uncertainty.

The important distinction between conditions of uncertainty and conditions of risk will be followed throughout this book. The decision rules employed by managers when outcomes are not certain differ under conditions of uncertainty and conditions of risk. We first address decisions characterized by uncertainty before turning to the more important topic of decisions involving risk.

6.2 DECISIONS UNDER UNCERTAINTY

Practically all economic theories about behavior in the absence of complete information deal with risk rather than uncertainty. Furthermore, decision science has little guidance to offer managers making decisions when they have no idea about the likelihood of various states of nature occurring. This should not be too surprising, given the nebulous nature of uncertainty. We will, however, present four rather simple decision rules that can help managers make decisions under uncertainty.

The Maximax Criterion

maximax rule
Identifying the best outcome for each possible decision and choosing the decision with the maximum payoff of all the best outcomes.

For managers who tend to have an optimistic outlook on life, the **maximax rule** provides a guide for making decisions when uncertainty prevails. Under the maximax rule, a manager identifies for each possible decision the best outcome that could occur, then chooses the decision that would give the maximum payoff of all the best outcomes. Under this rule a manager ignores all possible outcomes except the best outcome from each decision.

To illustrate the application of this rule, suppose the management at Dura Plastic is considering changing the size (capacity) of its manufacturing plant. Management has narrowed the decision to three choices. The plant's capacity will be either (1) expanded by 20 percent, (2) maintained at the current capacity, or (3) reduced by 20 percent. The outcome of this decision depends crucially upon how the economy performs during the upcoming year. Thus the performance of the economy is the "state of nature" in this decision problem. Management envisions three possible states of nature occurring: (1) the economy enters a period of recovery, (2) economic stagnation sets in, or (3) the economy falls into a recession.

payoff matrix
Table with rows corresponding to the various decisions, columns corresponding to various states of nature, and each cell giving the outcome or payoff associated with that decision and state of nature.

For each possible decision and state of nature, the managers determine the profit outcome, or payoff, shown in the *payoff matrix* in Table 6.1. A **payoff matrix** is a table with rows corresponding to the various decisions and columns corresponding to the various states of nature. Each cell in the payoff matrix in Table 6.1 gives the outcome (payoff) for each decision when a particular state of nature occurs. For example, if management chooses to expand the manufacturing plant by 20 percent and the economy enters a period of recovery, Dura Plastic is projected to earn profits of $5 million. Alternatively, if Dura Plastic expands plant capacity but the economy falls into a recession, it is projected that the company will lose $3 million. Since the managers do not know which state of nature will actually occur, nor the probabilities of occurrence, the decision to alter plant capacity is made under conditions of uncertainty. In order to apply the maximax rule to this decision, management first identifies the best possible outcome for each of the three decisions. The best payoffs are:

$5 million for Expand plant size by 20 percent
$3 million for Maintain plant size
$2 million for Reduce plant size by 20 percent

Each best payoff occurs if the economy recovers. Under the maximax rule management would decide to expand its plant.

While the maximax rule is simple to apply, it fails to consider "bad" outcomes in the decision-making process. The fact that two out of three states of nature result in losses when management decides to expand plant capacity, and neither of the other decisions would result in a loss, is overlooked when using the maximax criteria. Only managers with optimistic natures are likely to find the maximax rule to be a useful decision-making tool.

The Maximin Criterion

maximin rule
Identify the worst outcomes for each decision and choose the decision with the maximum worst-payoff.

For managers with a pessimistic outlook on business decisions, the *maximin rule* may be more suitable than the maximax rule. Under the **maximin rule**, the manager identifies the worst outcome for each decision and makes the decision associated with the maximum worst-payoff. For Dura Plastic, the worst outcomes for each decision from Table 6.1 are:

–$3 million for Expand plant size by 20 percent
$0.5 million for Maintain plant size
$0.75 million for Reduce plant size by 20 percent

TABLE 6.1
The Payoff Matrix for Dura Plastic, Inc.

	States of nature		
Decisions	Recovery	Stagnation	Recession
Expand plant capacity by 20%	$5 million	–$1 million	–$3.0 million
Maintain same plant capacity	$3 million	$2 million	$ .5 million
Reduce plant capacity by 20%	$2 million	$1 million	$ .75 million

Using the maximin criterion, Dura Plastic would choose to reduce plant capacity by 20 percent. The maximin rule is also simple to follow, but it fails to consider any of the "good" outcomes.

Minimax Regret Criterion

potential regret
For a given decision and state of nature, the improvement in payoff the manager could have experienced had the decision been the best one when that state of nature actually occurs.

Managers concerned about their decisions not turning out to be the best *once the state of nature is known* (i.e., after the uncertainty is resolved) may make their decisions by minimizing the potential regret that may occur. The **potential regret** associated with a particular decision and state of nature is the improvement in payoff the manager could have experienced had the decision been the best one when that state of nature actually occurred. To illustrate, we calculate from Table 6.1 the potential regret associated with Dura Plastic's decision to maintain the same level of plant capacity if an economic recovery occurs. The best possible payoff when recovery occurs is $5 million, the payoff for expanding plant capacity. If a recovery does indeed happen and management chooses to maintain the same level of plant capacity, the payoff is only $3 million, and the manager experiences a regret of $2 million (= $5 – $3 million).

minimax regret rule
Determine the worst-potential regret associated with each decision. Then choose the decision with the minimum worst-potential regret.

Table 6.2 shows the potential regret for each combination of decision and state of nature. Note that every state of nature has a decision for which there is no potential regret. This occurs when the correct decision is made for that particular state of nature. To apply the **minimax regret rule**, which requires managers to make a decision with the minimum worst potential regret, management identifies the maximum possible potential regret for each decision from the matrix:

$3.75 million for Expand plant size by 20 percent
$2 million for Maintain plant size
$3 million for Reduce plant size by 20 percent

Management chooses the decision with the lowest worst potential regret: maintain current plant capacity. For Dura Plastic, the minimax regret rule results in management choosing to maintain the current plant capacity.

Equal Probability Criterion

In situations of uncertainty, managers have no information about the probable state of nature that will occur and sometimes simply assume that each state of nature is equally likely to occur. In terms of the Dura Plastic decision, manage-

TABLE 6.2
Potential Regret Matrix for Dura Plastic, Inc.

	States of nature		
Decisions	Recovery	Stagnation	Recession
Expand plant capacity by 20%	$0	$3 million	$3.75 million
Maintain same plant capacity	$2 million	$0	$ .25 million
Reduce plant capacity by 20%	$3 million	$1 million	$0

ment assumes each state of nature has a one-third probability of occurring. When managers assume each state of nature has an equal likelihood of occurring, the decision can be made by considering the *average* payoff for each equally possible state of nature. This approach to decision making is often referred to as the **equal probability rule**. To illustrate, the manager of Dura Plastic calculates the average payoff for each decision as follows:

equal probability rule Assume each state of nature is equally likely to occur and compute the average payoff for each equally likely possible state of nature. Make the decision with the highest average payoff.

$.33 million [= (5 + (−1) +(−3))/3] for Expand plant size
$1.83 million [= (3 + 2 + 0.5)/3] for Maintain plant size
$1.25 million [= (2 + 1 + 0.75)/3] for Reduced plant size

Under the equal probability rule, the manager's decision is to maintain the current plant capacity since this decision has the maximum average return.

The four decision rules discussed here do not exhaust the possibilities for managers making decisions under uncertainty. We present these four rules primarily to give you a feel for decision making under uncertainty and to show the imprecise or "unscientific" nature of these rules. Recall that management could choose any of the courses of action depending upon which rule was chosen. These and other rules are meant only to be guidelines to decision making and are not substitutes for the experience and intuition of management.

6.3 MEASURING RISK WITH PROBABILITY DISTRIBUTIONS

Decisions under risk occur when a decision maker can assign a probability to each potential outcome or payoff from a decision or course of action. Because it is possible to assign a probability to each outcome, decisions under risk are more straightforward and can be analyzed more scientifically than decisions under uncertainty. The remainder of this chapter is concerned with decision making under risk. However, before we can discuss and set forth rules for decision making under risk, we must first discuss how risk can be measured. The most direct method of measuring risk involves the characteristics of a probability distribution of outcomes associated with a particular decision. This section will describe these characteristics.

Probability Distributions

probability distribution Table or graph showing all possible outcomes or payoffs of a decision and the probabilities that each outcome will occur.

A **probability distribution** is a table or graph showing all possible outcomes (payoffs) for a decision and the probability that each outcome will occur. The probabilities can take values between 0 and 1, or alternatively they can be expressed as percentages between 0 and 100 percent.[1] If *all possible* outcomes are assigned probabilities, the probabilities must sum to one (or 100 percent); that is, the probability that some other outcome will occur is zero because there is no other possible outcome.

[1]If the probability of an outcome is 1 (or 100 percent), the outcome is certain to occur and no risk exists. If the probability of an outcome is 0, then that particular outcome will not occur and need not be considered in decision making.

To illustrate a probability distribution, we assume that the director of advertising at a large corporation believes the firm's current advertising campaign may result in any one of five possible outcomes for corporate sales. The probability distribution for this advertising campaign is

Outcome (sales)	Probability (percent)
47,500 units	10
50,000 units	20
52,500 units	30
55,000 units	25
57,500 units	15

Each outcome has a probability greater than 0 but less than 100 percent, and the sum of all probabilities is 100 percent (=10 + 20 + 30 + 25 + 15). This probability distribution is represented graphically in Figure 6.1.

From a probability distribution (either in tabular or graphical form), the riskiness of a decision is reflected by the variability of outcomes indicated by the different probabilities of occurrence. For decision-making purposes, managers often turn to mathematical properties of the probability distribution to facilitate a formal analysis of risk. The nature of risk can be summarized by examining the

FIGURE 6.1
The Probability Distribution for Sales Following an Advertising Campaign

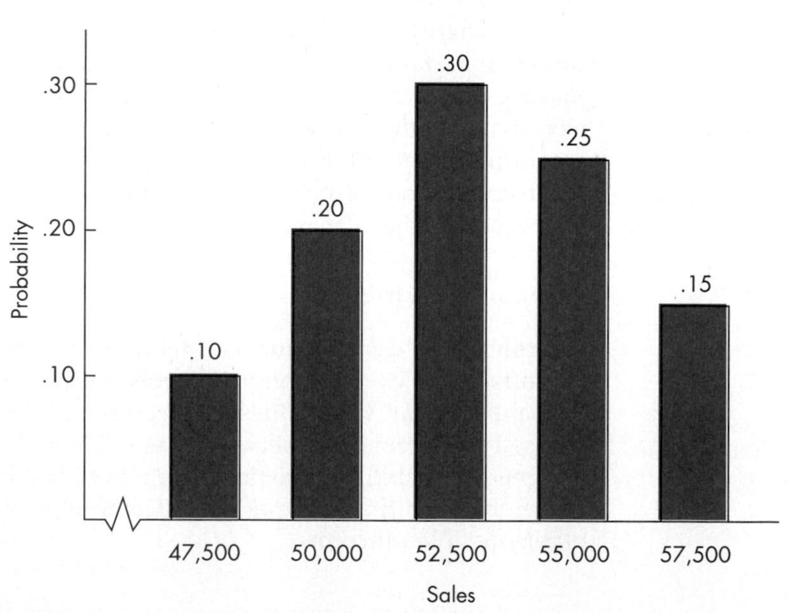

central tendency of the probability distribution, as measured by the expected value of the distribution, and by examining the dispersion of the distribution, as measured by the standard deviation and coefficient of variation. We discuss first the measure of central tendency of a probability distribution.

Expected Value of a Probability Distribution

expected value
The weighed average of the outcomes with the probabilities of each outcome serving as the respective weights.

The **expected value** of a probability distribution of decision outcomes is the weighted average of the outcomes with the probabilities of each outcome serving as the respective weights. The expected value of the various outcomes of a probability distribution is

$$E(X) = \text{Expected value of } X = \sum_{i=1}^{n} p_i X_i$$

where X_i is the ith outcome of a decision, p_i is the probability of the ith outcome, and n is the total number of possible outcomes in the probability distribution. Note that the computation of expected value requires the use of fractions or decimal values for the probabilities p_i, rather than percentages. The expected value of a probability distribution is often referred to as the **mean of the distribution.**

mean of the distribution
The expected value of the distribution.

The expected value of sales for the advertising campaign associated with the probability distribution shown in Figure 6.1 is

$$\begin{aligned} E(\text{sales}) &= (.10)(47{,}500) + (.20)(50{,}000) + (.30)(52{,}500) + \\ &\quad (.25)(55{,}000) + (.15)(57{,}500) \\ &= 4{,}750 + 10{,}000 + 15{,}750 + 13{,}750 + 8{,}625 \\ &= 52{,}875 \end{aligned}$$

While the actual sales that occur as a result of the advertising campaign is a random variable possibly taking values of 47,500, 50,000, 52,500, 55,000, or 57,500 units, the expected level of sales is 52,875 units. If only one of the five levels of sales can occur, the level that actually occurs will not equal the expected value of 52,875, but expected value does indicate what the *average* value of the outcomes would be if the risky decision were to be repeated a large number of times.

Dispersion of a Probability Distribution

variance
The probability-weighted sum of the squared deviations about the expected value of X.

As you may recall from your statistics classes, probability distributions are generally characterized not only by the expected value (mean) but also by the variance. The **variance** of a probability distribution measures the dispersion of the distribution about its mean. Figure 6.2 shows the probability distributions for the profit outcomes of two different decisions, A and B. Both decisions, as illustrated in Figure 6.2, have identical expected profit levels but different variances. The larger variance associated with making decision B is reflected by a larger dispersion (a wider spread of values around the mean). Because distribution A is more compact (less spread out) A has a smaller variance.

FIGURE 6.2
Two Probability Distributions with Identical Means but Different Variances

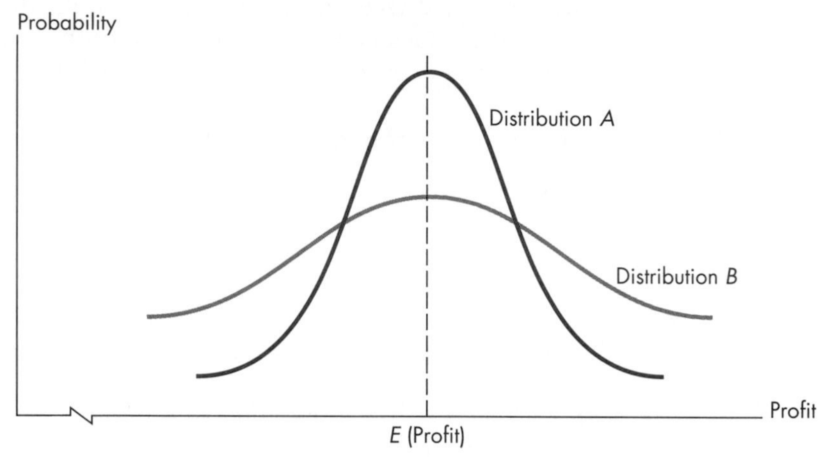

The variance of a probability distribution of the outcomes of a given decision is frequently used to indicate the level or degree of risk associated with that decision. If the expected values of two distributions are the same, the distribution with the higher variance is associated with the riskier decision. Thus in Figure 6.2, decision *B* has more risk than decision *A*. Furthermore, variance is often used to compare the riskiness of two decisions even though the expected values of the distributions differ.

Mathematically, the variance of a probability distribution of outcomes X_i, denoted by σ_x^2, is the probability-weighted sum of the squared deviations about the expected value of *X*:

$$\text{Variance } (X) = \sigma_x^2 = \sum_{i=1}^{n} p_i[X_i - E(X)]^2$$

For example, consider the two distributions illustrated in Figure 6.3. As is evident from the graphs and demonstrated in the table that follows, the two distributions have the same mean, 50. Their variances differ, however. Decision *A* has a smaller variance than decision *B*, and is therefore less risky. The calculation of the expected values and variance for each distribution are shown in the following table:

	Decision A			Decision B		
Profit X_i	Probability p_i	p_iX_i	$[X_i - E(X)]^2p_i$	Probability p_i	p_iX_i	$[X_i - E(X)]^2p_i$
30	.05	1.5	20	.10	3	40
40	.20	8	20	.25	10	25
50	.50	25	0	.30	15	0
60	.20	12	20	.25	15	25
70	.05	3.5	20	.10	7	40
		$E(X) = 50$	$\sigma_A^2 = 80$		$E(X) = 50$	$\sigma_B^2 = 130$

FIGURE 6.3
Probability Distributions with Different Variances

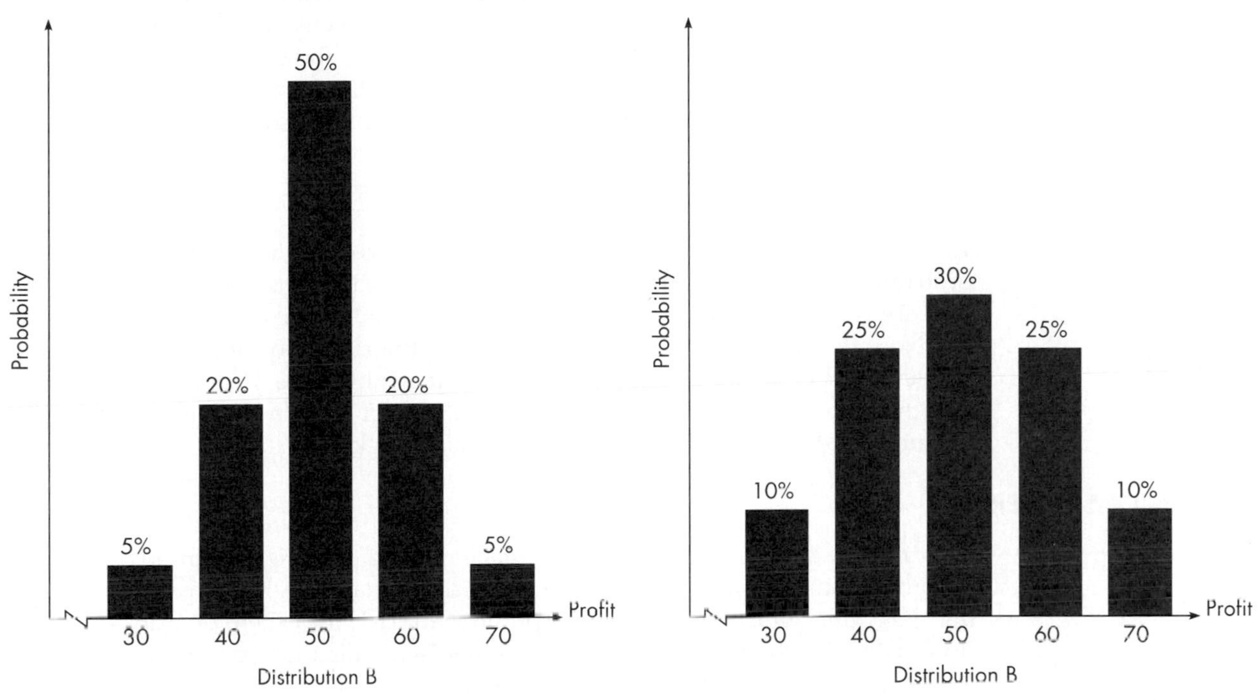

standard deviation
The square root of the variance.

Because variance is a squared term, it is usually much larger than the mean. To avoid this scaling problem, the standard deviation of the probability distribution is more commonly used to measure dispersion. The **standard deviation** of a probability distribution, denoted by σ_x, is the square root of the variance:

$$\sigma_x = \sqrt{\text{Variance } (X)}$$

The standard deviations of the distributions illustrated in Figure 6.3 and in the above table are $\sigma_A = 8.94$ and $\sigma_B = 11.40$. As in the case of the variance of a probability distribution, the higher the standard deviation, the more risky the decision.

Managers can compare the riskiness of various decisions by comparing their standard deviations, as long as the expected values are of similar magnitudes. For example, if decisions *C* and *D* both have standard deviations of 52.5, the two decisions can be viewed as equally risky if their expected values are close to one another. If however, the expected values of the distributions differ substantially in magnitude, it can be misleading to examine only the standard deviations. Suppose decision *C* has a mean outcome of $400 and decision *D* has a mean outcome of $5,000, but the standard deviations remain 52.5. The dispersion of outcomes for decision D is much smaller *relative to its mean value of $5,000* than is the dispersion of outcomes for decision C *relative to its mean value of $400*.

When the expected values of outcomes differ substantially, managers should measure the riskiness of a decision *relative* to its expected value. One such measure of relative risk is the coefficient of variation for the decision's distribution. The **coefficient of variation**, denoted by υ, is the standard deviation divided by the expected value of the probability distribution of decision outcomes,

coefficient of variation
The standard deviation divided by the expected value of the probability distribution.

$$\upsilon = \frac{\text{Standard deviation}}{\text{Expected value}} = \frac{\sigma}{E(X)}$$

The coefficient of variation measures the level of risk *relative* to the mean of the probability distribution. In the preceding example, the two coefficients of variation are $\upsilon_C = 52.5/400 = .131$ and $\upsilon_D = 52.5/5{,}000 = .0105$.

Now that we have shown how to measure the risk associated with making a particular managerial decision, we will discuss how these measures of risk can help managers make decisions under conditions of risk. In the next section, we set forth three rules to guide managers making risky decisions.

6.4 DECISIONS UNDER RISK

One important task of managers is to make choices or decisions, frequently with the goal of maximizing profit. When managers make choices or decisions under risk, they must somehow incorporate this risk into their decision-making process. Unfortunately, there is no single decision rule that managers can follow to guarantee that profits will actually be maximized. Indeed, no decision rule can eliminate the risk surrounding a decision. Decision rules just provide tools for systematically including risk into the decision-making process. It is certainly possible that two managers facing identical situations could have very different profits at the end of the year because of good or bad luck rather than good or bad decision-making skills. With this caveat in mind, we will now discuss some of the various decision rules used by managers who lack complete knowledge about outcomes.

Maximization of Expected Value

Information about the likelihood of the various possible outcomes, while quite helpful in making decisions, does not solve the manager's decision-making problem. How should a manager choose among various decisions when each decision has a variety of possible outcomes? One rule or solution to this problem, called the **expected value rule**, is to choose the decision with the highest expected value. The expected value rule is easy to apply. Unfortunately, this rule uses information about only one characteristic of the distribution of outcomes, the mean. It fails to incorporate the riskiness (dispersion) associated with the probability distribution of outcomes into the decision. Therefore, the expected value rule is not particularly useful in situations where the level of risk differs across decisions—unless the decision maker does not care about the level of risk associated with a decision and is concerned only with expected value. (Such a

expected value rule
Choosing the decision with the highest expected value.

decision maker is called *risk neutral*, a concept we will discuss later in this chapter.) Also, the expected value rule is only useful to a manager when the decisions have *different* expected values. Of course, if decisions happen to have identical expected values, the expected value rule offers no guidance for choosing between them, and, considering only the mean, the manager would be indifferent to a choice among them. The expected value rule *cannot* be applied when decisions have identical expected values and *should not* be applied when decisions have different levels of risk, except in the circumstance noted above.

To illustrate the expected value rule (and other rules to be discussed later), consider the owner and manager of Chicago Rotisserie Chicken, who wants to decide where to open one new restaurant. Figure 6.4 shows the probability distributions of possible weekly profits if the manager decides to locate the new restaurant in either Atlanta (Panel A), Boston (Panel B), or Cleveland (Panel C). The expected values, standard deviations, and coefficients of variation for each distribution are displayed in each panel.

Based on past experience, the manager calculates that weekly profit in Atlanta will take one of four values: $3,000 or $4,000 per week each with a 30 percent chance of occurring, and $2,000 or $5,000 a week each with a 20 percent change of occurring. The expected weekly profit in Atlanta is $3,500. If the manager decides to open a restaurant in Boston, the weekly profits may be any of six indicated values ranging from $1,000 to $6,000 weekly with the indicated probabilities and an expected value of $3,750. For Cleveland, the manager assigns a probability of 30 percent to weekly profits of $1,000 and $6,000 and a probability of 10 percent to each of the profits, $2,000, $3,000, $4,000, and $5,000 with an expected value of $3,500 for the distribution. If the manager is not concerned with risk (is risk neutral) and follows the expected value rule, the new restaurant will be opened in Boston, with the highest expected profit of $3,750. Note that if the manager had been choosing between only the Atlanta and Cleveland locations the expected value rule could not have been applied because each has an expected value of $3,500. In such cases some other rule may be used.

Mean-Variance Analysis

Managers who choose among risky alternatives using the expected value rule are, in effect, ignoring risk (dispersion) and focusing exclusively on the mean outcome. An alternative method of making decisions under risk uses both the mean *and* the variance of the probability distribution, which incorporates information about the level of risk into the decisions. This method of decision making, commonly known as **mean-variance analysis**, employs both the mean and variance (or standard deviation) to make decisions according to the following rules.

mean-variance analysis
Method of decision making that employs both the mean and variance to make decisions.

Given two risky decisions (designated *A* and *B*), the *mean-variance rules* for decisions under risk are:

1. If decision *A* has a higher expected outcome *and* a lower variance than decision *B*, decision *A* should be made.

FIGURE 6.4
Probability Distributions for Weekly Profit at Three Restaurant Locations

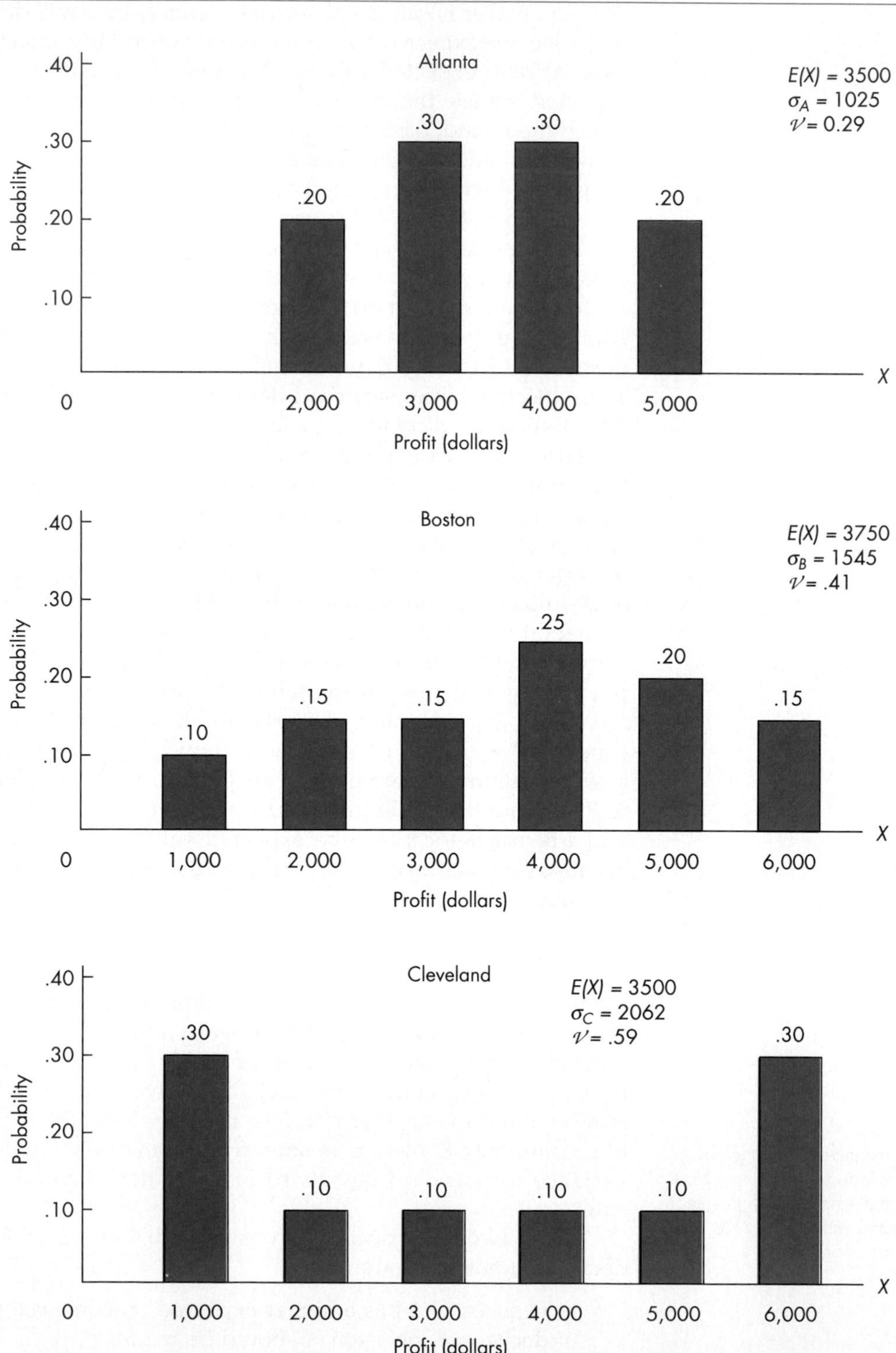

2. If both decisions A and B have identical *variances* (or standard deviations), the decision with the higher expected value should be made.
3. If both decisions A and B have identical *expected values*, the decision with the lower variance (standard deviation) should be made.

The mean-variance rules are based on the assumption that a decision maker prefers a higher expected return to a lower, other things equal, and a lower risk to a higher, other things equal. It therefore follows that the *higher* the expected outcome and the *lower* the variance (risk), the more desirable a decision will be. Under rule 1, a manager would always choose a particular decision if it has *both* a greater expected value *and* a lower variance than other decisions being considered. With the same level of risk, the second rule indicates managers should choose the decision with the higher expected value. Under rule 3, if the decisions have identical expected values, the manager chooses the less risky (lower standard deviation) decision.

Returning to the problem of Chicago Rotisserie Chicken, no location dominates both of the other locations in terms of any of the three rules of mean-variance analysis. Boston dominates Cleveland because it has both a higher expected value and a lower risk (rule 1). Atlanta also dominates Cleveland in terms of rule 3 because both locations have the same expected value ($3,500) but Atlanta has a lower standard deviation—less risk ($\sigma_A = 1025 < 2062 = \sigma_c$).

If the manager compares the Atlanta and Boston locations, the mean-variance rules cannot be applied. Boston has a higher weekly expected profit ($3,750 > $3,500) but Atlanta is less risky ($\sigma_A = 1025 < 1{,}545 = \sigma_B$). Therefore, when making this choice, the manager must make a trade-off between risk and expected return, so the choice would depend on the manager's valuation of higher expected return versus lower risk. We will now set forth an additional decision rule that uses information on both the expected value and dispersion, and can be used to make decisions involving trade-offs between expected return and risk.

Coefficient of Variation Analysis

As we noted in the discussion about measuring the riskiness of probability distributions, variance and standard deviation are measures of *absolute* risk. In contrast, the coefficient of variation ($\sigma/E(X)$) measures risk *relative* to the expected value of the distribution. The coefficient of variation, therefore, allows managers to make decisions based on relative risk instead of absolute risk. The **coefficient of variation rule** states: "When making decisions under risk, choose the decision with the smallest coefficient of variation ($\sigma/E(X)$). This rule takes into account both the expected value and the standard deviation of the distribution. The lower the standard deviation and the higher the expected value, the smaller the coefficient of variation. Thus a desired movement in either characteristic of a probability distribution moves the coefficient of variation in the desired direction.

coefficient of variation rule
Choosing the decision with the smallest coefficient of variation.

ILLUSTRATION 6.1

Lowering Risk by Diversification

Although investors can't do much about the amount of risk associated with any specific project or investment, they do have some control over the amount of risk associated with their entire portfolio of investments. *The Wall Street Journal* (April 8, 1993) advised " . . . for anyone who doesn't need . . . money right away, this may be a good time to broaden your investment horizon. The best strategy, investment advisors say, is to diversify by spreading your money among a wide variety of stocks, bonds, real estate, cash, and other holdings."

The *Journal* pointed out that you will have to expect the value of your holdings to fluctuate with changes in the economy or market conditions. The returns should comfortably beat those from CDs, and the ups and downs should be a lot smaller than if you simply put all of your money in the stock market. One investment advisor stated, "Diversified portfolios of stocks and bonds had much less risk while providing nearly as much return as an all-stock portfolio during the past 15, 20, and 25 years. During the period since 1968, stocks soared in five years but were losing investments in six years. Investors who put a third of their money in stocks, a third in Treasury bonds, and a third in "cash equivalent" investments would have lost money in only four years, with the largest annual loss being less than five percent. The annual compound return over the 25 years in that investment would have been 9 percent, compared with 10.56 percent in an all stock portfolio, 8.26 percent in all bonds, and 9.89 percent in 60 percent stock and 40 percent bonds. But the more diversified investment would have been less risky.

The theoretical arguments in the *WSJ* article are based on portfolio theory. The core of portfolio theory is deceptively simple: As more securities are added to an investor's portfolio, the portfolio risk (the standard deviation of portfolio returns) declines. A particular security or investment is subject to two types of risk: market risk and unique risk. Market risk is the risk faced due to economy-wide changes, such as economic fluctuations and fluctuations in the market rate of interest. Unique risk is the risk associated with the particular security or investment, such as fluctuations in the sales of a particular firm or region relative to the entire economy.

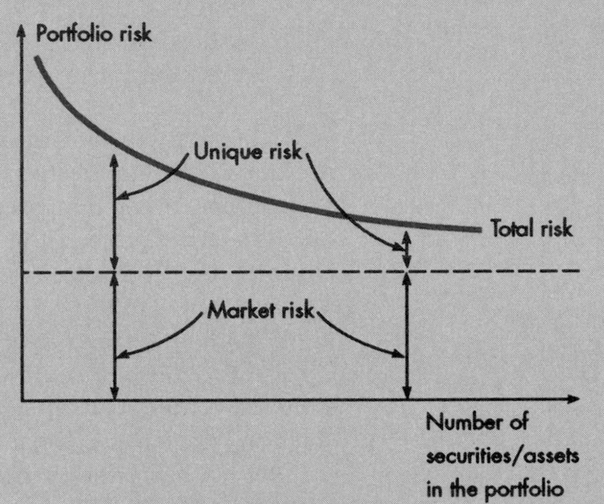

As different securities are added to a portfolio, the unique risk associated with a specific security is diversified away. That is, as more securities are added, the entire portfolio is less subject to the unique risk associated with a given stock. As the number of securities or assets is increased, unique risk decreases and the total risk of the portfolio (the standard deviation) approaches the market risk.

Source: Tom Herman, "The First Rollovers of Spring Bring Advice on Diversification," *The Wall Street Journal*, April 8, 1993.

We return once more to the decision facing the manager of Chicago Rotisserie Chicken. The coefficients of variation for each of the possible location decisions are

$$\upsilon_{\text{Atlanta}} = 1{,}025/3{,}500 = 0.29$$
$$\upsilon_{\text{Boston}} = 1{,}545/3{,}750 = 0.41$$
$$\upsilon_{\text{Cleveland}} = 2{,}062/3{,}500 = 0.59$$

The location with the smallest coefficient of variation is Atlanta, which has a coefficient of 0.29. Notice that the choice between locating in either Atlanta or Boston, which could not be made using mean-variance rules, is now resolved using the coefficient of variation to make the decision. Atlanta wins over Boston with the smaller coefficient of variation (.29 < .41), while Cleveland comes in last.

Which Rule Is Best?

At this point, you may be wondering which one of the three rules for making decisions under risk is the "correct" one? After all, the manager of Chicago Rotisserie Chicken reached either a different decision or reached no decision at all depending upon which rule was used. Using the expected value rule, Boston was the choice. Using the coefficient of variation rule, Atlanta was chosen. According to mean-variance analysis, Cleveland was out, but the decision between Atlanta and Boston could not be resolved using mean-variance analysis. If the decision rules do not all lead to the same conclusion, a manager must decide which rule to follow.

When a decision is to be made repeatedly, with identical probabilities each time, the expected value rule provides managers with the most reliable rule for maximizing (expected) profit. The average return of a given risky course of action repeated many times will approach the expected value of that action. Therefore, the average return of the course of action with the highest expected value will tend to be higher than the average return of any course of action with a lower expected value, when carried out a large number of times. Situations involving repeated decisions can arise, for example, when a manager must make the same risky decision once a month, or even once every week. Or, a manager at corporate headquarters may make a decision that directs activities of dozens, maybe even hundreds, of corporate offices in the country or around the world. When the risky decision is repeated many times, the manager at corporate headquarters believes strongly that each of the alternative decision choices will probably result in an average profit level that is equal to the expected value of profit, even though any one corporate office might experience either higher or lower returns. In practice, then, the expected value rule is justifiable when a decision will be repeated many times under identical circumstances.

When a manager makes a one-time decision under risk, there will not be any follow-up repetitions of the decision to "average out" a bad outcome (or a good outcome). Unfortunately, there is no best rule to follow when decisions are not repetitive. The rules we present for risky decision making should be used by managers to help *analyze* and *guide* the decision-making process. Ultimately, making decisions under risk (or uncertainty) is as much an art as it is a science.

The "art" of decision making under risk or uncertainty is closely associated with a decision maker's preferences with respect to risk taking. Managers can differ greatly in their willingness to take on risk in decision making. Some managers are quite cautious, while others may actually seek out high-risk situations. For convenience, economists generally classify decision makers into three categories, according to their attitudes toward risk. These three categories are (1) *risk averse*, (2) *risk loving*, and (3) *risk neutral*. The risk category of a person is determined according to the following rule:

> A person must choose between two alternatives: (A) take a risky course of action with a known expected value and a positive variance, or (B) receive the expected value of that course of action with certainty.

1. A **risk-averse** person would choose to receive with certainty the expected value of the risky course of action (alternative B).
2. A **risk-loving** person would choose the risky course of action (alternative A).
3. A **risk-neutral** person would be indifferent between the two alternative decisions.

risk averse
A decision maker who chooses to receive with certainty the expected value of a risky decision rather than undertaking the risky decision.

risk loving
A decision maker who chooses to undertake a risky decision rather than receive with certainty the expected value of the risky decision.

risk neutral
A decision maker who is indifferent about taking on a risky decision or alternatively receiving with certainty the expected value of that risky decision.

For example, suppose someone offers to flip a coin once and give you $100 if it comes up heads and nothing if it comes up tails (alternative A) or simply give you $50, the expected value of the risky course of action, but not flip the coin (alternative B). You are risk averse if you choose the $50 with certainty, risk loving if you choose to flip, and risk neutral if you are indifferent (equally satisfied) between the two options.

The decision or decision-making rule would differ depending upon the decision maker's attitude toward risk. For example, when faced with decisions involving uncertainty, a risk lover may very well choose to follow the maximax rule while the risk-averse person would follow the maximin rule. Or a risk lover may choose decisions with highly profitable outcomes even though the likelihood of an extremely high payoff is small. A risk-averse person would possibly choose a distribution with a small variance but little or no likelihood of a huge payoff.

To repeat the answer to the question at the beginning of this discussion: "Which rule is best?" There is no "best" rule. The judgment and attitude toward risk of the decision maker determine the rule to follow. As noted above, we set forth these rules only as guidelines and to give you a feel for decision making under risk or uncertainty.

6.5 FINDING THE OPTIMAL LEVEL OF A RISKY ACTIVITY

In the introduction to this chapter, we explained briefly why we devote so much space in this text to decision making under certainty, when a large portion of actual decision making is done under conditions of uncertainty or risk. First, the marginal rules of Chapter 4 and the theoretical material throughout the text form the basic foundation of decision making with incomplete information. Second, the theory of optimization under complete information can be easily adapted and applied to optimization under risk when marginal benefits and marginal costs are not known with certainty. We will now show how optimization theory can be used in a straightforward manner in situations where the decision maker has incomplete information about the marginal costs and benefits of an activity, but does have information on the expected value of marginal costs and marginal benefits for different levels of the activity. We will also discuss how regression estimates of the marginal benefits and costs of an activity generally meet all of the criteria needed for finding the optimal level of the activity. As you will see, the rules you learned in Chapter 4 can easily be modified to handle situations involving risk.

Maximizing Expected Net Benefits

Recall from Chapter 4 that the optimal level of an activity is the level of activity that maximizes net benefit, where net benefit is the difference between total benefit and total cost ($NB = TB - TC$). When the activity varies continuously, the optimal level occurs where marginal benefit equals marginal cost ($MB = MC$). If the activity only varies discretely, the optimal level of activity is the last level of activity for which marginal benefit exceeds marginal cost ($MB > MC$).

For decision-making situations in which benefits and costs are random variables, net benefit is also a random variable. For each level of activity, the net benefit may take on a range of values in a random fashion, and there is a probability distribution for net benefit at each level of activity. Figure 6.5 shows the expected value of an activity, X, over a range of the activity and the probability distribution for three levels of activity, 100, 200, and 300. If the manager chooses 100 units of X, net benefit may take on a range of values as indicated by the bell-shaped probability distribution shown at 100 units of activity X. The expected value of net benefits at that level is $40,000. If the manager repeatedly chooses 100 units of activity X a large number of times, net benefit will, on average, equal

FIGURE 6.5
Probability Distributions for the Net Benefits Associated with a Risky Activity

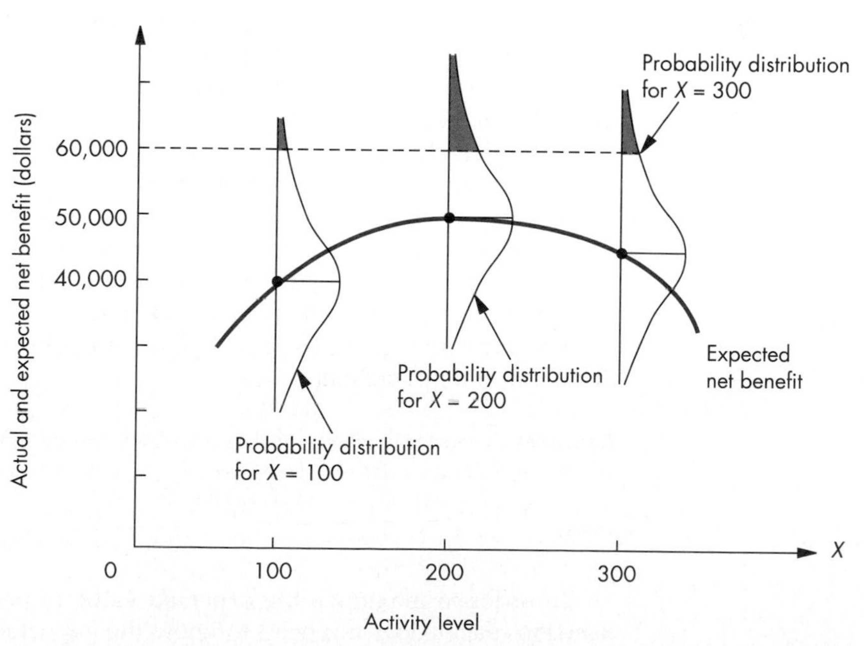

expected net benefit curve
The locus of expected values of net benefit for all relevant levels of activity X.

optimal level of a risky activity
The level of activity that maximizes the expected net benefit $E(NB)$ of the activity.

$40,000. At an activity level of 200 units, the expected value of net benefits is $50,000. The **expected net benefit curve**, shown in Figure 6.5, represents the locus of expected values of net benefit for all relevant levels of activity X. The **optimal level of a risky activity** is the level that maximizes the *expected net benefit* of the activity. In Figure 6.5, a manager would choose 200 units of the activity since the expected value of net benefit is maximized at that level.

As long as the probability distribution for net benefit has the same variance at each level of activity—a topic we discuss further below—maximizing the expected net benefit is optimal regardless of whether the manager is risk neutral, risk loving, or risk averse. This is obvious for a risk-neutral manager who is, by the definition of a risk-neutral decision maker, indifferent between choosing to accept the random return from the decision or receiving the expected value of the decision. Since only the expected value of net benefit matters to a risk-neutral manager, the manager would clearly prefer the highest expected value to any lower expected value.

A risk-loving manager wants to choose the level of activity that maximizes the probability of earning high returns. Since the variance is assumed constant at each activity level, the level with the highest expected return is associated with the greatest probability of achieving a high return. For example, suppose the manager wants to choose X in such a way as to maximize the probability of earning a net benefit of at least $60,000. As you can see in Figure 6.5, it is possible that net benefit might equal $60,000 or more at any of the possible activity levels. But the activity level that maximizes the likelihood of at least a $60,000 payoff (net benefit) is 200 units of the activity—as you see by comparing the shaded area above $60,000 in each of the three probability distributions in Figure 6.5. If the risk-loving manager chooses an activity level of 100 or 300 units, the manager needlessly reduces the probability of earning $60,000 or more. The probability of earning at least $60,000 is highest at 200 units of the activity, the level of maximum expected value.

Alternatively, suppose a risk-averse manager wants to choose the level of X that minimizes the probability of earning $40,000 or less. As you can see from the figure, the probability distribution with the smallest portion lying below $40,000 is that associated with 200 units of X. If this manager chooses 100 or 200 units of X, the probability of receiving $40,000 or less is needlessly increased. Therefore, no matter what the attitude toward risk, the manager should choose the activity level that maximizes the expected value of net benefit. We now summarize this discussion in a principle:

Principle When the variance of the probability distribution on net benefit is constant at all relevant levels of activity, the optimal level of a risky activity is the level of activity with the highest expected net benefit, regardless of whether the decision maker is risk neutral, risk loving, or risk averse.

In order to maximize the expected value of net benefits from an activity, a decision maker does not need to know the expected net benefits and the probability distribution on net benefit at each level of activity. For an activity that varies continuously, expected net benefit reaches its maximum value at the level of the activity at which the *expected* marginal benefit of the activity equals the *expected* marginal cost.[2] When the activity varies discretely, the expected value of net benefits is maximized at the last value of the activity for which expected marginal benefits exceed expected marginal cost.

Figure 6.6 shows the expected marginal benefit and expected marginal cost curves for activity X that correspond to the expected net benefit curve shown in Figure 6.5. The probability distribution of marginal benefit and marginal cost are shown for 100, 200, and 300 units of the activity. The two expected marginal curves in Figure 6.6 are derived from expected total benefit and expected total cost curves (not shown), which also are used to derive the expected net benefit curve in Figure 6.5. The decision maker, following the $E(MB) = E(MC)$ rule, would choose 200 units of activity for which expected marginal benefit equals expected marginal cost at $20. Engaging in 200 units of activity X yields expected net benefit of $50,000, the maximum point on the expected net benefit curve. If the manager repeatedly engages in 200 units of activity a large number of times, the actual net benefit incurred will vary randomly, but the firm will *on average* earn $50,000 net benefit.

Regression Analysis and Maximizing Expected Net Benefits

You might be a bit skeptical about whether a manager can actually use the analysis in this section to make decisions under risk, such as finding the level of sales, advertising, or input usage to maximize the expected value of profits. It appears at first that actually estimating expected marginal benefits and cost would pose an insurmountable problem. Fortunately, however, this task is rather simple.

You may recall from the discussion in Chapter 5 on basic estimation techniques that a regression equation such as $Y = a + bX$ shows the *average* or *expected value* of the dependent variable, Y, for a given level of the independent variable, X. We emphasized that the regression equation has a random error term to capture the effect of random influences on Y. Because the variation in Y is due to random effects as well as variation in X, the *exact* value of Y cannot be predicted. The value of Y predicted by the regression equation is the value Y would take, on average, after being observed a large number of times for a constant level of X. Thus, the predicted value of the dependent variable given by a regression equation is correctly interpreted as the expected value of the dependent variable Y for a given level of X.

In later chapters we will show how to use regression analysis to estimate the marginal benefit and marginal cost functions for an activity—for example, a firm's output level. These estimated marginal functions can be interpreted to show the expected values for marginal benefit and marginal cost. We will also show how easy it is to derive the expected total benefit and expected total cost functions from the marginal functions. And, of course, subtracting expected total

[2] A mathematical proof of this statement is presented in the appendix for this chapter.

FIGURE 6.6
Expected Marginal Benefit and Expected Marginal Cost

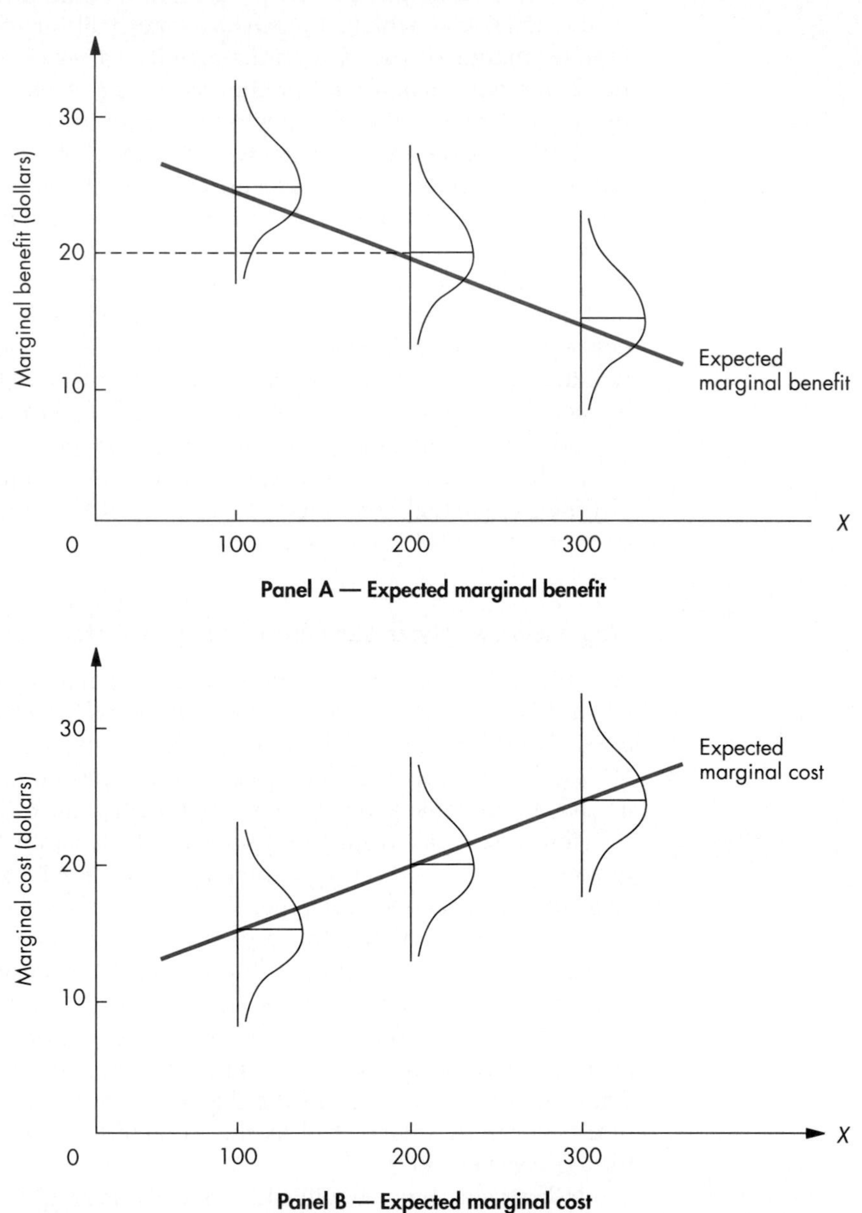

cost from expected total benefits at any level of activity gives expected net benefits—for example, expected profits—for that level of the activity.

Earlier in this section, we demonstrated that, if the expected net benefit function has a constant variance, it makes no difference whether the decision maker is risk neutral, risk averse, or risk loving. In each case, the decision maker should choose the level of activity at which expected net benefit is maximized. The regression estimates of expected marginal benefit and expected marginal cost are generally assumed to have a constant variance at all levels of activity X.[3] When the expected marginal functions—$E(MB)$ and $E(MC)$—have constant variances at all activity levels, the expected net benefit function—$E(NB)$—has a constant variance as well.[4] Therefore, equating the *estimated* $E(MB)$ to the *estimated* $E(MC)$ does indeed locate the level of activity that maximizes $E(NB)$, no matter what the risk preference of the decision maker.

6.6 SUMMARY

This chapter presented some basic rules for managers to help them make decisions under conditions of uncertainty and risk. Conditions of *risk* occur when a manager must make a decision for which the outcome is not known with certainty. However, he can make a list of all possible outcomes and assign probabilities to the various outcomes. *Uncertainty* exists when a decision maker cannot list all possible outcomes and/or cannot assign probabilities to the various outcomes.

In the case of uncertainty, decision science can provide very little guidance to managers beyond offering them some simple decision rules to aid them in their analysis of uncertain situations. Four basic rules for decision making under uncertainty are presented in this chapter: (1) the maximax rule, (2) the maximin rule, (3) the minimax regret rule, and (4) the equal probability rule. Table 6.3 summarizes each of these rules.

In order to measure the risk associated with a decision, the manager can examine several characteristics of the probability distribution of outcomes for the decision. A probability distribution is a table or graph showing all possible outcomes (payoffs) for a decision and the proba-

TABLE 6.3
Summary of Decision Rules under Conditions of Uncertainty

Maximax rule	Identify the best outcome for each possible decision and choose the decision with the maximum payoff.
Maximin rule	Identify the worst outcomes for each decision and choose the decision associated with the maximum worst-payoff.
Minimax regret rule	Determine the worst potential regret associated with each decision, where the potential regret associated with any particular decision and state of nature is the improvement in payoff the manager could have experienced had the decision been the best one when that state of nature actually occurred. The manager chooses the decision with the minimum worst potential regret.
Equal probability rule	Assume each state of nature is equally likely to occur and compute the average payoff for each equally likely possible state of nature. Make the decision with the highest average payoff.

[3] In regression analysis, researchers typically assume the variance of the error term, and by implication, the variance of the dependent variable are constant for all values of the explanatory variables. However, when the problem of heteroscedasticity is encountered, the variance of the error term and the dependent variable are not constant. Appendix 5C in Chapter 5 briefly discusses heteroscedasticity. Heteroscedasticity can usually be corrected using special estimation techniques typically taught in econometrics courses.

[4] Some rather unusual circumstances can occur under which the expected marginal functions $E(MB)$ and $E(MC)$ could have constant variances even though the expected total functions $E(TB)$ and $E(TC)$ and expected net benefit function $E(NB)$ do not have constant variances. A discussion of these exceptions is beyond the scope of this text.

TABLE 6.4
Summary of Decision Rules under Conditions of Risk

Expected value rule	Choose the decision with the highest expected value.
Mean-variance rules	Given two risky decisions A and B:
	If decision A has a higher expected outcome *and* a lower variance than decision B, decision A should be made.
	If both decisions A and B have identical *variances* (or standard deviations), the decision with the higher expected value should be made.
	If both decisions A and B have identical *expected values*, the decision with the lower variance (standard deviation) should be made.
Coefficient of variation rule	Choose the decision with the smallest coefficient of variation.

bility that each outcome will occur. The various rules for making decisions under risk require information about several different characteristics of the probability distribution of outcomes: (1) the expected value (or mean) of the distribution, (2) the variance and standard deviation, and (3) the coefficient of variation.

The expected value (or mean) of a probability distribution is

$$E(X) = \text{Expected value of } X = \sum_{i=1}^{n} p_i X_i$$

where X_i is the ith outcome of a decision, p_i is the probability of the ith outcome, and n is the total number of possible outcomes in the probability distribution. The variance of a probability distribution measures the dispersion of the outcomes about the mean outcome. The variance is calculated as

$$\text{Variance } (X) = \sigma_x^2 = \sum_{i=1}^{n} p_i (X_i - E(X))^2$$

Because the variance is a squared term and usually much larger than the mean, the standard deviation is often used to measure the dispersion of a probability distribution:

$$\sigma_x = \sqrt{\text{Variance } (X)}$$

When the expected values of outcomes differ substantially, managers should measure riskiness of a decision relative to its expected value using the coefficient of variation:

$$\upsilon = \frac{\text{Standard deviation}}{\text{Expected value}} = \frac{\sigma}{E(X)}$$

The coefficient of variation measures the level of risk relative to the mean of the probability distribution.

When managers make decisions under risk they must incorporate the risk into their decision-making process. While there is no single decision rule that managers can follow to guarantee that profits are actually maximized, there are a number of decision rules that managers can use to help them make decisions under risk: (1) the expected value rule, (2) the mean-variance rules, and (3) the coefficient of variation rule. These three rules are summarized in Table 6.4. Like the rules for decision making under uncertainty, these rules can only guide managers in their analysis of risky decision making.

The actual decisions made by a manager will depend in large measure upon the manager's willingness to take on risk. Managers' propensity to take on risk can be classified in one of three categories: risk averse, risk loving, or risk neutral. These categories of risk preference are defined according to how that manager would choose between the following two alternatives:

A. Take a risky course of action with a known expected value and a positive variance.

B. Receive the expected value of that course of action with certainty.

A *risk-averse* person would choose to receive with certainty the expected value of the risky course of action (alternative B). A *risk-loving* person would choose the risky course of action (alternative A). A *risk-neutral* person would be indifferent between the two alternative decisions.

When managers wish to find the optimal level of a risky activity, they follow the same rule no matter what their preference for risk. When the variance of the probability on net benefit is constant at all relevant levels of activity, the optimal level of a risky activity is the level of activity with the highest expected net benefit, regardless of whether the manager is risk neutral, risk loving, or risk averse. For activities that vary continuously, expected net benefit reaches its maximum value at the level of activity for which the expected marginal benefit equals the expected marginal cost:

$$E(MB) = E(MC)$$

When the activity varies discretely, the optimal level of activity occurs at the last level of activity for which $E(MB)$ exceeds $E(MC)$.

The expected marginal benefit and expected marginal cost curves can be obtained using the techniques of regression analysis presented in Chapter 5. As explained there, the predicted value of Y is correctly interpreted as the expected value of Y given a particular value of X. Thus, the optimal level of a risky activity can be found by equating marginal benefit and marginal cost curves that are estimated using regression analysis.

TECHNICAL PROBLEMS

1. Consider the following two probability distributions for sales:

Sales (in 1,000 units)	Distribution 1 probability (percent)	Distribution 2 probability (percent)
50	10	10
60	20	15
70	40	20
80	20	30
90	10	25

   a. Graph the two distributions shown in the above table. What are the expected sales for the two probability distributions?
   b. Calculate the variance and standard deviation for both distributions. Which distribution is more risky?
   c. Calculate the coefficient of variation for both distributions. Which distribution is more risky?

* 2. A firm is making its production plans for next quarter, but the manager of the firm does not know what the price of the product will be next month. He believes that there is a 40 percent probability the price will be $15 and a 60 percent probability the price will be $20. The manager must decide whether to produce 7,000 units or 8,000 units of output. The following table shows the four possible profit outcomes, depending on which output management chooses and which price actually occurs.

	Profit (loss) when price Is	
	$15	$20
Option A: produce 7,100	−$3,730	+$31,770
Option B: produce 8,000	−$6,000	+$34,000

   a. If the manager chooses the option with the higher expected profits, which output is chosen?
   b. Which option is the more risky?

c. What is the decision if the manager uses the mean-variance rules to decide between the two options?
d. What is the decision using the coefficient of variation rule?

3. Suppose in the above problem that the price probabilities are reversed: The manager expects a price of $15 with a probability of 60 percent and a price of $20 with a probability of 40 percent. Answer all parts of problem 2 under the assumption of these reversed probabilities. What would the probabilities have to be to make the expected values of the two options equal?

* 4. Suppose the manager in problem 2 has absolutely no idea about the probabilities of the two prices occurring. Which option would the manager choose under each of the following decision rules?
a. Maximax rule
b. Maximin rule
c. Minimax regret rule
d. Equal probability rule

5. A project with a higher standard deviation in returns is said to be a more risky project than one with a lower standard deviation.
a. In what sense is it more risky?
b. What kinds of risks are not captured by this definition of risk?
c. Can you think of another, perhaps better, definition of risk than standard deviation using the term "risk" in its general definition? If it is a better definition, why?

6. The following table shows the expected marginal benefits and expected marginal costs associated with 100, 200, 300, and 400 units of an activity and the associated variances for each level of activity.

	Marginal benefit		Marginal cost	
Activity level	Expected *MB*	Variance of *MB*	Expected *MC*	Variance of *MC*
100	$62	756	$50	336
200	58	756	55	336
300	52	756	56	336
400	46	756	60	336

a. If the decision maker is risk neutral, what level of the activity would be chosen?
b. How might the decision change (if it would change) if the manager is risk loving?
c. How might the decision change if the manager is risk averse?

7. Consider a firm that is deciding whether to operate plants only in the United States or also in either or both Mexico and Canada. Congress is currently discussing an overseas investment in new capital (OINC) tax credit for US firms that operate plants outside the country. If Congress passes OINC in 1996, management expects to do well if it is operating plants in Mexico and Canada. If OINC does not pass in 1996 and the firm does operate plants in Mexico and Canada, it will incur rather large losses. It is also possible that Congress will table OINC in 1996 and wait until 1997 to vote on it. The profit payoff matrix (profits in 1996) is shown below:

	States of nature		
	OINC passes	OINC fails	OINC stalls
Operate plants in US only	$10 million	−$1 million	$2 million
Operate plants in US and Mexico	$15 million	−$4 million	$1.5 million
Operate plants in US, Mexico, Canada	$20 million	−$6 million	$4 million

Assuming the managers of this firm have no idea about the likelihood of Congressional action on OINC in 1996, what decision should the firm make using the following rules?

a. Maximax rule
b. Maximin rule
c. Minimax regret rule
d. Equal probability rule

APPLIED PROBLEMS

1. Suppose your company's method of making decisions under risk is "making the best out of the worst possible outcome." What rule would you be forced to follow?
2. "A portfolio manager needs to pick winners—assets or securities with high expected returns and low risk." What is wrong with this statement?
3. Remox Corporation is a British firm that sells high-fashion sportswear in the United States. Congress is currently considering the imposition of a protective tariff on imported textiles. Remox is considering the possibility of moving 50 percent of its production to the United States to avoid the tariff. This would be accomplished by opening a plant in the United States. The table below lists the profit outcomes under various scenarios:

	Profit in 1996	
	No tariff	Tariff
Option A: Produce all output in Britain	1,200,000	800,000
Option B: Produce 50 percent in the United States	875,000	1,000,000

Remox hires a consulting firm to assess the probability that a tariff on imported textiles will in fact pass a congressional vote and not be vetoed by the president. They forecast the following probabilities:

	Probability
Tariff will pass	30 percent
Tariff will fail	70 percent

a. Compute the expected profits for both options.
b. Based upon the expected profit only, which option should Remox choose?
c. Compute the probabilities that would make Remox indifferent between options A and B using that rule.
d. Compute the standard deviations for options A and B facing Remox Corporation.
e. What decision would Remox make using the mean-variance rule?
f. What decision would Remox make using the coefficient of variation rule?

4. Using the information in Problem 3 what decision would Remox make if it had no idea of the probability of a tariff using the following rule.
   a. Maximax
   b. Maximin
   c. Minimax regret
   d. Equal probability criterion
5. Return to Technical Problem 7 and suppose the managers of the firm decide on the following subjective probabilities of congressional action on OINC:

OINC passes	40 percent
OINC fails	10 percent
OINC stalls	50 percent

   a. Compute the expected profits for all three decisions.
   b. Using the expected value rule, which option should the managers choose?
   c. Compute the standard deviations for all three decisions. Using the mean-variance rules does any one of the decisions dominate? If so, which one?
   d. What decision would the firm make using the coefficient of variation rule?

APPENDIX Maximization of Expected Net Benefit

Let total benefit (TB) and total cost (TC) be random variables. Net benefit is a random variable equal to the difference between total benefit and total cost:

$$NB = TB - TC$$

Following the summation rule for expected values which is presented in any textbook on mathematical statistics, the expected net benefit is equal to the difference between expected total benefit and expected total cost:

$$E(NB \mid X) = E(TB \mid X) - E(TC \mid X)$$

where $E(\cdot \mid X)$ denotes the expected value of benefits or costs *given* the level of activity X.

The first order condition for a maximum of $E(NB \mid X)$ is

$$d[E(NB \mid X)]/dX = d[E(TB \mid X)]/dX - d[E(TC \mid X)]/dX = 0$$

which can also be expressed as

$$E(dTB/dX) - E(dTC/dX) = 0$$

and

$$E(dTB/dX) = E(dTC/dX)$$

Thus, maximizing expected net benefit requires the level of activity be chosen so that expected marginal benefit equals expected marginal cost.

PART

Demand

Theory and Empirical Analysis

CHAPTER 7

Theory of Consumer Behavior

Managers are obviously interested in obtaining information about the demand for the goods and services they sell. Firms spend a great deal of time and money trying to estimate and forecast the demand for their products. Even government policymakers are interested in the demand for certain products, such as energy, housing, agricultural products, health care, and government services.

Obtaining accurate estimates of demand requires a thorough understanding of the underpinnings of demand functions. Such understanding requires a certain amount of familiarity with the theory of consumer behavior. The theory of consumer behavior explains why consumers choose the goods and services they purchase, why they choose the particular *amounts* of the products they purchase, and why different consumers make different choices. Therefore, the theory of consumer behavior provides the foundation for the study of consumer demand.

This chapter sets forth the most important aspects of the theory of consumer behavior. As you will see, the basic theory of consumer behavior is really quite simple. It follows directly from the theory of constrained maximization described in Chapter 4. (As you read this chapter, you may want to look back at Chapter 4 to see how closely the analysis here follows that general framework.) Few, if any, people have incomes sufficient to buy as much as they desire of every good or service. Consumers are constrained by the amount of their incomes. Therefore, consumers attempt to maximize their satisfaction from the goods and services they purchase, given the constraint of a limited income.

Before explaining why people choose the particular combination of goods and services they buy, rather than some other combination, we will develop two new tools of analysis. These tools are indispensable for the graphical analysis of consumer behavior. The first tool, indifference curves, depicts consumer preferences graphically by showing the rate at which consumers are willing to substitute one good for another. The second tool, budget lines, shows graphically the various combinations of goods that a consumer is able to purchase with a given money income at given prices of the goods. You might recall that a demand function indicates how much of a good a consumer is both willing and able to purchase at each price. Combining indifference curves and budget lines illustrates what a consumer is willing and able to do. We will therefore put the two together in order to develop the theory of consumer behavior and show how the theory is related to demand functions.

We will also use the theory of consumer behavior to explain more rigorously than we did in Chapter 2 why demand curves are downward sloping. We end the chapter with an analysis of consumer behavior under risk, that is, when the consumer does not have complete information about a purchasing decision. In this discussion we make use of the methods of risk analysis developed in Chapter 6.

When you finish this chapter, you will have a good understanding of why consumers choose to purchase a particular bundle of products and why they do not choose some other bundle. You will therefore understand the underpinnings of demand functions, which will give some insight into the way managers can estimate and forecast the demand for their products, the subject of the next two chapters.

7.1 UTILITY

We noted in the introduction to this chapter that the theory of consumer behavior is based upon the principle of constrained maximization as set forth in Chapter 4. Recall that constrained maximization means that a decision maker chooses the levels of activities in order to attain the most benefits possible within a given constraint. For a consumer, the constraint is obvious—the consumer's income and the prices that must be paid for the activities, which are the amounts of goods and services the consumer purchases. In this section, we will first address the problem of measuring the benefits obtained from consuming goods and services. We will then develop the concept of a utility function—a key concept in the analysis of consumer behavior.

The Problem of Measuring Benefits from Consumption

We have thus far referred to the benefits forthcoming from the consumption of goods and services as "satisfaction." Satisfaction, however, is not really a good word. Is anyone ever completely satisfied with what is presently being consumed? Most people always want more, and this is natural. "Happiness" is another word that might describe the benefits from consumption. But some people never seem happy, no matter what they can purchase. Others appear happy in almost any circumstance.

utility
Benefits consumers obtain from the goods and services they consume.

For want of a better name, economists have traditionally named the benefits consumers obtain from the goods and services they consume **utility**. This is not completely descriptive either. Utility implies usefulness, and many of the products most of us consume may not be particularly useful. Many people are willing to pay a lot more for a Mercedes or BMW than they would pay for a Geo, which may well be just as useful. And people can differ drastically over what is and is not useful. A child would probably consider a Nintendo game more useful than new clothes, while the parents would have the opposite opinion. Most people probably buy a lot of things that others would not consider particularly useful. Nonetheless, we will follow tradition and refer to the benefits obtained from goods and services as utility. If you can come up with a better name, feel free to use it.

Settling on a name for the benefits does not solve the problem of how to measure these benefits from consumption. Who could say how many units of benefit, or how much utility, they receive by consuming an ice cream cone, or a pizza, or from a visit to the dentist? After all, it is not possible to plug a "utility meter" into a consumer's ear and measure the amount of utility generated by consuming some good or service. And even if we could measure utility, what units or denomination would we use? In previous classes, we have used terms such as "utils," which is too serious, "globs," which is too frivolous, "bushels," which is too precise, and others we need not mention. Over time, we have settled on the phrase "units of utility," which is certainly pedestrian and dull, but it seems as good a name as any.

The Utility Function

utility function
Shows an individual's perception of the level of utility that would be attained from consuming each conceivable bundle of goods: $U = f(X, Y)$.

The concept of consumer utility is best expressed as a **utility function**. A utility function shows an individual's perception of the level of utility that would be attained from consuming each conceivable bundle or combination of goods and services. A simple form of a utility function for a person who consumes only two goods, X and Y, might be

$$U = f(X,Y)$$

where X and Y are, respectively, the amounts of goods X and Y consumed, f means "a function of" or "depends upon," and U is the amount of utility the person receives from each combination of X and Y. Thus, utility depends upon the quantities consumed of X and Y.

The actual numbers assigned to the levels of utility are arbitrary. It is inconceivable that anyone could actually assign specific numbers for the amount of utility received from consuming every possible combination of goods. Therefore, a utility function is a theoretical concept that proves useful in analysis. We need only say that if a consumer prefers one combination of goods, say $20X$ and $30Y$, to some other combination, say $15X$ and $32Y$, the amount of utility derived from the first bundle is greater than the amount from the second. It makes no difference if the amount of utility assigned to the first bundle is 150 and the amount to the second is 100, or if the first number if 90 and the second is 80. The only thing that matters is that

$$U = f(20,30) > U = f(15,32)$$

Later in this section, we will return to the assumption that a consumer can rank different bundles of goods in order of preference without being able to assign specific numbers to the amount of utility.

For analytical simplicity and graphical convenience we will analyze the case of a consumer choosing between only two goods or services. The utility function will therefore be specified as above. We could express a utility function with any number of goods and services. Such a utility function would be

$$U = f(X_1, X_2, X_3, \ldots, X_n)$$

where X_i is the amount of the ith good or service, and U is an index of utility depending on the quantities consumed of goods $X_1, X_2, X_3, \ldots, X_n$. We should emphasize, however, that the two-good approach enables us to derive every important theoretical concept that can be derived from the n-good model and is far less complex analytically.

Assumptions about Utility Functions

As with all economic models, the theory of consumer behavior employs some simplifying assumptions. These assumptions permit us to go directly to the fundamental determinants of consumer behavior and to abstract away from the less important aspects of the consumer's decision process. Let us briefly describe these assumptions.

Complete information

We assume for now that consumers have complete information pertaining to their consumption decisions. They know the full range of goods and services available and the capacity of each to provide utility. Further, the price of each good is known exactly, as is each consumer's income during the time period in question.

Admittedly, to assume perfect knowledge is an abstraction from reality, but the assumption of complete information does not distort the relevant aspects of real-world consumer decisions. It allows us to concentrate on how real consumption choices are made without becoming bogged down with extraneous details. Later in the chapter, we will relax the assumption of complete information and examine consumer behavior when consumers must devote time and money to search for information about product prices and quality.

Preference ordering

The second assumption is that consumers are able to rank all conceivable bundles of commodities on the basis of the ability of each bundle to provide utility. When confronted with two or more bundles of goods, consumers can determine their order of preference among them.

As an example, suppose a consumer is confronted with two bundles consisting of different combinations of two goods. Bundle A consists of five candy bars and one soft drink. Bundle B consists of three candy bars and three soft drinks.

Ranking the two bundles, the person can make one of three possible responses: (1) I prefer bundle A to bundle B, (2) I prefer bundle B to bundle A, or (3) I would be equally satisfied with either.

The same is true when ranking any two bundles of goods and services. The consumer either prefers one bundle to the other or is indifferent between the two. A consumer who is indifferent between two bundles clearly feels that either bundle would yield the same level of utility. A preferred bundle would yield more utility than the other, less-preferred bundle. We can summarize this discussion in a principle:

Principle Consumers have a preference pattern that (1) establishes a rank ordering of all bundles of goods and (2) compares all pairs of bundles, indicating that bundle *A* is preferred to bundle *B*, *B* is preferred to *A*, or the consumer is indifferent between *A* and *B*. In a three- (or more) way comparison, if *A* is preferred (indifferent) to *B*, and *B* is preferred (indifferent) to *C*, *A* must be preferred (indifferent) to *C*.

7.2 INDIFFERENCE CURVES AND MAPS

indifference curve
A locus of points, representing different bundles of goods and services, each of which yields the same level of total utility or satisfaction.

A fundamental tool for the analysis of consumer behavior is an **indifference curve**, defined as a locus of points, representing different bundles of goods and services, each of which yields an individual the same level of total utility or satisfaction. Indifference curves provide a means of depicting graphically the preferences of a consumer.

For simplicity we will continue to assume that the consumer chooses among bundles consisting of only two goods. This assumption enables us to explain and analyze consumer behavior using two-dimensional graphs.

Figure 7.1 shows a representative indifference curve with the typically assumed slope. The quantity of some good X is plotted along the horizontal axis; the quantity of good Y is plotted along the vertical axis.

All combinations of goods X and Y along indifference curve I yield the consumer the same level of utility. In other words, the consumer is indifferent among all points such as A, with 10 units of X and 60 units of Y; point B, with $20X$ and $40Y$; point C, with $40X$ and $20Y$; and so on. At any point on I, it is possible to take away some amount of X and add some amount of Y (though not necessarily the same amount) and leave the consumer with the same level of utility. Conversely, we can add X and take away just enough Y to make the consumer indifferent between the two combinations.

An indifference curve is downward sloping. This assumption reflects the fact that the consumer obtains utility from both goods. Thus, if more X is added, some Y must be taken away in order to maintain the same level of utility. If the curve in Figure 7.1 would begin to slope upward at, say, 70 units of X, it would mean that the consumer has so much X that any additional X would reduce utility if the quantity of Y remains constant. In such a case, to keep the consumer at the same level of utility when X is added, more Y would have to be added to compensate for the lost utility from having more X. Likewise, if the curve begins to bend backward at, say, 75 units of Y, it would mean that the consumer experiences reduced levels of utility with increases in Y.

FIGURE 7.1
A Typical Indifference Curve

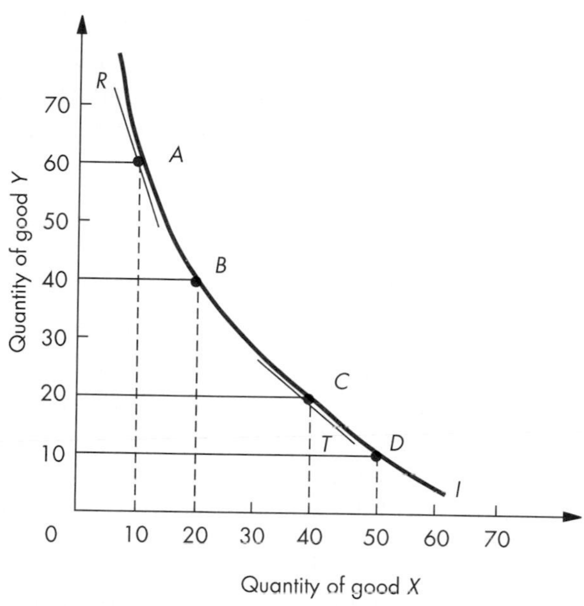

Indifference curves are convex. This shape requires that as the consumption of X is increased relative to Y, the consumer is willing to accept a smaller reduction in Y for an equal increase in X, in order to stay at the same level of utility. This property is apparent in Figure 7.1. Begin at point A with 10 units of X and 60 units of Y. In order to increase the consumption of X by 10 units, to 20, the consumer is willing to reduce the consumption of Y by 20 units, to 40. Given indifference curve I, the consumer will be indifferent between the two combinations represented by A and B. Next begin at C, with 40X and 20Y. From this point, to gain an additional 10 units of X (move to point D), the consumer is willing to give up only 10 units of Y, much less than the 20 units willingly given up to obtain 10 more units of A. The convexity of indifference curves implies a diminishing marginal rate of substitution, to which we now turn.

Marginal Rate of Substitution

marginal rate of substitution The marginal rate of substitution measures the number of units of Y that must be given up per unit of X added so as to maintain a constant level of utility.

An important concept in indifference curve analysis is the marginal rate of substitution. The **marginal rate of substitution** of X for Y measures the number of units of Y that must be given up per unit of X added so as to maintain a constant level of unity. For extremely small changes in X and Y, the marginal rate of substitution is given by the negative of the slope of an indifference curve at a point. It is defined only for movements along a given curve.

Returning to Figure 7.1, you can see that the consumer is indifferent between combinations A (10X and 60Y) and B (20X and 40Y). Thus the rate at which the consumer is willing to substitute is

$$\frac{\Delta Y}{\Delta X} = \frac{60 - 40}{10 - 20} = -\frac{20}{10} = -2$$

The marginal rate of substitution is 2, meaning that the consumer is willing to give up 2 units of Y for each unit of X added. Since it would be cumbersome to have the minus sign on the right side of the equation, the marginal rate of substitution is defined as

$$MRS = -\frac{\Delta Y}{\Delta X} = 2$$

For the movement from C to D along I, the marginal rate of substitution is

$$MRS = -\frac{\Delta Y}{\Delta X} = -\frac{(20 - 10)}{(40 - 50)} = \frac{10}{10} = 1$$

In this case the consumer is willing to give up only 1 unit of Y per additional unit of X added.

Therefore, the marginal rate of substitution diminishes along an indifference curve. When consumers have a small amount of X relative to Y, they are willing to give up a lot of Y to gain another unit of X. When they have less Y relative to X, they are willing to give up less Y in order to gain another unit of X.

The marginal rate of substitution is, as noted, the negative of the slope of an indifference curve for small changes in X and Y. For example, the negative of the slope of the tangent R at point A is the marginal rate of substitution at that point. This slope indicates how much Y the consumer is willing to give up if X is increased by a very small amount. The same is the case for tangent T at point C. Looking at these tangents, it is easily seen that the slope of the indifference curve, and hence the marginal rate of substitution, declines as X is increased relative to Y.

Relation Indifference curves are negatively sloped and convex. Therefore, if the consumption of one good is increased, consumption of the other must be reduced to maintain a constant level of utility. The marginal rate of substitution—the negative of the slope of the indifference curve—diminishes as the consumer moves downward along an indifference curve, increasing X relative to Y.

Indifference Maps

An indifference map is simply a graph showing a set of two or more indifference curves. Figure 7.2 shows a typical indifference map, made up of four indifference curves, *I*, *II*, *III*, and *IV*. Any indifference curve lying above and to the right of another represents a higher level of utility. Thus any combination of X and Y on *IV* is preferred to any combination on *III*, any combination on *III* is preferred to any on *II*, and so on. All bundles of goods on the same indifference curve are equivalent; all combinations lying on a higher curve are preferred.

The indifference map in Figure 7.2 consists of only four indifference curves. We could have drawn many, many more. In fact, the X-Y space actually contains an infinite number of indifference curves. Each point in the space lies on one and only one indifference curve; that is, indifference curves cannot intersect.

FIGURE 7.2
Indifference Map

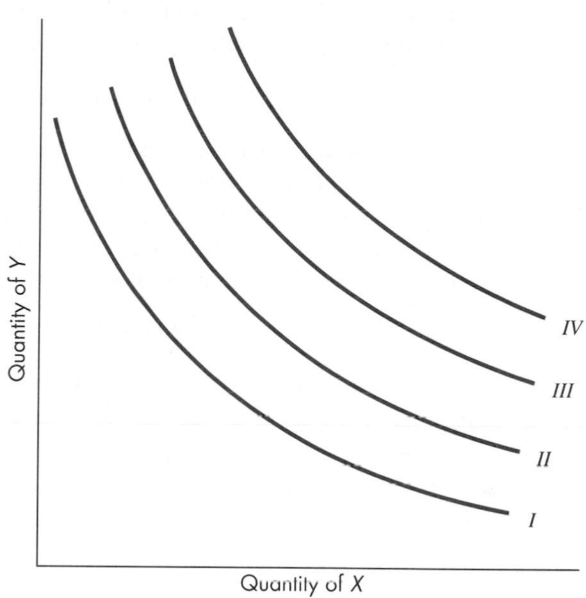

Relation An indifference map consists of several indifference curves. The higher (or further to the right) an indifference curve, the greater the level of utility associated with the curve. Combinations of goods on higher indifference curves are preferred to combinations on lower curves.

A Marginal Utility Interpretation of *MRS*

marginal utility
The addition to total utility that is attributable to the addition of one unit of a good to the current rate of consumption, holding constant the amounts of all other goods consumed.

The concept of *marginal utility* can give additional insight into the properties of indifference curves, particularly the slope of indifference curves. **Marginal utility** is the addition to total utility that is attributable to consuming one more unit of a good, holding constant the amounts of all other goods consumed. Economists typically assume that as the consumption of a good increases, the marginal utility from an additional unit of the good dimimishes. While diminishing marginal utility cannot be proven theoretically, falling marginal utility appears to characterize the pattern of consumption for most people with most goods.

Just imagine how you feel about the soft drinks you consume at a football game on a hot day. The first soft drink boosts your utility by a substantial amount. The second soft drink does taste good, and it increases your utility, but the increase in utility is not as great as it was for the first soft drink. So while the marginal utility of the second soft drink is positive, it is smaller than the marginal utility of the first soft drink. Similarly, the third and fourth soft drinks also make you feel better (i.e., increase your utility), but by successively smaller amounts. This illustrates the concept of diminishing marginal utility.

While some economists object to the concept of marginal utility on the grounds that utility is not measurable, many other economists find it useful to relate marginal utility to the marginal rate of substitution along an indifference curve. The change in total utility that results when both X and Y change by small amounts is related to the marginal utilities of X and Y as[1]

$$\Delta U = (MU_x \times \Delta X) + (MU_y \times \Delta Y)$$

where MU_x and MU_y are the marginal utilities of X and Y, respectively. To illustrate this relation, suppose a consumer increases consumption of X by two units ($\Delta X = 2$) and decreases consumption of Y by one unit ($\Delta Y = -1$). Further suppose the marginal utility of X is 25 for each additional unit of X, and the marginal utility of Y is 10. The amount by which utility changes is computed as

$$\Delta U = (25 \times 2) + (10 \times -1) = 40$$

Consuming two more X and one less Y causes total utility to rise by 40 units of utility.

For points on a given indifference curve, all combinations of goods yield the same level of utility, so ΔU is zero for all changes in X and Y that would keep the consumer on the same indifference curve. From the above equation, if $\Delta U = 0$, it follows that

$$\Delta U = 0 = (MU_x \times \Delta X) + (MU_y \times \Delta Y)$$

Therefore, solving for $-\Delta Y/\Delta X$,

$$-\frac{\Delta Y}{\Delta X} = \frac{MU_x}{MU_y}$$

where $-\Delta Y/\Delta X$ is the negative of the slope of the indifference curve, or the marginal rate of substitution. Thus, we have shown that the marginal rate of substitution can be interpreted as the ratio of the marginal utility of X divided by the marginal utility of Y:

$$MRS = MU_x/MU_y$$

7.3 THE CONSUMER'S BUDGET CONSTRAINT

Indifference curves are derived from the preference patterns of consumers. As such, they provide a method of analyzing what consumers are willing to do. Recall from Chapter 2 that demand functions indicate what consumers are both *willing and able* to do. Consumers are constrained in what they are able to do by the market-determined prices and their income. We now turn to an analysis of the constraint that consumers face.

[1]Note that we have stretched one of the assumptions in this analysis. Recall that marginal utility is the increase in utility from a one-unit increase in the rate of consumption in a good, holding the consumption of all other goods constant. In this example, we speak of marginal utility while letting the consumption of both goods change at the same time. However, if the change in each is small, this presents little or no problem.

Budget Lines

If consumers had unlimited money incomes there would be no problem of economizing. People could buy whatever they wanted and would have no problem of choice. But this is not generally the case.

Consumers normally have limited incomes. Their problem is to spend this limited income in a way that gives the maximum possible utility. The constraint faced by consumers can be illustrated graphically.

Continue to assume the consumer buys only two goods, bought in quantities X and Y. The consumer has a fixed money income of \$1,000, which is the maximum amount that can be spent on the two goods. For simplicity, assume the entire income is spent on X and Y.[2] If the price of X is \$5 per unit and the price of Y is \$10 per unit, the amount spent on X ($\$5 \times X$) plus the amount spent on Y ($\$10 \times Y$) must equal the \$1,000 income constraint:

$$\$5X + \$10Y = \$1{,}000$$

Alternatively, solving for Y in terms of X,

$$Y = \frac{\$1{,}000}{\$10} - \frac{\$5}{\$10}X = 100 - \frac{1}{2}X$$

budget line The locus of all bundles of goods that can be purchased at given prices if the entire money income is spent.

The graph of this equation, shown in Figure 7.3, is a straight line, and is called the *budget line*. A **budget line** is the locus of all combinations or bundles of goods that can be purchased at given prices if the entire money income is spent.

To purchase any one of the bundles of X and Y on the budget line AB in Figure 7.3, the consumer spends exactly \$1,000. If the consumer decides to spend all \$1,000 on good Y and spend nothing on good X, 100 (= \$1,000/\$10) units of Y can be purchased (point A in Figure 7.3). If the consumer spends all \$1,000 on X and buys no Y, 200 (= \$1,000/\$5) units of X can be purchased (point B). In Figure 7.3, consumption bundles C, with $40X$ and $80Y$, and D, with $120X$ and $40Y$, represent two other combinations of goods X and Y that can be purchased by spending exactly \$1,000, because ($80 \times \$10$) + ($40 \times \$5$) = \$1,000 and ($40 \times \$10$) + ($120 \times \$5$) = \$1,000.

The slope of the budget line, $-1/2$ ($=\Delta Y/\Delta X$), indicates the amount of Y that must be given up if one more unit of X is purchased. For every additional unit of X purchased, the consumer must spend \$5 more on good X. To continue meeting the budget constraint, \$5 less must be spent on good Y; thus the consumer must give up 1/2 of a unit of Y. To illustrate this point, suppose the consumer is currently purchasing bundle D, but wishes to move to bundle E, which is composed of one more unit of X and 1/2 a unit less of Y (see the blowup in Figure 7.3). Bundles D and E both cost \$1,000 to purchase, but the consumer must trade off 1/2 of a unit of good Y for the extra unit of good X in bundle E. Note also that

[2]More advanced theories permit consumers to save and borrow between periods. We shall address these more complicated topics later when we analyze the effect of time and the interest rate.

FIGURE 7.3

A Consumer's Budget Constraint

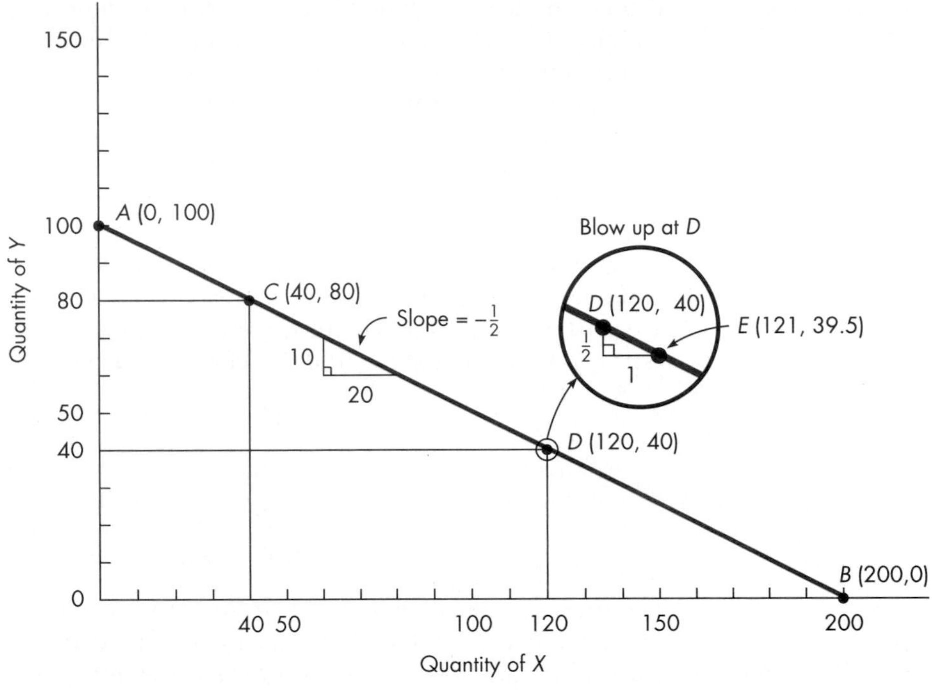

if the consumer buys one *fewer* unit of X, then an *additional* 1/2 unit of Y can be purchased with the same money income.

The rate at which the consumer can trade off Y for one more unit of X is equal to the price of good X (here \$5) divided by the price of good Y (here \$10); that is,

$$\text{the slope of the budget line} = -P_x/P_y$$

where P_x and P_y are the prices of goods X and Y, respectively. In Figure 7.3, the slope of the budget line is –1/2, which equals –\$5/\$10.

The relation between money income (M) and the amount of goods X and Y purchased can be expressed in general as:

$$M = P_xX + P_yY$$

This equation can be rewritten in the form of a straight line,

$$Y = \frac{M}{P_y} - \frac{P_x}{P_y}X$$

The first term, M/P_y, gives the amount of Y the consumer can buy if no X is purchased. As noted, $-P_x/P_y$ is the slope of the budget line and indicates how much Y must be given up for an additional unit of X.

FIGURE 7.4
A Typical Budget Line

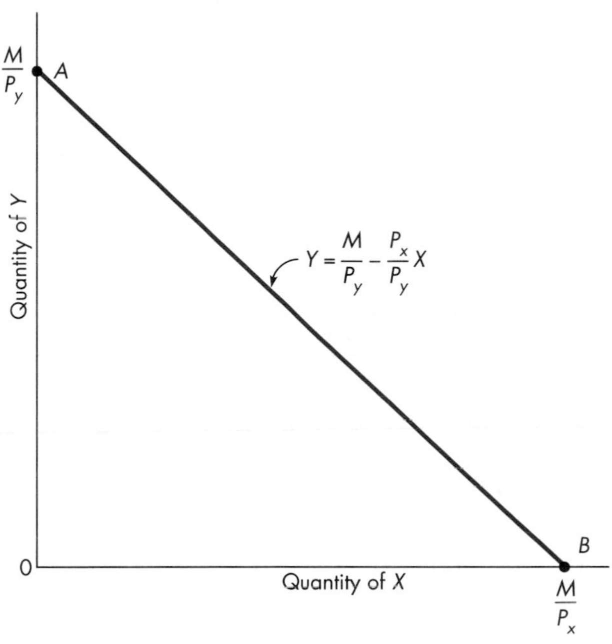

The general form of a typical budget line is shown in Figure 7.4. The line *AB* shows all combinations of *Y* and *X* that can be purchased with the given money income (*M*) and given prices of the goods (P_x and P_y). The intercept on the *Y* axis, *A*, is M/P_y; the horizontal intercept, *B*, is M/P_x. The slope of the budget line is $-P_x/P_y$. Note that this slope can be derived by the typical "rise-over-run" formula, $-(M/P_y \div M/P_x) = -P_x/P_y$.

Shifting the Budget Line

If money income (*M*) or the price ratio (P_x/P_y) changes, the budget line must change. Panel A of Figure 7.5 shows the effect of changes in income. Begin with the original budget line, *AB*, which corresponds to $1,000 money income and prices of *X* and *Y* of $5 and $10, respectively. Next let money income increase to $1,200, holding the prices of *X* and *Y* constant. Since the prices do not change, the slope of the budget line remains the same (–1/2). But since money income increases, the vertical intercept (M/P_y) increases (shifts upward) to 120 (= $1,200/$100). That is, if the consumer now spends the entire income on good *Y*, 20 more units of *Y* can be purchased than was previously the case. The horizontal intercept (M/P_x) also increases (to 240 = $1,200/$5). The result of an increase in income is, therefore, a parallel shift in the budget line from *AB* to *RN*. The increase in income increases the set of combinations of the goods that can be purchased.

FIGURE 7.5
Shifting Budget Lines

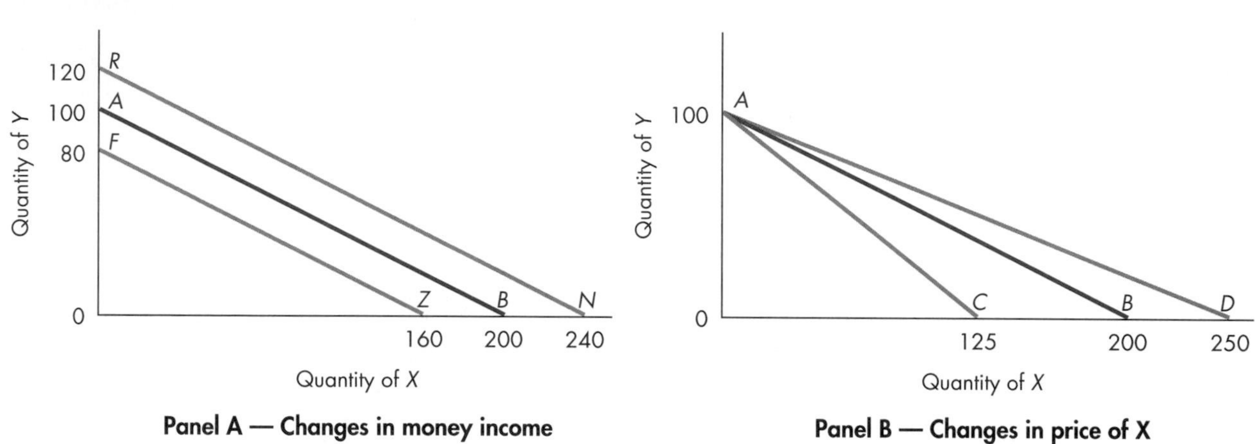

Panel A — Changes in money income

Panel B — Changes in price of X

Alternatively, begin once more with budget line *AB*, then let money income decrease to \$800. In this case the set of possible combinations of goods decreases. The vertical and horizontal intercepts decrease to 80 and 160, respectively, causing a parallel shift in the budget line to *FZ*, with intercepts of 80 and 160.

Panel B shows the effect of changes in the price of good *X*. Begin as before with the original budget line *AB* , then let the price of *X* fall from \$5 to \$4 per unit. Since M/P_y does not change, the vertical intercept remains at *B* (100 units of *Y*). However, when P_x decreases, the absolute value of the slope (P_x/P_y) falls to 4/10 (= \$4/\$10). In this case, the budget line becomes less steep. After the price of *X* falls, more *X* can be purchased if the entire money income is spent on *X*. Thus the horizontal intercept increases from 200 units to 250 units of *X*. In Panel B the budget line pivots (or rotates) from *AB* to *AD*.

An increase in the price of good *X* to \$8 causes the budget line to pivot backward, from *AB* to *AC*. The intercept on the horizontal axis decreases to 125 (= \$1,000/\$8). When P_x increases to \$8, the absolute value of the slope of the line, P_x/P_y, increases to 8/10 (= \$8/\$10). The budget line becomes steeper when P_x rises, while the vertical intercept remains constant.

Relation An increase (decrease) in money income causes a parallel outward (backward) shift in the budget line. An increase (decrease) in the price of *X* causes the budget line to pivot backward (outward) around the original vertical intercept.

7.4 UTILITY MAXIMIZATION

We have now set forth the tools needed to analyze the utility maximization problem. The budget line shows all bundles of commodities that are available to the consumer, given the limited income and market-determined prices. The in-

FIGURE 7.6
Constrained Utility Maximization

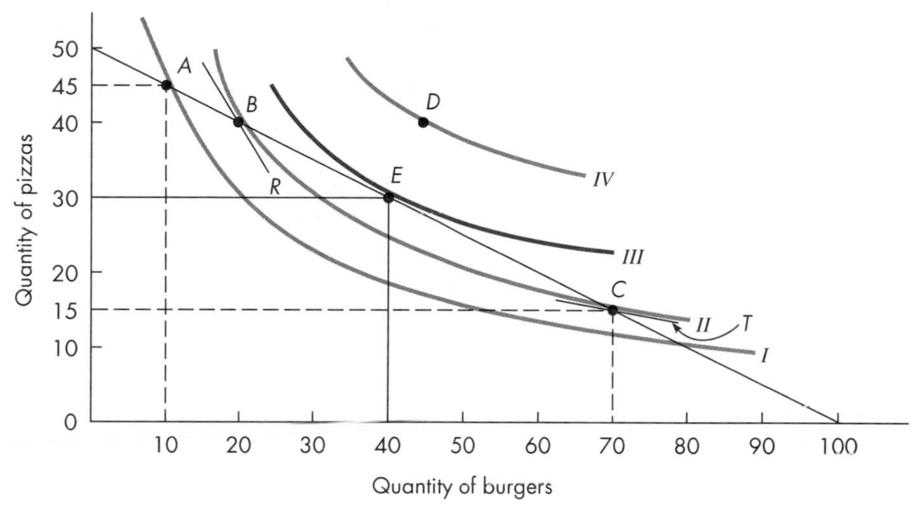

difference map shows the preference ordering of all conceivable bundles of goods. The consumer's task is to choose, from all available combinations of goods, the combination that yields the highest attainable level of utility.

Maximizing Utility Subject to a Limited Money Income[3]

We will illustrate the maximization process graphically with the use of a rather farfetched example. Joan Johnson is a young, overworked, underpaid management trainee working for a large corporation. Johnson's monthly food budget is $400, which, because she works such long hours, is spent only on pizzas and burgers. The price of a pizza is $8, and the price of a burger is $4. The water, with which she washes down the burgers and pizzas, is free. Johnson's task is to determine the combination of pizzas and burgers that yields the highest level of utility possible from the $400 food budget at the given prices.

The maximization process is shown graphically in Figure 7.6. Indifference curves *I* through *IV* represent a portion of Johnson's indifference map between pizzas, plotted along the vertical axis, and burgers, plotted along the horizontal axis. Her budget line, from 50 pizzas to 100 burgers, shows all combinations of the two fast foods that Johnson can consume during a month. If she spends the entire $400 on pizzas at $8 each, she can consume 50 pizzas. If she spends the entire $400 on burgers at $4 each, she can consume 100 burgers. Or she can consume any other combination on the line. The slope of the budget line is the price of burgers divided by the price of pizzas, or $P_B/P_P = \$4/\$8 = 1/2$. The slope

[3]A mathematical approach to constrained utility maximization is provided in the appendix to this chapter.

indicates that to consume one additional $4 burger, Johnson must give up 1/2 of an $8 pizza. Alternatively, one more pizza can be bought at a cost of two burgers.

As is clear from the graph, the highest possible level of utility is reached when Johnson purchases 30 pizzas and 40 burgers a month. This combination is represented by point *E*, at which the budget line is tangent to indifference curve *III*. Many other combinations of the two fast foods, such as 40 pizzas and 45 burgers at point *D* on indifference curve *IV*, are preferable to the combination at *E*, but these other combinations cannot be purchased at the given prices and the $400 income. For example, 40 pizzas and 45 burgers would cost $500. All such bundles lie outside of Johnson's budget constraint.

Johnson can purchase many combinations along her budget line other than the one at point *E*. These other combinations all lie on lower indifference curves and are therefore less preferred. Consider the combination at point *A*, consisting of 45 pizzas and 10 burgers. This combination can be purchased with the $400 income but, because it is on indifference curve *I*, it clearly gives a lower level of utility than combination *E* on indifference curve *III*. If Johnson is consuming the combination at point *A*, she can increase the number of burgers, decrease the number of pizzas at the rate of one more burger for 1/2 less pizza, and move down the budget line. This substitution leads to higher and higher levels of utility—for example, 40 pizzas and 20 burgers (combination *B*) are on indifference curve *II* and therefore provide more utility than combination *A* on curve *I*. Johnson should not stop at *B*. She should continue substituting pizzas for burgers until point *E* on curve *III* is attained. Thus, every combination on the budget line above point *E* represents a lower level of utility than can be attained by consuming 30 pizzas and 40 burgers.

Alternatively, suppose Johnson is consuming 15 pizzas and 70 burgers—combination *C*. This combination is on indifference curve *II*, which is below *III* and therefore represents a lower level of utility than combination *E*. Johnson can increase the number of pizzas and decrease the number of burgers at the rate of 1/2 pizza for every burger given up, and move to higher indifference curves. She should continue substituting pizzas for burgers until combination *E* is reached. Thus, every combination on the budget line below *E* represents a lower level of utility than is attainable with 30 pizzas and 40 burgers.

By elimination, we have shown that every other combination on the budget line yields less utility than combination *E*. Thus, utility is maximized with the given income and prices when Johnson consumes at point *E*, the point at which the budget line is tangent to indifference curve *III*, the highest attainable indifference curve. It therefore follows that the highest attainable level of utility is reached by consuming the combination at which the marginal rate of substitution (the slope of the indifference curve) equals the price ratio (the slope of the budget line).

We can use this relation between the *MRS* and the price ratio, or slope of the budget line, to provide more insight into why every other combination on the budget line yields less utility than the combination at point *E* (Figure 7.6). Consider again the combination at *B*, with 40 pizzas and 20 burgers. At this combination, the *MRS* (the slope of indifference curve *II*) is greater than the slope of the budget line, $P_B/P_P = 1/2$. Suppose the *MRS* at *B* is 2 (the slope of tangent *R* equals 2). This means that Johnson, in order to obtain one more burger, is *just* willing to exchange two pizzas. Exchanging two pizzas for one more burger leaves Johnson at the same level of utility—she is made no better and no worse off by this exchange. If Johnson could get one burger and give up *less* than two pizzas, she would be better off. Since burgers cost only 1/2 as much as pizzas, the market allows Johnson to obtain one more burger while only giving up 1/2 of a pizza. Obtaining an extra burger for only 1/2 of a pizza clearly makes Johnson better off. Giving up 1/2 a pizza to get one more burger is a much more favorable exchange rate than the exchange rate she is just willing to make (giving up two pizzas for one burger). Thus, Johnson moves to a higher indifference curve by trading only 1/2 a pizza for an additional burger.

As you can see, at every other combination on the budget line above *E*, the slope of the indifference curve—the *MRS*—must be greater than the slope of the budget line. Therefore, at each of these combinations, Johnson, by the same argument, can raise her utility by adding a burger and giving up less pizza than she would be willing to give up in order to gain the additional burger. Thus, all combinations above *E*, at which the *MRS* is greater than 1/2, leads to less utility than combination *E*.

At any combination on the budget line below *E*, the slope of the indifference curve, *MRS*, is obviously less than the slope of the budget line. Suppose the *MRS* at combination *C* is 1/10 (the slope of tangent *T* equals 1/10) meaning that Johnson is just willing to give up 10 burgers in order to obtain an additional pizza. Since the slope of the budget line is 1/2, she can obtain the additional pizzas by giving up only two burgers. She clearly becomes better off by sacrificing the two burgers for the additional pizza.

At every point on the budget line below *E*, the *MRS* is less than 1/2, and Johnson can obtain the additional pizza by giving up fewer burgers than the amount she is just willing to give up. Thus, she should continue reducing the number of burgers and increasing the number of pizzas until utility is maximized at *E* with 30 pizzas and 40 burgers. Again we have shown that all combinations other than *E* yield less utility from the given income.

The marginal rate of substitution is the rate at which the consumer is *willing* to substitute one good for another. The price ratio is the rate at which the consumer is *able* to substitute one good for the other in the market. Thus, equilibrium occurs where the rate at which the consumer is willing to substitute equals the rate at which he or she is able to substitute. We can summarize the concept of consumer utility maximization with the following:

Principle A consumer maximizes utility subject to a limited money income at the combination of goods for which the indifference curve is just tangent to the budget line. At this combination, the marginal rate of substitution (the absolute value of slope of the indifference curve) is equal to the price ratio (the absolute value of the slope of the budget line):

$$-\frac{\Delta Y}{\Delta X} = MRS = \frac{P_X}{P_Y}$$

Marginal Utility Interpretation of Equilibrium

As noted at the beginning of this chapter, the theory of constrained utility maximization is a straightforward application of the theory of constrained maximization developed in Chapter 4. Recall from Chapter 4 that a decision maker attains the highest level of benefits possible within a given cost constraint when the marginal benefit per dollar spent on each activity is the same and the cost constraint is met.

As shown above, a consumer attains the highest level of utility from a given income when the marginal rate of substitution for any two goods, say goods X and Y, is equal to the ratio of the prices of the two goods: that is, $-\Delta Y/\Delta X = MRS = P_x/P_y$. Recall that the marginal rate of substitution is equal to the ratio of the marginal utilities of the two goods. Therefore, utility-maximizing equilibrium occurs when the entire income is spent and

$$MRS = -\frac{\Delta Y}{\Delta X} = \frac{MU_x}{MU_y} = \frac{P_x}{P_y}$$

or, by rearranging this equation,

$$\frac{MU_x}{P_x} = \frac{MU_y}{P_y}$$

This second expression means that the marginal utility per dollar spent on the last unit of good X equals the marginal utility per dollar spent on the last unit of good Y. For example, if $MU_x = 10$ and $P_x = \$2$, $MU_x/P_x = 5$, meaning that one additional dollar spent on X (which buys only 1/2 of a \$2 unit of X) increases utility by 5 units, or one less dollar spent on X decreases utility by 5 units.[4]

To see why marginal utilities per dollar spent must be equal for the last unit consumed of both goods, suppose the condition did not hold and that

$$\frac{MU_x}{P_x} < \frac{MU_y}{P_y}$$

The marginal utility per dollar spent on good X is less than the marginal utility per dollar spent on Y. The consumer can take dollars away from X and spend them on Y. As long as the inequality holds, the lost utility from each dollar taken away from X is less than the added utility from each additional dollar spent on Y, and the consumer continues to substitute Y for X. As the consumption of X decreases, we would expect the marginal utility of X to rise. As Y increases, its marginal utility would decline. The consumer continues substituting until MU_x/P_x equals MU_Y/P_y.

A simple numerical example should make this concept more concrete. Suppose a customer with an income of \$140 is spending it all on 20 units of X priced at \$4 each and 30 units of Y priced at \$2 each: $(\$4 \times 20) + (\$2 \times 30) = \$140$. Further suppose that the marginal utility of the last unit of X is 20 and the marginal

[4]To be precise, the change in utility is only "approximately" equal to 5 units because we have ignored diminishing marginal utility as X increases.

utility of the last unit of Y is 16. The ratio of marginal utilities per dollar spent on X and Y are

$$\frac{MU_x}{P_x} = \frac{20}{4} = 5 < 8 = \frac{16}{2} = \frac{MU_y}{P_y}$$

The consumer should reallocate spending on X and Y because it is possible to increase utility while still spending only \$140. To see how this can be done, let the consumer spend one more dollar on Y. Buying another dollar's worth of good Y causes utility to increase by 8 units.[5] In order to stay within the \$140 budget, the consumer must also reduce spending on good X by one dollar. Spending one dollar less on good X causes utility to fall by 5 units. Since the consumer loses 5 units of utility from reduced consumption of good X but gains 8 units of utility from the increased consumption of good Y, the consumer experiences a net gain in utility of 3 units while still spending only \$140.

The consumer should continue transferring dollars from X to Y as long as $MU_x/P_x < MU_y/P_y$. Because MU_x increases as less X is purchased and MU_y decreases as more Y is purchased, the consumer will reach utility-maximizing equilibrium when $MU_x/P_x = MU_y/P_y$, and no further changes should be made.

Alternatively, if

$$\frac{MU_x}{P_x} > \frac{MU_y}{P_y}$$

the marginal utility per dollar spent on X is greater than the marginal utility per dollar spent on Y. The consumer takes dollars away from Y and buys additional X, continuing to substitute until the equality holds.

Principle To obtain maximum satisfaction from a limited money income, a consumer allocates money income so that the marginal utility per dollar spent on each good is the same for all commodities purchased, and all income is spent.

Finding the Optimal Bundle of Hot Dogs and Cokes

The following numerical example will illustrate the points made in this section. Suppose your boss decides that you have been working too hard and gives you the rest of the day off and a ticket to the afternoon baseball game. After getting seated at the stadium, you discover that you have only \$20, and the concessionaire won't take American Express (or Visa, for that matter). Hot dogs and Cokes are the only snack items you plan to consume while at the game, but it's a hot day, you missed lunch, and \$20 is not going to be enough money to buy all the Cokes and hot dogs you would want to consume. The only rational thing to do is to maximize your utility subject to your \$20 budget constraint.

[5] Even though one extra dollar of expenditure on Y only allows the consumer to purchase 1/2 a unit of Y, and producers may only be willing to sell integer amounts (i.e., you can't buy 1/2 of a burger at most fast-food restaurants), Y is in fact measuring the *rate* of consumption of good Y per unit of time and can include fractional units. If, for example, 12 burgers are consumed weekly, the number of burgers consumed daily is a fraction—1.71 (= 12/7) burgers per day.

On the back of your baseball program you make a list of the marginal utility you expect to receive from various levels of hot dog and Coke consumption. You then divide the marginal utilities by the prices of hot dogs and Cokes, \$2.50 and \$2, respectively. The back of your baseball program looks like this:

Unit per game	Marginal utility of hot dogs MU_H	$\frac{MU_H}{P_H}$	Marginal utility of Cokes MU_C	$\frac{MU_C}{P_C}$
1	20	8	60	30
2	15	6	40	20
3	12.5	5	20	10
4	10	4	16	8
5	7.5	3	8	4
6	5	2	4	2

Using this information, you can now figure out how to get the most satisfaction from consuming hot dogs and Cokes, given your budget constraint.

Should you buy a Coke or a hot dog first? The first unit of Coke increases total utility by 30 units for each dollar spent (on the first Coke), while the first hot dog only increases total utility by 8 units per dollar spent (on the first hot dog). You buy the first Coke and have \$18 left. After finishing the first Coke, you consider whether to buy the first hot dog or the second Coke. Since 8 ($= MU_H/P_H$) < 20 ($= MU_C/P_C$), you buy the second Coke and have \$16 left. Using similar reasoning, you buy the third Coke.

The fourth Coke and the first hot dog both increase total utility by 8 units per dollar spent. You buy both of them and note that the marginal utilities per dollar spent both equal 8. This is not yet optimal, however, because you have spent only \$10.50 (one hot dog and four Cokes). You continue using marginal analysis until you end up buying four hot dogs and five Cokes, at which $MU_H/P_H = 4 = MU_C/P_C$. And you have spent the entire \$20 on the four hot dogs and five Cokes. No other combination of Cokes and hot dogs that you could have purchased for \$20 would have yielded more total utility.

A General Graphical Summary of Consumer Utility Maximization

Figure 7.7 summarizes graphically the fundamental principles of utility maximization under a budget constraint. A consumer purchases two goods, X and Y, with a given income, M. The prices of X and Y are, respectively, P_x and P_y. The budget line is the line AB, from M/P_y (the maximum amount of Y attainable if no X is purchased) to M/P_x (the maximum amount of X attainable if no Y is purchased). The slope of the budget line is $-P_x/P_y$, which gives the rate at which X can be substituted for Y in the market, holding the level of spending constant.

The marginal rate of substitution of X for Y measures the number of units of Y the consumer is willing to give up per additional unit of X, holding the level of utility constant. MRS is equal to the absolute value of the slope of the indifference curve:

FIGURE 7.7
Utility Maximization with a Budget Constraint

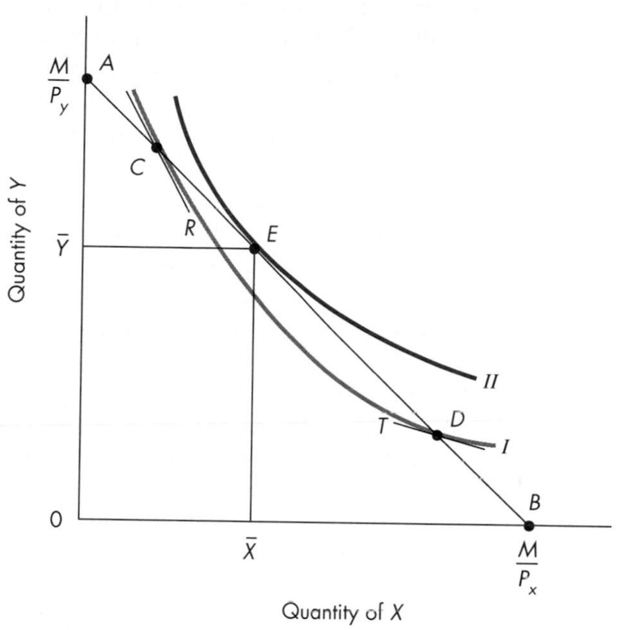

$$MRS = -\Delta Y/\Delta X = -\text{ slope of line tangent to indifference curve}$$

The highest level of utility with the given budget line is achieved with $\overline{X}$ units of X and $\overline{Y}$ units of Y. At this combination, budget line AB is tangent to indifference curve II at point E, which is the highest curve with at least one combination on the budget line. At this combination, the slope of the indifference curve equals the slope of the budget line:

$$MRS = P_x/P_y$$

and

$$P_x\overline{X} + P_y\overline{Y} = M$$

At any combination on the budget line above the point of equilibrium (point E), the indifference curve through that combination crosses the budget line from above, and thus is steeper than the budget line. This implies

$$MRS > P_x/P_y$$

At point C, for example, tangent line R is steeper than the budget line, so that $MRS > P_x/P_y$ at this point. If the consumer gives up MRS units of Y to get an extra unit of X, the consumer is made no better (or worse) off. In market transactions, the consumer must only give up P_x/P_y units of Y to get one more unit of X. Consequently, buying one more X and P_x/P_y fewer units of Y in the marketplace leaves the consumer on the budget line, while increasing utility because the consumer gives up less Y than the amount that would leave the consumer just indifferent. The consumer would continue to give up Y and increase X, moving down the budget line, until the point of tangency is reached.

At any combination on the budget line below the equilibrium combination E, the budget line is steeper than the indifference curve. At point D, for example, the budget line is steeper than tangent line T. At points on AB below E, $MRS < P_x/P_y$. If the consumer gives up one unit of X, P_x/P_y more units of Y can be purchased in the market and still satisfy the budget constraint. The consumer is just willing to give up one unit of X in exchange for MRS additional units of Y. Buying one less unit of X and P_x/P_y more units of Y leaves the consumer on the budget line, while increasing consumer satisfaction because the consumer gets more Y than the amount that would leave the consumer just indifferent. The consumer would continue to give up X and increase Y, moving up the budget line, until the point of tangency is reached.

The marginal utility interpretation of consumer equilibrium provides an alternative way to show that equilibrium must occur at point E by comparing the marginal utilities per dollar spent on each of the two goods X and Y. Since MRS equals MU_x/MU_y along an indifference curve, the equilibrium condition can also be expressed as

$$\frac{MU_x}{P_x} = \frac{MU_y}{P_y}$$

This equilibrium condition implies that the marginal utility per dollar spent on the last unit of each good is the same.

At any combination on the budget line above point E, $MRS > P_x/P_y$ and hence,

$$\frac{MU_x}{P_x} > \frac{MU_y}{P_y}$$

Good X gives the consumer greater additional utility per dollar spent than does good Y. By spending one more dollar on good X, the consumer gains MU_x/P_x additional units of utility. In order to remain on the budget line, the consumer must spend one less dollar on good Y, causing utility to fall by MU_y/P_y units. Since $MU_x/P_x > MU_y/P_y$, the net effect of reallocating a dollar of the budget from Y to X is to increase utility. The consumer continues to reallocate spending to good X away from good Y until the marginal utilities per dollar spent are equal for the last units consumed of X and Y. This occurs at point E.

At any combination on the budget line below point E, $MRS < P_x/P_y$, and hence,

$$\frac{MU_x}{P_x} < \frac{MU_y}{P_y}$$

Good Y gives the consumer more additional utility per dollar spent than does good X. By spending one more dollar on good Y, the consumer gains MU_y/P_y additional units of utility. In order to remain on the budget line, the consumer must spend one less dollar on good X, causing utility to fall by MU_x/P_x units. Since $MU_x/P_x < MU_y/P_y$, the net effect of reallocating a dollar of the budget from X to Y is to increase utility. The consumer continues to reallocate spending to good Y away from good X until the marginal utilities per dollar spent are equal for the last units consumed of X and Y. Again, this occurs at point E.

Thus far, for graphical purposes, we have assumed that the consumer purchases only two goods. The analysis is easily extended, although not graphically, to any number of goods. Since the above equilibrium conditions must apply to *any* two goods in a consumer's consumption bundle, they must apply to all goods in the bundle. Therefore, if a consumer purchases N goods, X_1, X_2, X_3, . . . , X_N with prices P_1, P_2, P_3, . . . , P_N from a given income M, utility maximization requires

$$P_1X_1 + P_2X_2 + P_3X_3 + \cdots + P_NX_N = M$$

and

$$-\frac{\Delta X_i}{\Delta X_j} = MRS = \frac{P_j}{P_i}$$

for any two goods, X_i and X_j. Alternatively, in terms of marginal utilities per dollar spent,

$$\frac{MU_1}{P_1} = \frac{MU_2}{P_2} = \frac{MU_3}{P_3} = \cdots = \frac{MU_N}{P_N}$$

In this way the maximization principle is expanded to cover any number of goods.[6]

7.5 AN INDIVIDUAL CONSUMER'S DEMAND CURVE

We can now use the theory of consumer utility maximization to derive a demand curve for a consumer. In this way we will provide a complete analysis of the underpinnings of demand, which were briefly discussed in Chapter 2. Recall from Chapter 2 that demand was defined as the quantity of a good the consumer is willing and able to purchase at each price in a list of prices, holding other things constant. You have just seen that consumers maximize utility when the rate at which they are *willing* to substitute one good for another just equals the rate at which they are *able* to substitute. It would seem, therefore, that the two theories are closely related, and they are. The theory of demand can be easily developed from the theory of consumer behavior.

We use Figure 7.8 to show this relation and how an individual consumer's demand curve is obtained. Begin with a money income of $1,000 and prices of good X and good Y both equal to $10. The corresponding budget line is given by budget line 1, from 100Y to 100X, in the upper panel of the figure. From the

[6]We should mention that a consumer may choose to consume zero units of some good Z, if all income is spent and the marginal utility per dollar spent on the first unit of some good Z is less than the marginal utility per dollar spent on the last unit of all the other goods purchased: $MU_z/P_z < MU_A/P_A = MU_B/P_B = \ldots = MU_N/P_N$.

FIGURE 7.8
Deriving a Demand Curve

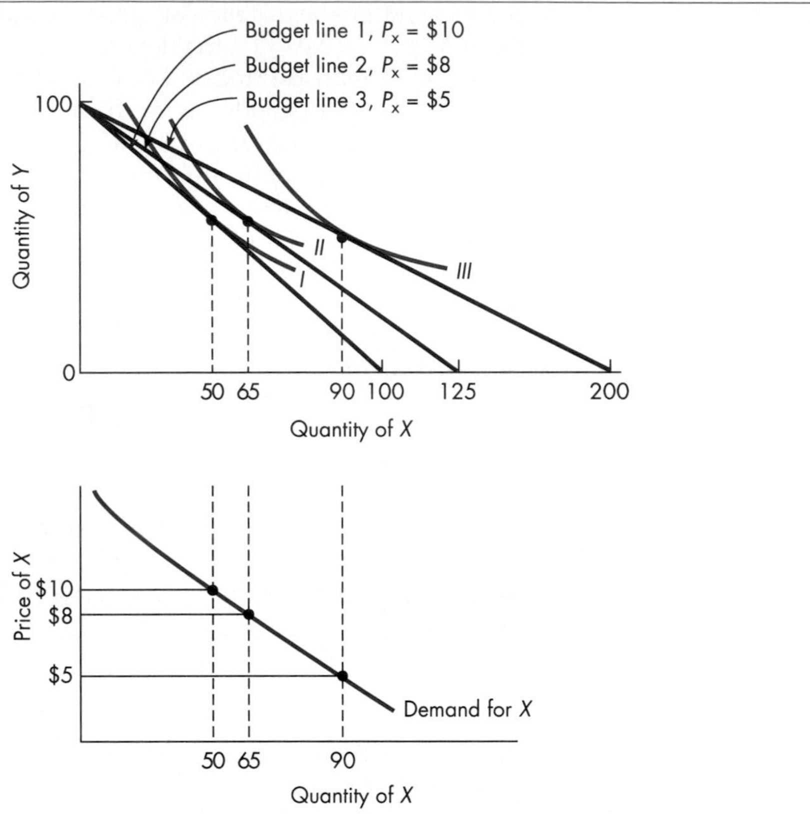

previous analysis, you know the consumer maximizes utility where budget line 1 is tangent to indifference curve *I*, consuming 50 units of *X*. Thus, when income is $1,000, one point on this consumer's demand for *X* is $10 and 50 units of *X*. This point is illustrated on the price-quantity graph in the lower panel of Figure 7.8.

Following the definition of demand, we hold money income and the price of the other good, *Y*, constant, while letting the price of *X* fall from $10 to $8. The new budget line is the less steep budget line 2. Since money income and the price of *Y* remain constant, the vertical intercept does not change, but, because the price of *X* has fallen, the budget line must pivot outward along the *X*-axis. The new *X*-intercept for budget line 2 is 125 (= $1,000/$8). With this new budget line, the consumer now maximizes utility where budget line 2 is tangent to indifference curve *II*, consuming 65 units of *X*. Thus another point on the demand schedule in the lower panel must be $8 and 65 units of *X*.

Next, letting the price of *X* fall again, this time to $5, the new budget line is budget line 3, from 100 to 200. Again the price of *Y* and money income are held constant. The new equilibrium is on indifference curve *III*. At the price $5, the consumer chooses 90 units of *X*, another point on this consumer's demand curve.

Thus we have derived the following demand schedule for good *X*.

Price	Quantity demanded
$10	50
8	65
5	90

This schedule with other points so generated is graphed as a demand curve in price-quantity space in the lower part of Figure 7.8. This demand curve is downward sloping. As the price of *X* falls, the quantity of *X* the consumer is willing and able to purchase increases, following the rule of demand. Furthermore, we followed the definition of demand, holding money income and the price of the other good (goods) constant. Thus an individual's demand for a good is derived from a series of utility-maximizing equilibrium points. We only used three such points, but we could easily have used more in order to obtain more points on the demand curve. We can summarize this section with the following:

Principle The demand curve of an individual for a specific commodity relates utility-maximizing equilibrium quantities purchased to market prices, holding constant money income and the prices of all other goods. The slope of the demand curve illustrates the law of demand: quantity demanded varies inversely with price.

7.6 SUBSTITUTION AND INCOME EFFECTS

As emphasized in Chapter 2, when the price of a good decreases, consumers tend to substitute more of that good for other goods, since the good in question has become cheaper relative to other goods. Conversely, when the price of a good rises, it becomes more expensive relative to other goods, and consumers tend to substitute some additional amounts of the other goods for some of the good with the now higher price. This is called the *substitution effect*.

There is also another effect, called the *income effect*. If a good becomes cheaper, people who are consuming that good are made better off. Since the price of that good has fallen, people can consume the same amount as before, but, because of the reduced price, they have some income left over which can be spent on the good with the now lower price and on other goods as well. The opposite happens when the price of a good increases. Consumers are worse off in the sense that they now cannot afford the bundle they originally chose. They must consume less of the now more expensive good, less of other goods, or less of both. This is called the income effect. We will analyze each effect in turn.

substitution effect
The substitution effect of a price change is the change in consumption of the good that would result if the consumer remained on the same indifference curve after the price change.

Substitution Effect

We begin the analysis of the substitution effect with a more precise definition. The **substitution effect** of a change in the price of a good is the change in the consumption of the good that would result if the consumer remained on the original indifference curve after the price change.

FIGURE 7.9
The Substitution Effect

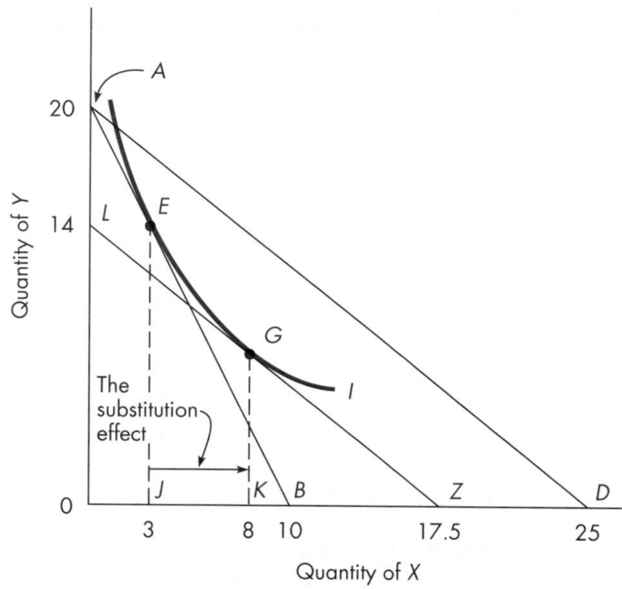

We develop the substitution effect formally in Figure 7.9. Begin with the original budget line *AB* that corresponds to money income of $150, P_y = $7.50, and P_x = $15. The consumer is originally in equilibrium where budget line *AB* is tangent to indifference curve *I* at three units of X (point *E*). Now let the price of X decrease to $6 so that the new budget line pivots outward to *AD*, because $150/$6 = 25.

The consumer, being better off because more choices are now available, can move to an indifference curve higher than *I*. But, the substitution effect concerns changes along the *same* indifference curve. To this end, we theoretically take away just enough of the consumer's income to force a new budget line, with the same slope as *AD* to reflect the lower price of X, to become tangent to the original indifference curve *I*. This is shown as the parallel shift of the budget line *AD* to the adjusted budget line *LZ*. It is important to note that the slope of *LZ*, 4/5 (= $6/$7.50), reflects the new, lower price of X, but is associated with a lower money income than is the original budget line *AB*. Since budget line *LZ* is tangent to indifference curve *I* at point *G*, the consumer now chooses to purchase eight units of X. Note that the consumer's adjustment from point *E* to point *G*, which takes place along the original indifference curve *I*, is a theoretically conceived (or hypothetical) adjustment in consumption. It is the change in the optimal consumption that would occur when the price of X relative to the price of Y falls from 2 (= 15/7.50) to .8 (= 6/7.50) *and* the consumer is forced by a *hypothetical* reduction in income to remain on the same indifference curve.

The substitution effect is shown as the distance JK (five additional units of X), resulting from the movement along I from E to G. It is clear that this effect is negative—a decrease in price must result in an increase in consumption of the good when utility is held constant. This must always be the case, given the shape of indifference curves. When the price of X falls from \$15 to \$6, the budget line becomes flatter; so the budget line, after taking away some income, must be tangent to the original indifference curve at a point with a less steep slope (MRS) than was the case at the original equilibrium. This can only occur with increased consumption of X.

Principle The substitution effect is the change in the consumption of a good after a change in its price, when the consumer is forced by a change in money income to consume at some point on the original indifference curve. Considering the substitution effect only, the amount of the good consumed must vary inversely with its price.

Income Effect

income effect
The income effect of a price change is the change in the consumption of a good resulting strictly from the change in purchasing power.

The direction of the income effect is not unambiguous, as was the case for the substitution effect. Before we analyze the income effect, let us define it. The **income effect** from a price change is the change in the consumption of a good resulting strictly from the change in purchasing power.

We noted earlier that a decrease in the price of a good makes a consumer of that good better off in the sense of being able to purchase the same bundle of goods and have income left over; that is, the consumer can move to a higher indifference curve. An increase in the price of a good makes a consumer worse off because he or she is unable to purchase the original bundle; that is, the consumer must move to a lower indifference curve. Since the consumer moves to a higher or lower indifference curve, depending upon the direction of the price change, and the substitution effect takes place along the original indifference curve, the income effect is simply the difference between the total effect of the price change—the movement from one indifference curve to another—and the substitution effect.

Figure 7.10 illustrates how to isolate the substitution and income effects for a decrease in the price of X. First consider (in Panel A) the case of a normal good. The consumer initially faces the budget line AB (M = \$150, P_x = \$15, and P_y = \$7.50), and maximizes utility subject to budget line AB at point E on the indifference curve I. Let the price of X fall from \$15 to \$6, so that the budget line pivots to AD. The new equilibrium is at point F on indifference curve II. The total effect of the price decrease is to increase the consumption of X from 3 units to 12 units.

As explained earlier, the substitution effect is the change in consumption of X that would result if the consumer remained on the same indifference curve after the change in price. At the new price ratio P_x/P_y = \$6/\$7.50 = .8, we again temporarily take away just enough income to keep the consumer on the original indifference curve. This reduction in income causes the budget line to shift downward to LZ. In this example, income must be reduced to \$105 (= \$7.50 × 14 = \$6 × 17.5) to isolate the substitution effect. On the adjusted budget line LZ,

FIGURE 7.10
Income and Substitution Effects: A Decrease in P_x

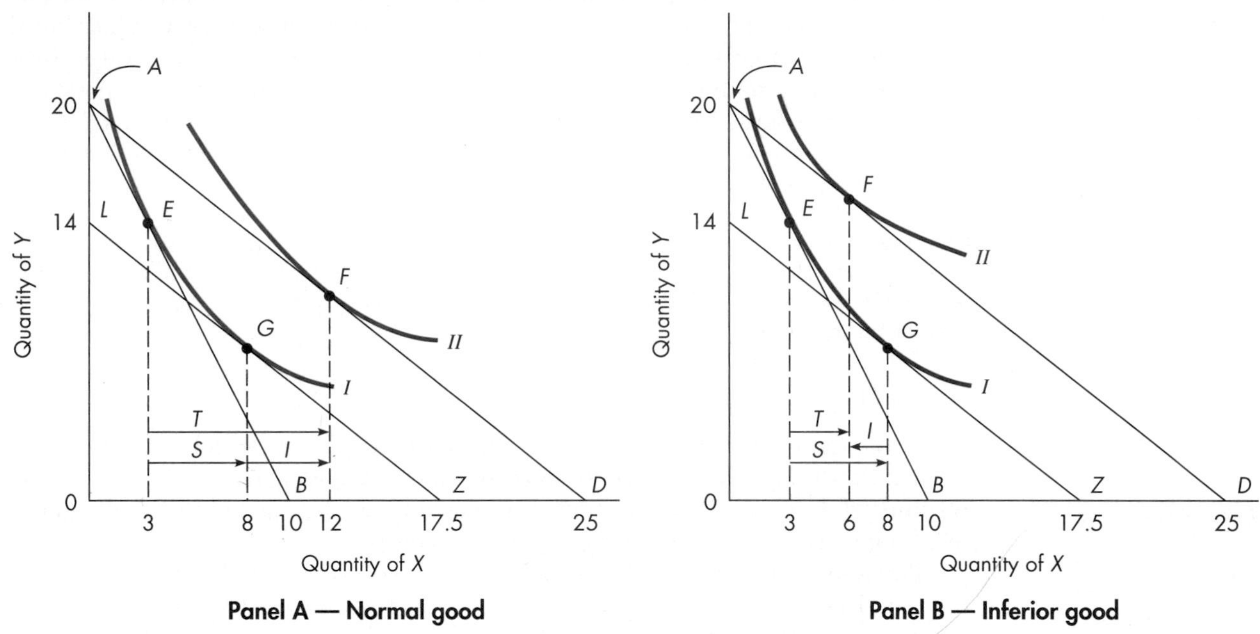

$MRS = P_x/P_y$ at point G. The substitution effect of the price *reduction* is an *increase* in consumption of X by 5 units. For the substitution effect alone, the price and consumption of X move in opposite directions.

Recall from Chapter 2 that consumption of a normal good increases when income increases, prices held constant. This is exactly what happens when the hypothetical reduction in income is restored and the budget line shifts from LZ back to AD. When the income that was hypothetically taken away to isolate the substitution effect is returned, the consumer increases the consumption of X by 4 units. You can see in Panel A that good X is a normal good because the increase in income from \$105 to \$150 (LZ to AD) causes consumption of X to increase from 8 to 12.

When the price of X *falls*, both the substitution effect and the income effect cause the consumer to purchase *more* of the good—the income effect reinforces the substitution effect. Both of these effects cause consumption of X to move in the opposite direction of the change in price. The **total effect** of the decrease in price is equal to the sum of the substitution and income effects:

total effect
The total effect of a price change is equal to the sum of the substitution and income effects.

Total effect of price decrease	=	Substitution effect	+	Income effect
9	=	5	+	4

The situation is different for an inferior good. Recall from Chapter 2 that if a good is inferior, an increase in income (holding prices constant) causes less of the good to be consumed. The case of an inferior good is illustrated in Panel B of Figure 7.10. Begin, as before, with budget line *AB*. Equilibrium is at *E* on indifference curve *I* with 3 units of *X* being consumed. Let the price of *X* fall from $15 to $6, which causes the budget line to pivot outward to *AD*. The new equilibrium is at *F* on indifference curve *II* with 6 units of *X* being consumed. The total effect of the price decrease is an increase of 3 units in the consumption of *X*.

In Panel B, the substitution effect is isolated in exactly the same way as in Panel A and is again equal to 5 units of *X* . Note that the substitution effect is greater than the total effect. It is apparent that the income effect has partially offset the substitution effect. This will always be true for inferior goods because the income effect for inferior goods moves in the opposite direction as the substitution effect. When the budget line moves back to *AD* from *LZ*, the increase in income causes the consumption of *X* to *fall* from 8 to 6 units of *X* , and thus, the income effect is –2 units of *X*. The total effect of the decrease in the price of *X* is

Total effect of price decrease	= Substitution effect	+ Income effect
3	= 5	+ (–2)

Figure 7.11 shows the substitution, income, and total effects for an increase in the price of good X. Panel A illustrates the case of a normal good. The initial budget line is *AR* (M = $60, P_x = $2.40, and P_y = $4), and the consumer initially maximizes utility at point *E* on indifference curve *II*. When the price of *X* increases from $2.40 to $6, the budget line pivots to *AS* and the new equilibrium is at point *F* on indifference curve *I*. The substitution effect is isolated by temporarily increasing income to $84 (the adjusted budget line is *LZ*). The substitution effect of the price *increase* is a *reduction* in the consumption of *X* by 5 units. When income is returned to $60, the adjusted budget line shifts back to *AS*, and the consumer reduces consumption by 2 more units of *X*. The total effect of the increase in price is

Total effect of price increase	= Substitution effect	+ Income effect
–7	= –5	+ (–2)

Note that income and substitution effects reinforce each other since *X* is a normal good.

In Panel B, good *X* is inferior. The substitution effect is the same as in Panel A, but now the income effect partially offsets the substitution effect. When the budget line shifts backward from *LZ* to *AS*, income falls from $84 to $60, and consumption of the inferior good *X* increases from 5 to 6 units. The total effect of the increase in price is

Total effect of price increase	= Substitution effect	+ Income effect
–4	= –5	+ 1

FIGURE 7.11
Income and Substitution Effects: An Increase in P_x

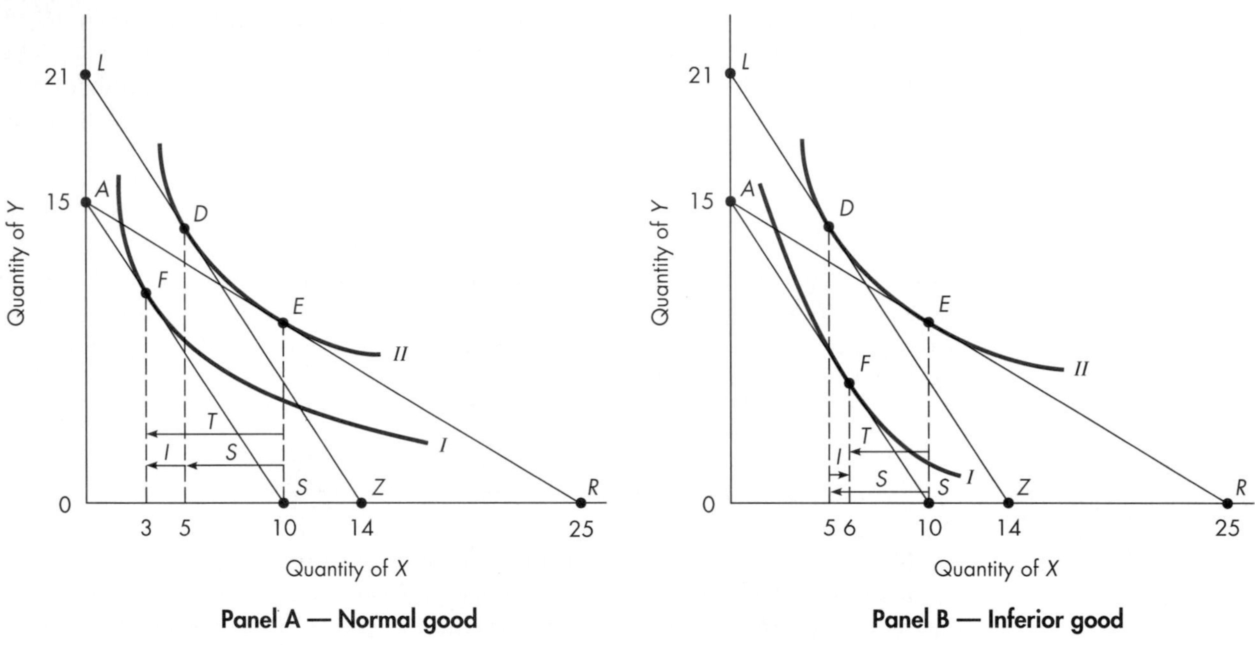

Because X is inferior in Panel B, the substitution and income effects move in opposite directions. These effects are summarized in Table 7.1 and the following relation.

Relation Considering the substitution effect alone, an increase (decrease) in the price of a good causes less (more) of the good to be demanded. For a normal good, the income effect—from the consumer's being made better or worse off by the price change—adds to or reinforces the substitution effect. The income effect in the case of an inferior good offsets or takes away from the substitution effect.

Why Demand Slopes Downward

In the case of a normal good, it is clear why price and quantity demanded are negatively related along demand. From the substitution effect alone, a decrease in price is accompanied by an increase in quantity demanded. (An increase in price decreases quantity demanded.) For a normal good, the income effect must add to the substitution effect. Since both effects move quantity demanded in the same direction, demand must be negatively sloped.

In the case of an inferior good, the income effect does not move in the same direction, and to some extent offsets the substitution effect. However, looking at

TABLE 7.1
Summary of Substitution and Income Effects for a Change in the Price of X

Price of X decreases	Substitution effect	Income effect
Normal good	X rises	X rises
Inferior good	X rises	X falls
Price of X increases		
Normal good	X falls	X falls
Inferior good	X falls	X rises

Panel B in Figures 7.10 and 7.11 again, you can see that the income effect only *partially* offsets the substitution effect, so that quantity demanded still varies inversely with price. This is generally the case: Even if the commodity is inferior, the substitution effect almost always dominates the income effect and the demand curve still slopes downward.

Giffen good
A good for which the demand curve is upward sloping.

It is *theoretically* possible that the income effect for an inferior good could dominate the substitution effect. In this case—the so-called **Giffen good**—quantity demanded would vary directly with price and the demand curve would be upward sloping. However, in this text, we will ignore Giffen goods. While experimental economists have suggested that a Giffen good may exist for an individual, we have as yet seen no convincing evidence of the existence of a Giffen good for a group of consumers.

7.7 MARKET DEMAND CURVES

market demand
A list of prices and the quantities consumers are willing and able to purchase at each price in the list, other things being held constant.

Managerial decision makers are typically more interested in the market demand for a product than in the demand of an individual consumer. Nonetheless, the behavior of individual consumers in the market determines market demand. Recall that in Chapter 2 we defined **market demand** as a list of prices and the corresponding quantity consumers are willing and able to purchase at each price in the list, holding constant money income, the prices of other goods, tastes, price expectations, and the number of consumers. When deriving individual demand in this chapter, we pivoted the budget line around the vertical intercept, therefore holding income and the prices of other goods constant. Since the indifference curves remained constant, tastes were unchanged.

Thus the discussion here conforms to the conditions of market demand. To obtain the market demand function we need only to aggregate the individual demand functions of all potential consumers in the market. We now demonstrate this aggregation.

Suppose there are only three individuals in the market for a particular commodity. The quantities demanded by each consumer at each price in column 1 are shown in columns 2, 3, and 4 of Table 7.2. Column 5 shows the sum of these quantities demanded at each price and is therefore the market demand. Since the demands for each consumer are negatively sloped, market demand is negatively sloped also. Quantity demanded is inversely related to price.

TABLE 7.2
Aggregating Individual Demands

Price	Quantity demanded			Market demand
	Consumer 1	Consumer 2	Consumer 3	
$6	3	0	0	3
5	5	1	0	6
4	8	3	1	12
3	10	5	4	19
2	12	7	6	25
1	13	10	8	31

FIGURE 7.12
Derivation of Market Demand

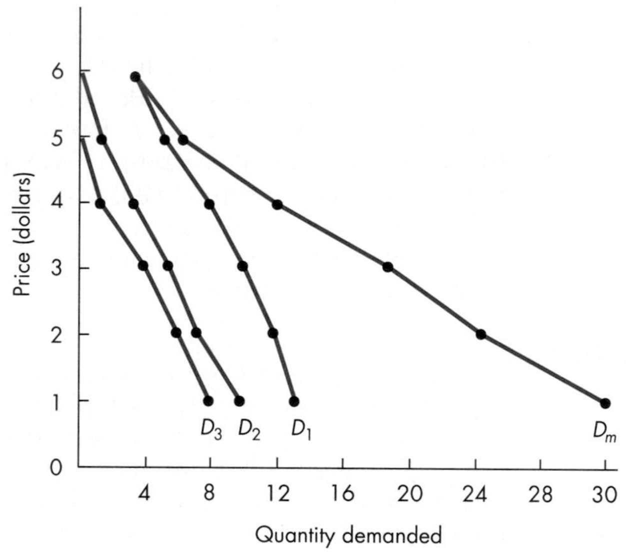

Figure 7.12 shows graphically how a market demand curve can be derived from the individual demand curves. The individual demands of consumers 1, 2, and 3 from Table 7.2 are shown graphically as D_1, D_2, and D_3, respectively. The market demand curve, D_m, is simply the sum of the quantities demanded at each price. At $6 consumer 1 demands 3 units. Since the others demand nothing, 3 is the quantity demanded by the market. At every other price D_m is the horizontal summation of the quantities demanded by the three consumers. And if other consumers came into the market, their demand curves would be added to D_m to obtain the new market demand.

Relation The market demand curve is the horizontal summation of the demand curves of all consumers in the market. It therefore shows how much all consumers demand at each price over the relevant range of prices.

7.8 IMPERFECT INFORMATION ABOUT PRICE AND QUALITY

Thus far in this chapter, we have assumed that consumers have complete information about the price and quality of the goods and services available in the market. In most cases, consumers probably do not have complete information about the prices of all the products that are available, and they may not be fully aware of the amount of utility they will receive from these products—that is, they may not know about product quality. Because information is not complete, consumers must engage in search activities to gather information. Consumers gather information about prices and quality in many ways: for example, by reading research or trade magazines (such as *Consumer Reports, Car & Driver, PC Computing,* etc.), visiting stores and talking with sales clerks, talking to friends, and watching the newspapers for advertisements that convey information about prices and quality.

All of these search activities take time and sometimes money. Even if no monetary expenditure is involved with the search, the time itself required to search for information has value to consumers. Economists refer to the costs of gathering information about price and quality as **search costs**. It is important for managers to understand how and why consumers search for price and quality information. To the extent that managers can reduce the search costs associated with buying their products, they can expect to sell more units. In this section and the next, we will discuss some theories about how consumers decide how much to search for information.

search costs
The costs of gathering information about product prices or product quality.

Consumer Search Theory

When consumers engage in search activities for information about product prices and quality, they incur both benefits and costs. As it turns out, the theory of searching for information is essentially the same regardless of whether it is price or quality information. To illustrate how consumers determine how much search activity to undertake, we will consider a consumer that needs information about product price. The results of this discussion can be directly applied to determining how much time to spend searching for quality information. Since search activity involves both costs and benefits, and there is no constraint on the amount of search activity undertaken, the consumer's search problem is an unconstrained maximization problem. Using the theory of optimization developed in Chapter 4, we know that the optimal level of search occurs at the point where the marginal benefit of search just equals the marginal cost of search.

The marginal benefit from searching one more hour is the reduction in the price the consumer must pay for the good. For now, we will assume the consumer knows with certainty the marginal benefit associated with various levels of search activity. Obviously, consumers usually do not know with certainty how much lower a price they will find if they search an extra hour. In most situations, search involves risk. We will introduce risk into the analysis of search once we show you how to find the optimal level of search when marginal benefit is known with certainty. To illustrate the search decision, consider the problem facing Mark Smith, who is shopping for a 486 personal computer. Mark knows

FIGURE 7.13
Finding the Optimal Level of Search

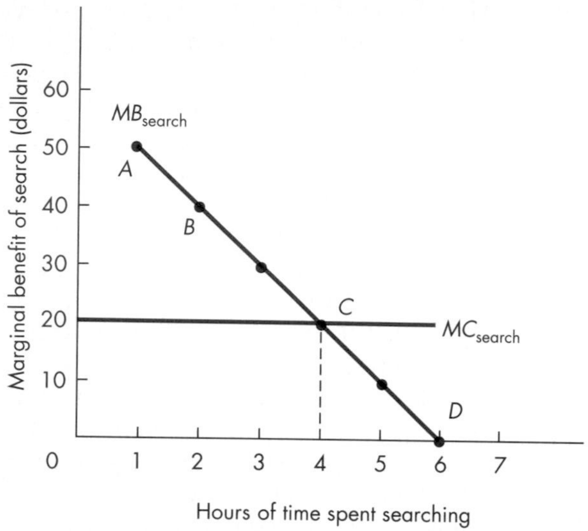

exactly what features he needs in a PC (i.e., quality is known) and is going to buy the cheapest brand of PC with these features he can find in the amount of time he decides to spend shopping. Figure 7.13 shows the (known) marginal benefit curve for additional hours Mark spends searching for a lower priced 486 PC.

Mark knows he can buy a PC from a mail-order firm that advertises in *PC Computing* magazine, and pay a price of $2,000 with no search activity. As shown by point *A* in Figure 7.13, Mark can spend one hour shopping at various stores and can get a personal computer with the same features for $50 less than the mail-order price (i.e., the no-search price). If Mark wants to shop for a second hour, he can save another $40 (point *B*) and get a computer for $90 (= $50 + $40) less than the mail-order price. Mark can continue finding a lower price by searching up to six hours. Once Mark has spent six hours shopping around town, he will have found the lowest price in town (point *D*). While it might seem optimal to search for the lowest price, consumers generally quit shopping before they have found the lowest possible price because search is costly.

Mark recognizes that searching for a lower price is using up some of his valuable leisure time, which he values at $20 per hour. Thus, Mark's marginal cost of search is $20 per hour. For the first hour of search that Mark undertakes, he saves $50 by finding a lower price on the computer, but he spends $20 worth of his time. Clearly, Mark is better off by using $20 worth of time to save $50. For the second extra hour spent shopping Mark can reduce price by another $40, but again he gives up $20 worth of his time. Again, this extra hour of search makes Mark better off. Mark will continue searching until the marginal cost of an extra hour of search exceeds the marginal benefit. In Figure 7.13, Mark will increase his search time up to 4 hours, the point at which the marginal benefit of search equals the marginal cost of search (point C). This example treats search time as a continuous variable. Had search time been a discrete variable, Mark would have continued to increase the search up to the last level for which the marginal benefit exceeded the marginal cost of search. We can summarize the rule for consumer search in the following principle.

Principle When the marginal benefit of search is known with certainty, the consumer maximizes the net benefit by increasing search activity up to the point where the marginal benefit of search equals the marginal cost of search. If the consumer must choose among discrete levels of activity, the consumer maximizes net benefit by increasing search activity up to the last level of search for which the marginal benefit of search exceeds the marginal cost of search.

Consumer Search under Conditions of Risk

In most cases, a consumer will not know with certainty the marginal benefit from searching an additional hour. Instead, a consumer is likely to view the search as a random process that may yield a range of different possible price savings. The consumer is often able to determine subjectively a probability distribution for the various possible savings outcomes from spending an additional hour of time searching for a lower price. When consumers face a probability distribution of possible marginal benefits from search, the optimal amount of time to spend searching for price information is a decision that is made under conditions of risk.

Recall from Chapter 6 (section 6.5), that the optimal level of a risky activity occurs where the expected marginal benefit just equals the expected marginal cost of the activity. We can apply this rule of optimization under risk to the search problem facing a consumer. Since the marginal cost of search is known and constant, only marginal benefit is risky. In order to maximize the expected net benefit of search, a consumer should increase the time spent searching for a lower price as long as the expected marginal benefit exceeds the (certain) marginal cost of search. The optimal level of search occurs where

$$E(MB_{\text{search}}) = MC_{\text{search}}$$

To illustrate how this rule can be applied by consumers, we return to the problem faced by Mark Smith in his search for price information on 486 personal computers. In the previous discussion, we assumed Mark knew with certainty both the marginal benefit and the marginal cost of searching additional hours. Now suppose Mark does not know with certainty how much he will save if he spends an extra hour searching, but he does know with certainty that an extra hour will cost him $20 worth of his leisure time.

While Mark is not willing to undertake an in-depth statistical analysis of the probability distribution of possible savings associated with each extra hour of search time (i.e., determine objective probabilities), he does have a "gut feeling" about the likelihood of saving $10, $20, $30, $40, $50, or $60 by shopping one more hour—that is, he can determine subjective probabilities. The process of determining subjective probability distributions is a sequential process that

ILLUSTRATION 7.1

First Chicago Shows Customers "How to Lose Wait"

As we will point out in section 7.9, managers use informative advertising to reduce the search costs consumers incur when they gather information about price and product quality. Since the full price paid by the consumer is equal to the money price plus the search costs (per unit purchased), one way informative ads can increase sales of the product is by reducing the search cost component of this total price. Another way that managers can reduce the full price to their customers is to reduce the time the consumers must spend completing a purchase—primarily time spent locating items in the store and waiting in check-out lines. The time consumers spend completing a transaction represents a cost to consumers, and this cost of waiting must be added to the money price of the good (just as search costs are added) when computing the full price of a product.

Leonard Berry and Linda Cooper, in an article in *Business* magazine,* report that consumers today feel a "poverty of time." Recent studies reveal that Americans feel as though time is becoming increasingly scarce. A 1987 Newspaper Advertising Bureau study found that 76 percent of working women and 58 percent of all Americans felt pressured for time. In a 1987 *USA Today* poll, 70 percent of two-income households surveyed claimed they did not have enough time to do all the things they wished to do. Given the increasing value consumers place on their time, it is not surprising to find many business managers searching for ways to reduce the time cost component of their product's full price. According to Berry and Cooper, managers today view "convenience" as a key component of their strategic plans for competing with rival firms. Managers are relying on convenience as a way to reduce the full price consumers pay for their product.

An example of a firm that uses reductions in waiting time to enhance its competitiveness is the First National Bank of Chicago (First Chicago). Deregulation of financial institutions in the early 1980s substantially increased the competitiveness of the banking services industry. During the early to middle 1980s, First Chicago lost customers to credit unions, savings and loan associations, and security brokerage houses that became direct competitors of the bank when deregulation allowed other types of financial institutions to begin offering financial services that previously only commercial banks could offer. In a

involves updating the distribution of possible savings for the next hour of search time *based upon the outcome of all previous hours spent searching*.

Mark's subjective evaluation of the benefits from searching a *second* hour depend upon how well things turn out *after the first hour* of search is completed. If Mark finds a *large* price reduction in the first hour of search, he may feel optimistic about a second hour of search—he expects a second hour may turn up even further (large) price reductions. Or, after discovering the substantially lower price in the first hour, Mark may feel pessimistic about the second hour of search—he thinks it unlikely, though still possible, that he will find an even lower price. Alternatively, if Mark finds only a *small* price reduction in the first hour of search, he may decide success is improbable in a second hour, or he may think he just had bad luck in the first hour and feels more confident of finding a large price reduction in the second hour of search. No matter how things turn out in the first hour, Mark's subjective probability distribution of possible savings associated with a second hour of search will change, or be updated, at the end of the first hour.

move that further heated up competition in the Chicago banking market, Citicorp entered the Chicago market by acquiring a failed savings and loan association in 1984. First Chicago found itself facing a major new competitor, one with a history of aggressive pricing. In formulating a strategy to prosper in this more competitive market, managers at First Chicago decided to undertake a multifaceted program to increase convenience by reducing consumer waiting time. First Chicago planned to decrease its full price by saving its customers time.

The actions taken by First Chicago to reduce waiting time, and hence full price, are explained in detail by Berry and Cooper. We summarize some of these actions here. The bank installed a new IBM terminal system, which consolidated all information on each account so that tellers could more quickly and completely handle customers' banking transactions. An electronic queuing system was implemented to measure and display, for both employees *and customers* to see, the number of customers in line, the number of teller windows open, and the average time a customer is waiting. First Chicago also added cash dispatching machines that eliminated the need for tellers to count money, thereby saving almost 30 seconds on each transaction. The job descriptions of managers were revised in a way that made managers responsible for the front side of the teller counter as well as the back side. Managers began "floor-walking" to expedite customer flow.

First Chicago managers also began paying higher wages to attract premium tellers to work peak-load time periods (around noon and before holidays). Management began recognizing and rewarding teller productivity. In order to ensure that consumers take advantage of these time-saving measures, First Chicago distributed brochures to customers titled "How to Lose Wait," which informed customers about when the bank was busiest and how to avoid delays.

First Chicago made a dramatic commitment to reducing waiting time of consumers. The purpose was to reduce the full price consumers pay for banking services at First Chicago Bank. In markets where time costs are a significant fraction of the full price of a product, managers can effectively use time-saving measures to increase sales.

*The information in this illustration is drawn from Leonard L. Berry and Linda R. Cooper, "Competing with Time-Saving Services," *Business* (April/June, 1990).

Figure 7.14 shows Mark's subjective probability distributions for the marginal benefit of searching the first hour (MB_1), the second hour (MB_2), and the third hour (MB_3). Mark bases his probability distributions for the second and third hours on the assumption that his search in the first hour will yield exactly the expected marginal benefit [$E(MB_1) = \$42$], and his search in the second hour will also yield exactly the expected marginal benefit [$E(MB_2) = \$34$]. As discussed above, Mark will update or revise his subjective probability distributions for the second hour once the first hour of search is complete. Likewise, the probability distribution for the marginal benefit of a third hour will be revised after (and if) a second hour of search is completed. Before beginning to search, Mark believes the expected marginal benefit of search decreases with each additional hour of time spent shopping: $E(MB_1) = \$42$, $E(MB_2) = \$34$, and $E(MB_3) = \$16.50$.

Mark determines the optimal level of shopping time by making a series of optimizing decisions. First, Mark decides if he should order the computer from the mail-order company (i.e., pay \$2,000 and engage in no search) or spend one

FIGURE 7.14

Probability Distributions for Marginal Benefits of Search

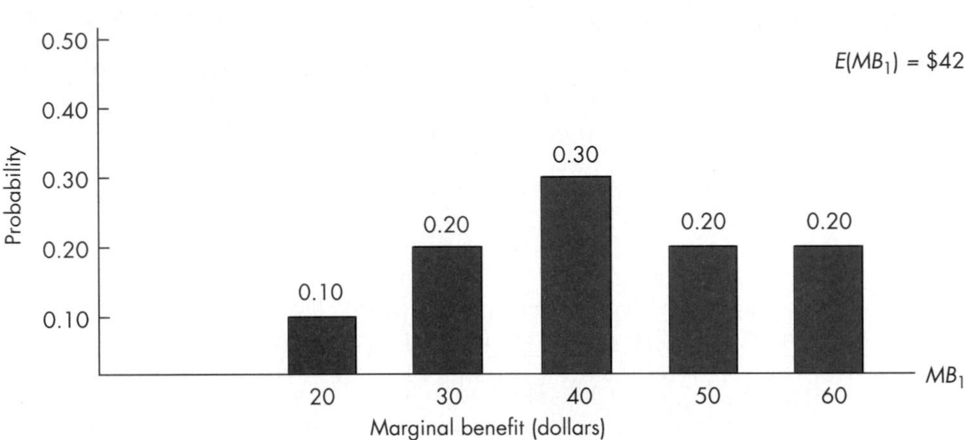

Panel A — Marginal benefit of first hour of search

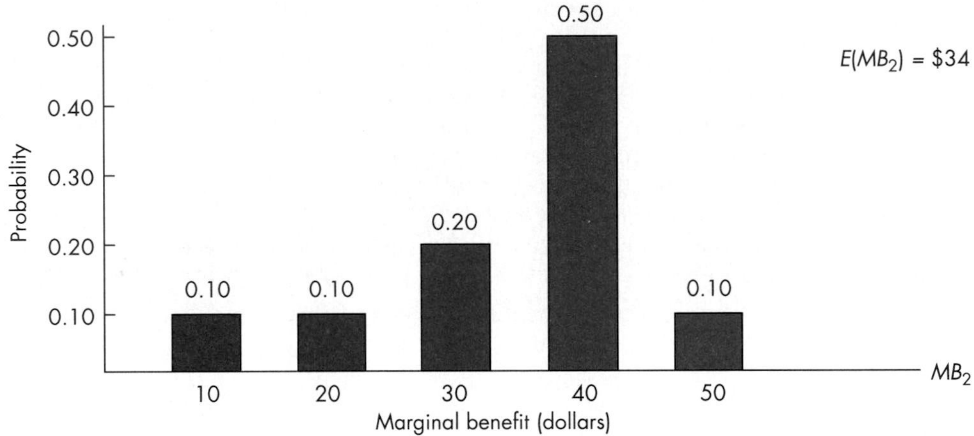

Panel B — Marginal benefit of second hour of search

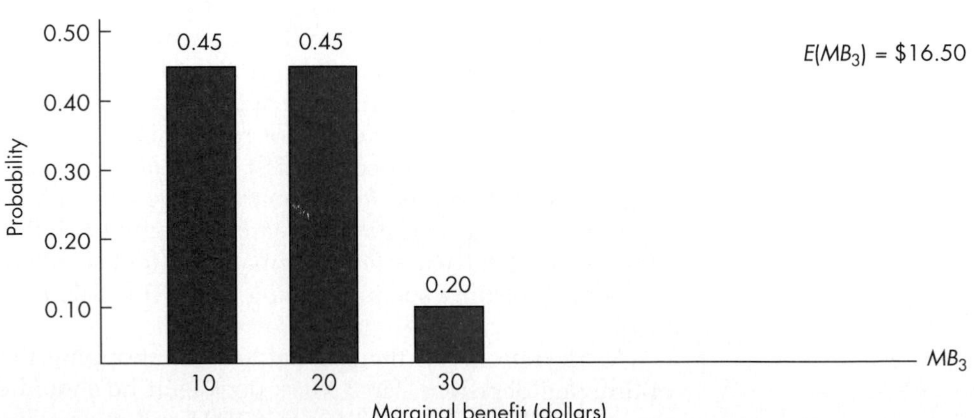

Panel C — Marginal benefit of third hour of search

hour searching around town for a lower price. Since the expected savings from search is $42 [= $E(MB_1)$ for the first hour and the marginal cost is $20, Mark will undertake the first hour of search. Now suppose that Panel B in Figure 7.14 shows Mark's subjective probability distribution for MB_2 *after completing the first hour of search.*[7] Mark would choose to engage in a second hour of search since $34 (= $E(MB_2)$) is greater than $20 (=$MC_{search}$). If Mark's subjective probability distribution for MB_3 *after a second hour of search* looks like Panel C, a third hour of search would not be undertaken because the expected marginal benefit (= $16.50) is less than the marginal cost of another hour of search ($20). Thus, the optimal amount of time for Mark to shop for a lower price is two hours.

In this example Mark did not update his prior subjective probabilities for the marginal benefits of search. In the more common situation where consumers do update their future subjective probability distributions for marginal benefits, consumers still follow the same rule for finding the optimal level of search—increase search if the *new* (or updated) expected marginal benefit of search exceeds the marginal cost of extra search, and stop searching otherwise.

In the discussion above, Mark is behaving in a risk-neutral fashion since he is following the decision rule for maximizing expected net benefit (see Section 6.5). If Mark is instead a risk-loving decision maker, then he may undertake *more* hours of search than if he is risk neutral. Alternatively, if Mark is risk averse, he may undertake *fewer* hours of search than if he is risk neutral.

We can summarize the search rules of a consumer in the following principle

Principle A consumer who wishes to maximize the expected net benefit from searching for information about price or product quality should continue to spend more time searching for information up to the point where the expected marginal benefit from more information just equals the marginal cost of searching for additional information:

$$E(MB_{search}) = MC_{search}$$

7.9 IMPERFECT INFORMATION AND ADVERTISING

Advertising is big business. A number of US corporations spend more than $1 billion annually on advertising for the purpose of increasing sales. While many consumers may feel that they are bombarded with superficial and sometimes annoying advertising, a significant amount of advertising actually improves knowledge about product prices and quality. Some advertising even succeeds in convincing people that certain goods or services are more desirable than they had previously believed. Indeed, advertising does increase sales; otherwise, firms wouldn't advertise.

To illustrate how advertising improves and alters the information that consumers use in making consumption decisions, we classify advertising as either

[7]Panel B requires no updating or revision if, by assumption, Mark's first hour of search yields the expected marginal benefit of $42. If the first hour of search results in a marginal benefit different from $42, Mark's updated probability distribution for MB_2 would look different than the one shown in Panel B.

purely informative advertising
Advertising designed primarily to convey price, quality, or availability information about a product.

image advertising
Advertising that conveys an image about a product.

(1) purely informative or (2) image advertising. **Purely informative advertising** is designed primarily to convey information about product quality and product price. **Image advertising** conveys an image about the product that is designed to alter and enhance consumers' perception of a good.

Purely Informative Advertising

Purely informative advertising conveys quality and price information. Examples of this type of advertising are newspaper ads for grocery and drug stores, catalog ads, and ads in technical publications. In most of this chapter, we have assumed that consumers have complete information about both product price and the ability of goods to satisfy their wants. If this were always the case, there would be no need for informative advertising. Complete information, however, is frequently not available. As noted in the previous section, consumers do not have full information about prices or the quality of all products and may decide to engage in activities that increase their knowledge about prices and qualities.

As you may recall from our discussion of utility maximization, the higher the marginal utility per dollar spent on a good (MU/P), the more of a good the consumer will wish to purchase for any given level of income. Informative advertising can affect either, or both, marginal utility and price. Marginal utility can be increased by providing information on product quality, and the average price paid can be lowered by giving shoppers information about prices.

First consider the effect of informative advertising on marginal utility. When informative ads convey information to buyers about the desirable attributes of a product, the consumers' perception of product quality rises, causing the perceived marginal utility to increase. For a given price, an increase in marginal utility causes MU/P to rise, and consumers will buy more of the product.

Next consider the effect of informative advertising on the price paid by consumers for the product. As emphasized in the previous section, searching for price and quality information is costly. Not only do consumers spend valuable time in the search for information, many decide to purchase magazines such as *Consumer Reports* and *Motor Trend* for information on automobiles and other durable goods, or *The Wall Street Journal* for information on financial products and services, or various catalogs, computer data bases, etc. When consumers incur search costs, the price they consider in making their consumption decision is *full price*. The **full price (P_F)** a consumer pays for a unit of a product equals the money price per unit purchased (P) plus the search costs per unit (S):

full price
The money price per unit purchased plus the search costs per unit.

$$P_F = P + S$$

For example, if the money price of a good is \$5 per unit and a consumer spends \$2 worth of resources searching for price and quality information about that good before making a purchase, the full price of the good is equal to \$7 (= \$5 + \$2), and the marginal utility per dollar spent on the good is $MU/\$7$.

Managers use informative advertising to reduce the search costs (S) for their products. To the extent that informative ads reduce the full price consumers pay for a product, full price falls, MU/P_F rises, and consumers buy more of that

ILLUSTRATION 7.2

Some Perils of Image Advertising

When it succeeds, image advertising can be an extremely powerful and cost-effective method of persuading consumers to buy a company's product. Image advertising campaigns can, however, fail spectactularly. Image advertising increases sales by enhancing consumers' perception of the marginal utility of the product. Since the advertised image is intended literally to become a characteristic of the product, the success or failure of an image advertising campaign depends crucially upon finding and projecting an image that consumers will want "to buy." Even highly paid advertising agencies cannot guarantee that an image advertising campaign will be successful, for it can backfire if the projected image turns out to be unpopular with consumers.

Subaru of America learned just how perilous image advertising can be when it launched a bold advertising campaign designed to link Subaru cars with the image of practicality and reverse snobbery. * According to the Subaru ad, "A car is a car. If it improves your standing with the neighbors, then you live among snobs with distorted values. A car is steel, electronics, rubber, plastic, and glass. A machine." Subaru believed a trend was underway in the United States of rejecting "1980s style greed" in favor of practicality and basic values. When the first ad appeared in the fall of 1991, advertising critics thought it was sensational. Six months later, however, Subaru sales had fallen sharply and began a lengthy decline.

According to *The Wall Street Journal*, Subaru "misjudged how important status is for car buyers willing to fork over $13,000 or more, and underestimated the powerful emotions involved in choosing a car." Subaru's image of practicality just didn't sell. By May of 1992, Subaru abandoned its unsuccessful image advertising in favor of an informative advertising campaign that emphasized the special features of Subaru cars.

Image ads frequently employ celebrities to enhance the image of a company or product; however, this can be risky since celebrity images can change over time. Corporations may spend millions designing an image advertising campaign around a celebrity only to see the celebrity's popularity fade, or in some cases, even become negative or undesirable. Executives at Pepsi have undoubtedly lost a lot of sleep over the alleged misdeeds of Madonna and Michael Jackson. The Florida Department of Citrus, which employed Burt Reynolds to promote Florida orange juice, decided to cancel its television commercials because Burt's highly publicized divorce from Loni Anderson was tarnishing Burt's image and had reduced the effectiveness of the commercials.

The riskiness of using celebrities in image advertising can be substantially reduced by resurrecting celebrities who are dead.† Many companies, such as PepsiCo, the Gap, and McDonald's, are featuring deceased celebrities in their ads in order (practically) to eliminate the risk of embarrassment. The Gap features Humphrey Bogart, Orson Wells, Rock Hudson, Sammy Davis Jr., and Marilyn Monroe in its ads for khaki trousers. McDonald's plans to create an ad campaign featuring actors portraying Abbott and Costello. Pepsi uses a Buddy Holly look-alike in television ads overseas.

While this illustration shows that image advertising can, and does, backfire on occasion, you should not conclude that purely informative advertising is somehow better, or less risky, than image advertising. Both forms of advertising involve some degree of risk, and neither type of advertising can be guaranteed to increase demand.

*Joanne Lipman, "Subaru's New Ad Campaign Isn't Working," *The Wall Street Journal*, March 31, 1992.

†Kevin Goldman, "Dead Celebrities Are Resurrected as Pitchmen," *The Wall Street Journal*, January 7, 1994.

product. In addition, informative ads can lower the marginal costs of search. As discussed in the previous section, the lower the marginal cost of additional search, the greater the amount of time spent searching for a lower price, and the actual money price paid (P) is likely to be lower. Thus, informative ads can lower both P and S causing P_F to fall, MU/P_F to rise, and sales to increase.

Image Advertising

Image advertising is designed to change the consumer's preference patterns so that the consumer perceives a higher marginal utility associated with the good. Examples of image advertising are the ads for Chrysler's New Yorker, which show the car parked on the driveway of an elegant mansion, or the ads for Merrill Lynch, which often show a bull to create the image of a strong company "bullish" on the stock market. By enhancing the image of a good or service, the marginal utility increases, causing the marginal utility per dollar spent on the good (MU/P) to increase. As explained earlier, an increase in MU/P, for a given level of income, will cause a consumer to buy more of a good. Thus, image advertising causes an increase in the demand by increasing the perceived marginal utility of the good or service. In contrast to informative advertising, image advertising does not affect price.

7.10 SUMMARY

This chapter has provided the theoretical underpinnings for demand analysis. We began with a utility function,

$$U = U(X,Y)$$

and the fact that the consumers can rank various bundles of consumption goods as to whether they prefer one bundle to another or are indifferent between the two. We then constructed an indifference curve showing all combinations of two commodities among which a consumer is indifferent. The collection of all indifference curves—the consumer's indifference map—shows what the consumer is willing to purchase: consumers gain utility by consuming more of the commodities. On a more technical level, we discussed why the marginal rate of substitution diminishes as more of good X is consumed and why the slope of the indifference curve—the marginal rate of substitution—is equal to the ratio of the marginal utilities of the two commodities:

$$MRS = MU_x/MU_y$$

The consumer's budget line determines what the consumer is able to consume. The budget line is a straight line with a slope equal to the ratio of the prices of the two commodities:

$$Y = (M/P_y) - (P_x/P_y)X$$

As income changes, the budget line shifts. As price changes the budget line rotates.

The consumer maximizes utility subject to the constraint of a limited income by consuming that combination of the two commodities at which the budget line is tangent to an indifference curve. At that point, the slope of the budget line is equal to the slope of the highest attainable indifference curve, so the equilibrium condition can be expressed as:

$$MRS = MU_x/MU_y = P_x/P_y$$

or

$$\frac{MU_x}{P_x} = \frac{MU_y}{P_y}$$

An individual consumer's demand curve can be derived by holding income and the prices of all other commodities constant, then altering the price of one commodity and observing how the constrained utility-maximizing consumption of that commodity changes. Price changes have two effects: a substitution effect and an income effect. The substitution effect of a price change upon the consumption of that good is always negative; that is, quantity demanded varies inversely with price, holding utility constant and considering the substitution effect only. If the good is normal, the income effect reinforces the substitution effect. If the good is inferior, the income effect offsets to some extent the substitution effect.

The market demand curve is the horizontal summation of the demand curves of all consumers in the market. It shows how much all consumers demand at each price in the relevant range of prices.

When consumers have imperfect information about prices and product quality, they must engage in search for information. The optimal level of search is found by considering both the benefits from searching for more information and the search costs associated with gathering price or quality information. When the marginal benefit from search and the marginal cost of search are both known with certainty, the consumer will continue to search up to the point where

$$MB_{\text{search}} = MC_{\text{search}}$$

While the marginal cost of search is generally known to a consumer, the marginal benefit from search is often not known with certainty, which creates a decision-making problem involving risk. When the marginal benefit from search is random, a risk-neutral consumer will increase the amount of time spent searching for information up to the point where the *expected* marginal benefit just equals the (known) marginal cost:

$$E(MB_{\text{search}}) = MC_{\text{search}}$$

At this level of search, the expected net benefit from search is maximized.

The purpose of advertising is to increase sales. Advertising can be classified as either purely informative advertising or image advertising. Informative advertising conveys information about the product price and product quality. The higher the marginal utility per dollar spent on a good (MU/P), the more of the good the consumer will buy. Information about product quality can enhance the perceived marginal utility of a good, increasing MU/P, and increasing sales. Informative advertising can also lower consumer information search costs. This, in turn, lowers the full price (money price plus the search costs) of the good or service and increases sales. Image advertising conveys an image about a product that is designed to increase the consumer's perception of the marginal utility of the good. Increasing marginal utility causes MU/P to increase for the good. Thus, image advertising increases demand.

TECHNICAL PROBLEMS

1. Suppose that two units of X and eight units of Y give a consumer the same satisfaction as four units of X and two units of Y. Over this range:
   a. If the consumer obtains one more unit of X, how many units of Y must be given up in order to keep utility constant?
   b. If the consumer obtains one more unit of Y, how many units of X must be given up in order to keep utility constant?
   c. What is the marginal rate of substitution?
   d. What is the ratio of the marginal utility of X to the marginal utility of Y?
2. Use the following graph to answer this question.

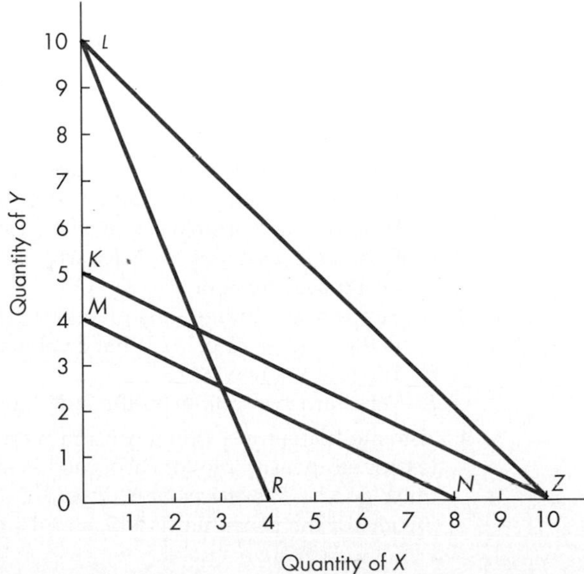

a. The equation of budget line *LZ* is $Y =$ _____ $-$ _____ X.
b. The equation of budget line *LR* is $Y =$ _____ $-$ _____ X.
c. The equation of budget line *KZ* is $Y =$ _____ $-$ _____ X.
d. The equation of budget line *MN* is $Y =$ _____ $-$ _____ X.

3. Suppose a consumer has the indifference map shown in the following graph. The relevant budget line is *LZ*. The price of good *Y* is $10.

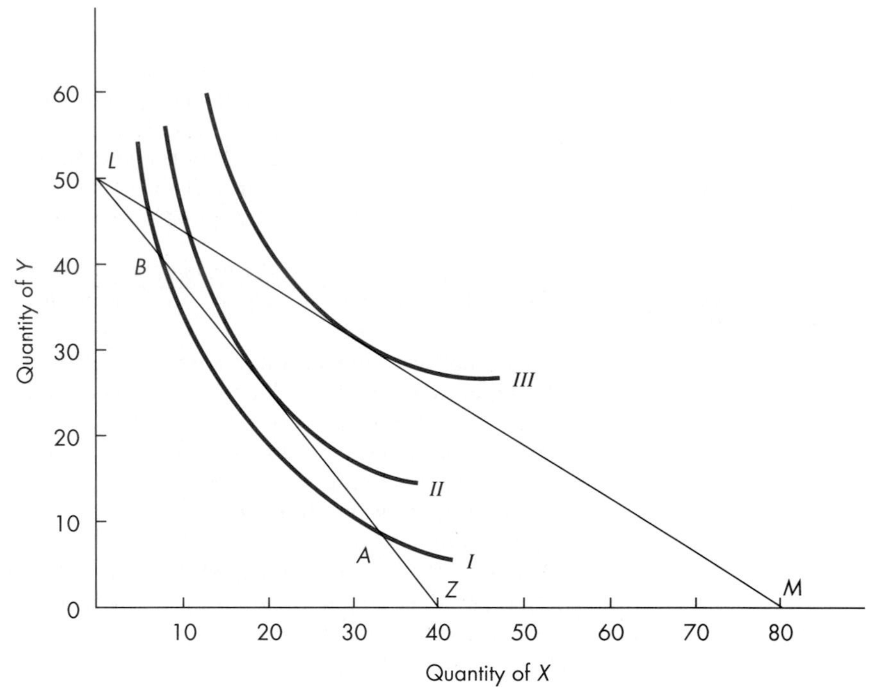

a. What is the consumer's income?
b. What is the price of *X*?
c. Write the equation for the budget line *LZ*.
d. What combination of *X* and *Y* will the consumer choose? Why?
e. What is the marginal rate of substitution at this combination?
f. Explain in terms of the *MRS* why the consumer would not choose combinations designated by *A* or *B*.
g. Suppose the budget line pivots to *LM*, money income remaining constant. What is the new price of *X*? What combination of *X* and *Y* is now chosen?
h. What is the new *MRS*?
i. What are two points on the individual's demand curve for *X*?

* 4. Assume that an individual consumes three goods, *X*, *Y*, and *Z*. The marginal utility (assumed measurable) of each good is independent of the rate of consumption of other goods. The prices of *X*, *Y*, and *Z* are respectively $1, $3, and $5. The total income of the consumer is $65, and the marginal utility schedule is as follows:

Units of good	Marginal utility of X (units)	Marginal utility of Y (units)	Marginal utility of Z (units)
1	12	60	70
2	11	55	60
3	10	48	50
4	9	40	40
5	8	32	30
6	7	24	25
7	6	21	18
8	5	18	10
9	4	15	3
10	3	12	1

a. Given a $65 income, how much of each good should the consumer purchase to maximize utility?
b. Suppose income falls to $43 with the same set of prices; what combination will the consumer choose?
c. Let income fall to $38; let the price of X rise to $5 while the prices of Y and Z remain at $3 and $5. How does the consumer allocate income now? What would you say if the consumer maintained that X is not purchased because he or she could no longer afford it?

5. Suppose that the marginal rate of substitution of X for Y is 2, the price of X is $3, and the price of Y is $1.
   a. If the consumer obtains one more unit of X, how many units of Y must be given up in order to keep utility constant?
   b. If the consumer obtains one more unit of Y, how many units of X must be given up in order to keep utility constant?
   c. What is the rate at which the consumer is willing to substitute X for Y?
   d. What is the rate at which the consumer is able to substitute X for Y?
   e. Is the consumer making the utility-maximizing choice? Why or why not? If not, what should the consumer do? Explain.
6. A person's marginal rate of substitution between X and Y is 4. The price of X is $12 and the price of Y is $3. The consumer is in equilibrium. The price of X rises to $15 and the price of Y rises to $5. Income is varied to restrict the consumer to the original level of utility. Does the person choose more X and less Y or less X and more Y? Explain.

* 7. The graph that follows shows a portion of a consumer's indifference map. If the consumer faces the budget line LZ and the price of X is $20 then:
   a. The consumer's income = $_____.
   b. The price of Y is = $_____.
   c. The equation for the budget line LZ is _____.
   d. What combination of X and Y does the consumer choose? Why?
   e. The marginal rate of substitution for this combination is _____.
   f. Explain in terms of MRS why the consumer does not choose either combination A or B.
   g. What combination is chosen if the budget line pivots to MZ?
   h. The new price of Y = $ _____.
   i. The new price of X = $ _____.
   j. The new MRS is _____.

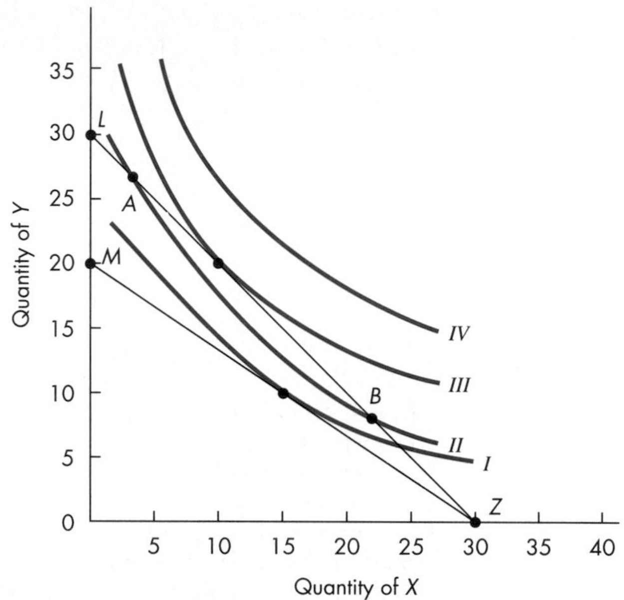

8. In the graph below, indifference curves *I*, *II*, and *III* make up a portion of an individual's indifference map. The consumer's income is \$1,000; the price of *Y* is \$20. Derive three points on the individual's demand curve for good *X* corresponding to prices of \$67, \$20, and \$11 for good *X*.

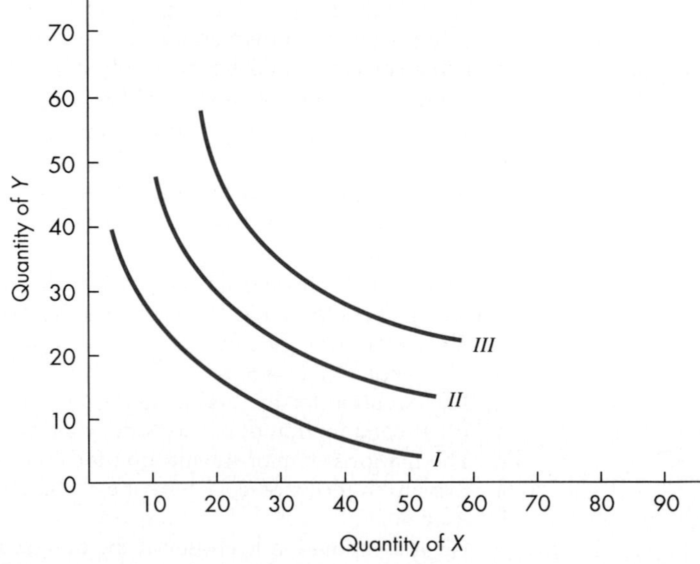

9. In the following graph the consumer begins in equilibrium with an income of \$5,000 facing the prices P_x = \$50 and P_y = \$25.

a. In equilibrium, ______ units of X are consumed.

Now let the price of X fall to \$20, income and the price of Y remaining constant.

b. In the new equilibrium, ______ units of X are consumed.

c. In order to isolate the substitution effect, \$ ______ must be taken away from the consumer.

d. The total effect of the price decrease is ______. The substitution effect is ______. The income effect is ______.

e. Good X is ______, but not ______.

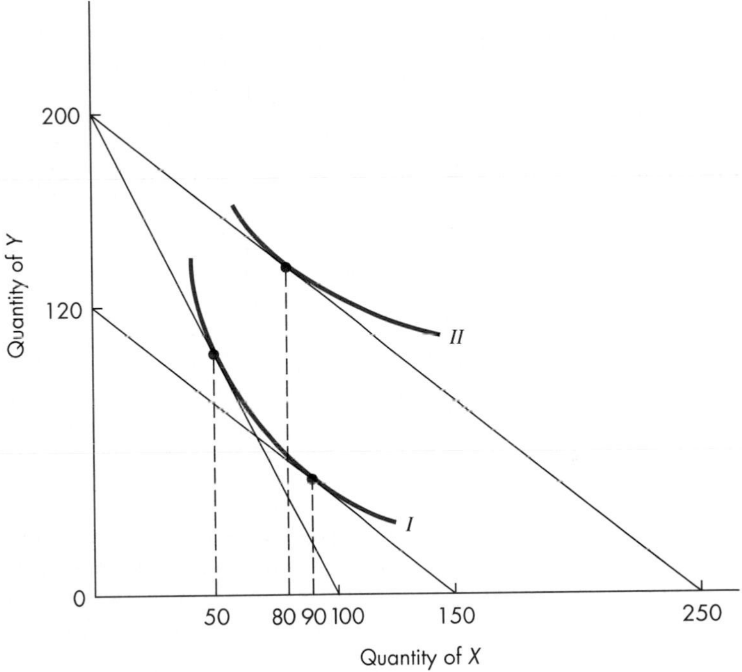

10. Suppose there are only three consumers in the market for good X. The quantities demanded by each consumer at each price between \$1 and \$9 are shown in the table below:

Price of X	Quantity demanded			Market demand
	Consumer 1	Consumer 2	Consumer 3	
9	0	5	10	______
8	0	10	20	______
7	10	15	30	______
6	20	20	40	______
5	30	25	50	______
4	40	30	60	______
3	50	35	70	______
2	60	40	80	______
1	70	45	90	______

a. Using the following graph, draw the demand curve for each of the three consumers. Label the three curves D_1, D_2, and D_3, respectively.
b. Fill in the blanks in the table for the market quantity demanded at each price.
c. Construct the market demand curve in the graph, and label it D_m.

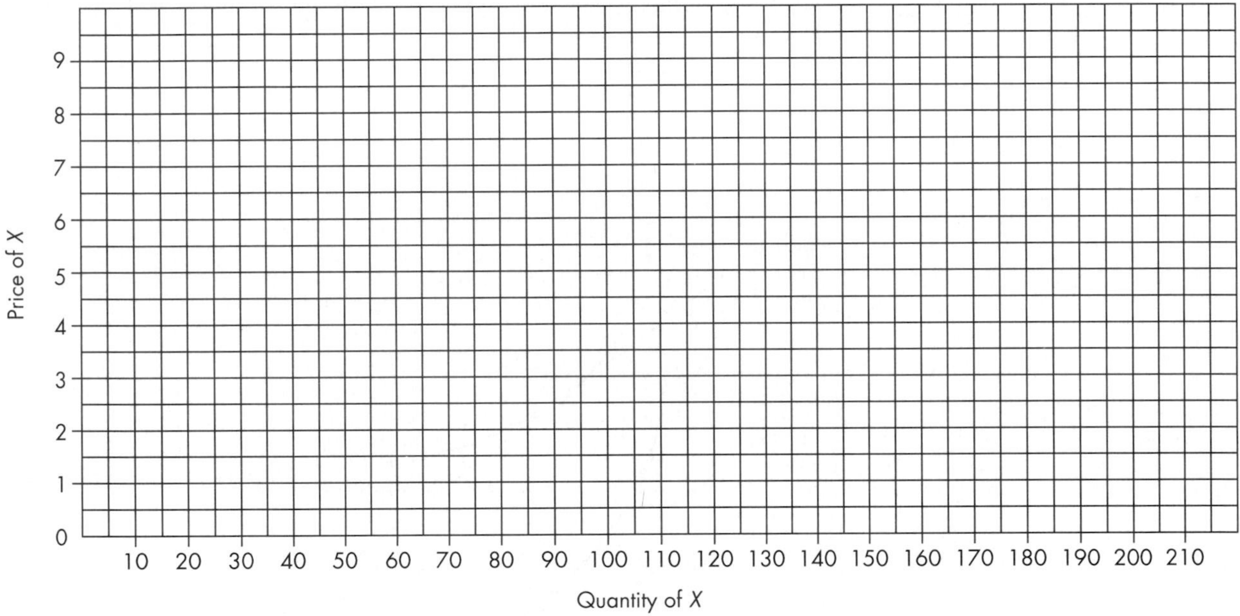

11. The following graph shows the (known) marginal benefit curve for a consumer searching for price information. The consumer's leisure time is worth $15 per hour.

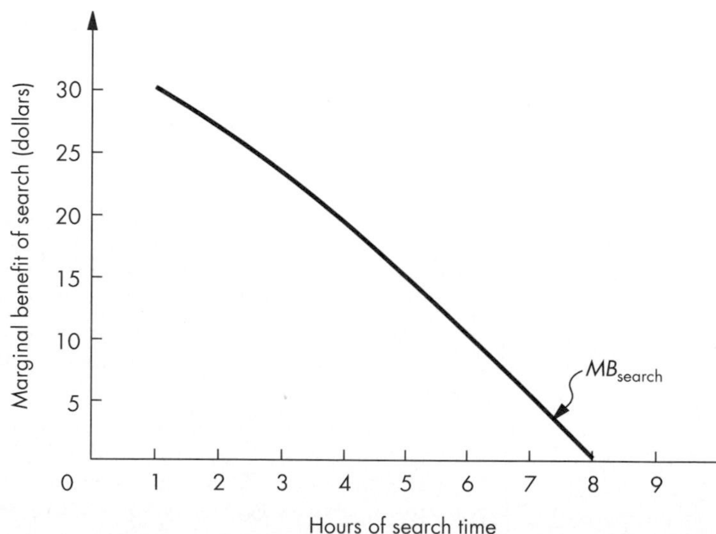

a. If the consumer wishes to obtain the lowest possible price, _____ hours should be spent searching for a lower price.

b. On the graph above, draw the marginal cost curve for search.

c. The consumer maximizes the net benefit of search by spending _____ hours searching for a lower price. The optimal level of search is the level for which _____ equals _____.

d. If the consumer's leisure time is worth only $5 per hour, the optimal level of search is _____ hours.

APPLIED PROBLEMS

1. Gigi has a limited income and consumes only wine and cheese; her current consumption choice is 4 bottles of wine and 10 pounds of cheese. The price of wine is $10 per bottle and the price of cheese is $4 per pound. The last bottle of wine added 50 units to Gigi's utility, while the last pound of cheese added 40 units.
   a. Is Gigi making the utility-maximizing choice? Why or why not?
   b. If not, what should she do instead? Why?
2. Suppose Bill is on a low carbohydrate diet. He can eat only three foods: Rice Krispies, cottage cheese, and popcorn. The marginal utilities for each food are tabulated below. Bill is allowed only 167 grams of carbohydrates daily. Rice Krispies, cottage cheese, and popcorn provide 25, 6, and 10 grams of carbohydrates per cup, respectively.

Units of food (cups/day)	Marginal utility of Rice Krispies	Marginal utility of cottage cheese	Marginal utility of popcorn
1	175	72	90
2	150	66	80
3	125	60	70
4	100	54	60
5	75	48	50
6	50	36	40
7	25	30	30
8	25	18	20

   a. Given that Bill can only consume 167 grams of carbohydrates daily, how many cups of each food will he consume daily? Show your work.
   b. Suppose Bill's doctor tells him to further reduce his carbohydrate intake to 126 grams per day. What combination will he consume?
3. What methods, other than advertising, can firms use to shift consumers' indifference curves or change the marginal rates of substitution between the product they sell and substitute products?
4. Grocery store ads are examples of informative advertising. They generally contain nothing more than price and availability information. Why is no quality information presented? For what kind of products would we be likely to find no quality information in the ad? What kind of products require that quality information be presented?

5. Can you think of hypothetical cases in which someone would not give up a single unit of a good, no matter what is offered in exchange? What type of goods would these extreme examples be?
6. The beef association, dairy farmers, the potato growers association, the US textile industry, and the Florida citrus growers often run ads designed to increase the demand for a product. Why are trade associations, rather than individual firms, placing these ads?
7. The manager/owner of Good Guys Enterprises obtains utility from income (profit) and from having the firm behave in a socially conscious manner, such as making charitable contributions or civic expenditures. Can you set up the problem and derive the equilibrium conditions if the manager/owner wishes to obtain a specific level of utility at the lowest possible cost? Do these conditions differ from the utility-maximizing conditions?
8. Joan Quant decides to buy a used car. She is known for carefully and intelligently making her consumption decisions. After carefully considering a number of various makes of autos, she has decided to buy a compact car driven no more than 75,000 miles. Joan lives in a rather large urban area that has several newspapers, as well as a publication specializing in used cars. Given that search is costly, how could Joan determine the amount of time to spend searching for the best price? In what sense is this the best price?
9. In terms of the consumer theory set forth in this chapter, can you explain the meaning of the following expressions?
   a. I think you get more for your money from Nike than from Reebok.
   b. I wanted to buy an RX-7 rather than a Mazda 626 but it just wasn't worth it.
   c. You pick the restaurant, but after dinner I'd rather see *Rambo VIII* than *Dances with Wolves*.
   d. "I'd like to go to Mexico over spring break, but I just can't afford it," said Don. Jill asked, "Don't you have enough money in your account?" Don replied, "Yeah, but I can't afford to go."
   e. Jack had to flip a coin to decide whether to buy chocolate chip or coffee ice cream.
10. On April 23, 1991, the Air Force awarded a $93 billion (or more) contract to a group led by Lockheed, Boeing, and General Dynamics to build the new fighter plane for the 21st century, the YF-22 Lightning 2. A group headed by Northrop and McDonnell Douglas, which had spent over $1 billion on development for their alternative YF-23, lost out on the contract. That evening on CNN's "Crossfire," Secretary of Defense Cheney explained that the Lockheed group got the contract because their "quality for the price per plane was higher." He didn't elaborate. In terms of the theory set forth in this chapter, did he mean
    a. The Lockheed quality was higher?
    b. The Lockheed price was lower?
    If neither, what did he mean?
11. *The Wall Street Journal* (January 22, 1992) reported that the "laws of economics often don't apply in (the) health-care field" citing numerous examples of consumers that paid higher prices than necessary for health care, and in some cases, also received lower quality care at the higher price. Despite widely varying prices and qualities, patients rarely comparison shop among doctors and hospitals. Using consumer search theory, explain why patients may spend little or no time searching for price and quality information when seeking medical help.

APPENDIX Utility Maximization Subject to an Income Constraint

In the text of this chapter, we considered the problem of maximizing utility subject to an income (budget) constraint. We provided both a graphical and a verbal description of the constrained optimization problem. For the student with a mathematical background, this problem can be solved easily using the tools of differential calculus.

The consumer maximizes utility,

$$U = U(X, Y)$$

subject to the income (budget) constraint,

$$M = P_xX + P_yY$$

Thus, the Lagrangian function to be maximized is

$$\mathcal{L} = U(X, Y) + \lambda(M - P_xX - P_yY)$$

Maximization of this function with respect to the levels of consumption of X and Y requires that the partial derivatives be equal to zero:

$$\frac{\partial \mathcal{L}}{\partial X} = \frac{\partial U}{\partial X} - \lambda P_x = 0$$

and

$$\frac{\partial \mathcal{L}}{\partial Y} = \frac{\partial U}{\partial Y} - \lambda P_y = 0$$

Combining the two equations, the necessary condition for maximizing utility subject to the income constraint is

$$\frac{\partial U/\partial X}{\partial U/\partial Y} = \frac{P_x}{P_y}$$

Note that $\partial U/\partial X$ and $\partial U/\partial Y$ are the marginal utilities of the two goods; their ratio is the marginal rate of substitution. The ratio P_x/P_y is the absolute value of the slope of the budget line. Hence, the necessary condition for income-constrained utility maximization is that the marginal rate of substitution between the two commodities be equal to the ratio of their prices.

C H A P T E R

8

Empirical Demand Functions

Information about demand is essential for making pricing and production decisions. Managers need to understand how quantity demanded is affected by changes in variables such as the price of the good, household income, the price of substitute goods, or any of the other variables that determine demand. Managers also need to be able to forecast prices and sales in the future. From the discussion in Chapter 7 and in previous chapters, it should be clear why knowledge about the demand function is important to a manager. In planning and making policy decisions, managers must have some idea about the characteristics of the demand for their products in order to attain the objectives of the firm.

empirical demand functions Demand equations derived from market data.

In order to accomplish their goals, managers frequently rely on empirical demand functions for decision-making purposes. **Empirical demand functions** are demand equations derived from actual market data. This chapter and the next show you how managers can estimate the demand for their products and forecast prices and sales. As you will see in later chapters, empirical demand functions can be extremely useful in making pricing and production decisions.

We begin with a description of some of the more direct methods of demand estimation—consumer interviews and market studies. We deal rather briefly with these methods, attempting only to point out the strengths and weaknesses in each. The primary topic of the chapter is the use of regression analysis to estimate demand functions. As always, our fundamental concern is how an analyst can use regression analysis and interpret the results, rather than with the precise statistical concepts underlying the estimation. To this end, we will provide some examples to show how actual demand functions have been estimated and interpreted.

This chapter about demand estimation and the next chapter about demand forecasting are intended to provide you with an introductory treatment of empirical demand analysis. While our discussion of statistical demand estimation (and statistical demand forecasting) is limited to the simpler methods, these methods are widely used in business to analyze market demand. Almost all of the more advanced techniques of empirical demand analysis that you will encounter in your marketing research, advanced statistics, and econometrics courses are extensions of, or related to, the methods we will present in the next two chapters.

8.1 DIRECT METHODS OF DEMAND ESTIMATION

Direct methods of demand estimation are techniques that do not involve regression analysis. After reading about some of these direct methods of estimation, you may get the impression that direct estimation techniques are quite simple and straightforward. This is far from correct. Many of the techniques used in making direct estimates of demand are quite sophisticated and require a great deal of experience and expertise in order to estimate demand accurately. This section is designed only to give an overview of some of the methods that can be used and is not meant to teach you how to make these types of estimates. Such instruction is left to more advanced marketing courses.

Consumer Interviews

Since consumers themselves should be the most knowledgeable about their individual demand functions for particular commodities, the most straightforward method of demand estimation would be simply to ask potential buyers how much of the commodity they would buy at different prices with alternative values for the determinants of demand (i.e., the price of substitute commodities, the price of complement commodities, and so on). At the simplest level, this might be accomplished by stopping shoppers and asking them how much of the product they would buy at various prices. At a more sophisticated level, this procedure would entail administering detailed questionnaires to a selected sample of the population by professional interviewers. While this procedure appears very simple, there exist several substantial problems. Among these problems are (1) the selection of a representative sample, (2) response bias, and (3) the inability of the respondent to answer accurately. Let's look at each of these problems briefly.

When selecting a sample of the population for a survey, the resulting demand estimation is reliable only if the survey uses a representative sample. A **representative sample** has the same characteristics of the population as a whole. A representative sample is typically obtained by *randomly* selecting members for the sample from the general population. For example, if 52 percent of the population is female, and if 35 percent have annual incomes over $65,000, then a representative sample must have approximately 52 percent females and 35 percent persons with incomes over $65,000. In actuality, it is very difficult to obtain a truly representative sample.

representative sample
A sample, usually drawn randomly, that has characteristics that accurately reflect the population as a whole.

A classic illustration of what can happen if the sample is not random occurred during the presidential campaign of 1948. A survey was performed that predicted an overwhelming victory for Thomas Dewey. In fact, Harry Truman won the election. The problem with the survey was that the sample was drawn from the subscription list of a particular magazine. The subscribers were not representative of the entire population of the United States; they were instead a subgroup of the voting population and had some important characteristics in common. Thus, the biased sample led to biased results. In 1936, in a similar but less celebrated election forecast error, a popular magazine predicted Franklin Roosevelt would lose that election and were wrong because the pollsters used a telephone survey and only wealthy people were able to afford phones at that time. Today, election forecasting has become so accurate—in large part due to the advanced sampling techniques now employed by pollsters—that television networks are not allowed to project winners until the polls are all closed on election day.

Another example of a biased sample yielding misleading results occurred at a home-building convention, during which Owens-Corning Fiberglas Corporation commissioned a survey to determine the industry's outlook for future sales. The results were startling. The survey indicated that builders were planning to increase housing starts by an amazing 30 percent. When asked to interpret the bullish forecast, Michael Sumichrast, chief economist for the National Association of Home Builders, replied that "it shows when you ask stupid questions, you get stupid answers." Apparently, the survey did not use a representative sample. According to *The Wall Street Journal*, the survey was taken only among the builders who attended the convention, and these builders tend to be the larger and more aggressive companies which would naturally be more bullish in their outlook.[1]

response bias
The difference between the response given by an individual to a hypothetical question and the action the individual takes when the situation actually occurs.

A **response bias** can result simply from the fact that those interviewed are giving hypothetical answers to hypothetical questions. The answers do not necessarily reflect what the individual will do; rather, they may reflect intentions or desires. More importantly, however, the responses may be biased by the manner in which the question is asked. In many cases, the questions may be such that the respondents give what they view as a more socially acceptable response, rather than reveal their true preferences.

One example of response bias is found in a survey by an automobile manufacturer taken many years ago—during the time of cheap gasoline. Potential consumers were asked if they would be interested in buying small economical cars (i.e., fuel-efficient cars) which were not flashy, fast, or showy. A large number of people said they would indeed buy such a car. On the basis of this survey, the manufacturer introduced a small, fuel-efficient car—with disastrous results. Perhaps had the respondents—who indicated that they wanted economy cars—been asked whether their *neighbors* would buy such cars they might have provided more valid responses. It's easier to say that your neighbor wants a flashy

[1]See "Stupid Questions," *The Wall Street Journal*, February 7, 1984.

car than to admit that you do. The point is that the wrong question was asked. The way the question was asked induced a response bias.

Past surveys by food manufacturers have yielded bad results because of response bias. The food industry has a lot riding on the claims that people make about what they eat. Food companies have, in the past, conducted their market research by asking people what they eat. Based on the results of these surveys, the food manufacturers would develop new products. But, as noted in *The Wall Street Journal*, there is one big problem: "People don't always tell the truth."[2] As Harry Balzer, the vice president of a market research firm, said: "Nobody likes to admit he likes junk food." In other words, a response bias exists in such surveys. Instead of answering truthfully, a consumer is likely to give a socially acceptable answer. Asking a sweets-eater how many Twinkies he eats "is like asking an alcoholic if he drinks much."

Finally, it is quite possible that the respondent is *simply unable to answer accurately the question posed.* Conceptually, the firm performing the survey may want to know about the elasticity of demand for its products. Thus, the firm is interested in the response of consumers to incremental changes in price and some other variable. For example, the firm needs to know how the consumers would react to such things as a 1, 2, or 3 percent increase (or decrease) in price or a 5 percent increase (decrease) in advertising expenditures. Obviously, most people interviewed are not able to answer such questions precisely.

Although the survey technique is plagued with these inherent difficulties, it can still be an extremely valuable tool for a manager to use in quantifying demand. The trick in doing a survey is to avoid the pitfalls, and, as the following discussion indicates, it can be done.

Market Studies and Experiments

A somewhat more expensive and difficult technique for estimating demand and demand elasticity is the controlled market study or experiment. The analyst attempts to hold everything constant during the study except for the price of the good.

Those carrying out these market studies normally display the products in several different stores, generally in areas with different characteristics, over a period of time. They make certain that there are always sufficient amounts available in every store at each price to satisfy demand. In this way the effect of changes in supply is removed. There is generally no advertising. During the period of the experiment, price is changed in relatively small increments over a range, and sales are recorded at each price. In this way, many of the effects of changes in other things can be removed, and a reasonable approximation of the actual demand curve can be estimated.

An example of such an approach is a study conducted by M&M/Mars using 150 stores over a 12-month period to determine the optimal weights for its candy

[2]See Betsy Morris, "Study to Detect True Eating Habits Finds Junk-Food Fans in Health-Food Ranks," *The Wall Street Journal*, February 3, 1984.

bars.[3] Instead of altering the price from store to store, the company kept price constant and altered the size of the product. As the director of sales development reported, in stores where the size was increased "sales went up 20 percent to 30 percent almost overnight." As a result, M&M/Mars decided to change much of its product line.

A relatively new technique for estimating demand is the use of experiments performed in a laboratory or in the field. Such experiments are a compromise between market studies and surveys. In some types of laboratory experiments, volunteers are paid to simulate actual buying conditions without going through real markets. Volunteer consumers are given money to go on simulated market trips. The experimenter changes relative prices between trips. After many shopping trips by many consumers an approximation of demand is obtained. The volunteers have the incentive to act as though they are really shopping, because there is a probability that they may keep their purchases.

Going a step further, some economists have conducted experiments about consumer behavior—with the help of psychologists—in mental institutions and in drug centers, by setting up token economies (which incidentally are supposed to have therapeutic value). Patients receive tokens for jobs performed. They can exchange these tokens for goods and services. The experimenters can change prices and incomes and thus generate demand curves, the properties of which are compared with the theoretical properties of such curves.

In field experiments, the researchers want to be able to change the price of goods and actually observe the behavior of the consumers. To illustrate this type of experiment, let us give you an example. Some economists at Texas A&M were interested in estimating the own-price elasticity of the demand of electric energy.[4] They recruited a sample of 100 households to participate in their experiment. The objective of the study was to observe these households' weekly consumption of electric power. After first establishing the households' baseline levels of usage, the researchers experimentally changed the price of electric power for part of their sample by paying rebates for reductions in weekly electricity usage.

For example, in one of their subgroups, the researchers paid the household 1.3 cents for every kilowatt-hour (kwh) reduction in weekly usage. At the time this study was conducted, the cost of electrical power to the residential consumers was 2.6 cents per kwh. Therefore, for this subgroup, the price of consuming an additional kwh was increased: To consume an additional kwh, the household not only had to *pay* 2.6 cents but also had to *forgo* the rebate of 1.3 cents they could have received had they conserved rather than consumed electricity.

---

[3]See John Koten, "Why Do Hot Dogs Come in Packs of 10 and Buns in 8s or 12s?", *The Wall Street Journal*, September 21, 1984.

[4]This example is taken from Raymond C. Battalio, John H. Kagel, Robin C. Winkler, and Richard A. Wineh, "Residential Electricity Demand: An Experimental Study," *The Review of Economics and Statistics*, May 1979, pp. 180–89.

Hence, for this subgroup, the price of electricity increased by 50 percent, from 2.6 to 3.9 cents per kwh.

Other subgroups were given other rebate schedules. And one subgroup—the control group—was given no rebate. The researchers could then actually measure the reduction in electricity consumption due to the experimentally imposed price increase by comparing the change in the consumption of the subgroup receiving the rebate with the change in the consumption of the control group.

The results of this experimental study indicated that the maximum own-price elasticity of the residential demand for electricity was 0.32. That is, the experiment indicated that the residential demand for electricity was price inelastic. However, as the researchers indicated, this study measured an extremely short-run elasticity. (As we noted in Chapter 3, we would expect the price elasticity to increase as the time period for adjustment gets longer.)

The experimental approach to estimating the demand for products has rapidly moved out of the laboratories and off the college campuses to the real-world applications more of interest to Wall Street and Main Street. The rapid growth of microcomputers and cable television systems has made possible market experiments that could only have been dreamed of a few years ago.

8.2 SPECIFICATION OF THE EMPIRICAL DEMAND FUNCTION

Managers can use the techniques of regression analysis outlined in Chapter 5 to obtain estimates of the demand for their firm's product. The theoretical foundation for specifying and analyzing empirical demand functions is provided by the theory of consumer behavior, which was presented in Chapter 7. In this section, we will show you two possible specifications of the demand function to be estimated. Again, we do not intend to teach you statistics or econometrics. Instead, we want to give you an idea of how these techniques of demand estimation can provide useful information for managerial decision making.

As we will discuss later in this chapter (section 8.3), the statistical method used to estimate the parameters of a *market* demand function differs from the method used to estimate the demand curve for a *single firm*. Despite the differences in the way the parameters are estimated for market and firm demand functions, the way that empirical demand functions are specified and interpreted for market and firm demand equations is essentially the same. Thus, the two empirical demand specifications that we discuss in the following paragraphs can be applied to the estimation of either market or firm demand functions.

A General Empirical Demand Specification

In order to estimate a demand function for a product it is necessary to use a specific functional form. Here we will consider both linear and nonlinear forms. Before proceeding, however, we must simplify the general demand relation. Recall that quantity demanded depends on the price of the product, consumer income, the price of related goods, consumer tastes or preferences, expected price, and the number of buyers. Given the difficulties inherent in quantifying taste and price expectations, we will ignore these variables—as is commonly done in many empirical demand studies—and write the general demand function as

$$Q_x = f(P_x, M, P_R, N)$$

where

Q_x = quantity purchased of commodity X
P_x = price of X
M = consumers' income
P_R = price(s) of related good(s)
N = number of buyers

While this general demand specification seems rather simple and straightforward, the task of defining and collecting the data for demand estimation requires careful consideration of numerous factors. For example, it is important to recognize the geographic boundaries of the product market. Suppose a firm sells its product only in California. In this case, the consumer income variable (M) should measure the buyers' incomes in the state of California. Using average household income in the United States would be a mistake unless California's household income level matches nationwide income levels and trends. It is also crucial to include the prices of all substitute and complement goods that affect sales of the firm's product in California. While we will illustrate empirical demand functions using just one related good (either a substitute or complement), there are often numerous related goods whose prices should be included in the specification of an empirical demand function. Whether the market is growing (or shrinking) in size is another consideration. Researchers frequently include a measure of population in the demand specification as a proxy variable for the number of buyers. As you can see from this brief discussion, defining and collecting data to estimate even a simple general demand function requires careful consideration.

A Linear Empirical Demand Specification

The simplest demand function is one that specifies a linear relation. In linear form, the empirical demand function is specified as

$$Q_x = a + bP_x + cM + dP_R + eN$$

In this equation, the parameter b measures the change in quantity demanded that would result from a one-unit change in the price of X. That is, $b = \Delta Q_x/\Delta P_x$, which is assumed to be negative. Also,

$$c = \Delta Q_x/\Delta M \gtrless 0 \text{ if } X \text{ is a } \begin{cases} \text{normal good} \\ \text{inferior good} \end{cases}$$

and

$$d = \Delta Q_x/\Delta P_R \gtrless 0 \text{ if commodity } R \text{ is a } \begin{cases} \text{substitute} \\ \text{complement} \end{cases}$$

Using the techniques of regression analysis, this linear demand function can be estimated to provide estimates of the parameters *a, b, c, d,* and *e*. Then *t*-tests are performed to determine if these parameters are statistically significant.

As stressed in Chapter 3, the elasticity of demand is an important aspect of demand. The elasticities of demand—with respect to own-price, income, and the prices of related commodities—can be calculated from a linear demand function without much difficulty. Consider first the own-price elasticity, defined as

$$E = \frac{\Delta Q_x}{\Delta P_x} \cdot \frac{P_x}{Q_x}$$

In the linear specification set forth in the previous text, $b = \Delta Q_x/\Delta P_x$, so the *estimated* own-price elasticity is

$$\hat{E} = \hat{b} \cdot \frac{P_x}{Q_x}$$

As you know from the discussion of demand elasticity in Chapter 3, the elasticity depends upon where it is measured along the demand curve (note the P_x/Q_x term in the formula above). The elasticity should be evaluated at the price and quantity values that correspond to the point on the demand curve being analyzed. If no particular point on demand is specified, then it is customary to evaluate the elasticity at the mean values in the sample for price and output (i.e., $\overline{P}_x$ and $\overline{Q}_x$). If *b* is statistically significant, the estimated elasticity ($\hat{E}$) will also be statistically significant.

In similar manner, the income elasticity may be estimated as

$$\hat{E}_M = \hat{c} \cdot \frac{M}{Q_x}$$

Likewise, the estimated cross-price elasticity is

$$\hat{E}_{XR} = \hat{d} \cdot \frac{P_R}{Q_x}$$

A Nonlinear Empirical Demand Specification

The most commonly employed nonlinear demand specification is the log-linear (or constant elasticity) form. A log-linear demand function is written as

$$Q_x = aP_x^b M^c P_R^d N^e$$

The obvious potential advantage of this form is that it provides a better estimate if the true demand function is indeed nonlinear. Furthermore, as you may recall from Chapter 5, this specification allows for the direct estimation of the elasticities. Specifically, the value of parameter *b* measures the own-price elasticity of demand. Likewise, *c* and *d*, respectively, measure the income elasticity and cross-price elasticity of demand.[5]

[5]See Appendix A to this chapter for the derivation of the elasticities associated with the log-linear demand specification.

ILLUSTRATION 8.1

Demand for Imported Goods in Trinidad and Tobago: A Log-Linear Estimation

Trinidad and Tobago, two small developing countries in the Caribbean, rely heavily on imports from other nations to provide their citizens with consumer and capital goods. Policymakers in these two countries need estimates of the demand for various imported goods to aid them in their trade-related negotiations and to make forecasts of trade balances in Trinidad and Tobago. The own-price elasticities and income elasticities of demand are of particular interest.

In a recent empirical study, John S. Gafar estimated the demand for imported goods in the two countries, using a log-linear specification of demand.* According to Gafar, the two most common functional forms used to estimate import demand are the linear and log-linear forms. As we noted, the choice of functional form is often based on the past experience of experts in a particular area of empirical research. Gafar chose to use the log-linear specification because a number of other import studies "have shown that the log-linear specification is preferable to the linear specification."† Gafar notes that he experimented with both the linear and log-linear forms and found the log-linear model had the higher R^2.

In his study, Gafar estimates the demand for imports of eight groups of commodities. The demand for any particular group of imported goods is specified as

$$Q_d = aP^bM^c$$

where Q_d is the quantity of the imported good demanded by Trinidad and Tobago, P is the price of the imported good (relative to the price of a bundle of domestically produced goods), and M is an income variable. Taking natural logarithms of the demand equation results in the following demand equation to be estimated:

$$\log Q_d = \log a + b \log P + c \log M$$

Recall from the discussion in the text, b, is the own-price elasticity of demand, and c is the income elasticity of demand. The sign of $\hat{b}$ is expected to be negative and the sign of $\hat{c}$ can be either positive or negative. The results of estimation are presented in the table on the next page.

Only two of the estimated parameters are *not* statistically significant at the 95 percent level of

As you learned in Chapter 5, to obtain estimates from a log-linear demand function, you must convert it to logarithms. Thus, the function to be estimated is linear in the logarithms;

$$\log Q_x = \log a + b \log P_x + c \log M + d \log P_R + e \log N$$

Although we have presented only two functional forms (linear and log-linear) as possible choices for specifying the empirical demand equation, there are many possible functional forms from which to choose. As noted in Chapter 5, choosing an incorrect functional form of the equation to be estimated results in biased estimates of the parameters of the equation.

Unfortunately, the exact functional form of the demand equation generally is not known to the researcher. Choosing the functional form to use is, to a large degree, a matter of judgment and experience. Nevertheless, there are some things a manager can do to suggest the best choice of functional form. A manager should consider the functional form used in similar empirical studies of demand. If a linear specification has worked well in the past or has worked well

Estimated Own-Price and Income Elasticities in Trinidad and Tobago

Product group	Own-price elasticity estimates ($\hat{b}$)	Standard error of $\hat{b}$	Income elasticity estimates ($\hat{c}$)	Standard error of $\hat{c}$
Food	−0.6553	0.1632	1.6411	0.1281
Beverages and tobacco	−0.0537[n]	0.1165	1.8718	0.1591
Crude materials (except fuel)	−1.3879	0.3287	4.9619	0.4424
Animal and vegetable oils and fats	−0.3992	0.1427	1.8688	0.2049
Chemicals	−0.7211	0.1255	2.2711	0.1154
Manufactured goods	0.2774[n]	0.2566	3.2085	0.3692
Machinery and transport equipment	−0.6159	0.4239	2.9452	0.4982
Miscellaneous manufactured articles	−1.4585	0.3671	4.1997	0.3201

confidence (denoted by "n" in the table). Note that all the product groups have the expected sign for $\hat{b}$, except manufactured goods, for which the parameter estimate is not statistically significant. The estimates of $\hat{c}$ suggest that all eight product groups are normal goods ($\hat{c} > 0$). As you can see, with the log-linear specification, it is much easier to estimate demand elasticities than with a linear specification.

*This illustration is based on the paper by John S. Gafar, "The Determinants of Import Demand in Trinidad and Tobago: 1967–84," *Applied Economics* 20, (1988).

†Ibid.

for other products that are similar, specifying a linear demand function may be justified. In some cases a manager may have information or some type of experience that indicates whether the demand function is either linear or curvilinear, and this functional form is then used to estimate the demand equation.

Finally, if the estimated coefficients have the wrong signs, or if they are not statistically significant, the specification of the model may be wrong. Researchers often try estimating some new specifications, using the same data, to search for a specification that gives significant coefficients with the expected signs.[6]

Since the process of choosing the correct functional form is more of an art than a science, we have chosen to present just the linear and log-linear forms. These two functional forms of demand have proven to be quite popular in the empirical analysis of demand.

[6]In a strict statistical sense, it is incorrect to estimate more than one model specification with the same set of data.

8.3 ESTIMATING MARKET DEMAND

While most managers will never need to estimate the *market* demand for a good or service, sometimes managers at large corporations will have a staff of professional econometricians or statisticians who do estimate market demand and supply curves in order to study industry-wide price and output trends. Our purpose in this section is to familiarize you with the process of estimating market demand, and to show you some of the problems that can arise when market demand curves are estimated using regression analysis. It is important for you to know something about how market demand curves are estimated, even though you will probably never estimate a market demand curve yourself. This knowledge will help you avoid being intimidated by the jargon that econometricians are fond of using around managers. After we discuss the complications involved with estimating a market demand curve in this section, we will show you in the following section that estimating the demand curve for a *single firm* is much easier than estimating *market* demand. This is fortunate, since most managers are primarily concerned with estimating the demand for their own firm's output. We turn now to a discussion of the basic problem of simultaneity which makes estimating market demand curves difficult.

The Nature of the Simultaneity Problem

A fundamental difficulty arises in estimating market demand curves because the observed quantity and price data used in regression analysis are determined simultaneously by the intersection of both demand and supply. Consequently, the observed variation in market quantity is caused by all the factors that cause *both* demand *and* supply to change. As discussed in the previous section, the empirical specification of demand relates quantity demanded to changes in market price, income, prices of related goods, and the number of buyers. Since the variation in market quantity (and market price) is caused by changes in both demand *and supply*, market demand cannot, in general, be correctly estimated by regressing Q on P, M, P_R, and N. The problem of estimating market demand which arises because market quantity and price are simultaneously determined by both demand and supply is known as the **simultaneity problem**. The simultaneity problem can be viewed as a combination of two separate, but related, problems—the *identification problem* and the *simultaneous equations bias problem.*

simultaneity problem
The problem in estimating market demand that arises because variation in observed values of market quantity and price are simultaneously determined by changes in *both* demand and supply.

To illustrate the nature of the simultaneity problem, let's consider the following market demand and market supply functions for a good:

$$\text{Demand: } Q = 1{,}500 - 500P + 5M$$
$$\text{Supply: } Q = 11{,}000 + 2{,}000P - 1{,}000P_L$$

where P and Q are price and quantity, M is consumer income, and P_L is the price of the labor input used in production. These two equations make up a system of two simultaneous equations with two *endogenous* variables. The variables whose values are determined by the system are called the **endogenous variables** of the

endogenous variables
Variables whose values are determined by a system of equations.

system. Q and P are the endogenous variables in this system of equations. The values of the other economic variables in the system (M and P_L in this example) are determined outside this system of equations. Variables determined outside the market under consideration are called **exogenous variables.** M and P_L are exogenous variables in the simultaneous system of demand and supply equations set forth above.

exogenous variables Variables in a system of equations that are determined outside the system.

In the above demand and supply model, suppose the exogenous variables initially take the values M = \$2,300 per month and P_L = \$18 per hour. Then the initial demand and supply equations, D_1 and S_1, are

$$D_1\text{: } Q = 1{,}500 - 500P + (5 \times 2{,}300)$$
$$= 13{,}000 - 500P$$
$$S_1\text{: } Q = 11{,}000 + 2{,}000P - (1{,}000 \times 18)$$
$$= -7{,}000 + 2{,}000P$$

These two equations are shown graphically as D_1 and S_1 in Figure 8.1. The market price and output are determined by the intersection of demand and supply. When the exogenous variables are M = \$2,300 and P_L = \$18, the market price and quantity are \$8 and 9,000 units, as shown by point A in Figure 8.1.

Now let the exogenous variables change values to M = \$2,800 and P_L = \$13. The change in the exogenous variables causes demand and supply to shift to new locations as determined by the demand and supply equations, D_2 and S_2:

FIGURE 8.1
The Problem of Simultaneity

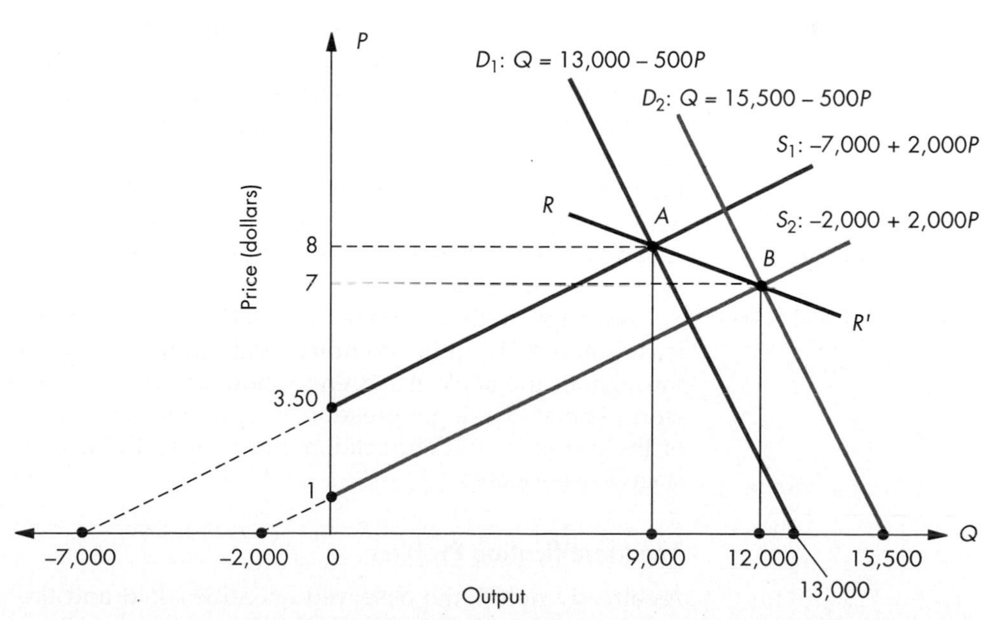

$$D_2\text{: } Q = 1{,}500 - 500P + (5 \times 2{,}800)$$
$$= 15{,}500 - 500P$$
$$S_2\text{: } Q = 11{,}000 + 2{,}000P - (1{,}000 \times 13)$$
$$= -2{,}000 + 2{,}000P$$

The new market price and quantity are \$7 and 12,000 units, as shown by the intersection of D_2 and S_2 at point B in Figure 8.1. Notice that the values of the endogenous variables (P and Q) are determined by the values of the exogenous variables in *both* the demand and supply equations—M and P_L in this example. In Figure 8.1, the variation in market quantity and price between points A and B is caused by simultaneous shifts in both demand and supply.

Suppose an econometrician attempts to estimate market demand by fitting a straight line between points A and B (shown as line RR' in Figure 8.1). The slope of this "demand curve" is –2,000 [$= \Delta Q/\Delta P = (9{,}000 - 12{,}000)/(8 - 7)$]. As you can see from either D_1 or D_2, the true demand curve has a slope of –500. By failing to account for the fact that the observed variation in market quantity and price are caused simultaneously by changes in both demand and supply, the market demand curve is incorrectly estimated in this example.

The possibility that observed changes in market quantity are being caused by changes in both demand and supply must be addressed in order to estimate accurately the parameters of the demand (or supply) function. The problem of determining whether or not the variation in the observed market quantity sold and the observed market price represent the true underlying demand relation is called the **identification problem**. As you will see, it is usually possible to solve the identification problem and correctly estimate market demand even though market quantities and prices are simultaneously determined by demand and supply.

identification problem
The problem of knowing whether or not the variation in the observed data on quantity and price reflect the underlying demand curve.

Once a researcher determines that the demand equation can indeed be identified by the market data, a second problem must be addressed concerning the suitability of the least-squares method of estimating the parameters of the (identified) demand equation. As it turns out, the least-squares method of estimating the parameters of the demand equation is not generally appropriate when the demand equation is a *market* demand equation. A different estimation method, called **two-stage least-squares (2SLS)**, must be used to estimate the parameters of a market demand function.

two-stage least-squares (2SLS)
A method of estimating the parameters of a *market* demand function.

A complete discussion of the identification problem and the use of two-stage least-squares is quite complex and unnecessary for our purpose, which, throughout the book, has been to show you how to use and interpret the parameters estimated using regression analysis. We turn now to an intuitive discussion of the problem of identification and then to the use and interpretation of two-stage least-squares.

The Identification Problem

As already noted, the observed quantities sold and the observed prices are not simply points on a specific demand curve, but rather points of market equilibrium that occur at the intersection of the demand and supply curves. As you saw in Figure 8.1, the observed price-quantity combinations may not trace out a picture of the underlying demand curve. In order to discover the circumstances under which the observed data points can identify a demand curve, we must examine the four possible situations that could be generating the observed data points in a sample:

1. Both the demand and supply functions are stable (i.e., nothing causes either demand or supply to shift.)
2. The supply function is stable, but the demand function is shifting (perhaps due to changes in income).
3. The demand function is stable, but the supply function is shifting (perhaps due to changes in the price of inputs).
4. Both the demand and supply functions are shifting.

Let us examine each one of these situations in turn to see what happens if the demand function is estimated by simply regressing observed quantity sold on observed price.

Case 1 is illustrated in Panel A of Figure 8.2. If both demand and supply are stable, the equilibrium price and quantity will be subject only to random variation around the point of intersection of demand and supply. The observed price and quantity points would be shown by the scatter of points in this figure. If output is regressed on price in this situation, the regression results would indicate no statistically significant relation between quantity and price—the estimated demand curve is flat. Clearly, such an interpretation would be a serious error.

Case 2 is illustrated in Panel B. In this case demand shifts from D_1 to D_2 and then to D_3 (as would be the case if the good is normal and income increases). Thus, there are three points of equilibrium. As before, since the actual price-quantity points are subject to random variation about the equilibrium, the observed points would be similar to the scatter presented in Panel B. In this instance, attempting to obtain an estimate of the demand function by simply regressing output on price would result in a positive relation between price and output. More specifically, in this case, such a simple estimation would result in an estimate of the supply function rather than the demand function. As in Case 1, interpreting this line as a demand function would be a serious error.

In case 3, shown in Panel C of Figure 8.2, supply shifts from S_1 to S_2 then to S_3 (as a result, for instance, of increasing input prices), while demand remains stable. Again, the actual observed price and quantity points are scattered about the equilibrium points. Regressing output on price will indeed result in a good estimation of the demand function. That is, in this case, fitting a regression line through the illustrated scatter of points provides an estimate of the true demand function, D.

Finally, Panel D illustrates the situation when both the demand and supply functions shift. Let's suppose that D_1 is the demand curve when income is \$35,000 and D_2 is the demand curve when income is \$45,000. Also suppose supply shifts because the wage rate takes on three different values. In this case

FIGURE 8.2
The Identification Problem

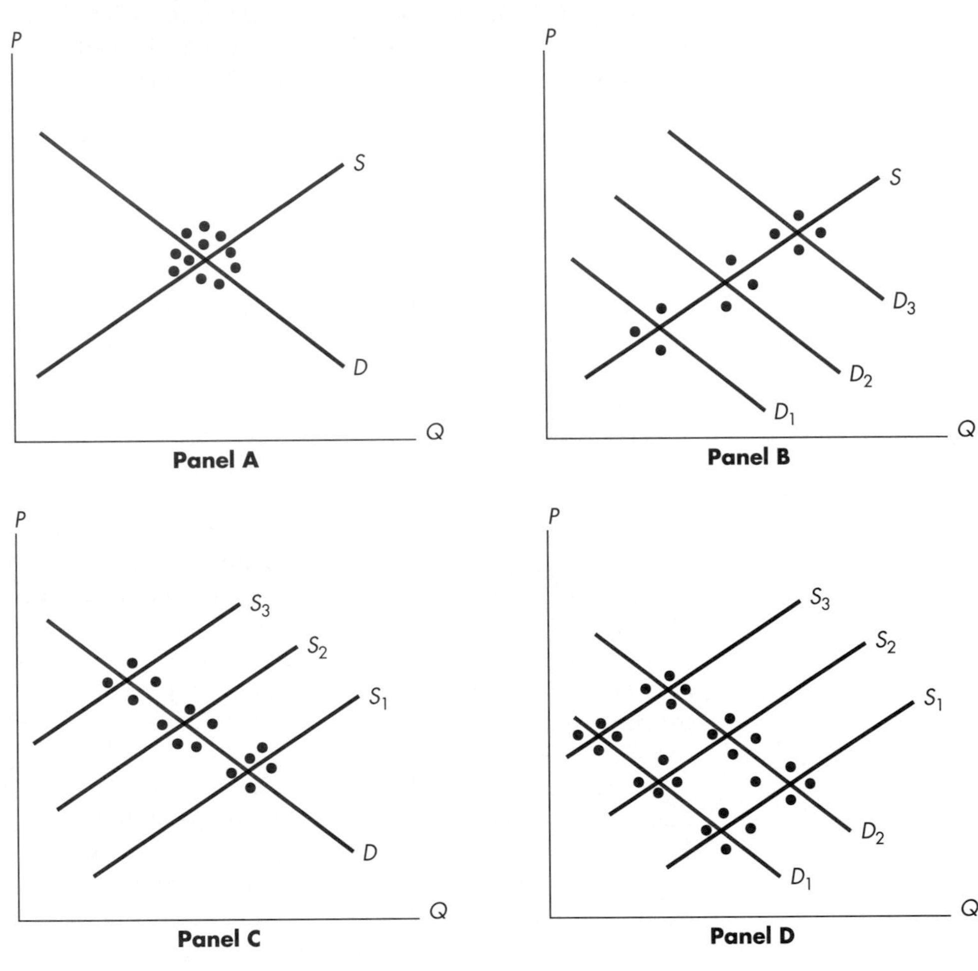

there are six equilibrium points (the intersections of the two demand curves and three supply curves) with the observed price-quantity points scattered randomly around each of these equilibria. It is easily seen that the shifts in supply trace out the two demand curves—one associated with an income level of \$35,000 and another one associated with an income level of \$45,000. When quantity is regressed on price and income in a multiple regression equation,

$$Q = a + bP + cM,$$

the parameter b does, in the case illustrated in Panel D, measure the change in quantity demanded per unit change in price when income is held constant. The effect of a change in income (price held constant) is measured by the parameter c. Thus, a multiple regression model of demand that includes income as an explanatory variable can be applied to the data shown in Panel D to estimate the underlying demand relation generating the observed price-quantity points. Demand is identified in this situation even though both supply and demand are shifting because for any given level of income, the shifts in supply trace out demand.[7]

From the preceding discussion, you can see that demand is identified only when shifts in supply result in the equilibrium points tracing out the underlying demand curve. This situation occurs whenever the supply equation is specified to include variables that will cause supply to shift without simultaneously causing demand to shift. As long as the supply equation includes at least one supply shifting variable that does not also appear in the demand equation, the demand equation will be identified. Typically, the identification problem is solved by specifying that quantity supplied is a function of price and at least one of the supply shifting variables discussed in Chapter 2 (technology, input prices, prices of goods related in production, price expectations, or the number of sellers). Since a supply-shifting variable will not be included in the demand equation, the demand function is therefore identified.

Relation A demand equation is *identified* when it is possible to estimate the true demand function using observations on market output and market price. A demand equation is identified when the supply equation includes at least one exogenous explanatory variable that is not also included in the demand equation.

Estimation of Demand Using Two-Stage Least-Squares (2SLS)

In order for the least-squares method of estimating the parameters of a regression equation to yield unbiased estimates of the regression parameters, the right-hand side explanatory variables cannot be correlated with the random error term of the equation. We did not mention this fact in our discussion of regression analysis in Chapter 5 because virtually all of the applications covered in this book involve explanatory variables that are not likely to be correlated with the random error. There is one important exception, however, and that exception involves the estimation of market demand.

All demand functions will have price as one of the explanatory variables. Because random variations in either the demand or supply equations will cause a random variation in market price, market price will be correlated to the random error term in the demand (and supply) equation. Consequently, when price is an endogenous variable—as it will be for market demand equations—price will be correlated with the random error term in the demand equation, and the least-squares estimates of the parameter of the demand equation will be biased.[8]

[7]Demand will only be identified in this situation if the shifts in demand and supply are caused by changes in a *different* shift-variable. If, for example, both quantity demanded and quantity supplied were each specified to be functions of the wage rate, then a change in the wage rate would cause both demand and supply to shift simultaneously, and the consequent shift in supply would not occur along a stable demand curve.

[8]The fact that market price is correlated with the error term of the demand and supply equations is demonstrated in Appendix B.

Recall that a parameter estimate is biased if the average (or expected) value of the estimate obtained in repeated samples does not equal the true value of the parameter. The bias that occurs when the least-squares estimation method is employed to estimate parameters of an equation for which one or more of the right-hand side variables (price in this case) is an endogenous variable is called a **simultaneous equations bias**.

simultaneous equations bias Bias in estimation that occurs when the least-squares method of estimation is used to estimate the parameters of an equation for which one or more of the explanatory variables is an endogenous variable.

As we mentioned earlier, econometricians employ an estimation technique called *two-stage least-squares* (2SLS) to eliminate simultaneous equations bias. As its name suggests, estimation of the parameters proceeds in two steps. In the first stage, a proxy variable for the endogenous variable market price is created in such a way that the proxy variable is correlated with market price but uncorrelated with the random error term in the demand equation. In the second stage, market price is replaced with the proxy variable created in the first stage, and the usual least-squares procedure is then employed to estimate the parameters of the demand equation.[9] Two-stage least-squares can be applied only to demand equations that are identified. If demand is not identified, there is no estimation technique that will correctly estimate the parameters of the demand equation.

Once the estimates for the parameters of a demand equation have been obtained from the second stage of the regression, they can be tested for significance using a t-test in precisely the same manner as for any other regression equation. However, due to the manner in which 2SLS estimates are calculated, the R^2 and F-statistics are not meaningful. Indeed, these statistics are usually not even reported in the output of standard regression packages.

We should again remind you that estimating market demand curves is a rather challenging task even for trained econometricians, and we don't expect you to do this estimation yourself. However, if you ever do wish to try your hand at estimating market demand functions, you will be happy to know that many regression programs are available—even for personal computers—that have a two-stage least-squares routine, and these 2SLS packages perform the two stages of estimation automatically. It is normally necessary for the user to specify only which variables are endogenous and which are exogenous in the system of equations.

Relation Since market price is an endogenous variable, it will be correlated with the random error term in the demand equation causing a simultaneous equations bias if the ordinary least-squares method of estimation is applied. To eliminate simultaneous equations bias, the two-stage least-squares method of estimation (2SLS) can be employed if the demand equation is identified.

The World Demand for Copper: Estimating Market Demand Using 2SLS

To illustrate how a market demand function is estimated using two-stage least-squares, we estimate the world demand for copper (i.e., the market demand for all countries buying copper). In its simplest form, the world demand for copper

[9]A more complete presentation of 2SLS estimation is presented in Appendix B.

is a function of the price of copper, income, and the price of any related commodities. Using aluminum as the related commodity, because it is the primary substitute for copper in manufacturing, the demand function can be written as

$$Q_{\text{copper}} = f(P_{\text{copper}}, M, P_{\text{aluminum}})$$

As noted, either a linear or a nonlinear demand function can be specified. A linear form is used in this example:

$$Q_{\text{copper}} = a + bP_{\text{copper}} + cM + dP_{\text{aluminum}}$$

It is tempting to simply regress consumption on the price of copper, income, and the price of aluminum. Because of the identification problem, such a procedure is normally not appropriate. It is first necessary to identify the demand function, and this requires that the supply function be specified.

Let the quantity supplied of copper depend on the price of copper and the level of available technology. In the market for copper, inventories are also of particular importance. When inventories rise, current production usually falls. Therefore, an additional variable to reflect inventory changes must be added. We define the ratio of consumption to production in the preceding period (denoted simply as X) to be this variable. As consumption declines relative to production, X will fall, and current production is expected to decline. Thus, the supply function becomes

$$Q_{\text{copper}} = g(P_{\text{copper}}, T, X)$$

or, using a linear specification,

$$Q_{\text{copper}} = e + fP_{\text{copper}} + gT + hX$$

Now we must address the question of whether or not the demand function is identified. Since the supply function includes two exogenous variables that are excluded from the demand equation (T and X), the demand function is identified and may be estimated.

The data needed to estimate demand are: (1) The world consumption (sales) of copper in 1,000 metric tons, (2) the price of copper and aluminum in cents per pound, deflated by a price index to obtain the real (i.e., constant dollar) prices, (3) an index of real per capita income, and (4) the world production of copper (in order to calculate the inventory variable, X). Time serves as a proxy for available technology (i.e., this assumes that the level of technology increased steadily over time). The resulting data set is presented in Table 8C.1 in Appendix 8C.

Using these data, the demand function is estimated using 2SLS. In this estimation, the endogenous variable P_{copper} is first regressed on all of the exogenous variables: M, P_{aluminum} X, and T. Then, as described earlier, this estimation is used to generate the predicted value of P_{copper}. Finally, consumption Q_{copper}, is regressed on this predicted price of copper as well as on income and the price of aluminum. The results of these estimations are:

```
SECOND STAGE STATISTICS

DEPENDENT VARIABLE: QC

OBSERVATIONS: 25

                      PARAMETER    STANDARD
VARIABLE              ESTIMATE      ERROR       T-RATIO

INTERCEPT            -6837.800    1264.500      -5.408
PC.HAT                 -66.495      31.534      -2.109
M                    13997.000    1306.300      10.715
PA                     107.660      44.510       2.419
```

Note that the computer output provides only the results of the second-stage estimation, that is, estimation of the demand function using a proxy for price, denoted by $\hat{P}$. Indeed, this printout indicates that a proxy variable for price was used, since it denotes the price of copper as *PC.HAT* rather than *PC*. Note further that, since R^2 and F values are not meaningful in 2SLS, they are not reported.

Before estimating the demand equation, we determine whether the estimated coefficients $\hat{b}$, $\hat{c}$, and $\hat{d}$ should be positive or negative based on theoretical considerations. We expect that (1) due to a downward-sloping demand curve for copper, $b < 0$; (2) since copper is a normal good, $c > 0$; and (3) since copper and aluminum are substitutes, $d > 0$. The estimated coefficients conform to this sign pattern:

$$\hat{b} = -66.495 < 0$$
$$\hat{c} = 13997.0 > 0$$
$$\hat{d} = 107.66 > 0$$

In order to test for the statistical significance of these parameter estimates, the t-ratios are compared to the critical value of t. Since four parameters are estimated ($\hat{a}$, $\hat{b}$, $\hat{c}$, and $\hat{d}$), there are $25 - 4$ degrees of freedom, and the critical value of t at a 95 percent confidence level is 2.08. The absolute value for the calculated values of t for each of the parameter estimates exceeds the critical value of t; thus the estimated parameters are statistically significant.

Now, we calculate the elasticities of demand. While the elasticity can be evaluated at any point on the demand curve, we use the sample means. The means of the variables under consideration are calculated using the data from Table 8C.1. They are

$$\overline{Q}_c = 5433.63 \quad \overline{M} = 0.87$$
$$\overline{P}_c = 37.17 \quad \overline{P}_A = 24.29$$

The own-price elasticity of demand evaluated at the sample mean is

$$E = \hat{b}\,\frac{\overline{P}_c}{\overline{Q}_c} = (-66.495)\left(\frac{37.17}{5433.63}\right)$$
$$= -0.45$$

Similarly, the income elasticity of demand at the sample mean is

$$E_M = \hat{c}\left(\frac{\overline{M}}{\overline{Q}_c}\right) = 13997\left(\frac{0.87}{5433.63}\right)$$
$$= 2.24$$

and the cross-price elasticity of demand at the sample mean is

$$E_{CA} = \hat{d}\left(\frac{\overline{P}_A}{\overline{Q}_c}\right) = 107.66\left(\frac{24.29}{5433.63}\right)$$
$$= 0.48$$

Thus, the demand for copper—when evaluated at the sample means $\overline{P}_C$, $\overline{Q}_C$, $\overline{M}$, and $\overline{P}_A$—is inelastic ($|E| < 1$), copper is a normal good ($E_M > 0$), and copper is a substitute for aluminum ($E_{CA} > 0$). Note that copper is a rather poor substitute for aluminum since a 10 percent increase in the price of aluminum increases the quantity demanded of copper by only 4.8 percent.

8.4 ESTIMATING DEMAND FACING AN INDIVIDUAL FIRM

In most situations, the price and output data used to estimate a market demand function are generated by the simultaneous market forces of demand and supply. As you saw in the previous discussion, it is necessary for an econometrician to make sure the demand function is indeed identified. If the demand equation is identified, then the estimation of the demand equation is accomplished using the 2SLS regression technique. As it turns out, estimating the demand curve facing an individual firm is in many cases much easier than estimating a market demand equation because the problem of simultaneity may not arise when estimating a *firm's* demand function. This section begins with a brief discussion of *price-taking* and *price-setting* firms and explains why estimating a demand curve for a price-setting firm does not require checking for identification of demand nor estimation using 2SLS. We then present an example of how a price-setting pizza firm can estimate the demand for its pizza.

Price-Taking Firms and Price-Setting Firms

Not all managers have the power to set the price of their product. In some industries, each firm in the industry produces a product that is *identical* to the output produced by all the rest of the firms in the industry. The price of the good in such a situation is not determined by any *one* firm or manager, but rather by the impersonal forces of the marketplace—the intersection of market demand and supply. If a manager attempts to raise price above the market-determined price, the firm loses all of its sales to the other firms in the industry. After all,

ILLUSTRATION 8.2

Estimating the Demand for Corporate Jets

Given the success that many of our former students have experienced in their careers and the success we predict for you, we thought it might be valuable for you to examine the market for corporate aircraft. Rather than dwell on the lackluster piston-driven and turboprop aircraft, we instead focus this illustration on the demand for corporate jets. In a recent empirical study of general aviation aircraft, McDougall and Cho estimated the demand using techniques that are similar to the ones in this chapter.* Let's now look at how regression analysis can be used to estimate the demand for corporate jets.

In order to estimate the demand for corporate jets, McDougall and Cho specified the variables that affect jet aircraft sales and the general demand relation as follows.

$$Q_J = f(P, P_R, M, D)$$

where

Q_J = the number of new corporate jets purchased,
P = the price of a new corporate jet,
P_R = the price of a used corporate jet,
M = the income of the buyer, and
D = a so-called dummy variable to account for seasonality of jet sales.

Since the market for used jets is extensively used by corporations, the price of used jets (a substitute) is included in the demand equation. We should note that P and P_R are not the actual prices paid for the aircraft but are instead the user-costs of an aircraft. A jet aircraft provides many miles of transportation, not all of which are consumed during the first period of ownership. The user-cost of a jet measures the cost per mile (or per hour) of operating the jet by spreading the initial purchase price over the lifetime of jet transportation services and adjusting for depreciation in the value of the aircraft.

The income of the buyer (M) is approximated by corporate profit since most buyers of small jet aircraft are corporations. The data used to estimate the demand equation are quarterly observations (1981I–1985III). Many corporations purchase jets at year-end for tax purposes. Consequently, jet sales tend to be higher in the fourth quarter, all else constant, than in the other three quarters of any given year. Adjusting for this pattern of seasonality is accomplished by adding a variable called a dummy variable, which takes on values of 1 for observations in the fourth quarter and 0 for observations in the other three quarters. In effect, the dummy variable shifts the estimated demand equation rightward during the fourth quarter. A complete explanation of the use of dummy variables to adjust for seasonality in data is presented in Chapter 9 of this text.

The following linear model of demand for corporate jets is estimated:

$$Q_J = a + bP + cP_R + dM + eD_4$$

McDougall and Cho estimate this demand equation using least-squares estimation rather than two-stage least squares because they note that the supply curve for aircraft is almost perfectly elastic or horizontal. If the supply of jets is horizontal, the supply price of new jets is constant no matter what the level of output. Since the market price of jets is determined by the position of the (horizontal) jet supply curve, and the position of supply is fixed by the exogenous determinants of supply, the price of jets is itself exogenous. If jet price (P) is exogenous, least-squares regression is appropriate. The computer output obtained by McDougall and Cho from estimating this equation is

buyers do not care from whom they buy this identical product and would be unwilling to pay more than the going market price for the product. In such a situation, the firm is a **price-taker** and cannot set the price of the product it sells.

price-taker
A firm that cannot set the price of the product it sells since price is determined strictly by the market forces of demand and supply.

We will discuss price-taking firms in detail in Chapters 13 and 14, and you will see that the demand curve facing a price-taking firm is horizontal (perfectly elastic) at the price determined by the intersection of *market* demand and supply.

DEPENDENT VARIABLE: QJ F-RATIO: 20.35

OBSERVATIONS: 18 R-SQUARE: 0.8623

VARIABLE	PARAMETER ESTIMATE	STANDARD ERROR	T-RATIO
INTERCEPT	17.33	43.3250	0.40
P	-0.00016	0.000041	-3.90
PR	0.00050	0.000104	4.81
M	-0.85010	0.7266	-1.17
D4	31.99	8.7428	3.66

Theoretically, the predicted signs of the estimated coefficients are (1) $\hat{b} < 0$, since demand for corporate jets is expected to be downward sloping, (2) $\hat{c} > 0$, since new and used jets are substitutes, (3) $\hat{d} > 0$, because corporate jets are expected to be normal goods, and (4) $\hat{e} > 0$, because the tax effect at year-end should cause jet demand to increase (shift rightward) during the fourth quarter. All the estimates, except $\hat{d}$, match the expected signs.

To test for statistical significance, the t-values are compared to the critical value. The critical t-value for $18 - 5 = 13$ degrees of freedom at a 95 percent confidence level is 2.16. The absolute value of the t-values exceeds the critical values for all the estimated slope parameters, except $\hat{d}$. Thus, all the variables in the model play a statistically significant role in determining sales of jet aircraft, except corporate profits.

The model as a whole does a good job of explaining the variation in sales of corporate jets—86 percent of the variation in sales is explained by the model ($R^2 = 0.8623$). The F-ratio easily exceeds the critical value of 3.18 (4 and 13 degrees of freedom at a 95 percent confidence level).

McDougall and Cho estimate the own-price and cross-price elasticities of demand using the values of Q_J, P, and P_R in the third quarter of 1985:

$$E = \hat{b}\,\frac{P_{1985III}}{Q_{1985III}} = -3.95$$

$$E_{NU} = \hat{c}\,\frac{P_{R,1985III}}{Q_{1985III}} = 6.41$$

where E_{NU} is the cross-price elasticity between new and used jets sales and the price of used jets. The own-price elasticity estimate suggests that the quantity demanded of new corporate jets is quite responsive to changes in the price of new jets ($|E| > 1$). Furthermore, a 10 percent decrease in the price of used jets is estimated to cause a 64.1 percent decrease in sales of new corporate jets. Given this rather large cross-price elasticity, used jets appear to be viewed by corporations as extremely close substitutes for new jets, and for this reason, we advise all of our managerial economics students to look closely at the used jet market before buying a new corporate jet.

*The empirical results in this illustration are taken from Gerald S McDougall and Dong W Cho, "Demand Estimates for New General Aviation Aircraft: A User-Cost Approach," *Applied Economics* 20, (1988).

price-setting firm
A firm that can raise its price without losing all of its sales. Demand for a price-setting firm is downward sloping.

Thus, estimating the demand for a price-taking firm requires estimation of *market* demand, which entails addressing both the problem of identification and simultaneous equations bias as previously discussed.

In contrast to price-taking firms, the manager of a **price-setting firm** does set the price of the product. Price-setting firms have the ability to raise price without losing all sales because the product is somehow differentiated from rivals' products, or perhaps because the geographic market area in which the product is sold has only one (or just a few) sellers of the product. At higher prices, the firm sells less of its product; and at lower prices the firm sells more of its product. The demand curve for a price-setting firm is downward sloping, and the firm can operate at any point (price and quantity demanded combination) it wishes on the firm's demand curve.

Recall that the problem of simultaneity arises when estimating market demand because the observed data on prices and quantities are generated by the intersection of both market demand and supply. Standard least-squares regression is not appropriate for estimating market demand because the observed data may not trace out the underlying market demand curve (creating an identification problem), and market price (an explanatory variable) will be correlated with the random error term (creating a simultaneous equations bias). If the firm is a price-setting firm, however, there is no simultaneity problem involved with estimating the firm's demand curve because the manager is setting the price along a firm's demand curve, rather than price being determined by the intersection of market demand and supply.[10]

Figure 8.3 illustrates why estimating a demand curve for a price-setting firm can be accomplished using the standard least-squares regression technique. Suppose a price-setting firm faces the demand function labeled "D_{Firm}" in the figure. The manager of the firm sets four different prices over a one-year time period. The table in Figure 8.3 shows the actual level of monthly sales at each price over the twelve-month period. For example, a price of $2 was charged in the months of October, November, and December with corresponding sales of 2,125, 1,875, and 1,750 units, respectively. (Recall from the discussion of the random error term in Chapter 5 that random variation in sales will occur due to a variety of random effects that cannot reasonably be included in the demand specification.) Because the various prices set by the manager trace out the underlying demand curve, the standard least-squares method of estimation can be employed to estimate the demand curve for a price-setting firm. The problem of simultaneous equations bias causes no trouble now because price, which is set by the manager, is not likely to be correlated with the random error. Thus, the demand curve for a price-setting firm can generally be estimated using the standard least-squares technique.

Relation When a firm is a price-taking firm, estimating the demand curve facing a single firm in the industry requires estimating the market demand curve. The market demand equation must be identified and 2SLS estimation must be employed. When a firm is a price-setting firm, the problem of simultaneity vanishes, and the demand curve for the firm can be estimated using the standard least-squares method of estimation.

[10]In the case of an oligopoly market, which will be discussed in Chapter 16, rival firms recognize a mutual interdependence. Each manager recognizes that its own choice of product price will affect its rivals' choice of product price. In the presence of mutual interdependence, managers do not choose prices independently of one another, and thus the problem of simultaneity is present and must be addressed in estimating the demand facing a single oligopolistic firm. The methods of modeling this interdependence and estimating oligopoly demand go well beyond the scope of a managerial economics textbook.

FIGURE 8.3
Estimating a Price-Setting Firm's Demand

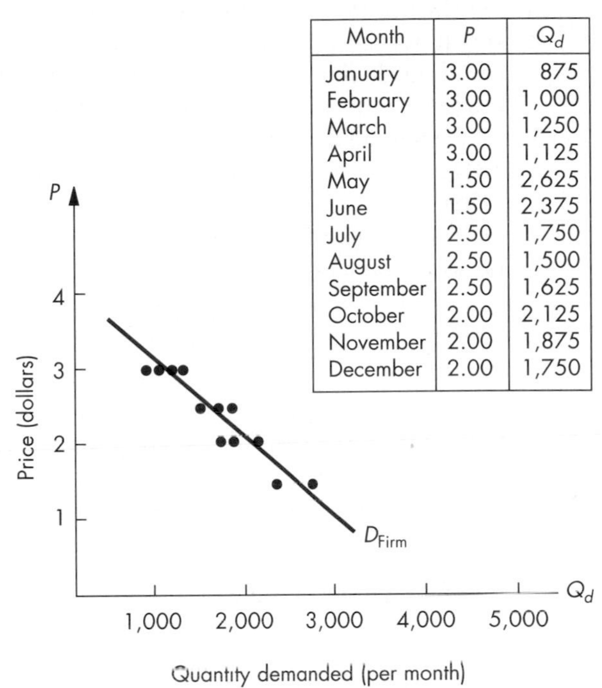

Month	P	Q_d
January	3.00	875
February	3.00	1,000
March	3.00	1,250
April	3.00	1,125
May	1.50	2,625
June	1.50	2,375
July	2.50	1,750
August	2.50	1,500
September	2.50	1,625
October	2.00	2,125
November	2.00	1,875
December	2.00	1,750

Estimating Demand for Pizzas: An Example

We will now illustrate how a firm with price-setting power can estimate the demand equation for its output. Consider Checkers Pizza, one of only two home delivery pizza firms serving the Westbury neighborhood of Houston. The manager and owner of Checkers Pizza, Ann Chovie, knows that her customers are rather price conscious. Pizza buyers in Westbury pay close attention to the price she charges for a home-delivered pizza and the price her competitor, Al's Pizza Oven, charges for a similar home-delivered pizza.

Ann decides to estimate the empirical demand function for her firm's pizza. She collects data on the last 24 months of pizza sales from her own company records. She knows the price she charged for her pizza during that time period, and she also has kept a record of the prices charged at Al's Pizza Oven. Ann is able to obtain average household income figures from the Westbury Small Business Development Center. The only other competitor in the neighborhood is the local branch of the McDonald's hamburger chain. Ann is able to find the price of a Big Mac for the last 24 months from advertisements in old newspapers. Ann adjusts her price and income data for the effects of inflation by deflating the dollar figures, using a deflator she obtained from the *Survey of Current Business*.

(She had to make a trip to the University of Houston library.) To measure the number of buyers in the market area (N), Ann collected data on the number of residents in Westbury. As it turned out, the number of residents had not changed during the last 24 months, so Ann dropped N from her specification of demand. The data she collected are presented in Table 8C.2 in Appendix 8C.

Since the price of pizza at Checkers Pizza is set by Ann, and therefore is an exogenous variable, she can estimate the empirical demand equation using the standard techniques of regression analysis—2SLS is not required. Ann first estimates the following linear specification of demand using 24 monthly observations:

$$Q = a + bP + cM + dP_{\text{Al}} + eP_{\text{BMac}}$$

where

Q = the sales of pizza at Checkers Pizza,
P = the price of a pizza at Checkers Pizza,
M = the average annual household income in Westbury,
P_{Al} = the price of a pizza at Al's Pizza Oven, and
P_{BMac} = the price of a Big Mac hamburger at McDonald's.

The following computer printout shows the results of her least-squares regression:

DEPENDENT VARIABLE: Q F-RATIO: 153.17

OBSERVATIONS: 24 R-SQUARE: 0.9699

VARIABLE	PARAMETER ESTIMATE	STANDARD ERROR	T-RATIO
INTERCEPT	-346.856	413.886	-0.838
P	-196.000	11.036	-17.760
M	0.075	0.010	7.500
PAL	174.500	31.698	5.505
PBMAC	81.086	22.155	3.660

Ann tests the four estimated slope parameters ($\hat{b}$, $\hat{c}$, $\hat{d}$, and $\hat{e}$) for statistical significance at the 99 percent level of confidence. The critical t-value for 19 degrees of freedom ($n - k = 24 - 5$) at the 99 percent confidence level is 2.861. The t-ratios for all four slope parameters exceed 2.861, and thus the coefficients are all statistically significant.

The own-price, income, and cross-price elasticities can be calculated using the mean values of Q, P, M, P_{AL}, and P_{BMac} in the sample (calculated from the data in Table 8C.2 in Appendix 8C):

$$\overline{Q} = 1{,}731 \qquad \overline{P}_{\text{Al}} = 10.12$$

$$\overline{P} = 9.05 \qquad \overline{P}_{\text{BMac}} = 1.15$$

$$\overline{M} = 26{,}614$$

The elasticities for the linear demand specification are calculated in the now familiar fashion:

$$E = \hat{b}(\overline{P}/\overline{Q}) = (-196)(9.05/1{,}731) = -1.025$$
$$E_M = \hat{c}(\overline{M}/\overline{Q}) = 0.075(26{,}614/1{,}731) = 1.153$$
$$E_{Al} = \hat{d}(\overline{P}_{Al}/\overline{Q}) = 174.5(10.12/1{,}731) = 1.020$$
$$E_{BMac} = \hat{e}(\overline{P}_{BMac}/\overline{Q}) = 81.086(1.15/1{,}731) = 0.054$$

Ann's estimated elasticities show that she prices her pizzas just slightly higher than the price at which demand is unit elastic. A one percent increase in average household income will cause sales to rise by 1.15 percent—pizzas are a normal good in Westbury. The estimated cross-price elasticity E_{Al} suggests that if Al's Pizza Oven raises its pizza price by 1 percent, sales of Checkers' pizzas will increase by 1.02 percent. While the price of a Big Mac does play a statistically significant role in determining sales of Checkers' pizzas, the impact is estimated to be quite small. Indeed, a *ten* percent decrease in the price of a Big Mac will only decrease sales of Checkers' pizzas by one-half of one percent (.54 percent). Apparently families in Westbury aren't very willing to substitute a Big Mac for a home-delivered pizza from Checkers Pizza.

While Ann is satisfied that a linear specification of demand for her firm's pizza does an outstanding job of explaining the variation in her pizza sales, she decides to estimate a nonlinear model just for comparison. Ann chooses a log-linear demand specification of the form

$$Q = aP^bM^cP_{Al}^dP_{BMac}^e$$

which can be transformed (by taking logarithms) into the following estimable form:

$$\log Q = \log a + b \log P + c \log M + d \log P_{Al} + e \log P_{BMac}$$

The regression results from the computer are presented below:

```
DEPENDENT VARIABLE: LOGQ    F-RATIO: 114.25

OBSERVATIONS: 24            R-SQUARE: 0.9600

                     PARAMETER       STANDARD
       VARIABLE      ESTIMATE          ERROR          T-RATIO

      INTERCEPT       -2.422           0.823           -2.943
      LOGP            -0.981           0.065          -15.092
      LOGM             1.194           0.187            6.385
      LOGPAL           1.304           0.215            6.065
      LOGPBMAC         0.055           0.015            3.667
```

While the *F*-ratio and R^2 for the log-linear model are just slightly smaller than for the linear specification, the log-linear specification certainly performs just as well. Recall that the slope parameter estimates in a log-linear model are elasticities. While the elasticity estimates from the log-linear model come extremely close to the elasticity estimates from the linear model (evaluated at the sample means), linear and log-linear specifications may not always produce such similar elasticity estimates. In this case, Ann Chovie could use either one of the empirical demand functions in her business decision making.

8.5 SUMMARY

This chapter presented the basic techniques of estimating demand functions. Consumer interviews and market studies are direct methods of estimating demand. Consumer interviews attempt to estimate demand by administering detailed questionnaires to a selected sample of the population in order to determine how much of the commodity they would buy at different prices with alternative values for the determinants of demand. When estimating demand using consumer interviews, managers may encounter problems with the selection of a representative sample, with biases in the responses of consumers, and with the inability of consumers to answer questions accurately. An alternative method of directly estimating demand involves controlled market studies or experiments. In a typical market study, a product is displayed at a number of different stores, each store having its own particular characteristics. Price is varied over time and sales recorded for each price, thereby producing an approximation of the actual demand curve for the product. In some cases, experiments are used to simulate consumer choice in a laboratory (controlled) environment.

While consumer interviews and market studies provide managers with valuable information about consumer demand, actual estimation of demand functions is most often accomplished using the technique of regression analysis. The method of estimating demand depends upon whether *market* demand or *firm* demand is being estimated. Estimating the market demand for a product is rather complicated because of the problem of simultaneity that arises when market price is an endogenous variable. The problem of simultaneity is that the observed variation in market output and market price is the result of changes in the determinants of both demand and supply. Because market output and price are determined jointly by the forces of supply and demand, two econometric problems arise when we try to employ regression analysis on observed values of *P* and *Q* to estimate an empirical demand equation: the identification problem and the simultaneous equations bias problem.

The identification problem refers to the problem of determining whether or not the variation in the observed market quantity sold and the observed market price represent the underlying demand relation. In other words, a demand equation is *identified* when it is possible to estimate the true demand function using observations on market output and market price. Demand is identified when the supply equation includes at least one exogenous explanatory variable that is not also included in the demand equation.

The second problem that arises when price is an endogenous variable is the problem of simultaneous equations bias. In order for the standard least-squares regression procedure to yield unbiased parameter estimates, all explanatory variables must be uncorrelated with the random error term. An endogenous variable is always correlated with the error term in both the demand and supply equations. Since price is an explanatory variable in the demand equation, and an endogenous variable in the case of market demand, then a simultaneous equations bias will result when the standard least-squares procedure is employed to estimate the parameters of a market demand equation. The simultaneous equations bias is eliminated by estimating the parameters of a market demand equation using two-stage least-squares (2SLS).

When estimating the demand curve facing an individual firm, the problem of simultaneity does not exist for price-setting firms—those firms whose managers set the price of the product off of a downward sloping firm demand curve. Consequently, the standard method of least-squares is appropriate for estimating the parameters of a price-setting firm's demand curve. If the firm is a price-taking firm—market forces of demand and supply determine product price—the problem of simultaneity remains, and the parameters of the identified demand curve must be estimated using 2SLS.

When demand is specified to be linear in form, the coefficients on each of the explanatory variables measure the rate of change in quantity demanded as that explanatory variable changes, holding all other explanatory variables constant. For example, if the demand for a good is specified to be linearly related to its own price (P), consumer income (M), and the price of some related good R (P_R),

$$Q = a + bP + cM + dP_R$$

then $b = \Delta Q/\Delta P$, $c = \Delta Q/\Delta M$, and $d = \Delta Q/\Delta P_R$. The expected signs of the coefficients can be deduced from consumer theory. Given the law of demand, b is expected to be negative. If the good is normal (inferior), c is expected to be positive (negative). If the two goods X and Y are substitutes (complements), d is expected to be positive (negative). The elasticities of demand are computed as:

$$\hat{E} = \hat{b} \cdot \frac{P}{Q}$$

$$\hat{E}_M = \hat{c} \cdot \frac{M}{Q}$$

and

$$\hat{E}_{XR} = \hat{d} \cdot \frac{P_R}{Q}$$

As in any regression analysis, the estimated coefficients must be tested for statistical significance using the usual t-test. If the coefficient estimates are statistically significant, the estimated elasticities are statistically significant.

When demand is specified as log-linear, the demand function is written as

$$Q = aP^bM^cP_R^d$$

In order to estimate the log-linear demand function, it is converted to logarithms:

$$\log Q_X = \log a + b \log P + c \log M + d \log P_R$$

In log-linear form, the elasticities of demand are constant, and

$$E = b$$

$$E_M = c$$

and

$$E_{XR} = d$$

In this chapter you have learned how to estimate and interpret the demand function facing a firm. In the next chapter you will see how to forecast the demand conditions in future time periods. Clearly managers must know about the future demand in order to plan for future production and to make investment decisions concerning new plants and equipment.

TECHNICAL PROBLEMS

1. Cite the three major problems with consumer interviews or surveys and provide an example of each.
2. For each of the following sets of demand and supply functions, determine if the demand function is identified and explain why or why not.
   a. D: $Q = a + bP$
   S: $Q = e + fP$
   b. D: $Q = a + bP + cM$
   S: $Q = e + fP$
   c. D: $Q = a + bP$
   S: $Q = e + fP + gT$
   d. D: $Q = a + bP + cM$
   S: $Q = e + fP + gT + hP_F$
3. Evaluate the following statement:
   If a demand equation is not identified, then two-stage least-squares (2SLS) must be used to estimate the demand equation.

4. The estimated market demand for good X is:

$$Q = 70 - 3.5P - .6M + 4P_R$$

where Q = units of good X, P = price of good X, M = income, and P_R = price of related good Z. (All coefficients are stastically significant.)
   a. Is X a normal or an inferior good? Explain.
   b. Are X and Z substitutes or complements? Explain.
5. A linear demand function of the form

$$Q = a + bP + cM + dP_R$$

was estimated using 2SLS. (Obviously, this demand function was first identified by specifying the supply function.) The results of this estimation are as follows:

SECOND STAGE STATISTICS

DEPENDENT VARIABLE: Q

OBSERVATIONS: 30

VARIABLE	PARAMETER ESTIMATE	STANDARD ERROR	T-RATIO
INTERCEPT	68.38	12.65	5.41
P.HAT	-6.50	3.15	-2.06
MM	13.926	1.306	10.66
PR	-10.77	2.45	-4.40

The sample means of the variables are as follows:

$$\overline{Q} = 125$$
$$\overline{P} = 25$$
$$\overline{M} = 20$$
$$\overline{P}_R = 25$$

a. Are the signs of $\hat{b}$ and $\hat{c}$ as would be predicted theoretically?
b. What does the sign of $\hat{d}$ imply about the relation between commodity X and the related commodity?
c. Are the parameter estimates $\hat{a}$, $\hat{b}$, $\hat{c}$, and $\hat{d}$ statistically significant?
d. Using the sample means, calculate
   (1) The own-price elasticity of demand.
   (2) The income elasticity.
   (3) The cross-price elasticity.

6. The following log-linear demand curve for an individual firm is estimated using the method of least-squares.

$$Q = aP^bM^cP_R^d$$

The results of this estimation are:

DEPENDENT VARIABLE: LOG Q		F-RATIO: 89.165	
OBSERVATIONS: 48		R-SQUARE: 0.781	
VARIABLE	PARAMETER ESTIMATE	STANDARD ERROR	T-RATIO
INTERCEPT	6.77	4.01	1.69
LOG P	-1.68	0.70	-2.40
LOG M	-0.82	0.22	-3.73
LOG PR	1.35	0.75	1.80

a. The supply curve for X is $Q = e + fP + gW$, where W is the price of labor. Is the demand curve identified?

b. The estimated demand equation can be expressed in logarithms as log Q = _____ .

c. Does the parameter estimate for b have the expected sign? Explain.

d. Given these parameter estimates, is good X a normal or inferior good? Explain. Are goods X and R substitutes or complements? Explain.

e. Which of the parameter estimates are statistically significant at the 95 percent level of confidence?

f. Find the following elasticities:
(1) The own-price elasticity of demand.
(2) The cross-price elasticity of demand.
(3) The income elasticity of demand.

g. A 10 percent decrease in household income, holding all other things constant, will cause quantity demanded to _____ by _____ percent.

h. All else constant, a 10 percent increase in price causes quantity demanded to _____ by _____ percent.

i. A 5 percent decrease in the price of R, holding all other variables constant, causes quantity demanded to _____ by _____ percent.

* 7. In the example dealing with the world demand for copper, we estimated the demand elasticities (at the sample means). Using these estimates, evaluate the impact on the world consumption of copper of:

a. The formation of a worldwide cartel in copper that increases the price of copper by 10 percent.

b. The onset of a recession that reduces world income by 5 percent.

c. A technical breakthrough that is expected to reduce the price of copper by 10 percent.

d. A 10 percent reduction in the price of aluminum.

APPLIED PROBLEMS

1. Sharp Econometrics, a consulting firm in San Francisco, has been hired by Nitax Cameras, Inc. to estimate the demand for their single lens reflex (SLR) cameras. Nitax provides the econometricians at Sharp with data from 45 states during 1992 on the quantity of Nitax SLRs purchased, the price of a Nitax in each state, average household income in each state, and the average price of 35mm film in each state.
   a. Is this data set sufficient to identify the demand function? Why or why not?

   Sharp Econometrics is also employed by Knoxville Slugger Baseball Bats to estimate the demand for baseball bats. Sharp has data over the last five years on the quantity of Knoxville Slugger baseball bats sold, consumers' income, the price of baseballs, and the price of lumber.
   b. Is this data set sufficient to identify the demand function? Why or why not?
2. The manager of We-Rent-All, a tool rental business, wants to estimate the demand for its airless paint sprayers, using data from last year. The manager, while collecting the needed data, discovers that during the past year, the store had only three sprayers to rent, and the three units were rented all of the time. Consequently, the supply curve for airless sprayers was perfectly inelastic over the range of prices We-Rent-All charged to rent these machines. Can the manager estimate the demand for airless sprayers using data from last year? Why or why not? Explain by using a graph.
3. Wilpen estimates the demand for its tennis balls by using the following linear specifications:

$$Q = a + bP + cM + dP_R$$

   where Q = cans of tennis balls (millions), P = real price of tennis balls (dollars/can), M = consumers' income ($1,000 per capita), and P_R = the average real price of tennis rackets (dollars/racket). The least-squares regression results are as follows:

DEPENDENT VARIABLE: Q		F-RATIO: 28.750	
OBSERVATIONS: 20		R-SQUARE: 0.6415	
VARIABLE	PARAMETER ESTIMATE	STANDARD ERROR	T-RATIO
INTERCEPT	80.64	25.03	3.22
P	-25.93	8.77	-2.96
M	10.24	2.51	4.08
PR	-1.52	0.36	-4.22

   a. Are the estimates $\hat{a}$, $\hat{b}$, $\hat{c}$, and $\hat{d}$ statistically significant?
   b. Are the signs of $\hat{b}$, $\hat{c}$, and $\hat{d}$ consistent with the theory of demand?
   c. Wilpen plans to price its tennis balls at $3 per can. The average real price of a tennis racket is $70, and consumers' income is $15,000 per capita ($M$ = $15).
   (1) What is the estimated number of cans of tennis balls demanded?

(2) What are the values of the own-price, income, and cross-price elasticities of demand?
(3) What will happen to the number of cans of tennis balls demanded if the price of tennis balls decreases 15 percent?
(4) What will happen to the number of cans of tennis balls demanded if consumers' income doubles?
(5) What will happen to the number of cans of tennis balls demanded if the price of tennis rackets increases 20 percent?

4. In the examination of world demand for copper, we used a linear specification. However, we could have estimated a log-linear specification. That is, we could have specified the copper demand function as

$$Q_c = aP_c^b M^c P_A^d$$

or

$$\log Q_c = \log a + b \log P_c + c \log M + d \log P_A$$

The results of such an estimation, using the data in Table 7.1, are presented below.

SECOND STAGE STATISTICS

DEPENDENT VARIABLE: LOG QC

OBSERVATIONS: 25

VARIABLE	PARAMETER ESTIMATE	STANDARD ERROR	T-RATIO
INTERCEPT	9.0072	0.97059	9.28
LOG PC.HAT	-0.68233	0.30635	-2.23
LOG M	2.5265	0.28963	8.72
LOG PA	0.75246	0.23498	3.20

a. Are the parameter estimates consistent with the theoretical predictions made about the signs of *b*, *c*, and *d*?
b. Are the parameter estimates statistically significant?
c. What are the values of the own-price, income, and cross-price elasticities of demand?
d. How do these results compare with those obtained from the linear specification?

5. In a recent article, a researcher reported that he had found that the demand curve for kerosene sloped upward—as the price of kerosene rose, the quantity demanded of kerosene increased. What questions might you have for this researcher?

6. The sales director of Nutra Dinner, Inc., a company producing high-nutrition, low-fat, low-salt microwave dinners, wishes to estimate demand for one of the firm's latest additions—asparagus gumbo. The sales director sets up a booth at a health foods convention in order to conduct consumer interviews to estimate demand for the asparagus gumbo dinner. A few of the questions asked are (1) How many times a day do you actually eat asparagus? and (2) Would you rather eat a dinner of liver,

asparagus, and herbal tea or a turkey dinner with mashed potatoes, corn-on-the-cob, and wine? What three problems are likely to affect the validity of the consumer interview method of estimating demand? Explain each one.

APPENDIX 8A Derivation of Elasticity Estimates for Log-Linear Demand

As demonstrated in Chapter 3, the own-price elasticity of demand is

$$E = \frac{\partial Q_x}{\partial P_x} \cdot \frac{P_x}{Q_x}$$

With the linear specification of the demand function,

$$Q_x = a + bP_x + cM + dP_R$$

the statistic b is an estimate of the partial derivative of quantity demanded with respect to the price of the product,

$$\hat{b} = \text{Estimate of} \left(\frac{\partial Q_x}{\partial P_x}\right)$$

Hence for any price-quantity demanded combination (P_x, Q_x), the estimated own-price elasticity of that point on the demand function is

$$\hat{E} = \hat{b} \cdot \left[\frac{P_x}{Q_x}\right]$$

With the log-linear specification of the demand function,

$$Q_x = aP_x^b M^c P_R^d$$

the partial derivative of quantity demanded with respect to own price is

$$\frac{\partial Q_x}{\partial P_x} = baP_x^{b-1} M^c P_R^d = \frac{bQ_x}{P_x}$$

Hence, $\hat{b}$ is an estimate of own-price elasticity

$$\hat{E} = \frac{\hat{b}Q_x}{P_x} \cdot \frac{P_x}{Q_x} = \hat{b}$$

Using the same methodology estimates of income and cross-price elasticities can be obtained. The estimates are summarized in the following:

Elasticity	Definition	Estimate from linear specification	Estimate from log-linear specification
Own-price	$E = \frac{\partial Q_x}{\partial P_x} \cdot \frac{P_x}{Q_x}$	$\hat{b} \cdot \left[\frac{P_x}{Q_x}\right]$	$\hat{b}$
Income	$E_M = \frac{\partial Q_x}{\partial M} \cdot \frac{M}{Q_x}$	$\hat{c} \cdot \left[\frac{M}{Q_x}\right]$	$\hat{c}$
Cross-price	$E_{XR} = \frac{\partial Q_x}{\partial P_R} \cdot \frac{P_R}{Q_x}$	$\hat{d} \cdot \left[\frac{P_R}{Q_x}\right]$	$\hat{d}$

Note that the elasticity estimates from the linear specification depend on the point on the demand curve at which the elasticity estimate is evaluated. In contrast, the log-linear demand curve exhibits constant elasticity estimates.

APPENDIX 8B Simultaneous Equations Bias and Two-Stage Least-Squares Estimation

Simultaneous Equations Bias

Consider the following system of demand and supply equations

$$\text{Demand: } Q_d = a + bP + cM + \epsilon_d$$
$$\text{Supply: } Q_s = d + eP + fP_I + \epsilon_s$$

where P and Q are the endogenous variables, M and P_I are the exogenous variables, and ϵ_d and ϵ_s are the random error terms for demand and supply. We now solve for the *reduced form equations* which show how the values of the endogenous variables are determined by the exogenous variables and the random error terms. First we set $Q_d = Q_s$ and solve for P*:

$$a + bP + cM + \epsilon_d = d + eP + fP_I + \epsilon_s$$
$$P(b - e) = d - a + fP_I - cM + \epsilon_s - \epsilon_d$$
$$P^* = \frac{d - a}{b - e} + \frac{f}{b - e} P_I + \frac{-c}{b - e} M + \frac{\epsilon_s - \epsilon_d}{b - e}$$

Next, we substitute P^* into either demand or supply and solve for Q^*:

$$Q^* = \frac{bd - ae}{b - e} + \frac{bf}{b - e} P_I + \frac{-ce}{b - e} M + \frac{b\epsilon_s - e\epsilon_d}{b - e}$$

The reduced form equations for P* and Q* can be expressed in a simpler, more general form as follows:

$$P^* = f(P_I, M, \epsilon_d, \epsilon_s)$$
$$Q^* = g(P_I, M, \epsilon_d, \epsilon_s)$$

The reduced form equations show

(1) The problem of simultaneity. Each one of the endogenous variables, P^* and Q^* in this case, are clearly determined by all of the exogenous variables in the system and by all of the random error terms in the system. Thus the observed variation in both P and Q are reflecting variations in both demand- and supply-side determinants.

(2) The simultaneous equations bias. In order for the ordinary least-squares estimation procedure to produce unbiased estimates of a, b, and c in the demand equation, the explanatory variables (P and M) must *not* be correlated with the error term in the demand equation, ϵ_d (for a proof of this statement, see Gujarati*). The reduced form equations show us clearly that all endogenous variables are functions of all random error terms in the system. P is an endogenous variable and we have seen that P is a function of ϵ_d. Thus, P will be correlated with the error term in the demand equation, and the estimates of a, b, and c will be biased if the ordinary least-squares procedure is employed. This bias that results because P is an endogenous explanatory variable is called *simultaneous equations bias*.

Two-Stage Least-Squares Estimation

If a market demand equation is identified, it can be estimated using any number of available techniques. Perhaps the most widely used of these techniques—and the one that is most likely to be preprogrammed into the available regression packages—is two-stage least-squares (2SLS).

As shown above, the estimates of the parameters of the demand equation will be biased if ordinary least-squares is employed because price is an endogenous variable that is on the right-hand side of the demand equation. Because price is endogenous, it will be correlated with the error term in the demand equation causing simultaneous equations bias.

Conceptually, the endogenous right-hand side variable (in this case, price) must be made to behave as if it is exogenous; traditional regression techniques are used to obtain estimates of the parameters. In the linear example we have been using, we have a system of two simultaneous equations:

$$\text{Demand: } Q = a + bP + cM + \epsilon_d$$
$$\text{Supply: } Q = d + eP + fP_I + \epsilon_s$$

In these equations, P is an endogenous variable. To obtain unbiased estimates of a, b, and c, the estimation of the demand function proceeds in two steps or stages, which is why the technique is called two-stage least squares.

Stage 1

The endogenous right-hand side variable is regressed on all of the exogenous variables in the system:

$$P = \alpha + \beta M + \gamma P_I$$

From this estimation, we obtain estimates of the parameters, that is, $\hat{\alpha}$, $\hat{\beta}$, and $\hat{\gamma}$. Using these estimates and the *actual values* of the exogenous variables, we generate a *new* price series—predicted price—as follows

$$\hat{P} = \hat{\alpha} + \hat{\beta}M + \hat{\gamma}P$$

Note how the predicted price, $\hat{P}$, is obtained. $\hat{P}$ is simply a linear combination of the exogenous variables, so it follows that $\hat{P}$ now is also exogenous. However, given the way that the predicted price series is obtained, the values of $\hat{P}$ will correspond closely to the original values of P. In essence, this first stage forces price to behave as if it were exogenous.

Stage 2

We then use the predicted price variable ($\hat{P}$) in the demand function we wish to estimate. That is, in the second stage, we estimate the regression equation:

$$Q = a + b\hat{P} + cM$$

Note that this estimation uses the exogenous variable constructed in the first stage. We use predicted price, $\hat{P}$, rather than the actual price variable, P, in the final regression.

---

*Damodar N Gujarati, *Basic Econometrics.* (New York: McGraw-Hill, 1988).

APPENDIX 8C Data Used in Chapter 8 Examples

TABLE 8C.1
The World Copper Market*

Year	(Q_C) World consumption	(P_C) Real price copper	(M) Index of real income	(P_A) Real price aluminum	X	T
1	3,173.0	26.56	0.70	19.76	0.97679	1
2	3,281.1	27.31	0.71	20.78	1.03937	2
3	3,135.7	32.95	0.72	22.55	1.05153	3
4	3,359.1	33.90	0.70	23.06	0.97312	4
5	3,755.1	42.70	0.74	24.93	1.02349	5
6	3,875.9	46.11	0.74	26.50	1.04135	6
7	3,905.7	31.70	0.74	27.24	0.97686	7
8	3,957.6	27.23	0.72	26.21	0.98069	8
9	4,279.1	32.89	0.75	26.09	1.02888	9
10	4,627.9	33.78	0.77	27.40	1.03392	10
11	4,910.2	31.66	0.76	26.94	0.97922	11
12	4,908.4	32.28	0.79	25.18	0.99679	12
13	5,327.9	32.38	0.83	23.94	0.96630	13
14	5,878.4	33.75	0.85	25.07	1.02915	14
15	6,075.2	36.25	0.89	25.37	1.07950	15
16	6,312.7	36.24	0.93	24.55	1.05073	16
17	6,056.8	38.23	0.95	24.98	1.02788	17
18	6,375.9	40.83	0.99	24.96	1.02799	18
19	6,974.3	44.62	1.00	25.52	0.99151	19
20	7,101.6	52.27	1.00	26.01	1.00191	20
21	7,071.7	45.16	1.02	25.46	0.95644	21
22	7,754.8	42.50	1.07	22.17	0.96947	22
23	8,480.3	43.70	1.12	18.56	0.98220	23
24	8,105.2	47.88	1.10	21.32	1.00793	24
25	7,157.2	36.33	1.07	22.75	0.93810	25

*The data presented are actual values for 1951–1975.

TABLE 8C.2
Data for Checkers Pizza

Observation	Q	P	M	P_{Al}	P_{BMac}
1	1773	8.65	25500	10.55	1.25
2	1863	8.65	25600	10.45	1.35
3	1798	8.65	25700	10.35	1.55
4	1775	8.65	25970	10.30	1.05
5	1796	8.65	25970	10.30	0.95
6	1786	8.65	25750	10.25	0.95
7	1916	7.50	25750	10.25	0.85
8	1997	7.50	25950	10.15	1.15
9	2008	7.50	25950	10.00	1.25
10	2012	7.50	26120	10.00	1.75
11	1864	8.50	26120	10.25	1.75
12	1884	8.50	26150	10.25	1.85
13	1762	8.50	26200	9.75	1.50
14	1398	9.99	26350	9.75	1.10
15	1480	9.99	26450	9.65	1.05
16	1458	9.99	26350	9.60	1.25
17	1469	9.99	26850	10.00	0.55
18	1525	10.25	27350	10.25	0.55
19	1587	10.25	27350	10.20	1.15
20	1554	10.25	27950	10.00	1.15
21	1622	9.75	28159	10.10	0.55
22	1717	9.75	28264	10.10	0.55
23	1755	9.75	28444	10.10	1.20
24	1731	9.75	28500	10.25	1.20

CHAPTER

9 Demand Forecasting

A knowledge of future demand conditions can be extremely useful to managers when they are planning production schedules, inventory control, advertising campaigns, output in future periods, and investment, among other things. This chapter will describe some techniques that managers can use to forecast future demand conditions. The range of forecasting techniques is so wide that a complete discussion is quite beyond the scope of this text. Instead, we confine ourselves to a brief description of some of the more widely used techniques. For convenience, we divide forecasting methods into two groups—qualitative models and statistical models.

qualitative model
A model that does not employ explicit models or methods that can be replicated by another analyst.

Qualitative models are more difficult to describe since there exists no explicit model or method that can serve as a reference point. There is no model that can be used to replicate the initial forecast with a given set of data, and this feature, above all others, distinguishes this approach. It has been said by some that a qualitative model is essentially a "rule-of-thumb" technique. However, you should not infer from this description that qualitative forecasts are naive or unsophisticated. Indeed, it is the very complexity of this method that makes replication so difficult, since such forecasts are typically based on at least some subjective factors. In the final analysis, qualitative forecasts are often based on *expert opinion*. The forecaster examines the available data, solicits the advice of others, then sifts through this amalgamation of evidence to formulate a forecast. The weights assigned to the various bits and pieces of information are subjectively determined and, we might add, separate the neophyte from the expert.

statistical model
A model that employs explicit models or methods that can be replicated by other analysts.

In contrast, a **statistical model** employs explicit models or methods that can be replicated by another analyst. The results of statistical models can be reproduced by different researchers. An additional advantage of this approach is the existence of reasonably well-defined standards for evaluating such models. The final advantage of statistical models is the ability to use them in simulation models. (Basically, simulation models are models in which a researcher can obtain alternative forecasts for the future values of the endogenous variable, given alternative future trends in the exogenous variables.) Statistical models can be further subdivided into two categories—time-series models and econometric models.

We begin with a discussion of qualitative forecasts. Next, we describe some basic time-series techniques. We then introduce econometric models and show how to use simulation procedures to examine the impact on future demand of changes in the exogenous variables of the model. We close this chapter with a note on some of the more important problems involved in forecasting.

9.1 QUALITATIVE FORECASTING TECHNIQUES

As noted, qualitative forecasting methods are rather difficult to describe due to the subjective elements involved. Forecasters combine available data with their knowledge of the firm and industry and, assigning subjective weights to these pieces of evidence, obtain a forecast. While qualitative forecasting may indeed be the best technique, it is difficult, if not impossible, to teach these techniques. In truth, we do not actually know how people are successful at qualitative forecasting. We can only say that those who are successful understand economics and know a great deal about their industries.

Skillful forecasters do use data to make these forecasts. While it is impossible to set forth the manner in which their subjective weights are assigned to the data they use, we can describe some of the data that forecasters may observe and use.

It is possible that the analyst has observed through experience (or, perhaps, using regression techniques) that a relation exists between the sales of the firm and the movement in certain aggregate economic variables over time. More specifically, managers know that changes in certain economic variables *lead* the changes in the firm's sales. If managers know these variables, they can use these leading indicators as a barometer to predict changes in the sales of the firm. The problem then is the isolation of these indicators and the collection of appropriate data.

This problem of data identification and collection has been simplified immensely through the work of the National Bureau of Economic Research and the US Department of Commerce. The US Department of Commerce publishes, monthly, *Business Conditions Digest*, which contains data on a large number of indicators. (*Business Conditions Digest* contains almost 200 data series that could be used as indicators.) Of these, 11 variables considered particularly important as leading indicators are presented in Table 9.1.

If a forecaster can relate the firm's sales to one or more of the leading indicators, it can then be possible to generate short-term forecasts on the basis of these published data. For example, a firm that manufactures dishwashers would be interested in the index of new building permits. An increase in building permits

TABLE 9.1
The 11 Leading Indicators

1. Average workweek, production workers, manufacturing (hours).
2. Average weekly initial claims, state unemployment insurance—inverted* (thousands).
3. New orders for consumer goods and materials in 1972 dollars (billion dollars).
4. Vendor performance, companies receiving slower deliveries (percent).
5. University of Michigan's Index of Consumer Expectations.
6. Contracts and orders for plant and equipment in 1972 dollars (billion dollars).
7. New building permits, private housing units (index: 1967 = 100).
8. Change in inventories on hand and on order in 1972 dollars, smoothed† (annual rate, billion dollars).
9. Change in sensitive materials prices, smoothed† (percent).
10. Stock prices, 500 common stocks (index: 1941 – 43 = 100).
11. Money supply (M2) in 1972 dollars (billion dollars).

*This series is inverted, hence a decrease in unemployment claims will lead to an increase in the indicator.

†*Smoothed* means that irregularities in the data have been removed. The purpose in this procedure is to demonstrate the trend in the variable. Many variables exhibit considerable short-term (or seasonal) variation. In order to ascertain the trend in the variable, it is necessary to remove the effects of the short-term variation, that is, smooth the data series.

Source: US Department of Commerce, *Business Conditions Digest.*

precedes housing starts, which precede the purchase of dishwashers. An experienced forecaster could combine this information with personal knowledge about the firm (e.g., its share of the market) and about the market (e.g., the percentage of new houses that have dishwashers) to provide a forecast of sales for the firm. Again, it is impossible for us to determine the weights that should be assigned to these various pieces of information.

There are also more complex situations in which more than one indicator is used. In some instances, the different indicators could provide conflicting forecasts. To handle this difficulty, two multiple indicator methods are commonly employed. One method is to calculate a composite index, that is, a weighted average of individual indicators. Indeed, the US Department of Commerce itself publishes several composite indicators, one of which is the weighted average of the 11 leading indicators. In Figure 9.1, we have provided a graph of the behavior of this composite index over the period 1965–1993. In this figure, it is easy to see why these are leading indicators. Note how the index turned down prior to the recessions of 1969–70, 1973–75, 1980, 1981–1983, and 1991–1992. Likewise, the upturn in this composite index preceded—led—the upturn in general economic activity.

Multiple indicators are also used to calculate a diffusion index. Using this approach, one would calculate the percentage of the indicators that are rising. For example, if 5 of the 11 leading indicators were rising, the diffusion index would be $\frac{5}{11}$ or 46 percent. Using a diffusion index, one normally defines a critical percentage (usually 50 percent). If the diffusion index is above this critical percentage, one would say that economic activity is rising. Likewise, if the diffusion index is below the critical value, economic activity is said to be declining. In Figure 9.2 we have provided a graph of the diffusion index for the 11 leading indicators for the period 1965–1993, and compared it to periods of recession.

FIGURE 9.1

Composite Index of the 11 Leading Indicators (1965–1993)

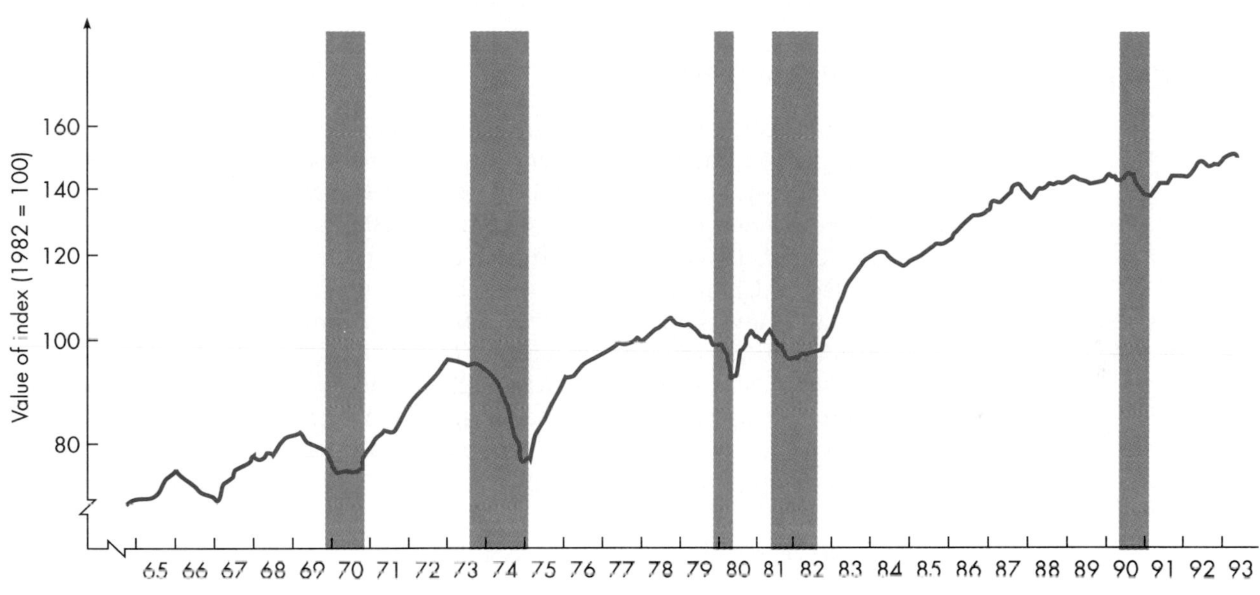

Note: Periods shaded are periods of recession as determined by the National Bureau of Economic Research (e.g., the 1969–70 recession covered the period December 1969 through November 1970).

Source: US Department of Commerce, *Survey of Current Business.*

FIGURE 9.2

Diffusion Index for the 11 Leading Indicators: Percent of Components Rising over 6-month Span

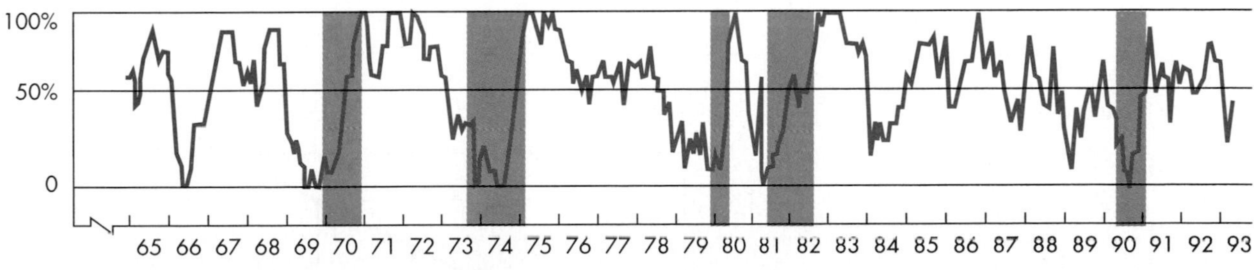

Source: US Department of Commerce, *Survey of Current Business.*

Again, let us stress that the procedures outlined above require a great many subjective decisions by forecasters. The analyst must determine the appropriate indicators, then interpret them in light of the conditions that will exist in their particular markets and firms. First, these indicators do not always indicate changes in another economic variable (and there also exists some random month-to-month variation in these indicators). Second, the lead times are not necessarily constant. Third, and most important, since these leading indicators predict the *direction rather than the magnitude of changes*, the responsibility for assigning a magnitude rests with the forecaster.

9.2 TIME SERIES FORECASTS OF SALES AND PRICE

Statistical forecasting is more analytical than qualitative forecasting because the models can be replicated by another researcher. Statistical forecasting uses empirical data in basic statistical models to generate forecasts about economic variables. There are two categories of statistical methods: time series models and econometric models. We begin with time series models.

time-series model
A statistical model that shows how a time-ordered sequence of observations on a variable are generated.

As noted in Chapter 5, a *time series* is simply a time-ordered sequence of observations on a variable. In general, a **time-series model** uses only the time-series history of the variable of interest to predict future values. Time-series models describe the process by which these historical data were generated. Thus, to forecast using time series analysis, it is necessary to specify a mathematical model that represents the generating process. We will first discuss a general forecasting model, and then give examples of price and sales forecasts.

Linear Trend Forecasting

A linear trend is the simplest time-series forecasting method. Using this type of model, one could posit that sales or price increases or decreases linearly over time. For example, a firm's sales for period 1984–1993 are shown by the 10 data points in Figure 9.3. The straight line that best fits the data scatter, calculated using simple regression analysis, is illustrated by the solid line in the figure. The fitted line indicates a positive trend in sales. Assuming that sales in the future will continue to follow the same trend, sales in any future period can be forecast by extending this line and picking the forecast values from this *extrapolated*

FIGURE 9.3
A Linear Trend Forecast

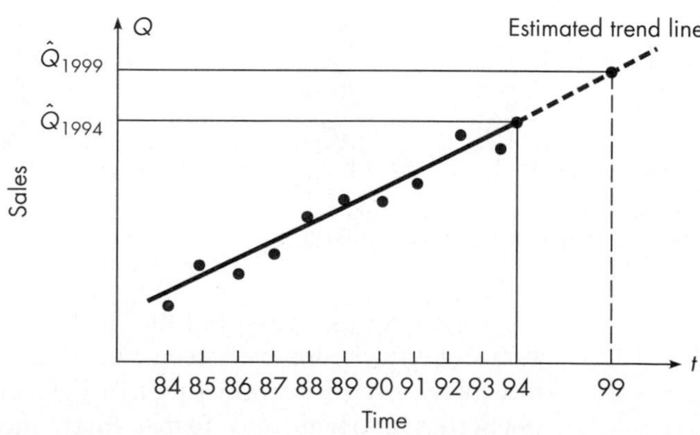

dashed line for the desired future period. We have illustrated sales forecasts for 1994 and 1999 ($\hat{Q}_{1994}$ and $\hat{Q}_{1999}$) in Figure 9.3.

Summarizing this procedure, we assumed a linear relation between sales and time:

$$Q_t = a + bt$$

Using the 10 observations for 1984–1993, we regressed time, the independent variable expressed in years, on sales, the dependent variable expressed in dollars, to obtain the estimated trend line

$$\hat{Q}_t = \hat{a} + \hat{b}t$$

This line best fits the historical data. It is important to test whether there is a statistically significant positive or negative trend in sales. As shown in Chapter 5, it is easy to determine if $\hat{b}$ is significantly different from zero by using a t-test for statistical significance. If $\hat{b}$ is positive and statistically significant, sales are trending upward over time. If $\hat{b}$ is negative and statistically significant, sales are trending downward over time. However, if $\hat{b}$ is not statistically significant, one would assume that $b = 0$, and sales are constant over time. That is, there is no relation between sales and time, and any variation in sales is due to random fluctuations.

If the estimation indicates a statistically significant trend, you can then use the estimated trend line to obtain forecasts of future sales. For example, if a manager wanted a forecast for sales in 1994, the manager would simply insert 1994 into the estimated trend line:

$$\hat{Q}_{1994} = \hat{a} + \hat{b} \times (1994)$$

A Sales Forecast for Terminator Pest Control

In January 1993, Arnold Schwartz started Terminator Pest Control, a small pest-control company in Atlanta. Terminator Pest Control serves mainly residential customers citywide. At the end of March 1994, after 15 months of operation, Arnold decides to apply for a business loan from his bank to buy another pest-control truck. The bank is somewhat reluctant to make the loan, citing concern that sales at Terminator Pest Control did not grow significantly over its first 15 months of business. In addition, the bank asks Arnold to provide a forecast of sales for the next three months (April, May, and June).

Arnold decides to do the forecast himself using a time-series model based on past sales figures. He collects the data on sales for the last 15 months—sales are measured as the number of homes serviced during a given month. Since data are collected monthly, Arnold creates a continuous time variable by numbering the months consecutively as January 1993 = 1, February 1993 = 2, etc. The data for Terminator and a scatter diagram are shown in Figure 9.4.

Arnold estimates the linear trend model

$$Q_t = a + bt$$

FIGURE 9.4
Forecasting Sales for Terminator Pest Control

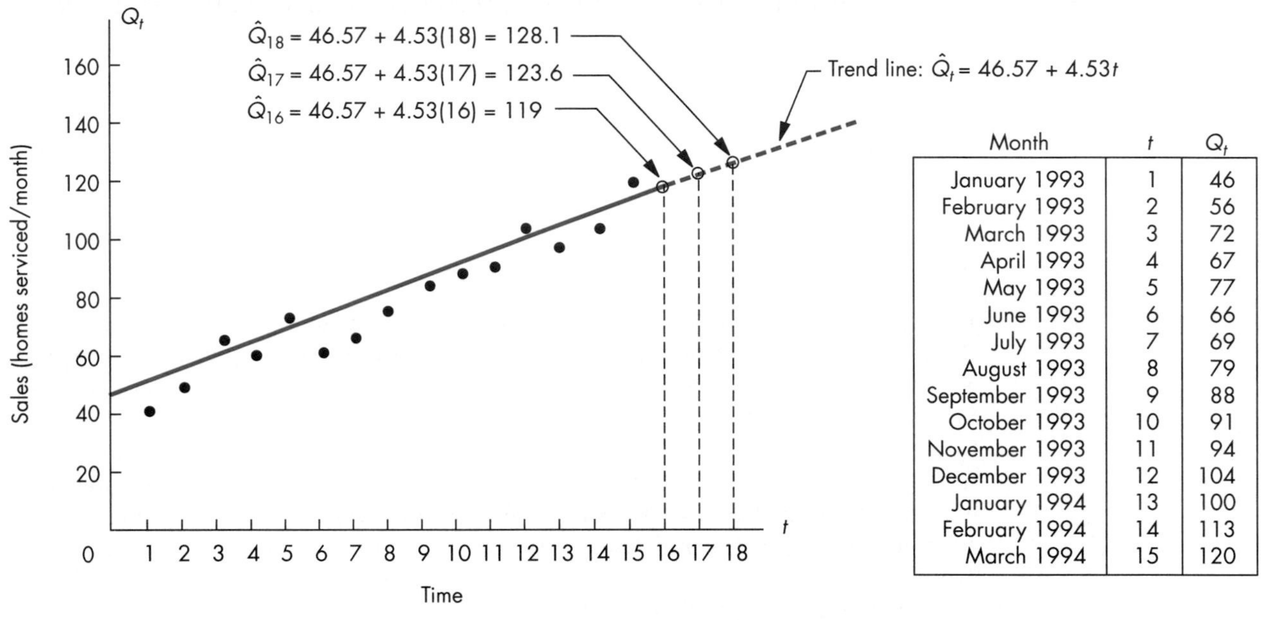

Month	t	Q_t
January 1993	1	46
February 1993	2	56
March 1993	3	72
April 1993	4	67
May 1993	5	77
June 1993	6	66
July 1993	7	69
August 1993	8	79
September 1993	9	88
October 1993	10	91
November 1993	11	94
December 1993	12	104
January 1994	13	100
February 1994	14	113
March 1994	15	120

and gets the following printout from the computer:

```
DEPENDENT VARIABLE: Q        F-RATIO:   156.11

OBSERVATIONS: 15             R-SQUARE: 0.9231

                        PARAMETER       STANDARD
     VARIABLE           ESTIMATE          ERROR            T-RATIO

     INTERCEPT            46.57            3.29             14.16
     T                     4.53            0.36             12.58
```

The t-ratio for the time variable, 12.58, exceeds the critical t of 3.012 for 13 degrees of freedom (= 15 – 2) at the 99 percent level of confidence. Thus, the sales figures for Terminator suggest a statistically significant upward trend in sales. The sales forecasts for April, May, and June of 1994 are

$$\text{April 1994:}\quad \hat{Q}_{16} = 46.57 + (4.53 \times 16) = 119$$
$$\text{May 1994:}\quad \hat{Q}_{17} = 46.57 + (4.53 \times 17) = 123.6$$
$$\text{June 1994:}\quad \hat{Q}_{18} = 46.57 + (4.53 \times 18) = 128.1$$

The bank decided to make the loan to Terminator Pest Control in light of the statistically significant upward trend in sales and the forecast of higher sales in the three upcoming months.

A PRICE FORECAST: LUMBER PRICES IN MIAMI

In December 1992, after hurricane Andrew demolished the small town of Homestead, as well as severely damaging parts of Miami and the surrounding areas, the price of all types of lumber products began to increase sharply. Suppose you work for a large lumber producer in south Florida, and your manager wants you to forecast the price of lumber for the next two quarters. Information about the price of a ton of lumber is readily available. Using quarterly lumber prices since 1992 III, you estimate a linear trend line for lumber prices through the 1994 II time period. Your computer output for the linear time trend model on lumber price is:

DEPENDENT VARIABLE: P		F-RATIO: 18.71	
OBSERVATIONS: 8		R-SQUARE: 0.5500	
VARIABLE	PARAMETER ESTIMATE	STANDARD ERROR	T-RATIO
INTERCEPT	2066	794.62	2.60
T	25	8.62	2.90

Both parameter estimates, $\hat{a}$ and $\hat{b}$, are significant at the 95 percent confidence level since both t-ratios exceed 2.447, the critical t for the 95 percent confidence level. Thus, the real (inflation adjusted) price for a ton of lumber has exhibited a statistically significant trend upward since the third quarter of 1992. Lumber prices have risen, on average, \$25 per ton each quarter over the range of this sample period.

To forecast the price of lumber for the next two quarters, you make the following computations:

$$\hat{P}_{1994\text{III}} = 2066 + (25 \times 9) = \$2{,}291 \text{ per ton}$$
$$\hat{P}_{1994\text{IV}} = 2066 + (25 \times 10) = \$2{,}316 \text{ per ton}$$

As you can see by the last two hypothetical examples, the linear trend method of forecasting is a simple procedure for generating forecasts for either sales or price. Indeed, this method can be applied to forecast any economic variable for which a time series of observations is available.

9.3 SEASONAL (OR CYCLICAL) VARIATION

seasonal or cyclical variation
The regular variation that time-series data frequently exhibit.

Time-series data may frequently exhibit regular, **seasonal or cyclical variation** over time, and the failure to take these regular variations into account when estimating a forecasting equation would bias the forecast. Frequently, when using quarterly or monthly sales to forecast sales, seasonal variation may occur—the sales of many products vary systematically by month or by quarter. For example, in the retail clothing business, sales are generally higher before Easter and Christmas. Thus, sales would be higher during the second and fourth quarters of the year. Likewise, the sales of hunting equipment would peak during early fall, the third quarter. In such cases, you would definitely wish to incorporate these systematic variations when estimating the equation and forecasting future sales. We shall describe the technique most commonly employed to handle cyclical variation. The reader interested in additional techniques should look at the references cited at the end of the text.

Correcting for Seasonal Variation Using Dummy Variables

Consider the simplified example of a firm producing and selling a product for which sales are consistently higher in the fourth quarter than in any other quarter. A hypothetical data scatter is presented in Figure 9.5. In each of the four years, the data point in the fourth quarter is much higher than in the other three. While a time trend clearly exists, if the analyst simply regressed sales against time, without accounting for the higher sales in the fourth quarter, too large a trend would be estimated (i.e., the slope would be too large). In essence, there is an upward shift of the trend line in the fourth quarter. Such a relation is presented in Figure 9.6. In the fourth quarter, the intercept is higher than in the other quarters. In other words, a', the intercept of the trend line for the fourth-quarter data points, exceeds a, the intercept of the trend line for the data points in the other quarters. One way of specifying this relation is to define a' as $a' = a +$

FIGURE 9.5
Sales with Seasonal Variation

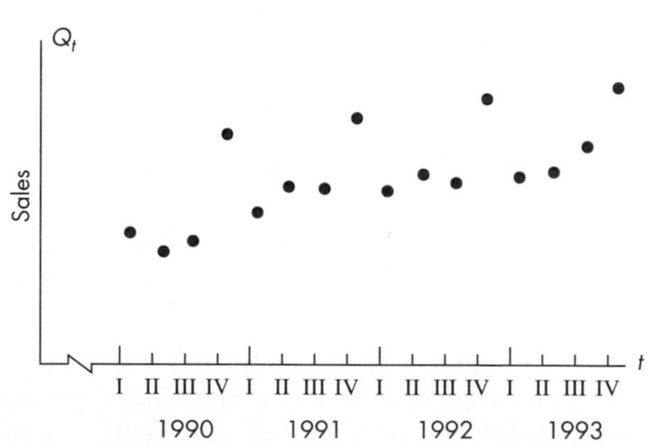

c, where c is some positive number. Therefore, the regression line we want to estimate will take the form:

$$\hat{Q}_t = a + bt + c$$

where $c = 0$ in the first three quarters.

dummy variable
A variable that takes only values of 0 and 1.

To estimate the preceding equation, statisticians use what is commonly referred to as a *dummy variable* in the estimating equation. A **dummy variable** is a variable that can take on only the values of *zero* or *one*. In this case, we would assign the dummy variable (D) a value of one if the sales observation is from the fourth quarter and zero in the other three quarters. The data are shown in Table 9.2, where Q_t represents the sales figure in the tth period and $D = 1$ for quarter IV and zero otherwise. Since quarterly data are being used, time is converted into integers to obtain a continuous time variable. Using these data, the following equation is estimated:

$$\hat{Q}_t = a + bt + cD$$

The above specification produces two equations like those shown in Figure 9.6. The estimated slope of the two equations would be the same ($\hat{b}$). For quarters I, II, and III the estimated intercept is $\hat{a}$, while for the fourth quarter the estimated intercept is $\hat{a} + \hat{c}$. This estimation really means that for any future period t, the sales forecast would be

$$\hat{Q}_t = \hat{a} + \hat{b}t$$

unless period t occurs in the fourth quarter, in which case the sales forecast would be

$$\hat{Q}_t = \hat{a} + \hat{b}t + \hat{c} = (\hat{a} + \hat{c}) + \hat{b}t$$

For example, referring to the data in Table 9.2, when a manager wishes to forecast sales in the third quarter of 1994, the manager uses the equation

$$\hat{Q}_{1994(III)} = \hat{a} + \hat{b}\,(19)$$

FIGURE 9.6
The Effect of Seasonal Variation

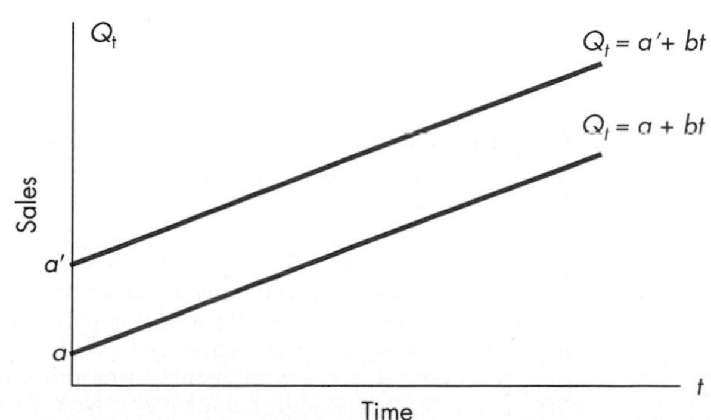

TABLE 9.2

Creating a Dummy Variable

Q_t	t	D
$Q_{1990(I)}$	1	0
$Q_{1990(II)}$	2	0
$Q_{1990(III)}$	3	0
$Q_{1990(IV)}$	4	1
$Q_{1991(I)}$	5	0
$Q_{1991(II)}$	6	0
$Q_{1991(III)}$	7	0
$Q_{1991(IV)}$	8	1
$Q_{1992(I)}$	9	0
$Q_{1992(II)}$	10	0
$Q_{1992(III)}$	11	0
$Q_{1992(IV)}$	12	1
$Q_{1993(I)}$	13	0
$Q_{1993(II)}$	14	0
$Q_{1993(III)}$	15	0
$Q_{1993(IV)}$	16	1

If a manager wishes to forecast sales in the fourth quarter of 1994, the forecast is

$$\hat{Q}_{1994(IV)} = (\hat{a} + \hat{c}) + \hat{b}\,(20)$$

In other words, when the forecast is for quarter IV, the forecast equation adds the amount $\hat{c}$ to the sales that would otherwise be forecast.[1]

Going a step further, it could be the case that there exist quarter-to-quarter differences in sales (i.e., in Figure 9.6 there would be four trend lines). In this case, three dummy variables are used: D_1 (equal to one in the first quarter and zero otherwise), D_2 (equal to one in the second quarter and zero otherwise), and D_3 (equal to one in the third quarter and zero otherwise).[2] Then, the manager estimates the equation

$$Q_t = a + bt + c_1D_1 + c_2D_2 + c_3D_3$$

In quarter I the intercept is $a + c_1$, in quarter II it is $a + c_2$, in quarter III it is $a + c_3$, and in quarter IV it is a only.

[1]Throughout this discussion, we have assumed that trend lines differ only with respect to the intercepts—the slope is the same for all of the trend lines. Dummy variables can also be used to reflect differences in slopes. This technique is beyond the scope of this text, and we refer the interested reader to the references cited at the end of this text.

[2]Likewise, if there were month-to-month differences, 11 dummy variables are used to account for the monthly change in the intercept. Note that in using dummy variables, you must always use one fewer dummy variable than periods being considered. For further explanation, see the references at the end of this chapter.

To obtain a forecast for some future quarter, it is necessary to include the coefficient for the dummy variable for that particular quarter. For example, predictions for the third quarter of a particular year would take the form

$$\hat{Q}_t = \hat{a} + \hat{b}t + \hat{c}_3$$

Perhaps the best way to explain how these dummy variables can be used to account for cyclical variation is to provide an example.

The Dummy Variable Technique: An Example

Jean Reynolds, the sales manager of Statewide Trucking Company, wishes to predict sales for all four quarters of 1994. The sales of Statewide Trucking are subject to seasonal variation and also have a trend over time. Reynolds obtains sales data for 1990–1993 by quarter. The data collected are presented in Table 9.3. Note that since quarterly data are used, time is converted into a continuous variable by numbering quarters consecutively in Column 4 of the table.

Reynolds knows, from a college course in managerial economics, that the desired sales forecast requires her to estimate an equation containing three dummy variables—one fewer than the number of time periods in the annual cycle. She chooses to estimate the following equation:

$$Q_t = a + bt + c_1D_1 + c_2D_2 + c_3D_3$$

where D_1, D_2, and D_3 are, respectively, dummy variables for quarters I, II, and III.[3] Using the data in Table 9.3, she estimates the preceding equation and the results of this estimation are:

DEPENDENT VARIABLE: QT F-RATIO: 794.126

OBSERVATIONS: 16 R-SQUARE: 0.9965

VARIABLE	PARAMETER ESTIMATE	STANDARD ERROR	T-RATIO
INTERCEPT	139.63	1.7436	80.081
T	2.7375	0.12996	21.064
D1	-69.788	1.6895	-41.307
D2	-58.755	1.6643	-35.303
D3	-62.013	1.6490	-37.606

[3]This is only one of the specifications that is appropriate. Equally appropriate is

$$Q_t = a + bt + c_2D_2 + c_3D_3 + c_4D_4$$
$$Q_t = a + bt + c_1D_1 + c_3D_3 + c_4D_4$$

or

$$Q_t = a + bt + c_1D_1 + c_2D_2 + c_4D_4$$

It is necessary only to have *any three* of the quarters represented by dummy variables.

TABLE 9.3
Quarterly Sales Data for Statewide Trucking Company (1990–1993)

(1) Year	(2) Quarter	(3) Sales ($000)	(4) t	(5) D_1	(6) D_2	(7) D_3
1990	I	$ 72	1	1	0	0
	II	87	2	0	1	0
	III	87	3	0	0	1
	IV	150	4	0	0	0
1991	I	82	5	1	0	0
	II	98	6	0	1	0
	III	94	7	0	0	1
	IV	162	8	0	0	0
1992	I	97	9	1	0	0
	II	105	10	0	1	0
	III	109	11	0	0	1
	IV	176	12	0	0	0
1993	I	105	13	1	0	0
	II	121	14	0	1	0
	III	119	15	0	0	1
	IV	180	16	0	0	0

Upon examining the estimation results, Reynolds notes that a positive trend in sales is indicated ($\hat{b} > 0$). In order to be sure that the trend is statistically significant, a t-test must be performed on $\hat{b}$. The calculated t-value for $\hat{b}$ is $t_{\hat{b}} = 21.064$. With $16 - 5 = 11$ degrees of freedom, the critical value of t (using a 95 percent confidence level) is 2.201. Since $21.064 > 2.201$, $\hat{b}$ is statistically significant, and Reynolds has evidence of a significant positive trend in sales.

Next, Reynolds calculates the estimated intercepts of the trend line for each of the four quarters. In the first quarter,

$$\begin{aligned}\hat{a} + \hat{c}_1 &= 139.63 - 69.788 \\ &= 69.842\end{aligned}$$

in the second quarter

$$\begin{aligned}\hat{a} + \hat{c}_2 &= 139.63 - 58.775 \\ &= 80.855\end{aligned}$$

in the third quarter

$$\begin{aligned}\hat{a} + \hat{c}_3 &= 139.63 - 62.013 \\ &= 77.617\end{aligned}$$

and in the fourth quarter

$$\hat{a} = 139.63$$

These estimates indicate that the intercepts, and thus sales, are lower in quarters I, II, and III than in quarter IV. The question that always must be asked is: Are these intercepts *significantly* lower?

To answer this question, Reynolds decides to compare quarters I and IV. In quarter I, the intercept is $\hat{a} + \hat{c}_1$; in quarter IV, it is $\hat{a}$. Hence, if $\hat{a} + \hat{c}$ is significantly lower than $\hat{a}$, it is necessary that $\hat{c}_1$ be significantly less than zero. That is, if

$$\hat{a} + \hat{c}_1 < \hat{a}$$

it follows that $\hat{c}_1 < 0$. Reynolds already knows that $\hat{c}_1$ is negative; to determine if it is significantly negative, she must perform a t-test. The calculated value of t for $\hat{c}_1$ is –41.307. Since $|-41.307| > 2.201$, $\hat{c}_1$ is significantly less than zero. This indicates that the intercept—and the sales—in the first quarter is less than in the fourth. The t-values for $\hat{c}_2$ and $\hat{c}_3$, –35.315 and –37.606, respectively, are both greater (in absolute value) than 2.201 and are significantly negative. Thus, the intercepts in the second and third quarters are also significantly less than the intercept for the fourth quarter. Hence, Reynolds has evidence that there is a significant increase in sales in the fourth quarter.

She can now proceed to forecast sales by quarters for 1994. In the first quarter of 1994, $t = 17$, $D_1 = 1$, $D_2 = 0$, and $D_3 = 0$. Therefore, the forecast for sales in 1994 would be

$$\begin{aligned}\hat{Q}_{1994(\text{I})} &= \hat{a} + \hat{b} \times 17 + \hat{c}_1 \times 1 + \hat{c}_2 \times 0 + \hat{c}_3 \times 0 \\ &= \hat{a} + \hat{b} \times 17 + \hat{c}_1 \\ &= 139.63 + 2.7375 \times 17 - 69.788 \\ &= 116.3795\end{aligned}$$

Using precisely the same method, the forecasts for sales in the other three quarters of 1994 are as follows:

1994 II:

$$\begin{aligned}\hat{Q}_{1994(\text{II})} &= \hat{a} + \hat{b} \times 18 + \hat{c}_2 \\ &= 139.63 + 2.7375 \times 18 - 58.775 \\ &= 130.13\end{aligned}$$

1994 III:

$$\begin{aligned}\hat{Q}_{1994(\text{III})} &= \hat{a} + \hat{b} \times 19 + \hat{c}_3 \\ &= 139.63 + 2.7375 \times 19 - 62.013 \\ &= 129.6295\end{aligned}$$

1994 IV:

$$\begin{aligned}\hat{Q}_{1994(\text{IV})} &= \hat{a} + \hat{b} \times 20 \\ &= 139.63 + 2.7375 \times 20 \\ &= 194.38\end{aligned}$$

ILLUSTRATION 9.1

Forecasting New Home Sales: A Time-Series Forecast

Suppose that in January of 1991, the market analyst of a national real estate firm wanted to forecast the total number of new homes that would be sold in the United States in March of 1991. Let's examine how this analyst could have used time-series techniques to forecast sales of new homes. The actual data on the total number of new homes sold monthly during the years 1989–1990 are presented in the table (columns 1–3) and are shown by the line (Q_t) in the graph.

Suppose the market analyst forecasts sales using a linear trend, and the following linear specification is estimated:

$$Q_t = a + bt$$

where Q_t is the number of new homes sold in the nth month (measured in thousands of new homes), and $t = 1, 2, \ldots, 24$. Note that because these are monthly data, the analyst must convert time into integers as shown in column 4 of the table (ignore column 5 for now). When the analyst runs a regression analysis on the 24 time-series observations on new home sales, the following computer output results:

```
DEPENDENT VARIABLE: QT    F-RATIO:
                            28.871

OBSERVATIONS: 24         R-SQUARE:
                            0.5675

              PARAMETER   STANDARD
VARIABLE      ESTIMATE    ERROR

INTERCEPT     61.3369     2.5447
T             -0.9570     0.1781
```

Monthly Sales of New Homes in the United States (1989–1990)

(1) Year	(2) Month	(3) Sales*	(4) t	(5) D_t
1989	1	52	1	0
	2	51	2	0
	3	58	3	1
	4	60	4	1
	5	61	5	1
	6	58	6	1
	7	62	7	1
	8	61	8	1
	9	49	9	0
	10	51	10	0
	11	47	11	0
	12	40	12	0
1990	1	45	13	0
	2	50	14	0
	3	58	15	1
	4	52	16	1
	5	50	17	1
	6	50	18	1
	7	46	19	1
	8	46	20	1
	9	38	21	0
	10	37	22	0
	11	34	23	0
	12	29	24	0

*Thousands of new homes sold

Source: US Department of Housing and Urban Development.

The estimated forecast equation, $Q_t = 61.3369 - 0.9570t$, is labeled $\hat{Q}_t$ in the figure.

The estimate of b is negative ($\hat{b} = -0.9570$), indicating sales were decreasing over the time period 1989–

In this example, we have confined our attention to quarterly variation. However, exactly the same techniques can be used for monthly data, or any other type of seasonal or cyclical variation. In addition to its application to situations involving seasonal and cyclical variation, the dummy variable technique can be

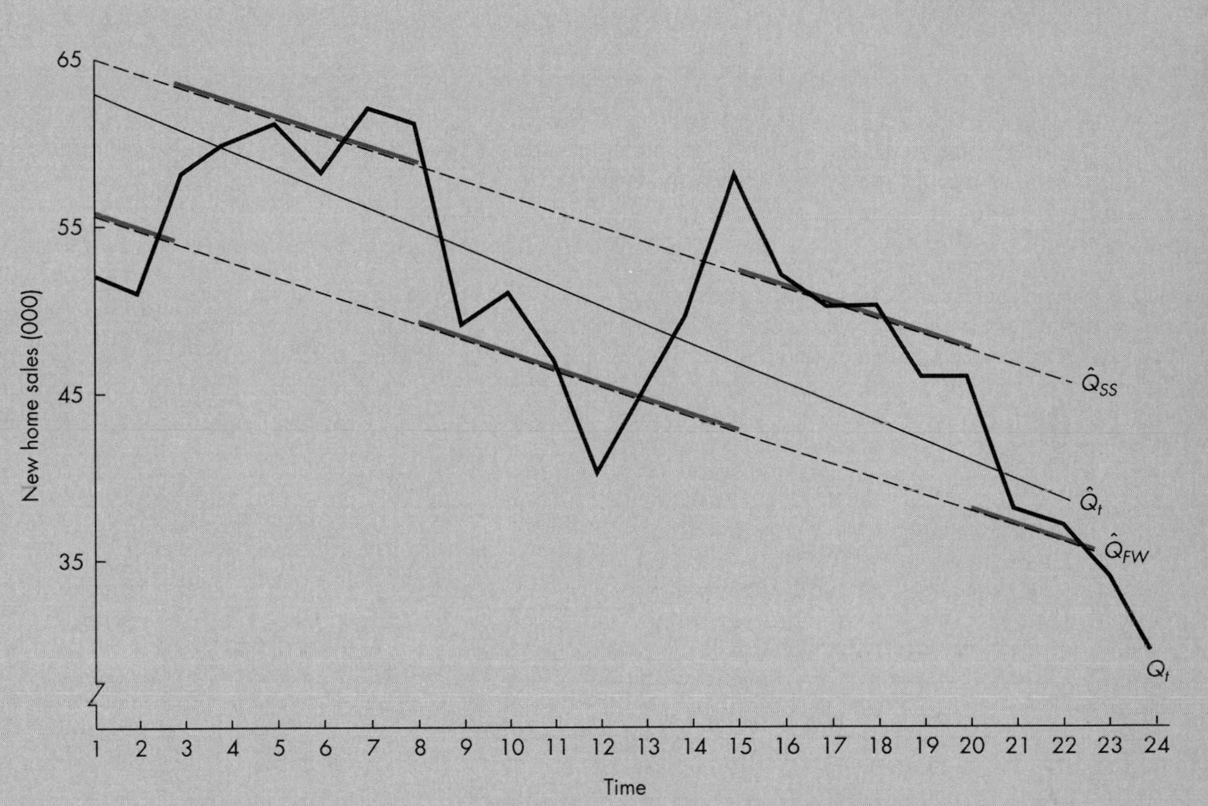

1990. The analyst needs to test for statistical significance of $\hat{b}$. The calculated value of the t-statistic for $\hat{b}$ is

$$t_{\hat{b}} = \frac{-0.9570}{0.1781} = -5.37$$

Since $|-5.37| > 2.819$ (the critical value for t with $24 - 2 = 22$ degrees of freedom at a 99 percent confidence level), the negative trend in new home sales over the period 1989–1990 is statistically significant.

Note that the value of R^2 indicates a rather loose fit, as can be seen in the figure as well, even though the model as a whole is statistically significant ($F = 28.871 > 7.88$).

Using the estimated linear trend line, the market analyst can forecast sales for March 1991 ($t = 27$) by substituting the value 27 for t:

$$\hat{Q}_{\text{March 1991}} = 61.3369 - 0.9570\,(27)$$
$$= 35.50$$

used to account for changes in sales (or any other economic variable that is being forecast) due to forces such as wars, bad weather, or even strikes at a competitor's production facility. We summarize the dummy variable technique with the following:

ILLUSTRATION 9.1

(*continued*)

Using linear trend analysis, the number of new homes sold in March 1991 is forecast to be 35,500. The number of homes actually sold in March 1991 turned out to be 51,000. The analyst's forecast, using a trend line technique, underestimates the actual number of homes sold by 30.4 percent, a rather sizable error.

The market analyst could improve the forecast by modifying the forecast equation to reflect the seasonality of new home sales. Sales of new homes tend to vary seasonally. In the spring and summer months, new home sales tend to be higher than in other months as families try to relocate while school is out of session. Let's examine how adding a dummy variable to account for this seasonality can substantially improve the market analyst's sales forecast.

To account for the seasonal increase in new home sales during the spring and summer months (March through August), the analyst can define a dummy variable, D_t, to be equal to 1 when $t = 3, 4, 5, 6, 7, 8$, and 15, 16, 17, 18, 19, 20. The dummy variable is equal to zero for all other months. The values of the dummy variable are shown in column 5 of the table. Adding this dummy variable to the trend line results in the following equation to be estimated:

$$Q_t = a + bt + cD_t$$

Again using the sales data for 1989–1990, a regression analysis results in the following computer output:

DEPENDENT VARIABLE: QT		F-RATIO: 74.379
OBSERVATIONS: 24		R-SQUARE: 0.8763
VARIABLE	PARAMETER ESTIMATE	STANDARD ERROR
INTERCEPT	55.1111	1.6371
T	-0.8539	0.0985
D	9.8755	1.3641

As was the case when no adjustment was made for seasonality, a statistically significant downward trend in sales is present ($\hat{b} < 0$). The calculated t for $\hat{b}$ ($t_{\hat{b}} = |-0.8534/0.0985| = 8.66$) easily exceeds the critical t (2.819). Note that after accounting for seasonal variation, the trend line is less steep ($|-0.8539| < |-0.9570|$).

Relation When seasonal variation causes the intercept of the demand equation to vary systematically from season to season, dummy variables can be added to the estimated forecasting equation to account for the cyclical variation. If there are N seasonal time periods to be accounted for, $N - 1$ dummy variables are added to the demand equation. Each of these dummy variables accounts for one of the seasonal time periods by taking a value of 1 for those observations that occur during that season, and a value of 0 otherwise. Used in this way, dummy variables allow the intercept of the demand equation to vary across seasons.

Before leaving the discussion of time series models, we should mention that the linear trend model is just one—and probably the simplest—of many different types of time-series models that can be used to forecast economic variables. More advanced time-series models fit cyclical patterns, rather than straight lines, to the scatter of data over time. These techniques, which involve moving average models, exponential smoothing models, and Box-Jenkins models, go well beyond the scope of a managerial textbook. In fact, you may take entire courses in

The estimated intercept for the trend line is 55.1111 for fall and winter months ($D_t = 0$). During the spring and summer buying season, the estimated intercept of the trend line is

$$\hat{\alpha} + \hat{c} = 55.1111 + 9.8755$$
$$= 64.9866$$

To check for statistical significance of $\hat{c}$, we calculate the t-statistic $t_{\hat{c}}$ as

$$t_{\hat{c}} = \frac{9.8755}{1.3641} = 7.24$$

which exceeds the critical t for 21 degrees of freedom and a 99 percent confidence level (2.831). Thus the statistical evidence suggests that there is a significant increase in sales of new homes during the spring and summer months. The increase in the average number of new homes sold in March through August compared to September through February is about 9,875 more homes per month.

The estimated trend lines representing the spring and summer months ($\hat{Q}_{SS}$) and the fall and winter months ($\hat{Q}_{FW}$) are shown in the figure above. Note that the spring and summer trend line is parallel to the fall and winter line, but the sales intercept is higher during spring and summer months. The estimated trend line for the fall and winter months is the solid portion of the lower trend line. For the spring and summer months, the estimated trend line is the solid portion of the upper trend line. Note how much better the line fits when it is seasonally adjusted. Indeed, the R^2 increased from 0.5675 to 0.8763.

We now determine whether adding the dummy variable improves the accuracy of the market analyst's forecast of sales in March 1991. Using the estimated trend line accounting for seasonal variation in sales, the sales forecast for March 1991 ($t = 27$) is now

$$\hat{Q}_{\text{March 1991}} = 55.1111 - 0.8539\ (27) + 9.8755$$
$$= 41.93$$

Clearly, this forecast is an improvement over the unadjusted forecast, compared to the previous 30.4 percent underestimate. The sales forecast that accounts for seasonality underestimates the actual level of sales by 9,070 homes, or 17.8 percent. Compare this to the previous forecast of 35,500, which underestimated actual sales by 30.4 percent. In order to further improve the accuracy of the forecast, the analyst might try using one of the more complicated time-series techniques, which fit cyclical curves to the data, thereby improving the fit (R^2) and the forecast. As already noted, these techniques are well beyond the scope of this text.

business forecasting that will teach how to implement some of these more sophisticated time-series forecasting techniques.

9.4 ECONOMETRIC MODELS

econometric model A statistical model that employs an explicit structural model to explain the underlying economic relations.

Another method used in statistical forecasting and decision making is econometric modeling. The primary characteristic of **econometric models**, which differentiates this approach from the preceding approaches, is the use of an explicit structural model that attempts to *explain* the underlying economic relations. More specifically, if we wish to employ an econometric model to forecast future sales, we must develop a model that incorporates those variables that actually determine the level of sales (e.g., income, the price of substitutes, and so on). This approach is in marked contrast to the qualitative approach, in which a loose relation was posited between sales and some leading indicators, and the time-series approach, in which sales are assumed to behave in some regular fashion over time.

The use of econometric models has several advantages. First, econometric models require analysts to define explicit causal relations. This specification of an explicit model helps to eliminate problems such as spurious (false) correlation between normally unrelated variables and may make the model more logically consistent and reliable.

Second, this approach allows analysts to consider the sensitivity of the variable to be forecasted to changes in the exogenous variables. Using estimated elasticities, forecasters can determine which of the variables are most important in determining changes in the variable to be forecasted. Therefore, the analyst can examine the behavior of these variables more closely.

Forecasting the Demand Function

In addition to wanting to know the current demand for their product, managers frequently want to forecast what demand will be during some future period. After all, decisions about price and output are generally made prior to actual production and sales. Such pricing and output decisions require a prior knowledge about what demand will be when production and sales actually take place.

Suppose that the estimated general demand relation for a firm's product is

$$\hat{Q} = \hat{a} + \hat{b}P + \hat{c}M + \hat{d}P_R$$

where Q is quantity demanded, P is price, M is income, and P_R is the price of a good related in consumption. For specific values of the exogenous variables, $M = M'$ and $P_R = P_R'$, the estimated demand function is

$$\hat{Q} = (\hat{a} + \hat{c}M' + \hat{d}P_R') + \hat{b}P = \hat{a}' + \hat{b}P$$

The intercept term, $\hat{a}'$, captures the effect of all the exogenous variables and the constant term; that is, changes in either or both of the exogenous variables cause the intercept term $\hat{a}'$ to change value. This is just another way of saying that the demand curve shifts when either or both M and P_R change value.

Assume that the above demand equation is estimated in 1994, but the manager wants to forecast what demand will be in 1996. Assume also that the manager believes that the parameters of the demand function ($\hat{a}$, $\hat{b}$, $\hat{c}$, and $\hat{d}$) will not change significantly between 1994 and 1996. The manager does, however, believe that income and the price of the related good will change over this time period. In order to forecast the demand in 1996, the manager must obtain forecast values for both the exogenous variables in 1996, M_{96} and $P_{R,96}$. Forecasted values of the exogenous variables are generally obtained from one of two sources: (1) the firm's own time-series forecast of the exogenous variables, or (2) commercial vendors selling forecasts from macroeconomic (econometric) models that forecast the values of many aggregate economic variables.[4]

[4]Numerous private firms—Data Resources, Inc., Chase Econometrics, or Wharton Econometrics, to name the larger ones—are in the business of selling macroeconomic forecasts of dozens of economic variables to businesses. While businesses wish to forecast the price and sales of their own product, they do not wish to undertake the formidable task of building a large, simultaneous equations model of the US or world economy in order to be able to forecast for the next four quarters such exogenous variables as the rate of inflation, interest rates, or the level of household income.

Once forecasts for the exogenous variables are obtained, the "location" of the demand curve in 1996 can be determined by substituting the values of the forecasted exogenous variables into the estimated demand relation:

$$\hat{Q}_{96} = (\hat{a} + \hat{c}M_{96} + \hat{d}P_{R,96}) + \hat{b}P$$
$$= \hat{a}'_{96} + \hat{b}P$$

The forecasted values of the exogenous variables determine where the demand curve intersects the quantity axis (i.e., the "location" of demand).

To illustrate this process of forecasting future demand, we turn to a numerical example. Suppose a firm estimates its general demand relation to be

$$\hat{Q} = 250 - 15P + 10M - 4P_R$$

Since $\hat{c}$ is positive, the good is normal; and since P_R is negative, the related good is a complementary good. The firm obtains forecasts of the exogenous variables, M and P_R, 18 months in the future. The forecasts are $M' = 50$ (thousands of dollars in household income) and $P_R' = \$100$. The forecasted demand equation 18 months from now is

$$\hat{Q} = [250 + (10 \times 50) + (-4 \times 100)] - 15P$$
$$= 350 - 15P$$

Again let us emphasize that it is changes in the future values of the exogenous variables that cause the demand function in the future to be different from the demand function in the current time period. The parameters of the demand function are assumed to be constant; that is, a, b, c, and d do not change value; rather it is M and P_R that change demand.

Simultaneous Equations Forecasts

Using econometric models to forecast future price and sales in a market is slightly more complicated and requires more information than forecasting future demand. To forecast price and sales an analyst must have an estimate not only of demand but also of supply. Nonetheless, the idea behind simultaneous equations forecasting is really quite simple.

We introduce and illustrate the methodology to be used to forecast price and sales with Figure 9.7. Suppose that, using regression analysis, we have estimated the demand function

$$Q = \hat{a} + \hat{b}P + \hat{c}M + \hat{d}P_R$$

and the supply function

$$Q = \hat{e} + \hat{f}P + \hat{g}P_I$$

where Q is quantity, P is the price, M is income, P_R is the price of a good related in consumption; and P_I is the price of an input used in production. (Note again that the hats on the parameters indicate that these are estimates.) Suppose we know the actual 1994 values for the exogenous variables M_{94} and $P_{R,94}$. Therefore, we know where the demand function is located in 1994. Likewise, if $P_{I,94}$ is also known, we know where the supply function is located in 1994. These demand

FIGURE 9.7
Simultaneous Equations Forecasting

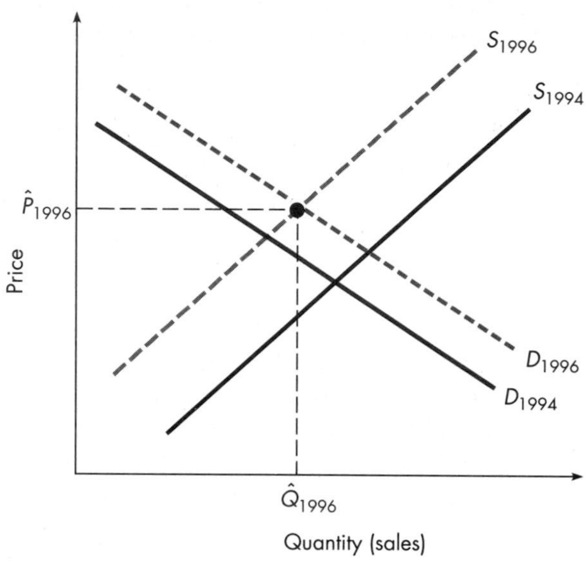

and supply functions are illustrated in Figure 9.7. Note that their intersection indicates price and sales in 1994.

Suppose that in 1994 we want to forecast sales for 1996. To obtain this sales forecast, we must know where the demand and supply functions will be located in 1996; that is, we must determine the values of the exogenous variables in 1996. In the case of the estimated demand function, the values of income and the price of the related good in 1996 will determine the location of the 1994 demand function. For simplicity, suppose that over the period 1994–1996, the price of the related good is expected to remain unchanged,

$$P_{R,\,96} = P_{R,\,94},$$

but income is expected to rise,

$$M_{96} > M_{94}$$

Because the good is a normal good, demand would increase and the location of the demand curve in 1996 would be as indicated in Figure 9.7.

In the case of the supply function, its location in 1996 is determined by the predicted value of P_I. Suppose P_I is expected to rise:

$$P_{I,\,96} > P_{I,\,94}$$

The increase in the input price will cause a decrease in supply, as illustrated by the 1996 supply curve in Figure 9.7.

Finding the location of the future demand and supply functions requires the future, or forecasted, values of the exogenous variables for the time period of the forecast. As already mentioned, a manager can obtain forecasted values of exogenous variables by either using time-series techniques to generate predicted values of the exogenous variables or purchasing forecasts of the exogenous variables from forecasting firms.

Once forecasts for the exogenous variables are obtained, the locations of the 1996 demand and supply functions are determined from the their specifications. The intersection of the 1996 demand and supply curves then provides the forecasted values of price and sales (output) in 1996. In Figure 9.7, these forecasts are denoted as $\hat{P}_{1996}$ and $\hat{Q}_{1996}$.

Relation The technique of forecasting with simultaneous equations involves three steps. First, the current (or prevailing) demand and supply functions are estimated using currently available data. Then, future (forecasted) values of the exogenous variables are substituted into the current demand and supply equations to obtain the demand and supply functions in the forecast time period. Finally, the intersection of future demand and supply provides the forecast of future price and sales (output).

The World Market for Copper: A Simultaneous Equations Forecast

As an example of forecasting with simultaneous equations, we use the copper data presented in Chapter 8 to forecast future copper sales in year 26. To this end, we will follow the three steps outlined in the discussion of simultaneous equations forecasting:

Step 1: Estimate the current demand and supply equations. We begin with the demand and supply functions for copper. The world demand function for copper was specified as

$$Q_{copper} = a + bP_{copper} + cM + dP_{aluminum}$$

and the world supply function as

$$Q_{copper} = e + fP_{copper} + gT + hX$$

where time (T) is a proxy for the level of available technology and X is the ratio of consumption of copper to production of copper in the preceding period to reflect inventory changes. Both of these functions are identified and were estimated in Chapter 8 using two-stage least squares. The estimated demand for copper is

$$\hat{Q}_{copper} = -6{,}837.8 - 66.495\ P_{copper} + 13{,}997M + 107.66\ P_{aluminum}$$

and the estimated supply function is

$$\hat{Q}_{copper} = 145.623 + 18.154\ P_{copper} + 213.88T + 1{,}819.8X$$

Step 2: Locate the demand and supply functions for time period 26. To locate demand and supply in year 26, we obtained forecast values for the exogenous variables in year 26. Since time is a proxy for technology, the period 26 value for T is simply $T_{26} = 26$. As previously noted, the value of X in any period is the ratio of consumption to production in the preceding period. Since both of these values are known (consumption was 7,157.2 and production was 8,058.0), $\hat{X}_{26} = 0.88821$

(= 7,157.2/8,058.0). For the other two exogenous variables, M and P_R, values must be obtained using time-series forecasting.

To obtain values for $\hat{M}_{26}$ and $\hat{P}_{R,\,26}$, a linear trend method of forecasting was used to obtain

$$\hat{M}_{26} = 1.13 \text{ and } \hat{P}_{R,\,26} = 23.79$$

Using $\hat{M}_{26}$ and $\hat{P}_{R,\,26}$, the demand function in time period 26 is

$$\begin{aligned}\hat{Q}_{\text{copper, 26}} &= -6{,}837.8 - 66.495\ P_{\text{copper, 26}} + 13{,}997(1.13) + 107.66(23.79)\\ &= 11{,}540.04 - 66.495\ P_{\text{copper, 26}}\end{aligned}$$

Likewise, using $\hat{T}_{26} = 26$ and $\hat{X}_{26} = 0.88821$, the supply function in time period 26 is

$$\begin{aligned}\hat{Q}_{\text{copper, 26}} &= 145.623 + 18.154\ P_{\text{copper, 26}} + 213.88(26) + 1{,}819.8(0.88821)\\ &= 7{,}322.868 + 18.154\ P_{\text{copper, 26}}\end{aligned}$$

Step 3: Calculate the intersection of the demand and supply functions. We set quantity demanded equal to quantity supplied and solve for equilibrium price:

$$\begin{aligned}11{,}540.04 - 66.495\ P_{\text{copper, 26}} &= 7{,}322.868 + 18.154\ P_{\text{copper, 26}}\\ P_{\text{copper, 26}} &= 49.819\end{aligned}$$

The sales forecast is then found by substituting $P_{\text{copper, 26}}$ into either the demand or supply equation. Using the demand function,

$$\begin{aligned}Q_{\text{copper, 26}} &= 11{,}540.04 - 66.495\ (49.819) = 7{,}322.868 + 18.154\ (49.819)\\ &= 8{,}227.3\end{aligned}$$

Thus, we forecast that sales of copper in year 26 will be 8,227.3 metric tons.[5] The price of copper in year 26 is forecast to be 49.8 cents per pound.

9.5 ECONOMETRIC FORECASTING UNDER RISK

Since the values of the exogenous variables in the forecast time period determine the location of demand and supply, forecasts of price and sales are determined by the forecast values of the exogenous variables. Consequently, different forecasts of the values of the exogenous variables produce different forecasts of demand and supply and the endogenous variables, price and sales. Analysts would probably not know what the values of the exogenous variables will actually be in a future period. They may, however, be able to assign probabilities to the occurrence of specific values of the variables (as discussed in Chapter 6). In such cases, the decision to use one forecast or another is a risky decision.

We begin our discussion of forecasting under risk by showing how to forecast demand when one or more of the exogenous variables in the demand equa-

[5] As we noted in Chapter 8, the data we used for the copper market illustration are the actual data for the period 1951–75. Hence, our forecast for year 26 can be interpreted as the forecast for 1976. The actual value for copper consumption in 1976 was 8,174.0, so the forecast error in this example was 0.54 percent—about $\frac{1}{2}$ of 1 percent.

tion is not known with certainty. We assume that the forecaster is able to determine the probability that an exogenous variable will take on various values. After illustrating the process of forecasting demand with random exogenous variables, we demonstrate how to generate probabilistic forecasts by calculating the expected values of price and sales in a future time period. Later in the text, we will show how probabilistic forecasts of price and sales can be used by managers to make profit-maximizing decisions under conditions of risk.

Demand Forecasting with Risky Variables

Assume once again the firm's general demand relation is estimated to be

$$\hat{Q} = 250 - 15P + 10M - 4P_R$$

As before, assume the manager forecasts income to be 50 (thousand dollars) in 1996—a forecast the manager feels is certain. The forecasted price of the complement good (the coefficient on P_R is negative) in 1996 is not known with certainty. The manager's best estimate of the price of the complement good is \$100—the most likely value of P_R in 1996. In fact, the manager believes there is a 60 percent probability that P_R will equal \$100 in 1996. The manager believes a low price of \$90 may occur with a 10 percent probability, and a high price of \$120 may occur with a 30 percent probability. Since P_R is a risky exogenous variable (i.e., the 1996 value of P_R is a random variable for which the manager knows the probability distribution), the process of forecasting demand now involves risk.

The forecasted demand function for 1996 may take on any one of the three different functional specifications depending upon the value of the random exogenous variable P_R. Using the manager's best estimate of the price of the related good in 1996 (P_R = 100), the forecasted demand equation in 1996 is

$$\begin{aligned}\hat{Q} &= [250 + (10 \times 50) + (-4 \times 100)] - 15P \\ &= 350 - 15P\end{aligned}$$

Using the manager's low price estimate of P_R (P_R = 90), the forecasted demand equation in 1996 is

$$\begin{aligned}\hat{Q} &= [250 + (10 \times 50) + (-4 \times 90)] - 15P \\ &= 390 - 15P\end{aligned}$$

And finally, for the high price estimate of P_R (P_R = 120), the forecasted demand in 1996 is

$$\begin{aligned}\hat{Q} &= [250 + (10 \times 50) + (-4 \times 120)] - 15P \\ &= 270 - 15P\end{aligned}$$

These three forecasted demand functions for 1996 are illustrated in Figure 9.8. The rightmost forecasted demand curve (passing through points *D* and *A* in Figure 9.8) has a 10 percent chance of being the correct demand curve in 1996. The middle forecasted demand is the best estimate and has a 60 percent chance of being correct in 1996. The leftmost forecasted demand (passing through points *F* and *C*) has a 30 percent chance of being the correct demand curve in 1996.

Simultaneous Equations Forecasts with Risky Variables

Forecasts of price and quantity require not only forecasts of demand but also forecasts of supply. The procedure for forecasting supply is identical to that of forecasting demand. Once both demand and supply have been forecast, the forecasts of price and sales are found by solving mathematically for the equilibrium values of P and Q in the future time period. We now illustrate simultaneous equations forecasting by adding a risky supply forecast to the risky demand forecast obtained above.

Suppose the manager determines the general supply relation to be

$$\hat{Q} = 190 + 26P - 20P_I$$

where P_I is the price of the labor input used in production. Currently, labor is earning a wage of \$12 per hour ($P_I = 12$), but a union contract comes up for renegotiation in 1995 and wages may rise in 1996. Management plans to resist any increase in wages, but realizes the union may win a wage dispute. In light of these circumstances, the manager forecasts that wages will either remain at \$12 in 1996, if management prevails in the negotiations, or wages will rise to \$16 in 1996 if the labor union is successful in the 1995 contract negotiations. The manager believes the outcome of the 1995 labor negotiations is too close to project and assigns a 50 percent probability to wages being \$12 in 1996, and a 50 percent probability to wages being \$16 in 1996.

If wages remain at \$12 in 1996, the forecasted supply equation is

$$\begin{aligned}\hat{Q} &= 190 + (-20 \times 12) + 25P \\ &= -50 + 25P\end{aligned}$$

If wages increase to \$16 in 1996, the forecasted supply equation is

$$\begin{aligned}\hat{Q} &= 190 + (-20 \times 16) + 25P \\ &= -130 + 25P\end{aligned}$$

Both of these forecasted supply curves are shown in Figure 9.8. Each one of the supply curves has a 50 percent chance of being the correct supply curve for 1996.

Since forecasted demand may be any one of the three demand curves shown in Figure 9.8 and forecasted supply may be either one of the two supply curves shown in Figure 9.8, there are six possible forecasts for the 1996 values of price and sales. The six possible equilibria are located at points $A, B, \ldots, F$ in the figure. Given the known probability distributions for the random exogenous variables P_R and P_I, the manager calculates the probabilities associated with each one of the six points of intersection. Table 9.4 shows the probabilities that equilibrium occurs at each of the six points shown in Figure 9.8. The manager assumes the two random variables are independent so that the joint probability is calculated as the product of the individual probabilities. For example, the joint probability that $P_R = 90$ and $P_I = 12$ is equal to the product of the independent probabilities:

$$\begin{aligned}\text{Prob}(P_R = 90 \text{ and } P_I = 12) &= \text{Prob}(P_R = 90) \times \text{Prob}(P_I = 12) \\ &= .10 \times .5 \\ &= .05\end{aligned}$$

FIGURE 9.8
Econometric Forecasting under Risk

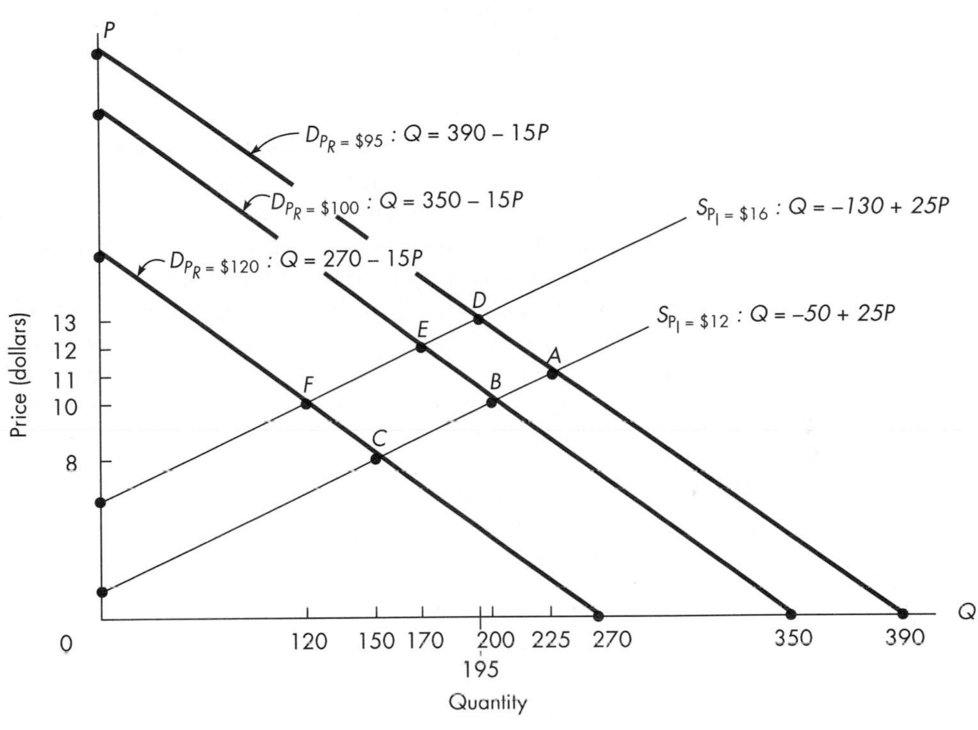

TABLE 9.4
Simultaneous Equations Forecasts with Risky Variables

Random exogenous variables				*Forecasts*	
P_R	P_I	Equilibrium point	Probability	$\hat{P}$	$\hat{Q}$
90	12	A	.05	11	225
100	12	B	.30	10	200
120	12	C	.15	8	150
90	16	D	.05	13	195
100	16	E	.30	12	170
120	16	F	.15	10	120

Thus, there is a 5 percent chance that the price of the related good will be $90 and the wage rate will be $12 in 1996. The rest of the probabilities in Table 9.4 are calculated similarly.

In order to use the forecast information generated by the simultaneous equations forecasts shown in Figure 9.8 and Table 9.4, the manager computes the expected value of the six price forecasts and the six sales (quantity) forecasts:

$$E(\hat{P}) = .05(11) + .30(10) + .15(8) + .05(13) + .30(12) + .15(10)$$
$$= \$10.50$$
$$E(\hat{Q}) = .05(225) + .30(200) + .15(150) + .05(195) + .60(170) + .15(120)$$
$$= 172$$

Thus, using the simultaneous equations method of forecasting, the manager expects the price of the product to be $10.50 in 1996 and sales in 1996 are expected to be 172 units. The manager recognizes that $10.50 and 172 are only *expected values*, and the actual values of P and Q in 1996 may differ substantially from the expected values. Indeed, forecasted price ranges in value from $8 to $13 and forecasted sales range in value from 120 units to 225 units.

The manager can use the expected value of price and sales, as calculated above, to calculate the expected profit in 1996. We will discuss how this is done later in this text.

9.6 SOME FINAL WARNINGS

We have often heard it said about forecasting that "he who lives by the crystal ball ends up eating ground glass." While we do not make nearly so dire a judgment, we do feel that you should be aware of the major limitations of and problems inherent in forecasting. Basically, our warnings are concerned with three issues—confidence intervals, specification, and change of structure.

To illustrate the issue of confidence intervals in forecasting, consider once again the simple linear trend model,

$$Q_t = a + bt$$

In order to obtain the prediction model, we must estimate two coefficients, a and b. Obviously, we cannot estimate these coefficients with certainty. Indeed, the estimated standard errors reflect the magnitude of uncertainty (i.e., potential error) about the values of the parameters.

In Figure 9.9, we have illustrated a situation in which there are observations on sales for periods t_1 through t_n. Due to the manner in which it is calculated, the regression line will pass through the sample mean of the data points $(\bar{Q}, \bar{t})$. In Panel A, we have illustrated as the shaded area our confidence region if there exist errors only in the estimation of the slope, b. In Panel B, the shaded area represents the confidence region if an error exists only in the estimation of the intercept, a. These two shaded areas are combined in Panel C. As you can see, the further the value of t is from the mean value of t, the wider this zone of uncertainty becomes.

Now consider what happens when we use the estimated regression line to predict future sales. At a future time period, t_{n+k}, the prediction for sales will be a point on the extrapolated regression line (i.e., $\hat{Q}$). However, note what happens to the region of uncertainty about this estimate. The further one forecasts into the future, the wider is this region of uncertainty, and this region increases geometrically rather than arithmetically.

FIGURE 9.9
Confidence Intervals

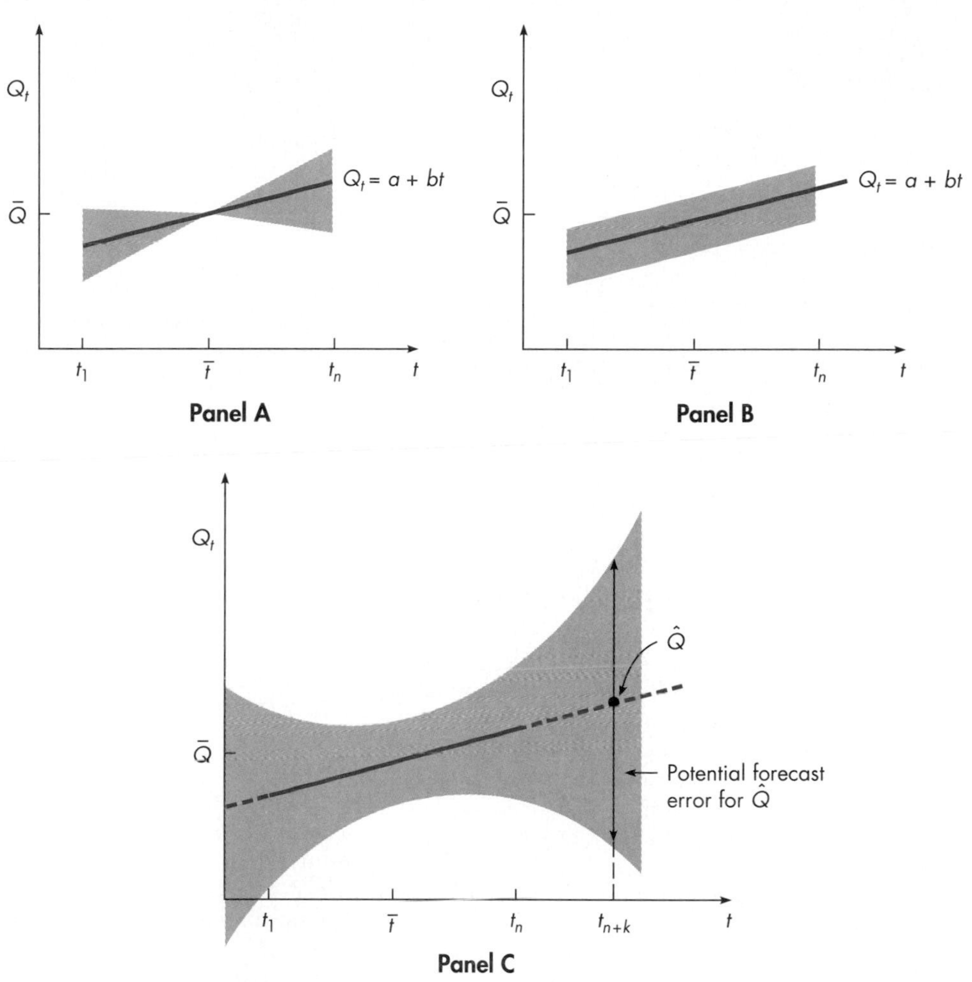

This warning applies not just to time-series models. It applies to all statistical techniques. The further the variables used in the forecasts are from the mean values used in the regression, the wider will be the region of uncertainty, and therefore, the less precise the forecast will be. For example, consider the econometric forecasting model for copper. If we attempt to forecast copper sales using a value of per capita income that is much higher than the mean in the data set, the confidence interval for the forecast will be much wider than would be the case if the value of income used in the forecast was close to the mean value in the data set.

We mentioned the problem of incorrect specification in our discussion of demand estimation, but we feel that it is important enough to deserve another mention here. In order to generate reliable forecasts, the model used must

ILLUSTRATION 9.2

The Perils of Forecasting

As we have noted, the forecasting of sales and price is not as precise and scientific as it might appear when one is learning the techniques. A recent article in *The Wall Street Journal* (December 9, 1992) illustrates some of the pitfalls involved with forecasting retail sales.

"During November and December, many retailers ring up a third of their annual sales and half of their profits. Yule receipts can turn a good year . . . into a great one. And a bad season can stop the show . . . " Most chains begin planning for Christmas by early February, when merchants make their holiday sales forecasts. They base their forecasts on, among other things, their hunches, based on last year's results and the future economic outlook. They place their orders four to eight months in advance, leaving some flexibility for possible changes in orders and unexpected delays in shipping. It is important to have enough of what customers want because running out of stock early would cost many lost sales. On the other hand, stores don't want to have too much stock either. Either carrying over large inventories or resorting to huge markdowns can ruin profits for the entire year.

In five out of the past ten years, the early forecast for Christmas sales turned out to be rather close to what actually occurred. In the other five years, the forecasts were the *opposite* of what actually happened—in some cases drastically missing the mark. According to the *Journal*, there are several factors that help determine just how full Santa's bag will be for retailers.

The first is economics. In several seasons, unexpected changes in the economy—outside of the control of retailers—had a substantial effect on sales. For example, Christmas 1991 was a disaster for many merchants because they weren't expecting the slump in the economy. By fall, when consumer demand dropped, they had already stocked up inventories, forcing them to discount prices heavily in December. The 1985 season was much smoother. Even though many chains had flat holiday sales, profits were good because there were few emergency markdowns. Even though sales were not great, retailers made money because their forecasts turned out to be right.

Good planning, based on economic forecasts, is the second factor. The chief economist at J.C. Penney noted that anticipating what consumer demand will be is critical. Since stores must order so far in advance, they must forecast what merchandise to order even if they are right about what the state of the economy will be. This complicates the problem even more.

The third factor is timing. Even though retailers urge consumers to shop early, they must generally wait until the two weeks before Christmas for 40 percent of their holiday sales. Thus successful forecasts must not only predict the correct magnitude but also the timing of sales.

Timing is important because of the fourth factor, the so-called "panic button." Many retailers have slashed prices too early when sales slip a little. Profits are therefore needlessly reduced. The *Journal* points out that the decision to go into "alarm-bell" mode is usually made at the highest level of the management structure.

Finally, even though forecasters have done the best job possible, there are numerous factors that are beyond their control. For example, the stock market crash in October 1987 or the Iraq invasion of Kuwait in the summer of 1991 both sent consumer confidence plunging. And there is always the weather. Merrill Lynch & Co. contends that a two-degree temperature difference, plus or minus, from the norm is enough to affect sales. Retailers say that this is especially true during the Christmas season.

So forecasting is not always as scientific as it seems. Unexpected things can and do happen. Of course, if you make a forecast and miss, you can always blame unforeseen events. As noted in the *Journal*, "Retailers have been known to blame slow sales on unseasonably warm weather or unseasonably cold weather, rain, sleet, and snow."

incorporate the appropriate variables. The quality of the forecast can be severely reduced if important explanatory variables are excluded or if an improper functional form is employed (e.g., using a linear form when a nonlinear form is appropriate).

We have saved what we feel to be the most important problem for last. This problem stems from potential changes in structure. Forecasts are widely, and often correctly, criticized for failing to predict turning points—sharp changes in the variable under consideration. If it were the case that these changes were only the result of radical changes in the exogenous variables, the simulation approach should be able to handle the problem. However, it is often the case that such changes are the result of changes in the structure of the market itself.

For example, in our consideration of the copper market, there exists the potential for a major change in structure. A major consumer of copper is the telecommunications industry. This industry has been replacing copper transmitting cables with glass fibers. As this change occurs, the demand for copper will be affected significantly. More specifically, any temporal or econometric relation estimated using data before such a change occurred would be incapable of correctly forecasting quantity demanded after the change. In the context of a demand function, the coefficients would be different before and after the change.

Unfortunately, we know of no satisfactory method of handling this problem of "change in structure." Instead, we must simply leave you with the warning that changes in structure are likely. The further you forecast into the future, the more likely it is that you will encounter such a change.

9.7 SUMMARY

This chapter sets forth some of the basic methods of forecasting demand. The purpose of the chapter was to show some of the simpler techniques that can be used to forecast demand in future time periods. A complete treatment of demand forecasting is a course in itself. The emphasis in this chapter was on understanding the nature of the forecasting problem and on how to interpret the results of demand forecasts. You can learn more about demand forecasting by taking advanced courses in marketing, statistics, and econometrics.

Forecasting models are either qualitative models or statistical models. Qualitative forecasting involves combining the available data with a heavy dose of expert opinion about the firm and industry. Qualitative forecasting is complex and not easily replicated. It is difficult to teach qualitative forecasting techniques because the subjective or judgment component of the forecast depends upon the experience and knowledge of the forecaster.

Statistical forecasting models can be subdivided into two categories—time-series models and econometric models. Time-series forecasts use the time-ordered sequence of historical observations on a variable to develop a model for predicting future values of that variable. Time-series models specify a mathematical model representing the generating process, then use statistical techniques to fit the historical data to the mathematical model.

The simplest time-series forecast is a linear trend forecast where the generating process is assumed to be the linear model $Q_t = a + bt$. Using time-series data on Q, regression analysis is used to estimate the trend line that best fits the data. If b is greater (less) than zero, sales are increasing (decreasing) over time. If b equals zero, sales are constant over time.

When data exhibit cyclical variation, such as seasonal patterns, dummy variables can be added to the time-series model to account for the seasonality. If there are N seasonal time periods to be accounted for, $N - 1$ dummy variables are added to the demand equation. Each dummy variable accounts for one of the seasonal time periods. The dummy variable takes a value of 1 for those observations that occur during the season assigned to that dummy variable, and a value of 0 otherwise. This type of dummy variable allows the intercept of the demand equation to take on different values for each season—the demand curve can shift up and down from season to season.

In contrast to time-series models, econometric models use an explicit structural model to *explain* the underlying economic relations. Simultaneous equations forecasting uses both a demand and supply equation to model price and output (sales) determination. The technique of forecasting with simultaneous equations involves three steps. First, the current (or prevailing) demand and supply functions are estimated using currently available data. Then, future (forecasted) values of the exogenous variables are substituted into the current demand and supply equations to obtain the demand and supply functions in the forecast time period. Finally, the intersection of future demand and supply provides the forecast of future price and sales (output).

Econometric models can be used to forecast price and sales under conditions of risk. When a manager knows the probability distributions for the future values of the exogenous variables, the future demand and supply equations can be determined with a probability attached to each one giving the likelihood that a particular demand or supply equation will be the correct one in the forecast period. Then probabilities are determined for each intersection of forecasted demand and supply. Using the forecasts and the associated probabilities, the expected price and expected level of sales (output) can be calculated.

When making forecasts, analysts must be careful to recognize that the further into the future the forecast is made, the wider the confidence interval or region of uncertainty. Incorrect specification of the demand equation (as well as supply in the case of simultaneous equation forecasts) can seriously undermine the quality of a forecast. An even greater problem for accurate forecasting is posed by the occurrence of structural changes that cause turning points in the variable being forecast. Forecasts often fail to predict turning points. While there is no satisfactory way to account for unexpected structural changes, forecasters should note that the further into the future you forecast, the more likely it is that a structural change will occur.

This chapter concludes Part II of the text on demand analysis. In Part III of the text, we will present the theory of production and cost. We also will describe the empirical techniques used to estimate production functions and the various cost equations used by managers to make output and investment decisions.

TECHNICAL PROBLEMS

1. Contrast and compare qualitative and statistical forecasting methods.

* 2. A linear trend equation for the sales of the form

$$Q_t = a + bt$$

was estimated for the period 1979–1993 (i.e., t = 79, 80, . . . , 93). The results of the regression are as follows:

DEPENDENT VARIABLE: QT		F-RATIO: 13.1792	
OBSERVATIONS: 15		R-SQUARE: 0.8786	
VARIABLE	PARAMETER ESTIMATE	STANDARD ERROR	T-RATIO
INTERCEPT	73.7146	10.1315	7.276
T	3.7621	1.0363	3.630

a. Test the estimated coefficients for statistical significance at a 95 percent confidence level. Does this estimation indicate a significant trend?
b. Perform an *F*-test for significance of the equation at a 95 percent confidence level.
c. Using this equation, forecast sales in 1994 and 1999.
d. Comment on the precision of these two forecasts.

* 3. Consider a firm subject to quarter-to-quarter variation in its sales. Suppose that the following equation was estimated using quarterly data for the period 1985–1993 (the time variable goes from 1 to 36). The variables D_1, D_2, and D_3 are, respectively, dummy variables for the first, second, and third quarters (e.g., D_1 is equal to one in the first quarter and zero otherwise).

$$Q_t = a + bt + c_1D_1 + c_2D_2 + c_3D_3$$

The results of the estimation are presented below:

DEPENDENT VARIABLE: QT		F-RATIO: 761.133	
OBSERVATIONS: 36		R-SQUARE: 0.9761	
VARIABLE	PARAMETER ESTIMATE	STANDARD ERROR	T-RATIO
INTERCEPT	51.234	7.163	7.153
T	3.127	0.524	5.968
D1	-11.716	2.717	-4.312
D2	-1.424	0.836	-1.703
D3	-17.367	2.112	-8.223

a. Perform *t*- and *F*-tests to check for statistical significance of the coefficients and the equation.
b. Calculate the intercept in each of the four quarters. What do these values imply?
c. Use this estimated equation to forecast sales in the four quarters of 1994.

4. Supply and demand functions were specified for commodity *X*:

$$\text{Demand: } Q_X = a + bP + cM + dP_R$$
$$\text{Supply: } Q_X = e + fP + gP_I$$

where *M* is in \$1,000 units, *Q* is in 1,000 units, and all prices are in dollars. Using quarterly data for the period 1987(I) through 1994(IV), these functions were estimated (via 2*SLS*). The resulting parameter estimates are presented in the following estimated equations. (All estimated coefficients are statistically significant.)

$$\text{Demand: } Q_X = 50 - 30P + 100M - 20P_R$$
$$\text{Supply: } Q_X = -40 + 20P - 10P_I$$

The predicted values for the exogenous variables (M, P_R, and P_I) for the first quarter of 1996 were obtained from a macroeconomic forecasting model. These predicted values are:

Income (M) = 10
The price of the commodity related in consumption (P_R) = 20
The price of inputs (P_I) = 6.

a. Are the signs of the estimated coefficients as would be predicted theoretically? Explain.
b. Predict the sales of commodity X in the first quarter of 1996.
c. Perform a simulation analysis to determine the sales of commodity X in 1996(I) if income were $9,000 and $12,000.

5. Describe the major shortcomings of time-series models.
6. Suppose that you have an estimate of the demand function

$$Q = a + bP + cM + dP_R$$

Obviously you could use a historical trend to forecast the values for *all* of the right-hand side variables and thereby obtain a prediction for sales. What is the major shortcoming in such an approach?

7. In the final section of this chapter we provided warnings about three problems which frequently arise. List, explain, and provide an example of each.
8. A firm estimates its general demand relation to be

$$\hat{Q} = 250 - 15P + 10M - 4P_R$$

where M is measured in $1,000 units. The manager knows with certainty that the price of the complementary good will be $120 in 1997. He believes there is a 30 percent chance income will be $42,000 in 1997 and a 70 percent chance income will be $50,000 in 1997. The manager estimates the general supply relation to be

$$\hat{Q} = 190 + 26P - 20P_I$$

and he believes there is a 50 percent chance that the price of the input (P_I) will be $16 in 1997 and a 50 percent chance P_I will be $12 in 1997.

a. Sketch a graph showing the two demand curves and the two supply curves that can occur in 1997 in the risky forecasting situation described above. Label the four points of equilibrium *A*, *B*, *C*, and *D* as listed in column 3 in the table below.
b. Calculate and write the probabilities for each of the four possible equilibrium points in column 4 of the table below. Assume the probability distributions for M and P_I are independent.
c. Calculate forecasts for P and Q in 1997 for the different possible values the random exogenous variables M and P_I can take in 1997. Write the forecasts of P and Q in columns 5 and 6 of the table.
d. Calculate forecasts for the expected price and quantity in 1997:

$E(P_{1997})$ = ______
$E(Q_{1997})$ = ______

(1) Random Exogenous Variables	(2)	(3)	(4)	(5) Forecasts	(6)
M	P_I	Equilibrium point	Probability	$\hat{P}_{1997}$	$\hat{Q}_{1997}$
$50	$12	A	______	______	______
$50	$16	B	______	______	______
$42	$12	C	______	______	______
$42	$16	D	______	______	______

APPLIED PROBLEMS

1. Freeze Tech, a manufacturer of refrigerators and freezers, is concerned about near-term economic conditions and wishes to obtain a qualitative forecast of sales in the upcoming quarter. If you are the market analyst for Freeze Tech and you plan to use the 11 leading indicators published by the US Department of Commerce to formulate your qualitative forecast, explain how each of these indicators might affect future sales. (For example, if the average workweek of production workers in manufacturing increased, explain the effect on Freeze Tech's sales.) Which of these indicators would be most important in formulating your qualitative forecast?
2. Cypress River Landscape Supply is a large wholesale supplier of landscaping materials in Georgia. Cypress River's sales vary seasonally; sales tend to be higher in the spring months than in other months.
   a. Suppose Cypress River estimates a linear trend *without* accounting for this seasonal variation. What effect would this omission have on the estimated sales trend?
   b. Alternatively, suppose there is, in fact, no seasonal pattern to sales, and the trend line is estimated using dummy variables to account for seasonality. What effect would this have on the estimation?
3. Rubax, a US manufacturer of athletic shoes, estimates the following linear trend model for shoe sales:

$$Q_t = a + bt + c_1D_1 + c_2D_2 + c_3D_3$$

where

Q_t = sales of athletic shoes (measured in 1,000 units) in the tth quarter,
t = 1, 2, . . . , 28 (1987I, 1987II, . . . , 1993IV),
D_1 = 1 if t is quarter I (winter); 0 otherwise,
D_2 = 1 if t is quarter II (spring); 0 otherwise,
D_3 = 1 if t is quarter III (summer); 0 otherwise,

The regression analysis produces the following results:

DEPENDENT VARIABLE: QT			F-RATIO: 159.01
OBSERVATIONS: 28			R-SQUARE: 0.9651
VARIABLE	PARAMETER ESTIMATE	STANDARD ERROR	T-RATIO
INTERCEPT	184.50	10.31	17.90
T	2.10	0.34	6.18
D1	3.28	2.17	1.51
D2	6.25	2.22	2.82
D3	7.01	1.58	4.44

a. Is there sufficient statistical evidence of an upward trend in shoe sales? Perform the appropriate test at the 95 percent level of confidence.

b. Do these data indicate a seasonal pattern of sales for Rubax shoes? If so, what is the seasonal pattern exhibited by the data? Perform the appropriate tests at the 95 percent confidence level.

c. Using the estimated forecast equation, forecast sales of Rubax shoes for 1994III and 1995II.

d. How might you improve this forecast equation?

4. The automobile industry relies heavily on sales forecasts. If an automobile firm produces too many cars, the costs of holding them in inventory are substantial. If too few cars are produced, sales are lost and substantial profits are forgone. As is evident from the recent experience of U.S. automobile manufacturers, such forecasting is not yet precise.

   a. If you were to provide a qualitative forecast, which of the 11 leading indicators would be most relevant? Why?

   b. How well would you expect time-series forecasting to work in forecasting the automobile market?

   Suppose you decide to use an econometric forecasting model for this market.

   c. Specify the demand and supply functions you think would be appropriate and explain why.

   d. In our examination of the copper market, the values of the exogenous variables were forecast using historical trends. Such an approach might not be advisable in the automobile market—particularly in the case of the complementary good, gasoline. The real (deflated) price of gasoline fell during most of the 1960s. Only after the mid-1970s did gasoline prices begin to rise rapidly with its subsequent decline through most of the 1980s. Then, the Persian Gulf War caused gasoline prices to rise rather significantly for a few months in the fall of 1990, after which prices again declined. With this history in mind, suggest a methodology for forecasting automobile sales in the future.

5. Suppose you are the market analyst for a major US bank and the bank president asks you to forecast the median price of new homes and the number of new homes that will be sold in 1997. You specify the following demand and supply functions for the US housing market:

$$\text{Demand: } Q_H = a + bP_H + cM + dP_A + eR$$
$$\text{Supply: } Q_H = f + gP_H + hP_M$$

   where the endogenous variables are measured in the following way:

   Q_H = thousands of units sold quarterly, and
   P_H = median price of a new home in thousands of dollars

   The exogenous variables are median income in dollars (M), average price of apartments (P_A), mortgage interest rate as a percent (R), and the price of building materials as an index (P_M).

   a. Is the demand equation identified? Is the supply equation identified?

   b. What signs do you expect each of the estimated coefficients to have? Explain.

   Using quarterly data for the period 1985I through 1994I, you estimate these equations using two-stage least squares. All the coefficients are statistically significant and the estimated equations are

$$\text{Demand: } Q_H = 504.5 - 10.0\, P_H + 0.01\, M + 0.5\, P_A - 11.75\, R$$
$$\text{Supply: } Q_H = 326.0 + 15P_H - 1.8\, P_M$$

The predicted values for the exogenous variables for the first quarter of 1997 are obtained from a private econometrics firm. The predicted values are:

Median Income (M) = 26,000
Average Price of Apartments (P_A) = 400
Mortgage Interest Rate (R) = 14
Price of Building Materials (P_M) = 320 (an index)

c. Using these predicted values of the exogenous variables, forecast the median price and sales of new homes in 1997.

d. Suppose you feel that the predicted mortgage interest rate for 1997, 14 percent, is much too high. Determine how changing the forecast interest rate to 10 percent affects the forecast price and sales for 1997.

6. A number of prominent economic forecasters believe the price of scrap metal—left-over copper from pipes, steel from wrecked cars, and aluminum from old beverage cans—is more useful in predicting the future path of the economy than many government statistics (*The Wall Street Journal*, April 27, 1992). Why would scrap-metal prices be a useful leading indicator? In what type of forecasts would these prices be valuable?

PART

IV

Production and Cost

Theory and Empirical Analysis

CHAPTER 10

Theory of Production and Cost in the Short Run

Managers must have information about the cost structure of their firms because the cost of producing the goods and services they sell provides the foundation for some of the most important decisions a manager makes: whether to operate or shut down a production facility; how much to produce if the firm does operate; how much to invest in capital equipment; and, frequently, even the price to charge for the product. Knowledge of the cost structure of the organization is also important for managers in government and in nonprofit organizations. As you will see in this chapter and in Chapter 11, the structure of a firm's costs is determined by the nature of the production process that transforms inputs into goods and services, and the prices of the inputs used in producing the goods or services.

Managers face two different types of decision-making frameworks: short-run decisions and long-run decisions. Short-run decision making takes place when the level of usage of one or more inputs is fixed at a specific level. In a typical short-run situation, the manager has a fixed amount of plant and equipment with which to produce the firm's output. The manager can change production levels by hiring more or less labor and purchasing more or less raw materials, but the size of the plant is viewed by the manager as essentially unchangeable or fixed for the purposes of making production decisions in the short run.

Long-run decision making concerns the same types of decisions as the short run with one important distinction—the usage of all inputs can be either increased or decreased. In the long run, a manager can choose to operate in any size plant with any amount of capital equipment. Once a firm builds a new plant or changes the size of an existing plant, the manager is once more in a short-run decision-making framework. Sometimes economists think of the short run as the time period during which production actually takes place, and the long run as the planning horizon during which future production will take place. As it turns out, the structure of costs differs in rather crucial ways depending upon whether production is taking place in the short run or whether the manager is planning for a particular level of production in the long run.

This chapter sets forth the fundamentals of the theory of production and the theory of cost in the short run. We will show how the theory of short-run cost is based upon the theory of short-run production. Using production theory, managers determine how much of the variable input(s) to use in combination with the fixed input(s) to produce a particular level of output. This chapter develops the theory of production in the short run when the usage of only one input can be changed. This may at first seem like an unreasonably simple assumption. However, most of the concepts developed within the framework of this assumption will be important later when we analyze production with more than one variable input. Furthermore, a large number of actual production decisions are made when it is feasible to change the usage of only one input, labor, which is generally the most important input of all in terms of the proportion of labor cost compared to the proportion of cost going to other inputs.

After we set forth the theory of production in the short run, we derive the structure of the firm's costs in the short run. By applying the concepts of production theory, the manager can determine the combination of inputs to use to produce a given amount of output at the lowest total cost. Given input prices and the amount of each input that will be purchased, it is a straightforward task to determine the total cost of production.

10.1 SOME BASIC CONCEPTS OF PRODUCTION THEORY

production
The creation of goods and services from inputs or resources.

Production is the creation of goods and services from inputs or resources, such as labor, machinery and other capital equipment, land, raw material, and so on. Obviously, when a company such as Ford makes a truck or car or when Exxon refines a gallon of gasoline, it is production. But production goes much further than that. A doctor produces medical services, a teacher produces education, and a singer produces entertainment. So production involves services as well as making the goods people buy. Notice also that we said in the introduction that managers organize the production of their "organizations" not just the production of their "business firms." Governments and nonprofit *organizations* produce goods and services also. A city police department produces protection, a public school produces education, and a hospital produces health care.

In the following chapters, as in most of this text, we will analyze production within the framework of business firms using inputs to produce goods, rather than services. Such an approach is more simple and straightforward than the study of the production of services or production by agencies of the government. It is conceptually easier to visualize the production of cars, trucks, or refrigerators than the production of education, health, or security, which are hard to measure but even harder to define. Nonetheless, throughout the discussion, remember that the concepts developed here apply to services as well as goods and to government production as well as firm production.

Most of production theory is based upon efficiency—producing the maximum output possible with a given level of input usage or producing a given level of output at the lowest possible cost. That is, production describes how resources are organized to produce in the most efficient way. Since a substantial part of a manager's responsibilities involves production of one type or another, and since most managers are concerned with efficiency, it is important that managers understand the fundamentals of production theory.

Production Functions

A production function is the link between levels of input usage and attainable levels of output. That is, the production function formally describes the relation between physical rates of output and physical rates of input usage. With a given state of technology, the attainable quantity of output depends on the quantities of the various inputs employed in production.

production function
A schedule (or table or mathematical equation) showing the maximum amount of output that can be produced from any specified set of inputs, given the existing technology.

A **production function** is a schedule (or table, or mathematical equation) showing the maximum amount of output that can be produced from any specified set of inputs, given the existing technology or state of the art of production. In short, the production function is a catalog of output possibilities.

Many different inputs are used in production. So, in the most general case, we can define maximum output, Q, to be a function of the level of usage of the various inputs, X. That is,

$$Q = f(X_1, X_2, \ldots, X_n)$$

But in our discussion we will generally restrict attention to the simpler case of one product being produced using either one input or two inputs. As examples of the two inputs, we will normally use capital and labor. Hence the production function we will usually be concerned with is

$$Q = f(L, K)$$

where L and K represent, respectively, the amounts of labor and capital used in production. However, we must stress that the principles to be developed apply to situations with more than two inputs and, as well, to inputs other than capital and labor.

Technical Efficiency and Economic Efficiency

technical efficiency
When the firm produces the maximum level of output that can be obtained from a given combination of inputs.

Before proceeding, we want to distinguish between *technical efficiency* and *economic efficiency*. **Technical efficiency** is achieved when the maximum possible amount of output is being produced with a given combination of inputs. The definition of a production function assumes that technical efficiency is being achieved because the production function gives the *maximum* output level that can be achieved for any particular combination of inputs. Thus, technical efficiency is implied by the production function.

To illustrate the concept of technical efficiency, consider a firm that manufactures electric generators using an assembly-line process that begins with workers manually performing five steps before the generator reaches a computer-controlled drill press. At this stage, the computer-controlled drill makes 16 holes that are required for final assembly. In the process of drilling 16 holes almost one pound of iron is removed. Using this production process, the firm employs 10 assembly-line workers and one computer-controlled drill press and produces 140 generators each day. A production engineer studying this process discovers that moving the computer-controlled drill press to the beginning of the assembly line, ahead of five steps that are performed manually, will save laborers energy each day—the generators weigh one pound less when they get to the workers on the assembly line. By moving the drilling to the beginning of the production process, the same 10 workers and one drill press can produce 150 generators per day. The production engineer is unable to find any other change in the production process that would further increase output. Now the firm is operating in a technically efficient manner; 150 generators is the maximum number of generators that can be produced daily using 10 laborers and one drill press.

economic efficiency
Using the combination of inputs that permits a firm to produce a given amount of output at the lowest possible cost.

Economic efficiency is achieved when the firm is producing a given amount of output at the lowest possible cost. As you will recall from Chapter 4, this is a constrained optimization problem. The optimization rules discussed there and those to be developed in Chapter 11 lead a producer to an economically efficient method of production.

One should be careful about labeling a particular production process inefficient. Certainly a process would be technically inefficient if another process can produce the same amount of output using less of one or more inputs and the same amounts of all others. If, however, the second process uses less of some inputs but more of others, the economically efficient method of producing a given level of output depends on the prices of the inputs. Even when both are technically efficient, one process might cost less—be economically efficient—under one set of input prices, while the other may be economically efficient at other input prices.

Short Run and Long Run

fixed input
An input for which the level of usage cannot readily be changed.

variable input
An input for which the level of usage may be changed quite readily.

When analyzing the process of production, it is convenient to introduce the classification of inputs as *fixed* or *variable*. A **fixed input** is one for which the level of usage cannot readily be changed. To be sure, no input is ever absolutely fixed, no matter how short the period of time under consideration. However, the cost of immediately varying the use of an input may be so great that, for all practical purposes, the input is fixed. For example, buildings, major pieces of machinery, and managerial personnel are inputs that generally cannot be rapidly augmented or diminished. A **variable input**, on the other hand, is one for which the level of usage may be changed quite readily in response to desired changes in output. Many types of labor services as well as certain raw and processed materials would be in this category.

short run
That period of time in which the level of usage of one or more of the inputs is fixed.

As mentioned in the introduction, economists distinguish between the *short run* and the *long run*. The **short run** refers to that period of time in which the level of usage of one or more of the inputs is fixed. Therefore, in the short run, changes in output must be accomplished exclusively by changes in the use of the variable inputs. Thus, if producers wish to expand output in the short run, they must do so by using more hours of labor (a variable service) and other variable inputs, with the existing plant and equipment. Similarly, if they wish to reduce output in the short run, they may discharge only certain inputs. They cannot immediately "discharge" a building or a blast furnace (even though its use may fall to zero). In the context of our simplified production function, we might consider capital to be the fixed input and write the resulting short-run production function as

$$Q = f(L, \overline{K})$$

where the bar over capital means that it is fixed. Furthermore, since capital is fixed, output depends only on the level of usage of labor, so we could write the short-run production function as simply

$$Q = f(L)$$

long run
That period of time (or planning horizon) in which all inputs are variable.

The **long run** is defined as that period of time (or planning horizon) in which all inputs are variable. The long run refers to that time in the future when output changes can be accomplished in the manner most advantageous to the producers. For example, in the short run a producer may be able to expand output by operating the existing plant for more hours per day. In the long run, it may be more economical to install additional productive facilities and return to the normal workday.

Fixed or Variable Proportions

Most of the discussion in this chapter and Chapter 11 refers to production functions that allow at least some substitution of one input for one another in reaching an output target. When substitution is possible, we say inputs may be used in *variable proportions*. As a consequence, producers must determine not only the optimal level of output to produce but also the optimal combination of inputs. **Variable proportions production** means that output can be changed in the short run by changing the variable inputs without changing the fixed inputs. And, it means that the same output can be produced using different combinations of inputs.

variable proportions production
When a given level of output can be produced with more than one combination of inputs.

Most economists regard production under conditions of variable proportions as typical of both the short and long run. There is certainly no doubt that proportions are variable in the long run. When making an investment decision, for instance, a producer may choose among a wide variety of different production processes. As polar opposites, an automobile can be practically handmade or it can be made by assembly-line techniques. In the short run, however, there may be some cases where there is little opportunity for substitution among inputs.

fixed proportions production
There is one, and only one, ratio or mix of inputs that can be used to produce a good.

Fixed proportions production means that there is one, and only one, ratio or mix of inputs that can be used to produce a good. If output is expanded or contracted, all inputs must be expanded or contracted at the same rate to maintain the fixed input ratio. At first glance, this might seem the usual condition: one worker and one shovel produce a ditch; two parts hydrogen and one part oxygen produce water. Adding a second shovel or a second part of oxygen will not augment the rate of production. In such cases, the producer has little discretion about what combination of inputs to employ. The only decision is how much to produce.

In actuality, examples of fixed proportions production are hard to come by. Certainly some "ingredient" inputs are often used in relatively fixed proportions to output. Otherwise, the quality of the product would change. There is so much leather in a pair of shoes of a particular size and style. Use less leather, and we have a different type of shoe. There is so much tobacco in a cigarette, and so on. In these cases, the producer has little choice over the quantity of input per unit of output. But fixed-ingredient inputs are really only a short-run problem. Historically, when these necessary ingredients have become very expensive, businesses have invented new processes, discovered new ingredients, or somehow overcome the problem of a given production function and increasingly scarce ingredients. As a consequence, we will direct attention here to production when the producer has some control over the mix of inputs and concentrate on production with variable proportions.

10.2 PRODUCTION IN THE SHORT RUN

We begin the analysis of production in the short run with the simplest kind of short-run situation: only *one* variable input and *one* fixed input:

$$Q = f(L, \overline{K})$$

The firm has chosen the level of capital (made its investment decision) so capital is fixed in amount. Once the level of capital is fixed, the only way the firm can change its output is by changing the amount of labor it employs.

Total Product

Suppose a firm with a production function of the form $Q = f(L, K)$ can, in the long run, choose levels of both labor and capital between 0 and 10 units. A production function giving the maximum amount of output that can be produced from every possible combination of labor and capital is shown in Table 10.1. For example, from the table, 4 units of labor combined with 3 units of capital can produce a maximum of 325 units of output; 6 labor and 6 capital can produce a maximum of 655 units of output; and so on. Note that with zero capital, no output can be produced regardless of the level of labor usage. Likewise, with zero labor, there can be no output.

Once the level of capital is fixed, the firm is in the short run, and output can be changed only by varying the amount of labor employed. Assume now that the capital stock is fixed at two units of capital. The firm is in the short run and can

TABLE 10.1
A Production Function

Units of labor (L) \ Units of capital (K)	0	1	2	3	4	5	6	7	8	9	10
0	0	0	0	0	0	0	0	0	0	0	0
1	0	25	52	74	90	100	108	114	118	120	121
2	0	55	112	162	198	224	242	252	258	262	264
3	0	83	170	247	303	342	369	384	394	400	403
4	0	108	220	325	400	453	488	511	527	535	540
5	0	125	258	390	478	543	590	631	653	663	670
6	0	137	286	425	523	598	655	704	732	744	753
7	0	141	304	453	559	643	708	766	800	814	825
8	0	143	314	474	587	679	753	818	857	873	885
9	0	141	318	488	609	708	789	861	905	922	935
10	0	137	314	492	617	722	809	887	935	953	967

TABLE 10.2
Total, Average, and Marginal Products of Labor (with capital fixed at two units)

(1) Number of workers (L)	(2) Total product (Q)	(3) Average product ($AP = Q/L$)	(4) Marginal product ($MP = \Delta Q/\Delta L$)
0	0	—	—
1	52	52	52
2	112	56	60
3	170	56.7	58
4	220	55	50
5	258	51.6	38
6	286	47.7	28
7	304	43.4	18
8	314	39.3	10
9	318	35.3	4
10	314	31.4	–4

vary output only by varying the usage of labor (the variable input). The column in Table 10.2 under 2 units of capital gives the total output, or total product of labor, for 0 through 10 workers. This column, for which $K = 2$, represents the short-run production function when capital is fixed at two units.

These total products are reproduced in column 2 of Table 10.2 for each level of labor usage in column 1. Thus, columns 1 and 2 in Table 10.2 define a production function of the form $Q = f(L, \overline{K})$, where $\overline{K} = 2$. In this example, total product (Q) rises with increases in labor up to a point (nine workers) and then declines. While total product does eventually *fall* as more workers are employed, a manager would not (knowingly) hire additional workers if he knew output would fall. In Table 10.2, for example, a manager can hire either 8 workers or 10 workers to produce 314 units of output. Obviously, the economically efficient amount of labor to hire to produce 314 units is 8 workers.

Average and Marginal Product

average product of labor (AP)
Total product (output) divided by the number of workers ($AP = Q/L$).

marginal product of labor (MP)
The additional output attributable to using one additional worker with the use of all other inputs fixed ($MP = \Delta Q/\Delta L$).

Average and marginal products are obtained from the production function and may be viewed merely as different ways of looking at the same information. The **average product of labor** is the total product divided by the number of workers,

$$AP = Q/L$$

In this example, average product, shown in column 3, first rises, reaches a maximum at 56.7, then declines thereafter.

The **marginal product of labor** (MP) is the additional output attributable to using one additional worker with the use of all other inputs fixed (in this case at two units of capital). That is,

$$MP = \Delta Q/\Delta L$$

where Δ means "the change in." The marginal product schedule associated with the production function in Table 10.2 is shown in column 4 of the table. Because no output can be produced with zero workers, the first worker adds 52 units of output; the second adds 60 units (that is, increases output from 52 to 112), and so on. Note that increasing the amount of labor from 9 to 10 actually decreases output from 318 to 314. Thus the marginal product of the 10th worker is negative. In this example, marginal product first increases as the amount of labor increases, then decreases, and finally becomes negative. This is a pattern frequently assumed in economic analysis.

In this example, the production function assumes that labor, the variable input, is increased one worker at a time. But we can think of the marginal product of an input when more than one unit is added. At a fixed level of capital, suppose that 20 units of labor can produce 100 units of output, and 30 units of labor can produce 200 units of output. In this case, output increases by 100 units as labor increases by 10. Thus

$$MP = \frac{\Delta Q}{\Delta L} = \frac{100}{10} = 10$$

Output increases by 10 units for each additional worker hired.

We might emphasize that we speak of the marginal product of labor, not the marginal product of a particular laborer. We assume that all workers are the same, in the sense that if we reduce the number of workers from 8 to 7 in Table 10.2, total product falls from 314 to 304 regardless of which of the eight workers is released. Thus the order of hiring makes no difference; a third worker adds 58 units of output no matter who is hired.

Figure 10.1 shows graphically the relations among the total, average, and marginal products set forth in Table 10.2. In Panel A, total product increases up to nine workers, then decreases. Panel B incorporates a common assumption made in production theory: average product first rises then falls. When average

FIGURE 10.1

Total, Average, and Marginal Product ($\bar{K}$ = 2)

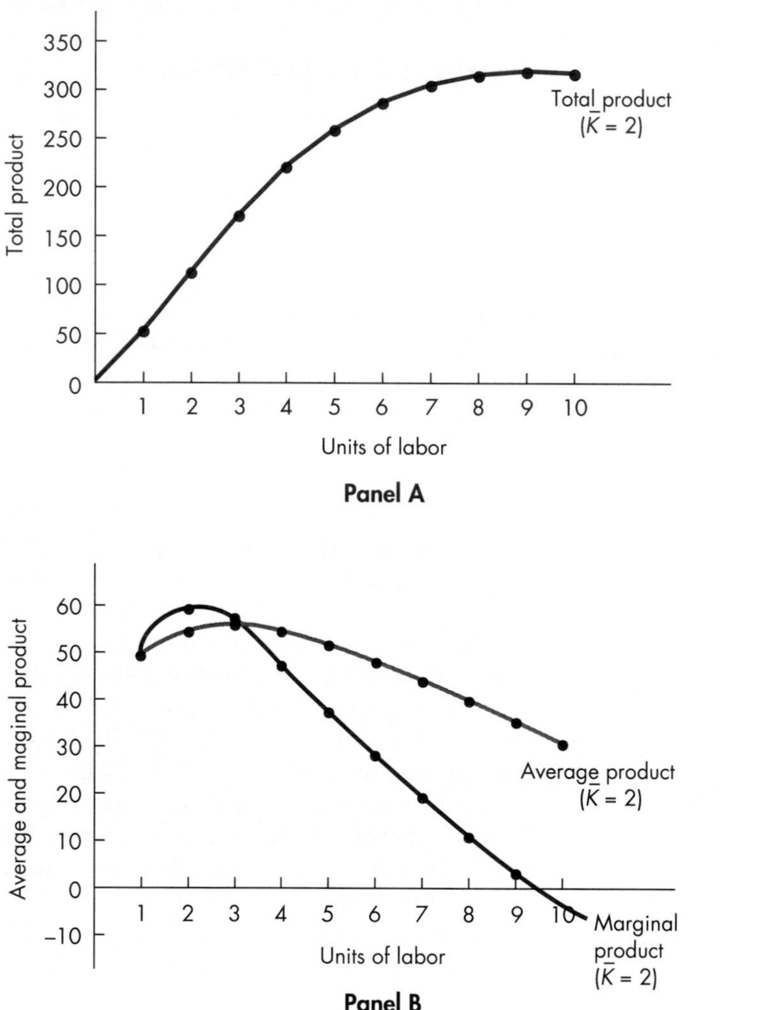

product is increasing, marginal product is greater than average product (after the first worker, at which they are equal). When average product is decreasing, marginal product is less than average product. This result is not peculiar to this particular production function; it occurs for any production function for which average product first increases then decreases.[1]

An example might help demonstrate that for any average and marginal schedule, the average must increase when the marginal is above the average and decrease when the marginal is below the average. If you have taken two tests

[1]This relation is demonstrated mathematically in the appendix to this chapter.

and made grades of 70 and 80, your average grade is 75. If your third test grade is higher than 75, the marginal grade is above the average, so your average grade increases. Conversely, if your third grade is less than 75—the marginal grade is below the average—your average would fall. In production theory, if each additional worker adds more than the average, average product rises; if each additional worker adds less than the average, average product falls.

As shown in Figure 10.1, marginal product first increases then decreases, becoming negative after nine workers. The maximum marginal product occurs before the maximum average product is attained. When marginal product is *increasing*, total product increases at an *increasing* rate. When marginal product begins to *decrease* (after two workers), total product begins to increase at a *decreasing* rate. When marginal product becomes negative (10 workers), total product declines.

We should note another important relation between average and marginal product that is not obvious from the table or the graph, but does follow directly from the discussion. If labor is allowed to vary continuously rather than in discrete units of one, as in the example, marginal product equals average product when average is at its maximum. This follows because average product must increase when marginal is above average and decrease when marginal is below average. The two, therefore, must be equal when average is at its maximum.

Law of Diminishing Marginal Product

law of diminishing marginal product
As the number of units of the variable input increases, other inputs held constant, a point will be reached beyond which the marginal product decreases.

The slope of the marginal product curve in Panel B of Figure 10.1 illustrates an important principle, **the law of diminishing marginal product**. As the number of units of the variable input increases, other inputs held constant, there exists a point beyond which the marginal product of the variable input declines. When the amount of the variable input is small relative to the fixed inputs, more intensive utilization of fixed inputs by variable inputs may initially increase the marginal product of the variable input as this input is increased. Nonetheless, a point is reached beyond which an increase in the use of the variable input yields progressively less additional output. Each additional unit has, on average, fewer units of the fixed inputs with which to work.

To illustrate the concept of diminishing marginal returns, consider the kitchen at Mel's Hot Dogs, a restaurant that sells hot dogs, french fries, and soft drinks. Mel's kitchen has one gas range for cooking the hot dogs, one deep-fryer for cooking french fries, and one soft drink dispenser. One cook in the kitchen can prepare 15 meals (consisting of a hot dog, fries, and soft drink) per hour. Two cooks can prepare 35 meals per hour. The marginal product of the second cook is 20 meals per hour, five more than the marginal product of the first cook. One cook possibly concentrates on making fries and soft drinks while the other cook prepares hot dogs. Adding a third cook results in 50 meals per hour being produced, so the marginal product of the third worker is 15 (= 50 – 35) additional meals per hour.

Therefore, after the second cook, the marginal product of additional cooks begins to decline. The fourth cook, for example, can increase the total number of

ILLUSTRATION 10.1

The Sometimes Impossible Task of Measuring Productivity

To anyone concerned with the performance of the economy, a particular industry, or a particular firm, trends in labor productivity are of the utmost importance. In some segments of the economy, however, measuring productivity can pose an almost insurmountable problem, even at the level where one might expect that managers would have large amounts of data on labor productivity. In manufacturing, the task is relatively simple. For example, take the case of a bicycle manufacturer. The average product of labor would be calculated as the total number of bicycles produced in a period, divided by the number of workers, possibly adjusted for the production of bicycles of different quality. For firms that sell services, the problem of measurement is much more difficult.

The Wall Street Journal recently discussed some problems the US government faces when measuring productivity in the service sector.* Measures of productivity in service industries are important because of the large, and expanding, role of services in the economy—employing more than three-fourths of the labor force—and because economists have long been troubled by lackluster productivity in the service sector. The *WSJ* article noted that data for the most recent quarter indicated that productivity in service-type businesses fell at a 2.3 percent annual rate while manufacturing productivity rose 4.7 percent. The falling productivity in services was worrisome to many observers because rising productivity plays a key role in the economy's ability to generate higher living standards.

Some experts feel that the service industry gets a bum rap, and productivity in services rises faster than the data suggest. Many prominent economists believe that because of the difficulty of measuring service productivity, no accurate evaluation can be made, and service productivity might be rising faster than that of manufacturing. The chief of productivity research at the Bureau of Labor Statistics stated that productivity in many services is "simply impossible to measure." As an example, he cited the insurance industry: "Do higher premiums, which tend to boost an insurance company's revenues, also serve to boost its productivity? Or are higher premiums merely a sign of higher policy risks?" So the BLS provides no productivity statistics for the insurance sector. Other service industries whose productivity the BLS finds it impossible to measure include health care, real estate, and stock and bond brokerage. Services for which no productivity figures are available employ nearly 70 percent of all people with service jobs.

Notwithstanding the measurement difficulties, many experts believe that service productivity is rising much more rapidly than is generally believed. A Federal Reserve Board economist noted that pay for bankers had risen sharply. Since compensation growth is linked to productivity in the long run, why would employers be willing to grant consistently large pay increases where unionization is low if productivity is so poor? Capital spending rose a strong 8 percent over the past year, hardly a sign of stagnating productivity. The United States has enjoyed large foreign trade surpluses in services for several years, a possible indicator of rising productivity.

Some reasons for the tendency of the BLS to understate productivity in services can be seen in the following examples from specific industries. One is retailing. An 11-ounce can of shaving cream sells for $1.49 in one small drug store and for $1.29 in a larger,

meals prepared to 60 meals per hour—a marginal product of just 10 additional meals. A fifth cook adds only 5 extra meals per hour, an increase to 65 meals. While the third, fourth, and fifth cooks increase the total number of meals prepared each hour, their marginal contribution is diminishing because the amount of space and equipment in the kitchen is fixed (i.e., capital is fixed). Mel could increase the size of the kitchen or add more cooking equipment to increase the productivity of all workers. The point at which diminishing returns set in would then possibly occur at a higher level of employment.

newer store nearby. The larger store can sell the product at a lower price because of faster turnover and customer self-service, but government statistics treat the cheaper product at the newer store as an entirely new product, rather than as a product being sold more efficiently. Banking productivity statistics ignore the large increases in banking volume, which, if included, would surely indicate productivity increases. Computers in large trucks have decreased ton-miles per driver when they are used—surely an increase in productivity—but the decrease in ton-miles indicates a statistical decrease in productivity.

The *WSJ* article points out that services sometimes get undeserved credit for productivity gains. The growth of self-service allows retailers to increase their productivity as consumers do work previously done by employees, but the statistics fail to account for the decline in quality of service.

A later article in *The Wall Street Journal*† cites a new study by a management consultant firm and concludes, "US workers in major service sectors are more productive than their counterparts overseas—except in restaurants, where the French excel." The study, based on some new statistical methodologies, concludes that "the United States has a slightly higher level of overall productivity [in services] than Germany and France and a significantly higher level than Japan and the United Kingdom." The consulting firm stated that the US edge reflects both the way management organizes operations and the degree to which government allows competition to force businesses to be efficient. Surprisingly, worker skills and the amount of financial investment make little difference. So it appears that management has a big impact.

We thought you might be interested in some of the statistical comparisons. Comparisons in the restaurant industry are complicated because Americans spend much more than the French or Germans on full-service meals and on fast foods. So, simply counting the number of meals, American restaurants are more productive. However, a meal at a premier French restaurant such as Tour d'Argent is not the same as eating a Big Mac. Adjusting for quality differences in food and services, the study concludes that productivity in French restaurants is 4 percent higher than in those in the United States, and productivity in German restaurants is 8 percent lower. US retailers are 4 percent more productive than German retailers, 18 percent more than British, 31 percent more than French, and 56 percent more than Japanese.

Taking into account all employees, airline employees in Europe are 28 percent less productive than those in the United States. The reason for this difference, according to the study, is the deregulation of US airlines. German bank employees are 32 percent less productive and British 36 percent less than their US counterparts. The study credits automatic tellers and the widespread use of computers in the United States for these results. In the business of telecommunications, labor productivity is about equal in the United States, France, and Japan, but 20 percent less in Germany and 40 percent less in the United Kingdom. We should mention, before you take these statistics as absolute facts, recall the previous discussion of the pitfalls of productivity measurement of services.

*Alfred Malabre, Jr. and Lindley Clark, Jr., "Productivity Statistics for the Service Sector May Understate Gains," *The Wall Street Journal*, August 12, 1992.

†David Wessel, "US Workers Excel in Productivity Poll," *The Wall Street Journal*, October, 13, 1992.

The marginal product of additional cooks can even become negative. For example, adding a sixth cook reduces the number of meals from 65 to 60. The marginal product of the sixth cook is –5. Do not confuse *negative* marginal product with *diminishing* marginal product. Diminishing marginal product sets in with the third cook, but marginal product does not become negative until the sixth cook is hired. Obviously, the manager would not want to hire a sixth cook since output would fall. The manager would hire the third, or fourth, or fifth cook, even though marginal product is decreasing, if more than 35, 50, or 60 meals must be prepared. As we will demonstrate, managers do in fact employ variable inputs beyond the point of diminishing returns but not to the point of negative marginal product.

The law of diminishing marginal product is a simple statement concerning the relation between marginal product and the rate of production that comes from observing real-world production processes. While the eventual diminishing of marginal product cannot be proved or refuted mathematically, it is worth noting that a contrary observation has never been recorded. That is why the relation is called a law.

Changes in Fixed Inputs

The production function shown in Figure 10.1 and also in Table 10.2 was derived from the production function shown in Table 10.1 by holding the capital stock fixed at two units ($\bar{K} = 2$). As can be seen in Table 10.1, when different amounts of capital are used, total product changes for each level of labor usage. Indeed, each column in Table 10.1 represents a different short-run production function, each corresponding to the particular level at which capital stock is fixed. Because the output associated with every level of labor usage changes when capital stock changes, a change in the level of capital causes a *shift* in the total product curve for labor. Since total product changes for every level of labor usage, average product and marginal product of labor also must change at every level of labor usage.

Referring once more to Table 10.1, notice what happens when the capital stock is increased from 2 to 3 units. The total product of three workers increases from 170 to 247, as shown in column 3. The average product of three workers increases from 56.7 to 82.3 (= 247/3). The marginal product of the third worker increases from 58 to 85 ($\Delta Q/\Delta L = (247 - 162)/1 = 85$). Table 10.3 shows the total, average, and marginal product schedules for two levels of capital stock, $\bar{K} = 2$

TABLE 10.3
The Effect of Changes in Capital Stock

	$\bar{K} = 2$			$\bar{K} = 3$		
L	*Q*	*AP*	*MP*	*Q*	*AP*	*MP*
0	0	—	—	0	—	—
1	52	52	52	74	74	74
2	112	56	60	162	81	88
3	170	56.7	58	247	82.3	85
4	220	55	50	325	81.3	78
5	258	51.6	38	390	78	65
6	286	47.7	28	425	70.8	35
7	304	43.4	18	453	64.7	28
8	314	39.3	10	474	59.3	21
9	318	35.3	4	488	54.2	14
10	314	31.4	–4	492	49.2	4

FIGURE 10.2
Shifts in Total, Average, and Marginal Product Curves

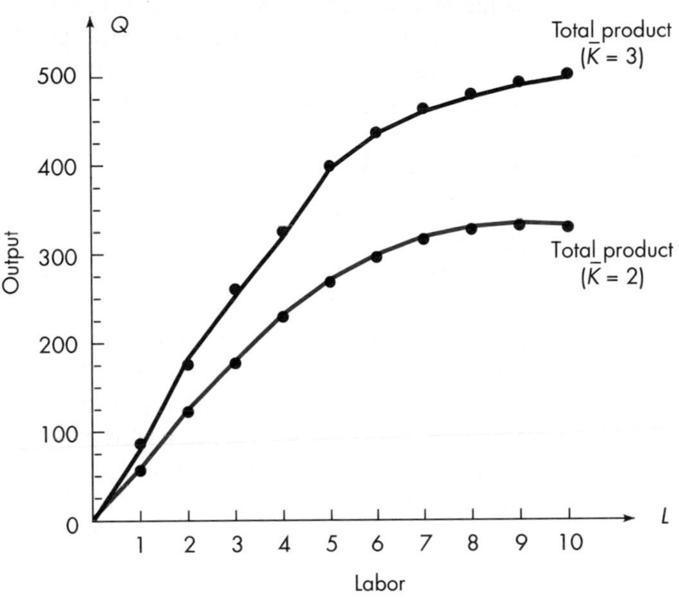

Panel A — Shift in total product

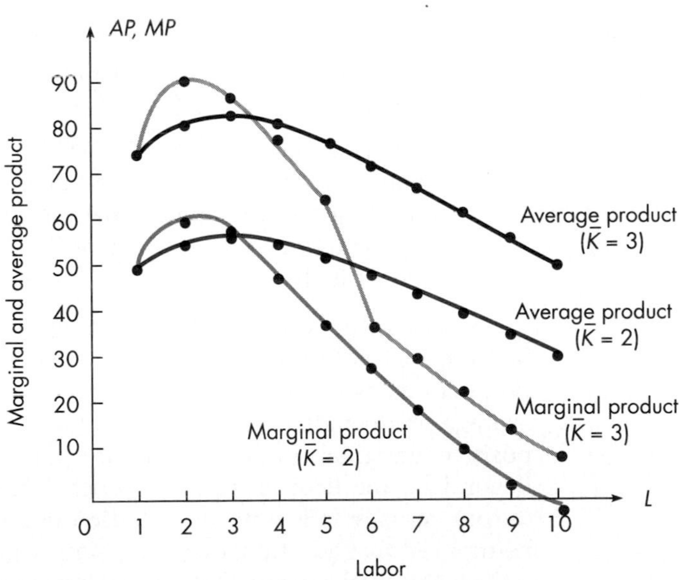

Panel B — Shifts in ***MP*** and ***AP***

and $\overline{K} = 3$. As you can see, *TP*, *AP*, and *MP* all increase at each level of labor usage as *K* increases from two to three units. Figure 10.2 shows how a change in the fixed amount of capital shifts the product curves. In Panel A, increasing $\overline{K}$ causes the total product curve to shift upward, and in Panel B, the increase in $\overline{K}$ causes both *AP* and *MP* to shift upward.

10.3 SUMMARY OF SHORT-RUN PRODUCTION

The production function gives the maximum amount of output that can be produced from any given combination of inputs, given the state of technology. The production function assumes technological efficiency in production, because technological efficiency occurs when the firm is producing the maximum possible output with a given combination of inputs. Economic efficiency occurs when a given output is being produced at the lowest possible total cost.

In the short run, at least one input is fixed. In the long run, all inputs are variable. This chapter examines the short-run situation when only one input is variable and one fixed. Panel A of Figure 10.3 shows a typical total product curve when labor is the only variable input. This curve gives the maximum amount of output that can be produced by each amount of labor when combined with the fixed inputs. The total product curve reflects the following relations:

1. No output can be produced with zero workers.
2. Output first increases at an increasing rate until L_0 workers are employed producing Q_0 units of output. Over this range marginal product is increasing.
3. Total product then increases but at a decreasing rate when the firm hires between L_0 and L_2 workers. Over this range *MP* is decreasing.
4. Average product reaches its maximum value at L_1 where *AP* equals *MP*.
5. Finally a point will be reached beyond which output will decline, indicating a negative marginal product. In Figure 10.3 this occurs for employment levels greater than L_2. The maximum possible total product is thus Q_2.

The corresponding average and marginal product curves are shown in Panel B. Note that both curves first rise, reach a maximum, then decline. Marginal product attains a maximum (at L_0) at a lower input level than the level at which average product attains its maximum (at L_1). While the average product is always positive, marginal product is zero at L_2 units of labor and is negative thereafter. Beyond L_2, the firm is using so much labor (relative to the fixed inputs) that output actually falls with the addition of more units. Possibly so much labor is being used that additional workers simply get in each other's way, and therefore reduce the total output that can be produced. The falling portion of the total product curve (*MP* is negative) is not economically efficient since any output for which total product is falling can be produced using less labor, and thus, at a lower cost.

When marginal product is greater than average product, average product is increasing. When marginal product is less than average product, average product

FIGURE 10.3
Total, Average, and Marginal Product Curves

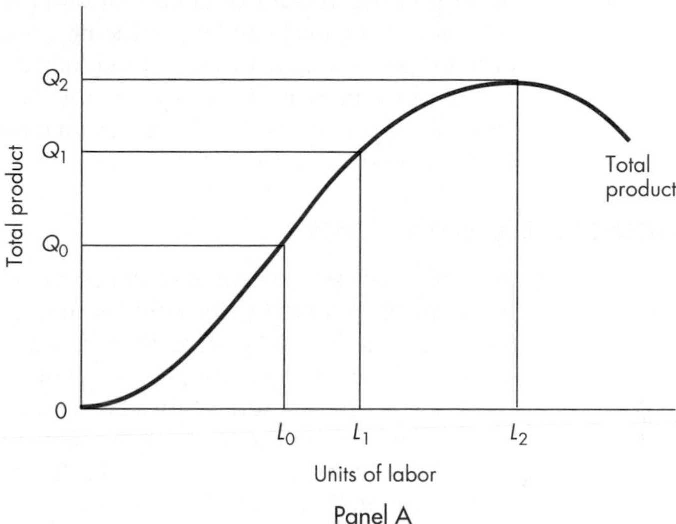

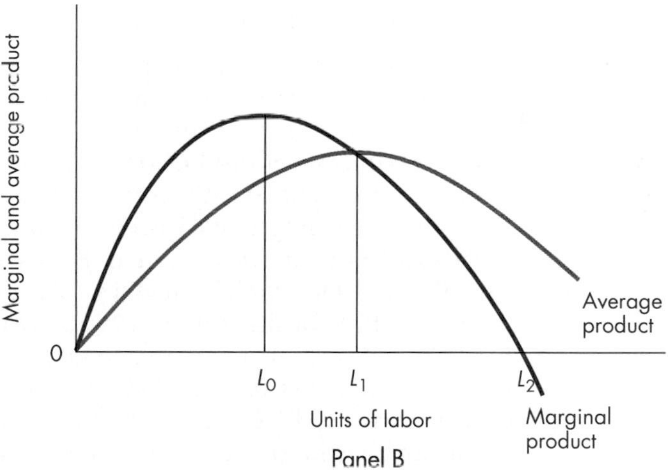

is falling. When average product is at its maximum, that is, neither rising nor falling, marginal product equals average product. The reason for this was discussed previously. The concepts of average and marginal product will become quite important later, when we analyze how firms decide how much of an input to hire.

We are now ready to derive the cost structure of the firm in the short run. For any level of output the manager wishes to produce, the economically efficient amount of labor to combine with the fixed amount of capital is found from the total product curve. In Figure 10.3, if the manager wishes to produce Q_0 units of output, the amount of labor that will produce Q_0 units at the lowest total cost is L_0 units. The total cost of producing Q_0 units is found by multiplying the price of labor per unit times L_0 to get the total expenditure on labor, then this amount is added to the cost of the fixed input. This computation can be done for every level of output to get the short-run total cost of production. We turn now to the costs of production in the short run.

10.4 THE NATURE OF ECONOMIC COSTS

We will devote the next few pages to an explanation of what cost means to economists. You might think this is unnecessary because everyone knows what "cost" means. But the economic meaning of cost is much broader than the common meaning. If someone asks you how much your new VCR cost, you might answer $298, the amount of the check you wrote. An economist would think that it probably cost you more, possibly much more. Because of the different meanings of cost, we are going to explain the economic concept of opportunity cost, and, incidentally, try to convince you that the economic usage of the term "cost" is more meaningful.

Explicit and Implicit Costs

opportunity cost
What the firm's owners give up to use a resource; the sum of explicit and implicit costs.

The cost of using resources to produce a good or service is the **opportunity cost** to the owners of the firm using those resources. The opportunity cost to the firm's owners of using a resource is what the owners must give up to use the resource. All costs of production are opportunity costs, and for decision-making purposes, it is opportunity costs that matter.

explicit cost
An out-of-pocket monetary payment for the use of a resource.

The opportunity cost of using an input or a resource is classified as either an *explicit cost* or an *implicit cost*. **Explicit costs** are what most people mean when they think of the cost of something. An explicit cost is the monetary payment made by a firm for the use of an input owned or controlled by other individuals. Explicit costs are also referred to as accounting costs. For example, if a firm purchases 40 hours of unskilled labor services for $8 per hour, an explicit (accounting) cost of $320 is incurred by the firm. The $320 payment is the amount the firm's owners give up to use the 40 hours of labor. Other types of explicit costs include the costs of purchasing raw materials, leasing a building, purchasing advertising, and leasing a plot of land. Incidentally, the explicit cost of the VCR in the previous example was $298.

implicit cost
The foregone return the firm's owners could have received had they used their own resources in their best alternative use.

Firms frequently use some resources that do not involve explicit monetary payments. Even though the firm does not make an explicit monetary payment for the use of such an input, the opportunity cost of using this input is not zero.[2] These nonmonetary opportunity costs are called **implicit costs**. An implicit cost is the opportunity cost of using resources that are owned or controlled by the

[2]The opportunity cost to a firm of using a resource is only equal to zero if the market value of the resource is zero; that is, if no other firm would be willing to pay anything for the use of that resource.

owners of the firm. The implicit cost is the foregone return the owners of the firm could have received had they used their own resources in their best alternative use rather than using the resources for their own firm's production. Implicit costs typically take two forms: (1) the opportunity cost of using land or capital owned by the firm, or (2) the opportunity cost of the owner's time spent managing the firm or working for the firm in some other capacity. These implicit costs are just as real and important in decision making as the firm's out-of-pocket explicit costs.

To illustrate the implicit cost of using capital owned by the firm, suppose Alpha Corporation and Beta Corporation are two manufacturing firms that produce a particular good and are in every way identical, with one exception. The owner of Alpha Corporation rents the building in which the good is produced. The owner of Beta Corporation inherited the building the firm uses and therefore pays no rent. Which firm has the higher costs of production? The costs are the same, even though Beta makes no explicit payment for rent. The reason the costs are the same is that using the building to produce goods costs the owner of Beta the amount of income that could have been earned had the building been leased at the prevailing rent. Since these two buildings are the same, presumably the market rentals would be the same. In other words, Alpha incurred an explicit cost for the use of its building, whereas Beta incurred an implicit cost for the use of its building. Regardless of whether the payment is explicit or implicit, the opportunity cost of using the building resource is the same for both firms.

The opportunity cost or implicit cost of using capital equipment or land that is owned by the firm (that is, owned by the firm's owners) is the return that could have been received if this resource had not been used by the firm but instead employed in its best alternative use. This sacrificed return can be measured in one of two ways. As in the above example, the sacrificed return is what could have been earned from leasing or renting the resource to some other firm. Alternatively, the sacrificed return can be measured as the amount the owner could earn if the resource, such as the building, were sold and the payment invested at the market rate of interest. The sacrificed interest is the implicit cost. These two measures of implicit cost are frequently the same, but if they are not equal, the true opportunity cost is the *best* alternative return.[3]

We should note that the opportunity cost of using land or capital owned by the firm may not bear any relation to the amount the firm paid for the land or capital. The opportunity cost reflects the current market value of the resource. If the firm paid $1 million for a plot of land two years ago, but the market value of the land has since fallen to $500,000, the implicit cost is the best return that could be earned if the land is sold for $500,000, not $1 million (which would be impossible under the circumstances), and the proceeds are invested. Similarly, if the market value has risen to $2 million, the implicit cost is the best possible return on $2 million, not $1 million. If the value of the land has fallen to zero, the

[3]The implicit cost of an owner's land or capital is frequently the same as the amount the firm would have to pay if it leased an identical piece of land or capital, although this is not always the case.

implicit cost of using it is zero—there is no alternative return. Note that the implicit cost is not what the resource could be sold for but the best return that could be earned by selling the resource and investing this amount in the best way possible. In the above example, if the $2 million could be invested at 10 percent, the implicit cost is $200,000.

Another example of an implicit cost is the value of a firm owner's time that is used to manage the business. Presumably, if the owners of firms are not managing their businesses or working for their firms in another capacity, they could obtain a job with some other firm, possibly as managers. The salary that could be earned in this alternative occupation is an implicit cost that should be considered as part of the total cost of production, because it is an opportunity cost to these owners. Incidentally, the value of the time you spent searching for the VCR is an implicit cost.

The implicit cost of an owner's time spent managing a firm or working for the firm in some other capacity is frequently, though not always, the same as the payment that would be necessary to hire an equivalent manager or worker if the owner does not work for the firm. As an extreme example of a case in which these amounts would not be the same, suppose Shaquille O'Neal retires from basketball and opens a sporting goods store that he manages himself. Presumably, he could hire an equivalent manager for about $50,000 to $70,000 a year. Mr. O'Neal's opportunity cost, however, is the $10 to $12 million he could earn from playing basketball and endorsing products. In most other cases that are not so farfetched, the two amounts would be similar.

The Importance of Implicit Costs

We want to reemphasize that implicit costs are just as real as explicit costs and must be considered when making decisions. To reinforce this assertion, we want you to consider another farfetched scenario. Suppose you are attending college full-time. Your explicit costs are your direct payments for books, tuition, and so on, which amount to $8,000 per year. Your implicit cost is the amount you give up by not working and attending school. Suppose this yearly implicit cost is the $30,000 that you could earn working for a bank. You choose to attend college and sacrifice the $30,000 for the chance to earn more in the future and for the pleasure of getting an education. Now suppose Spike Lee or Stephen Spielberg sees you walking across the campus and is so impressed that he offers you a $2 million contract to appear in his next movie. What happens to the opportunity cost of going to college? How would this change in opportunity cost affect your decision to continue school? It would probably make you give the decision some additional thought, so this implicit cost is certainly a real cost of college.

The total cost of using resources for production is the sum of all explicit costs and all implicit costs. Both are real opportunity costs. Throughout the remainder of this chapter, and in later chapters, when we refer to a firm's cost we include both explicit and implicit costs, even though we will not explicitly divide them into two separate categories. In all cases, cost will mean the entire opportunity cost.

Principle The opportunity cost to a firm of using resources is the amount the firm gives up by using these resources. Opportunity costs are explicit or implicit. An explicit opportunity cost is the payment the firm makes to a resource owner to hire, rent, or lease that resource. Implicit opportunity costs are the forgone earnings from using resources owned by the firm in the firm's own production process. These resources are typically any land or capital owned by the firm and an owner's time spent working for the firm. The implicit cost is the return that could have been earned in the best alternative use of the resources.

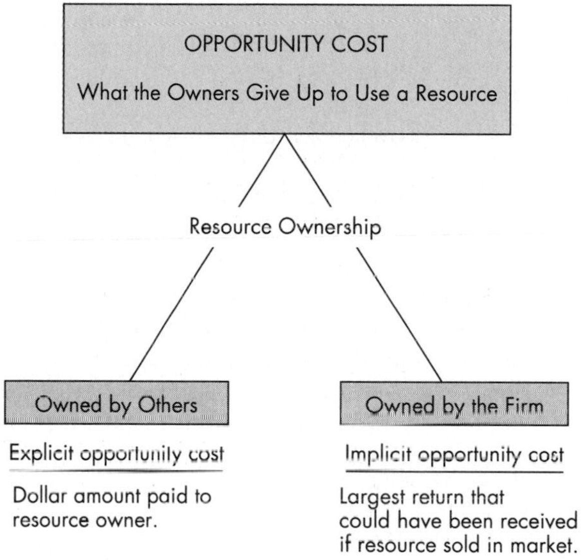

Fixed and Variable Costs

In the short run some inputs are fixed. Since these inputs have to be paid regardless of the level of output produced, these payments to the fixed inputs remain constant no matter what level of output is produced. Such payments are called *fixed costs*. An example of a fixed cost is a machine that is leased for one year at a cost of $500 per month. The cost of the machine is $500 every month for one year regardless of how many units of output are produced using the machine. Even if the firm shuts down for a month and does not use the machine, the firm still must pay $500 for the machine that month.

The payments to variable inputs are called *variable costs*. Producing more output requires more variable inputs. Thus, variable costs increase as the level of output increases. Examples of variable costs would be the payments for many types of labor, ingredient inputs or raw materials, or the energy used in production.

10.5 SHORT-RUN TOTAL COSTS

total fixed cost (*TFC*)
The total amount paid for fixed inputs. Total fixed cost does not vary with output.

As noted above, in the short run the levels of use of some inputs are fixed, and the costs associated with these fixed inputs must be paid regardless of the level of output produced. Other costs vary with the level of output. **Total fixed cost (TFC)** is the sum of the short-run fixed costs that must be paid regardless of the

ILLUSTRATION 10.2

Implicit Costs and Household Decision Making

As we explained in the text, the implicit opportunity cost to the firm of using a resource owned by the firm equals the best possible foregone payment the firm could have received if it had rented or leased the resource to another firm or had chosen to sell the resource in the market and invest the returns from the sale rather than retain the input for its own use. Producers decide how much of a resource to use based on the opportunity cost of the resource, regardless of whether that opportunity cost is an explicit cost or an implicit cost. You should not get the impression that opportunity costs, particularly implicit costs, are relevant only to decisions about production. All decision makers, including household decision makers, must consider both explicit and implicit costs in order to get the most from their limited resources.

Consider homeowners who pay off their mortgages early. Suppose a homeowner wins the state lottery and decides to pay off a $100,000 balance on a home mortgage. After "burning the mortgage," the homeowner no longer must make monthly mortgage payments, an explicit cost of homeownership. Ignoring maintenance costs and changes in the market value of the home, is the cost of owning the home now zero? Certainly not. By using his or her own financial resources to pay off the mortgage, the homeowner must forgo the income that could have been earned if the $100,000 had been invested elsewhere. If the homeowner could earn 7.5 percent on a certificate of deposit, the implicit cost (opportunity cost) of paying off the mortgage is $7,500 per year. Smart lottery winners do not pay off their mortgages if the interest rate on the mortgage is less than the rate of interest they can earn by putting their money into investments no more risky than homeownership. They do pay off their mortgage if the rate on the mortgage is higher than the rate they can earn by making investments no more risky than homeownership.

Another example of how implicit costs affect decisions made by households involves a story in *The St. Petersburg Times* about Jamie Lashbrook, an 11-year-old boy from Brooksville, Florida. Jamie won two tickets to Super Bowl XXV by kicking a field goal before a Tampa Bay Buccaneers game. Jamie quickly discovered that using the two "free" tickets does in fact involve an opportunity cost.* Less than one day after winning the tickets, Jamie's father had received more than a dozen requests from people who were willing to pay as much as $1,200 for each ticket. While the boy *obtained* the tickets at little or no cost, *using* these tickets involved an implicit cost—the payment Jamie could have received if he had sold the tickets in the marketplace rather than using them himself. We don't know if Jamie actually went to the Super Bowl or not, but even this 11-year-old decision maker knew better than to ignore the opportunity cost of using a resource.

*Bill Adair, "Wanted: The Hottest Ticket in Town," *The St. Petersburg Times*, January 6, 1991.

total variable cost (*TVC*) The amount paid for variable inputs. Total variable cost increases with increases in output.

total cost (*TC*) The sum of total fixed cost and total variable cost. Total cost increases with increases in output ($TC = TFC + TVC$).

level of output produced. **Total variable cost (TVC)** is the sum of the amounts spent for each of the variable inputs used. Total variable cost increases as output increases. Short-run **total cost (TC)**, which also increases as output increases, is the sum of total variable and total fixed cost:

$$TC = TVC + TFC$$

A Numerical Example

To show the relation between output (Q) and total cost in the short run, we present the simplest case. A firm uses two inputs, capital and labor, to produce output. The total fixed cost paid for capital is $6,000 per period. In Table 10.4, column 2, the total fixed cost (*TFC*) for each of seven possible levels of output is

TABLE 10.4
Short-Run Total Cost Schedules

(1) Output (*Q*)	(2) Total fixed cost (*TFC*)	(3) Total variable cost (*TVC*)	(4) Total cost (*TC*) *TC* = *TFC* + *TVC*
0	$6,000	$ 0	$ 6,000
100	6,000	4,000	10,000
200	6,000	6,000	12,000
300	6,000	9,000	15,000
400	6,000	14,000	20,000
500	6,000	22,000	28,000
600	6,000	34,000	40,000

FIGURE 10.4
Total Cost Curves

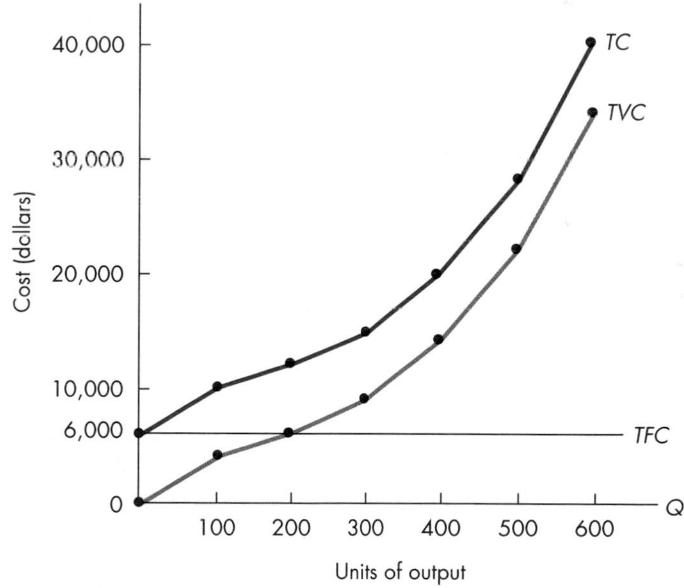

$6,000, including zero units of output. Column 3 shows the total variable cost (*TVC*) for each level of output. Total variable cost is zero when output is zero because the firm hires none of the variable input, labor, if it decides not to produce. As the level of production rises, more labor must be hired, and total variable cost rises as shown in column 3. Total cost (*TC*) is obtained by adding total fixed and total variable cost. Column 4 in Table 10.4, which shows the total cost of production for various levels of output, is the sum of columns 2 and 3.

Figure 10.4 shows the total cost curves associated with the total cost schedules in Table 10.4. The total fixed cost curve is horizontal at $6,000 indicating that *TFC* is constant for all levels of output. Total variable cost starts at the origin since the firm incurs no variable costs if production is zero, and *TVC* rises thereafter as output increases because to produce more the firm must use more resources which increases cost. Since total cost is the sum of *TFC* and *TVC*, the *TC* curve lies above the *TVC* curve by an amount exactly equal to $6,000 (*TFC*) at each output level. Consequently, *TC* and *TVC* are parallel and have identical shapes.

Average and Marginal Costs

average fixed cost (*AFC*) Total fixed cost divided by output (*AFC* = *TFC*/*Q*).

A more useful way of depicting the firm's cost structure is through the behavior of short-run average and marginal costs. Table 10.5 presents the average and marginal costs derived from the total cost schedules in Table 10.4. First, consider average fixed cost (*AFC*), given in Column 2. **Average fixed cost (*AFC*)** is total fixed cost divided by output,

$$AFC = TFC/Q$$

Average fixed cost is obtained by dividing the fixed cost (in this case $6,000) by output. Thus *AFC* is high at relatively low levels of output; since the denominator increases as output increases, *AFC* decreases over the entire range of output. If output would continue to increase, *AFC* would approach zero as output became extremely large.

average variable cost (*AVC*) Total variable cost divided by output (*AVC* = *TVC*/*Q*).

Average variable cost (*AVC*) is total variable cost divided by output

$$AVC = TVC/Q$$

TABLE 10.5
Average and Marginal Cost Schedules

(1) Output (*Q*)	(2) Average fixed cost (*AFC*) *AFC* = *TFC*/*Q*	(3) Average variable cost (*AVC*) *AVC* = *TVC*/*Q*	(4) Average total cost (*ATC*) *ATC* = *TC*/*Q*	(5) Marginal cost (*SMC*) *SMC* = Δ*TC*/Δ*Q*
0	—	—	—	
				$ 40
100	$60	$40	$100	
				20
200	30	30	60	
				30
300	20	30	50	
				50
400	15	35	50	
				80
500	12	44	56	
				120
600	10	56.7	66.7	

The average variable cost of producing each level of output in Table 10.5 is shown in Column 3. *AVC* at first falls to $30, then increases thereafter.

average total cost (*ATC*) Total cost divided by output or the sum of average fixed cost plus average variable cost ($ATC = TC/Q = AFC + AVC$).

Average total cost (*ATC*) is short-run total cost divided by output,

$$ATC = TC/Q$$

The average total cost of producing each level of output is given in Column 4 of Table 10.5. Since total cost is total variable plus total fixed cost,

$$ATC = \frac{TC}{Q} = \frac{TVC + TFC}{Q} = AVC + AFC$$

The average total cost in the table has the same general structure as average variable cost. It first declines, reaches a minimum at $50, then increases thereafter. The minimum *ATC* is attained at a larger output (between 300 and 400) than that at which *AVC* attains its minimum (between 200 and 300). This result is not peculiar to the cost schedules in Table 10.5; as we shall show later, it follows for all average cost schedules of the general type shown here.

short-run marginal cost (*SMC*) The change in either total variable cost or total cost per unit change in output ($\Delta TVC/\Delta Q = \Delta TC/\Delta Q$).

Finally, **short-run marginal cost (*SMC*)** is defined as the change in either total variable cost or total cost per unit change in output:

$$SMC = \frac{\Delta TVC}{\Delta Q} = \frac{\Delta TC}{\Delta Q}$$

The two definitions are the same because, when output increases, total cost increases by the same amount as the increase in total variable cost. Thus, since $TC = TFC + TVC$,

$$SMC = \frac{\Delta TC}{\Delta Q} = \frac{\Delta TFC}{\Delta Q} + \frac{\Delta TVC}{\Delta Q} = 0 + \frac{\Delta TVC}{\Delta Q} = \frac{\Delta TVC}{\Delta Q}$$

The short-run marginal cost is given in column 5 of Table 10.5. It is the per unit change in cost resulting from a change in output when the use of the variable input changes. For example, when output increases from 0 to 100, both total and variable costs increase by $4,000. The change in cost per unit of output is, therefore, $4,000 divided by the increase in output, 100, or $40. Thus the marginal cost over this range is $40. It can be seen that *MC* first declines, reaches a minimum of $20, then rises. Note that minimum marginal cost is attained at an output (between 100 and 200) below those at which either *AVC* or *ATC* attains its minimum. Marginal cost equals *AVC* and *ATC* at their respective minimum levels. We shall return to the reason for this result below.

The average and marginal cost schedules in columns 3, 4, and 5 are shown graphically in Figure 10.5. Average fixed cost is not graphed because it is a curve that simply declines over the entire range of output and because, as you will see, it is irrelevant for decision making. The curves in Figure 10.5 depict the properties of the cost schedules we have discussed. All three curves decline at first, then rise. Marginal cost equals *AVC* and *ATC* at each of their minimum levels. Marginal cost is below *AVC* and *ATC* when they are declining and above them when they are increasing. Since *AFC* decreases over the entire range of output and since $ATC = AVC + AFC$, *ATC* becomes increasingly close to *AVC* as output

FIGURE 10.5
Average and Marginal Cost Curves

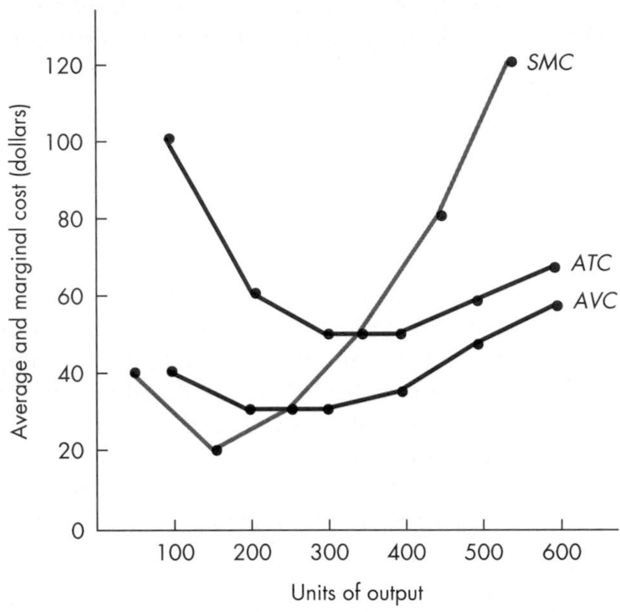

increases. As we show below, these are the general properties of typically assumed average and marginal cost curves.

General Short-Run Average and Marginal Cost Curves

Most of the properties of cost curves set forth thus far in this section were derived by using the specific cost schedules in Tables 10.4 and 10.5. These properties also hold for general cost curves when output and therefore cost vary continuously rather than discretely. These typical average and marginal cost curves are shown in Figure 10.6. These curves show the following:

Relations (1) *AFC* declines continuously, approaching both axes asymptotically (as shown by the decreasing distance between *ATC* and *AVC*). (2) *AVC* first declines, reaches a minimum at Q_2, and rises thereafter. When *AVC* is at its minimum, *SMC* equals *AVC*. (3) *ATC* first declines, reaches a minimum at Q_3, and rises thereafter. When *ATC* is at its minimum, *SMC* equals *ATC*. (4) *SMC* first declines, reaches a minimum at Q_1, and rises thereafter. *SMC* equals both *AVC* and *ATC* when these curves are at their minimum values. Furthermore, *SMC* lies below both *AVC* and *ATC* over the range for which these curves decline; *SMC* lies above them when they are rising.

In general, the reason marginal cost crosses *AVC* and *ATC* at their respective minimum points follows from the definitions of the cost curves. If marginal cost is below average variable cost, each additional unit of output adds less to cost

FIGURE 10.6
Short-Run Average and Marginal Cost Curves

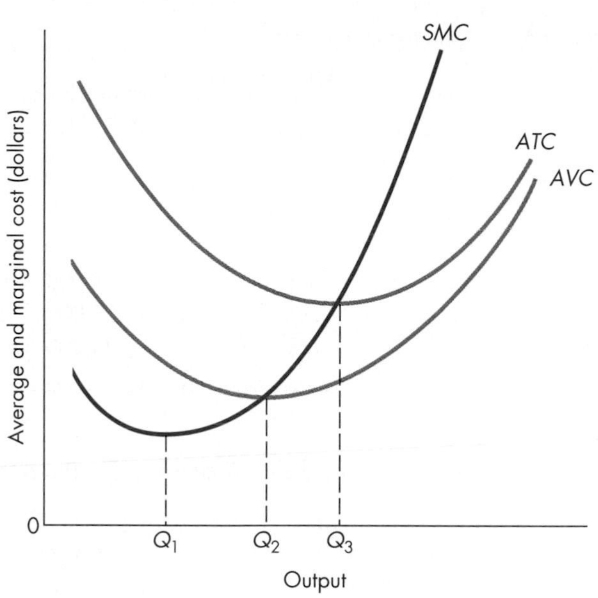

than the average variable cost of that unit. Thus, average variable cost must decline over this range. When *SMC* is above *AVC*, each additional unit of output adds more to cost than *AVC*. In this case, *AVC* must rise.

So when *SMC* is less than *AVC*, average variable cost is falling; when *SMC* is greater than *AVC*, average variable cost is rising. Thus *SMC* must equal *AVC* at the minimum point on *AVC*.[4] Exactly the same reasoning can be used to show that *SMC* crosses *ATC* at the minimum point on the latter curve.

10.6 RELATIONS BETWEEN SHORT-RUN COSTS AND PRODUCTION

We will now describe, in some detail, exactly how the short-run cost curves set forth in the preceding section are derived. As you will recall, once the total variable cost (*TVC*) and the total fixed cost (*TFC*) are developed, all of the other costs—*TC*, *ATC*, *AVC*, *AFC*, and *MC*—can be derived directly from the simple formulas that define these costs. Total fixed cost is simply the sum of the payments to the fixed inputs. As we will now show, total variable cost is derived directly from the short-run production function. In addition to deriving *TVC* from the total product curve, we also show how average variable cost can be derived from average product, and how marginal cost can be derived from marginal product.

[4]This relation is derived mathematically in the appendix to this chapter.

TABLE 10.6

Short-Run Production and Short-Run Total Costs

Short-run production		Short-run total costs		
(1) Labor (L)	(2) Output (Q)	(3) Total variable cost ($TVC = wL$)	(4) Total fixed cost ($TFC = rK$)	(5) Total cost ($TC = wL + rK$)
0	0	0	$6,000	$ 6,000
4	100	$ 4,000	6,000	10,000
6	200	6,000	6,000	12,000
9	300	9,000	6,000	15,000
14	400	14,000	6,000	20,000
22	500	22,000	6,000	28,000
34	600	34,000	6,000	40,000

Total Costs and the Short-Run Production Function

We begin with the short-run production function shown in columns 1 and 2 in Table 10.6. If 4 units of labor are employed, the firm can produce (a maximum of) 100 units; if 6 units of labor are employed, the firm's maximum output is 200 units; and so on. (Remember, the production function assumes technical efficiency.) For this example, we assume the wage rate—the price of a unit of labor services (w)— is $1,000. Total variable cost for any given level of output is simply the amount of labor employed multiplied times the wage rate:

$$TVC = w \times L$$

Column 3 shows the total variable costs associated with the various levels of output. Obviously, *TVC* is derived directly from the short-run production function. Note that *TVC* is derived for a particular wage rate. If the wage rate increases, *TVC* must increase at each level of output.

To see how total fixed cost is determined, assume that the short-run production function in columns 1 and 2 is derived for a firm using three units of capital in the short run ($\bar{K} = 3$) and that capital costs $2,000 per unit to employ. Thus, the total fixed cost is

$$TFC = r \times K = \$2{,}000 \times 3 = \$6{,}000$$

where r is the price of a unit of capital services. Column 4 shows the total fixed cost for each level of output.

Short-run total cost (*TC*) is the sum of the total variable cost and total fixed costs of production:

$$TC = wL + rK$$

Column 5 in Table 10.6 shows the total cost of producing each level of output in the short run when the firm's level of capital is fixed at three units. Note that these total cost schedules are the same as the ones in Table 10.4. Using the formulas set forth earlier in this chapter, we could easily derive *AVC* and *MC*

TABLE 10.7

Average and Marginal Relations between Cost and Production

Short-run production				Short-run costs	
(1) Labor	(2) Q	(3) AP (Q/L)	(4) MP (ΔQ/ΔL)	(5) AVC (w/AP)	(6) SMC (w/MP)
0	0	—	—	—	—
			25		$ 40
4	100	25		$40	
			50		20
6	200	33.33		30	
			33.33		30
9	300	33.33		30	
			20		50
14	400	28.57		35	
			12.50		80
22	500	22.73		44	
			8.33		120
34	600	17.65		56.67	

from the *TVC* schedule and *ATC* from the *TC* schedule. However, we can give you more of an understanding of the reasons for the typical shape of these curves by showing the relation between *AVC* and *AP* and *MC* and *MP*, which we discuss next.

Average Variable Cost and Average Product

Table 10.7 reproduces the production function in columns 1 and 2 of in Table 10.6. The average product of labor ($AP = Q/L$) is calculated in column 3 of Table 10.7. The relation between *AVC* and *AP* can be seen as follows. Consider the 100 units of output that can be produced by four workers. The total variable cost of using four workers is found by multiplying $1,000—the wage rate—times the four workers employed:

$$TVC = \$1{,}000 \times 4$$

The 100 units of output produced by the four workers can be found by multiplying 25—the average product—times the four workers employed:

$$Q = 25 \times 4$$

Since *AVC* is *TVC* divided by *Q*,

$$AVC = \frac{TVC}{Q} = \frac{\$1{,}000 \times 4}{25 \times 4} = \frac{\$1{,}000}{25} = \frac{w}{AP} = \$40$$

From this numerical illustration, you can see that *AVC* can be calculated as either *TVC/Q* or *w/AP*. It is easy to show that this relation holds in general for any production function with one variable input. In general,

$$AVC = \frac{TVC}{Q} = \frac{w \times L}{AP \times L} = \frac{w}{AP}$$

In Table 10.7, column 5 shows the value of average variable cost calculated by dividing $1,000 by average product at each level of output. You should verify that the computation of *AVC* in Table 10.7 ($AVC = w/AP$) yields the same values for *AVC* as the values obtained for *AVC* in Table 10.5 ($AVC = TVC/Q$).

Marginal Cost and Marginal Product

The relation between marginal cost and marginal product is also illustrated in Table 10.7. Column 4 shows the marginal product associated with the additional labor employed to increase production in 100-unit intervals. For example, to increase production from 100 to 200 units, two additional workers are required (an increase from 4 to 6 units of labor), so the marginal product is 50 units per additional worker. The change in total variable cost associated with going from 100 to 200 units of output is $2,000—$1,000 for each of the two extra workers. So,

$$SMC = \frac{\Delta TVC}{\Delta Q} = \frac{\$1{,}000 \times 2}{50 \times 2} = \frac{w}{MP} = \$20$$

Repeating this calculation for each of the 100-unit increments to output, you can see that the marginal cost at each level of output is the wage rate divided by the marginal product, and this will be true for any production function with one variable input, since,

$$SMC = \frac{\Delta TVC}{\Delta Q} = \frac{\Delta(w \times L)}{\Delta Q} = w\frac{\Delta L}{\Delta Q} = \frac{w}{MP}$$

You can verify that the values for marginal cost calculated as w/MP in Table 10.7 are identical to the values for marginal cost calculated as $\Delta TC/\Delta Q$ in Table 10.5.

The Graphical Relation between *AVC*, *MC*, *AP*, and *MP*

Figure 10.7 illustrates the relation between cost curves and product curves. We have constructed a typical set of product and cost curves in Panels A and B, respectively. Assume the wage rate is $21, and consider first the product and cost curves over the range of labor usage from zero to 500 units of labor. In Panel A, marginal product lies above average product over this range, so average product is rising. Since marginal cost is inversely related to marginal product ($MC = w/MP$) and average variable cost is inversely related to average product ($AVC = w/AP$), and since both *MP* and *AP* are rising, both *MC* and *AVC* are falling as output rises when labor usage increases (up to points *A* and *B* in Panel A). Marginal product reaches a maximum value of 9 at 500 units of labor usage (point *A*). The level of output that corresponds to using 500 units of labor is found by using the relation $AP = Q/L$. Since $AP = 6.5$ and $L = 500$, *Q* must be 3,250 (= 6.5 × 500). Thus, marginal product reaches its *maximum* value

FIGURE 10.7
Short-Run Production and Cost Relations

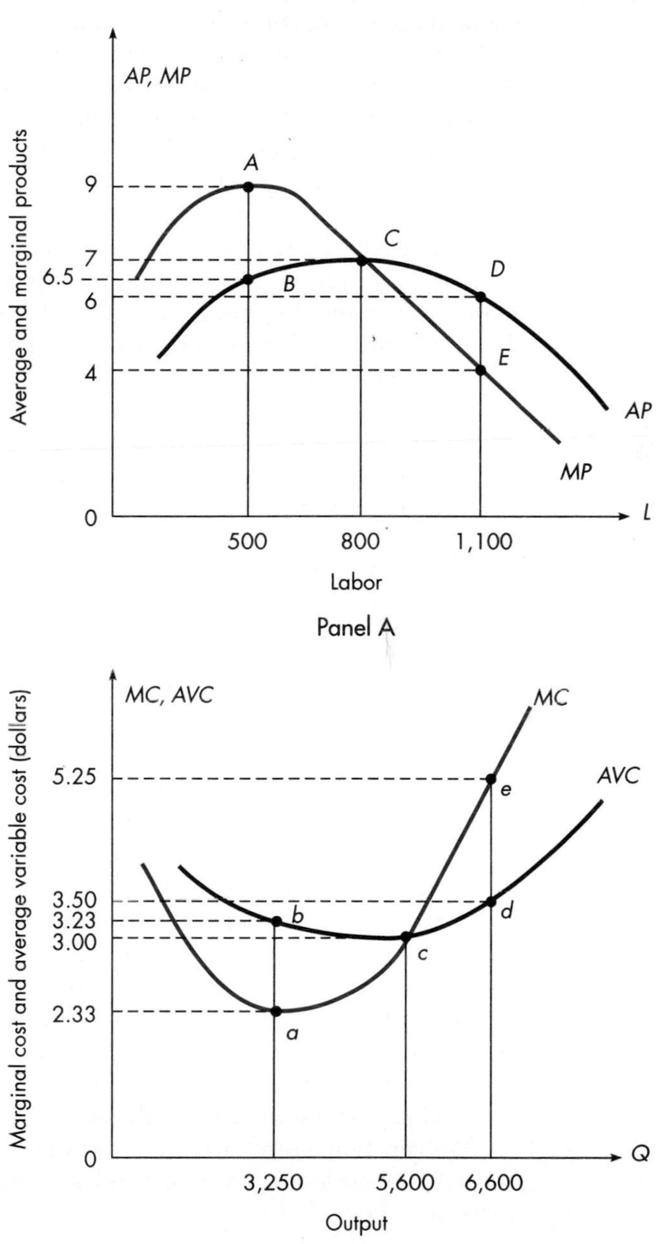

at 3,250 units of output, and, consequently, marginal cost must reach its *minimum* value at 3,250 units of output. At 3,250 units, marginal cost is equal to \$2.33 (= w/MP = \$21/9), and average variable cost is equal to \$3.23 (= w/AP = \$21/6.5). Points *A* and *B* in Panel A correspond to points *a* and *b* in Panel B of Figure 10.7.

One of the most important relations between production and cost curves in the short run involves the effect of the law of diminishing marginal product on the marginal cost of production. While marginal product generally rises at first, the law of diminishing marginal product states that, when capital is fixed, a point will eventually be reached beyond which marginal product must begin to fall. As marginal product begins to fall, marginal cost begins to rise. In Figure 10.7, marginal product begins to fall beyond 500 units of labor (beyond point *A* in Panel A). Marginal cost begins to rise beyond 3,250 units of output (beyond point *a* in Panel B).

Consider the range of labor usage between 500 and 800 units of labor. Marginal product is falling, but while marginal product still lies above average product, average product continues to rise up to point *C* where $MP = AP$. At point *C*, average product reaches its maximum value at 800 units of labor. When 800 units of labor are employed, 5,600 units of output are produced (5,600 = $AP \times L = 7 \times 800$). Thus, at 5,600 units of output, marginal cost and average variable cost are both equal to \$3:

$$MC = w/MP = \$21/7 = \$3$$
$$AVC = w/AP = \$21/7 = \$3$$

So, at 5,600 units of output, average variable cost reaches its minimum and is equal to marginal cost.

Finally, consider the cost and product relations as labor usage increases beyond 800 units. Marginal product falls below average product, and average product continues to decrease but never becomes negative. Marginal product will eventually become negative, but a manager who wishes to minimize costs would never hire an amount of labor that would have a negative marginal product. If marginal product is negative, the manager could *increase* output by *decreasing* labor usage, and this would also decrease the firm's expenditure on labor. Points *D* and *E* in Panel A correspond to points *d* and *e* in Panel B. At 1,100 units of labor, average product is 6, and output is 6,600 units (= $AP \times L = 6 \times 1{,}100$). You should verify for yourself that marginal cost is \$5.25 and average variable cost is \$3.50 when 6,600 units are produced.

We can now summarize the discussion of the relation between production and cost by restating the two fundamental relations between product and cost variables:

$$SMC = w/MP \text{ and } AVC = w/AP$$

Thus the following relations must hold:

Relations When marginal product (average product) is increasing, marginal cost (average variable cost) is decreasing. When marginal product (average product) is decreasing, marginal cost (average variable cost) is increasing. When marginal product equals average product at maximum *AP*, marginal cost equals average variable cost at minimum *AVC*.

As we explained in section 10.2, when the fixed inputs are allowed to change, all the product curves, *TP*, *AP*, and *MP*, shift. This, of course, will shift the short-run cost curves.

10.7 SUMMARY OF SHORT-RUN COST

In the short run when some inputs are fixed, short-run total cost (*TC*) is the sum of total variable cost (*TVC*) and total fixed cost (*TFC*):

$$TC = TVC + TFC$$

Average fixed cost is total cost divided by output:

$$AFC = TFC/Q$$

Average variable cost is total variable cost divided by output:

$$AVC = TVC/Q$$

Average total cost is total cost divided by output:

$$ATC = TC/Q = AVC + AFC$$

Short-run marginal cost (*SMC*) is the change in either total variable cost or total cost-per-unit change in output:

$$SMC = \Delta TVC/\Delta Q = \Delta TC/\Delta Q$$

A typical set of short-run cost curves is characterized by the following features: (1) *AFC* decreases continuously as output increases, (2) *AVC* is U-shaped, (3) *ATC* is U-shaped, (4) *SMC* is U-shaped and crosses both *AVC* and *ATC* at their minimum points, and (5) *SMC* lies below (above) both *AVC* and *ATC* over the output range for which these curves fall (rise).

The link between product curves and cost curves in the short run when one input is variable is reflected in the following relations:

$$SMC = w/MP$$

and

$$AVC = w/AP$$

When *MP* (*AP*) is increasing, *SMC* (*AVC*) is decreasing. When *MP* (*AP*) is decreasing, *SMC* (*AVC*) is increasing. When *MP* equals *AP* at *AP*'s maximum value, *SMC* equals *AVC* at *AVC*'s minimum value. Similar but not identical relations hold when more than one input is variable.

TECHNICAL PROBLEMS

* 1. Fill in the blanks in the following table.

Units of labor	Total product	Average product	Marginal product
1	____	40	____
2	____	____	48
3	138	____	____
4	____	44	____
5	____	____	24
6	210	____	____
7	____	29	____
8	____	____	–27

2. The following table shows the amount of total output produced from various combinations of labor and capital.

Units of labor	Units of capital 1	2	3	4
1	50	120	160	180
2	110	260	360	390
3	150	360	510	560
4	170	430	630	690
5	160	480	710	790

a. Calculate the marginal product and average product of labor when capital is held constant at two units. When the average product of labor is increasing, what is the relation between the average product and marginal product? What about when the average product of labor is decreasing?

b. Calculate the marginal product of labor for each level of the capital stock. How does the marginal product of the second unit of labor change as the capital stock increases? Why?

3. "When a manager is using a technically efficient input combination, the firm is also producing in an economically efficient manner." Evaluate this statement.

4. The first two columns in the table below give a firm's short-run production function when the only variable input is labor, and capital (the fixed input) is held constant at 5 units. The price of capital is $2,000 per unit and the price of labor is $500 per unit.

Units of labor	Units of output	Average product	Marginal product	Cost: Fixed	Cost: Variable	Cost: Total	Average cost: Fixed	Average cost: Variable	Average cost: Total	Marginal cost
0	0	____	____	____	____	____	____	____	____	____
20	4,000	____	____	____	____	____	____	____	____	____
40	10,000	____	____	____	____	____	____	____	____	____
60	15,000	____	____	____	____	____	____	____	____	____
80	19,400	____	____	____	____	____	____	____	____	____
100	23,000	____	____	____	____	____	____	____	____	____

a. Complete the table.
b. Graph the average variable cost, average total cost, and marginal cost curves.
c. What is the relation between average variable cost and marginal cost? Between average total cost and marginal cost?
d. What is the relation between average product and average variable cost? Between marginal product and marginal cost?

* 5. Fill in the blanks in the following table.

Output	Total cost	Total fixed cost	Total variable cost	Average fixed cost	Average variable cost	Average total cost	Marginal cost
100	260	_____	60	_____	_____	_____	_____
200	_____	_____	_____	_____	_____	_____	.30
300	_____	_____	_____	_____	.50	_____	_____
400	_____	_____	_____	_____	_____	1.05	_____
500	_____	_____	360	_____	_____	_____	_____
600	_____	_____	_____	_____	_____	_____	3.00
700	_____	_____	_____	_____	1.60	_____	_____
800	2,040	_____	_____	_____	_____	_____	_____

6. Assume that labor—the only variable input of a firm—has the average and marginal product curves shown in the graph below. Labor's wage is $2 per unit.

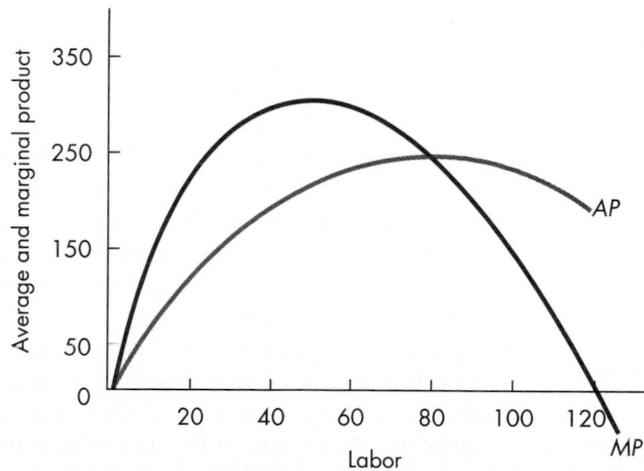

a. When the firm attains minimum average variable cost, how many units of labor is it using?
b. What level of output is associated with minimum average variable cost?
c. What is the average variable cost of producing this output?
d. Suppose the firm is using 100 units of labor. What is output? What is marginal cost? What is average variable cost?

7. Suppose that a firm is currently employing 20 workers, the only variable input, at a wage rate of $60. The average product of labor is 30, the last worker added 12 units to total output, and total fixed cost is $3,600.
   a. What is marginal cost?
   b. What is average variable cost?
   c. How much output is being produced?
   d. What is average total cost?
   e. Is average variable cost increasing, constant, or decreasing? What about average total cost?
8. Assume average variable cost is constant over a range of output. What is marginal cost over this range? What is happening to average total cost over this range?
9. Economists frequently say that the firm plans in the long run and operates in the short run. Explain.
10. Refer to Table 10.2 and explain precisely why using 10 units of labor and 2 units of capital is not economically efficient.

APPLIED PROBLEMS

1. At a management luncheon, two managers were overheard arguing about the following statement: "A manager should never hire another worker if the new person causes diminishing returns." Is this statement correct? If so, why? If not, explain why not.
2. Explain why it would cost Boris Becker or Steffi Graf more to leave the professional tennis tour and open a tennis shop than it would for the coach of a university tennis team to do so.
3. You are the adviser to the president of a university. A wealthy alumnus buys, then gives, a plot of land to the university to use as an athletic field. The president says that, as far as the land is concerned, it does not cost the university anything to use the land as an athletic field. What do you say?
4. Suppose that you manage a business and have to make business trips of two to four days at least once a month. What factors determine the total cost of a trip? What factors would you consider when deciding whether your salespeople should travel by automobile or airplane? Are these necessarily the same factors that determine the cost of your own travel?
5. Until recently you worked as an accountant, earning $30,000 annually. Then you inherited a piece of commercial real estate bringing in $12,000 in rent annually. You decided to leave your job and operate a video rental store in the office space you inherited. At the end of the first year, your books showed total revenues of $60,000 and total costs of $30,000 for video purchases, utilities, taxes, and supplies. What is your economic profit for the year?
6. When Burton Denson graduated with honors from the American Trucking Academy, his father gave him a $350,000 tractor-trailer rig. Recently, Burton was boasting to some fellow truckers that his revenues were typically $25,000 per month, while his operating costs (fuel, maintenance, and depreciation) amounted to only $18,000 per month. Tractor-trailer rigs identical to Burton's rig rent for $15,000 per month. If Burton was driving trucks for one of the competing trucking firms, he would earn $5,000 per month.

a. How much are Burton Denson's explicit costs per month? How much are his implicit costs per month?
b. What is the dollar amount of the opportunity cost of the resources used by Burton Denson each month?
c. Burton is proud of the fact that he is generating a net cash flow of $7,000 (= $25,000 – $18,000) per month, since he would only be earning $5,000 per month if he were working for a trucking firm. What advice would you give Burton Denson?

7. The famous financial analyst, Jane Bryant Quinn, in her *Newsweek* column (February 8, 1993) gave the following advice:

> "But you can't 'buy and forget' the new stocks any more than you could the old . . . you have to make continuous judgments on when to hold and when to sell. You also need a fix on companies other than the ones you own. Stocks need to be judged not just for themselves but in relation to what you could earn by switching money somewhere else."

According to Ms. Quinn, what is the implicit opportunity cost of holding a stock share? State her advice in terms of opportunity cost. If her advice is sound, and it is, why don't the most astute investors evaluate, buy, and sell stocks continuously? Answer in terms of opportunity cost and information costs.

APPENDIX: Mathematical Derivation of Production and Cost Relations

Mathematical Derivation of the Relation Between MP and AP

Define the two-input production function as

$$Q = f(L, K).$$

In the short run, hold capital constant at $\overline{K}$:

$$Q = f(L, \overline{K}) = g(L)$$

Thus, $Q = g(L)$ is the short-run production function when capital is fixed at $\overline{K}$ units.
Average product of labor is

$$AP = Q/L$$

Marginal product of labor is

$$MP = \frac{dQ}{dL} = \frac{dg(L)}{dL}$$

When AP is increasing (decreasing), marginal product is greater (less) than average product. $MP = AP$ when AP attains its maximum value.

Differentiating average product with respect to L yields

$$\frac{d(AP)}{dL} = \frac{d(Q/L)}{dL} = \frac{L(dQ/dL) - Q}{L^2}$$

$$= \frac{1}{L}(MP - AP)$$

If AP is rising, $d(AP)/dL > 0$; thus $MP > AP$. If AP is falling, $d(AP)/dL < 0$; thus $MP < AP$. And if AP is at its maximum value, $d(AP)/dL = 0$; thus MP = AP.

Mathematical Derivation of the Relation between *MC*, *AVC*, and *ATC*

Define short-term total cost (C) as

$$C = C(Q) = V(Q) + F$$

where $V(Q)$ is total variable cost and F is total fixed cost. Short-run marginal cost (SMC) is

$$SMC = \frac{dC}{dQ} = \frac{dV(Q)}{dQ}$$

Average total cost is

$$ATC = \frac{C}{Q} = \frac{V(Q)}{Q} + \frac{F}{Q}$$

When *AVC* is decreasing (increasing), *SMC* is below (above) *AVC*. *SMC* = *AVC* at minimum *AVC*. This same relation holds between SMC and ATC.

Differentiating average variable cost with respect to *Q* yields

$$\frac{d(AVC)}{dQ} = \frac{d[V(Q)/Q]}{dQ} = \frac{Q(dV/dQ) - V(Q)}{Q^2}$$

Rewriting this condition, we have

$$\frac{d(AVC)}{dQ} = \frac{1}{Q}\left(\frac{dV}{dQ} - \frac{V(Q)}{Q}\right)$$
$$= \frac{1}{Q}(MC - AVC)$$

If *AVC* is falling, $d(AVC)/dQ < 0$; thus $SMC < AVC$. If *AVC* is rising, $d(AVC)/dQ > 0$; thus $SMC > AVC$. And if *AVC* is at its minimum value, $d(AVC)/dQ = 0$; thus $SMC = AVC$.

By similar mathematical derivation, $d(ATC)/dQ$, and *MC* and *ATC* are related just as *MC* and *AVC* are related:

If *ATC* is falling, $d(ATC)/dQ < 0$; thus $SMC < ATC$. If *ATC* is rising, $d(ATC)/dQ > 0$; thus $SMC > ATC$. And if *ATC* is at its minimum value, $d(ATC)/dQ = 0$; thus $SMC = ATC$.

CHAPTER

11 Theory of Production and Cost in the Long Run

We will now analyze the situation in which there are two or more variable inputs, a situation that is both more complex and more interesting than production with only one variable input. As emphasized in the last chapter, every point on the total product curve (the short-run production function) is both technically and economically efficient. This is not the case when many different combinations of inputs can produce each level of output, as is true when production takes place under the typical conditions of variable proportions. As it turns out, only one of the many technically efficient combinations of inputs is economically efficient—that is, capable of producing a given level of output at the lowest possible total cost. The problem facing a manager is to choose the single input combination that is economically efficient from the many input combinations capable of producing a given output in a technically efficient manner.

When analyzing production with more than one variable input, we cannot simply use sets of average and marginal product curves, such as those discussed in Chapter 10, because these curves were derived holding the use of all other inputs constant (fixed) and letting the use of only one input vary. As noted, if the level of usage of the fixed input changes, the total, average, and marginal product curves shift. In the case of two variable inputs, changing the use of one input would cause a shift in the marginal and average product curves of the other input. For example, an increase in capital would probably result in an increase in the marginal and average product of labor over a wide range of labor use.

The primary objective of this chapter is to develop the principles of cost minimization (and output maximization) when more than one input is variable.

We will restrict the analysis to the two-input case for simplicity and for ease of graphical analysis. However, the same principles apply when more than two inputs are variable.

The analysis of production set forth here can be considered long run if capital and labor are the only inputs the firm employs—no inputs are fixed. In the short run, however, when two or more inputs are variable, the economically efficient choice of variable inputs is also determined using the same analytical techniques presented in this chapter. It is crucial for you to keep in mind that while we will typically refer to production in this chapter as "long-run" production, it applies to the short-run situation when a firm combines more than one variable input with its fixed inputs to produce a good or service.

We first develop some tools to be used later in the exposition, then derive and set forth the principles of cost minimization at a given level of output. As will become apparent, these principles follow directly from the principles of constrained minimization and constrained maximization set forth in Chapter 4. Once we show how the economically efficient input combination is found for producing various levels of output, it is a straightforward task to derive the long-run total cost schedule or curve. We then analyze several important concepts concerning costs of production in the long run.

11.1 PRODUCTION ISOQUANTS

isoquant
A curve showing all possible combinations of inputs physically capable of producing a given fixed level of output.

An important tool of analysis when two inputs are variable is the *production isoquant* or simply *isoquant*. An **isoquant** is a curve (or locus of points) showing all possible combination of the inputs physically capable of producing a given (fixed) level of output. Each point on an isoquant is technically efficient; that is, for each combination on the isoquant, the maximum possible output is that associated with the given isoquant. The concept of an isoquant implies that it is possible to substitute some amount of one input for some of the other, say labor for capital, while keeping output constant. Therefore, if the two inputs are continuously divisible, as we will assume, there are an infinite number of input combinations capable of producing each level of output.

To explain the concept of an isoquant, return for a moment to Table 10.1 in the preceding chapter. This table shows the maximum output that can be produced by combining different levels of labor and capital. Now note that several levels of output in this table can be produced in two ways. For example, 108 units of output can be produced using either 6 units of capital and 1 worker or 1 unit of capital and 4 workers. Thus these two combinations of labor and capital are two points on the isoquant associated with 108 units of output. And if we assumed that labor and capital were continuously divisible, there would be many more combinations on this isoquant.

Other input combinations in Table 10.1 that can produce the same level of output are:

$Q = 258$: using $K = 2, L = 5$ or $K = 8, L = 2$
$Q = 400$: using $K = 9, L = 3$ or $K = 4, L = 4$
$Q = 453$: using $K = 5, L = 4$ or $K = 3, L = 7$

$Q = 708$: using $K = 6$, $L = 7$ or $K = 5$, $L = 9$
$Q = 753$: using $K = 10$, $L = 6$ or $K = 6$, $L = 8$

These pairs of combinations of K and L are two of the many combinations associated with each specific level of output. They demonstrate that it is possible to increase capital and decrease labor (or increase labor and decrease capital) while keeping the level of output constant. For example, if the firm is producing 400 units of output with nine units of capital and three units of labor, it can increase labor by one, decrease capital by five, and keep output at 400. Or if it is producing 453 units of output with $K = 3$ and $L = 7$, it can increase K by two, decrease L by three, and keep output at 453. Thus, an isoquant shows how one input can be substituted for another while keeping the level of output constant.

Characteristics of Isoquants

We now set forth the typically assumed characteristics of isoquants when labor, capital, and output are continuously divisible. Figure 11.1 illustrates three such isoquants. Isoquant Q_1 shows all the combinations of capital and labor that will yield 100 units of output. As shown, the firm can produce 100 units of output by using 10 units of capital and 75 of labor, or 50 units of capital and 15 of labor, or by using any other combination of capital and labor on isoquant Q_1. Similarly, isoquant Q_2 shows the various combinations of capital and labor that can be used to produce 200 units of output. And, isoquant Q_3 shows all combinations that can produce 300 units of output. Each capital-labor combination can be on only one isoquant. That is, isoquants cannot intersect.

FIGURE 11.1
Typical Isoquants

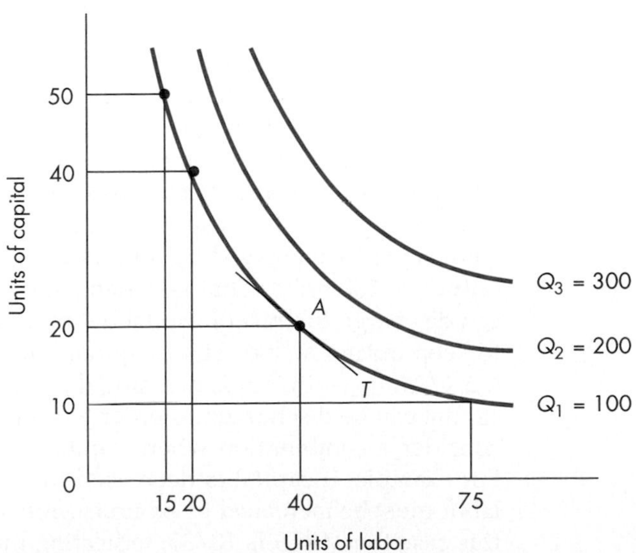

Isoquants Q_1, Q_2, and Q_3 are only three of an infinite number of isoquants that could be drawn. A group of isoquants is called an isoquant map. In an isoquant map, all isoquants lying above and to the right of a given isoquant indicate higher levels of output. Thus in Figure 11.1 isoquant Q_2 indicates a higher level of output than isoquant Q_1, and Q_3 indicates a higher level than Q_2.

We should also note that combinations other than those on a given isoquant can be used to produce the given level of output, but such combinations would not reflect the "maximum-amount-of-output" concept we introduced in the definition of a production function. Clearly, 100 units of output *could* be produced using *more than* 10 units of capital and *more than* 75 units of labor, but such production would involve wasting some inputs. In contrast, it is impossible to produce 100 units of output using less than 10 units of capital with 75 units of labor, or vice versa. For any combination along an isoquant, if the usage level of either input is reduced and the other is held constant, output must decline.

Marginal Rate of Technical Substitution

As depicted in Figure 11.1, isoquants slope downward over the relevant range of production. This negative slope indicates that if the firm decreases the amount of capital employed, more labor must be added in order to keep the rate of output constant. Or, if labor use is decreased, capital usage must be increased to keep output constant. Thus, the two inputs can be substituted for one another to maintain a constant level of output.

Great theoretical and practical importance is attached to the rate at which one input must be substituted for another in order to keep output constant. This rate at which one input is substituted for another along an isoquant is called the **marginal rate of technical substitution (*MRTS*)**, and is defined as

marginal rate of technical substitution (*MRTS*)
The rate at which one input is substituted for another along an isoquant $\left(-\frac{\Delta K}{\Delta L}\right)$.

$$MRTS = -\frac{\Delta K}{\Delta L}$$

The minus sign is added in order to make *MRTS* a positive number, since $\Delta K/\Delta L$, the slope of the isoquant, is negative.

Over the relevant range of production the marginal rate of technical substitution diminishes. That is, as more and more labor is substituted for capital while holding output constant, the absolute value of $\Delta K/\Delta L$ decreases. This can be seen in Figure 11.1. If capital is reduced from 50 to 40 (a decrease of 10 units) labor must be increased by 5 units (from 15 to 20) in order to keep the level of output at 100 units. That is, when capital is plentiful relative to labor, the firm can discharge 10 units of capital but must substitute only 5 units of labor in order to keep output at 100. The marginal rate of technical substitution in this case is $-\Delta K/\Delta L = -(-10)/5 = 2$, meaning that for every unit of labor added, two units of capital can be discharged in order to keep the level of output constant. However, consider a combination where capital is more scarce and labor more plentiful. For example, if capital is decreased from 20 to 10 (again a decrease of 10 units) labor must be increased by 35 units (from 40 to 75) to keep output at 100 units. In this case the *MRTS* is 10/35, indicating that for each unit of labor added, capital can be reduced by slightly more than one-quarter of a unit.

Thus, as capital decreases and labor increases along an isoquant, the amount of capital that can be discharged for each unit of labor added declines. Or, put another way, the amount of labor that must be added for each unit of capital eliminated, holding output constant, must increase. This relation is seen in Figure 11.1. As the change in labor and the change in capital becomes extremely small around a point on an isoquant, the slope of a tangent to the isoquant at that point is the *MRTS* ($-\Delta K/\Delta L$) in the neighborhood of that point. For example, in Figure 11.1, the slope of tangent T to isoquant Q_1 at point A shows the marginal rate of technical substitution at that point. Thus, the slope of the isoquant reflects the rate at which labor can be substituted for capital. It is easy to see that the isoquant becomes less and less steep with movements downward along the isoquant. Thus *MRTS* declines along an isoquant as labor increases and capital decreases.

Relation of *MRTS* to Marginal Products

For very small movements along an isoquant, the marginal rate of technical substitution equals the ratio of the marginal products of the two inputs. We will demonstrate why this comes about.

The level of output, Q, depends upon the use of the two inputs, L and K. Since Q is constant along an isoquant, ΔQ must equal zero for any change in L and K that would remain on a given isoquant. Suppose that, at a point on the isoquant, the marginal product of capital (MP_K) is 3 and the marginal product of labor (MP_L) is 6. If we add 1 unit of labor, output would increase by 6 units. To keep Q at the original level, capital must decrease just enough to offset the six-unit increase in output generated by the increase in labor. Because the marginal product of capital is 3, 2 units of capital must be discharged in order to reduce output by six units. In this case the $MRTS = -\Delta K/\Delta L = -(-2)/1 = 2$, which is exactly equal to $MP_L/MP_K = 6/3 = 2$.

Or, if we were to increase capital by one unit, output would rise by 3. Labor must decrease by one-half a unit to offset the increase of 3 units of output and keep output constant, since $MP_L = 6$. In this case, the $MRTS = -\Delta K/\Delta L = -(1)/(-1/2) = 2$, which is again equal to MP_L/MP_K.

In more general terms, we can say that, when L and K are allowed to vary slightly, the change in Q resulting from the change in the two inputs is the marginal product of L times the amount of change in L plus the marginal product of K times its change. Put in equation form,

$$\Delta Q = (MP_L)(\Delta L) + (MP_K)(\Delta K)$$

In order to remain on a given isoquant, it is necessary to set ΔQ equal to zero. Then, solving for the marginal rate of technical substitution, yields[1]

$$MRTS = -\frac{\Delta K}{\Delta L} = \frac{MP_L}{MP_K}$$

[1]This relation is demonstrated mathematically in the appendix to this chapter.

Using this relation, the reason for diminishing *MRTS* is easily explained. As additional units of labor are substituted for capital, the marginal product of labor diminishes. Two forces are working to diminish labor's marginal product: (1) less capital causes a downward shift of the marginal product of labor curve, and (2) more units of the variable input (labor) cause a downward movement along the marginal product curve. Thus, as labor is substituted for capital the marginal product of labor must decline. For analogous reasons the marginal product of capital increases as less capital and more labor are used. The same two forces are present in this case: a movement along a marginal product curve and a shift in the location of the curve. In this situation, however, both forces work to increase the marginal product of capital. Thus, as labor is substituted for capital the marginal product of capital increases. Combining these two conditions, as labor is substituted for capital, MP_L decreases and MP_K increases, so MP_L/MP_K will decrease.[2]

11.2 ISOCOST CURVES

isocost curves
Lines that show the various combinations of inputs that may be purchased for a given level of expenditure at given input prices.

Producers must consider relative input prices in order to find the least-cost combination of inputs to produce a given level of output. An extremely useful tool for analyzing the cost of purchasing inputs is an isocost curve. An **isocost curve** shows all combinations of inputs that may be purchased for a given level of total expenditure at given input prices. As you will see in the next section, isocost curves play a key role in finding the combination of inputs that produce a given output level at the lowest possible total cost.

Before we develop the concept of isocost curves, we need to discuss briefly how input prices are determined. For most managers, the price of each input is determined in the market for that input by the intersection of the demand for the input and the supply of the input. In such cases, the manager simply takes the market-determined price of the input as given when deciding how much of the input to purchase for production. In some cases, however, managers may be large enough buyers of resources that they can bargain with sellers of the resource to get a better price. They may, for example, get a lower price on the input if they buy a greater quantity of the input. In this case, the price of the input is not constant, but rather, declines as more of the input is purchased. While some managers may have the ability to negotiate lower prices for their inputs, we concentrate upon producers who are relatively small purchasers, so we treat input prices as constant.

Characteristics of Isocost Curves

Suppose a manager must pay $25 for each unit of labor services and $50 for each unit of capital services employed. The manager wishes to know what combinations of labor and capital can be purchased for $400 total expenditure on inputs.

[2]Note that we have violated our assumption about marginal product somewhat. The marginal product of an input is defined as the change in output per unit change in the input, the use of other inputs held constant. In this case we allow the usage of both inputs to change; thus the marginal product is really an approximation. But we are speaking only of slight or very small changes in use. Thus violation of the assumption is small and the approximation approaches the true variation for small changes.

FIGURE 11.2
An Isocost Curve (w = $25 and r = $50)

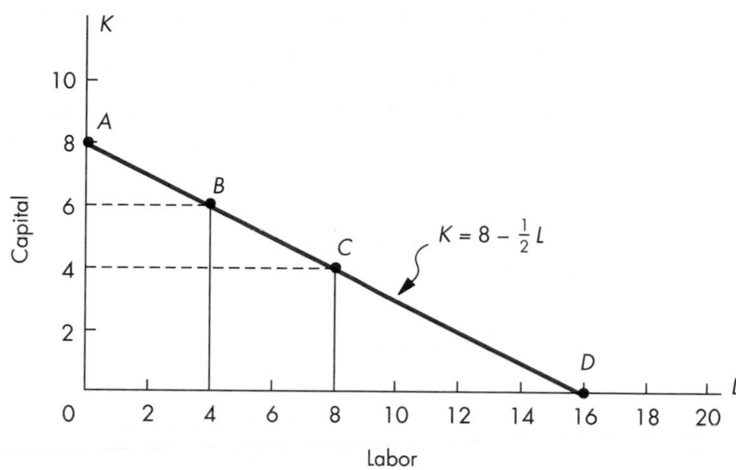

Figure 11.2 shows the isocost curve for $400 when the price of labor is $25 and the price of capital is $50. Each combination of inputs on this isocost curve costs $400 to purchase. Point *A* on the isocost curve shows how much capital could be purchased if no labor is employed. Since the price of capital is $50, the manager can spend all $400 on capital alone and purchase eight units of capital and zero units of labor. Similarly, point *D* on the isocost curve gives the maximum amount of labor—16 units—that can be purchased if labor costs $25 per unit and $400 is spent on labor alone. Points *B* and *C* also represent input combinations that cost $400. At point *B*, for example, $300 (= $50 × 6) is spent on capital and $100 (= $25 × 4) is spent on labor, which represents a total cost of $400.

If we continue to denote the quantities of capital and labor by *K* and *L*, and denote their respective prices by *r* and *w*, total cost, *C*, is $C = wL + rK$. Total cost is simply the sum of the cost of *L* units of labor at *w* dollars per unit and of *K* units of capital at *r* dollars per unit:

$$C = wL + rK$$

In the example above, the total cost function is $400 = 25L + 50K$. Solving this equation for *K*, you can see the combinations of *K* and *L* that can be chosen: $K = \frac{400}{50} - \frac{25}{50}L = 8 - 1/2L$. More generally, if a fixed amount $\overline{C}$ is to be spent, the firm can choose among the combinations given by

$$K = \frac{\overline{C}}{r} - \frac{w}{r}L$$

If $\overline{C}$ is the total amount to be spent on inputs, the most capital that can be purchased (if no labor is purchased) is $\overline{C}/r$ units of capital, and the most labor that can be purchased (if no capital is purchased) is $\overline{C}/w$ units of labor.

The slope of the isocost curve is equal to the negative of the relative input price ratio, $-w/r$. This ratio is important because it tells the manager how much capital must be given up if one more unit of labor is purchased. In the example given above and illustrated in Figure 11.2, $-w/r = -\$25/\$50 = -1/2$. If the manager wishes to purchase one more unit of labor at \$25, 1/2 unit of capital, which costs \$50, must be given up in order to keep the total cost of the input combination constant. If the price of labor happens to rise to \$50 per unit, r remaining constant, the slope of the isocost curve is $-\$50/\$50 = -1$, which means the manager must give up one unit of capital for each additional unit of labor purchased in order to keep total cost constant.

Shifts in Isocost Curves

If the constant level of total cost associated with a particular isocost curve changes, the isocost curve shifts parallel. Figure 11.3 shows how the isocost curve shifts when the total expenditure on resources ($\overline{C}$) increases from \$400 to \$500. The isocost curve shifts out parallel, and the equation for the new isocost curve is

$$K = 10 - 1/2L$$

The slope is still $-1/2$ because $-r/w$ does not change. The K-intercept is now 10, indicating that a maximum of 10 units of capital can be purchased if no labor is purchased and \$500 is spent.

In general, an increase in cost, holding input prices constant, leads to a parallel upward shift in the isocost curve. A decrease in cost, holding input prices constant, leads to a parallel downward shift in the isocost curve. An infinite number of isocost curves exist, one for each level of total cost.

FIGURE 11.3
Shift in an Isocost Curve

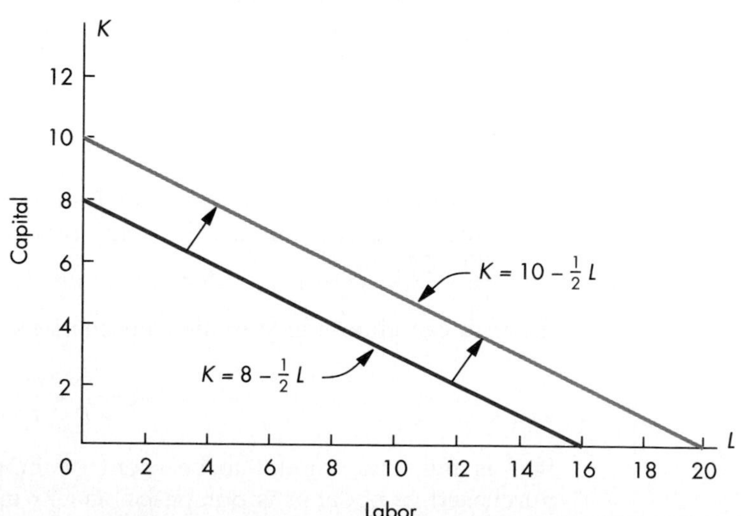

Relation At constant input prices, w and r for labor and capital, a given expenditure on inputs ($\bar{C}$) will purchase any combination of labor and capital given by the following equation, called an isocost curve:

$$K = \frac{\bar{C}}{r} - \frac{w}{r}L$$

11.3 FINDING THE OPTIMAL COMBINATION OF INPUTS

As explained in the introduction to this chapter, a manager who wishes to maximize profit must first decide how much output to produce and then how to produce that amount at the lowest possible total cost. We have shown that any given level of output can be produced by many combinations of inputs—as illustrated by isoquants. When a manager wishes to produce a given level of output at the lowest possible total cost, the manager chooses the combination on the desired isoquant that costs the least. This is a constrained minimization problem that a manager can solve by following the rule for constrained optimization set forth in Chapter 4. The ability to find the cost-minimizing combination of inputs is a fundamental skill a manager must master if profit is to be maximized.

While managers whose goal is profit-maximization are generally and primarily concerned with searching for the least-cost combination of inputs to produce a given (profit-maximizing) output, managers of nonprofit organizations may face an alternative situation. In a nonprofit situation, a manager may have a budget or fixed amount of money available for production and wish to maximize the amount of output that can be produced. As we have shown using isocost curves, there are many different input combinations that can be purchased for a given (or fixed) amount of expenditure on inputs. When a manager wishes to maximize output for a given level of total cost, the manager must choose the input combination on the isocost curve that lies on the highest isoquant. This is a constrained maximization problem; the rule for solving it was set forth in Chapter 4.

Whether the manager is searching for the input combination that minimizes cost for a given level of production or maximizes total production for a given level of expenditure on resources, the optimal combination of inputs to employ is found using the same rule. We first illustrate the fundamental principles of cost minimization with an output constraint, then we will turn to the case of output maximization given a cost constraint.

Production of a Given Output at Minimum Cost[3]

The principle of minimizing the total cost of producing a given level of output is illustrated in Figure 11.4. The manager wants to produce 10,000 units of output at the lowest possible total cost. All combinations of labor and capital capable of producing this level of output are shown by isoquant Q_1. The price of labor (w) is \$40 per unit and the price of capital (r) is \$60 per unit.

[3]Conditions for minimizing total cost subject to an output constraint are derived mathematically in the appendix to this chapter.

FIGURE 11.4
Optimal Input Combination to Minimize Cost for a Given Output

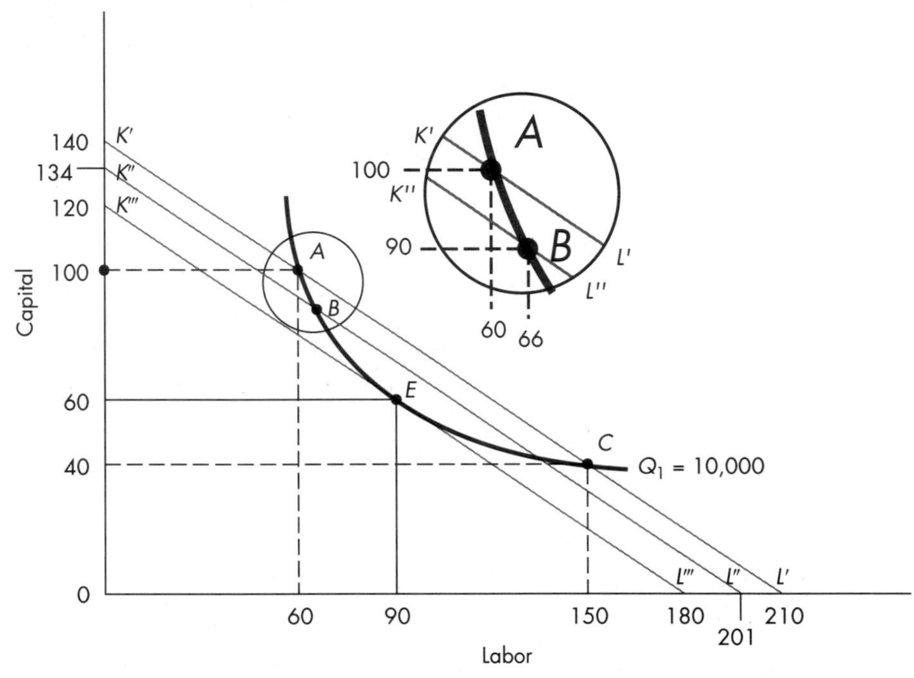

Consider the combination of inputs 60 L and 100 K, represented by point A on isoquant Q_1. At point A, 10,000 units can be produced at a total cost of $8,400, where the total cost is calculated by adding the total expenditure on labor and the total expenditure on capital:[4]

$$C = wL + rK = (\$40 \times 60) + (\$60 \times 100) = \$8{,}400$$

The manager can lower the total cost of producing 10,000 units by moving down along the isoquant and purchasing input combination B, because this combination of labor and capital lies on a lower isocost curve ($K''L''$) than input combination A, which lies on $K'L'$. The blowup in Figure 11.4 shows that combination B uses 66L and 90K. Combination B costs $8,040 [= ($40 × 66) + ($60 × 90)]. Thus, the manager can decrease the total cost of producing 10,000 units by $360 (= $8,400 – $8,040) by moving from input combination A to input combination B on isoquant Q_1.

Since the manager's objective is to choose the combination of labor and capital on the 10,000-unit isoquant that can be purchased or the lowest possible cost,

[4]Alternatively, you can calculate the cost associated with an isocost curve as the maximum amount of labor that could be hired at $40 per unit if no capital is used. For $K'L'$, 210 units of labor could be hired (if $K = 0$) for a cost of $8,400. Or 140 units of capital can be hired at $60 (if $L = 0$) for a cost of $8,400.

the manager will continue to move downward along the isoquant until the lowest possible *isocost* curve is reached. Examining Figure 11.4 reveals that the lowest cost of producing 10,000 units of output is attained at point E by using 90 units of labor and 60 units of capital on isocost curve $K'''L'''$, which shows all input combinations that can be purchased for $7,200. Note that at this cost-minimizing input combination:

$$C = wL + rK = (\$40 \times 90) + (\$60 \times 60) = \$7{,}200$$

No input combination on an isocost curve below the one going through point E is capable of producing 10,000 units of output. The total cost associated with input combination E is the lowest possible total cost for producing 10,000 units when $w = \$40$ and $r = \$60$.

Suppose the manager chooses to produce using 40 units of capital and 150 units of labor—point C on the isoquant. The manager could now increase capital and reduce labor along isoquant Q_1, keeping output constant and moving to lower and lower isocost curves, and hence lower costs, until point E is reached. Regardless of whether a manager starts with too much capital and too little labor (such as point A) or too little capital and too much labor (such as point C), the manager can move to the optimal input combination by moving along the isoquant to lower and lower isocost curves until input combination E is reached.

At point E, the isoquant is tangent to the isocost curve. Recall that the slope (in absolute value) of the isoquant is the $MRTS$, and the slope of the isocost curve (in absolute value) is equal to the relative input price ratio, w/r. Thus, at point E, $MRTS$ equals the ratio of input prices. In cost minimizing equilibrium,

$$MRTS = \frac{w}{r}$$

To minimize the cost of producing a given level of output, the manager employs the input combination for which $MRTS = w/r$.

The Marginal Product Approach to Cost Minimization

Recall from the discussion in Chapter 4 that finding the optimal levels of two activities A and B in a constrained optimization problem involved equating the marginal benefit per dollar spent on each of the activities (MB/P). A manager compares the marginal benefit per dollar spent on each activity to determine which activity is the "better deal"; that is, which activity gives the highest marginal benefit per dollar spent. In constrained equilibrium, both activities are equally good deals ($MB_A/P_A = MB_B/P_B$) and the constraint is met.

The tangency condition for cost minimization, $MRTS = w/r$, is equivalent to the condition of equal marginal benefit per dollar spent set forth in Chapter 4. Recall that $MRTS = MP_L/MP_K$; thus the cost-minimizing condition can be expressed in terms of marginal products:

$$MRTS = MP_L/MP_K = w/r$$

After a bit of algebraic manipulation, the equilibrium condition may be expressed as

$$\frac{MP_L}{w} = \frac{MP_K}{r}$$

The marginal benefits of hiring extra units of labor and capital are the marginal products of labor and capital. Dividing each marginal product by its respective input price tells the manager the additional output that will be forthcoming if one more dollar is spent on that input. Thus, at point E in Figure 11.4, the marginal product per dollar spent on labor is equal to the marginal product per dollar spent on capital, and the constraint is met ($Q = 10{,}000$ units).

To illustrate how a manager uses information about marginal products and input prices to find the least-cost input combination, we return to point A in Figure 11.4 where $MRTS$ is greater than w/r. Assume that at point A, $MP_L = 160$ and $MP_K = 80$; thus $MRTS = 2$ $(= MP_L/MP_K = 160/80)$. Since the slope of the isocost curve is $2/3$ $(= w/r = 40/60)$, MRTS is greater than w/r, and

$$\frac{MP_L}{w} = \frac{160}{40} = 4 > 1.33 = \frac{80}{60} = \frac{MP_K}{r}$$

The firm should substitute labor, which has the higher marginal product per dollar, for capital, which has the lower marginal product per dollar. For example, an additional unit of labor would increase output by approximately 160 units while increasing labor cost by \$40.[5] To keep output constant, two units of capital must be released, causing output to fall 160 units (the marginal product of each unit of capital released is approximately 80), but the cost of capital would fall by \$120, which is \$60 for each of the two units of capital released. Output remains constant at 10,000 because the higher output from one more unit of labor is just offset by the lower output from two fewer units of capital. However, because labor cost rises by only \$40 while capital cost falls by \$120, the total cost of producing 10,000 units of output falls by \$80 (= \$120 – \$40).

This example shows that when MP_L/w is greater than MP_K/r, the manager can reduce cost by increasing labor usage while decreasing capital usage just enough to keep output constant. Since $MP_L/w > MP_K/r$ for every input combination along Q_1 from point A to point E, the firm should continue to substitute labor for capital until it reaches point E. As more labor is used, MP_L falls because of diminishing marginal product. As less capital is used, MP_K rises for the same reason. As the manager substitutes labor for capital, $MRTS$ falls until equilibrium is reached.

Now consider point C, where $MRTS$ is less than w/r, and consequently MP_L/w is less than MP_K/r. The marginal product per dollar spent on the last unit of labor is less than the marginal product per dollar spent on the last unit of capital. In this case, the manager can reduce cost by increasing capital usage and decreasing labor usage in such a way as to keep output constant. To see this

[5]Note that we use "approximately" because we have ignored the possibility of diminishing marginal product.

point, assume that at point C, $MP_L = 40$ and $MP_K = 240$, and thus $MRTS = 40/240 = 1/6$, which is less than w/r (= 2/3). If the manager uses one more unit of capital and six fewer units of labor, output stays constant while total cost falls by \$180. (You should verify this yourself.) The manager can continue moving upward along isoquant Q_1, keeping output constant but reducing cost until point E is reached. As capital is increased and labor decreased, MP_L rises and MP_K falls until, at point E, MP_L/w equals MP_K/r. We have now derived the following:

Principle In order to produce a given level of output at the lowest possible cost when two inputs (L and K) are variable and the prices of the inputs are, respectively, w and r, a manager chooses the combination of inputs for which

$$MRTS = \frac{MP_L}{MP_K} = \frac{w}{r}$$

which implies that

$$\frac{MP_L}{w} = \frac{MP_K}{r}$$

In cost-minimizing equilibrium, the isoquant associated with the desired level of output (the slope of which is the $MRTS$) is tangent to the isocost curve (the slope of which is w/r) at the optimal combination of inputs. This equilibrium condition also means that the marginal product per dollar spent on the last unit of each input is the same.

Production of Maximum Output with a Given Level of Cost[6]

As discussed earlier, in most cases managers choose the firm's level of production and then choose the input combination that permits production of that output at least cost. There may be times, however, when managers can spend only a fixed amount on production and wish to attain the highest level of production consistent with that amount of expenditure. This is a constrained maximization problem and, as we showed in Chapter 4, the equilibrium condition for constrained maximization is the same as for constrained minimization. In other words, the input combination that maximizes the level of output for a given level of total cost of inputs is that combination for which

$$MRTS = w/r \quad \text{or} \quad \frac{MP_L}{w} = \frac{MP_K}{r}$$

This is the very same condition that must be satisfied by the input combination that minimizes the total cost of producing a given output level.

This situation is illustrated in Figure 11.5. The isocost line KL shows all possible combinations of the two inputs that can be purchased for the level of total cost (and input prices) associated with this isocost curve. Suppose the manager chooses point R on the isocost curve and is thus meeting the cost constraint. While 500 units of output are produced using L_R units of labor and K_R

[6]Conditions for output maximization subject to a cost constraint are derived mathematically in the appendix to this chapter.

FIGURE 11.5
Output Maximization for a Given Level of Cost

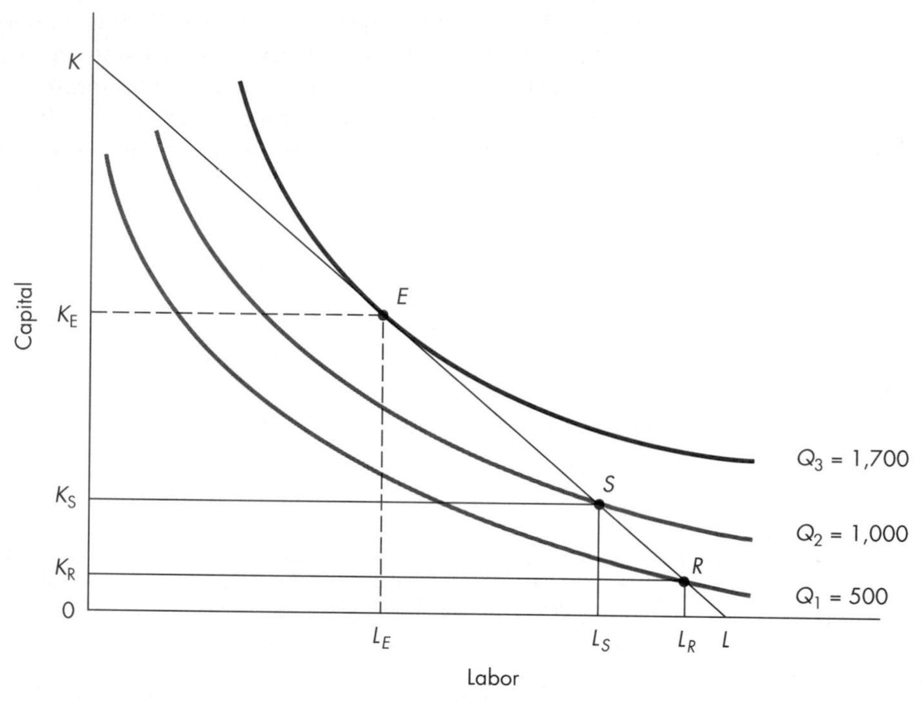

units of capital, the manager could produce more output at no additional cost by using less labor and more capital.

This can be accomplished, for example, by moving up the isocost curve to point *S*. Point *S* and point *R* lie on the same isocost curve and consequently cost the same amount. Point *S* lies on a higher isoquant, Q_2, allowing the manager to produce 1,000 units without spending any more than the given amount on inputs (represented by isocost curve *KL*). The highest level of output attainable with the given level of cost is 1,700 units (point *E*), which is produced by using L_E labor and K_E capital. At point *E*, the highest attainable isoquant, isoquant Q_3, is just tangent to the given isocost, and $MRTS = w/r$ or $MP_L/ = MP_K/r$—the same conditions that must be met to minimize the cost of producing a given output level.

To see why MP_L/w must equal MP_K/r in order to maximize output for a given level of expenditures on inputs, suppose that this optimizing condition does not hold. Specifically, assume that $w = \$2$, $r = \$3$, $MP_L = 6$, and $MP_K = 12$, so that

$$\frac{MP_L}{w} = \frac{6}{2} = 3 < 4 = \frac{12}{3} = \frac{MP_K}{r}$$

The last unit of labor adds three units of output per dollar spent; the last unit of capital adds four units of output per dollar. If the firm wants to produce the maximum output possible with a given level of cost, it could spend $1 less on labor, thereby reducing labor by one-half a unit and hence output by three units. It could spend this dollar on capital, thereby increasing output by four. Cost would be unchanged and total output would rise by one unit. And the firm would continue taking dollars out of labor and adding them to capital so long as the inequality holds. But as labor is reduced, its marginal product will increase, and as capital is increased, its marginal product will decline. Eventually the marginal product per dollar spent on each input will be equal.

We have established the following:

Principle In the case of two variable inputs, labor and capital, the manager of a firm maximizes output for a given level of cost by using the amounts of labor and capital such that the marginal rate of technical substitution (*MRTS*) equals the input price ratio (w/r). In terms of a graph, this condition is equivalent to choosing the input combination where the slope of the given isocost curve equals the slope of the highest attainable isoquant. This equilibrium condition implies that the marginal product per dollar spent on the last unit of each input is the same.

11.4 OPTIMIZATION AND COST

Using Figure 11.4 we showed how a manager can choose the optimal (least cost) combination of inputs to produce a given level of output. We also showed how the total cost of producing that level of output is calculated. When the optimal input combination for each possible output level is determined and total cost is calculated for each one of these input combinations, a total cost curve (or schedule) is generated. In this section, we illustrate how any number of optimizing points can be combined into a single graph and how these points are related to the firm's cost structure.

An Expansion Path

In Figure 11.4 we illustrated one optimizing point for a firm. This point shows the optimal (least cost) combination of inputs for a given level of output. However, as you would expect, there exists an optimal combination of inputs for every level of output the firm might choose to produce. And, the proportions in which the inputs are used need not be the same for all levels of output. To examine several optimizing points at once, we use the *expansion path.*

expansion path
The curve or locus of points that shows the cost-minimizing input combination for each level of output with the input price ratio held constant.

The **expansion path** shows the cost-minimizing input combination for each level of output with the input-price ratio held constant. It therefore shows how input usage changes as output changes. Figure 11.6 illustrates the derivation of an expansion path. Isoquants Q_1, Q_2, and Q_3 show, respectively, the input combinations of labor and capital that are capable of producing 500, 700, and 900 units of output. The price of capital (r) is $20 and the price of labor (w) is $10. Thus any isocost curve would have a slope of $10/20 = 1/2$.

The three isocost curves KL, $K'L'$, and $K''L''$, each of which has a slope of 1/2, represent the minimum costs of producing the three levels of output, 500, 700, and 900, because they are tangent to the respective isoquants. That is, at equilibrium points A, B, and C, $MRTS = w/r = 1/2$. In the figure, the expansion path connects these points of equilibrium and all other points so generated.

FIGURE 11.6
An Expansion Path

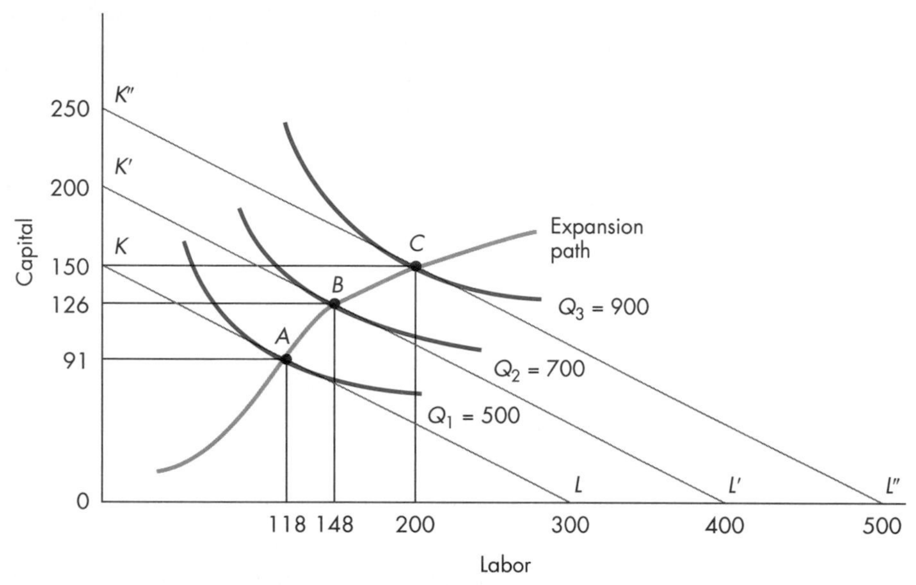

Note that points A, B, and C are also points indicating the combinations of inputs that can produce the maximum output possible at each level of cost given by isocost curves KL, $K'L'$, and $K''L''$. The optimizing condition, as emphasized, is the same for cost minimization with an output constraint and output maximization with a cost constraint. For example, to produce 500 units of output at the lowest possible cost, the firm would use 91 units of capital and 118 units of labor. The lowest cost of producing this output is therefore \$3,000 (from the vertical intercept, $\$20 \times 150 = \$3{,}000$). Likewise, 91 units of capital and 118 units of labor is the input combination that can produce the maximum possible output (500 units) under the cost constraint given by \$3,000 (isocost curve KL). Each of the other points of equilibrium along the expansion path also shows an input combination that is the cost-minimizing combination for the given output or the output maximizing combination for the given cost. At every point along the expansion path,

$$MRTS = \frac{MP_L}{MP_K} = \frac{w}{r}$$

and

$$\frac{MP_L}{w} = \frac{MP_K}{r}$$

Therefore, the expansion path is the curve or locus of points along which the marginal rate of technical substitution is constant and equal to the input price ratio. It is a curve with a special feature: It is the curve or locus along which the firm will expand output when input prices are constant.[7]

Relation The expansion path is the curve along which a firm expands (or contracts) output when input prices remain constant. Each point on the expansion path represents an efficient (least-cost) input combination. Along the expansion path, the marginal rate of technical substitution equals the constant input price ratio. The expansion path indicates how input usage changes when output or cost changes.

The Expansion Path and the Structure of Cost

An important aspect of the expansion path that was implied in this discussion and will be emphasized in the remainder of this chapter is that the expansion path gives the firm its cost structure. The lowest cost of producing any given level of output can be determined from the expansion path. Thus, the structure of the relation between output and cost is determined by the expansion path.

Recall from the discussion of Figure 11.6 that the lowest cost of producing 500 units of output is $3,000, which was calculated as the price of capital, $20, times the vertical intercept of the isocost curve, 150. Alternatively, the cost of producing 500 units can be calculated by multiplying the price of labor times the amount of labor used plus the price of capital times the amount of capital used:

$$wL + rK = (\$10 \times 118) + (\$20 \times 91) = \$3{,}000$$

Using the same method, we calculate the lowest cost of producing 700 and 900 units of output, respectively, as

$$(\$10 \times 148) + (\$20 \times 126) = \$4{,}000$$

and

$$(\$10 \times 200) + (\$20 \times 150) = \$5{,}000^{8}$$

Similarly, the sum of the quantities of each input used times the respective input prices gives the minimum cost of producing every level of output along the expansion path. As you will see later in this chapter, this allows the firm to relate its cost to the level of output used.

[7]We should note that thus far in our discussion of the expansion path we have assumed that as the firm expands output, it increases its usage of all inputs. This need not be the case. It is possible that as a firm expands, it actually decreases the usage of one or more—though not all—inputs over the relevant range. For example, in the two-input case, a firm may increase output by using more capital and less labor. In this case, labor would be called an *inferior input*. An input is said to be inferior if, over a range, increased output causes less of the input to be used. In such cases, the expansion path curves backward if the quantity of the inferior input is plotted along the horizontal axis, or curves downward if the quantity of the inferior input is plotted along the vertical. Since this phenomenon is not of particular theoretical or empirical importance, we will not consider it further in our analysis.

[8]As you can verify, these are the same costs that would be obtained by multiplying the price of capital (labor) times the vertical (horizontal) intercept of the relevant isocost curve.

11.5 RETURNS TO SCALE

We will now describe the effect of a proportional increase in all inputs on the level of output produced. For example, if the firm's usage of all inputs doubles, output would increase. The question is: By how much? The answer to this question depends upon the concept of returns to scale.

constant returns to scale When all inputs are increased by the same proportion and output also increases by that exact proportion.

increasing returns to scale When all inputs are increased by the same proportion and output increases by more than this proportion.

decreasing returns to scale When all inputs are increased by the same proportion and output increases by less than this proportion.

Assume the usage of all inputs increases by 25 percent. If output increases by exactly 25 percent, the production function exhibits **constant returns to scale.** If, however, output increases by more than 25 percent, the production function exhibits **increasing returns to scale**. Alternatively, if output increases by less than 25 percent, the production function is characterized by **decreasing returns to scale.**

These relations can be illustrated using Figure 11.7. Begin with an arbitrary level of capital and labor at K_0 and L_0. This combination of capital and labor produces some level of output, Q_0. For purposes of illustration, we define Q_0 to be 100 units. Now, double the level of input usage to $2K_0$ and $2L_0$. Output increases to Q_1. The question is the magnitude of the increase. Input usage has increased by 100 percent. If Q_1 is equal to 200, output would have exactly doubled (increased by 100 percent) in response to the doubling of input usage, so constant returns to scale are indicated. If Q_1 is greater than 200 units (for example, 215), increasing returns to scale are indicated. If Q_1 is less than 200 units (for example, 180), the production function exhibits decreasing returns to scale.

Returns to scale are defined more analytically by writing the production function in functional form as

$$Q = f(L,K)$$

FIGURE 11.7
Returns to Scale

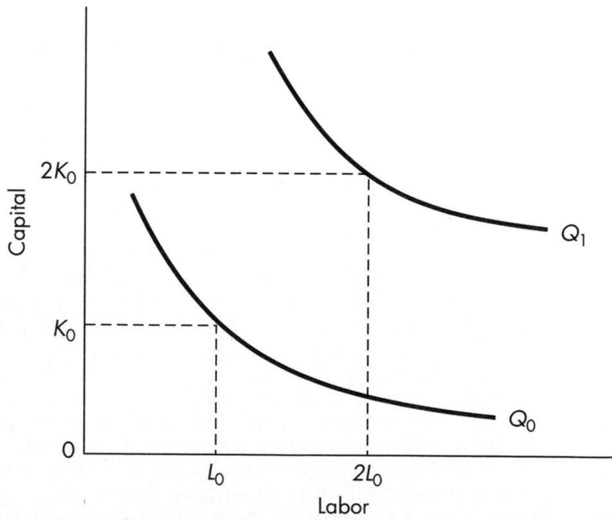

If input usage increases by a constant proportion (for example, c) and the proportionate change in output is z,

$$f(cL, cK) = zQ$$

Again remember that c and z represent proportionate increases in the level of input usage and level of output, respectively.

We have noted, in the case of constant returns to scale, that if inputs are increased by a given percent, output rises by the same percent, that is, $z = c$. More generally, if all inputs increase by a factor of c and output goes up by a factor of z, then a firm experiences:

1. Increasing returns to scale if $z > c$. (Output goes up proportionately more than the increase in input usage.)
2. Constant returns to scale if $z = c$. (Output goes up by the same proportion as the increase in input usage.)
3. Decreasing returns to scale if $z < c$. (Output goes up proportionately less than the increase in input usage.)

Do not deduce from this discussion of returns to scale that firms with variable-proportions production functions actually expand output by increasing their usage of every input in exactly the same proportion. As you have seen, the very concept of variable proportions means that they do not necessarily expand inputs in the same proportions. The expansion path may twist and turn in many directions. However, the concept of returns to scale does enter into some aspects of production and cost theory, and you should be familiar with this term.

11.6 SUMMARY OF LONG-RUN PRODUCTION

In the long run, all inputs are variable. Figure 11.8 summarizes graphically the long-run production decision. In the figure, isoquants Q_1, Q_2, and Q_3 show all possible combinations of labor and capital capable of producing three of the infinite number of output levels that the firm may choose to produce. Isoquants are downward sloping to reflect the fact that if larger amounts of labor are used, less capital is required to produce the same output level. The marginal rate of technical substitution (*MRTS*) is the absolute value of the slope of an isoquant and measures the rate at which the two inputs can be substituted for one another while maintaining a constant level of output: $MRTS = -\Delta K/\Delta L$. The marginal rate of technical substitution can be expressed as the ratio of the two marginal products:

$$-\frac{\Delta K}{\Delta L} = MRTS = \frac{MP_L}{MP_K}$$

As labor is substituted for capital, MP_L declines and MP_K rises causing *MRTS* to diminish along the isoquant.

The isocost curves show the various combinations of inputs that may be purchased for a given dollar outlay. The equation of an isocost curve is given by:

$$K = \frac{\overline{C}}{r} - \frac{w}{r}L$$

FIGURE 11.8
Summary of Cost Minimization and Output Maximization

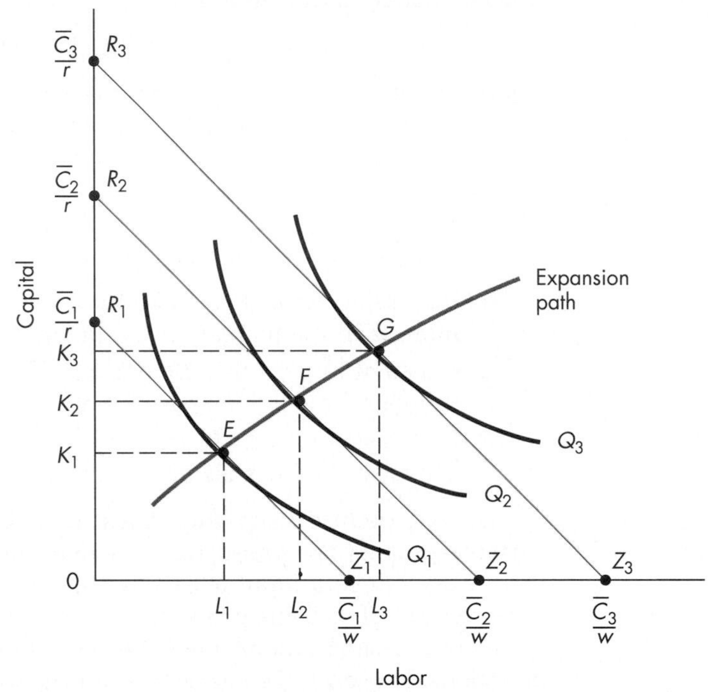

where $\overline{C}$ is the cost of any of the input combinations on this isocost curve; and w and r are the prices of labor and capital, respectively. The slope of an isocost curve is the negative of the input price ratio $(-w/r)$. The isocost curve intersects the capital (or vertical) axis at $\overline{C}/r$, which represents the amount of capital that may be purchased when all $\overline{C}$ dollars are spent on capital and no labor is purchased. The isocost curve intersects the labor (or horizontal) axis at $\overline{C}/w$. The cost associated with any particular isocost curve can be determined by multiplying the price of capital times $\overline{C}/r$ or the price of labor times $\overline{C}/w$.

A manager minimizes the total cost of producing a given level of output or maximizes output for a given level of cost (expenditure on inputs) by choosing an input combination at the point of tangency between the relevant isoquant and isocost curves. Points *E, F, G* are points of tangency between each of the three isoquants and the *lowest* isocost curve that includes an input combination that is capable of producing the output level given by that isoquant. Alternatively, these points of tangency indicate the combination of inputs on each isocost curve that can produce the largest output (the highest isoquant) that is attainable from any combination on the given isocost curve.

Since the cost-minimizing or output-maximizing input combination occurs at the point of tangency between the isoquant and the isocost curve, the slopes of the two curves are equal in equilibrium. The equilibrium condition may be expressed as

$$MRTS = \frac{MP_L}{MP_K} = \frac{w}{r}$$

or

$$\frac{MP_L}{w} = \frac{MP_K}{r}$$

Thus, the marginal product per dollar spent on the last unit of each input is the same. Equating marginal product per dollar spent on all variable inputs is the rule managers should follow both in the long run when all inputs are variable and in the short run when two or more inputs are variable.

The expansion path shows the equilibrium (or optimal) input combination for every level of output. Figure 11.8 shows a typical expansion path. An expansion path is derived for a specific price of labor (w) and price of capital (r). An expansion path shows how input usage changes when output changes, input prices remaining constant. Along the expansion path the marginal rate of technical substitution is constant, since the ratio of input prices (w/r) is constant.

All points on the expansion path are both cost-minimizing and output-maximizing combinations of labor and capital. For example, consider the input combination consisting of K_2 units of capital and L_2 units of labor (combination F in Figure 11.8). Combination F lies on the lowest possible isocost curve for which Q_1 units of output can be produced. Thus, the minimum cost for producing Q_2 units of output is $\bar{C}_2$ (= $wL_2 + rK_2$). Similarly, the minimum cost of producing Q_1 units is $\bar{C}_1$, and the minimum cost for Q_3 units is $\bar{C}_3$.

Input combination F also lies on the highest possible isoquant (Q_2) costing only $\bar{C}_2$. Thus, L_2 units of labor and K_2 units of capital is the input combination that maximizes output when only $\bar{C}_2$ can be spent on inputs. Similarly, Q_1 and Q_3 are the maximum levels of output that can be produced when only $\bar{C}_1$ and $\bar{C}_3$, respectively, can be spent on inputs.

Returns to scale, a long-run concept, involves the effect on output of changing all inputs by equiproportionate amounts. If all inputs are increased by a factor of c and output goes up by a factor of z, then a firm experiences: Increasing returns to scale if $z > c$; constant returns to scale if $z = c$; and decreasing returns to scale if $z < c$.

Now that we have demonstrated how a manager can find the cost-minimizing input combination when more than one input is variable, we can derive the cost curves facing a manager in the long run. The structure of long-run cost curves is determined by the structure of long-run production, as reflected in the expansion path.

11.7 LONG-RUN COSTS

Recall from Chapter 10 that the long run is not some particular date in the future. The long run simply means that all inputs are variable to the firm. One of the first decisions to be made by the firm is to determine the scale of operations, that is, the size of the firm. To make this decision, a manager must know the cost of producing each relevant level of output. As emphasized above, just as short-run cost is derived from the short-run production function, long-run cost is derived from the long-run expansion path, to which we now turn.

Derivation of Cost Schedules from a Production Function

As we have throughout this chapter, we assume that the firm's levels of usage of the inputs do not affect the prices that must be paid for the inputs—the manager takes input prices as given. We also continue to assume that the only two inputs used in production are labor and capital. We begin the discussion with a situation in which the price of labor (w) is \$5 per unit and the price of capital (r) is \$10 per unit. Figure 11.9 shows a portion of the firm's expansion path. Isoquants Q_1, Q_2, and Q_3 are associated, respectively, with 100, 200, and 300 units of output.

For the given set of input prices, the isocost curve with intercepts of 12 units of capital and 24 units of labor, which clearly has a slope of –5/10 (= $-w/r$), shows the least cost method of producing 100 units of output: use 10 units of labor and 7 units of capital. If the firm wants to produce 100 units, it spends \$50 (\$5 × 10) on labor and \$70 (\$10 × 7) on capital, giving it a total cost of \$120.

long-run average cost (*LAC*) Long-run total cost divided by output ($LAC = LTC/Q$).

long-run marginal cost (*LMC*) The change in long-run total cost per unit change in output ($LMC = \Delta LTC/\Delta Q$).

Similar to the short run, we define **long-run average cost** as

$$LAC = \frac{\text{Long-run total cost } (LTC)}{\text{Output } (Q)}$$

and **long-run marginal cost** as

$$LMC = \frac{\Delta LTC}{\Delta Q}$$

Therefore at an output of 100,

$$LAC = \frac{LTC}{Q} = \frac{\$120}{100} = \$1.20$$

Since there are no fixed inputs in the long run, there is no fixed cost when output is zero. Thus, the long-run marginal cost of producing the first 100 units is

FIGURE 11.9
Long-Run Expansion Path

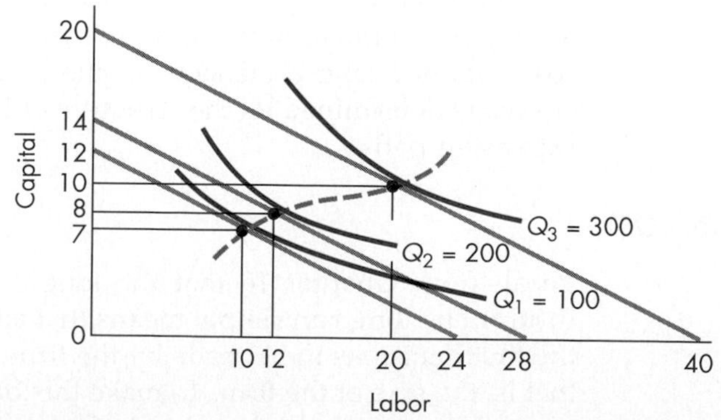

$$LMC = \frac{\Delta LTC}{\Delta Q} = \frac{\$120 - 0}{100 - 0} = \$1.20$$

The first row of Table 11.1 gives the level of output, the least-cost combination of labor and capital that can produce that output, and the long-run total, average, and marginal costs when output is 100 units.

Returning to Figure 11.9, you can see that the least-cost method of producing 200 units of output is to use 12 units of labor and 8 units of capital. Thus, producing 200 units of output costs \$140 (= \$5 × 12 + \$10 × 8). The average cost is \$0.70 (= \$140/200) and, since producing the additional 100 units increases total cost from \$120 to \$140, the marginal cost is \$0.20 (= \$20/100). These figures are shown in the second row of Table 11.1, and they give additional points on the firm's long-run total, average, and marginal cost curves.

Figure 11.9 shows that the firm will use 20 units of labor and 10 units of capital to produce 300 units of output. Using the same method as before, we calculate total, average, and marginal costs, which are given in row 3 of Table 11.1.

Figure 11.9 shows only three of the possible cost-minimizing choices. But, if we were to go on, we could obtain additional least-cost combinations, and in the same way as above, we could calculate the total, average, and marginal costs of these other outputs. This information is shown in the last four rows of Table 11.1 for output levels from 400 through 700.

Thus, at the given set of input prices and with the given technology, column 4 shows the long-run total cost schedule, column 5 the long-run average cost schedule, and column 6 the long-run marginal cost schedule. The corresponding long-run total cost curve is given in Panel A, Figure 11.10. This curve shows the least cost at which each quantity of output in Table 11.1 can be produced when no input is fixed. Its shape depends exclusively on the production function and the input prices.

This curve reflects three of the commonly assumed characteristics of long-run total cost. First, because there are no fixed costs, *LTC* is zero when output is zero. Second, cost and output are directly related; that is, *LTC* has a positive

TABLE 11.1

Derivation of a Long-Run Cost Schedule

(1)	(2) Least cost combination of	(3)	(4)	(5)	(6)
Output	Labor (units)	Capital (units)	Total cost (w = \$5, r = \$10)	Average cost (*LAC*)	Marginal cost (*LMC*)
100	10	7	\$120	\$1.20	\$1.20
200	12	8	140	0.70	0.20
300	20	10	200	0.67	0.60
400	30	15	300	0.75	1.00
500	40	22	420	0.84	1.20
600	52	30	560	0.93	1.40
700	60	42	720	1.03	1.60

FIGURE 11.10
Long-Run Total, Average, and Marginal Cost

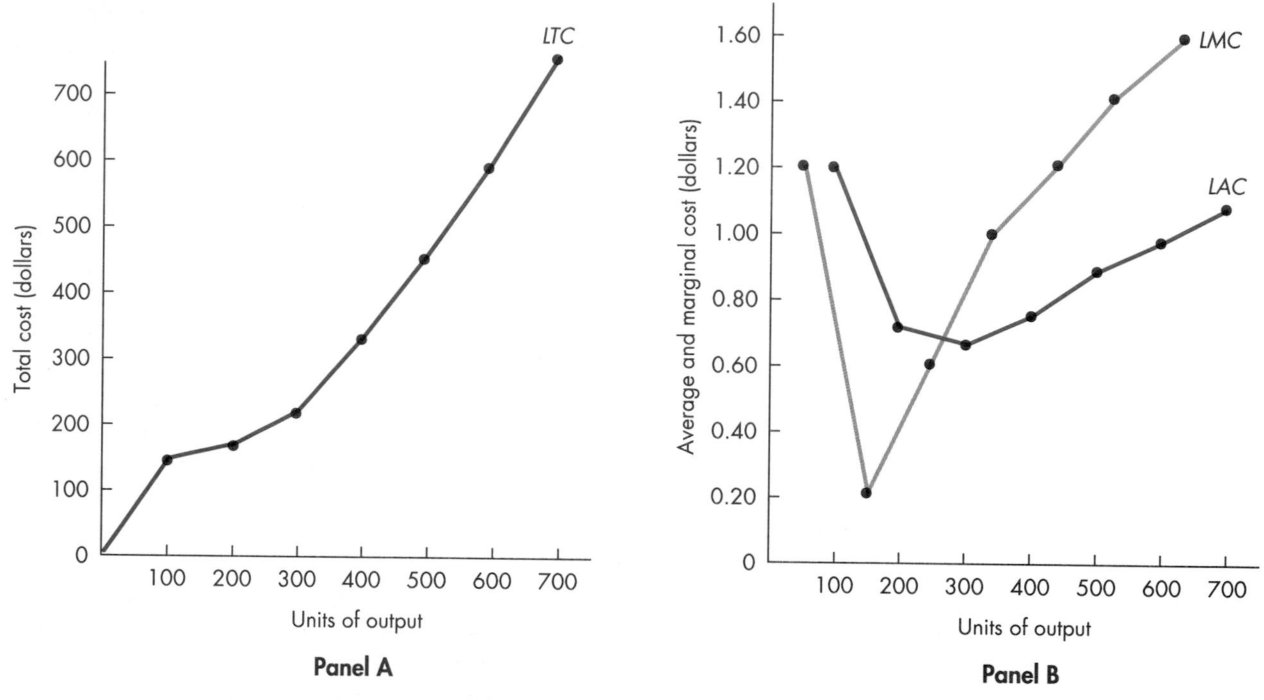

slope. It costs more to produce more, which is to say that resources are scarce or that one never gets something for nothing. Third, *LTC* first increases at a decreasing rate, then increases at an increasing rate. This implies that marginal cost first decreases, then increases.

Turn now to the long-run average and marginal cost curves derived from Table 11.1 and shown in Panel B of Figure 11.10. These curves reflect the characteristics of typical *LAC* and *LMC* curves. They have essentially the same shape as in the short run—but, as we shall show below, for different reasons. Long-run average cost first decreases, reaches a minimum (at 300 units of output), then increases. Long-run marginal cost first declines, reaches its minimum at a lower output than that associated with minimum *LAC* (between 100 and 200 units), then increases thereafter.

In Figure 11.10, marginal cost crosses the average cost curve at approximately the minimum of average cost. As we will show below, when output and cost are allowed to vary continuously, *LMC* crosses *LAC* at exactly the minimum point on the latter. (It is only approximate in Figure 11.10 because output varies discretely in the table.)

The reasoning is the same as that given for short-run average and marginal cost curves. When marginal cost is less than average cost, each additional unit

FIGURE 11.11
Long-Run Average and Marginal Cost Curves

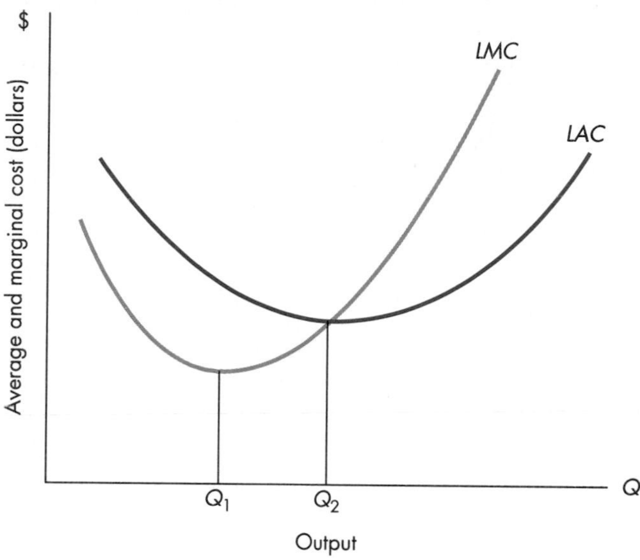

produced adds less than average cost to total cost, so average cost must decrease. When marginal cost is greater than average cost, each additional unit of the good produced adds more than average cost to total cost, so average cost must be increasing over this range of output. Thus, marginal cost must be equal to average cost when average cost is at its minimum.

Figure 11.11 shows long-run marginal and average cost curves that reflect the typically assumed characteristics when output and cost can vary continuously.

Relations As illustrated in Figure 11.11, (1) Long-run average cost, defined as

$$LAC = \frac{LTC}{Q}$$

first declines, reaches a minimum (here at Q_2 units of output), then increases. (2) When *LAC* is at its minimum, long-run marginal cost, defined as

$$LMC = \frac{\Delta LTC}{\Delta Q}$$

equals LAC. (3) *LMC* first declines, reaches a minimum (here at Q_1, less than Q_2), then increases. *LMC* lies below *LAC* over the range in which *LAC* declines; it lies above *LAC* when *LAC* is rising.

Economies and Diseconomies of Scale

Thus far we have concentrated exclusively on describing the generally assumed shapes of the long-run cost curves as depicted in Figure 11.11. We are now ready to analyze the economic forces behind these shapes. The economic forces that

ILLUSTRATION 11.1

Downsize, Upsize: What is the Right Size?

Our discussion of why economies and diseconomies of scale exist may have given you the impression that economies and diseconomies are unavoidable and beyond the control of a firm's management. To some extent this is correct; the production function and the state of technology determine the range of economies and diseconomies of scale. The manager of a firm does, however, choose the size of the firm which, in turn, determines where the firm will operate on the long-run average cost curve. The manager's choice of firm size is often subject to a great deal of uncertainty, since the precise shape of *LAC* is not known with certainty. Firm management sometimes makes decisions about firm size that turn out to be incorrect, and may choose a size or scale that is either too small or too large. A number of recent business articles in *The Wall Street Journal* illustrate how firms have been affected by past decisions about firm size. Some of these decisions turned out well, others did not turn out well.

What can firms too small to compete effectively with larger firms in the market do to enhance their competitive position? For two personal computer manufacturers the answer was to merge their businesses. In May 1993, AST Research, the eighth largest US PC producer, agreed to acquire the personal computer business of Tandy Corporation, the seventh largest US producer. This merger would move AST into fourth place in the industry. Recent price wars had hurt the two firms, and according to one industry analyst, "Computer makers like AST have been forced to look to high volume sales for profit [with the] focus on turning out [units] more efficiently and at lower cost."

According to the *WSJ*, the acquisition of Tandy's business would provide some innovative new products and better economies of scale for AST. The economies would come from AST's acquired ability to expand into new markets and increase its market share. The merger would help it establish a direct consumer sales channel through Tandy's 6,600 Radio Shack stores and other chains of computer stores. In essence, AST wanted Tandy's sales capacity in order to achieve previously unattainable economies of scale, thereby leading to lower costs and enhanced ability to compete by reducing prices.

Sometimes firms are actually too big to compete successfully with smaller rivals that have lower per unit costs. *The Wall Street Journal* reports that many of Japan's biggest steel producers have become too large and are being outperformed by smaller, more efficient firms. Nippon Steel Corporation, the biggest steelmaker in the world's number one steel-producing country, symbolizes the problem facing firms that grow too large. Close to Nippon's largest mill, the little Tokyo Steel Company opened a plant that was 1/20 the size of traditional Japanese steel mills but five times as efficient. The new mill undercut the prices of Nippon and other big steelmakers by 39 percent. According to the *WSJ*, Tokyo Steel planned to build two more "minimills." Other small Japanese steel producers were following suit with more small mills. Big Steel in Japan was beginning to look like Big Steel in the US had a decade before. Net profits in Japan's largest three steel producers were down between 77 percent and 92 percent. And, according to a study by

explain the shape of long-run cost curves are economies and diseconomies of scale.

economies of scale
Occur when long-run average cost falls as output increases.

diseconomies of scale
Occur when long-run average cost rises as output increases.

Economies of scale occur when long-run average cost falls as output increases. In Figure 11.11, economies of scale exist over the range of output from zero units up to Q_2 units of output. **Diseconomies of scale** occur when the long-run average cost rises as output increases. Diseconomies of scale set in beyond Q_2 units of output in Figure 11.11. We first discuss why economists believe economies of scale exist, and then we present some reasons why firms may eventually experience diseconomies of scale.

Paine-Webber, Nippon's largest mill did not even rank among the 40 lowest cost steel producers in the world.

The trend was worldwide. "Large, high-volume 'integrated' plants with disjointed production lines are giving way to small plants with faster, cheaper production methods that can adjust quickly to demand variations." The president of the world's second largest steelmaker said, "It's quite sure that in the future the largest part of steel will be produced in smaller mills." The chairman of another large steel firm observed, "If the integrated [plants] take this chance to restructure, they can keep their position. If not, newcomers will take it." But, the *Journal* was less optimistic for the huge firms: "Unlike nimbler minimill operators, however, many old-line makers remain saddled with slow-moving corporate cultures, bloated staffs, and huge investments in increasingly outdated mills." It appears then that the largest steelmakers had become too large and inflexible because of, among other things, serious managerial diseconomies of scale.

During the 1980s and early 1990s many huge corporations that had become too large and unwieldy and were moving into the range of serious diseconomies of scale began trying a new plan: decentralized management. This involved breaking the company into smaller, semi-autonomous units that would presumably become more flexible and more responsive to consumer demand. It didn't always work out that way. *The Wall Street Journal* stated, "A growing number of US companies are now reasserting central authority over a range of corporate activities."

In many cases decentralization had left the corporation in worse shape than it had been with highly centralized management. The *Journal* pointed out some prominent examples. Two years previously, Kentucky Fried Chicken, in a quality improvement plan, established autonomous regional divisions. They failed, however, to coordinate plans and ended up with three different plans in different parts of the country to improve service. A vice president complained, "There was so much redundance [that] the process became dysfunctional." Levi Strauss was replacing six order-processing computer systems with one system under centralized control. Retailers were complaining that they had to deal with too many different divisions, each with its own procedures.

For many firms, decentralization has led to considerable duplication and increases in cost. Businesses had expected that decentralization would save money. But as the CEO of a Boston concern noted, "The notion that you can reduce the overhead by dispersing it just hasn't worked out. You don't reduce costs by dividing the problem up and shipping it out of town."

These illustrations are intended to show that finding the "correct size" can be elusive and tricky in many cases. Just because a correct size may exist, finding it may prove quite difficult. Finding the correct size for the firm is one of the key strategic decisions that determines the firm's competitive strength.

Ken Yamada and Kyle Pope, "AST to Acquire PC Business of Tandy Corporation," *The Wall Street Journal*, May 27, 1993.

Dana Milbank, "Big Steel is Threatened by Low-Cost Rivals, Even in Japan, Korea," *The Wall Street Journal*, February 2, 1993.

Gilbert Fuchsberg, "Decentralized Management Can Have Its Drawbacks," *The Wall Street Journal*, December 9, 1992.

Probably the most fundamental reason for economies of scale is that larger scale firms are able to take greater advantage of opportunities for specialization and division of labor. When the number of workers is expanded in the short run, with a fixed stock of capital equipment, the opportunities for specialization and division of labor are rapidly exhausted. The marginal product curve rises, to be sure, but not for long. It very quickly reaches its maximum and declines. But, in the long run, when workers and equipment are expanded together, very substantial gains may be reaped by division of jobs and the specialization of workers in one job or another.

Proficiency is also gained by concentration of effort. If a plant is small and employs only a small number of workers, each worker will usually have to perform several different jobs in the production process. In doing so, a worker is likely to have to move about the plant, change tools, and so on. Not only are workers not highly specialized but a part of their work time is consumed in moving about and changing tools. Thus, important savings may be realized by expanding the scale of operation. A larger plant with a larger work force may permit each worker to specialize in one job, gaining proficiency and decreasing or eliminating time-consuming interchanges of location and equipment. There naturally will be corresponding reductions in the unit cost of production.

Technological factors constitute a second force contributing to economies of scale. If several different machines, each with a different rate of output, are required in a production process, the operation may have to be quite sizable to permit proper meshing of equipment. Suppose only two types of machines are required, one that produces the product and one that packages it. If the first machine can produce 30,000 units per day and the second can package 45,000 units per day, output will have to be 90,000 units per day in order to utilize fully the capacity of each type of machine.

Another technological element is the fact that the cost of purchasing and installing larger machines is usually proportionately less than the cost of smaller machines. For example, a printing press that can run 200,000 papers per day does not cost 10 times as much as one that can run 20,000 per day—nor does it require 10 times as much building space, 10 times as many people to operate it, and so forth. Again, expanding size tends to reduce the unit cost of production.

A final technological element is perhaps the most important of all: as the scale of operation expands, there is usually a qualitative, as well as a quantitative, change in equipment. Consider ditchdigging. The smallest scale of operation is one worker and one shovel. But as the scale expands beyond a certain point, the firm does not simply continue to add workers and shovels. Shovel and most workers are replaced by a modern ditch-digging machine. In like manner, expansion of scale normally permits the introduction of various types of automation devices, all of which tend to reduce the unit cost of production.

Thus two broad forces, (1) specialization and division of labor and (2) technological factors, enable producers to reduce unit cost by expanding the scale of operation.[9] These forces give rise to the negatively sloped portion of the long-run average cost curve.

You may wonder why the long-run average cost curve would ever rise. After all possible economies of scale have been realized, why doesn't the curve become horizontal?

---

[9]This discussion of economies of scale has concentrated on physical and technological forces. There are financial reasons for economies of scale as well. Large-scale purchasing of raw and processed materials may enable the buyer to obtain more favorable prices (quantity discounts). The same is frequently true of advertising. As another example, financing of large-scale businesses is normally easier and less expensive: a nationally known business has access to organized security markets, so it may place its bonds and stocks on a more favorable basis. Bank loans also usually come easier and at lower interest rates to large, well-known corporations.

The rising portion of *LAC*, or diseconomies of scale, is generally attributed to limitations to efficient management. Managing any business entails controlling and coordinating a wide variety of activities—production, transportation, finance, sales, and so on. To perform these managerial functions efficiently, a manager must have accurate information, otherwise the essential decision making is done in ignorance.

As the scale of plant expands beyond a certain point, top management necessarily has to delegate responsibility and authority to lower echelon employees. Contact with the daily routine of operation tends to be lost, and efficiency of operation declines. Red tape and paperwork expand; management is generally not as efficient. Thus, the cost of the managerial function increases, as does the unit cost of production.

It is difficult to determine just when diseconomies of scale set in and when they become strong enough to outweigh the economies of scale. In businesses where economies of scale are negligible, diseconomies may soon become of paramount importance, causing *LAC* to turn up at a relatively small volume of output. Panel A of Figure 11.12 shows a long-run average cost curve for a firm of this type. In other cases, economies of scale are extremely important. Even after the efficiency of management begins to decline, technological economies of scale may offset the diseconomies over a wide range of output. Thus the *LAC* curve may not turn upward until a very large volume of output is attained. This case is illustrated in Panel B of Figure 11.12.

In many actual situations, however, neither of these extremes describes the behavior of *LAC*. A very modest scale of operation may enable a firm to capture all of the economies of scale, and diseconomies may not be incurred until the volume of output is very great. In this case, *LAC* would have a long horizontal section as shown in Panel C of Figure 11.12. Some economists and business

FIGURE 11.12
Various Shapes of *LAC*

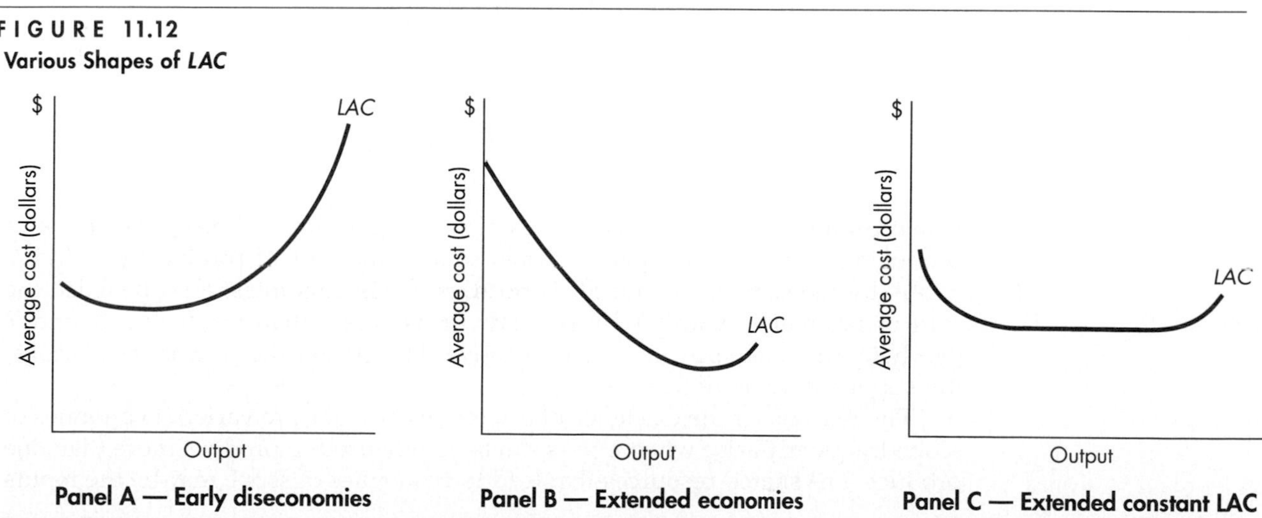

executives feel that this type of *LAC* curve describes many production processes in the American economy. For analytical purposes, however, we will assume a representative *LAC*, such as that illustrated earlier in Figure 11.11.

Economies of Scope

Many firms produce a number of different products. These multiproduct firms use inputs that contribute simultaneously to the production of two or more goods—a citrus orchard produces both oranges and grapefruit, an oil well produces both crude oil and natural gas, an automotive plant produces both cars and trucks, and commercial banks use the same assets to provide a variety of different financial services. Whenever it is less costly for a single firm to produce two or more products together rather than for separate firms to produce the same level of output for each product, **economies of scope** are said to exist.

economies of scope
Exist when the joint cost of producing two or more goods is less than the sum of the separate costs of producing the goods.

For example, consider Precision Mufflers, a firm that installs replacement mufflers and also repairs brakes. This firm uses inputs that simultaneously contribute to the production of two different services. Precision Mufflers can replace 25 mufflers and perform 10 brake jobs a day for a total cost of $1,400. A firm that specializes in muffler replacement can only install 25 replacement mufflers at a total cost of $1,000. Another firm that specializes in brake repair can perform 10 brake jobs for a total cost of $600. Since the joint cost of replacing 25 mufflers and fixing the brakes on 10 cars ($1,400) is less than the total cost of two separate firms producing the same level of outputs ($1,600 = $1,000 + $600), economies of scope exist.

Let $C(X)$ be the total cost of producing a given level of some good X by a single-product firm and $C(Y)$ be the total cost of producing a given level of another good Y by a single-product firm. If $C(X, Y)$ represents the cost of a single firm jointly producing the same levels of X and Y, economies of scope exist when

$$C(X,Y) < C(X) + C(Y)$$

The degree to which economies of scope exist (SC) can be measured by the fraction:

$$SC = \frac{C(X) + C(Y) - C(X, Y)}{C(X, Y)}$$

When production involves economies of scope, the sum of the separate costs of producing X and Y by separate firms exceeds the cost of producing X and Y jointly by the same firm, and SC is positive. If diseconomies of scope exist, the sum of producing X and Y by separate firms is less than producing X and Y jointly by the same firm, and SC is negative. The greater the economies of scope, the larger the value of SC.

The reasons for the existence of economies of scope are varied. Economies of scope frequently arise when inputs can be jointly used to produce more than one product. The shared resources that lead to economies of scope may be the inputs

ILLUSTRATION 11.2

Economies of Scale and Scope in Banking

During the 1980s, the banking industry in the United States experienced an unprecedented period of deregulation. One of the key results of this deregulation has been widespread legislative changes by state legislatures allowing interstate banking activities. By 1990, only three states completely prohibited interstate banking. One of the most controversial effects of interstate banking is the consolidation currently taking place through mergers and acquisitions of local banks by large, out-of-state banks. According to Robert Goudreau and Larry Wall, the primary incentives for interstate expansion appear to be to gain market power, to diversify earnings, and to exploit economies of scale and scope.* To the extent that significant economies of scale exist in banking, large banks will have a cost advantage over small banks. If there are economies of scope in banking, then banks offering more banking services (products) will have lower costs than banks that provide a small number of services.

Two recent empirical studies have attempted to measure both economies of scale and scope in the financial services industry. John Murray and Robert White studied 61 credit unions in British Columbia.† They found significant economies of scale in the credit union industry. Larger credit unions had lower long-run average costs than smaller ones. They also found evidence of economies of scope for credit unions offering a full line of consumer loans and mortgage loans. Thus, those credit unions that offered automobile loans as well as home mortgage loans could provide mortgage loans and automobile loans at a lower cost than credit unions specializing only in home mortgages or only in automobile loans.

In another study, Thomas Gilligan, Michael Smirlock, and William Marshall examined 714 commercial banks to determine the extent of economies of scale and scope in commercial banking.‡ They conclude that economies of scale in banking are exhausted at relatively low output levels. In other words, the long-run average cost curve (*LRAC*) for commercial banks is shaped like *LRAC* in Panel C of Figure 11.12. When *LRAC* reaches its minimum value at relatively low levels of output, small banks are not necessarily at a cost disadvantage when they compete with large banks. Economies of scope also appear to be present for banks producing the traditional set of bank products (various types of loans and deposits). Given their empirical evidence that economies of scale do not extend over a wide range of output, Gilligan, Smirlock, and Marshall argue that public policy makers should not encourage bank mergers on the basis of cost savings. They also point out that government regulations restricting the types of loans and deposits that a bank may offer can lead to higher costs, given their evidence of economies of scope in banking.

*Robert Goudreau and Larry Wall, "Southeastern Interstate Banking and Consolidation: 1984–90," *Economic Review*, Federal Reserve Bank of Atlanta, November/December 1990, pp. 32–41.

†John Murray and Robert White, "Economies of Scale and Economies of Scope in Multiproduct Financial Institutions: A Study of British Columbia Credit Unions," *Journal of Finance*, June 1983, pp. 302–21.

‡Thomas Gilligan, Michael Smirlock, and William Marshall, "Scale and Scope Economies in the Multi-Product Banking Firm," *Journal of Monetary Economics* 13, (1984), pp. 393–405.

used in the manufacture of the product, whereas in some cases it may involve only the administrative and marketing resources of the firm. In other cases, the production process may involve joint products for which the production of one good results in the production of another good at little or no extra cost. Examples of joint products are beef and leather, wood and mutton, chickens and fertilizer, and sometimes crude oil and natural gas.

Relation Economies of scope exist when the joint cost of producing two or more goods is less than the sum of the separate costs of producing the goods. In the case of two goods X and Y, economies of scope are measured by

$$SC = \frac{C(X) + C(Y) - C(X, Y)}{C(X, Y)}$$

where SC is greater (less) than zero when (dis)economies of scope exist.

11.8 RELATIONS BETWEEN SHORT-RUN AND LONG-RUN COST

We can summarize the discussion of cost thus far by noting that firms *plan* in the long run and *operate* in the short run. Indeed, we call the long run the firm's planning horizon. The long-run cost function gives the most efficient (the least cost) method of producing any given level of output, because all inputs are variable. But once a particular firm size is chosen and the firm begins producing, the firm is in the short run. Plant and equipment have already been constructed. Now if the firm wishes to change its level of output, it can't vary the usage of all inputs. Some inputs, the plant and so forth, are fixed to the firm. Thus the firm cannot vary all inputs optimally and therefore cannot produce this new level of output at the lowest possible cost.

Such a situation is shown in Figure 11.13 where LAC is the firm's long-run average cost curve. Suppose that when making its plans, the firm had decided that it wanted to produce Q_0 units of output per period. It chooses the optimal combination of inputs to produce this output at the lowest possible cost. At this least cost, the average cost of producing Q_0 units is LTC_0 in the figure. Since it would not wish to vary any of its inputs so long as it continues to produce Q_0—and so long as input prices and technology remain the same—the short-run

FIGURE 11.13

Long-Run and Short-Run Average Cost Curves

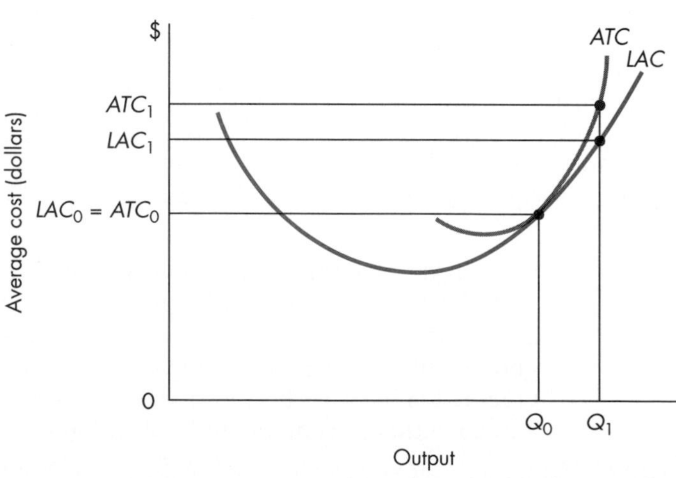

average total cost of producing Q_0 is the same as the long-run average cost ($ATC_0 = LAC_0$).

Thus the short-run average total cost curve, *ATC*, equals and is tangent to *LAC* at Q_0. But, since some inputs are fixed in the short run, if the firm wants to vary its output in the short run, it cannot produce this new output at the lowest possible cost. At any output other than Q_0, the short-run input combination is not the least-cost combination; it would result in a higher total and average cost than the combination that would be chosen if all inputs were variable.

Suppose, for example, that the firm wants to increase its output from Q_0 to Q_1. If all inputs were variable, it could produce this output at an average cost of LAC_1. But if plant and some other inputs are fixed, *ATC* gives the average cost of producing Q_1. This average cost is ATC_1, which is clearly higher than LAC_1 because total cost is greater in the short run than in the long run. And, because total cost is greater in the short run than in the long run at any output other than Q_0, *ATC* will be higher than *LAC*. Only at Q_0 are the two average costs the same.

Figure 11.14 shows the typical relation between short- and long-run average and marginal cost curves. In this figure, *LAC* and *LMC* are the long-run average and marginal cost curves. Three short-run situations are indicated by the three sets of curves: ATC_1, SMC_1; ATC_2, SMC_2; and ATC_3, SMC_3.

First look at ATC_1 and SMC_1. These are the short-run curves for the plant size designed to produce output Q_S optimally. The long-run and short-run average cost curves are tangent at this output. Since marginal cost, $\Delta C/\Delta Q$, is given by the slope of the total cost curve, long-run marginal cost equals short-run marginal cost at the output given by the point of tangency, Q_S. Finally, short-run marginal cost crosses short-run average cost at the latter's minimum point. Note that because Q_S is on the decreasing portion of *LAC*, ATC_1 must be decreasing also at the point of tangency.

FIGURE 11.14
Long-Run and Short-Run Average and Marginal Costs

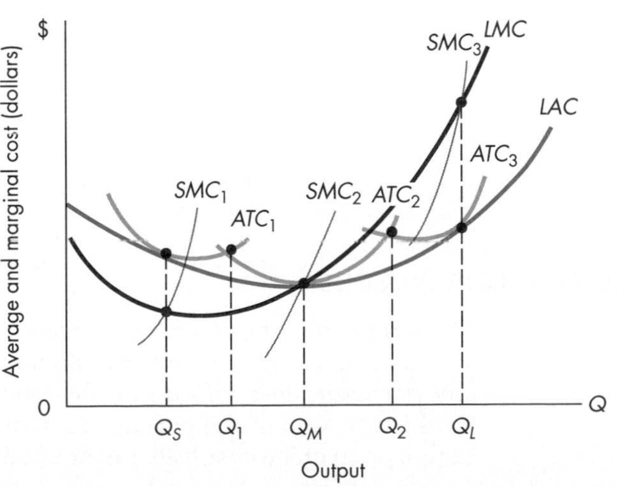

ATC_3 and SMC_3 show another short-run situation—a different plant size. Here tangency occurs at Q_L on the increasing part of LAC. Thus, ATC_3 is increasing at this point also. Again the two marginal curves are equal at Q_L, and SMC_3 crosses ATC_3 at the minimum point on the latter.

Finally, ATC_2 is the short-run average cost curve corresponding to the output level—plant size—at which long-run average cost is at its minimum. At output level Q_M, the two average cost curves are tangent. The two marginal cost curves, SMC_2 and LMC, are also equal at this output. And, since both average cost curves attain their minimum at Q_M, the two marginal cost curves must intersect the two average cost curves. Thus, all four curves are equal at output Q_M. That is, at Q_M, $LAC = ATC_2 = SMC_2 = LMC$.

If the firm is limited to producing with only one of the three short-run cost structures shown in Figure 11.14, it would choose the cost structure—plant size—given by ATC_1 to produce outputs from zero to Q_1, because the average cost, and hence the total cost, of producing each output over this range is lower under this cost specification. If it wishes to produce any output between Q_1 and Q_2 it would choose the plant size given by ATC_2. This average cost curve lies below either of the other two for any output over this range. It would choose the cost structure shown by ATC_3 for any level of output greater than Q_2

But typically the firm is not limited to three sizes—large, medium, or small. In the long run it can build the plant of the size that leads to lowest average cost at whatever level of output is chosen. The long-run average cost curve is a planning device, because this curve shows the least cost of producing each possible output. Managers therefore are normally faced with a choice among a wide variety of plant sizes.

The long-run planning curve, LAC, is a locus of points representing the lowest possible unit cost of producing the corresponding output. The manager determines the desired size of plant by reference to this curve, selecting the short-run plant that yields the lowest unit cost of producing the volume of output desired.

Relations (1) *LMC* intersects *LAC* when the latter is at its minimum point. There exists some short-run plant size for which the minimum *ATC* coincides with minimum *LAC*. (2) At each output where a particular *ATC* is tangent to *LAC*, the relevant *SMC* equals *LMC*. At outputs below (above) the tangency output, the relevant *SMC* is less (greater) than *LMC*. (3) For all *ATC* curves, the point of tangency with *LAC* is at an output less (greater) than the output of minimum *ATC* if the tangency is at an output less (greater) than that associated with minimum *LAC*.

11.9 SUMMARY OF LONG-RUN COST

The long-run cost curves are derived from the expansion path. Since the expansion path gives the efficient combination of labor and capital used to produce any particular level of output, the long-run total cost of producing that output level is the sum of the optimal amounts of labor and capital times their prices. Long-run average cost (LAC) is defined as

$$LAC = LTC/Q$$

and is U-shaped. Long-run marginal cost (*LMC*) is defined as

$$LMC = \Delta LTC/\Delta Q$$

and is also U-shaped. *LMC* lies below (above) *LAC* over the output range for which *LAC* is decreasing (increasing). *LMC* crosses *LAC* at the minimum point on *LAC*. When *LAC* is decreasing, economies of scale are present. When *LAC* is increasing, diseconomies are present.

When a firm produces more than one good or service, economies of scope may be present. Economies of scope exist when the joint cost of producing two or more goods is less than the sum of the separate costs of producing the goods. In the case of two goods *X* and *Y*, economies of scope are measured by

$$SC = \frac{C(X) + C(Y) - C(X, Y)}{C(X, Y)}$$

where *SC* is greater (less) than zero when (dis)economies of scope exist.

We have distinguished between cost in the short run and cost in the long run. The relations between long-run and short-run cost can be summarized by the following points: (1) at each output at which a particular *ATC* is tangent to *LAC*, the relevant *SMC* equals *LMC*; (2) there exists some short-run plant size for which the minimum *ATC* coincides with minimum *LAC*; and (3) except for the output level at which *ATC* = *LAC*, cost is always higher in the short run than in the long run for every short-run situation.

While the cost of production is important to business firms and to the economy as a whole, it is only half the story. Cost gives one aspect of economic activity; it is the obligation to pay out funds. The other aspect is revenue or demand. To the individual manager, revenue constitutes the flow of funds from which the obligation may be met.

Thus, both demand and cost must be taken into consideration. After discussing empirical estimation of production and cost in the next chapter, we will combine our theories of demand and cost to analyze firms' supply decisions.

TECHNICAL PROBLEMS

1. Suppose a firm is currently using 500 laborers and 325 units of capital to produce its product. The wage rate is \$25, and the price of capital is \$130. The last laborer adds 25 units to total output, while the last unit of capital adds 65 units to total output. Is the manager of this firm making the optimal input choice? Why or why not? If not, what should the manager do?
2. An expansion path can be derived under the assumption either that the manager attempts to produce each output at minimum cost or that the manager attempts to produce the maximum output at each level of cost. The paths are identical in both cases. Explain why.
3. In the graph on the following page, *LZ* is the isocost curve and Q_1 is an isoquant.
   a. For input combination *A*, MP_L/w is ________ than MP_K/r. Explain, in terms of MP_L/w and MP_K/r, why combination *A* is not efficient.

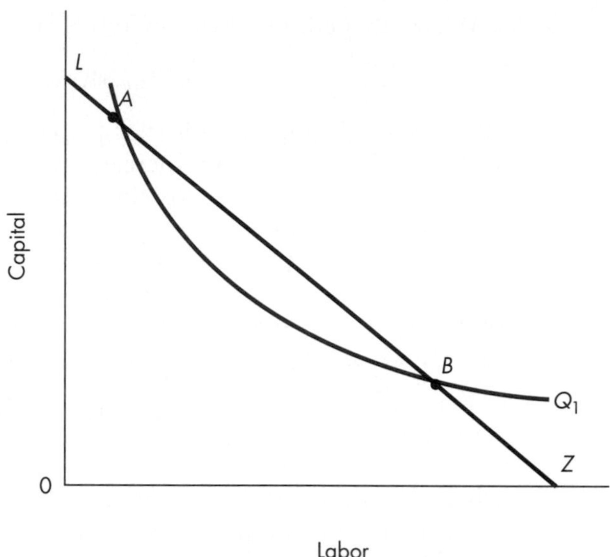

b. For input combination B, MP_L/w is ________ than MP_K/r. Explain, in terms of MP_L/w and MP_K/r, why combination B is not efficient.

c. In the graph, find and label the optimal input combination for producing the output designated by isoquant Q_1. (Hint: You need to use the straight edge of a ruler.)

* 4. In the following graph, the price of capital is $100 per unit.

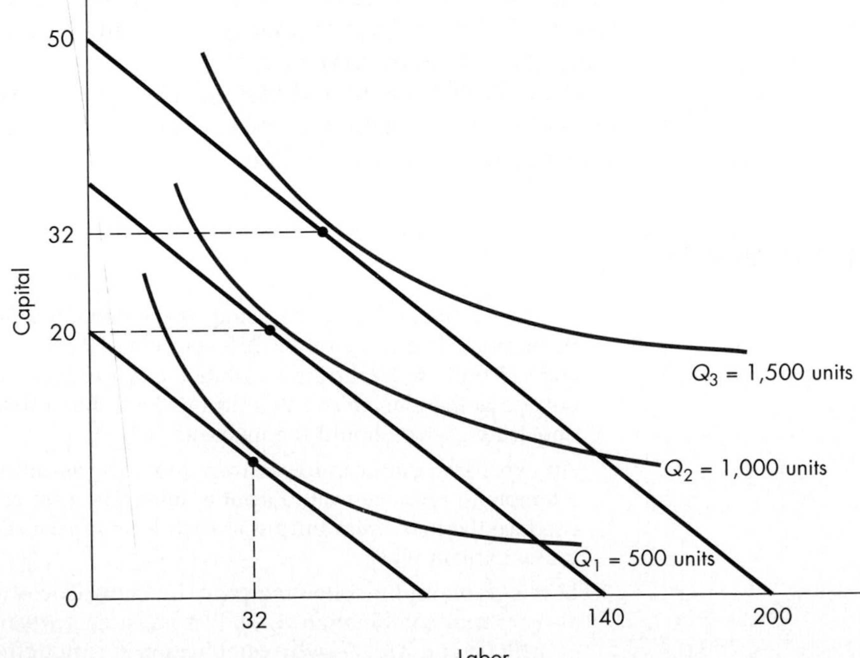

a. The price of labor is $________.

b. To produce 500 units efficiently, a manager would use ________ units of labor and ________ units of capital. The minimum cost of producing 500 units is $________.

c. To produce 1,000 units efficiently, a manager would use ________ units of labor and ________ units of capital. The minimum cost of producing 1,000 units is $________.

d. To produce 1,500 units efficiently, a manager would use ________ units of labor and ________ units of capital. The minimum cost of producing 1,500 units is $________.

e. In the graph, construct the expansion path.

f. Along the expansion path constructed in question *e*, the marginal rate of technical substitution is equal to ________.

5. In the following graph, the isoquants Q_1, Q_2, and Q_3 are associated with, respectively, 1,000, 2,000, and 3,000 units of output. The price of capital is $2 and the price of labor is $1.

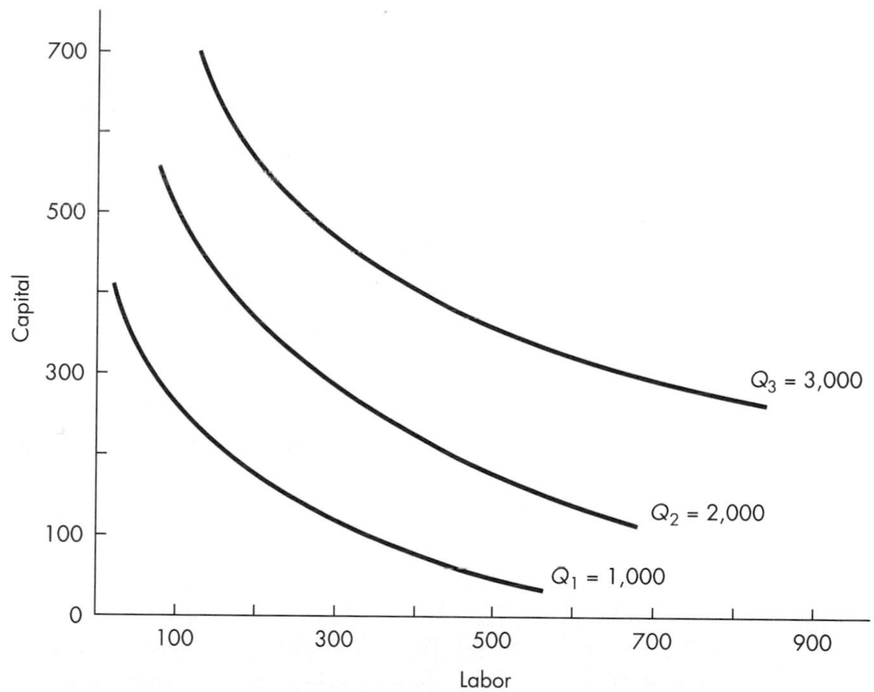

a. Find the least-cost input combination for 1,000, 2,000, and 3,000 units of output. (Hint: Use a ruler to construct the appropriate isocost curves.)

b. Construct the expansion path. What is the marginal rate of technical substitution along this path?

c. What is the minimum cost of producing each level of output?

d. Now let the price of labor be $2 and the price of capital be $1. Construct the new expansion path. What is the minimum cost of producing each level of output?

* 6. The graph below shows five points on a firm's expansion path when the price of labor is $25 per unit and the price of capital is $100 per unit.

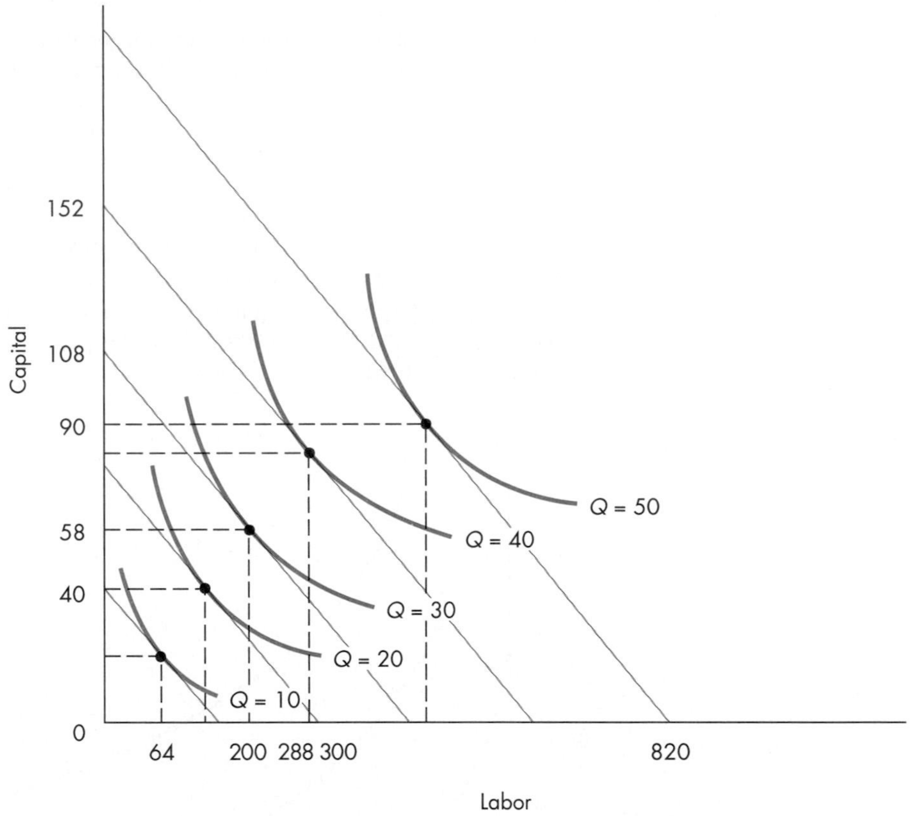

a. From this graph, fill in the blanks in the following table.

Q	*L*	*K*	*LTC*	*LAC*	*LMC*
10	____	____	____	____	____
20	____	____	____	____	____
30	____	____	____	____	____
40	____	____	____	____	____
50	____	____	____	____	____

b. Economies of scale exist over the range of output _______ to _______ units.
Diseconomies of scale exist over the range of output _______ to _______ units.

7. Explain why long-run average cost first falls, then rises. Why does short-run average variable cost first fall, then rise?
8. Explain why short-run marginal cost is greater than long-run marginal cost beyond the point at which they are equal.
9. Explain why short-run average cost can never be less than long-run average cost.

10. Using the example in the text concerning Precision Muffler, calculate the degree to which economies of scope exist (*SC*) when producing 25 muffler replacements and 10 brake jobs. Are there economies or diseconomies of scope?

APPLIED PROBLEMS

1. A study by the Computer Manufacturers Association of America analyzed the significant increase in the usage of computers by business firms in the United States over the last two decades. In terms of production theory, one might say the computer-labor ratio has risen.
   a. Using production theory, provide a rationale for this trend.
   b. Given the falling prices of business computers, what types of changes in business offices would you expect to have occurred?
2. The Largo Publishing House uses 400 printers and 200 printing presses to produce books. A printer's wage rate is \$20, and the price of a printing press is \$5,000. The last printer added 20 books to total output, while the last press added 1,000 books to total output. Is the publishing house making the optimal input choice? Why or why not? If not, how should the manager of Largo Publishing House adjust input usage?
3. How does the theory of efficient production apply to managers of government bureaus or departments that are not run for profit? How about nonprofit clubs that collect just enough dues from their members to cover the cost of operation?
4. The MorTex Company assembles garments entirely by hand even though a textile machine exists which can assemble garments faster than a human can. Workers cost \$50 per day, and each additional laborer can produce 200 more units per day (i.e., marginal product is constant and equal to 200). Installation of the first textile machine on the assembly line will increase output by 1,800 units daily. Currently the firm assembles 5,400 units per day.
   a. The financial analysis department at MorTex estimates that the price of a textile machine is \$600 per day. Can management reduce the cost of assembling 5,400 units per day by purchasing a textile machine and using less labor? Why or why not?
   b. The Textile Workers of America is planning to strike for higher wages. Management predicts that, if the strike is successful, the cost of labor will increase to \$100 per day. If the strike is successful, how would this affect the decision in question *a* to purchase a textile machine? Explain.
5. Gamma Corporation, one of the firms that retains you as a financial analyst, is considering buying out Beta Corporation, a small manufacturing firm that is now barely operating at a profit. You recommend the buyout because you believe that new management could substantially reduce production costs, and thereby increase profit to a quite attractive level. You collect the following product information in order to convince the CEO at Gamma Corporation that Beta is indeed operating inefficiently:

$$MP_L = 10 \qquad P_L = \$20$$
$$MP_K = 15 \qquad P_K = \$15$$

   Explain how these data provide evidence of inefficiency. How could the new manager of Beta Corporation improve efficiency?

6. Engineers at a national research laboratory built a prototype automobile that could be driven 180 miles on a single gallon of unleaded gasoline. In mass production, they estimated that the car would cost $40,000 per unit to build. The engineers argued that Congress should force US automakers to build this energy-efficient car.
   a. Is energy efficiency the same thing as economic efficiency? Explain.
   b. Under what circumstances would the energy-efficient automobile described above be economically efficient?
   c. If the goal of society is to get the most benefit from its limited resources, then why not ignore economic efficiency and build the energy-saving automobile?
7. *Business Week*, in an article dealing with management (October 22, 1984, p. 156), wrote "When he took over the furniture factory three years ago . . . [the manager] realized almost immediately that it was throwing away at least $100,000 a year worth of wood scrap. Within a few weeks, he set up a task force of managers and workers to deal with the problem. And within a few months, they reduced the amount of scrap to $7,000 worth." Was this necessarily an *economically efficient* move?
8. Government at all levels sometimes imposes regulations on business firms, such as pollution controls on the amount of emissions, safety regulations for workers, and requirements on access for handicapped workers or customers.
   a. How might such regulations be thought of as being negative technological change—that is, technological deterioration rather than technological improvement?
   b. What effect would such regulations be expected to have?
   c. Given your answer to part *b* of this question, is it still possible for such regulations to be efficient from the point of view of society? Explain.
9. We frequently hear several terms used by businesspersons. What do they mean in economic terminology?
   a. Spreading the overhead.
   b. A break-even level of production.
   c. The efficiency of mass production.
10. The production engineers at Impact Industries have derived the expansion path shown in the following figure. The price of labor is $100 per unit.

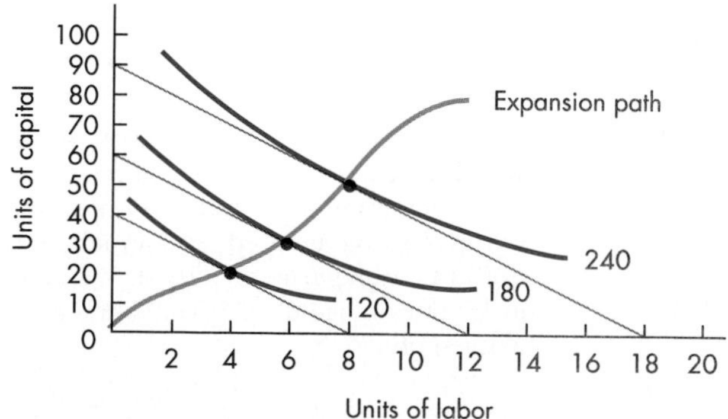

   a. What price does Impact Industries pay for capital?
   b. If the manager at Impact decides to produce 180 units of output, how much labor and capital should be used in order to minimize total cost?

c. What is the total cost of producing 120, 180, and 240 units of output in the long run?

d. Impact Industries originally built the plant (i.e., purchased the amount of capital) designed to produce 180 units optimally. *In the short run with capital fixed,* if the manager decides to expand production to 240 units, what is the amount of labor and capital that will be used? (Hint: How must the firm expand output in the short run when capital is fixed?)

e. Given your answer to part *d,* calculate average variable, average fixed, and average total cost in the short run.

11. Commercial bakeries typically sell a variety of products (breads, rolls, muffins, cakes, etc.) to local grocery stores. There are substantial economies of scale in production of each one of the bakery products, which makes it cost effective for bakeries to specialize in the production of just one product. Grocery stores, however, prefer to buy from multiproduct bakeries that sell a full line of bakery products. How might managers organize production to take advantage of the economies of scale and scope in production and marketing that exist in the baking industry?

12. *The Wall Street Journal* (February 26, 1993) reported that many members of the National Association of Home Builders were worried about the price of lumber, which had risen 85 percent since October. A poll found that 40 percent of builders indicated they would be using engineered wood and 9 percent said they would use some steel instead of wood. The *Journal* noted that steel and engineered wood still cost more than traditional lumber, but their prices were more stable. One builder noted that he could get a guaranteed price for engineered wood six months in advance compared to sometimes only a day for conventional lumber. Why would a cost-minimizing firm perhaps prefer stable but higher prices, to unstable but lower prices for inputs? Recall the previous discussion of uncertainty and risk.

APPENDIX Mathematical Derivation of Long-Run Production and Cost Relations

1. The marginal rate of technical substitution (*MRTS*) along an isoquant is the ratio of the marginal products of the two inputs.

Define the two-input production function as

$$Q = f(K,L)$$

The marginal products of the two inputs are

$$MP_L = \partial Q/\partial L \text{ and } MP_K = \partial Q/\partial K$$

Take the total differential of the production function and set $dQ = 0$ to force output to remain constant along a particular isoquant:

$$dQ = \frac{\partial Q}{\partial K}dK + \frac{\partial Q}{\partial L}dL = 0$$

Solving for the *MRTS*,

$$MRTS = -\frac{dK}{dL} = \frac{\partial Q/\partial L}{\partial L/\partial K} = \frac{MP_L}{MP_K}$$

2. Cost minimization requires that the *MRTS* equals the input-price ratio.

The firm wants to minimize cost, $C = rK + wL$, subject to the constraint that output is fixed at a specified level, $\overline{Q} - f(K,L)$. It is necessary to set up the Lagrangian function

$$\mathcal{L} = rK + wL + \lambda[\overline{Q} - f(K,L)]$$

where λ is the Lagrangian multiplier. Minimization with respect to the usage of capital and labor requires that the partial derivatives be equal to zero:

$$\frac{\partial \mathcal{L}}{\partial K} = r - \lambda\frac{\partial Q}{\partial K} = 0$$

$$\frac{\partial \mathcal{L}}{\partial L} = w - \lambda\frac{\partial Q}{\partial L} = 0$$

Combining these two conditions, it follows that the necessary condition for minimizing the cost of producing a given level of output is

$$\frac{r}{w} = \frac{\partial Q/\partial K}{\partial Q/\partial L}$$

or

$$\frac{\partial Q/\partial L}{\partial Q/\partial K} = \frac{MP_L}{MP_K} = MRTS = \frac{w}{r}$$

3. Output maximization requires that the *MRTS* equals the input-price ratio.

In this case, the firm wishes to maximize output, $Q = f(K,L)$, subject to a given level of expenditure, $\bar{C} = rK + wL$. We set up the Lagrangian function

$$\mathcal{L} = f(K,L) + \lambda(\bar{C} - rK - wL)$$

Maximization requires that the partial derivatives with respect to the choice variables, *K* and *L*, be set equal to zero:

$$\frac{\partial \mathcal{L}}{\partial K} = \frac{\partial Q}{\partial K} - \lambda r = 0$$

$$\frac{\partial \mathcal{L}}{\partial L} = \frac{\partial Q}{\partial L} - \lambda w = 0$$

Combining these necessary conditions, we obtain precisely the same result we obtained for cost minimization,

$$\frac{\partial Q/\partial K}{\partial Q/\partial L} = \frac{r}{w}$$

4. When long-run average cost, *LAC*, is increasing (decreasing), long-run marginal cost, *LMC*, is greater (less) than long-run average cost. *LMC* = *LAC* when *LAC* reaches its minimum value.

Let $LTC = C(Q)$. Thus, $LMC = d[C(Q)]/dQ$ and $LAC = C(Q)/Q$. Differentiating *LAC* with respect to *Q* yields:

$$\frac{d(LAC)}{dQ} = \frac{d(C/Q)}{dQ} = \frac{Q(dC/dQ) - C(Q)}{Q^2} = \frac{1}{Q}(LMC - LAC)$$

If *LAC* is rising, $d(LAC)/dQ > 0$; thus $LMC > LAC$. If *LAC* is falling, $d(LAC)/dQ < 0$; thus $LMC < LAC$. And if *LAC* is at its minimum value, $d(LAC)/dQ = 0$; thus, $LAC = LMC$.

CHAPTER

12 Empirical Analysis of Production and Cost

Managers use estimates of production and cost functions to make output, pricing, hiring, and investment decisions. Chapters 10 and 11 set forth the basic theories of production and cost. We will now show you some statistical techniques that can be used to estimate production and cost functions. The focus will be on estimating short-run production functions and short-run cost functions. These are the functions that managers need to make a firm's pricing, output, and hiring decisions. Although long-run production and cost functions can help mangers make long-run decisions about investments in plant and equipment, most of the analysis in this text concerns short-run operational decisions. Application of regression analysis to the estimation of short-run production and cost functions is a rather straightforward task. However, because of difficult problems with the data that are required to estimate long-run production and cost functions—as well as the more complex regression equations required—managers typically restrict their use of regression analysis to estimation of short-run production and cost functions.

empirical production function
The mathematical form of the production function to be estimated.

We begin by showing how to use regression analysis to estimate short-run production functions. The first step in estimating a production function and the associated product curves (such as average product and marginal product) is to specify the **empirical production function**, which is the exact mathematical form of the equation to be estimated. We discuss how to specify a cubic equation to estimate short-run production functions when only one input, labor, is variable. As you will see, the cubic equation has the properties of the theoretical short-run production function discussed in Chapter 10. Next, we explain how to estimate the parameters of the short-run production function and test for statistical significance.

After developing the techniques of empirical production analysis, we turn to estimation of short-run cost equations. The cubic specification is also employed to estimate the short-run cost functions. The analysis of empirical cost functions begins with a brief discussion of some general issues concerning the nature of estimating cost functions, such as adjusting for inflation and measurement of economic cost. We then explain how to estimate the various short-run cost functions derived in Chapter 10: the average variable cost (*AVC*), marginal cost (*MC*), and total variable cost (*TVC*) curves. Then we demonstrate how to estimate and test the parameters of these cost functions.

We must stress at the outset that the purpose here is not so much to teach you how to do the actual estimations of the functions, but rather to show how to use and interpret the estimates of production and cost equations. As emphasized in Chapter 5, the computer will do the tedious calculations involved with estimation. However, you must tell it what to estimate. Therefore, you should learn how to choose the particular function that is best suited for the purpose at hand.

As already noted, this chapter focuses primarily on short-run production and cost estimation. However, we have set forth the techniques used to estimate long-run production and cost functions in Appendix 12B at the end of this chapter. Once you see that application of regression analysis to short-run functions is rather easy, you may wish to tackle this more difficult appendix treating long-run empirical analysis.

12.1 SPECIFICATION OF THE SHORT-RUN PRODUCTION FUNCTION

Before describing how to estimate short-run production functions, we will first specify an appropriate functional form for the long-run production function. Recall from Chapter 10 that the short-run production function is derived from the long-run production function when holding the levels of some inputs constant. Once the fixed inputs are held constant at some predetermined levels and only one input is allowed to vary, the production equation to be estimated should have the theoretical characteristics set forth in Chapter 10.

In this chapter, we will continue to consider the case of two variable inputs, labor and capital. The most general form of such a production function is

$$Q = f(L, K)$$

In this form, the production function can be viewed as a **long-run production function** since both labor (L) and capital (K) are variable inputs. In the short run, when the level of capital usage is fixed at $\bar{K}$, the **short-run production function** is expressed in general form as

long-run production function
A production function in which all inputs are variable.

short-run production function
A production function in which at least one input is fixed.

$$Q = f(L, \bar{K}) = f(L)$$

The exact mathematical form of this production function is frequently referred to as the *estimable form* of the production function. In general, an **estimable form** of an equation—whether it is a production equation, cost equation, or any other type of equation—is the exact mathematical form of the equation that can be estimated using regression analysis. We will now specify an estimable form for the production function. We will first show you why a linear specification of the

estimable form
The form of an equation that can be estimated using regression analysis.

estimable form is inappropriate; then we will describe an appropriate nonlinear specification of the long-run and short-run production function.

Shortcomings of a Linear Specification

Given our earlier discussion of regression techniques, the mathematical form for the *long-run* production function that might first come to mind is a simple linear form,

$$Q = aK + bL$$

There are, however, two major problems with using this linear functional form for the long-run production function. First, in this form, it is not necessary to use positive amounts of both inputs in order to produce a positive level of output. For instance, let K equal zero. Output would then be equal to bL, which is greater than zero when any (positive) amount of labor is employed. Thus, production can take place without using any capital. (The same is true for labor.) A second problem arises because the isoquants are straight lines. While the isoquants would slope downward, they would not be convex, so the marginal rate of technical substitution (*MRTS*) is not diminishing.[1] These two problems indicate that a linear specification does not conform to the necessary theoretical characteristics of a long-run production function.

Consider also the linear specification for the *short-run* production function. Since capital is constant in the short run, the short-run production function is

$$\begin{aligned} Q = f(L, \bar{K}) &= a\bar{K} + bL \\ &= c + bL \end{aligned}$$

where $c = a\bar{K}$. Two problems make this linear production function an unsuitable specification of a *short-run production function*. First, when no labor is used, positive output is produced (when $L = 0$, $Q = c$). Second, because the marginal product of labor in this specification is

$$MP = \frac{\Delta Q}{\Delta L} = b$$

the marginal product of labor is constant. Hence, the law of diminishing marginal product is violated. As in the long-run specification, the linear form also fails to conform to the theoretical characteristics of a short-run production function. These problems render the simple linear specification unsuitable as a functional form for estimating either a long-run or a short-run production function.

---

[1]For any given level of output, Q', the various combinations of L and K which will produce exactly Q' units is

$$Q' = aK + bL$$

Thus, the equation for the Q' isoquant is

$$K = \frac{Q'}{a} - \frac{b}{a}L$$

which is linear with a constant slope of $-b/a$.

A Cubic Production Function

Although a linear specification of a production function is not tractable, many other specifications are theoretically suitable. A particularly useful *nonlinear* functional form, which can be transformed into a linear form for easy estimation, is the **cubic production function**:

cubic production function A production function of the form $Q = aK^3L^3 + bK^2L^2$.

$$Q = aK^3L^3 + bK^2L^2$$

For this form of the production function, both inputs are required in order to produce output. If either capital or labor usage equals zero, no output is produced. Furthermore, the cubic production function has convex isoquants so the marginal rate of technical substitution diminishes as required by the theory of production. (All of the mathematical properties of cubic production functions set forth in this chapter are mathematically derived in Appendix 12A.)

Holding capital constant at $\bar{K}$ units ($K = \bar{K}$), the **short-run cubic production function** is

short-run cubic production function A production function of the form $Q = AL^3 + BL^2$.

$$\begin{aligned} Q &= a\bar{K}^3L^3 + b\bar{K}^2L^2 \\ &= AL^3 + BL^2 \end{aligned}$$

where $A = a\bar{K}^3$ and $B = b\bar{K}^2$, and both A and B are constant when $\bar{K}$ is constant. The average and marginal products for the cubic short-run production function are, respectively,

$$AP = \frac{Q}{L} = AL^2 + BL$$

and

$$MP = \frac{\Delta Q}{\Delta L} = 3AL^2 + 2BL$$

As shown in Appendix 12A, in order for average and marginal product to first rise, reach a maximum, then fall (as illustrated in Chapter 10), A must be negative and B must be positive. It is also shown in Appendix 12A that the level of labor usage beyond which marginal product begins to fall, and diminishing returns set in, is

$$L_m = -\frac{B}{3A}$$

When marginal product equals average product and average product is at its maximum (as discussed in Chapter 10),[2]

[2]The level of labor usage at which AP reaches its maximum value, L_a, can be found algebraically. First, set AP equal to MP:

$$AL^2 + BL = 3AL^2 + 2BL$$

or

$$0 = 2AL^2 + BL$$

Solving for L, the level of labor usage at which average product is maximized is $L_a = -B/2A$.

FIGURE 12.1
Marginal and Average Product Curves for the Short-Run Cubic Production Function:
$Q = AL^3 + BL^2$

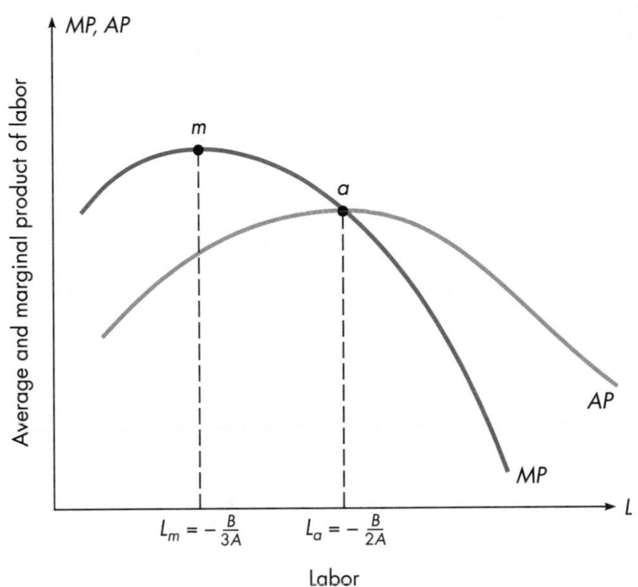

$$L_a = -\frac{B}{2A}$$

Recall that A is negative ($A < 0$) so that both L_m and L_a are positive. These two relations are illustrated in Figure 12.1.

Note that when the fixed level of capital changes, both A ($= a\bar{K}^3$) and B ($= b\bar{K}^2$) change in value and all three product curves (TP, AP, and MP) shift.[3] Also note that once estimates of A and B are obtained for any one of the three product equations (TP, AP, and MP), the other two have also been estimated; that is, A and B are the only two parameters that need to be estimated to get all three equations.

The short-run cubic production function exhibits all of the theoretical properties discussed in Chapter 10. Table 12.1 summarizes the cubic specification of the short-run production function.

12.2 ESTIMATION OF A SHORT-RUN CUBIC PRODUCTION FUNCTION

Now that we have specified a cubic form for the short-run production function, we can discuss how to estimate this production function. As you will see, only the simple techniques of regression analysis presented in Chapter 5 are needed to estimate the cubic production function in the short run when capital is fixed. We illustrate the process of estimating the production function with an example.

[3]Recall from Table 10.3 in Chapter 10 that capital is held constant in any given column. The entire marginal and average product schedules change when capital usage changes.

TABLE 12.1
Summary of the Short-Run Cubic Production Function

	Short-run cubic production function
Total product	$Q = AL^3 + BL^2$ where $A = a\bar{K}^3$, $B = b\bar{K}^2$
Average product	$AP = AL^2 + BL$
Marginal product	$MP = 3AL^2 + 2BL$
Diminishing marginal returns	Beginning at $L_m = -\dfrac{B}{3A}$
Diminishing average product	Beginning at $L_a = -\dfrac{B}{2A}$
Restrictions on parameters	$A < 0$, $B > 0$

FIGURE 12.2
Scatter Diagram

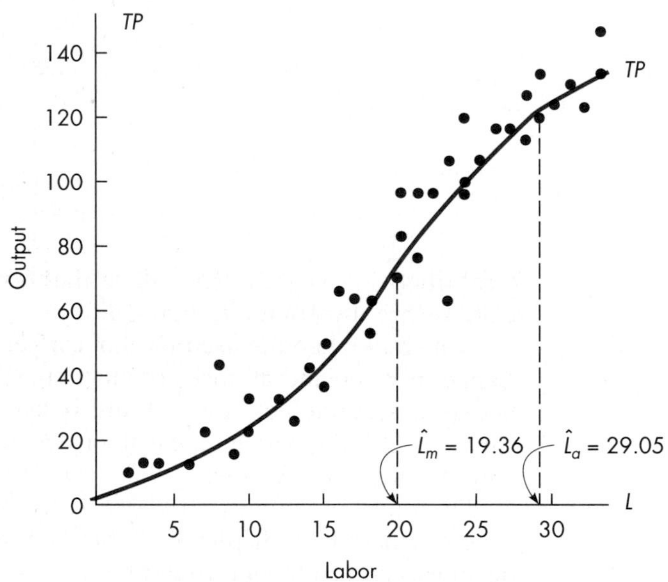

Suppose a small plant uses labor with a fixed amount of capital to assemble a product. There are 40 observations on labor usage (hours per day) and output (number of units assembled per day). The manager wishes to estimate the production function and the marginal product of labor. Figure 12.2 presents a scatter diagram of the 40 observations.

The scatter diagram suggests that a cubic specification of short-run production is appropriate because the scatter of data points appear to have an S-shape, similar to the theoretical total product curve set forth in Chapter 10. For such a curve, the slope first increases, then decreases, indicating that the marginal product of labor first increases, reaches a maximum, then decreases. Both the marginal product and average product curves should take on the inverted-U-shape described in Chapter 10, and shown in Figure 10.3.

Since it seems appropriate to estimate a cubic production function in this case, we specify the following estimable form:

$$Q = AL^3 + BL^2$$

Following the procedure discussed in Chapter 5, we transform the cubic equation into a linear form for estimation:

$$Q = AX + BW$$

where $X = L^3$ and $W = L^2$. In order to correctly estimate the cubic equation, we must account for the fact that the cubic equation does not include an intercept term. In other words, the estimated regression line must pass through the origin; that is, when $L = 0$, $Q = 0$. **Regression through the origin** simply requires the analyst to specify in the computer routine that the intercept term be "suppressed." Most computer programs for regression analysis provide the user with a simple way to suppress the intercept term. After using a regression routine to estimate a cubic equation for the 40 observations on output and labor usage (and suppressing the intercept), the following computer output is forthcoming:

regression through the origin
A regression in which the intercept term is forced to equal zero.

DEPENDENT VARIABLE: Q		F-RATIO: 1148.83	
OBSERVATIONS: 40		R-SQUARE: 0.9837	
VARIABLE	PARAMETER ESTIMATE	STANDARD ERROR	T-RATIO
L3	-0.0047	0.0006	-7.833
L2	0.2731	0.0182	15.0055

The F-ratio and the R^2 for the cubic specification are quite good.[4] The critical value of F with $k - 1 = 1$ and $n - k = 38$ degrees of freedom is 4.1 at the 95 percent confidence level. The following parameter estimates are obtained from the printout:

$$\hat{A} = -0.0047$$

and

$$\hat{B} = 0.2731$$

[4]For purposes of illustration, the hypothetical data used in this example were chosen to fit closely an S-shaped cubic equation. In most real-world applications, you will probably get smaller values for the F-ratio, R^2, and t-statistics.

The estimated short-run cubic production function is

$$\hat{Q} = -0.0047\ L^3 + 0.2731\ L^2$$

The parameters theoretically have the correct signs; $\hat{A} < 0$ and $\hat{B} > 0$. We must test to see if $\hat{A}$ and $\hat{B}$ are significantly negative and positive, respectively. The computed t-ratios allow us to test for statistical significance:

$$t_{\hat{a}} = -7.83 \quad \text{and} \quad t_{\hat{b}} = 15.00$$

The absolute values of both t-statistics exceed the critical t-value for 38 degrees of freedom at a 95 percent level of confidence (2.021). Hence, $\hat{A}$ is significantly negative, and $\hat{B}$ is significantly positive. Both estimates satisfy the theoretical characteristics of a cubic production function.

The estimated marginal product of labor is

$$\begin{aligned}\widehat{MP} &= 3\hat{A}L^2 + 2\hat{B}L \\ &= 3(-0.0047)L^2 + 2(0.2731)L \\ &= -0.0141L^2 + 0.5462L\end{aligned}$$

The level of labor usage beyond which diminishing returns set in (after MP_L reaches its maximum) is estimated as

$$\hat{L}_m = -\frac{\hat{B}}{3\hat{A}} = -\frac{0.2731}{3(-0.0047)} = 19.36$$

Note in Figure 12.2 that L_m is at the point where total product no longer increases at an increasing rate, but begins increasing at a decreasing rate. The estimated average product of labor is

$$\begin{aligned}\widehat{AP} &= \hat{A}L^2 + \hat{B}L \\ &= (-0.0047)L^2 + (0.2731)L\end{aligned}$$

The maximum average product is attained when $AP = MP$ at the estimated level of labor usage:

$$\hat{L}_a = -\frac{\hat{B}}{2\hat{A}} = -\frac{0.2731}{2(-0.0047)} = 29.05$$

Maximum AP, as expected, occurs at a higher level of labor usage than maximum MP (see Figure 12.2). The evidence indicates that the cubic estimation of the production function from the data points in Figure 12.2 provides a good fit and has all of the desired theoretical properties.

12.3 SHORT-RUN COST ESTIMATION: SOME PROBLEMS WITH MEASURING COST

The techniques of regression analysis can also be used to estimate cost functions. Cost depends upon the level of output being produced, as well as the prices of the inputs used in production. This relation can be expressed mathematically as

$$C = C(Q;\, w,\, r)$$

where we continue to let w denote the price of a unit of labor services and r the price of a unit of capital services. Before describing procedures used in estimating short-run cost functions, we must discuss two important considerations that arise when measuring the cost of production—the problem of inflation and that of measuring economic cost.

When estimating short-run cost functions, the data will necessarily be such that the level of usage of one (or more) of the inputs is fixed. In the context of the two-input production function employed in Chapter 10, this restriction could be interpreted to mean that the firm's capital stock is fixed while labor usage is allowed to vary. In most cases, a manager will be using a time-series set of observations on cost, output, and input prices to estimate the short-run cost function. The time period over which the data are collected should be short enough so that at least one input remains fixed. For instance, an analyst might collect monthly observations over a two-year period in which the firm did not change its basic plant (i.e., capital stock). Thus, the analyst could obtain 24 observations on cost, output, and input prices. When using a time-series data set of this type, an analyst should be careful to adjust the cost and input price data (which are measured in dollars) for inflation and to make sure the cost data measure economic cost. We now discuss these two possible problems.

Correcting Data for the Effects of Inflation

While output is expressed in physical units, cost and input prices are expressed in nominal dollars. Hence, the **nominal cost data** would include the effect of inflation. That is, over time, inflation would cause reported costs to rise, even if output remained constant. Such a situation is depicted in Figure 12.3. As you can

nominal cost data
Data that have not been corrected for the effects of inflation.

FIGURE 12.3
The Problem of Inflation

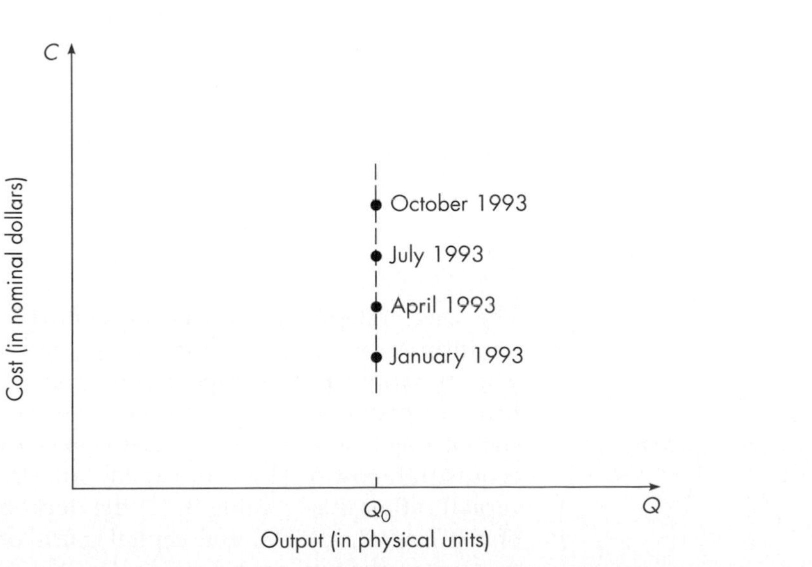

see in this figure, estimation based on a data set affected by inflation will indicate that cost rises more steeply than it would if inflation did not exist in the data. In order to accurately measure the real increase in cost caused by increases in output, it is necessary to eliminate the effects of inflation.

deflating The method of correcting for the influence of inflation by dividing nominal cost data by a price index.

Correcting for the effects of inflation is easily accomplished by **deflating** nominal cost data into constant (or real) dollars using a price index. To convert nominal cost into a constant dollar amount, the nominal cost data are divided by the appropriate price index for the period under consideration. Price indexes can be obtained from the *Survey of Current Business*, published by the US Department of Commerce. We will illustrate the process of deflating nominal cost data later in this chapter.

Inflation also can affect input prices, but for short-run cost estimation this is seldom a problem. As long as inflation affects all input prices and cost equally—that is, all input prices and cost rise equiproportionately—the effect of inflation on cost estimation is fully corrected for by deflating nominal cost. For example, if there is a 4 percent increase in cost and in the prices of both labor and capital, deflating cost by 4 percent will remove the effect of inflation, even when the prices of the inputs are not included in the cost equation. Therefore, it is a fairly common practice to omit input prices in short-run cost estimation because the span of the time-series data set is generally short enough that changes in the real input prices do not occur or are quite small. Thus, we will concentrate on showing how to adjust for inflation in the cost data and not be concerned with the effects of inflation on input prices.

Problems Measuring Economic Cost

Another potentially troublesome problem can result from the difference between the accounting definition of cost and the economic definition of cost. As stressed in Chapter 10, the cost of using resources in production is the opportunity cost of using the resources. Since accounting data are of necessity based on expenditures, opportunity cost may not be reflected in the firm's accounting records. To illustrate this problem, suppose a firm owns its own machinery. The opportunity cost of this equipment is the income that could be derived if the machinery were leased to another firm, but this cost would not be reflected in the accounting data.

In a two-input setting, total cost at a given level of outputs is

$$C = wL + rK$$

The wage rate should reflect the opportunity cost of labor to the firm; so, expenditures on labor, wL (including any additional compensation not paid as wages), would reflect opportunity cost. The problem is the calculation of the firm's opportunity cost of capital. The cost of capital, r, must be calculated in such a way that it reflects the **user cost of capital**. User cost includes not only the acquisition cost of a unit of capital but also (1) the return forgone by using the capital rather than renting it, (2) the depreciation charges resulting from the use of the capital, and (3) any capital gains or losses associated with holding the particular type of capital. Likewise, the measurement of the capital stock, K,

user cost of capital The firm's opportunity cost of using capital.

must be such that it reflects the stock actually owned by the firm. For example, you might want the capital variable to reflect the fact that a given piece of capital has depreciated physically or embodies a lower technology than a new piece of capital. While these problems are difficult, they are not insurmountable. The main thing to remember is that such opportunity cost data would be expected to differ greatly from the reported cost figures in accounting data.

12.4 ESTIMATION OF A SHORT-RUN COST FUNCTION

As is the case when estimating a production function, specification of an appropriate equation for a cost function must necessarily precede the estimation of the parameters using regression analysis. The specification of an empirical cost equation must ensure that the mathematical properties of the equation reflect the properties and relations described in Chapter 10. Figure 12.4 illustrates again the typically assumed total variable cost, average variable cost, and marginal cost curves.

Since the shape of any one of the three cost curves determines the shape of the other two, we begin with the average variable cost curve. Because this curve is U-shaped, the simplest possible form, the linear specification, $AVC = a + bQ$, cannot be used. Because the simple linear form won't work, we use the slightly more complex specification,

$$AVC = a + bQ + cQ^2$$

FIGURE 12.4
Representative Short-Run Cost Curves

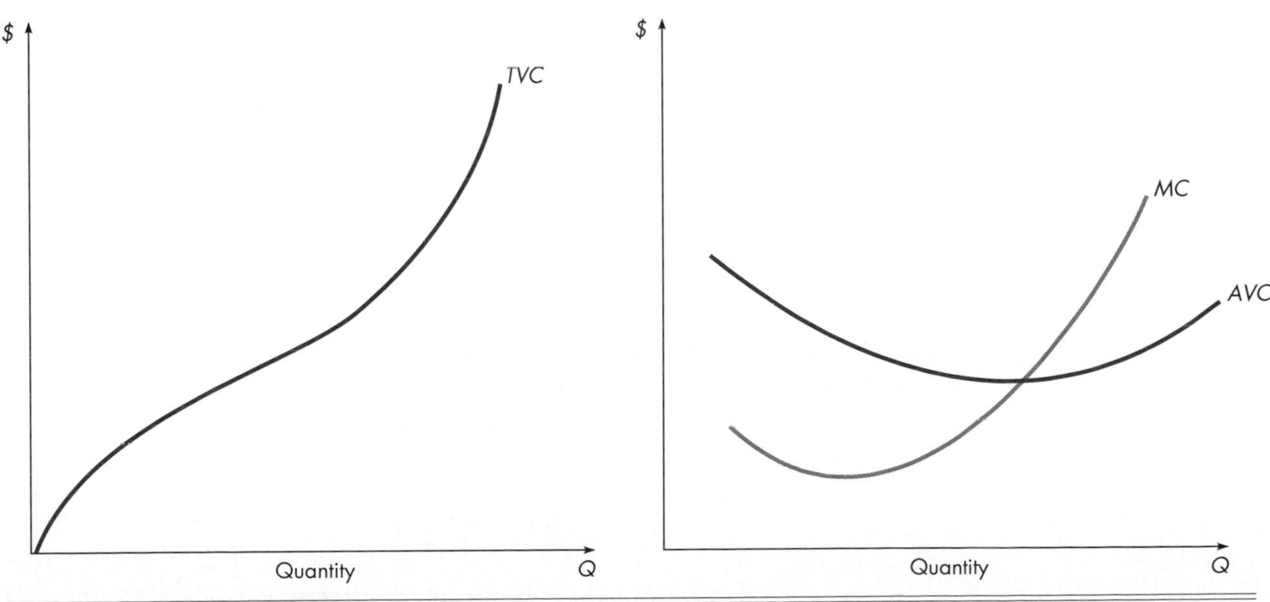

As explained earlier, input prices are not included as explanatory variables in the cost equation because the input prices (adjusted for inflation) are assumed to be constant over the relatively short time span of the time-series data set. In order for the *AVC* curve to be U-shaped, a must be positive, b must be negative, and c must be positive; that is, $a > 0$, $b < 0$, and $c > 0$.[5]

Given the specification for average variable cost, the specifications for total variable cost and marginal cost are straightforward. Since $AVC = TVC/Q$, it follows that

$$TVC = AVC \times Q = (a + bQ + cQ^2)Q = aQ + bQ^2 + cQ^3$$

Note that this equation is a cubic specification of *TVC*, which conforms to the S-shaped *TVC* curve in Figure 12.4.

The equation for marginal cost is somewhat more difficult to derive. It can be shown, however, that the marginal cost equation associated with the above *TVC* equation is

$$MC = a + 2bQ + 3cQ^2$$

If, as specified for *AVC*, $a > 0$, $b < 0$, and $c > 0$, the marginal cost curve will also be U-shaped.

Because all three of the cost curves, *TVC*, *AVC*, and *MC*, employ the same parameters, it is only necessary to estimate any one of these functions in order to obtain estimates of all three. For example, estimation of *AVC* provides estimates of a, b, and c, which can then be used to generate the marginal and total variable cost functions. The total cost curve is trivial to estimate; simply add the constant fixed cost to total variable cost.

As for the estimation itself, ordinary least-squares estimation of the total (or average) variable cost function is usually sufficient. Once the estimates of a, b, and c are obtained, it is necessary to determine whether the parameter estimates are of the hypothesized signs and statistically significant. The tests for significance are again accomplished using t-tests.

Using the estimates of a total or average variable cost function, we can also obtain an estimate of the output at which average cost is a minimum. Remember that when average variable cost is at its minimum, average variable cost and marginal cost are equal. Thus we can define the minimum of average variable cost as the output at which

$$AVC = MC$$

Using the specifications of average variable cost and marginal cost presented above, we can write this condition as

$$a + bQ + cQ^2 = a + 2bQ + 3cQ^2$$

or

$$bQ + 2cQ^2 = 0$$

[5]Appendix 12B derives the mathematical properties of a cubic cost function.

TABLE 12.2
Summary of a Cubic Specification for Total Variable Cost

	Cubic total variable cost function
Total variable cost	$TVC = aQ + bQ^2 + cQ^3$
Average variable cost	$AVC = a + bQ + cQ^2$
Marginal cost	$MC = a + 2bQ + 3cQ^2$
AVC reaches minimum point	$Q_m = -b/2c$
Restrictions on parameters	$a > 0$ $b < 0$ $c > 0$

FIGURE 12.5
A Potential Data Problem

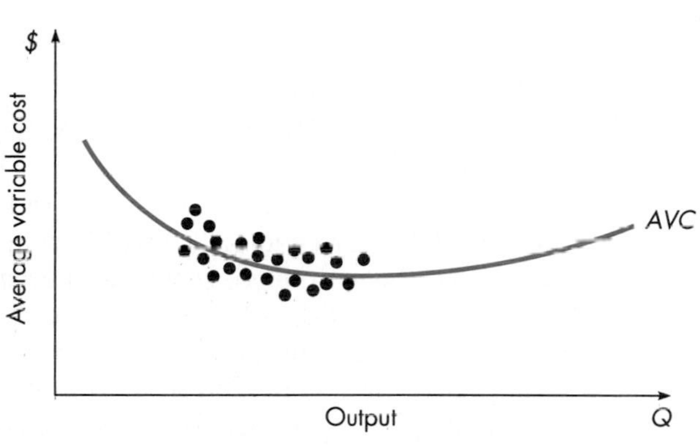

Solving for Q, the level of output at which average variable cost is minimized is

$$Q_m = -b/2c$$

Table 12.2 summarizes the mathematical properties of a cubic specification for total variable cost.

Before estimating a short-run cost function, we want to mention a potential problem that can arise when the data for average variable cost are clustered around the minimum point of the average cost curve, as shown in Figure 12.5. If the average variable cost function is estimated using data points clustered as shown in the figure, the result is that while $\hat{a}$ is positive and $\hat{b}$ is negative, a t-test would indicate that $\hat{c}$ is not statistically different from zero. This result does not mean that the average cost curve is not U-shaped. The problem is that because there are no observations for the larger levels of output, the estimation simply cannot determine whether or not average cost is rising over that range of output.

Estimation of Short-Run Costs at Rockford Enterprises: An Example

In January 1994, the manager at Rockford Enterprises decided to estimate the total variable, average variable, and marginal cost functions for the firm. The capital stock at Rockford has remained unchanged since the fourth quarter of 1991. The manager collected quarterly observations on cost and output over this period and the resulting data were as follows:

Quarter	Output (1,000 units)	Average variable cost ($)
1991IV	30	$50
1992I	10	52
1992II	15	38
1992III	25	38
1992IV	40	64
1993I	20	45
1993II	35	61
1993III	45	80
1993IV	50	90

Average variable cost was measured in nominal (i.e., current) dollars, and the cost data were subject to the effects of inflation. Over the period for which cost was to be estimated, costs had increased due to the effects of inflation. The manager's analyst decided to eliminate the influence of inflation by deflating the nominal costs. Recall that such a deflation involves converting nominal cost into constant-dollar cost by dividing the nominal cost by an appropriate price index. The analyst used the Consumer Price Index (CPI) published in the *Survey of Current Business*. The following values for the CPI were used to deflate the nominal cost data:

Quarter	Consumer price index (1982–84 = 1.000)
1991IV	1.379
1992I	1.393
1992II	1.402
1992III	1.413
1992IV	1.419
1993I	1.436
1993II	1.444
1993III	1.451
1993IV	1.458

To obtain the average variable cost (measured in constant dollars) for the 30,000 units produced in the fourth quarter of 1991, $50 is divided by 1.379 to obtain $36.26. Repeating this computation for each of the cost figures, the manager obtained the following data set:

Quarter	Output (1,000 units)	Deflated average variable cost ($)
1991IV	30	$36
1992I	10	37
1992II	15	27
1992III	25	27
1992IV	40	45
1993I	20	31
1993II	35	42
1993III	45	55
1993IV	50	62

Given these inflation-adjusted data, the manager estimated the cost functions. As shown above, it is sufficient to estimate any one of the three cost curves in order to obtain the other two because each cost equation is a function of the same three parameters—a, b, and c. The manager decided to estimate the average variable cost function:

$$AVC = a + bQ + cQ^2$$

and obtained the following printout from the estimation of this equation:

```
DEPENDENT VARIABLE:  AVC            F-RATIO:   51.404

OBSERVATIONS:   9                   R-SQUARE:   0.9449

                    PARAMETER       STANDARD
VARIABLE            ESTIMATE        ERROR              T-RATIO

INTERCEPT             44.35          6.17                7.188
Q                     -1.44          0.46               -3.130
Q2                     0.04          0.008               5.000
```

After the estimates were obtained, the manager determined that the estimated coefficients had the theoretically required signs: $\hat{a} > 0$, $\hat{b} < 0$, and $\hat{c} > 0$. To determine whether these coefficients are statistically significant, the usual t-tests were performed, in this case with $9 - 3 = 6$ degrees of freedom. From the t-table, the critical value of t at a 95 percent level of confidence is 2.447. Next, the manager compared the t-ratios with the critical t-value of 2.447. Since the absolute values of these calculated t-statistics all exceed the critical value of t, the coefficients all have the correct sign and are statistically significant.

The estimated average variable cost function for Rockford Enterprises is, therefore,

$$\widehat{AVC} = 44.35 - 1.44Q + 0.04Q^2$$

which conforms to the shape of the average variable cost curve in Figure 12.4. As emphasized above, the marginal cost and total variable cost equations are easily determined from the estimated parameters of *AVC*, and no further regression analysis is necessary. In this case

$$\widehat{MC} = \hat{a} + 2\hat{b}Q + 3\hat{c}Q^2$$
$$= 44.35 - 2.88Q + 0.12Q^2$$

and

$$\widehat{TVC} = \hat{a}Q + \hat{b}Q^2 + \hat{c}Q^3$$
$$= 44.35Q - 1.44Q^2 + 0.04Q^3$$

To illustrate the use of the estimated cost equations, suppose the manager wishes to calculate the marginal cost, average variable cost, and total variable cost when Rockford is producing 27,000 units of output.[6] Using the estimated marginal cost equation, the marginal cost associated with 27,000 units is

$$MC = 44.35 - 2.88(27) + 0.12(27)^2$$
$$= 44.35 - 77.76 + 87.48$$
$$= \$54.07$$

Average variable cost for this level of output is

$$AVC = 44.35 - 1.44(27) + 0.04(27)^2$$
$$= 44.35 - 38.88 + 29.16$$
$$= \$34.63$$

and total variable cost for 27,000 units of output is

$$TVC = AVC \times Q$$
$$= 34.63 \times 27{,}000$$
$$= \$935{,}010$$

Total cost of 27,000 units of output would, of course, be $935,010 plus fixed cost.

Finally, the output level at which average variable cost is minimized can be computed as

$$Q_m = -b/2c$$

In this example,

$$\hat{Q}_m = \frac{1.44}{2 \times 0.04} = 18$$

At Rockford Enterprises, average variable cost reaches its minimum at an output level of 18,000 units, when

[6]Normally, the marginal cost refers to the cost of producing the last unit—the 27,000th unit. However, since the data were expressed in 1,000 units, the marginal cost is interpreted as the additional cost *per unit* for producing the last 1,000 units—the cost per unit for the 26,001st through 27,000th unit.

$$AVC = 44.35 - 1.44(18) + 0.04(18)^2$$
$$= 44.35 - 25.92 + 12.96$$
$$= \$31.39$$

As you can see by this example, estimation of short-run cost curves is just a straightforward application of cost theory and regression analysis. Many firms do, in fact, use regression analysis to estimate their costs of production in the short-run. In Part V of this book, we will examine theoretically how managers make production, pricing, and hiring decisions to maximize the profit of a firm. We will also show how to implement the theoretical rules by using empirically estimated demand and cost functions. You will see that the estimated set of cubic cost functions plays a crucial role in finding the profit-maximizing levels of output, price, and labor employment.

12.5 SUMMARY

In this chapter you have learned how to specify and estimate a popular form of production and cost functions—the cubic specification. We discussed how to use the results of the estimations to investigate a variety of production and cost issues that are relevant to managerial decision making, such as finding the point of diminishing returns and estimating the values of marginal products and marginal costs.

As we showed, simple linear specifications are not appropriate for the estimation of production functions or cost functions because linear models do not conform to the various theoretical characteristics of long-run or short-run production and cost functions. Instead, we employed a slightly more complicated nonlinear specification, the cubic specification. The mathematical properties of the short-run cubic production and cost specification are summarized again for you in Table 12.3.

Estimation of the short-run cubic production function involves estimating the two parameters A and B. This is accomplished by regressing output on L^3 and L^2 using the technique of regression through the origin.

TABLE 12.3
Summary of the Short-Run Cubic Production and Cost Specification

	Short-run cubic production equations
Total product	$Q = AL^3 + BL^2$
Average product of labor	$AP = AL^2 + BL$
Marginal product of labor	$MP = 3AL^2 + 2BL$
Diminishing marginal returns	beginning at $L_m = -B/3A$
Restrictions on parameters	$A < 0$ $B > 0$

	Short-run cubic cost equations
Total variable cost	$TVC = aQ + bQ^2 + cQ^3$
Average variable cost	$AVC = a + bQ + cQ^2$
Marginal cost	$MC = a + 2bQ + 3cQ^2$
Average variable cost reaches minimum at	$Q_m = -\frac{b}{2c}$
Restrictions on parameters	$a > 0$, $b < 0$, $c > 0$

Once A and B are estimated, the estimated t-ratios are examined to test that A is significantly negative and B is significantly positive. Once estimates of A and B are obtained for any one of the three product equations (TP, AP, and MP), the other two product equations will also have been estimated since A and B are the only two parameters in all three equations. The cubic production function exhibits all of the theoretical properties discussed in Chapter 10.

When estimating cost equations, researchers must be careful to adjust for the effects of inflation. The effects of inflation are removed from the data by "deflating" using price indexes, which can be obtained from a variety of sources including the *Survey of Current Business*, published by the US Department of Commerce and available at most libraries (US government documents section). Researchers must also be careful to use economic costs, rather than accounting costs, to measure the cost of production.

A suitable specification for estimating a set of short-run cost curves (TVC, AVC, and MC) is a cubic TVC equation with the associated AVC and MC equations summarized in Table 12.3. If $a > 0$, $b < 0$, and $c > 0$, the total variable cost curve has the typical S-shape, and average variable and marginal cost are U-shaped. Average variable cost reaches its minimum value at an output level of $Q_m = -b/2c$.

This chapter concludes Part IV of this text, which discussed production and cost. Now that revenue and cost relations have been presented, we are ready to proceed with the analysis of managerial decision making in the context of a profit-maximizing firm. In Parts V and VI of this text, you will learn how output, price, and investment decisions are made by managers. The crucial consideration in all decisions made by the manager is economic profit. You now have the tools to estimate both the revenue and cost equations needed for business decision making.

TECHNICAL PROBLEMS

1. Consider the linear long-run production function,

$$Q = aK + bL$$

Calculate the marginal rate of technical substitution and explain why this functional form does not conform to the theoretical properties of a production function.

2. Let the production function be

$$Q = 4K + 5L.$$

The isoquant for 200 units of output for this production function is shown in the figure on the following page. It is derived by setting $Q = 200$ and solving for K:

$$200 = 4K + 5L,$$

so

$$K = 50 - 5/4L$$

Notice the intercepts are at $K = 200/4 = 50$ and $L = 200/5 = 40$.

a. Assume the price of capital (r) is \$60 and the price of labor (w) is \$30. Plot a representative isocost curve and then find the cost-minimizing combination of labor and capital.

b. Assume now that r = \$25 and w = \$50. Using the above technique, find the cost-minimizing combination of labor and capital.

c. Assume that r = \$16 and w = \$20. Find the cost-minimizing combination(s) of labor and capital.

d. Give a general rule about the cost-minimizing problem for straight-line production functions and isoquants. Why don't we assume such isoquants?

* 3. The following cubic equation is a long-run production function for a firm:

$$Q = -0.002K^3L^3 + 6K^2L^2$$

Suppose the firm employs 10 units of capital.

a. What are the equations for the total product, average product, and marginal product of labor curves?

b. At what level of labor usage does the marginal product of labor begin to diminish?

c. Calculate the marginal product and average product of labor when 10 units of labor are being employed.

Now suppose the firm doubles capital usage to 20 units.

d. What are the equations for the total product, average product, and marginal product of labor curves?

e. What happened to the marginal and average product of labor curves when capital usage increased from 10 to 20 units? Calculate the marginal and average products of labor for 10 units of labor now that capital usage is 20 units. Compare your answer to part *c*. Did the increase in capital usage affect marginal and average product as you expected?

4. Consider the multiplicative production function

$$Q = \gamma LK$$

a. Does production require positive amounts of both inputs?

b. What are the marginal products? Do they diminish?

c. Does the marginal rate of technical substitution diminish?

5. A firm estimates its cubic production function of the following form

$$Q = AL^3 + BL^2$$

and obtains the following estimation results:

DEPENDENT VARIABLE: Q		F-RATIO: 126.1	
OBSERVATIONS: 25		R-SQUARE: 0.841	
VARIABLE	PARAMETER ESTIMATE	STANDARD ERROR	T-RATIO
L3	-0.002	0.0005	-4.0
L2	0.40	0.08	5.0

a. What are the estimated total, average, and marginal product functions?
b. Are the parameters of the correct sign and are they significant?
c. At what level of labor usage is average product at its maximum?

Now recall the following formulas derived in Chapter 10: $AP = Q/L$, $AVC = w/AP$, and $MC = w/MP$. Assume that the wage rate for labor (w) is \$200.

d. What is output when average product is at its maximum?
e. At the output level for part *d*, what are average variable cost and marginal cost?
f. When the rate of labor usage is 120, what is output? What are *AVC* and *MC* at that output?
g. Conceptually, how could you derive the relevant cost curves from this estimate of the production functions?

* 6. Consider estimation of a short-run average variable cost function of the form

$$AVC = a + bQ + cQ^2$$

Using time-series data, the estimation procedure produces the following computer output:

DEPENDENT VARIABLE: AVC		F-RATIO: 4.230	
OBSERVATIONS: 15		R-SQUARE: 0.4135	
VARIABLE	PARAMETER ESTIMATE	STANDARD ERROR	T-RATIO
INTERCEPT	30.420202	6.465900	4.7047
Q	-0.079952	0.030780	-2.5975
Q2	0.000088	0.000032	2.7500

a. Do the parameter estimates have the correct signs? Are they statistically significant?
b. At what level of output do you estimate average variable cost reaches its minimum value?
c. What is the estimated marginal cost curve?

d. What is the estimated marginal cost when output is 700 units?
e. What is the estimated average variable cost curve?
f. What is the estimated average variable cost when output is 700 units?

APPLIED PROBLEMS

1. You are planning to estimate a short-run production function for your firm, and you have collected the following data on labor usage and output:

Labor usage	Output
3	1
7	2
9	3
11	5
17	8
17	10
20	15
24	18
26	22
28	21
30	23

Does a cubic equation appear to be a suitable specification given these data? You may wish to construct a scatter diagram to help you answer this question.

2. Dimex Fabrication Co., a small manufacturer of sheet-metal body parts for a major US automaker, estimates its long-run production function to be

$$Q = -0.015625\ K^3L^3 + 10\ K^2L^2$$

where Q is the number of body parts produced daily, K is the number of sheet-metal presses in its manufacturing plant, and L is the number of man-hours per day of sheet-metal workers employed by Dimex. Dimex is currently operating with 8 sheet-metal presses.

a. What is the total product function for Dimex? The average product function? The marginal product function?
b. Managers at Dimex can expect the marginal product of additional workers to fall beyond what level of labor employment?
c. Dimex plans to employ 50 workers. Calculate total product, average product, and marginal product.

3. The chief economist for Argus Corporation, a large appliance manufacturer, estimated the firm's short-run cost function for vacuum cleaners using an average variable cost function of the form:

$$AVC = a + bQ + cQ^2$$

where AVC = dollars per vacuum cleaner and Q = number of vacuum cleaners (millions). Total fixed cost is \$30 million. The following results were obtained:

DEPENDENT VARIABLE: AVC		F-RATIO: 39.428	
OBSERVATIONS: 19		R-SQUARE: 0.736	
VARIABLE	PARAMETER ESTIMATE	STANDARD ERROR	T-RATIO
INTERCEPT	81.93	17.81	4.60
Q	-3.05	0.94	-3.24
Q2	0.24	0.08	3.00

a. Are the estimates $\hat{a}$, $\hat{b}$, and $\hat{c}$ statistically significant?
b. Do the results indicate that the average variable cost curve is U-shaped? How do you know?
c. If Argus Corporation produces 3 million vacuum cleaners, what is estimated average variable cost? Marginal cost? Total variable cost? Total cost?
d. Answer part c, assuming that Argus produces 10 million vacuum cleaners.
e. At what level of output will average variable cost be at a minimum? What is minimum average variable cost?

APPENDIX 12A The Cubic Production Function

In Chapter 12, the cubic production function was introduced:

$$Q = aK^3L^3 + bK^2L^2$$

This functional form is best suited for short-run applications, rather than long-run applications. When capital is fixed ($K = \bar{K}$), the short-run cubic production function is

$$\begin{aligned} Q &= a\bar{K}^3L^3 + b\bar{K}^2L^2 \\ &= AL^3 + BL^2 \end{aligned}$$

where $A = a\bar{K}^3$ and $B = b\bar{K}^2$. This appendix presents the mathematical properties of the short-run cubic production function.

Input usage

In order to produce output, some positive amount of labor is required:

$$Q(0) = A(0)^3 + B(0)^2 = 0$$

Marginal product

The marginal product function for labor is

$$\frac{dQ}{dL} = Q_L = 3AL^2 + 2BL$$

The slope of marginal product is

$$\frac{d^2Q}{dL^2} = Q_{LL} = 6AL + 2B$$

In order for marginal product of labor to first rise, then fall, Q_{LL} must first be positive, then negative. Q_{LL} will be positive, then negative (as more labor is used) when A is negative and B is positive. These are the only restrictions on the short-run cubic production function:

$$A < 0 \text{ and } B > 0$$

Marginal product of labor reaches its maximum value at L_m units of labor usage. This occurs when $Q_{LL} = 0$. Setting $Q_{LL} = 0$, and solving for L_m:

$$L_m = -B/3A$$

Average product

The average product function for labor is

$$AP = \frac{Q}{L} = AL^2 + BL$$

Average product reaches its maximum value at L_a units of labor usage. This occurs when $\frac{dAP}{dL} = 2AL + B = 0$. Solving for L_a:

$$L_a = -\frac{B}{2A}$$

APPENDIX 12B The Cubic Cost Function

The cubic cost function,

$$TVC = aQ + bQ^2 + cQ^3$$

generates average and marginal cost curves that have the typical U-shapes set forth in Chapter 10. Since $AVC = TVC/Q$,

$$AVC = a + bQ + cQ^2$$

The slope of the average variable cost function is

$$\frac{dAVC}{dQ} = b + 2cQ$$

Average variable cost is at its minimum value when $\frac{dAVC}{dQ} = 0$, which occurs when $Q = -b/2c$. To guarantee a minimum, the second derivative,

$$\frac{d^2AVC}{dQ^2} = 2c$$

must be positive, which requires c to be positive.

When $Q = 0$, $AVC = a$, which must be positive. In order for average variable cost to have a downward sloping region, b must be negative. Thus, the parameter restrictions for a short-run cubic cost function are

$$a > 0,\ b < 0, \text{ and } c > 0$$

The marginal cost function is

$$MC = \frac{dTVC}{dQ} = a + 2bQ + 3cQ^2$$

APPENDIX 12C The Cobb-Douglas Production Function

In Chapter 12, we used a cubic specification for estimating the production function. In this appendix, we show you another nonlinear specification of the production function that has been widely used in business economics applications. We will describe the mathematical properties of both the long-run and short-run Cobb-Douglas production function and explain how to estimate the parameters using regression analysis. In order to help you distinguish between the Cobb-Douglas form and the cubic form, we will use Greek letters to represent the parameters of the Cobb-Douglas functions.

The Long-Run Cobb-Douglas Production Function: $Q = \gamma K^{\alpha}L^{\beta}$

Input usage

In order to produce output, both inputs are required.

$$Q(0,L) = \gamma 0^{\alpha}L^{\beta} = Q(K,0) = \gamma K^{\alpha}0^{\beta} = 0$$

Marginal products

The marginal product functions for capital and labor are

$$\frac{\partial Q}{\partial K} = Q_K = \alpha\gamma K^{\alpha-1}L^{\beta} = \alpha\frac{Q}{K}$$

and

$$\frac{\partial Q}{\partial L} = Q_L = \beta\gamma K^{\alpha}L^{\beta-1} = \beta\frac{Q}{L}$$

In order that the marginal products be positive, α and β must be positive. The second derivatives,

$$\frac{\partial^2 Q}{\partial K^2} = Q_{KK} = \alpha(\alpha - 1)\ \gamma K^{\alpha-2}L^{\beta}$$

and

$$\frac{\partial^2 Q}{\partial L^2} = Q_{LL} = \beta(\beta - 1)\ \gamma K^{\alpha}L^{\beta-2}$$

demonstrate that, if the marginal products are diminishing (i.e., Q_{KK} and $Q_{LL} < 0$), α and β must be less than one.

Marginal rate of technical substitution

From Chapter 9, the *MRTS* of L for K is Q_L/Q_K. In the context of the Cobb-Douglas function,

$$MRTS = \frac{Q_L}{Q_K} = \frac{\beta}{\alpha}\frac{K}{L}$$

Note first that the *MRTS* is invariant to output,

$$\frac{\partial MRTS}{\partial Q} = 0$$

Hence, the Cobb-Douglas production is *homothetic*—the production function has a straight-line expansion path and changes in the output level have no effect on relative input usage. Moreover, the *MRTS* demonstrates that the Cobb-Douglas production function is characterized by convex isoquants. Taking the derivative of the *MRTS* of L for K with respect to L,

$$\frac{\partial MRTS}{\partial L} = -\frac{\beta}{\alpha}\cdot\frac{K}{L^2}$$

Hence, the *MRTS* diminishes as more and more capital is replaced with labor: the isoquants are convex.

Output elasticities

Output elasticities are defined as

$$E_K = \frac{\partial Q}{\partial K}\cdot\frac{K}{Q} = Q_K\cdot\frac{K}{Q}$$

and

$$E_L = \frac{\partial Q}{\partial L}\cdot\frac{L}{Q} = Q_L\cdot\frac{L}{Q}$$

Using the Cobb-Douglas specification

$$E_K = \left(\alpha\frac{Q}{K}\right)\cdot\frac{K}{Q} = \alpha$$

and

$$E_L = \left(\beta\frac{Q}{L}\right)\cdot\frac{L}{Q} = \beta$$

The function coefficient

Begin with a production function, $Q = Q(K,L)$. Suppose that the levels of usage of both inputs are increased by the same proportion (λ); i.e., $Q = Q(\lambda K, \lambda L)$. The definition of the function coefficient ($\mathscr{E}$) is

$$\mathscr{E} = \frac{dQ/Q}{d\lambda/\lambda}$$

Take the total differential of the production function

$$dQ = Q_K dK + Q_L dL$$

and rewrite this as

$$dQ = Q_K K\frac{dK}{K} + Q_L L\frac{dL}{L}$$

Since K and L were increased by the same proportion, $dK/K = dL/L = d\lambda/\lambda$. Thus,

$$dQ = \frac{d\lambda}{\lambda}(Q_K K + Q_L L)$$

Using this expression, the function coefficient is

$$\mathscr{E} = Q_K\cdot\frac{K}{Q} + Q_L\cdot\frac{L}{Q} = E_K + E_L$$

In the context of the Cobb-Douglas production function, it follows that

$$\mathscr{E} = \alpha + \beta$$

Estimating the Long-Run Cobb-Douglas Production Function

The mathematical properties of the Cobb-Douglas production function make it a popular specification for estimating long-run production functions. After converting to logarithms, the estimable form of the Cobb-Douglas function ($Q = \gamma K^{\alpha}L^{\beta}$) is

$$\log Q = \log\gamma + \alpha\log K + \beta\log L$$

Recall from the previous discussion that $\hat{\alpha}$ and $\hat{\beta}$ are estimates of the output elasticities of capital and labor, respectively. Recall also that the estimated marginal products,

$$\widehat{MP}_K = \hat{\alpha}\frac{Q}{K} \text{ and } \widehat{MP}_L = \hat{\beta}\frac{Q}{L}$$

are significantly positive and decreasing (the desired theoretical property) if the t-tests on $\hat{\alpha}$ and $\hat{\beta}$ indicate that these coefficients are significantly positive but less than one in value.

The function coefficient is estimated as

$$\hat{\xi} = \hat{\alpha} + \hat{\beta}$$

and provides a measure of returns to scale. In order to determine whether or not $\hat{\alpha} + \hat{\beta}$ is significantly greater (less) than one, a t-test is performed. If $\hat{\alpha} + \hat{\beta}$ is not significantly greater (less) than one, we cannot reject the existence of constant returns to scale. To determine whether the sum, $\hat{\alpha} + \hat{\beta}$, is significantly different from one, we use the following t-statistic:

$$t_{\hat{\alpha} + \hat{\beta}} = \frac{(\hat{\alpha} + \hat{\beta}) - 1}{S_{\hat{\alpha} + \hat{\beta}}}$$

where the value 1 indicates that we are testing "different from" and $S_{\hat{\alpha} + \hat{\beta}}$ is the estimated standard error of the sum of the estimated coefficients $(\hat{\alpha} + \hat{\beta})$. After calculating this t-statistic, it is compared to the critical t-value from the table. Again note that since the calculated t-statistic can be negative (when $\hat{\alpha} + \hat{\beta}$ is less than 1), it is the absolute value of the t-statistic that is compared to the critical t-value.

The only problem in performing this test involves obtaining the estimated standard error of $\hat{\alpha} + \hat{\beta}$. The available regression packages will provide the analyst, upon request, with variances and covariances of the regression coefficients, $\hat{\alpha}$ and $\hat{\beta}$, in a variance-covariance matrix.[1] Traditionally, variances of $\hat{\alpha}$ and $\hat{\beta}$ are denoted as $\text{Var}(\hat{\alpha})$ and $\text{Var}(\hat{\beta})$ and the covariance between $\hat{\alpha}$ and $\hat{\beta}$ as $\text{Cov}(\hat{\alpha}, \hat{\beta})$. As you may remember from a statistics course,

$$\text{Var}(\hat{\alpha} + \hat{\beta}) = \text{Var}(\hat{\alpha}) + \text{Var}(\hat{\beta}) + 2\,\text{Cov}(\hat{\alpha}, \hat{\beta})$$

The estimated standard error of $\hat{\alpha} + \hat{\beta}$ is

$$S_{\hat{\alpha} + \hat{\beta}} = \sqrt{\text{Var}(\hat{\alpha}) + \text{Var}(\hat{\beta}) + 2\text{Cov}(\hat{\alpha}, \hat{\beta})}$$

The Short-Run Cobb-Douglas Production Function

When capital is fixed in the short run at $\bar{K}$, the short-run Cobb-Douglas production function is

$$Q = \gamma \bar{K}^{\alpha} L^{\beta} = \delta L^{\beta}$$

where $\delta = \gamma \bar{K}^{\alpha}$. Note that if L is 0, no output is forthcoming. In order for output to be positive, δ must be positive. The marginal product of labor is

$$Q_L = \delta \beta L^{\beta - 1}$$

In order for marginal product to be positive, β must be positive. The second derivative

$$Q_{LL} = \beta(\beta - 1)\delta L^{\beta - 2}$$

reveals that if the marginal product of labor is diminishing, β must be less than one. Thus, the restrictions for the Cobb-Douglas production in the short run are

$$\delta > 0$$

and

$$0 < \beta < 1$$

Estimating the Short-Run Cobb-Douglas Production Function

As in the case of the long-run Cobb-Douglas production function, the short-run Cobb-Douglas production function must also be transformed into a linear form by converting it to logarithms. The equation actually estimated is

$$\log Q = \tau + \beta \log L$$

where $\tau = \log \delta$. Recall that β must be positive for the marginal product of labor to be positive and less than one for the marginal product to be decreasing (i.e., $0 < \beta < 1$). It is common practice to test that $\beta > 0$ and $\beta < 1$ using the t-test.

[1]The variance-covariance matrix is a listing (in the form of a matrix on the computer printout) of the estimated variances and covariances of all the estimated coefficients. For example, in the regression of $Y = \alpha + \beta X$, the variance-covariance matrix provides estimates of $\text{Var}(\hat{\alpha})$, $\text{Var}(\hat{\beta})$, and $\text{Cov}(\hat{\alpha}, \hat{\beta})$. As noted in Chapter 5, the variance of a regression coefficient provides a measure of the dispersion of the variable about its mean. The covariance of the regression coefficients provides information about the joint distribution, that is, the relation between the two regression coefficients.

APPENDIX 12D Estimation of a Long-Run Cost Function

Since the general form for the long-run cost function with two inputs is

$$C = f(Q, w, r)$$

and since cross-sectional data are generally used for long-run estimation, the empirical specification of a long-run cost function must, as emphasized above, include the prices of inputs as explanatory variables. At first glance, it would appear that the solution would be simply to add the input prices as additional explanatory variables in the cost function developed above and express total cost as

$$TC = aQ + bQ^2 + cQ^3 + dw + er$$

This function, however, fails to satisfy a basic characteristic of cost functions. A total cost function can be written as $TC = wL + rK$. If both input prices double, holding output constant, input usage will not change, but total cost will double. Letting TC' denote total cost after input prices double,

$$\begin{aligned} TC' &= (2w)L + (2r)K \\ &= 2(wL + rK) \\ &= 2TC \end{aligned}$$

The long-run cost function suggested above does not satisfy this requirement. For a given output, if input prices double,

$$\begin{aligned} TC' &= aQ + bQ^2 + cQ^3 + d(2w) + e(2r) \\ &= aQ + bQ^2 + cQ^3 + dw + er + (dw + er) \\ &= TC + dw + er \end{aligned}$$

and TC' is not equal to $2TC$.

Therefore, an alternative form for estimating a long-run cost function must be found. The most commonly employed form is a log-linear specification such as the Cobb-Douglas specifications. With this type of specification, the total cost function is expressed as

$$TC = \alpha Q^{\beta} w^{\gamma} r^{\delta}$$

Using this functional form, when input prices double while holding output constant:

$$\begin{aligned} TC' &= \alpha Q^{\beta}(2w)^{\gamma}(2r)^{\delta} \\ &= 2^{(\gamma + \delta)} (\alpha Q^{\beta} w^{\gamma} r^{\delta}) \\ &= 2^{(\gamma + \delta)} TC \end{aligned}$$

If $\gamma + \delta = 1$, doubling input prices indeed doubles the total cost of producing a given level of output—the required characteristic of a cost function. Hence, it is necessary to *impose* this condition on the proposed log-linear cost function by defining δ as $1 - \gamma$; so

$$\begin{aligned} TC &= \alpha Q^{\beta} w^{\gamma} r^{1-\gamma} \\ &= \alpha Q^{\beta} w^{\gamma} r^{-\gamma} r \\ &= \alpha Q^{\beta} (w/r)^{\gamma} r \end{aligned}$$

The parameter restrictions are $\alpha > 0$, $\beta > 0$, and $0 < \gamma < 1$, which ensure that total cost is positive and increases when output and input prices increase.

To estimate the above total cost equation, it must be converted to logarithms:

$$\log TC = \log \alpha + \beta \log Q + \gamma \log \left(\frac{w}{r}\right) + 1 \log r$$

While we can estimate the parameters α, β, and γ, this formulation requires that the coefficient for log r be *precisely* equal to one. If we were to estimate this equation, such a value cannot be guaranteed. To impose this condition on the empirical cost function, we simply move log r to the left-hand side of the equation to obtain

$$\log TC - \log r = \log \alpha + \beta \log Q + \gamma \log (w/r)$$

which, using the rules of logarithms, can be rewritten as

$$\log \left[\frac{TC}{r}\right] = \log \alpha + \beta \log Q + \gamma \log (w/r)$$

This equation is then estimated in order to obtain an estimate of the long-run cost function.

As noted earlier, the primary use of the long-run cost function is in the firm's investment decision. Therefore, once the above cost equation is estimated, its most important use is determining the extent of economies of scale. From the discussion of log-linear functions in Chapter 5, the coefficient β indicates the **elasticity of total cost** with respect to output; that is,

$$\beta = \frac{\text{Percentage change in total cost}}{\text{Percentage change in output}}$$

When $\beta > 1$, cost is increasing more than proportionately to output (e.g., if the percentage change in output is 25 percent and the percentage change in cost is 50 percent, β would be equal to 2); therefore long-run average cost

TABLE 12D.1

Summary of the Cobb-Douglas Specification for Long-Run Total Cost

Long-run total cost	$TC = \alpha Q^{\beta} w^{\gamma} r^{1-\gamma}$ $= \alpha Q^{\beta} \left(\frac{w}{r}\right)^{\gamma} r$
Estimable form	$\log\left[\frac{TC}{r}\right] = \log \alpha + \beta \log Q + \gamma \log\left(\frac{w}{r}\right)$
Elasticity of total cost	$\beta = \frac{\%\Delta TC}{\%\Delta Q}$
If $\begin{Bmatrix} \beta < 1 \\ \beta = 1 \\ \beta > 1 \end{Bmatrix}$ there exist	$\begin{Bmatrix} \text{economies of} \\ \text{constant returns to} \\ \text{diseconomies of} \end{Bmatrix}$ scale
Restrictions on parameters	$\alpha > 0$ $\beta > 0$ $0 < \gamma < 1$

would be increasing. Hence if $\beta > 1$, the estimates indicate diseconomies of scale. If $\beta < 1$, total cost increases proportionately less than the increase in output and economies of scale would be indicated. Furthermore, note that the magnitude of the estimate of β indicates the "strength" of the economies or diseconomies of scale. Finally, if $\beta = 1$, there are constant returns to scale. The statistical significance of β is tested in the manner outlined earlier. Table 12D.1 summarizes the mathematical properties of the Cobb-Douglas specification for long-run total cost.

PART

V

Perfect Competition

CHAPTER

13 Theory of Perfectly Competitive Firms and Industries

This is the first in a series of chapters that address an important question facing all managers: What can I do to achieve the highest possible profits for my firm? Although the answer sometimes differs, depending on the type of market in which the firm sells its products, the fundamental principles are quite similar for all firms. These principles were developed in the theory of unconstrained maximization in Chapter 4. The decision maker chooses the level of an activity or activities so as to maximize the net benefits—total benefits minus total costs. To maximize net benefits, marginal benefits must equal marginal cost for the last unit of the activity. In the case of firms, the net benefits are called profits. Profit is the difference between total revenue and total cost. Thus profit is maximized where marginal revenue equals marginal cost for the last unit of the activity undertaken. As we will show in this chapter, a manager can choose either the level of output or the level of employment of inputs to maximize profits. As you will see, choosing either the output level or the level of input usage will lead to the same maximum profit outcome.

This chapter and Chapter 14 set forth the theory of profit maximization for firms selling in perfectly competitive markets. Such markets are the simplest and most straightforward of all market structures. Perfectly competitive markets consist of a large number of small firms, each of which sells a product that is identical to the products sold by every other firm in the market. Each firm is small enough that its sales have absolutely no effect on the market price. Each firm believes that it can sell all the output it produces at the going market price.

Within the framework of profit maximization, managers of perfectly competitive firms—firms selling in perfectly competitive markets—look at price and cost conditions facing their firm in order to answer three fundamental questions: (1) Should the firm produce or shut down? (2) If the firm produces, what is the optimal level of production? (3) What are the optimal levels of each input to employ? The major part of this chapter is devoted to presenting the theory of how such decisions are made to maximize the firm's profits. Notice that since the perfectly competitive firm takes the market price as given, the manager is not faced with the decision concerning what price to charge. Later chapters will address the pricing decision within other types of market structures in which the manager of a business must decide what price to charge.

The theory of perfect competition is important for two reasons. First, the theory describes important segments of an economy, the most important of which are the markets for most agricultural products. Typically, in agricultural markets, there are a large number of firms that are small relative to the entire market—each firm produces only a small fraction of the total industry output. Each agricultural producer recognizes that the price of the product is determined by the market forces of demand and supply, and thus cannot be set by an individual producer. In addition to agricultural products, many other products are also sold in markets that are perfectly competitive, or nearly perfectly competitive.

A second reason the theory of perfect competition is important is that the conclusions derived from it frequently permit accurate explanation and prediction of real world phenomena. The theory often works well as a model of economic processes even though it does not precisely describe the firms and industries under consideration. Therefore, the fundamentals of the theory are useful not only to economists but to managerial decision makers as well. Managers can profitably use the conclusions of the theory, even though all of its assumptions do not exactly fit the characteristics of their firms.

To summarize, although relatively few markets are perfectly competitive, the behavior of many markets closely approximates the model of perfect competition. Thus, we can use the model as an approximation of real-world markets that are *close* to being perfectly competitive.

13.1 CHARACTERISTICS OF PERFECT COMPETITION

Because firms in perfectly competitive markets produce identical products and face a given market price, the essence of the theory is that producers do not recognize any competitiveness among themselves; that is, no direct competition among firms exists. Therefore, the theoretical concept of competition in these markets is diametrically opposed to the generally accepted concept of competition. We could say that the automobile industry or the personal computer industry is quite competitive since each firm in these industries must consider what its rivals will do before it makes a decision about advertising campaigns, design changes, quality improvements, and so forth. However, that type of market is far removed from the theory of perfect competition, which permits no personal rivalry. ("Personal" rivalry is personal in the sense that firms consider the reactions of other firms in determining their own policy.) In perfect competition all relevant economic magnitudes are determined by impersonal market forces.

perfect competition
A market structure that exists when (1) all firms produce a homogeneous product, (2) each firm is so small it cannot affect price, (3) entry and exit are unrestricted, and (4) each firm has complete knowledge about production and prices.

Several important conditions define **perfect competition**:

1. The product of each firm in a perfectly competitive market is identical to the product of every other firm. This condition ensures that buyers are indifferent as to the firm from which they purchase. Product differences, whether real or imaginary, are precluded under perfect competition. Thus, the market is characterized by a homogeneous (or perfectly standardized) commodity.
2. Each firm in the industry must be so small relative to the total market that it cannot affect the market price of the good it produces by changing its output. If all producers act together, changes in quantity will definitely affect market price. But, if perfect competition prevails, each producer is so small that individual changes will go unnoticed. Neither is any individual firm able to affect the price of any input by its usage of that input. Again all producers could, under certain conditions, change their usage of an input and affect its price. In other words, the actions of any individual firm do not affect the market supply of the product produced or the market demand for any input.
3. There exists unrestricted entry and exit into and out of the industry. Hence, there can be no artificial restrictions on the number of firms in the industry. New firms do not require huge amounts of capital equipment and investment to enter perfectly competitive industries.
4. Each firm has full and complete knowledge about the product and the market. Thus each firm knows the best—least cost—method of production, the price of output, and input prices. Even potential entrants know whether or not firms in the industry are making economic profits. This assumption of complete information is made for analytical convenience only and is not necessary for the development of the theory.

13.2 BASIC PRINCIPLES OF PROFIT MAXIMIZATION

In order to explain and predict how managers can and do make decisions about production levels, employment of inputs, or the price to charge (for firms operating in markets *not* perfectly competitive), we must begin with an assumption about how a manager behaves. A fundamental behavioral assumption underlying the theory of perfect competition, and for that matter, theories of behavior of firms selling in *all* types of market structures, is that managers make decisions with the objective of maximizing the amount of profit to be earned. While this assumption has been widely used by economists to model the decision making of managers, you might be concerned that profit maximization is a bit too restrictive to describe the motivation of *all* managers *all* the time. Managers of firms may from time to time pursue goals other than profit maximization. Indeed, economists have suggested a number of alternatives to profit maximization as the goal of managers.

It has been suggested that the salaries of many managers are linked to the level of sales—or possibly the rate of growth of sales—instead of the level of profit earned by the firm. In such situations, managers may be more interested in maximizing sales than maximizing profit. (We will show later that maximizing sales revenue does not, in general, maximize profit.) Another alternative to the profit maximization assumption is to view a manager as making decisions that maximize the manager's utility—that is, managers might seek to maximize their own utility by using the firm's resources to provide themselves with generous perks such as luxurious offices, private club memberships, entertainment expense accounts, company cars, or expensive health insurance. Some managers have been known to promote their favorite social causes (but not necessarily favorites of all the owners of the firm). Naturally, the owners (stockholders) of the firm would object to such behavior by managers, but it is costly and sometimes difficult to oversee managers to make sure they are indeed maximizing profits.[1]

Despite these and other situations in which managers may find themselves pursuing a goal other than profit maximization, the assumption of profit maximization generally leads to the best predictions and explanations about the way actual markets and firms function. Most managers do seek higher profits most of the time. It would be an unusual manager who was completely uninterested in profits or who did not include them as an important goal of the firm. As you will see in this chapter, firms operating in perfectly competitive markets will be forced to maximize profit if they are to survive in the long run. Therefore, we will follow tradition in this textbook and assume that all firms attempt to maximize profit even though we recognize that there may be some exceptions.

Economic Profit and Normal Profit

Before examining the basic principles of profit maximization, we should briefly discuss the meaning of economic profit and introduce the concept of normal profit. **Economic profit** is the amount by which total revenue exceeds total economic cost, where total economic cost is the total opportunity cost of all resources used by the firm. As discussed in Chapter 10, the opportunity cost of using resources owned by others is equal to the dollar amount paid to the resource owners. For the resources used by the firm that are owned by the firm, the opportunity cost is equal to the largest payment that the owner could have received if that resource had been leased or sold in the market. Therefore, if the owner manages the firm, the greatest income the owner could have earned in alternative employment must be included as a cost of production. Or, if the owner invested personal resources in purchasing the capital used in the firm's production process, the maximum return that could be earned elsewhere if the capital is sold or leased is an opportunity cost of production.

economic profit
The difference between total revenue and total economic cost, including both explicit and implicit cost:
$\pi = TR - TC$.

[1]When the owners of a firm do not manage a firm themselves, and instead hire a manager to run the firm, the manager acts as an *agent* for the owners of the firm—the owners being the *principal* in this situation. Owners typically expect managers to maximize the profit of the firm. When managers pursue a goal other than profit maximization, the so-called *principal-agent problem* arises. We will discuss the principal-agent problem later in Chapter 19.

normal profit
The opportunity cost of owner-supplied resources.

Economists frequently refer to the opportunity cost of using the owner's own resources as a **normal profit**. Normal profit is just another name for the implicit opportunity cost that a firm incurs when it employs owner-supplied resources such as financial capital and management services. In contrast to economic profit, which is computed by subtracting total cost from total revenue, normal profit is in no way related to total revenue. Normal profit is simply a part of total cost. As a part of total cost, normal profit does play a role in determining the economic profit of the firm:

$$\begin{aligned}\text{Economic profit} &= \text{Total revenue} - \text{Total economic cost}\\ &= \text{Total revenue} - \text{Explicit costs} - \text{Normal profit}\end{aligned}$$

Any return to the owner over and above a normal profit is economic profit. When total revenue just covers total economic cost, economic profit is zero, and the firm's owner earns just a normal profit.

To illustrate the concepts, assume a firm has revenues of $5 million and explicit costs of $3 million. The owner of the firm has provided $1 million of capital to the firm. If the owner could have earned a 10 percent return on the $1 million in the best alternative investment (of similar risk), the normal profit is $100,000. Economic profit is $1.9 million (= $5 million – $3 million – $.1 million). Sometimes normal profit is expressed as a rate of return. In this example, the normal rate of return is 10 percent. Suppose this same firm only received a total revenue of $3.1 million; then the firm would be earning only a normal profit (or just a **normal rate of return**), and economic profit is zero. In this text, when we use the term *profit*, we mean pure or economic profit; that is, profit over and above the return on the owner's resources.

normal rate of return
A firm earns only a normal rate of return when economic profit is zero and only a normal profit is being earned.

When the owners of a firm earn positive economic profit, they earn more than a normal profit on their owner-supplied resources. If owners earn just a normal profit (i.e., economic profit is zero), then their resources are earning only as much as could be earned if these resources were employed in their best alternative. When less than a normal profit is being earned (i.e., economic profit is negative), the owners will not wish to stay in the market since their resources could be earning more in an alternative market. As you will see later in this chapter, when economic profit becomes negative and firms earn less than a normal profit, firms will exit an industry in the long run.

Relation Normal profit is the opportunity cost of the owner's resources, which are used by the firm. Normal profit is added to explicit costs to obtain the total economic cost of production. When economic profit is zero, the firm is just earning a normal profit or a normal rate of return. When economic profit is positive (negative), the firm earns a higher (lower) than normal rate of return.

Choosing the Level of Output or Input Usage to Maximize Profit

The basic principles of profit maximization are straightforward and follow from the discussion of optimization in Chapter 4. The economic profit earned by a firm is equal to the difference between total revenue (*TR*) and total economic cost of production (*TC*). Both total revenue and total cost are determined by the level of output the manager of the firm chooses to produce:

$$TR = R(Q)$$

and

$$TC = C(Q)$$

where $R(Q)$ and $C(Q)$ mean total revenue and total cost are functions of the level of output (Q). A manager, then, can view the level of output as the choice variable for determining the value of the firm's objective function, which is profit. Since the manager's choice of output determines the amount of profit earned by the firm, profit (π) itself is a function of output:

$$\begin{aligned}\pi &= R(Q) - C(Q) \\ &= \pi(Q)\end{aligned}$$

As shown in Chapter 10, the level of output is determined by the level of usage of resources. If, for example, only two inputs (labor and capital) are used in production, the production function,

$$Q = f(L, K)$$

indicates the maximum output that can be produced by a given amount of labor and capital. Because labor and capital usage determine output, which in turn determines the level of profit, the manager can view labor and capital as the choice variables that determine the level of profit:[2]

$$\begin{aligned}\pi &= \pi(Q) \\ &= \pi[Q(L, K)] \\ &= \pi(L, K)\end{aligned}$$

A manager can view maximizing profit as the problem of finding either (1) the optimal level of output, or (2) the optimal level of input usage. The two approaches are equivalent since choosing either the profit-maximizing levels of labor and capital or the profit-maximizing level of output lead to the same level of profit.[3]

Relation Since both total revenue and total cost are functions of output, profit is a function of output, and the manager can view output as a choice variable for maximizing profit. Alternatively, since output itself is a function of input usage (through the production function), the manager can also treat the level of usage of inputs as the choice variables for maximizing profit.

[2]We are referring to a long-run situation here since capital is being treated as a variable input. In a short-run situation, when capital is a fixed input, the manager can affect profit only through changes in labor usage: $\pi = \pi(L)$.

[3]The equivalency of choosing either the level of input usage or the level of output is based on the assumption that the optimal level of output will, in fact, be produced efficiently (i.e., at minimum total cost).

Choosing Output to Maximize Profit

Suppose the manager treats output as the choice variable for maximizing the firm's profit. You may recall from the discussion in Chapter 4 on optimization theory, that the manager should increase any activity so long as the additional revenue from the increase exceeds the additional cost of the increase. The firm will decrease the activity if the additional revenue is less than the additional cost. Thus a manager who wishes to maximize profit should choose the level of the activity at which the additional revenue just equals the additional cost.

When the activity or choice variable is the firm's level of output, the rules of optimization apply in a straightforward way. As the firm increases its level of output, each additional unit adds to the total revenue of the firm. The additional revenue attributable to producing one more unit of output is called marginal revenue. As the firm increases its level of output, each unit increase in output increases the firm's total cost. The additional cost of producing one more unit of output is called marginal cost.

This chapter is concerned with the special case in which the price of the commodity is given to the firm by the market. In this special case, marginal revenue equals price. For example, if the firm produces plywood, and the market price of plywood is $300 per 1,000 square feet, the marginal revenue from each additional thousand square feet is $300. The owner of the firm would increase plywood production as long as the marginal cost of each additional thousand square feet is less than $300. The owner would not increase production if each additional thousand square feet costs more than $300 to produce.

Thus, the firm will choose to expand output so long as the added revenue from the expansion (marginal revenue) is greater than the added cost of the expansion (marginal cost). The firm will decrease output if marginal cost is greater than marginal revenue. In order to maximize profit, the manager chooses to produce the level of output for which marginal revenue equals marginal cost ($MR = MC$). Profit maximization is, therefore, based upon the following principle:

Principle If an increase in output adds more to revenue than to cost, the increase in output adds to profit. If the increase in output adds less to revenue than to cost, the increase in output subtracts from profit. The firm, therefore, chooses the level of output at which marginal revenue equals marginal cost. This level of output maximizes total profit.

Choosing Input Usage to Maximize Profit

As mentioned above, profit maximization can also be analyzed through the firm's choice of the level of input usage. Again the principle is simple and follows directly from the analysis in Chapter 4. The firm will expand its usage of any input (or factor of production) so long as additional units of the input add more to the firm's revenue than to cost. The firm would not increase the usage of the input if hiring more units increases the firm's cost more than its revenue.

marginal revenue product ($MRP = \Delta TR/\Delta I$) The additional revenue earned when the firm hires one more unit of the input.

The extra revenue added by another unit of the input is called the **marginal revenue product (MRP)** of that input:

$$MRP = \frac{\Delta TR}{\Delta I}$$

where TR is the firm's total revenue and I is the level of usage of a particular input. As before, the "Δ" symbol means "change in." Thus, if the marginal revenue product of the tenth worker is $150, this means the additional output attributable to hiring the tenth worker adds $150 to total revenue when it is sold. The additional cost to the firm of hiring another unit of an input is called the **marginal factor cost (*MFC*)** of that input:

marginal factor cost ($MFC = \Delta TC/\Delta I$)
The additional cost to the firm when it hires one more unit of the input.

$$MFC = \frac{\Delta TC}{\Delta I}$$

If, for example, labor can be hired for $15 per hour, the marginal factor cost of hiring another unit of labor is $15. So long as MRP is greater than MFC, the manager should continue to increase usage of the input. In order to maximize profit, all inputs are hired up to the point where marginal revenue product equals marginal factor cost ($MRP = MFC$).

Suppose a manufacturing firm can hire all of the labor it wishes at $10 an hour, or $80 per day. The firm would increase labor usage so long as it expects each additional worker hired to add more than $80 a day to the firm's revenue ($MRP > MFC$). It would not increase the number of laborers hired if an additional laborer would add less than $80 a day to revenue ($MRP < MFC$). The firm would hire labor up to the point where the marginal revenue product is just equal to $80 ($MRP = MFC$). In this way profit is maximized. When input usage is the choice variable for profit maximization, the procedure for maximizing profit is set forth in the following principle:

Principle If an increase in the usage of an input in the production process adds more to revenue than to cost, the increase in input usage adds to profit. If an increase in usage of the input adds less to revenue than to cost, the increase in usage reduces profit. The firm, therefore, chooses the level of input usage at which the additional revenue per unit change in the input—called marginal revenue product (*MRP*)—equals the additional cost per unit of the input added—called marginal factor cost (*MFC*).

13.3 DEMAND FACING A PERFECTLY COMPETITIVE FIRM

Suppose you are the owner-manager of a small citrus orchard that specializes in the production of oranges, which your firm then processes to be sold as frozen concentrate. You wish to determine the maximum price you can charge for various levels of output of frozen concentrate; that is, you wish to find the demand schedule facing your firm. After consulting *The Wall Street Journal*, you find that the market-determined price of orange juice concentrate is $1.20 per pound. You have 50,000 pounds of concentrate to sell, which makes your output minuscule compared to the tens of millions of pounds of orange juice concentrate sold in the market as a whole. On top of that, you realize that buyers of orange juice concentrate don't care about whom they buy from since all orange juice concentrate is virtually identical (homogenous).

FIGURE 13.1
Demand and Marginal Revenue Facing a Citrus Producer

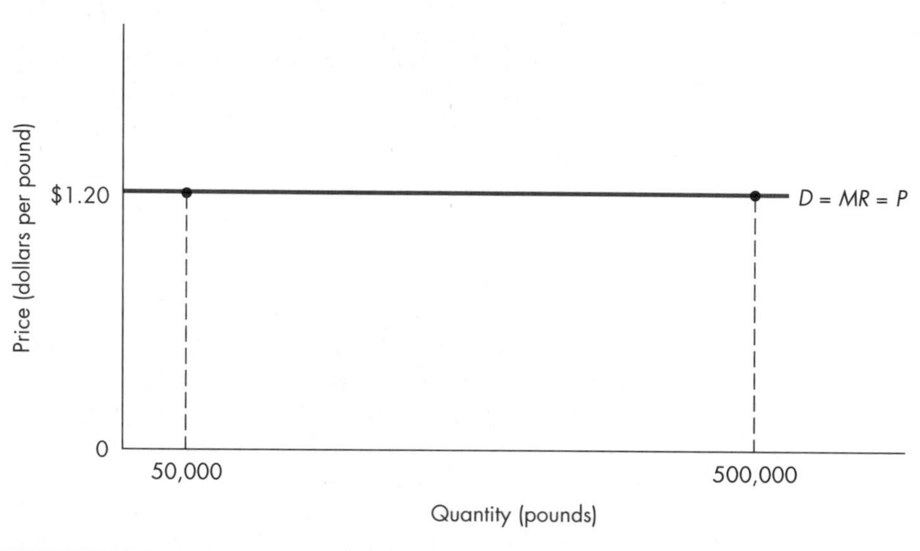

All at once it hits you like a ton of oranges: You can sell virtually all the orange juice concentrate you wish at the going market price of $1.20 per pound. Even if you increased your output tenfold to 500,000 pounds, you could still find buyers willing to pay you $1.20 per pound for the entire 500,000 pounds because your output, by itself, is not going to affect (shift) market supply in any perceptible way. Indeed, if you lowered the price to sell more oranges, you would be needlessly sacrificing revenue. You also realize that you cannot charge a price higher than $1.20 per pound because buyers will simply buy from one of the thousands of other citrus producers that produce orange juice concentrate identical to your own.

By this reasoning, you realize that the demand curve facing your citrus grove can be drawn as shown in Figure 13.1. The demand for your firm's product is horizontal at a price of $1.20 per pound of orange juice concentrate. The demand price for any level of orange juice concentrate is $1.20, no matter how many pounds you produce. This means that every extra pound sold contributes $1.20 to total revenue, and hence, the market price of $1.20 is also the marginal revenue for every pound of orange juice concentrate sold. The demand curve facing the citrus producer is also its marginal revenue curve.

We can generalize the above discussion to apply to *any* firm that is perfectly competitive. When a market is characterized by a large number of (relatively) small producers, each producing a homogeneous product, the demand curve facing the manager of each individual firm is horizontal at the price determined by the intersection of the *market* demand and supply curves. In addition, the horizontal demand curve is also the marginal revenue curve facing the manager.

FIGURE 13.2
Derivation of Demand for a Perfectly Competitive Firm

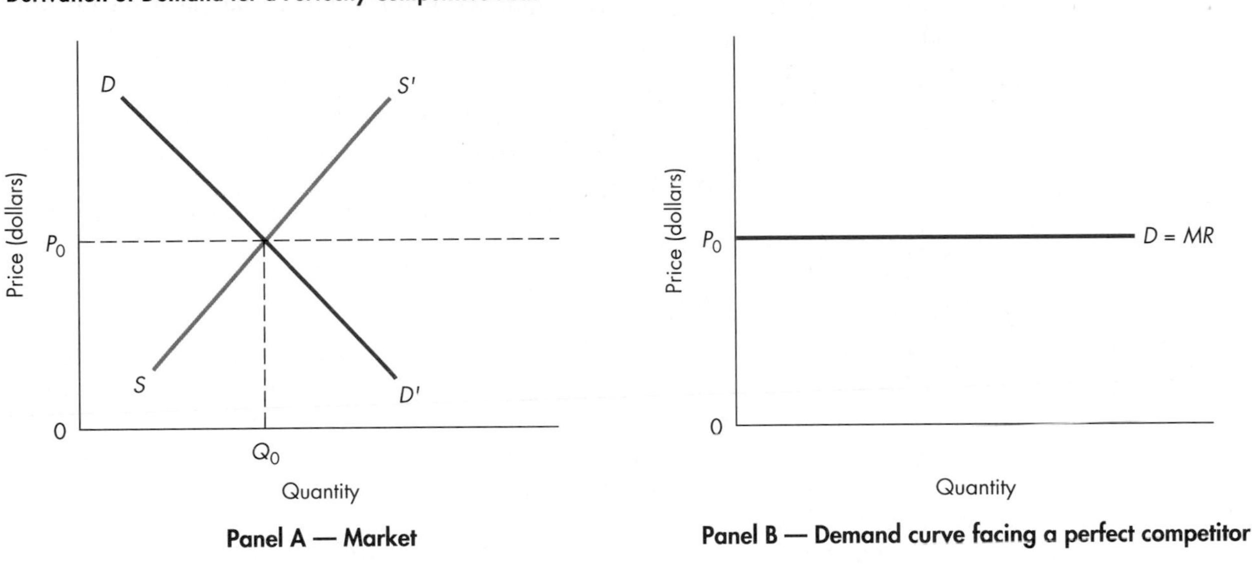

Panel A — Market

Panel B — Demand curve facing a perfect competitor

Figure 13.2 illustrates the derivation of demand for a perfectly competitive firm. Note, in Figure 13.2, that the *market* demand curve *DD′* in Panel A is downward sloping, which the law of demand always requires of a demand curve. It is the demand curve faced by a single firm that is horizontal, as shown in Panel B of Figure 13.2. Recall from Chapter 2 that demand price is the maximum price buyers can be charged for a given amount of the good. The demand price is constant, and equal to P_0, for any level of output produced by the firm. Since each additional unit sold adds exactly P_0 to total revenue, marginal revenue equals P_0 for all output levels for the firm, as shown in Panel B in Figure 13.2.

The horizontal demand curve facing an individual firm selling in a perfectly competitive market is frequently called a *perfectly* (or infinitely) *elastic demand*. Recall from Chapter 3 that the point elasticity of demand is measured by $E = P/(P - a)$, where a is the price-intercept of the demand curve. Measured at any given price, as demand becomes flatter, $|P - a|$ becomes smaller, and $|E|$ becomes larger. In the limit when demand is horizontal, $P - a = 0$, and $|E| = \infty$. Thus, for a horizontal demand, demand is said to be infinitely elastic or perfectly elastic.

Looked at another way, the product sold by a perfectly competitive firm has a large number of *perfect* substitutes—the identical (homogeneous) products sold by the other firms in the industry. As we stressed in Chapter 3, the better the substitutes for a product, the more elastic the demand for the product. The perfectly competitive firm's product, with many perfect substitutes, therefore has a perfectly elastic demand.

Again, we emphasize the fact that perfectly competitive firms face a perfectly elastic or horizontal demand does not mean that the law of demand does not apply to perfectly competitive markets. It does. The *market demand* for the product is downward sloping.

Relation The demand curve facing the manager of an individual perfectly competitive firm is horizontal or perfectly elastic at the price determined by the intersection of the *market* demand and supply curves. Since marginal revenue equals price for a perfectly competitive firm, the demand curve is also simultaneously the marginal revenue curve under perfect competition (i.e., $D = MR$). The firm can sell all it wants at the market price. Each additional unit of sales adds an amount equal to price to the firm's total revenue.

13.4 PROFIT MAXIMIZATION IN THE SHORT RUN

We now turn to the output decision facing the manager of a firm in a perfectly competitive industry in the short run. Recall that the short run is that time period of decision making during which the firm has at least one of its inputs fixed in quantity. In the short-run period of analysis, the manager has fixed costs that must be paid regardless of the level of output and variable costs that vary with the level of output.

shut down
When a firm produces zero output but must still pay for fixed inputs.

In the short run, a manager must make two decisions. The first decision is whether to produce or shut down during the period. By **shut down**, we mean the manager decides to produce zero output and to hire none of the variable inputs. When production is zero, the only costs incurred by the firm are the fixed costs. If the first decision is to produce (rather than shut down), the second decision is the choice of the optimal level of output. As noted earlier, when a firm is in a perfectly competitive industry, the manager has no control over price and therefore does not have a pricing decision.

In this section, we first discuss the firm's output decision, assuming that the decision to produce rather than shut down has been made. We then give the conditions under which the manager should choose to shut down rather than produce. Next, a numerical example is presented to emphasize that fixed costs are completely irrelevant for managerial decision making. After briefly summarizing the firm's output decision in the short run, the supply curve for a perfectly competitive firm is derived, and the firm's supply curve is then used to derive the short-run supply curve for a perfectly competitive industry.

The Manager's Output Decision

We begin by assuming the manager has already decided to produce rather than shut down, and must now find the optimal level of output to produce. Using the terminology presented in Chapter 4, the optimal level of output is that level of output that maximizes the objective function, which is economic profit:

$$\pi = TR - TC$$

Under some circumstances, which we discuss later, a firm will choose to make losses (i.e., profit is negative) yet continue to produce rather than shut down. In

FIGURE 13.3
Finding the Profit-Maximizing Output Level: $P = MC$

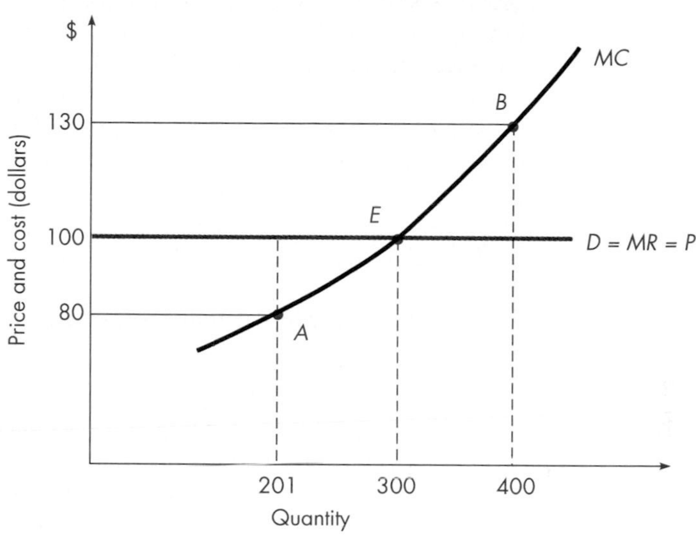

such a situation, the manager chooses the level of output that *minimizes* the loss of the firm. Since minimizing a loss is equivalent to maximizing a (negative) profit, the decision rule for finding the optimal level of output is exactly the same regardless of whether profit is positive or negative. For this reason, we will speak of profit maximization in deriving the rule for finding the optimal level of output even though the same rule applies to the firm that is minimizing a loss.

As emphasized, a manager of a profit-maximizing firm will increase its output as long as the marginal revenue (which is equal to price) from selling another unit exceeds the marginal cost of producing that unit. Figure 13.3 illustrates the output decision of a manager. The firm faces a market-determined price of $100, which is the marginal revenue, and the marginal cost curve is *MC*. Suppose that the firm is producing 200 units of output, which it can sell for a price of $100 per unit, and the marginal cost of the 201st unit is $80 (see point *A* in Figure 13.3). By choosing to produce and sell the 201st unit, the manager adds $100 to revenue and only $80 to cost, thereby adding $20 to the firm's profit. By this same reasoning, the manager would continue to increase production so long as *MR* (= *P*) is greater than *MC*. In Figure 13.3, output would be increased to 300 units, the output level for which $P = MR = MC =$ $100 (point *E* in Figure 13.3).

If, on the other hand, a mistake has been made and the firm is producing an output of 400 units at which marginal revenue (price) is less than marginal cost, the manager can increase the firm's profit by reducing output. For example, the marginal cost of producing the 400th unit is $130, while the price remains $100 (see point *B* in Figure 13.3). The manager could decrease output by one unit and reduce its cost by $130 (the cost of the extra resources needed to produce the 400th unit). The lost sale of that unit would reduce revenue by only $100, so the firm's profit would increase by \$30. By the same reasoning, the manager would continue to decrease production so long as MR (= P) is less than MC (up to point E in Figure 13.3). It follows, then, that the manager maximizes profit by choosing that level of output where MR (= P) = MC. This rule is, of course, the rule for unconstrained maximization set forth in Chapter 4 ($MB = MC$).

We obviously don't mean to imply that the firm begins with zero output, then expands by actually producing and selling the first unit, then the second, and so on until it produces and sells the last unit, at which MR equals MC. The manager makes the short-run production decision after looking at price and the firm's cost structure. It then chooses the optimal level of output to produce.

The Output Decision: Positive Economic Profit

Figure 13.4 shows a typical set of short-run cost curves—marginal cost (MC), average total cost (ATC), and average variable cost (AVC). (Average fixed cost is omitted for convenience and because, as we will demonstrate, it is irrelevant for the output decision.) Suppose that the market-determined price, and therefore the marginal revenue, is \$10 per unit. Marginal revenue equals marginal cost at point E, with 600 units of output being produced and sold.

The firm would not produce less than 600 units. At any lower output, an additional unit sold would add \$10 to the firm's revenue, but, since marginal cost

FIGURE 13.4
Profit-Maximization in the Short Run

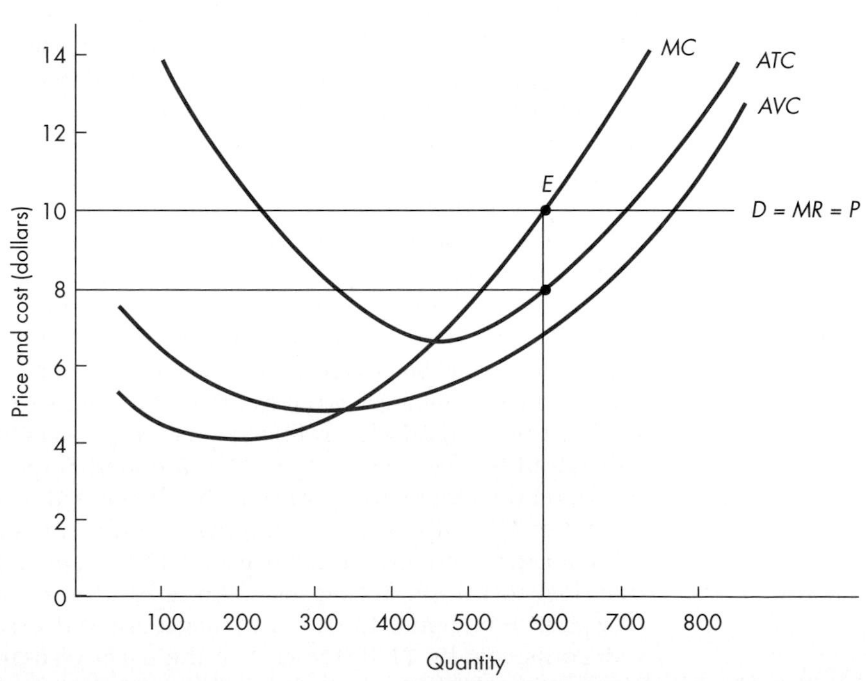

is less than $10 for this unit of output, the cost of producing this additional unit is less than the additional revenue. Thus, at any output lower than 600 units, producing and selling an additional unit of output would increase profit. Likewise, the firm would not produce more than 600 units. Beyond 600 units, a reduction in output would increase profit, because one less unit of output would reduce cost by more than $10, the lost revenue. Thus, producing any output less than or greater than 600 units is not profit maximizing.

Therefore the firm maximizes profit by producing and selling 600 units of output per period of time. The average total cost of producing 600 units is $8 per unit, as shown from *ATC* in the figure. Thus, the total cost of production is average total cost times quantity, or $8 × 600 = $4,800. Total revenue, price times quantity, is $10 × 600 = $6,000. The maximum possible profit is, therefore, $6,000 – $4,800 = $1,200.

Looking at Figure 13.4, suppose that the market price is higher than $10. The perfectly elastic demand facing the firm would rise and the profit-maximizing level of output would also rise. If price is higher, the firm will produce a greater output. Conversely, if price is lower, the firm will produce a lower output. It follows then that the firm's output varies directly with price. For example, if price is $12, the firm would produce almost 700 units (where *MC* = $12); if price is $8, the firm would produce slightly more than 500 units (where *MC* = $8). Clearly the higher the price, the more profit earned by the firm.

Since the $4,800 total cost includes the normal profit or opportunity cost of the resources provided by the firm's owners, the owners are earning $1,200 more than they could if they had employed their resources in their best alternative use. The $1,200 economic profit is a return to the owners *in excess* of what they could have earned in their best alternative. As explained earlier, when a firm earns positive economic profit, it is earning more than a normal profit or more than a normal rate of return.

The Output Decision: The Firm Operates at a Loss

In the short run, when the manager of a perfectly competitive firm faces a market-determined price that is less than average total cost ($P < ATC$) at every level of output, total revenue must be less than total cost at every level of output and the firm will make a loss no matter what output it produces. Therefore, the manager must decide whether to produce the output that leads to the smallest loss, or shut down the firm, produce zero output, and lose all of its fixed cost. The decision rule is simple: The firm should produce a positive output and suffer a loss only if that loss is smaller than the loss the firm would incur by producing nothing (shutting down). The firm should shut down and produce nothing if the loss at zero output is less than the smallest loss it could incur by producing a positive level of output. When a firm produces nothing, it loses an amount equal to its total fixed cost ($\pi = -TFC$). The firm's total revenue is zero, and its total cost is equal to its fixed cost since variable cost is zero.

Figure 13.5, with the same cost curves as those shown in Figure 13.4, illustrates the manager's decision to produce or to shut down. Suppose the manager

FIGURE 13.5
Loss Minimization in the Short Run

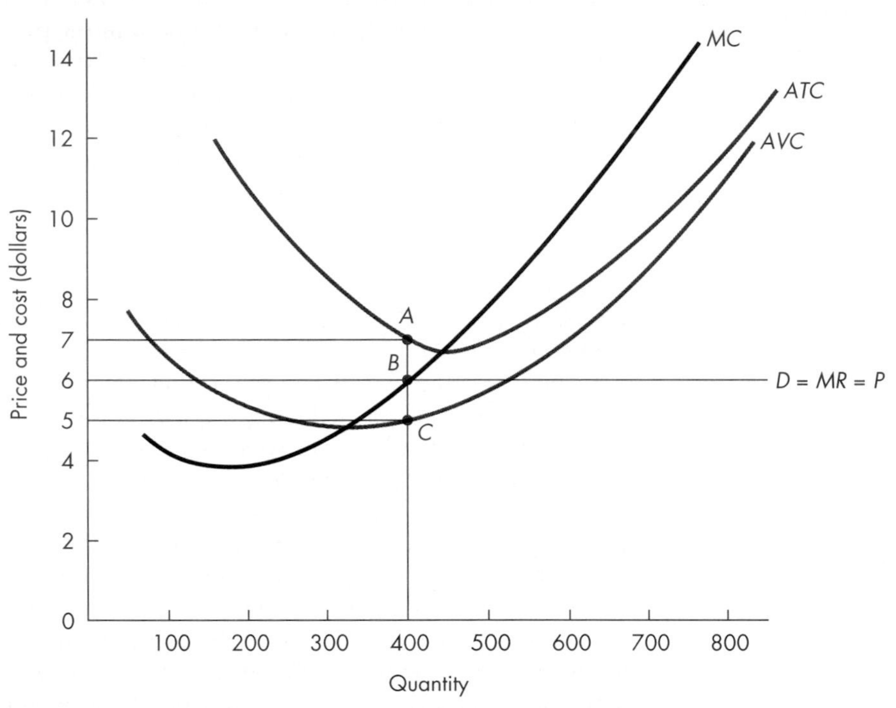

faces a price of \$6. The firm must suffer a loss at every output level because \$6 is less than average total cost ($P < ATC$) at all levels of output. If the manager does decide to produce, rather than shut down, the firm should produce 400 units where MR (= P) = MC = \$6. At 400 units of output, total revenue is \$2,400 (= \$6 × 400), total cost is \$2,800 (= \$7 × 400), and the firm earns a (negative) profit equal to –\$400 (= \$2,400 – \$2,800). The manager should choose to produce 400 units at a loss of \$400 only if the firm would lose more than \$400 by producing nothing.

To compute the total fixed cost (the loss when $Q = 0$), recall that $TFC = AFC \times Q$. Also recall that $AFC = ATC - AVC$. You can see in Figure 13.5 that AFC = \$2 (the distance from A to C, or \$7 – \$5), so TFC = \$2 × 400 = \$800. The manager should produce 400 units at a loss of \$400 rather than produce zero units (shut down) and lose \$800.

In a short-run situation when a firm cannot earn positive economic profit ($P < ATC$), a manager should make the decision to produce or to shut down production using the following rule: If price exceeds average variable cost ($P > AVC$), the firm should produce the level of output where $P = MC$ rather than produce nothing at all. When $P > AVC$, total revenue exceeds total variable cost ($TR > TVC$). The firm generates enough revenue to pay all of its variable costs and has some revenue left over to apply toward its fixed costs. Consequently, the loss incurred from production must be less than total fixed cost, which is the amount lost if nothing is produced.

Again consider Figure 13.5. At 400 units, price ($6) exceeds average variable cost ($5) by $1. Thus, on 400 units of output, total revenue ($2,400) exceeds total variable cost ($5 × 400 = $2,000) by $400 ($2,400 – $2,000). The $400 revenue left over after paying variable costs can then be applied toward paying a part of the $800 fixed cost. The remainder of the fixed costs that are not covered represent the loss to the firm ($400 = $800 – $400).

When price is less than minimum average variable cost ($P < AVC$), TR is less than TVC, and the firm would lose all of its fixed costs plus the portion of its variable costs not covered by revenues if it produces. The firm could improve its earnings situation by producing nothing and losing only fixed cost. We can summarize the manager's decision to produce or not to produce with a principle.

Principle In the short run, the manager of a firm will choose to produce, rather than shut down, so long as total revenue more than covers the total variable costs of production ($TR > TVC$), or equivalently, price exceeds average variable cost ($P > AVC$). If price is less than average variable cost ($P < AVC$), the manager will produce nothing and lose only fixed costs.

The Irrelevance of Fixed Costs

When managers make production decisions, they decide how much to produce (if they do produce) by choosing the level of output where price equals marginal cost. They decide whether or not to produce that output by comparing price with average variable cost. If $P > AVC$, the firm should produce (even at a loss) the output level at which $P = MC$. Thus, fixed costs play absolutely no role in the manager's output decision.

To provide you with more insight into why fixed costs do not matter in decision making, we remind you that the marginal cost curve is unaffected by changes in fixed cost. Recall from Chapter 10 that the U-shape of the marginal cost curve is determined by the S-shape of the total variable cost curve or the ∩-shape of the marginal product curve. In Figure 13.5, for example, any change whatsoever in fixed cost has no effect on the marginal cost curve. If total fixed costs double, MC does not shift or change shape, and marginal revenue still intersects marginal cost at the same level of output. No matter what the level of fixed costs, 400 units is the profit-maximizing level of output when price is $6.

To illustrate that fixed costs do not affect the decision to produce or not to produce, we chose five different levels of total fixed costs and examined the shutdown decision for a firm with the MC and AVC curves shown in Figure 13.5. Keeping market price at $6, Table 13.1 shows all of the relevant revenue, cost, and profit information for each of the five levels of fixed cost. First note that the optimal level of production for any of the five levels of fixed cost is 400 units because MC equals $6 at 400 units, no matter what the level of fixed costs. In all cases shown in Table 13.1, total revenue is $2,400, total variable cost is $2,000, and after paying all variable costs, $400 remains to apply toward the fixed costs.

TABLE 13.1
The Irrelevance of Fixed Costs

(1) Total fixed cost	(2) Price	(3) Output	(4) Total revenue	(5) Total variable costs	(6) Revenue remaining after paying variable costs	(7) Profit (loss) if Q = 400	(8) Profit (loss) if Q = 0
$ 200	$6	400	$2,400	$2,000	$400	$ 200	$ –200
800	6	400	2,400	2,000	400	–400	–800
1,000	6	400	2,400	2,000	400	–600	–1,000
5,000	6	400	2.400	2,000	400	–4,600	–5,000
100,000	6	400	2,400	2,000	400	–99,600	–100, 000

When fixed cost is only $200, economic profit is positive because revenue exceeds all costs. Obviously the manager chooses to produce and earn a profit, rather than produce nothing and lose its fixed cost. For each of the other four cases, the revenue remaining after paying variable cost is not enough to pay all the fixed cost, and profit is negative. Columns 7 and 8, respectively, show the loss if the firm produces 400 units (where $P = MC$) and the loss if the firm produces nothing and loses its fixed cost.

Note that in all cases when the firm makes a loss, the loss from producing 400 units is $400 less than the loss if the firm shuts down. No matter how high the total fixed cost, the firm loses $400 less by producing a positive amount of output than by producing nothing (shutting down). The level of fixed cost has no effect on the firm's decision to produce.

Summary of the Manager's Output Decision in the Short Run

Figure 13.6 summarizes three possible short-run situations for the firm. First, if the market-established price is P_1, the demand and marginal revenue facing the firm are D_1 and MR_1. The optimal output for the firm to produce is at point A, where $MC = P_1$, and the firm will produce q_1 units of output. Since ATC is less than price at q_1 the firm makes an economic profit.

Next let the market price fall to P_2. Price equals MC at point C. Because average total cost is greater than price at this output, total cost is greater than total revenue, and the firm suffers a loss. The amount of loss is the loss per unit (CR) times the number of units produced (q_2).

When price is P_2 and demand is $D_2 = MR_2$, there is simply no way the firm can earn a profit. At every output level, average total cost exceeds price. The firm will continue to produce if, and only if, it loses less by producing than by closing the plant entirely. If the firm produced zero output, total revenue would also be zero and total cost would be the total fixed cost. The loss would thus be equal to total fixed cost. If the firm produces where $MC = MR$ (point C), total revenue is greater than total variable cost, because $P_2 > AVC$ at q_2 units of output. The firm covers all of its variable cost and still has CD times

FIGURE 13.6
Profit, Loss, or Shutdown in the Short Run

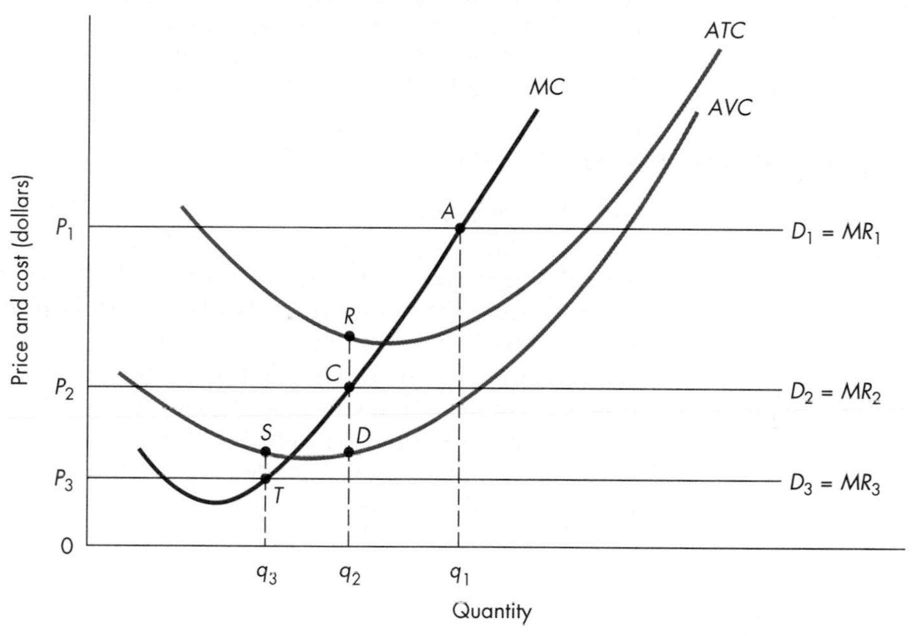

the number of units produced (q_2) left over to pay part of its fixed cost. A smaller loss is suffered when production takes place than if the firm were shut down. The loss is that part of fixed cost not covered by revenue and is clearly less than the entire fixed cost.

Finally, in Figure 13.6, suppose that the market price is P_3. Demand is given by $D_3 = MR_3$. If the firm were to produce, its equilibrium would be at T where $MC = P_3$. Output would be q_3 units per period of time. However, since the average variable cost of production exceeds price, not only would the firm lose all of its fixed costs, it would also lose ST dollars per unit on its variable costs as well. The firm could improve its earnings situation by producing nothing and losing only fixed cost. Thus when price is below average variable cost at every level of output, the short-run, loss-minimizing output is zero.

As discussed in Chapter 10 and as shown in Figure 13.6, average variable cost reaches its minimum at the point at which marginal cost and average variable cost intersect. If price is less than the minimum average variable cost, the loss-minimizing output is zero. For any price equal to or greater than minimum average variable cost, equilibrium output is determined by the intersection of marginal cost and price.[4]

[4]This result is demonstrated mathematically in the appendix to this chapter.

Principle (1) Average variable cost tells whether to produce; the firm ceases to produce—shuts down—if price falls below minimum *AVC*. (2) Marginal cost tells how much to produce; if $P >$ minimum *AVC*, the firm produces the output at which $MC = P$. (3) Average total cost tells how much profit or loss is made if the firm decides to produce; profit equals the difference between *P* and *ATC* multiplied by the quantity produced and sold.

13.5 SHORT-RUN SUPPLY FOR THE FIRM AND INDUSTRY

Using the concepts developed in the preceding discussion, it is possible to derive the short-run supply curve for an individual firm in a perfectly competitive market. Figure 13.7 illustrates the process. In Panel A, points *a, b,* and *c* are the profit-maximizing equilibrium points for the firm at prices of $5, $9, and $17, respectively. That is, the marginal cost curve above average variable cost indicates the quantity the firm would be willing and able to supply at each price, which is the definition of supply. Panel B shows 80, 110, and 150 units of output as the quantities supplied from Panel A when market price is $5, $9, and $17, respectively. For a market price lower than minimum average variable cost, quantity supplied is zero.

FIGURE 13.7
Derivation of a Short-Run Supply Curve for an Individual Firm

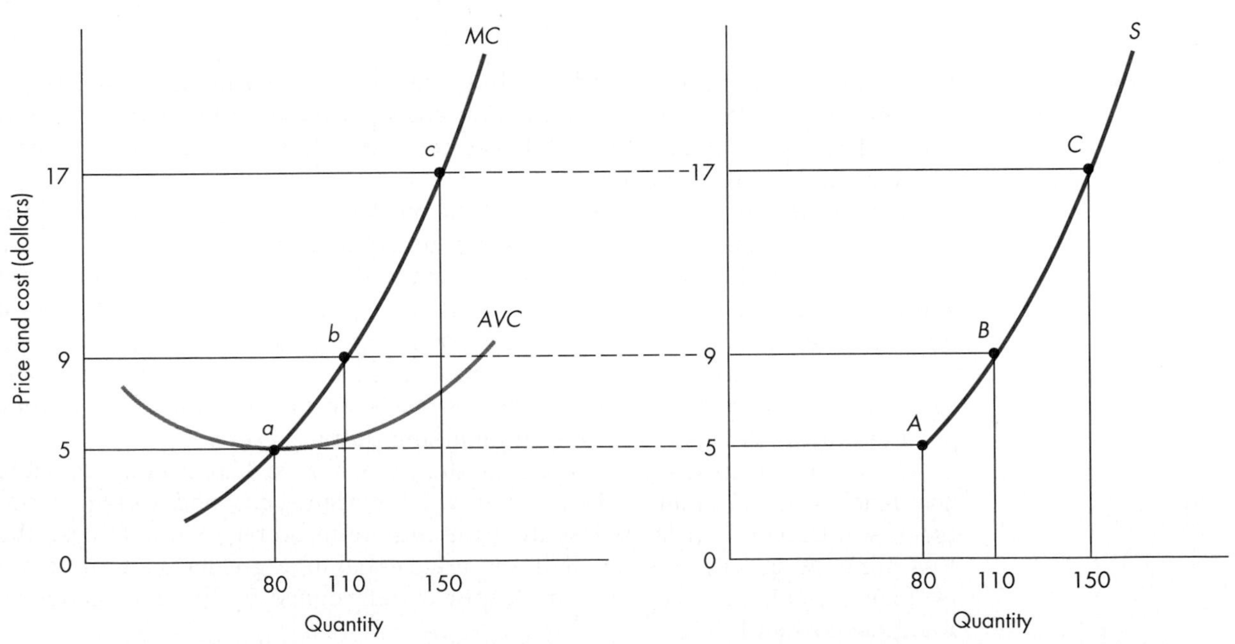

Panel A — Profit maximization for the firm

Panel B — Supply curve for the firm

Relation The short-run supply curve for an individual firm in a perfectly competitive market is the portion of the firm's marginal cost curve above minimum average variable cost. For market prices less than minimum average variable cost, quantity supplied is zero.

In contrast to market demand curves of consumers, described in Chapter 7, the industry supply curve cannot always be obtained by simply summing (horizontally) the marginal cost curves of each producer. The reason is that the short-run supply curve for each firm is derived assuming that the prices of variable inputs are constant. No change in input usage by an individual firm acting alone can change an input's unit cost to the firm, because a single competitive firm is so small relative to all users of the resource. But if all producers in an industry *simultaneously* expand output and thereby their usage of inputs, there may be a noticeable increase in the demand for some inputs. When all firms attempt to increase output, the prices of some variable inputs may be bid up, and the increase in these input prices causes an increase in all firms' cost curves, including marginal cost. Consequently, the industry's short-run supply curve usually is somewhat more steeply sloped and somewhat less elastic when input prices increase in response to an increase in industry output than when input prices remain constant (as would be the presumption if we simply summed the marginal cost curves). In any case, in the short run, quantity supplied by the industry varies directly with price.

Before concluding this discussion of supply, we should note that any change that shifts the firm's marginal cost curve shifts each firm's supply curve and hence the industry's supply curve. For example, an increase in the wage rate would increase (shift upward) each firm's marginal cost curve, since labor is usually a variable input. With the higher wage the marginal cost of producing each additional unit of output would rise, so each firm would supply less at each price of the product.

Relation The short-run supply curve for a competitive industry cannot, in general, be obtained by horizontally summing the supply curves of all the individual firms in the industry. Since increases in industry output may cause input prices to rise, which in turn shifts each firm's marginal cost curve upward, the industry supply curve tends to be more steeply sloped (less elastic) than the horizontal summation would be. Short-run supply for a perfectly competitive industry is always upward sloping.

This concludes our analysis of a perfectly competitive firm's short-run profit-maximizing output decision. As you saw, the firm can make an economic profit or a loss in the short run, depending on market price. Certainly a firm would not go on indefinitely suffering a loss in each period. In the long run, a firm would exit from the industry if it could not cover its total cost with its revenue. Or, even if the firm is making a profit in the short run, it may wish to change its plant size or capacity in the long run in order to earn even more profit. We will now analyze the profit-maximizing output decision of perfectly competitive firms in the long run when all inputs, and therefore all costs, are variable.

13.6 PROFIT MAXIMIZATION IN THE LONG RUN

In the short run, the manager's production decisions are limited because some of the inputs used by the firm are fixed for the short-run time period of production. Typically, the key input that a manager views as fixed in the short run is the amount of capital available to the firm in the form of plant or equipment. In the long run, all inputs are variable, and a manager can choose to employ any size plant—amount of capital—required to produce most efficiently the level of output that will maximize profit. The choice of plant size is often referred to as the "scale of operation." The scale of operation may be fixed in the short run, but in the long run, it can be altered as economic conditions warrant.

The long run can also be viewed as the planning stage, prior to a firm's entry into an industry. In this stage the firm is trying to decide how large a production facility to construct, that is, the optimal scale of operation. Once the plans have congealed (a particular size plant is built), the firm operates in a short-run situation. Recall that a fundamental characteristic of perfect competition is unrestricted entry and exit of firms into the industry. As you will see in this section, the entry of new firms, which is possible only in the long run, plays a crucial role in long-run analysis of competitive industries.

In the long run, just as in the short run, the firm attempts to maximize profits. Exactly the same approach is used, except in this case there are no fixed costs; all costs are variable. As before, the firm takes a market-determined price as given. This market price is again the firm's marginal revenue. As in the preceding section, the firm would increase output as long as the marginal revenue from each additional unit is greater than the marginal cost of that unit. It would decrease output when marginal cost exceeds marginal revenue. The firm maximizes profit by equating marginal cost and marginal revenue.

Profit-Maximizing Equilibrium for the Firm in the Long Run

Suppose that an entrepreneur is considering entering a competitive industry in which the firms already in the industry are making economic profits. The prospective entrant, knowing the long-run costs and the product price, expects to make an economic profit also. Since all inputs are variable, the entrant can choose the scale or plant size for the new firm. We examine the decision graphically.

In Figure 13.8, *LAC* and *LMC* are the long-run average and marginal cost curves. The firm's perfectly elastic demand, *D*, indicates the equilibrium price ($17) and is the same as marginal revenue. As long as price is greater than long-run average cost, the firm can make a profit. Thus, in Figure 13.8, any output between 20 units and 290 units yields some economic profit. The points of output *B* and *B′* are sometimes called the break-even points. At these two points, price equals long-run average cost, economic profit is zero, and the owners of the firm earn only a normal profit (or rate of return).

Maximum profit occurs at 240 units of output (point *S*) where marginal revenue equals long-run marginal cost. The firm would want to select the plant size to produce 240 units of output. Note that the firm would not, under these

FIGURE 13.8
Profit-Maximizing Equilibrium for the Firm in the Long Run

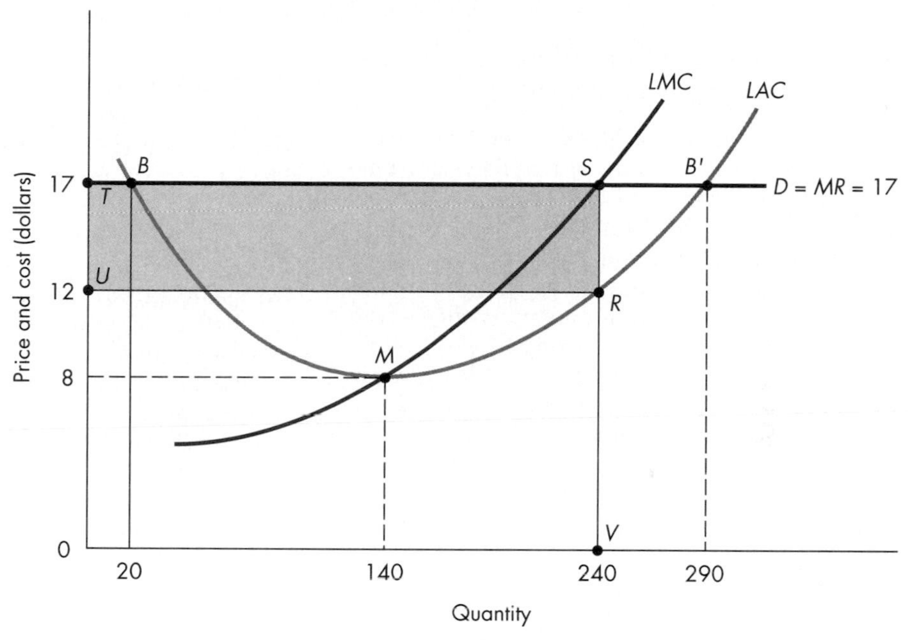

circumstances, want to produce 140 units of output at point M, the minimum point of long-run average cost. At M, marginal revenue exceeds marginal cost, so the firm can gain by producing more output. As shown in Figure 13.8, total revenue (price times quantity) at 140 units of output is equal to \$4,080 (= \$17 × 240), which is the area of the rectangle $0TSV$. The total cost (average cost times quantity) is equal to \$2,880 (= \$12 × 240), which is the area of the rectangle $0URV$. The total profit is \$1,200 [= (\$17 – \$12) × 240], which is the area of the rectangle $UTSR$.

Thus the firm would plan to operate at a scale (or plant size) such that long-run marginal cost equals price. This would be the most profitable situation under the circumstances. But, as we shall show, these circumstances will change. If the firm illustrated in Figure 13.8 is free to enter the industry, so are other prospective entrants. And this entry will drive down the market price. We will now show how this occurs.

Long-Run Competitive Equilibrium for the Industry

While the individual firm is in long-run profit-maximizing equilibrium when $MR = LMC$ (as shown in Figure 13.8), the *industry* will not be in long-run equilibrium until there is no incentive for new firms to enter or incumbent firms to exit. The economic force that induces firms to enter into an industry or that drives firms out of an industry is the existence of economic profits and economic losses, respectively.

ILLUSTRATION 13.1

A Roller Coaster Ride: Long-Run Adjustment in the US Securities Brokerage Industry

When the Federal Reserve Bank of New York executes monetary policy by buying and selling government securities, it deals with an elite group of commercial banks and brokerage firms. These primary dealers buy and sell US Treasury securities directly from the New York Fed. Belonging to this group of primary brokers is widely viewed as a requirement for recognition as a global player in banking.

Despite all this prestige, and despite the fact that $100 billion of Treasury securities are bought and sold every day on Wall Street, the number of primary dealers is on the decline. *The Wall Street Journal*, July 18, 1990, reported that most primary bond dealers are no longer making a profit. In 1980, a primary dealer in Treasury notes could expect to earn $1,250 profit on each $1 million trade. In 1990, the profit on that same trade was only $312.

As it turns out, 1989 was the first year in a decade that primary bond dealers as a group posted a loss. Because entry into bond trading is essentially unrestricted (even foreign banks are now allowed to be primary brokers of US government securities), the theory of perfect competition would predict new firms would enter when the returns are high. The graph shows that significant entry did occur during the profitable period 1985–1988 (a 27 percent increase in the number of firms).

The increase in the number of firms would, of its own accord, have bid down brokers' margins and their profits. But at about the same time that profits were luring new firms into the industry, the demand for US Treasury securities decreased. When the US economy began to slow down in late 1989, many institutional investors decreased their holdings of Treasury securities. At the same time, the savings-and-loan crisis eliminated many of the thrift institutions that once actively participated in the government securities market. Finally, reduced volatility in interest rates removed much of the opportunity for bid spreads in trading. Dealers claim they must have volatility in markets in order to book "decent" trading margins.

Just as the theory of long-run adjustment in perfectly competitive markets would predict, *The Wall Street Journal* reported that many firms were exiting, from the prestigious primary brokerage industry. As the graph shows, only 42 firms remained in the industry in 1990. According to one dealer, "People are getting out because they can't make any money. This industry probably needs only 25 primary dealers." The falling profit from trading government securities provided a signal to potential new entrants not to enter the market. Reacting to these losses, several Japanese banks, some of them among the world's largest financial institutions, decided to cancel their plans to become primary dealers of US government securities.

This example illustrates how an industry adjusts when losses are being earned. Economic losses provide an incentive for some firms to exit, as well as sending a signal to potential entrants to look elsewhere for new markets. Eventually, after a sufficient number of firms have exited, brokers' margins will rise, and losses will be eliminated.

Number of Primary Dealers in US Government Securities

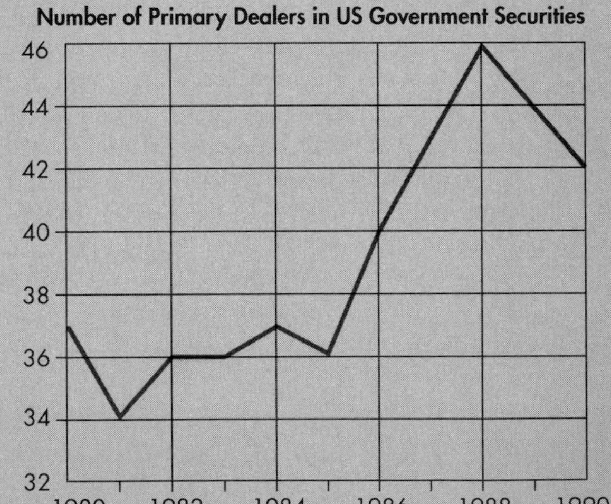

Source: Constance Mitchell, Tom Herman, and Michael R Sosit, "Treasury Market Takes No Prisoners," *The Wall Street Journal*, July 18, 1990.

Economic profits attract new firms into the industry and entry of these new firms increases industry supply. This increased supply drives down price. As price falls, all firms in the industry adjust their output levels in order to remain in profit-maximizing equilibrium. New firms continue to enter the industry, price continues to fall, and existing firms continue to adjust their outputs until all economic profits are eliminated. There is no longer an incentive for new firms to enter, and all firms in the industry earn only a normal rate of return.

Economic losses motivate some existing firms to exit, or leave the industry. The exit of these firms decreases industry supply. The reduction in supply drives up market price. As price is driven up, all firms in the industry must adjust their output levels in order to remain in profit-maximizing equilibrium. Firms continue to exit until economic losses are eliminated, and economic profit is zero; that is, firms earn only a normal rate of return.

long-run competitive equilibrium
All firms are producing where $P = LMC$ and economic profits are zero ($P = LAC$).

Long-run competitive equilibrium, then, requires not only that all firms be in profit-maximizing equilibrium, but also that economic profits be zero. These two conditions are satisfied when price equals marginal cost ($P = LMC$), so that firms are in profit-maximizing equilibrium, and price also equals average cost ($P = LAC$), so that no entry or exit occurs. These two conditions for equilibrium can be simultaneously satisfied only when price equals minimum LAC, at which point $LMC = LAC$.

Figure 13.9 shows a typical firm in long-run competitive equilibrium.[5] The long-run cost curves in Figure 13.9 are the same as those in 13.8. The difference between the two figures is that in Figure 13.8 the *firm* is in profit-maximizing equilibrium, but the industry is not yet in zero-profit equilibrium. In Figure 13.9, the firm is in profit-maximizing equilibrium (P equals LMC), and the industry is also in long-run competitive equilibrium because economic profit is zero ($P = LAC$).

Long-run equilibrium occurs at a price of $8 at point M. Each (identical) firm in the industry makes neither economic profit nor loss. There is no incentive for further entry because the rate of return in this industry is the normal rate of return, which is equal to the firm's best alternative. For the same reason, there is no incentive for a firm to leave the industry. The number of firms stabilizes, and each firm operates with a plant size represented by short-run marginal and average cost, SMC and ATC, respectively. We can now summarize long-run competitive equilibrium with a principle.

Principle In long-run competitive equilibrium, all firms are in profit-maximizing equilibrium ($P = LMC$), and there is no incentive for firms to enter or exit the industry because economic profit is zero ($P = LAC$). Long-run competitive equilibrium occurs because of the entry of new firms into the industry or the exit of existing firms from the industry. The market adjusts so that $P = LMC = LAC$, which is at the minimum point on LAC.

[5] We will assume that all firms in the industry have identical cost curves. For example Figures 13.8 and 13.9 show the cost curves of a typical firm. While it is not necessary to assume identical costs for all firms, this assumption substantially simplifies the theoretical analysis without affecting the conclusions.

FIGURE 13.9
Long-Run Equilibrium for a Firm in a Perfectly Competitive Industry

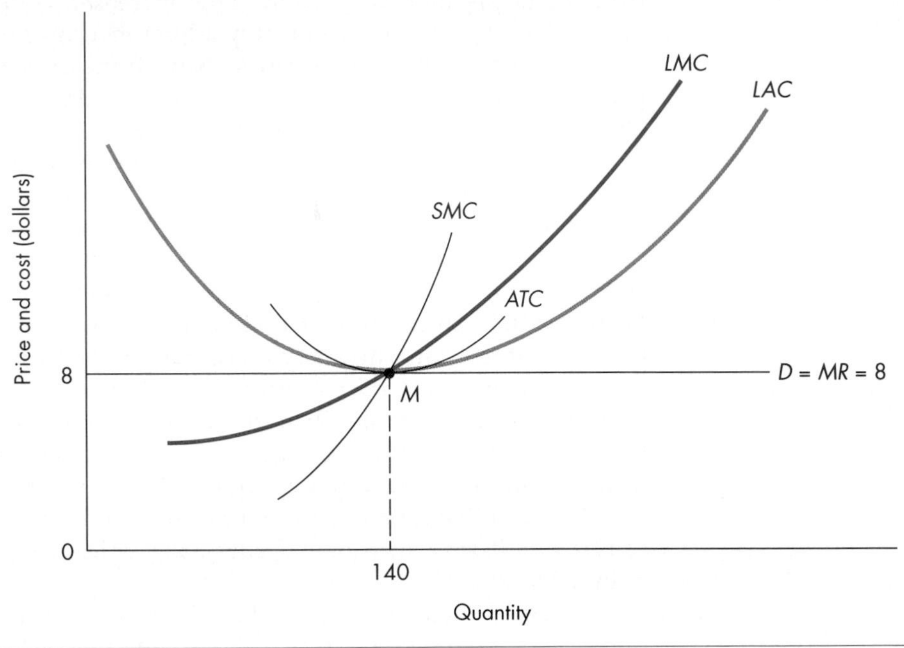

Long-Run Supply for a Perfectly Competitive Industry

In the short run when the amount of capital in an industry is fixed, as well as the number of firms, an increase in price causes industry output to increase. This increase is accomplished by each firm using its fixed capital more intensively, that is, each firm hires more of the variable inputs to increase output. As we discussed previously, the short-run industry supply curve is always upward sloping.

In the long run, when entry of new firms is possible, the industry's response to an increase in price takes on a new dimension: The industry's supply adjustment to a change in price is not complete until entry or exit results in zero economic profit. This means that for all points on the long-run industry supply curve, economic profit must be zero.

increasing-cost industry A industry in which input prices rise as all firms in the industry expand output.

constant-cost industry An industry in which input prices remain constant as all firms in the industry expand output.

To derive the industry supply curve in the long run, we must differentiate between two types of industries: (1) an increasing-cost industry, and (2) a constant-cost industry. An industry is an **increasing-cost industry** if, as all firms in the industry expand output and thus input usage, the prices of some inputs used in the industry rise. For example, if the personal computer industry expands production by 15 percent, the price of many specialized inputs (such as microprocessor chips, RAM boards, disk drives, and so on) will increase, causing marginal and average cost for all firms to shift upward. An industry is a **constant-cost industry** if, as industry output and input usage increase, all prices of

FIGURE 13.10
Long-Run Industry Supply for a Constant-Cost Industry

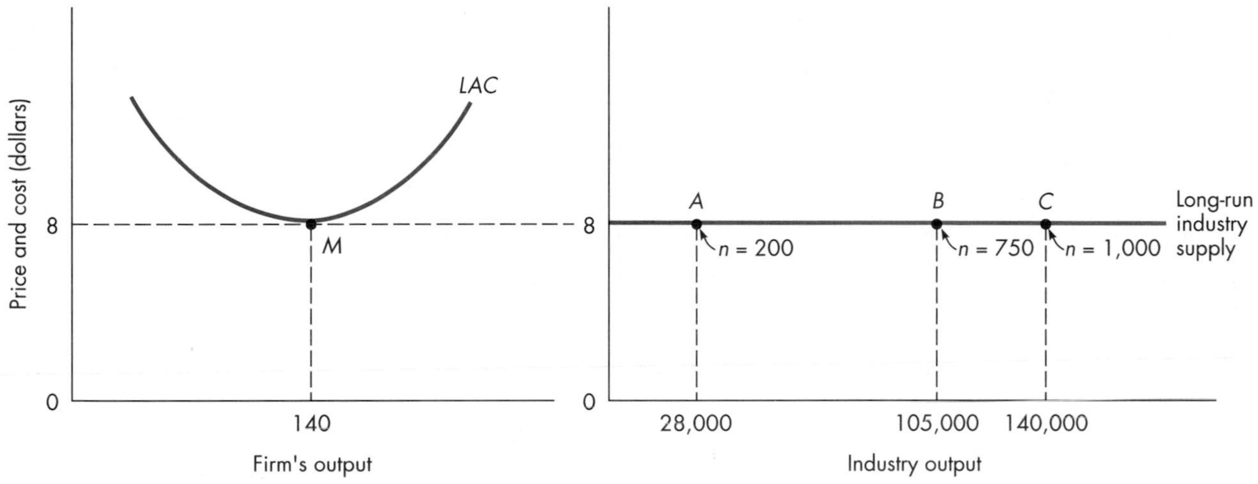

inputs used in the industry remain constant.[6] For example, the rutabaga industry is probably so small that its usage of inputs such as fertilizer, farm labor, and machinery have no effect on the prices of these inputs. This industry is therefore probably a constant-cost industry.

Figure 13.10 shows the relation between a typical firm (Panel A) in a constant-cost industry and the long-run industry supply curve (Panel B) for a constant-cost industry. Note that the supply price in the long run is constant and equal to $8 for all levels of industry output. This result follows from the long-run equilibrium condition that economic profit must be zero. The long-run supply price, $8, is equal to minimum long-run average cost for every level of output produced by the industry because the entry of new firms always bids price down to the point of zero economic profit (point *M* in Figure 13.10). Because the industry is a constant-cost industry, expansion of industry output does not cause minimum *LAC* (point *M*) to rise. Therefore, long-run supply price (= minimum *LAC*) is constant.

For example, if industry output expands from 28,000 units to 105,000 units through the entry of new firms, each firm (old and new) ends up producing 140 units of output at the minimum *LAC* of $8. No single firm expands output in the long run; output expands because there are more firms, each producing 140 units. When the industry produces 28,000, 105,000, and 140,000 units, the industry

[6]Theoretically it is possible that input prices might fall as industry output rises, in which case, there is a decreasing-cost industry. Decreasing-cost industries are so extremely rare that we will not consider them in this text.

FIGURE 13.11

Long-Run Industry Supply for an Increasing-Cost Industry

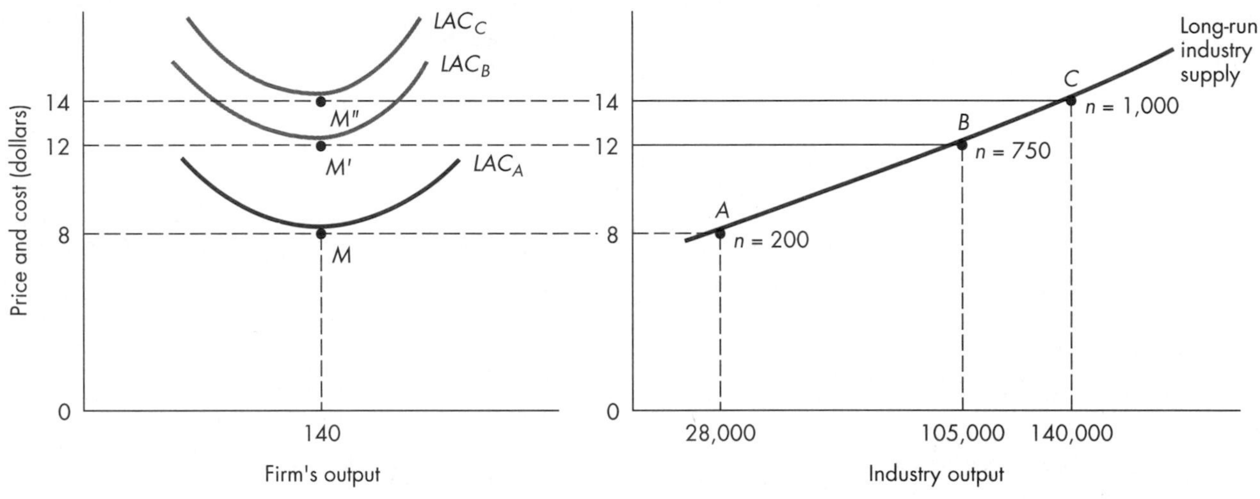

Panel A — A typical firm in long-run equilibrium **Panel B — The industry in long-run equilibrium**

is in long-run equilibrium with 200, 750, and 1,000 firms, respectively. Finally, note that at all points on long-run industry supply (*A*, *B*, and *C*, for example), economic profit is zero. For a constant-cost industry, long-run industry supply is perfectly elastic.

Next consider an increasing-cost industry. Figure 13.11 illustrates the relation between a typical firm (Panel A) in an increasing-cost industry and the long-run industry supply curve (Panel B). In contrast to the constant-cost case, the supply price for an increasing-cost industry rises as industry output increases.

Since the industry is an increasing-cost industry, as the industry expands output, resource prices rise, causing the long-run average cost in Panel A to shift upward. LAC_A, LAC_B, and LAC_C represent the increasingly higher long-run average costs associated with industry output levels of 28,000; 105,000; and 140,000 units, respectively. For example, when the industry output increases from 28,000 units, produced by 200 firms, to 105,000 units, input prices rise, causing minimum *LAC* to rise to *M'* (in Panel A). Each firm in the industry still produces 140 units, but there are now 750 firms producing a total industry output of 105,000 units.[7] Just as in the case of a constant-cost indus-

[7]In Figure 13.11 we have assumed that the minimum points on the higher *LAC* curves, LAC_B and LAC_C, remain at 140 units of output. Actually, *M'* and *M''* could also be at output levels either larger or smaller than 140 units; in this case, we would simply have to adjust the number of firms associated with points *B* and *C* in Panel B.

ILLUSTRATION 13.2

Competition in Riverboat Gambling: A Case of Fool's Gold*

Nobody remembers exactly which state governor first cried, "There's gold in them thar casinos," but most everyone now sees that the 1980s ushered in its own brand of gold fever. With government revenues falling in many states nationwide, many governors and state legislatures decided to legalize gambling—casinos, black-jack and poker parlors, state lotteries, and riverboats. Yes, even riverboat gambling is making a comeback on the Mississippi.

Desperate for jobs and tax revenues after a decade that witnessed a collapse in farming and manufacturing, Iowa Governor Terry Branstad decided it was time for Iowa to jump into the newly reborn market for gambling. In April 1991, the first excursion boats with casino gambling began paddling their way up the Mississippi River. Branstad has assured Iowans that gambling will bring prosperity without decadence. This promise is based on the strict limits that Iowa law places on how much gamblers can bet and how much they can lose. Governor Branstad promised to "protect the integrity of the state."

The dream of revitalizing the Iowa economy with revenues generated from casino gambling, particularly by tourists, is not likely to pan out. With unrestricted entry into riverboat gambling, many other state governors are now looking at the profits to be had from riverboat gambling. Just across the river, for example, Illinois politicians recently passed their own law legalizing riverboat gambling. In contrast to the Iowa law, the Illinois law places no limits on wagering. It appears that the entry of this new rival, with a gambling product more in tune with the desires of gamblers, will substantially reduce demand for Iowa's floating casinos. Governor Branstad of Iowa is going to have a tough time keeping limits on wagering when new entrants do not.

Just when Illinois politicians thought they were seeing gold, Mississippi's governor decided to launch a fleet of gambling boats. Worse still, Missouri, Wisconsin, Louisiana, Pennsylvania, and Minnesota are now considering riverboat gambling.

Yes, it appears the governors have been panning for fool's gold. Just as the theory of perfect competition predicts, profits lure new firms until firms earn only a normal rate of return. The economic truth about gambling is that entry is unrestricted when the competitors are the state legislatures themselves. As theory would predict: "The more gambling outlets there are, the less good they do in revitalizing downtrodden communities and helping state and local governments pay their bills."

It is interesting to note that even landlocked states are beginning to enter the gambling industry. In the fall of 1990, Colorado voted to allow $5-a-hand blackjack and poker, just as South Dakota had done in 1988. South Dakota is now contemplating boosting its limit to $100-a-hand to retaliate. Even Indian tribes have gold fever. Congress, in 1988, began allowing casino gambling on reservations.

With all this competition and relatively easy entry, William Eadington, an economics professor at the University of Nevada in Reno, predicts casino gambling will be available everywhere in the United States in the next 30 years. It appears that casino gambling is another market where the theory of perfect competition works rather well in explaining and predicting market behavior.

*"The Fool's Gold in Gambling," Paul Glastris and Andrew Bates, *US News & World Report*, April 1, 1991.

try, economic profit is zero at all points along the long-run supply curve. And similarly, when industry output increases from 105,000 to 140,000 units, input prices rise further, causing minimum LAC to rise to M''. At point C, 1,000 firms each produce 140 units at an average cost of \$14 per unit and earn zero economic profit.

Relations For a constant-cost industry, as industry output expands, input prices remain constant, and the minimum point on long-run average cost (*LAC*) is unchanged. Since long-run supply price equals minimum *LAC*, the long-run industry supply curve is perfectly elastic (horizontal) for a constant-cost industry. For an increasing-cost industry, as industry output expands, input prices are bid up, causing minimum *LAC* to rise, and long-run supply price to rise. The long-run industry supply curve for an increasing-cost industry is upward sloping. Economic profit is zero at all points on the long-run industry supply curve for both constant- and increasing-cost industries, and each firm earns just a normal profit or normal rate of return.

Managers of firms in industries that have the characteristics of perfect competition (in particular, low barriers to entry and homogeneous product) should expect to see economic profit competed away in the long run by the entry of new firms, regardless of whether constant or increasing costs characterize the industry. Likewise, managers should expect that losses in the short run will be eliminated in the long run as firms exit the industry and the price of the product rises. Managers can also expect to see entry of new firms driving up the prices they pay for inputs if they are operating in an increasing-cost industry that is expanding.

Rent and Long-Run Competitive Equilibrium

The fact that economic profit is zero in long-run competitive equilibrium does not mean that "nobody gets rich" in a competitive industry. Obviously, those with skills or talent that are greatly in demand can make a lot of money if the market salary or wage for people with those skills is high. Resource owners can earn a substantial return over and above owners of similar types of resources, if their resources are more productive than the others employed in the industry.

To illustrate, suppose that you are an experienced construction supervisor for a builder of median-priced homes, and you are exceptionally talented at organizing subcontractors—concrete workers, carpenters, bricklayers, plumbers, painters, and so forth. You can build a house in 10 percent less time than the typical experienced construction supervisor in the industry, and this saving of time reduces the average costs of constructing a house by $2,000.

The home construction industry in your market is in long-run equilibrium. Each firm in the market, including yours, is selling homes at the going market price of $90,000, which is the minimum long-run average cost for every other firm but your employer. Each of the other firms builds 30 houses a year and earns only a normal profit at the $90,000 price. Panel A of Figure 13.12 illustrates the situation for every other contractor in the market. Each of these produces at point *A* in the figure. Assume that an experienced construction contractor is typically paid $80,000 a year, which is what you are paid.

The situation for the firm that employees you is illustrated in Panel B. *LAC′* and *LMC′* are your firm's long-run average and marginal cost curves. At each level of output, *LAC′* is $2,000 below the long-run average cost for every other firm (*LAC* in Panel A) because you can construct a house for $2,000 less than any other contractor. Your firm produces where *LMC′* equals price ($90,000), and builds 36 houses per year, as shown by point *B* in Panel B. Your firm makes an

FIGURE 13.12
Economic Rent in Long-Run Competitive Equilibrium

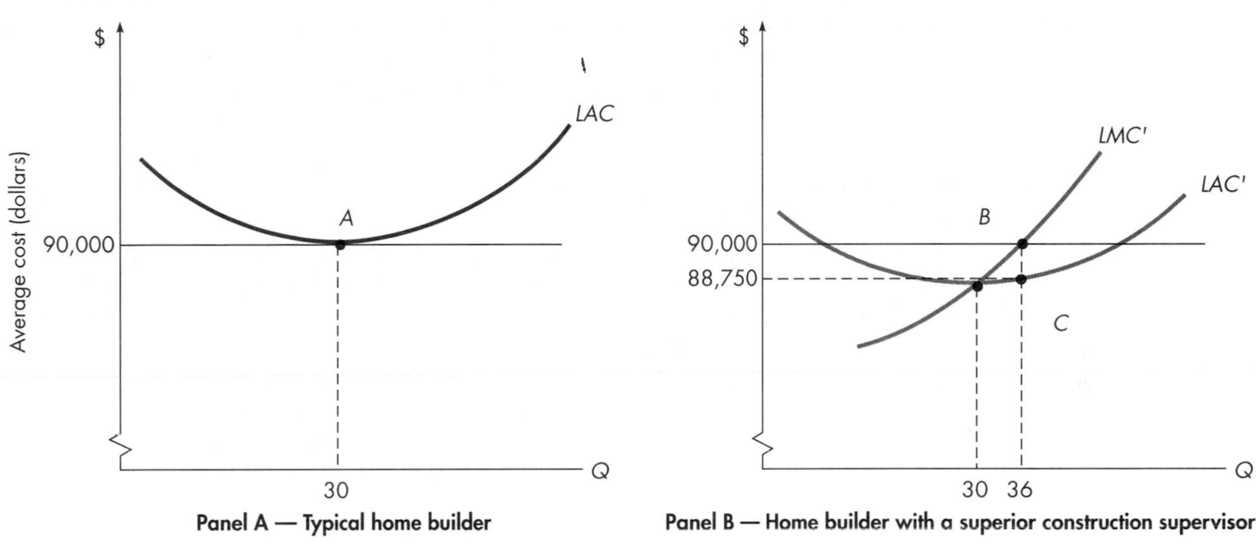

economic profit, a return over and above the normal profit included in cost, of $1,250 per house, or $45,000 (= $1,250 × 36). You are solely responsible for the $45,000 economic profit. Your firm is identical in every way to every other firm except for your superior skills. (As the famous football coach and philosopher Bum Phillips said about Don Shula, the brilliant coach of the Miami Dolphins, "He can take his'n and beat your'n and take your'n and beat his'n.") You could be the supervisor for any other firm in the market and earn $45,000 economic profit for that firm. You know it, and presumably the other firms know it also, as does the owner of the firm that employs you.

So what would you do? If we were your agents, we would advise you to ask for a raise, but you probably wouldn't need our advice. How much of a raise? Around $45,000 to a salary of $125,000 seems about right. You could get a raise of about $45,000 from other firms in the market because, presumably, you could lower their costs as well. Even if you didn't ask your employer for the raise, other firms, aware of your ability to lower costs, would try to lure you away by bidding up your salary.

Your employer, and any other employer in the market, really has little choice. A firm could pay you the additional $45,000 and earn only a normal profit because all economic profit would go toward your salary. Or your firm could refuse to pay the additional $45,000, causing you to move to another firm or perhaps start your own. The original employer would find that its costs had shifted back to *LAC* after you left and would consequently earn only a normal profit because it would be in the situation shown in Panel A. Thus, each firm in the market would earn only a normal profit whether it hires you at $125,000 or not. But you would earn a premium because of your superior skills.

economic rent (or rent)
A payment in excess of a resource's opportunity cost (the highest payment a resource could earn in an alternative use).

The additional payment you receive above the typical salary of $80,000 is called **economic rent** or simply **rent**. Rent is the payment to a superior or more productive resource over and above its opportunity cost (what the resource could earn in its best alternative use). The opportunity cost for experienced supervisors is what they could earn in their best alternative occupation—such as selling insurance or supervising a factory. If this opportunity cost is around $80,000, the other supervisors are earning zero rent and you are earning $45,000 rent after your salary increase.

This same type of analysis holds for any resource that, if compensated at only its opportunity cost, would result in that firm earning economic profit in long-run competitive equilibrium. The return to that resource will be bid up as in the above example. Therefore, even in a competitive industry, owners of particularly productive resources can earn substantial premiums even though economic profit is zero. While this example examined rents to superior skills of a manager, resources such as superior land, superior location, superior craftsmanship, or superior capital (that cannot be easily duplicated) can also earn economic rent for their owners.

You might be wondering about a situation in which the owner of a competitive firm is also the owner of the superior resource that causes the long-run average cost to be lower than the costs of other firms in the industry. Would this firm owner earn an economic profit when the industry is in long-run competitive equilibrium? The answer is no. The firm owner's opportunity cost rises because presumably the owner could sell the superior resource to another firm, and, consequently, *the firm's implicit cost increases*. The owner earns a premium (rent) as the resource owner but earns only a normal profit as the firm's owner. This classification is only a technicality that economists make in order to be consistent. The resource/firm owner makes no distinction as to what income is called when it is deposited in the bank.

Relation Economic rent is a payment to the owner of a resource in excess of the resource's opportunity cost. Firms that employ such exceptionally productive resources earn only a normal profit (economic profit is zero) in long-run competitive equilibrium because the potential economic profit from employing a superior resource is paid to the resource as rent.

13.7 PROFIT-MAXIMIZING INPUT USAGE

Thus far, we have analyzed the firm's profit-maximizing decision in terms of the output decision. But, as noted in the introduction, we can also consider profit maximization from the input side. Of course, when we determine the profit-maximizing level of output, we implicitly have determined the economically efficient level of input usage of the firm. Recall from Chapter 10 that the cost function is directly related to the production function. Thus, when we determine a unique profit-maximizing level of output, we also determine the cost-minimizing quantity of each input that is used in the production process.

It is possible, however, to determine a profit-maximizing equilibrium directly from the input decision. In this way, we can develop the theory of a competitive firm's demand for inputs or factors of production.

Marginal Revenue Product

Recall that in Section 13.2 we noted that a firm will increase its usage of an input so long as the addition to total revenue per unit increase in the input, which we called *marginal revenue product (MRP)*, exceeds the addition to total cost of hiring an extra unit of the input, which we called *marginal factor cost (MFC)*. Thus a manager will increase input usage when MRP exceeds MFC, and a manager will decrease input usage when MFC exceeds MRP.

The marginal revenue product of an input ($\Delta TR/\Delta I$) is equal to the product of the marginal revenue from selling the output produced times the marginal product of the input:[8]

$$MRP = \frac{\Delta TR}{\Delta I} = MR \times MP$$

For a competitive firm, the marginal revenue from the product of an input is equal to the price of the product, which *is* marginal revenue for a perfectly competitive firm, times the marginal product of the input:

$$MRP = P \times MP$$

For example, if one additional unit of an input, say labor, has a marginal product of 10 and the price at which the product can be sold for is \$5, the marginal revenue product for that unit of the input is \$50 (= $P \times MP$ = \$5 × 10). In other words, hiring the extra unit of labor adds 10 extra units of output which can each be sold for \$5 each, and thus the addition to total revenue attributable to hiring this extra unit of labor is \$50.[9]

As shown in Chapter 10, the "typical" marginal product curve first increases, reaches a maximum, then declines thereafter. Therefore, the MRP curve, which is simply price times marginal product, also rises then declines. At the level of input usage at which marginal product becomes negative, the value of marginal product becomes negative also. Since an input's marginal product depends on the usage of other inputs, the marginal revenue product also changes at each level of the input when the quantities of other inputs change.

A typical MRP schedule for a single variable input (I) is given in Table 13.2, assuming that the price of the product is \$10. Columns 1 and 2 show the firm's production function for 1 through 9 units of input usage. Column 3 shows that the marginal product of the input first rises through 3 units of input usage, then

---

[8]The appendix at the end of the chapter shows mathematically that $MRP = MR \times MP$.

[9]In the case of a perfectly competitive industry, the marginal revenue product of an input is sometimes referred to as the *value of marginal product* (VMP) since the additional revenue attributable to hiring an extra unit of the input is simply the market value of the additional output produced by the additional unit of the input. MRP and VMP are just different names for the precisely the same concept—both are measures of the increase in revenue attributable to hiring an extra unit of the input.

TABLE 13.2

Finding the Profit-Maximizing Level of Input Usage

(1) Units of variable input (I)	(2) Output (Q)	(3) Marginal product $\left(\frac{\Delta Q}{\Delta I}\right)$	(4) Marginal revenue product ($P \times MP$)	(5) Marginal cost $\left(\frac{w}{MP}\right)$	(6) Marginal revenue (= P)
1	20	20	$200	$ 5	$10
2	50	30	300	3.33	10
3	90	40	400	2.50	10
4	120	30	300	3.33	10
5	138	18	180	5.55	10
6	150	12	120	8.33	10
7	155	5	50	20	10
8	158	3	30	33.33	10
9	154	–4	–40	—	10

decreases, becoming negative at 9 units of the input. The marginal revenue product ($10 × *MP*) in column 4 also increases through 3 units of the input, then decreases, becoming negative at 9 units of the input. We will return to columns 5 and 6 later in this section. If the price of the product increases, *MRP* will increase for each level of input usage. If the price of the product falls, *MRP* falls also.

Marginal Revenue Product and the Hiring Decision

As we have emphasized, the quantity of a labor input a manager chooses to hire depends on the marginal revenue product and the marginal factor cost. Assume that a manager can hire as much of an input as is desired at a constant price—that is, the price that must be paid for the input is the same no matter how much or how little is hired. Thus, the marginal factor cost is equal to the price of the input.[10]

Suppose that labor is the input for which the *MRP* schedule is shown in Table 13.2. If the wage rate of labor is $100 per unit of labor, each additional unit of labor hired through the sixth adds more to revenue (*MRP* > $100) than it adds to cost. Each unit after the sixth adds less to revenue (*MRP* < $100) than it adds to cost; that is, each unit after the sixth adds less than the wage rate to revenue. Thus, with the given *MRP* schedule and wage rate, the manager hires 6 units of labor.

If the firm is hiring only 5 units, it could add the sixth unit of labor, and revenue would rise by $120 while cost would increase by $100; thus profit would increase $20. If the firm makes a mistake and employs 7 workers, it could increase profit by reducing labor usage by 1 unit. Eliminating the seventh worker would decrease revenue $50 as cost falls $100; profit would increase $50.

A general rule for a continuously variable input is illustrated graphically in Figure 13.13. In this example, labor is the only variable input, and only the decreasing portion of *MRP* is shown. The *MRP* curve is simply the *MP* curve

[10]In some instances, the price of an input may either rise or fall as a firm hires more of the input. When the price is not constant, marginal factor cost will not be equal to the price of the input.

FIGURE 13.13
A Competitive Firm's Demand for Labor

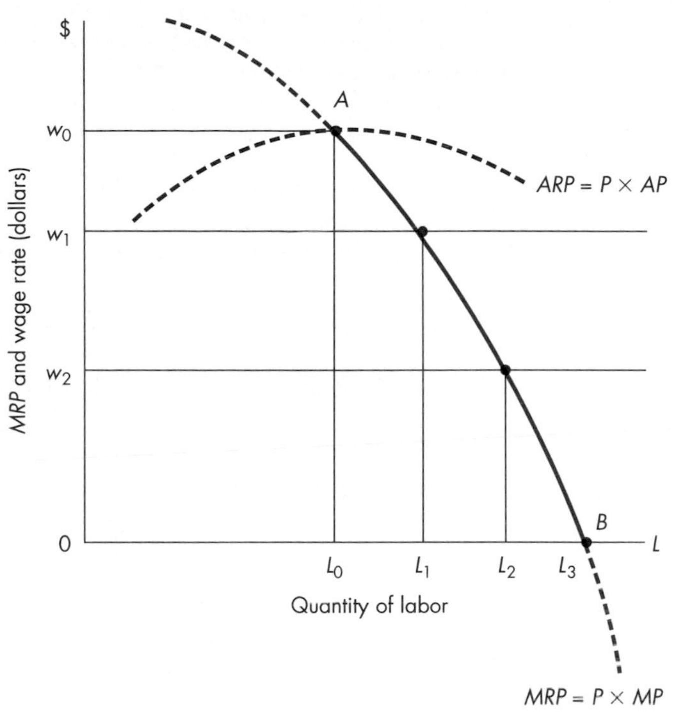

multiplied by the market price of the product produced at each level of labor usage over the relevant range. Therefore, if at a labor usage of $\overline{L}$ the marginal product is $\overline{MP}$, $\overline{MRP} = \overline{P} \times \overline{MP}$, where $\overline{P}$ is product price. This means that the $\overline{L}^{th}$ worker adds $\overline{MRP}$ to total revenue. If the wage rate is w_1, the manager would wish to hire L_1 units of labor. The manager would not stop short of L_1 because up to employment level L_1 an additional unit of labor would add more to revenue than to cost. The manager would not hire more than L_1, because beyond L_1 the added cost would exceed the added revenue. If the wage rate falls to w_2, the manager would increase its labor usage to L_2 units. Hence, if labor is the firm's only variable input, the manager maximizes profits or minimizes loss by employing the amount of labor for which the marginal revenue product of labor equals the wage rate:

$$MRP = w$$

This result holds for any variable input.[11]

[11]As noted, we did not include the upward-sloping portion of the *MRP* curve because this segment is not relevant to the hiring decision. If the wage equals *MRP* and *MRP* is increasing, the manager could hire additional units, and the marginal revenue product of these inputs would be greater than the wage. Therefore, this level of input use would not be profit maximizing. Later in this section we show that the relevant portion of *MRP* is that range of input usage for which $AP > MP$ and *MP* is positive.

Principle If the *MRP* of an additional unit of a variable input is greater than the price of that input, that unit should be hired. If the *MRP* of an additional unit adds less than its price, that unit should not be hired. If the usage of the variable input varies continuously, the manager should employ the amount of the input at which

$$MRP = \text{Input price}$$

The above principle is equivalent to the condition that the profit-maximizing, perfectly competitive firm will produce the level of output at which $P = MC$. Recall from Chapter 10 that cost minimization at any level of output requires that

$$MC = \frac{w}{MP}$$

Recall also that the profit-maximizing level of output is where

$$P = MC$$

But, from the cost-minimization condition when one input is variable,

$$P = MC = \frac{w}{MP}$$

or

$$P \times MP = w$$

which gives the profit-maximizing level of input usage. Thus the profit-maximizing, output-choice equilibrium condition, $P = MC$, is equivalent to the profit-maximizing, input-choice equilibrium condition, $MRP = w$. Each leads to the same level of output and the same level of input usage.

To illustrate numerically that the profit-maximizing decision for the manager is invariant to choosing either input usage or output, we now return to Table 13.2, in which we showed that 6 units of labor is the level of labor usage that maximizes profit. Marginal cost (column 5) is computed by dividing the wage rate ($100) by the marginal product for each unit of labor from 1 through 9. For example, the first 20 units of output are produced, using one unit of labor costing $100. Thus, the marginal cost per unit of the first 20 units of output is $5 ($= w/MP_L = \$100/20$). The other values for marginal cost in column 5 are calculated in the same way. The marginal revenue is equal to the price received for each unit of output, which is $10 in this example. Using the usual rules of marginal analysis for the output decision, a manager would increase production up to the 150th unit because *MR* exceeds *MC*. Beyond 150 units of output, marginal cost exceeds marginal revenue. Since the manager maximizes profit by hiring 6 units of labor to produce 150 units, it does not matter if the manager chooses input usage or output to maximize profit; the outcomes are identical.

We now want to be more precise about the range of *MRP* over which a manager would actually operate. Clearly, a manager never hires labor beyond the point at which *MRP* becomes negative—when *MRP* is negative, hiring more labor *decreases* total revenue. Furthermore, we will now demonstrate that a man-

average revenue product (*ARP*)
The average revenue per worker ($ARP = TR/L$).

ager shuts down operations (i.e., hires no labor) if the wage rate rises above the *average revenue product* of labor. The **average revenue product (*ARP*)** of labor is the average revenue per worker, $ARP = TR/L$, and it is easy to see that ARP can be calculated as price times average product:

$$ARP = \frac{TR}{L} = \frac{PQ}{L} = P\frac{Q}{L} = P \times AP$$

To see why a manager shuts down when $w > ARP$, suppose $MRP = w$—as necessary for profit-maximization—at a level of labor usage where ARP is less than the wage rate,

$$w > ARP$$

Substituting TR/L for ARP into this inequality results in the following expression:

$$w > TR/L$$

Now multiply both sides of the inequality by L and you can see that

$$wL > TR,$$

$$\text{or} \quad TVC > TR.$$

Thus total variable cost exceeds total revenue when $w > ARP$. From previous analysis, you know that the manager should shut down when total revenue does not cover total variable costs.[12] Therefore, no labor would be hired if the average revenue product is less than the wage rate.

In Figure 13.13, the firm's demand for labor is the MRP curve over the range of labor usage L_0 to L_3 (between points A and B). To maximize profit, the manager chooses the level of labor usage for which $MRP = w$. When wages rise above w_0 in Figure 13.13 at the level of labor usage for which $MRP = w$, the wage rate exceeds the average revenue product ($w > ARP$), and the manager will shut the firm down and hire no labor at all. At all wage rates above point A, the firm shuts down. Below point B, MRP is negative, and the manager would never hire more than L_3 units of labor. We now summarize the discussion in a principle.

Principle The demand for a single variable input by a perfectly competitive firm is the positive portion of the *MRP* curve over the range of input usage for which $MRP < ARP$. This portion of the *MRP* curve shows the quantity of variable input that a profit-maximizing manager should hire at each price of the input.

Before concluding the discussion of input demand, we should note that when there is more than one variable input, the firm's demand function for a particular input is slightly different. For example, if the quantities of other inputs are also variable, when wages fall from w_1 to w_2 in Figure 13.13, the firm will use more labor but it may use more or less of the other variable inputs as well. For this reason, the MRP curve of labor may shift—either outward or inward—

[12] This result is demonstrated mathematically in the appendix to this chapter.

because the changed usage of these other inputs shifts the *MP* curve. Thus, the firm may use more than or less than L_2 units of labor at wage w_2, but not less than L_1. The firm's demand for any variable input is negatively sloped.

Nevertheless, two things are certain: (1) the firm will hire more labor when the wage falls, and (2) it will hire labor up to the quantity at which the wage equals the marginal revenue product, even though *MRP* may shift. Thus, for every variable input, the firm will hire the quantity of the input at which its *MRP* equals its price. If, for example, the firm uses two variable inputs, denoted *I* and *J*, the firm will maximize profits by using both inputs at such levels that[13]

$$MRP_I = P_I$$
$$MRP_J = P_J$$

Since the marginal product of either input shifts according to the level of usage of the other, these conditions must hold *simultaneously*.

13.8 MAXIMIZING EXPECTED PROFIT UNDER RISK

Our discussion of managerial decision making in perfectly competitive markets has thus far assumed that the manager knows with certainty the revenue and cost conditions facing the firm. The manager of a perfectly competitive firm maximizes profit, under certainty, by choosing to produce the level of output for which the known price equals the known marginal cost. While the model of decision making under certainty is extremely useful in providing a manager with an understanding of how to use information about revenues and costs to maximize profit, we also want to apply the rules of decision making under risk, set forth in Chapter 6, to show how a manager can make decisions when risk is involved. In this section we focus on decisions made in the short-run period of production, but the techniques can be applied in identical fashion in the long run.

Assume that a manager can choose the level of output precisely; that is, output can be controlled and is known with certainty. For any chosen level of output, however, the manager does not know with certainty either the revenue or costs associated with that output level. On the revenue side, the manager does not know with certainty the price at which the product can be sold. Instead, the manager has a subjectively (or possibly objectively) determined probability distribution for price. Panel A of Figure 13.14 shows the probability distribution for product price. The expected value of price, $E(P)$, is also the expected marginal revenue for the perfectly competitive firm, $E(MR)$. Since a competitive firm can sell all the product it wishes at the going (expected) market price, the expected price (and expected marginal revenue) is constant for all levels of output. Panel B of Figure 13.14 illustrates how expected price and marginal revenue remain constant for all possible output levels. Regardless of whether the manager chooses to produce Q_1 units or Q_2 units—or any other level of output—the expected price is $\bar{P}$.

---

[13]It can be shown that when these results hold, the price of the product equals marginal cost.

FIGURE 13.14
Probability Distribution for Price

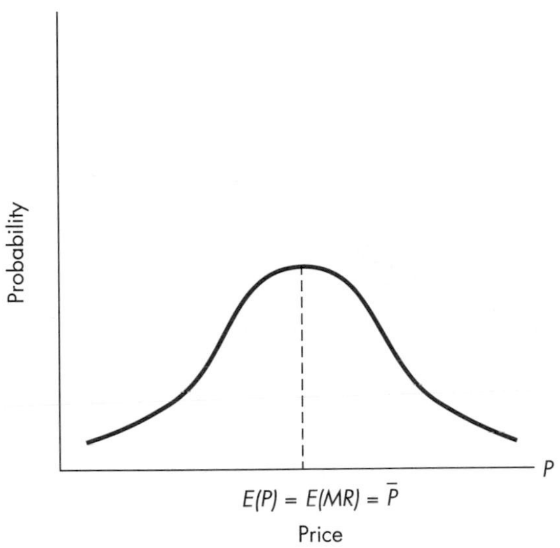

Panel A — Probability distribution for *P*

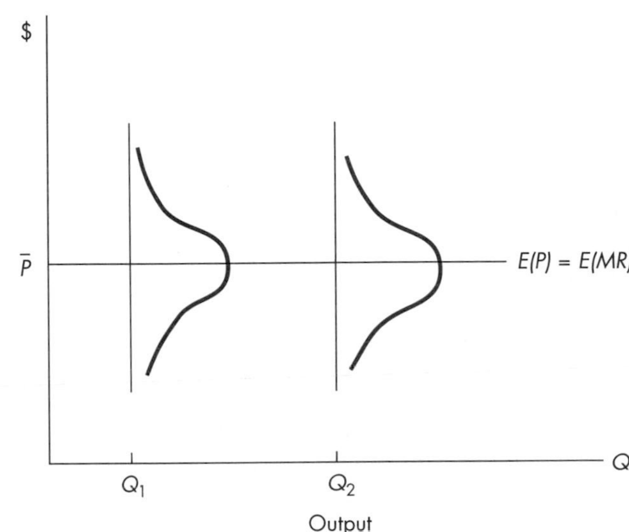

Panel B — The expected *MR* curve

On the cost side, the manager does not know with certainty the costs that will be associated with any given level of output. In order to choose output—either under conditions of certainty or risk—the manager needs information about marginal cost. Panel A in Figure 13.15 shows a probability distribution for the possible marginal cost associated with the production of a particular level of output, Q_1. The expected marginal cost of producing Q_1 units is $\overline{MC}_1$, as shown in Panel B. Because the marginal cost of production increases at higher levels of production, the expected marginal cost will rise for higher output levels, as shown in Panel B. In Panel B, the probability distribution for marginal cost has the same shape at different output levels, but the expected values of the probability distributions rise with higher production levels. In other words, the variance of marginal cost is constant across various output levels; only the expected marginal cost changes. For example, at Q_2 units of production, the expected marginal cost is $\overline{MC}_2$, which is higher than the expected marginal cost of producing Q_1 units.[14]

Recall from Section 6.5, which discusses finding the optimal level of a risky activity, that when the variance of net benefit is constant for all levels of activity,

[14]Recall from our discussion of regression analysis in Chapter 5 that the regression line gives the expected value of Y for a given level of X. When regression analysis is used to estimate the marginal cost curve, as shown in Chapter 12, the estimated marginal cost function actually gives the manager an estimate of the expected marginal cost of producing any given level of output.

FIGURE 13.15
Probability Distribution for Marginal Cost

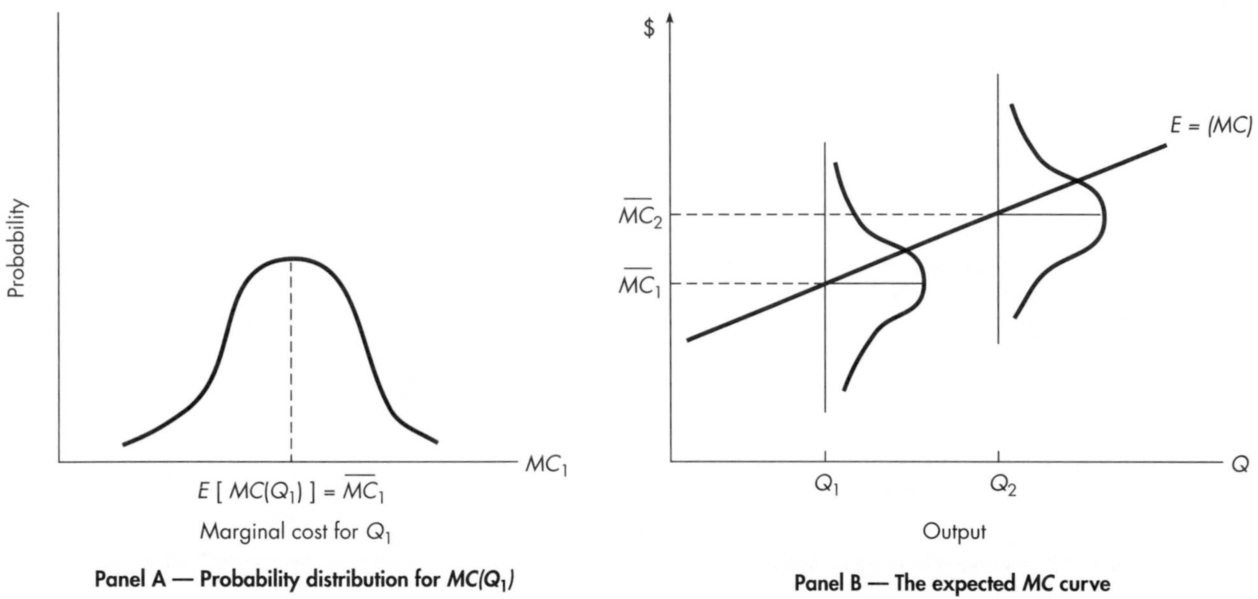

the optimal level of a risky activity is that level for which *expected* marginal benefit equals *expected* marginal cost—regardless of whether the decision maker is risk neutral, risk loving, or risk averse. According to this rule, the manager of a perfectly competitive firm, choosing output under conditions of risk, will maximize expected profit by choosing the level of output for which expected marginal revenue (expected price) equals expected marginal cost:

$$E(MR) = E(P) = E(MC)$$

Since we are assuming the variance of price and marginal cost are constant for different outputs, the variance of net benefit (profit) is constant, and the above rule applies to all managers. Figure 13.16 shows the level of output that will maximize expected profit. At Q^* units of production, the expected price, $\overline{P}$, equals the expected marginal cost of producing Q^* units of output (point A). We can summarize our discussion of maximizing expected profit in a principle:

Principle When the variance of profit is constant for all levels of output, a manager of a perfectly competitive firm will choose the level of output that maximizes expected profit, regardless of whether the manager is risk averse, risk loving, or risk neutral. The level of output that maximizes expected profit is the output level for which $E(MR) = E(P) = E(MC)$.

FIGURE 13.16
Maximization of Expected Profit:
***E*(*MR*) = *E*(*P*) = *E*(*MC*)**

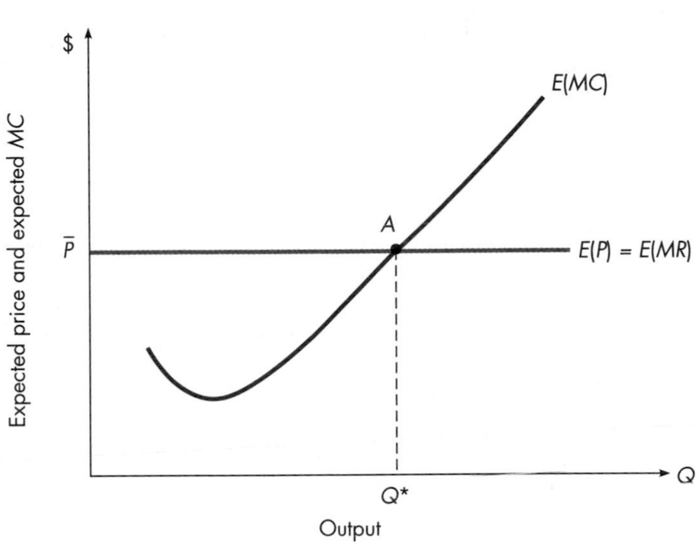

13.9 SUMMARY

Perfectly competitive markets exist when there are a large number of buyers and sellers, identical products, unrestricted entry and exit by producers, complete knowledge, and prices freely determined by the interaction of supply and demand. While these conditions do not exactly describe any real-world market, many markets function in ways that can be explained by using the theory of perfect competition. Managers that operate in markets where a large number of firms produce similar products, and entry into the industry is not restricted, will find that the theory of perfect competition is applicable to their decisions concerning production levels and input usage, as well as for predicting market conditions.

The profit-maximizing decision for a manager can take either one of two equivalent forms. The manager can choose the level of output that maximizes profit or the level of input usage that maximizes profit. The two approaches both lead to identical levels of input usage, output, and profit.

Economic profit is the difference between total revenue and total economic cost. Normal profit is the opportunity cost of the owners' resources that are used by the firm. Normal profit plus explicit costs equal total economic cost. Thus when economic profit is zero, the firm is earning just enough revenue to pay all explicit costs and pay the owners of the firm a normal profit.

A manager operating a firm in a competitive market faces a perfectly elastic demand curve. The firm's demand curve is a horizontal line at the market-determined price. Since marginal revenue equals price for a perfectly competitive firm, the firm's demand is also simultaneously the marginal revenue curve under perfect competition.

In the short run, a manager chooses to produce that level of output where marginal revenue (price) equals marginal cost, so long as price exceeds average variable cost. When price is less than average variable cost, total revenue is less than total variable cost. If the firm produces, it would lose an amount equal to all of its fixed costs plus some of its variable costs. Under these circumstances ($P < AVC$), the manager should shut down the firm and lose only fixed costs.

The supply curve for a perfectly competitive firm in the short run is the portion of the firm's marginal cost curve above minimum average variable cost. If all input prices are constant as industry output expands, the short-run supply curve for the industry is the horizontal summation of all the firms' marginal cost curves. If the industry's (although not the individual firm's) use of some inputs affects the prices of these inputs, industry supply is less elastic than this horizontal summation, but is still positively sloped.

In managerial decision making, fixed costs don't matter. Fixed costs play no role in determining the profit-maximizing level of output. The shutdown rule involves comparing total revenue and total variable cost (or equivalently, price and average variable cost). The optimal level of production is found by equating marginal revenue and marginal cost. Fixed costs have nothing to do with determining how much to produce or with the decision to shut down.

In the long run, the firm is in profit-maximizing equilibrium when MR (= P) equals long-run marginal cost (LMC). The industry is in long-run competitive equilibrium when economic profit is zero, eliminating any incentive for entry or exit, and all incumbent firms in the industry are in profit-maximizing equilibrium. Thus, industry equilibrium requires that all firms are satisfying the two conditions: $P = LMC$ and $P = LAC$. This occurs when the market-determined price is just equal to minimum long-run average cost.

The long-run industry supply curve for a competitive industry can be either upward sloping in the case of an increasing-cost industry or horizontal in the case of a constant-cost industry. When industry output expands, the prices of inputs may be bid up, causing the minimum point on LAC to rise. Since long-run supply price equals minimum LAC, an upward shift in LAC due to rising input prices causes supply price to increase. This is why the industry supply curve is upward sloping in the long run for an increasing-cost industry. If input prices are constant as industry output and input usage increase, minimum LAC remains constant, and the long-run supply curve is perfectly elastic for the constant-cost industry.

When choosing the profit-maximizing level of labor usage to maximize the profit of the firm, the manager hires labor up to the point where the marginal revenue product of labor ($MRP = P \times MP_L$) equals the wage rate, which is the marginal factor cost when the price of labor is given to the firm. Using this rule, the demand for a single variable input by a competitive firm is the positive portion of the MRP curve over the range of input usage for which ARP is greater than w. The input demand curve gives the quantity of the variable input that the manager will hire at each price of the input.

When a manager must decide how to produce under conditions of risk, the probability distributions for marginal revenue (price) and marginal cost are known to the manager. As long as the variance of profit is constant for all levels of output, a manager of a perfectly competitive firm will choose output to maximize expected profit. Expected profit is maximized at the output level for which the expected price (marginal revenue) is equal to the expected marginal cost: $E(P) = E(MR) = E(MC)$.

It should be emphasized that the theory of perfect competition is not designed to describe specific real-world firms. It is a theoretical model that is frequently useful in explaining real-world behavior and in predicting the economic consequences of changes in the different variables contained in the model. It is also useful as a guide for managerial decision making.

In the next chapter, we will show how a manager can implement the theory developed in this chapter to make profit-maximizing decisions concerning the level of output and level of usage of variable inputs. You will see how to combine the statistical techniques of cost estimation with price forecasts and the decision-making rules developed in this chapter to make decisions about whether to produce or shut down, as well as the optimal level of production and input usage.

TECHNICAL PROBLEMS

1. Answer the following questions using the cost curves for a perfectly competitive firm shown in the graph on the following page.
   a. If price is \$7 per unit of output, draw the marginal revenue curve. The manager should produce ____ units in order to maximize profit.
   b. Since average total cost is \$____ for this output, total cost is \$____.
   c. The firm makes a profit of \$____.
   d. Let price fall to \$3, and draw the new marginal revenue curve. The manager should now produce ____ units in order to maximize profit.
   e. Total revenue is now \$____ and total cost is \$____. The firm makes a loss of \$____.

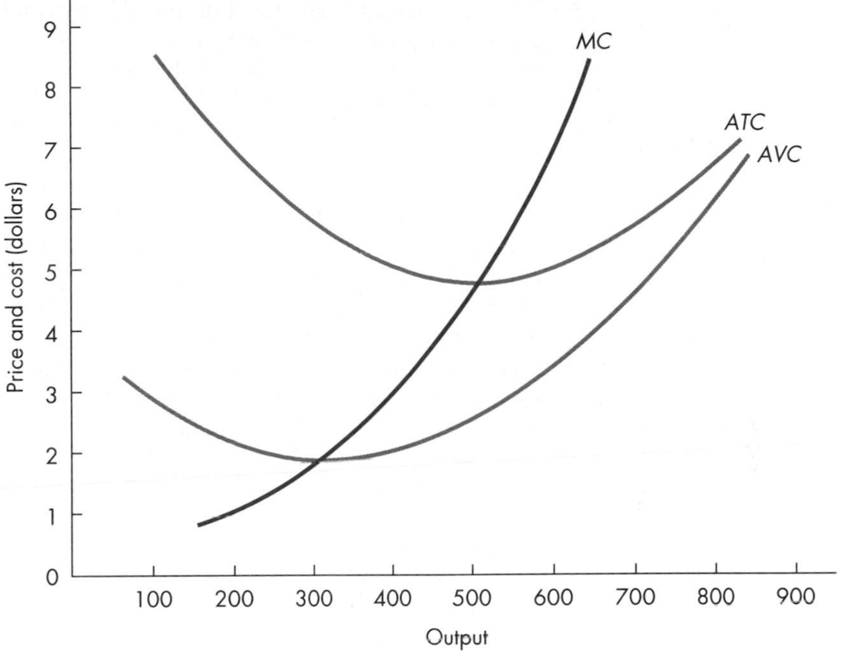

f. Total variable cost is $____, leaving $____ to apply to fixed cost.
g. If price falls below $____ the firm will produce zero output. Explain why.

2. Describe a position of long-run competitive equilibrium for a perfectly competitive firm and industry.
   a. How and why does such an equilibrium come about?
   b. How would a manager of a perfectly competitive firm know when the industry is in equilibrium?

* 3. Consider a perfectly competitive firm that has total fixed cost of $50 and faces a market-determined price of $2 per unit for its output. The wage rate is $10 per unit of labor, the only variable input. Using the table below, answer the following questions.

(1) Units of labor	(2) Output	(3) Marginal product	(4) Marginal revenue product	(5) Marginal cost	(6) Profit
1	5	____	____	____	____
2	15	____	____	____	____
3	30	____	____	____	____
4	50	____	____	____	____
5	65	____	____	____	____
6	77	____	____	____	____
7	86	____	____	____	____
8	94	____	____	____	____
9	98	____	____	____	____
10	96	____	____	____	____

a. Fill in the blanks in column 3 of the table by computing the marginal product of labor for each level of labor usage.

b. Fill in the blanks in column 4 of the table by computing the marginal revenue product for each level of labor usage.
c. How much labor should the manager hire in order to maximize profit? Why?
d. Fill in the blanks in column 5 of the table by computing marginal cost.
e. How many units of output should the manager produce in order to maximize profit? Why?
f. Fill in the blanks in column 6 with the profit earned at each level of labor usage.
g. Do your answers to parts *c* and *e* both maximize profit? Does it matter whether the manager chooses labor usage or chooses output in order to maximize profit? Why?
h. How much labor should the manager hire when the wage rate is $20? How much profit is earned? Is marginal product greater or less than average product at this level of labor usage? Why does it matter?

4. A typical firm in a perfectly competitive market made positive economic profits last period. What do you expect will happen this period to:
   a. The number of firms in the market.
   b. The market demand curve.
   c. The market supply curve.
   d. Market price.
   e. Market output.
   f. The firm's output.
   g. The firm's profit.
5. In a perfectly competitive industry the market price is $12. A firm is currently producing 50 units of output; average total cost is $10, marginal cost is $15, and average variable cost is $7.
   a. Draw a graph of the demand and cost conditions facing the firm and show where the firm is currently producing.
   b. Is the firm making the profit-maximizing decision? Why or why not? If not, what should the firm do?
   c. Consider another firm in a perfectly competitive industry that faces a market price of $25. This firm is producing 10,000 units of output, and average total cost, which is at its minimum value, is $25. Answer parts *a* and *b* for this firm.
6. The following graph shows a perfectly competitive firm's short-run cost structure.

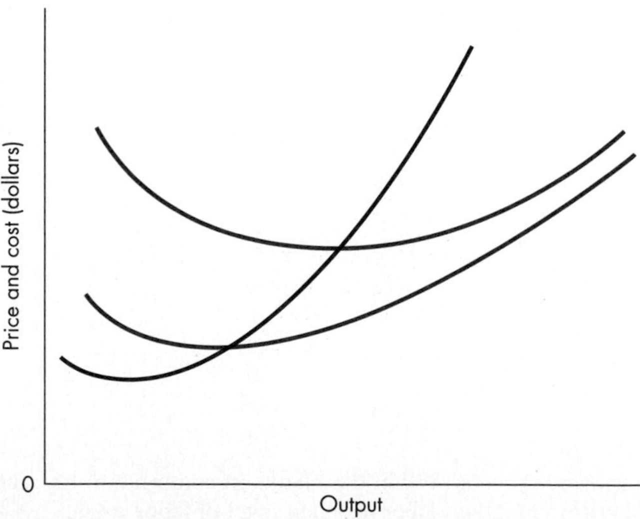

a. Label the three curves.
b. Show a price at which the firm would make a pure profit. Show the quantity it would produce and the amount of pure profit that would be earned.
c. Show a price at which the firm would continue to produce in the short run but would suffer losses. Show the output and losses at this price.
d. Show the price below which the firm would not produce in the short run.

* 7. Suppose that a perfectly competitive industry is in long-run competitive equilibrium. Then the price of a substitute good (in consumption) decreases. What will happen in the short run to:
a. The market demand curve.
b. The market supply curve.
c. Market price.
d. Market output.
e. The firm's output.
f. The firm's profit.

What will happen in the long run?

8. The following graph shows the relevant portion of the marginal product curve for labor (the only variable input) used by a perfectly competitive firm.

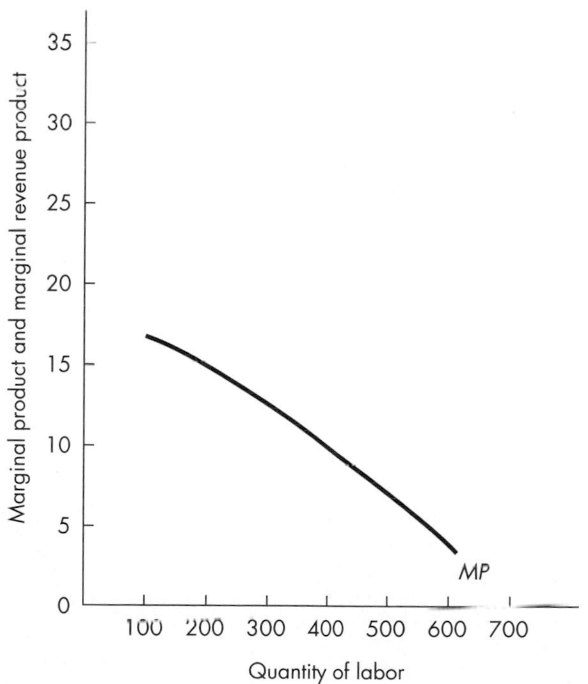

a. On the graph, draw the associated marginal revenue product curve over the relevant range of labor usage. The price of the product produced is $2 per unit.
b. At a wage rate of $30, how much labor will the firm hire? What if the wage rate falls to $20? What if the wage falls to $14?

c. Suppose the price of the product falls to $1. Draw the new *MRP* curve.
d. How much labor is hired now at each of the three wage rates?

9. Firm A and Firm B both have total revenues of $100,000 and total fixed costs of $50,000; Firm A has total variable costs of $80,000, while Firm B has total variable costs of $110,000.
   a. How much profit or loss is each firm earning? Should Firm A operate or shut down? What about Firm B? Why?
   b. Firms C and D both have total revenues of $200,000 and total costs of $250,000; Firm C has total fixed costs of $40,000, while Firm D has total fixed costs of $70,000. How much profit or loss is each firm earning? Should Firm C operate or shut down? What about Firm D? Why?

10. A manufacturing firm employs a superior plant manager to manage production at its plant. This plant manager is much more efficient than the typical plant manager employed at the rest of the firms in the industry, which is perfectly competitive. Typical plant managers make $5,000 per month in salary. By employing the superior plant manager, the firm faces the *LAC* and *LMC* curves shown in the following figure. In long-run equilibrium, the price of the product is $10.
    a. Minimum *LAC* for a firm with a typical plant manager is $_____. The typical firm earns economic profit of $_____.
    b. The firm with the superior plant manager earns economic profit of $_____.
    c. The superior plant manager earns a salary of $_____ per month, $_____ of which is economic rent.
    d. If the superior plant manager were also the owner of the manufacturing plant, how much profit would he earn? Explain.

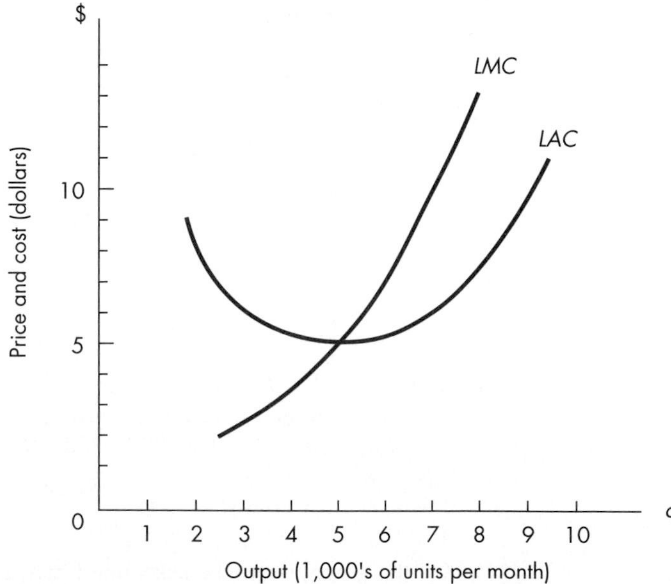

APPLIED PROBLEMS

1. The MidNight Hour, a local nightclub, earned $100,000 in accounting profit last year. This year the owner, who had invested $1 million in the club, decided to close the club. What can you say about economic profit (and the rate of return) in the nightclub business?
2. Grocery stores and gasoline stations in a large city would appear to be an example of perfectly competitive markets—there are numerous sellers, each seller is relatively small, and the products sold are quite similar. How could we argue that these markets are not perfectly competitive (leaving out the assumption of perfect knowledge)? Could each firm face a demand curve that is *not* perfectly elastic? What rate of return do you expect grocery stores and gasoline stations to earn in the long run?
3. The manager of All City Realtors wants to hire some real estate agents to specialize in selling housing units acquired by the Resolution Trust Corporation (RTC) in its attempt to bail out the savings and loan industry. The commission paid by the RTC to the company to sell these homes is a flat rate of $2,000 per unit sold, rather than the customary commission that is based on the sale price of a home. The manager estimates the following marginal product schedule for real estate agents dealing in government-owned housing:

Number of real state agents	Marginal product (number of additional units sold per year)	Marginal revenue product
1	20	______
2	17	______
3	15	______
4	12	______
5	8	______
6	4	______

   a. Construct the marginal revenue product schedule by filling in the blanks in the table above.
   b. If the manager of All City Realtors must pay a wage rate of $32,000 per year to get agents who will specialize in selling RTC housing, how many agents should the manager hire? Why?
   c. If the wage rate falls to $18,000 per year, how many agents should the manager hire?
   d. Suppose the RTC raises its commission to $3,000 per unit sold. Now what is the value of the marginal product for each real estate agent employed?
   e. Now that the RTC is paying $3,000 per unit sold, how many agents should the manager hire if the wage rate is $30,000?
4. HoneyBee Farms, a medium-size producer of honey, operates in a market that fits the competitive market definition relatively well. However, honey farmers are assisted by support prices above the price that would prevail in the absence of controls. The owner of HoneyBee Farms, as well as some fellow honey producers, complain that they can't make a profit even with these support prices. Explain why. Explain why even higher support prices would not help honey farmers in the long run.

5. Insurance agents receive a commission on the policies they sell. Many states regulate the rates that can be charged for insurance. Would higher or lower rates increase the incomes of agents? Explain, distinguishing between the short run and the long run.
6. If all of the assumptions of perfect competition hold, why would firms in such an industry have little incentive to carry out technological change or much research and development? What conditions would encourage research and development in competitive industries?
7. At a recent board meeting, the president and CEO got into a heated argument about whether or not to shut down the firm's plant in Miami. The Miami plant currently loses \$60,000 monthly. The president of the firm argued that the Miami plant should continue to operate, at least until a buyer is found for the production facility. The president's argument was based on the fact that the Miami plant's fixed costs are \$68,000 per month. The CEO exploded over this point, castigating the president for considering fixed costs in making the shutdown decision. According to the CEO, "Everyone knows fixed costs don't matter!"
   a. Should the Miami plant be closed or continue to operate at a loss in the short run?
   b. How would you explain to the incorrect party that he or she is wrong?
8. Suppose you own a home remodeling company. You are currently earning short-run profits. The home remodeling industry is an increasing-cost industry. In the long run, what do you expect will happen to
   a. Your firm's costs of production? Explain.
   b. The price you can charge for your remodeling services? Why?
   c. The rate of return in home remodeling? Why?
9. A commentator on the "CBS Evening News" reported, "The Pentagon has already invested \$3 million in the B-2 bomber. Cuts will drive prices up to \$1 billion each. But they can't afford to eliminate the program because so much has already been invested." Comment on this analysis.
10. Many state governments are offering huge benefits to large corporations if these corporations agree to open new offices or manufacturing facilities in those states. The benefits offered include lump sum cash payments, "forgivable" loans, free land for office sites, and lower taxes. In what sense are these benefits similar to economic rents for these firms? Other than the fortunate firms who receive these benefits, who else benefits from these payments?

APPENDIX Profit-Maximizing Conditions for a Perfectly Competitive Firm

1. A perfectly competitive firm will maximize profit by producing the output at which price equals marginal cost if $P \geq AVC$.

Let F = fixed cost, $C(Q)$ = variable cost, Q = output, and P = price. Thus profit is

$$\pi = PQ - C(Q) - F$$

Maximizing profit with respect to output requires

$$\frac{d\pi}{dQ} = P - \frac{dC}{dQ} = 0$$

Since dC/dQ is marginal cost for very small changes in Q, price equals marginal cost.

To analyze whether the firm should operate or shut down, write the profit function as

$$\pi = PQ - \frac{C(Q)}{Q}Q - F = \left(P - \frac{C(Q)}{Q}\right)Q - F$$

$$= (P - AVC)Q - F$$

If profit is positive when $P = MC$, the firm clearly would choose to operate. But suppose that profit is negative (the firm is making a loss) when $P = MC$.

The firm must pay the fixed cost, F, at any output, including zero. First, suppose that $P > AVC$ when $P = MC$. In this case, since $(P - AVC)Q - F > -F$, the firm should continue to produce. Its loss is less than $-F$, the fixed cost it would lose if its shuts down. That is, the positive term in the profit function, $(P - AVC)Q$, partially offsets the negative term, $-F$. But, if $P = MC$ and $P < AVC$, $(P - AVC)Q < 0$, and $(P - AVC)Q - F < -F$. Thus, the firm should shut down and lose only $-F$, its fixed cost. It loses less by shutting down than by operating.

2. The firm will hire a variable input at the point where the price of the input, w, equals the input's marginal revenue product. Let the only variable input be labor, L. The production function is $Q = f(L)$. Thus profit would be

$$\pi = Pf(L) - wL - F$$

where P is product price and F is fixed cost. Profit maximization requires

$$\frac{d\pi}{dL} = P\frac{dQ}{dL} - w = 0$$

where dQ/dL is labor's marginal product. Since the marginal revenue product is $P \cdot MP_L$,

$$MRP_L = w$$

if the firm produces a positive output.

The firm will shut down if at the point where $w = MRP$, $MRP > ARP$. Write the profit function as

$$\begin{aligned} \pi &= P\frac{Q}{L}L - wL - F \\ &= ARP \cdot L - MRP \cdot L - F \\ &= L\,(ARP - MRP) - F \end{aligned}$$

If $ARP < MRP$, the firm will lose only $-F$ if $L = 0$; that is, if it shuts down. It will lose $(PQ - wL) - F$, which is clearly a larger loss than $-F$, if $L > 0$ when ARP is less than MRP. If $ARP > MRP$ at the point where $MRP = w$, the firm will produce $(L > 0)$ even if it is making a loss because it would lose less than $-F$.

CHAPTER

14

Profit Maximization in Perfectly Competitive Markets:

Implementation of the Theory

Although managers should know the fundamentals of the theory of profit maximization, it is even more useful for them to know how to implement and use the theory. They should be able to use empirical estimates or forecasts of the relevant variables and equations to determine the actual values of the variables that maximize the firm's profit. As emphasized in Chapter 13, a manager can choose either the level of output or the level of input usage. The two approaches are equivalent because they both lead to the same levels of output, input usage, and profit. This chapter describes how to use empirical techniques to find the optimal level of output and inputs.

Using the statistical techniques for estimating demand, production, and cost functions, you will learn how to estimate or forecast the levels of output and input usage that maximize the firm's profit. You have spent a lot of time learning the techniques of estimating the various demand, production, and cost functions. Now you will learn how to use these empirical skills to answer an important question facing a manager: How can the theory of profit maximization be used in practice to make profit-maximizing decisions about production?

In most of the examples used here, the manager has complete information about all of the relevant variables and equations. In reality, managers will probably not have access to such ideal information. However, by showing how to make decisions about profit maximization under the most favorable circumstances, we can give you a feel for the way such decisions are made under conditions that are not so favorable—that is, when information is not complete.

We will first outline how managers can, in general, determine the optimizing conditions. This outline gives a pattern for situations in which numerical estimates of the variables and equations are available. Then we present examples of how a firm can use this approach to determine the optimal level of output and the optimal level of input usage. We demonstrate numerically that the two methods lead to the same results. We end with a discussion of how the presence of risk modifies the decision-making process.

14.1 IMPLEMENTING THE PROFIT-MAXIMIZING OUTPUT DECISION

In Chapter 13 we emphasized that a manager must answer two questions when choosing the level of output that maximizes profit. These two questions and the answers forthcoming from the theoretical analysis in Chapter 13 are summarized as follows:

1. Should the firm produce or shut down? *Produce as long as the market price is greater than or equal to minimum average variable cost—*$P \geq AVC_{min}$. *Shut down otherwise.*
2. If production occurs, how much should the firm produce? *Produce the output at which market price (which is marginal revenue) equals marginal cost—*$P = MC$.

It follows from these rules that to determine the optimal level of output, a manager must obtain estimates or forecasts of the market price of the good produced by the firm, the firm's average variable cost function, and the firm's marginal cost function. Based on the theoretical analysis presented in Chapter 13, the following steps can be followed to find the profit-maximizing rate of production and the level of profit the firm will earn:

Step 1: Forecast the price of the product

Output decisions are typically made for some period in the future: next week, next month, next quarter, etc. Therefore, in order to decide whether or not to produce and how much to produce, a manager must obtain a forecast of the price at which the completed product can be sold. Remember that a perfectly competitive firm does not face a downward-sloping demand curve but simply takes the market price as given. You learned in Chapter 9 how to use two statistical techniques—time-series forecasting and econometric forecasting—to forecast the price of the product.

Step 2: Estimate average variable cost (*AVC*) and marginal cost (*MC*)

As emphasized in Chapter 13, the cubic specification is the appropriate form for estimating a family of short-run cost curves. Thus the manager could estimate the following average variable cost function:

$$AVC = a + bQ + cQ^2$$

As demonstrated in Chapter 13, the marginal cost function associated with this average variable cost function is

$$MC = a + 2bQ + 3cQ^2$$

Step 3: Check the shutdown rule

When P is less than AVC, the firm loses less money by shutting down than it would lose if it produced where $P = MC$. A manager can determine the price below which a firm should shut down by finding the *minimum* point on the AVC curve, AVC_{min}. As long as price is greater than (or equal to) AVC_{min}, the firm will produce rather than shut down.[1] Recall from Chapter 12 that the average variable cost curve reaches its minimum value at $Q_m = -b/2c$. The minimum value of average variable cost is then determined by substituting Q_m into the AVC function:

$$AVC_{min} = a + bQ_m + c(Q_m)^2$$

The firm should produce as long as $P \geq AVC_{min}$. If the forecasted price is greater than (or equal to) minimum average variable cost ($P \geq AVC_{min}$), the firm should produce the output level where $P = MC$. If the forecasted price is less than the minimum average variable cost ($P < AVC_{min}$), the firm should shut down in the short run, and it loses an amount equal to its total fixed costs.

Step 4: If $P \geq AVC_{min}$, find the output level where $P = MC$.

A perfectly competitive firm should produce the level of output for which $P = MC$—if $P \geq AVC_{min}$. Thus, if the manager decides to produce in the short run, the manager maximizes profit by finding the output level for which $P = MC$. In the case of a cubic specification for cost, profit maximization or loss minimization requires that

$$P = MC = a + 2bQ + 3cQ^2$$

Solving this equation for Q gives the optimal output level for the firm—unless P is less than AVC, and then the optimal output level is zero.

Step 5: Computation of profit or loss

Once a manager determines how much to produce, the calculation of total profit or loss is straightforward. Profit (or loss) is equal to total revenue minus total cost. Total revenue for a competitive firm is price times quantity sold. Total cost is the sum of total variable cost and total fixed cost, where total variable cost is average variable cost times the number of units sold. Hence, total profit (loss) is

$$\begin{aligned} \pi &= TR - TC \\ &= (P \times Q) - [(AVC \times Q) + TFC] \\ &= (P - AVC)Q - TFC \end{aligned}$$

If $P < AVC_{min}$, the firm shuts down, and $\pi = -TFC$.

---

[1]When price exactly equals average variable cost ($P = AVC$), total revenue is just sufficient to cover total variable cost, and the firm loses an amount equal to total fixed cost. Losing an amount equal to total fixed cost is exactly what happens if the firm shuts down. Thus, when $P = AVC$ the firm is indifferent between producing or shutting down. As in Chapter 13, we continue to assume arbitrarily that the manager will choose to produce, rather than shut down, if price exactly equals average variable cost.

To illustrate how to implement these steps to find the profit-maximizing level of output and to forecast the profit to the firm, we now turn to a hypothetical firm that operates in a perfectly competitive market.

14.2 IMPLEMENTING THE PROFIT-MAXIMIZING OUTPUT DECISION: AN ILLUSTRATION

As an example, we use the output decision facing the manager of Beau Apparel, Inc., a clothing manufacturer that produces moderately priced men's shirts. Beau Apparel is only one of many firms that produce a fairly homogeneous product, and none of the firms in this moderate-price shirt market engages in any significant advertising. While the market for shirts does not exactly match all the conditions of perfect competition, it does, approximately, satisfy the conditions of a perfectly competitive industry. Consequently, the manager of Beau Apparel can employ the steps outlined above to find the level of shirt production that maximizes profit.

Price Forecasts

In mid-December 1994, the manager of Beau Apparel was preparing the firm's production plan for the first quarter of 1995. The manager wanted to obtain a forecast of the wholesale price of shirts for the first quarter of 1995. This price forecast would subsequently be used in making the production decision for Beau Apparel. Since the manufacturer sells shirts to retail clothing stores, the wholesale, rather than the retail price, is the relevant price.

The manager recognizes that in this particular segment of the shirt market, Beau Apparel is operating in a nearly perfectly competitive market. Consequently, the manager believed specifying a demand and supply model for the shirt market was appropriate. The manager specified the following demand and supply equations:

$$\text{Demand:} \quad Q = a + bP + cM$$

$$\text{Supply:} \quad Q = e + fP + gP_F$$

where Q represents both the quantity demanded and quantity supplied (since they are the same in equilibrium), P is wholesale price of a shirt (adjusted for the effects of inflation), M is per capita income, and P_F is the price of the variable input.[2]

Using quarterly data for the seven-year time period 1988I–1994IV, the manager estimated the demand and supply equations using the two-stage least-squares method of estimation to eliminate the simultaneous equations bias, as

[2]While there are usually many variable inputs used in production, it is not usually convenient (or necessary) to include in the supply equation the price of every one of the variable inputs employed by the firm. Instead, the effect of a change in input prices on supply can usually be adequately modeled by including the prices of only the most important inputs, where importance is determined by the share of total cost attributable to a particular input. Alternatively, a weighted average of input prices can be used for P_F, where the weights are computed as the share of the total cost accounted for by each input.

discussed in Chapter 8. Both demand and supply are identified, and the estimated demand and supply equations were

$$\text{Demand: } Q = 125 - 2P + 12.5M$$
$$\text{Supply: } Q = 250 + 8P - 3.125P_F$$

In this estimation, sales (Q) were expressed in units of 1,000, the wholesale price of shirts (P) in dollars per unit, per capita income (M) in thousands of dollars, and the price of the variable input (P_F) in dollars. Each of the estimated coefficients had the expected sign and was statistically significant at the 95 percent level of confidence.

Before the estimated demand and supply equations can be used to forecast price in the first quarter of 1995, values for the exogenous variables, income and price of the variable input, must be forecast for the first quarter of 1995. To obtain the necessary forecasts for the exogenous variables, the manager purchased forecasts of per capita income and input prices from a large econometric forecasting firm. The forecast for the price of the variable input in the first quarter of 1995 was \$16.

In the case of the income forecast, the forecasting firm believed that future levels of per capita income depended crucially upon the outcome of a major domestic economic policy matter currently being addressed by the US Congress. To reflect this uncertainty, the forecasting firm provided the manager of Beau Apparel with two different forecasts of income, each based on a different assumption about the outcome of the legislation pending in Congress. These income forecasts for the first quarter of 1995, which we shall refer to as the *low* and *high* forecasts were

$$\text{High} = \$22{,}000$$
$$\text{Low} = \$14{,}000$$

When forecasting the price of shirts in the first quarter of 1995, the manager of Beau Apparel had two alternative values of $\hat{M}_{1995I}$, 14 and 22.

To obtain forecasts of the price of shirts, the manager next substituted the forecasted values of the exogenous variables into the estimated demand and supply functions. Using the high forecast for income, the demand and supply equations in the first quarter of 1995 are

$$\text{Demand: } Q_{1995I} = 125 - 2P_{1995I} + 12.5(22)$$
$$= 400 - 2P_{1995I}$$
$$\text{Supply: } Q_{1995I} = 250 + 8P_{1995I} - 3.125(16)$$
$$= 200 + 8P_{1995I}$$

To calculate the equilibrium price, the manager set quantity demanded equal to quantity supplied,

$$400 - 2P_{1995I} = 200 + 8P_{1995I}$$

to obtain

$$\hat{P}_{1995I} = 20$$

For the case of the high income forecast ($22,000), the forecasted wholesale price of shirts in the first quarter of 1995 was $20 per unit.

In exactly the same way, the manager then calculated a forecast for product price using the low income forecast ($14,000) and obtained a wholesale price of $10 per unit. Thus, the econometric method of forecasting generated two forecasts for the wholesale price of shirts in the first quarter of 1995, $10 and $20 per unit.

The manager decided to obtain one more price forecast by using a time-series model. Specifically, the manager specified a linear trend model with a dummy variable to correct for seasonal variation in shirt prices. The time-series model for shirt prices was

$$P_t = a + bt + cD_t$$

where P_t is the inflation-adjusted price of shirts in time period t, and D_t is a dummy variable to account for seasonal variations in the price of shirts. The dummy variable, D_t, equals one in the winter and summer quarters (I and III) when stores usually stock up shirts for the spring and fall buying seasons, and equals zero in the spring and fall quarters (II and IV) when stores are primarily concerned with selling the shirts they purchased in the winter and summer quarters.

The linear trend equation was estimated using quarterly data for the seven-year period 1988I–1994IV. Since the textile industry is an increasing-cost industry and textile demand had generally been increasing over the last seven years, the manager of Beau Apparel expected the estimated value of b to have a positive sign, indicating an upward trend in the price of shirts. The estimated value of c was expected to be positive, reflecting the higher wholesale prices during the winter and summer quarters. The estimated trend line was

$$P_t = 6.25 + 0.2759t + 0.75D_t$$

The estimated coefficients were each statistically significant at the 95 percent level of confidence and each coefficient had the expected sign.

To forecast the wholesale price for the first quarter of 1995, the manager substituted the values $t = 29$ and $D_t = 1$ (since 1995I corresponds to time period 29 and the first quarter is a winter quarter) into the estimated trend line equation:

$$\begin{aligned} P_{1995I} = \hat{P}_{29} &= 6.25 + 0.2759(29) + 0.75(1) \\ &= 15 \end{aligned}$$

Thus, the time-series model generated a forecast of $15 for the first quarter of 1995. With this forecast, the manager of Beau Apparel had three forecasts of the wholesale price of shirts in the first quarter of 1995:

Econometric model (high) = $20
Time-series model (medium) = $15
Econometric model (low) = $10

Estimation of Average Variable Cost and Marginal Cost

The manager of Beau Apparel chose a cubic specification of short-run cost for estimating the average variable cost and the marginal cost curves. Using time-series data over the seven-year time period 1988I–1994IV, during which Beau Apparel had the same size plant, the following average variable cost function was estimated:

$$AVC = 20 - 3Q + 0.25Q^2$$

where *AVC* was expressed in dollars, and output (*Q*) was expressed in units of 1,000. All of the estimated coefficients (20, –3, and 0.25) had the required sign and were statistically significant. The estimated average cost function provided the information needed for making the decision to produce or shut down. We will return to this decision after we discuss how the manager of Beau Apparel estimated the marginal cost function.

As explained in Chapter 12 and as reviewed in the previous section, the parameter estimates for the average variable cost function can be used to obtain the estimated marginal cost function:

$$MC = a + 2bQ + 3cQ^2$$

where *a*, *b*, and *c* are the estimated parameters (coefficients) for the *AVC* function. The manager used the estimated coefficients of the average variable cost equation to obtain the corresponding marginal cost function. Since the estimate of the average variable cost function for the shirt division was

$$AVC = 20 - 3Q + 0.25Q^2$$

the corresponding marginal cost function for shirts was

$$\begin{aligned} MC &= 20 + 2(-3)Q + 3(0.25)Q^2 \\ &= 20 - 6Q + 0.75Q^2 \end{aligned}$$

After obtaining forecasts of price and estimates of the average variable cost and marginal cost curves, the manager was able to answer the two production questions: (1) Should the firm produce or shut down?, and (2) If production is warranted, how much should the firm produce? We now can show how the manager of Beau Apparel made these two decisions and calculated the firm's forecasted profit.

The Shutdown Decision

Since the estimated average variable cost function for shirts was

$$AVC = 20 - 3Q + 0.25Q^2$$

AVC reaches its minimum value at

$$Q_m = -(-3)/2(0.25) = 6$$

or 6,000 units of output. Substituting this output level into the estimated average variable cost function, the value of average variable cost at its minimum point is

$$AVC_{\min} = 20 - 3(6) + 0.25(6)^2 = 11$$

Thus, average variable cost reaches its minimum value of \$11 at 6,000 units of output.

The manager of Beau Apparel then compared this minimum average variable cost with the three price forecasts for the first quarter of 1995. For the high forecast,

$$\hat{P}_{1995I} = \$20 > \$11 = AVC_{\min}$$

so the firm should produce in order to maximize profit or minimize loss. Likewise, with the time-series forecast,

$$\hat{P}_{1995I} = \$15 > \$11 = AVC_{\min}$$

and the firm also should produce. However, if the market-determined price of shirts turned out to be equal to the low forecast, the firm should shut down (produce zero output) since

$$\hat{P}_{1995I} = \$10 < \$11 = AVC_{\min}$$

In this case, total revenue would not cover all variable costs of production, and the firm would be better off shutting down and losing only its fixed costs. The manager, therefore, must determine only how much output to produce when price is either \$20 or \$15.

The Output Decision

Given the estimated marginal cost equation for Beau Apparel, profit maximization or loss minimization requires that

$$P = MC = 20 - 6Q + 0.75Q^2$$

The manager first considered the high forecast of wholesale shirt prices. After setting the \$20 forecasted price equal to estimated marginal cost, the optimal production of shirts when price is \$20 was found by solving

$$20 = 20 - 6Q + 0.75Q^2$$

Subtracting 20 from both sides of the equation and factoring out a Q term results in the following expression:

$$0 = Q(-6 + 0.75Q)$$

There are two solutions to this equation since the right-hand side of the equation is zero if either $Q = 0$ or if $Q = 8$. Since the manager of Beau Apparel had already determined that price was greater than $AVC_{\min}$ and production was warranted, the manager concluded that the profit-maximizing output level was 8,000 units (Q = 8 units of 1,000).

Using the time-series price forecast of $15, the manager again determined the optimal output by equating the forecasted price to estimated marginal cost

$$15 = 20 - 6Q + 0.75Q^2$$

or

$$0.75Q^2 - 6Q + 5 = 0$$

The solution to this equation is not as simple as was the preceding case, because the left-hand side of the equation cannot be factored. To solve a quadratic equation that cannot be factored, the quadratic formula must be used:[3]

$$Q = \frac{-(-6) \pm \sqrt{(-6)^2 - 4(0.75)(5)}}{2(0.75)} = \frac{6 \pm 4.6}{1.5}$$

The two solutions for this quadratic equation are $Q = 0.93$ and $Q = 7.1$.

To determine which solution is optimal, the manager computed the average variable cost for each level of output:

$$AVC_{Q = 0.93} = 20 - 3(0.93) + 0.25(0.93)^2 = \$17.43$$
$$AVC_{Q = 7.1} = 20 - 3(7.1) + 0.25(7.1)^2 = \$11.30$$

Since the price forecast of $15 is less than $17.43, the manager would not produce the output level $Q = 0.93$. If the wholesale price is expected to be $15, the manager would produce 7,100 units at which *AVC* is $11.30. We now consider the amount of profit or loss that Beau Apparel would earn at each of the optimal levels of output.

Computation of Total Profit or Loss

Total revenue for a competitive firm is price times quantity sold. Total cost is the sum of total variable cost and total fixed cost, where total variable cost is average variable cost times the number of units sold. Hence, total profit (loss) is

$$\begin{aligned}\pi &= TR - TC \\ &= (P \times Q) - [(AVC \times Q) + TFC]\end{aligned}$$

The manager expects total fixed costs for the shirt division for 1995I to be $30,000. The values for total revenue and total variable cost depend on the price forecast and corresponding optimal output. We now show how the manager of Beau Apparel computed profit or loss for each of the three forecasts of the wholesale price of shirts.

---

[3]For an equation of the form $aX^2 + bX + c = 0$, the two solutions, X_1 and X_2, are

$$X_1, X_2 = \frac{-b \pm \sqrt{b^2 - 4ac}}{2a}$$

High price forecast (P = \$20)

In this case, Beau Apparel's manager determined that the optimal level of production would be 8,000 units ($Q = 8$). The average variable cost when 8,000 units are produced is

$$AVC_{Q=8} = 20 - 3(8) + 0.25(8)^2 = \$12$$

Economic profit when price is \$20 would be

$$\pi = (\$20 \times 8{,}000) - [(\$12 \times 8{,}000) + \$30{,}000] = \$34{,}000$$

If the price of shirts is \$20 per unit in the first quarter of 1995, Beau Apparel should produce 8,000 units to earn a profit of \$34,000, which is the maximum profit possible given this price.

Middle price forecast (P = \$15)

If the price of shirts is \$15 in the first quarter of 1995, the optimal level of output is 7,100 units ($Q = 7.1$). The average variable cost is

$$AVC_{Q=7.1} = 20 - 3(7.1) + 0.25(7.1)^2 = \$11.30$$

Economic profit when price is \$15 would be

$$\pi = (\$15 \times 7{,}100) - [(\$11.30 \times 7{,}100) + \$30{,}000] = -\$3{,}730$$

When the price of shirts is \$15, the shirt division of Beau Apparel would be expected to suffer a *loss* of \$3,730 in the first quarter of 1995. Note that the firm should continue to produce since this is the minimum loss possible when price is \$15. If Beau Apparel shut down production when price is \$15, the firm would lose an amount equal to the total fixed cost of \$30,000—considerably more than the \$3,750 the firm loses by producing 7,100 units.

Low price forecast (P = \$10)

At a price of \$10 per shirt, the firm would shut down and produce zero output ($Q = 0$). In this case, economic profit would be equal to $-TFC$:

$$\pi = (\$10 \times 0) - [0 + \$30{,}000] = -\$30{,}000$$

Beau Apparel would minimize loss by producing nothing and losing only its fixed costs of \$30,000.

This extended example about Beau Apparel's production decision illustrates how the manager of a firm that sells in a perfectly competitive market can find the optimal level of output. Our purpose in using the three different price forecasts was to illustrate the decision-making rules developed in Chapter 12, where we showed that a firm makes one of the following choices in the short-run:

1. Produce a positive level of output and earn an economic profit (if $P > AVC$ and $P > ATC$).
2. Produce a positive level of output and suffer an economic loss less than the amount of total fixed cost (if $AVC \leq P < ATC$).
3. Produce zero output and suffer an economic loss equal to total fixed cost (if $P < AVC$).

The Beau Apparel example follows the theoretical analysis set forth in Chapter 13. However, by confronting the manager with three forecasts of price, we introduced the problem of risk into the profit-maximizing decision of the manager. The manager does not know which of the three prices will actually be the market price in the next time period, yet the manager must make a decision *now* about the level of output to produce in the future. We will return to the problem of making profit-maximizing decisions under risk at the end of this chapter.

14.3 IMPLEMENTATION OF THE PROFIT-MAXIMIZING INPUT DECISION

Managers may choose the level of input usage, rather than output, to maximize the profit of the firm. This section illustrates how to find the optimal level of input usage for a firm in a perfectly competitive market. We consider the case of a single variable input here, relegating the more complex case of more than one variable input to the appendix to this chapter.

To be consistent with the discussion in Chapter 13, we call the variable input labor, although the techniques shown here can be used for any variable input. As in the case of choosing output, the manager must answer two questions in order to find the level of input usage that maximizes profit. These two questions and the answers set forth in Chapter 13 are summarized here as follows:

1. Should the firm produce or shut down? *Produce as long as the wage rate is less than or equal to the maximum value of average revenue product—* $w \leq ARP_{max}$. *Otherwise, shut down and hire no labor.*
2. If production occurs, how much labor should the firm hire? *Hire the amount of labor at which the wage rate equals the marginal revenue product—* $w = MRP$.

Recall from Chapter 13 that the marginal revenue product is the price of the product times the marginal product of labor:

$$MRP = P \times MP$$

Because the wage rate is determined in the labor market, the manager treats the wage rate as given and can hire as much, or as little, labor as needed at the going market-determined wage rate.

In order to determine the optimal level of input usage from these rules, a manager must obtain estimates or forecasts of the market price of the firm's product, the wage rate, and the average revenue product and marginal revenue product functions of the variable input. Based on the theoretical analysis presented in Chapter 13, the following steps can be followed to find the profit-maximizing level of labor employment and the level of profit the firm will earn.

Step 1: Forecast the price of the product and the wage rate

Forecast the price of the product using one of the procedures from Chapter 9 and discussed under Step 1 for finding the profit-maximizing level of output. The wage rate must also be forecast either by time-series methods or by applying econometric modeling techniques to the market for labor. In order to know how to model the supply and demand for labor, you would need to take a course in labor economics. Most managers either use time-series techniques to forecast wages, or purchase wage forecasts from econometric forecasting firms. Note that the product price must be forecasted regardless of whether the manager wishes to choose output or input usage to maximize profit, but the wage rate is forecasted only when choosing input usage to maximize profit.

Step 2: Estimate average revenue product (*ARP*) and marginal revenue product (*MRP*)

To estimate the average revenue product and marginal revenue product functions of labor, the manager must specify and estimate a short-run production function. Following the procedure set forth in Chapter 11, the manager can specify a short-run cubic production function:

$$Q = AL^3 + BL^2$$

As shown in Chapter 12, the average product function and the marginal product function are

$$AP = AL^2 + BL$$
$$MP = 3AL^2 + 2BL$$

and the average revenue product and marginal revenue product functions ($ARP = P \times AP$ and $MRP = P \times MP$) are

$$ARP = P \times AP = PAL^2 + PBL$$
$$MRP = P \times MP = 3PAL^2 + 2PBL$$

Step 3: Check the shutdown rule.

When the wage rate exceeds average revenue product ($w > ARP$), the firm loses less money by shutting down than it would lose if it produced where $w = MRP$. A manager can determine the wage above which a firm should shut down by finding the value of *ARP* at the *maximum* point on the average revenue product curve, ARP_{max}. To find ARP_{max}, the manager first finds the level of labor usage for which *AP* reaches its maximum value. Recall from Chapter 12 that AP reaches its maximum value at $L_a = -B/2A$. Thus,

$$AP_{max} = A(L_a)^2 + BL_a$$
$$ARP_{max} = P \times AP_{max} = PA(L_a)^2 + PBL_a$$

The manager should produce as long as $w \leq ARP_{max}$.[4]

Step 4: If $w \leq ARP_{max}$, find the input level where $w = MRP$

In the case of a perfectly competitive firm, the manager should employ the amount of labor for which $w = MRP$—if $w \leq ARP_{max}$. Thus, if the decision is to

[4]When the wage rate exactly equals average revenue product ($w = ARP$), total revenue is just sufficient to cover total variable cost, and the firm loses an amount equal to fixed cost. Just as in the case when price is exactly equal to *AVC*, the firm is indifferent between producing or shutting down. As before, we continue to assume arbitrarily that the manager will choose to produce, rather than shut down, if the wage rate exactly equals average revenue product.

produce in the short run, profit is maximized at the level of labor usage for which $w = MRP$. In the case of a cubic specification for the production function, profit maximization or loss minimization requires that

$$w = MRP = P \times MP = 3PAL^2 + 2PBL$$

Solving this equation for L gives the optimal level of labor usage for the firm—unless $w > ARP$, then the optimal level of labor to hire is zero.

Step 5: Computation of profit or loss

Once the profit-maximizing level of labor usage is determined, the calculation of total profit or loss can be easily accomplished. First, total revenue is computed by determining the level of output that is produced using the profit-maximizing amount of labor and multiplying this output by price. This level of output, which must also be the profit-maximizing output level, is found by substituting the profit-maximizing level of labor usage (L^*) into the production function.

$$Q^* = A(L^*)^3 + B(L^*)^2$$

Total revenue is equal to price times the profit-maximizing level of output:

$$TR = P \times Q^* = PA(L^*)^3 + PB(L^*)^2$$

Total variable cost is found by multiplying the wage rate times the profit-maximizing level of labor usage:

$$TVC = w \times L^*$$

Hence, total profit (loss) is $\pi = TR - TVC - TFC$. If $w > ARP_{max}$, the firm shuts down, and $\pi = -TFC$.

We will illustrate these steps, and let the manager choose labor usage to maximize profit by returning to our previous example.

14.4 IMPLEMENTING THE PROFIT-MAXIMIZING INPUT DECISION: AN ILLUSTRATION

We now return to the hypothetical textile firm, Beau Apparel, Inc. to show how the manager could maximize profit by choosing the optimal level of labor usage, instead of choosing the optimal level of output. As you will see, the resulting level of output, profit, and labor employment is the same regardless of whether the manager chooses Q or L to maximize profit.

Price and Wage Forecasts

The manager of Beau Apparel wants to determine how much labor to hire in the first quarter of 1995. As discussed, the manager will need forecasts for the price of shirts and the wage rate in the first quarter of 1995. For this discussion, we will consider only the high price forecast, $\hat{P}_{1995I} = \$20$. For the wage forecast, the manager purchased a high and a low wage forecast for the region in which the Beau Apparel plant is located from an economic forecasting firm. The forecasted low wage rate was \$16 per hour; $\hat{w}_{1995I} = \$16$. The forecasted high wage was $\hat{w}_{1995I} = \$30$.

Estimation of Average Revenue Product and Marginal Revenue Product

Using the 28 quarterly observations on output and labor usage, the following estimated production equation was obtained using the appropriate regression techniques:

$$Q = -0.051846\ L^3 + 0.53330\ L^2$$

where Q is expressed in units of one thousand, and L is expressed in thousands of hours. Both coefficients have the correct signs ($A < 0$ and $B > 0$), and both are statistically significant at the 95 percent level of confidence.

The manager used the production estimates to obtain the following equation for the average product of labor (Q/L):

$$AP = AL^2 + BL = -0.051846\ L^2 + 0.53330\ L$$

At the wholesale price forecast of \$20, the average revenue product function was obtained:

$$\begin{aligned} ARP = P \times AP &= 20 \times (-0.051846\ L^2 + 0.53330\ L) \\ &= -1.03690\ L^2 + 10.6660\ L \end{aligned}$$

The marginal product of labor for Beau Apparel was also computed using the parameter estimates for A and B from the cubic production function:

$$\begin{aligned} MP = 3AL^2 + 2BL &= 3(-0.051846)L^2 + 2(0.53330)L \\ &= -0.155538\ L^2 + 1.0666\ L \end{aligned}$$

At the wholesale price forecast of \$20, the manager computed the marginal revenue product function as follows:

$$\begin{aligned} MRP = 20 \times MP &= 20 \times (-0.155538\ L^2 + 1.0666\ L) \\ &= -3.11076\ L^2 + 21.332\ L \end{aligned}$$

Figure 14.1 shows the average revenue product (ARP) and the marginal revenue product curve (MRP). Note that MRP and ARP have the expected ∩-shape, and MRP intersects ARP at ARP's maximum value (compare Figures 13.13 and 14.1).

The Shutdown Decision

To find the maximum value of ARP, the maximum value of average product (AP_{max}) was calculated. The level of labor usage at which AP reaches its maximum value (L_a) was 5.143 ($= -B/2A = -0.5333/2(-0.051846)$); thus the maximum value of the average product of labor was

$$\begin{aligned} AP_{max} &= -0.051846(5.143)^2 + 0.5333(5.143) \\ &= 1.3715 \end{aligned}$$

The maximum value of average revenue product was then calculated as

$$\begin{aligned} ARP_{max} &= 20 \times 1.3715 \\ &= 27.43 \end{aligned}$$

FIGURE 14.1
The Profit-Maximizing Labor Usage for Beau Apparel

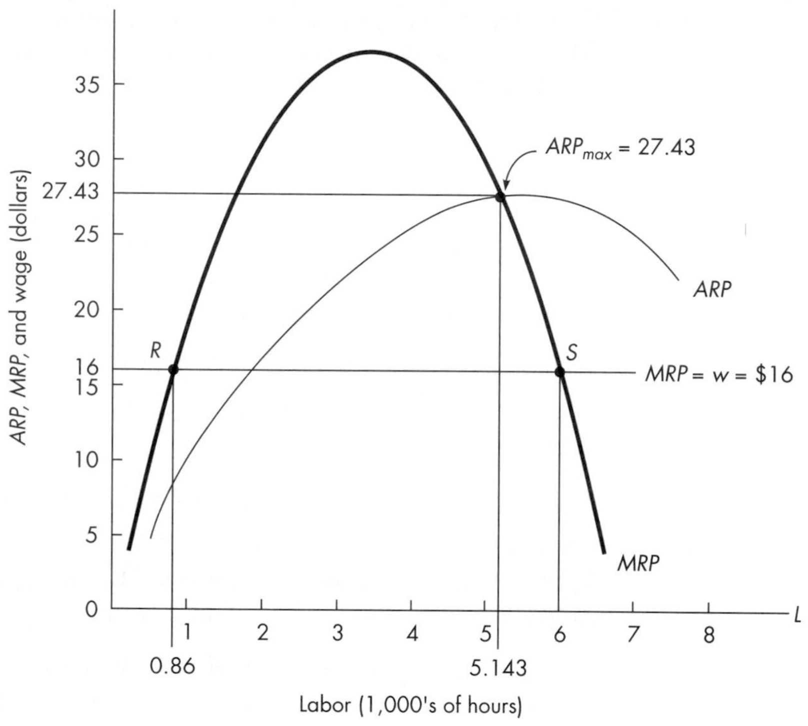

In Figure 14.1, the maximum point on *ARP* (point *T*) occurs at 5,143 (= 5.144 × 1,000) units of labor, and *ARP* equals 27.43 at this level of labor usage.

The manager of Beau Apparel compared the two forecasted wage rates to this maximum value of *ARP*. If the high wage forecast of $30 is correct, the manager would shut down operations and hire no labor since the wage rate exceeds the maximum value of average revenue product ($w > ARP$). If the low wage forecast of $16 turns out to be correct, the manager would decide to produce rather than shut down. Thus, the Beau Apparel manager would determine how much labor to hire only for the low wage forecast of $16.

The Labor Employment Decision

Given the estimated marginal revenue product equation for Beau Apparel, profit-maximization or loss-minimization requires that

$$w = 16 = -3.11076\ L^2 + 21.332\ L$$

or

$$-3.11076\ L^2 + 21.332\ L - 16 = 0$$

As you can see in Figure 14.1, there are two points (R and S) where MRP equals \$16. The solutions for these two levels of labor usage (L_1 and L_2) were obtained with the quadratic formula

$$L_1, L_2 = \frac{-21.3332 \pm \sqrt{(21.3332)^2 - 4(-3.11076)(-16)}}{2(-3.11076)}$$

$$= \frac{-21.3332 \pm 16}{-6.222}$$

The two levels of labor usage that satisfy the condition that MRP = \$16 are

$$L_1 = \frac{-5.3332}{-6.222} = 0.86$$

and

$$L_2 = \frac{-37.3332}{-6.222} = 6.00$$

To determine which of these two levels of labor employment does indeed maximize profit (or minimize loss), a manager should compare the average revenue product at both levels of labor employment to the wage rate of \$16. Only the level of labor usage for which ARP exceeds the wage rate will result in profit being maximized. The manager of Beau Apparel calculated the average revenue product for both L = .86 and L = 6:

$$ARP_{L=0.86} = -1.036920\ (0.86)^2 + 10.6660\ (0.86) = 8.41$$

$$ARP_{L=6} = -1.036920\ (6)^2 + 10.6660\ (6) = 26.60$$

Since $ARP < w$ for 0.86 units of labor, Beau Apparel would shut down rather than hire 860 hours of labor. For 6 units of labor, $ARP > w$. Thus, the profit-maximizing or loss-minimizing level of labor usage for the first quarter of 1995 is 6,000 hours.

Computation of Total Profit or Loss

When Beau Apparel employs 6 units of labor, the level of output is

$$Q = -0.051846(6)^3 + 0.5333(6)^2 = 8$$

The profit-maximizing level of output is 8,000 units. Total revenue is calculated by multiplying the output times the price:

$$TR = \$20 \times 8{,}000 = \$160{,}000$$

Total variable cost is \$96,000 (= $w \times L$ = 16 × 6,000), and total fixed cost is \$30,000, as before. Thus, Beau Apparel earns a profit of \$34,000:

$$\pi = \$160{,}000 - \$96{,}000 - \$30{,}000 = \$34{,}000$$

The Equivalence of Choosing Output or Input Usage

When the manager of Beau Apparel chose to employ 6,000 units of labor to maximize profit, the firm produced 8,000 units of output, which is the same output that was optimal when the manager set $P = \$20 = MC$ and chose Q rather than L to maximize profit. Because $MC = w/MP$ (as shown in Chapter 10) the marginal cost associated with using 6 units of labor is

$$MC = w/MP_{L=6} = 16/0.80 = \$20$$

This means that when the manager of Beau Apparel chose either $Q = 8{,}000$ or $L = 6{,}000$, *both* profit-maximizing conditions were simultaneously satisfied:

$$P = MC_{Q=8}$$

and

$$w = MRP_{L=6}$$

Satisfying either one of these conditions results in satisfying the other condition. Note also that the profit is the same as when the manager chose output to maximize profit:

$$\begin{aligned}\pi = PQ - wL - TFC &= (\$20 \times 8{,}000) - [(\$16 \times 6{,}000) + \$30{,}000]\\ &= \$34{,}000\end{aligned}$$

Before leaving the example of Beau Apparel, we should tell you that the equivalence of choosing either output or labor usage always holds when the functional forms of the cost and production equations are known exactly. When the cost curves and production curves must be estimated using regression analysis, the estimated coefficients usually differ from the true values of the parameters. Consequently, the error due to estimation will usually result in less than an exact equivalence between choosing Q and choosing L.[5]

14.5 PROFIT-MAXIMIZATION UNDER RISK

In most real world situations, a manager does not know with certainty what prices, wages, or for that matter anything else, will be in the next quarter, and much less even further down the road. Decisions about future plans must always be made under a certain amount of risk. Nonetheless, the best approach to the basics of implementing the profit-maximization decision is to examine the decision under conditions of complete information, as we have done thus far in this chapter. Now that we have established these foundations we can examine profit-maximizing decision making under risk. We will now take a final look at Beau Apparel in a situation in which price and cost are random, but the variance is the same at each level of output.

---

[5]In the hypothetical example concerning Beau Apparel, we made certain the estimated values were in fact equal to the values of the underlying cost and production functions.

In Chapter 13 we applied the rules of decision making under risk set forth in Chapter 6 to show how a manager of a perfectly competitive firm can make decisions when risk is involved. A risk-neutral manager chooses the level of output so as to maximize the expected value of profit. When the variance of the probability distribution of profit is constant for all levels of output, all managers, whether risk averse, risk loving, or risk neutral, would choose output to maximize expected profit. The manager of Beau Apparel can maximize *expected* profit by choosing the output level for which expected marginal revenue (i.e., expected price) equals expected marginal cost:

$$E(MR) = E(P) = E(MC)$$

We continue to assume that the manager can choose the level of output with certainty, but now the price and costs are not known with certainty. The manager had a subjective idea about the probability distribution of prices in the first quarter of 1995, which is shown in Figure 14.2. The expected price of shirts in 1995I was calculated to be $18:

$$E(P_{1995I}) = (16 \times .1) + (17 \times .20) + (18 \times .4) + (19 \times .2) + (20 \times .1) = \$18$$

Thus, the expected marginal revenue for Beau Apparel was $18, $E(MR_{1995I}) = E(P_{1995I})$.

The manager used regression analysis to estimate the marginal and average variable cost functions. As stressed in the discussion of regression analysis in Chapter 5, a regression line gives the expected value of Y for a given level of X.

FIGURE 14.2
Probability Distribution for Price in the First Quarter of 1995

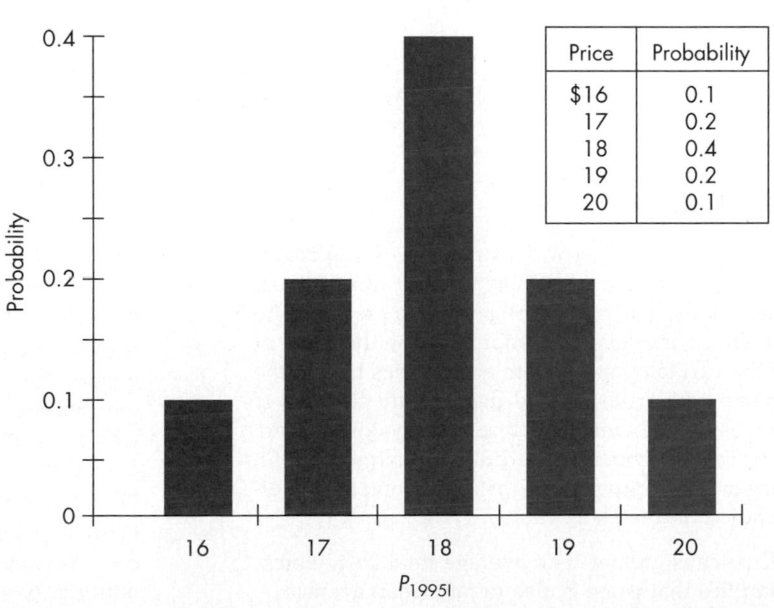

Price	Probability
$16	0.1
17	0.2
18	0.4
19	0.2
20	0.1

The estimated marginal cost function, therefore, is an estimate of the expected marginal cost for producing any given level of output. Thus, the previously estimated marginal cost function is interpreted as the *expected* marginal cost function:

$$E(MC) = 20 - 6Q + .75Q^2$$

Similarly, the estimated average variable cost function is an estimate of the *expected* average variable cost for any given level of production. Fixed costs are known with certainty to be $30,000.

The manager of Beau Apparel maximizes the expected profit by choosing the level of output for which $E(MR) = E(P) = E(MC)$:

$$18 = 20 - 6Q + 0.75Q^2$$

Solving for Q using the quadratic formula, the manager found two solutions, $Q = 0.35$ and $Q = 7.65$. When 350 units are produced, the expected average variable cost would be greater than the expected price, and the firm should not produce:

$$E(AVC_{Q=.35}) = 20 - 3(.35) + 0.25(.35)^2 = \$18.98 > \$18 = E(P_{1995I})$$

The level of output that maximizes the expected profit is 7,650 units because the expected average variable cost exceeds the expected price of $18:

$$E(AVC_{Q=7.65}) = 20 - 3(7.65) + .25(7.65)^2 = \$11.68 < \$18$$

The manager did not know with certainty how much profit would actually be earned in the first quarter of 1995, but by choosing to produce 7,650 shirts, the expected profit is maximized. The expected profit in 1995I was calculated as follows:

$$\begin{aligned} E(\pi_{1995I}) &= E(P_{1995}) \times Q - E(AVC_{1995I}) \times Q - TFC \\ &= (\$18 \times 7{,}650) - (\$11.68 \times 7{,}650) - \$30{,}000 \\ &= \$18{,}348 \end{aligned}$$

14.6 SUMMARY

This chapter illustrated how a manager can implement the theory of perfect competition to make profit-maximizing decisions. The manager can maximize profit by choosing either the level of production or the level of usage of the variable inputs. Both approaches lead to the same (maximum) profit for the firm, or in the case of short-run losses, the same (minimum) losses for the firm.

In the case of choosing output to maximize profit, the manager of a competitive firm makes one of the following choices in the short run:

1. If price is greater than average total cost, which implies that price is also greater than average variable cost, the manager will produce the level of output at which $P = MC$. The firm earns positive economic profit in this case.
2. If price is less than average total cost but greater than minimum average variable cost, the manager will produce the level of output at which $P = MC$. The firm makes a loss in this case, but a smaller loss than would occur if the firm produced nothing (shut down).
3. If price is less than minimum average variable cost, the manager will choose to produce nothing ($Q = 0$) and shut the firm down in the

short run. The firm suffers a loss equal to its total fixed costs, but this is the smallest loss possible when $P < AVC$.

In order to implement the above decisions, the manager must have forecasts of the price of the product, and estimates of the average variable cost and marginal cost functions. These estimates are obtained as explained in Chapters 9 and 12.

Once the required empirical work has been done, the manager compares the forecasted price ($\hat{P}$) with the estimated minimum value of average variable cost ($\widehat{AVC}_{min}$). If $\hat{P} \geq \widehat{AVC}_{min}$, the firm will produce a positive output. If $\hat{P} < \widehat{AVC}_{min}$, the manager will shut the firm down.

If the manager does decide to produce, the optimal level of output is determined by solving the following equation for Q:

$$\hat{P} = \widehat{MC}$$

Since marginal cost is U-shaped, $\hat{P} = \widehat{MC}$ at two levels of output. The optimal level of output is the one for which $\hat{P} > \widehat{AVC}$, which turns out to be the larger of the two values in every case.

In the case of choosing the level of variable inputs to maximize profit, we considered only the case of one variable input. The more complex case of multiple variable inputs is covered in the appendix to this chapter. For a single variable input, say labor, the manager of a perfectly competitive firm maximizes profit by choosing the level of labor usage for which the marginal revenue product (MRP) is equal to the wage rate:

$$w = MRP$$

To obtain the estimated marginal revenue product equation, the manager must first estimate the MP equation. Then the estimated MP is multiplied by the forecasted price of the product to obtain:

$$\widehat{MRP} = \hat{P} \times \widehat{MP}$$

The manager can use the methods of estimating production curves presented in Chapter 12. As noted, if a cubic equation is specified for either the cost or production function, then a cubic specification should be used to estimate the associated product or cost curves.

Since the marginal revenue product curve is ∩-shaped, the wage rate equals the marginal revenue product at two different levels of labor usage. The manager should choose the level of labor usage for which the average revenue product ($ARP = P \times AP$) exceeds the wage rate:

$$ARP > w$$

When $ARP > w$, total revenue will exceed total variable cost. When $ARP < w$, total revenue is less than total variable cost, and the manager should choose to hire no labor ($L = 0$) and shut down.

When choosing output to maximize profit under conditions of risk, the manager chooses to produce the level of output that maximizes the expected profit. As long as the variance of profit is the same for all output levels, the optimal output level is the same for risk-averse, risk-loving, and risk-neutral managers. Expected profit is maximized at the level of output for which expected marginal revenue, which is expected price, equals expected marginal cost: $E(MR) = E(P) = E(MC)$.

This chapter discussed only profit maximization in the short run. Long-run decision making involves making decisions about how much capital to employ. The decision to buy capital is an investment decision, which we will discuss in Chapter 20. We have now completed the analysis of perfectly competitive markets in which managers take the market-determined price as given. In Part V of the text, firms with some degree of power to set the price of the product they sell will be examined. These firms have market power, and their profit-maximizing behavior differs from perfectly competitive firms in some rather interesting ways.

TECHNICAL PROBLEMS

1. In a perfectly competitive market, the manager of a firm will
   a. Produce rather than shut down if the forecasted price of the product is greater than ______.
   b. Produce and make an economic profit if the forecasted price of the product is greater than ______.

c. Produce at a loss if the forecasted price is less than ______ but greater than ______.
d. Shut down if the forecasted price is less than ______.
e. Minimize loss by producing the level of output where ______ equals ______ when forecasted price is greater than ______ but less than ______.
f. Maximize profit by producing the level of output where ______ equals ______ when forecasted price is greater than ______.

* 2. Suppose that the manager of a firm operating in a perfectly competitive market has estimated the firm's average variable cost function to be

$$AVC = 10.0 - 3.0Q + 0.5Q^2$$

where *AVC* was expressed in dollars per unit and *Q* was measured in 100 units. Suppose that total fixed cost is $600.
a. What is the corresponding marginal cost function?
b. At what output is *AVC* at its minimum?
c. What is the minimum value for *AVC*?
If the forecasted market price of the firm's output is $10 per unit,
d. How much output will this firm produce in the short run?
e. How much profit (loss) is this firm expected to earn?
If the forecasted market price of the firm's output is $5 per unit,
f. How much output will this firm produce in the short run?
g. How much profit (loss) is this firm expected to earn?

3. Suppose the marginal cost function is estimated to be

$$MC = Q^2 - 10Q + 60.$$

The price of the product is forecasted to be $50.
a. The average variable cost equation is *AVC* = ______.
b. At what two levels of output does price equal marginal cost?
c. What is average variable cost at the two levels of output in part *b*? Which of the two output levels is optimal? Explain.

4. Consider a firm that uses only one variable input, labor, to produce a good. The firm can hire all the labor it wishes for $*w* per unit. In a perfectly competitive market, the manager of this firm will
a. Maximize profit or minimize loss by employing the amount of labor for which ______ equals ______ when the average revenue product of labor is ______ (greater, less) than the ______.
b. Minimize loss by shutting down if, at the level of labor usage for which ______ equals ______, the wage rate is ______ (greater, less) than the average revenue product of labor.

* 5. A firm sells its product in a perfectly competitive market. The product is produced using only one variable input, labor. The wage rate is $15 per unit of labor. The manager of the firm estimates the following cubic production function:

$$Q = -0.025\,L^3 + 1.45L^2$$

a. Find the estimated average product equation.
b. Find the estimated marginal product equation.
c. If the forecasted price of the product is $5, find the estimated marginal revenue product of labor function.

d. What two levels of labor usage would the manager consider to be optimal? Which one maximizes profit (or minimizes loss)? How do you know?

e. If total fixed costs are $1,000, compute the profit or loss for this firm when it employs the optimal amount of labor.

APPLIED PROBLEMS

1. Suppose that you are the manager of a firm. If you wanted to determine the profit-maximizing level of output or input usage for your firm, how might you decide whether or not the competitive model is appropriate?
2. The production manager of the ABC Co., a perfectly competitive firm, has just returned from a trade convention. On the basis of the presentations there, he believes that market price next period will be somewhere between $15 and $25, with $20 being the best guess.

   The firm's average variable cost function is

   $$AVC = 30 - 10Q + Q^2$$

   where *AVC* is dollars per unit, Q = number of units (1,000), and total fixed cost is $10,000.

   a. How much output should the firm produce and how much profit (loss) will it earn if price is $15? $20? $25?

   b. What is the shutdown price? How likely is it that the firm will have to shut down to minimize losses?

   c. If the manager's predictions are accurate, what is the range of expected profit?
3. During a coffee-room debate among several young MBAs who had recently graduated, one of the young executives flatly stated, "The most this company can lose on its Brazilian division is the amount it has invested (its fixed costs)." Not everyone agreed with this statement. In what sense is this statement correct? Under what circumstances could it be false? Explain.
4. EverKleen Pool Services provides weekly pool maintenance in Atlanta. Dozens of firms provide this service. The service is standardized; each company cleans the pool and maintains the proper levels of chemicals in the water. The service is typically sold as a four-month summer contract. The market price for the four-month service contract is $115.

   EverKleen Pool Services has fixed costs of $3,500. The manager of EverKleen has estimated the following marginal cost function for EverKleen, using data for the last two years:

   $$MC = 125 - 0.42\,Q + 0.0021\,Q^2$$

   where *MC* is measured in dollars, and Q is the number of pools serviced each summer. Each of the estimated coefficients is statistically significant at the 95 percent level of confidence.

   a. Given the estimated marginal cost function, what is the average variable cost function for EverKleen?

   b. At what output level does *AVC* reach its minimum value? What is the value of *AVC* at its minimum point?

   c. Should the manager of EverKleen continue to operate, or should the firm shut down? Explain.

d. The manager of EverKleen finds two output levels that appear to be optimal. What are these levels of output and which one is actually optimal?

e. How much profit (or loss) can the manager of EverKleen Pool Services expect to earn?

f. Suppose EverKleen's fixed costs rise to $4,000. How does this affect the optimal level of output? Explain.

APPENDIX Input Choice with a Cobb-Douglas Production Function

The Single Variable Input Case

The short-run Cobb-Douglas production function would have been a poor choice of specifications in the Beau Apparel example because the cost data suggested a U-shaped marginal cost curve, which then implied a ∩-shaped marginal product of labor curve. Thus, the cubic production function was the appropriate specification in the Beau Apparel example.

In cases where the sample data indicate only diminishing marginal product, a short-run Cobb-Douglas specification can be used to estimate the marginal product, average product, and marginal revenue product curves. We will now show how to use the Cobb-Douglas specification to find the profit-maximizing level of usage of a single variable input.

Recall from Chapter 11 that, for the Cobb-Douglas short-run production function, the total product function is

$$Q = \delta L^{\beta}$$

where δ is positive, and β is greater than zero but less than one ($0 < \beta < 1$). The marginal product of labor is

$$MP = \beta\delta L^{\beta - 1}$$

and marginal product diminishes over all levels of labor usage. Once the manager obtains a forecast of the price of the product (P), the wage rate (w), and estimates the marginal product equation, the profit-maximizing condition for the Cobb-Douglas specification is expressed as:

$$MRP = P \times \beta\delta L^{\beta - 1} = w$$

To find the profit-maximizing employment for labor, the manager simply solves this equation for L and checks to see that $w < ARP$ (i.e., shutdown is not warranted). To illustrate how this is done, let's look at an example.

Case Machine & Tool Company manufactures bearings that are widely used in oil field drilling equipment. The bearings are standardized and entry into the industry is unrestricted. Given the large number of firms producing these bearings, the manager of Case Machine & Tool views the market for bearings as perfectly competitive. The going price for the bearings has been $35 for the last two years, and, for planning purposes, is not expected to change.

The primary variable input used in the manufacturing process is the labor of skilled machinists. The machinists earn $19.41 per hour. The manager estimates a short-run Cobb-Douglas production function of the form

$$Q = \delta L^{\beta}$$

Using 10 quarterly observations, the following log-linear form was estimated:

$$\log Q = \log \delta + \beta \log L$$

where output (Q) was expressed in units of 1,000, and labor usage (L) was expressed in units of 1,000 hours. The estimation results were

$$\log Q = 1.004 + 0.6 \log L$$

The appropriate *t*-tests were performed, and the manager concluded that the estimate of β was significantly greater than zero but less than one.

Rewriting the estimated production function in its exponential form, the estimated empirical production function was

$$Q = 2.73\ L^{0.6}$$

From the estimated production function, the marginal and average product functions for labor were

$$MP = (0.6)(2.73)\ L^{0.6 - 1.0} = 1.638\ L^{-0.4}$$
$$AP = 2.73\ L^{-0.4}$$

Given the $35 price of bearings and a wage rate of $19.41, the profit-maximization condition ($P \times MP_L = w$) is

$$35 \times 1.638\ L^{-0.4} = 19.41$$

or

$$L^{-0.4} = 0.33856$$

Taking logarithms of both sides of the preceding equation,

$$-0.4 \log L = -1.0830$$
$$\log L = 2.708$$

and it follows that $L = 15$.[1] The profit-maximizing level of labor usage is 15,000 hours of machinist labor.

The firm would hire this amount of labor—15,000 units—only if the wage rate is less than the average revenue product of labor ($w < ARP$). In order to make sure $L = 15$ is indeed optimal, the manager substituted $L = 15$ into the estimated average product function

$$AP_{L=15} = 2.73(15)^{-0.4} = .9241$$

Then the manager calculated ARP and compared ARP to the wage rate:

$$ARP = P \times AP = \$35 \times .9241 = \$32.34 > w = \$19.41$$

Since ARP exceeds the wage rate, the manager hired 15,000 units of labor rather than shut down.[2]

Using this optimal level of employment, the number of ball bearings produced by Case Machine & Tool is computed as

$$Q = 2.73\ (15)^{0.6} = 13.862$$

The profit-maximizing level of output is 13,862 units. Since the level of labor usage and wage rate are both known, the manager can calculate total variable cost:

$$TVC = w \times L = \$19.41 \times 15{,}000 = \$291{,}150$$

If total fixed costs are \$100,000, the profit earned by Case Machine & Tool Company is

$$P = (\$35 \times 13{,}862) - (\$291{,}150 + \$100{,}000) = \$94{,}020.$$

We must emphasize once more that the choice between the cubic and Cobb-Douglas specification should be based on the nature of the data. If the data exhibit diminishing returns throughout the range of usage of the variable input, the Cobb-Douglas production function can be used to estimate the product curves. Alternatively, if the data indicate that marginal product at first rises, then falls, a cubic specification of the production function is a better choice than the Cobb-Douglas specification.

[1] Since natural logarithms were used, it follows that, if $\log L = 2.708$, then $L = e^{\log L} = e^{2.708} = 14.999$ (≈ 15).

[2] This was the expected result since MP is always less than AP for a Cobb-Douglas. Thus, $P \times MP$ is always less than $P \times AP$, and $w(= MRP) < ARP$.

The Profit-Maximizing Levels of Input Usage When Several Inputs Are Variable

If the firm hires several variable inputs, the profit-maximization condition remains unchanged. However, the profit-maximization conditions for the inputs must be solved simultaneously, so the computation is somewhat more complex.

Consider the case in which the firm has two variable inputs—capital and labor. The profit-maximization conditions require that the value of the marginal products for the inputs be equal to the respective input prices. That is,

$$P \times MP_L = w \text{ and } P \times MP_K = r$$

where r is the user cost of capital; i.e., the cost to the firm of using a unit of capital.

We have already discussed how the firm can obtain its price forecast ($\hat{P}$). And, the firm can obtain forecasts of the price of capital ($\hat{r}$) in much the same way it obtains forecasts for the wage rate ($\hat{w}$). Hence, the remaining question is the determination of the marginal product functions for labor and capital.

In this case, there is a two-input production function, $Q = f(K, L)$. As described in Chapter 12, we can use a Cobb-Douglas production function, so we can write the empirical production function as

$$Q = \gamma K^{\alpha} L^{\beta}$$

where $0 < \alpha, \beta < 1$. As noted in Chapter 11, with this production function, the marginal product functions are

$$MP_K = \alpha\frac{Q}{K} = \alpha\gamma K^{\alpha-1}L^{\beta}$$

$$MP_L = \beta\frac{Q}{L} = \beta\gamma K^{\alpha}L^{\beta-1}$$

Once the production function has been estimated (i.e., we have the estimates $\hat{A}$, $\hat{\alpha}$, and $\hat{\beta}$, it can be used in conjunction with the forecasts of the output price and the prices of inputs to express the two profit-maximizing conditions as

$$(\hat{P}) \times (\hat{\beta}\gamma K^{\hat{\alpha}}L^{\hat{\beta}-1}) = \hat{w}$$

and

$$(\hat{P}) \times (\hat{\alpha}\gamma K^{\hat{\alpha}-1}L^{\hat{\beta}}) = \hat{r}$$

To determine the profit-maximizing levels of labor and capital, the manager solves these two equations simultaneously for L and K. To make sure production is warranted, the manager calculates total revenue ($TR = P \times Q$) and total variable cost ($TVC = wL + rK$). If $TR > TVC$, the firm produces; if $TR < TVC$, the firm shuts down.

PART VI

Firms with Market Power

CHAPTER

15

Market Power and the Theory of Monopoly

market power
The ability of a firm to raise price without losing all of its sales.

This chapter and the following three chapters discuss the principles of profit maximization for firms that have market power. **Market power** is the ability of a firm to increase the price of its product without losing all of its sales. Market power is completely absent for managers of perfectly competitive firms that face a market-determined price and could not sell anything if they charged only slightly more than the price in the market. Firms with market power face demand curves for their product that are downward sloping. When such firms raise the price of their products, sales fall because of the law of demand, but sales do not fall to zero.[1]

All firms other than perfect competitors have some amount of market power, which allows them to choose the prices they charge. Firms do, however, differ greatly in the amount of market power they possess. An electric utility that is the only seller of electricity in a large city would have a great deal of latitude over the price it charges if it were not regulated. It consequently has a large amount of market power—which is why it is regulated. A grocery store, shoe store, or service station has some control over its prices and therefore has some market power. Its control over price is limited by the number of similar stores that are competitors, and thus it has only limited market power. Firms with market

[1]Economists frequently use the terms *monopoly power* and *market power* interchangeably, both terms meaning the firm has the ability to raise price without losing all sales. In this text, we will always use the term *market power*, instead of the term *monopoly power*, because we do not want you to have the mistaken impression that only monopoly firms have market power. Monopolies, monopolistic competitors, and oligopolies all face downward-sloping demand curves and consequently have market power.

power range in scope from virtual monopolies, such as the electric utility, to firms with a great deal of close competition and just a small amount of market power.

The first part of this chapter describes some ways of measuring market power that are more precise and concrete than terms such as "great deal" or "limited amount." We then discuss some of the determinants of the market power possessed by a firm and reasons why some firms have much more market power than others.

monopoly
A firm that produces a good for which there are no close substitutes and other firms are prevented from entering the market by a barrier to entry.

The major portion of the chapter is devoted to the theory of monopoly. A **monopoly** exists when a firm produces and sells a good or service for which there are no close substitutes, and other firms are prevented by some type of entry barrier from entering the market. A monopoly, consequently, has more market power than any other type of firm. Although there are few true monopolies in real world markets—and most of these are subject to some form of government regulation—the theory of monopoly is important in managerial economics for two reasons. First, a lot of firms, while not meeting all of the specifications of a monopoly, do have some of the characteristics. Many large and small firms possess a considerable amount of market power in the sense of having few close substitutes for the products they sell, and the monopoly model is useful for studying their behavior. Second, and perhaps more important, the theory of monopoly provides the basic analytical framework for the analysis of how managers of all firms with market power can make decisions to maximize their profit. As you will see in the next three chapters, theories that describe the behavior of all types of firms in the range between perfect competitors and monopolies require only small modifications of the theory of pure monopoly. Therefore, managers of all types of firms will find monopoly theory useful for their own decision making.

15.1 MEASUREMENT OF MARKET POWER

There is no single measurement of market power that is totally acceptable to economists, policy makers, and the courts. Indeed, there is not even an accepted degree of market power that determines whether a given firm is, or is not, a monopoly. Economists have come to rely on several measures of market power. These methods are widely used, frequently in antitrust cases which require objective measurement of monopoly power. The measurement of market power involves more than just determining that a firm can raise price without losing all sales; it involves determining the *degree* to which sales fall as price is increased. We now discuss three of the most important methods of measuring monopoly power.

Elasticity of Demand

One approach to measuring how much market power a firm possesses is to measure the elasticity of the firm's demand curve. Recall from Chapter 3 that a firm's ability to raise price without suffering a substantial reduction in unit sales is inversely related to the demand elasticity. The less elastic is demand, the smaller the percentage reduction in quantity demanded associated with any particular price increase. The more elastic is demand, the larger the percentage decrease in unit sales associated with a given increase in price. Also recall from Chapter 3 that the elasticity of demand is greater (i.e., more elastic) the larger the number of substitutes available for a firm's product. As demand becomes less elastic, consumers view the product as having fewer good substitutes.

Although a firm's market power is greater the less elastic is its demand, this does not mean a firm with market power chooses to produce on the inelastic portion of its demand. In other words, monopoly power does not imply that a manager produces where $|E| < 1$, but rather, the less elastic (or equivalently, the more inelastic) is demand, the greater the degree of monopoly power. We will emphasize later in this chapter that a monopolist always chooses to produce and sell on the elastic portion of its demand.

Relation The degree to which a firm possesses market power is inversely related to the elasticity of demand. The less (more) elastic the firm's demand, the greater (less) its degree of market power. The fewer the number of close substitutes consumers can find for a firm's product, the smaller the elasticity of demand, and the greater the firm's market power. When demand is perfectly elastic (demand is horizontal), the firm possesses no market power.

Cross-Price Elasticity of Demand

Another useful measure of market power is the cross-price elasticity of demand. Recall from Chapter 3 that cross-price elasticity measures the sensitivity of the quantity purchased of one good to a change in the price of another good. It indicates whether two goods are viewed by consumers as substitutes. A large, positive cross-price elasticity means that consumers consider the goods to be readily substitutable. Market power in this case is likely to be weak. If a firm produces a product for which there are no other products with a high (positive) cross-price elasticity, the firm is likely to possess a high degree of market power.

The cross-price elasticity of demand is often used in antitrust cases to help determine whether consumers of a particular firm's product perceive other products to be substitutes for that product. Using cross-price elasticities, antitrust officials try to determine which products compete with one another. For example, antitrust officials might wish to determine the degree of monopoly power enjoyed by Nike brand athletic shoes. Nike Corporation has spent a great deal of money advertising to establish a prominent position in the market for athletic shoes. To determine which other products compete with Nike, the cross-price elasticity of the quantity demanded of Nike shoes with respect to a change in the price of a potential rival's product can be calculated. Using such cross-price elasticities, antitrust officials can determine whether consumers view Nike as having any real competitors in the market for athletic shoes.

Relation If consumers view two goods to be substitutes, the cross-price elasticity of demand (E_{XY}) is positive. The higher the cross-price elasticity, the greater the perceived substitutability and the smaller the degree of market power possessed by the firms producing the two goods.

The Lerner Index

Lerner index
A ratio that measures the proportionate amount by which price exceeds marginal cost: $\frac{P - MC}{P}$.

Another method of measuring the degree of market power is to measure the extent to which price deviates from the price that would exist under perfect competition. The **Lerner index**, named for Abba Lerner who popularized this measure, is a ratio that measures the proportionate amount by which price exceeds marginal cost:

$$\text{Lerner index} = \frac{P - MC}{P}$$

Since price equals marginal cost under perfect competition, the Lerner index equals zero under perfect competition. The higher the value of the Lerner index, the greater the degree of market power.

The Lerner index can also be related to the elasticity of demand. In profit-maximizing equilibrium, marginal cost equals marginal revenue. Also recall from Chapter 3 that $MR = P(1 + 1/E)$. Thus, the Lerner index can be expressed as

$$\text{Lerner index} = \frac{P - MR}{P} = \frac{P - P(1 + \frac{1}{E})}{P} = 1 - (1 + \tfrac{1}{E})$$
$$= -\frac{1}{E}$$

In this form, it is easy to see that the less elastic is demand, the higher the Lerner index and the higher the degree of market power. The Lerner index is consistent with our earlier discussion showing that market power is inversely related to the elasticity of demand.

Relation The Lerner index, $\frac{P - MC}{P}$, measures the proportionate amount by which price exceeds marginal cost. Under perfect competition, the index is equal to zero, and the index increases in magnitude as market power increases. The Lerner index can be expressed as $-1/E$, which shows that the index, and market power, vary inversely with the elasticity of demand. The lower (higher) the elasticity of demand, the greater (smaller) the Lerner index and the degree of market power.

15.2 DETERMINANTS OF MARKET POWER

high (or strong) barrier to entry
Exists when it is difficult for new firms to enter a market in which economic profits are being earned.

Firms in a given market can possess a high degree of market power only if high barriers to the entry of new firms exist. A **high (or strong) barrier to entry** exists when it is difficult for new firms to enter a market in which economic profits are being earned. The easier it is for firms to enter a market, the better the substitutes for the products sold by firms in the market. Strong barriers to the entry of new firms make it difficult for new firms to begin selling a related product and protect the economic profits of firms already selling in the market.

An example of strong barriers to entry would be a television cable company that is granted the only cable franchise by a city government. This fortunate company will be protected from other firms competing away any economic profits and would be close to being a monopoly. Note that we said "close" to being a monopoly because the cable company has some outside competition even though it is the only cable company in town. Possible substitutes, though certainly not perfect ones, might be regular broadcast television, satellite dishes, radio, books and magazines, rental movies, and so on. Thus, the firm would be a monopoly if the cable TV market is the relevant market, but not if the entertainment market is the relevant market. We should note that in cases in which a government body protects a firm from entry by other firms into a market, it typically regulates the protected firm.

Low (or weak) barriers to entry generally exist in most retail markets. Retail stores typically do not have much market power because entry by other firms into the market is easy and there are good substitutes for the products of firms selling in the market. The products are not perfect substitutes, as is the case for perfect competition, because other firms cannot sell identical products or sell in the same location. However, firms can produce close substitutes. Therefore, even though perfect competition would not exist in such markets because products are not perfect substitutes, no firm has much market power since it cannot raise its price much above its rivals' without a substantial loss of sales. Many types of barriers to entry exist, but we will discuss here only a few of the most common types. The stronger these barriers are the more difficult it is for new firms to enter the market and the greater the market power of firms in the market.

Economies of Scale

An extremely important barrier to entry is created when the long-run average cost curve of a firm decreases over a wide range of output, relative to the demand for the product. Consequently, a new firm that wishes to enter this type of market must enter on a large scale in order to keep its costs as low as the large-scale firms already operating in the market. The necessity of entering on a large scale is usually not a barrier to entry by itself, but, when coupled with relatively small product demand, a strong barrier to entry can be created.

Consider an industry where four existing firms each produce about 200,000 units annually to take advantage of substantial economies of scale. At the current price of the product, annual sales are running at about 800,000 units per year. While many entrepreneurs could obtain the financial backing to enter this industry with a large-scale plant capable of producing 200,000 units, there is no room in the industry for five large-scale producers without a significant decline in the price of the product. Even though a firm could enter the industry producing approximately 50,000 units annually, the per-unit production costs would be much higher than competitors' costs because of the substantial economies of scale. There just isn't room for a new firm to enter this industry on a scale big enough to enjoy costs as low as those of rivals. In such situations, economies of scale create a barrier to entry.

Barriers Created By Government

An obvious entry barrier is government. Licensing and franchises are ways monopolies are created by government decree. For example, licenses are granted to radio and television stations by the Federal Communications Commission

(FCC), and only those stations possessing a license are allowed to operate. Locally, this confers immense market power on those stations that have FCC approval. New entrants can petition the FCC for a license to operate, but if those stations that are operating protest to the commission, the petition is frequently denied. Governments also grant exclusive franchises for city, county, and state services. For example, local telephone and cable television utilities have a great deal of market power in that they are the only regional producer of the product. By law, no other producer can exist.

Another legal barrier to competition lies in the patent laws. These laws make it possible for a person to apply for and obtain the exclusive right to produce a certain commodity, or to produce a commodity by means of a specified process that provides an absolute cost advantage. E. I. duPont de Nemours & Company enjoyed patent monopolies over many commodities, cellophane being the most notable. The Eastman Kodak Company continues to hold numerous patents on its camera equipment.

Despite examples to the contrary, holding a patent on a product or production process may not be quite what it seems in many instances. A patent does not preclude the development of closely related substitute goods or closely allied production processes. International Business Machines (IBM) has the exclusive right to produce their patented computers, but many other computers are available and there is competition in the computer market.

Input Barriers

Historically, an important reason for market power has been the control of raw-material supplies. If one firm (or perhaps a few firms) controls all of the known supply of a necessary ingredient for a particular product, the firm or firms can refuse to sell that ingredient to other firms at a price low enough for them to compete. Since no others can produce the product, monopoly results. For many years the Aluminum Company of America (Alcoa) owned almost every source of bauxite, a necessary ingredient in the production of aluminum, in North America. The control of resource supply, coupled with certain patent rights, provided Alcoa with an absolute monopoly in aluminum production. It was only after World War II that the federal courts effectively broke Alcoa's monopoly in the aluminum industry. At the present time, however, there are few examples of firms with considerable market power because of exclusive control of a raw material.

Another frequently cited input barrier arises in capital markets. Established firms, perhaps because of a history of good earnings, are able to secure financing at a more favorable rate than new firms. Imagine how far a typical person would get by walking into a bank and requesting a loan for $20 million to start a mainframe computer company. Most bankers would take a very dim view of this new company's survival. Knowing that the new firm would be in the same market as IBM and other well-established companies, bankers would probably turn down the loan application. If the loan was made available, the interest rate for a new company would be above that paid by established firms. Capital markets

ILLUSTRATION 15.1

Patents Are No Guarantee of Fat Monopoly Profits

As noted, holding a patent does not necessarily create substantial market power since a profitable product, even a patented one, will encourage potential rivals to develop close substitutes for the patented product or process. An illustration is provided by the recent introduction of a new substance named Simplesse, which was developed to replace fat in food.

It is no secret that fat is what gives many foods their taste; it makes Haagen-Dazs creamy and rich, Big Macs tasty, and real mayonnaise slippery. Dietary fat has been linked to heart disease, and many health-conscious Americans have reduced substantially their fat intakes. The new awareness of the ill effects of fat has created a demand for substances to replace fat so that food manufacturers can produce tasty foods low in calories and cholesterol.

Simplesse, an engineered mixture of skim milk and whipped egg whites, was developed and patented by a Canadian firm that then sold the new product (patent and all) to NutraSweet. NutraSweet, a division of Monsanto Company, needed a new product to take the place of its sugar substitute, the 1969 patent of which expired in 1992. Consultants for NutraSweet predicted that Simplesse would generate more than $200 million in profits annually by 1992. In light of the lucrative market for fake fat and the protection of a patent, Simplesse seemed a sure bet. According to one executive at NutraSweet, "Simplesse is going to succeed because it's the best technology for getting the fat out of food." Unfortunately for NutraSweet, the patent on Simplesse failed to create the expected market power and accompanying profits.

According to *The Wall Street Journal*, a top executive at NutraSweet made a strategic error during the company's unveiling of Simplesse to the press. The overconfident executive boasted that Simplesse would not need approval by the Food and Drug Administration (FDA) because it was an all natural substance. This statement irritated top administrators at the FDA. The FDA then spent two years reviewing Simplesse before it decided to approve its use in frozen desserts.

The delay imposed by the FDA approval process, coupled with NutraSweet's own internal difficulties in developing an imitation ice cream made with Simplesse, gave rival firms time to beat NutraSweet to the grocers' shelves with their own imitation ice cream. Kraft General Foods introduced Sealtest Free brand and Dreyers/Edy's introduced American Dream brand imitation ice cream.

By the time NutraSweet delivered its own product, called Simple Pleasures, to the grocers, the proliferation of other faux-fat ice creams had dramatically undercut NutraSweet. Even though the rival firms used only conventional gums, gels, and other ingredients to reduce the fat content of their brands of pseudo ice creams, NutraSweet failed to convince consumers of the value of using Simplesse as a fat-replacer. As pointed out by Yves Coleon, the vice president of marketing at Haagen-Dazs, "The value of [NutraSweet's] fat substitute was diluted by competitive entries."

The *Journal* reported that NutraSweet had been able to convince only four US companies to use Simplesse in the production of their frozen desserts. Despite the superiority of Simplesse over currently available fat-substitutes, many of the potentially large buyers of Simplesse have been working to invent their own substitute fat. In fact, Pfizer Incorporated and A.E. Staley Manufacturing Company have already produced FDA-approved substitutes for Simplesse.

The experience of NutraSweet with Simplesse illustrates how fleeting market power can be when profits create an incentive for rival firms to find a way to enter. Even the seemingly absolute protection afforded by patents can be quickly undermined by the development of close substitutes.

Source: Alix M Freedman and Richard Gibson, "Maker of Simplesse Discovers Its Fake Fat Elicits Thin Demand," *The Wall Street Journal*, July 31, 1991.

pose a barrier for new firms when a large investment is necessary to enter a market.

Brand Loyalties

On the demand side, older firms may have, over time, built up the allegiance of their customers. New firms can find this loyalty difficult to overcome. For example, no one knows what the service or repair policy of a new firm may be. The preference of buyers can also be influenced by a long successful advertising campaign; established brands, for instance, allow customers recourse if the product should be defective or fall short of its advertised promises. Although technical economies or diseconomies of scale may be insignificant, new firms might have considerable difficulty establishing a market organization and overcoming buyer preference for the products of older firms. A classic example of how loyalty preserves monopoly power can be found in the concentrated lemon juice market. ReaLemon lemon juice successfully developed such strong brand loyalties among consumers that rival brands evidently could not survive in the market. The situation was so serious that the courts forced ReaLemon to license its name to would-be competitors.

The role of advertising as a barrier to entry has long been a source of controversy. Some argue that advertising acts as a barrier to entry by strengthening buyer preferences for the products of established firms. On the other hand, consider the great difficulty of entering an established industry without access to advertising. A good way for an entrenched monopoly to discourage entry would be, in fact, to get the government to prohibit advertising. The reputation of the old firm would enable it to continue its dominance. A new firm would have difficulty informing the public about the availability of a new product unless it was able to advertise. Thus advertising may be a way for a new firm to overcome the advantages of established firms. The effect of advertising on entry remains a point of disagreement among economists.

The purpose of this discussion is to expose you to several of the most common types of entry barriers and to illustrate the diversity of factors that hinder entry into a market and, consequently, foster market power. It is noteworthy that several of the barriers mentioned are somewhat influenced by the firm with market power. The control of inputs and the development of consumer loyalties are effective barriers essentially erected by firms already producing in the market.

Yet despite the existence of barriers to entry, firms can lose and have lost their positions of extensive market power. Even quite strong barriers to entry can be overcome. A monopolist can become complacent in its protected position and allow inefficiencies to enter the production process. This raises the cost, and hence the price, and allows new, more efficient firms to enter the market. Some potential entrants are ingenious enough to find ways to lower cost, or (as noted above) get around patent protection, or overcome brand loyalty to the established firm. Thus barriers to entry do protect the established firm with great market power, but not completely.

ILLUSTRATION 15.2

Credit as an Entry Barrier

The Wall Street Journal reported, "1991 was the worst year for housing starts since World War II. The nation's largest builders should feel truly grateful. For when it comes to home building, this isn't an equal opportunity recession." Why should home builders feel grateful for a building slump? The article goes on to say, "The slump has stopped many small and midsized builders in their tracts, but it is allowing the better-financed large builders to improve their position . . . [to] grab more and more of the market."

The recession that was under way at the time, in combination with the aging of the baby-boom generation, contributed to slowing the formation of new households, and consequently, housing starts dropped dramatically. At the same time, the legacy of the savings-and-loan crisis also reduced the willingness of the banks and S&Ls to make construction loans. This particularly hurt the smaller builders who were accustomed to borrowing on a project-by-project basis. Midsized builders, the article points out, generally bought tracts, then developed them by putting in roads, sewers, and so forth, before building homes.

Many banks simply stopped making loans for such projects, often citing pressure from regulators. This reluctance to lend not only prevented many builders from starting new projects but also stopped some projects midway through development. When loans came due, banks were refusing to roll them over, forcing many builders to unload developed land at fire-sale prices.

According to the *Journal*, "Most large builders don't operate through project-by-project loans, and certainly don't borrow 100 percent of needed funds, as smaller builders often must. When they can't finance a project from cash on hand, the stronger firms may dip into a revolving credit line—which smaller builders rarely can get, lacking the track record and equity of many large publicly held firms." These credit lines were not secured by real estate. The executive vice-president of the National Association of Homebuilders said that the big banks did not consider the credit lines real estate loans, which many were reluctant to give, but instead, corporate loans. Furthermore, a large builder was less likely to borrow from a S&L than a smaller builder, who would be in trouble if the S&L failed, the Resolution Trust Company cut off credit, and then demanded that the builder make up the difference between the loan value and the reappraisal value of the property.

In addition to any technical or marketing economies of scale that the larger builders possessed, as a housing-market analyst observed, "Financing has become a barrier to entry now for builders to do anything more than a couple of houses a year." This story from the home-building industry graphically illustrates the way that financing, discussed briefly, can be a significant barrier to entry into the business.

Source: This illustration is based upon the article by Jim Carlton and Mitchell Pacelle, "Weak Home Market Confers an Advantage on Largest Builders," *The Wall Street Journal*, January 27, 1992.

15.3 PROFIT MAXIMIZATION UNDER MONOPOLY: THE OUTPUT AND PRICE DECISIONS

We will now analyze the profit-maximizing decision of firms that are pure monopolies. Keep in mind that the fundamentals of this monopoly decision apply to a large extent to all firms with market power. The manager of a monopoly treats the market demand curve as the firm's demand curve. As was the case for perfect competition, we assume that the manager wishes to maximize profit. Thus, the manager of a monopoly firm chooses the point on the market demand curve that maximizes the profit of the firm. While the manager of a monopoly does, in fact, determine the price of the good, price cannot be chosen independent of

FIGURE 15.1
Demand and Marginal Revenue Facing a Monopolist

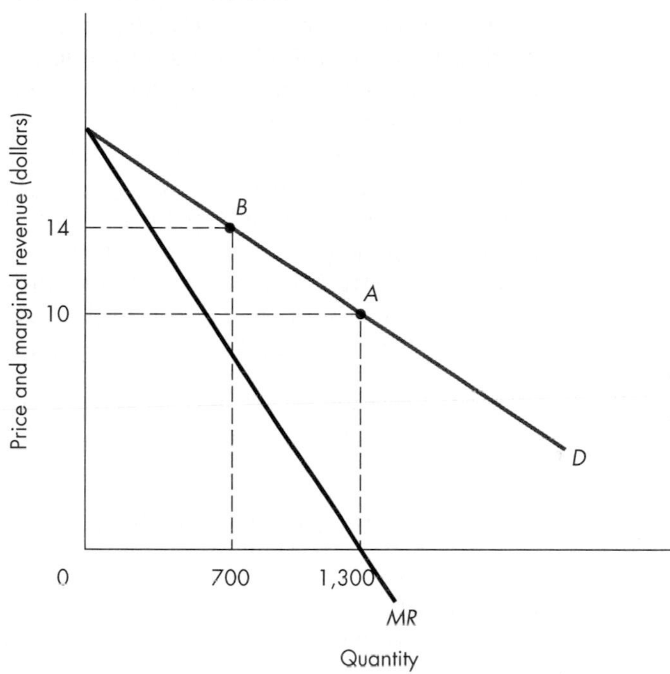

output. The manager must choose price and output combinations that lie on the market demand curve.

In Figure 15.1, for example, if the manager wishes to charge a price of $14 per unit, the monopoly firm can only sell (consumers will only buy) 700 units of the product. Alternatively, if the manager decides to sell 700 units, the highest price that can be charged for this output is $14. So, while the monopolist can choose both price and output, the two choices are not independent of one another.

In practice, some monopolists choose price and let market demand determine how many units will be sold, whereas other monopolists choose the level of output to produce and then sell that output at the highest price market demand allows. Consider your electric utility company. Electric utilities set the price of a unit of electricity, say eight cents per kilowatt-hour, and then stand ready to supply as many kilowatt-hours as consumers wish to buy at that price. You can be sure that your electric company has estimated its demand function and knows approximately how much electricity will be demanded at various prices.

Alternatively, consider an automobile manufacturer that decides to produce 300,000 cars of a particular model in a given year. The manufacturer sells these cars at the highest possible price given the existing market demand. Again, you can be sure that the automobile manufacturer has estimated the demand for its cars and knows approximately the average price at which each car can be sold.

Given the demand curve facing a monopolist, choosing price to maximize profit is equivalent to choosing output to maximize profit. To be consistent with our discussion of profit maximization under perfect competition, we will view the monopolist as choosing *output* to maximize profit.

The basic principle of profit maximization—profit is maximized by producing and selling the output at which marginal cost equals marginal revenue—is the same for the monopoly as for the competitive firm. A manager can increase profit by expanding output as long as the marginal revenue from the expansion exceeds the marginal cost of expanding output. A manager would reduce output if marginal revenue is less than marginal cost. The fundamental difference for a monopolist is that marginal revenue is not equal to price.

Principle A monopolist chooses the point on the market demand curve that maximizes profit. If marginal revenue exceeds marginal cost, a profit-maximizing monopolist increases output. If marginal revenue is less than marginal cost, the monopolist does not produce these additional units.

Demand and Marginal Revenue for a Monopolist

Under perfect competition, a firm can sell additional units of output without lowering its price. It follows that marginal revenue is equal to price for a competitive firm. A monopolist, facing a downward-sloping market demand curve, must *lower* price in order to sell additional units of output. As shown in Chapter 3, if the demand curve is downward sloping, the marginal revenue from each additional unit sold is less than price (beyond the first unit sold). Consequently, the marginal revenue curve lies below the market demand curve.

A typical demand and marginal revenue curve for a monopoly are shown in Figure 15.1. As emphasized in Chapter 3, when marginal revenue is positive, demand is elastic (at outputs between zero and 1,300 units). When marginal revenue is negative, demand is inelastic (at outputs greater than 1,300 units). We might again note that in the case of a straight-line demand curve (as in Figure 15.1), the marginal revenue curve has the same vertical intercept as demand and is twice as steep.

Relation The market demand curve is the demand curve for the monopolist. Because the monopolist must lower price in order to sell additional units of output, marginal revenue is *less* than price for all but the first unit of output sold. When marginal revenue is positive (negative), demand is elastic (inelastic). For a linear market demand, the monopolist's marginal revenue is also linear with the same vertical intercept as demand and is twice as steep.

Maximizing Profit at Southwest Leather Designs: An Example

Southwest Leather Designs specializes in the production of fashionable leather belts for women. Southwest's original designs are sometimes imitated by rival leather goods manufacturers, but the Southwest logo is a registered trademark that affords the company some protection from outright counterfeiting of its products. Consequently, Southwest Leather enjoys a degree of market power that

TABLE 15.1
Profit Maximization for Southwest Leather Designs

(1) Output (Q)	(2) Price (P)	(3) Total revenue ($1,000) ($TR = PQ$)	(4) Total cost ($1,000) ($TC$)	(5) Marginal revenue $\left(MR = \frac{\Delta TR}{\Delta Q}\right)$	(6) Marginal Cost $\left(MC = \frac{\Delta TC}{\Delta Q}\right)$	(7) Profit ($1,000) ($\pi$)
0	$40.00	0	40.00	—	—	−$40.00
1,000	35.00	35.00	42.00	$35.00	$4.20	−7.00
2,000	32.50	65.00	43.50	30.00	1.50	21.50
3,000	28.00	84.00	45.50	19.00	2.00	38.50
4,000	25.00	100.00	48.50	16.00	3.00	51.50
5,000	21.50	107.50	52.50	7.50	4.00	55.00
6,000	18.92	113.52	57.50	6.02	5.00	56.02
7,000	17.00	119.00	63.75	5.48	6.25	55.25
8,000	15.35	122.80	73.75	3.80	10.00	49.05
9,000	14.00	126.00	86.25	3.20	12.50	39.75

would not be present if imitators could make identical copies of its belts, trademark and all.

Table 15.1 presents the demand and cost conditions faced by the manager of Southwest Leather Designs. Columns 1 and 2 give the demand schedule for 1,000 through 9,000 units of output (leather belts) in discrete intervals of 1,000. Column 3 shows the associated total revenue schedule (price times quantity). The cost of producing each level of output is given in column 4. Total revenue and total cost are measured in units of $1,000. The manager computes profit or loss from producing and selling each level of output by subtracting total cost from total revenue. Profit, which is also measured in $1,000 units, is presented in column 7. Examination of the profit column indicates that the maximum profit ($56,020) occurs when Southwest Leather Designs sells 6,000 belts at a price of $18.92.

The manager of Southwest Leather Designs can reach the same conclusion using the marginal revenue–marginal cost approach. Marginal revenue and marginal cost are shown, respectively, in columns 5 and 6. The marginal revenue from selling additional leather belts exceeds the marginal cost of producing the additional belts until 6,000 units are sold. After 6,000 units the marginal revenue of the next 1,000 belts is $5.48 per belt while the marginal cost of the next 1,000 belts is $6.25 per belt. Clearly, increasing output and sales from 6,000 to 7,000 belts would lower profit. Thus profit must increase until 6,000 units are produced, then profit decreases thereafter. This is the same solution that was obtained by subtracting total cost from total revenue: an output of 6,000 belts maximizes profit.

The example in Table 15.1 is shown graphically in Figure 15.2. Since marginal revenue and marginal cost are per-unit changes in revenue and cost over discrete changes in output of 1,000 units, we plot these values in the middle of the 1,000-unit interval. For example, marginal revenue for the first 1,000 units sold is $35 per unit for each of these 1,000 units. We plot this value of marginal revenue

FIGURE 15.2
Profit Maximization for Southwest Leather Designs: Choosing Output

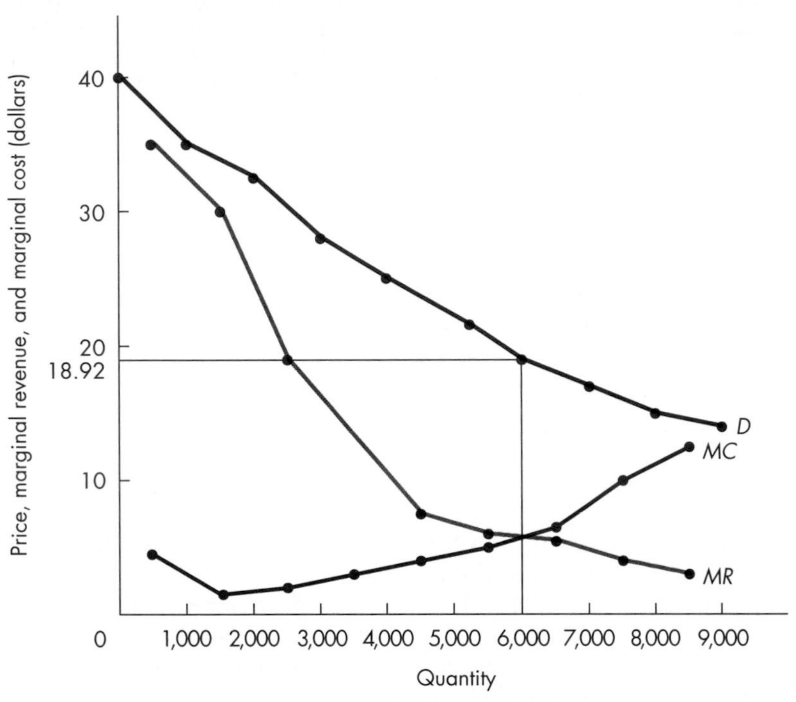

($35) at 500 units of output. We do this at all levels of output for both marginal revenue and marginal cost.

In Figure 15.2, marginal revenue equals marginal cost at 6,000 units of output, which, as you saw from the table, is the profit-maximizing level of output. The demand curve shows the price that Southwest Leather Designs will charge for the 6,000 belts is $18.92.

We turn now from a specific numerical example of profit maximization for a monopolist to a more general graphical analysis of a monopolist in the short run. In this case, we will assume for analytical convenience that output and price are continuously divisible.

Short-Run Equilibrium: Profit Maximization or Loss Minimization

A monopolist, just as a perfect competitor, attains maximum profit by producing and selling that rate of output for which the positive difference between total revenue and total cost is greatest; or, it attains a minimum loss by producing the rate of output for which the negative difference between total revenue and total cost is least. When price exceeds average variable cost, this condition occurs when marginal revenue equals marginal cost.[2] As for the perfectly competitive

[2]This result is derived mathematically in the appendix to this chapter.

FIGURE 15.3
Short-Run Profit-Maximizing Equilibrium under Monopoly

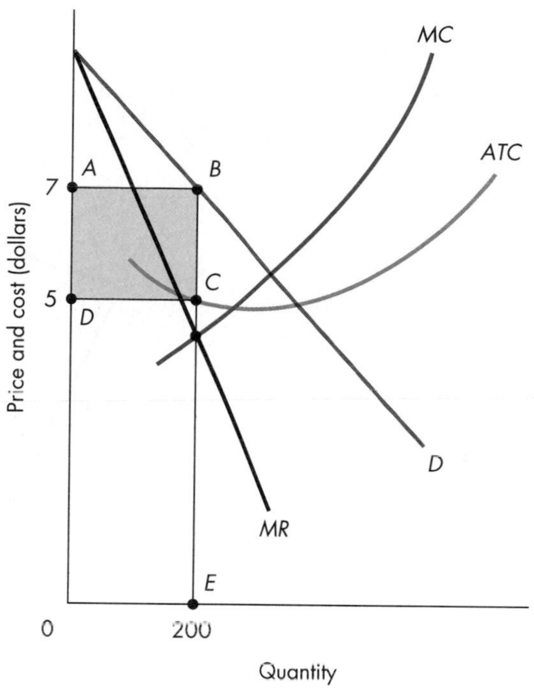

firm, when price is less than average variable cost, the manager shuts down production in the short run. We will first discuss profit maximization and then loss minimization.

The position of short-run equilibrium is easily described graphically. Figure 15.3 shows the relevant cost and revenue curves for a monopolist. Since *AVC* and *AFC* are not necessary for exposition, they are omitted. Note that demand is the downward-sloping market demand curve. Marginal revenue is also downward sloping and lies below the demand curve everywhere except at the vertical intercept. The short-run cost curves confronting a monopolist are derived in exactly the fashion described in Chapter 10 and have the typically assumed shapes. Figure 15.3 shows a situation where price exceeds average total cost, and thus the monopolist earns an economic profit.

The monopolist maximizes profit by producing 200 units of output where *MR* = *MC*. From the demand curve, the monopolist can (and will) charge $7 per unit. Total revenue is $1,400 (= $7 × 200), or the area of the rectangle 0*ABE*. The average total cost of producing 200 units of output is $5. Total cost of producing 200 units is $1,000 (= $5 × 200), or the area of the rectangle 0*DCE*. Economic profit is *TR* minus *TC*, $400 (= $1,400 – $1,000), or the shaded area *ABCD*. Since price is greater than average total cost at the equilibrium output of 200 units, the monopolist earns an economic profit. This need not be the case, however.

FIGURE 15.4
Short-Run Loss-Minimization under Monopoly

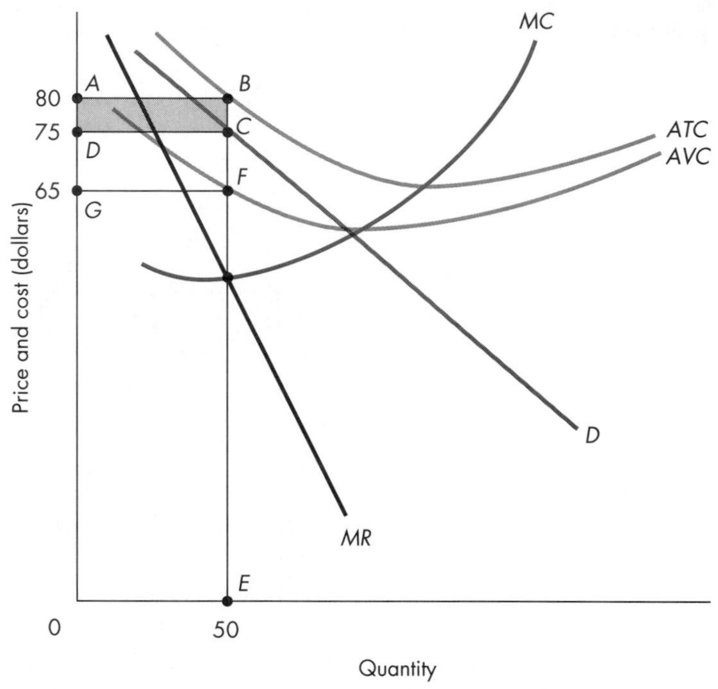

People often have the idea that all monopoly firms can always make a profit; if the firm is making losses, it can simply raise price until it makes a profit. It is, however, a misconception that all monopolies are assured a profit. Figure 15.4 illustrates a monopolist that makes losses in the short run. Marginal cost equals marginal revenue at 50 units of output, which, from the demand curve, can be sold for $75 each. Total revenue, then, is $3,750 (= $75 × 50), or the area 0*DCE*. Since average total cost is $80 per unit, total cost is $4,000 (= $80 × 50), or the area 0*ABE*. Since total cost exceeds total revenue, the firm makes a loss of $250 (= $4,000 – 3,750), which is the shaded area *ABCD*.

Note that in Figure 15.4 the monopolist would produce rather than shut down in the short run since total revenue (area 0*DCE*) exceeds the total variable cost of $3,250 (= $65 × 50), or area 0*GFE*. After all variable costs have been covered, there is still some revenue, $500 (area *GDCF*), left over to apply to fixed cost. Since total fixed cost in this example is $750 (= $15 × 50), or area *ABFG*, the firm loses less by producing 50 units than by shutting down. If the monopolist shuts down, it would, of course, lose its entire fixed cost of $750.

If demand decreases so that the monopolist could not cover all of its variable cost at any price, the firm would shut down and lose only fixed cost. This is exactly the same shutdown rule as that of the perfect competitor.

We should note that a monopolist would never choose a situation in which it was producing and selling an output on the inelastic portion of its demand.

When demand is inelastic, marginal revenue is negative. Since marginal cost is always positive, it must equal marginal revenue when the latter is also positive. Thus, the monopolist will always be on the elastic portion of demand.

In the short run, the primary difference between a monopoly and a perfect competitor lies in the slope of the demand curve. Either may earn a pure profit; either may incur a loss.

Relations In the short run a monopoly will produce a positive output if some price on the demand curve exceeds average variable cost. It maximizes profit or minimizes loss by producing the quantity for which $MR = MC$. The price for that output is given by the demand curve. If the price exceeds average total cost the firm makes a pure economic profit. If price is less than average total cost but exceeds average variable cost, the firm suffers an economic loss, but continues to produce in the short run. If demand falls below average variable cost at every output, the firm shuts down in the short run and loses only its fixed cost. If the firm produces a positive output, equilibrium price exceeds marginal cost, since the monopolist's demand curve is above its marginal revenue curve at every output.

Long-Run Equilibrium

We have said that a monopoly exists if there is only one firm in the market. Among other things, this statement implies that entry into the market is closed. Thus, if a monopolist earns a pure profit in the short run, no new producer can enter the market in the hope of sharing whatever pure profit potential exists. Therefore, economic profit is not eliminated in the long run, as was the case under perfect competition. The monopolist will, however, make adjustments in plant size as demand conditions warrant, in order to maximize profit in the long run.

Clearly, in the long run, a monopolist would choose the plant size designed to produce the quantity at which long-run marginal cost equals marginal revenue. Profit would be equal to the product of output times the difference between price and long-run average cost

$$\pi = P \times Q - LAC \times Q = Q\,(P - LAC).$$

New entrants cannot come into the industry and compete away profits—entry will not shift the demand curve facing the monopolist

Demand conditions may change for reasons other than the entry of new firms, and any such change in demand and marginal revenue causes a change in the optimal level of output in both the short run and long run. Suppose demand does change, due perhaps to a change in consumer income. In the short run, the manager will adjust output to the level where the new marginal revenue curve intersects the short-run marginal cost curve (or it will shut down if $P < AVC$). This short-run adjustment in output is accomplished without the benefit of being able to adjust the size of the plant to its optimal size. Recall from Chapter 10 that the plant size that minimizes the cost of production varies with the level of output. Hence, in the long run, the manager would adjust plant size to the level that minimizes the cost of producing the optimal level of output. If there is no plant size for which long-run average cost is less than price, the monopolist would not operate in the long run and would exit the industry.

FIGURE 15.5
Long-Run Profit-Maximization under Monopoly

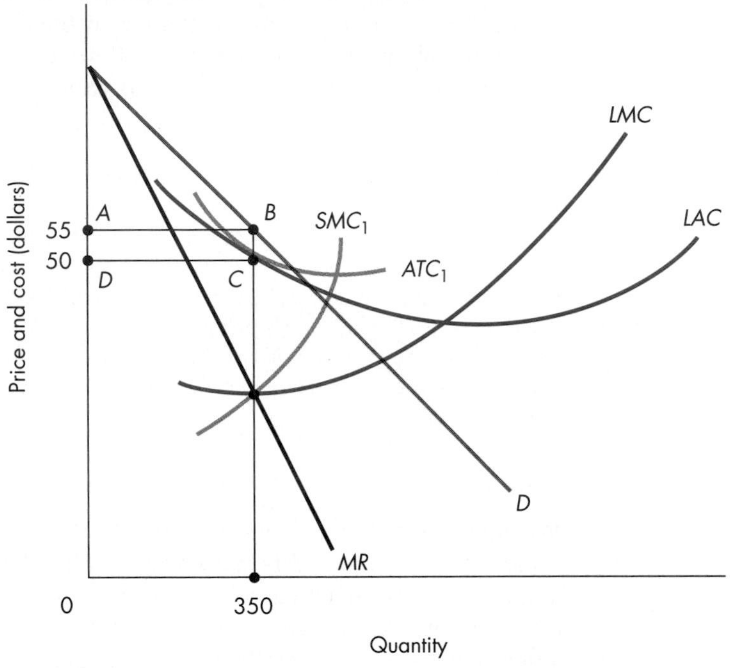

Principle The manager of a monopoly firm maximizes profit in the long run by choosing to produce the level of output where marginal revenue equals long-run marginal cost ($MR = LMC$), unless price is less than long-run average cost ($P < LAC$), in which case the firm exits the industry. In the long run, the manager will adjust plant size to the optimal level; that is, the optimal plant is the one with the short-run average cost curve tangent to the long-run average cost at the profit-maximizing output level.

This principle is illustrated in Figure 15.5. The level of output that maximizes profit in the long run is 350 units, the point at which $MR = LMC$. In the long run, the manager adjusts plant size so that 350 units are produced at the lowest possible total cost. In Figure 15.5, the optimal plant size is the one with short-run average total cost and marginal cost curves labeled ATC_1 and SMC_1, respectively. Thus, the average cost of producing 350 units is $50 per unit. The manager will sell the 350 units at a price of $55 in order to maximize profit. Long-run profit is $1,750 [$= Q \times (P - LAC) = 350 \times (\$55 - \$50)$], or the area *ABCD*. By the now familiar argument, this is the maximum profit possible under the given revenue and cost conditions.

15.4 PROFIT-MAXIMIZING INPUT USAGE

Thus far we have analyzed monopoly profit maximization in terms of the output decision. As was the case for perfect competition, the manager can also maximize profit by choosing the optimal level of input usage. Choosing the optimal level of input usage results in exactly the same output, price, and profit level as choosing the optimal level of output would. We now discuss the monopoly firm's input decision assuming that there is only one variable input.

Marginal Revenue Product for a Monopolist

marginal revenue product (*MRP*) The additional revenue attributable to hiring one additional unit of the input, which is also equal to the product of marginal revenue times marginal product, $MRP = MR \times MP$.

The analytical principles underlying the input decision for the manager of a monopoly are the same as for managers of perfectly competitive firms. But, since price does not equal marginal revenue for a monopoly, $P \times MP$ is not the correct measure of the **marginal revenue product (*MRP*)**—the increase in revenue attributable to hiring an additional unit of the variable input. Suppose a monopolist employs an additional unit of labor, which causes output to increase by the amount of the marginal product of labor. To sell this larger output, the manager must reduce the price of the good. Each additional unit adds marginal revenue (*MR*) to total revenue. Thus the additional unit of labor adds to total revenue an amount equal to marginal revenue times the marginal product of labor:

$$MRP = \Delta TR/\Delta L = MR \times MP$$

For example, suppose hiring the tenth unit of labor increases output by 20 units ($MP = 20$). To sell these 20 additional units of output, the monopolist must lower price. Further suppose that marginal revenue is \$5 per additional unit. Thus the additional revenue attributable to hiring the tenth unit of labor is the \$5 additional revenue received on each of the 20 additional units of output produced and sold, or \$100 (= \$5 × 20). The marginal revenue product of the tenth unit of labor is \$100.

Recall that in the case of perfect competition, marginal revenue product is measured by multiplying price (= *MR*) times the marginal product of labor. Also recall that *MRP* for a perfect competitor declines because marginal product declines. For a monopolist, marginal revenue product declines with increases in input usage not only because marginal product declines but also because marginal revenue declines as output is increased.

Marginal Revenue Product and the Hiring Decision

average revenue product (*ARP*) The ratio of total revenue to the total amount of the variable input hired, which is also equal to the product of price times average product of the variable input, $ARP = P \times AP$.

For the same reason that the *MRP* curve (over the relevant range) is the input demand curve for a perfectly competitive firm, the *MRP* curve (over the relevant range) is the input demand curve for a monopoly. We will establish the principle that the relevant range over which *MRP* serves as the monopolist's input demand curve is the downward-sloping, positive portion of *MRP* over which the **average revenue product (*ARP*)** of the variable input exceeds the marginal revenue product. As in the case of perfect competition, $ARP = TR/L = P \times AP$.

Figure 15.6 shows that the positive portion of *MRP* below *ARP* is the monopoly demand for a single variable input. The figure shows the relevant portion of the *MRP* curve for a monopolist employing labor as its only variable input. Suppose the wage rate is \$45. In order to maximize profit, the manager should hire 400 units of labor at a wage rate of \$45. To see why this is the optimal level of labor usage, suppose the manager hires only 300 units of labor. Hiring the 301st unit of labor adds slightly less than \$58 to total revenue, while adding only \$45 to

FIGURE 15.6
A Monopoly Firm's Demand for Labor

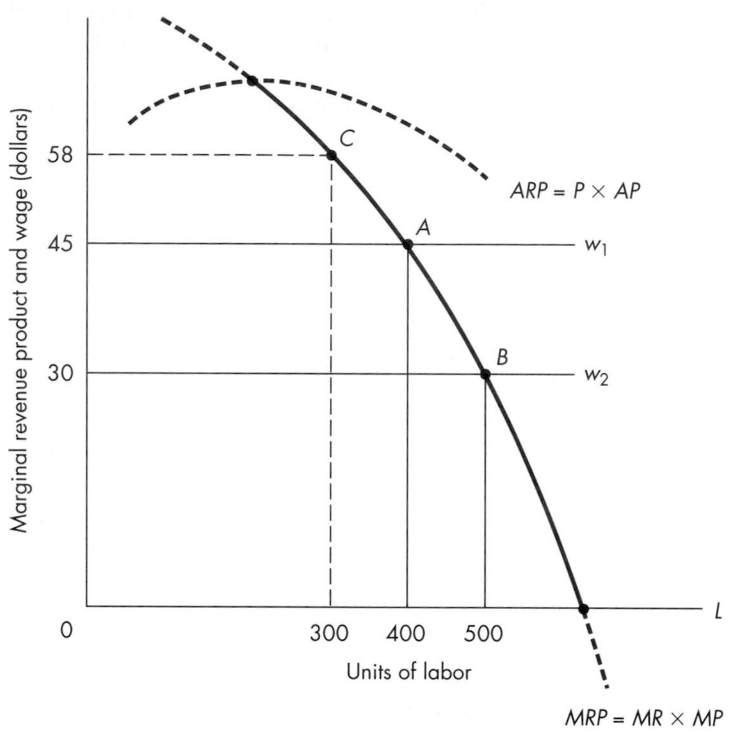

total cost. Clearly, hiring the 301st unit increases profit, in this case, \$13 (= \$58 – \$45). The manager should continue to hire additional units of labor until $MRP = w_1 = \$45$ at point *A* in Figure 15.6. If the manager mistakenly hired more than 400 units, say 500 units of labor, the additional revenue from hiring the last unit of labor (\$30 for the 500th unit) is less than the additional cost, \$45, and profit falls if the 500th worker is hired. Getting rid of the 500th worker lowers cost by \$45 but revenue falls by only \$30; thus, reducing labor by one unit increases profit by \$15. And, each additional one-unit reduction in labor similarly increases profit until labor usage is reduced down to the 400th worker.

If the wage rate falls to \$30 per unit (shown by the horizontal line w_2), the manager should hire 500 units of labor to maximize monopoly profit. Similarly, at a wage of \$58, the manager would hire 300 workers. Thus, you can see that over the relevant range, the *MRP* curve is the monopolist's demand curve for a single variable input.

We now show that a monopolist would never choose a level of variable input usage at which the average revenue product is less than the marginal revenue product ($ARP < MRP$). If, at the level of input usage where $MRP = w$,

$$MRP > ARP$$

then

$$w > PQ/L$$

and

$$wL > PQ$$

which implies that total variable cost exceeds total revenue, and the profit-maximizing monopolist would hire zero units of the variable input and shut down. Hence, the relevant range over which the *MRP* curve is the input demand curve is the downward-sloping portion that lies below the *ARP* curve.

Principle When producing with a single variable input, a monopolist will maximize profit by employing that amount of the input for which marginal revenue product (*MRP*) equals the price of the input when input price is given. Consequently, the *MRP* curve, over the relevant range, is the monopolist's demand curve for the variable input when only one variable input is employed. The relevant range of the *MRP* curve is the downward-sloping, positive portion of *MRP* for which $ARP > MRP$.

Equivalence of Choosing Input Usage or Output to Maximize Profit

Recall that, for a perfect competitor, the profit-maximizing condition that the marginal revenue product of labor equals the wage rate ($MRP = w$) is equivalent to the profit-maximizing condition that product price equals marginal cost ($P = MC$). By equivalent we mean that regardless of whether the manager chooses Q or L to maximize profit, the resulting levels of output, labor usage, and profit are identical. We will now demonstrate that, for a monopolist, the profit-maximizing condition that $MRP = w$ is equivalent to the profit-maximizing condition that $MR = MC$.

Suppose the manager of a monopoly firm chooses the level of output to maximize profit. The optimal output for the monopolist is where

$$MR = MC$$

Recall from Chapter 10 that

$$MC = \frac{w}{MP}$$

where MP_L is the marginal product of labor and w is its price. Substituting this equation for marginal cost, the profit-maximizing condition that $MR = MC$ can be expressed as

$$MR = \frac{w}{MP}$$

or

$$MR \times MP = w$$
$$MRP = w$$

Thus, you can see that the two profit-maximizing rules are equivalent: $MR = MC$ implies $MRP = w$ and vice versa.

Relation For a monopolist, the profit-maximizing condition that the marginal revenue product of the variable input must equal the price of the input ($MRP = w$) is equivalent to the profit-maximizing condition that marginal revenue must equal marginal cost ($MR = MC$). Thus, regardless of whether the manager chooses Q or L to maximize profit, the resulting levels of input usage, output, price, and profit are the same in either case.

We now illustrate the equivalency of maximizing profit by choosing either the level of output or input usage by returning to the numerical example involving Southwest Leather Designs. As you will see, the manager earns exactly the same level of profit in either case.

Maximizing Profit at Southwest Leather Designs: The Input Choice

Table 15.2 presents the production function for Southwest Leather Designs in columns 1 and 2. Using this production function, we computed the marginal product of labor, which is given in column 4. The price and marginal revenue from Table 15.1 are reproduced in Table 15.2 as columns 3 and 5, respectively. The marginal revenue product for each level of labor usage is computed by multiplying marginal revenue times marginal product ($MRP = MR \times MP$). MRP is given in column 6. In order to determine the relevant range over which MRP is the monopolist's demand for labor, we also computed average revenue product by multiplying price times the average product of labor shown in column 7 ($ARP = P \times AP$), which is presented in column 8.

As we have shown, the monopolist's demand for labor is the positive portion of MRP over the range of labor usage for which $ARP > MRP$. Hence, the monop-

TABLE 15.2
The Hiring Decision for Southwest Leather Designs

(1) Labor (L)	(2) Output (Q)	(3) Price (P)	(4) Marginal product $\left(MP = \frac{\Delta Q}{\Delta L}\right)$	(5) Marginal revenue (MR)	(6) Marginal revenue product ($MRP = MR \cdot MP$)	(7) Average product $\left(AP = \frac{Q}{L}\right)$	(8) Average revenue product ($ARP = P \cdot AP$)
0	0	$40.00	—	—	—	—	—
80	1,000	35.00	12.50	$35.00	$437.50	12.50	$437.50
140	2,000	32.50	16.67	30.00	500.10	14.29	464.43
220	3,000	28.00	12.50	19.00	237.50	13.64	381.92
340	4,000	25.00	8.33	16.00	133.28	11.76	294.00
500	5,000	21.50	6.25	7.50	46.88	10.00	215.00
700	6,000	18.92	5.00	6.02	30.10	8.57	162.14
950	7,000	17.00	4.00	5.48	21.92	7.37	125.29
1,350	8,000	15.35	2.50	3.80	9.50	5.93	91.02
1,850	9,000	14.00	2.00	3.20	6.40	4.86	68.04

olist's demand for labor schedule in Table 15.2 is the *MRP* schedule for levels of labor usage of 220 units or more when *ARP* > *MRP*.

Figure 15.7 presents the demand for labor curve for Southwest Leather Designs. Since *MRP* is the per-unit change in revenue over discrete changes in labor usage, we plot the values of *MRP* in the middle of the interval of labor usage. For example, marginal revenue product for the 160 units of labor in the interval between 340 units and 500 units of labor is $46.88. We plot this value of *MRP* ($46.88) at 420 units of labor, which is the midpoint between 340 and 500 units (see point *a* in Figure 15.7).

The wage rate earned by leather workers is $25. Using Figure 15.7, the manager of Southwest Leather Designs should hire 700 units of labor to maximize profit. The manager would not hire more than 700 units of labor because *MRP* is less than $25 beyond 700 units, and profit would decrease.

At 700 units of labor, you can see from the production function in Table 15.2 that 6,000 leather belts are produced, each of which can be sold for $18.92. The total variable cost of producing the 6,000 leather belts is $17,500 (= 700 × $25). Total fixed cost is $40,000, as you can see by looking at total cost when *Q* = 0 in Table 15.1. Total cost, then, is $57,500 (= $17,500 + $40,000). Subtracting total cost from the total revenue of $113,520 (= 6,000 × $18.92), economic profit is calculated to be $56,020 (= $113.520 – $57,500). Thus, when the manager chooses the amount of labor to maximize profit, the firm produces 6,000 belts using 700 units

FIGURE 15.7
Profit Maximization for Southwest Leather Designs: The Hiring Decision

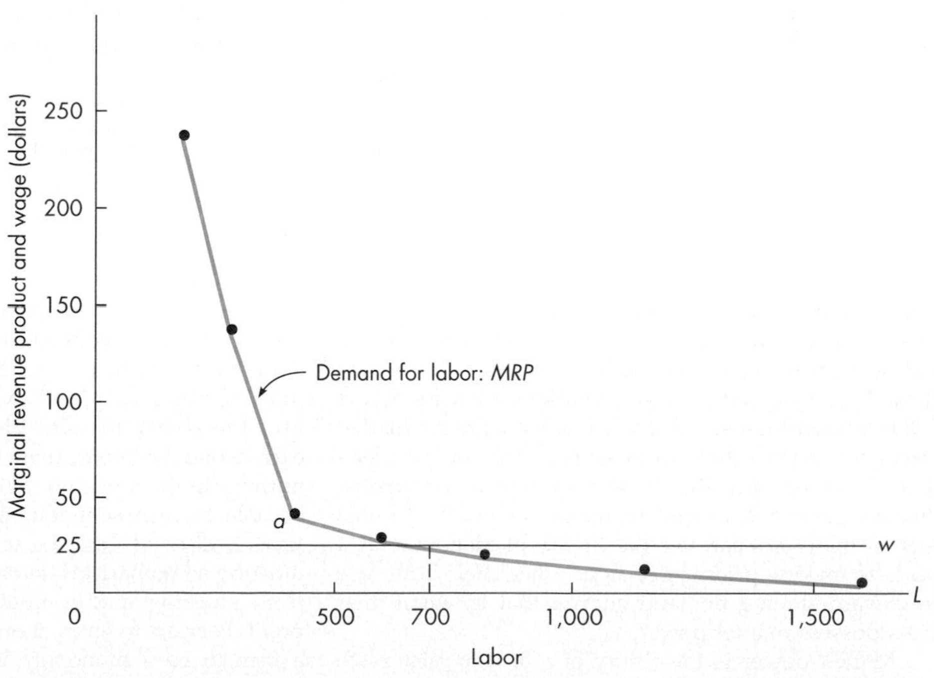

of labor, sells them for \$18.92 each, and earns an economic profit of \$56,020. This is exactly the same result obtained from Table 15.1 when the manager chooses the level of output to maximize profit using the rule $MR = MC$.

Input Demand: Several Variable Inputs

As was the case for perfect competition, the derivation of input demand curves is a bit more complicated when production involves more than one variable input. The *MRP* curve is no longer the demand for the productive service, because the inputs are interdependent in the productive process. A change in the price of any one input leads to a change not only in the usage of that input but also in the use of other inputs as well. Recall that the marginal product curve for an input is derived assuming the usage of all other inputs is held constant. Thus changes in the rates of usage of other inputs shift the *MRP* curve.

Nonetheless, the monopolist's demand for an input is still downward sloping. And, most important, the monopolist still uses the amount of each variable input at which its marginal revenue product equals its price.[3] For instance, if the monopoly firm uses three variable inputs—V_1, V_2, and V_3—which have given, market-determined prices—w_1, w_2, and w_3—the firm will maximize profit (or minimize loss) by employing each input so that

$$MRP_{V_1} = w_1$$
$$MRP_{V_2} = w_2$$
$$MRP_{V_3} = w_3$$

Since the inputs are interdependent in the production process, these conditions must hold simultaneously; the optimal levels of usage of the inputs must be determined simultaneously.

[3] The mathematical derivation of this result is in the appendix to this chapter.

15.5 SUMMARY

A monopoly exists if a single firm produces and sells a good or service for which there are no close substitutes and new firms are prevented from entering the market in the long run. While these conditions are seldom met in the real world, many firms do have a degree of market power that allows them to make price and output decisions in essentially the same way that a monopolist chooses price and output to maximize profit. For this reason, managers can use the theory of monopoly as a guide to making pricing decisions when their firms face downward-sloping demand curves; that is, when their firms possess market power.

Market power is the ability of a firm to raise price without losing all its sales. Any firm that faces a downward-sloping demand curve has market power. In contrast, a perfectly competitive firm, facing a horizontal demand curve, has no market power—any increase in price causes sales to fall to zero. Market power gives a firm the ability to raise price above average cost and earn economic profit, demand and cost conditions permitting. In the long run, a firm with market power may be able to earn economic profit because entry of new firms is difficult. In order to be a true monopolist, there must be some barriers to entry that prevent rival firms from entering and competing away the monopolist's profit. Barriers to entry, therefore, must exist in order for a firm to be a monopoly in the long run. Barriers to entry include economies of scale, barriers created by government, input barriers, and barriers resulting from brand loyalties.

Market power is never absolute. There are always substitutes for a monopolist's product, even if imperfect. And, even though monopolists have no *direct* competitors who sell an identical product, monopolists do compete indirectly with all goods and services for a place in the consumer's budget. Market power, then, is not possessed absolutely, but rather to varying degrees. The degree to which a firm possesses market power is inversely related to the availability of close substitutes for the firm's product, and thus, can be measured (approximately) by the own-price and cross-price elasticities of demand.

The less elastic the demand for the monopolist's product, the less available are good substitutes and the greater its degree of market power. The degree to which consumers view another good to be a substitute for the monopolist's good can be measured by the cross-price elasticity of demand. The higher the (positive) cross-price elasticity, the greater the perceived substitutability, and the smaller the degree of market power enjoyed by the monopolist. The Lerner index $\frac{P - MC}{P}$, measures the proportionate amount by which monopoly price exceeds marginal cost (i.e., the competitive price level). The higher the Lerner index, the greater the degree of market power. Because the Lerner index can be shown to be equal to the inverse of the own-price elasticity of demand $(-1/E)$, it follows that the Lerner index will be high when consumers perceive few readily substitutable goods and E is low.

As in the case of perfect competition, the profit-maximizing decision for a manager can take either one of two equivalent forms. The manager can choose either output or input usage to maximize profit using the rule $MR = MC$ or $MRP = w$, respectively. The two rules lead to identical prices, outputs, input usage, and profits.

In the short run, the manager of a monopoly firm maximizes profit by producing and selling that level of output for which $MR = MC$, so long as $P > AVC$ for this output level. If $P < AVC$ for all output levels, the manager should shut down in the short run. Alternatively, the manager of a monopoly that produces using a single variable input can maximize profit by hiring the amount of labor for which $MRP = w$, so long as average revenue product exceeds marginal revenue product. If ARP is less than MRP, the manager should shut down.

In the long run, the manager should produce the output level for which $MR = LMC$ and adjust plant size so that the optimal plant is used to produce the profit-maximizing output. The optimal plant is the one associated with the short-run average cost curve that is tangent to long-run average cost at the profit-maximizing output. If $P < LAC$ for all levels of output, the monopolist exits the industry. In the long run when all inputs are variable, the manager can maximize profit by choosing the levels of each input so that their marginal revenue products all equal their respective input prices *simultaneously*.

In the next chapter we will consider other market structures in which firms have some degree of market power but are not pure monopolies, specifically monopolistic competition and oligopoly markets. You will see that these market structures lie somewhere between the extremes of perfect competition and pure monopoly. Chapter 16 introduces two important new concepts that influence pricing behavior: product differentiation and strategic interaction.

TECHNICAL PROBLEMS

1. The graph on the following page shows the demand, marginal revenue, and cost curves facing a monopolist in the short run.
   a. The manager maximizes profit by charging a price equal to \$_____.
   b. The profit-maximizing level of output is _____ units.
   c. At the optimal level of output, total revenue is \$_____, total cost is \$_____, and profit is \$_____.
   d. The point elasticity of demand at the profit-maximizing price is _____. Should demand be elastic or inelastic at the point of profit maximization? Explain.

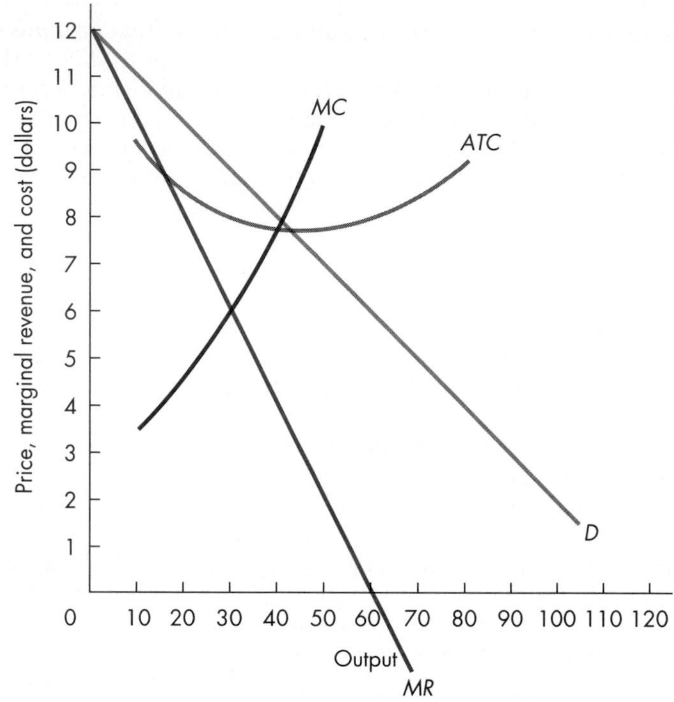

2. Compare the perfectly competitive firm and monopolist as to how each makes the following decisions:
   a. How much to produce.
   b. What price to charge.
   c. Whether or not to shut down in the short run.

* 3. A monopolist faces the following demand and cost schedules.

Price	Quantity	Total cost
$20	7	$36
19	8	45
18	9	54
17	10	63
16	11	72
15	12	81

   a. How much output should the monopolist produce?
   b. What price should the firm charge?
   c. What is the maximum amount of profit that this firm can earn?

4. A monopolist is producing a level of output, 500 units, at which price is $8, marginal revenue is $5, average total cost is $6, and marginal cost is $10.
   a. Draw a graph of the demand and cost conditions facing the firm.
   b. Is the firm making the profit-maximizing decision? Why or why not? If not, what should the firm do?

5. A monopolist faces the short-run cost structure shown below.

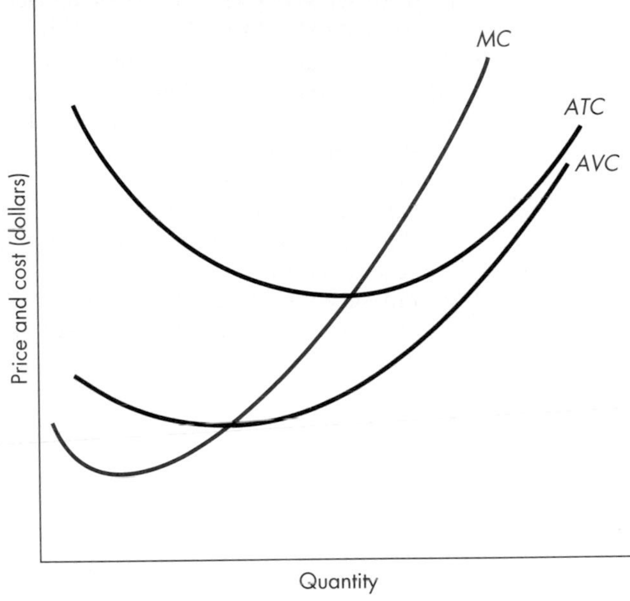

a. Show a demand curve (and associated marginal revenue curve) with which the monopolist earns a short-run economic profit. Show the price, quantity, and amount of profit being earned.

b. Show a demand curve (and associated marginal revenue curve) with which the monopolist earns losses but continues to operate in the short run. Show the price, quantity, and amount of loss. What will the firm do in the long run?

c. Show a demand curve (and associated marginal revenue curve) with which the monopolist shuts down in the short run. What will the firm do in the long run?

6. Explain why the manager of a profit-maximizing monopoly always produces and sells on the elastic portion of the demand curve. If costs are zero, what output will the manager produce? Explain.

7. Discuss the difference between a monopolist's demand for an input and the input demand for a perfectly competitive firm. In what sense is the demand for an input determined by the demand for the good or service produced by the firm?

* 8. In the following table, columns 1 and 2 make up a portion of the production function of a monopolist using a single variable input, labor. Columns 2 and 3 make up the demand function facing the monopolist over this range of output.

(1) Labor	(2) Quantity	(3) Price
9	50	$21
10	100	20
11	140	19
12	170	18
13	190	17
14	205	16
15	215	15

a. Derive and graph *MP*, *MR*, and *MRP* over this range.
b. If the wage rate is $60, how much labor would the manager hire? Why? What if the wage falls to $40?

9. Consider a monopoly firm with the demand and cost curves shown in the graph below. Assume that the firm is operating in the short run with the plant designed to produce 400 units of output optimally.
   a. What output should be produced?
   b. What will be the price?
   c. How much profit is made?
   d. If the firm can change plant size and move into the long run, what will be output and price?
   e. Will profit increase? How do you know?
   f. Draw in the new short-run average and marginal cost curves associated with the new plant size.

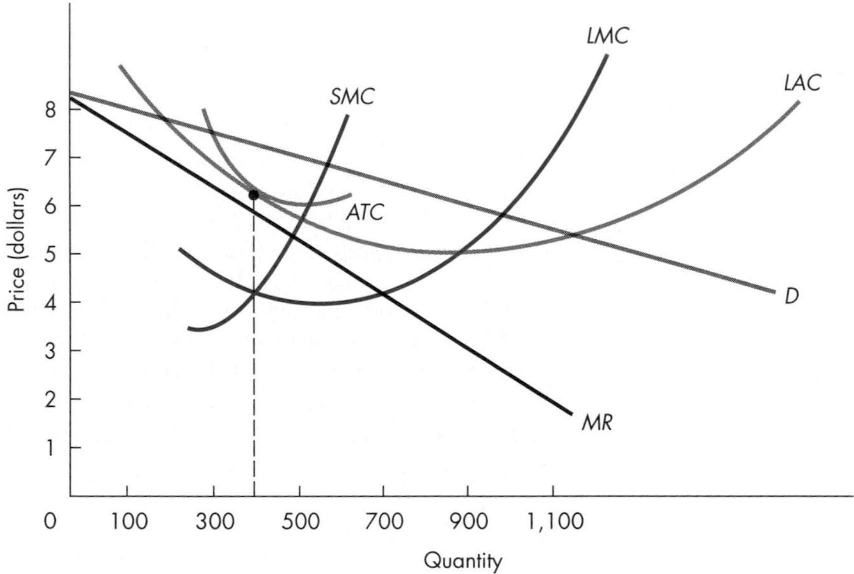

10. A manager of a monopoly faces the demand schedule given in columns 2 and 3 of the table on the following page. Column 1 shows the amount of the single variable input, labor, used to produce each of the output levels in the table. Total fixed cost is $50, and the price of labor is $5 per unit. Fill in the blanks in the table and answer the following questions:
    a. In order to maximize profit, the manager should produce ______ units of output and charge a price of $______. Explain why.
    b. At the optimal level of output, the monopolist earns a (profit, loss) of $______.
    c. Examine the profit schedule in Column 9. Does profit reach its maximum value at the level of output given in part *a*?

(1) Labor usage	(2) Output	(3) Price	(4) Total revenue	(5) Marginal revenue	(6) Total variable cost	(7) Total cost	(8) Marginal cost	(9) Profit
0	0	$8.00	____	—	____	____	—	____
8	10	7.50	____	____	____	____	____	____
12	20	7.00	____	____	____	____	____	____
17	30	6.50	____	____	____	____	____	____
24	40	6.00	____	____	____	____	____	____
33	50	5.50	____	____	____	____	____	____
44	60	5.00	____	____	____	____	____	____
57	70	4.50	____	____	____	____	____	____

11. Suppose the same manager in problem 10 decides to choose the level of input usage to maximize profit rather than choosing output to maximize profit. The same demand and production schedules from problem 10 are reproduced in the table below. Fixed cost and the wage rate are the same. Complete the table and answer the following questions:

(1) Labor usage	(2) Output	(3) Price	(4) Marginal product	(5) Average product	(6) Average revenue product	(7) Marginal revenue product
0	0	$8.00	–	—	—	—
8	10	7.50	____	____	____	____
12	20	7.00	____	____	____	____
17	30	6.50	____	____	____	____
24	40	6.00	____	____	____	____
33	50	5.50	____	____	____	____
44	60	5.00	____	____	____	____
57	70	4.50	____	____	____	____

a. In order to maximize profit, the manager should hire ____ units of labor. Explain.

b. This amount of labor will result in the production of ____ units of output, which can be sold at a price of $____. The firm earns a (profit, loss) of $____.

c. What does it mean to say that choosing output to maximize profit is equivalent to choosing labor usage to maximize profit? Use your results from this problem and problem 10 to illustrate this equivalency.

d. If the wage rate is $10, the manager should hire ____ units of labor. Explain.

e. If the wage rises to $15, the manager should hire ____ units of labor. The firm earns a (profit, loss) of $____. Explain.

APPLIED PROBLEMS

1. QuadPlex Cinema is the only move theater in Idaho Falls. The nearest rival movie theater, the Cedar Bluff Twin, is 35 miles away in Pocatello. Thus QuadPlex Cinema possesses a degree of market power. Despite having market power, QuadPlex Cinema is currently suffering losses. In a conversation with the owners of QuadPlex, the manager of the movie theater made the following suggestions: "Since

QuadPlex is a local monopoly, we should just increase ticket prices until we make enough profit."

a. Comment on this strategy.
b. How might the market power of QuadPlex Cinema be measured?
c. What options should QuadPlex consider in the long run?

2. The *El Dorado Star* is the only newspaper in El Dorado, New Mexico. Certainly, the *Star* competes with *The Wall Street Journal, USA Today,* and *The New York Times* for national news reporting, but the *Star* offers readers stories of local interest, such as local news, weather, sporting events, and so on. The *El Dorado Star* faces the revenue and cost schedules shown in the table which follows:

Q Number of newspapers per day	*TR* Total revenue (including advertising revenues) per day	*TC* Total cost per day
0	0	$2,000
1,000	$1,500	2,100
2,000	2,500	2,200
3,000	3,000	2,360
4,000	3,250	2,520
5,000	3,450	2,700
6,000	3,650	2,890
7,000	3,725	3,090
8,000	3,625	3,310
9,000	3,475	3,550

a. How many papers should the manager of the *El Dorado Star* print and sell daily?
b. How much profit (or loss) will the *Star* earn?
c. Graph the marginal revenue and marginal cost curves. Do these curves support your answer to part *a*? (Hint: Be sure to plot the values of *MR* and *MC* in the middle of the intervals over which they are computed.)
d. What is total fixed cost for the *El Dorado Star*? If total fixed cost increases to $5,000, how many papers should be printed and sold in the short run? What should the owners of the *Star* do in the long run?

3. Neighborhood grocery stores in a large city would appear to be an example of a perfectly competitive market—there are numerous sellers, each seller is small, and each store carries generally the same products (i.e., homogeneous outputs). However, it can be argued that these stores are monopolies or at least have monopoly power. Comment.
4. Tots-R-Us operates the only day-care center in an exclusive neighborhood just outside of Washington, DC. Tots-R-Us is making substantial economic profit, but the owners know that new day-care centers will soon learn of this highly profitable market and attempt to enter the market. The owners decide to begin spending immediately a rather large sum on advertising designed to decrease elasticity. Should they wait until new firms actually enter? Explain how advertising can be employed to allow Tots-R-Us to keep price above average cost without encouraging entry.
5. Antitrust authorities at the Federal Trade Commission are reviewing your company's recent merger with a rival firm. The FTC is concerned that the merger of two rival firms in the same market will increase market power. A hearing is scheduled for your company to present arguments that your firm has not increased its market

power through this merger. Is there any way you can do this? What kind of evidence might you wish to present at this hearing?

6. You own a small bank in a state that is now considering allowing interstate banking. You oppose interstate banking because it will be possible for the very large money center banks in New York, Chicago, and San Francisco to open branches in your bank's geographic market area. While proponents of interstate banking point to the benefits to consumers of increased competition, you worry that economies of scale might ultimately force your now profitable bank out of business. Explain how economies of scale (if significant economies of scale do in fact exist) could result in your bank being forced out of business in the long run.
7. In what sense is NASA a monopolist in the deployment of telecommunications satellites? In what sense is it not? Would you expect the elasticity of demand for NASA's deployment services to be large or small? Would you expect the cross-price elasticity of demand for NASA and private deployment services to be positive or negative? Large or small?

APPENDIX Profit-Maximizing Conditions for a Monopolist

1. A monopolist produces and sells the level of output at which marginal revenue equals marginal cost, as long as price exceeds average variable cost. The monopolist's profit function is

$$\pi = R(Q) - C(Q) - F$$

where $R(Q)$ and $C(Q)$ are, respectively, revenue and variable cost as functions of output, Q, and F is fixed cost.

Profit maximization requires

$$d\pi/dQ = dR/dQ - dC/dQ = 0$$

Since dR/dQ is marginal revenue and dC/dQ is marginal cost, $MR = MC$ in equilibrium.

Let $P = P(Q)$ be the monopolist's demand function, and let Q^* be the output at which $MR = MC$. If

$$\pi = P(Q^*)Q^* - C(Q^*) - F > 0$$

the firm makes an economic profit. If

$$P(Q^*) - C(Q^*)/Q^* > 0$$

that is, if price in equilibrium exceeds average variable cost, and if π at Q^* is negative,

$$|P(Q^*)Q^* - C(Q^*) - F| < F$$

Thus the firm produces Q^*. If price is less than average variable cost, the firm minimizes its loss by producing nothing and loses only fixed cost.

2. A monopolist using several variable inputs uses the amount of each variable input at which its marginal revenue product equals the price of that input.

Let the production function be

$$q = f(V_1, V_2, \ldots, V_n)$$

where q is output and V_i is the quantity used of the i-th input. The monopolist faces a demand for its product of

$$p = p(q) = p[f(V_1, V_2, \ldots, V_n)]$$

where $p' < 0$. Let w_i be the price of the i-th input. The firm's profit function is therefore

$$\pi = p[f(V_1, V_2, \ldots, V_n)]\, f(V_1, V_2, \ldots, V_n) - \sum_{i=1}^{n} w_i V_i$$

The firm maximizes π with respect to the n variable inputs, which requires

$$(dp/dq\; q + p)\, f_1 = w_1$$
$$(dp/dq\; q + p)\, f_2 = w_2$$
$$\vdots$$
$$(dp/dq\; q + p)\, f_n = w_n$$

Since total revenue is $p(q)q$, marginal revenue is

$$dTR/dq = dp/dq\; q + p$$

From above, profit maximization requires that for each input, V_i, $(dp/dq\; q + p)\, f_i = w_i$. Since f_i is the marginal product of the i-th input, profit maximization requires

$$MR \times MP_i = MRP_i = w_i = \text{input price}$$

CHAPTER 16 Imperfect Competition

Between the two extremes of perfect competition, in which a firm has the least market power—none—and monopoly, in which the firm has no close competition and hence the most market power, lies a vast spectrum of widely differing market structures, in which firms have greatly differing degrees of market power. These structures range from service stations and grocery stores in a city to the highly competitive personal computer and automobile industries, and to the soft drink, banking, and steel industries. Therefore firms in these intermediate markets range from Gucci and Payless shoe stores, through IBM and Toyota, to Coca Cola and USX.

imperfect competition All firms in a market have some market power but are not monopolies.

All of the intermediate markets, as different as they are, are typically lumped under the classification of *imperfect competition*. **Imperfect competition** means that firms in a market have some market power—the ability to raise price without losing all their sales—but they are not monopolies. As you would expect, economists have not been able to devise a general theory that would explain satisfactorily the behavior of such a vast array of firms and markets with such widely differing characteristics. Economists have, however, developed several behavioral models that explain how firms in different types of imperfectly competitive markets behave as they attempt to maximize their profit. This chapter will give you an overview of several of the most important of these models. We believe that you, as a future manager, will find it useful to see how firms in many types of situations try to maximize profits and circumvent problems that arise because of the type of competition under various market situations.

For analytical convenience, economists generally separate imperfect competition into two broad categories: *monopolistic competition* and *oligopoly*. Under

monopolistic competition An intermediate market structure consisting of a large number of firms selling a differentiated product with no barriers to entry.

oligopoly An intermediate market structure consisting of a small enough number of firms that each firm has a substantial share of the market and the firms recognize their mutual interdependence.

mutual interdependence Recognition by firms in an oligopoly market that the actions of any one firm will have an effect on other firms, who will react in turn.

monopolistic competition, the market consists of a large number of relatively small firms that produce similar but slightly differentiated products and therefore have some, but not much, market power. Monopolistically competitive markets are characterized by easy entry into and exit from the market. Most retail and wholesale firms and many small manufacturers are examples of monopolistic competition.

Under **oligopoly**, the market consists of a few relatively large firms that have varying degrees of market power and produce either differentiated or homogeneous products. There are typically moderate to high barriers to entry in oligopoly markets. The most important characteristic of oligopoly markets is that firms in these markets recognize their **mutual interdependence**, which means that the actions of any one firm will have an effect on other firms in the market, and these will react in turn. For example, if one firm in an oligopoly market is considering a price change or an expanded advertising campaign, it must take into account how other firms in the market will respond and make its plans accordingly. Hence, there is usually a large amount of uncertainty in such markets. We will devote considerable space in this chapter to analyzing the way oligopolies make decisions under such circumstances.

As you will see, firms in oligopoly markets exhibit many types of behavioral patterns. Some oligopoly markets are intensely competitive; some are not. Firms in some markets cooperate with one another. In other markets they do not. Some markets are characterized by a lot of price competition; some have little price competition but a great deal of advertising or product development competition. Examples of oligopolies that produce a homogeneous product are the steel, rubber, and aluminum markets. Examples of oligopolies that produce a differentiated product are soft drinks, beer, and electronics. Typically, when people think of oligopoly, what first comes to mind are the huge international firms such as those in the above examples. Oligopolies can, however, be relatively small. Some examples would be the few banks in a medium-sized city, the two or three newspapers in a city, or network TV stations in a particular area. As you will see, there is sometimes only a fine line between a market that would be classified as oligopolistic and one that would be classified as monopolistically competitive. In our discussion of oligopoly models, we will stress that the price and output decisions depend critically upon the assumptions made about the behavioral reactions of rival managers. Since many different assumptions can and have been made, many different solutions can and have been reached. Consequently, there is no single theory of oligopoly.

Nonetheless, economists do have a great deal to say about oligopolistic behavior, even though there is no single theory of oligopoly. A rather large part of the analysis of oligopoly consists of the study of strategic behavior among the firms in an oligopoly market. As you will see, the study of strategic behavior is quite similar to the study of players participating in a game of skill, such as chess or poker. This is why this important area of economic analysis is frequently referred to as game theory.

The discussion of oligopoly behavior in this chapter is designed to introduce you to and give you a feel for the way managers of firms in oligopolistic markets make decisions. Because strategic behavior is so important in managerial decision making, it is an important topic in managerial economics. However, in this text we can only scratch the surface of the broad range of topics in this area. A complete treatment of game theory and oligopoly strategic behavior would require several courses.

This chapter will analyze decision making under two intermediate market structures. We first discuss profit maximization under monopolistic competition, then turn to oligopoly. Keep in mind throughout the discussion that both types of firms have the same goal as that of perfect competitors and monopolists—to maximize profit. And, to maximize profit, each type of firm tries to equate marginal revenue and marginal cost. But complications arise under each structure. The complication under monopolistic competition is the combination of unrestricted entry and exit with some market power. The complication under oligopoly is the mutual interdependence of firms.

16.1 MONOPOLISTIC COMPETITION

The theory of monopolistic competition is designed to explain the behavior of firms selling in markets characterized by: (1) a large number of firms that are small relative to the total market, (2) unrestricted entry and exit of firms in the market, and most important (3) a product sold by each firm that is similar to, but somewhat different from, the products sold by other firms in the market. Thus, the only important difference between perfect competition and monopolistic competition is differentiated products in the latter structure. You will see that this modest change in the assumptions of perfect competition has a significant effect on the behavior of sellers in the market.

The reason for this change in behavior is that product differentiation in monopolistic competition will prevent the firm's demand from becoming horizontal. Real or perceived differences between goods, though slight, will make them less than perfect substitutes. For example, gasoline stations in a particular city are good, but not perfect, substitutes for one another. Your car would run on gasoline from any gasoline station, but stations differ in location, and people's tastes differ—some people prefer Texaco, some prefer Exxon, some prefer the service at Joe's, others prefer Julie's service. And the differentiating characteristics go on and on. The most important point is that although the products are similar, they are differentiated, causing each firm to have a small amount of market power.

We will first set forth the theory of monopolistic competition in its original form, as developed by Edward Chamberlin in the 1930s.[1] Because each firm in the market sells a slightly differentiated product, it faces a downward-sloping demand curve, which is relatively elastic but not horizontal. Any firm could raise its price slightly without losing all of its sales; or it could lower its price slightly without gaining the entire market. Under the original set of assumptions

[1] E. H. Chamberlin, *The Theory of Monopolistic Competition* (Cambridge, Mass.: Harvard University Press, 1933).

employed by Chamberlin, each firm's output is so small relative to the total sales in the market that the firm believes that its price and output decisions will go unnoticed by other firms in the market. It therefore acts independently.

As you will see, the theory of monopolistic competition is essentially a long-run theory; in the short run, there is virtually no difference between monopolistic competition and monopoly. In the long run, because of unrestricted entry into the market, the theory of monopolistic competition closely resembles the theory of perfect competition. After developing the short- and long-run equilibrium under the original assumptions, we will discuss why monopolistic competitors may not act independently when faced with competition from closely related firms, possibly because of close proximity, and in fact, exhibit a great deal of mutual interdependence and intense personal rivalry—that is, they behave like oligopolists. This change in assumptions will not alter the long-run conclusions of the theory, however.

Short-Run Equilibrium

With the given demand, marginal revenue, and cost curves, a monopolistic competitor maximizes profit or minimizes loss by equating marginal revenue and marginal cost. Figure 16.1 illustrates the short-run, profit-maximizing equilibrium

FIGURE 16.1
Short-Run Profit Maximization under Monopolistic Competition

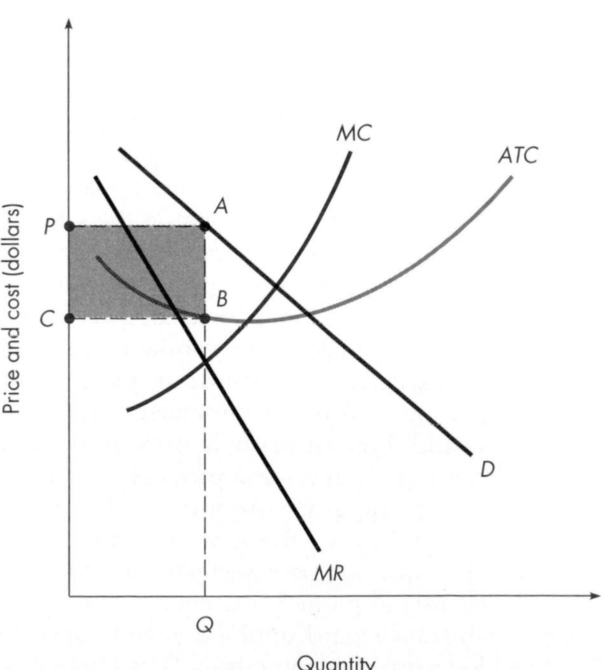

for a firm in a monopolistically competitive market. Profit is maximized by producing an output of *Q* and selling at price *P*.

In the situation illustrated, the firm will earn an economic profit, shown as the shaded area *PABC*. However, as was the case for perfect competition and monopoly, in the short run the firm could operate with a loss, if the demand curve lies below *ATC* but above *AVC*. If the demand curve falls below *AVC*, the firm would shut down.

In its original form, there appears to be little competition in monopolistic competition so far as the short run is concerned. Indeed Figure 16.1 is identical to one illustrating short-run equilibrium for a monopoly. In the long run, however, a monopoly cannot be maintained if there is unrestricted entry into the market. If firms are earning economic profit in the short run, other firms will enter and produce the product, and they will continue to enter until all economic profits are eliminated. This feature leads to a discussion of the long-run equilibrium for a monopolistically competitive firm.

Long-Run Equilibrium

While the short-run equilibrium for a firm under monopolistic competition is similar to that under monopoly, the long-run equilibrium is more closely related to the equilibrium position under perfect competition. Because of unrestricted entry, all economic profit must be eliminated in the long run. Such a zero-profit equilibrium can only occur at an output at which price equals long-run average cost. This occurs when the firm's demand is tangent to long-run average cost. The only difference between this equilibrium and that for perfect competition is that, for a firm in a monopolistically competitive market, the tangency cannot occur at minimum average cost. Since the demand curve facing the firm is downward sloping under monopolistic competition, the point of tangency must be on the downward-sloping range of long-run average cost. Thus, the long-run equilibrium output under monopolistic competition is less than that forthcoming under perfect competition in the long run.

This long-run result is shown in Figure 16.2. *LAC* and *LMC* are the long-run average and marginal cost curves for a typical monopolistically competitive firm. Suppose that the original demand curve is given by D_m. In this case the firm would be making substantial economic profits because demand lies above *LAC* over a wide range of output, and, if this firm is making profits, one would expect that other firms in the market are also earning economic profits. These profits would then attract new firms into the market. While the new firms would not sell exactly the same products as existing firms, their products would be very similar. So as new firms enter, the number of substitutes would increase and the demand facing the typical firm will shift backward and probably become more elastic (though not perfectly elastic). Entry will continue as long as there is some economic profit being earned. Thus entry causes each firm's demand curve to shift backward until a demand curve such as *D* in Figure 16.2 is reached. This long-run demand curve, *D*, is tangent to *LAC* at a price of $\overline{P}$ and output of $\overline{Q}$.

FIGURE 16.2
Long-Run Equilibrium under Monopolistic Competition

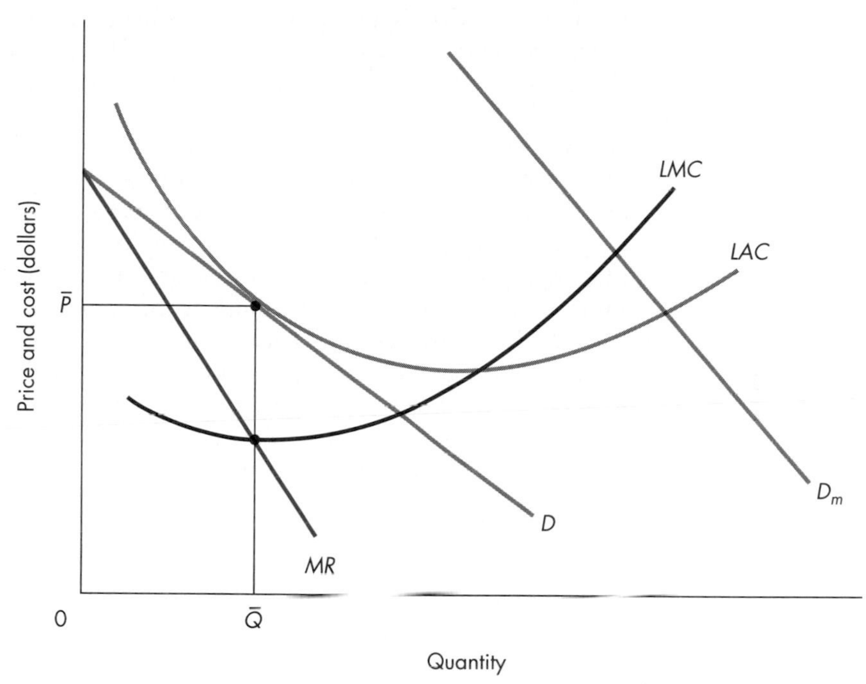

In such an equilibrium either an increase or a decrease in price by the firm would lead to losses. No further entry would occur since there are no economic profits to be earned in this market.

If too many firms enter the market, each firm's demand curve would be pushed so far back that demand falls below *LAC*. Firms would be suffering losses and exit would take place. As this happened, the demand curve would be pushed back up to tangency with *LAC*. Free entry and exit under monopolistic competition must lead to a situation where demand is tangent to *LAC*—where price equals average cost—and no economic profit is earned, but the firms earn a normal profit.

The equilibrium in Figure 16.2 must also be characterized by the intersection of *LMC* and *MR*. Only at output $\overline{Q}$ can the firm avoid a loss, so this output must be optimal. But the optimal output requires marginal cost to equal marginal revenue. Thus, at $\overline{Q}$, it must be the case that *MR* = *LMC*.

Relation Long-run equilibrium in a monopolistically competitive market is attained when the demand curve for each producer is tangent to the long-run average cost curve. Unrestricted entry and exit lead to this equilibrium. At the equilibrium output, price equals long-run average cost and marginal revenue equals long-run marginal cost.

Mutual Interdependence in Monopolistic Competition

In the theory discussed above, monopolistic competitors act independently, and in the short run behave like monopolists. This is a reasonable assumption under many circumstances. If there are many small shirt manufacturers producing similar but not identical apparel in a national market, each firm would probably believe, justifiably, that its own sales or pricing policy would have an insignificant effect on the total market. Similarly, no service station, grocery store, or bar in a large city would have much effect on its respective total citywide market.

However, in small segments of many markets, firms may believe, justifiably, that there is a great deal of mutual interdependence among firms within the same market segment. For example, the manager of an Exxon station on one corner of an intersection would know that if the station dropped its price it would have a substantial impact on the sales of the Chevron station across the street, and the Chevron manager would probably respond. But the Exxon manager would not know how the Chevron station would react. Chevron might exactly meet Exxon's new price, it might take an even larger price reduction, perhaps leading to a mutually ruinous price war, or it might cut price by a lesser amount.

If there were three or four bars across the street from a campus, one of them, Joe's bar, knows that if it has a promotion of three beers for the price of one during happy hour, Jane's bar next door would have to respond, perhaps by advertising four for the price of one. But Joe really doesn't know what Jane, or for that matter, the other bars, will do. In certain areas, the Albertson's grocery store puts the price charged by Kroger's or Appletree or another nearby grocery store on the same price marker as it posts its own price for certain products on the shelf—the competitor's price is obviously always higher when it is posted. This is intense personal rivalry and is indicative of a great deal of mutual interdependence.

In the above examples, Albertson's has no effect on stores in other parts of the city; Joe's price does not affect the sales of cocktail lounges in the large downtown hotels, and Exxon has little impact on gasoline sales along the interstate highway outside the city. Taken as a whole, the gasoline market, the lounge market, and the grocery market in the city are monopolistically competitive. But specific submarkets are quite oligopolistic in nature and exhibit the oligopoly characteristics discussed in the introduction. Firms in these types of submarkets can easily fit into one or another pattern of oligopoly behavior to be developed throughout the remainder of this chapter. We will not go into these patterns now because we will devote so much space to them later. But, when you read about these oligopoly models, be aware that they can easily apply to firms that would seem to exhibit all of the characteristics of monopolistic competition—*with one monumental exception that we must stress.*

This exception is *easy entry into monopolistically competitive markets.* Because firms can easily enter into these markets, generally at a rather small size, economic profit tends to be competed away in the long run even in the submarkets we have noted. This is not always a characteristic of oligopoly markets, which are frequently characterized by high barriers to the entry of new firms. Thus, economic profit may persist in many oligopoly markets even in the long run.

We might note that short of getting the government to prevent entry, there is nothing the firms in a monopolistically competitive market can do about having their profits competed away. Even if the firms were to conspire to fix a price, new firms would enter. Each firm would find its demand decreased and its sales reduced until price equaled average cost and economic profits were zero, although possibly at a higher price than would occur in the absence of the price-fixing agreement.

We have emphasized that, under monopolistic competition, profits are competed away in the long run. While this is correct in general, we do not mean to imply that there is no opportunity for astute managers to postpone this situation into the future by innovative decision making. Firms selling in monopolistically competitive markets can and do advertise and change product quality in an effort to lengthen the time period over which they earn economic profit. Those managers who are successful in their marketing strategy can sometimes earn profit for a long time. However, successful market strategies can be easily imitated by competitors who sell a product that is rather similar. Therefore, under monopolistic competition there is always a strong tendency for economic profit to be eliminated in the long run, no matter what strategies managers undertake.

16.2 CHARACTERISTICS OF OLIGOPOLY

The nature of an oligopoly industry cannot be captured by a uniform set of characteristics that apply to each and every case of oligopoly. As you will see in this section, there are certain characteristics that all oligopoly markets share. Other characteristics of oligopoly, however, may differ substantially from one oligopolistic industry to another. We first discuss several characteristics common to any oligopoly market: all oligopolies are characterized by the existence of (1) mutual interdependence, (2) market power, and (3) barriers to entry. We then will discuss two important dimensions in which oligopolies may differ: oligopolies can (1) produce either homogeneous or differentiated goods, and (2) behave either cooperatively or noncooperatively in making price, output, and other decisions.

Common Characteristics

A key characteristic that all oligopolies share is that there are few enough firms that each firm recognizes its mutual interdependence with the other firms. This is by far the most important characteristic, and the one that makes the analysis of oligopoly so complicated. An oligopolist knows that if it changes the price of its product, its rivals will notice. And, accordingly, they may or may not change their price. This then leads to uncertainty. If rivals change their prices, sales after the original price change will differ from sales if the rivals do not change their prices. This uncertainty about competitors' reactions leads to uncertainty about the oligopolist's demand and marginal revenue curves.

Firms in other market structures do not worry about rivals' reactions. They can set marginal revenue equal to marginal cost and maximize profit, even though in two of the other structures we have described, this profit is competed away in the long run. This absence of mutual interdependence makes these other structures easier to analyze. The oligopolist would like to equate marginal revenue to marginal cost. But since it is uncertain about the reactions of rivals, it is uncertain about its marginal revenue. And mutual interdependence and uncertainty are present in other oligopoly decisions, such as advertising campaigns, product design, and marketing strategies.

Another characteristic common to all oligopolies is that each firm has a certain amount of market power. If an oligopolist increases its price, it won't lose all of its sales; if it lowers its price, it won't gain the entire market. But, we must stress that how much sales are gained or lost depends on the behavior of rival firms.

Finally, oligopoly markets are characterized by moderate to high barriers to entry. Just as a monopoly must be protected by entry barriers to maintain its monopoly position, oligopolists must be similarly protected from entry. Otherwise the market would become much more like perfect competition or monopolistic competition.

Although the barriers to entry in a monopoly market may be stronger, entry barriers for oligopoly are quite similar in form. As in monopoly, economies of scale over a large range of output are probably the most important barrier in oligopoly markets. But in an oligopoly market the extent of these economies permits a few firms, rather than only one, to sell in the market without making losses. New firms would be forced to enter the market at a large size in order to compete with existing firms.

Other oligopoly entry barriers, similar to monopoly, are control of an essential raw material or the possession of protective patents by a few firms. Some entry barriers are the direct result of the strategic behavior of the oligopolistic firms selling in the market. For example, brand loyalty is quite an important barrier to entry in many, though not all, oligopoly markets. Buyer allegiance for durable goods can be built by establishing a reputation for service. No one knows what the service or repair policy of a new firm may be. Or, the allegiance of buyers can be built by a long, successful advertising campaign. (This type of allegiance is also probably more prevalent for durable goods.) New firms might have considerable difficulty establishing a market organization and overcoming buyer preferences for the established firms. Some barriers to entry arise because the pricing policy of established firms discourages the entry of new firms into the market. Such a policy is called entry limit pricing. Other oligopolies may increase their capacity or the size of their firm, in order to discourage entry. We will discuss strategic entry deterrence at some length in this chapter.

Differing Characteristics

Oligopolies can be classified by the type of product produced. In some oligopoly markets the products are homogeneous. Unless a buyer knows which firm sold the product, it would be impossible to determine the seller solely from the characteristics of the product itself. Some examples are markets such as steel, aluminum, and nickel. Other oligopoly markets are characterized by differentiated products. In varying degrees it is possible to determine who produced the product from the product itself or its package. Some examples are automobiles, major home appliances, breakfast cereals, and cigarettes. The type of product produced can affect the oligopolist's strategic behavior.

cooperative oligopolists Oligopolists who tend to follow changes initiated by rivals.

noncooperative oligopolists Oligopolists who do not accommodate price changes of other firms.

Broadly speaking, economists refer to two contrasting patterns of behavior for oligopolists: cooperative or noncooperative. **Cooperative oligopolists** tend to follow changes made by rival firms. For example, if a rival raises price, a cooperative oligopolist would go along with the move and raise price also. **Noncooperative oligopolists** on the other hand, do not accommodate such changes. If a rival firm raises price, other firms would keep prices low in order to attract sales away from the higher price producer.

But, oligopolists have ways other than price to compete. Some oligopolistic markets are characterized by a great deal of price competition. In others, firms don't compete extensively by price changes but do compete in other ways, such as advertising, product quality, and other marketing strategies.

Because of these differences in oligopoly markets, there are four general oligopolistic market structures. These are, first, a few noncooperative firms producing either (1) a homogeneous product, or (2) related but differentiated products; and, second, a few cooperative firms producing either (3) a homogeneous product, or (4) related but differentiated products.

The price and output decisions of an oligopolist depend to a large extent on the market structure. If an oligopolist produces a homogeneous product and does not cooperate, the market tends toward the competitive solution. Each firm's demand elasticity will be high because of the availability of close substitutes. If each firm's output exhausts all economies of scale, price will be close to minimum long-run average cost.

Cooperative oligopolists producing identical products tend to behave much like a monopoly. Firms tend to act as one; since buyers cannot distinguish among products, when price rises, it appears as though a monopoly actually controlled production.

Differentiated products make cooperation more difficult. In a cooperative agreement, price differences would have to be negotiated to account for quality differences. Added to the increased difficulty of setting prices is the opportunity to compete for sales by quality changes. This type of competition is difficult to control. The most visible sort of cooperation when products are differentiated is leadership by a dominant firm in price or model changes.

Oligopoly behavior is also determined by other factors. For example, if entry barriers are relatively moderate and new firms would find it fairly easy to enter, the gains from cooperation are small. High prices encourage new firms to enter the market. Prices in such oligopoly markets tend to be low, and cooperation tends to increase profit only minimally. When entry is extremely difficult, firms have a greater incentive to reach a cooperative agreement. Prices will tend to be higher in such markets.

The history of the industry and even the personalities of the top executives tend to affect oligopoly behavior. Over time firms learn something about how their rivals will react to changes. Some industries are characterized by a live and let live attitude. In others, firms compete far more aggressively and competitively. As noted, in some markets competition takes the form of price cutting. In others, firms compete much more by advertising and marketing strategy.

Again, the distinguishing characteristic of oligopoly is the recognition by each firm that its actions will have a noticeable effect upon other firms and that these rivals will react accordingly. Thus the potential reactions of other firms must be taken into account when an individual firm makes decisions, especially decisions about price and output. This is why there is no general theory of oligopoly. Oligopoly behavior depends on so many things that its forms are as numerous as the number of oligopolistic industries. Thus the best we can do in one chapter is give you a feel for some of the more important aspects of this market structure.

16.3 NONCOOPERATIVE OLIGOPOLY BEHAVIOR

In spite of the uncertainty about the reactions of rivals, the managers of oligopolies do use the marginal benefit–marginal cost rule when making decisions. A firm would reduce price and increase output as long as expected marginal revenue exceeds marginal cost. It would increase price and reduce output if expected marginal revenue is less than marginal cost.

The problem for an oligopolist is, of course, accurately forecasting its demand and marginal revenue if it changes its price. As emphasized, any change in price and output has a noticeable effect on the sales of other firms. These rivals may react by changing *their* prices and output; or they may not react at all. We begin our discussion of noncooperative oligopoly behavior with a hypothetical story to illustrate the problem with forecasting oligopoly demand.

The Problem with Oligopoly Demand: An Example

Suppose the marketing executives at Pepsi-Cola are meeting to decide whether or not the company should change the price of a six-pack of Pepsi. For several months both Pepsi and Coca-Cola have been charging the same price, \$3, for a six-pack. Over that period, Pepsi has been selling, on average, one million six-packs a day. The question is, should Pepsi change its price in an attempt to make more profit?

Some of the marketing vice presidents suggest raising the price of Pepsi to \$4, because they believe that the sales of Pepsi will not decline much, and the higher price will be more profitable. When questioned about how Coke will respond, they answer that Coke will probably raise its price to \$4 also, and, if in fact this is the case, Pepsi's sales will fall only to 800,000. There won't be much substitution away from Pepsi to Coke if Coke is selling at the same price. If these vice presidents are correct, the movement in Figure 16.3 will take place along demand curve *D* (labeled "Coke follows" in the figure) from point *C* to point *A*. As you can see, the \$1 price increase causes sales to fall by 200,000 six-packs.

Another group of vice presidents vehemently objects, saying that Coke would never follow the \$1 price increase. If Coke keeps its price at \$3, Pepsi will

FIGURE 16.3
The Problem with Oligopoly Demand

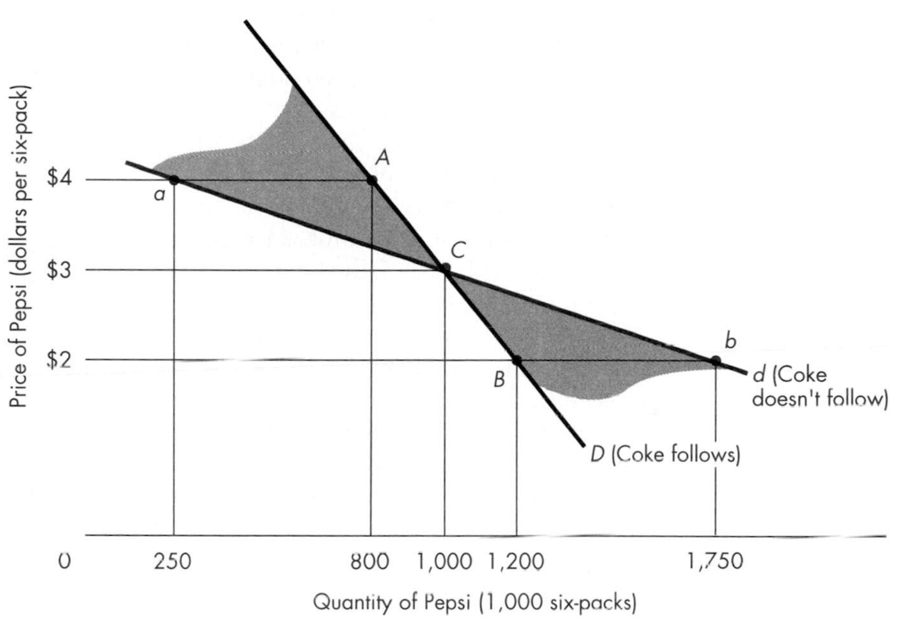

lose a huge amount of sales, probably falling to 250,000 six-packs. If this group is correct, the movement takes place along demand curve *d* (labeled "Coke doesn't follow" in the figure) from point *C* to point *a*. Under this assumption about Coke's response, sales fall by 750,000 six-packs to 250,000.

Because of the confusion about the effect of a $1 price increase, someone suggests a $1 price reduction to $2. Again, one group argues that Coke, not wishing to lose a large share of the market, would immediately follow with a $1 price decrease of their own, and thus Pepsi would enjoy a sales increase of only 200,000, to 1,200,000 six-packs. If this is correct, the movement is along demand curve *D*, from point *C* to point *B*. Pepsi picks up some sales, but not many when Coke responds with a lower price.

Then those who believe that Coke will not follow the price cut argue that the price reduction from $3 to $2 will increase Pepsi's sales by 750,000, to 1,750,000 six-packs. They maintain that the movement will take place along demand curve *d*, from point *C* to point *b*. Pepsi will take a huge share of Coke's market in this scenario.

After a considerable amount of arguing about which demand is the correct demand curve, a management trainee asks what would happen if Coke responds to Pepsi's price increase with less than a $1 increase of its own or to a price decrease with less than a $1 decrease of its own. Under these assumptions, couldn't Pepsi's actual demand be anywhere in the shaded area between demand curves D and d? Or following up that question, the trainee asks whether it is possible that Coke would choose *not* to follow a price increase, hoping to pick up a lot of sales when Pepsi raises its price; but, not wanting to lose a lot of sales if Pepsi lowers price, would Coke choose to follow a price decrease? Then wouldn't the demand curve for Pepsi be d for a price increase above $3 and D for a price decrease below $3. The meeting is adjourned when the senior marketing vice president announces that there will be no change in price anytime soon, unless of course, Coke changes its price, and then there will be another meeting.

So, there is the oligopoly problem. The firm would like to know what its demand actually is so that it can maximize profits under those demand and marginal revenue conditions. However, it can't do this, because the actual demand depends crucially on what rivals will do, and there is a considerable amount of uncertainty about this response. Certainly, in the above example, the CEO of Pepsi could call the CEO of Coke and work out a pricing agreement between the two firms. But, price fixing is illegal in the United States, and business executives have been fined or even sent to prison for doing just that.

So managers of oligopolies usually just have to live with the problem of oligopoly interdependence and the consequent uncertainty. Economists also have to live with the problem that they have no general theory to explain oligopoly behavior. Nonetheless, managers have found ways to deal with their problem, and economists have found ways to deal with theirs. The remainder of this chapter is directed at showing you a few ways that both managers and economists have tried to come to grips with the oligopoly problem.

Price Rigidity under Oligopoly

Some economists have argued that the very nature of the oligopoly problem—the expected reaction of rivals—causes oligopoly markets to be characterized by a great deal of price rigidity. That is, prices under oligopoly would not be very responsive to changes in demand or cost conditions.

Many theories have been set forth to explain why prices are supposedly inflexible in an oligopoly market structure. The most frequently cited hypothesis takes the following form: If one oligopolist increases its price, competing oligopolists will hold their prices constant, so the oligopolistic firm that raises its price will lose considerable sales to rivals. On the other hand, if one oligopolist lowers its price, the rival firms, fearing substantial losses in sales, will also lower their prices. Thus, the oligopolist that lowers price will experience only an insignificant increase in sales, because of the price competition. (Remember the question asked by the Pepsi trainee, the question that broke up the meeting when the CEO decided not to change price: what happens if Coke follows a decrease in price but not an increase?)

The nature of the problem is shown in Figure 16.4. Suppose that a firm in a noncooperative oligopolistic market structure has been producing 400 units of output per period and selling them at $5 each. Its total revenue is therefore $2,000. Also suppose that the firm is considering changing its price.

FIGURE 16.4
Price Rigidity under Oligopoly

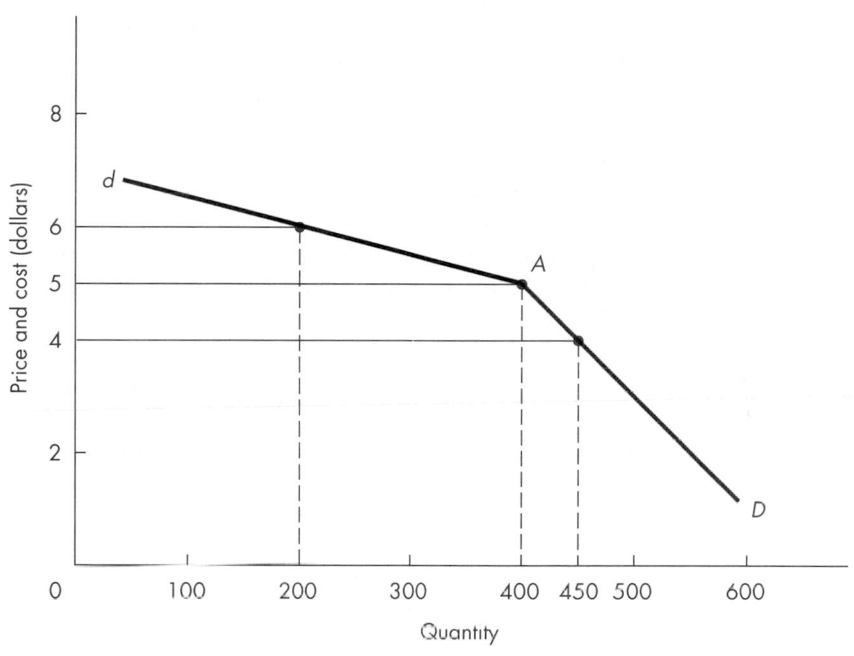

The firm believes that if it increases its price to $6, its rivals will not change their prices and the firm will lose a great deal of sales to them after the price increase. Thus it thinks it will be able to sell only 200 units after raising its price to $6. Its revenue would fall to $1,200. For any price increase that is unmatched by the other firms, this firm's demand is segment *dA*, which is quite elastic as is shown by the fall in revenue after the price increase. (Note that this is similar to the upper portion of demand *d* in Figure 16.3.)

But, suppose the firm decreases price from $5 to $4. Now the firm expects its rivals to match the price decrease so as not to lose sales. Thus the firm would gain few, if any, additional sales from its rivals by decreasing price. Sales would increase some because of the downward-sloping market demand for the products of all the firms, but not by much. In the figure sales increase only to 450 units when price is reduced to $4. Thus revenue decreases to $1,800. For any reduction in price from $5, the firm's demand is the inelastic segment *AD*, when rivals match the decrease. Thus the firm expects revenue to decline if price is changed in any direction, under its assumption about its rivals' behavior. (Note that this segment is similar to the lower portion of demand *D* in Figure 16.3.)

If the preceding hypothesis is true, oligopolists would have little motivation to change prices. Thus oligopoly is sometimes claimed to be less adaptable than other market structures, since prices are rigid. This theory is sometimes used by economists to explain why oligopoly markets are characterized by "sticky" prices; however, the theory does not explain why price is where it is in the first place. It must, therefore, be regarded as an ex post rationalization of market behavior rather than an ex ante explanation of market behavior. Furthermore, there is a certain amount of contradictory empirical evidence. Several studies have shown that, in general, oligopoly markets are characterized by as many price changes as both more competitive markets and markets characterized by monopoly.

There are many other theories designed to explain oligopoly price and output decisions, dating as far back as 1836. Yet none is accepted as a good general explanation of oligopoly price behavior when the firms are noncooperative. Nevertheless, we can say a good bit more about other aspects of noncooperative oligopolistic markets.

Nonprice Competition in Oligopoly Markets: Advertising

nonprice competition
A form of competition used by oligopolists that does not involve price changes by firms.

Although the preceding discussion indicates that there is a certain amount of debate among economists as to the amount of price competition in industries characterized by oligopoly, most would agree that oligopoly is characterized by considerable **nonprice competition**, particularly when the product is differentiated. The alternative forms of nonprice competition are as diverse as the minds of inventive managers can make them. Yet there is one central feature: an oligopoly frequently attempts to attract customers to its own product (and, therefore, away from that of rivals) by some means other than a price differential.

Nonprice competition accordingly involves differentiating a product, even when the product is fundamentally homogeneous. The ways of differentiating are diverse, but the two principal methods of nonprice competition are advertising and product quality.

Using advertising and product quality, the firm wishes to increase the demand for its product and make it less elastic. As you would expect, a firm chooses the amount of advertising and product quality at which the marginal cost of advertising (quality) equals the marginal revenue from increased advertising (quality). The oligopolist then allocates its advertising budget so that the marginal revenue per dollar spent is the same for all media.

Choosing the optimal level of advertising is not, however, always a simple straightforward decision. The problem is the same as that for price and quantity choices: any one firm's change in its advertising will have a noticeable effect on the sales of other firms, and these rivals would certainly react by changing their own advertising plans, which would of course require the originating firm to react, and so on.

We could just as easily have demonstrated the oligopoly interdependence problem with a story about Pepsi's advertising department meeting to discuss what Coke would do in response to a change in Pepsi's advertising, as we did with the marketing department and the price changes. Or perhaps Reebok would be debating what Nike will do in response to a new Reebok campaign. Or Miller and Bud, Ford and Chevrolet, Kellogg Cereal and Post Cereal, and on and on. Can't you imagine the Reebok advertising manager opening the meeting with, "Well, Nike has Michael Jordan and Shaquille O'Neal, so let's counter with John Elway and Joe Montana, but then they might come back with Patrick Ewing and Roger Clemens, then what could we do . . . ?"

So oligopoly advertisers face the same problem as that discussed for price and quantity decisions: How will my rivals react, and how will I, in turn, respond to their reaction? Each firm has to take into account the reactions of other firms when making its decisions. As was the case for price, this interdependence complicates the advertising decision considerably.

Nonprice Competition in Oligopoly Markets: Product Quality

As we mentioned, oligopolists also can use changes in product quality as a means of nonprice competition—that is, to differentiate their product from those of rival firms. The product quality change may be real or perceived. In either case, such decisions are made employing the same process as that used in the case of advertising or anything else—evaluating marginal revenue and marginal cost.

As was true for advertising and price, the firm must take into consideration the reaction of its rivals to any quality changes. Thus, quality changes that will be noticed by consumers but cannot be quickly copied by rivals are frequently attempted. A wine that is aged longer to give it a better taste, a few added inches between seats on an airplane, or fewer defective parts in a large shipment of equipment are quality changes not easily copied by rivals.

Product-quality competition is particularly intense in service oligopolies, where product quality is difficult to judge. Doctors and dentists, for instance, do not usually compete via the prices they charge patients, but the quality of their services and the waiting time in their offices vary a great deal.

The annual style change made by manufacturers of consumer durables is another method of product quality competition. We see such changes in automobiles, household appliances, TVs, stereos, and sporting goods. Until the new models are put on the market, these style changes are closely guarded secrets. If other firms do not know what the new model is going to look like, it may take a year or more for the rivals to copy it, if in fact, the style change is successful.

We could go on with many other examples, but we are sure you have seen the point. The types of quality competition are practically as numerous as the oligopolistic industries themselves.

But oligopolists have another way of using product quality as a method of competition, other than by simply improving the real or perceived quality of their product. Products can be thought of as a collection of attributes or characteristics. For example, an automobile can be described by its engine size, brakes, transmission, suspension, fuel efficiency, tires, head and trunk room, number of doors, color, and so on. These product features can differ among products and can be altered by the manufacturers to differentiate their products from others. How a producer selects these attributes determines the quality and nature of the product and the product's substitutability with other products in the market. A manufacturer who produces an automobile with most of the attributes that

FIGURE 16.5
Product Quality Measure

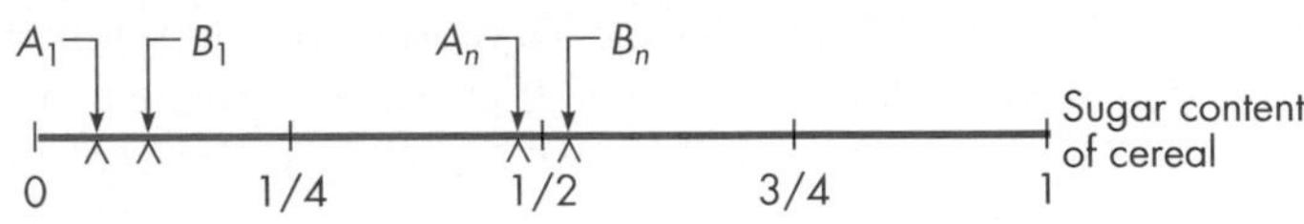

characterize a Cadillac Sedan DeVille will make a car that is an unlikely substitute for a Ford Mustang.

To illustrate how product attributes can serve as a competitive tool, we consider another hypothetical example. The basic idea is captured by letting all of the possible preferences consumer may have for a particular attribute be measured along a scale with end points 0 and 1, as shown in Figure 16.5. Assume that this product attribute is sugar on breakfast cereal; 0 is cereal with no sugar and 1 is cereal of virtually pure sugar cubes. The values 1/4, 1/2, and 3/4, mark equal distance points along this scale. Suppose that those who buy breakfast cereal are uniformly distributed along this scale so that the number of individuals who want no sugar on their cereal is equal to the number who want their cereal half-sugared and is equal to the number who want all sugar.

For the first firm that enters the cereal market, it does not matter how much sugar is put on its product. It is the only cereal consumers can buy. We arbitrarily locate firm A on the scale at A_1. Since sugar is expensive, firm A initially chooses a point on the lower end of the scale. We subscript the location because the firm may later want to change the sugar content of its cereal when other firms enter the market.

Rivalry begins when firm B decides to enter the market. The new seller knows the preferences of consumers, that is, the scale in Figure 16.5, and how much sugar A has on its product. The question is, how much sugar should B use to capture the largest share of the market? You can see in the figure that (with constant prices) firm B could capture most of the market by using a little more sugar than A. The best thing for B to do is enter with a product that is just to the right of A_1. We label this point B_1. Firm B captures all of the market to the right of A_1 in sugar content.

Firm A will, of course, not tolerate this for long. Its market share has been reduced to an insignificant part of the total market. Only those buyers with preferences between 0 and A_1 remain loyal to A's cereal. The firm could lower price or think about countering B's product by putting more sugar on its cereal. It can regain much of its lost market by moving just to the right of B_1. But then B will move to the right of A again, and A will then move to the right of B a second time. The leapfrogging will continue until one firm drops out of the market, or both firms end up with approximately equal market shares at the midpoint of the preference scale. After a large number of moves, firms will put approximately the same amount of sugar on their cereal and supply the amounts desired by the average buyer; that is, at A_n and B_n.

ILLUSTRATION 16.1

Who Cares about a Little Bit of Sugar?

You might be asking whether people care about product attributes. Who cares how much sugar a firm puts in its product? Several years ago a lot of people cared. On Wednesday, July 10, 1985, Coca-Cola announced that it was bringing back its old Coke with a little less sugar, now called Classic Coke, after switching to a sweeter version almost three months before. ABC interrupted its soap opera, "General Hospital," to break the news. Dan Rather, Peter Jennings, and Tom Brokaw had news stories on the CBS, ABC, and NBC evening news. ABC featured the story on "Nightline." Senator David Pryor expressed jubilation on the Senate floor during a debate on South Africa. *Time* covered the story in a prominent article.*

The story actually began on April 23, 1985, when Coca-Cola announced that, after extensive testing, it was changing the flavor of Coke for the first time in its 99-year history. In essence, Coca-Cola had added a little more sugar to the recipe, making Coke taste much more like Pepsi, which celebrated the occasion by declaring a company holiday. No one actually knows, but Coke may well have "jumped" Pepsi in the sugar war, as described in Figure 16.5. Coke's advertising agency reported that two-thirds of the nation heard the news within 24 hours.

The change caused a national furor. Coke had merely tried to move its product closer to its largest competitor on the flavor spectrum. But people thought it was like tampering with a national institution. Coca-Cola received as many as 1,500 phone calls a day as well as a multitude of protesting letters. "Save Coke" clubs were formed. And all of this was after by far the most extensive market testing program in the company's history.

After almost three months of protest, Coca-Cola decided to keep the new, sweeter Coke on the market but bring back the old flavor of Coke and call it Classic Coke.

Was it one of the dumbest marketing moves in history? Some thought so at the time. Or was it a giant hoax? Did Coke plan all along to reintroduce the Classic Coke and reap the benefits of all the publicity? After all, Coke had Pepsi almost surrounded in the sugar battle.

Donald R. Keough, the president of Coca-Cola, denied the stories that the new Coke was a deliberate plot to create support for the old product, saying, "Some critics will say Coca-Cola has made a marketing mistake. Some cynics say that we planned the whole thing. The truth is, we're not that dumb, and we're not that smart."

*"Coca-Cola's Big Fizzle," *Time*, July 22, 1985, pp. 48–52.

The situation gets more complicated when a third firm enters the market. With a little experimenting, you can discover that firms do not find an equilibrium; they continually change the amount of sugar on their cereals. This is not uncommon in the real world—think how many new and improved labels producers put on their products. Often these improvements are nothing more than a slight adjustment in a product attribute, a change the marketing personnel hope will place them near their rival, but on the side of the preference scale that gives them the largest market share.

We have oversimplified things a great deal by allowing product differentiation for only one product variable and assuming price competition does not take place at the same time. Realistically, there are all sorts of ways attributes can be mixed. Discovering the attributes that capture the largest share of the market requires sophisticated marketing techniques and, at times, just plain luck. The point of the simple model, though, is that product differentiation is a competitive tool that firms use to maximize profits. Differentiation can be as much a part of competition as price.

We have attempted to show that noncooperative oligopolists compete in many ways. They generally don't like price competition, but they use it. And they don't like nonprice competition much better, but they use it also. No matter what type of competition oligopolists use, there is always the problem of mutual interdependence among firms and the resulting uncertainty. This is a problem whether the competition involves price, advertising, or product quality.

We should mention in closing this section that mutual interdependence is not just a problem for the industrial giants we have used as examples—the GMs and Fords, the Coca-Colas and Pepsis. Markets served by much smaller firms can be just as oligopolistic and can face exactly the same problem of mutual interdependence. They can compete in as many different ways as the giants, even though they probably would not be discussed on the CBS evening news, in *Time*, or in *The Wall Street Journal*. Some examples of smaller oligopolists would be the major banks that serve a city, city newspapers, large department stores, and some manufacturers. All have decision-making problems similar to the ones discussed above.

Actually, we have, in this section, barely touched upon more specific ways oligopolists compete. We have limited the discussion to a more general exposition. The methods of competition actually employed by oligopolists depend not only on the structure of the market, but on the history of the industry and even on the personalities of the managers. Not surprisingly, a huge number of competitive patterns are possible.

As noted, we have classified nonprice competition into two broad general categories: advertising and product quality. There is, however, a relatively new type of oligopolistic competition that has become increasingly important in the last few years. Because this type of competition seems to defy classification and because its widespread use is so recent, we have not mentioned it in the text but its implications are discussed in Illustration 16.2.

16.4 STRATEGIC INTERACTION IN OLIGOPOLY MARKETS

Because oligopoly markets are characterized by mutual interdependence among firms, oligopoly is the only market structure in which firms must plan for and react to the behavior of their rivals. In all other structures, firms more or less take market conditions as given and try to maximize profits within the constraints imposed by these conditions. Certainly firms selling in other types of market structures might carry out innovations or attempt in some way or another to lower their costs or, in the case of monopoly or monopolistic competition, to expand their sales, perhaps by advertising. In doing so, however, the reactions and countermoves of other firms generally do not play as large a role in the decision-making process of monopolistic competitors. In oligopoly markets, the potential reactions and countermoves are extremely important.

We can make an analogy between firms in other market structures and a sprinter in a 100-meter dash or a swimmer in a 50-meter race. The sprinter or swimmer essentially runs or swims as fast as possible for a short distance without worrying much about the relative positions of the other racers. An oligopoly is analogous to a runner or swimmer in a 1,500-meter or longer race. A long-distance runner or swimmer generally plans tactics or strategy according to the relative positions of other competitors and may even change tactics during the race depending on what the other competitors are doing. Furthermore, runners or swimmers in longer races may have already planned, well before the race began, contingency tactics that can be used to counter tactics of the competitors. In fact, all of the competitors will plan moves and countermoves before and during the race. Similar plans and reactions to opponents by firms in oligopoly markets are called strategic interactions or **strategic behavior**.

strategic behavior
Actions taken by firms in oligopolistic markets to plan for and react to competition from rival firms.

game theory
An analytical tool used by economists to aid in explaining and predicting some strategic interactions of oligopolists.

In recent years, economists have increasingly relied on an analytical tool, called **game theory**, to explain and predict the strategic interactions of oligopolists. In this section we will give you a brief overview of how game theory is used and discuss why this approach is at times useful. We must mention that game theory is a rather complex, mathematical concept, and an in-depth understanding would require several graduate, level courses in economic theory. We do, however, want you to get a feel for the concept and how it could be useful for managerial decision making.

The Game Theory Approach to Oligopoly Behavior: An Example

We will use a hypothetical example to show how some oligopoly strategic behavior is similar to the behavior of players in a game of skill. Since we used Pepsi and Coke in previous examples, we will continue with these two firms.

Imagine Pepsi's marketing vice presidents in a meeting to decide future advertising strategy. The senior vice president summarizes, "We're strong now with Ray Charles and Michael J. Fox and we've just added Ricky Henderson for the sports customer. Coke has the ever reliable Bill Cosby and The New Kids on the Block for the young group. But they've called Henderson with Jose Canseco and raised with Steffi Graff. I think we've got to counter."

Another vice president suggests, "We should go for the country and western consumers with Garth Brooks and maybe raise with a big public figure." The senior vice president replies, "We might be able to throw in Rush Limbaugh but Coke would probably call with Oprah Winfrey, and I don't think Boris Yeltsin is available, but even so Coke might raise with President Clinton." Doesn't this sound a bit like poker?

Then the same trainee who broke up the last meeting might say, "It seems as though both companies are faced with a dilemma. We both keep paying huge amounts for more and more celebrities, and it sounds like we are going to end up bailing out Russia, and Coke will probably pay off the federal budget deficit. Yet neither company seems to increase its sales very much no matter how many celebrities are hired. Am I right?" All the executives agree that the trainee is right, but they all say, "We can't afford to cut back because if we do and Coke doesn't, we'll lose our shirts." We will return to this dilemma later.

ILLUSTRATION 16.2

Competition by Doing the Right Thing

Over the past decade, many major corporations have seemingly discovered social consciousness. Major oil companies have become more careful in protecting the environment in their drilling operations. Other extraction firms have followed suit. McDonald's changed from styrofoam packaging to paper, because styrofoam wasn't sufficiently biodegradable. McDonald's also has established a "hire-the-handicapped" program. Chicken of the Sea and the other two major tuna sellers don't use tuna from fishermen who may inadvertently catch dolphin. Major grocery chains offer consumers the choice between paper bags and plastic bags.

Newsweek reported in January 1991 that many large business firms have recently become socially conscious.* A huge advertising agency dropped its lavish Christmas parties; instead, employees worked in soup kitchens, renovated low-income housing, and wrapped presents for hospital patients. A seller of tanning beds and other yuppie playthings began selling *The Recycler's Handbook* and touted its own use of biodegradable packing material. Ivory soap commercials downplayed the emphasis of the soap's cleaning properties and featured handicapped youngsters training for the Special Olympics. AT&T received an award for its program to stop using ozone-depleting chlorofluorocarbons.

How many commercials have you seen in which the corporation promises to donate money to some worthy cause for each one of its products sold? Sometimes it appears that beer manufacturers are more interested in promoting responsible drinking behavior than in selling more beer. Soft drink companies warn consumers not to litter.

Why the sudden change? If a miraculous conversion seems rather unlikely, firm managers must believe that, given the current social climate, doing good will be good for business. *Newsweek* reported that the public is now paying more attention to corporate behavior. A Roper poll found that 52 percent of a sample of US consumers said they would pay 10 percent more for a socially responsible product, and 67 percent said that when they shopped they were concerned about a company's social performance. (Remember the problem with consumer interviews, discussed in Chapter 8?) Whether or not these consumers told the truth, many corporations have used their social consciousness to increase sales or to charge more for their products. Doing good was used, though not admitted, as a way to increase profits.

Judging from the advertising, and the article in *Newsweek*, oligopolists appear to be the firms that are most socially conscious. Clearly, perfect competitors would not tell consumers how much good they are doing. Because of homogeneous products, consumers wouldn't know whether they were buying from a socially conscious firm or not. A monopoly faces no good substitutes for its product and would not use this approach unless it was government regulated and wanted to please the regulators.

Oligopolies that sell a differentiated product to consumers would try to improve their image by informing people about their socially responsible behavior. This type of nonprice price competition has overtones of both advertising and product quality competition. The advertising conveys an image of the product; using the product makes a statement about the user's social responsibility. The image of corporate responsibility also is a way to change the quality

While the soft drink game sounds like poker, other oligopoly games sound more like chess: "If we move into the Southeast with a full marketing program, our rival will take advantage of our weakness in the Midwest and become so established that we will never become strong there." Or, "I wonder if my rival will lead off with a new model this year, or are they only bluffing, in the hope that I will play the wrong card?"

A huge number of books and articles have dealt with strategy in games of skill such as bridge, chess, and poker. A large part of oligopoly strategy is similar

of the product. The product is somehow better—gives more utility—if it was produced in a socially responsible way.

We do not mean to imply that the desirable behavior by corporations is solely motivated by profits, although *Newsweek* reported that some corporate observers were a bit skeptical about the motivations and about the long-term usefulness of such behavior, particularly as consumers' incomes fall in a recession. However, oligopolies—particularly those that sell a differentiated product to consumers—do appear to be the only types of firms that consistently tell about their social consciousness. It would appear that, to a greater or lesser extent, many oligopolies undertake such activities as a market tactic to gain sales from competitors.

We end this illustration by noting the plight of a truly socially conscious firm owner who gains absolutely no economic benefit from his behavior. A California peach and grape orchard owner, David Mas Manumoto, told his story of "political correctness" in *USA Today*.† According to Mr. Manumoto, he "farms organically, utilizing farm practices that sustain the land and air. [His] peach and grape farm is part of a renewable, natural system. [His] peaches are part of the environmental solution, not part of the problem. They don't add to landfills, compost piles love their peelings, and the trees provide habitat for wildlife. My produce is 'made in the USA' and grown by a minority (I'm Japanese-American) who employs 90 percent minorities. . . . [I don't] use toxic pesticides. . . . "

But the only benefit for Mr. Manumoto is "knowing my peaches are grown with a raised consciousness." As he notes, "The problem is that you won't think about this when you squeeze or smell my peaches in the grocery store. You won't ask the produce manager where the peaches came from or how they were grown. But you'll buy lots of peaches this summer because they're cheap."

Mr. Manumoto is a perfect competitor in the peach market. He sums up the problem of perfect competitors beautifully, "A simple law of economics drives agriculture: For us growers, there are just too damn many peaches out there. . . . Supply and demand deals a crushing blow to political correctness."

A perfectly competitive market doesn't value social responsibility. As you saw in Chapter 13, profits are driven to a normal return. Competitors who use socially responsible production methods that add to their cost will be driven out of business if other competitors in the market use the least-cost method of production.

As Mr. Manumoto states, "You can't fault me for wanting to make a profit. I can't farm very long just on social consciousness. . . . Until political correctness is valued more highly, price will still be the primary consideration when consumers decide to buy my peaches. What I believe in won't add much value in the marketplace."

So there is the difference between competitors and oligopolies that sell a differentiated product. And, there is the reason that the messages about politically correct production and distribution methods are coming from oligopolies.

*"Doing the Right Thing," *Newsweek*, January 7, 1991, pp. 42–3.

†"Politically Correct Peaches Confront Law of Supply and Demand," *USA Today*, July 2, 1991, p. 104.

to strategy in such games. Therefore, when economists analyze oligopoly strategy, they frequently treat oligopolists as though they were playing a game against their rivals, who are also playing the same game against them. The objective of the game is similar to that in poker—win money—but in the case of oligopolies it is to make as much profit as possible under the constraints. However, as you will see, sometimes the oligopolists actually find their profit reduced once they become involved in the game, as was implied in the above Coke/Pepsi example.

The outcome of the game and the amount of profits earned frequently depends on the assumptions made about the strategy of the participants and the method of playing the game. To introduce you to the concept of oligopoly games we begin with the grandfather of most economic games, which doesn't involve oligopoly behavior at all. This game is called the Prisoner's Dilemma.

The Prisoner's Dilemma

The model of the prisoner's dilemma is best illustrated by the story for which it is named. Suppose that a crime is committed and two suspects are apprehended and questioned by the police. Unknown to the suspects, the police do not have enough evidence to convict them unless one of them confesses. So the police separate them and make each one an offer that is known to the other. The offer is, if one suspect confesses to the crime and turns state's evidence, the one who confesses receives only a two-year sentence, while the other (who does not confess) will get 10 years. If both prisoners confess, each receives a two-year sentence. If neither confesses, the probability is very high both will go free. Thus, each prisoner could receive two years, 10 years, or go free, depending on what the other does.

Figure 16.6 shows the four possibilities. The upper-left and lower-right cells show the results if both, respectively, do not confess or confess. The upper-right and lower-left cells show the consequences if one confesses and the other does not.

The problem for the suspects is that they cannot collude. If they could, it is clear that neither would confess. However, they must make their decisions independently. The suspect who pleads innocent stands a chance of 10 years in prison if the other confesses. However, the worst that could happen if a suspect confesses to the crime is two years imprisonment regardless of what the other does.

We can approach the dilemma of the suspects in a slightly different way. Put yourself in the shoes of suspect 2, who knows that suspect 1 has only two alternatives, confess or not confess. If suspect 1 does not confess, the *worst* thing that can happen to suspect 2 is to confess and receive a two-year sentence. However, if suspect 2 confesses, the worst that suspect 1 can expect is 10 years, by not confessing, but by confessing, suspect 2 would receive only two years. Suspect 1

FIGURE 16.6
The Prisoner's Dilemma

		Suspect 1	
		Does not confess	Confesses
Suspect 2	Does not confess	A 1: 0 years 2: 0 years	B 1: 2 years 2: 10 years
	Confesses	C 1: 10 years 2: 2 years	D 1: 2 years 2: 2 years

faces exactly the same alternatives. If each suspect chooses the alternative that minimizes the maximum possible sentence, each will confess, and both will end up in cell D (no pun intended) serving two years. In game theory, such a strategy is called a **minimax strategy**, a strategy or choice that minimizes the worst thing that can occur.

minimax strategy
A strategy in game theory that involves minimizing the worst possible outcome.

The less each suspect knows about the other, regardless of whether the suspect committed the crime or not, the more likely the suspect will confess to the crime. In other words, the less information these accused criminals possess about each other, the less certainty they have about going free—settling in cell A. Each wants to avoid cells B and C. Each can get two years in prison with certainty by confessing. Thus, the safest tactic, or the minimax strategy, is for both to confess, and they end up in cell D.

An Advertiser's Dilemma

Oligopolists sometimes get caught in a similar dilemma in the case of both price and nonprice competition. A rather frequently encountered dilemma occurs when oligopolists compete in the level of advertising purchased. To illustrate the advertiser's dilemma we return to the hypothetical advertising war, or in this case a celebrity war, being fought by Pepsi and Coke. Recall that Pepsi and Coke were each escalating the amount of their advertising, to a large extent in response to the higher advertising expenses of their rival.

Suppose for simplicity and for illustrative purposes, each soft drink firm is limited to only two choices of advertising—a large advertising budget or a small advertising budget. Each firm must make its choice with little knowledge about what the other will do. Each firm knows that the outcome, the amount of profit earned from its choice, will depend crucially upon the choice of its rival.

Once again, let's consider Pepsi's alternatives. If Pepsi chooses a low level of advertising and Coke also chooses a low level, Pepsi knows that its profits will be large. The advertising of each firm attracts sales from the other but has a rather small effect on total soft drink sales. That is, total soft drink sales are relatively inelastic with respect to advertising. If Pepsi chooses a low level of advertising but Coke chooses a high level, total soft drink sales will not increase much, but Coke's advertising will attract a huge amount of sales away from Pepsi. Coke's profit will be quite high, but Pepsi will actually make a loss.

Alternatively, suppose Pepsi chooses a high advertising budget. If Coke chooses a low budget, Pepsi will take away a lot of Coke's sales; Pepsi will make a large profit, and Coke will make a loss. If Pepsi chooses a high level of advertising while Coke chooses a high advertising budget also, neither firm will increase its market share; and neither will increase its sales or its revenue much. Both will experience high advertising costs, so both will make some profit, but not nearly as much as would be the case for the firm that chooses the high budget when the other chooses the low budget.

The complete picture is illustrated in Figure 16.7, which shows the advertiser's dilemma. Pepsi's choices are shown along the top of the table and Coke's along the side of the table. The profits of Pepsi and Coke for each combination of

FIGURE 16.7
An Advertiser's Dilemma

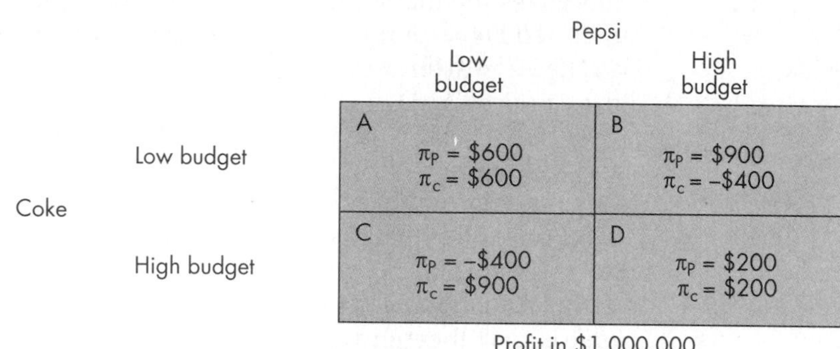

advertising choices (in millions of dollars) are shown, respectively, as π_p and π_c in each cell. In cell A, when both companies choose a low budget, each earns a profit of $600 million. In cells B and C, the firm with the high budget increases its profit to $900 million while the firm with the low budget makes a loss of $400. If both choose a large budget and end up in cell D, each will earn a $200 million profit, which is much lower than would be the case if both choose a low budget.

Clearly, the two firms would like to get together and agree to limit their advertising budgets and earn a substantial profit, if only they could trust each other. But such agreements are illegal and extremely hard to enforce (more on this later). If each follows a minimax strategy and minimizes the worst thing that can happen, both firms will advertise heavily and end up in cell D, earning a $200 million profit. High advertising is the minimax strategy for each firm, because the worst that could occur is for the rival to choose high advertising, and each earns $200 million. But, if the rival chooses low advertising, the firm with high advertising earns $900 million. Using a low advertising strategy can result in a $400 million loss, if the rival chooses high advertising, and is therefore not a minimax strategy, even though there is a possibility of a $600 million profit.

Each firm makes a choice and ends up in cell D, with lower profits than could be earned if both choose low budgets. From each seller's perspective, there is too much advertising. But once the choice of a high advertising budget is made, it is extremely difficult to get out of cell D. It is quite unlikely that the firms will move into cell A, unless they make an (illegal) explicit agreement to do so. Each firm knows that if it acts alone and reduces its advertising, the other firm would probably not reduce its advertising because its profit would rise substantially, while the firm that decreases its advertising would suffer a large loss. The uncertainty about a rival's behavior, inherent in an oligopoly market, can easily result in lower profits than might otherwise be earned for *both* firms.

A Pricing Dilemma

Firms may find themselves in dilemmas, not only with advertising or other nonprice competition, but also with price competition. To illustrate a pricing dilemma, consider the following example.

FIGURE 16.8
A Pricing Dilemma

		Diana's price: High ($10)	Diana's price: Low ($6)
Charles's price	High ($10)	A π_D = $1,000 π_C = $1,000	B π_D = $1,500 π_C = 0
	Low ($6)	C π_D = 0 π_C = $1,500	D π_D = $300 π_C = $300

Diana's Pizza Palace and Charles's Pizza Castle are located practically side by side across the street from a major university. Since the products of the Palace and the Castle are practically identical, their primary means of competition is pricing. For illustrative purposes, suppose each restaurant can choose between only two prices for its pizza: a high price of $10 and a low price of $6. Clearly the profit for each firm at each of the prices depends greatly on the price charged by the other firm.

Figure 16.8 illustrates the familiar dilemma in which Charles and Diana find themselves. Clearly, if both charge $10, each will do quite well, making $1,000 a week profit, as shown in cell A. If both lower their price to $6, sales will increase some, each will probably maintain its market share, and because of the lower price, the profit of each will fall to $300 a week, as shown in cell D. However, if either firm lowers its price to $6 while the other maintains its price at $10, the firm with the lower price will capture most of the other's business. The firm with the lower price will enjoy a $1,500 profit ($\pi_D$ in cell B or π_C in cell C), while the profits of the other fall to zero (π_C in cell B or π_D in cell C).

The minimax strategy for both Diana and Charles is to choose the price that minimizes the worst thing that can happen. For example, if Diana sets a high price, the worst that could happen to her is for Charles to set a low price, causing her profits to fall to zero. The worst thing that could happen if Diana sets a low price is for Charles to set a low price also, and her profits are $300 a week.

The Palace and Castle will quite likely end up in cell D, taking part in what their customers might call a "price war." Of course, the best solution is for the Castle and the Palace to merge or to reach an agreement under which both charge $10. The US Department of Justice probably would not actually prosecute two local pizza establishments for violation of antitrust laws if the firms cooperate and set price jointly. There may, however, be problems if one firm breaks or cheats on the agreement (a problem we will discuss later). More likely, if both set the high price, someone else will enter the market, charge a price lower than $10, and cause one or both to go out of business.

We have illustrated oligopolists' dilemmas for price and advertising. While these are the most familiar examples, dilemmas can arise in other forms of competition among oligopolies. Firms can introduce too many new models, or put too many features on their products. In all such cases, firms would be better off if they cooperated and agreed to compete less even though such agreements are generally illegal and hard to maintain. In the absence of such an agreement, firms will likely use a minimax strategy and carry on too much competition for their own good, thus ending up in a situation like cell D in the examples we discussed.

Reaction Functions

Thus far in this section we have assumed for simplicity that firms face only two alternatives and make a one-time decision, unaware of what a rival's decision will be. Once the decision is made, neither firm has an incentive to change if the other does not change. In the previous examples, cell D was the equilibrium situation. In practice, however, firms sometimes arrive at an equilibrium situation, which may or may not be optimal from the firms' point of view, by making a *series* of adjustments or changes in response to changes made by the rival firm. Economists have developed a tool, called **reaction functions**, to analyze and explain these adjustment paths.

reaction functions Functions or curves that indicate the best (usually profit maximizing) response to any changes made by a rival.

To illustrate the concept of reaction functions, we use an example of two oligopolists (generally called duopolists), which compete with each other through advertising, although we could have chosen an example of pricing, output, or other nonprice competition. Figure 16.9 illustrates the process of adjustment.

Suppose there are two oligopolists, firms A and B. These firms produce similar, but not identical, products and are the only firms in the relevant market. They charge approximately the same price and compete only by advertising. The more ads each runs in a month the higher its sales, other things equal. The number of ads purchased per month by B is plotted along the horizontal axis and the number of ads purchased per month by A along the vertical axis.

In the figure, B's reaction function for the amount of ads run by A is shown as R_B. B's reaction function shows the number of ads for B that would maximize B's profit, for each level of advertising chosen by A. For example, if A runs 30 ads per month (shown on the vertical axis), in order to maximize B's profit, B should run 45 ads, shown as point 3 on R_B. Or if A runs 15 ads, B would run 30 ads, at point 1 on R_B.

The reaction function for A is R_A; it shows the level of advertising by A that maximizes A's profit for each possible level of B's advertising. For example, if B runs 45 ads, A should run 37 ads, at point 4. Both reaction functions are upward sloping, indicating that the more ads used by one firm, the more ads the other should run in order to maximize its own profit.

We begin at the origin with neither firm advertising. Clearly, the optimal move for either firm is to run 15 ads if the other runs no ads. Arbitrarily, suppose A leads off and uses 15 ads. B sees this and counters by running 30 ads, point 1 on B's reaction curve. Now, 15 ads are no longer optimal for A, who then increases the number of ads to 30 (point 2 on R_A). Then B counters with 45 ads (at point 3), after which A increases to 37 ads (point 4).

You have the picture by now and should realize why these curves are called reaction functions. Firms B and A continue to react to one another's changes

FIGURE 16.9
Advertising Reaction Functions

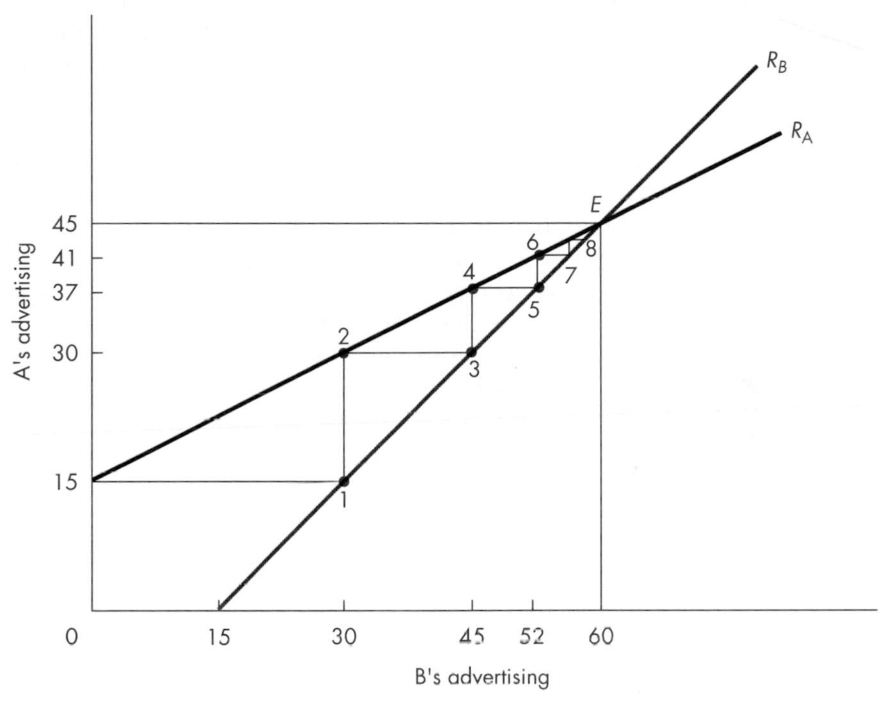

moving from 4 to 5 to 6 and so on until point E is reached. Firm B uses 60 ads and firm A uses 45 ads. This combination of advertising is an equilibrium because neither firm has an incentive to change the number of ads. From B's reaction function, 60 ads are optimal when A uses 45 ads. From A's reaction function, 45 ads are optimal when B uses 60 ads. The firms will continue with the same levels of advertising until some exogenous change occurs and shifts one or both reaction functions.

We must emphasize that point E in the figure is the point of equilibrium only because neither firm has any incentive to change if the other firm does not change. Point E is not necessarily the combination of advertising that maximizes the total or joint profit of the two firms.[2] Joint profit maximization may very well occur when each firm uses considerably less advertising. Actually, point E in Figure 16.9 may well be similar to cell D in the diagram showing the advertiser's dilemma. Neither firm is making as much profit as would be possible if both firms cooperated and moved back to a position similar to cell A in the advertiser's dilemma diagram.

[2]This type of equilibrium is often referred to as a Nash equilibrium, named after the game-theorist, John F. Nash. In Nash equilibrium, no firm can increase its profit given the current strategic choices of all other firms.

Although the final equilibrium using reaction functions may be similar to the final equilibrium in the advertiser's dilemma when both firms use a minimax strategy, we wanted to show that the theory need not be based solely on the assumption that each firm makes one once-and-for-all move simultaneously with the other firm.

As we mentioned at the beginning of this section, the discussion here is designed only to give you a feel for the theories of oligopoly strategic interactions. You have seen that under relatively realistic conditions it is possible for oligopolists to reach an equilibrium price below what may be optimal for the oligopolists, though not for consumers. In fact, when the products are similar, oligopolists may be so competitive that price falls almost to the perfectly competitive level, which is great for consumers but not so great for oligopolists.

You have also seen how oligopolists may end up choosing levels of advertising, or possibly quality or product design, that are not optimal from the oligopolists' point of view. Whether these levels are good or bad for consumers is debatable and depends on how much consumers value the advertising, quality, or product design. Finally, you have seen how oligopolists react to one another's moves and possibly, although not inevitably, reach an equilibrium.

As we end this section, we want once more to emphasize that economists do not have a general theory to explain oligopoly behavior. There are many theories of behavior, based on how firms attempt to solve the problem of mutual interdependence. Theories of strategic interaction make up one of the most promising branches of oligopoly theory.

16.5 STRATEGIC ENTRY DETERRENCE

Earlier in this chapter, we mentioned that a characteristic common to oligopoly markets is moderate to high barriers to the entry of new firms into the market. The barriers discussed are quite similar to the barriers that exist in monopoly markets: economies of scale over a wide range of output, ownership of important raw materials in the production process, governmentally erected barriers, such as patents or franchises, and consumers' brand loyalty to the products of established firms. With the exception of consumers' brand loyalty, these barriers are essentially technical in nature or, to some extent, beyond the control of the established firms. For example, economies of scale over a broad range of output exist because of properties of the production function.

In this section, we will discuss some barriers to the entry of new firms that are basically the result of the strategic behavior of existing firms. Such behavior is called **strategic entry deterrence**. The barriers to be discussed here are equally appropriate to both oligopoly or monopoly. We discuss these barriers here because strategic behavior is more characteristic of oligopoly than monopoly.

strategic entry deterrence Barriers to the entry of new firms into the market resulting from the strategic behavior of established firms.

The types of strategic behavior described in this section involve pricing policies, building excess capacity, and producing multiple products, all of which are designed to discourage the entry of new firms. The theories to explain such entry-limiting practices have been developed rather recently in both economic and business analysis.

Entry Limit Pricing

Under certain circumstances an oligopolist, or possibly a monopolist, may charge a price lower than the short-run profit-maximizing price in order to prevent or discourage new firms from entering the market. Such a strategy is called **entry limit pricing**. In order to practice entry limit pricing, an established firm must have a cost advantage over potential entrants into the market.

entry limit pricing
A price set lower than the short-run profit-maximizing price in order to prevent or discourage the entry of new firms into the market.

An example of a situation in which an established firm might lower its price below the profit-maximizing level is illustrated in Figure 16.10. Panel B shows the demand and marginal revenue curves for an established firm, along with the firm's long-run average and marginal cost curves, LAC_0 and LMC_0. To maximize profit, this firm would produce 60,000 units of output, where marginal revenue equals marginal cost, and set a price of $70, from the demand curve. The firm's profit would be $1,200,000 [= ($70 – $50) × 60,000].

The long-run average cost curve for a potential entrant into the market is shown as LAC_E in Panel A. If the established firm charges a price of $70, this firm could enter the market, perhaps at a price a little lower than $70, and make a profit. LAC_0 is lower than $70 over a broad range of output.

Note, however, that the long-run average cost curve of the potential entrant is higher than the long-run average cost curve of the established firm; LAC_E

FIGURE 16.10
Entry Limit Pricing

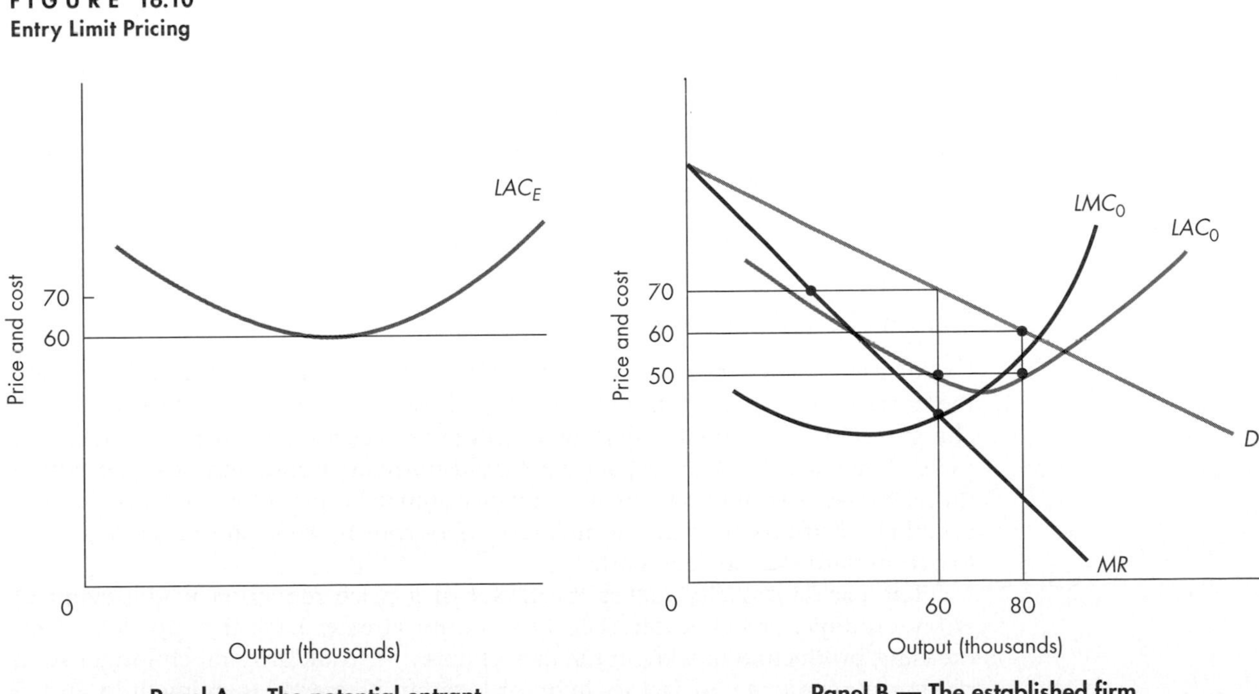

reaches a minimum at slightly more than \$60, while LAC_0 reaches its minimum at approximately \$45. Thus the established firm could charge a price slightly below the minimum long-run average cost of the potential entrant (\$60) but above its own long-run average cost and prevent the entry of the new firm, while continuing to make an economic profit.

Suppose, for example, that the established firm sets a price of \$60, and, from its demand, sells 80,000 units of output. The potential entrant could not cover its average cost at any level of output when the price is \$60. It would, therefore, be discouraged from entering the market, because if it did, it would make a loss. At a \$60 price, the established firm would sell 80,000 units of output and make less than the maximum profit of \$1,200,000. But, the firm would still make an economic profit of \$800,000 [= (\$60 – \$50) × 80,000].

This lower profit would, however, be higher than would be the case if the new firm had entered the market and taken away some of the sales of the established firm. Therefore, the firm is willing to sacrifice some immediate profit to prevent the entry of the new firm in order to earn a stream of lower, but protected, profits over a longer period of time. Of course, if the threat of entry is not great, the firm may not wish to sacrifice the stream of higher current profits. If entry is relatively easy, the firm may well be satisfied with lower profit. (We will consider in greater detail the decision to practice entry limit pricing later in the text when we develop techniques for dynamic analysis.)

We should note that the ability to practice entry limit pricing depends on the established firm having a cost advantage over potential entrants. If the established firm does not have a long-run average cost curve below that of the other firm, it could not lower its price below the minimum average cost of the potential entrant and continue to make an economic profit. Because the established firm shown in Figure 16.10 has a cost advantage, it can effectively block the entry of the other firm. Even though entry limit pricing is a form of strategic behavior, the feasibility of such behavior depends on technical conditions as well. Without a cost advantage, entry limit pricing is not feasible, and the firm would have to search for another way to impede entry—if that is possible.

Capacity Barriers to Entry

Under certain circumstances, it is possible for an established firm to discourage the entry of new firms into the market without actually decreasing the price it charges and consequently finding its profits reduced. The firm can maintain excess capacity, above the capacity it would normally build, and pose a credible threat to new entrants. The excess capacity signals to potential entrants that the established firm is prepared to increase its output by reducing its price if new firms prepare to enter the market.

The excess capacity makes the threat of a price reduction in the event of entry credible, or believable. The firm would already have the capacity of increasing production quickly in the face of entry. It would take much longer for a new firm to build a new factory in order to enter the market than it would for the established firm to gear up idle capacity. By the time the new entrant is ready for business, output in the market would be higher and price lower from the increased production. Thus new entrants would be discouraged. This is the nature of a **capacity barrier to entry**.

capacity barrier to entry
Holding excess capacity as a threat to potential entrants that the established firm is prepared to increase output and lower price if entry occurs.

Certainly holding idle capacity would add to a firm's costs, thereby reducing profits somewhat. However, compared to a pricing strategy that blocks entry, carrying idle capacity may be a less expensive (more profitable) way for a firm to hold its market share in the face of potential entry. The choice would depend on the expected relative stream of profit from excess capacity compared to the stream from entry limit pricing. If demand is not particularly elastic, a small increase in output would cause price to fall a great deal. In this case the required amount of idle capacity would be small, and excess capacity may be a less costly way to block entry. (We will discuss the dynamic aspects of this entry-blocking decision later in the text.)

Multiproduct Cost Barriers

The existence of economies of scope, discussed in Chapter 11, may enable a firm to make the entry of new competitors into the market more difficult. Recall that **economies of scope** mean that producing two goods together is less costly (either in terms of total cost or per unit cost) than producing the two goods separately. And it follows that producing three goods together is less costly than producing any other combinations of the goods. Therefore, if a firm produces two or more related goods together, it would have a cost advantage over any firm that produced the goods in another combination.

economies of scope
Exist when the cost of producing two or more goods together is less costly than producing the same goods separately.

To show how economies of scope can act as an entry deterrent, we use the following simplified example. Suppose there are three related goods, X, Y, and Z, each of which has constant average costs of production of \$20:

$$c(X) = c(Y) = c(Z) = \$20$$

where $c(X)$, $c(Y)$, and $c(Z)$ denote *average* costs of production.[3] Thus, the price of each good would have to exceed \$20 in order to cover costs when the goods are produced separately.

Now suppose that if any two of the goods are produced together, the average cost of the *pair* of goods is \$34:

$$c(X,Y) = c(X,Z) = c(Y,Z) = \$34$$

In this case, a firm producing any pair of the goods must charge a price for each good that (on average) exceeds \$17 (= \$34/2) in order to cover costs. Note that we are not saying the *profit-maximizing* price for each good in a pair should be the same (\$17). Obviously demand conditions must also be considered. We simply want to point out that unless the *average* price of the two goods is at least \$17, then costs will not be covered by revenue. Since a firm producing a pair of goods

[3]The assumption that all three goods have exactly the same average cost is made solely to simplify the discussion. The per unit costs almost certainly would differ in a real-world situation, but the analysis would be the same. Similarly, the assumption that average costs are constant for all output levels is for the purpose of simplification and does not affect the analysis.

has a lower per unit cost for each good than if either good were produced separately, economies of scope exist.

Further suppose a firm that produces all three goods together has an average cost for the *triplet* of goods of $48:

$$c(X,Y,Z) = \$48$$

This firm could sell the three goods at slightly under $17 each (on average) and undersell any firms that are producing the three goods either separately or in pairs. If the price is just under $17, the firm producing the three goods together would receive a revenue of just under $51, which would more than cover its costs.

Certainly, the firm in the above example would not necessarily block the entry of new firms, nor would any established firm producing multiple products under economies of scope. A new firm could enter the markets with the same cost structure if it also produced all three products together. However, it is generally more costly to enter all three markets and produce all three products than it is to enter one or even two markets. For one thing, the initial capital cost would probably be considerably higher. It is harder for new firms to raise investment capital. Consequently, the large capital investment required would tend to discourage some new firms from entering all three markets.

New Product Development as a Barrier to Entry

Sometimes established firms can block or at least discourage entry by producing substitutes for its own products in the market. Such a strategy is greatly preferred to seeing other firms introduce the new products.

Producing several related products crowds the market with choices. The wider the range of choices, the more substitutes there are for a given product. As you know, the more substitutes there are, the more elastic is the demand for any given product in the market. This makes it more difficult for a new firm to find its own niche in the market, because the demand for its own product would be lower. Its price and sales would be lower than would be the case if the established firm or firms had not introduced so many substitutes. It therefore is less likely under these conditions that new firms could cover their costs. In this way entry is discouraged.

There are many examples of oligopolists in consumer markets producing and selling a broad range of substitute products. Of course, we cannot say what their purpose in producing so many products actually is. Firms don't typically brag that they are trying to prevent new competition.

Nevertheless, the three largest breakfast cereal producers, General Mills, Kellogg, and Post, each produce a broad range of cereals. Some are aimed at children, some are aimed at adults, some are aimed at the health conscious, and so on. Coca-Cola sells regular Coke, Classic Coke, Diet Coke, Caffeine Free Coke, and Cherry Coke. Pepsi has its own broad range of beverages. The major beer producers, primarily Budweiser and Miller, sell regular beer, light beer, dry beer, and sometimes nonalcoholic beer. Automobile manufacturers sell a large array of cars under the same brand name. These different models can vary widely in price and are designed to appeal to different segments of the market. We are sure that you can think of other producers that sell a range of substitutes for their own products.

We have touched upon some of the more important ways that established firms can discourage the entry of new firms into the market. Such strategic entry deterrence is limited only by the ingenuity of the managers. Quite possibly the most effective way a new firm can discourage entry, and the most beneficial for consumers, is to continue producing an excellent product that people like, and carry out research and development that reduce costs, which enable the firm to lower price over a time. A good product at a low price may very well be the best way to discourage entry.

16.6 COOPERATIVE OLIGOPOLY BEHAVIOR

Thus far we have discussed oligopoly behavior under the assumption that rival firms do not cooperate or collude. We have described some of the many ways that oligopolies can compete—price, advertising, product quality, and so on. While firms compete in a myriad of ways, they generally don't like it, because of the uncertainty involved with mutual interdependence. You saw in the pricing and advertising dilemmas that noncooperating firms, under reasonable behavioral assumptions, can end up setting prices too low or doing too much advertising from their point of view, and ending up in a situation shown in cell D, making lower profit than would be possible if they cooperated and moved to cell A. Typically, if oligopolists cooperate, they can be better off than if they don't. In this section we will describe how oligopolists can cooperate to improve their profit situation, but we will also point out some problems that can arise when firms cooperate.

price fixing
When firms collude by explicitly agreeing upon the prices they will charge for their products. Price fixing is illegal in the United States.

Firms do, at times, cooperate and reach agreements to raise price and reduce output or to limit competition in other areas, even though explicit **price fixing** and other collusive behavior is illegal in the United States. Yet antitrust litigation still flourishes, indicating that such behavior is still thought to continue. In some other countries collusion is legal and, in some cases, even encouraged by government.

You have seen the effect of a price increase by an oligopolist when its rivals did not change their prices. The firm lost a great deal of its sales. But suppose all the other firms increase their prices by approximately the same amount. With the prices of rivals set higher, the demand of an individual firm would be much less elastic. Thus, if a firm could somehow convince its rivals to follow, it could increase its price without a substantial reduction in sales. Since total cost always falls when output falls, the firm could, it hopes, increase its profit.

Thus it may be possible for all firms to make themselves better off by cooperative agreements, even though these agreements may be illegal. Such cooperative arrangements are called collusive agreements. The most extreme form of collusion is a cartel.

Cartel Profit Maximization

A cartel is a group of firms with the objective of limiting competitive forces within a market. It may take the form of open collusion, with the member firms entering into contracts about price and other market variables. Or, the cartel may involve secret collusion among members with no explicit contract. One of the most famous cartels is OPEC (Organization of Petroleum Exporting Countries), an association of major oil-producing nations.

We first consider an *ideal* cartel. Suppose a group of firms producing a homogeneous commodity forms a cartel. A central management body is appointed, its function being to determine the uniform cartel price. The task, in theory, is relatively simple, as illustrated in Figure 16.11. Market demand for the homogeneous commodity is given by D, so marginal revenue is given by the dashed line MR. The marginal cost curve for the cartel must be determined by the management body. If all firms in the cartel purchase their inputs in perfectly competitive markets, the cartel marginal cost curve (MC_c) is simply the horizontal sum of the marginal cost curves of the member firms. Otherwise, allowance must be made for the increase in input price accompanying an increase in input usage; MC_c will be steeper than would be the case if all input markets were perfectly competitive. (Recall the discussion of short-run supply in Chapter 13.)

FIGURE 16.11
Cartel Profit Maximization

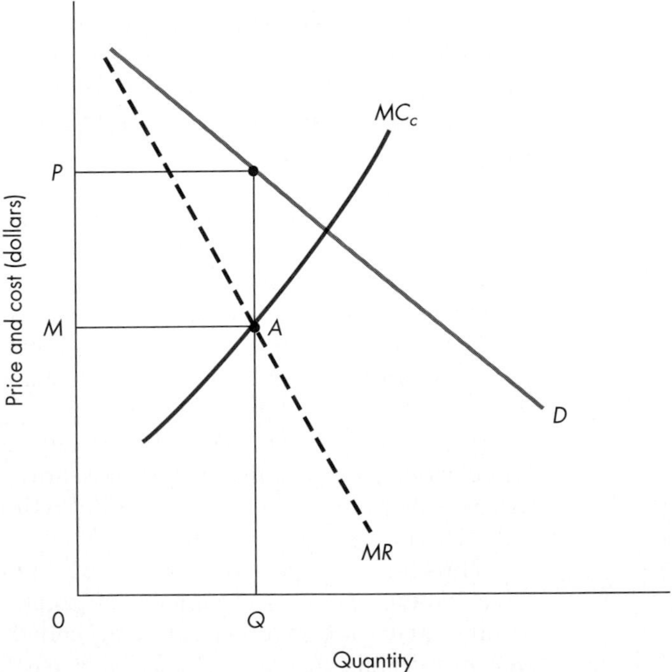

In either case, once the management group determines the cartel marginal cost curve (MC_c), the problem is the simple one of determining the price that maximizes cartel profit—the monopoly price. In Figure 16.11 marginal cost and marginal revenue intersect at A. This gives the level of output, Q, and the price, P, that maximizes total profit for the cartel.

Once the profit-maximizing price and output are determined, the problem confronting cartel management is how to allocate the output among the member firms. Two fundamental methods of allocation are possible: market sharing (or quotas) and nonprice competition.

There are several possible variants of market sharing or quotas. Indeed there is no uniform principle by which quotas can be determined. In practice, the bargaining ability of a firm and the importance of the firm to the cartel are likely to be extremely important elements in determining a quota. However, one method of allocating the market is to use either the relative sales of each firm in some pre-cartel period or the productive capacity of the firm as a basis for allocating shares of the cartel sales. As a practical matter, the choice of which pre-cartel period or what measure of capacity to use is a matter of bargaining among the members. The most skillful bargainer is likely to come out best.

While market sharing or quota agreements may be difficult in practice, we can set forth some guidelines. If the cartel produces a homogeneous product, a reasonable objective for the cartel is to produce the optimal output at the minimum total cost. In this way, total cartel profit is maximized.

Minimum cartel cost is achieved when each firm produces that output for which its marginal cost equals the common cartel marginal cost and marginal revenue. Returning to Figure 16.11 each firm would produce the amount at which its marginal cost is equal to M. Summing to obtain MC_c, total cartel output will be Q, and total profit is maximized.

To reinforce this conclusion, suppose that two firms in the cartel are producing at different marginal costs, that is, assume

$$MC_1 > MC_2$$

for firms 1 and 2. In this case the cartel manager could transfer sales from the higher-cost firm 1 to the lower-cost firm 2. So long as the marginal cost of producing in firm 2 is lower, total cartel cost can be lowered by transferring production. For example, suppose MC_1 equals \$20 and MC_2 equals \$10. One unit of output taken away from firm 1 lowers the cartel's cost \$20. Producing that unit in firm 2 increases cartel cost by \$10. Thus the total cost of production falls \$10. And the cartel would continue taking output away from firm 1 and increasing the output of firm 2, thus lowering total cost, until $MC_1 = MC_2$. This equality would result because MC_1 would fall as the output of firm 1 decreases, and MC_2 would increase as the output of firm 2 increases. Thus in equilibrium the marginal costs will be equal for all firms in the cartel.[4]

[4]This point is demonstrated mathematically in the appendix to this chapter.

Principle In order to produce the profit-maximizing output at the minimum total cost, a cartel should allocate production among its various producers so that the marginal costs of all producers are equal. In profit-maximizing equilibrium, marginal revenue equals the common marginal cost.

The difficulty involved with this method of allocation is that, if firms differ in their cost structures, the lower-cost firms obtain the bulk of the market and therefore the bulk of the profits. To make this method of allocation acceptable to all members, a profit sharing system, more or less independent of the sales quota, must be devised.

In some cases, it will be easy for the member firms to agree upon the share of the market each is to have. This is illustrated in Figure 16.12 for an ideal situation. Suppose only two firms are in the market and they decide to divide the market evenly. The market demand curve is D, so the half-share curve for each firm is d, which lies halfway between D and the vertical axis. The marginal revenue curve for d is the line MR, the half-share marginal revenue for each firm. Suppose each firm has identical costs, represented by ATC and MC.

With these individual marginal revenue, marginal cost, and demand curves, each firm will decide to produce Q units of output, where MR and MC intersect. A uniform price of P is established on each firm's demand. At P a total output of

FIGURE 16.12
Ideal Market Sharing

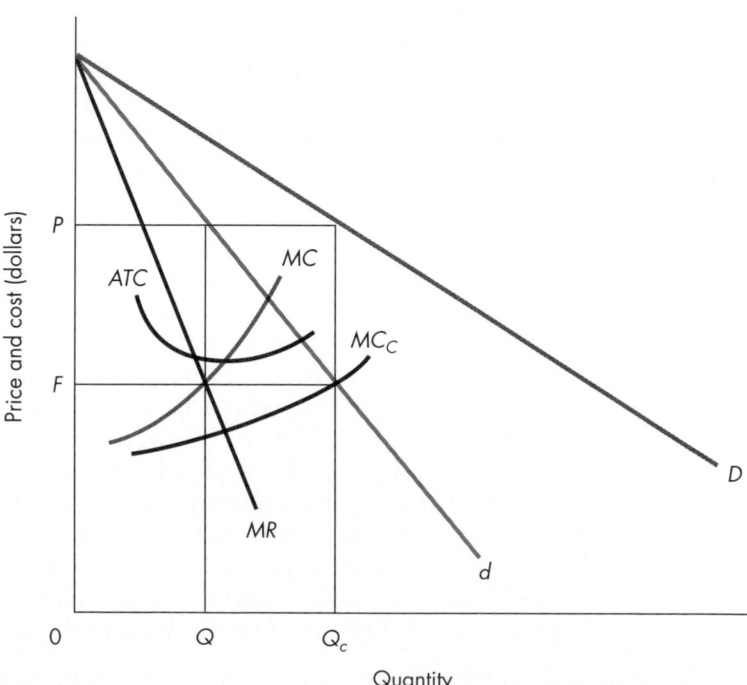

Q_C is supplied (Q_C is twice Q, the output of each firm). This is a tenable solution because the market demand is consistent with the sale of Q_C units at a price of P.

To see this, let's approach the problem in another way. Suppose a cartel management group is formed and given the task of maximizing cartel profit. With the demand curve D, the cartel management views d as the marginal revenue curve; d lies halfway between market demand, D, and the vertical axis. Next, summing the identical marginal cost curves, the manager obtains cartel marginal cost MC_C. The intersection of cartel marginal cost and cartel marginal revenue occurs at the level F, corresponding to output Q_C and price P. Since this is the same solution arrived at by the identical firms, the firms' decision to share the market equally is consistent with the objective of the cartel.

In this example we have assumed firms with identical cost functions. The solution is more complex when cost conditions differ, as noted above. Nonetheless, cartel profit is maximized when total cartel output is chosen so that market marginal revenue equals the horizontal sum of all firms' marginal costs—the cartel's marginal cost curve. Price is determined from the market demand curve at the chosen output. Output is allocated to the firms so that each firm's marginal cost equals market marginal revenue (which is also equal to the cartel's marginal cost) at the chosen level of output.

Ideal situations such as the one described above are rare. More likely, cost conditions will differ among firms. Yet another problem arises when firms produce a differentiated product. In such cases a cartel frequently allocates sales through nonprice competition. This type of allocation is generally associated with loose cartels.

In such cases, a uniform price is fixed and each firm is allowed to sell all it can at that price. The only requirement is that firms do not reduce price below the cartel price. There are many examples of this type of cartel organization in the United States today. For instance, in many localities both medical doctors and lawyers have associations whose code of ethics is frequently the basis of price agreement. The patient market, for example, is divided among the various doctors on the basis of nonprice competition: each patient selects the doctor of his or her choice. Similarly, the generally uniform prices of haircuts, major brands of gasoline, and movie tickets do not result from perfect competition within the market. Rather, they result from tacit, and sometimes open, agreement upon a price. The sellers compete with one another in various ways, but not by price variations. This type of cartel arrangement is rather common in the sale of services. We will discuss tacit (or silent) collusion after pointing out the major problem facing all cartels, both formal and informal. This is the problem of cheating.

The Problem of Cheating

Unless backed by strong enforcement mechanisms, cartel agreements are quite likely to collapse from internal pressure. That is, cartel members, particularly in times of weakened demand, have a strong incentive to cheat on the agreement in an effort to increase profits. A few large, geographically concentrated firms producing a relatively homogeneous commodity may form a successful cartel and maintain it, at least during prosperous times. But the greater the number of firms in the cartel, the more the products are differentiated, and the greater the geographical dispersion of the firms, the greater is the incentive to cheat on the cartel agreement. When profits are low or even negative, firms have a increased incentive to increase output and reduce price.

A typical cartel is characterized by a high (perhaps monopoly) price, a relatively low output, and a sales distribution that cause most firms to produce an output less than that associated with minimum long-run average cost. In this situation, any one firm, acting alone, can profit tremendously from secret price concessions leading to increased sales. As we will demonstrate, this incentive to cheat on the agreement typically causes the cartel to break up.

The incentive of a cartel member to cheat can be explained using the previously developed theory of sticky prices. Figure 16.13 shows the potential gain for a single member of the cartel. Assume the price is fixed at P_0; this particular cartel member sells Q_0, but output may vary among members.

The firm knows that if it reduces price slightly, say to P_1, and other cartel members do not detect the reduced price, it can increase its own sales tremendously. In this case, the firm believes that an unmatched price reduction to P_1 would increase sales to Q_2, resulting in a substantial increase in profit. Thus the firm believes that the segment of its demand for an *undetected* price reduction is *Ad*.

This demand segment is quite elastic, because the firm knows that an unmatched price reduction would allow it to gain sales from the other, obedient members of the cartel. This situation is most likely when the number of members in the cartel is large and the product is differentiated.

But the price reduction is unlikely to go unmatched for very long. In the first place, even in a cartel with a large number of firms, other members are likely to notice their decreases in sales and find out that a rival has lowered price. A

FIGURE 16.13
The Incentive to Cheat

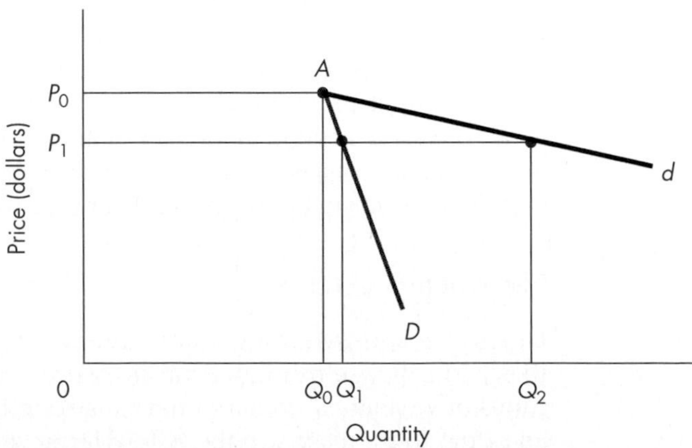

reasonable reaction would be to match the lower price. This would protect their market share and punish the cheater by reducing its sales. In most cartels that is the only means of enforcement. In the second place, if this firm has the incentive to reduce price and increase sales, so do all of the other firms in the cartel. And this incentive is reinforced because every firm knows that every other firm has the same incentive. So there is the strong temptation to be the first to reduce price and gain at least a temporary increase in sales and profits before the others begin to cheat.

If rivals match the price cut or if they all cheat on the agreement, the firm's demand is the inelastic segment *AD*. Customers would have no reason to change sellers if they all sell at the lower price, P_1. Thus the firm's gain in sales is small; output increases from Q_0 to Q_1 rather than to Q_2. This increase is due mainly to increased total market sales because of the lower price charged by everyone in the cartel.

The increase in sales from Q_1 to Q_2 represents sales that would have been attracted away from rivals. A huge increase in the output of one firm while others are losing sales at the cartel price is, however, a strong signal of cheating. Rivals will suspect that someone has lowered the price. So a potentially large increase in sales from an undetected price cut is the incentive for cheating, but, at the same time, it is the signal to others that someone is cheating.

For these reasons, even strong cartels are likely to break up, particularly during times when the economy is weak. All have the incentive to cheat on the agreement, and firms generally do.

Tacit Collusion

tacit collusion Cooperation among oligopoly firms that does not involve an explicit agreement.

A less extreme form of cooperation among oligopoly firms is **tacit collusion**—agreement without explicit communication. For instance, the producers in a market may restrict their sales to specific geographical regions without meeting and explicitly designating marketing areas on a map. One firm's market area is understood from the ongoing relations it has had with its rivals. As opposed to the formation of a cartel in an attempt to monopolize a market, tacit collusion is not per se (categorically) illegal. However, evidence of agreement would quickly tip the legal balance against accused participants.

Examples consistent with tacit collusion are evident among manufacturers of consumer durables. For instance, oligopolists will often act together (cooperatively) by changing their models annually at the same time. Washing machines, refrigerators, cooking ranges, and lawn mowers have annual model changes that are announced by manufacturers at nearly the same time. Without any known agreement, there is a surprising amount of uniformity in such behavior. The same holds true for fashions, that is, when spring and fall designs are announced. Why do makers of soft drinks and beer all use the same size cans and bottles (or makers of breakfast cereal package their product in the same size boxes)? Certainly, all consumers do not have a preference for the 12-ounce size. But, as far as anyone knows, cereal makers and bottlers have no explicit agreement that only certain container sizes are allowable.

ILLUSTRATION 16.3

When Is Price "Signaling" Really Price Fixing?

As we noted in the text, price fixing is illegal in the United States. Nevertheless, numerous cases of innovative methods of secretly fixing prices are discovered each year by the Justice Department. *The Wall Street Journal* reported in October 1990 that the Justice Department was conducting several investigations into possible price fixing by airlines.

At the heart of these investigations is the alleged practice by airlines of "signaling." Signals apparently take place in the thousands of fare changes that are submitted each day to the computer network that manages air fare information. An example of price signaling was provided by Steven B. Elkins, a senior director of marketing at Northwest Airlines, during courtroom testimony in the Justice Department's investigations into possible price fixing. According to Elkins, when Northwest lowered price on certain night flights out of Minneapolis, Continental responded by cutting fares in important Northwest markets. The Continental fares, however, were scheduled to expire one or two days after they were introduced.

Elkins interpreted Continental's extraordinarily brief fare reduction as "(telling) us that they weren't serious about wanting to sell those fares . . . We felt what they were doing was trying to send us a message that they didn't want us reducing night coach fares in these markets." Northwest apparently didn't feel like retracting its night-fare reductions in Minneapolis and signaled this to Continental by offering new cheap fares from Houston to California, *again using short expiration dates*. Houston is an essential market for Continental, and they got the message.

While some economists and antitrust attorneys view this type of back-and-forth exchange by airlines as a routine competitive business practice, critics believe signaling may, in fact, be just another innovative way of fixing prices. The most controversial aspect of price signaling is its use in disciplining airlines that cut fares. In an internal pricing memo at Northwest Airlines that surfaced in Elkin's testimony, Northwest clearly revealed that it wished to avoid price competition in the worst way:

> When you get right down to it pricing is really a very poor competitive weapon in our marketing arsenal. It suffers the same limitations as the atomic bomb. Its potential is so dangerous that none of us can permit our competitors to wield it unchallenged. Attempts to use price to improve market share will be countered immediately and rendered ineffective.

Price signaling, legal or not, is clearly a mechanism by which airlines attempt to coordinate pricing decisions in a way that will be less damaging to their oligopoly profits that outright price competition would be.

We now want to pass on to you some good advice, based on a more recent article in *The Wall Street Journal* (July 30, 1993) on airline signaling: Think twice before buying airline tickets on a weekend. According to the *WSJ*, "Many carriers these days test fare increases by raising prices on Friday nights, Saturdays, and Sundays, when few tickets are sold. If their competitors don't go along with the increases, the fares come down on Monday."

Airlines had previously signaled planned fare increases in computer reservation systems, then waited to see whether all other airlines followed. A single defector could scuttle an increase because the other airlines would not take the risk of losing customers to a rival that didn't increase prices. But a consent decree by the Justice Department prohibited carriers from signaling price actions. As the *Journal* reported, "The weekend fare rates are a way to accomplish the

Probably the strongest evidence consistent with tacit collusion is found in the prices oligopolists charge. Particularly in the service sector of the economy, there is surprising price uniformity, even though there is a wide variance in the quality of services. For instance, lawyers and real estate agents by and large charge the same prices for their services even though the quality of services

same purpose with limited risk: Even if competitors don't match the increase, the higher-priced carriers won't lose much business over a weekend and can back down on Monday morning."

The results: Airlines raised fares on one weekend, and these fares stuck. The following weekend saw full coach fares rise 5 percent; those fares also stuck. But the next weekend many carriers again raised advance-purchase prices 5 percent, but pulled back on Monday because some airlines didn't follow. Fliers who bought tickets on Saturday or Sunday paid 5 percent more than if they had bought the same tickets on the Friday before or the Monday after. In addition, many airlines increased the fee to reissue a ticket at a cheaper fare. A year before, cut-rate tickets had been refundable.

The *Journal* noted that weekend price increases could become routine, because airlines need to raise prices to improve their balance sheets. Full coach fares, used by businesses, were expected to rise. One airline executive said that the higher weekend fares were fairly widespread, but most denied any type of collusion. Other airlines blamed the "phantom" fares on the Justice Department. The weekend increases were simply the "industry's way of operating under the constraints of a consent decree."

So what is the moral? Well, when signaling practices used to avoid getting trapped in the "wrong" box of the prisoners dilemma are restricted, managers will find other methods of signaling.

In an interview in *Forbes* magazine, Barry Nalebuff, a professor of Organization and Management at Yale, pointed out another way airlines try to signal and reduce unwanted price competition. The interviewer at *Forbes* asked Professor Nalebuff, who teaches a managerial decision-making course that focuses to some extent on how to avoid the prisoner's dilemma, "I . . . understand my payoffs, but my competitors don't. They start a price war. What do I do now?" Professor Nalebuff suggested doing what TWA was trying to do—change the competitive playing field. TWA was ripping out seats in its planes to offer more leg room for passengers. Instead of competing only on price, TWA was offering quality as well. As Nalebuff pointed out, "If competitors decide to match TWA, all passengers will be more comfortable and the industry will have less capacity. Cutting the excess capacity will help restore price stability and improve the profits of all airlines. TWA is trying to change the game from zero-sum to 'positive-sum' competition—everyone benefits."

We rather doubt that this will work out very well, but Professor Nalebuff also offers other examples of signaling or (legal) methods of getting out of the "bad box." We aren't going to make any recommendations. We do suggest you might want to read the article (or take Nalebuff's course). But we believe that as long as interdependence, uncertainty, and restrictions against collusion exist, astute managers will develop ways to cooperate (legally or otherwise) rather than resort to intense price competition, or, for that matter, advertising or other types of competition. We also believe that, as long as these conditions exist, oligopolists will end up competing intensely and earning less profit than would be possible with cooperation. This may be good for consumers but is bad for the oligopolists. It is not because managers are stupid or ignorant about what they are doing. Far from it. We simply believe that the rules of the game and the constraints determine the way the game is played.

Sources: Asra Q Nomani, "Fare Warning: How Airlines Trade Price Plans," *The Wall Street Journal*, October 9, 1990. James Hirsch, "Fliers Discover They Don't' Fare Well on the Weekends," *The Wall Street Journal*, July 30, 1993. Rita Koselka, "Businessman's Dilemma," *Forbes*, October 11, 1993.

varies from lawyer to lawyer and broker to broker. Explicit collusion is illegal in these industries and presumably does not take place, but a substantial amount of price uniformity exists.

How does tacit collusion arise? What makes oligopolists cooperate without an explicit arrangement? The answer lies in the consequences of noncooperation.

As you know, each oligopolist realizes that what it does will cause its rivals to react. The expected reaction is likely to leave sellers no better off than they were before the move. Oligopolists know that they are related to rivals in what we referred to earlier as the prisoner's dilemma. A new style or a lower price may increase profits in the short run, but may reduce profits in the long run.

Thus, whether or not an oligopolist makes a change depends upon the relative expected costs and benefits of making the change. Profits may increase substantially at first as a result of a change, but decrease after rivals react. How quickly rivals react in large measure determines how profitable a change will be. Moreover, since each oligopolist knows that its rivals may have the same motivation to make a change, there is the temptation to move first.

In many cases *patterns of behavior* are established among rivals. Oligopolists cooperate because, given the expected reaction of rivals to one firm's attempt to raise profits, long-run profits are more likely maximized by stable behavior. This is particularly true because other behavior in the long run will raise the costs to producers, and revenues are not likely to go up after rivals have adjusted.

Price Leadership

price leadership
One firm in an oligopoly market sets a price that the other firms match.

Another cooperative solution to the oligopoly problem is **price leadership**. This solution does not require open collusion, but the firms in the market must tacitly agree to the solution. Price leadership has been quite common in certain industries. It was characteristic of the steel industry some time ago. At times it has characterized the tire, oil, and cigarette industries.

Any firm in an oligopoly market can be the price leader. While it is frequently the dominant firm in the market, it may be simply the firm with a reputation for good judgment. There could exist a situation in which the most efficient—the least cost—firm is the price leader, even though this firm is not the largest. In any case, the price leader sets a price that will maximize industry profits, and all firms in the industry compete for sales through advertising and other types of marketing. The price remains constant until the price leader changes the price, or one or more other firms break away.

Possibly the simplest form of price leadership is *barometric* price leadership. In this case the price leader is a firm with a reputation for good decision making. (In reality, most price leaders have been one of the larger firms.) The price leader acts as a barometer for prevailing market conditions and sets the price so as to maximize profits under these conditions. For example, if consumers' incomes increase (and the commodity in question is normal), the price leader would note an increase in demand and would respond by raising price. If all of the other firms in the industry follow with price increases, the result will be that the industry moves to a new position of equilibrium with a minimum of interfirm competition. It is important to note that, in this case, the price leader has no power to coerce the other firms into following its lead. Instead, the rival firms will follow this lead only so long as they believe that the price leader's behavior accurately and promptly reflects changes in market conditions.

A much more structured form of price leadership is *dominant firm* price leadership. In this case, there is one firm in the oligopoly market that has the capability of becoming a monopoly. Hence the market is composed of one dominant firm and numerous small ones.

The dominant firm could possibly eliminate all its rivals by a price war. But in addition to being costly, this would establish the firm as a monopoly, with its attendant legal problems. Possibly a more desirable course of action for the dominant firm is to become the price leader and set the market price so as to maximize its own profit, at the same time letting the small firms sell all they wish at that price. Note that, given the size of the dominant firm, in this type of price leadership the price leader—the dominant firm—does have the ability to enforce the price it sets. It does not have to rely on its reputation or the trust of the smaller firms. The small firms, recognizing their position, will behave as do perfectly competitive firms. That is, they will regard their demand curve as a horizontal line at the price set by the dominant firm and sell that amount for which marginal cost equals price. Notice, however, that this does not necessarily entail the long-run, zero-profit solution for the smaller firms, because the dominant firm may set price above the (minimum) average cost of some firms.

There are many variations of dominant firm price leadership. One may allow for the existence of two or more dominant firms, for product differentiation, for geographically separated sellers, for transportation costs, and so on. In all cases, however, the dominant firm is allowed to set price, since it controls such a large share of the market.

This completes our discussion of cooperative oligopoly behavior, although it by no means exhausts the topic. Methods of cooperation are diverse. Different types of cooperative behavior arise because of differences in products and markets, in the history of firms and industry, and in the personalities of managers.

Two fundamental themes are an integral part of all types of oligopoly cooperation. First, firms in an oligopoly market are strongly motivated to cooperate because of the problem of uncertainty about the reactions of rivals if firms do not cooperate. Competition of any type, as you have seen, lowers firms' profits. Second, once firms cooperate, there is a strong temptation for them to break the agreement. The cheating motive causes any type of agreement to become extremely fragile and likely to break down.

16.7 SUMMARY

We have covered a huge amount of territory in a small amount of space. First we briefly developed the theory of monopolistic competition. The key feature of monopolistic competition is that in the long run, the firm's economic profit is competed away, even though each firm has some market power. The firm's demand is downsloping because each firm sells a product that is somewhat differentiated from that of every other firm in the market. In the short run, a monopolistic competitor simply acts like a monopoly. In the long run, the entry of new firms causes each firm's demand to become tangent to the long-run average cost curve.

Oligopoly is much more complex. We have treated oligopoly rather briefly, but not because economists do not have a great deal to say about oligopoly. They have said a great deal, much more than is discussed in this chapter. Economists just have yet to develop a definitive theory of oligopoly. Mutual interdependence makes derivation of a general theory of oligopoly elusive at best and perhaps unattainable at worst.

As we have tried to demonstrate, the oligopoly market structure is perhaps more realistic than perfect competition or monopoly, but this increase in realism cannot be gained without a cost. The increased complexity of the firm's decisions in an oligopoly market effectively precludes straightforward solutions.

We have emphasized that the primary feature differentiating oligopoly from the other market structures is that the *firms recognize their mutual interdependence*. In contrast to the other market structures, it is not sufficient for a firm in an oligopoly market to make its output and pricing decisions on the basis of its own demand and cost conditions. In addition, an oligopolist must consider the potential reactions of its rivals. In this chapter we discussed some possible ways in which the oligopoly firms could resolve this difficulty. However, as you have seen, the determination of the profit-maximizing levels of output and price for a specific firm becomes extremely difficult. Furthermore, oligopolistic firms frequently compete with one another on a nonprice basis. Typically, the best solution for oligopolists is to collude with each other, but this is frequently impossible, illegal, or both.

The important point then is that, for the oligopoly market structure, economists are unable to provide a simple profit-maximization rule of the type presented in Chapters 13 and 15. In the oligopoly market, the answer to the question of the profit-maximizing levels of output and price is: "It depends." In the cases of perfect competition and monopoly we could show you the forest. In our discussion of the oligopoly market, the best we have been able to do is to bump into several of the trees.

TECHNICAL PROBLEMS

1. Describe the features of monopolistic competition:
   a. How is it similar to monopoly?
   b. How is it similar to perfect competition?
   c. What are the characteristics of short-run equilibrium?
   d. What are the characteristics of long-run equilibrium?
   e. How is long-run equilibrium attained?
2. The following graph shows the long-run average and marginal cost curves for a monopolistically competitive firm.

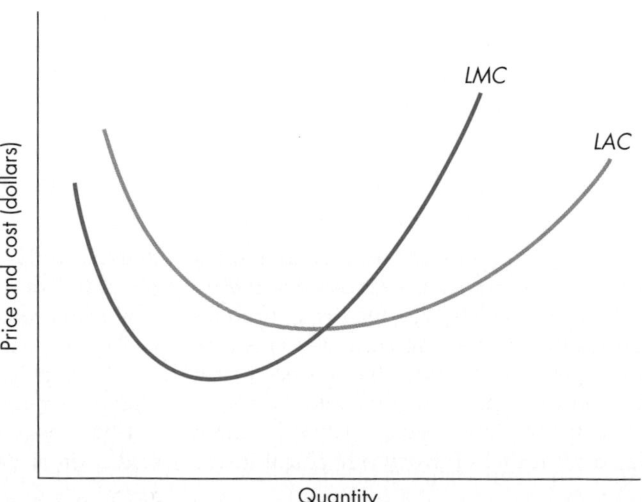

a. Assume the firm is in the short run and making profits. Draw in the demand and marginal revenue curves. Show output and price.
b. Now let the firm reach long-run equilibrium. Draw in precisely the new demand and marginal revenue curves. Show output and price.
c. Why must $MR = MC$ at *exactly* the same output at which LAC is tangent to demand?
d. Contrast this firm's output and price in long-run equilibrium with the price and output if this firm was a perfect competitor.

3. It has been argued that a higher price and lower output in the long run in monopolistic competition is the price society must pay for product diversity. Otherwise, people would have to consume the same products. Explain.
4. Monopolistic competitors may face intense, almost oligopolistic competition from a few firms in the market, while being practically independent from the actions of most other firms. Explain and give examples. Along this line, discuss conditions in which monopolistic competitors may face the same problems as those of oligopolists.
5. Even if the firms in a monopolistically competitive market collude successfully and fix price, economic profit will still be competed away if there is unrestricted entry. Explain. Will price be higher or lower under such an agreement in long-run equilibrium than would be the case if firms didn't collude? Explain.
6. Suppose that a monopolistically competitive industry is in long-run equilibrium. Then consumers' incomes increase (the firms are producing a normal good).
   a. In the short run, what will happen to:
      (1) The demand facing a typical firm.
      (2) The amount of output produced by a typical firm.
      (3) The amount of profit earned by a typical firm.
   b. What will happen in the long run?
7. Why would a monopolistic competitor advertise while a perfect competitor would not?
8. Compare and contrast oligopoly with perfect competition, pure monopoly, and monopolistic competition. What is the principal distinguishing characteristic of oligopolies?
9. Barriers to entry play a crucial role in the behavior of oligopoly firms.
   a. What are the important technical barriers to entry? Which of these involve some strategic behavior on the part of the firms? Explain.
   b. What are the important strategic barriers to entry? Which of these are, to some degree, technical in nature? Explain.
10. As you saw in Illustration 16.3, Northwest Airlines strongly opposed the use of price competition as a means of competing. Most oligopolists feel the same way about price competition.
    a. What types of nonprice competition might oligopolists use? Why would oligopolists be more likely to use nonprice competition than firms in other market structures?
    b. Are oligopolists that produce differentiated products more or less likely to engage in price competition than oligopolists that produce homogeneous products? Explain.
11. The graph on the following page shows segments of an oligopolist's demand. The firm charges a price of P and sells an output of Q. The firm's rivals are also charging a price of approximately P.

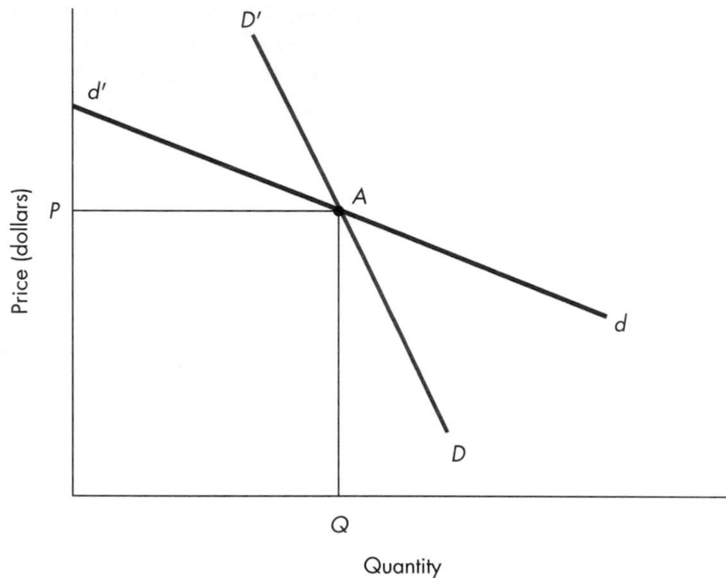

a. Explain the assumption underlying each of the demand segments, *d′A*, *D′A*, *Ad*, and *AD*.
b. What would be the relevant segments of the demand if the sticky price theory is relevant to this firm? Explain why.
c. Why would price be sticky at *P* if the sticky price theory is relevant here?
d. Are the demand segments shown here the only possible segments? Explain.

12. The diagram below shows the situation for two oligopolists, A and B, in an advertising dilemma. π_A and π_B are the relevant profits.

		Firm A	
		Low budget	High budget
Firm B	Low budget	1. π_A = \$100, π_B = \$100	2. π_A = \$180, π_B = −\$50
	High budget	3. π_A = −\$50, π_B = \$180a	4. π_A = \$30, π_B = \$30

a. Under what conditions would firms end up in cell 4?
b. If firms are in cell 4, does either firm have any incentive to move? Explain.
c. Why does cell 4 give lower profits than cell 1, when cells 2 and 3 yield the high advertiser more profits than are attainable in cell 1?
d. Under what conditions would firms end up in cell 1? Explain. Does either firm have an incentive to change if both are in cell 1?

e. If the firms are in cell 2 or 3, does either have an incentive to change? Explain. Where would the firms end up?

* 13. In the graph below, MC_1 and MC_2 are the marginal cost curves for two firms that have formed a cartel. D and MR represent market demand and marginal revenue, respectively, for the cartel, and MC_T is the cartel's marginal cost curve.

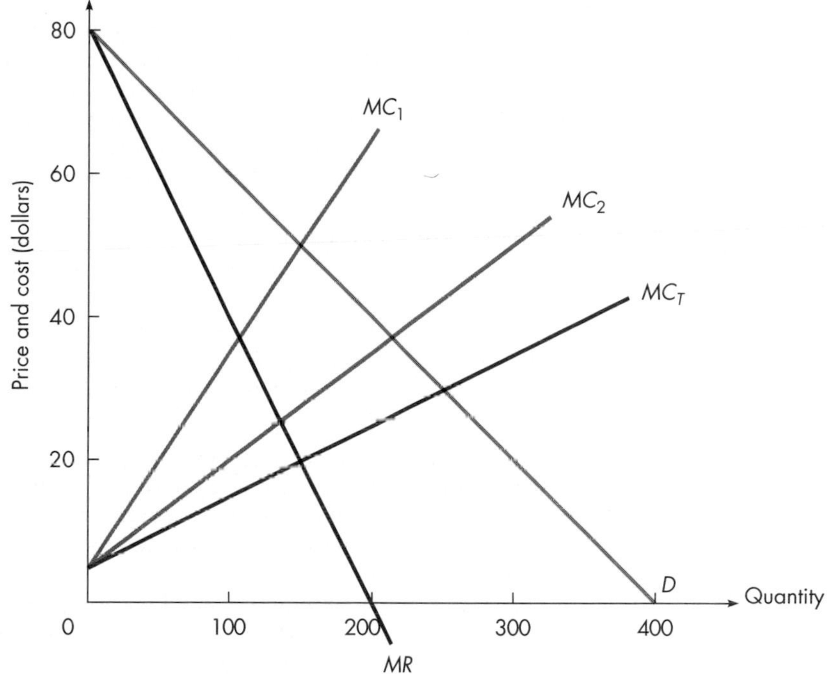

a. What is the profit-maximizing level of cartel output? How should it be allocated between the two firms? What price should the cartel set?

b. Suppose the firms are each producing and selling 75 units of output. What is marginal cost for each firm? Is this optimal? Why or why not? If not, what should the firms do instead?

c. Under what conditions might this cartel break up?

* 14. What is tacit collusion? How would the behavior of the firms differ from that of members of a cartel? Why would tacit collusion exist?

APPLIED PROBLEMS

1. "One sure test that an industry is competitive is the absence of any economic profit." Comment.

2. An industry said to be characterized by monopolistic competition is the apparel industry. Suppose you were hired as a consultant by a firm in this industry. How

would you advise the firm as to the levels of output, price, input usage, and levels of advertising? What problems might you encounter?

3. Some states have had laws restricting the sale of most goods on Sunday. Consumers, by and large, oppose such laws because they find Sunday afternoon a convenient time to shop. Paradoxically, retail trade associations frequently support the laws. Discuss the reasons for merchants supporting these laws. (You may find the prisoner's dilemma useful.)

4. MegaCorp is a large manufacturer of household robots used as mechanical servants for wealthy families. MegaCorp has considerable market power—it invented the household robot—but is facing some potential competition from some new firms. MegaCorp is considering entry limit pricing, increasing its capacity, or simply maximizing profits until the new firms enter.
   a. What factors should the firm consider when making its plans? In your answer, discuss the length of the time horizon, the time new firms would require to enter the market, any possible cost advantage MegaCorp may have, the financial backing the new firms might have, brand loyalty of consumers, and any other factors you think may be relevant.
   b. Suppose MegaCorp decides it doesn't have a sufficient cost advantage to practice entry limit pricing, so it decides on a strategy of building excess capacity. Under what conditions might some new firms enter the market? What do you think may happen under this circumstance?

5. The travel agents in a large city have long had a pricing agreement on the fees they charge. During a rather severe recession, residents of the city cut back on their travel and most travel agents were soon making losses. A medium-sized agency, Fly-By-Night, is trying to decide whether to cut its fees in order to turn its loss into a profit.
   a. What conditions would probably induce Fly-By-Night to cut its fees? Explain.
   b. What conditions would probably discourage Fly-By-Night from cutting its fees? Explain.

6. The Sweetbreath Company produces two rather successful mouthwashes: one is strong and has a medicinal taste and the other is more gentle and has a sweet taste. Sweetbreath is thinking about introducing an intermediate brand of mouthwash that tastes like ice cream. Discuss the pros and cons for Sweetbreath introducing a new product.

7. Suppose you were attempting to establish a price-fixing cartel in an industry.
   a. Would you prefer many or few firms? Why?
   b. How could you prevent cheating (price cutting) by cartel members? Why would members have an incentive to cheat?
   c. Would you keep substantial or very few records? What are the advantages and disadvantages of each?
   d. How could you prevent entry into the industry?
   e. How could government help you prevent entry and even cheating?

8. Many economists argue that more research, development, and innovation occur in the oligopolistic market structure than in any other. Why might this conclusion be true?

9. In light of the discussion about product quality as a form of nonprice competition, could you explain the common complaint that TV programs are all alike?

APPENDIX Profit Maximization for a Cartel

If a cartel is maximizing total profit, the marginal costs of all firms are equal.

Assume two firms in a cartel. Their outputs are Q_1 and Q_2; the respective cost functions are $C_1(Q_1)$ and $C_2(Q_2)$. The industry demand is $P = P(Q_1 + Q_2) = P(Q)$. Total industry profit is

$$\pi_T = P(Q_1 + Q_2) \times (Q_1 + Q_2) - C_1(Q_1) - C_2(Q_2)$$

Maximizing π with respect to the outputs of the two firms gives the first order conditions:

$$\frac{\partial \pi_T}{\partial Q_1} = \frac{\partial P}{\partial Q}(Q) + P - \frac{\partial C_1}{\partial Q_1} = MR_T - MC_1 = 0$$

$$\frac{\partial \pi_T}{\partial Q_2} = \frac{\partial P}{\partial Q}(Q) + P - \frac{\partial C_2}{\partial Q_2} = MR_T - MC_2 = 0$$

It therefore follows that, for maximizing total industry profit,

$$MR_T = MC_1 = MC_2$$

C H A P T E R

17

Profit Maximization for Firms with Market Power:

Implementation of the Theory

We will now demonstrate how managers of firms with market power can use estimates of their cost, demand, and marginal revenue functions to determine the firm's optimal price and level of output. The objective is to show how to combine the theoretical principles set forth in the preceding two chapters with relatively simple empirical analysis to obtain forecasts or estimates that will aid in maximizing the firm's profit. This objective does not mean that we want to teach you to be a mathematician. Rather, we want you to understand how the principles of profit maximization can be implemented for firms with market power.

In most of the examples used to demonstrate the process of implementing the profit-maximizing decision, we assume that a manager has accurate information about, and precise estimates of, all of the relevant variables and equations. For most managers, such exact estimates would seldom be available at any reasonable cost. However, the assumption of complete and accurate information allows us to show how the profit-maximizing results are obtained under the best of circumstances. This process can then be adapted to situations in which less accurate information is available.

We will begin by examining the price and output decisions for a monopoly. As we stressed in Chapter 15, the decision-making process for a monopoly is applicable to any firm with market power, with perhaps a few modifications for changes in the form of the demand and marginal revenue functions to account for differences in the market structure. Then we discuss implementing the profit-maximization decision under risk. We will examine the situation facing an oligopolist that does not know how rivals will react to changes in price, as discussed in Chapter 16. Finally, we set forth an alternative pricing rule that is sometimes used by firms that do not have complete information about the demand for their product.

17.1 A GUIDE TO IMPLEMENTING THE PROFIT-MAXIMIZING OUTPUT DECISION

Recall from Chapter 15 that the profit-maximizing or loss-minimizing output for a monopoly, or for any firm with market power, is the output level at which marginal revenue equals marginal cost. Once the optimal level of output is determined, the manager finds the optimal price from the demand curve. The firm should produce in the short run if price is greater than average variable cost. The situation in which a monopoly produces in the short run and makes an economic profit is reviewed in Figure 17.1. The profit-maximizing level of output, Q^*, occurs at point A where $MR = MC$. The profit-maximizing price, P^*, is found by locating the point on demand associated with Q^* units of output—point B in Figure 17.1. Since P^* exceeds average variable cost, the monopolist should produce rather than shut down. The maximum value of economic profit is calculated by multiplying the profit per unit, $P^* - ATC$, times the profit-maximizing level of output: $\pi^* = (P^* - ATC) \times Q^*$. The shaded area shown in the figure represents the

FIGURE 17.1
Short-Run Profit Maximization for Monopoly

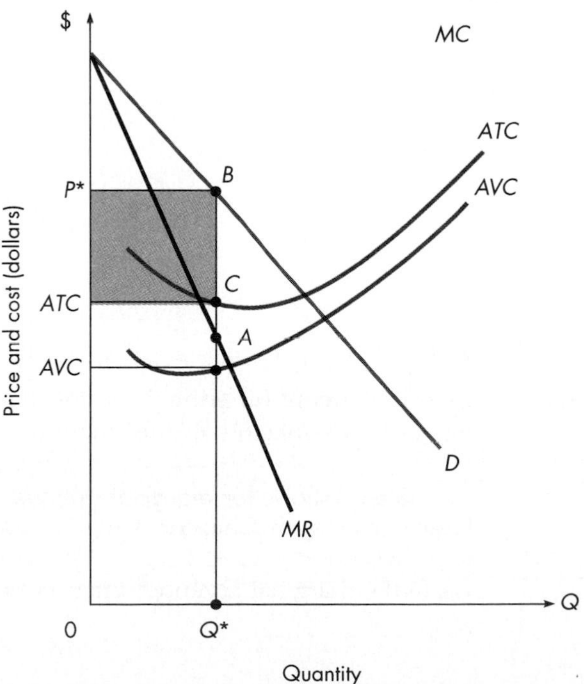

maximum value of profit. Based on this theoretical analysis, we can summarize the process of finding Q^*, P^*, and π^* with the following step-by-step procedure:

Step 1: Estimate the demand equation

To determine the optimal level of output, the manager must estimate the marginal revenue function. Since marginal revenue is derived from the demand equation, the manager begins by estimating demand. In the case of a linear demand specification, the empirical demand function facing the monopolist can be written as

$$Q = a + bP + cM + dP_R$$

where Q is output, P is price, M is income, and P_R is the price of a good related in consumption. As discussed in Chapter 9, in order to obtain the estimated demand curve for the relevant time period, the manager must have forecasts for the values of the exogenous variables, M and P_R, for that time period. Once the empirical demand equation has been estimated, the forecasts of M and P_R (denoted $\hat{M}$ and $\hat{P}_R$) are substituted into the estimated demand equation, and the demand function is expressed as

$$Q = a' + bP$$

where $a' = a + c\hat{M} + d\hat{P}_R$.

Step 2: Find the inverse demand equation

Before we can derive the marginal revenue function from the demand function, the demand function must be expressed so that price is a function of quantity: $P = f(Q)$. This is accomplished by solving for P in the estimated demand equation in Step 1:

$$\begin{aligned} P &= \frac{-a'}{b} + \frac{1}{b}Q \\ &= A + BQ \end{aligned}$$

where $A = \frac{-a'}{b}$ and $B = \frac{1}{b}$. This form of the demand equation is called the **inverse demand function**. Now the demand equation is expressed in a form that makes it possible to solve for marginal revenue in a straightforward manner.

inverse demand function The demand function with demand price expressed as a function of output, $P = f(Q)$.

Step 3: Solve for marginal revenue

Now recall from Chapter 3 that when demand is expressed as $P = A + BQ$, marginal revenue is $MR = A + 2BQ$. Using the inverse demand function, we can write the marginal revenue function as

$$\begin{aligned} MR &= A + 2BQ \\ &= \frac{-a'}{b} + \frac{2}{b}Q \end{aligned}$$

Step 4: Estimate average variable cost (AVC) and marginal cost (MC).
We have already discussed in detail the empirical techniques for estimating cubic cost functions. There is nothing new or different about estimating *MC* and *AVC* for a monopoly firm. The usual forms for the *AVC* and *MC* functions, when *TVC* is specified as a cubic equation, are

$$AVC = a + bQ + cQ^2$$
$$MC = a + 2bQ + 3cQ^2$$

You may wish to review this step by returning to Chapter 12 or to Chapter 14 (step 2).

Step 5: Find the output level where *MR* = *MC*
To find the level of output that maximizes profit or minimizes losses, the manager sets marginal revenue equal to marginal cost and solves for *Q*:

$$A + 2BQ = a + 2bQ + 3cQ^2$$

Solving this equation for *Q* gives the optimal level of output for the firm—unless *P* is less than *AVC*, and then the optimal level of output is zero.

Step 6: Find the optimal price.
Once the optimal quantity, Q^*, has been found in Step 5, the profit-maximizing price is found by substituting Q^* into the inverse demand equation to obtain the optimal price, P^*:

$$P^* = A + BQ^*$$

This price and output will be optimal only if price exceeds average variable cost.

Step 7: Check the shutdown rule.
For any firm, with or without market power, if price is less than average variable cost, the firm will shut down ($Q^* = 0$) because it makes a smaller loss producing nothing than it would lose if it produced any positive amount of output. The manager calculates the average variable cost at Q^* units:

$$AVC^* = a + bQ^* + cQ^{*2}$$

If $P^* \geq AVC^*$, then the monopolist produces Q^* units of output and sells each unit of output for P^* dollars. If $P^* < AVC^*$, then the monopolist shuts down in the short run.

Step 8: Computation of profit or loss.
To compute the profit or loss, the manager makes the same calculation regardless of whether the firm is a monopolist, oligopolist, or perfect competitor. Total profit or loss is

$$\begin{aligned}\pi &= TR - TC \\ &= (P \times Q) - [(AVC \times Q) + TFC]\end{aligned}$$

If $P < AVC$, the firm shuts down, and $\pi = -TFC$.

To illustrate how to implement these steps to find the profit-maximizing price and output level and to forecast profit, we now turn to a hypothetical firm that possesses a degree of market power.[1]

17.2 MAXIMIZING PROFIT AT AZTEC ELECTRONICS: AN EXAMPLE

By virtue of several patents, Aztec Electronics possesses substantial market power in the market for advanced stereo headphones. In December 1995, the manager of Aztec wished to determine the profit-maximizing price and output for its stereo headphones for 1996.

Estimation of Demand and Marginal Revenue

The demand for headphones was specified as a linear function of the price of headphones, income of the buyers, and the price of stereo tuners (a complement good),

$$Q = f(P, M, P_R)$$

Using data available for the period 1985–95, a linear form of the demand function was estimated. The resulting estimated demand function was

$$Q = 41 - 0.5P + 0.6M - 0.0225P_R$$

where output (Q) is measured in 10,000 units, average annual family income (M) in \$1,000 units, and the two prices (P and P_R) in \$1 units. Each estimated parameter has the expected sign and is statistically significant at the 90 percent level of confidence. The R^2 and F-statistics were both quite high, indicating the linear model specification does an excellent job of explaining the variation in quantity demanded.[2]

From an economic consulting firm, the manager obtained 1996 forecasts for income and the price of the complementary good (stereo tuners) as, respectively, \$45,000 and \$800. Using these values—$\hat{M} = 45$ and $\hat{P}_R = 800$—the estimated (forecasted) demand function in 1995 was

$$Q = 41 - 0.5P + 0.6(45) - 0.0225(800) = 50 - 0.5P$$

The inverse demand function for the estimated (empirical) demand function was obtained by solving for P:

$$P = 100 - 2Q$$

From the inverse demand function, the manager of Aztec Electronics obtained the estimated marginal revenue function:

$$MR = 100 - 4Q$$

[1]The monopolist can choose input usage rather than output in order to maximize profit. Appendix B shows how to find the profit-maximizing level of input usage for a firm with market power.

[2]Recall from Chapter 8 that when a firm is a price-setting firm (i.e., possesses some degree of market power), the problem of simultaneity vanishes. Thus, the demand for a monopolist can be estimated using the standard method of least-squares estimation—two-stage least-squares is not necessary.

FIGURE 17.2
Demand and Marginal Revenue for Aztec Electronics

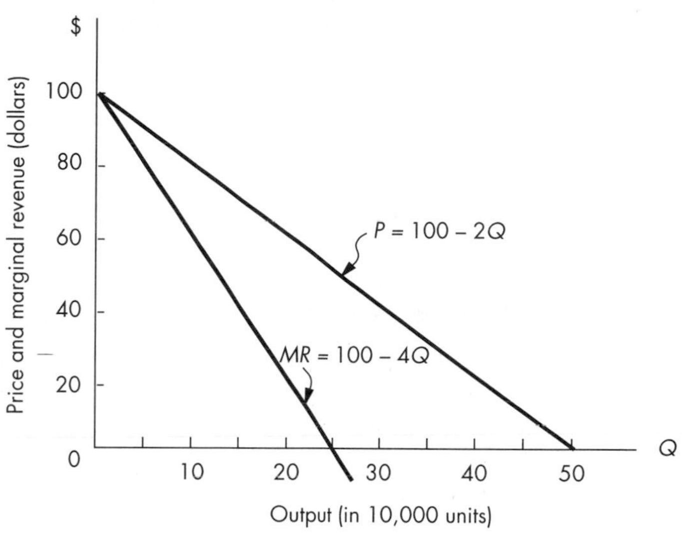

We should note that if the parameters of the demand equation are statistically significant, so are the parameters of the marginal revenue equation.

Figure 17.2 illustrates the estimated linear demand and marginal revenue curves for Aztec Electronics.

Estimation of Average Variable Cost and Marginal Cost

The manager of Aztec Electronics obtained an estimate of the firm's average variable cost function using a short-run cubic specification (as described in Chapter 12). The estimated average variable cost function was

$$AVC = 28 - 5Q + Q^2$$

For this estimation, AVC was measured in dollar units, and Q was measured in units of 10,000 to conform to the units in the demand specification. Given the estimated average variable cost function, the marginal cost function is

$$MC = 28 - 10Q + 3Q^2$$

As you can see, the specification and estimation of cost functions is the same regardless of whether a firm is perfectly competitive or possesses a degree of market power.

The Output Decision

Once the manager of Aztec obtained estimates of the marginal revenue function and the marginal cost function, the determination of the optimal level of output was accomplished by equating the estimated marginal revenue equation with the estimated marginal cost equation and solving for Q^*. Setting MR equal to MC results in the following expression:

$$100 - 4Q = 28 - 10Q + 3Q^2$$

Solving this equation for Q, the manager of Aztec finds two solutions: $Q = 6$ and $Q = -4$. Since $Q = -4$ is an irrelevant solution—negative outputs are impossible—the optimal level of output is $Q = 6$. That is, the profit-maximizing (or loss-minimizing) number of stereo headphones to produce and sell in 1996 is 60,000 units—if the firm chooses to produce rather than shut down.

The Pricing Decision

Once the manager of Aztec Electronics has found the optimal level of output, determining the profit-maximizing price is really nothing more than finding the price on the monopolist's demand curve that corresponds to the profit-maximizing level of output. The optimal output level, Q^*, is substituted into the inverse demand equation to obtain the optimal price. Substituting $Q = 6$ into the inverse demand function, the optimal price, P^*, is

$$P^* = 100 - 2(6) = \$88$$

Thus, Aztec will charge \$88 for a set of headphones in 1995.

The Shutdown Decision

To see if Aztec Electronics should shut down production in 1996, the manager compared the optimal price of \$88 to the average variable cost of producing 60,000 units. Average variable cost for 60,000 units was computed as

$$AVC^* = 28 - 5(6) + 6^2 = \$34$$

Since \$88 is greater than \$34, if these forecasts prove to be correct in 1996, all of the variable costs will be covered, and the manager should operate the plant rather than shut it down. Note that Aztec's expected total revenue in 1996 is \$5,280,000 (= \$88 × 60,000) and estimated total variable cost was \$2,040,000 (= \$34 × 60,000). Since total revenue exceeds total variable cost ($TR > TVC$), the manager would produce rather than shut down.

Computation of Total Profit or Loss

Computation of profit is straightforward process once the manager has estimated total revenue and all costs. The manager of Aztec has already estimated price and average variable cost for 1996, but total fixed cost is needed to calculate total profit or loss. On the basis of 1995 data, the manager of Aztec Electronics estimated that fixed costs would be \$2,700,000 in 1996. The profit for 1996 was calculated to be

$$\begin{aligned}\pi &= TR - TVC - TFC \\ &= \$5{,}280{,}000 - \$2{,}040{,}000 - \$2{,}700{,}000 \\ &= \$540{,}000\end{aligned}$$

FIGURE 17.3
Profit Maximization at Aztec Electronics

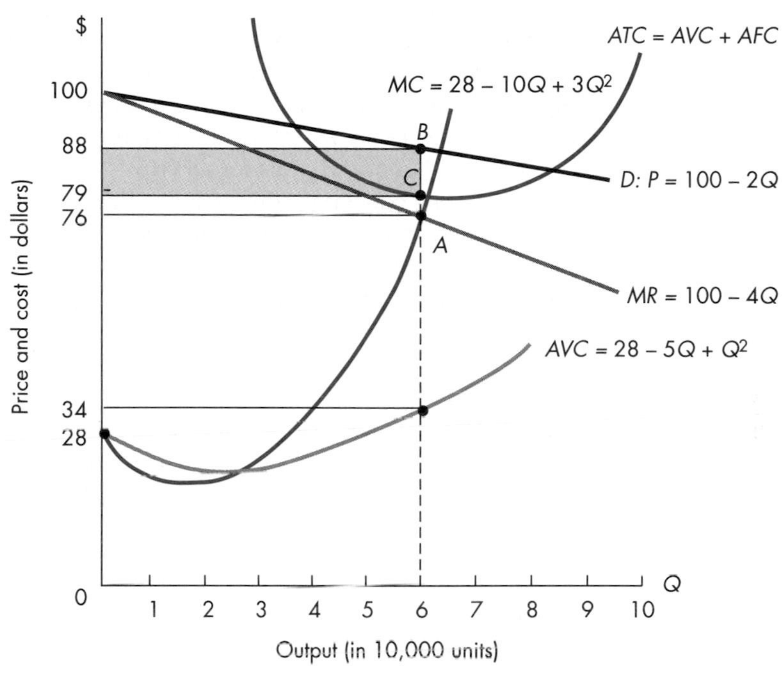

If projected fixed costs for 1996 had been \$3,500,000, Aztec would have predicted losses of \$260,000 for 1996. Despite the losses, Aztec should continue operations in 1995 because if it shuts down it loses an amount equal to its fixed costs \$3,500,000). Losing \$260,000 is obviously better than losing \$3,500,000. As always, fixed costs do not matter when making the output (or pricing) decision. No matter how high fixed costs are, Aztec will not shut down since $P > AVC$.

Figure 17.3 shows the estimated equations for 1996 and the profit-maximizing price and output. At point *A*, $MR = MC$, and the profit-maximizing level of output is 60,000 units ($Q = 6$). At point *B*, the profit-maximizing price is \$88, the price at which 60,000 units can be sold. At point *C*, *ATC* is \$79, which was calculated as

$$ATC = TC/Q = (\$2{,}040{,}000 + \$2{,}700{,}000)\ /\ 60{,}000$$
$$= \$79$$

The total profit earned by Aztec is represented by the area of the shaded rectangle.

17.3 COST-PLUS PRICING: AN ALTERNATIVE PRICING RULE

It should be clear by now that the short-run pricing decision based upon the equality of marginal revenue and marginal cost yields the maximum profit (or minimum loss) for a firm. However, there is some evidence to suggest that many firms use some other types of rules to determine price and output, particularly when it is difficult to obtain an accurate estimate of their demand function. Examples of such cases might be when a firm's demand is a function of the prices and levels of advertising of several close rivals. One prominent alternative pricing technique is called **cost-plus pricing**. Firms using cost-plus pricing determine their price by setting price equal to average total cost plus a percentage of average total cost (*ATC*) as a markup.

cost-plus pricing
A method of determining price by setting price equal to average total cost plus a percentage of *ATC* as a markup.

The basic concept is deceptively simple. In cost-plus pricing, the firm determines its average total cost then adds a percentage markup (or margin). Thus, price is

$$P = ATC + (m \cdot ATC)$$
$$= (1 + m) \cdot ATC$$

where m is the markup on cost. For example, if the markup is 20 percent, price would be $1.2 \times ATC$.

This very basic description of cost-plus pricing glosses over two major difficulties. First, how does the firm determine average total cost? Second, how does the firm select the appropriate markup (or margin)?

Because costs vary with the level of output produced, determination of average cost requires that the firm first specify the level of output that will be produced. Obviously, a precise determination of this output would require consideration of the prevailing demand conditions—a feature not incorporated in cost-plus pricing. Instead, firms typically specify some standard volume of production, based on some assumption about the percentage of the firm's capacity that will be utilized. Furthermore, the costs used are derived from accounting data. As noted in earlier chapters, the use of accounting data may not be valid, since accounting costs do not always reflect opportunity costs. Also, such historical data would not reflect recent or potential changes in input prices.

Notwithstanding the difficulties involved in determining average cost, a potentially more troublesome problem is the selection of the markup percentage. While the firm might arbitrarily select some target rate of return on invested capital, recent empirical evidence suggests that firms use a more subjective approach. It appears that the markups for different products differ according to such factors as the degree of competitiveness in the market and the price elasticity of demand. Apparently, managers employ knowledge about the market to determine the markup that maximizes profits.

Cost-plus pricing has been criticized on two grounds. First, it employs average rather than marginal cost. As you know from Chapter 4, marginal (or incremental) cost rather than total cost should be used in making any optimizing decision. Second, cost-plus pricing does not incorporate a consideration of prevailing demand conditions. Using the $MR = MC$ pricing rule, demand conditions enter explicitly through the marginal revenue function, but cost-plus pricing does not embody this information.

Although these criticisms are valid, it should be noted that, *under certain circumstances*, cost-plus pricing may approximate $MR = MC$ pricing. Let us show you how this can occur. As was shown in an earlier chapter, marginal revenue may be written as

$$MR = P\left(1 + \frac{1}{E}\right)$$

where E is the own-price elasticity of demand. Setting marginal revenue equal to marginal cost, the optimization condition may be written as

$$P\left(1 + \frac{1}{E}\right) = MC$$

so that

$$P = \left(\frac{E}{1 + E}\right) MC$$

If the firm has a horizontal average cost curve (e.g., if the firm's long-run cost relation is characterized by constant returns to scale), average cost is constant and is equal to marginal cost. In this case, the preceding condition can be expressed as

$$P = \left(\frac{E}{1 + E}\right) LAC$$

Note the similarity between this equation and the equation for cost-plus pricing, $P = (1 + m)LAC$. Setting these equations equal (i.e., assuming that cost-plus pricing is equivalent to $MR = MC$ pricing) and solving for m, the markup would be

$$m = -\frac{1}{1 + E}$$

That is, if firms are using cost-plus pricing as an approximation to pricing based on profit maximization, the markup would be determined by the price elasticity of demand—precisely the relation indicated in the empirical investigations mentioned earlier. While a firm with market power is limited to the elastic portion of the demand function (i.e., where $|E| > 1$), this formulation indicates that, as the demand curve becomes more elastic (i.e., as $|E|$ increases), the profit-maximizing markup decreases. For example, if $|E| = 2$, the profit-maximizing markup would be 100 percent. However, if the demand curve were more elastic, say, $|E| = 5$, the profit-maximizing markup would fall to 25 percent. The point is that if the firm's average cost is constant, cost-plus pricing *could* be equivalent to pricing based on profit maximization. Moreover, the size of the markup would depend on the own-price elasticity of demand, which of course depends upon the availability of good substitutes for the product. The easier it is for consumers to substitute, the lower the markup.

Relation When a manager practices cost-plus pricing, the price of the product is determined as

$$P = (1 + m)ATC$$

where m is the markup on average total cost (ATC). Cost-plus pricing is not, in general, equivalent to the profit-maximizing price determined by equating marginal revenue and marginal cost. In the special case in which the markup is related to the elasticity of demand as

$$m = -\frac{1}{1 + E}$$

and when average cost is constant, cost-plus pricing is equivalent to pricing based on profit maximization.

17.4 MAXIMIZING OLIGOPOLY PROFIT WITH A RISKY DEMAND

Recall that the most important characteristic of oligopoly, which also creates a serious problem for managers trying to maximize oligopoly profit, is the mutual interdependence that exists among firms. The manager of each oligopoly firm realizes that changes in its own price and output will affect the demand (and profit) of all of its rivals, and the managers of these rival firms will likely respond by adjusting their own prices and outputs, which in turn will affect the demand (and profit) of the firm that originated the price change. While managers can be rather certain that rivals will notice changes in price, they generally do not know with certainty how their rivals will react to the changes.

We illustrated the interdependence problem with an example of a manager considering a price change. The oligopoly firm faced two or more demands—and hence, two or more marginal revenue functions—depending upon how rival firms actually responded to the price change. At the extremes, the manager recognized two demand curves: one demand curve assuming that rivals follow the manager's price change; and the other demand curve assuming that rivals do not change their prices in response to a price change.

Which demand is the "correct" one for decision-making purposes? Clearly, there is no "correct" demand *before* the firm acts. A manager facing a risky demand situation cannot know what the true demand is until after it changes price or takes some other action, and the rival firms have had time to react, if they so desire. In order to make plans, managers should have some idea about the way rivals will respond and, therefore, some idea about the firm's demand. The principles of decision making under risk give one possible method that a manager can use when there is incomplete information about how rivals will react to a price change. We will now show you a simple example to illustrate this approach, but we must emphasize that there are many other methods of approaching this problem.

Suppose Atlas Corporation and Butler Industries are the only two firms in a market producing close substitutes—a market structure called "duopoly"—and both firms are charging a price of $40 ($P_A = P_B = \$40$). The manager of Atlas Corporation estimates its demand to be

$$Q_A = 6{,}000 - 300P_A + 225P_B$$

In the current situation, both firms are charging a price of $40, and Atlas's sales are 3,000 [= 6,000 – (300 × 40) + (225 × 40)] units. The manager of Atlas Corporation does not believe selling 3,000 units at a price of $40 is maximizing the firm's profit, and is considering a price change.

If Butler Corporation does not match Atlas's new price and continues to charge a price of $40, then Atlas's demand when Butler does not follow a price change ($D_{\text{doesn't follow}}$) is

$$\begin{aligned} Q_A &= 6{,}000 + (225 \times 40) - 300P_A \\ &= 15{,}000 - 300P_A \qquad (D_{\text{doesn't follow}}) \end{aligned}$$

Alternatively, if Butler Corporation exactly matches any price charged by Atlas ($P_A = P_B$), then Atlas faces the following demand

$$\begin{aligned} Q_A &= 6{,}000 - 300P_A + 225P_A \\ &= 6{,}000 - 75P_A \qquad (D_{\text{follows}}) \end{aligned}$$

The manager at Atlas believes there is a 40 percent probability that Butler will maintain a constant price of $40 and believes there is a 60 percent probability that Butler will match any price change made by Atlas. For any price chosen by the manager at Atlas, the expected quantity demanded at each price, $E(Q_A)$, is

$$E(Q_A) = .4 \times (15{,}000 - 300P_A) + .6 \times (6{,}000 - 75P_A) = 9{,}600 - 165P_A$$

Note that if Atlas's manager is correct in assuming that Butler will make one of only two responses to a price change, then Atlas's actual sales after a price change will never equal the expected sales, $E(Q_A)$. The actual quantity sold will lie on one of the two demands, $D_{\text{doesn't follow}}$ or D_{follows}. If Atlas changes price a large number of times, the average level of sales will lie on the expected quantity demanded curve, $E(Q_A)$. Figure 17.4 shows the two demand curves facing the manager of Atlas Corporation, depending upon the price response from its rival. The expected quantity demanded, $E(Q_A)$, is shown by the dotted line between the two demand curves.

In order to maximize *expected* profit, the manager at Atlas will decide how much to produce and what price to charge by equating *expected* marginal revenue and *expected* marginal cost. In order to obtain the expected marginal revenue function, the inverse function for $E(Q_A)$ must be found:[3]

$$P_A = [9{,}600 - E(Q_A)]/165 \approx 58 - 0.006\ E(Q_A)$$

The expected marginal revenue function is

$$E(MR) \approx 58 - 0.012\ E(Q_A)$$

[3]This is not an expected price. Alpha's manager chooses a given expected quantity from its expected quantity function and will charge exactly that price in order to maximize profit. In other words, the manager knows with certainty the price the firm will receive for each unit sold, but once the price has been chosen, the actual level of sales is the risky variable.

FIGURE 17.4
Profit Maximization with Risky Demand

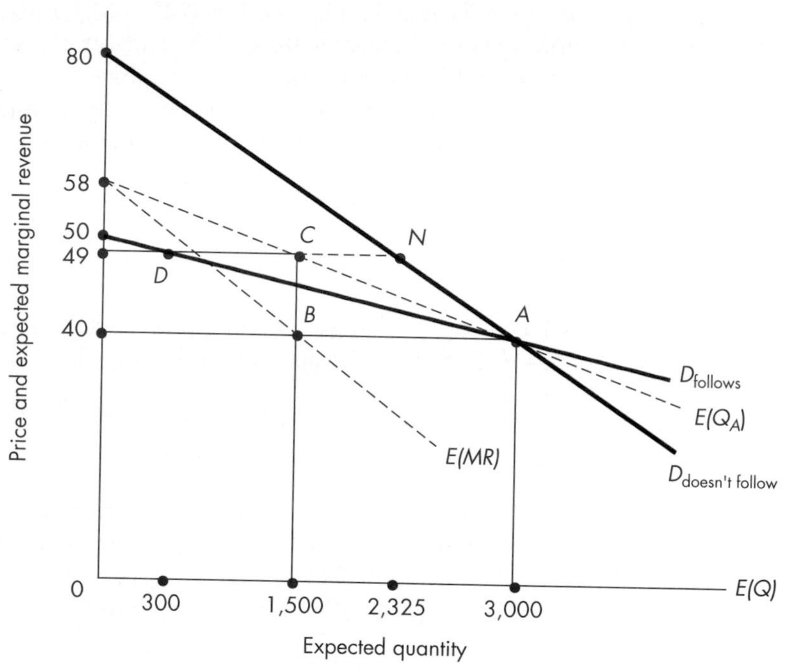

This function is the *expected* marginal revenue because once the manager chooses a price, the sales depend upon the reaction of the rival. Thus, marginal revenue also depends on the rival's reaction.

Atlas Corporation faces a constant marginal cost that is known with certainty to be equal to $40. To find the level of output that maximizes expected profit, the manager at Atlas Corporation sets expected marginal revenue equal to expected marginal cost, which is known with certainty in this example:

$$E(MR) = 58 - .012\ E(Q_A) = 40$$

and solves for $E(Q_A)$,

$$E(Q_A) = 1{,}500$$

Thus, the manager should choose the (certain) price that will generate expected sales of 1,500 units. This price is determined from the inverse function:

$$P_A = 58 - (0.006 \times 1{,}500) = \$49$$

The *actual* sales will be 300 [= 15,000 – (300 × 49)] units if Butler Corporation does not match Atlas's new price and keeps their price at $40. The *actual* sales will be 2,325 [= 6,000 – (75 × 49)] units if Butler does match the price change and sets its own price at $49.

Figure 17.4 illustrates this numerical example. When Atlas sets a price of $40 (as does Butler), it sells 3,000 units (point *A*). The demand curves when Butler does and does not follow are, respectively, D_{follows} and $D_{\text{doesn't follow}}$. The expected sales at each price are given by the dashed inverse demand, $E(Q_A)$. The expected marginal revenue at any price on $E(Q_A)$ is given by the dashed line, $E(MR)$.

If the firm sets $E(MR) = MC =$ \$40 (point *B*), expected sales are 1,500 units and the manager of Atlas sets a price of $49, given by $E(Q_A)$ at point *C* in Figure 17.4. Atlas will sell 300 units if demand is actually D_{follows} (point *D*) and 2,325 units if demand is actually $D_{\text{doesn't follow}}$ (point *N*).

This simple example is not intended to demonstrate precisely how an oligopolist with incomplete information about its rivals' reaction to price changes actually makes its profit-maximizing decision. It is designed only to show how a manager can take risk into account in decision making. The actual process would probably be more complex. Nonetheless, a manager can use objectively or subjectively determined probabilities about demand in estimating rivals' reactions.

17.5 SUMMARY

This chapter showed how a manager of a firm with market power can use estimates of demand and cost functions to make profit-maximizing decisions. The steps a manager follows to find the price and output that maximize profit or minimize losses are summarized below:

1. The demand curve facing the firm is estimated. Then the inverse demand function—which is used to derive the marginal revenue function—is derived.
2. The cost curves are estimated in order to estimate the marginal cost function facing the firm.
3. Set the estimated marginal revenue equal to the estimated marginal cost and solve for the profit-maximizing level of output.
4. The profit-maximizing price is then found by substituting the optimal level of output into the inverse demand function.
5. The optimal price is then compared to average variable cost at the optimal output level to make sure the firm should actually produce. The firm should produce if $P \geq AVC$, and the firm should shut down if $P < AVC$.
6. The profit or loss earned by the firm is calculated by subtracting total cost from total revenue: $\pi = TR - TC = P \times Q - [(AVC \times Q) + TFC]$.

Sometimes it is difficult, or perhaps impossible, to estimate the demand conditions when there is mutual interdependence in a market. In such cases, the $MR = MC$ rule cannot be applied, and some managers resort to alternative pricing techniques. One such technique is cost-plus pricing, where the price charged represents a markup (margin) over average cost determined as follows:

$$P = (1 + m)ATC$$

Two problems exist with this approach: (1) the appropriate output level at which to measure *ATC* is unknown, and (2) the appropriate margin (*m*) is unknown. However, when the firm's cost curve is relatively flat, cost-plus pricing can approximate profit maximization if the markup is equal to $\frac{-1}{1+E}$, where *E* is the own-price elasticity of demand.

One method of estimating oligopoly demand under mutual interdependence is to assign probabilities to rivals' responses to the firm's action. In this way a manager can at least obtain an expected sales function and use this function to maximize expected profit. There are, of course, problems with this approach, in particular, assigning probabilities to rival responses. Nonetheless, there are problems associated with most oligopoly decision making in the absence of complete information.

TECHNICAL PROBLEMS

* 1. The manager of a monopoly firm obtained the following estimate of the market demand function for its output:

$$Q = 26 - 1P + 2M - 5P_R$$

where Q was measured in 100 units, prices in dollars per unit, and income (M) in thousand dollar units. From an econometric forecasting firm, the manager obtained forecasts for the 1995 values of M and P_R as, respectively, $20,000 and $2. For 1995 what is

a. The forecasted demand function?
b. The inverse demand function?
c. The marginal revenue function?

* 2. For the firm in problem 1, the manager estimated the average variable cost function as

$$AVC = 20 - 7Q + 1Q^2$$

where AVC was measured in dollars per unit and Q was measured in 100 units.

a. What is the estimated marginal cost function?
b. What is the optimal level of production in 1995?
c. What is the optimal price in 1995?
d. Check to make sure that the firm should actually produce in the short run rather than shut down.

In addition, the manager expects fixed costs in 1995 to be $22,500.

e. What is the firm's expected profit or loss in 1995?

3. Cost-plus pricing is a method of price determination used predominantly by monopolistically competitive firms.

a. Why is cost-plus pricing used mainly by monopolistic competitors and not often used by monopolists?
b. Under what condition(s) would cost-plus pricing be equivalent to profit-maximizing pricing, that is, $MR = MC$ pricing?
c. If the condition(s) in part *b* are satisfied and if the own-price elasticity of demand facing the firm is 1.5, what is the profit-maximizing markup?
d. What is the profit-maximizing markup if the own-price elasticity is equal to 3?

APPLIED PROBLEMS

1. The Ali Baba Co. is the only supplier of a particular type of Oriental carpet. The estimated demand for their carpets is

$$Q = 112 - .5P + 5M$$

where Q = number of carpets (1,000), P = price of carpets (dollars per unit), and M = consumers' income per capita ($1,000).

The estimated average variable cost function for Ali Baba's carpets is

$$AVC = 200 - 12Q + 2Q^2$$

Consumers' income per capita is expected to be $20,000 and total fixed cost is $100,000.

a. How many carpets should the firm produce in order to maximize profit?

b. What is the profit-maximizing price of carpets?

c. What is the maximum amount of profit that the firm can earn selling carpets?

d. Answer parts *a* through *c* if consumers' income per capita is expected to be $30,000 instead.

2. Dr. Leona Williams, a well-known plastic surgeon, has a reputation for being one of the best surgeons for reconstructive nose surgery. Dr. Williams enjoys a rather substantial degree of market power in this market. Dr. Williams has estimated demand for her work to be

$$Q = 480 - 0.2P$$

where Q is the number of nose operations performed monthly, and P is the price of a nose operation.

a. What is the inverse demand function for Dr. Williams's services?

b. What is the marginal revenue function?

The average variable cost function for reconstructive nose surgery is estimated to be

$$AVC = 2Q^2 - 15Q + 400$$

where AVC is average variable cost (measured in dollars), and Q is the number of operations per month. The doctor's fixed costs each month are $8,000.

c. If the doctor wishes to maximize her profit, how many nose operations should she perform each month?

d. What price should Dr. Williams charge to perform a nose operation?

e. How much profit does she earn each month?

3. The Pluto Corporation makes toy space vehicles. It has one close rival, Red Planet, Inc., which also makes toy space vehicles but of lower quality. Red Planet therefore generally charges a lower price than Pluto, but the toys are substitutes. Pluto's demand is estimated as

$$Q = 1{,}000 - 8P + 4P_R$$

where P_R is the price set by Red Planet. Currently Red Planet is selling its toys for $80. Pluto is charging $140 and selling 200 per period. Pluto's marginal cost is constant at $65.

a. What are Pluto's inverse demand and marginal revenue functions in this situation?

b. Is Pluto maximizing its profit?

Pluto's management is deciding whether or not to change price, but the manager is not certain about how Red Planet will respond. From past experience, it is believed that if Pluto changes, there is a 20 percent probability Red Planet will not change price, a 50 percent probability it will set its price at one-half of Pluto's price, and a 30 percent probability it will set its price three-fourths of Pluto's price.

c. What is the expected sales function?

d. What is the inverse demand function? The expected marginal revenue function?

e. What price should Pluto set to maximize expected profits?

f. What are Pluto's expected sales at the profit-maximizing price?

g. What will Pluto's actual range of sales be at this price?

APPENDIX 17A Estimation of Marginal Revenue with a Log-Linear Demand

In this appendix, we show how to specify a log-linear demand function for a monopoly and estimate the associated marginal revenue function.

First, the log-linear form of the demand function must be estimated:

$$Q = aP^bM^cP_R^d$$

Once the parameters a, b, c, and d are estimated (by transforming to logs and running a regression), and forecast values for the exogenous variables ($\hat{M}$ and $\hat{P}_R$) are obtained, the demand function can be expressed as

$$Q = AP^b$$

where $A = a\hat{M}^c\hat{P}_R^d$. Next, solve for the inverse demand function as

$$P = A^{-1/b}Q^{1/b}$$

Total revenue ($TR = P \times Q$) is expressed as

$$TR = (A^{-\frac{1}{b}}Q^{\frac{1}{b}})\,Q = A^{-\frac{1}{b}}Q^{\left(\frac{1}{b}\right)+1}$$

Marginal revenue is obtained by taking the derivative of total revenue:

$$\begin{aligned} MR = \frac{dTR}{dQ} &= \left[\left(\frac{1}{b}\right)+1\right]A^{-\frac{1}{b}}Q^{\frac{1}{b}} \\ &= \left[\left(\frac{1}{b}\right)+1\right]P \\ &= \frac{b+1}{b}P \end{aligned}$$

Thus, marginal revenue is a function of output or price.

We consider now an example showing how a monopolist can estimate marginal revenue when the empirical demand specification is log-linear.

Estimating Marginal Revenue at Allied Cable: An Example

In preparation for forecasting the optimal level of service and the optimal monthly service fee for 1995, the manager of Allied Cable TV, Inc., elected to estimate a demand function of the form

$$Q = aP^bM^c$$

The manager was able to obtain a cross-section data set in which Q was measured as the number of households served (in thousands), P as the (monthly) service fee, and M as the average annual family income of households in the service area (in thousand dollars). Using these data, the estimated demand function was

$$\log Q = 2.785 - 2.0 \log P + 3.0 \log M$$

Since the antilog of 2.785 is 16.2, the estimated demand function can be expressed as

$$Q = 16.2P^{-2}M^3$$

From an economic consulting firm, the manager obtained a forecast of average annual family income for Allied's service area in 1995 of $20,000; that is, $M = 20$. Using this forecast in the estimated demand function, the forecasted demand function for Allied Cable TV in 1995 was

$$Q = 16.2P^{-2}(20)^3 = 129{,}600P^{-2}$$

Solving this equation for P, the inverse demand function for 1995 was

$$P = 360Q^{-1/2}$$

Forecasted total revenue is $P \times Q = 360Q^{1/2}$, so the forecasted marginal revenue function was

$$\begin{aligned} MR &= \left(\frac{b+1}{b}\right)P = \left(\frac{-2+1}{-2}\right)360Q^{-\frac{1}{2}} \\ &= 180\,Q^{-\frac{1}{2}} \end{aligned}$$

As in the previous example, the firm's manager would set this estimated marginal revenue function equal to the estimated marginal cost and solve for Q^*. From the demand function, $P = 360\,Q^{*-1/2}$, the manager would determine the optimal price, P^*. If P^* is greater than AVC at Q^*, the firm would produce this optimal output. If not, the firm would shut down. If the firm produces, its profit or loss would be TR ($= 360\,Q^{*1/2}$) minus variable cost minus fixed cost.

APPENDIX 17B Profit-Maximizing Input Usage

Just as in the case of perfectly competitive firms, managers of firms with market power also can make their profit-maximization (or loss-minimization) decision by selecting the optimal levels of usage of their inputs. To see how this can be done—and to demonstrate that this situation is quite similar to the case of perfect competition—we consider the case in which a firm employs a single variable input and pays a given, market-determined price for that input.

Consider a firm that has market power—its demand curve is downward sloping. The firm employs a single variable input, labor, which it purchases at the market-determined wage rate. As you saw in Chapter 15, the optimal level of employment of any input is the level at which the marginal revenue product of the input is equal to the price of the input. Since we are using labor as an example, the condition for optimal employment can be expressed as

$$MRP = w$$

where MRP is the marginal revenue product of labor and w is the market-determined wage rate. Recall from Chapter 15 that for a firm with market power, MRP is equal to the product of marginal revenue times marginal product for the input:

$$MRP = MR \times MP$$

The relevant range of MRP is the range of labor usage for which ARP exceeds MRP and MRP is positive.

To illustrate how to find the profit-maximizing level of input usage, we will specify product demand to be log-linear and the production function to be log-linear (i.e., the short-run Cobb-Douglas function). While we could have chosen to employ a linear specification for demand or a cubic specification for the production function, the computations required to calculate the marginal revenue product are extremely tedious with either of these two alternative specifications.* These complications did not arise in the case of perfect competition because MR does not vary with output and labor usage for perfect competitors; MR is constant and equal to P. The case we are going to present here—log-linear marginal revenue and log-linear marginal product—will be sufficient to illustrate how MRP can actually be estimated and used to find the optimal level of input usage.

First, the manager must estimate the short-run Cobb-Douglas production function in order to obtain an estimated marginal product function. The single input version of the Cobb-Douglas production function is

$$Q = \delta L^{\beta}$$

where $0 < \beta < 1$ and $\delta > 0$. The associated marginal product of labor function is

$$MP = \beta\delta L^{\beta-1}$$

The log-linear demand function is

$$Q = aP^{b}M^{c}P_{R}^{d}$$

As we demonstrated earlier in this chapter, after estimating the parameters and obtaining forecasts for M and P_R, the forecasted demand function may be written as

$$Q = AP^{b}$$

where again

$$A = aM^{c}P_{R}^{d}$$

and the marginal revenue function as

$$MR = \left(\frac{b+1}{b}\right) A^{-1/b}Q^{1/b}$$

However, to solve for the optimal usage of labor, the marginal revenue function must be expressed in terms of L rather than Q. To accomplish this, substitute the production function ($Q = \delta L^{\beta}$) into the MR function. After this substitution, the marginal revenue function becomes

$$\begin{aligned} MR &= \left(\frac{b+1}{b}\right)A^{-1/b}(\delta L^{\beta})^{1/b} \\ &= \left(\frac{b+1}{b}\right)A^{-1/b}\delta^{1/b}L^{\beta/b} \end{aligned}$$

The marginal revenue product function is then obtained by multiplying:

$$MRP = MR \times MP$$

*The mathematical complications that arise when either MR or MP is *not* specified in a multiplicative form (i.e., log-linear form) can, data availability permitting, be avoided by estimating the marginal revenue product directly. Direct estimation of MRP by regressing $\Delta TR/\Delta L$ on L is not, however, without its own econometric difficulties, which go beyond the scope of this text.

where the MR and MP functions are those derived above. Then, to determine the optimal level of usage of labor, equate this marginal revenue product function to the price of labor, w, and solve for L. Also check to see if ARP ($= P \times AP$) is greater than MRP. If ARP is less than MRP, no labor is hired, and the firm shuts down. To make this seemingly complicated procedure more clear, let's look at an example.

The Employment Decision at Allied Cable TV: A Numerical Example

Allied Cable TV, Inc., is a local monopolist with substantial market power. Allied employs a single variable input, labor, and pays the market-determined wage rate, $18 an hour for each worker. The manager of Allied wants to determine the optimal level of labor usage for 1995. As you know, in order to make this determination, the manager must have estimates of the marginal product of labor function, the marginal revenue function, and the wage rate for 1995.

From the earlier numerical example in this Appendix, the forecasted inverse demand function for 1995 was

$$P = 360\ Q^{-1/2}$$

(where price is expressed in dollars per household per month and output is expressed in thousands of households serviced per month) and the associated marginal revenue function was

$$MR = 180\ Q^{-1/2}$$

Next, as noted above, the production function must be substituted into the marginal revenue function so that MR is a function of L. To this end, the manager used historical data to estimate a short-run production function of the form

$$Q = \delta L^{\beta}$$

Measuring output in thousands of households serviced and labor usage in thousands of hours per month, the estimated production function was

$$\log Q = 3.892 + 0.4 \log L$$

Rewriting this function in its exponential form, the production function is

$$Q = 49L^{0.4}$$

Using the relation set forth above, the corresponding marginal product function is

$$MP = (0.4)(49)L^{0.4-1} = 19.6\ L^{-0.6}$$

Next, the production function must be substituted into the previously derived marginal revenue equation so that MR is a function of L:

$$\begin{aligned} MR &= 180(49L^{0.4})^{-1/2} \\ &= 25.714L^{-0.2} \end{aligned}$$

Using these estimates of MP and MR, the manager of Allied Cable TV calculated the marginal revenue product of labor as

$$MRP = MR \times MP = (25.714L^{-0.2}) \times (19.6L^{-0.6}) = 504L^{-0.8}$$

As noted, the forecasted wage rate was $18 per hour. To determine the optimal monthly employment of labor for Allied Cable TV in 1995, the manager equated the forecasts for MRP and w:

$$504L^{-0.8} = 18$$

Solving this equation for L,

$$L^{-0.8} = 0.0357$$

and therefore $L = 64.4$. The optimal monthly level of labor usage in 1995 is forecasted to be 64,400 hours, or an annual level of usage of 772,800 hours. (This is approximately 386 full-time employees.)

Given $L = 64.4$, the output of the firm in 1995 would be obtained from the above production function as

$$Q = 49(64.4)^{0.4} = 259.3$$

That is, the forecasted number of households to be serviced is 259,300. Then, the price of the output is, from the inverse demand function,

$$P = 360\ Q^{-1/2} = 360(259.3)^{-1/2} = 22.36$$

To make sure Allied should not shut down in the short run, the manager checks to see if ARP is greater than MRP. ARP is calculated as follows:

$$\begin{aligned} ARP = P \times AP &= P(Q/L) \\ &= \$22.36\ (259.3/64.4) \\ &= \$90.03 \end{aligned}$$

Since MRP equals $18 (the wage rate) at the optimal level of labor usage, ARP does exceed MRP. These estimates, then, indicate that Allied Cable TV should serve 259,300 households and charge a monthly fee of $22.36. Total fixed costs are expected to be $2.5 million in 1995. Allied will earn an economic profit of $2,138,748, computed as follows:

$$\begin{aligned}\pi &= PQ - wL - TFC \\ &= (22.36)(259{,}300) - (18)(64{,}400) - 2{,}500{,}000 \\ &= \$2{,}138{,}748\end{aligned}$$

Note that since Allied is earning economic profit in this example, it would not be necessary to check to see that *ARP* is greater than *MRP*. We did so in this case simply to illustrate the procedure.

Before leaving this numerical example, we wish to show you that using the $MRP = w$ rule to maximize profit is equivalent to using the $MR = MC$ rule to maximize profit. To see that a manager would get the same price, output, and profit, let's apply the $MR = MC$ rule to the decision facing Allied Cable TV. Let the manager of Allied find the optimal level of output rather than the optimal level of input.

The manager first estimates demand and marginal revenue, which, of course, are the same as before:

$$TR = 360\ Q^{1/2}$$

and

$$MR = 180\ Q^{-1/2}$$

Next, the manager must obtain an estimate for the marginal cost. Since the wage rate is \$18, total variable cost is

$$TVC = 18L$$

The production function was estimated to be

$$Q = 49L^{0.4}$$

From the estimated production function, the manager can take the inverse of the production function to obtain

$$L^{0.4} = Q/49 \text{ and}$$
$$L = Q^{2.5}/49^{2.5}$$

By substituting this expression for L, the manager can express total variable cost as a function of output:

$$TVC = 18\left(\frac{Q^{2.5}}{49^{2.5}}\right)$$

The marginal cost function associated with this total variable cost function is

$$MC = \frac{(2.5)(18)}{49^{2.5}}\ Q^{1.5}$$

While this marginal cost function does not take the cubic form set forth in Chapter 12, it is, nevertheless, a valid form for a marginal cost function.

The manager then equates marginal revenue and marginal cost to find the optimal level of output:

$$\begin{aligned}MR &= MC \\ 180Q^{-\frac{1}{2}} &= \frac{(2.5)(18)}{49^{2.5}}\ Q^{1.5} \\ Q^2 &= \frac{(49^{2.5})(180)}{(2.5)(18)} = 67{,}228 \\ Q &= 259.3\end{aligned}$$

This is the same level of output that was optimal when the manager used the $MRP = w$ rule to maximize profit. Since the optimal level of output is the same, the same price will be charged. The optimal level of labor to employ is

$$\begin{aligned}L &= \frac{(259.3)^{2.5}}{49^{2.5}} \\ &= 64.4\end{aligned}$$

As expected, this is the same amount of labor that was optimal when the $MRP = w$ rule was used. Since P, Q, and L are all the same as before, Allied earns the same amount of profit whether the manager chooses to produce 259,300 units of output or chooses to hire 64,400 hours of labor services.

CHAPTER

18 Multiple Plants, Markets, and Products

Until now we have considered—at least implicitly—only a rather simple firm. This firm has a single plant in which it produces a single product that is sold in a single market. Although the simpler models give great insight into a firm's decision process, this is frequently not the type of situation faced by many real-world firms or corporations.

In this chapter, we will show how some complications, such as multiple plants, multiple markets, and multiple products, affect the profit-maximization conditions set forth in previous chapters. The discussion of each of these topics will of necessity be brief. It is not our intention to provide an exhaustive discussion of these complications. Rather, we want to show that these complications do not alter the principles of profit maximization already set forth: The firm continues to produce that output at which marginal revenue equals marginal cost or to choose the level of input usage at which marginal revenue product is equal to marginal factor cost. The effect of these complications does, however, make the implementation of these principles somewhat more complex computationally: "The rule's the same but the arithmetic's a little harder."

In this discussion, we limit our attention to firms with market power—monopoly, oligopoly, and monopolistic competition. Since we will be concerned with the firm's output and pricing decision in the short run, these market structures are analytically the same. Hence, in our discussion, we will normally consider a monopoly firm, but the conclusions also apply to monopolistic competition and oligopoly, with perhaps a few modifications.

We begin with a discussion of multiplant firms. This will be followed by a discussion of firms that sell in multiple markets and then a discussion of firms that produce multiple products. For clarity of exposition, we treat these extensions of the theory as separate topics without trying to integrate them. Keep in mind, however, that firms frequently fall into two or even all three of the categories. That is, a firm such as an automobile manufacturer would produce several different products in several different plants and may well sell in several different markets. This extension would further complicate what is already a somewhat complex analysis. We do, however, end with a discussion of why firms would want to produce multiple products.

18.1 MULTIPLANT FIRMS

A firm with market power often produces output in more than one plant. In this situation, it is likely that the various plants will have different cost conditions. The problem facing the firm is how to allocate the firm's desired level of production among these plants so that the total cost is minimized.

For simplicity, we assume there are only two plants, A and B. Suppose at the desired level of output, the following situation holds:

$$MC_A < MC_B$$

for the last unit of output produced in each plant. In this situation, the manager should transfer output from the higher cost Plant B to the lower cost Plant A. If the last unit produced in Plant B costs \$10, but one more unit produced in Plant A adds only \$7 to A's cost, that unit should be transferred from B to A. The transfer results in a cost reduction of \$3. In fact, output should be transferred from B to A until

$$MC_A = MC_B$$

Equality eventually occurs because of increasing marginal cost. As output is transferred out of B into A, the marginal cost in A rises, and the marginal cost in B falls. It is simple to see that exactly the opposite occurs in the case of

$$MC_A > MC_B$$

Output is taken out of Plant A and produced in Plant B until

$$MC_A = MC_B$$

The total output decision is easily determined. The horizontal summation of all plants' marginal cost curves is the firm's total marginal cost curve. This total marginal cost curve is equated to marginal revenue in order to determine the profit-maximizing output and price. This output is divided among the plants so that the marginal cost is equal for all plants.[1] The solution is identical to that for a cartel dividing production among firms.

The two-plant case is illustrated in Figure 18.1. Demand facing the firm is *D*, and marginal revenue is *MR*. The marginal cost curves for Plants A and B are, respectively, MC_A and MC_B. The total marginal cost curve for the firm is the

[1]For a mathematical demonstration, see Appendix A to this chapter.

FIGURE 18.1
A Multiplant Firm

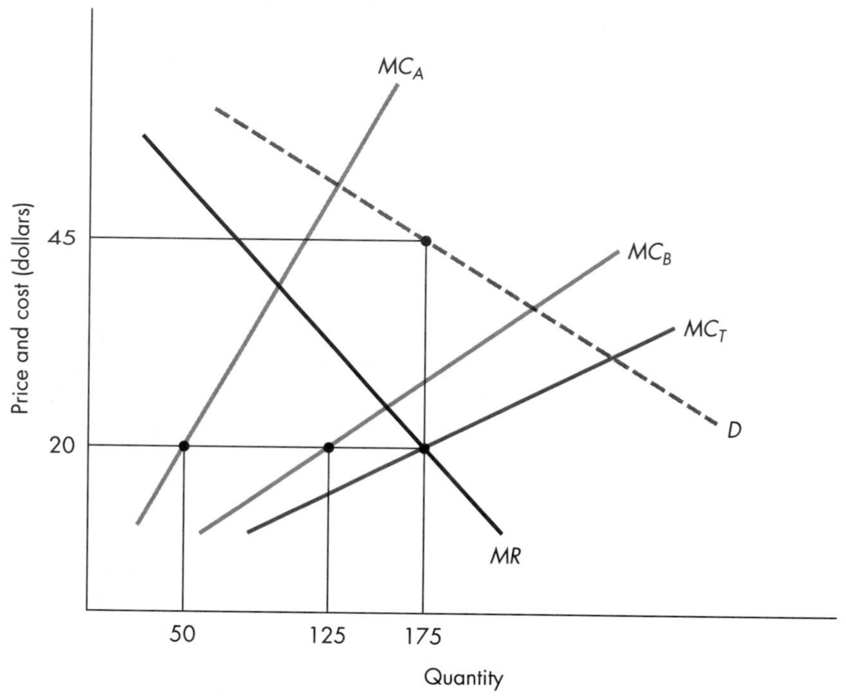

horizontal summation of MC_A and MC_B, labeled MC_T. Profit is maximized at that output level where MC_T equals marginal revenue, at an output of 175 units and a price of \$45. Marginal cost at this output is \$20. Equalization of marginal cost requires Plant A to produce 50 units and Plant B to produce 125 units, which of course sums to 175 since MC_T is the horizontal summation of MC_A and MC_B. This allocation equalizes marginal cost and consequently minimizes the total cost of producing 175 units.

To further illustrate the principle of optimally allocating output in a multiplant situation, we turn now to a numerical illustration. As you will see, the algebra is somewhat more complex than for the single plant case, but the principle is the same: The manager maximizes profit by producing the output level for which marginal revenue equals marginal cost.

Principle For a firm that produces using two plants, A and B, with marginal costs MC_A and MC_B, respectively, the total cost of producing any given level of total output Q_T (= $Q_A + Q_B$) is minimized when the manager allocates production between the two plants so that the marginal costs are equalized:

$$MC_A = MC_B$$

Multiplant Production of Mercantile Enterprises

Mercantile Enterprises—a firm with some degree of market power—produces its product in two plants. Hence, when making production decisions, the manager of Mercantile must decide not only how much to produce but also how to allocate the desired production between the two plants.

The production engineering department of Mercantile was able to provide the manager with simple, linear estimates of the incremental (marginal) cost functions for the two plants:

$$MC_A = 28 + 4Q_A \qquad MC_B = 16 + 2Q_B$$

where the marginal costs were measured in dollars per unit and output was measured in thousand units. Note that the estimated marginal cost function for Plant A (a plant built in 1968) is higher for every output than that for Plant B (a plant built in 1990); Plant B is more efficient.

The equation for the total marginal cost function (the horizontal sum of MC_A and MC_B), can be derived algebraically using the following procedure. First, solve for both inverse marginal cost functions:

$$Q_A = \frac{1}{4} MC_A - 7$$

and

$$Q_B = \frac{1}{2} MC_B - 8$$

Next, Q_T (= $Q_A + Q_B$) is found by summing the two inverse marginal cost functions. Recall, however, that the horizontal summing process requires that $MC_A = MC_B = MC_T$ for all levels of total output Q_T. Thus, it follows that

$$Q_A = \frac{1}{4} MC_T - 7$$

and

$$Q_B = \frac{1}{2} MC_T - 8$$

Summing the two inverse marginal cost functions results in the inverse *total* marginal cost function:

$$Q_T = Q_A + Q_B = \frac{3}{4} MC_T - 15$$

which, after taking the inverse to express marginal cost once again as a function of output, results in the total marginal cost function:

$$MC_T = 20 + \frac{4}{3} Q_T$$

FIGURE 18.2

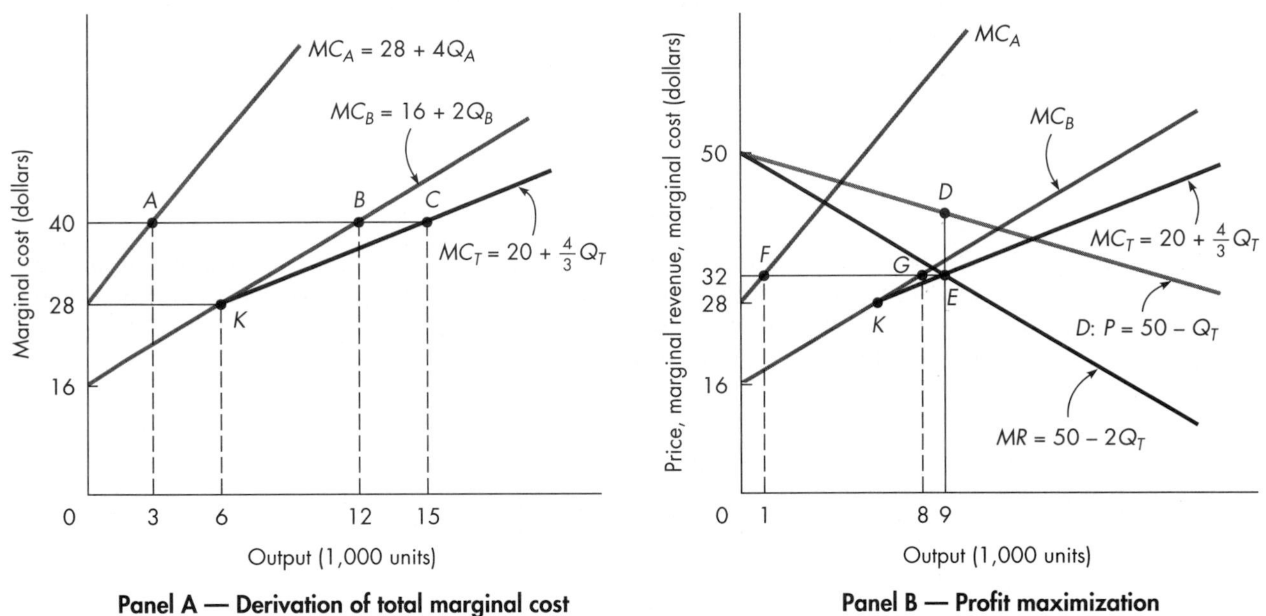

Panel A — Derivation of total marginal cost

Panel B — Profit maximization

The marginal cost functions for Plants A and B and the associated total marginal cost function are shown in Panel A of Figure 18.2. The process of horizontal summation can be seen by noting that when MC = \$40, Q_A = 3,000 units (point A), Q_B = 12,000 units (point B), and $Q_T = Q_A + Q_B$ = 15,000 units (point C). Thus, if 15,000 units are to be produced, the manager should allocate production so that 3,000 units are produced in Plant A and 12,000 units are produced in Plant B. This allocation of production between the two plants minimizes the total cost of producing a total of 15,000 units.

Note that when Q_T is less than 6,000 units, Plant A is shut down, and only Plant B is operated. Until Mercantile increases total production to 6,000 units or more (point K), the marginal cost of producing any output at all in Plant A is greater than the marginal cost of producing additional units in Plant B. For output levels in the zero to 6,000 unit range, MC_B is the relevant total marginal cost curve since Q_A = 0. For total output levels greater than 6,000 units, Mercantile Enterprises will operate *both* plants and MC_T is the total marginal cost function.

Suppose that the estimated demand curve for Mercantile's output is

$$Q = 50 - P$$

where output is measured in thousand units, and price is measured in dollars per unit. The inverse demand function is

$$P = 50 - Q$$

and marginal revenue is

$$MR = 50 - 2Q$$

Equating marginal revenue and total marginal cost,

$$50 - 2Q = 20 + \frac{4}{3}Q$$

and solving for Q, the profit-maximizing level of output for Mercantile Enterprises is $Q = 9$ (9,000 units). At this output level, marginal revenue and total marginal cost are both \$32 at point E in Panel B of Figure 18.2. In order to minimize the cost of producing 9,000 units, the production of the 9,000 units should be allocated between Plants A and B so that the marginal cost of the last unit produced in either plant is \$32:

$$MC_A = 28 + 4Q_A = 32 \qquad MC_B = 16 + 2Q_B = 32$$

Hence, for Plant A, $Q_A = 1$, so 1,000 units will be produced in Plant A. For Plant B, $Q_B = 8$, so 8,000 units will be produced in Plant B.

Now suppose that forecasted demand decreases and a new forecast of the demand for Mercantile's output is

$$Q = 40 - P$$

Given that the corresponding marginal revenue function is

$$MR = 40 - 2Q$$

the firm's profit-maximizing output (where $MR = MC_T$) declines to 6,000 units. At this output, marginal revenue and marginal cost are both \$28. Equating MC_A and MC_B to \$28, the manager found that for Plant A, $Q_A = 0$, and for Plant B, $Q_B = 6$. With the new (lower) forecast of demand, Plant A will be shut down and all of the output will be produced in Plant B. As you can verify, if demand declines further, Mercantile would still produce, using only Plant B. So for output levels of 6,000 or fewer units, the total marginal cost function is MC_B.

In effect, the total marginal cost function has a "kink" at point K in the figure. The kink at point K represents the total output level below which the high-cost plant is shut down. A kink occurs when marginal cost in the low-cost plant equals the minimum level of marginal cost in the high-cost plant, thereby making it optimal to begin producing with an additional plant. The output at which the kink occurs is found by setting marginal cost in the *low*-cost plant equal to the minimum value of marginal cost in the *high*-cost plant:

$$MC_B = 28 = 16 + 2Q$$

so the high-cost plant begins operating when Q exceeds 6,000 units.

The preceding discussion and example show how a manager should allocate production between two plants to minimize the cost of producing the level of output that maximizes profit. The principle of equating marginal costs applies in exactly the same fashion to the case of three or more plants: Marginal cost is the same in all plants that produce. The only complication arises in the derivation of total marginal cost.

Once the total marginal cost function is derived, either by summing the individual plants' marginal cost curves graphically or by solving algebraically, the manager uses the total marginal cost function to find the profit-maximizing level of total output.

Principle A manager who has *n* plants that can produce output will maximize profit when the firm produces the level of total output and allocates that output among the *n* plants so that

$$MR = MC_T = MC_1 = \ldots = MC_n$$

18.2 FIRMS WITH MULTIPLE MARKETS—PRICE DISCRIMINATION

price discrimination Firms charge different groups of customers different prices for the same good or service.

Thus far we have treated demand as simply the horizontal summation of the demands of all consumers, and every consumer is charged the same price for the product. But, since consumers are different, their demands differ. At times, firms can take advantage of these differences in demand in order to increase their profit. Price discrimination is the method by which this is accomplished. **Price discrimination** means that the firm charges different consumers different prices for the same good (when there are no corresponding differences in costs). For example, price discrimination can occur when a firm charges different prices in its domestic and foreign markets or when a movie theater charges adults a higher price to see a movie than it charges children.

Certain conditions are necessary for the firm to be *able* to price discriminate. First, the firm obviously must possess some market power. Economists normally think of price discrimination in the context of a monopoly firm, but, since they have market power, monopolistic competitors and oligopolists may also be able to price discriminate. Second, the demand functions for the individual consumers or groups of consumers must differ. As we will demonstrate later, this statement can be made more specific to require that the own-price elasticities must be different. Third, the different markets must be separable. The firm must be able to identify the individuals or groups of individuals and effectively separate them into submarkets. Finally, purchasers of the product must not be able to resell it to other customers. If consumers could buy and sell the product among themselves, there is no way that the firm can keep the submarkets separated. (Firms don't want the low-price buyers to sell their product to the high-price buyers.)

Normally, economists speak of three degrees of price discrimination. However, because we only want to provide a brief overview of price discrimination, we will limit our discussion to what is referred to as third-degree price discrimination. This is the form most commonly observed and is the form that best illustrates our primary concern in this section: profit maximization with multiple markets.

TABLE 18.1
Allocation of Sales Between Two Markets

Quantity	Marginal revenue in Market 1	Order of sales	Marginal revenue in Market 2	Order of sales
1	$45	(1)	$34	(3)
2	36	(2)	28	(5)
3	30	(4)	22	(7)
4	22	(6)	13	(10)
5	17	(8)	10	(12)
6	15	(9)	8	
7	10	(11)	7	
8	7		4	
9	4		2	
10	0		1	

Allocation of Sales in Two Markets to Maximize Revenue

The analysis of price discrimination is a straightforward application of the $MR = MC$ rule. As a first step in that analysis, assume that a firm has two separate markets for its product. Demand conditions in each market are such that the marginal revenues from selling specified quantities are as given in Table 18.1. Assume also that the manager has decided to produce 12 units. How should the manager allocate sales between the two markets in order to maximize the total revenue from the sale of 12 units? Clearly, revenue from selling the chosen level of output must be maximized if profit is to be maximized.

Consider the first unit; the firm can increase revenue by $45 by selling it in Market 1 or by $34 by selling in Market 2. Obviously, the firm will sell the first unit in Market 1. So, the first unit (1) is sold in Market 1. The second unit is also sold in Market 1 since its sale there increases revenue by $36, whereas it would only increase revenue by $34 in Market 2. Since $34 can be gained in Market 2 but only $30 in Market 1, unit three is sold in Market 2. Similar reasoning shows that the fourth unit goes to Market 1 and the fifth to Market 2. Since unit six adds $22 to revenue in either market, it makes no difference where it is sold; six and seven go one to each market. Eight and 9 are sold in Market 1 because they yield higher marginal revenue there; 10 goes to Market 2 for the same reason. Unit 11 can go to either market, since the additional revenues are the same, and unit 12 goes to the other. Thus the 12 units will be divided so that the marginal revenue is the same for the last unit sold in each market; the firm sells seven units in Market 1 and five in Market 2. Thus, the price discriminating firm allocates a given output in such a way that the marginal revenues in each market are equal.[2]

[2]For a mathematical demonstration, see Appendix A to this chapter.

The results from Table 18.1 indicate that a manager will maximize profit when output is allocated in such a way that

$$MR_1 = MR_2$$

This condition should not be surprising since it is just another application of the principle of constrained optimization presented in Chapter 4. If a manager wants to maximize total revenue subject to the constraint that there is only a limited number of units to sell, the manager should allocate sales so that the marginal revenues (marginal benefits) per unit are equal in the two markets. The marginal cost of selling one unit in Market 1 is the one unit not available for sale in Market 2 ($MC_1 = MC_2 = 1$ unit).

Principle A manager who wishes to maximize the total revenue from selling a given amount of output in two separate markets (*A* and *B*) should allocate sales between the two markets so that

$$MR_A = MR_B$$

and all units are sold.

Although the marginal revenues in the two markets are equal, the prices charged are not. The higher price will be charged in the market with the less elastic demand; the lower price will be charged in the market having the more elastic demand. In the more elastic market, price could be raised only at the expense of a large decrease in sales. In the less elastic market higher prices bring less reduction in sales.

This assertion can be demonstrated as follows. Let the prices in the two markets be P_1 and P_2. Likewise, let E_1 and E_2 denote the respective own-price elasticities. As shown in Chapter 3 marginal revenue can be expressed as

$$MR = P\left(1 + \frac{1}{E}\right)$$

As shown above, managers will maximize revenue if they allocate output so that $MR_1 = MR_2$. That is,

$$MR_1 = P_1\left(1 + \frac{1}{E_1}\right) = P_2\left(1 + \frac{1}{E_2}\right) = MR_2$$

Since MR_1 and MR_2 must both be positive, E_1 and E_2 must both be greater (in absolute value) than one (i.e., demand must be elastic in each market). Assume that

$$P_1 < P_2$$

when $MR_1 = MR_2$. By manipulating the equation above,

$$\frac{P_1}{P_2} = \frac{\left(1 + \frac{1}{E_2}\right)}{\left(1 + \frac{1}{E_1}\right)} < 0$$

Therefore, since

$$\left(1 + \frac{1}{E_2}\right) < \left(1 + \frac{1}{E_1}\right)$$

it must be the case that

$$\left|\frac{1}{E_2}\right| > \left|\frac{1}{E_1}\right|$$

so that

$$|E_1| > |E_2|$$

The market with the lower price must have the higher elasticity at that price. Therefore, if a firm price discriminates, it will always charge the lower price in the market having the more elastic demand curve.

Principle A manager who price discriminates in two separate markets, A and B, will maximize total revenue for a given level of output by charging the lower price in the more elastic market and the higher price in the less elastic market. If $|E_A| > |E_B|$, then $P_A < P_B$.

Profit Maximization with Price Discrimination

Thus far we have assumed that the price discriminating firm wishes to allocate a *given level of output* among its markets in order to maximize the revenue from selling that output. Now we discuss how a manager determines the profit-maximizing level of output and the prices to charge in the different markets.

As you probably expected, the manager maximizes profit by equating marginal revenue with marginal cost. The firm's marginal cost curve is no different from that of a nondiscriminating firm with market power. So the problem is to derive the marginal revenue curve.

With discrete data such as in Table 18.1, we would simply increase sales as discussed above, then determine the total marginal revenue from the allocation of each unit of output to the market with the higher marginal revenue. Thus total marginal revenue from Table 18.1 would be $45 for the first unit sold, $36 for the second (both in Market 1), $34 for the third (in Market 2), $30 for the fourth, and so on.

For continuous demand and marginal revenue curves in each submarket, the total marginal revenue curve for a price discriminating firm is simply the horizontal summation of the marginal revenues in each market. Assume that the firm sells in two markets, 1 and 2. The demand and marginal revenue curves in Markets 1 and 2 are shown, respectively, as D_1 and MR_1 in Panel A of Figure 18.3 and as D_2 and MR_2 in Panel B. In Panel C of the figure, the total marginal revenue, MR_T, is the horizontal summation of MR_1 and MR_2.

From the above discussion, a manager will allocate any given output between the two markets so that MR_1 equals MR_2. For example, if the firm produces 300 units of output at which MR equals $30, it will sell 100 units in Market 1 and 200 in Market 2. At 100 units of output (from Panel A), MR_1 equals $30. At 200 units of output (from Panel B), MR_2 also equals $30. Thus, no matter which

FIGURE 18.3
Deriving Total Marginal Revenue

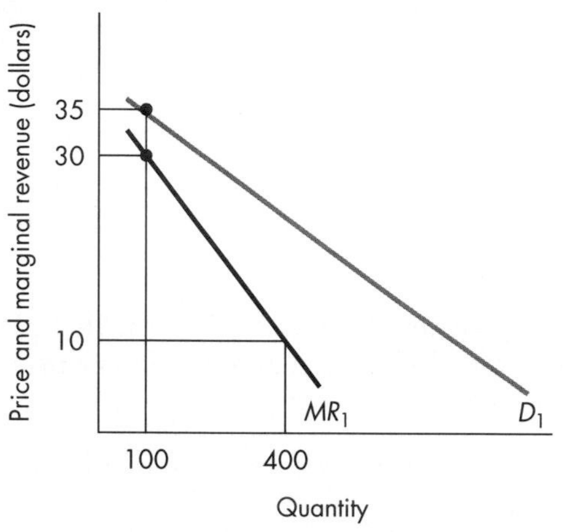

Panel A — Demand and marginal revenue: Market 1

Panel B — Demand and marginal revenue: Market 2

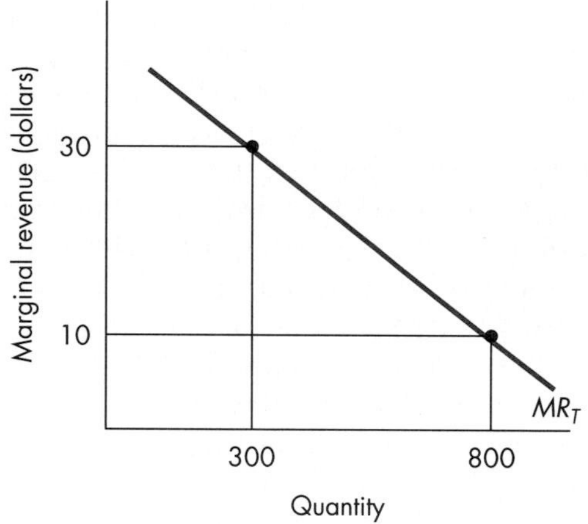

Panel C — Total marginal revenue

market unit 300 is sold in, the firm's marginal revenue is \$30, as shown in Panel C. And this is the only allocation of 300 total units that equates the marginal revenues in the two markets. Likewise, if the firm wants to sell 800 units, it will sell 400 in Market 1 and 400 in Market 2; as shown in the figure, the marginal revenue is \$10 in each market. Thus for 800 units of output the total marginal revenue is \$10. At every other output, the marginal revenue in Panel C (MR_T) is obtained in the same way.

FIGURE 18.4
Profit Maximization with Two Markets

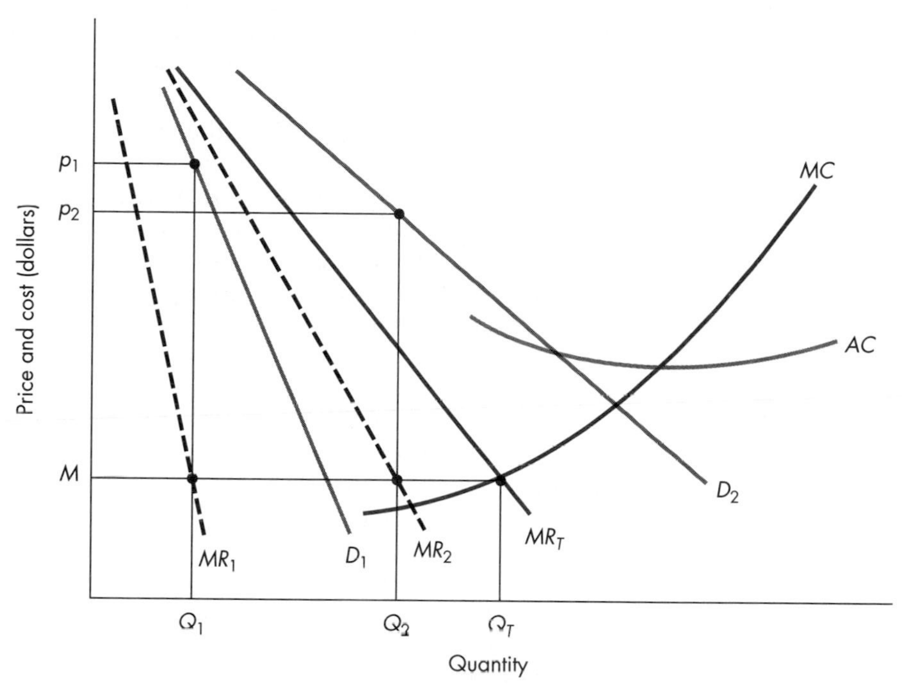

For each level of output, the price in each market is given by the demand in that market. For example, if a total of 300 units are sold, from D_1 the price of the 100 units sold in Market 1 is $35; from D_2 the price of the 200 units sold in Market 2 is $40. (The horizontal sum of D_1 and D_2 was not graphed since this curve is irrelevant for the price discriminating firm.)

The only decision remaining is how much total output the firm should produce to maximize its profits. To see how this decision is made, consider Figure 18.4 in which all of the relations are generalized graphically. Again the firm is selling a product in two markets: D_1 and MR_1 are demand and marginal revenue in Market 1; D_2 and MR_2 are demand and marginal revenue in Market 2. MR_T is the horizontal summation of the two marginal revenue curves. For convenience, all these curves are shown on the same graph, along with the firm's average cost (*AC*) and marginal cost (*MC*) curves.

As always, the firm maximizes profit by producing the output at which total marginal revenue equals marginal cost. In this case, Q_T, where *MC* equals MR_T, is the total output. The marginal revenue and marginal cost are both equal to the dollar amount *M* in Figure 18.4.

The market allocation rule, previously determined, requires that marginal revenue be the same in each submarket. Since the total market marginal revenue is the added revenue from selling the last unit in either submarket, $MR_1 = MR_2 =$

M. At a marginal revenue of M, the quantity sold in Market 1 is Q_1, in Market 2, Q_2. Since MR_T is the horizontal summation of MR_1 and MR_2, $Q_1 + Q_2 = Q_T$, the total output. Furthermore, from the relevant demand curves, the price associated with output Q_1 in Market 1 is p_1, and the price associated with Q_2 in Market 2 is p_2.

Summarizing these results, if the aggregate market for a firm's product can be divided into submarkets with different price elasticities, the firm can profitably practice price discrimination. Total output is determined by equating marginal cost with total marginal revenue. The output is allocated among the submarkets so as to equate marginal revenue in each submarket with total marginal revenue at the profit-maximizing level of output. With two markets, the profit-maximization rule for the price-discriminating firm is

$$MR_T = MC = MR_1 = MR_2$$

Price in each submarket is determined from the submarket demand curve.

Examples of price discrimination are not hard to find. Many drugstores offer discounts on drugs to persons 65 and over. Thus, the drugstores price discriminate. Retired persons probably have a more elastic demand for drugs, because the market value of their time is lower. Retired persons would tend to shop around more for lower prices, and differences in price among different age-groups can be explained by different price elasticities, resulting from different evaluations of time.

Movies, plays, concerts, and similar forms of entertainment practice price discrimination according to age. Generally, younger people pay lower prices. Supposedly, in such cases, younger people have more elastic demands for tickets, possibly because of the availability of more substitute forms of entertainment. (It is not correct to say that different ticket prices for afternoon and evening performances are evidence of price discrimination. These are different products in the eye of the consumer.)

Airlines frequently discriminate between vacation and business travel. Vacation travelers would have a more elastic demand than business travelers, probably because the value of time in business travel is greater. Other examples of price discrimination are electric companies that charge lower rates to industrial users than to households (although this may be, in part, due to differences in costs), and university bookstores that charge lower prices to faculty than to students. On the other hand, students frequently are charged a lower price for subscriptions to newspapers and magazines.

Manufacturers and sellers of durable goods, such as automobiles and large appliances, sometimes practice price discrimination also. Automobiles with exactly the same characteristics all have the same window or sticker price (excluding the shipping charge). But as you probably know, dealers generally discount these prices on many models. Except for extremely hot sellers, people seldom pay the listed price. However, everyone does not pay the same price for the same vehicle. Ms. Jones may pay a lower price than Mr. Smith because Ms. Jones is willing to bargain longer or possibly the dealer recognized that Mr. Smith is already sold on the car. Perhaps Mr. Smith came into the showroom, saw the list price, and said, "Wow, is that all you're charging for that great car?" In any case, Mr. Smith probably has the less elastic demand. We should note, however, that this is a slightly different form of price discrimination than that discussed above. In this case the dealer treats each potential consumer as a separate market, and charges as much as the consumer is willing to pay, if possible.

In order to implement profit maximization with multiple markets, it would be necessary for the manager to estimate demand and marginal revenue functions for each of the markets. After summing to obtain a total marginal revenue function, total output would be that at which total marginal revenue is equal to marginal cost. Then, this output will be allocated to the various markets so that the marginal revenues are all equal to total marginal revenue at the profit-maximizing output. We illustrate this procedure with a simple algebraic example.

Multiple Market Pricing at Galactic Manufacturing

The manager of Galactic Manufacturing—a firm with substantial monopoly power—knows that the firm faces two distinct markets. Using the techniques described earlier in this text, the demand curves for these two markets were forecasted to be

$$\text{Mkt 1: } Q_1 = 100 - 2P_1 \quad \text{and} \quad \text{Mkt 2: } Q_2 = 50 - .5P_2$$

where output is measured in thousand units and price in dollars per unit. Solving for the inverse demand functions in the two markets,

$$\text{Mkt 1: } P_1 = 50 - .5Q_1 \quad \text{and} \quad \text{Mkt 2: } P_2 = 100 - 2Q_2$$

The marginal revenue functions associated with these inverse demand functions are:

$$\text{Mkt 1: } MR_1 = 50 - 1Q_1 \quad \text{and} \quad \text{Mkt 2: } MR_2 = 100 - 4Q_2$$

To obtain the total marginal revenue function, $MR_T = f(Q_T)$, we follow steps identical to those employed in the algebraic derivation of the total marginal cost function. First, the inverse marginal revenue functions are obtained for both markets in which Galactic Manufacturing sells its product:

$$\text{Mkt 1: } Q_1 = 50 - MR_1 \qquad \text{Mkt 2: } Q_2 = 25 - \frac{1}{4}MR_2$$

For any given level of total output, $MR_1 = MR_2 = MR_T$, thus

$$\text{Mkt 1: } Q_1 = 50 - MR_T \qquad \text{Mkt 2: } Q_2 = 25 - \frac{1}{4}MR_T$$

Since $Q_T = Q_1 + Q_2$, the inverse of total marginal revenue is obtained by summing the two inverse marginal revenue curves to get:

$$Q_T = Q_1 + Q_2 = (50 - MR_T) + \left(25 - \frac{1}{4}MR_T\right) = 75 - \frac{5}{4}MR_T$$

FIGURE 18.5
Galactic Manufacturing

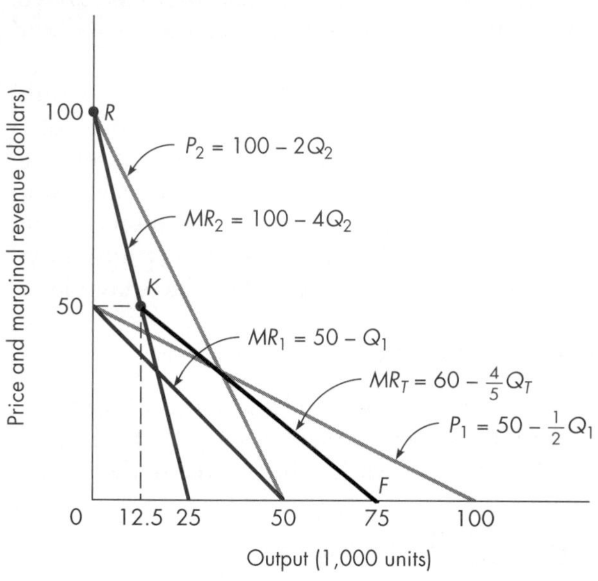

Panel A — Derivation of total marginal revenue

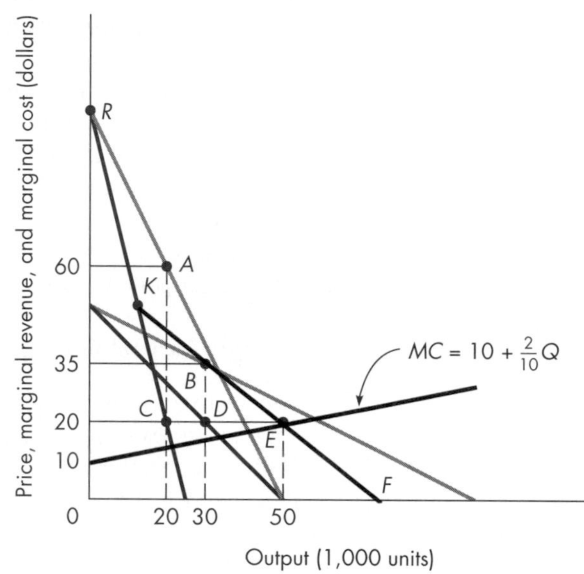

Panel B — Profit maximization

Taking the inverse, we obtain the total marginal revenue function facing Galactic Manufacturing:

$$MR_T = 60 - \frac{4}{5}Q_T$$

Panel A of Figure 18.5 illustrates graphically the derivation of total marginal revenue for Galactic Manufacturing. Panel A shows graphs of the demand and marginal revenue functions in Markets 1 and 2. The total marginal revenue function is the line (*RKF*). If total output is less than 12.5 (12,500 units), every unit produced should be sold in Market 2 in order to maximize revenue (for that output level) because MR_2 exceeds MR_1 until Galactic chooses to sell more than 12,500 units. Thus, total marginal revenue has a kink at 12.5 (point *K*) and MR_2 is the total marginal revenue function since $Q_1 = 0$ when total output is 12,500 units or less.

The manager of Galactic Manufacturing obtained from the engineering department a linear estimate of the firm's marginal cost function:

$$MC = 10 + \frac{2}{10}Q$$

where Q is measured in units of 1,000. Equating estimated total marginal revenue and marginal cost,

$$60 - \frac{4}{5}Q = 10 + \frac{2}{10}Q$$

the manager of Galactic solved for Q and determined the profit-maximizing level of output to be 50 (50,000 units). As you can see in Panel B of Figure 18.5, MR_T intersects MC at 50,000 units (point E). At 50,000 units of output, total marginal revenue and marginal cost both equal \$20. To find the optimal allocation of 50,000 units between the two markets, the manager allocates sales so that marginal revenues are equated across the two markets at a value of \$20. The manager must solve the following two equations:

$$\text{Mkt 1: } 20 = 50 - Q_1 \qquad \text{and} \qquad \text{Mkt 2: } 20 = 100 - 4Q_2$$

The solution is to sell 30,000 units in Market 1 and 20,000 units in Market 2. These points where $MR_1 = MR_2 = MR_T$ are shown in Panel B by points C, D, and E.

The manager determines the price to charge in the two markets by substituting the optimal quantities into the demand equations in each of the markets. The manager finds that profit is maximized by selling the 30,000 units of output in Market 1 at a price of \$35 and the 20,000 units of output in Market 2 at a price of \$60. Points A and B in Panel B show the optimal pricing solution for Galactic Manufacturing.

Principle A manager who wishes to sell output in n separate markets will maximize profit if the firm produces the level of total output and allocates that output among the n separate markets so that

$$MR_T = MR_1 = \ . \ . \ . \ = MR_n = MC$$

The optimal prices to charge in each market are determined from the demand functions in each of the n markets.

18.3 FIRMS SELLING MULTIPLE PRODUCTS

Even the most cursory survey of firms operating in the United States shows that many firms produce several different products or at least several different models in their product line. While in some cases the firm's products are unrelated, in most cases the products are related either in consumption or production. When the products that a firm produces are related, the firm's output and pricing decision must incorporate the interrelations in order to maximize total profit.

This section provides a brief overview of how managers make profit-maximizing decisions for multiple-product firms. Three possible cases are considered. First, the products are related in consumption. Second, the products are complements in production. Third, the products are substitutes in production.

ILLUSTRATION 18.1

Sometimes It's Hard to Price Discriminate

In the theoretical discussion of price discrimination, we made two important points: 1) Firms must separate the markets according to demand elasticity, and 2) Firms must be able to separate markets so as to keep buyers in the higher-price market from buying in the lower-price market. In some of the market examples we used it was relatively easy to separate the markets. For example, at movie theaters it is fairly simple, and relatively inexpensive, to prevent an adult from entering the theater with a lower-priced child's ticket. In other cases of price discrimination, it is rather difficult or costly to separate the markets. If it is impossible or expensive to separate markets, price discrimination will not be profitable, and the monopolist will charge a single price to all customers.

One of the most frequently cited examples of a market in which separation is difficult is the airline market. It is no secret that airlines attempt to charge leisure fliers lower fares than business travelers. The story of such an attempt recently by Northwest Airlines illustrates the difficulty of separating markets.

The Wall Street Journal reported that "Northwest Airlines, seeking to entice families and groups of leisure travelers who often wait for deep fare cuts before flying, has introduced a permanent discount fare. The new supersaver fare will offer savings of 20 percent to 40 percent anytime *groups of two or more people* travel together." According to a Northwest vice-president, "We're trying to decouple the leisure fares from the rest of the fare market by offering fares low enough so that it won't pay for them to wait for a special fare sale."

The *Journal* noted that this change would be likely to stimulate family travel but would also eliminate the use of supersaver fares by business travelers. Previously, many business travelers purchased round-trip supersaver tickets when fares dropped below 50 percent, then threw away the return portion of the ticket or used it later. Northwest was planning to raise or do away with its other supersaver fares designed to attract leisure travelers. Most business travelers fly alone and would not be able to take advantage of the new lower fares requiring groups of two or more. The Northwest executive also predicted that business people would not abuse these tickets. Should the plan stick and spread, he said, it will allow airlines to maintain an attractive offering for the most price-sensitive travelers, while allowing the basic supersaver fares to continue rising along with business rates.

This reasoning was a bit optimistic on the part of the airline. The *WSJ* noted that groups of business travelers could work around the restrictions that currently applied to supersavers. The president of one travel agency said, "Groups of business people going to company meetings or conventions might be able to save thousands." One airline official expressed concern that travel agents would match travelers who did not know each other who were going to the same destination. Clearly there were many ways to defeat the airline's attempts to price discriminate effectively.

But Northwest knew about the problems and tried to make the practice of cross-buying difficult. Travelers were required to book their flights together, check in together, and follow identical itineraries in order to qualify for the group discounts. The fares were nonrefundable, required a Saturday night stay, and booking 14 days in advance—practices that business travelers typically would find difficult to accomplish. Of course, some of these restrictions designed to weed out business travelers could discourage many leisure travelers, the very people the new discounts were designed to attract. And obviously single leisure travelers would be left out.

As you can see, the problem of separating markets—preventing customers in the higher-priced market from buying in the lower-priced market—can be an extremely challenging task for the would-be price discriminator. For airlines, it would be much easier if passengers came with signs saying "business traveler" or "leisure traveler." As previously noted, in markets where separating the higher-price buyers from the lower-price buyers is too difficult or too expensive, price discrimination will not be profitable.

Source: Brett Pulley, "Northwest Cuts Fares to Boost Leisure Travel," *The Wall Street Journal*, January 12, 1993.

Multiple Products Related in Consumption

Recall that the demand for a particular commodity depends not only on the price of the product itself but also on the prices of related commodities, incomes, tastes, and so on. For simplicity, we ignore the other factors and write one demand function as

$$Q_X = f(P_X, P_Y)$$

where Q_X is the quantity demanded of commodity X, P_X is the price of X, and P_Y is the price of a related commodity Y—either a substitute or complement.

In the discussion so far in the text, we have treated P_Y as if it were given to the firm. That is, we assumed P_Y to be a parameter determined outside of the firm. Thus, the firm would maximize its profits by selecting the appropriate level of production and price for X. If, however, the firm in question produces *both* commodities X and Y, the price of the related commodity Y is no longer exogenous but is controlled by the firm. The profitability of X then depends on the price of Y and vice versa.

In order to maximize profit, the levels of output and prices for the related commodities must be determined *jointly*. For a two-product firm, the profit maximizing conditions remain the same,

$$MR_X = MC_X \quad \text{and} \quad MR_Y = MC_Y$$

However, the marginal revenue of X will be a function of the quantities of both X and Y, as will the marginal revenue of Y. Hence, these marginal conditions must be satisfied *simultaneously*. (Note that in this case the products are not related in production, so MC_X and MC_Y depend only upon, respectively, the output of X and the output of Y.) To show how a manager would maximize profit under these circumstances, we will use another hypothetical example. In this example we will look at a firm that produces products that are substitutes in consumption, but the same technique applies for products that are complements in consumption.

Producing Multiple Products (substitutes) at Zicon Manufacturing

Zicon Manufacturing produces two types of automobile vacuum cleaners. One, which we denote as product X, plugs into the cigarette lighter receptacle; the other—product Y—has rechargeable batteries. Assuming that there is no other relation between the two products other than the apparent substitutability in consumption, the manager of Zicon wanted to determine the profit-maximizing levels of production and price for the two products.

Using the techniques described in this text, the demand functions for the two products were forecasted to be

$$Q_X = 80 - 8P_X + 6P_Y \quad \text{and} \quad Q_Y = 40 - 4P_Y + 4P_X$$

where the outputs were measured in thousand units and the prices in dollars per unit. Solving these two forecasted demand functions simultaneously, the manager obtained the following functions in which prices are a function of both quantities.[3]

$$P_X = 70 - \frac{1}{2}Q_X - \frac{3}{4}Q_Y \quad \text{and} \quad P_Y = 80 - 1Q_Y - \frac{1}{2}Q_X$$

The marginal revenue functions were[4]

$$MR_X = 70 - \frac{3}{4}Q_Y - 1Q_X \quad \text{and} \quad MR_Y = 80 - \frac{1}{2}Q_X - 2Q_Y$$

As noted earlier, MR_X is a function of both Q_X and Q_Y, as is MR_Y.

The production manager obtained estimates of the marginal cost functions.

$$MC_X = 10 + \frac{1}{2}Q_X \quad \text{and} \quad MC_Y = 20 + \frac{1}{4}Q_Y$$

where output was again measured in thousand units.

To determine the output that will maximize profit, the manager of Zicon equated MR and MC for the two products.

$$70 - 1Q_X - \frac{3}{4}Q_Y = 10 + \frac{1}{2}Q_X$$

$$80 - 2Q_Y - \frac{1}{2}Q_X = 20 + \frac{1}{4}Q_Y$$

Solving these equations simultaneously for Q_X and Q_Y (see footnote 3), the profit-maximizing outputs were found to be $Q_X = 30$ (i.e., 30,000 units) and $Q_Y = 20$ (i.e., 20,000 units). Finally, using these outputs in the price functions, the manager of Zicon found that the profit-maximizing prices for X and Y were

$$P_X = 70 - \frac{1}{2}(30) - \frac{3}{4}(20) = \$40$$

and

$$P_Y = 80 - 1\,(20) - \frac{1}{3}(30) = \$45$$

---

[3]One way to solve these two equations simultaneously is to use the method of substitution. First, solve one demand function for P_X in terms of Q_X and P_Y and the other demand function for P_Y in terms of Q_Y and P_X. Then substitute the equation for P_Y into the equation for P_X, and vice versa. These two equations can then be solved for P_X and P_Y in terms of Q_X and Q_Y.

[4]As noted several times, the marginal revenue curve associated with a straight-line demand curve has the same intercept and is twice as steep as the demand curve. The intercepts for MR_X and MR_Y are, respectively, $(70 - 3/4Q_Y)$ and $(80 - 1/2Q_X)$. Thus,

$$MR_X = \left(70 - \frac{3}{4}Q_Y\right) - (2)\left(\frac{1}{2}\right)Q_X = 70 - \frac{3}{4}Q_Y - 1\,Q_X$$

and

$$MR_Y = \left(80 - \frac{1}{2}Q_X\right) - (2)\,(1)\,Q_Y = 80 - \frac{1}{2}Q_X - 2\,Q_Y$$

From the preceding discussion and following illustration, the point we wish to stress is that if a firm produces products that are related in consumption, profit maximization requires that output levels and prices be determined jointly. Specifically, in such a firm, the profit-maximizing price for a particular commodity will be determined not only by the demand and cost conditions for that commodity, but also by those of any related commodities the firm produces.

Principle When a firm produces two products, X and Y, that are related in consumption either as substitutes or complements, the manager of the multiple-product firm maximizes profit by producing and selling the amounts of X and Y for which

$$MR_X = MC_X$$

and

$$MR_Y = MC_Y$$

are *simultaneously* satisfied. The profit-maximizing prices, P_X and P_Y, are determined by substituting the optimal levels of X and Y into the demand functions and solving for P_X and P_Y.

Multiple Products That Are Complements in Production

complements in production Two goods that are produced using a common input.

To examine products that are related in production, we begin by considering a firm that produces outputs that are **complements in production**. Complementarity in production typically occurs when an ingredient input is used to produce two or more products. One of the classic examples is that of beef carcasses and hides. The food products produced with the beef carcasses and the leather products produced with the hides are complement goods in production. Furthermore, the joint production of the two products is characterized by fixed proportions—for each additional beef carcass produced, one additional hide is produced also.

Petroleum refining has similar characteristics. With an existing refinery and a given mix of input crude oils, production of an additional barrel of one of the lighter distillates, such as gasoline, requires that the refinery produce some additional amount of the heavy distillates, such as fuel oil. Complementarity in production can also be observed in mineral extraction. Frequently, two or more metals are found together in the same ore deposit. When the ore goes into the smelter, more than one metal is produced. For example, since nickel and zinc frequently are in the same deposit, the smelters are designed to produce both metals from the same ore.

Since complements in production frequently result when one raw material is used to produce two or more products, this type of joint production results in the product being produced in fixed proportions from the ingredient. If the firm produces outputs that are complements in production and characterized by fixed proportions production, the profit-maximizing firm will select the level of output of the joint product at which total marginal revenue equals total marginal cost. Given this level of production, the prices for the individual products would

ILLUSTRATION 18.2

Cannibalization by Saturn Concerns General Motors Corporation

As noted in the previous analysis, when a firm produces multiple products that are related in consumption, the demand and marginal revenue functions for each product depend on the levels of output for all the other related goods. Since the multiproduct firm can control production levels, and hence prices of the various products, the manager of this type of firm must account for such interdependencies when choosing the profit-maximizing prices and outputs.

When a multiproduct firm produces related goods that are substitutes, the pricing decision places the management in a rather pernicious position. Lowering price on one product to increase sales will cause a reduction in sales of the substitute good, which is also produced by the same firm. This complication in pricing substitute goods is sometimes referred to as cannibalization.

A recent example of the cannibalization problem involves General Motors Corporation's pricing decision regarding its new Saturn line of automobiles. The Saturn Corporation is GM's $3 billion project aimed at producing a high-quality, price-competitive car that would make GM more competitive with Japanese imports. The Saturn plant, in Spring Hill, Tennessee, began production in 1991 with three Saturn sedans and one coupe priced between $8,000 and $12,000.

A few problems have arisen in the early stages of getting the new Saturn plant operating. Management at Saturn decided to begin production at the new plant by concentrating on production of sedans rather than coupes. In fall 1990, managers at Saturn reasoned that with winter approaching, sedans sell better than the sportier coupes. Apparently, management was wrong. According to newspaper reports, Saturn dealers have been "howling" for coupes as demand for coupes relative to sedans was much higher than forecasted.

A more vexing problem for management at Saturn and the parent corporation, GM, is the problem posed by cannibalization. The low-to-moderately priced Saturn is taking sales away from Chevrolet, GM's other low-to-moderately priced line of automobiles. GM management had predicted that 20 percent of Saturn's sales would come from cannibalization of other GM models. By summer 1991, the cannibalization rate reached approximately 33 percent. One-third of Saturn's sales, which came mostly at the expense of Chevrolet, did nothing to expand GM's market share with respect to the Japanese (or, for that matter, any other automaker).

This example illustrates the complexity of pricing and output decisions that face managers of multiple product firms. As this example shows, even when management recognizes in concept that cannibalization is going to occur, it may be very difficult to predict the degree to which it will occur. You can be sure that a corporation like GM, which has always faced the problem of pricing substitute goods, is as well equipped as any firm to estimate the impact of cannibalization among its various products. Their forecast error indicates just how complex the decision actually is for real-world managers.

Source: The information for this illustration is from "After Early Snags, Saturn in Orbit," *The Tampa Tribune*, August 1, 1991, p. 8.

be taken from the individual demand curves. (Complementarity in production is illustrated in Appendix B to this chapter.)

Multiple Products That Are Substitutes in Production

substitutes in production Goods produced by the same firm that compete for limited production facilities.

While the case of products that are complements in production is clearly possible, a more common situation is the multiproduct firm that produces outputs that are **substitutes in production**. This situation is commonly encountered when a firm produces several models of the same basic product. These different models compete for the limited production facilities of the firm and are therefore substitutes in the firm's production process. In the long run, the firm can adjust its production facility in order to produce the profit-maximizing level of each product. However, in the short run, the firm must determine how to allocate its limited production capacity among the competing products in order to maximize profit.

The short-run case is another example of constrained optimization. The firm must maximize profit subject to the constraint imposed by the limited production facility. For simplicity, we consider a firm that produces only two products, which we will denote as X and Y. Further, we assume that the two products are produced using the same production facility and that the cost of operating this facility is invariant to the product produced. The marginal benefit accrued from producing an additional unit of either product is the marginal revenue that is generated. In the case of product X, this is MR_X. The marginal cost of producing an additional unit of one product is the reduction in output of the competing product. For product X, the marginal cost is the corresponding reduction in the production of Y, ΔY. Conversely, the marginal cost of producing an additional unit of Y is ΔX. As we demonstrated in Chapter 4, a firm will maximize its objective function subject to a constraint when the ratios of marginal benefit to marginal cost are equal for all decision variables. In this case, profit will be maximized when the levels of production of the two products are such that

$$\frac{MR_X}{\Delta Y} = \frac{MR_Y}{\Delta X}$$

To see how this condition can be utilized, let's look at a simplified example.

Multiple-Product Production at Surefire Products

A division of Surefire Products, Inc., manufactures two products, X and Y, that are unrelated in consumption but are substitutes in production. More specifically, these two products are produced on the same assembly line, so they compete for the limited time available. The question facing the manager of the parent company—Surefire Products—is: How should an eight-hour production day be allocated between the production of X and the production of Y?

The demand functions for the two products were forecasted to be

$$Q_X = 60 - \frac{1}{2} P_X \quad \text{and} \quad Q_Y = 40 - \frac{2}{3} P_Y$$

where the quantities were the number of units demanded per day and the prices were expressed in dollars per unit. From these forecasted demand functions, the marginal revenue functions were

$$MR_X = 120 - 4Q_X \quad \text{and} \quad MR_Y = 60 - 3Q_Y$$

Discussions with the plant supervisor indicated that, in one hour of production time, either two units of X or four units of Y could be produced. In a sense, the production functions for the two products are

$$Q_X = 2H_X \quad \text{and} \quad Q_Y = 4H_Y$$

where H_X and H_Y denote, respectively, hours of assembly line time in the production of X and Y. From this, the marginal cost of using an additional hour in the production of X is $\Delta Y = 4$. That is, if this plant devotes an additional hour to the production of X, it must forgo the production of four units of Y. Likewise, the marginal cost of an additional hour in the production of Y is $\Delta X = 2$.

Hence, the firm will maximize profit subject to the limitation of the eight-hour production day if it produces amounts of X and Y such that the condition

$$\frac{MR_X}{\Delta Y} = \frac{120 - 4Q_X}{4} = \frac{60 - 3Q_Y}{2} = \frac{MR_Y}{\Delta X}$$

is satisfied. This condition requires that $Q_X = \frac{3}{2}Q_Y$. Using the production functions above, this profit-maximization condition can be rewritten in terms of the hours devoted to the production of the two products:

$$Q_X = 2H_X = \frac{3}{2}Q_Y = \frac{3}{2}(4\ H_Y)$$

solving for H_X in terms of H_Y,

$$H_X = 3H_Y$$

To maximize profit, the firm should devote assembly line time to X and Y in the ratio of 3:1.

Using this optimality condition with the time constraint (i.e., $H_X + H_Y = 8$), it follows that to maximize profits, six hours will be devoted to product X and two hours to product Y. That means that Surefire Products will produce 12 units of X per day and 8 units of Y; from the demand functions, the optimal prices are \$96 per unit for X and \$48 per unit for Y.

Actually, there is another way of expressing the optimization condition for the allocation of the production facility between the production of X and Y. Suppose F is the level of usage of the production facility. Thus, $\Delta X/\Delta F$ is the marginal product of the production facility in the production of X (MP_X). Likewise, $\Delta Y/\Delta F$ is the marginal product of the production facility in the production of Y (MP_Y). We can now show that the optimization condition for allocating the production facility, $\frac{MR_X}{\Delta Y} = \frac{MR_Y}{\Delta X}$, can be expressed in terms of marginal revenue products for X and Y: By the above optimization condition,

$$(MR_X) \times (\Delta X) = (MR_Y) \times (\Delta Y)$$

Now divide both sides of this relation by ΔF,

$$(MR_X) \times \left(\frac{\Delta X}{\Delta F}\right) = (MR_Y) \times \left(\frac{\Delta Y}{\Delta F}\right)$$

Thus,

$$(MR_X) \times (MP_X) = (MR_Y) \times (MP_Y)$$

or

$$MRP_X = MRP_Y$$

MRP_X and MRP_Y are, respectively, the marginal revenue products of F in the production of X and Y. With a given level of usage of the production facility, the firm will maximize profit by allocating the facility so that its marginal revenue product in producing each good is the same.

Optimal Usage of a Production Facility

Next, suppose the firm can vary the total number of hours it can use its production facilities. In Figure 18.6, the horizontal axis measures the level of usage of the production facilities. The figure shows the marginal revenue product curves for the production facility in the production of the two products and, summing horizontally, the total marginal revenue product curve. In this situation, we continue to consider a single marginal cost curve—that is, costs are assumed to depend only on the level of usage of the production facility and are not affected by the type of product produced. Profit will be maximized at the point at which marginal cost is equal to total marginal revenue product. Thus, the usage level of the production facility will be F_T. The question then becomes how this level of usage (e.g., machine-hours) is to be divided between the two products.

From the discussion to this point, the answer is probably obvious. If the allocation were such that $MRP_X > MRP_Y$, profit could be increased by reallocating

FIGURE 18.6
Profit-Maximizing Allocation of Production Facilities

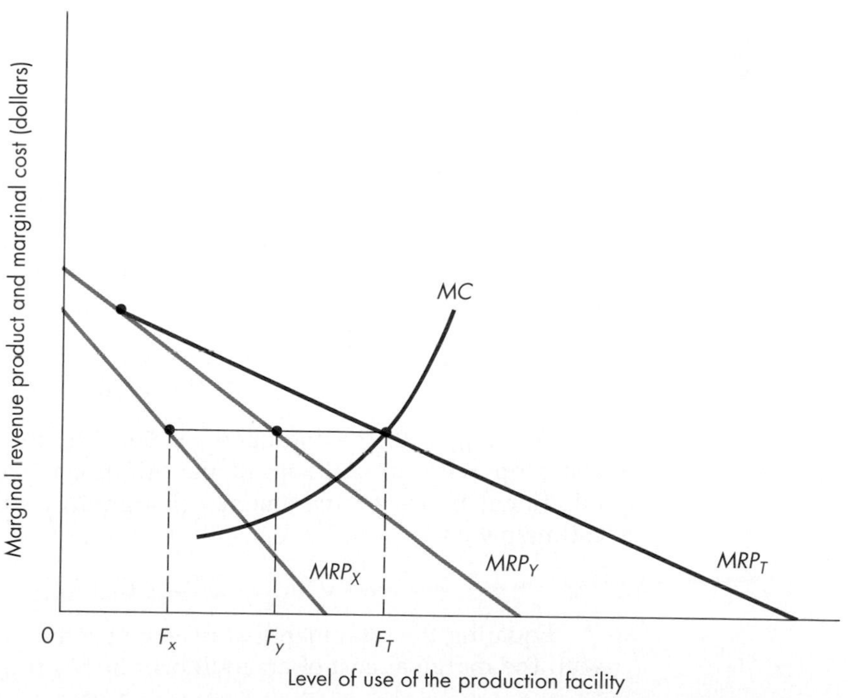

away from the production of Y to the production of X. This would reduce MRP_X and increase MRP_Y. Such a reallocation would continue until the marginal revenue products are equal, $MRP_X = MRP_Y$. Further, since the total marginal revenue product curve is simply the horizontal sum of the two individual curves, the profit-maximizing condition is

$$MRP_T = MC = MRP_X = MRP_Y$$

Thus, profits will be maximized when production is allocated such that the marginal additions to revenue are the same for the two products; F_X is devoted to the production of X and F_Y to the production of Y; and $F_X + F_Y = F_T$. To show how this decision rule could be implemented, let's return to our example.

Optimal Usage of a Production Facility at Surefire Products

The manager of Surefire Products, Inc., wanted to consider changing the daily production schedule for the plant producing X and Y from a strict eight-hour-per-day schedule. That is, the manager wanted to know the answers to two questions: (1) What is the optimal level of usage (hours of operation) of the plant? (2) How should this level of usage be allocated between the production of the two products?

Using the demand forecasts and the estimates of the production functions provided by the plant supervisor, estimates of the marginal revenue product of the production facility in the production of X and Y were

$$\begin{aligned} MRP_X &= MR_X \times MP_X = [120 - 4\,(2H_X)] \times (2) \\ &= 240 - 16H_X \end{aligned}$$

and

$$\begin{aligned} MRP_Y &= MR_Y \times MP_Y = [60 - 3\,(4H_Y)] \times (4) \\ &= 240 - 48H_Y \end{aligned}$$

To obtain the total marginal revenue product function, these two curves were summed horizontally, that is, these functions were inverted to find H_X and H_Y, the hours were summed ($H_T = H_X + H_Y$), then the inverse was taken once again. The resulting total MRP was

$$MRP_T = 240 - 12H_T$$

Working with the engineers for Surefire, the plant supervisor was able to come up with an estimate of the additional cost of operating the plant an additional hour—an incremental (marginal) cost for usage of the plant. This estimate was

$$MC = 72 + 2H_T$$

Equating the total marginal revenue product of an hour's usage of the plant with the marginal cost of an additional hour's usage,

$$240 - 12H_T = 72 + 2H_T$$

the manager then solved for H_T and found that the optimal level of usage of the plant was 12 hours per day. At this level of usage, $MRP_T = MC = \$96$. To allocate these hours between the production of X and Y, the marginal revenue products for the production facility in the production of X and Y must both be equal to $96:

$$240 - 16H_X = 96 \quad \text{and} \quad 240 - 48H_Y = 96$$

Since $H_X = 9$ and $H_Y = 3$, the optimal allocation would be nine hours in the production of X and three hours in the production of Y.

18.4 WHY MULTIPLE PRODUCTS?

The preceding discussion simply assumed that firms produce not one, but several products, then described the conditions of production under several sets of product characteristics. No attempt was made to answer why firms would want to produce multiple products. In some cases the answer is obvious, in others it is not so obvious. Certainly firms produce multiple products for a multitude of reasons. We can only summarize a few of the most common reasons.

Complements in Consumption

complements in consumption
Products that are used together and are frequently purchased together.

It is rather easy to see why a firm would produce and sell two or more products that are **complements in consumption**. These products are used together and are frequently purchased together. The firm would be able to set prices and quantities that maximize the total profit from the products.

For example, single firms manufacture razors and the blades that fit the razors. The firm has control over both design and prices. It may well want to set a very low price for the razor to increase sales and extend the future market for its blades. It can also advertise the two together.

Another example is a firm such as Coleman, which produces several commodities that are complementary—tents, lanterns, stoves, ice chests, and so forth. Consumers of outdoor recreational equipment frequently wish to purchase this bundle of commodities. Therefore, we would expect the sales of, say, lanterns to depend to some extent on the price charged for goods that are used in conjunction; for example, tents. It follows that the price charged for tents would affect the profits of the division producing lanterns, and those of the firm as a whole. And, even if the goods were not purchased at the same time, buyer loyalty can carry over for the next purchase. A family that was well satisfied with a Coleman tent would be likely to choose a Coleman product when it purchased a stove.

Similar examples of complementary goods produced and sold by the same firm are golf clubs and golf balls, tennis rackets and tennis balls, and baseball equipment. In all such cases the firm will set output and price to maximize total profits rather than the profit from a single item. Therefore, as stressed in Section 18.3, the firm must determine the output and price for all the products simultaneously.

Complements in Production

The discussion of complements in production in Section 18.3 and in the appendix deals specifically with the fixed proportions production of two or more products from the same ingredient input. We mentioned as examples the production of beef carcasses and hides, a refinery that produces several final products from crude oil, and a smelter that obtains different minerals from the same ore. But there are more subtle examples of complementarity in production for which the final products need not be produced in fixed proportions.

Less obvious examples arise from capital expenditures that contribute to the production of more than one product. Railroads, for instance, offer both freight and passenger transportation over the same tracks and between the same depots. These inputs are shared. The postal service shares its capital in sorting and delivering parcels and letters. Finally, telephone companies use the same lines and switching gear to place local and long-distance calls. In these instances, a single investment contributes to the production of more than one product. This is a common phenomenon among multiproduct firms.

Whenever it is less costly to produce products together than separately, economies of scope exist. Recall from the discussion of economies of scope in Chapters 11 and 16 that multiproduct firms enjoy a cost advantage over single-product rivals when there are economies of scope in production. With economies of scope, a multiproduct firm not only benefits from higher profits due to lower costs, but, as discussed in Chapter 16, the economies of scope can provide a barrier to entry that enhances market power and profit.

There are other examples of the production of goods that are complementary in production. But we can summarize the majority of such cases simply by saying that when such complementarity exists it is less costly to produce the goods together than to produce them separately.

Substitution in Consumption and Production

One reason many firms produce products that are good substitutes for other products they sell, even when these products compete for time and space on a firm's production facilities, was discussed at some length in Chapter 16. As noted there, a firm can sometimes block entry or gain a competitive advantage by introducing substitutes for its own product in the market. Such a maneuver is frequently preferred to seeing new entrants or old rivals introduce them. Producing related products crowds the market with choices. As the demand for each individual product decreases and becomes more elastic, a new firm finds it more difficult to enter that segment of the market because it would face a smaller demand.

Certainly not all firms that produce multiple products that are substitutes in consumption do so to strengthen their market power. Many oligopolists are caught in a product quality dilemma, similar to the advertiser's dilemma discussed in Chapter 16. If they don't enter a particular segment of the market, they will lose a considerable market share to their rivals. It is possible that each of the

ILLUSTRATION 18.3

Multiproduct Firms: Diversification to Reduce Risk

In our discussion of why firms diversify and produce several different products, we did not mention the problem of dealing with risk. It is a well-known theorem in portfolio theory that an investor can reduce the variability of a portfolio of investments by diversification—increasing the number of different types of investments. Many manufacturing firms try to follow this advice by increasing the number of different products they produce, particularly when the firms previously had "all their eggs in one basket" but the basket went into a slump. In this illustration, we show you how two market leaders in two vastly different industries added new products to their lines to reduce risk.

At the end of the cold war in the early 1990s many companies that had specialized in sales to the military experienced large declines in sales with the reduction of US military expenditures. One such firm was the Canadian firm, CAE Inc., the world's largest producer of aircraft simulators. The firm's traditional customers had been the military and the airline industry. Military sales had fallen, perhaps permanently, and airline sales had slumped. CAE was determined to become much less dependent on the military segment of its market.

The company was trying to capitalize on its most productive resource, expertise in high-tech simulation, to develop a host of novel products. According to CAE's president, "The markets we're now serving don't offer the growth we'd like to see. So we have to seek new products and new markets." Among the wide range of new products introduced were a simulator system for hospitals to train anesthetists without risking anyone's life, other types of simulators to train medical practitioners in emergency procedures, the first commercial version of a totally implantable artificial heart, a "telerobotic" that would allow a miner to perform work underground without leaving the surface, and a simulator to train refinery workers.

The goal of the company was to reverse a three-year decline in sales. All in all, CAE had about 20 major initiatives in new product areas. According to a senior vice president, the plan was showing promise: "Although the airline business has been slow over the last few years, our annual sales haven't been decreasing. We've managed to smooth it because we have a lot of different strengths to our bow."

In an entirely different industry, a leading toy manufacturer also reduced risk by increasing the number of products offered. During the 1980s, the conventional wisdom in the toy industry was that a firm should concentrate its marketing on a few major toys, in the hope of coming up with a roaring success which would carry the company with large profits. During that period, the fortunes of many toy companies rose and fell on mega-hits and mega-misses. In the early 1990s, Hasbro, the industry leader, began bucking that wisdom by diversifying. Hasbro had grown from a tiny firm to the largest toymaker by 1985 with blockbusters such as G.I. Joe. But its growth stalled in the late 1980s with a series of losers.

By 1992, Hasbro was no longer dependent on a handful of toys. Six years before, three toys had accounted for 45 percent of the company's sales. By 1992, no toy accounted for more than 5 percent. Even a major flop would not have hurt the overall profit picture much. An analyst at Salomon Brothers stated that Hasbro was "no longer like a traditional toy company where unpredictability is an issue, but they've become more like a consumer products franchise, where stability and dependability are key words."

Source: This illustration is based on Larry M. Greenberg, "Shrinking Aircraft Market Forces CAE to Branch Out," *The Wall Street Journal*, August 24, 1993, and Joseph Pereira, "Hasbro Enjoys Life Off the Toy-Market Roller Coaster," *The Wall Street Journal*, May 5, 1992.

oligopolists would be better off if each offered fewer products. In spite of this possible problem, producing a variety of differentiated yet similar products that are substitutes is simply another way that firms, particularly oligopolists, compete among themselves.

18.5 SUMMARY

In this chapter we have looked at a lot of special cases. While it might seem that we have introduced a lot of new conditions, we really have not. Essentially, all we have done is apply the basic principles of profit maximization to instances in which the firm has more than one plant or market or product. To show that the resulting roles for profit maximization have much in common, we review them briefly:

1. Multiple plants

If a firm produces in two plants, A and B, it should allocate production between the two plants so that $MC_A = MC_B$. The optimal total output for the firm is that at which $MR = MC_T$. Hence, for profit maximization, the firm should produce the level of output and allocate the production of this output between the two plants so that

$$MR = MC_T = MC_A = MC_B$$

2. Multiple markets

If a firm sells in two distinct markets, 1 and 2, it should allocate output (sales) between the two markets such that $MR_1 = MR_2$. The optimal level of total output for the firm is that at which $MR_T = MC$. Hence, for profit maximization, the firm should produce the level of output and allocate the sales of this output between the two markets so that

$$MR_T = MC = MR_1 = MR_2$$

3. Multiple products/related in consumption

Defining the two products to be X and Y, the firm will produce and sell those levels of output for which

$$MR_X = MC_X \text{ and } MR_Y = MC_Y$$

Since the products are related in consumption, MR_X is a function not only of Q_X but also of Q_Y, as is MR_Y. Therefore, the marginal conditions for the two products must be satisfied simultaneously.

4. Multiple products/substitutes in production

If a firm produces two products, X and Y, that compete for the firm's limited production facilities, the firm should allocate the production facility so that the marginal revenue product of the production facility is equal for the two products, $MRP_X = MRP_Y$. If in the long run the firm can vary its usage of or size of the production facility, the optimal level of usage of the facility is that at which $MRP_T = MC$. Hence, for profit maximization the firm should select the level of usage of its production facility and allocate this level of usage between the production of the two products so that

$$MRP_T = MC = MPR_X = MRP_Y$$

Note, in particular, the similarities between cases 1, 2, and 4. All of these are allocation problems, so they share a common solution. Case 3 requires only that the basic profit-maximization conditions for the related products be solved simultaneously.

So, the view we want to leave you with is that the complications introduced in this chapter do not change the basic rules of profit maximization. As we noted at the outset, the only thing these real-world complications do is to make profit maximization a little more computationally complex.

TECHNICAL PROBLEMS

1. In the following graph, D represents the demand for dishwashers facing the Allclean Company. The firm manufactures dishwashers in two plants; MC_1 and MC_2 are their marginal cost curves.
   a. How many dishwashers should the firm produce?
   b. What price should the firm set?
   c. How should the output be allocated between the two plants so as to maximize profit?
2. A hotel serves both business and vacation travelers. In the following figure, D_1 is the demand for business travelers and D_2 is the demand for vacation travelers. The firm wishes to price discriminate. Suppose that the total marginal revenue for the firm is \$20 at the profit-maximizing level of *total* output.

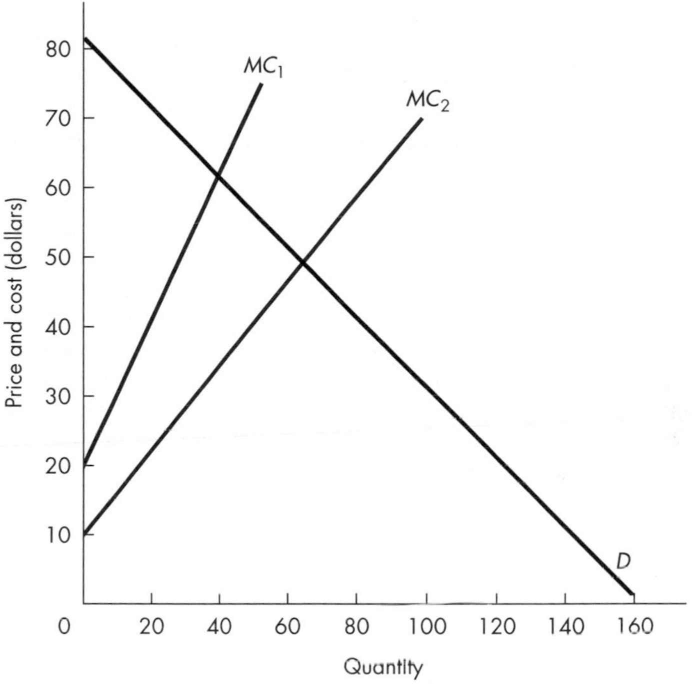
Price and cost (dollars)
Quantity
MC1
MC2
D
0
10
20
30
40
50
60
70
80
20
40
60
80
100
120
140
160

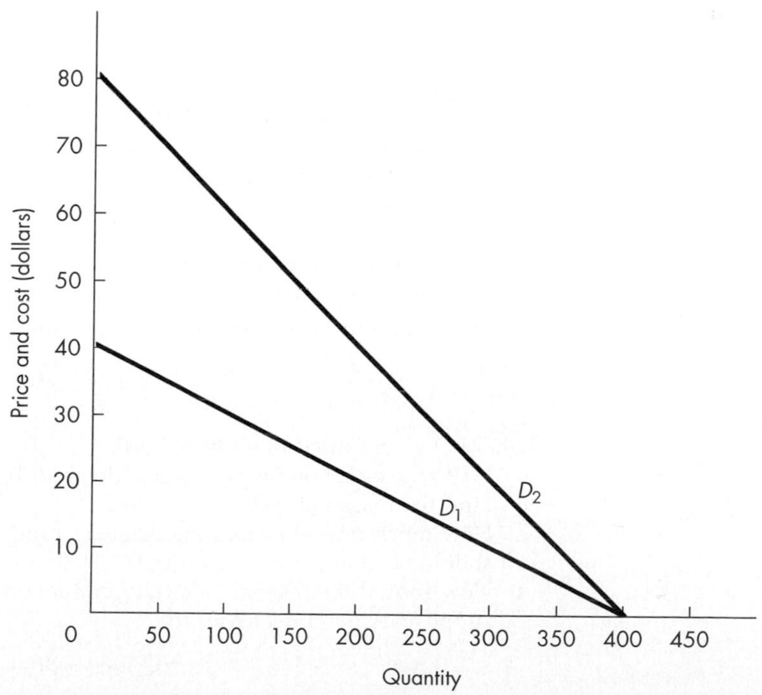
Price and cost (dollars)
Quantity
D1
D2
0
10
20
30
40
50
60
70
80
50
100
150
200
250
300
350
400
450

a. What is the profit-maximizing number of business travelers to serve? Vacation travelers?
b. What price should be charged to each?
c. Answer part *a* and *b*, assuming that $30 is the marginal revenue at the profit-maximizing level of *total* output.

* 3. Consider a firm that produces, using two plants, A and B, with marginal cost functions:

$$MC_A = 10 + \frac{1}{10} Q_A$$

$$MC_B = 4 + \frac{3}{10} Q_B$$

where Q_A and Q_B are measured in units of 1,000.
a. Find the inverse marginal cost functions.
b. Set $MC_A = MC_T$ and $MC_B = MC_T$, and find the algebraic sum $Q_A + Q_B = Q_T$.
c. Take the inverse of the horizontal sum in part *b* to get the total marginal cost (MC_T) expressed as a function of total output (Q_T).
d. Beyond what level of output will the firm use both plants in production? (Hint: Find the output level where MC_T kinks.)
e. If the manager of this firm wished to produce 140,000 units at the least possible total cost, should 70,000 units be produced in each plant? Why or why not? If not, what should the allocation be?
f. Draw a graph of MC_A, MC_B, and MC_T. Check your algebraic derivation of total marginal cost with your graph. Check your answer to part *e*.

4. A manager faces two separate markets. The estimated demand functions for the two markets are

$$Q_A = 16 - \frac{4}{5} P_A$$

$$Q_B = 24 - P_B$$

where output is measured in units of 100.
a. Find the inverse marginal revenue functions.
b. Find the total marginal revenue function.
c. Draw a graph of MR_A, MR_B, and MR_T. Check your algebraic derivation of total marginal revenue.
d. If the manager has a total of 650 units to sell ($Q = 6.5$), how should the 650 units be allocated to maximize total revenue?

5. Suppose the firm in problem 3 faces the following demand function:

$$Q = 400 - \frac{25}{2} P$$

where Q is measured in units of 1,000.
a. Write the equation for the inverse demand function.
b. Find the marginal revenue function.
c. How much output should the manager produce to maximize profit? What price should be charged for the output?
d. How should the manager allocate production between plants A and B? Now suppose demand decreases to

$$Q = 80 - 8P$$

e. How many units should the manager produce in order to maximize profit?
f. How should the manager allocate production between plants A and B?

6. Suppose the manager in problem 4 decides to price discriminate. The marginal cost is estimated to be

$$MC = 3 + \frac{7}{11}Q$$

where Q is measured in units of 100.
a. How many units should the manager produce and sell?
b. How should the manager allocate the profit-maximizing output between the two markets?
c. What prices should the manager charge in the two markets?
d. Which market has the more elastic demand?

7. A firm with two factories, one in Michigan and one in Texas, has decided that it should produce a total of 500 units in order to maximize profit. The firm is currently producing 200 units in the Michigan factory and 300 units in the Texas factory. At this allocation between plants, the last unit of output produced in Michigan added $5 to total cost, while the last unit of output produced in Texas added $3 to total cost.
a. Is the firm maximizing profit? If so, why? If not, what should it do?
b. If the firm produces 201 units in Michigan and 299 in Texas, what will be the increase (decrease) in the firm's total cost?

8. Using the example dealing with profit maximization in multiple markets (Galactic Manufacturing), what price would be charged if the firm does not price discriminate? Demonstrate that the firm will have a higher profit if it price discriminates than if it charges the same price in both markets.

* 9. Suppose a firm serves two distinct markets. The forecasted demand functions in the two markets are:

$$\text{Mkt 1: } Q_1 = 50 - 0.25P_1 \text{ and Mkt 2: } Q_2 = 100 - 1.0P_2$$

and the firm's marginal cost function has been estimated to be

$$MC = 20 + 0.4Q$$

a. What is the profit-maximizing total level of output?
b. How should this output be allocated between the two markets?
c. What are the profit-maximizing prices in the two markets?
d. Which market has the more elastic demand?

10. How would the profit-maximizing decision for a firm that produces two products that are related in consumption differ from that for a firm whose two products are unrelated?

11. Look again at Zicon Manufacturing—a firm that produces products that are substitutes in consumption. Suppose that the production manager changed the estimates of the marginal cost functions to

$$MC_X = 20 + \frac{1}{4}Q_X \quad \text{and} \quad MC_Y = 16 + \frac{1}{2}Q_Y$$

Calculate the new profit-maximizing levels of output and price for the two products.

12. Look again at the division of Surefire Products, Inc., that produces two products that are substitutes in production. Suppose that the forecasted demand function for X was changed to

$$Q_X = 76 - \frac{1}{2} P_X$$

a. How will an eight-hour production day be allocated between the production of the two products?
b. What will be the daily outputs?
c. What prices will be charged?

13. In the example dealing with the optimal usage of a production facility (Surefire Products, Inc.), suppose that the plant supervisor changes the estimate of the marginal cost for usage of the plant to

$$MC = 150 + 3H_T$$

a. What is the optimal level of usage for the plant (hours per day)?
b. How will this level of usage be allocated between the production of the two products?
c. What will be the daily outputs?
d. What prices will be charged?

14. A bar offers female patrons a lower price for a drink than male patrons. The bar will maximize profit by selling a total of 200 drinks (a night). At the current prices, male customers buy 150 drinks, while female customers buy 50 drinks. At this allocation between markets, the marginal revenue from the last drink sold to a male customer is $1.50, while the marginal revenue from the last drink sold to a female customer is $0.50.
a. What should the bar do about its pricing?
b. If the bar sells 151 drinks to males and 49 to females instead, what will be the increase (decrease) in total revenue?

APPLIED PROBLEMS

1. *The Financial Herald*, a weekly newspaper specializing in corporate financial news, is purchased by both business people and students. A marketing research firm has estimated the two linear marginal revenue functions shown in the figure below. MR_B is the estimated marginal revenue for the business readers, and MR_S is the estimated marginal revenue for the student readers. The production department at *The Financial Herald* estimates a linear marginal cost function for newspaper production, which is also graphed in the figure below. All quantities are in units of 1,000 per week.
a. How many total copies should *The Financial Herald* print each week?
b. How many copies should be sold to business readers? How many copies should be sold to students?
c. What price should business readers be charged? What price should students be charged?

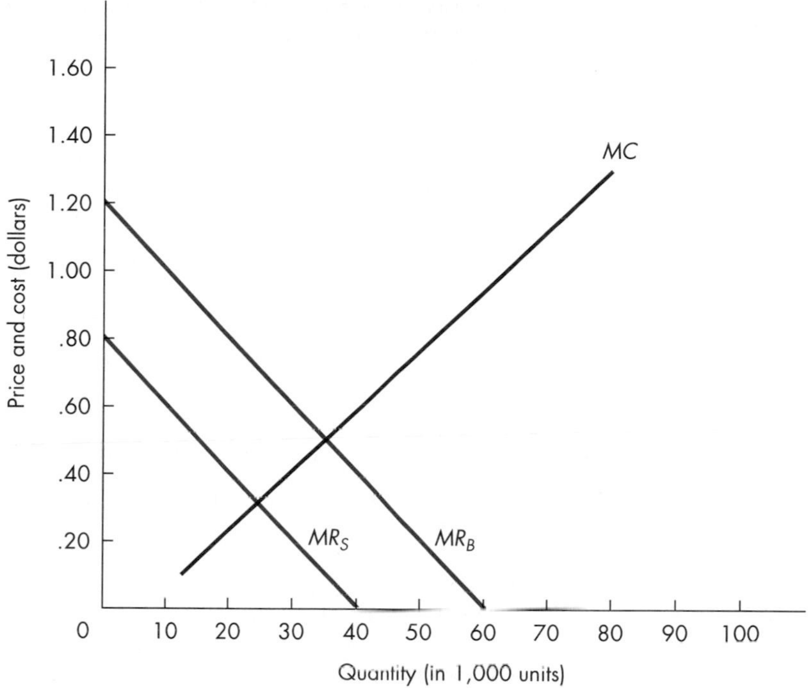

2. The board of directors of R & B Root Beer Corporation recently called a meeting of the managers of the five regional bottling companies. The reason for calling the meeting was to consider closing the Milwaukee bottling plant. Over the past decade, the Milwaukee facility's marginal costs of production have increased to the point where its marginal cost of production now exceeds that of each of the other four bottling companies at every level of output. Several members of the board of directors and two of the managers favored closing the Milwaukee plant. The manager of the Milwaukee bottling plant pointed out that, while the Milwaukee plant is the oldest of the five, with the oldest capital equipment, it would be inefficient to close it given the current growth rate in sales. Only if sales fell by a rather substantial amount would it be profit maximizing to shut the Milwaukee plant. Draw a graph and defend the manager of the Milwaukee plant.
3. Although there is relatively little difference in the cost of producing hardcover and paperback books, these books sell for very different prices. Explain this pricing behavior.
4. *The Wall Street Journal* once reported on dating services, noting that the fees were \$300 for men and \$250 for women. The owner of the service said that the difference in fees was to compensate for inequalities in pay scales for men and women. Can you suggest any alternative reasons for this difference?
5. In the mid 1980s, many observers of the automobile industry were saying that GM was producing cars that were too much alike. Many GM executives agreed. Why would this be a problem for GM?
6. Caytel Products manufactures two models of a particular product—the "good" model (G) and the "best" model (B). The two models are substitutes in production,

and must share Caytel's production facilities. Caytel has determined that the production functions for the two models are:

$$\text{Good Model: } Q_G = 4.0H_G$$
$$\text{Best Model: } Q_B = 4.0H_B$$

where H_G and H_B measure the number of hours per month Caytel's plant spends producing the good and best models, respectively. The demand functions for the two models are forecasted to be:

$$Q_G = 4{,}000 - 256P_G$$

and

$$Q_B = 600 - 4P_B$$

The marginal cost of using Caytel's plant is estimated to be:

$$MC = 5.0 + 0.05H, \text{ where } H = H_G + H_B$$

a. In order to maximize profit, how many hours per month should Caytel's plant operate?
b. How should the manager allocate production time between the good model and the best model?
c. How many units of the good model should be produced to maximize Caytel's profit? How many units of the best model?
d. What prices should Caytel charge for the two models?

7. Airlines practice price discrimination by charging leisure travelers and business travelers different prices. Different customers pay varying prices for essentially the same coach seat because some passengers qualify for discounts and others do not. Since the discounts are substantial in many cases, the customer who qualifies for a discount pays a significantly lower airfare.
   a. Which group of customers tends to pay the higher price—business travelers or leisure travelers?
   b. Why would business travelers generally have a different elasticity of demand for air travel than leisure travelers? Is the more elastic market paying the lower or higher price? Is this consistent with profit maximization?

   Airlines rely on an assortment of restrictions that travelers must meet in order to qualify for the discounted fares. In effect, these restrictions roughly sort flyers into business travelers and leisure travelers.
   c. Explain how each of the following restrictions sometimes used by airlines tends to separate business and leisure travelers:
      (1) Advance purchase requirements, which require payment at least 14 days before departure.
      (2) Weekend stay requirements, which require travelers to stay over a Saturday night before returning.
      (3) Time of day restrictions, which disallow discounts for travel during peak times of the day
   d. In each of the above cases, which group of passengers effectively pays a higher price for air travel? Is this consistent with profit maximization?
8. For many years American Express had charged a fee (generally higher than Visa or MasterCard) to each merchant accepting its credit cards. The fees were a percentage of each sale, and American Express charged all merchants the same fee. Many merchants who accepted American Express cards complained that the fees were too

high, discouraged customers from using the card, and some even stopped accepting the card. The president of the company's card division announced that American Express would lower its fees, but a merchant with a lower than industry average charge volume on American Express would get a lower fee than those with a higher than average charge volume. This was supposed to lower the fee the most on each transaction "where the value of accepting American Express is not present." (*The Wall Street Journal*, Feb. 24, 1992).

Is this price discrimination? If not, why not? If so, on what basis is American Express basing its discrimination?

9. A woman complained to "Dear Abby" that a laundry charged $1.25 each to launder and press her husband's shirts, but for her shirts—the same description, only smaller—the laundry charged $3.50. When asked why, the owner said, "Women's blouses cost more." Abby suggested sending all the shirts in one bundle and enclosing a note saying, "There are no blouses here—these are all shirts."
   a. Is the laundry practicing price discrimination or is there really a $2.25 difference in cost?
   b. Assuming the laundry is engaging in price discrimination, why do men pay the lower price and women the higher?
   c. Could the laundry continue to separate markets if people followed Abby's advice? What about the policing costs associated with separating the markets?

APPENDIX 18A Mathematical Demonstration of Results

1. To maximize profit, a multiplant firm will produce the level of output at which the horizontal sum of each plant's marginal cost equals marginal revenue. Each plant will produce the output at which the marginal costs of all plants are equal.

   Assume the firm has two plants, A and B, whose total cost functions are respectively $C_A(Q_A)$ and $C_B(Q_B)$. The firm's total revenue function is $R(Q_A + Q_B) = R(Q)$. Thus the firm's profit function is

$$\pi = R(Q) - C_A(Q_A) - C_B(Q_B)$$

   Maximizing profit with respect to Q_A and Q_B requires

$$\frac{\partial \pi}{\partial Q_A} = \frac{\partial R}{\partial Q} - \frac{\partial C_A(Q_A)}{\partial Q_A} = 0$$

$$\frac{\partial \pi}{\partial Q_B} = \frac{\partial R}{\partial Q} - \frac{\partial C_B(Q_A)}{\partial Q_B} = 0$$

   Combining these conditions, profit is maximized when

$$MR = MC_A = MC_B$$

2. A price-discriminating firm maximizing profit will produce the level of output at which marginal revenue in each market equals marginal cost. The price in each market is given by the demand in that market.

   Assume the firm sells its output in two markets. The demands in these markets are

$$P_1(Q_1) \text{ and } P_2(Q_2)$$

   Cost is a function of total output:

$$C = C(Q_1 + Q_2) = C(Q)$$

   The firm maximizes profit,

$$\pi = P_1(Q_1)Q_1 + P_2(Q_2)Q_2 - C(Q)$$

   with respect to the levels of output sold in the two markets.

   Thus, the first-order conditions for profit maximization are

$$\frac{\partial P_1}{\partial Q_1} Q_1 + P_1 - \frac{dC}{dQ} = MR_1 - MC = 0$$

$$\frac{\partial P_2}{\partial Q_2} Q_2 + P_2 - \frac{dC}{dQ} = MR_2 - MC = 0$$

   Thus, profit maximization requires that the marginal revenues in the two markets be equal and equal to marginal cost. Once Q_1 and Q_2 are determined, P_1 and P_2 are given by the demand functions.

APPENDIX 18B Multiple Products That Are Complements in Production

In the text we discussed rather briefly how a firm would maximize profit when producing products that are complements in production and are produced in fixed proportions from an ingredient input. We did not develop the profit-maximizing conditions in the text because the graphical analysis is more complex than that in the rest of the chapter and because this type of multiproduct firm is not as widely encountered as the others. We will examine these conditions here.

Assume that the firm produces only two products, X and Y, in fixed proportions. The problem is to determine the level of output and the price for each of these complementary products.

In Figure 18.A1, we have provided a graphical analysis of this problem. In this figure, the demand curves for the two products are denoted as D_X and D_Y and the corresponding marginal revenue curves are shown as the dashed lines MR_X and MR_Y. The marginal cost curve shown is the marginal cost of producing the joint product.

In order to determine how much of the joint product to produce, we need to obtain the demand curve and the marginal revenue curve for the joint product. To obtain the joint product demand curve, we sum the individual demand curves *vertically*: For example, given some level of production of beef carcasses and hides, the total price received is equal to the sum of the prices received for the carcasses and hides, since the number of carcasses must equal the number of hides.

The marginal revenue curve for the joint product is also obtained via the *vertical* summation of MR_X and MR_Y, but there is one major difference. In Figure 18.A1, note that MR_Y becomes zero at an output denoted as Q_Y. For sales of commodity Y in excess of Q_Y, the marginal revenue for Y would be negative. Clearly, no firm would wish to sell a unit of a product for which the marginal revenue is negative, so the maximum amount of Y the firm will *sell* is Q_Y. Therefore, the marginal revenue curve for the joint product is the vertical sum of MR_X and MR_Y until MR_Y equals zero. For outputs in excess of Q_Y, the excess units of Y would be discarded and, only commodity X would be sold; the joint marginal revenue curve corresponds to MR_X. The result is the kinked joint product marginal revenue curve shown in Figure 18.A1.

The profit-maximizing level of production for the firm is determined at that level of output at which the joint marginal revenue is equal to the joint marginal cost. In Figure 18.A1, this means that the firm will produce Q units of the joint product. The firm will then sell Q units of product X at a price of P_X and Q units of product Y at a price of P_Y.

To see how the firm can implement profit maximization with joint products, we turn to a stylized example.

A firm produces refined chemicals. In one of its divisions a joint product is produced. That is, as it refines the raw chemical input, the processes will yield equal amounts of two products, which we will denote simply as products X and Y. The question facing the manager is, of course, how much of products X and Y should the firm sell and at what prices?

The demand functions for the two products had been forecasted as

$$Q_X = 285 - P_X \text{ and } Q_Y = 150 - 2P_Y$$

where the outputs were measured in thousand pounds and the prices in cents per pound. The marginal revenue curves associated with these demand functions are

$$MR_X = 285 - 2Q_X \text{ and } MR_Y = 75 - Q_Y$$

Note that the marginal revenue function for Y is equal to zero at an output of 75 (i.e., 75,000 pounds). So, for output levels of the joint product less than or equal to 75, the marginal revenue function for the joint product is the vertical summation of the two marginal revenues,

$$MR = 360 - 3Q$$

For output levels in excess of $Q = 75$, the joint product marginal revenue function is the same as MR_X.

Given the existing capital stock, the incremental (marginal) cost function for refining the raw chemical input was estimated to be

$$MC = 10 + 2Q$$

where marginal cost is measured in cents per pound and output (Q) is in thousand pounds.

Equating marginal revenue and marginal cost for the joint product,

$$360 - 3Q = 10 + 2Q$$

the profit-maximizing level of production of the joint product is $Q = 70$ (i.e., 70,000 pounds). Using $Q = 70$ in the two demand curves, the manager determined that the firm should sell 70,000 pounds of X at $2.15 per pound and 70,000 pounds of Y at $0.40 per pound.

So far, our results have indicated that the firm will produce *and sell* equal amounts of the two products. This need not always be the case. The joint product nature of

FIGURE 18.A1
Profit Maximization with Joint Products

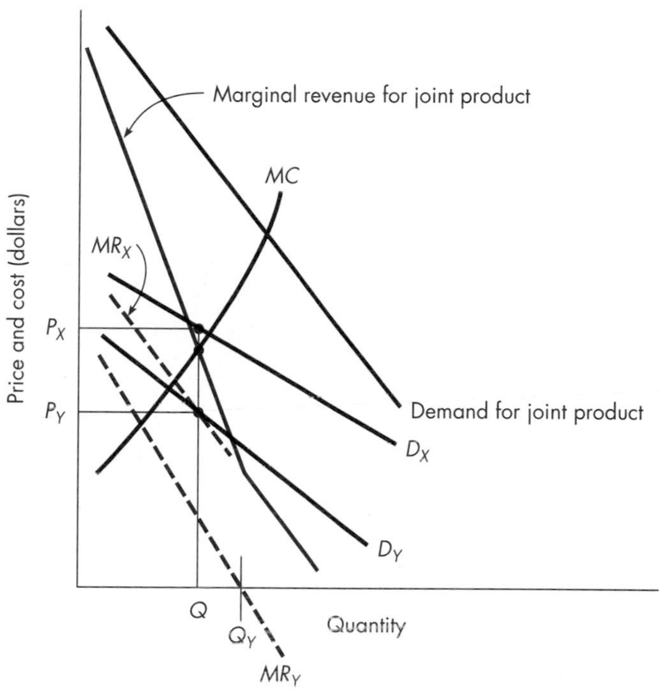

the production relation we have been considering does require that the firm will always *produce* equal amounts of the two products. (You can't produce an additional beef carcass without producing an additional hide.) But, there is nothing that requires the firm to *sell* equal amounts of the two products.

We have illustrated this situation in Figure 18.A2. The only difference between this figure and Figure 18.A1 is the location of the marginal cost curve for the joint product. In this case, the firm will *produce* Q' units of the joint product. And, since MR_X is positive at Q', the firm will *sell* Q' units of X at the price P'_X. However, at Q', MR_Y is negative. Clearly the firm will not sell Q' units of Y. Instead, the firm will *sell* only Q_Y units of commodity Y at the price of P'_Y. Since it has produced Q' units of Y but only sells Q_Y units, what will the firm do with the remainder (i.e., $Q' - Q_Y$ units of Y)? The answer is simple: the firm will destroy the remainder, since marketing these units would reduce the firm's revenues.

Look again at the decision faced by the manager in the above numerical example. Suppose that the engineers had instead estimated the incremental (marginal) cost of refining the joint product to be

$$MC = 80 + \frac{1}{2}Q$$

Setting this marginal cost function equal to the joint product marginal revenue function used before,

$$360 - 3Q = 80 + \frac{1}{2}Q$$

the *implied* optimal output would be $Q = 80$. However, as the manager is aware, at this production level, the marginal revenue for product Y would be negative. Hence, in this range of production, the joint product marginal revenue function coincides with MR_X, so to determine optimal production, the manager must equate marginal cost to the marginal revenue for product X,

$$285 - 2Q = 80 + \frac{1}{2}Q$$

Hence, in this situation, the optimal level of production of the joint products is $Q = 82$. That is, the firm will produce 82,000 pounds of chemicals X and Y.

FIGURE 18.A2
Profit Maximization with Joint Products— Destruction of One Product

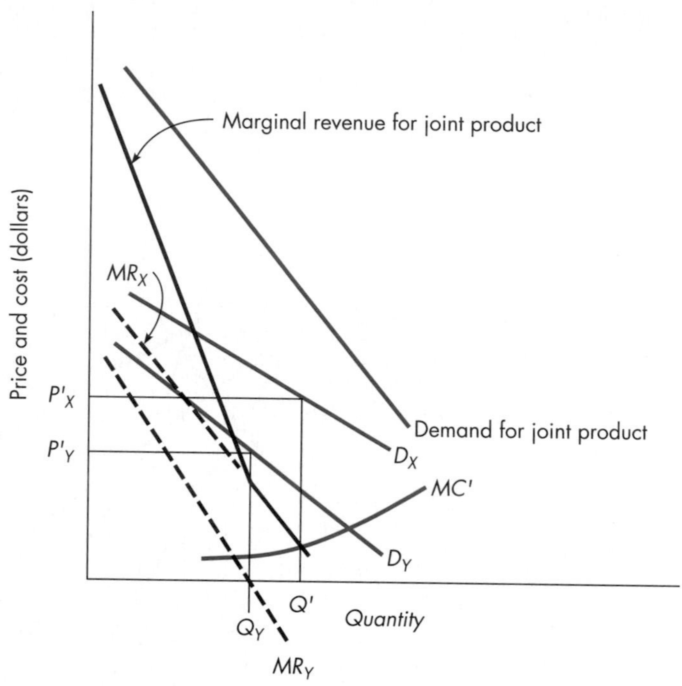

Since MR_X is positive at $Q = 82$, the firm will sell the 82,000 pounds of X. From the demand function for X, the price charged will be \$2.03 per pound.

However, the firm will sell chemical Y only to that point at which its marginal revenue is zero. That is, since $MR_Y = 0$ when $Q = 75$, the firm will sell only 75,000 pounds of chemical Y and will destroy the remaining 7,000 pounds. From the demand function for Y, the price that will be charged for the 75,000 pounds of Y that is sold is 37.5 cents per pound.

PART

VII

Decision Making over Time

CHAPTER

19 Profit Maximization over Time

In this and the following chapter, we will analyze the decision-making process of a firm with a time horizon of not just one period but several periods into the future. Furthermore, the firm under consideration is owned by many shareholders rather than by a single owner who also manages the firm. Such a firm would seem to be a radical departure from the owner-managed firm with a single-period horizon that we have considered throughout most of the text.

In a sense, this change in assumptions does represent a substantial departure, and the analysis of such a firm appears to be a large order for only two chapters. Given this space limitation, we will merely scratch the surface of a number of issues. However, for someone who understands the principles of optimization set forth in Chapter 4 and the optimization analysis already described in a large part of the text, this material should be nothing new. What you have seen in the theories of the firms described thus far are applications of the marginal benefit equals marginal cost rule, and that is what you will also see in the remainder of the text.

Before we proceed with the analysis of a firm's multi-period decision-making process, we want to reassure you that we have not cheated you by devoting so much space to profit maximization by a firm with a single-period time horizon. Most firm and managerial decision making can be analyzed and understood just as fruitfully within the single-period framework without adding the complexity of the time dimension. For some firms' decisions, however, the additional time dimension is not only useful but necessary. Some important examples of this are the firm's investment decisions and profit-maximization decisions, when such decisions made in one period affect decisions made in future periods.

After introducing the concepts of present value and maximization of the value of the firm, we will analyze the profit-maximization decision when decisions in one period affect decisions in future periods. We will demonstrate that in a large number of cases, multi-period optimization is identical to single-period maximization. We will also demonstrate that the rule of marginal benefit equals marginal cost still applies even though the time horizon has been extended. In the following chapter, we will use the multi-period framework to address the firm's investment decision. In all of the examples to follow, you will see that there is one simple rule for the profit-maximizing firm to follow: *Maximize the present value of the firm.*

19.1 NET PRESENT VALUE

present value (*PV*)
The value at the present time of a return to be received at some time in the future.

net present value (*NPV*)
The difference between the present value of the net cash flow(s) from an asset and the cost of the asset.

Multi-period decision making is based upon the concepts of present value and net present value. **Present value** is the value at the present time of a payment or stream of payments to be received some time in the future. **Net present value** is the difference between the present value of a future return or stream of returns from an asset or project and the cost of that asset or project. Before using the concept of net present value to analyze a firm's decision making, we will describe how net present value is calculated.

Present Value of a Single Payment in the Future

First consider how much someone would pay today for a project that will return \$100 in one year. There is no risk or uncertainty, so the \$100 return is a sure thing. An alternative to this risk-free project is investing in other riskless activities, the best example of which is US government securities. Suppose that one-year government bonds are paying 6 percent annually. How much would have to be invested in these bonds to get \$100 at the end of the year? Investing $\$X$ today at an interest rate of 6 percent will return $\$X(1.06)$ in one year. If this investment is worth \$100 at the end of one year,

$$\$X(1.06) = \$100$$

It follows that the amount one must invest today is \$94.34(= \$100/1.06). That is, the present value of \$100 in one year with an interest rate—a discount rate—of 6 percent is \$94.34.

Now suppose that the project would return the \$100 not in one year, but in two years. Again, suppose that the annual interest rate on two-year US government bonds is 6 percent. Investing $\$X$ at 6 percent would yield $\$X(1.06)$ at the end of year one and, at the end of year two, $[\$X(1.06)](1.06) = \$X(1.06)^2$. Thus, for an investment to be worth \$100 in two years,

$$\$X(1.06)^2 = \$100$$

Thus, the amount that must be invested today is $\$89.00[=\$100/(1.06)^2]$. The present value of \$100 in two years with a discount rate of 6 percent is \$89.00.

Clearly a pattern is emerging: The present value of $100 in one year at 6 percent is

$$PV = \frac{\$100}{(1.06)} = \$94.34$$

The present value of $100 in two years at 6 percent is

$$PV = \frac{\$100}{(1.06)^2} = \$89.00$$

Therefore, the present value of $100 to be received in t years (t being any number of years) with a discount rate of 6 percent is

$$PV = \frac{\$100}{(1.06)^t}$$

This relation can be made even more general to determine the present value of some net cash flow (*NCF*) to be received in t years at a prevailing interest rate of r. By *net cash flow*, we obviously mean the cash received in time period t, net of any costs or expenses that must be paid out of the cash inflow. Also note that if the interest rate is 6 percent, for example, r is expressed as 0.06.

Relation The present value (*PV*) of $*NCF* to be received in t years at a discount rate of r is

$$PV = \frac{\$NCF}{(1 + r)^t}$$

As illustrated above, the present value of a cash flow declines the further in the future it is to be received—for example, the present value of $100 at 6 percent was $94.34 in one year and only $89.00 in two years. As should be evident from the more general statement of present value, the present value of a cash flow is inversely related to the discount rate—for example, the present value of $100 to be received in two years is $89.00 with a discount rate of 6 percent, but only $85.73[=$100/(1.08)^2] with a discount rate of 8 percent. Obviously the present value of a cash flow increases as the size of the cash flow increases—for example, using one year to maturity and a discount rate of 6 percent the present value of $200 is $188.68, rather than the $94.34 for a $100 cash flow. These relations are summarized in the following relation, the first two parts of which are illustrated graphically in Figure 19.1.

Relation There is an inverse relation between the present value of a cash flow and the time to maturity—the present value of cash flow $*NCF* to be received in t years is greater than that for the same cash flow to be received in $t + i$ years.

There is an inverse relation between the present value of a cash flow and the discount rate—the present value of cash flow $*NCF* discounted at r is greater than that for the same cash flow discounted at $r + j$.

There is a direct relation between the present value of a cash flow and the size of the cash flow—using the same times to maturity and discount rates, the value of cash flow $*NCF* is less than that for cash flow $(*NCF* + *k*).

FIGURE 19.1

The Present Value of $100: Changes in the Discount Rate and Time to Maturity

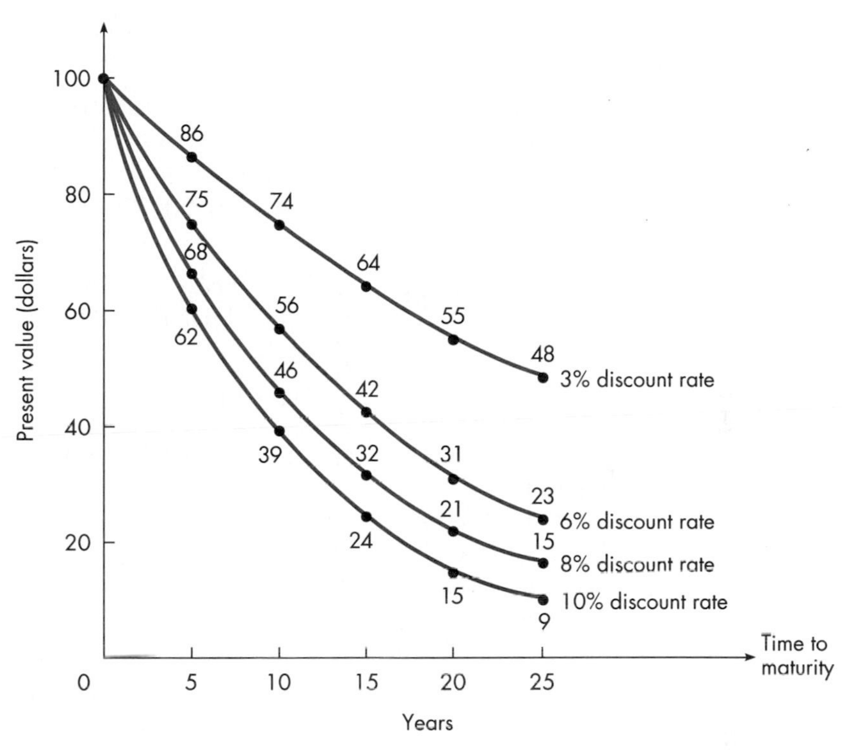

Present Value of a Stream of Payments

So far we have considered the present value of a project that returns a single payment. We now extend the analysis to consider the value of an investment that makes a number of payments in the future: for example, the value of a riskless project that pays $100 in one year and $100 in two years. As you know, the present value of each of these payments depends on the relevant discount rates; and, since the project is riskless, the discount rate is the interest rate for government securities. Suppose that the annual interest rate for a one-year government security is 6 percent and the rate for a two-year security is 7 percent. The present value of the first payment would then be

$$\frac{\$100}{(1.06)} = \$94.34$$

and the present value of the second payment would be

$$\frac{\$100}{(1.07)^2} = \$87.34$$

Thus, the present value of the project is

$$PV = \frac{\$100}{(1.06)} + \frac{\$100}{(1.07)^2} = \$181.68$$

From the preceding, you should be able to see that the present value of a project that has a number of cash flows is equal to the sum of the present values of the net cash flows. Let us put this a little more precisely: The present value of a stream of cash flows, where $\$NCF_t$ is the cash flow received or paid in period t is given by

$$PV = \frac{\$NCF_1}{(1 + r_1)} + \frac{\$NCF_2}{(1 + r_2)^2} + \frac{\$NCF_3}{(1 + r_3)^3} + \ldots + \frac{\$NCF_T}{(1 + r_T)^T}$$
$$= \sum_{t=1}^{T} \frac{\$NCF_t}{(1 + r_t)^t}$$

where r_t is the discount rate for period t, and T is the life span of the stream of cash flows.

Once the present value of a project has been calculated it is a simple matter to find the net present value of the project. The *net present value (NPV)* is the present value of the returns from the project minus the current cost of the project. The net present value of a project (asset) is the difference between the present value of the net cash flows of the project and its current cost:

$$NPV = PV - \text{Cost of project}$$

Calculation of Net Present Value: An Example

At the end of 1994, the management of Metroplex Properties was offered a one-third share in a six-year limited partnership on a new office building. Construction was to begin on January 1, 1995, with completion on December 31, 1995. The price of the one-third partnership to Metroplex Properties was $450,000. Scheduled occupancy, total rental income, and total expenses were as follows:

Year	Occupancy rate (percent)	Rental income	Expenses	Net cash flow
1996	60	$325,000	$200,000	+$125,000
1997	80	425,000	250,000	+ 175,000
1998	100	525,000	300,000	+ 225,000
1999	100	525,000	300,000	+ 225,000
2000	100	525,000	325,000	+ 200,000

Note: For simplicity, we assume that payments and receipts occur at the end of the year.

At the end of 2000, the value of the building would be $1,000,000. These cash flows are known with certainty.

Clearly, the management of Metroplex needed to determine the value of the project. They found the annual interest rates for one-, two-, . . . , six-year government securities to be

Maturity	Interest rate (percent)
Dec. 1995	5.75
Dec. 1996	6.00
Dec. 1997	6.25
Dec. 1998	6.50
Dec. 1999	6.75
Dec. 2000	7.00

Using these rates, and the above net cash flows, they calculated the present value of the project as

$$
\begin{aligned}
PV &= \frac{\$125{,}000}{(1.06)^2} + \frac{\$175{,}000}{(1.0625)^3} + \frac{\$225{,}000}{(1.065)^4} + \frac{\$225{,}000}{(1.0675)^5} + \frac{\$200{,}000}{(1.07)^6} + \frac{\$1{,}000{,}000}{(1.07)^6} \\
&= \$111{,}250 + \$145{,}899 + \$174{,}898 + \$162{,}309 + \$133{,}268 + \$666{,}342 \\
&= \$1{,}393{,}966
\end{aligned}
$$

Since the management of Metroplex Properties had been offered a 33 percent share of the six-year partnership for a price of \$450,000, the net present value of the deal to Metroplex Properties is calculated as

$$
\begin{aligned}
NPV &= (0.33)(\$1{,}393{,}966) - \$450{,}000 \\
&= \$10{,}009
\end{aligned}
$$

19.2 MAXIMIZING THE VALUE OF THE FIRM—ANOTHER MARGINAL RULE

As shown in the preceding section, present value is additive. For example, the present value of a project returning \$100 after one year and \$125 after two years is equivalent to the sum of the present values of a project returning \$100 in one year and another project returning \$125 in two years. In more general terms, the present value of the portfolio of two projects, A and B, is equal to the sum of the present values of Projects A and B: $PV(A + B) = PV(A) + PV(B)$.

worth of a firm
A firm's present value.

Going a step further, a firm is really nothing more than a portfolio of projects (assets). The **worth of a firm** is the price the firm would bring if it were sold, and is, therefore, simply its present value. The present value of this portfolio of projects is the sum of the present values of the individual projects.

If the objective is to maximize the present value of the firm, what behavior is required? Think about the firm as a portfolio of n projects. Now consider whether it should grow by acquiring an additional (marginal) project, the $n + 1$ project. From the principles of optimization, you know that the present value of the firm will increase if the marginal benefit (the present value of the additional project) exceeds the marginal cost (the cost of the additional project). Put another way, an additional project will increase the value of the firm if the present value of the additional project is greater than the cost of the project (i.e., if the net present value of the project is positive).

Now consider whether a firm would be better off by shrinking. That is, would the value of a firm increase by selling off a project? Using the optimization principles, the value of the firm would rise as a result of selling off a project if the present value of the divested project was less than its market value (the price the firm could get for it). That is, the value of the firm will rise if it sells projects that have negative net present values. For example, suppose one of the firm's assets has a present value of \$1 million, and it could sell this asset for \$1.5 million. The net present value of the asset is −\$500,000. Consequently, the value of the firm would increase \$500,000 if it sold the asset. Thus, the value of the firm will increase if it divests projects or assets for which the net present value is negative.

Although this principle seems correct in theory, it may sound a little strange. You might wonder why someone else would be willing to pay more for an asset/project/subsidiary than it is worth to the firm itself? The reason has to be that the project fits better with the portfolio of projects of the acquiring firm than with the divesting firm, most likely because of product complementarities such as those discussed in Chapter 18.

In the previous example of Metroplex Properties, the price for the investment project was \$450,000, and the net present value for the project was \$10,009. Clearly, Metroplex should accept this project, because it will increase the value of the firm. However, if the price Metroplex had to pay for the 33 percent share in the office building project was \$470,000, the net present value of the project would be negative: $NPV = (0.33)(\$1{,}393{,}966) - 470{,}000 = -\$9{,}991$. In this instance, the management of Metroplex should reject the project. Accepting a project with a negative net present value would reduce the value of the firm, for the same reason as selling a project with a negative net present value would increase the value of the firm.

Combining the two preceding principles produces a general rule for the behavior of a value-maximizing firm:

Principle *The Net Present Value Rule* for maximizing the value of the firm is to accept projects (acquire assets) for which the net present value is positive and reject projects for which the net present value is negative. The firm should divest projects for which the net present value is negative.

19.3 MAXIMIZING THE VALUE OF THE FIRM VERSUS SINGLE-PERIOD PROFIT MAXIMIZATION

In this chapter we have added a time dimension to managerial decision making, and we have argued that the proper objective of the firm is to maximize its value. But, most of the space in this text is devoted to the principles of maximizing the profit of the firm. We must now pause to show you how the two seemingly different objectives compare. As it turns out, single-period profit maximization is consistent with maximizing the value of the firm in most, but not all, cases. Recall that the present value of a firm is defined as the sum of the discounted net cash flows over the relevant time horizon:

$$PV = \sum_{t=1}^{T} \frac{NCF_t}{(1 + r_t)^t}$$

ILLUSTRATION 19.1

What Is the Value of a Firm?

The previous discussion of the value of a firm may have seemed a bit abstract, more suited for discussions in economic theory than for the use of sophisticated investors. Not so, as a column "Smart Money" in *Business Week* illustrates.

This column begins by noting that investment analysts use a vast collection of tools to select stocks and one of their handier devices is the dividend discount model, or DDM. "The DDM works on the premise that an investment is worth the present value of its future cash flows. So to value a stock, you'll need the current annual dividend, a projected growth rate, and a 'discount rate'."

The *Business Week* column used Exxon to illustrate the necessary calculation. At the time, the annual dividend was $2.20, which can be obtained from a newspaper. It was expected to grow at a 7 percent annual rate, according to *Value Line Investment Survey*. This information could also be obtained from a broker. To calculate the discount rate, the *Business Week* column used the current rate on long-term government bonds, at the time about 9.2 percent. The column suggested adding an equity risk premium to compensate for the added risk of owning stocks. The premium was said to range between 2 and 5 percent, depending on the riskiness of the stock. For a blue chip such as Exxon, the author suggested about 3 percent, yielding a 12.2 percent discount factor.

To calculate the effective discount rate, subtract the 7 percent growth rate of the Exxon dividend from the discount rate of 12.2 percent to obtain 5.2 percent. Then convert 5.2 percent into decimal form (0.052) and divide the decimal value into the $2.20 dividend to obtain a present value of $42.30. The column pointed out that Exxon stock at the time was selling for $46, and, therefore, by this measure was overpriced. But the model is sensitive to the estimated values of discount and growth rates used in the calculation. A small change in the discount or growth rate produces a big difference in the present value of Exxon stock.

The DDM allows investors to ask, "What if?" questions. For example, as the author points out, "If you think interest rates will fall, lower your discount rate by, say, a percentage point. That would value Exxon at $52, signaling a buy." Or, the column went on to say, "if the discount rate is raised a point, that would value Exxon at $35, indicating you should wait for the price to fall."

According to the author, some pros recast the DDM by dividing the dividend by the stock price to get the current yield. Then they add the growth rate to get the stock's implied rate of return. (It was 11.8 percent for Exxon at the time.) The implied rates of return for several stocks can then be ranked by potential return, and only the growth rate must be estimated.

Before you plunge deeply into the market, we must warn you that the columns pointed out that the DDM has limitations. "It works best on slow growing, mature companies that are consistent dividend payers." The model doesn't work well on high-flying biotech stocks, and it may make asset-rich stocks appear overpriced when takeover artists are willing to pay much more.

Source: This illustration is based on Jeffrey Laderman, "Smart Money: Fast Figuring for Stock Handicappers," *Business Week*, August 1, 1988, p. 103.

As demonstrated in the preceding section, the net cash flow in period t can be decomposed into the difference between the revenue in that period (R_t) and the costs in period t (C_t). Hence, we can write present value as

$$PV = \sum_{t=1}^{T} \frac{R_t - C_t}{(1 + r_t)^t}$$

Since $R_t - C_t$ is profit in period t, the maximum present value will be attained by maximizing profit in each period. That is, the preceding indicates that single-period profit maximization and maximizing the value of the firm are equivalent means to the same end: maximizing profit in each period will result in the maximum value of the firm and maximizing the value of the firm requires maximizing profit in each period.

The equivalence of single-period profit maximization and maximizing the value of the firm holds only when the revenue and cost conditions in one time period are independent of revenue and costs in future time periods. As we shall discuss in the next section, when today's decisions affect net cash flows in future time periods, price or output decisions that maximize profit in each (single) time period will not maximize the value of the firm.

To illustrate his point further, recall that profit maximization in any period, say period t, requires that $MR_t = MC_t$, which determines the profit-maximizing output in that period (Q_t^*). At Q_t^*, the difference between R_t and C_t is at its maximum. Thus $\pi_t = NCF_t = R_t - C_t$ is maximized. The present value of the stream of *maximum* profits or net cash flows must be higher than the present value of any other stream of *lower* net cash flows. Thus, maximizing single-period profit, under these circumstances, maximizes the present value of the firm.

Principle If cost and revenue conditions in any period are independent of decisions made in other time periods, a manager will maximize the value of a firm (the present value of the firm) by making decisions that maximize profit in every single time period.

19.4 SOME CASES WHEN VALUE AND PROFIT MAXIMIZATION ARE NOT EQUIVALENT

As we discussed, maximizing the value of a firm can be accomplished through single-period maximization of profit, *in most cases*. Under certain conditions, however, inconsistencies between single-period profit maximization and present value maximization can occur. Such inconsistencies develop when revenues and/or costs in one period are not independent of the rate of output in other periods. Some examples might illustrate this seemingly complicated point.

Learning By Doing

learning by doing
When a firm's employees, by producing in the present, become more productive or more efficient in future periods, thereby lowering future costs.

One example where value and profit maximization are not equivalent is **learning by doing**. A firm's employees become more productive, more efficient, in future periods by producing more output in earlier periods. In such cases, the more a firm produces in the present, the lower its cost, and hence marginal cost, will be in the future. Therefore, current output will have a positive effect on future output and profit, and the firm's management should take this future effect into account when planning current production. The current output would then differ from (be larger than) the output that the firm would choose if the only objective is to maximize the profit in the current period.

To illustrate the effect on optimal decision making under the above conditions, suppose the firm's planning horizon extends only over two periods. The cost functions in periods 1 and 2 are

$$C_1 = C_1(q_1) \quad \text{and} \quad C_2 = C_2(q_2, q_1)$$

where q_1 and q_2 are output levels in periods 1 and 2. Cost in period 1 depends only upon output in period 1, but cost in period 2 depends upon output in period 2 and output in period 1. The cost of producing a total of $q_1 + q_2$ units is equal to the sum of the costs in the two periods:

$$C(q_1 + q_2) = C_1(q_1) + C_2(q_2, q_1)$$

The marginal cost of production in periods 1 and 2 is

$$\frac{\Delta C}{\Delta q_1} = \frac{\Delta C_1}{\Delta q_1} + \frac{\Delta C_2}{\Delta q_1}$$

and

$$\frac{\Delta C}{\Delta q_2} = \frac{\Delta C_2}{\Delta q_2}$$

Because production in period 1 lowers cost in period 2, $\Delta C_2/\Delta q_1$ is negative, so that $\Delta C/\Delta q_1 < \Delta C_1/\Delta q_1$. If the firm maximizes single-period profit only, it would choose the output in period 1 at which marginal revenue equals $\Delta C_1/\Delta q_1$. If it maximizes the value of the firm, it would set MR equal to $(\Delta C_1/\Delta q_1 + \Delta C_2/\Delta q_1)$, which is lower than $\Delta C_1/\Delta q_1$. Therefore, the firm would produce more in period 1 under the latter conditions.

The situation in period 1 is illustrated in Figure 19.2, in which MR_1 is the firm's marginal revenue curve in period 1 and MC_1 is the period 1 marginal cost curve, considering only the effect of current production on current cost. If the firm is interested only in single-period profits, it would produce q_1, where $MR_1 = MC_1$. If the firm maximizes present value and hence considers the effect current output has on future cost, $\overline{MC}_1$ is the relevant marginal cost curve (MR_1 would not be affected); $\overline{MC}_1$ is below MC_1 because current production lowers future cost: that is, $\Delta C_2/\Delta q_1 < 0$. In this case, the firm would produce $\bar{q}_1$ if it maximizes present value, and current output would be higher.[1]

Alternatively, if current production has the effect of increasing cost in the future, maximizing present value would result in a lower current output than maximizing single-period profit. In such cases, maximizing single-period profit also is not equivalent to maximizing present value. One example of higher current production raising future cost would occur if higher rates of output in the present cause capital equipment to depreciate faster and become less productive in the future. Another relatively important example occurs in extractive industries

[1]Note that the effect of q_1 on C_2 would have to be discounted by the relevant interest rate for complete accuracy. We did not discount because we were interested only in showing that period 1 production is affected, and not how much it is affected. Thus there was no reason to further complicate the analysis.

FIGURE 19.2
Single-Period Profit Maximization versus Present Value Maximization

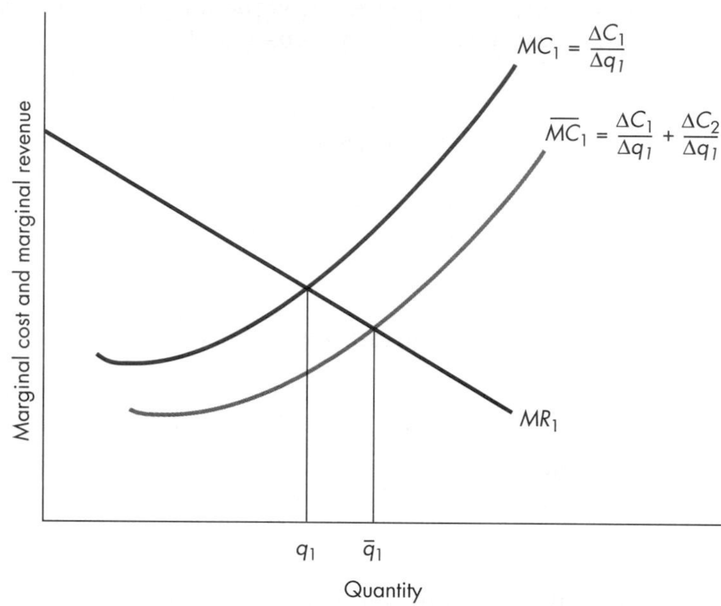

such as mining and oil production. The higher the rate of extraction or pumping in the present time period, the more costly it is, in general, to extract ore from a mine or pump oil from a well in the future. Miners typically must dig deeper the more that has been previously extracted. As oil is pumped from a well, the well loses pressure, and pumping additional oil costs more, sometimes because of the different techniques that must be used. In any case, present production affects future costs.

Despite these examples of inconsistencies between the two types of maximization, it is generally the case that there is little difference between the conclusions of single-period profit maximization (the topic of most of this text) and present value maximization (the topic of this chapter). Thus, single-period profit maximization is generally the most useful approach to the analysis of maximization over time.

Entry Limit Strategies over Time

The discussion thus far has concerned situations in which a firm's costs are not independent over time. Another situation in which present value maximization is not equivalent to single-period maximization occurs when firms practice entry limit pricing or use excess capacity as a barrier to the entry of new firms into the market. These strategies were discussed in Chapter 16, but we did not analyze these strategies in a multiperiod framework. Rather than discussing the effect over time, we limited the discussion to single-period analysis, while noting that we would add a time dimension later. We now turn to this task.

As noted in Chapter 16, entry limit pricing and excess capacity are two possible strategies available to an established firm that wishes to prevent or discourage the entry of new firms into the market. As we just mentioned, these strategies involve decision making over time and, therefore, might cause a divergence between the maximization of profit in each period and maximization of present value. We will now present a hypothetical example showing how a manager can determine whether entry limit pricing is a better strategy than maximizing profit in each period and letting entry occur. We will postpone discussion of capacity as an entry-blocking strategy, in order to simplify the example by considering only two choices.

Zephyr Products—a firm providing industrial services—was the first firm to enter a new market and therefore enjoys the position of being the established firm. The manager of Zephyr has determined the single-period profit-maximizing price to be $2,000. With this price, annual profit is $80,000.

However, the manager knows that, if price is set at $2,000, additional firms will enter the market. Entry would gradually drive price to $1,200 and, over time, Zephyr's annual profit would fall to $30,000. Using experience in other markets, the manager believes Zephyr's profits over its five-year planning horizon would be:

Year:	1	2	3	4	5
Profit:	$80,000	$50,000	$40,000	$30,000	$30,000

Alternatively, Zephyr can practice entry limit pricing. The manager of Zephyr believes that if price is set at $1,400, no firms would enter the market. With this price, Zephyr's annual profit would be $50,000 in each year over the five-year planning horizon.

Hence, the manager of Zephyr is faced with a choice of two strategies—two income streams. The manager will obviously select that stream of income that has the higher present value. Using the prevailing US Treasury rates provided earlier in this chapter, the present values of the two possible streams are as follows:

Maximize single-period profit and permit entry:

$$PV = \frac{\$80{,}000}{(1.0575)} + \frac{\$50{,}000}{(1.06)^2} + \frac{\$40{,}000}{(1.0625)^3} + \frac{\$30{,}000}{(1.065)^4} + \frac{\$30{,}000}{(1.0675)^5}$$
$$= \$75{,}650 + \$44{,}500 + \$33{,}348 + \$23{,}320 + \$21{,}641$$
$$= \$198{,}459$$

Entry limit price:

$$PV = \frac{\$50{,}000}{(1.0575)} + \frac{\$50{,}000}{(1.06)^2} + \frac{\$50{,}000}{(1.0625)^3} + \frac{\$50{,}000}{(1.065)^4} + \frac{\$50{,}000}{(1.0675)^5}$$
$$= \$47{,}281 + \$44{,}500 + \$41{,}685 + \$38{,}866 + \$36{,}069$$
$$= \$208{,}401$$

In this example, the value of Zephyr Products is maximized by entry limit pricing. We have, of course, made several assumptions that allow Zephyr to be able to practice this strategy. First, as was discussed at length in Chapter 16, the limit price must be below the minimum point on the long-run average cost curve of all potential entrants. Also, because Zephyr continued making profits at the limit price, Zephyr's long-run average cost must be below the limit price over a range of output.[2] Thus, Zephyr must have a cost advantage over potential entrants, a point emphasized in Chapter 16.

One final assumption is implicit in this example: Zephyr must have the capacity to increase its output in order to sell the increased quantity demand forthcoming at the lower price. Thus Zephyr may have been able to use this excess capacity already in place as an entry deterrent without having to actually lower its price. Potential entrants, knowing about this excess capacity, would possibly be discouraged from entering the market because they know that if they prepared to enter, Zephyr would have the capacity to increase output by decreasing its price. If the firm does not already have the capacity to increase sales, the cost of adding this extra capacity during early periods would have to be considered when comparing present values under single-period maximization, entry limit pricing, and capacity deterrence. The computation would be the same as that used in the above comparison of present values. In any case, when an entry-limiting strategy is employed, single-period profit maximization may not be the same as value maximization.

19.5 CONFLICTS BETWEEN SHAREHOLDERS (OWNERS) AND MANAGERS

In the simple firms described throughout most of this text, the entrepreneur was both the owner (shareholder) and the manager; what was good for the owner was, by definition, good for the manager. If this owner-manager identity does not exist, conflicts are likely between shareholders and the managers they have hired to operate the firm. In general, these conflicts arise because of differences between the objectives of the shareholders and the managers. More specifically, the conflicts can most often be traced to the contracts between the shareholders and the management teams. Such conflicts, frequently referred to as the *principal-agent problem* or simply the *agency problem*, are currently receiving a great deal of attention from economists and corporate analysts.

principal-agent problem
The conflict that arises when the goals of management (the agent) do not match the goals of the owner (the principal).

A principal in an agreement contracts with an agent to perform tasks designed to further the principal's objectives. The **principal-agent problem** arises when the agents have objectives that differ from those of the principal; the principal has difficulty enforcing the contract with the agent; or the principal finds it difficult to learn whether or not the agent is actually carrying out the agreement and furthering the principal's objectives. Although there are a multitude of examples of the principal-agent problem—whenever one party contracts with an-

[2] If entry was deterred at the price of single-period profit maximization—if the minimum average cost of potential entrants was above $2,000—we would say entry is blockaded: Zephyr could maximize single-period profit without attracting entrants.

other party to perform a function—we are concerned here with the shareholder-manager problem. The shareholders are obviously the principals and the managers are the agents. The agency problem occurs because of the existence of *moral hazard*.

Moral Hazard

Moral hazard
Exists when either party to an agreement has an incentive not to abide by all provisions of the agreement.

Moral hazard exists when either party to an agreement has an incentive not to abide by all provisions of the agreement, and one party finds it difficult, perhaps impossible, to find out if the other party is abiding by the agreement, or to actually enforce the agreement even when the information is available. Moral hazard arises in a large number of principal-agent agreements. Workers may shirk on the job, lawyers may not put forth their best effort for their clients, and a firm might sell goods or services that are below standard with deficiencies that are difficult to detect. Here, however, we are concerned only with moral hazard in the case of firm management working for shareholders.

We have tried to demonstrate that shareholders have a single, straightforward objective: maximize the value of the firm. Managers may or may not share this objective. They could desire to attain other goals and may be willing to sacrifice some of the firm's value in order to pursue these other objectives. Several conflicting managerial objectives have been proposed. For example, managers may want amenities that cut into the firm's profit: luxurious office buildings in prestigious locations, elegant dining and entertainment facilities, corporate automobiles and airplanes, business trips to exotic locations. Managers may wish to use more of the firm's income for charitable, civic, or political contributions. Such contributions can enhance the manager's stature in the city, the state, or the nation.

Sometimes managers are willing to sacrifice some of the firm's profit for increased revenue. How much business a firm does or its share of the market is frequently a source of prestige to a firm's CEO. As you know, profit is maximized by producing where marginal revenue equals marginal cost. Revenue can be increased by producing beyond the profit-maximizing equilibrium as long as marginal revenue is positive—that is, demand is elastic. Beyond the equilibrium, marginal revenue is less than marginal cost and, as you know, profit is not being maximized because the firm is producing too much. During the slump of the early 1990s, firms that were experiencing a drastic decline in business frequently tried to remedy the problem by downsizing. These firms were simply too large. All of the conflicting goals we have mentioned, as well as some others, pose agency problems.

You may be wondering why the shareholders don't simply tell the managers to begin maximizing the value of the firm, and, if they don't comply, replace them with new managers. This process is a lot more complex and difficult than it would appear at first glance. The large modern corporation is an extremely complicated institution. The upper management of a firm is much more familiar with the functioning of the corporation than most or even all of the stockholders are. Stockholders would not even know, in many cases, whether management is or is not attempting to maximize the value of the firm or its profits, especially when business is good and the price of the stock is rising. They get their information about the firm primarily from that same management.

In the case of large corporations, any given shareholder typically holds a relatively small proportion of the total outstanding stock. The stockholders are generally broadly diversified and would have difficulty organizing into a group that could actually affect the firm's policies. Furthermore, an individual stockholder would probably not have the incentive to find the necessary information about the firm, and then attempt to monitor management. The cost of obtaining and processing the required information would be huge, while the benefits to an individual shareholder would be small, even if the monitoring were successful. Shareholders usually have diversified portfolios in which no individual stock looms particularly large, relative to their total holdings. They frequently don't have much of an interest in one particular stock. Therefore, the owners of large corporations have a difficult time policing the managers.

Some Solutions to the Agency Problem

All of this discussion of moral hazard is not meant to imply that shareholders are completely helpless in the face of managers who aren't doing what the shareholders expect them to do. Obviously, if shareholders are unhappy about a firm's performance, they can sell their stock in the firm and buy equity in other corporations. Such action, if taken by a relatively large number of stockholders, would tend to depress the price of a company's stock. This would generally be detrimental to the managers, who typically own stock in the firm themselves. This possibility would tend to limit egregious, conflicting behavior by the managers. However, if the price of the stock has been falling because of poor performance, stockholders would also experience some decline in wealth.

Stockholders often try to solve the agency problem by tying managers' income to fulfilling the goals of the stockholders. As an example of a poor compensation plan, suppose stockholders want to guarantee a firm's long-term growth in the industry; they might set up a managerial compensation plan based on net operating income, growth in sales, and the relative rank of the firm in the industry. Then if income is available after paying dividends, management would be motivated to reinvest these cash flows in new projects. If the firm gets larger, management gets better bonuses. Such a plan could work well for the stockholders if the market continues to grow. Dividends would continue to be high, as the price of the stock is driven up by the growth of the company.

However, if business begins to decline, the net present value of new investment projects would decline. Because of the bonus arrangement, management might even invest free cash flows into projects for which the net present value is negative. The management would be happy, but the shareholders would be unhappy as the value of the stock declined. The problem is that the shareholders gave management a compensation plan based on the goal of sales or size maximization rather than value maximization.

Resolving the conflict between managerial and stockholder objectives requires a compensation plan that induces management to maximize the value of the firm. The simplest approach is to change the compensation plan from one based on accounting revenues to one based on economic profitability. In such cases, management bonuses would be directly linked to increases in dividends and the value of the stock. Managers would then have the same objectives as shareholders.

It's easy to propose a sweeping change in compensation plans as a solution to the agency problem. In the real world of corporate politics, it may not be so easy to implement this type of change. It could well be the case that a management team likes the compensation system they have, and have enough clout with the board of directors to keep it in place. Furthermore, any attempts by shareholders to alter the method of compensation runs squarely into the previously discussed problems of shareholders attempting to police the firm and convince management to change its policies. Shareholders are small, numerous, and diversified, and an individual shareholder would not have much incentive or the capability of changing compensation policies.

Corporate takeovers are an important possible solution to the conflict between shareholders and managers who do not maximize the value of the firm. If the value of the firm is less with the present set of managers than it would be with another, there is a profit incentive for others to acquire the firm and replace the management team with a new set of managers. For example, in the above example of the poor compensation scheme, another company, or group of corporate raiders, believing its management could do a better job, might take over the firm by purchasing enough shares to take control. When the acquisition plan is announced, the firm's stock would probably increase in value, and the shareholders would once again be happy.

In this example, the new owners would benefit from the takeover. However, it should also be made clear that, in any takeover motivated by maximizing the present value of the firm, the shareholders of the target firm will also benefit. Indeed, it has been estimated that in merger and acquisition deals during the 1980s, the shareholders of the target firms realized huge increases in the values of their holdings. It is not surprising to see articles in business publications, such as *The Wall Street Journal*, telling of substantial increases in the price of a firm's stock after a takeover bid has been announced. Even though most of the media, many politicians, and certainly the managers of the takeover targets were outraged, such takeovers, frequently called "hostile," act as a check on the powers of incompetent managers to create inefficiency, and also on managers who are less interested in maximizing profits, since they are not major owners, than they are in expanding their corporate domain. Thus, takeovers can sometimes resolve to some extent the conflict between managers and shareholders. (For further discussion of hostile takeovers, see Illustration 19.2).

ILLUSTRATION 19.2

What's Wrong with Hostile Takeovers?

We briefly alluded to corporate takeovers as a possible solution to the conflict between shareholders and managers who do not maximize the corporation's present value. During the 1980s, and to a somewhat lesser extent in the 1990s, there was a wave of mergers and hostile takeovers (hostile at least to the managers involved) along with a certain amount of illegal insider trading. The media and many politicians were outraged over this seeming affront to entrenched corporate managers. Two columns by *Newsweek* columnist Robert J. Samuelson, published in 1985 and 1986, put the takeover movement in perspective, show how the takeover movement was related to the conflict of shareholders and managers, and explain some of the insider trading that was taking place.

According to Samuelson, corporate raiders were parodied as capitalism's juvenile delinquents, engaged in hostile takeovers financed by junk bonds. "In fact, hostile takeovers . . . represent a crude check on the power of corporate managers to waste wealth and create inefficiency. I doubt that those in Congress who condemn [T. Boone] Pickens [a prominent corporate raider at the time] and want to regulate takeovers understand [this]."

He went on to point out that, when corporate managers are not the major owners of their companies—as most are not—their loyalties become confused. "They may be less interested in maximizing profits than in preserving and expanding their corporate domain." This was the point of our discussion in the text.

Now recall the discussion in the text of the hypothetical corporation. Samuelson says, "As long as a company's primary business is thriving, the conflict may lie dormant. Managers can maximize profits and expand simultaneously. But this happy marriage rarely lasts forever." Then as the business matures, management may diversify into a new business, where the company may have no special knowledge or talent. And, "Hostile takeovers arise mainly to exploit profit opportunities created when corporations cannot cope with their growth dilemma." Samuelson emphasized that today's hostile takeovers represent a corrective for yesterday's abuses, and that many corporations have become cumbersome empires and cannot motivate workers or be managed efficiently. These companies are the potential takeover targets. He also argues, that even the distant *threat* of a takeover can be therapeutic. "Companies are furiously selling unwanted divisions and subsidiaries." According to these arguments, corporate raiders keep managers much more in line with the wishes of stockholders, and, to the extent that they improve companies' efficiency, they benefit consumers and the public as well.

In a later column, Samuelson reiterates the advantages or benefits of corporate takeovers but points out why illegal insider trading, particularly by the most prominent insider at the time who allegedly made billions illegally, gave beneficial takeovers a bad name. According to Samuelson, "Many companies are excessively bureaucratic or excessively diversified. They would operate more efficiently if broken up into their constituent business . . . or put under better management. . . . Fragmented shareholders are passive; directors are complacent." And, "short of bankruptcy, top executives have enjoyed huge job security. . . . Hostile takeovers shatter this security."

Samuelson notes that the resulting stock market speculation over possible takeover candidates really reflects mismanagement. Suppose a company's stock sells at $10, and someone plans a takeover at $13 (takeover premiums average between 25 and 50 percent). The takeover group thinks better management can raise the stock's value to $17. "At a crude level, the gap between $10 and $17 (if attained) is mismanagement."

Then there enter traders with illegal inside information, such as Ivan Boesky, the prominent trader referred to above. With a tip about the takeover, an insider trader can buy the stock at $10 and sell it at $13. Samuelson argues, however, "Nothing in Boesky's scam diminishes the real gains possible from replacing bad management with good." He also argues that even though the number of actual hostile takeovers is small, even the threat of a takeover spurs many managers to improve their efficiency. As noted in the text, takeovers can resolve to some extent the conflict between managers and shareholders.

Source: This illustration is based on Robert J. Samuelson, "In Praise of Boone," *Newsweek*, May 6, 1985, p. 59, and "The Super Bowl of Scandal," *Newsweek*, Dec. 1, 1986, p. 64.

19.6 SUMMARY

The value today of a cash flow to be received in the future is its present value. The *present value* (PV) of a net cash flow ($\$NCF$) to be received with certainty in t periods is

$$PV = \frac{\$NCF}{(1 + r)^t}$$

where r is the riskless interest rate in time period t—also known as the discount rate. The present value increases as (1) The size of the cash flow increases, (2) The time to receipt decreases, or (3) The discount rate decreases.

For a project or asset with a stream of cash flows over T periods of time, the present value is

$$PV = \sum_{t=1}^{T} \frac{\$NCF_t}{(1 + r_t)^t}$$

where NCF_t is the net cash flow received in period t, and r_t is the t-period discount rate. The *net present value* (NPV) of a project or asset is the difference between its present value and its cost,

$$NPV = PV - \text{Cost of the project or asset}$$

A firm can be thought of as a portfolio of projects or assets. Consequently, the value of the firm is the sum of the present values of all of its projects or assets. In order to maximize the value of the firm, the manager need only follow the *Net Present Value Rule* for maximizing the value of the firm:

> Accept projects (acquire assets) for which the net present value is positive and reject projects for which the net present value is negative. The manager should divest the firm of any projects for which the NPV is negative.

As long as revenues and costs are independent over time, single-period profit maximization is equivalent to maximizing the value of the firm. Inconsistencies occur when the firm's output decision in one period affects costs or revenues in subsequent time periods.

A principal-agent problem arises when managers have incentives that are different from those of shareholders. If there are many relatively small shareholders, as is the case for most large corporations, shareholders have a difficult time forcing managers to maximize the firm's value. Possible solutions are tying managers' income to profit, and takeovers that replace old managers with new managers.

TECHNICAL PROBLEMS

In the following five problems, use the term structure of US Treasury securities for the riskless interest rates below:

Time to maturity (years)	Interest rate (percent)
1	5.75
2	6.00
3	6.25
4	6.50
5	6.75

* 1. Calculate the present value of $1,000 to be received in

a. One year.
b. Two years.
c. Three years.
d. Four years.
e. Five years.

2. What is the present value of the following income stream from a project? (Treat all cash flows as paid or received at year-end.)

Year	Net cash flow
1	–$10,000
2	$20,000
3	$50,000
4	$75,000
5	$50,000

* 3. If the purchase price of the project described in problem 2 is $125,000, what is the project's net present value? What is the project's net present value if its purchase price is $150,000?

4. If the purchase price of the project outlined above is $125,000, should the firm undertake the project? What if the price is $150,000? What is the maximum amount the firm should pay for this project?

5. Look again at the discussion dealing with Zephyr Products's decision about whether to limit price. Reevaluate this decision if

   a. Entry occurred slower than originally presumed—that is:

Year	1	2	3	4	5
Profits	$80,000	$60,000	$50,000	$40,000	$30,000

   b. The limit price annual profits were $45,000 rather than $50,000.

   c. The US Treasury interest rates were 1 percent higher—that is:

Years to maturity	1	2	3	4	5
Interest rate	6.75%	7.0%	7.25%	7.5%	7.75%

6. Financial assets (e.g., shares of stock) are said to be zero net present value projects. Why? If an asset like a share of stock is a zero *NPV* project, noninterest-bearing checking accounts look like negative *NPV* projects. However, firms do hold such assets. Why?

7. What types of firms would you expect to be able to use entry limit pricing? What types either could not or would not use this strategy? Provide some examples of industries in which you might expect entry limit pricing and some for which such pricing would not be expected.

8. An oil deposit is discovered in your backyard. Your stream of royalty income will be as follows (all payments are made at year-end):

Year	Royalty payment
1	$20,000
2	$20,000
3	$15,000
4	$10,000
5	$ 2,000

Suppose you want your money now. What is the maximum price someone would be willing to pay for your future royalty income with a prevailing interest rate of 11 percent?

APPLIED PROBLEMS

1. The Environmental Protection Agency (EPA) is charged with regulating the amount of pollutants that firms can emit into the environment. The EPA can force firms to cease polluting beyond some acceptable level or it can impose fines upon polluting firms. The Hardrock Mining Co. operates a metal refining plant—a smelter—near a small city. In the process of refining the ore, the smelter is emitting sulfur dioxide (SO_2) into the air at the rate of 10 parts per million (molecules). The EPA regulation states that the firm will be fined $50,000 a year for every part per million in excess of five parts per million. The chief executive officer of Hardrock Mining asks his engineering department to investigate the problem and propose some solutions.

   In their report, the engineering department notes that the firm will have an entirely new plant in five years, so the solution to the present problem will be short run. They report that there are two possible solutions. The first is to put in a new air purification process, which will reduce the sulfur dioxide below five parts after it is installed. The cost will be $1,050,000, payable now. The second solution is to install scrubbers—that is, modify the present plant and equipment. This will reduce pollution to eight parts the first two years, and to seven parts thereafter. This will cost $250,000 at the end of the first year and $250,000 at the end of the second. Of course, the firm would have to pay a fine each year.

   The CEO adds a third alternative by noting that the firm could do nothing and pay the fine. The fine would be $250,000 a year, since five parts of sulfur dioxide above the maximum would be emitted each year.

   Prepare a report for the CEO ranking the three alternatives using the interest rates provided in the text.

2. The hypothetical example in which one firm acquired another firm that was not doing well occurred often in the oil business during the early 1980s. One oil company acquired another—and its reserves—at "a bargain basement price."

   These (often hostile) takeovers led to a great deal of criticism of takeover activity. As many press reports put it, Wall Street was undervaluing oil reserves and was wasting resources in nonproductive merger and acquisition activity. If you were working on Wall Street, how would you answer?

3. Taxicabs in New York City are licensed—in order to pick up passengers in the five boroughs of NYC, you must have a medallion displayed on the hood of your taxi. There are no new medallions available. If you want a medallion, you have to buy it from someone who owns one.

   If you were to purchase an NYC taxicab company, what is it you are purchasing? How would you calculate the value of the taxicab company?

   In October 1986, Mayor Ed Koch suggested that the number of NYC taxicab medallions be increased. What was the reaction to this suggestion? Why?

4. Gemini Robotics, Inc.—a monopoly firm in the market for home robots—must decide whether or not to limit price. The owner-manager of Gemini has determined the single-period profit-maximizing price to be $130,000 per robot. At this price,

economic profit will result and other firms will enter the market. Gemini's manager expects that entry will cause the 5-year profit stream to be:

Year	Profit
1	$3,500,000
2	$2,500,000
3	$1,750,000
4	$1,000,000
5	$ 750,000

If Gemini follows a limit pricing strategy by setting a price of $75,000 per robot, then no firms can enter the market. At this price Gemini can earn annual profit of $2,000,000 for the next five years.

a. If the interest rate is 10 percent, should Gemini limit price?
b. If the interest rate is 6 percent, should Gemini limit price?

5. Eveready Trucking Company runs a fleet of 10 tractor-trailer rigs in California. The California State Environmental Protection Administration informs Eveready that its five older trucks do not meet the state's air pollution standards. The annual license fee for each of these five trucks will be increased by $3,000 (effective immediately) until the trucks meet the California emission standards.

   Emission control devices cost $10,000 apiece. Unfortunately the five older trucks will have no useful life after four more years of service. Retiring the five trucks now would reduce profit by the following amounts over the next four years:

Year	Profit lost
1	$22,000
2	$16,000
3	$10,000
4	$ 9,000

   The manager of Eveready Trucking is considering three options:
   Option 1 Pay the fine (the increased license fee) on all five trucks.
   Option 2 Buy the emission control devices for all five trucks.
   Option 3 Retire all five trucks now.
   At a 12 percent rate of interest, what is the present value of the cost of each of the three options? Which option should the manager choose?

6. An article in *The Wall Street Journal* (October 13, 1992) discusses a trend among some large US corporations to base the compensation of outside members of their boards of directors partly on the performance of the corporation. "This growing practice more closely aligns the director to the company. [Some] companies link certain stock or stock-option grants for directors to improved financial performance, using a measure such as annual return on equity."

   How would such a linkage tend to reduce the agency problem between managers and shareholders as a whole? Why could directors be more efficient than shareholders in improving managerial performance and changing their incentives?

7. An article in *The Wall Street Journal* reported that large hotel chains, such as Marriott, are tending to reduce the number of hotels that they franchise to outside owners and increase the number the chain owns and manages itself. Some chains

are requiring private owners or franchisees to make upgrades in their hotels, but are having a difficult time enforcing the policy. Marriott says this upgrading is important because "We've built our name on quality."

a. What type of agency problem is involved here?

b. Why would Marriott worry about the quality of the hotels it doesn't own but franchises?

c. Why would a chain such as Marriott tend to own its hotels in resort areas, such as national parks, where there is little repeat business, and franchise hotels in downtown areas, where there is a lot of repeat business? Think of the reputation effect and the incentive of franchises to maintain quality.

8. The *National Enquirer* reported that in their divorce settlement Burt Reynolds offered Loni Anderson $10 million spread evenly over 10 years but Loni Anderson demanded $5 million now. If the interest rate is 8 percent which alternative is best for Burt and which for Loni? What if the interest rate is 20 percent?

CHAPTER 20

The Investment Decision

A large part of this text has been concerned with the basic questions of the profit-maximizing level of output for a business—what price to charge, and what level of variable inputs to employ. We will now address the question of how managers can make decisions about investment projects in order to maximize the value of the firm. Investment projects may involve purchasing new equipment for a plant, expanding the size of a production facility, adding a new product to the firm's product line, or even buying another firm.

Investment decisions involve cash flows over multiple periods of time in the future. These cash flows are inherently risky—they are obviously not known with certainty. To make investment decisions, managers must examine the present value of the stream of revenues and costs associated with the many investment projects available. As you will see, investment decision making requires using the analysis of present value developed in Chapter 19, as well as the optimization theory first set forth in Chapter 4 and the risk analysis discussed in Chapter 6.

We begin the analysis of investment decisions by describing how managers can determine the value of a stream of risky cash flows received over a period of time. Then we apply the net present value rule developed in Chapter 19 to the investment decision. As always, this analysis is an extension of the marginal benefit–marginal cost rule first set forth in Chapter 4. We discuss the various methods of finding the appropriate discount rate for making investment decisions. Next, we present some critiques and several alternative investment criteria—payback, return on investment, and the internal rate of return—that are sometimes used by managers to make investment decisions. Finally, we examine the manager's investment decision when the firm's investment funds are constrained by budgetary limits imposed either by banks or by the firm itself. This is the problem of capital rationing.

The topics covered in this chapter on investment decisions will be covered, in much greater detail, in the finance courses you will take, or may have already taken. Since investment decision making is a critical component of a manager's decision-making responsibilities, and since these decisions are typically made using the basic techniques of microeconomic analysis, managerial economics courses traditionally cover investment decision making. We follow tradition by including this chapter.

20.1 VALUING RISKY CASH FLOWS

When discussing the valuation of a *riskless* project (asset) in Chapter 19, we demonstrated that the value of the project is given by its present value. To obtain the present value of some specific project, *j*, we employed the valuation equation

$$PV_j = \sum_{t=1}^{T} \frac{NCF_{j,t}}{(1 + r_t)^t}$$

where $NCF_{j,t}$ is the net cash flow generated by project j in year t and r_t is the riskless discount rate in year t (the interest rate on US government securities). We will now examine the way this valuation equation changes when project j is a *risky* project.

Risky Cash Flows

Obviously, when cash flows are risky, the numerator of the present value equation must change. The cash flows from project j are no longer known with certainty. Instead of a single, known value of $NCF_{j,t}$, there exists a probability distribution for the cash flow from project j in year t, an illustration of which is provided in Figure 20.1. Since the probability distribution for the *NCF* is known, the manager can calculate the expected value of the net cash flow in each time period t for project j, $E(NCF_{j,t})$. Recall from Chapter 6 that decisions involving risk typically require calculating the expected value of random outcomes. For investment decisions, the manager is interested in the expected value of risky net cash flows.

A Discount Rate Reflecting Risk

A less obvious change in the valuation equation when risk is present is the change required in the denominator. For the riskless project, the appropriate discount rate was the riskless rate. Since there was no question about the size of the cash flow, the only thing that mattered was when the cash flows would be received (paid).

However, as is clear from Figure 20.1, the probability distribution for the cash flows from the risky project j has a nonzero variance. Because the variance

FIGURE 20.1
Cash Flows from a Risky Project

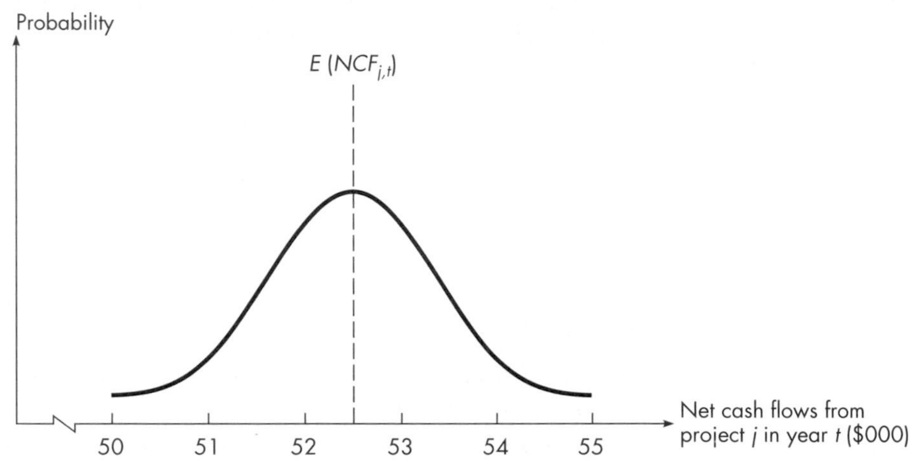

is a measure of risk, the cash flows from this project are risky in the sense that the size of the cash flow varies. The larger the variance (standard deviation) of the cash flows from a project, the riskier is the project.

Since the risk associated with the variance in the probability distribution for cash flows is not accounted for in the numerator of the valuation equation (*NCF*) it must be accounted for in the denominator. Thus, this risk must be reflected in the discount rate used. The riskless rate is clearly not appropriate: neither is some common or general discount rate for risky projects. Project *j* has some level of risk associated with the probability distribution of its cash flows and this risk is not necessarily the same as the risk for some other project *k*—even if the two projects have the same expected net cash flows. Therefore, there will exist a specific discount rate that reflects the risk associated with project *j*. We denote this specific discount rate for cash flows received (paid) from project *j* in year *t* as $r_{j,t}$.

Combining the discussions of uncertain cash flows and a risk-adjusted discount rate, it should be clear that, for a risky project *j*, the *expected* present value is

$$E(PV_j) = \sum_{t=1}^{T} \frac{E(NCF_{j,t})}{(1 + r_{j,t})^t}$$

Just as the present value equation provides the value of a riskless project, this equation can be used to value a risky project.

It should be clear now how a manager could estimate a probability distribution for cash flows from a project, then, using the appropriate discount rate, determine the expected net cash flows. Choosing the appropriate discount rate to reflect the riskiness of a project is not always a simple matter. We will now discuss the problem of finding the appropriate discount rate.

20.2 THE APPROPRIATE DISCOUNT RATE FOR A RISKY PROJECT

To discount the expected net cash flows from a risky project j, a manager should use a discount rate that compensates the firm for bearing the additional risk. Thus, the discount rate should be higher than the riskless rate. The appropriate discount rate for cash flows from risky project j in year t could be expressed as

$$r_{j,t} = r_t + (\text{risk premium})_j$$

where r_t is the riskless rate and the second term is the appropriate risk premium for project j.[1]

We will now show how to determine the appropriate risk premium. Several methods exist. We will describe two that are used most often: risk-adjusted discount rates and the weighted average cost of capital. After defining and briefly discussing these two rules of thumb, we will present a simple numerical example to illustrate their use.

The Risk-Adjusted Discount Rate

risk-adjusted discount rate
The riskless rate plus a risk premium.

The preceding equation illustrates the discounting problem quite clearly: a risk premium must be attached to the riskless rate. The **risk-adjusted discount rate** approach does that directly, simply by adding a specific risk premium directly to the riskless rate. Apparently simple, the risk-adjusted discount rate methodology is complicated by an obvious problem: How does the manager determine the appropriate risk premium? Elegant mathematical formulas have been presented by Franco Modigliani and Merton Miller and by J. Miles and R. Ezzell. However, the risk-adjusted discount rates remain rules of thumb and are at the discretion of the manager.

The Weighted Average Cost of Capital

weighted average cost of capital
The rate at which the firm can borrow, weighted by the ratio of debt to net worth, plus the rate of return required by stockholders, weighted by the ratio of equity to net worth: $r_{WACC} = r_D[D/(D + E)] + r_E[E/(D + E)]$.

The weighted-average-cost-of-capital (WACC) approach to finding the appropriate risk premium reflects market conditions more than the risk-adjusted discount rate approach. In essence, the weighted-average-cost-of-capital method is based on the assumption that the appropriate discount rate for new projects is the interest rate currently paid by the firm in the market; that is, a weighted average rate at which the firm can borrow funds, and the rate of return required by the firm's shareholders. Following this approach, the **weighted average cost of capital** for a firm, denoted as r_{WACC}, is calculated as[2]

$$r_{WACC} = r_D\left(\frac{D}{D + E}\right) + r_E\left(\frac{E}{D + E}\right)$$

[1]The risk discussed here deals with variation in the size of the cash flow. It should not be confused with default (performance) risk, which is imbedded in the numerator: $E(NCF)$ will incorporate any probabilities of default.

[2]This formula neglects corporate taxes. If corporate taxes were included

$$r_{WACC} = (1 - CTR)\left[r_D\left(\frac{D}{D + E}\right) + r_E\left(\frac{E}{D + E}\right)\right]$$

where CTR is the marginal corporate income tax rate.

where D and E are the current market values of the firm's outstanding debt and equity and r_D and r_E are, respectively, the current rate at which the firm can borrow and the rate of return on equity required by the firm's shareholders to induce them to hold the shares of stock.

In the above equation, D plus E is the net worth of the firm. Thus the first term is the rate at which the firm can borrow, weighted by the proportion of net worth that is represented by debt. The second term is the rate of required return on equity, weighted by the proportion of net worth represented by equity. Hence the term, weighted average cost of capital.

The weighted-average-cost-of-capital approach is intuitively appealing, and, in some cases, it actually works. Specifically, the WACC approach is appropriate (1) if the project being considered is just like the rest of the firm, and (2) if the project is to be financed with the same mix of debt and equity prevailing in the rest of the firm. The WACC approach is not appropriate for projects that are more or less risky than the firm's existing portfolio of projects. Likewise, the WACC approach is not appropriate if acceptance of the project would cause the firm's debt/equity ratio to change.

Perhaps because it is more intuitively appealing than the risk-adjusted discount rate approach, the weighted-average-cost-of-capital approach is widely used. For example, in 1978, almost half the firms surveyed used WACC as the appropriate discount rate.[3] However, like the risk-adjusted discount rate weighted average cost of capital is only a rule-of-thumb.

Estimating the Probability Distribution of Cash Flows and Discount Rates: A Numerical Example

We will now show how a firm can estimate a probability distribution for the cash flows from a project and determine the net cash flows. Suppose the managers of Zeus Manufacturing are considering the acquisition of machinery to produce a new product line. The machinery has a five-year time horizon. (At the end of the five years, the project has no scrap value.) The firm obtained low, best, and high estimates for the net cash flows from the project in each of its five years. The resulting table of outcomes is presented below:

	Net cash flow estimates ($ million)		
Year	Low	Best	High
1	−2	0	4
2	1	3	5
3	4	5	6
4	4	5	6
5	2	4	5

Management subjectively assigned probabilities to these outcomes as low—20 percent, best—70 percent, high—10 percent.

[3]See Harold Bierman, Jr., *Implementation of Capital Budgeting—Survey and Synthesis* (New York: Financial Management Association, 1986), p. 25.

Using these probabilities, the expected net cash flow in year 1 is zero:

$$E(NCF_1) = (-2)(0.2) + (0)(0.7) + (4)(0.1)$$
$$= -.4 + 0 + .4 = 0$$

Calculated in the same way, the expected net cash flows for years 2 through 5 are (in million dollars)

$$E(NCF_2) = 2.8$$
$$E(NCF_3) = 4.9$$
$$E(NCF_4) = 4.9$$
$$E(NCF_5) = 3.7$$

The managers of Zeus now want to determine the expected present value of this project. Their policy has been to attach a risk premium based on their evaluation of how risky the project is. The risk premiums they use are as follows:

Project riskiness	Risk premium (percent)
Low-risk project	3
Average-risk project	6
High-risk project	9

In their judgment, the project being considered was an average-risk project. Hence, the rates used to discount the expected cash flows are obtained by adding this risk premium to the riskless rate (the interest rate for US government securities):

Years to maturity	Riskless rate (percent)	Risk premium (percent)	Risk-adjusted discount rate (percent)
1	5.75	6	11.75
2	6.00	6	12.00
3	6.25	6	12.25
4	6.50	6	12.50
5	6.75	6	12.75

Using these risk-adjusted discount rates, the expected present value of the project is

$$E(PV_j) = \frac{0}{(1.1175)^1} + \frac{2.8}{(1.12)^2} + \frac{4.9}{(1.1225)^3}$$
$$+ \frac{4.9}{(1.125)^4} + \frac{3.7}{(1.1275)^5}$$
$$= 0 + 2.232 + 3.464 + 3.059 + 2.031$$
$$= 10.786$$

That is, the expected present value of the new machinery is \$10,786,000, using a risk-adjusted discount rate.

Now suppose the managers of Zeus want to compare this expected present value with an expected present value calculated with a discount rate reflecting the WACC method. To calculate the weighted average cost of capital for Zeus Manufacturing, the managers first needed the current market value of Zeus's debt and equity. The market value of Zeus's equity was the easier of the two: there were 1,200,000 shares of stock currently selling at $27.25 per share, so

$$E = 1{,}200{,}000 \times \$27.25 = \$32{,}700{,}000$$

Zeus had issued debt with a face value of $95 million. Currently, these corporate bonds are being traded at 92 percent of their face (par) value, so

$$D = 0.92 \times \$95{,}000{,}000 = \$87{,}400{,}000$$

The managers also needed Zeus's current borrowing rate and the rate of return required by its shareholders. Using data on the general performance of the stock market and a subjective assessment of the riskiness of Zeus, the finance director estimated that Zeus's shareholders require a return of 18 percent,

$$r_E = 0.18$$

Using the market valuation of Zeus's debt issues and prevailing interest rates, the finance director calculated that the current yield on Zeus's debt—the interest rate Zeus would have to pay to borrow money today—is 7 percent,

$$r_D = 0.07$$

Hence, the weighted average cost of capital for Zeus Manufacturing is

$$\begin{aligned} r_{\text{WACC}} &= 0.07\left(\frac{87.4}{87.4 + 32.7}\right) + 0.18\left(\frac{32.7}{87.4 + 32.7}\right) \\ &= 0.05 + 0.05 = 0.10 \end{aligned}$$

Using this discount rate to discount the expected net cash flows of the project under consideration,

$$\begin{aligned} E(PV_j) &= \frac{0}{(1.1)^1} + \frac{2.8}{(1.1)^2} + \frac{4.9}{(1.1)^3} + \frac{4.9}{(1.1)^4} + \frac{3.7}{(1.1)^5} \\ &= 0 + 2.314 + 3.681 + 3.347 + 2.297 \\ &= 11.639 \end{aligned}$$

That is, the expected present value of the project is $11,639,000, using a WACC discount rate. The latter method yields an expected present value for the project that is $853,000 higher than the first method of calculation, because it discounts with a lower rate than the risk-adjusted rate.

20.3 MAKING INVESTMENT DECISIONS TO MAXIMIZE THE VALUE OF THE FIRM

In Chapter 19 we explained that a firm can be thought of as a portfolio of projects. When net cash flows are known with certainty, a manager maximizes the value of a firm by following the net present value rule: Accept projects or purchase assets that have a positive net present value ($NPV > 0$) and reject projects or sell assets that have a negative net present value ($NPV < 0$). To make investment decisions to maximize the value of the firm, the net present value rule must be modified to account for the risk associated with investment projects. This modification will result in an *expected* net present value rule for investment decision making.

The Expected Net Present Value Rule for Investment

As you saw in the last section, the risk associated with a particular project can be accounted for by discounting the *expected* net cash flow using a discount rate that includes a risk premium. Accordingly, we define the expected net present value of investment project j as[4]

$$E(NPV_j) = E(PV_j) - \text{Cost of investment project } j$$
$$= \sum_{t=1}^{T} \frac{E(NCF_{j,t})}{(1 + r_{j,t})^t} - C_0$$

where the numerator is the expected value of the net cash flow in time period t, and $r_{j,t}$ is the risk-adjusted discount rate for project j in time period t.

The expected net present value rule for investment projects is to accept projects for which the expected net present value is positive, and reject those for which the net present value is negative:

$$E(NPV_j) > 0 \ldots \text{Accept}$$
$$E(NPV_j) < 0 \ldots \text{Reject}$$

Implementation of the expected net present value rule is a straightforward application of the techniques we have described in this text:

1. Forecast demand to obtain estimates of expected revenues from the project, $E(R_{j,t})$.
2. Forecast (estimate) costs to provide estimates of the expected future costs associated with the project, $E(C_{j,t})$.
3. Combine the expected revenues and costs to obtain estimates of expected net cash flows for the project,
$$E(NCF_{j,t}) = E(R_{j,t}) - E(C_{j,t})$$
4. Determine the appropriate discount rate, $r_{j,t}$.
5. Discount the expected net cash flows to obtain the expected present value of the project.
6. Subtract the current cost of the project to obtain expected net present value.

To show how this might be accomplished, we present the following example.

[4]We continue to consider a simple investment project for which the only outlay for the project occurs in the current period (C_0). However, it would not be difficult to generalize this expression to incorporate an investment project that requires outlays in future periods as well as the current period.

Investment Decision Making at Trenton Enterprises: An Example

The manager of Trenton Enterprises is considering the purchase of a new production facility for a price of $5.3 million. The manager expects to use the production facility for five years, then resell it. Investment analysts at Trenton determined expected revenues and costs, and the expected resale value of the plant. Using these data, the manager obtained the following expected net cash flows for the firm's investment in a new production facility:

Year	Expected revenues*	Expected resale value*	Expected cost*	Expected net cash flows*
1	$10.2	—	$10.4	$–0.2
2	10.2	—	10.4	–0.2
3	14.2	—	11.6	2.6
4	16.3	—	13.2	3.1
5	16.3	$3.5	13.2	6.6

*In million dollars per year.

Using the weighted-average-cost-of-capital method of determining the appropriate discount rate, the manager obtained the following discount rates for each of the next five years:

Year	Discount rate (percent)
1	13.13
2	13.38
3	13.63
4	13.88
5	14.13

Discounting each of the expected net cash flows by the appropriate discount rate and summing, the manager obtained the expected present value of the new plant:

Year	Expected net cash flow ($ million per year)	Discount rate (percent)		Expected present value ($ million per year)
1	$–0.2	13.13		$–0.18
2	–0.2	13.38		–0.16
3	2.6	13.63		1.77
4	3.1	13.88		1.84
5	6.6	14.13		3.41
			Total	$ 6.68

Subtracting the cost of the project, $5.3 million, from the expected present value of the project, $6.68 million, the expected net present value of the plant is $1.38

million. Since the expected net present value of the project is positive, the project should be undertaken.

As should be obvious, the discount rate plays a key role in determining the expected net present value and, therefore, in the investment decision. The expected net present value equation indicates (and Applied Problem 1 at end of the chapter will reinforce) the inverse relation between the expected net present value and the discount rate: As the discount rate rises, the expected net present value of the project will fall.

For example, consider a one-year investment project that currently costs $100,000 and will generate an expected net cash flow of $108,000 at the end of one year. With a risk-adjusted discount rate of 7 percent, the expected net present value of this project is $935. If the discount rate falls to 6 percent, the expected net present value of the project rises to $1,887. If the discount rate rises to 8 percent, the expected net present value of the project falls to zero. And, if the discount rate rises further, to 9 percent, the net present value of the project becomes negative, –$917. This relation between the expected net present value of this project and the discount rate—sometimes referred to as the expected net present value profile—is illustrated in Figure 20.2. This profile clearly shows that the expected net present value falls as the discount rate rises.

FIGURE 20.2
An Expected Net Present Value Profile

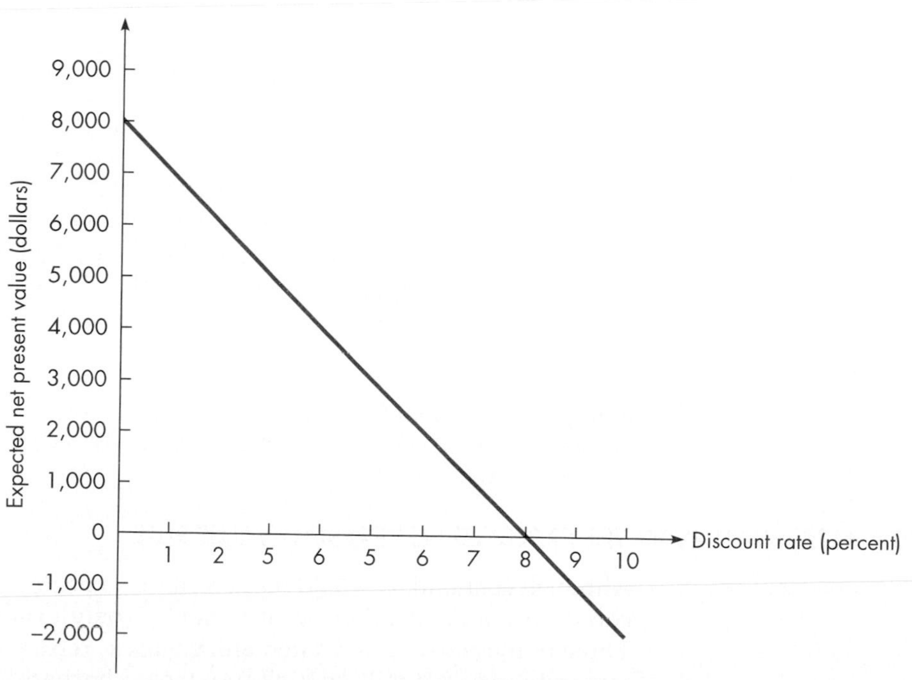

ILLUSTRATION 20.1

Do Income Taxes Affect Managerial Decision Making?

Throughout this text we have essentially ignored any effects of income taxes or corporate taxes in our analysis of managerial decision making. To be sure, we did demonstrate the effect of excise taxes on market prices and quantities sold early in the text. Excise taxes raise prices and decrease quantities sold, the extent of which depends on elasticity and the size of the tax. But we have not yet mentioned the effect of an income tax or corporate profit tax on price and sales, even though these are the taxes that are typically foremost in many people's minds. When we discussed managerial decision making and optimization there was no reason to consider the effect of income taxes—until now.

To put things into perspective, we will quote briefly from a column by Michael Kinsley, in *The New Republic*, September 6, 1993. Mr. Kinsley was commenting on Congressional and media debate over the effect on small businesses of President Clinton's proposal to increase tax rates for upper income taxpayers. He pointed out that many politicians and small business owners had been complaining that the higher taxes would put their businesses at a disadvantage when competing with foreign companies—presumably because of resulting price increases—and force them to eliminate jobs—presumably because of reduced production.

Mr. Kinsley comments, "Neither [complaint] makes economic sense. The income tax is levied on a businessperson's net profits. [The rate of the tax] has no effect on the question of how best to maximize those profits: how much to produce, what prices to charge, how many people to hire, etc. To be sure, higher tax rates can reduce the *incentive* to work and invest for small business people, like any other people."

Now we will take a look at those different effects to explain why we have ignored income taxes thus far. First, consider the effect on profit-maximizing decisions: output, price, and hiring. As we have emphasized throughout the text, profit is maximized in a given situation when price and output are chosen so that $MR = MC$ or when the usage of variable inputs is chosen so the MRP = Price of the input. Suppose a firm is choosing an output and price to maximize profit, but there is no income tax. If an income tax of t percent is levied, the firm would still choose the price and output that maximize profit—$MR = MC$—because the owners prefer to receive $(100 - t)$ percent of the maximum possible profit to $(100 - t)$ percent of any lower profit at which MR is not equal to MC. There is no incentive to change output, price, or, for that matter, the usage of any input. For example, suppose the income tax rate is 25 percent and the maximum before-tax profit is $1 million. The firm pays $250,000 in taxes and keeps $750,000. If the tax rate rises to 35 percent, paying taxes of $350,000 on the maximum before-tax profit of $1 million and keeping $650,000 is better than any alternative that would reduce before-tax profit.

Principle When evaluating risky investment projects, the firm should accept projects with a positive expected net present value and reject projects with a negative expected net present value.

20.4 ALTERNATIVES TO THE EXPECTED NET PRESENT VALUE RULE

Although economists would argue that the expected net present value rule is the correct investment criterion, it is not the only criterion available to managers. Three of the most widely cited are: payback, return on investment, and internal rate of return. We will now discuss these alternative criteria to show how they compare to the net present value rule.

Therefore, the reason that we have ignored the discussion of income taxes until now is that we have been concerned with the way firms maximize profit under given conditions and the tax rates have no effect on decision making under these circumstances. But now we are considering the investment decision, and, as Mr. Kinsley points out, taxes can have an effect on the incentives to work and invest. We will consider here only the effect on the incentive to invest, and will ignore the incentive to work.

As we have stressed in this chapter, the *NPV* rule provides the foundation for investment decision making. If *E*(*PV*) is greater than the cost of a project, *E*(*NPV*) is positive and the project should be undertaken. But the return that investors are interested in is the after-tax expected net present value. In an extreme case, suppose there is a 99 percent tax on yearly cash flows. This would presumably reduce the after-tax *NPV* of most prospective investments below their costs and substantially reduce the number of investments with a positive *E*(*NPV*). Alternatively, when choosing price and quantity, an owner would prefer one percent of maximum profit over one percent of a lesser amount, as we discussed. So the tax would probably have a large effect on investment and no effect on price.

As the tax rate is reduced, the after-tax expected cash flows from investment projects would increase; and more and more projects would change from negative *E*(*NPV*) to positive *E*(*NPV*)—assuming the cost of the project does not change. However, since the cost of an investment can be a tax deduction when financed with retained earnings, the costs may change when the tax rate changes. Nonetheless, the basic conclusion is the same. Increases in the tax rate reduce investment by reducing after-tax expected net cash flows, and decreases in the tax rate increase investment by increasing after-tax expected net cash flows. There are some additional factors influencing *E*(*NPV*) so the extent of the effect on tax rates is basically an empirical question, and depends to some extent on the characteristics of individual investors.

There is another way in which the tax structure, combined with inflation, may have a negative effect on investment. Under the present tax structure, nominal, not real, income is subject to taxation. Therefore, if someone purchases an asset and sells it later, all gains are subject to taxation, even though most, or even all, of the gain could be due to inflation. For example, suppose a firm purchases an asset for $100,000. The value of the asset increases during a year at the same rate as the rate of inflation, 5 percent. If the firm sells the asset for $105,000, realizing a net gain of $5,000 which, for sake of illustration, is taxed at a 34 percent rate, the after-tax return is $3,300. The firm, in real terms, has lost $1,700 (.34 × $5,000), because the $105,000 is worth only $100,000 in year-one dollars. In order to receive $105,000 after inflation and taking taxes into account, the rate of return must be about 7.6 percent.

Payback Period

payback period
Time required for the firm to recover its initial investment.

The **payback period** for an investment project is the time required for the firm to recover its initial investment. For example, if a project costs $1 million and it is expected to return $250,000 per year, the payback period is four years; if expected returns are $500,000 per year, the payback period is two years.

Using the payback criterion, the payback period for the investment project is calculated and compared to some maximum payback period set by the firm. If the project's payback period is less than this maximum, the project is accepted.

For example, returning to Trenton Enterprises, suppose the manager has set the maximum payback period for investment projects as three years. The payback period for the previously discussed prospective production facility is calculated from the cumulative expected net cash flows from the project:

Year	Expected net cash flow*	Cumulative expected net cash flow*
1	$–0.2	$–0.2
2	–0.2	–0.4
3	2.6	2.2
4	3.1	5.3
5	6.6	11.9

*In $ million.

The cumulative expected net cash flows equal (or exceed) the cost of the investment ($5.3 million) at the end of the fourth year. Hence, the payback period for this project is four years. And, since the payback period is longer than the maximum set by the firm, the project would be judged unacceptable using this criterion.

As this example makes clear, the major problem with the payback criterion is that it can lead to the rejection of positive net present value projects—projects that will increase the value of the firm. Conversely, this rule could lead to accepting negative net present value projects. (This point will be reinforced by Technical Problem 2.)

As should be clear from the discussion to this point, the reason the payback rule can lead to this value-reducing situation is that the cash flows are not discounted. Hence, the payback criterion gives too much weight to near returns and too little weight to distant returns: with the payback rule, net cash flows received after the maximum payback period have no value. This criterion ignores the time value of money and the time pattern of the cash flows generated by the investment project.

Interestingly, Harold Bierman noted from his survey results that many users of the payback criterion think of the payback period as a measure of risk. However, as Bierman correctly pointed out, gambling at the tables in Las Vegas may have a shorter payback period than purchasing a US government security, but that doesn't mean the crap tables in Las Vegas are less risky than T-bills.

Return on Investment (ROI)

return on investment (ROI) Average return from an investment divided by the average investment in a project.

The average **return on an investment (ROI)** project is defined as average returns from the investment divided by the average investment in the project. Then, using the ROI criterion, the decision whether or not to invest in the project is made by comparing the ROI for the project with the firm's target return.

For example, suppose Trenton Enterprises requires a rate of return on investment of 60 percent. The manager wanted to look at the prospective investment again with this criterion in mind. As shown in previous calculations, the cumulative net cash flows from the project amounted to $11.9 million for the five years of the project's lifetime. Hence, the average net cash flow was \$11.9/5 = \$2.38 million. Dividing this average income by the amount the firm would invest in the project, \$5.3 million, the average return on the investment (ROI) is

$$2.38/5.3 = 45\%$$

Since this ROI is less than the firm's target return of 60 percent, the project would be rejected using the rate of return on investment as the criterion.

As in the case of payback, the ROI criterion could result in positive net present value projects not being undertaken. And, also like the payback criterion, the problem with the return on investment criterion is that the cash flows are not discounted. However, unlike the payback criterion which gives *too little* weight to distant cash flows, the ROI criterion gives distant cash flows *too much* weight. With the ROI criterion, distant cash flows are treated as equivalent to current cash flows.

Internal Rate of Return (*IRR*)

In order to understand the concept of the internal rate of return, consider again the single-period investment project we discussed earlier and illustrated in Figure 20.2:

Cost of investment	\$100,000
Net cash flow at end of year 1	\$108,000

The rate of return on this investment project is 8 percent,

$$\frac{108{,}000 - 100{,}000}{100{,}000} = 0.08 = 8\%$$

Hence, for this single-period investment project, a criterion that is equivalent to the net present value rule is: accept the project if the discount rate for the project is less than 8 percent; reject the project if the discount rate is more than 8 percent.

Indeed, for any single-period investment project, the *NPV* rule is implemented by comparing the project's rate of return with its discount rate:

$$\text{Rate of return} > \text{Discount rate} \rightarrow NPV > 0 \rightarrow \text{Accept project}$$
$$\text{Rate of return} < \text{Discount rate} \rightarrow NPV < 0 \rightarrow \text{Reject project}$$

From this, it follows that the internal rate of return on the project is the discount rate that makes the net present value of the project equal to zero:

$$NPV = 0 \rightarrow \text{Rate of return} = \text{Discount rate}$$

For investment projects with longer lifetimes (multiple-period projects), the internal rate of return becomes more difficult to determine. Nonetheless, the definition of the internal rate of return (*IRR*) is simply a generalization of the

internal rate of return (*IRR*) The discount rate that makes the net present value of a project equal to zero.

preceding relation: The **internal rate of return** for an investment project is the discount rate that makes the net present value of the project equal to zero.

Solving for the *IRR* is not an easy arithmetic problem, since it involves solving for the discount rate at which the *NPV* of the project is zero. Operationally, that means that the equation

$$NPV = \sum_{t=1}^{T} \frac{NCF_t}{(1 + IRR)^t} - C_0 = 0$$

is solved for *IRR*. Given (1) the complexity of this solution and (2) the wide acceptance of the *IRR* criterion, it is probably not surprising that most business calculators are preprogrammed to calculate this value.

From the discussion of the single-period investment project, it should be clear that the investment criterion associated with the internal rate of return is to accept the project if the cost of capital to the firm is less than the *IRR* and reject the project if the cost of capital to the firm exceeds the *IRR*.

The *IRR* criterion can be illustrated graphically by looking at the net present value profile for an investment project. A generalized profile is presented in Figure 20.3. As long as the internal rate of return exceeds the discount rate—the opportunity cost of capital—the *NPV* of the project is positive and the project should be undertaken. However, if the *IRR* is less than the discount rate, the *NPV* of the project will be negative and the project should be rejected.

As an example of the use of the internal rate of return as an investment criterion, we return once again to Trenton Enterprises and its investment decision. The manager determined that the cost to Trenton of raising additional capital is 13.5 percent. That is, to raise money to finance investment projects,

FIGURE 20.3
A Generalized Net Present Value Profile

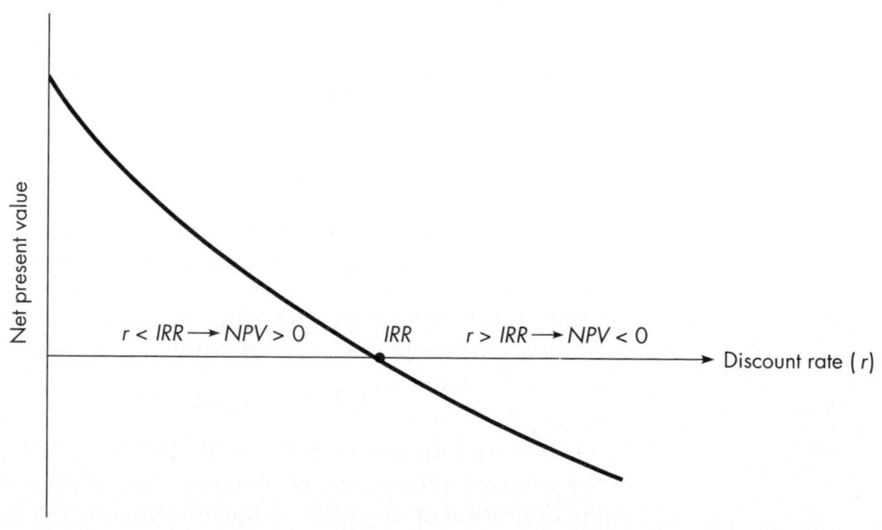

Trenton will have to pay 13.5 percent annually. He then reevaluated the proposed acquisition of the facility by looking at the project's rate of return relative to Trenton's opportunity cost of capital.

The internal rate of return for the project is the single discount rate (the *IRR*) that would make the *NPV* of the project equal to zero. This is found by solving the following for the *IRR*:

$$NPV = \frac{-0.2}{(1 + IRR)} + \frac{-0.2}{(1 + IRR)^2} + \frac{2.6}{(1 + IRR)^3} + \frac{3.1}{(1 + IRR)^4} + \frac{6.6}{(1 + IRR)^5} - 5.3 = 0$$

The resulting value for the *IRR* is 20.2 percent. Therefore, since the *IRR* for the project exceeded the firm's opportunity cost of capital, the project should be undertaken.

Note that, in contrast to the payback and return on investment criteria, the *IRR* criterion led to acceptance of the hypothetical investment project. In the context of this simple example it appears as though the *IRR* criterion and the *NPV* criterion are equivalent rules. And they are: as long as the *NPV* of the project declines smoothly as the discount rate rises—as is illustrated in Figure 20.3—the two criteria are functionally equivalent (for evaluating single projects).

Thus, as long as the relation between *NPV* and the discount rate is smooth and negative, the *NPV* rule and the *IRR* rule will give the same results. However, there are times when the *IRR* rule does not work.

Nonequivalence of *IRR* and *NPV* Rules

If the net present value profile does not look like that in Figure 20.3, the *IRR* rule and *NPV* rule will no longer be equivalent. Most investment projects are like lending money: an original outflow is made in return for a stream of inflows thereby generating down-sloping net present value profiles like that in Figure 20.3. However, this need not always be the case; it is not always the case that the largest expenditures on the project occur in the initial period. It is possible that the inflows occur earlier than the outflows—the investment project could look more like borrowing than lending. In this case the net present value profile would look like that illustrated in Panel A of Figure 20.4, where the discount rate, *r*, is plotted along the horizontal axis. Or, it could be the case that the investment project will require net cash outflows both initially and in some subsequent period; for example, the project may require a retrofit at some date in the future. In this case, the net present value profile will look like that illustrated in Panel B of Figure 20.4. In either case, the *IRR* criterion is no longer equivalent to the *NPV* criterion.

Another case in which the *IRR* and *NPV* rules do not necessarily provide the same recommendation is when the decision concerns mutually exclusive projects. Consider a firm deciding whether to replace or refit a machine—decisions that are clearly mutually exclusive. Suppose the net cash flows from these two projects are as presented in the following table:

FIGURE 20.4
Net Present Value Profiles That Do Not Decline Smoothly as the Discount Rate Rises

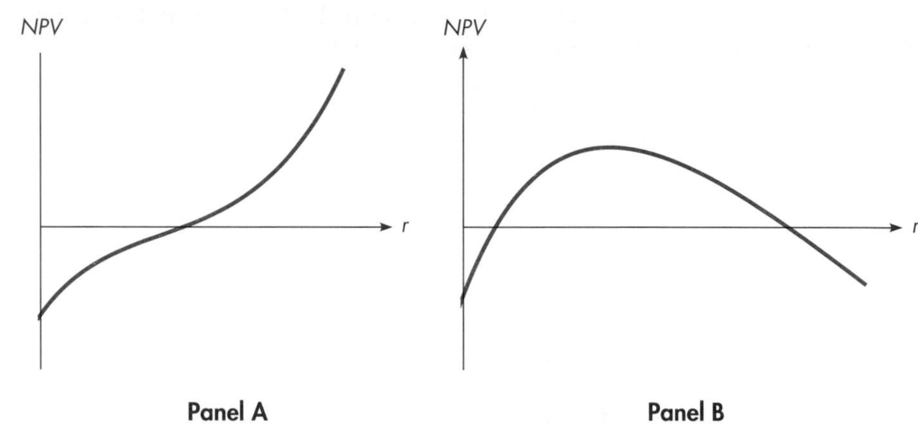

	Refit	Replace
Current cost	$100,000	$250,000
Net cash flow, year 1	75,000	125,000
Net cash flow, year 2	50,000	175,000

Looking at the internal rates of return,

	Refit	Replace
IRR	17.5%	12.3%

it seems as if refitting is the better choice. And, if the firm's cost of capital is greater than 12.3 percent but less than 17.5 percent, refitting is the correct decision. But, suppose the firm's opportunity cost of capital is less than 12.3 percent. Is refitting always the best choice? Suppose the discount rate is 9 percent. Looking at the net present values using a 9 percent discount rate,

	Refit	Replace
NPV (r = 9%)	$10,900	$12,000

the choice is reversed; the better choice now is to replace the machine.

The reason for the inconsistency is illustrated in Figure 20.5. For discount rates in excess of 9.45 percent, the *IRR* criterion and the *NPV* criterion will be consistent. That is, with the discount rate in excess of 9.45 percent, the project with the higher *IRR* will have the higher *NPV*. However, for discount rates below 9.45 percent, the *IRR* is no longer a useful criterion. With a discount rate less than 9.45 percent, the project with the higher *IRR* has the lower *NPV*. And, with these lower discount rates, the *IRR* criterion would lead to selecting the project with the lower, not higher, *NPV*.

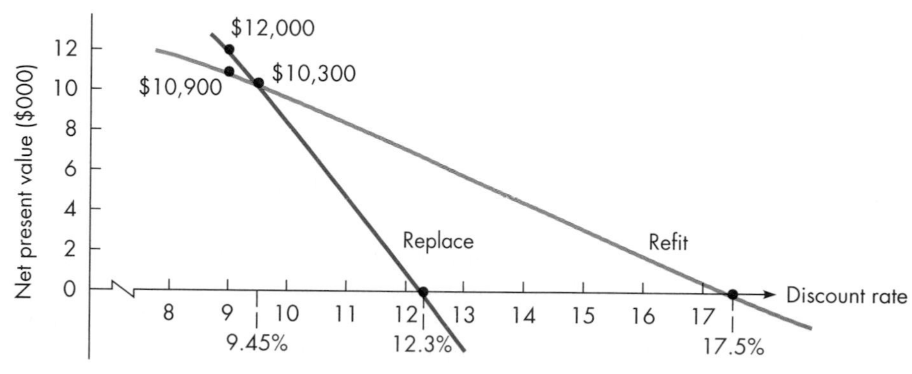

FIGURE 20.5
Net Present Value Profiles for Mutually Exclusive Projects

Finally, you may have noted a methodological difference. When we worked with net present value, we used different discount rates for different periods; payments received early were discounted at a different rate than those received late. The internal rate of return approach does not permit that differentiation. With the *IRR* approach, there is a single discount rate—payments received early are discounted using the same discount rate as those received late.

20.5 CAPITAL RATIONING

In the broadest perspective, capital rationing by the manager of a firm should not occur; there is no *external* constraint on the number of projects a firm can undertake. If the firm has available a project that will increase the value of the firm, the project should be undertaken. The capital constraint (the limit of available monies to finance the project) can always be eliminated by the credit market. If going to the credit market means that the firm will have to pay a higher and higher price for its capital (if the opportunity cost of capital is rising), the net present value of the project will decline. Indeed, if the opportunity cost of capital rises, some projects will no longer have a positive net present value. But in this case we are simply looking at the investment decision, not capital rationing.

From a more pragmatic perspective, most firms ration capital; most firms are subject to a constraint on the number of investment projects they can undertake. However, it is important to recognize that the constraint is, by and large, a *self-imposed constraint*. For some reason, the managers must believe that they will be unable to fund all of the investment projects available. And, if this is the case, they need some way to determine which projects to undertake.

When confronted by this constraint, many managers first think of the internal rate of return as a means of ranking the competing projects. However, we hope we have convinced you of the problems involved in using the *IRR* to choose among competing projects.

Then why not just rank projects according to their net present values? Suppose the firm had available the three projects ranked below by their net present values:

Project	*NPV* ($ million)	Rank
A	$10	1
B	7	2
C	5	3

Project A has the highest *NPV*. But, if the combination of Projects B and C costs less than A alone, it would be preferable to invest in the combination, since investing in both B and C would give a higher total *NPV* than would A alone. It is not sufficient to think simply about the project's net present value; a manager should think about the *NPV* per dollar spent on the project.

This shouldn't be at all surprising. This is a constrained optimization problem: the manager wants to maximize the value of the firm subject to the capital limitation. The rule for constrained optimization is to allocate so that the marginal benefit (the *NPV*) per dollar spent is equal among the competing activities. Hence, the most straightforward approach to the problem is to determine a **profitability index**—the ratio of the present value of the investment project to its cost. Presented below are additional data for the three projects introduced above.

profitability index
The ratio of the present value of an investment project to its cost.

Project	*NPV* ($ million)	Cost ($ million)	Present value ($ million)	Profitability index
A	$10	$5	$15	3.0
B	7	3	10	3.3
C	5	3	8	2.7

Given the values of the profitability index, the firm would allocate the first $3 million to Project B, since it has the largest ratio of marginal benefits to cost. The second project to be undertaken would be Project A. Project C would be undertaken only if the capital constraint is lifted.

The profitability index is, however, not without its own limitations. This approach fails if there is more than one constraint; for example, if the capital constraint is imposed in more than one period. It is also unreliable when the projects are mutually exclusive or when one project is dependent on another being undertaken. For such cases, more complicated techniques, including a linear programming approach, have been developed. (For these techniques the interested reader should see the references at the end of the text.)

20.6 SUMMARY

The investment decision combines decision making over time and under conditions of risk. A fundamental problem faced by all firms making investment decisions is the valuation of risky net cash flows generated by risky projects, assets, or investments. When dealing with risky cash flows, a manager must consider the *expected present value* of the project:

$$E(PV_j) = \sum_{t=1}^{T} \frac{E(NCF_{j,t})}{(1 + r_{j,t})^t}$$

where $E(NCF_{j,t})$ is the expected net cash flow generated by this jth project in period t and $r_{j,t}$ is the t period discount rate, which reflects the riskiness of project j.

The primary difficulty in evaluating the expected present value of a project is the determination of the appropriate discount rate for a risky project. Put another way, the problem is the determination of the *risk premium* for the *j*th project,

$$r_{j,t} = r_t + (\text{Risk premium})_j$$

We first considered two rules of thumb. With a *risk-adjusted discount rate*, some premium associated with the (total) variability in returns to the project is used. With the weighted-average-cost-of-capital approach, the firm's borrowing and equity costs are weighted by their relative shares to provide the discount rate for the firm,

$$r_{\text{WACC}} = r_D\left(\frac{D}{D+E}\right) + r_E\left(\frac{E}{D+E}\right)$$

The investment decision-making rule consistent with maximizing the value of the firm is simply the expected net present value rule. The expected net present value rule for investment projects is to accept those projects for which the expected net present value is positive, and reject those for which the expected net present value is negative:

$$E(NPV_j) > 0 \ldots \text{Accept}$$
$$E(NPV_j) < 0 \ldots \text{Reject}$$

The expected net present value of a project is calculated as

$$\begin{aligned} E(NPV) &= E(PV) - \text{Cost of the project} \\ &= \sum_{t-1}^{T} \frac{E(NCF_t)}{(1+r_t)^t} - C_0 \end{aligned}$$

where r_t is the risk-adjusted discount rate for the project in time period *t*.

To implement the expected net present value rule, the manager must (1) forecast revenues, (2) forecast (estimate) operating costs for the project, and (3) determine the appropriate discount rate for the project. Particular emphasis was placed on the relation between expected net present value and the discount rate, a relation depicted graphically by the expected net present value profile.

While the expected net present value rule is the theoretically and analytically correct investment criterion, other rules continue to be used. Two rules of thumb were considered.

- **The Payback Rule** The payback period is the time required for the firm to recover its initial investment. The investment criterion is to accept only those projects that have a payback period less than some arbitrary maximum set by the firm.

- **The Return on Investment (ROI) Rule** The average return on investment is the ratio of average net cash flows to average investment. If the *ROI* for the project is larger than the firm's arbitrary target return, the investment project will be undertaken.

The primary shortcoming with these two ad hoc rules is that the net cash flows are not discounted; these rules ignore the time value of money. The payback rule gives too much weight to cash flows that will be received early; the *ROI* rule gives too much weight to distant cash flows. A preferable alternative investment criterion is the internal rate of return rule.

- **The Internal Rate of Return (*IRR*) Rule** The *IRR* is the discount rate that makes the *NPV* of the investment project equal to zero. The project should be accepted if the *IRR* is greater than the firm's opportunity cost of capital.

As long as the expected net present value profile is a smooth, downward-sloping function, the *IRR* and expected *NPV* rules are functionally equivalent. However, the *IRR* rule can provide erroneous recommendations when mutually exclusive projects are considered. And, the *IRR* methodology requires that all net cash flows are discounted by the same rate—early and late cash flows are discounted using the same discount rate.

The constraint of limited funding for investment projects and the resulting capital rationing problem are, by and large, self-imposed by the management of the firm. Nonetheless, this is yet another constrained optimization problem: the solution must involve the ratio of marginal benefits to marginal costs (dollar expenditures). In this case, the profitability index is the ratio of the present value of the investment project (the marginal benefit from undertaking the project) to its cost. In order to maximize the value of the firm, managers will respond to the capital rationing problem by undertaking investment projects in the order of their profitability indexes.

TECHNICAL PROBLEMS

1. Consider an investment project costing $162,500 that is expected to generate net cash flows of $100,000 in years 1 and 2.
   a. Calculate the expected *NPV* for this project using discount rates of 10 percent, 15 percent, and 20 percent.
   b. Sketch the expected *NPV* profile for this project.
   c. What is the *IRR* for this project?
2. Your supervisor has asked you to evaluate two potential investment projects. Both of these projects cost $2 million. The net cash flows from the two projects are presented below.

	Net cash flows ($ million)	
Year	Project A	Project B
1	2	1.0
2	0	0.8
3	0	0.6
4	0	0.4

   The firm's policy is that the maximum payback period for an investment project is two years.
   a. Evaluate Projects A and B using the criterion that two years is the maximum payback period.
   b. Evaluate the two projects using the expected *NPV* criterion with a discount rate of 10 percent.
   c. Compare the recommendations in parts *a* and *b*.
3. * Your firm has a target rate of return on investment of 35 percent. Using this criterion, you have been asked to evaluate two investment projects, both of which cost $20.5 million and have four-year lifetimes. The net cash flows from the two projects are provided below.

	Net cash flows ($ million)	
Year	Project A	Project B
1	$10	$ 4
2	8	6
3	6	9
4	4	11

   a. Which, if either, of the two projects would be accepted using the ROI criterion?
   b. Reevaluate the two projects using the expected *NPV* criterion and a discount rate of 15 percent.
   c. Compare the two recommendations. What report would you forward on these two projects?
4. In general, when would the *IRR* and expected *NPV* investment criteria give conflicting recommendations?

5. Explain why the payback rule gives too little weight to distant net cash flows and the ROI rule gives them too much weight.
6. The capital rationing problem is, by and large, self-imposed. Explain why this is so. What could the management of a firm do to eliminate the constraint? Why do so many firms ration capital?
7. Consider an investment project with the following expected net cash flow:

Year	Expected net cash flow
1	$20,000
2	15,000
3	10,000
4	10,000
5	5,000

The investment will cost the firm $45,000. The appropriate discount rate is 10 percent.

a. What is the expected net present value?

b. Should the firm undertake this project? Briefly explain.

c. Suppose the appropriate discount rate is 18 percent. What is the expected net present value now?

d. At 18 percent, will this investment project increase the present value of the firm?

e. Compute the expected net present value for the following discount rates:

Discount rate (percent)	*E(NPV)*
9.5	
11.0	
13.25	

f. What is the internal rate of return (*IRR*) for this project? How do you know?

8. Reconsider the investment project in problem 7.

a. What is the payback period for this project?

b. If corporate policy is to accept only those projects with payback periods shorter than 30 months, will management accept this project?

c. Under what circumstances will management's decision under the payback rule be consistent with maximization of the firm's present value?

* 9. Your firm has available four investment projects, the cost and expected net present values of which are presented below.

Project	Expected *NPV*	Cost
A	$20	$10
B	17	10
C	12	5
D	8	5

a. Calculate the profitability index for each of the projects.
b. Which projects will be undertaken if the firm has an expenditure (funding) constraint of $5? $10? $15? $20?

10. Suppose that a firm used a single discount rate—the firm's cost of capital—to discount all projects. What error is the firm making?

APPLIED PROBLEMS

1. Consider a risky project under consideration by Sharp Investments that will produce a single net cash flow at the end of two years. The probability distribution for the net cash flow is:

Net cash flow (in $1,000)	Probability (percent)
25	5
30	5
35	20
40	30
45	30
50	10

a. Calculate the expected net cash flow for this project.
b. Suppose the interest rates on US government securities are currently:

Maturity	Interest rate (percent)
6 month	6.0
1 year	6.5
2 years	7.0
3 years	7.78

Compare the expected value for this project using the appropriate risk-free interest rate. Is the risk-free rate the appropriate discount rate to use? Why or why not?
c. Suppose Sharp Investments's current borrowing rate is 8.5 percent and its current outstanding debt is $20 million. Shareholders expect to earn 10 percent on equity, which amounts, in total, to $40 million. Compute the weighted average cost of capital (r_{WACC}). Using r_{WACC} for the discount rate, compute the expected present value of this project.

2. The fact that you are attending a college or university indicates that you have made an investment decision. What kind of investment decision is this? What factors did you (at least implicitly) evaluate when making this decision? In what way would the decision to go to graduate school differ?
3. In this chapter we concentrated on investment projects, implicitly talking about investments in plant and equipment. However, the same techniques could be used to evaluate other investment projects, including new products.

Down-Home Eatin' is considering the introduction of Diet Grits. The proposal is to test market the new project for one year in two regions—Macon, Georgia, and northwest Bergen County, New Jersey. If the test markets are successful, the product will be introduced nationwide.

How would the investment decision be structured? What data are required to make the decision? How would the necessary data be obtained?

For problems 4 through 7, use the following data: Argonaut Enterprises had available four potential investment projects that would all begin in 1992. The characteristics of these projects are summarized in the table below.

Project:	A	B	C	D
Cost:	$123,000	$89,200	$56,600	$55,800
Net cash flow*				
1992	30,000	50,000	20,000	40,000
1993	30,000	50,000	20,000	20,000
1994	30,000	0	20,000	10,000
1995	30,000	0	20,000	0
Scrap or resale value at end of 1995:	50,000	0	10,000	0

*At year-end.

4. Evaluate these projects using the expected *NPV* criterion and a discount rate of 15 percent.
5. The expected *NPV* evaluation did not sit very well with the vice president for operations, for whom Project A was a particular favorite. He argued that the discount rate used in the calculation of the net present values was too high. In response, the board of directors asked to see the internal rates of return for each of the projects. Provide these values and an evaluation based on these values.
6. The vice president for operations came back to the board of directors with another argument: He believes that the resale value for Project A was underestimated and that the resale value should be $70,000 rather than $50,000. If this is true, should this project be undertaken, using 15 percent as the relevant discount rate? Use the net present value of the project to support your answer.
7. It turns out that Project B also has a supporter. The director of new-product development argues that the capital outlay necessary for Project B is $86,800 rather than $89,200. If this is true, what would be the internal rate of return for Project B? Would this project be undertaken, using 15 percent as the relevant opportunity cost of capital?

A P P E N D I X

Statistical Tables

STUDENT'S *t*-DISTRIBUTION

Following is a table that provides the critical values of the *t*-distribution for three levels of confidence—90 percent, 95 percent, and 99 percent. It should be noted that these values are based on a two-tailed test for significance: tests to determine if an estimated coefficient is significantly *different* from zero (or one). For a discussion of one-tailed hypothesis tests, a topic not covered in this text, the reader is referred to R. J. Wonnacott and T. H. Wonnacott, *Econometrics*, 2d ed. (New York: John Wiley & Sons, 1979).

To illustrate the use of this table, return to an example presented in Chapter 5. In this example, 30 observations were used to estimate three coefficients, *a, b,* and *c.* Therefore, there are 30 − 3 = 27 degrees of freedom. Then, the critical *t*-value for a 95 percent confidence level can be obtained from the table as 2.052. If a higher confidence level is required, the researcher can use the 99 percent confidence level column to obtain a critical value of 2.771. Conversely, if a lower confidence level is acceptable, the researcher can use the 90 percent confidence level column to obtain a critical value of 1.703.

THE *F*-DISTRIBUTION

Presented below is a table that provides the critical value of the *F*-distribution at both 95 percent and 99 percent confidence levels. To illustrate the manner in which this table is used, we return to an example presented in Chapter 5. Again 30 observations were employed to estimate three coefficients—that is, $n = 30$ and

Critical *t*-Values

Degrees of freedom	Confidence level			Degrees of freedom	Confidence level		
	90%	95%	99%		90%	95%	99%
1	6.314	12.706	63.657	18	1.734	2.101	2.878
2	2.920	4.303	9.925	19	1.729	2.093	2.861
3	2.353	3.182	5.841	20	1.725	2.086	2.845
4	2.132	2.776	4.604	21	1.721	2.080	2.831
5	2.015	2.571	4.032	22	1.717	2.074	2.819
6	1.943	2.447	3.707	23	1.714	2.069	2.807
7	1.895	2.365	3.499	24	1.711	2.064	2.797
8	1.860	2.306	3.355	25	1.708	2.060	2.787
9	1.833	2.262	3.250	26	1.706	2.056	2.779
10	1.812	2.228	3.169	27	1.703	2.052	2.771
11	1.796	2.201	3.106	28	1.701	2.048	2.763
12	1.782	2.179	3.055	29	1.699	2.045	2.756
13	1.771	2.160	3.012	30	1.697	2.042	2.750
14	1.761	2.145	2.977	40	1.684	2.021	2.704
15	1.753	2.131	3.947	60	1.671	2.000	2.660
16	1.746	2.120	2.921	120	1.658	1.980	2.617
17	1.740	2.110	2.898	∞	1.645	1.960	2.576

Source: Adapted with permission from R. J. Wonnacott and T. H. Wonnacott, *Econometrics*, 2d ed. (New York: John Wiley & Sons, 1979).

$k = 3$. The appropriate *F*-statistic has $k - 1$ degrees of freedom for the numerator and $n - k$ degrees of freedom for the denominator. Thus, in the example, there are 2 and 27 degrees of freedom. From the table the critical *F*-value corresponding to a 95 percent confidence level is 3.35. If a 99 percent confidence level is desired, the critical value is 5.49.

Critical *F*-Values

Note: The values corresponding to a 95 percent confidence level are printed in light face type and the values corresponding to a 99 percent confidence level are printed in bold face type.

Degrees of freedom for denominator $(n - k)$	Degrees of freedom for the numerator $(k - 1)$																			
	1	2	3	4	5	6	7	8	9	10	11	12	14	16	20	24	30	40	50	∞
1 . . .	161	200	216	225	230	234	237	239	241	242	243	244	245	246	248	249	250	251	252	254
	4052	**4999**	**5403**	**5625**	**5764**	**5859**	**5928**	**5981**	**6022**	**6056**	**6082**	**6106**	**6142**	**6169**	**6208**	**6234**	**6258**	**6286**	**6302**	**6366**
2 . . .	18.51	19.00	19.16	19.25	19.30	19.33	19.36	19.37	19.38	19.39	19.40	19.41	19.42	19.43	19.44	19.45	19.46	19.47	19.47	19.50
	98.49	**99.01**	**99.17**	**99.25**	**99.30**	**99.33**	**99.34**	**99.36**	**99.38**	**99.40**	**99.41**	**99.42**	**99.43**	**99.44**	**99.45**	**99.46**	**99.47**	**99.48**	**99.48**	**99.50**
3 . . .	10.13	9.55	9.28	9.12	9.01	8.94	8.88	8.84	8.81	8.78	8.76	8.74	8.71	8.69	8.66	8.64	8.62	8.60	8.58	8.53
	34.12	**30.81**	**29.46**	**28.71**	**28.24**	**27.91**	**27.67**	**27.49**	**27.34**	**27.23**	**27.13**	**27.05**	**26.92**	**26.83**	**26.69**	**26.60**	**26.50**	**26.41**	**26.30**	**26.12**
4 . . .	7.71	6.94	6.59	6.39	6.26	6.16	6.09	6.04	6.00	5.96	5.93	5.91	5.87	5.84	5.80	5.77	5.74	5.71	5.70	5.63
	21.20	**18.00**	**16.69**	**15.98**	**15.52**	**15.21**	**14.98**	**14.80**	**14.66**	**14.54**	**14.45**	**14.37**	**14.24**	**14.15**	**14.02**	**13.93**	**13.83**	**13.74**	**13.69**	**13.46**
5 . . .	6.61	5.79	5.41	5.19	5.05	4.95	4.88	4.82	4.78	4.74	4.70	4.68	4.64	4.60	4.56	4.53	4.50	4.46	4.44	4.36
	16.26	**13.27**	**12.06**	**11.39**	**10.97**	**10.67**	**10.45**	**10.27**	**10.15**	**10.05**	**9.96**	**9.89**	**9.77**	**9.68**	**9.55**	**9.47**	**9.38**	**9.29**	**9.24**	**9.02**
6 . . .	5.99	5.14	4.76	4.53	4.39	4.28	4.21	4.15	4.10	4.06	4.03	4.00	3.96	3.92	3.87	3.84	3.81	3.77	3.75	3.67
	13.74	**10.92**	**9.78**	**9.15**	**8.75**	**8.47**	**8.26**	**8.10**	**7.98**	**7.87**	**7.79**	**7.72**	**7.60**	**7.52**	**7.39**	**7.31**	**7.23**	**7.14**	**7.09**	**6.88**
7 . . .	5.59	4.74	4.35	4.12	3.97	3.87	3.79	3.73	3.68	3.63	3.60	3.57	3.52	3.49	3.44	3.41	3.38	3.34	3.32	3.23
	12.25	**9.55**	**8.45**	**7.85**	**7.46**	**7.19**	**7.00**	**6.84**	**6.71**	**6.62**	**6.54**	**6.47**	**6.35**	**6.27**	**6.15**	**6.07**	**5.98**	**5.90**	**5.85**	**5.65**
8 . . .	5.32	4.46	4.07	3.84	3.69	3.58	3.50	3.44	3.39	3.34	3.31	3.28	3.23	3.20	3.15	3.12	3.08	3.05	3.03	2.93
	11.26	**8.65**	**7.59**	**7.01**	**6.63**	**6.37**	**6.19**	**6.03**	**5.91**	**5.82**	**5.74**	**5.67**	**5.56**	**5.48**	**5.36**	**5.28**	**5.20**	**5.11**	**5.06**	**4.86**
9 . . .	5.12	4.26	3.86	3.63	3.48	3.37	3.29	3.23	3.18	3.13	3.10	3.07	3.02	2.98	2.93	2.90	2.86	2.82	2.80	2.71
	10.56	**8.02**	**6.99**	**6.42**	**6.06**	**5.80**	**5.62**	**5.47**	**5.35**	**5.26**	**5.18**	**5.11**	**5.00**	**4.92**	**4.80**	**4.73**	**4.64**	**4.56**	**4.51**	**4.31**
10 . . .	4.96	4.10	3.71	3.48	3.33	3.22	3.14	3.07	3.02	2.97	2.94	2.91	2.86	2.82	2.77	2.74	2.70	2.67	2.64	2.54
	10.04	**7.56**	**6.55**	**5.99**	**5.64**	**5.39**	**5.21**	**5.06**	**4.95**	**4.85**	**4.78**	**4.71**	**4.60**	**4.52**	**4.41**	**4.33**	**4.25**	**4.17**	**4.12**	**3.91**
11 . . .	4.84	3.98	3.59	3.36	3.20	3.09	3.01	2.95	2.90	2.86	2.82	2.79	2.74	2.70	2.65	2.61	2.57	2.53	2.50	2.40
	9.65	**7.20**	**6.22**	**5.67**	**5.32**	**5.07**	**4.88**	**4.74**	**4.63**	**4.54**	**4.46**	**4.40**	**4.29**	**4.21**	**4.10**	**4.02**	**3.94**	**3.86**	**3.80**	**3.60**
12 . . .	4.75	3.89	3.49	3.26	3.11	3.00	2.92	2.85	2.80	2.76	2.72	2.69	2.64	2.60	2.54	2.50	2.46	2.42	2.40	2.30
	9.33	**6.93**	**5.95**	**5.41**	**5.06**	**4.82**	**4.65**	**4.50**	**4.39**	**4.30**	**4.22**	**4.16**	**4.05**	**3.98**	**3.86**	**3.78**	**3.70**	**3.61**	**3.56**	**3.36**

13 . . .	4.67	3.80	3.41	3.18	3.02	2.92	2.84	2.77	2.72	2.67	2.63	2.60	2.55	2.51	2.46	2.42	2.38	2.34	2.32	2.21
	9.07	**6.70**	**5.74**	**5.20**	**4.86**	**4.62**	**4.44**	**4.30**	**4.19**	**4.10**	**4.02**	**3.96**	**3.85**	**3.78**	**3.67**	**3.59**	**3.51**	**3.42**	**3.37**	**3.16**
14 . . .	4.60	3.74	3.34	3.11	2.96	2.85	2.77	2.70	2.65	2.60	2.56	2.53	2.48	2.44	2.39	2.35	2.31	2.27	2.24	2.13
	8.86	**6.51**	**5.56**	**5.03**	**4.69**	**4.46**	**4.28**	**4.14**	**4.03**	**3.94**	**3.86**	**3.80**	**3.70**	**3.62**	**3.51**	**3.43**	**3.34**	**3.26**	**3.26**	**3.00**
15 . . .	4.54	3.68	3.29	3.06	2.90	2.79	2.70	2.64	2.59	2.55	2.51	2.48	2.43	2.39	2.33	2.29	2.25	2.21	2.18	2.07
	8.68	**6.36**	**5.42**	**4.89**	**4.56**	**4.32**	**4.14**	**4.00**	**3.89**	**3.80**	**3.73**	**3.67**	**3.56**	**3.48**	**3.36**	**3.29**	**3.20**	**3.12**	**3.07**	**2.87**
16 . . .	4.49	3.63	3.24	3.01	2.85	2.74	2.66	2.59	2.54	2.49	2.45	2.42	2.37	2.33	2.28	2.24	2.20	2.16	2.13	2.01
	8.53	**6.23**	**5.29**	**4.77**	**4.44**	**4.20**	**4.03**	**3.89**	**3.78**	**3.69**	**3.61**	**3.55**	**3.45**	**3.37**	**3.25**	**3.18**	**3.10**	**3.01**	**2.96**	**2.75**
17 . . .	4.45	3.59	3.20	2.96	2.81	2.70	2.62	2.55	2.50	2.45	2.41	2.38	2.33	2.29	2.23	2.19	2.15	2.11	2.08	1.96
	8.40	**6.11**	**5.18**	**4.67**	**4.34**	**4.10**	**3.93**	**3.79**	**3.68**	**3.59**	**3.52**	**3.45**	**3.35**	**3.27**	**3.16**	**3.08**	**3.00**	**2.92**	**2.86**	**2.65**
18 . . .	4.41	3.55	3.16	2.93	2.77	2.66	2.58	2.51	2.46	2.41	2.37	2.34	2.29	2.25	2.19	2.15	2.11	2.07	2.04	1.92
	8.28	**6.01**	**5.09**	**4.58**	**4.25**	**4.01**	**3.85**	**3.71**	**3.60**	**3.51**	**3.44**	**3.37**	**3.27**	**3.19**	**3.07**	**3.00**	**2.91**	**2.83**	**2.78**	**2.57**
19 . . .	4.38	3.52	3.13	2.90	2.74	2.63	2.55	2.48	2.43	2.38	2.34	2.31	2.26	2.21	2.15	2.11	2.07	2.02	2.00	1.88
	8.18	**5.93**	**5.01**	**4.50**	**4.17**	**3.94**	**3.77**	**3.63**	**3.52**	**3.43**	**3.36**	**3.30**	**3.19**	**3.12**	**3.00**	**2.92**	**2.84**	**2.76**	**2.70**	**2.49**
20 . . .	4.35	3.49	3.10	2.87	2.71	2.60	2.52	2.45	2.40	2.35	2.31	2.28	2.23	2.18	2.12	2.08	2.04	1.99	1.96	1.84
	8.10	**5.85**	**4.94**	**4.43**	**4.10**	**3.87**	**3.71**	**3.56**	**3.45**	**3.37**	**3.30**	**3.23**	**3.13**	**3.05**	**2.94**	**2.86**	**2.77**	**2.69**	**2.63**	**2.42**
21 . . .	4.32	3.47	3.07	2.84	2.68	2.57	2.49	2.42	2.37	2.32	2.28	2.25	2.20	2.15	2.09	2.05	2.00	1.96	1.93	1.81
	8.02	**5.78**	**4.87**	**4.37**	**4.04**	**3.81**	**3.65**	**3.51**	**3.40**	**3.31**	**3.24**	**3.17**	**3.07**	**2.99**	**2.88**	**2.80**	**2.72**	**2.63**	**2.58**	**2.36**
22 . . .	4.30	3.44	3.05	2.82	2.66	2.55	2.47	2.40	2.35	2.30	2.26	2.23	2.18	2.13	2.07	2.03	1.98	1.93	1.91	1.78
	7.94	**5.72**	**4.82**	**4.41**	**3.99**	**3.76**	**3.59**	**3.45**	**3.35**	**3.26**	**3.18**	**3.12**	**3.02**	**2.94**	**2.83**	**2.75**	**2.67**	**2.58**	**2.53**	**2.31**
23 . . .	4.28	3.42	3.03	2.80	2.64	2.53	2.45	2.38	2.32	2.28	2.24	2.20	2.14	2.10	2.04	2.00	1.96	1.91	1.88	1.76
	7.88	**5.66**	**4.76**	**4.26**	**3.94**	**3.71**	**3.54**	**3.41**	**3.30**	**3.21**	**3.14**	**3.07**	**2.97**	**2.89**	**2.78**	**2.70**	**2.62**	**2.53**	**2.48**	**2.26**
24 . . .	4.26	3.40	3.01	2.78	2.62	2.51	2.43	2.36	2.30	2.26	2.22	2.18	2.13	2.09	2.02	1.98	1.94	1.89	1.86	1.73
	7.82	**5.61**	**4.72**	**4.22**	**3.90**	**3.67**	**3.50**	**3.36**	**3.25**	**3.17**	**3.09**	**3.03**	**2.93**	**2.85**	**2.74**	**2.66**	**2.58**	**2.49**	**2.44**	**2.21**
25 . . .	4.24	3.38	2.99	2.76	2.60	2.49	2.41	2.34	2.28	2.24	2.20	2.16	2.11	2.06	2.00	1.96	1.92	1.87	1.84	1.71
	7.77	**5.57**	**4.68**	**4.18**	**3.86**	**3.63**	**3.46**	**3.32**	**3.21**	**3.13**	**3.05**	**2.99**	**2.89**	**2.81**	**2.70**	**2.62**	**2.54**	**2.45**	**2.40**	**2.17**

Critical *F*-Values (*continued*)

Degrees of freedom for denominator $(n - k)$	Degrees of freedom for the numerator $(k - 1)$																			
	1	2	3	4	5	6	7	8	9	10	11	12	14	16	20	24	30	40	50	∞
26 . . .	4.22	3.37	2.89	2.74	2.59	2.47	2.39	2.32	2.27	2.22	2.18	2.15	2.10	2.05	1.99	1.95	1.90	1.85	1.82	1.69
	7.72	5.53	4.64	4.14	3.82	3.59	3.42	3.29	3.17	3.09	3.02	2.96	2.86	2.77	2.66	2.58	2.50	2.41	2.36	2.13
27 . . .	4.21	3.35	2.96	2.73	2.57	2.46	2.37	2.30	2.25	2.20	2.16	2.13	2.08	2.03	1.97	1.93	1.88	1.84	1.80	1.67
	7.68	5.49	4.60	4.11	3.79	3.56	3.39	3.26	3.14	3.06	2.98	2.93	2.83	2.74	2.63	2.55	2.47	2.38	2.33	2.10
28 . . .	4.20	3.34	2.95	2.71	2.56	2.44	2.36	2.29	3.24	2.19	2.15	2.12	2.06	2.02	1.96	1.91	1.87	1.81	1.78	1.65
	7.64	5.45	4.57	4.07	3.76	3.53	3.36	3.23	3.11	3.03	2.95	2.90	2.80	2.71	2.60	2.52	2.44	2.35	2.30	2.06
29 . . .	4.18	3.33	2.93	2.70	2.54	2.43	2.35	2.28	2.22	2.18	2.14	2.10	2.05	2.00	1.94	1.90	1.85	1.80	1.77	1.64
	7.60	5.52	4.54	4.04	3.73	3.50	3.33	3.20	3.08	3.00	2.92	2.87	2.77	2.68	2.57	2.49	2.41	2.32	2.27	2.03
30 . . .	4.17	3.32	2.92	2.69	2.53	2.43	2.34	2.27	2.21	2.16	2.12	2.09	2.04	1.99	1.93	1.89	1.84	1.79	1.76	1.62
	7.56	5.39	4.51	4.02	3.70	3.47	3.30	3.17	3.06	2.98	2.90	2.84	2.74	2.66	2.55	2.47	2.38	2.29	2.24	2.01
32 . . .	4.15	3.30	2.90	2.67	2.51	2.40	2.32	2.25	2.19	2.14	2.10	2.07	2.02	1.97	1.91	1.86	1.82	1.76	1.74	1.59
	7.50	5.34	4.46	3.97	3.66	3.42	3.25	3.12	3.01	2.94	2.86	2.80	2.70	2.62	2.51	2.42	2.34	2.25	2.20	1.96
34 . . .	4.13	3.28	2.88	2.65	2.49	2.38	2.30	2.23	2.17	2.12	2.08	2.05	2.00	1.95	1.80	1.84	1.80	1.74	1.71	1.57
	7.44	5.29	4.42	3.93	3.61	3.38	3.21	3.08	2.97	2.89	2.82	2.76	2.66	2.58	2.47	2.38	2.30	2.21	2.15	1.91
36 . . .	4.11	3.26	3.86	2.63	2.48	2.36	2.28	2.21	2.15	2.10	2.06	2.03	1.89	1.93	1.87	1.82	1.78	1.72	1.69	1.55
	7.39	5.25	4.38	3.89	3.58	3.35	3.18	3.04	2.94	2.86	2.78	2.72	2.62	2.54	2.43	2.35	2.26	2.17	2.12	1.87
38 . . .	4.10	3.25	2.85	2.62	2.46	2.35	2.26	2.19	2.14	2.09	2.05	2.02	1.96	1.92	1.85	1.80	1.76	1.71	1.67	1.53
	7.35	5.21	4.34	3.86	3.54	3.32	3.15	3.02	2.91	2.82	2.75	2.69	2.59	2.51	2.40	2.32	2.22	2.14	2.08	1.84
40 . . .	4.08	3.23	2.84	2.61	2.45	2.34	2.25	2.18	2.12	2.08	2.04	2.00	1.95	1.90	1.84	1.79	1.74	1.69	1.66	1.51
	7.31	5.18	4.31	3.83	3.51	3.29	3.12	2.99	2.88	2.80	2.73	2.66	2.56	2.49	2.37	2.29	2.20	2.11	2.05	1.81
42 . . .	4.07	3.22	2.83	2.59	2.44	2.32	2.24	2.17	2.11	2.06	2.02	1.99	1.94	1.89	1.82	1.78	1.73	1.68	1.64	1.49
	7.27	5.15	4.29	3.80	3.49	3.26	3.10	2.96	2.86	2.77	2.70	2.64	2.54	2.46	2.35	2.26	2.17	2.08	2.02	1.78
44 . . .	4.06	3.21	2.82	2.58	2.43	2.31	2.23	2.16	2.10	2.05	2.01	1.98	1.92	1.88	1.81	1.76	1.72	1.66	1.63	1.48
	7.24	5.12	4.26	3.78	3.46	3.24	3.07	2.94	2.84	2.75	2.68	2.62	2.52	2.44	2.32	2.24	2.15	2.06	2.00	1.75

46 . . .	4.05	3.20	2.81	2.57	2.42	2.30	2.22	2.14	2.09	2.04	2.00	1.97	1.91	1.87	1.80	1.75	1.71	1.65	1.62	1.46
	7.21	**5.10**	**4.24**	**3.76**	**3.44**	**3.22**	**3.05**	**2.92**	**2.82**	**2.73**	**2.66**	**2.60**	**2.50**	**2.42**	**2.30**	**2.22**	**2.13**	**2.04**	**1.98**	**2.72**
48 . . .	4.04	3.19	2.80	2.56	2.41	2.30	2.21	2.14	2.08	2.03	1.99	1.96	1.90	1.86	1.79	1.74	1.70	1.64	1.61	1.45
	7.19	**5.08**	**4.22**	**3.74**	**3.42**	**3.20**	**3.04**	**2.90**	**2.80**	**2.71**	**2.64**	**2.58**	**2.43**	**2.40**	**2.28**	**2.20**	**2.11**	**2.02**	**1.96**	**1.70**
50 . . .	4.03	3.18	2.79	2.56	2.40	2.29	2.20	2.13	2.07	2.20	1.98	1.95	1.90	1.85	1.78	1.74	1.69	1.63	1.60	1.44
	7.17	**5.06**	**4.20**	**3.72**	**3.41**	**3.18**	**3.02**	**2.88**	**2.78**	**2.70**	**2.62**	**2.56**	**2.46**	**2.39**	**2.26**	**2.18**	**2.10**	**2.00**	**1.94**	**1.68**
55 . . .	4.02	3.17	2.73	2.54	2.38	2.27	2.18	2.11	2.05	2.00	1.97	1.93	1.88	1.83	1.76	1.72	1.67	1.61	1.58	1.41
	7.12	**5.01**	**4.16**	**3.68**	**3.37**	**3.15**	**2.98**	**2.85**	**2.75**	**2.66**	**2.59**	**2.53**	**2.43**	**2.35**	**2.23**	**2.15**	**2.06**	**1.96**	**1.90**	**1.64**
60 . . .	4.00	3.15	2.76	2.52	2.37	2.25	2.17	2.10	2.04	1.99	1.95	1.92	1.86	1.81	1.75	1.70	1.65	1.59	1.56	1.39
	7.08	**4.98**	**4.13**	**3.65**	**3.34**	**3.12**	**2.95**	**2.82**	**2.72**	**2.63**	**2.56**	**2.50**	**2.40**	**2.32**	**2.20**	**2.12**	**2.03**	**1.93**	**1.87**	**1.60**
65 . . .	3.99	3.14	2.75	2.51	2.36	2.24	2.15	2.08	2.02	1.98	1.94	1.90	1.85	1.80	1.73	1.68	1.63	1.57	1.54	1.37
	7.04	**4.95**	**4.10**	**3.62**	**3.31**	**3.09**	**2.93**	**2.79**	**2.70**	**2.61**	**2.54**	**2.47**	**2.37**	**2.30**	**2.18**	**2.09**	**2.00**	**1.90**	**1.84**	**1.56**
70 . . .	3.98	3.13	2.74	2.50	2.35	2.32	2.14	2.07	2.01	1.97	1.93	1.80	1.84	1.79	1.72	1.67	1.62	1.56	1.53	1.35
	7.01	**4.92**	**4.08**	**3.60**	**3.29**	**3.07**	**2.91**	**2.77**	**2.67**	**2.59**	**2.51**	**2.45**	**2.35**	**2.28**	**2.15**	**2.07**	**1.98**	**1.88**	**1.82**	**1.53**
80 . . .	3.96	3.11	2.72	2.48	2.33	2.21	2.12	2.05	1.99	1.95	1.91	1.88	1.82	1.77	1.70	1.65	1.60	1.54	1.51	1.32
	6.95	**4.88**	**4.04**	**3.56**	**3.25**	**3.04**	**2.87**	**2.74**	**2.64**	**2.55**	**2.48**	**2.41**	**2.32**	**2.24**	**2.11**	**2.03**	**1.94**	**1.84**	**1.78**	**1.49**
100 . . .	3.94	3.09	2.70	2.46	2.30	2.19	2.10	2.03	1.97	1.92	1.88	1.85	1.79	1.75	1.68	1.63	1.57	1.51	1.48	1.28
	6.90	**4.82**	**3.98**	**3.51**	**3.20**	**2.99**	**2.82**	**2.69**	**2.59**	**2.51**	**2.43**	**2.36**	**2.26**	**2.19**	**2.06**	**1.98**	**1.89**	**1.79**	**1.73**	**1.43**
125 . . .	3.92	3.07	2.68	2.44	2.29	2.17	2.08	2.01	1.95	1.90	1.86	1.83	1.77	1.72	1.65	1.60	1.55	1.49	1.45	1.25
	6.84	**4.78**	**3.94**	**3.47**	**3.17**	**2.95**	**2.79**	**2.65**	**2.56**	**2.47**	**2.40**	**2.33**	**2.23**	**2.15**	**2.03**	**1.94**	**1.85**	**1.75**	**1.68**	**1.37**
150 . . .	3.91	3.06	2.67	2.43	2.27	2.16	2.07	2.00	1.94	1.89	1.85	1.82	1.76	1.71	1.64	1.59	1.54	1.47	1.44	1.22
	6.81	**4.75**	**3.91**	**3.44**	**3.13**	**2.92**	**2.76**	**2.62**	**2.53**	**2.44**	**2.37**	**2.30**	**2.20**	**2.12**	**2.00**	**1.91**	**1.83**	**1.72**	**1.66**	**1.33**
200 . . .	3.89	3.04	2.65	2.41	2.26	2.14	2.05	1.98	1.92	1.87	1.83	1.80	1.74	1.69	1.62	1.57	1.52	1.45	1.42	1.19
	6.76	**4.71**	**3.88**	**3.41**	**3.11**	**2.90**	**2.73**	**2.60**	**2.50**	**2.41**	**2.34**	**2.28**	**1.17**	**2.09**	**1.97**	**1.88**	**1.79**	**1.69**	**1.62**	**1.28**
400 . . .	3.86	3.02	2.62	2.39	2.23	2.12	2.03	1.96	1.90	1.85	1.81	1.78	1.72	1.67	1.60	1.54	1.49	1.42	1.38	1.13
	6.70	**4.66**	**3.83**	**3.36**	**3.06**	**2.85**	**2.69**	**2.55**	**2.46**	**2.37**	**2.29**	**2.23**	**2.12**	**2.04**	**1.92**	**1.84**	**1.74**	**1.64**	**1.57**	**1.19**
1000 . . .	3.85	3.00	2.61	2.38	2.22	2.10	2.02	1.95	1.89	1.84	1.80	1.76	1.70	1.65	1.58	1.53	1.47	1.41	1.36	1.03
	6.66	**4.62**	**3.80**	**3.34**	**3.04**	**2.82**	**2.66**	**2.53**	**2.43**	**2.34**	**2.26**	**2.20**	**2.09**	**2.01**	**1.89**	**1.81**	**1.71**	**1.61**	**1.54**	**1.11**
∞	3.84	2.99	2.60	2.37	2.21	2.09	2.01	1.94	1.88	1.83	1.79	1.75	1.69	1.64	1.57	1.52	1.46	1.40	1.35	1.00
	6.64	**4.60**	**3.78**	**3.32**	**3.02**	**2.80**	**2.64**	**2.51**	**2.41**	**2.32**	**2.24**	**2.18**	**2.07**	**1.99**	**1.87**	**1.79**	**1.69**	**1.59**	**1.52**	**1.00**

Source: Adapted with permission from R. J. Wonnacott and T. H. Wonnacott, *Econometrics*, 1st ed. New York: John Wiley & Sons, Inc., 1970).

A P P E N D I X

Linear Programming

Linear programming is a mathematical technique used to determine the optimal solutions to certain specific problems. This tool is frequently used to find the least-cost combinations of inputs necessary to produce some desired level of output; that is, cost minimization problems. However, the same technique can be used to solve other types of optimization problems, such as the optimal level of inventory, the least cost method of transporting commodities, and so on.

Basic Concepts

Let's begin with a practical problem: A firm produces two products, X_1 and X_2, which it can sell at fixed prices, P_1 and P_2. The production of X_1 and X_2 requires the use of three different types of machines, which can be used for eight hours a day. The firm currently owns three type-1 machines, two type-2 machines, and five type-3 machines. Therefore, given the daily capacity of each machine, the firm has available 24 type-1 machine-hours, 16 type-2 machine-hours, and 40 type-3 machine-hours per period. In the short run, the firm cannot buy or sell any machines; but it can employ various amounts of labor or other inputs at prevailing market prices.[1]

Since labor and other inputs are obtainable in unlimited supplies, the firm first calculates the gross profit on each product net of labor and other input costs from the market prices for X_1 and X_2. These net prices,

[1]Outputs and inputs are assumed to be infinitely divisible, and the outputs are produced according to fixed proportions, constant-returns-to-scale processes.

$$p_1 = P_1 - \text{Labor cost per unit of } X_1 - \text{Other costs per unit of } X_1$$
$$p_2 = P_2 - \text{Labor cost per unit of } X_2 - \text{Other costs per unit of } X_2$$

are the accountant's measure of gross profit. The problem for the firm is to choose the output combination that maximizes total (gross) profit.

To solve this problem, we must first know something about the actual productive capacity of each machine. Suppose that the number of type-1 machine-hours required per unit of X_1 is six, while only three type-1 machine-hours are required to produce a unit of X_2. Likewise, suppose each unit of X_1 requires two type-2 machine-hours and X_2 requires four hours per unit. Finally, suppose that eight type-3 machine-hours are required to produce a unit of either X_1 or X_2. Given the respective fixed quantities of machine-hours per period, these production relations may be written in the form of constraints,

$$6X_1 + 3X_2 \leq 24$$
$$2X_1 + 4X_2 \leq 16$$
$$8X_1 + 8X_2 \leq 40$$

which show the possible combinations of X_1 and X_2, given machine availability. For example, the first constraint indicates that, if no X_2 is produced, the maximum daily production of X_1 is four units because each unit of X_1 requires six hours of type-1 machine and only 24 hours of type-1 are available. Similarly from the first constraint, if four units of X_2 are produced, only 12 hours of type-1 machine time are left to produce X_1; thus, only two units of X_1 can be produced. The other two constraints are interpreted similarly. Thus, all three constraints put a limit on the combinations of X_1 and X_2 that the firm can produce daily.

Suppose that the net prices of X_1 and X_2 are \$12 and \$8 per unit, respectively. The problem facing the firm is to choose the combination of X_1 and X_2 (X_1 and X_2 are the *choice variables*) that maximizes total gross income

$$\pi = 12X_1 + 8X_2$$

subject to the physical constraints imposed by the production processes and the limited availability of machines.

In general, we write this type of problem, a *linear program*, as

$$\begin{aligned} \max \pi &= p_1X_1 + p_2X_2 \\ \text{subject to } & a_{11}X_1 + a_{12}X_2 \leq r_1 \\ & a_{21}X_1 + a_{22}X_2 \leq r_2 \\ & a_{31}X_1 + a_{32}X_2 \leq r_3 \\ & X_1, X_2 \geq 0 \end{aligned}$$

where a_{ij} ($i = 1, 2, 3; j = 1, 2$) is the required number of type-i machine-hours per unit of output j and r_i represent the restrictions on the program—in our example, the fixed quantities of machine-hours available. Of course, it should be noted that there could be any number of choice variables and constraints in any given linear program.

The first equation in the program, the total (gross) profit function, constitutes the objective function of the linear program; that is, it is the firm's *objective* to maximize total gross profits per production period. The three inequalities that follow are the *constraints* imposed on the linear program by the technological relation and the restrictions. Finally, by the last two inequalities ($X_1, X_2 \geq 0$), referred to as the *nonnegativity restrictions*, we impose the restriction that negative outputs are impossible. Therefore, there are three essential ingredients to every linear program: an objective function, a set of constraints, and a set of nonnegativity restrictions.

Returning to our specific example, we may write our problem in this general form:

$$\begin{aligned} \max \pi &= 12X_1 + 8X_2 \\ \text{subject to } 6X_1 + 3X_2 &\leq 24 \\ 2X_1 + 4X_2 &\leq 16 \\ 8X_1 + 8X_2 &\leq 40 \\ X_1, X_2 &\geq 0 \end{aligned}$$

Since our problem involves only two choice variables, X_1 and X_2, the linear program may be solved graphically. In Figure A.1 we plot X_1 along the horizontal

FIGURE A.1

Linear Constraints

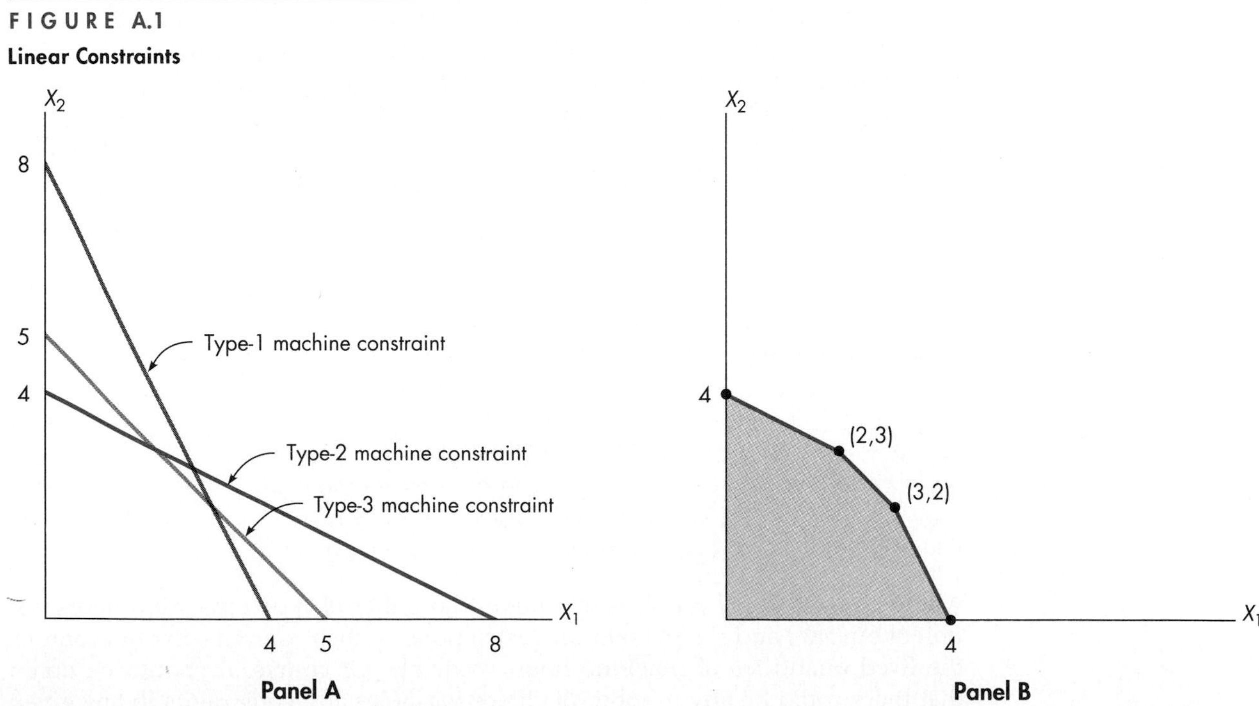

axis and X_2 along the vertical axis. Because of the nonnegativity restrictions, we need only concern ourselves with the positive (nonnegative) quadrant.

To see what the constraints look like graphically, first treat them as equalities and plot them as straight lines as in Panel A. Since each constraint is of the "less-than-or-equal-to" type, only the points lying on the line or below it will satisfy the constraint. To satisfy all three constraints simultaneously, we can only accept those points that lie interior to all three constraint lines. The collection of all points that satisfy all three constraints simultaneously is called the *feasible region*, shown as the shaded region in Panel B. Each individual point in that region is known as *feasible solution*. It should be noted that the feasible region includes the points on the *boundary*, or the heavy line in Panel B. Note that in the present (two-dimensional) case, the corner points on the boundary are called *extreme points*. They occur either at the intersection of two constraints [(2,3) and (3,2)] or at the intersection of one constraint and one of the axes [(0,4) and (4,0)].

The feasible region contains all output combinations satisfying all three constraints and the nonnegativity restrictions. However, some of these points may entail a lower level of total profits than others. To maximize profits, we must consider the objective function. To plot the profit function in (X_1,X_2) space we rewrite it as

$$X_2 = \frac{\pi}{8} - \frac{3}{2}X_1$$

This equation represents a family of parallel straight lines corresponding to different levels of profits or values of π. Since each of these lines is associated with a specific value of π, they are sometimes called *isoprofit curves*. Three isoprofit curves are shown in Figure A.2 as dashed lines, labeled I, II, and III.

The firm's objective is, of course, to attain the highest possible isoprofit curve while still remaining in the feasible region. In Figure A.2, isoprofit curve II satisfies this objective. While isoprofit curve III represents the highest level of profits, the combinations of X_1 and X_2 on this line are not in the feasible region, so this level of profit cannot be attained. Combinations on isoprofit line I clearly lie in the feasible region; however, a higher level of profit can be reached. Isoprofit line II represents the highest possible profit level that still incorporates a point in the feasible region. It coincides with the output combination of three units of X_1 and two units of X_2. Thus, the point (3,2) is the *optimal solution* to our linear program. Total profits for this optimal output combination can easily be obtained by using the values $X_1 = 3$ and $X_2 = 2$ in the objective function to yield the maximum profit, $\pi = \$52$ per production period.

Note that the optimal solution is an extreme point. In fact, the optimal solution to *any* linear program is always an extreme point. This fact will prove useful in developing a general solution methodology for linear programs.

General Solution Method

With two choice variables, the graphical method provided an optimal solution with little difficulty. This situation holds regardless of the number of constraints; additional constraints simply increase the number of extreme points, not the

FIGURE A.2
An Optimal Solution

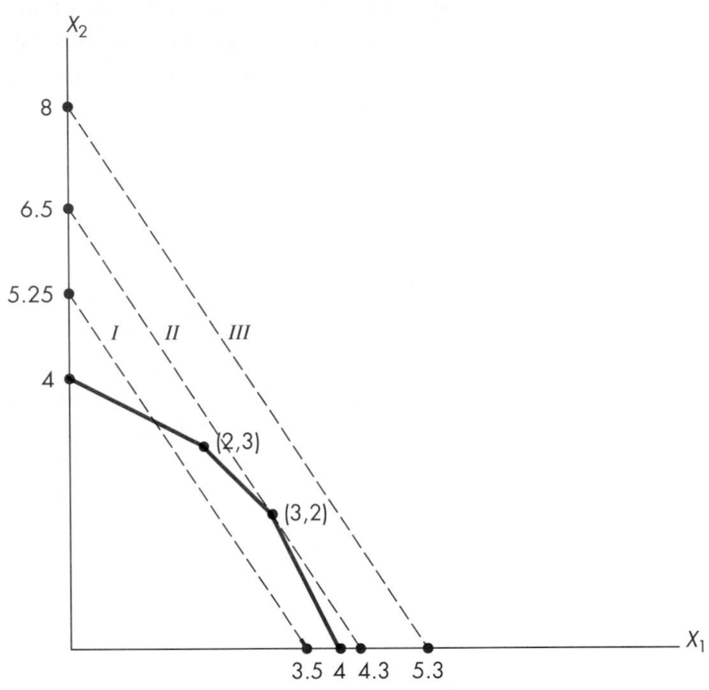

dimension of the diagram. When there are more than three choice variables, however, the graphical method becomes intractable, since we cannot draw a four-dimensional graph. Therefore, we need an analytical method to find the optimal solution to linear programs involving any number of choice variables.

As suggested above, the optimal solution of a linear program is one of the extreme points. Given a two-dimensional feasible region, it is relatively easy to find its extreme points, but finding them for the nongraphable n-variable case is more complex. Before considering the n-variable case, it will be instructive to return to our example. In Figure A.2, note that there are five extreme points—(0,4), (2,3), (3,2), (4,0), and (0,0)—all of which can be placed in one of three general categories.

The first category consists of those extreme points occurring at the intersection of two constraints. In our example, these points are (3,2) and (2,3). While such points exactly fulfill two of the three constraints, the remaining constraint is inexactly fulfilled. Consider the output combination (3,2). While the type-1 and type-3 machine constraints are exactly fulfilled, (3,2) lies inside the type-2 machine constraint and hence there is *slack* (or underutilization) in the use of type-2 machines.

Extreme points in the second category, illustrated by (0,4) and (4,0), occur at the intersection of a constraint and one of the axes. Because they are located on only one of the constraints, these points exactly fulfill only one constraint and, therefore, at such points there will be slack in the two remaining constraints. Lastly, the third category of extreme points consists of a single output combination, the origin (0,0), where there exists slack in all the constraints.

The point is that, whenever the number of constraints exceeds the number of choice variables, every extreme point will involve slack in at least one of the constraints. Furthermore, as is evident from Panel A of Figure A.1, the magnitude of the slack in any particular constraint can be calculated. Therefore, when we choose a particular extreme point as the optimal solution, we are not only choosing the optimal output combination (X_1, X_2) but also the optimal amount of slack in at least one constraint. Let us consider these slacks explicitly and denote the slack in the ith constraint ($i = 1, 2, 3$ in our example) by S_i. We call these S_i's *slack variables*. Since we now explicitly consider the possible slack in each constraint, we can transform each inequality constraint into a strict equality by adding these S_i's to the left-hand side of the ith constraint.

Returning to our example and adding a slack variable to each constraint, we may rewrite our linear program as

$$\begin{aligned} \max \pi &= 12X_1 + 8X_2 \\ \text{subject to } 6X_1 + 3X_2 + S_1 &= 24 \\ 2X_1 + 4X_2 + S_2 &= 16 \\ 8X_1 + 8X_2 + S_3 &= 40 \\ X_1, X_2, S_1, S_2, S_3 &\geq 0 \end{aligned}$$

There are now five choice variables: X_1, X_2, S_1, S_2, and S_3. When $S_i > 0$ there is slack in the ith constraint (a *nonbinding* constraint); if $S_i = 0$, there is no slack and the ith constraint is exactly fulfilled (a *binding* constraint). Slack in a constraint for this particular problem could best be thought of as excess capacity or overcapitalization of a certain type of machine.

It is easy to determine the values of the slacks implied by each extreme point. If we start with the origin (0,0), we substitute $X_1 = 0$ and $X_2 = 0$ into the transformed constraints and find that $S_1 = 24$, $S_2 = 16$, and $S_3 = 40$. Thus, the extreme point (0,0) in output space can be mapped into *solution space* as the point

$$(X_1, X_2, S_1, S_2, S_3) = (0, 0, 24, 16, 40)$$

Similarly, we may map each extreme point in outer space into solution space. The results are presented in Table A.1.

From Table A.1 the profit contribution at each extreme point can be calculated by inserting the values for X_1 and X_2 into the objective function. The point that yields the maximum profit is the constrained profit-maximizing output point—the solution to our linear-programming problem. The profit contributions of each point in solution space are shown in Table A.2. Again, we confirm that output combination (3,2) is the profit-maximizing point. Note that $S_2 > 0$ at the optimum indicates that the constraint on the type-2 machine is nonbinding.

The procedure described above is used in solving more complex linear programming problems. Computer programs are available which find solution

TABLE A.1

Extreme Points in Output Space

Output space (X_1, X_2)	Solution space $(X_1, X_2, S_1, S_2, S_3)$
(0,0)	(0, 0, 24, 16, 40)
(0,4)	(0, 4, 12, 0, 8)
(4,0)	(4, 0, 0, 8, 8)
(3,2)	(3, 2, 0, 2, 0)
(2,3)	(2, 3, 3, 0, 0)

TABLE A.2

Profit Contribution of Extreme Points

Solution at extreme point	Value of variable					Total profit contribution
	X_1	X_2	S_1	S_2	S_3	
(0,0)	0	0	24	16	40	0
(0,4)	0	4	12	0	8	32
(4,0)	4	0	0	8	8	48
(3,2)	3	2	0	2	0	52
(2,3)	2	3	3	0	0	48

values for the variables at all extreme points, evaluate total profits at each potential extreme point, and then determine the extreme point at which the objective function is maximized.

The Dual in Linear Programming

For every maximization problem in linear programming there exists a symmetrical minimization problem and vice versa. The original programming problem is referred to as the *primal* program and its symmetrical counterpart is referred to as the *dual* program. The concept of this duality is quite significant because the optimal values of the objective functions in the primal and in the dual are always identical. Therefore, the analyst can pick the program, the primal or the dual, that is easiest to solve.

The linear program we have been using as an illustration—our *primal*—is a maximization problem: we wish to maximize total (gross) profit subject to the constraints imposed by the technology and machine time availability.

Primal

$$\max \pi = 12X_1 + 8X_2$$
$$\text{subject to } 6X_1 + 3X_2 \le 24$$
$$2X_1 + 4X_2 \le 16$$
$$8X_1 + 8X_2 \le 40$$
$$X_1, X_2 \ge 0$$

Corresponding to this maximization problem there exists a *dual* minimization problem: Minimize the (opportunity) cost of using available machine-hours for the three machines subject to the constraints imposed by the production process and (gross) profitability of the two outputs.

Dual

$$\begin{aligned} \min \pi^\circ &= 24y_1 + 16y_2 + 40y_3 \\ \text{subject to } 6y_1 + 2y_2 + 8y_3 &\geq 12 \\ 3y_1 + 4y_2 + 8y_3 &\geq 8 \\ y_1, y_2, y_3 &\geq 0 \end{aligned}$$

In the primal, the choice variables X_1 and X_2 are the output levels of the two products. In the dual, the choice variables y_1, y_2, and y_3 represent the shadow prices (or premiums) for the inputs. For example, the variable y_1 is the shadow price of using one hour of machine type-1, and, since we have 24 type-1 hours, the total cost of using machine type-1 is $24y_1$. A shadow price can be viewed as the implicit value to the firm of having one more unit of the input; that is, the marginal profit contribution of the input. We then attempt to determine minimum values, or shadow prices, for each of the inputs, such that these shadow prices will be just sufficient to absorb the firm's total profit. In other words, we seek to assign values to each input so as to minimize the total inputed value of the firm's resources.

In the primal, the constraints reflected the fact that the total hours of each type of machine used in the production of X_1 and X_2 could not exceed the available number of hours of each type of machine. In the dual, the constraints state that the value assigned the inputs used in the production of one unit of X_1 or one unit of X_2 must not be less than the profit contribution provided by a unit of these products. Recall that \$12 is the (gross) profit per unit of X_1 and \$8 is the profit per unit of X_2. The constraints require that the shadow prices of the different types of machines times the hours of each type required to produce a unit of X_1 or X_2 must be greater than or equal to the gross (unit) profit of X_1 or X_2.

To solve the dual we again introduce slack variables, which allow us to write the constraint inequalities as strict equalities. Notice that in constrained minimization problems the constraints are of the "greater than or equal to" variety. Therefore, we introduce slack variables to the left-hand side of the constraints with a negative sign. (These negative S_i's used in the solution of minimization programs are often referred to as *surplus* variables.) We can then write the dual program as:

$$\begin{aligned} \min \pi^\circ &= 24y_1 + 16y_2 + 40y_3 \\ \text{subject to } 6y_1 + 2y_2 + 8y_3 - S_1 &= 12 \\ 3y_1 + 4y_2 + 8y_3 - S_2 &= 8 \\ y_1, y_2, y_3, S_1, S_2 &\geq 0 \end{aligned}$$

Since there are three choice variables (y_1, y_2, and y_3), a graphical solution would require a three-dimensional figure. Instead of such a complex diagram let's use the general techniques described above to find the solution space, evaluate the objective function for each feasible solution, and find that solution which minimizes the objective function.

A general rule illustrated in Table A.1 is that the maximum number of nonzero values in any solution is equal to the number of constraints. (In Table A.1, the number of constraints is three; so the maximum number of nonzero values in any solution is three.) Since there are two constraints in this dual problem, a maximum of two nonzero-valued variables define any solution point. Therefore, we can solve for the solutions by setting three of the variables—y_1, y_2, y_3, S_1, S_2—equal to zero and solving the constraint equations for the values of the remaining two.

For example, we can set y_1, y_2, and y_3 equal to zero and solve for S_1 and S_2. Using the first constraint,

$$6 \times 0 + 2 \times 0 + 8 \times 0 - S_1 = 12$$

so $S_1 = -12$. Likewise, using the second constraint,

$$3 \times 0 + 4 \times 0 + 8 \times 0 - S_2 = 8$$

and $S_2 = -8$. However, since S_1 and S_2 cannot be negative, this solution is outside the feasible region. Alternatively, setting y_1, y_2, and S_1 equal to zero, $y_3 = 1.5$ and $S_2 = 4$. Since all of the values in this solution are positive, the solution lies in the feasible region. All of the potential solutions are presented in Table A.3.

It is apparent from the table that not all the solutions lie within the feasible region. Only solutions 3, 5, 7, 9, and 10 meet the nonnegativity restrictions; that is, these are the only feasible solutions.

Each of the feasible solutions is then used to calculate a corresponding value of the objective function. For example, using solution 3, the value of the objective function is

$$\pi^\circ = 24 \times 0 + 16 \times 0 + 40 \times 1.5 = 60$$

All of these values are summarized in Table A.4.

TABLE A.3
Potential Solutions to Dual Problem

Solution number	Value of variable					Feasible?
	y_1	y_2	y_3	S_1	S_2	
1	0	0	0	−12	−8	No
2	0	0	1	−4	0	No
3	0	0	1.5	0	4	Yes
4	0	2	0	−8	0	No
5	0	6	0	0	16	Yes
6	0	−2	2	0	0	No
7	2.66	0	0	4	0	Yes
8	2	0	0	0	−2	No
9	1.33	0	0.5	0	0	Yes
10	1.8	0.66	0	0	0	Yes

With solution 9, the objective function—the total value inputed to the different types of machines—is minimized. As mentioned earlier, and confirmed in this example, the optimal value of the dual objective function is equal to the optimal value of the primal objective function (see Table A.2).

Note that at the optimum, the shadow price of type-2 machine-hours is zero. A zero shadow price implies that the input in question has a zero marginal value to the firm; adding another type-2 machine-hour adds nothing to the firm's maximum attainable profit. Thus, a zero shadow price for type-2 machines is consistent with our findings in the solution to the primal: the type-2 machine constraint is nonbinding. Excess capacity exists with respect to type-2 machines, so additional hours will not result in increased production of either X_1 or X_2. Analogously, we see that the shadow prices of type-1 and type-3 machines are positive. A positive shadow indicates that the fixed number of these machines' hours imposes a binding constraint on the firm and that, if an additional hour of type-1 (type-3) machine work is added, the firm can increase its total profit by \$1.33 (\$0.50).

The dual solution has thus far not indicated the optimal output combination (X_1, X_2); however, it does provide all the information we need to determine these optimal values. Note first that the solution to the dual tells us that the type-2 machine constraint is nonbinding. Furthermore, it tells us that, at the optimal output combination, $\pi = \pi^\circ = \$52$. Now consider the three constraints in the primal, which we rewrite here for convenience.

$$6X_1 + 3X_2 + S_1 = 24 \quad \text{type-1}$$
$$2X_1 + 4X_2 + S_2 = 16 \quad \text{type-2}$$
$$8X_1 + 8X_2 + S_3 = 40 \quad \text{type-3}$$

From the solution to the dual we know that the type-1 and type-3 constraints are binding, because the dual found these inputs to have positive shadow prices. Accordingly, S_1 and S_3 equal zero in the primal program, and the binding constraints can be rewritten as

$$6X_1 + 3X_2 = 24$$
$$8X_1 + 8X_2 = 40$$

TABLE A.4

Value of Objective Function in Dual Problem

Solution	(y_1, y_2, y_3)	Value of objective function	(S_1, S_2)
3	(0,0,1.5)	60	(0,4)
5	(0,6,0)	96	(0,16)
7	(2.66,0,0)	64	(4,0)
9	(1.33,0,0.5)	52	(0,0)
10	(1.8,0.66,0)	53.75	(0,0)

These two equations may be solved simultaneously to determine the optimal output combination. In this example, the solution is $X_1 = 3$ and $X_2 = 2$, the same output combination that was obtained in the primal problem.

Let us stress the two major points of this discussion and example. First, the choice between solving the primal or the dual of a linear programming problem is arbitrary, since both yield the same optimal value for the objective function. Second, the optimal solution obtained from the dual provides the information necessary to obtain the solution for the primal and vice versa. Thus, as we mentioned at the outset, one can elect to solve either the primal or the dual, depending on which one is easier to solve.

Activity Analysis: Linear Programming and Production Planning for a Single Output

As emphasized in Chapters 10 and 11, a decision problem faced by all firms is how to determine the least-cost combination of inputs needed to produce a particular product. If the production process satisfies certain regularity conditions, linear programming may be applied to solve the cost minimization problem.

Suppose that a firm produces a single product, Q, using two inputs, capital (K) and labor (L). As long as the production processes are subject to fixed proportions and constant returns to scale, we can characterize the relation between input usage and output as linear functions and thereby use linear programming to obtain a solution.

To illustrate how this is accomplished, consider the four production processes depicted in Figure A.3. Since production is characterized by fixed proportions, the relations between input usage and output are shown by a straight line from the origin. These lines are referred to as *activity rays*—hence the title *activity analysis*.

In Figure A.3, production process A requires four units of K and four units of L to produce one unit of Q. This requirement is illustrated by point A_1. Process B uses four units of L and two units of K to produce one unit of output. Similarly, Process C uses one and a half units of K and five units of L, while Process D requires eight units of L and one unit of K to produce one unit of output. These input-output relations are illustrated by B_1, C_1, and D_1, respectively. If we recall the definition of an isoquant, that is, different input combinations for which the level of output is constant, we can connect points A_1 through D_1 and derive an isoquant corresponding to a level of output equal to one unit of Q. In Figure A.3 this piecewise linear isoquant is labeled Q_1. With constant returns to scale, doubling the amount of both inputs employed results in output also doubling. In our graph, this doubling of inputs is illustrated by points A_2, B_2, C_2, and D_2. Connecting these points, we derive an isoquant corresponding to two units of output; it is labeled Q_2. Similarly, we may find isoquants Q_3 and Q_4 for three and four units of output, respectively.

Suppose that you are asked to determine the least-cost combination of L and K for an output level of four units when a unit of labor costs \$4 (say the hourly wage rate is \$4) and a unit of capital costs \$8 (say it costs \$8 to run a machine for

FIGURE A.3
Piecewise Liner Isoquants

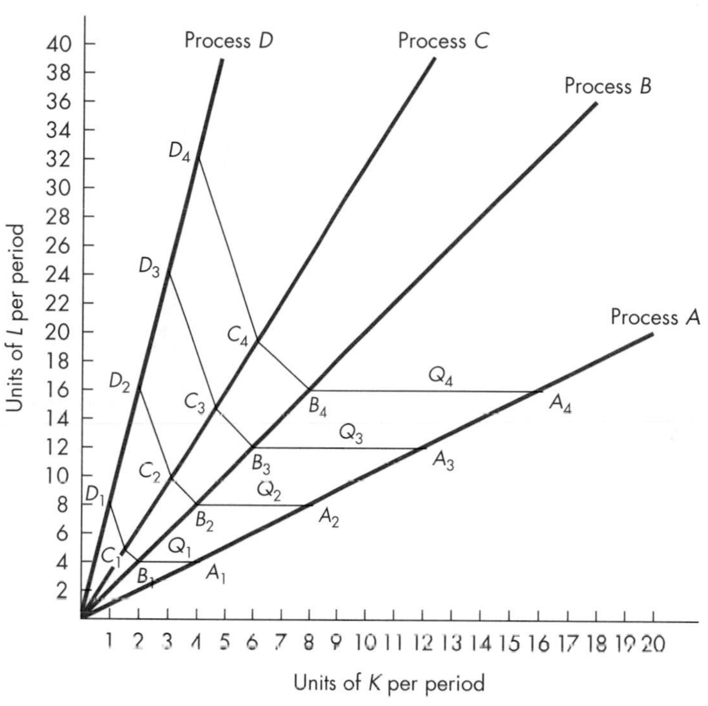

one hour). This problem is simply a constrained minimization problem, that is, we want to minimize the total cost of producing four units of output. Accordingly, we may translate the problem into a linear programming problem. For illustrative purposes we will solve this program first graphically then solve it using our general algebraic method developed above.

The isoquant for four units of output is reproduced in Figure A.4. Since we know the price of a unit of K is \$8 and the price of a unit of labor is \$4 we can plot on this graph a family of *isocost* curves corresponding to different levels of total cost. These curves are derived by solving the total cost function $C = 8K + 4L$ to obtain

$$L = \frac{C}{4} - 2K$$

Recall from Chapter 11 that we used a tangency rule to find the least-cost combination of inputs: we find the isocost curve that it just tangent to the isoquant and, therefore, the closest to the origin. At that point of tangency, corresponding to a particular combination of inputs, total cost of production is minimized. In linear programming, the same process is used.

In Figure A.4 isocost curves (I_1, I_2, I_3, I_4) are drawn through points B_4, C_4, D_4, and A_4. It is easy to see that isocost I_1 through point B_4 (8,16) is closest to the

FIGURE A.4
Solution to a Cost Minimization Problem

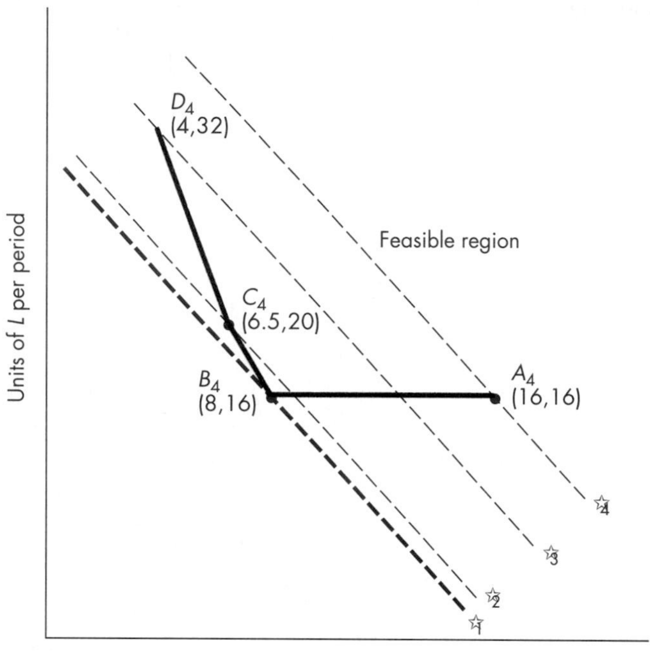

TABLE A.5
Total Cost at Extreme Points

Extreme point	Value of variable K	Value of variable L	Total cost
(4,32)	4	32	$160
(6.5,20)	6.5	20	132
(8,16)	8	16	128
(16,16)	16	16	192

origin and, therefore, represents the least cost possible of producing four units of output. If we use 8 units of K and 16 of L in our cost equation, we obtain a minimum total cost of production of $128.

We can use our algebraic method to solve the same problem. First note that there is only one constraint—the isoquant representing four units of output. Therefore, at the optimum there will be no slack or surplus in the constraint and we can determine the solution simply by substituting the values for the extreme points into the cost function (our objective function in this program). The results are shown in Table A.5. Since our objective is to minimize total cost, we pick the input combination that does just that. Again we confirm our result from the graphical solution; the combination of 8 units of capital and 16 units of labor minimizes the total cost of producing 4 units of Q.

TECHNICAL PROBLEMS

1. Solve the following linear programming problem graphically.

$$\begin{aligned} \text{maximize } \pi &= 2X_1 + 3X_2 \\ \text{subject to } \quad X_1 &\le 8 \\ X_2 &\le 6 \\ X_1 + 4X_2 &\le 16 \\ X_1, X_2 &\ge 0 \end{aligned}$$

2. In problem 1, how would the optimal solution change if the restrictions imposed (i.e., the r_i's) were all cut in half?
3. Solve the following linear programming problem using the general solution method.

$$\begin{aligned} \text{minimize } C &= 3X_1 + 4X_2 \\ \text{subject to } \quad X_1 + X_2 &\ge 2 \\ 2X_1 + 4X_2 &\ge 5 \\ X_1, X_2 &\ge 0 \end{aligned}$$

4. Form the dual to the linear programming problem presented in problem 3, then solve it to obtain the optimal values of X_1 and X_2.
5. Provide an explanation of the nonnegativity constraints for the problem of minimizing cost subject to a desired level of output.
6. Give some examples of managerial decisions for which linear programming can provide useful information. For each of these, suggest the type of analysis that would be employed.
7. Suppose you were hired by a firm that produces several products. This firm needs to know the amounts of the different products it should produce to maximize total profit. What information would you require? How would you analyze this problem?

ANSWERS TO SELECTED TECHNICAL PROBLEMS

Chapter 2

3. *a.* No change in demand.
   b. Demand increases.
   c. Demand decreases.
   d. Demand increases.
   e. Demand decreases.
   f. Demand decreases.
   g. Demand increases.
   h. Current demand increases.
   i. Current demand decreases.

11. *a.* At equilibrium, $Q_d = Q_s$. So $50 - 8P = -17.5 + 10P$, $P_E = \$3.75$, and $Q_E = 20$.
    b. When $P = \$2.75$, $Q_d = 28$ and $Q_s = 10$; there is a shortage of 18 units. Due to the excess demand, consumers will bid up the price, decreasing quantity demanded and increasing quantity supplied. Consumers will bid up price until it reaches \$3.75, the price at which quantity demanded equals quantity supplied.
    c. When $P = \$4.25$, $Q_d = 16$ and $Q_s = 25$; there is a surplus of 9 units. Producers will lower price in order to avoid accumulating unwanted inventories. The price will fall (reducing the excess supply) until equilibrium is attained at a price of \$3.75.
    d. At equilibrium, $59 - 8P = -17.5 + 10P$: $P_E = \$4.25$ and $Q_E = 25$.
    e. At equilibrium, $50 - 8P = -40 + 10P$: $P_E = \$5$ and $Q_E = 10$.

Chapter 3

3. *a.* $-0.5 = (-400/1{,}600) \div (2/4)$.
   b. + \$2,800 (= \$2 × 1,400); − \$1,200 (= \$3 × 400); increase; \$1,600.
   c. \$7,000 (= \$5 × 1,400); \$5,400 (= \$3 × 1,800); 400 units; $MR = \Delta TR/\Delta Q = (5{,}400 - 7{,}000)/400 = -4$.
   d. negative; less.
   e. $MR = 4\left(1 + \frac{1}{-.5}\right) = 4\,(1 - 2) = -4$.

11. $Q_d = 2{,}400 - 200P$; $MR = 12 - 0.01Q$; $E = -1$ at $P = \$6$; $MR = 0$ at $Q_d = 1{,}200$.

Chapter 4

4. *a.* \$47.50; \$42.50; greater; increases; \$5 (= 47.50 − 42.50).
   b. \$40; \$50; less; increases; \$10 (= 50 − 40).
   c. 200; \$45; \$45.
   d. \$9,500; \$8,500; \$1,000.
   e. Yes, the net benefit curve reaches its peak at 200 units of activity.

8. *a.* $X = 3$ and $Y = 2$.
   b. $TB_x + TB_y = 72 + 190 = 262$.
   c. $X = 4$ and $Y = 5$; $TB_x + TB_y = 84 + 400 = 484$.

Chapter 5

6. *a.* $n - k = 25 - 2 = 23$.
   b. 2.069.
   c. For $\hat{a}$: $t = 443.72/124.82 = 3.55 > 2.069$; statistically significant.
   For $\hat{b}$: $t = .80572/.06776 = 11.89 > 2.069$; statistically significant.
   d. $R^2 = .8347$ tells us that 83.47% of the total variation in Y is explained by the regression equation (i.e., by variation in X). 16.53% of the variation is unexplained.
   e. $k - 1 = 2 - 1 = 1$ and $n - k = 23$, so at a 95% confidence level, the critical value of F is 4.28. The regression equation is statistically significant because the F-ratio (141.391) is greater than the critical value of F.
   f. 443.72 + .80572 (100) = 524.29; 443.72 + .80572 (0) = 443.72.

7. *a.* The intercept, a, measures the level of sales with no advertising. The parameter b measures the change in sales from a one-unit change in newspaper advertising ($b = \Delta S/\Delta N$), and c measures the change in sales from a one-unit change in radio advertising ($c = \Delta S/\Delta R$).
   b. $a > 0$; $b > 0$; $c > 0$
   c. The parameter a is a multiplicative constant that reflects the overall effect of advertising on sales. The parameters b and c are elasticities—they measure the percent change in sales from a one percent change in newspaper and radio advertising, respectively.
   d. Take the logarithm of the function to obtain

$$\log S = \log a + b(\log N) + c(\log R)$$

Chapter 6

2. *a.* Expected value of option A = .4(–\$3,750) + .6(\$31,770) = \$17,562.
   Expected value of option B = .4(–\$6,000) + .6(\$34,000) = \$18,000.
   Option A has the higher expected value.
   b. Variance of option A = $.4(-3{,}750 - 17{,}562)^2 + .6(31{,}770 - 17{,}562)^2 = 302{,}800{,}896$.
   Variance of option B = $.4(-6{,}000 - 18{,}000)^2 + .6(34{,}000 - 18{,}000)^2 = 384{,}000{,}000$.

$$\sigma_A = \sqrt{302{,}800{,}896} = 17{,}401$$
$$\sigma_B = \sqrt{384{,}000{,}000} = 19{,}596$$

   Option B is more risky since its variance (or standard deviation) is higher than option A's variance (standard deviation).
   c. Option A is chosen since it has a higher expected payoff and a lower variance.
   d. $\upsilon_A = 17{,}401 \div 17{,}562 = 0.99$
   $\upsilon_B = 19{,}596 \div 18{,}000 = 1.09$
   Based on the coefficient of variation rule, option A is chosen.
4. *a.* Option B
   b. Option A
   c. Option A, because potential regret for A is \$2,230 while potential regret for B is \$2,270.
   d. Option A (\$14,020 > \$14,000).

Chapter 7

4. *a.* 8*X*, 9*Y*, 6*Z*.
   b. 5*X*, 6*Y*, 4*Z*.
   c. 0*X*, 6*Y*, 4*Z*; Since the price of *X* is \$5 and income is \$38, the consumer can indeed *afford* to buy *X*. The consumer chooses not to purchase *X* because MU_x/P_x is so small relative to MU_y/P_y and MU_z/P_z that zero consumption of *X* maximizes utility subject to the budget constraint.
7. *a.* 30 × \$20 = \$600.
   b. $P_y = \$20$.
   c. $Y = 30 - X$.
   d. 20*Y* and 10*X* (or $20X + 20Y = 600$).
   e. $MRS = 1 = P_x/P_y = 20/20$.
   g. 15*X* and 10*Y*.
   h. $P_y = \$30$.
   i. \$20.
   j. $MRS = \frac{2}{3}$.

Chapter 8

5. *a.* The theory of demand predicts that price and quantity demanded will be inversely related and that income and quantity demanded will be directly related for a normal good. The estimates of *b* and *c* thus are consistent with economic theory and imply that *X* is a normal good.
   b. A negative coefficient of the price of related good *R* means that the price of *R* and the quantity of *X* demanded are inversely related. In other words, *X* and *R* are complements.
   c. For a 95% confidence level with 26 (30 – 4) degrees of freedom, the critical value of *t* is 2.06. The *t*-statistics are: 68.38/12.65 = 5.41 for $\hat{a}$, –6.50/3.15 = –2.06 for $\hat{b}$, 13.926/1.306 = 10.66 for $\hat{c}$, and –10.77/2.45 = –4.40 for $\hat{d}$. All the parameter estimates are statistically significant because the absolute value of each *t*-statistic is greater than the critical value of *t*.
   d. (1) $E = b(P_x/Q_x) = (-6.50)(25/125) = -1.30$.
   (2) $E_M = c(M/Q_x) = (13.926)(20/125) = 2.23$.
   (3) $E_{XR} = d(P_R/Q_x) = (-10.77)(25/125) = -2.15$.
7. *a.* The quantity of copper demanded will decrease 4.5% if the price of copper increases 10%.
   $[E = -.45 = \%\Delta QC/\%\Delta PC \Rightarrow \%\Delta QC = -(.45)(10\%) = -4.5\%]$
   b. The quantity of copper demanded will decrease 11.2% if income decreases 5%.

$[E_M = 2.24 = \%\Delta QC/\%\Delta M \Rightarrow \%\Delta QC = (2.24)(-5\%) = -11.2\%]$

c. The quantity of copper demanded will increase 4.5% if the price of copper decreases 10%.

$[E = -.45 = \%\Delta QC/\%\Delta PC \Rightarrow \%\Delta QC = -(.45)(-10\%) = 4.5\%]$

d. The quantity of copper demanded will decrease 4.8% if the price of aluminum decreases 10%.

$[E_{CA} = .48 = \%\Delta QC/\%\Delta PA \Rightarrow \%\Delta QC = (.48)(-10\%) = -4.8\%]$

Chapter 9

2. *a.* For a 95% confidence level with 13 (15 – 2) degrees of freedom, the critical value of t is 2.16. The calculated t-statistics are: 73.7146/10.1315 = 7.276 for $\hat{a}$ and 3.7621/1.0363 = 3.630 for $\hat{b}$. Both estimates are statistically significant, and sales exhibit a significantly positive trend over time (i.e., $b > 0$).

   b. For a 95% confidence level with 1 (2 – 1) and 13 (15 – 2) degrees of freedom, the critical value of F is 4.67. The regression equation is statistically significant because the F-ratio (13.1792) is greater than the critical value of F.

   c. $Q(1994) = 73.7146 + (3.7621)(94) = 427.35$
   $Q(1999) = 73.7146 + (3.7621)(99) = 446.16$

   d. The farther the values of the variables in the forecast are from the mean values of the regression, the less precise the forecast will be. Thus the forecast for 1999 will be less precise than the forecast for 1994.

3. *a.* For a 95% confidence level with 31 (36 – 5) degrees of freedom, the critical value of t is about 2.04. The calculated t-statistics are: 51.234/7.163 = 7.15 for $\hat{a}$, 3.127/.524 = 5.97 for $\hat{b}$, −11.716/2.717 = −4.31 for $\hat{c}_1$, −1.424/.836 = −1.70 for $\hat{c}_2$, and −17.367/2.112 = 8.22 for $\hat{c}_3$. All the estimates, except c_2, are statistically significant. For a 95% confidence level with 4 (5 – 1) and 31 (36 – 5) degrees of freedom, the critical value of F is about 2.68. The regression equation is statistically significant because the F-ratio (761.133) is greater than the critical value of F.

   b. The intercepts are: 51.234 – 11.716 = 39.518 for the first quarter, 51.234 – 1.424 = 49.81 for the second quarter, 51.234 – 17.367 = 33.867 for the third quarter, and 51.234 for the fourth quarter. These values imply a cyclical trend in sales; after accounting for trend, sales fall in the first quarter, rise in the second, fall in the third, and rise again in the fourth quarter. Note that even if $c_2 = 0$ (as it is not statistically significant), sales still exhibit cyclical behavior, rising relative to the trend in the second and fourth quarter, falling relative to the trend in the first and third quarters.

   c. $Q(1994I) = 51.234 + (3.127)(37) - 11.716 = 155.217$
   $Q(1994II) = 51.234 + (3.127)(38) - 1.424 = 168.636$
   $Q(1994III) = 51.234 + (3.127)(39) - 17.367 = 155.82$
   $Q(1994IV) = 51.234 + (3.127)(40) = 176.314.$

Chapter 10

1.

Units of labor	Total product	Average product	Marginal product
1	40	40	40
2	88	44	48
3	138	46	50
4	176	44	38
5	200	40	24
6	210	35	10
7	203	29	–7
8	176	22	–27

5.

Q	*TC*	*TFC*	*TVC*	*AFC*	*AVC*	*ATC*	*MC*
100	260	200	60	2.00	.60	2.60	.60
200	290	200	90	1.00	.45	1.45	.30
300	350	200	150	.67	.50	1.17	.60
400	420	200	220	.50	.55	1.05	.70
500	560	200	360	.40	.72	1.12	1.40
600	860	200	660	.33	1.10	1.43	3.00
700	1,320	200	1,120	.29	1.60	1.89	4.60
800	2,040	200	1,840	.25	2.30	2.55	7.20

Chapter 11

4. *a.* $w = \$25(= \$5{,}000/200)$

   b. 32; 12; $2,000

   c. 60; 20; $3,500

   d. 72; 32; $5,000

   e. The expansion path passes through each and every tangency point.

   f. $MRTS = 0.25$

6. *a.*

Q	L	K	LTC	LAC	LMC
10	64	24	4,000	400	400
20	140	40	7,500	375	350
30	200	58	10,800	360	330
40	288	80	15,200	380	440
50	460	90	20,500	410	530

b. Economies of scale exist for 0 to 30 units of output; there are diseconomies of scale for 30 to 50 units of output.

Chapter 12

3. *a.* Total Product:

$$Q = -.002\ (10)^3L^3 + 6\ (10)^2L^2$$
$$= -2L^3 + 600L^2.$$

Letting $A = -2$ and $B = 600$,

$$AP = AL^2 + BL = -2L^2 + 600L$$
$$MP = 3AL^2 + 2\ BL = -6L^2 + 1{,}200L$$

b. $L_m = -\dfrac{B}{3A} = -\dfrac{600}{-6} = 100\ L$

c. $AP_{10} = -2(10)^2 + 600(10) = 5{,}800$
$MP_{10} = -6(10)^2 + 1{,}200(10) = 11{,}400$

6. *a.* Yes, all three coefficients have the correct signs. All three coefficients are statistically significant at the 95% level of confidence because the absolute value of each *t*-ratio exceeds the critical *t*-value (12 degrees of freedom) of 2.179:

$$|t_{\hat{a}}| = |30.420202/6.465900| = |4.70| > 2.179$$
$$|t_{\hat{b}}| = |-0.079952/0.030780| = |-2.60| > 2.179$$
$$|t_{\hat{c}}| = |0.000088/0.000032| = |2.75| > 2.179$$

b. $\hat{Q}_m = -\dfrac{\hat{b}}{2\hat{c}} = -\dfrac{-0.079952}{2(0.000088)} = 454.27$

c. $\widehat{MC} = \hat{a} + 2\hat{b}Q + 3\hat{c}Q^2$
$= 30.420202 - 0.159904\ Q + 0.000264\ Q^2$

d. $\widehat{MC}_{700} = 30.420202 - 0.159904\ (700) + 0.000264\ (700)^2$
$= \$47.85$

e. $\widehat{AVC} = \hat{a} + \hat{b}Q + \hat{c}Q^2$
$= 30.420202 - 0.079952\ Q + 0.000088\ Q^2$

f. $\widehat{AVC}_{700} = 30.4202 - 0.079952\ (700) + 0.000088\ (700)^2$
$= \$17.57$

Chapter 13

3. Your table should be:

(1) Units of labor	(2) Output	(3) Marginal product	(4) MRP	(5) MC $\left(\frac{10}{MP}\right)$	(6) Profit
1	5	5	$10	2	−$50
2	15	10	20	1	−40
3	30	15	30	0.67	−20
4	50	20	40	0.50	10
5	65	15	30	0.67	30
6	77	12	24	0.83	44
7	86	9	18	1.11	52
8	94	8	16	1.25	58
9	98	4	8	2.50	56
10	96	−2	−4	—	42

c. Profit is maximized by hiring 8 units of labor. If more than 8*L* are hired, $MRP < w$ (= \$10) and profit falls. If fewer than 8*L* are hired, $MRP > w$, and increasing *L* will increase profit.

e. 94, because *MR* (= \$2) will be less than *MC* if output is increased by hiring the ninth worker.

f. See column 6 in table above.

g. 8*L* or 94*Q* both result in a maximum profit of \$58. It doesn't matter whether the manager chooses *L* or *Q* to maximize profit. $MR = MC$ and $MRP = w$ are equivalent rules for profit maximization.

h. 6 *L*; $\pi = -\$16$; $MP_6 = 12 < 12.83 = AP_6$; If $AP < MP$, the firm would shut down in the short run.

7. *a.* If the price of a substitute good decreases, market demand will decrease.

b. Initially market supply will be unaffected.

c. Market supply is unchanged and market demand has decreased: market price will decrease.

d. Market output will decrease.

e. A profit-maximizing firm's output will decrease.

f. At the original price, economic profit was zero. Now the firm suffers economic losses.

Chapter 14

2. *a.* $MC = 10 + (2)(-3)Q + (3)(.5)Q^2 = 10 - 6Q + 1.5Q^2$.

b. $Q_{min} = -b/2c = -(-3)/(2)(.5) = 3$ (300 units).

c. $AVC_{min} = 10 - 3(3) + .5(3)^2 = \$5.50$.

d. $P = \$10 > AVC_{min} = \$5.50$: $P = MC \Rightarrow 10 = 10 - 6Q + 1.5Q^2$. $\Rightarrow Q^* = 4$ (400 units).

e. $AVC = 10 - 3(4) + .5(4)^2 = \$6$, $TVC = AVC \cdot Q = (\$6)(400) = \$2{,}400$, $\pi = (P \cdot Q) - (TVC + TFC) = (\$10)(400) - (\$2{,}400 + 600) = \$1{,}000$.

f. $P = \$5 < AVC_{min} = \$5.50$: $Q^* = 0$.

g. $\pi = -TFC = -\$600$.

5. *a.* $AP = -0.025L^2 + 1.45L$.

b. $MP = 0.075L^2 + 2.90L$.

c. $MRP = P \cdot MP = 5(-0.075L^2 + 2.90L) = -0.375 L^2 + 14.5L$.

d. Set *MRP* equal to *w* and solve for *L*:

$-0.375 L^2 + 14.5L = 15$

$-0.375 L^2 + 14.5L - 15 = 0$

Using the quadratic formula, the two values of *L* where *MRP* = *w* are

$$L_1, L_2 = \frac{-14.5 \pm \sqrt{(14.5)^2 - (4)(-0.375)(-15)}}{2(-0.375)}$$

$$= \frac{-14.5 \pm \sqrt{187.75}}{-0.75} = \frac{-14.5 \pm 13.7}{-0.75}$$

and

$L_1 = 1.067$

$L_2 = 37.6$.

The profit-maximizing level of labor usage is 37.6 since $AP_{37.6} = 19.18 > 3.0 = MP_{37.6}$. L_1 is *not* profit maximizing because $AP < MP$ and the firm should shut down.

e. $\pi = P \cdot Q - wL - TFC$

First, compute $Q^* = -0.025(37.6)^3 + 1.45(37.6)^2 = 721$

$\pi = \$5 \cdot 721 = 15 \cdot 37.6 - \$1{,}000 = 3{,}605 - 564 - 1{,}000 = \$2{,}041$

Chapter 15

3. *a.* $Q^* = 9$; the eighth and ninth units of output should be produced because they add more to *TR* than to *TC* (*MR* > *MC*), but producing the tenth unit would decrease profit (*MC* > *MR*).

b. $P^* = \$18$

c. $\pi = (\$18)(9) - (54) = \$108$

8. *a.*

L	*Q*	*P*	*MP*	*MR*	*MRP*
9	50	$21	—	—	—
10	100	20	50	19.00	950
11	140	19	40	16.50	660
12	170	18	30	13.33	400
13	190	17	20	8.50	170
14	205	16	15	3.33	50
15	215	15	10	−5.50	−55

b. If the wage rate is $60, the monopolist will employ 13 units of labor. Through the 13th unit, each unit of labor adds more to TR than to *TC* (*MRP* > *w*); employing the 14th unit of labor would decrease profit (*MRP* < *w*). If the wage rate falls to $40, the 14th unit of labor now adds more to *TR* than to *TC* and so should be hired. Regardless of the wage rate, no more than 14 units of labor will be employed—the firm will never hire a unit of labor with negative *MP*.

Chapter 16

13. *a.* $Q_T^* = 150$ (where $MR = MC_T$); $Q_1^* = 50$ and $Q_2^* = 100$ (where $MC_1 = MC_2$); $P^* = \$50$ (from the demand curve).

b. When $Q_1 = Q_2 = 75$, $MC_1 \approx \$28 > MC_2 \approx \$17$. This is not the cost-minimizing allocation of cartel output: moving one unit of output from firm 1 to firm 2 will leave the cartel's output and total revenue unchanged, but will decrease total cost and thus increase profit by $11 ($28 – 17). The cartel should shift output from firm 1 to firm 2, keeping total output unchanged, until $MC_1 = MC_2$. Only when marginal cost is the same for both firms is cost minimized and thus profit maximized for a given level of cartel output.

14. Tacit collusion is unspoken cooperation among firms. The behavior of firms that tacitly collude can approximate the behavior of members of a cartel—pricing tends to be uniform among firms. Tacit collusion, often based on historical patterns of interaction among firms, exists when firms believe that profit will be maximized by stable behavior.

Chapter 17

1. *a.* $Q = 26 - P + 2M - 5P_R = 26 - P + (2)(20) - (5)(2) = 56 - P$.

b. $P = 56 - Q$.
c. $MR = 56 - 2Q$.

2. *a.* $MC = 20 - 2(7Q) + 3(Q^2) = 20 - 14Q + 3Q^2$.
b. $MR = MC \Rightarrow 56 - 2Q = 20 - 14Q + 3Q^2 \Rightarrow Q^* = 6$ (600 units).
c. $P^* = 56 - Q^* = 56 - 6 = \$50$.
d. The firm should operate. For $Q = 6$, $AVC = 20 - 7Q + Q^2 = 20 - 7(6) + (6)^2 = \$14$, so $P^* = \$50 > AVC = \$14$.
e. $TR = P \cdot Q = (\$50)(600) = \$30{,}000$; $TVC = AVC \cdot Q = (\$14)(600) = \$8{,}400$; $\pi = TR - (TVC + TFC) = \$30{,}000 - (8{,}400 + 22{,}500) = -\$900$.

Chapter 18

3. *a.* $Q_A = 10MC_A - 100$.
$$Q_B = \frac{10}{3} MC_B - \frac{40}{3}.$$
b. $$Q_T = Q_A + Q_B = (10\, MC_T - 100) + \left(\frac{10}{3} MC_T - \frac{40}{3}\right) = \frac{40}{3} MC_T - \frac{340}{3}.$$
c. $$MC_T = \frac{3}{40} Q_T + 8.5.$$
d. Set marginal cost in plant B (the low-cost plant) equal to the minimum value of marginal cost in plant A (the high-cost plant):
$$MC_B = 4 + \frac{3}{10} Q_T = 10$$
so $Q_T = 20$. Beyond 20 units of total output, both plants are used.
e. At 70 units, $MC_A = 10 + \frac{1}{10}(70) = \$17$ and $MC_B = 4 + \frac{3}{10}(70) = \$25$. Since $MC_A < MC_B$, production should be shifted from plant B to plant A until $MC_A = MC_B$; this minimizes total cost.

9. *a.* $MR_1 = 200 - 8Q_1$
$MR_2 = 100 - 2Q_2$
$MR_T = 120 - 1.6Q$
Set $MR_T = MC$, $Q = 50$.
b. At $Q = 50$, $MR_T = \$40$. Setting $MR_1 = MR_2 = \$40$, $Q_1 = 20$ and $Q_2 = 30$.
c. $P_1 = 200 - 4(20) = \$120$.
$P_2 = 100 - 30 = \$70$.
d. $|E_2|$ must be greater than $|E_1|$ because P_2 is less than P_1 (price is lower in the market with the more elastic demand). More formally, $MR = P[1 + (1/E)]$, so $|E_1| = 3/2 < |E_2| = 7/3$.

Chapter 19

1. *a.* $PV = NCF/(1 + r)^t = \$1{,}000/(1.0575) = \$945.63$.
b. $PV = \$1{,}000/(1.06)^2 = \$890.00$.
c. $PV = \$1{,}000/(1.0625)^3 = \$833.71$.
d. $PV = \$1{,}000/(1.065)^4 = \$777.32$.
e. $PV = \$1{,}000/(1.0675)^5 = \$721.37$.

3. NPV of project = PV – cost of project.
$NPV_1 - \$144{,}397 - 125{,}000 = \$19{,}397$.
$NPV_2 = \$144{,}397 - 150{,}000 = -\$5{,}603$.

Chapter 20

3. *a.* Project A: Cumulative *NCF*s = \$10 + 8 + 6 + 4 = \$28
Average *NCF* = \$28/4 = \$7
ROI = average *NCF*/average amount invested
= \$7/\$20.5 = 34%
Project B: Cumulative *NCF*s = \$4 + 6 + 9 + 11 = \$30
Average *NCF* = \$30/4 = \$7.5
ROI = \$7.5/\$20.5 = 37%

Using the ROI criterion with a targer rate of return on investment of 35%, project A would be rejected and project B accepted.
b. Project A: $E(PV) = \$10/1.15 + 8/(1.15)^2 + 6/(1.15)^3 + 4/(1.15)^4 = \$21.0$
$E(NPV) = \$21.0 - 20.5 = \$.5$
Project B: $E(PV) = \$4/1.15 + 6/(1.15)^2 + 9/(1.15)^3 + 11/(1.15)^4 = \$20.2$
$E(NPV) = \$20.2 - 20.5 = -\$.3$
The recommendation is reversed under the expected *NPV* criterion: accept project A, reject project B. The ROI method treats current and future cash flows equivalently. The recommendation based on the expected *NPV* rule should be used because following the ROI criterion would reduce the value of the firm.

9. *a.*

Project	Expected *NPV*	Cost	*PV*	Profitability index	Rank
A	20	10	30	3.0	2
B	17	10	27	2.7	3
C	12	5	17	3.4	1
D	8	5	13	2.6	4

b.

Expenditure constraint	Projects undertaken
5	C
10	C and D (or A)
15	C and A
20	C, A, and D

SUGGESTED REFERENCES

Chapter 4

Allen, R. D. G. *Mathematical Analysis for Economists.* New York: St. Martin's Press, 1938.

Chiang, A. C. *Fundamental Methods of Mathematical Economics,* 3rd ed. New York: McGraw-Hill, 1984.

Chapter 5

Brown, William S. *Introducing Econometrics.* New York: West, 1991.

Gujarati, Damodar N. *Basic Econometrics.* New York: McGraw-Hill, 1988.

Johnston, J. *Econometric Methods.* New York: McGraw-Hill, 1984.

Kmenta, Jan. *Elements of Econometrics.* New York: Macmillan, 1986.

Mendenhall, William, and Terry Sincich, *A Second Course in Business Statistics: Regression Analysis.* San Francisco: Dellen, 1989.

Chapter 6

Bierman, H., C. Bonini and W. Hausman. *Quantitative Analysis for Business Decisions,* eighth edition. Burr Ridge, IL: Richard D. Irwin, Inc., 1991.

Takayama, Akira. *Analytical Methods in Economics.* Ann Arbor, MI: University of Michigan Press, 1993.

Chapter 8

Gujarati, Damodar N. *Basic Econometrics.* New York: McGraw-Hill, 1988.

Intrilligator, Michael D. *Econometric Models, Techniques, and Applications.* Englewood Cliffs: Prentice Hall, 1978.

Kmenta, Jan. *Elements of Econometrics.* New York: Macmillan, 1986.

Pindyck, Robert S., and Daniel L. Rubinfeld. *Econometric Models and Economic Forecasts.* New York: McGraw-Hill, 1981.

Chapter 9

Box, G. E. P., and G. M.. Jenkins. *Time Series Analysis, Forecasting and Control.* San Francisco: Holden-Day, 1970.

Granger, C. W. J. *Forecasting in Business and Economics.* New York: Academic Press, 1980.

Montgomery, D. C., and L. A. Johnson. *Forecasting and Time Series Analysis.* New York: McGraw Hill, 1976.

Pindyck, R. C., and D. L. Rubinfeld. *Econometric Models and Economic Forecasts.* New York: McGraw-Hill, 1981.

Chapter 12

Chambers, Robert G. *Applied Production Analysis: A Dual Approach.* Cambridge University Press, 1988.

Gujarati, D. *Basic Econometrics.* New York: McGraw-Hill, 1988.

Intrilligator, M. D. *Economic Models, Techniques, and Applications.* Englewood Cliffs, N.J.: Prentice Hall, 1978.

Maddala, G. S. *Introduction to Econometrics.* New York: Macmillan, 1988.

Chapter 20

For a general discussion of the investment decision, see:

Bierman, Harold, Jr., *Implementation of Capital Budgeting Techniques,* Financial Management Survey and Synthesis Series. New York: Financial Management Association, 1986.

Brealey, Richard, and Stewart Myers. *Principles of Corporate Finance.* New York: McGraw-Hill, 1984.

The linear programming approach to the capital rationing problem was pioneered by H. M. Weingartner.

Weingartner, H. M. *Mathematical Programming and the Analysis of Capital Budgeting Problems.* Englewood Cliffs, N.J.: Prentice Hall, 1963.

Appendix

Archibald, G. C., and R. G. Lipsey. *An Introduction to Mathematical Economics: Methods and Applications.* New York: Harper & Row, 1976.

Bierman, H., C. Bonini and W. Hausman. *Quantitative Analysis for Business Decisions,* eighth edition. Burr Ridge, IL: Richard D. Irwin, Inc., 1991.

Baumol, W. J. *Economic Theory and Operations Analysis.* Englewood Cliffs, N.J.: Prentice Hall, 1977.

Chiang, A. C. *Fundamental Methods of Mathematical Economics.* New York: McGraw-Hill, 1974.

Intriligator, M. D. *Econometric Models, Techniques, and Applications.* Englewood Cliffs, N.J.: Prentice Hall, 1978.

Takayama, A. *Analytical Methods in Economics.* Ann Arbor, MI: University of Michigan Press, 1993.

INDEX

D

E

J

K

L

N

S